TORT LAW

by

B. S. MARKESINIS & S. F. DEAKIN

Fourth Edition

CLARENDON PRESS · OXFORD

OXFORD
UNIVERSITY PRESS

Great Clarendon Street, Oxford OX2 6DP

Oxford University Press is a department of the University of Oxford.
It furthers the University's objective of excellence in research, scholarship,
and education by publishing worldwide in

Oxford New York

Athens Auckland Bangkok Bogotá Buenos Aires Calcutta
Cape Town Chennai Dar es Salaam Delhi Florence Hong Kong Istanbul
Karachi Kuala Lumpur Madrid Melbourne Mexico City Mumbai
Nairobi Paris São Paulo Singapore Taipei Tokyo Toronto Warsaw

with associated companies in Berlin Ibadan

Oxford is a registered trade mark of Oxford University Press
in the UK and certain other countries

Published in the United States
by Oxford University Press Inc., New York

British Library Cataloguing in Publication Data

Data available

Library of Congress Cataloging in Publication Data

Markesinis, B. S.
Tort law / by B.S. Markesinis & S.F. Deakin.—4th ed.
p. cm.
Includes bibliographical references and index.
1. Torts—Great Britain. 2. Liability (Law)—Great Britain.
I. Deakin, S. F. (Simon F.) II. Title.
KD1949.M37 1999 346.4103—dc21 99–21236

ISBN 0–19–876507–X
ISBN 0–19–876506–1 (pbk.)

1 3 5 7 9 10 8 6 4 2

Typeset in Swift
by Hope Services (Abingdon) Ltd.,
Printed in Great Britain
on acid-free paper by
Bookcraft Ltd., Midsomer Norton, Somerset

Preface to the Fourth Edition

Tort Law, in its fourth edition, still remains a student textbook. So the description of the English law of torts, with as much clarity and (relative) completeness as is possible, remains its prime aim. But like all creatures it has, with age, acquired a greater independence of mind. In this edition, the authors' desire to go beyond description to criticism and to the presentation of some personal ideas about the subject thus proved irresistible. In fact, criticism and creativity, if we expressed the first and attained the second to the degree that is appropriate in a textbook and not a monograph, both led us in the same direction. This is that tort law is not, as some would like us to believe, becoming unmanageably wide but, on the contrary, is being restricted by a number of developments. Some stem from the perennial fear of opening the floodgates of litigation. Others are the result of extending immunities to an ever-growing number of State agencies on the grounds, not always convincing, of economic efficiency. Yet others are the inevitable result of a shrinking Welfare State which, it is said, we can no longer afford. A final group of restrictions of tort liability can be traced to the effective killing of all attempts to let strict liability develop as it has in other systems. All these phenomena are handled in this edition in a more open and, at times, assertive manner in the belief that the modern student desires not only a description of the subject but also a stimulus for further reflection. We hope that these changes will help achieve the new targets that we set ourselves; and if they do, they may also provide food for thought to any practitioner who chooses to consult this book.

The above (partial) reorientation, coupled with the wealth of new material that has appeared since the last manuscript went to the press five years ago, have necessitated substantial rewriting (and not a mere updating) of the text. But we sincerely hope that the basic features of the book, which enabled it to go through four editions in the space of approximately twenty years, are still there for all to see.

In this edition as, in the earlier ones, we have been fortunate to have had the help and co-operation of Professors David Anderson, Andrew Grubb, and David Robertson, each of whom has kindly updated the sections of the book for which he assumed responsibility two editions ago. All three have brought to the book not just their teaching skills and profound scholarship but also a rich comparative dimension. To this we have ourselves occasionally added the European, which we predict will go on growing, especially as our practitioners become more adroit at exploiting the ideas that are coming into our law from Luxembourg and Strasbourg. To the above colleagues, as well as to the staff of the Oxford University Press, we again extend our grateful thanks. The law is stated as at 1 October 1998, although we have been able to make brief reference to two important judgments handed down after that date, namely the decision of the House of Lords in *White* v. *Chief Constable of South Yorkshire* and that of the European Court of Human Rights in *Osman* v. *United Kingdom*.

Basil Markesinis
Simon Deakin
Oxford and Cambridge, *3 October 1998*

Outline Table of Contents

Contents

1 INTRODUCTION

2 GENERAL PRINCIPLES OF NEGLIGENCE

3 SPECIAL FORMS OF NEGLIGENCE

4 Interference with the Person

5 Interference with Property and Economic Interests

6 Stricter Forms of Liability

Table of Cases

Table of Cases from Other Jurisdictions

CANADA

EUROPEAN COURT OF HUMAN RIGHTS

EUROPEAN COURT OF JUSTICE

US

Table of United Kingdom Legislation

Table of Legislation from Other Jurisdictions

Table of International Instruments

Abbreviations

ALJR	Australian Law Journal Reports
All ER (EC)	All England Law Reports (European Court)
All ER Rev.	All England Law Reports Review
ALR	Australian Law Reports
Am. J. Comp. L.	American Journal of Comparative Law
Amer. Bar Found. Res. J.	American Bar Foundation Research Journal
Anglo-Am. LR	Anglo-American Law Review
Aust. BR	Australian Business Review
Aust. Bus. LJ	Australian Business Law Journal
Aust. Bus. LR	Australian Business Law Review
Aust. LJ	Australian Law Journal
BCLR	British Columbia Law Reports
BLR	Building Law Reports
BMJ	British Medical Journal
BMLR	British Medical Law Reports
Buffalo LR	Buffalo Law Review
Building L Rep.	Building Law Reports
Cal. LR	California Law Review
Can. BR	Canadian Bar Review
Can. Bus. LJ	Canadian Business Law Journal
Chicago-Kent LR	Chicago-Kent Law Review
City of London LR	City of London Law Review
CL	Current Law
CLJ	Cambridge Law Journal
CLP	Current Legal Problems
CLR	Commonwealth Law Reports
CLY	Current Law Yearbook
CMLR	Common Market Law Reports
Col. LR	Columbia Law Review
Con. LR	Construction Law Reports
Const. LJ	Construction Law Journal
Conv.	Conveyancer
Conv. (NS)	Conveyancer (New Series)
Cornell L. Rev.	Cornell Law Review
Cornell LQ	Cornell Law Quarterly
Cr. App. Rep.	Criminal Appeal Reports
Crim. LR	Criminal Law Review
Denning LJ	Denning Law Journal

Dickinson J. Int. Law	Dickinson Journal of International Law
DLR	Dominion Law Reports
Dublin University LJ	Dublin University Law Journal
ECR	European Court Reports
EG	Estates Gazette
EGLR	Estates Gazette Law Reports
EHRLR	European Human Rights Law Review
EHRR	European Human Rights Reports
EMLR	Entertainment and Media Law Reports
Eur. Bus. LR	European Business Law Review
European J. of Health Law	European Journal of Health Law
FLR	Family Law Reports
FSR	Fleet Street Patent Law Reports
Harv. LR	Harvard Law Review
Hastings Int. & Comp. LR	Hastings International and Comparative Law Review
HLR	Housing Law Reports
HMC	Hospital Medical Council
ICR	Industrial Cases Reports
ILJ	Industrial Law Journal
Ill. LR	Illinois Law Review
ILRM	Irish Law Reports
ILT	Irish Law Times
Int. Encl. Comp. L	International Encyclopaedia of Comparative Law
Iowa LR	Iowa Law Review
Ir. Jur.	Irish Jurist
IRLR	Industrial Relations Law Reports
J. Law & Econ.	Journal of Law and Economics
JBL	Journal of Business Law
JC	Justiciary Cases (Scotland)
JEL	Journal of European Law
Jo. LS	Journal of Legal Studies
JP	Justice of the Peace and Local Government Review
JSWL	Journal of Social Welfare Law
KIR	Knight's Industrial Reports
La. LR	Louisiana Law Review
Law and CP	Law and Contemporary Problems
Leg. Stud.	Legal Studies
LGR	Local Government Reports
LIEI	Legal Issues in European Integration
LJNCCR	Law Journal Newspaper County Court Reports
LMCLQ	Lloyds Maritime and Commercial Law Quarterly
Louis. LR	Louisiana Law Review
LQR	Law Quarterly Review
LR Ir.	Law Reports, Ireland

LS	*Legal Studies*
McGill LJ	*McGill Law Journal*
Malaya LR	*Malaya Law Review*
Med. L. Rev.	*Medical Law Review*
Med. LR	*Medical Law Reports*
Mich. LR	*Michigan Law Review*
Minn. LR	*Minnesota Law Review*
Miss. LJ	*Mississippi Law Journal*
MLR	*Modern Law Review*
MULR	*Melbourne University Law Review*
NBR	*New Brunswick Reports (Canada)*
NCB	*National Coal Board*
NEJM	*New England Journal of Medicine*
New LJ	*New Law Journal*
NILJ	*Northern Ireland Law Journal*
NILQ	*Northern Ireland Legal Quarterly*
NLJ	*New Law Journal*
NSWLR	*New South Wales Law Reports (Australia)*
NWUL Rev.	*Northwestern University Law Review*
NYULR	*New York University Law Review*
NZLR	*New Zealand Law Reports*
NZULR	*New Zealand Universities Law Review*
OJLS	*Oxford Journal of Legal Studies*
Ont.	*Ontario Reports (Canada)*
Oregon LR	*Oregon Law Review*
Osgoode Hall LJ	*Osgoode Hall Law Journal*
PIQR	*Personal Injuries and Quantum Reports*
PL	*Public Law*
PN	*Professional Negligence*
RHA	*Regional Health Authority*
RPC	*Reports of Patent Cases*
RTR	*Road Traffic Reports*
S. Cal. LR	*Southern California Law Review*
SASR	*South Australian State Reports*
SC	*Session Cases (Scotland)*
SCR	*Supreme Court Reports (Canada)*
SJ	*Solicitors' Journal*
SLR	*Scottish Land Reports*
SLT	*Scots Law Times*
SR (NSW)	*State Reports, New South Wales (Australia)*
Stan. LR	*Stanford Law Review*
Syd. LR	*Sydney Law Review*
Tenn. LR	*Tennessee Law Review*
Texas LR	*Texas Law Review*

Tort LR	*Tort Law Review*
Tulane LR	*Tulane Law Review*
U. Fla. LR	*University of Florida Law Review*
U. Pa. LR	*University of Pennsylvania Law Review*
UBCLR	*University of British Columbia Law Review*
UCLA L. Rev.	*University of California Los Angeles Law Review*
UCLR	*University of Chicago Law Review*
UTLJ	*University of Toronto Law Journal*
Vanderbilt LR	*Vanderbilt Law Review*
Virginia LR	*Virginia Law Review*
VR	*Victoria Reports (Australia)*
WN	*Weekly Notes (Reports)*
WN (NSW)	*Weekly Notes, New South Wales (Australia)*
WWR	*Western Weekly Reports (Canada)*
Yale LJ	*Yale Law Journal*

1

Introduction

1. TORT AT THE CROSSROADS

Today the law of tort is mainly, though not exclusively, concerned with 'accidents' arising in countless ways. However, it by no means provides their main, let alone exclusive, source of compensation. In a modern industrial and mechanised society the number of accidents is great and, in some areas at least, seems destined to keep rising. The Pearson Committee reported in 1978 that the number of people who obtained compensation through the tort system was just over 200,000 a year.[1] This represents a small fraction of the total number of injuries (estimated, at that time, at around 3 million). Yet, this 6.66 per cent of the total number succeeded in obtaining through the tort system about 25 per cent of the amount of compensation paid to accident victims from *all* sources of compensation, including, for example, insurance and social security.[2] Thus, though the tort system has been accused, probably fairly, of being slow, cumbersome, and expensive, its study still possesses undoubted theoretical and practical significance, especially when properly related to the other systems of compensation (about which more in Section 7, below).

The continuing importance of the law of tort is due not only to the increase in the number of accidents, but also to the fact that the more developed a society becomes the more willing it apparently is to look sympathetically at a wider spectrum of complaints. The phenomenon is particularly pronounced in the United States, where one knowledgeable observer has remarked that: 'Few Americans, it seems, can tolerate more than five minutes of frustration without submitting to the temptation to sue.'[3] That is not the case in Britain; and national temperament and judicial caution are likely to ensure that we never quite emulate the more extreme features of the American system. Besides, the American system possesses some special features (such as the use of juries in civil trials and the almost total absence of a Welfare-State safety net) which are absent from our system and may thus ensure a more balanced approach towards the problem of accident compensation. On the other hand, on the intellectual/cultural level what happens in the United States has the habit of reaching our shores (in one way or another) after an interval of ten or fifteen years. Some signs thus do exist, both in Britain and the Continent of Europe, of an increased willingness to assert one's rights in a legal way. This may put our

---

[1] Cmnd. 7054–I, table 4.

[2] No study as thorough as that conducted by the Pearson Committee has taken place since the publication of that Report. But such, mainly circumstantial, evidence that is available suggests that the general trends remain unchanged and, hence, the Pearson Committee figures retain considerable interest.

[3] Quoted by J. Fleming, *The American Tort Process* (Select Bibliography), 2.

legal system under new pressures; but, on the other hand, to the extent that it suggests that victims are more informed about their rights, it might not necessarily be a bad development.

The above trends are not really surprising. A primitive legal system, because of its lack of techniques and inclination, concerns itself mainly with the murderer, the footpad, and those who disturb the 'King's peace'. In the Middle Ages civil liability for nervous shock received no attention in a world accustomed to unbelievable physical suffering. Liability for intentional false statements was unthought-of until much later; and liability for careless false statements was not generally accepted until 1963 (and we are still struggling to keep it within reasonable bounds). The recovery of damages for disappointment over a ruined holiday[4] today represents a very advanced stage of development, which not everyone would regard as 'progress'. Generally speaking, the common law, especially the English common law, tends to follow a pattern of evolution that consists of two steps forward followed by one step backwards. As we shall note in the second chapter on negligence, the present phase is one of retraction, following an expansionist phase in the late 1970s and early 1980s. However, it would not be at all surprising if this trend were reversed by the time of a new edition of this book.

Despite the ebb and flow of modern tort law the fact remains that nowadays, as stated, our willingness to put up with losses seems to have decreased, and this may account for the success of claims unthought-of even fifty years ago. The weakening of family, religious, and neighbourhood bonds may be making people less able to cope with the ordinary vicissitudes of life. On the other hand, losses may also be greater and more frequently inflicted. Toxic torts are a new problem; and so is widespread pollution. Digging in a populous area with a mechanical excavator when cables and pipelines lie beneath the surface of a road is also likely to cause more damage than the digging with a pickaxe by a single worker a hundred years ago in a small town or village. Not that long ago the Court of Appeal of the Fifth Circuit in the United States was called upon to decide a case of a spillage of a toxic chemical which led to the 'closing' by the authorities of a vast area of the Mississippi estuary. The closure had disastrous effects on the business interests of such local concerns as restaurants, commercial fishermen, cargo-terminal operators, and bait and tackle shops.[5] In the event only forty-one suits were brought against the polluter. Presumably, they were 'test' actions; and thousands more might have followed had the original claimants been successful; but one cannot be sure. Incidentally, though these claims involved pure financial loss—a type of harm which, we shall see, causes much concern to common lawyers—this opening of the 'floodgates of litigation' can also occur where personal injury has occurred. Thus, the American manufacturers of the intra-uterine contraceptive device the Dalcon Shield were sued by over 200,000 women—including 3–4,000 in Britain. They complained of suffering serious pelvic infection, sterility, or ectopic pregnancies as a result

---

[4] *Ichard* v. *Frangoulis* [1977] 1 WLR 556; *Jackson* v. *Horizon Holidays Ltd.* [1975] 1 WLR 1468 (a contract action).

[5] *State of Louisiana* v. *M/V Testbank*, 752 F.2d 1019 (1985) discussed by Atiyah in (1985) 3 *OJLS* 485.

of a defect in the product (there were also a few instances of death). The product was withdrawn from sale in 1974; by 1985 the manufacturers had been forced into bankruptcy; and by the end of that decade an offer for £1.3 billion had been made to the victims as part of a financial reorganisation plan for the manufacturers. Similar claims for physical injuries, suffered as a result of, say, defective heart valves have also been the subject of vast, world-wide settlements. In these cases, no one has raised the floodgates argument, which makes one wonder whether there is some other reason which makes the 'economic loss' claims so controversial.

The increase in tort claims is not only due to our greater ability to cause more and greater harm and our reduced willingness to put up with the normal vicissitudes of life. Other factors are also at play. Thus, the greater likelihood and potential magnitude of such losses have also encouraged people to seek to spread them as widely as possible, especially since modern insurance makes it easier to do this.[6] Modern insurance, developed mainly in order to protect defendants, has ended up also assisting and encouraging plaintiffs. Insurance has thus made the imposition of liability more frequent in certain areas of the law—especially traffic accidents and products liability—and has induced some strange twists in traditional concepts as a consequence. As we shall point out below, some authors[7] have criticised this trend and have argued that, in any event, the courts are ill-equipped to undertake such very specialised exercises. Yet, overall, there is no denying the fact that, as a result of modern insurance practices, the notions of 'duty' (and causation) are at times used to conceal insurance dictates and the term 'negligence' is employed in contexts where the defendant could not humanly have avoided the accident in question. Thus, in Section 4 below (and in other parts of this book), we shall be arguing that, despite the difficulties inherent in such exercises, our courts would be well advised (and our students well served) to consider these insurance arguments more openly. For, not only has this approach gained acceptance in modern life whether we like it or not, it also provides a useful tool (along with others) in solving the problems posed by modern tort cases.

There are other reasons behind this growing importance of tort litigation. The contingent-fee practice, which allows a lawyer to take his remuneration as a percentage of the successful claim, is (for most intents and purposes) not (yet) used in this country. In the United States, on the other hand, it is common practice in tort litigation and, though this may enable poor victims to sue (in a way that, perhaps, our ever-diminishing legal-aid system does not), it also makes the lawyer a party to the litigation. For many, this not only may impair the lawyer's objectivity; it *may* also be encouraging the growth of litigation. In the United States, jury awards, often of unbelievable dimensions,[8] have also encouraged

---

[6] Though in the so-called 'cable cases' (below, Section 3) it is not clear who that person should be, whether the contractor/defendant or the property-owner/plaintiff.

[7] Most recently, Professor Jane Stapleton in (1995) 58 *MLR* 820. Cf. Professor Bob Hepple in (1997) 50 *Current Legal Problems*, 69, esp. at 81 ff.

[8] Tunc, op. cit. (Select Bibliography), 3–4, gives many, often amazing, illustrations. Fleming's *The American Tort Process* is also replete with interesting statistics and stimulating observations about the American tort system in practice.

recourse to the courts and have led to unnecessary complication of the law. The law of product liability in the United States has arguably suffered from both these factors; and medical malpractice is currently the favourite example of those who believe that tort law in the United States is in a state of acute crisis. In this country damages are no longer determined by juries but by judges, and this has produced uniformity and, for many years, a relative moderation in the size of awards.[9] Even so, in recent times there has been a growing number of awards and settlements in personal injuries cases well over the £1 million mark; and the new 'structured settlement' mechanism, discussed in more detail in Chapter 8, below, has made such mega awards more frequent. Naturally such results are welcome to victims; but they will also raise new problems of their own. For example, can medical insurance societies go on increasing premiums? Can young doctors afford them? Will local authorities, which foot large awards against hospitals, be able to absorb such increased costs? There are legal difficulties that also have to be faced. For instance, in these medical cases one has to decide whether a doctor is guilty of 'negligence', or only of a regrettable but statistically inevitable error. Sympathy for the victim could lead English courts to follow the American example and draw the line in the latter's favour. This certainly happens in traffic-accident cases where statistically inevitable errors are described as 'negligence', thus providing victims with much-needed funds but without ruining the defendants. The resulting confusion between two distinct concepts, 'negligence' and 'error', is, as we shall note further down, unfortunate. But, as stated, if an award is great, it also means that the hospital (in practice the local health authority or trust) will be asked to bear the costs, which leads either to higher rates or higher insurance premiums or both. However, a glance at American insurance coverage for medical malpractice reveals some fairly disturbing facts. In the United States the percentage of physicians sued nearly tripled in the period between 1978 and 1983. In 1983 there were 16 malpractice claims for every 100 doctors, compared with 1 for 65 in 1956; 60 per cent of gynaecologists reported having been sued, 20 per cent three or more times. Moreover, awards have skyrocketed: the number of million dollar verdicts (1,963) doubled between 1972 and 1983, the average award in 1985 being $950,000. So did settlements: in 1982 more than 250 exceeded $1 million, a tenfold increase in four years.[10] The trend has not changed in the years that have followed these studies (though some types of litigation, notably product liability litigation, have shown important, regional decreases).[11]

The costs—financial and social—of such developments are equally disturbing. Doctors, especially obstetricians and neurosurgeons practising in New York or Florida, may have to pay insurance premiums that run into six figures. Much of this is, of course, passed on in patients' fees; but that is not the end of the

---

[9] Or so the Law Commission thought in its Report No. 225 entitled *Personal Injury Compensation: How Much is Enough?* (1994).

[10] Fleming, *The American Tort Process* (Select Bibliography), 16–17.

[11] For some interesting studies on this theme see: Eisenberg and Henderson, 'Inside the Quiet Revolution in Products Liability' 39 *UCLA L. Rev.* 731 (1992); Clermont and Eisenberg, 'Trial by Jury or Judge; Transcending Empiricism' 77 *Cornell L. Rev.* (1992).

story. Greater willingness to make doctors liable *may*[12] mean that they are forced to practise what is called 'defensive medicine' and order costly, complicated, and often unnecessary tests. Caesarean section operations are frequently preferred to normal child births; and by 1985 more than 10 per cent of the country's obstetricians and gynaecologists had either given up practice, apparently because of these developments, or were practising without insurance cover. Should our system follow a similar path? To decide in favour of the doctor simply because we wish to avoid such a trend in our country can cause injustice to the victim. On the other hand, to liberalise the rules in favour of patients without having studied the possible implications[13] might carry risks of a different nature, though potentially just as serious. The truth of the matter is that while American law may be excessively pro-patient, English law probably overprotects doctors. The search for the *via media* is not easy; but it must be pursued.[14] This example, incidentally, raises another problem of modern tort law and, of course, tort books; one can no longer study these types of problems only from a purely legal and conceptual point of view. The problems must be tackled in an interdisciplinary way. Yet how can one even attempt to do this in the confines of a single textbook? And how can an overworked judge even be persuaded to attempt the task, especially if our indigenous literature on this subject is still so poor? These are not easily answerable questions. On the other hand, the difficulty of answering them must not lead us to pretend that they do not exist.

This last example is as good as any to show the importance of modern insurance in the law of torts;[15] it also demonstrates how, as already stated, traditional tort concepts, such as 'negligence', can be moulded to accommodate this new reality. Finally, it underlines how in such cases the tort system manages to be unfair either to one party or to the other, or even to both. In addition, it is costly and slow, and capricious in so far as the successful outcome of a case often depends on the quality of the lawyer handling it and on such imponderables as the memories of witnesses. Not surprisingly, therefore, the whole tort system has come under attack in the last twenty years or so. Paradoxically, the great growth of the system has coincided with increasing criticisms of its efficiency, at any rate in the area of personal injuries that provide the bulk of tort litigation.

Doubts as to whether a tort system is the best means of solving problems have persuaded some legal systems to remove substantial areas of liability for accidents away from the tort system. In France, for example, accidents at work lie largely outside the law of civil responsibility, and, though the administration and financing of such claims is differently arranged, the same is true of Germany. With us, as we shall see, a mixed system prevails. Though many have

---

[12] It is surprising to assert that there does not seem to exist any reliable (statistical) survey on this subject (see Dewees, Duff, and Trebilcock, *Exploring the Domain of Accident Law* (1996), 111). Opinion in the United States is thus sharply divided on whether excessive medical tests are ordered in order to protect oneself against a law suit or conceal financial factors which exist in the United States because of the way medical services are paid for.

[13] Some of these were referred to by Lord Denning MR in *Whitehouse* v. *Jordan* [1980] 1 All ER 650, 658.

[14] These points are further pursued in Chapter 3.   [15] Discussed below, Section 7(3).

argued for a change, the position is unlikely to be altered in the near future, leaving us in the meantime with considerable duplication of effort and expenditure, to say nothing of the complication of the entire compensation system.[16] In other countries, Sweden for example, the role of tort has greatly diminished in the domain of personal injuries; while in New Zealand a system of social security was substituted for it in 1972. More recently, this system in its turn has been dismantled, and tort law partly reinstated as the basis for accident compensation. Many of these problems were considered by the Pearson Committee, which some authors writing in the mid-1970s believed would herald a similar end to our tort law, at any rate in the area of personal injuries. In the event the proposals of the Committee, which will be referred to briefly in the appropriate parts of this book, were nowhere near as radical as had been anticipated; and even their moderation did not save them from the cruel fate of being ignored by successive governments.[17] Over twenty-five years later the tort system is still alive and kicking, and the number of House of Lords' decisions on the subject is increasing (alas, also in size). The fact, however, that the tort system is still 'alive' in no way means that it is 'well'. As we shall see in various parts of this book, many of the criticisms voiced against it in the 1960s and 1970s are just as valid today as they were then.

The law of tort also faces another crisis. The French refer to this branch as the law of *individual responsibility*; but how much of this is true of *individual* responsibility? As a result of insurance and the extension of vicarious liability, a large number of actual wrongdoers, especially drivers and employees, are rarely called upon to meet the consequences of their conduct since these are shouldered by some insurance company or by the employers, usually companies. Today the law of torts is thus largely concerned with the liability of 'innocent absentees'. To some extent this development is inevitable, and even desirable. But it also represents a change of emphasis and direction for the law of torts from a branch of the law conceived to deal with human beings to a complex set of rules regulating impersonal legal entities or the possible liability of innocent absentees. As we shall see in Section 5, developments such as these have thrown into doubt the fault basis of tortious liability though one still finds tort lawyers who are willing to justify most tort rules by reference to rules of morality.[18] To be more precise, while it is right that fault should lead to liability, the converse, that there should be no liability in the absence of fault, is today in doubt. This shift from individual to corporate litigants has also played havoc with our law of defamation.

We can summarise this section by saying that tort law is nowadays at a crossroads. In the words of a leading comparative lawyer:[19]

---

[16] The reader of this book will get a glimpse of this complexity in Chapter 6, Section 3, dealing with the liability of employers towards their injured employees.

[17] They are discussed in the essays included in *Accident Compensation After Pearson* (ed. Allen, Bourn, and Holyoak, 1979); see also J. A. Weir, *Compensation for Personal Injuries and Death: Recent Proposals for Reform*, The Cambridge Tilburg Lectures (1978).

[18] For instance Professor Peter Cane in *The Anatomy of Tort Law* (1997).

[19] Tunc, op. cit. (Select Bibliography), 7.

In some respects people are more responsible than ever. Their capacity to cause damage, as indeed their capacity to come to the aid of their neighbour, has been greatly increased as a result of scientific and technological progress. On the other hand, given the increased importance of social security and insurance, their (individual) responsibility is in decline.

A supplementary conclusion for the novice reader would be that one could find support, both judicial and academic, for almost any proposition one might wish to put forward. That is why some have accused tort law of being a subject void for uncertainty. We shall be arguing in this book that this uncertainty accounts for the subject's special intellectual fascination. For the litigant, however, it is a cause of great and legitimate concern.

Select Bibliography

ATIYAH, P., *The Damages Lottery* (1997).
CANE, P., *Atiyah's Accidents, Compensation and the Law* (5th edn., 1993).
FLEMING, J. G., *An Introduction to the Law of Torts* (2nd edn., 1985), ch. 1.
—— *The American Tort Process* (1988), chs. 1, 2, and 4.
HARLOW, C., *Understanding Tort Law* (2nd edn., 1995), chs. 1 and 2.
HEPPLE, B., 'Negligence: The Search for Coherence', (1997) 50 *Current Legal Problems*, 69.
JAMES, FLEMING, 'Tort Law in Midstream: Its Challenge to the Judicial Process', 8 *Buffalo LR* 315 (1959).
JOLOWICZ, J. A., 'Liability for Accidents' [1968] *CLJ* 50.
RABIN, R. L., *Perspectives on Tort Law* (1976).
Report of the Royal Commission, *On Civil Liability and Compensation for Personal Injury* (The Pearson Committee Report) (Cmnd. 7054–I, 1978), chs. 3 and 4.
TUNC, A., *Int. Enc. Comp. L.* xi, ch. 1, Introduction (updated in French under the title *La Responsabilité civile* (1981)).
WILLIAMS, G. L. and HEPPLE, B. A., *Foundations of the Law of Tort* (2nd edn., 1984).

2. TORT AND CONTRACT

It is customary to compare and contrast the notion of tort with those of contract, crime, and trust,[20] but little of practical value is gained by the kind of abstract and cursory comparisons often attempted in introductory chapters. To say, for example, that crime and tort share a common past but are now subject to different rules and pursue different aims adds little to knowledge. In any case, compensation and punishment surface when we talk about the purposes

---

[20] One might also add restitution, since its relationship with tort can give rise to interesting areas of overlap. But, as Professor Birks has observed: 'The bulk of the law of restitution is not concerned with the menu of remedies available for wrongs but with the causes of action which, not being wrongs, nevertheless entitle a plaintiff to restitution of enrichment received by the defendant at his expense.' See: *Civil Wrongs: A New World*, Butterworth Lectures 1990–91 (1992), 109. An excellent illustration can be found in the case of payment made by mistake. Restitution gives the plaintiff the right to recover, but this right is not based on a wrong committed by the defendant. More about the relationship with restitution is said in Section 5, below.

of the law of torts and again when we consider penal damages. Given the limitations of space, such discussions can be avoided without much loss and the reader is referred to some of the older editions of tort textbooks for further details. However, the relationship between tort and contract is conceptually more difficult to define, and can have important practical implications; it may also help to explain and, perhaps, reinstate some of the tort rules that were formulated mainly in the late 1970s and are currently under attack. For clarity's sake the material in this section can be divided into three parts: (1) the theoretical division between contract and tort; (2) the escape 'into' tort prompted by a rather rigidly conceived law of contract; and (3) the attempt to escape 'out' of contract into the domain of tort.

1. The Division Between Contract and Tort

In his oft-quoted definition of tortious liability Winfield laid stress on the fact that liability in tort arises from the breach of an obligation primarily fixed by law, whereas in contract it is fixed by the parties themselves.[21] This distinction may have been acceptable when contract liability was regarded as stemming from an exchange of promises only and not, as is often the case today, from the mere fact that the plaintiff has conferred a benefit on the defendant, or has incurred loss by relying on the latter's behaviour. But basing contractual obligations exclusively on the prior promises of the parties is questioned by some influential modern contract lawyers; and to the extent that this new approach is correct, it makes the division between voluntarily assumed and legally imposed obligations[22] an 'oversimplification' of the issue.

It is not only contract lawyers who doubt this conceptual division. Tort lawyers, as well, have experienced difficulties in dealing with certain cases of liability which are regarded as tortious, but in which the duties imposed on the defendant flow from the fact that he and the plaintiff have entered into a particular relationship. For example, the relation between an occupier of land and his lawful visitors gives rise to a duty in the former to take care. In the absence of consideration (e.g. payment of a fee), the relationship cannot be regarded as contractual. However, there is an agreement or understanding between the parties in so far as the entrant is permitted to be there, so it is impossible to say that the will of the parties is totally irrelevant to the existence of the obligation to take care. Similarly the maker of a gratuitous but careless false statement may be liable partly because he voluntarily undertook to offer advice, and partly because the plaintiff, to his knowledge, relied on it.[23] The reliance element here plays a crucial role, but since it can be found increasingly both in contract and tort situations it makes the dividing line between these two concepts very vague.[24]

---

[21] *The Province of the Law of Tort*, 32.   [22] Atiyah, (Select Bibliography, see below) *passim.*

[23] *Hedley Byrne & Co. Ltd.* v. *Heller and Partners Ltd.* [1964] AC 465. The way we now understand the notions of 'assumption of responsibility' by the defendant and 'reliance' by the plaintiff may have taken this process further, notably by extending liability towards certain third parties. See the discussion of *Henderson* v. *Merret Syndicates Ltd.* [1995] 2 AC 145 and *White* v. *Jones* [1995] 2 AC 207 in Chapter 2, below.

[24] Another area where tort and contract come close to a complete overlap is that of defective products, as is seen most clearly in American and French law.

Another reason for scepticism about the decisive role of consent in contract and its absence in tort is that contracts are concluded or avoided on the strength of objective criteria and impersonal considerations. Moreover, even the presumed intention of the parties is losing ground in areas such as frustration, where, for a long time, it had exercised considerable influence. Conversely, consent may play an important role in tort, even where there is no overlap with contract. For example, a hurt sustained in the course of sport and in accordance with the rules of the game will not always be actionable. Whether consent can remove tortious liability in all cases of grievous bodily harm is doubtful, and one can envisage a number of borderline areas (e.g. emergency surgical operations) where a more cautious answer would be called for.[25] Still, consent may in this type of case prevent the rise of liability in tort.

A more subtle approach to this distinction is to say that it is not the existence of the duty, but its content, that is determined by the law in tort and by the parties in contract. There is a great deal of truth in this since in a contract for the sale of goods, for example, the quantity, price, and other terms will be determined in accordance with the declared or presumed intention of the parties, whereas the duties in tort are fixed by law. Even this variation, however, is not wholly true. This is because the content of tort duties can be avoided or varied by means of consent, warnings, etc. (i.e. by some manifestation of the will of the parties). Additionally, an increasing number of statutes require that certain obligations be implied by law in certain contracts, for example sale of goods or hire purchase.[26] In fairness to Winfield, however, it should be pointed out that he said only that tortious liability arises out of the breach of a duty *primarily* fixed by law. Hence, even in his day a distinction between tort and contract along the line we have been discussing was only an approximate one.

Winfield's second distinction, that tort duties are owed to the world at large (duties *in rem*) whereas in contract they are owed to a specific person (*in personam*), also needs careful examination. For although at the primary level, that is to say before a tort has been committed, this distinction is certainly valid, it is of rather academic importance. For a tort comes into existence only where there has been a breach of primary duty, which then brings into play the duty to pay damages, and this is as much *in personam*, i.e. owed to a specific person (the victim), as any contractual duty.

To establish a distinction between the two concepts on the basis of the difference of their avowed aims is perhaps more promising. For this may help explain, though not necessarily justify, the reluctance of the common law (*a*) to impose liability for omissions and (*b*) to decree compensation for pure economic loss. Thus, tort law primarily aims at protecting life and property, whereas the law of contract is, in a sense, there to promote the further development of a person's interests. As one writer[27] expressed this idea: 'Contract is

---

[25] Skegg, 'Consent to Medical Proceedings on Minors' (1973) 36 *MLR* 370; id., 'A Justification for Medical Procedures Performed without Consent' (1974) 90 *LQR* 512.

[26] E.g. Sale of Goods Act 1979, ss. 12–15, 55; Supply of Goods (Implied Terms) Act 1973, ss. 8–11; Unfair Contract Terms Act 1977, s. 20.

[27] Weir, (Select Bibliography, see below), 5.

productive, tort law protective. In other words, tortfeasors are typically liable for making things worse, contractors for not making them better.' If this statement is taken as descriptive of a certain attitude of the English common law it is accurate. However, the author's frequently expressed opposition to the use of tort law as a way of compensating negligently inflicted economic loss lends credence to the interpretation that he would also like his readers to take it prescriptively: this is what has been happening *and how things should remain*. We have here, therefore, a theoretical reason why we should leave the compensation of pure economic loss to contracts, which supports some of the more pragmatic objections (e.g. the 'floodgates' argument) against the compensability through tort of pure financial harm.

One wonders, however, whether economic loss can be really placed so firmly on the one side of this apparently rigid divide. Weir is conscious of the difficulties of his proposed division, so he cautiously added the word 'typically' in his statement. In fact he goes further by admitting that 'a man who makes a thing worse is also not making it better'. This, however, does not go far enough since it fails to address another question, namely: 'is a man who is not making a thing better making it in any sense worse?' The reader need not spend much time on these tongue-twisters but merely reflect on some of the cases that we will encounter later on. In the legal malpractice situation, has the intended beneficiary who has lost through the lawyer's negligence the benefit of the will made by the testator been made poorer or not made richer? Similarly in the construction type of contract, which was at the basis of the *Junior Books* v. *Veitchi*[28] litigation, has the negligence of the subcontractor that has affected the employer made the latter poorer or has it merely failed to make him richer? The same doubts can be raised in the context of shipping cases such as *The Aliakmon*[29]—discussed in Chapter 2—and thus make one wonder at the universal validity of the proposed basis for distinction.

Still, it is reasoning such as the above (and historical reasons coupled with nineteenth-century ideological beliefs) that also account for another important tort rule, namely that, statute apart, contract alone can create affirmative duties of action.[30] For contract's avowed aim to promote the plaintiff's desire to increase his wealth can explain why a defendant who has promised to do something in this respect will be made to pay damages if he fails to keep his promise. A glance at contract textbooks, however, will show that contract law not only protects expectations, but also reliance interests, and, as stated, Weir's formulation refers to tortfeasors being *typically* liable for making things worse and contractors *typically* liable for not making things better. We are, in other words, again talking of the traditional paradigm contract[31]—the executory sale— where failure by the seller to deliver the goods will deprive the buyer of a gain. This approach, however, fails to pay adequate heed to the case which is both breach of contract and a tort, for example, a dentist who has extracted the

---

[28] [1983] 1 AC 520.   [29] [1986] AC 785.
[30] The historical reasons behind this distinction are examined by Milsom, 'Not Doing is No Trespass', [1954] *CLJ* 105.
[31] Not now accepted by everyone: see Atiyah, op. cit. (Select Bibliography).

wrong tooth, or a carrier who has damaged the goods being transported. Where contractual liability is imposed because of detrimental reliance by the plaintiff, the latter is likely to complain that he is left worse off rather than not being made richer. Can it really be said that where there is such overlap between tort and contract the solution should in all instances be governed by formal categories shaped by tradition, and that the plaintiff's rights should depend on whether his action was framed in the one branch or the other? An affirmative answer does not commend itself; and it becomes ludicrous when one remembers that until recently the choice between the contractual or tortious set of rules was determined in a manner which, though historically explicable,[32] was little short of being capricious. The recent tendency of allowing plaintiffs a choice between the contractual or tortious remedies[33] must be seen as a move towards attenuating the difference between contract and tort. The even more recent attempt to assimilate the rules on remoteness of damage in certain cases[34] could also be seen in the same light. Yet, as we shall see, the judicial pronouncements do not all point in one direction and there undoubtedly exist different tendencies among different judges.

Why then, in view of these doubts, are contract and tort still kept so rigidly apart? A number of explanations could be offered. The first is that traditional thinking takes time to wear out.[35] Moreover, extensive government intervention in the economy is a comparatively modern phenomenon.[36] The inevitable time-lag between political and social change and consequential change in the law may partly explain the slowness of the reaction against the traditional schematisation. A second and more technical reason is that, despite the modern tendency to accept that at the *primary* level the frontier between the two notions is no longer that clear, at the *secondary* level (i.e. that of consequences) the law still contains a number of different rules for contract and tort. Two can be mentioned here briefly, though others do exist.[37]

The first is that the period of time after which a cause of action is barred starts to run in contract from the moment of the conduct constituting breach, whereas in tort it starts to run from the, often much later, moment when the plaintiff sustains his damage. The second rule relates to the service of writs outside the jurisdiction.[38] Such service depends on permission being granted by

[32] See Poulton (Select Bibliography, see below).

[33] *Esso Petroleum Co. Ltd.* v. *Mardon* [1976] QB 801, 819; *Batty* v. *Metropolitan Property Realizations Ltd.* [1978] QB 554, 566; *Midland Bank Trust Co. Ltd.* v. *Hett, Stubbs & Kemp* [1979] Ch. 384; *Henderson* v. *Merrett Syndicates Ltd.* [1995] 2 AC 145.

[34] *Parsons (Livestock) Ltd.* v. *Uttley Ingham & Co. Ltd.* [1978] QB 791.

[35] This is a theme of a series of essays by Watson, *Society and Legal Change* (1977). Professor A. W. B. Simpson, in his most readable *Invitation to Law* (1988), 85, states most appositely: 'Ways in which the law was classified in the past tend to persist, even though they may not be ideal for the conditions of today . . . For everything in the law, like everything in literature, is affected by the past.'

[36] Weir, op. cit. (Select Bibliography), 4.

[37] For instance, the range of remedies is greater for breach of contract than for the commission of a tort; the measure of damages is different for these two notions; the liability of the Crown is wider in contract than it is in tort; conversely, in the case of minors their tortious liability can be more extensive than their liability in contract. But in practice it is the two procedural issues discussed in the text above which have tested most the attempt to bring the two notions closer to one another.

[38] Rules of the Supreme Court, Orders 11, r. 1. (1) (b) and (f).

the High Court, and the Rules of the Supreme Court generally make it easier to obtain leave to serve a writ outside the jurisdiction if an action is framed in contract rather than in tort.

Another reason advanced in favour of keeping separate the treatment of contract and tort has been the following. The fusion of the two notions would create an 'unmanageably large' course and, by implication, an unmanageably large book. This is true. But quite apart from the fact that a pedagogic reason of this kind should not impede the development of the law, the fact remains that the value of such 'pragmatic' objections can also be exaggerated. For, first, one is not necessarily talking of a complete overlap of the two breaches of the law of obligations. Thus, some sections of contract, for example, offer and acceptance, need have no place in such a course. Secondly, a book need not be exhaustive. This is self evident, though it must, at least, lay down the right signposts warning its readers of the uncertain boundaries of its subject. Thus, we shall note further down that this is not the only frontier area of tort law that is vague. The old jurisdictional battles between common law and equity have also left outside the area of tort many 'wrongs' that have for traditional reasons been handled by the law of trusts—typically the area of constructive trusts. But let us return to the relation between contract and tort that is the main focus of this discussion.

It is arguable that a more unified approach in one book (and one course) would be of benefit to the student (and, even, practitioner)—even at the price of losing some detail. For example, let us not forget the difficulties that have resulted from the fact that both courts and the legislature have shared this traditional division of the law of obligations. One has only to see the changes in the law concerning negligent statements to see how these two agents of law reform approached the problem independently and with little effort to co-ordinate the new sets of rules. It is submitted, therefore, that a rigid distinction between contract and tort, and their separate exposition in separate courses, is becoming unfashionable and inadvisable. As stated, however, this applies only to those aspects where there is overlap. Where none exists, contract and tort must continue to be treated separately. In the remaining part of this section we shall thus focus on two particular ways in which the interaction between contract and tort has taken place. When many of these cases come up for reconsideration in the next chapter (on negligence) the reader would be well advised to bear these preliminary points in mind.

In the first group of cases, the courts are discovering tort duties where they could be promoting contractual solutions. Here the flight 'into tort' is taking place simply because the tort rules provide the least resistance for the creation of a remedy which the 'sense of justice' requires. It could be strongly argued that in most of these cases the less 'open-ended' contract law would have provided the better 'peg' for the legal solution demanded by justice and proposed by our courts. However, the rigidity of the doctrine of consideration made this impossible. So tort has been 'stretched' to make up for the rigidity of contract. But this subterfuge should not surprise us. For our tort law is accustomed to performing this residual, gap-filling role, as Lord Devlin himself acknowledged in precisely this context in his classic judgment in *Hedley Byrne & Co.* v. *Heller & Partners*.[39]

In the second group of cases we see the reverse. There is an attempt by the plaintiff to 'escape' into tort as a way of going 'beyond' what has been agreed in the contract. This is a far more problematic area of the law; and the dangers of abusing the advantages of a flexible approach towards the problem of demarcation are considerable. To make matters worse, the proposed division between these two types of cases is not waterproof. It is also fair to admit to the reader the fact that the multiple dicta on the subject are irreconcilable. While this will not come as a surprise to seasoned tort lawyers, students may find it disconcerting to be warned of such uncertainty in such a crucial area of the law of Negligence. Yet false certainty is bad certainty. For, as Professor Birks has remarked, 'When people follow a course, their vision is forever affected by what they are told at the start.'[40] The decisions typically advocated by textbooks have not so much formed the legal mind over decades as deceived it into underdevelopment.

2. The Escape 'Into' Tort Prompted by a Rigidly Conceived Law of Contract

In the common-law systems a person cannot enforce a promise which is not under seal unless he can show that he (the promisee) has suffered some detriment or, conversely, that he has conferred some benefit on the promisor. For this purpose, mutual promises of future performance are deemed to be sufficient. This is the requirement of *consideration* that evinces the presence of a bargain, which according to traditional thinking at least, justifies the enforcement of promises. One important side-effect of this is that a person who is not a party to the bargain in the sense of having personally given consideration cannot enforce it. Strict adherence to this notion by the English (but not American) common law has thus meant that contracts in favour of third parties are not valid in the sense that they give no rights to the third party to demand that the promisor carries out his promise. This rather rigid structuring of the English law of contract, explicable though it is in historical terms, contrasts sharply with other (e.g. modern European and Commonwealth) systems. More importantly, it accounts for some interesting fluctuations in the boundaries between contract and tort—hence the inclusion of this topic in the present discussion.

Generally speaking one could say that in earlier times contract used to expand to make up for the fact that tort law was still in a state of (relative) infancy. In *De la Bere* v. *Pearson Ltd.*,[41] for example, the defendants advertised in their newspaper that their finance editor was willing to answer relevant inquiries by the readers. The plaintiff asked for the name of a stockbroker and

---

[39] [1964] AC 465, though from time to time academic lawyers forget this and suggest that other parts of the law (e.g. the law of succession) might serve as a better vehicle for law reform. Thus, see, Weir 'The Damnosas Hereditas' (1995) 111 *LQR* 357, and for criticism of this see Cretney (1997) 113 *LQR* at 525.

[40] *Civil Wrongs: A New World*, Butterworth Lectures 1990–91 (1992), 110.

[41] [1908] 1 KB 280.

was inadvertently given that of an undischarged bankrupt who misappropriated his money. A contractual action against the defendants succeeded even though it is by no means obvious that the doctrine of consideration was satisfied. In reality the presence of a contract was assumed, for without it the plaintiff would have been without a remedy. On other occasions contracts were discovered during the pre-contractual phase when, by definition, there should not be one. So in *Dick Bentley Productions Ltd.* v. *Harold Smith (Motors) Ltd.*[42] the plaintiffs told the defendants that they were looking for a 'well-vetted' car. The defendants showed them a Bentley with an (apparently) low mileage (20,000 miles) which the plaintiffs bought. The statement as to the mileage turned out to be false, the car was unsatisfactory, so the plaintiffs claimed and were awarded damages for breach of contract. The difficulty about this case was that the statement on which the claim was based was made prior to the conclusion of the contract; and it was by no means clear that it had been turned into a contractual term. Lord Justice Salmon overcame the difficulty by arguing that:[43]

In effect [the defendant had] said: 'If you enter into a contract to buy this motor car from me . . . I undertake that you will be getting a motor car which has done no more than twenty thousand miles since it was fitted with a new engine and new gearbox.' This device is known as a 'collateral contract'.

Contract theory was here advancing into the pre-contractual phase achieving results almost identical to those of a negligence action.[44] In yet other instances, contracts have been invented in order to extend to third parties the operation of contractual exemption clauses;[45] or in order to correct the defect of specific legislative provisions such as section 1 of the Bills of Lading Act 1855.[46] Finally, contractual reasoning was employed in what, in today's terms would be described as a product liability case to make the manufacturer of a product which did not possess the advertised qualities liable to its ultimate purchaser.[47]

Other cases—typically of more recent vintage—reveal the opposite trend: a preference for pegging the solution on the law of torts which, as we shall note in the next chapter, has witnessed in the post-war years an unprecedented growth. *De la Bere*'s case, for example, would nowadays almost certainly be handled as a tort case falling under the rule in *Hedley Byrne & Co. Ltd.* v. *Heller & Partners Ltd.*[48] Other examples, where the plaintiff succeeded in tort, include *Ross* v. *Caunters*[49] and *Junior Books Ltd.* v. *Veitchi Co. Ltd.*[50] and, of course, the offshoots of *Donoghue* v. *Stevenson*[51] which switched the entire law of product liability from contract to tort.[52] *Leigh and Sillavan Ltd.* v. *The Aliakmon Shipping Co.*

---

[42] [1965] 1 WLR 623.   [43] Ibid., 629.
[44] See *Esso Petroleum* v. *Mardon* [1976] QB 801.
[45] *New Zealand Shipping Co. Ltd.* v. *A. M. Satterthwaite and Co. Ltd. (The Eurymedon)* [1975] AC 154.
[46] *Brandt* v. *Liverpool Brazil and River Plate Steam Navigation Co.* [1924] 1 KB 575.
[47] *Carlill* v. *Carbolic Smoke Ball Co.*, [1892] 2 QB 484; [1893] 1 QB 256.   [48] [1964] AC 465.
[49] [1980] Ch. 297.   [50] [1983] 1 AC 520.   [51] [1932] AC 562.
[52] That the law of product liability could have gone down the contractual (instead of tort) path can be seen from most of the early decisions on the subject both in the USA (which started from the common-law position) and French law (which was unincumbered by consideration) and chose to base its early product liability law on an expanded notion of the contract of sale.

Ltd. (The Aliakmon),[53] on the other hand, offers an intriguing but unsuccessful attempt by the plaintiff to base his action in tort. The non-availability of a contractual answer in this case led to the kind of vacuum which legal systems dislike and, in the event, a statutorily based solution.[54] All these cases will be discussed in greater detail in Chapter 2, below, as they form part of the complicated fabric of the law of negligence in the 1980s. Here we shall limit our observations to a few comments relevant to the topic under discussion, namely the relation between contract and tort. Student readers, however, may be well advised to reconsider these comments after they have read the text of Chapter 2.

Ross v. *Caunters*[55] offers a good illustration.[56] In that case a solicitor was hired by a testator to prepare his will. They did so and sent it to him for execution, failing to warn him that the will would be invalid if witnessed by the spouse of one of the beneficiaries. This is precisely what occurred, and when the plaintiff was deprived of the benefits under the will he sued the solicitors for their admitted negligence. Sir Robert Megarry VC gave judgment for the plaintiff relying on the wider dicta of *Donoghue* v. *Stevenson*[57] rather than the narrower rule in *Hedley Byrne & Co. Ltd.* v. *Heller & Partners Ltd.*[58] The differences between the two will be explained in Chapter 2. Here suffice it to say that the successful course of action was framed in tort. The same result (but through different reasoning) was more recently reached by the House of Lords in *White* v. *Jones*.[59] A contractual approach would have avoided the open-endedness of the notion of duty of care. It would also have ensured that the any exemption clauses available to protect the negligent attorney/promisor in a (possible) action by his client (promisee) would have also protected him in an action by the plaintiff (third-party beneficiary).[60] Finally, it would have avoided the criticisms levelled against the majority judgment for using the (vague) notion of assumption of responsibility. But for practical reasons the case was not pleaded in contract; and it was, clearly, decided in tort. For present purposes, however, these cases are particularly illuminating examples of the thesis advanced in this section: if considerations of justice require that a remedy be found, and one cannot be based on contract because of the rigidity engendered by the doctrine of

---

[53] [1986] AC 785.   [54] Carriage of Goods by Sea Act 1992.   [55] [1980] Ch. 297.
[56] So does the much maligned decision in *Junior Books* v. *Veitchi* [1983] 1 AC 520.
[57] [1932] AC 562.   [58] [1964] AC 465.   [59] [1995] 2 AC 207.
[60] In one sense the crux of these decisions is not so much whether the defendant (solicitor, subcontractor in the *Junior Books* case) should be liable towards the plaintiff (third party beneficiary or site owner), but whether he should be made to pay more to them than he would have had to pay had he been successfully sued by his co-contractor (testator, main contractor). This point was clearly identified by Lord Justice Goff in his judgment in *The Aliakmon* in the Court of Appeal. A contractual explanation (some kind of contract in favour of third parties) solves this problem instantly. For in such contracts the promisor (attorney, subcontractor) can oppose against the third party (beneficiary, site owner) all the exemptions and defences that he has against the promisee (testator, contractor). The contractual explanation also helps ensure that the nature of the relationship between plaintiff and defendant (in our examples owner/subcontractor, beneficiary/lawyer) is the same (contractual rather than tortious) as that of the defendant and his co-contractor (in our examples subcontractor/contractor, lawyer/testator). For if the two sets of relationships were different then they might be subject to different rules concerning such matters as jurisdiction, damages, limitation period, liability for omissions, and many others. These points have yet to receive proper consideration by our highest court.

consideration, then our courts will be tempted to resort to tort in order to fill the vacuum.[61] Academic purists are then left to vent their disagreement in learned journals in the hope that next time around they might bring greater doctrinal clarity in a subject that remains so endearingly casuistic.

3. The Escape 'Out' of Contract into the Domain of Tort

It is here that the contract/tort overlap has proved even more complicated; and wide dicta from some judges have not, it is submitted, helped clarify matters. For example, in *Tai Hing Cotton Mill Ltd.* v. *Liu Chong Hing Bank Ltd.*[62] Lord Scarman maintained that:

Their Lordships [did] not believe that there [was] anything to the advantage of the law's development in searching for a liability in tort where the parties are in a contractual relationship.

This was a bank–customer dispute, and his Lordship was eager to stress that his above-quoted comment was 'particularly' apt to commercial relationships. But later judgments, it is submitted unfortunately, seemed to have paid less attention to this proviso. So, in *Johnstone* v. *Bloomsbury Health Authority*[63] Sir Nicolas Browne-Wilkinson (as he then was) felt that the *Tai Hing* case:

shows that where there is a contractual relationship between the parties their respective rights and duties *have to be* analysed wholly in contractual terms and not as a mixture of duties in tort and contract.[64]

Below, when we discuss the case in the context of the employer's liability towards his employees, we shall argue that this approach, *in the context of that type of relationship*, may be particularly dangerous. For, if accepted and taken to its logical extremes, it could completely displace the law of employers' liabilities and put their employees at a disadvantage that may not be acceptable to modern society. In other words, the principle that in *commercial* transactions the contractual allocation of risks should not be disturbed by a subsequent escape 'out of contract' and 'into tort' (as has happened in many instances and with unfortunate consequences in the USA)[65] may be fully acceptable.[66] The same is true where the plaintiff is attempting to expand the defendant's duties beyond what is envisaged both by the express and implied terms of the contract *and* the accepted boundaries of the law of torts. So, in *Reid* v. *Rush & Tompkins Group plc*[67] an attempt to saddle employers with tortious liability for failing to provide their employee (who was working overseas) with personal

---

[61] Some authors have argued that the solution to the problem of the disappointed, intended legatee should be found in the law of succession. Thus, Weir (1995) 111 *LQR* 357. There may be something in this idea *de lege ferenda*; but *de lege lata*, it does not seem to be supportable. See Professor Cretney's remarks in (1996) 112 *LQR* 54–5. Thus, not for the first time, our law of torts has been called upon to rectify the deficiencies—real or perceived—of different parts of our private law.

[62] [1986] AC 80, 107.   [63] [1992] 1 QB 333.   [64] Ibid., 350 (emphasis added).

[65] For a brief discussion see Fleming, *The American Tort Process* (1988), *passim*.

[66] E.g. *National Bank of Greece SA* v. *Pinios Shipping Co (No. 1)* [1989] 3 WLR 185 (reversed on grounds not affecting this point: [1990] 1 AC 627); *Bank of Nova Scotia* v. *Hellenic Mutual War Risks Association (Bermuda) Ltd.* [1990] 1 QB 818; cf. *Canadian Pacific Hotels Ltd.* v. *Bank of Montreal* (1988) 40 DLR (4th) 385.

[67] [1989] 3 All ER 228.

accident insurance[68] was not successful since no such duty arose from contract nor could it be based on any existing tort rule. But the escape out of the contract regime into tort may be justifiable in other contexts where what one could call 'public policy' arguments would not favour the exclusion of rules deriving from the existing general law by the law of contract.[69]

Another area where Lord Scarman's pronouncement may also carry less weight (and, thus, recourse to the potentially more generous tort rules may be allowed) is that of concurrent contractual and tortious liability. This could be especially significant in the context of relationships between professionals and clients, for example, solicitors,[70] doctors,[71] insurance brokers,[72] and the like; and this position does not seem to have been undermined by wider dicta in such important House of Lords' decisions as *Pirelli*[73] and *Murphy*.[74] On the contrary, the concurrence rule was reaffirmed by the House of Lords in the important decision of *Henderson* v. *Merrett Syndicates Ltd.*[75] where Lord Goff said that:

. . . in the present context, the common law is not antipathetic to concurrent liability and . . . there is no sound basis for a rule which automatically restricts the claimant to either a tortious or a contractual remedy. The result may be untidy; but given that the tortious duty is imposed by the general law, and the contractual duty is attributable to the will of the parties, I do not find it objectionable that the claimant may be entitled to take advantage of the remedy which is most advantageous to him, subject only to ascertaining whether the tortious duty is so inconsistent with the applicable contract that, in accordance with ordinary principle, the parties must be taken to have agreed that the tortious remedy is to be limited or excluded.[76]

Select Bibliography

ATIYAH, P. S., 'Contracts, Promises and the Law of Obligations' (1978) 94 *LQR* 93.
BARTLETT, A. V. B., 'Concurrent Liability after *Murphy*' (1991) 7 *PN* 20.
BURROWS, A., 'Solving the Problem of Concurrent Liability' *Current Legal Problems* (1995), 103 ff.

[68] Or, alternatively, to advise him to obtain such insurance himself.

[69] The aforementioned *Johnstone* case offers an example. The same justification can be found in cases dealing with the liability of professionals (discussed in the next paragraph in the text) for, as Clerk and Lindsell correctly observe (7th edn., no. 1.08): 'It is highly unlikely that most plaintiffs in any sense voluntarily agree to forfeit such a benefit [i.e. deriving from the tort rules] when they enter into the relevant contract.'

[70] *Midland Bank Trust Co. Ltd.* v. *Hett, Stubbs & Kemp* [1979] Ch. 384.

[71] *Thake* v. *Maurice* [1986] QB 644.

[72] *Youell* v. *Bland Welch & Co. Ltd. (No. 2)* [1990] 2 Lloyd's Rep. 431, 459.

[73] *Pirelli General Cable Works Ltd.* v. *Oscar Faber and Partners* [1983] 2 AC 1.

[74] *Murphy* v. *Brentwood District Council* [1992] 1 AC 378.

[75] [1995] 2 AC 145 at 93–4. The reasoning of Oliver J (as he then was) in *Midland Bank Trust Co.* v. *Hett, Stubbs & Kemp* [1979] Ch. 384 was reaffirmed and the ambit of the Scarman dicta from *Tai Hing* further circumscribed.

[76] *Concurrent* thus does not imply that the two sets of duties (arising from contract and tort) will also be *co-extensive*; and it is precisely because the tort duty may be wider than the contract duty that the plaintiff may wish to rely upon it in preference to the contractual duty. This will be allowed provided there is nothing in the contract excluding such a tortious duty. See *Holt* v. *Payne Skillington (a firm)*, *The Times*, 22 Dec. 1995.

FRIDMAN, G. H. L., 'The Interaction of Tort and Contract' (1977) 93 *LQR* 422.

GUEST, A. G., 'Tort or Contract?' (1961) 3 *Malaya LR* 191.

HADDEN, T., 'Contract, Tort and Crime: The Forms of Legal Thought' (1971) 87 *LQR* 240.

HOLYOAK, J., 'Tort and Contract after *Junior Books*' (1983) 99 *LQR* 591.

—— 'Concurrent Liability in Tort and Contract' (1990) 6 *PN* 113.

MARKESINIS, B. S., 'An Expanding Tort Law—The Price of a Rigid Contract Law' (1987) 103 *LQR* 354.

—— 'Doctrinal Clarity in Tort Litigation' *The International Lawyer* 1992, vol. 25, no. 1, 953–66.

POULTON, W. D. C., 'Tort or Contract' (1966) 82 *LQR* 346.

REYNOLDS, F., 'Tort Actions in Contractual Situations' (1985) II *NZULR* 215.

WEIR, T., 'Complex Liabilities' in *Int. Encl. Comp. L.* xi. ch. 12 (1976).

WINFIELD, P. H., *The Province of the Law of Tort* (1931).

—— 'The Foundation of Liability in Tort' 27 *Col. LR* 1 (1927) (repr. in *Select Legal Essays*, 3 (1952)).

3. ELEMENTS OF WRONGDOING AND THE ROLE OF POLICY

The phrase 'law of contract' refers to the characteristics shared by every contract and not to the details of different types of contract. It is not possible to speak of a 'law of torts' in a similar sense. Though every tort is the breach of some legal duty, this gives little indication of the requirements of any particular tort. 'Duty' means a prohibition of a certain form of behaviour in a given kind of situation (e.g. you ought not to injure a person by a careless act, which means that the law recognises that there *could* be liability in a given kind of situation). 'Breach of duty' is constituted by the defendant's conduct violating this prohibition, which generally (but not always) has to be blameworthy in some way. In view of these vagaries, therefore, it might be thought appropriate to speak of a 'law of torts' rather than a 'law of tort', for there is no common set of characteristics which every tort has to possess. A few torts are complete without damage, for example, trespass and libel. These are said to be actionable *per se* and the absence of damage is not relevant to liability since, in these instances, the prime function of tort law is to vindicate private rights and not necessarily to compensate the victim. (Of course, if the victim has suffered actual damage he will also be awarded damages.) Other torts are complete without fault (blameworthiness) although, as we shall see, liability without fault remains the exception rather than the rule.

The majority of torts are complete and compensation must be made when there is conduct, causation, fault, and damage—an equation enshrined in a programmatic way in the famous article 1382 of the French Civil Code. What each of these elements means will be discussed as we proceed in appropriate sections of this book: it will suffice here to make two general points with regard to conduct. The first is that 'conduct' covers acts and omissions. An act in law is a bodily movement controllable by will, sometimes described as 'voluntary', as opposed to an unwilled movement that is involuntary. 'Voluntary' does not connote willingness, but only controllability. It is a basic element of liability that an act should be voluntary in this sense. Thus, in one case a man who was carried onto the plaintiff's land did not act and so was not liable in trespass; whereas a man who was induced by threats to do so was liable because, although he acted under threat, his mind still controlled his movement.[77] The second point is that the common law, unlike the modern civil-law systems, has, up to now, evinced a marked reluctance to assimilate liability for omissions into liability for wrongful acts. The matter will be discussed more fully in Chapter 2, where it presents its greater interest, though it is also of importance to the law of nuisance.

With regard to fault—which, incidentally, is not a term of art in English law—one should note that it assumes three forms: malice, intention (including recklessness), and negligence. The first, the most reprehensible state of mind, has assumed different meanings in different contexts, but it could broadly be equated to spite. Only a few torts make malice an ingredient of liability though proof of it in others can increase the plaintiff's compensation, while in some torts, for example defamation, it can negative one of the accepted defences. Intention signifies the state of mind of a person who foresees and desires a particular result (or is deemed to have foreseen and desired an inevitable result). It is often bracketed with recklessness where the actor foresees, but does not desire, a particular result that is not regarded as inevitable. Negligence, discussed in the next chapter, in one sense refers to the state of mind of a person who fails to advert to the foreseeable consequences of his conduct, as a reasonable man would have done. In another sense it refers to careless behaviour, which is the failure to act as a reasonable man who, having foreseen the consequences, would have acted. Yet a third use of 'negligence' denotes a separate tort of that name (and, in this book, whenever confusion might arise over the use of the term in this sense, we have capitalised the word). It is with the last two meanings that the law of tort is mainly concerned. These terms are not always used in the same way or with precision by writers or by courts, and the student should learn to understand the meaning of each term in its context.

The pattern of liability resulting from the complex interplay of the above requirements is difficult to grasp. It may therefore be helpful in conveying at least a general idea to present it in diagrammatic form (see Fig. 1.1).

The important feature of the common law of tort is that even if the requirements of conduct, fault, causation, and damage are present, it still does not follow that there will be liability.[78] For instance, the kind of harm sustained by the plaintiff may not be recognised as attracting liability. Thus, mental suffering (in the form of mere pain or grief), as distinguished from nervous shock, has, traditionally, not been recognised and hence it has not been compensated; and even shock was recognised by the courts only step by step. The same has been true with pure economic loss, though, as we shall see in Chapter 2, courts have

---

[77] Compare *Smith* v. *Stone* (1647), Style 65; 82 ER 533 (not liable) and *Gilbert* v. *Stone* (1647), Style 72; 82 ER 539 (liable).

[78] This point was the subject of a debate between Salmond, who talked of a law of torts, and Winfield, who believed in a law of tort. The history of the dispute, along with a suggested compromise, can be found in Williams's article in [1939] *CLJ* 111.

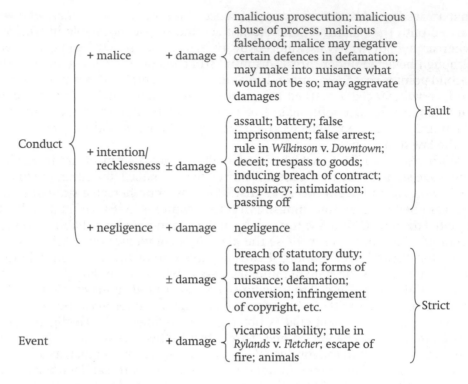

Fig. 1.1 Patterns of Liability

vacillated on this matter and have now moved towards a mixed regime. Alternatively, one or other of the parties to the action may not be recognised by the law. For policy reasons the 'Queen's enemies' are not recognised as capable of suing in respect of injuries inflicted on them. More significantly, as we shall see in Chapter 3, no one can sue in respect of a breach of statutory duty unless it can be shown that the statute in question recognises the category of persons to which that person belongs. For historical reasons, until the enactment of the Crown Proceedings Act 1947, the Crown could not be liable in tort. Trade unions used to enjoy extensive immunity from tortious liability when acting in contemplation or furtherance of trade disputes, but this was considerably reduced by the several Acts of Parliament in the 1980s.[79] Barristers, too, enjoy immunity in respect of work done in court, though this immunity may be on its way out, especially in view of the fact that liability insurance is now obligatory. If diplomats commit torts they cannot be sued, but their insurance companies can be made liable.[80] International comity demands that diplomats shall remain immune from suit;[81] justice demands that victims shall receive compensation; and insurance makes it possible to give effect to both considerations

---

[79] See Chapter 5.   [80] *Dickinson* v. *Del Solar* [1930] 1 KB 376; *Zoernsch* v. *Waldock* [1964] 1 WLR 675.
[81] A diplomat is under a legal duty to pay, which is unenforceable against him, but such a duty is a sufficient basis on which to ground the liability of the insurance company.

via the legal device of the 'unenforceable duty'—a striking example of the manipulation of concepts to give effect to policy decisions.

It will be noted that in all these cases the courts were not concerned with individual plaintiffs or defendants, but were expressing a dictate of general policy that there is to be no prima-facie liability. The device used by the common law to embody policy decisions as to whether liability should even be countenanced in the kind of situation in question is that of 'duty' or 'duty-situation'. In Professor Fleming's words[82]

Though fashions have shifted . . . the prevailing pattern is to express in terms of 'duty' judicial policies of a more or less generalised nature . . . leaving to 'remoteness of damage' the evaluation of more contingent and random features of each particular case.

The student can find many examples where liability was not imposed because, as the courts put it, there was no legal 'duty'. The notion of 'duty' has thus played a cardinal role in the common law of torts, but since it is talked about most frequently in relation to the law of negligence, namely, as a 'duty to take care', its detailed consideration will be deferred until Chapter 2. Yet, as will become clearer in Chapter 2, duty, carelessness, and remoteness are nothing more than verbal devices that help courts in formulating decisions, but do not really explain them. What is important is that the student should realise that all these concepts are tools to be used as necessary; they are means towards an end, not the end itself. Attachment to concepts as such, to the exclusion of the socio-economic pressures that guide the way in which they are used, can distract lawyers from the real policy issues that lie behind them. The brief discussion we have included in Section 4 on the important Canadian decision of *Norsk Pacific Steamship Co. Ltd.* v. *Canadian National Railway Co.* will make these points more obvious and facilitate the treatment of this subject in the next chapter (on negligence).

In accordance with what has just been said, we shall point out in the next chapter that which concept is chosen to justify a particular result will often (though not always) be a matter of personal choice by the judge. In some cases, however, a particular aim may dictate the adoption of one concept instead of another. *Rondel* v. *Worsley*[83] shows that an important reason (allegedly) in favour of a barrister's immunity from liability for his conduct of a case is the danger that action against him might be an indirect retrial of the previous case, which has exhausted the possibility of appeal. This aim could only be achieved through the terminology of 'no duty-situation'. If the 'lack of care' approach had been adopted instead of 'duty', as the plaintiff had urged upon the court, the result in that particular case might still have been the same (since it was by no means clear that the defendant barrister had been careless). However, the overall policy aim of not clogging up the courts with claims from disgruntled clients would not have been achieved. For it would have left open the possibility that some other frustrated litigant might sue his legal adviser and concentrate on the latter's lack of care, thereby bringing in the rights and wrongs of the earlier decision.

[82] *The Law of Torts* (8th edn., 1992), 136.   [83] [1969] 1 AC 191.

Another case of importance is *Smith* v. *Littlewoods Corp.*,[84] which will be discussed later in the chapters on negligence and nuisance. Here suffice it to say that Lord Mackay LC decided the case on what, in textbook terms, could be described as the element of carelessness, whereas Lord Goff relied on the notion of duty of care. The practical difference between these two judgments is that the first does not exclude in categorical terms the possibility of recovery in the case of omissions (in general), whereas the second one, which has prevailed in practice, does.

Nowadays writers and judges are increasingly prepared to bring policy issues into the open. For example, the so-called 'opening of the floodgates to litigation' argument used to play a dominant role in denying liability for nervous shock[85] and economic loss.[86] One can understand the fear that if such losses were to become automatically compensatable, the courts might be inundated with claims. This kind of argument, however, is questionable when it leads to a *blanket*[87] denial of justice. Also, it can be accorded more significance than it deserves, since experience has shown that even where liability has been recognised (thus creating new duty-situations) the corresponding increase in litigation has not, on the whole, been as great as had been feared. For the courts do possess other means of keeping liability under control. We shall see, for example, that allowing trespassers an action in negligence against occupiers of land does not deprive the courts of their ability to refuse claims by non-meritorious entrants.[88] But it has enabled them to do justice in other instances where in the past this was not possible because trespassers used not to be recognised as capable of suing in negligence at all. Some decisions of the House of Lords in the early 1980s on nervous shock and economic loss suggest that this 'floodgates' argument was losing favour with the courts,[89] though more recent decisions show that the fears associated with it have not yet been eradicated. The so-called 'cable cases' offer a good illustration of how policy arguments can help determine the outcome of litigation. The floodgates argument has been successfully invoked in these cases.

Another policy factor at work has been the role of insurance practice. Again the *Norsk* case contains one of the best discussions currently available on this

---

[84] Discussed by Markesinis in (1989) 105 *LQR* 104.

[85] See now *McLoughlin* v. *O'Brian* [1983] 1 AC 410.

[86] E.g. *Spartan Steel & Alloys Ltd.* v. *Martin & Co. (Contractors) Ltd.* [1973] QB 27, 38–9, per Lord Denning MR.

[87] As will be noted in Chapter 2, below, English law has a tendency to create 'blanket' immunities and then to justify them by reference to various policy factors. This is, nowadays, happening with increasing frequency in the case of various public authorities such as the social security services, local authorities, the police, the Crown Prosecution Service, etc. It remains to be seen, however, whether they will survive a challenge—inevitable we believe—under Strasbourg law or the Human Rights Act, 1998. The first pronouncement of the Strasbourg Court on this matter came in *Osman* v. *United Kingdom*—*The Times*, 5 Nov. 1998—and was related to the (apparently) blanket immunity given to the police under the House of Lords' ruling in *Hill* v. *Chief Constable of West Yorkshire Police* [1989] AC 53. This suggests that such immunities may be seen as 'disproportionate restriction on [a litigant's] right of access to a court, in breach of article 6.1 of the European Convention on Human Rights. We shall return to this topic in Chapters 2 and 3, but here we draw the reader's attention to the growing 'Europeanisation' of our tort law.

[88] Chapter 3, Section 3(2)(f).

[89] *McLoughlin* v. *O'Brian* [1983] 1 AC 410; *Junior Books Ltd.* v. *Veitchi Co. Ltd.* [1983] AC 520. The fear, however, has resurfaced in more recent cases.

subject; and it is to be regretted that we have no equivalent decision from a British court to hold out to our students as a model of a stimulating analysis of the law. Generally speaking, however, it would appear highly advisable that before extensions (or limitations) of liability are considered one should study their economic and insurance implications and weigh these against the advantage of making the negligent person liable.

All such matters, however, cannot be evaluated properly as long as we do not look beyond the formal conceptualism of the law—something that British judges and academics seem averse to doing. Overwork may be a reason; but not an entirely convincing one—at any rate as far as our highest court is concerned (and, certainly, not convincing as far as academics are concerned.) Having said that, however, we should at the same time never lose sight of the fact that all extra-legal dimensions only become meaningful in the light of the law itself. While a study of the law alone will yield but an incomplete picture of the problem with which it has to deal, to wander into the economic and social surroundings without a clear grasp of the rules and limits of the law will fail even to reveal what those problems are. So nothing we have said thus far should be understood to diminish the prime need to know the law and to acquire a sufficient mastery of its techniques. The purpose of this Introduction is to give some idea of the wider context, an appreciation of which, we contend, is essential for the full understanding and further sensible development of the law.

Select Bibliography

EHRENZWEIG, A. A., 'Assurance Oblige—A Comparative Study' 15 *Law and CP* 445 (1950).
FLEMING, J. G., 'Remoteness and Duty: The Control Devices in Liability for Negligence' 31 *Can. BR* 471 (1953).
GREEN, L., 'Tort Law Public Law in Disguise' 38 *Texas LR* 257 (1959).
JAMES, FLEMING, 'Accident Liability Reconsidered: The Impact of Liability Insurance' 57 *Yale LJ* 549 (1948).
—— and THORNTON, J. K., 'The Impact of Insurance on the Law of Torts' 15 *Law and CP* 431 (1950).
MARKESINIS, B. S., 'Policy Factors and the Law of Torts', *The Cambridge Lectures* (1981) 199.
SYMMONS, C. R., 'The Duty of Care in Negligence: Recently Expressed Policy Elements' (1971) 34 *MLR* 394, 528.

4. ECONOMIC ANALYSIS OF TORT LAW

1. Some General Remarks

In the last few years, common-law courts, particularly in the United States, have made increasing use of techniques of economic analysis in decision-making.[90] These techniques derive from welfare economics, which see the

---

[90] For a prediction of the growing influence of economic analysis in legal doctrine, see Ackerman, *Reconstructing American Law* (1984).

legal system as a potential means of enhancing the efficient allocation of society's resources. From this point of view, the law is 'a giant pricing machine' in which 'laws act as prices or taxes which provide incentives',[91] thereby complementing the allocative mechanisms of the market. The law of tort, and specifically the torts of nuisance and negligence, were the focus for many of the early breakthroughs in the economic theory of law,[92] and it has continued to provide fertile ground for scholarship and debate throughout the common-law world. However, very little of this academic effort has filtered through to the English courts, although this might (just conceivably) begin to change. Certainly, the judgment of Lord Hoffman in *Stovin* v. *Wise*,[93] which used economic reasoning to help explain the limited extent of duties of affirmative action in the tort of negligence, could serve as a model for further imitation.

There may be good reasons for this limited judicial reception of economic ideas. A great deal of economic writing in this area is difficult for non-specialists to penetrate. Having said that, there are now several texts and articles which are clearly written and reasonably accessible to the non-specialist.[94] A more serious objection is that the line taken in particular by the Chicago School and its followers has proved controversial. The 'law and economics movement' has been variously criticised for applying economic principles in an inconsistent and deficient way.[95] It has also been accused for failing to recognise the value judgments which are inherent in economic analysis;[96] and for seeking to advance the radical political agenda of the New Right at the expense of other points of view.[97] Whatever the rights and wrongs of these claims, under these circumstances it is far from clear that the economic approach to law could be adopted by the bench, which in this respect is no better qualified than academics are, to choose between the competing claims of the protagonists.

To take this view would, however, make the mistake of identifying just one school of thought—the Chicago School—as encompassing the whole field of law and economics. In reality this field is extremely diverse and the pioneering work of writers such as the Nobel Laureate Ronald Coase has been applied in a wide range of contexts.[98] At the same time, most analysts share enough com-

---

[91] C. Veljanovski, *The Economics of Law: An Introductory Text*, Institute of Economic Affairs, Hobart Paper 114 (1990).

[92] See, in particular, G. Calabresi, 'Some Thoughts on Risk Distribution and the Law of Torts' (1961) 70 *Yale LJ* 400, and *The Cost of Accidents: A Legal and Economic Analysis* (1970); and R. Posner, 'A Theory of Negligence' (1972) 1 *Jo. LS* 29. Ronald Coase used examples from nuisance law in his seminal article 'The Problem of Social Cost' (1960) 3 *J. Law & Econ.* 1.

[93] [1996] 1 AC 923, 944.

[94] In particular, in this field, Landes and Posner, *The Economic Structure of Tort Law* (1987).

[95] G. Cohen, 'Posnerian Jurisprudence and the Economic Analysis of Law: The View from the Bench', (1985) 133 *U. Pa. LR* 1, 117.

[96] This is a point frequently made by the critical legal studies school. See e.g. M. Kelman, 'Consumption Theory, Production Theory, and Ideology in the Coase Theorem' (1979) 52 *S. Cal. LR* 669.

[97] L. Caplan, 'Does Good Economics Make Good Law?' *California Lawyer* (May 1985), 28, cited in B. White, 'Coase and the Courts: Economics for the Common Man' (1987) 72 *Iowa LR* 577, at 579.

[98] For recent discussion of Coase's work and its relationship to the Chicago School see R. Ellickson, 'The Case for Coase and against "Coaseanism" ' (1989) 99 *Yale LJ* 611, discussing Donahue, 'Diverting the Coasean River: Incentive Schemes to Reduce Unemployment Spells' (1989) 99 *Yale LJ* 549. See also G. Calabresi, 'The Pointlessness of Pareto: Carrying Coase Further' (1991) 100 *Yale LJ* 1211, for discussion of the tensions between regulatory and libertarian aspects of Coase's work.

mon ground to make the application of economic techniques a realistic possibility in certain parts of the law. It is not necessary to share Judge Richard Posner's view (expressed in his academic capacity) that economic analysis can be a universal solvent for legal and ethical problems,[99] to see that for some issues at least economic techniques can provide a useful, additional tool to courts. One of Judge Posner's more forceful critics has written that 'economic analysis by itself, unencumbered by value choices, can be an effective aid in analysing the issues presented in legal disputes, clarifying when a value choice must be made, and identifying what choices are available'.[100]

2. The 'Coase Theorem' and the Concept of Transaction Costs

The starting-point for economic analysis of law is the proposition known as the 'Coase Theorem', which can be stated as follows: the assignment of legal rights and liabilities has no implications for economic efficiency as long as the parties involved in a particular dispute can bargain costlessly, that is to say, with *zero transaction costs*, to resolve that dispute. This surprising result—surprising, at least, to lawyers—is explained by Coase by the example of a rancher whose cattle trespass on to the adjoining land of a farmer, damaging his crops. If the right to graze cattle is worth more to the rancher than the farmer's right to keep his crops free from interference is worth to him, it is irrelevant that a court might give the farmer the legal right to enjoin the cattle trespass. In a world without transaction costs the party valuing the right the most highly will buy it from the other. Such an exchange will lead to a welfare gain since, by definition, it will make both parties better off than they were before the exchange. The court's assignment of legal liability has *distributional* implications and so will affect the relative *private* wealth of the two parties, but it does not, under these assumptions, affect the net *social cost* of the activity one way or the other.[101]

To appreciate this point it is necessary to bear in mind that economic analysis of the law focuses on the net cost to society *both* of certain harmful activities *and* of the legal intervention designed to offset them. Free exchange, based on contract, is seen as the normal means of enhancing the value of economic resources. This, of course, is on the (important) assumption that both parties to the exchange are acting rationally to pursue their own self-interest, and that their contract is not vitiated by force or fraud. Then, the exchange will necessarily make them both better off than they were before. Tort law, by contrast, sets up a series of income transfers from one party to another through liability

---

[99] See in particular *The Economics of Justice* (1981), for an attempt to make a wide ethical justification for the use of economic analysis in law.

[100] Professor Barbara Ann White, op. cit. (Select Bibliography), 579.

[101] See Coase, 'The Problem of Social Cost', 104: 'It is necessary to know whether the damaging business is liable or not for damage caused, since without the establishment of this initial delimitation of rights there can be no market transactions to transfer and recombine them. But the ultimate result (which maximizes the value of production) is independent of the legal position if the pricing system is assumed to work without cost.' If the assumption of zero transaction costs is maintained, any *wealth effect* which results from the transfer of legal liability to one side as opposed to another will, in the end, be unable to counter the movement of resources to their most efficient use: see Calabresi, 'Transaction Costs, Resource Allocation and Liability Rule—A Comment' (1968) 11 *J. Law & Econ.* 67; and Coase, 'Notes on the Problem of Social Cost', ch. 6 in *The Firm, the Market and the Law* (1988), at 170–4.

rules requiring the payment of compensation. An income transfer, dictated by a court, cannot be assumed to create economic surplus value in the same way that a contract would. Indeed, because of the administrative costs of income-transfer systems such as tort law or social security, it is possible that it will impose a net cost on society. Tort is therefore supplementary to contract in ensuring an efficient allocation of economic resources; but the primacy of contract does not necessarily hold in a situation where market-based exchange is inhibited by high transaction costs.

The Coase Theorem, then, reminds lawyers that decisions on legal liability are only the starting-point of a process of resource allocation, which is continued via the market. As a proposition, the 'theorem' is essentially tautologous, in that it follows from the way in which Coase appears to define 'transaction costs' very widely to include all barriers to private exchange. However, it is clear that Coase did not set out just to restate the basic axioms of welfare economics. His point in using the model of costless exchange was to illustrate the economic functions of legal rules in the real-life situations where transaction costs are high:

If market transactions were costless, all that matters (questions of equity apart) is that the rights of the various parties should be well defined and the results of legal actions easy to forecast. But as we have seen, the situation is quite different when market transactions are so costly as to make it difficult to change the arrangement of rights established by the law. In such cases the courts directly influence economic activity. It would therefore seem desirable that the courts should understand the economic consequence of their decisions and should, in so far as this is possible without creating too much uncertainty about the legal position itself, take these consequences into account when making their decisions.[102]

Thus the concept of transaction costs is central to Coasean analysis. In terms of contracting *process*, transaction costs may usefully be described as the costs of arriving at an agreement, monitoring it during performance, and enforcing it through legal or other sanctions.[103] More fundamentally, though, transaction costs include anything which prevents a competitive market equilibrium being arrived at through exchange: they include externalities, information costs, strategic behaviour, monopoly, 'small numbers bargaining', adverse selection, and all the other causes of incomplete or failed exchange identified by economic theory.[104] The Coase Theorem may look like a tautology, but this is irrelevant since the purpose of the concept of transaction costs is not, in the end, to examine the state of competitive equilibrium. Their purpose is, instead, to direct attention to the institutional arrangements that arise by virtue of the failure of the free market to arrive at this state unaided.

Coase's 1960 paper 'The Problem of Social Cost' laid out a basic framework for analysing the way in which different types of legal intervention interact with economic activity. This was later extended and developed by Guido

---

[102] 'The Problem of Social Cost', 119.
[103] C. J. Dahlman, 'The Problem of Externality' (1979) 22 *J. Law & Econ.* 148, approved by Coase, *The Firm, the Market and the Law*, 6.
[104] Hovenkamp, 'Marginal Utility and the Coase Theorem' (1990) 75 *Cornell L. Rev.* 783, 787.

Calabresi and Douglas Melamed in a paper entitled 'Property Rules, Liability Rules and Inalienability: One View of the Cathedral'.[105] At one level, the state can facilitate private exchange simply by instituting a system of *property rights*, which then form the subject-matter of private agreements.[106] If an 'entitle-ment' is protected by a 'property rule' in the form of an injunction or criminal sanction against interference, the effect is that it may be appropriated from its owner only through exchange. This is the least intrusive level of state inter-vention since it remains up to the parties to set the value of the entitlement. By contrast, in the case of a 'liability rule' the asset may be taken in return for the payment of damages representing what a court considers to be its value. In the case of an 'inalienable' entitlement, the law prevents its sale even between will-ing buyers and sellers; thus rules such as the ban on personal servitude simul-taneously 'protect' the entitlement while limiting its grant. Transaction-cost analysis can help to indicate why certain entitlements receive these particular forms of legal protection. Accident law protects the right to life and limb through liability rules, on the whole, because of the prohibitive costs of pre-accident bargaining between, for example, all road users and pedestrians. High transaction costs may mean that an accurate market evaluation cannot be made—the market assessment 'is either unavailable or too expensive com-pared to a collective valuation'[107]—and that bargaining over the entitlement is impossible, so that 'an initial entitlement, though incorrect in terms of eco-nomic efficiency, will not be altered in the marketplace'.[108] In these cases a lia-bility rule is preferable to a property rule which could cement in place an inefficient allocation. This model has been used for the analysis of nuisance and other areas of tort and property law.

Legal intervention, then, can enhance efficiency in situations where private bargaining will not lead to an optimal outcome. Coase is vague as to how the courts should achieve this goal, and proceeds by way of examples drawn from nuisance law, rather than through the formulation of a single, general princi-ple. However, in his discussion of the cases, it is possible to discern the rule later formulated more precisely by Judge Posner, namely that in circumstances of high transaction costs the court should allocate a legal right to *the party who values it the most highly*. In this way the court reproduces the outcome which the market would have arrived at under circumstances of pure competition (and which will therefore be welfare maximising).[109] Finally, Coase considers the possibility that the state will act through regulation or criminal legislation, restricting the scope of private activity. The point is not that regulation is nec-essarily illegitimate, but rather that it must be shown to be superior to the use of other methods in achieving the intended goal:

[105] (1972) 85 *Harv. LR* 1089.
[106] This is the theme of Coase's 1959 paper, 'The Federal Communications Commission' (1959) 2 *J. Law & Econ.* 1.
[107] Calabresi and Melamed (1972) 85 *Harv. LR* 1089, 1110. [108] Ibid., 1089, 1119.
[109] See Coase, 'The Problem of Social Cost', 119–33; Posner, *Economic Analysis of Law* (1972), 13–14, 45; and see the critique of B. White, 'Coase and the Courts: Economics for the Common Man' (1987) 72 *Iowa LR* 577.

From these considerations it follows that direct governmental regulations will not necessarily give better results than leaving the problem to be solved by the market or the
firm. But equally, there is no reason why, on occasion, such governmental administrative action should not lead to an improvement in economic efficiency. This would seem
particularly likely when, as is normally the case with the smoke nuisance, a large number of people is involved and when therefore the costs of handling the problem through
the market or the firm may be high.[110]

3. Accident Compensation and the Internalisation of Social Costs

Legal intervention may affect economic behaviour by, amongst other things,
'internalising' the social costs of dangerous and harmful activities to those
responsible for them:

Externalities are situations where the costs influencing individual behaviour diverge significantly from the costs to society. As a result the actions of rational individuals lead to
inefficient outcomes—those activities which impose (uncompensated) external costs are
over-expanded and those which supply uncompensated external benefits are under-
expanded. The law, by shifting these costs and by creating incentives, can cause individuals to consider these external effects ('internalise' them). In the case of external
harms the efficiency goal of the law is to impose third-party losses on those who could
bear them most cheaply.[111]

The result is a price structure which more accurately reflects the net costs of
various kinds of economic activity.

In this regard, Calabresi's book *The Costs of Accidents* illustrates the variety of
goals which may be imputed to the law of negligence. Instead of viewing tort
law in the conventional way as a means of satisfying the claims of individual
accident victims to compensation for their injuries, Calabresi insists that 'apart
from the requirements of justice [it is] axiomatic that the principal function of
accident law is to reduce the sum of the costs of accidents and the costs of
avoiding accidents'.[112] The costs of avoidance and the costs of administering
compensation systems must be taken into account, just as much as the injuries
and economic losses sustained by victims. The goal of overall cost-reduction can
be achieved through a variety of means—spreading the risk of loss as widely as
possible, imposing liability on defendants with 'deep pockets', or seeking to
deter careless behaviour through market incentives ('general deterrence')—and
through a variety of systems of compensation—fault-based liability with private insurance, social insurance, enterprise liability, or regulation. For
Calabresi, the purpose of economic analysis is not to dictate any particular system of compensation, but to 'indicate the questions we must ask in deciding
whether one system is preferable to another'.[113]

---

[110] 'The Problem of Social Cost', 118.
[111] Harris and Veljanovski, 'Liability for Economic Loss in Tort', in Furmston (ed.), *The Law of Tort: Policies
and Trends in Liability for Damage to Property and Economic Loss* (1986), 48.
[112] *The Costs of Accidents*, 26.
[113] Ibid., 312–13.

One way in which tort law may promote allocative efficiency is by identifying the 'least cost avoider' as the appropriate party to be assigned liability. This frequently means assigning liability to the 'deep pocket' defendant or 'best briber', since he or she will have the resources to initiate further exchanges in the market if the court cannot make a definitive allocation based on efficiency. Given the limited information which the court has available, this is more likely than not to be the case. For example, where an enterprise causes pollution damage to residents of a district, it may be more feasible to envisage the enterprise buying out the residents rather than vice versa. If the right to enjoin the pollution is accorded to the residents, the enterprise will buy them out if it values the right to pollute more highly than they do. But if the court grants the enterprise the right to carry on polluting, it is unlikely that the residents, given their lack of resources and access to contracting expertise, will bargain to buy the right from the enterprise even if they do value it more highly.

Calabresi makes no dogmatic insistence on the primacy of market solutions. Distributional questions are seen as important, not just because the law may have goals other than allocative efficiency, but because an unequal distribution of resources places constraints upon the effectiveness of any market-based approach. He thus maintains that 'unless the distribution of income—and therefore of goods and services—is satisfactory, it may be foolish to say that society is better off if all consumers can choose what they want for themselves after seeing what the true costs of their possible choices are.'[114] *The Costs of Accidents* concludes with a substantial indictment of the fault system, which is found to be defective both as a loss spreader and as a system of primary cost control.

4. The Theory of the Inherent Efficiency of the Common Law

The work of Judge Richard Posner demonstrates how price-theoretic economic techniques can be applied to non-market situations, such as family relations, crime and punishment, and the administration of the legal system. It is this wide-ranging and novel application of economic analysis, beyond the traditional areas of anti-trust and market regulation, which is said to account for the distinctive character of the 'new law and economics'.[115] Posner's second distinctive claim is to have revealed the implicit 'economic structure' or logic of the common law. In contrast to Calabresi's open discussion of policy-making, Posner aims to provide a 'positive' economic theory of the law. Central to this is his argument that the common-law courts tend to pursue the goal of welfare efficiency, even if they do not necessarily do so explicitly. One illustration is the fault principle in negligence, the 'dominant function' of which, Posner suggests, 'is to generate rules of liability that if followed will bring about, at least approximately, the efficient—the cost-justified-level of accidents'.[116] More

---

[114] *Costs of Accidents*, 78; see also G. Calabresi and P. Bobbit, *Tragic Choices* (1976), 32.

[115] Veljanovski, *The Economics of Law*, op. cit. (n. 91 above), 14–15.

[116] 'A Theory of Negligence' (1972) 1 *Jo. LS* 29, 33. This thesis is developed more systematically with William S. Landes in Posner and Landes, *The Economic Structure of Tort Law* (1987). An early analysis which contradicts the focus of Landes and Posner on the fault principle is J. P. Brown, 'Toward an

precisely, the so-called Hand formula[117] provides a mechanism for setting standards of care, which serves to minimise the total costs to society of any accident. The principles of causation and contributory negligence, and the calculation of damages, can also be seen as maximising the relevant incentives on parties to take the appropriate level of care, although here Posner criticises twentieth-century statutory developments reducing the importance of contributory negligence and altering the basis for calculating damages for wrongful death.[118] The answer to the question of why the common law should produce positive outcomes for efficiency when legislation, by and large, does not, lies in the nature of legal process, which can itself be analysed in an economic way. The case-law system in effect creates a 'market' for legal ideas in which concepts and rules are thrown into competition with each other (precedents are a 'capital stock'). The possibility of litigation means that parties themselves will seek to have inefficient rules overturned. Courts do not have the power to issue general rules of redistribution, and litigation generally takes the form of the assertion of individual rights, not general group interests. By contrast, Posner uses the arguments of the 'public choice' school to argue that the legislative process encourages collective action by pressure groups to bring about redistributive measures at the expense of the general good.[119]

Posner uses criteria of efficiency borrowed from welfare economics. According to the criterion of 'Pareto efficiency', a reallocation of resources will be welfare enhancing if it makes at least one person better off without making anyone else worse off. By definition, this will normally be achieved through exchange. An allocation is 'Pareto optimal' when no further change is possible without making somebody worse off, a kind of 'unanimity principle'. For most of his analyses Posner utilises a variation of the Pareto principle known as 'Kaldor-Hicks efficiency'. According to this principle, an allocation is efficient if it leads to a net welfare gain out of which winners could compensate the losers if they chose to (hence the use of the expression 'potential Pareto efficiency' to describe Kaldor-Hicks).[120] The use of Kaldor-Hicks is justified by the restrictiveness of the Pareto 'unanimity' principle. However, its use takes Posner a long way from libertarian positions on the value of freedom of contract; if the courts are applying some version of the Kaldor-Hicks principle, then 'the efficient solution is coercively imposed after some third party determination of costs and benefits'.[121] Following the direction hinted at by Coase, Posner argues that welfare will be maximised in a situation of high transaction costs by a court transferring the right in question to the party who values it most highly. For

Economic Theory of Liability' (1973) 2 *Jo. LS* 323; and see also S. Shavell, *Economic Analysis of Accident Law* (1987); I. Ayres, 'A Theoretical Fox Meets Empirical Hedgehogs: Competing Approaches to Accident Economics' (1988) 82 *NWUL Rev.* 387.

[117] Which measures breach of a duty of care by comparing the cost of precautions against the magnitude of the harm and likelihood of its occurring.

[118] Posner, 'A Theory of Negligence', op. cit.; and *Economic Analysis of Law*, ch. 6.

[119] *Economic Analysis of Law*, chs. 19–20. For criticism, see A. I. Ogus, 'Legislation, the Courts and the Demand for Compensation', ch. 6, in R. C. O. Matthews (ed.), *Economy and Democracy* (1986).

[120] *Economic Analysis of Law*, 12–15.

[121] Veljanovski, 'The New Law and Economics: A Research Review', Oxford Centre for Socio-Legal Studies (1982), repr. in Ogus and Veljanovski (eds.), *Readings in the Economics of Law and Regulation*, op. cit., 21.

this purpose value is defined by willingness to pay, so that in effect the right is allocated to the party who can make the highest bid for it. In this way the court 'mimics' the outcome of the market. The result may well be (in most cases, must be) to redistribute income from poor to rich. This analysis has been criticised as tending to define away questions of distribution and inequality. The result is that: 'the transfers that come about against a background of wealth inequality are fine; any that come about against a background of inequality in strength, or the power to organise and apply strength, are unjustifiable. Some inequalities are apparently more equal than others—and all without reference to any apparent normative criterion at all.'[122] Posner's work remains the most comprehensive and thought provoking, but also the most controversial application of economic techniques to the analysis of law.

5. Empirical Studies of the Effects of Tort Law

The pioneering studies of the economics of tort law were largely conceptual and theoretical. Increasingly, though, the emphasis within tort law scholarship has turned towards empirical studies. Some of these are referred to in later chapters of this book. In 1996 a major study by lawyers and economists from the University of Toronto was published which draws together the diverse evidence on the economic effects of tort, making it possible for the first time to assess the overall impact of economic research in this field.[123] The authors conclude that, taken as whole, tort law does not perform well when evaluated against the three normative criteria of deterrence, compensation, and corrective justice. Where tort performs a deterrent function, it tends to do so in conjunction with certain aspects of the insurance system (such as the varying of insurance premiums according to the risk of damage occurring). Similarly, tort, on its own, fails to ensure effective compensation, particularly for the consequences of product-related accidents and medical injuries. But, as the authors accept, 'tort cannot be meaningfully evaluated except by reference to its alternatives',[124] and it not always clear that no-fault compensation schemes or social insurance, taken in the round, can be said to perform better. Although they argue that tort law systems of the kind which prevail in most common-law jurisdictions should shrink, to be replaced by no-fault insurance schemes and wider dependence on universal health service provision, changes of this kind require legislative intervention which, in most systems, does not seem imminent. Moreover, legislative interventions may lead to problems of their own, including high administrative costs and the blunting of deterrence effects. Concerns such as these led to retrenchment, in the early 1990s, of the New Zealand scheme, which in the 1970s had replaced tort law with a form of state-backed social insurance as the principal source of compensation for accidents.

---

[122] A. A. Leff, 'Economic Analysis of Law: Some Realism about Nominalism' (1974) 60 *Virginia LR* 451, at 481 and 459 respectively.

[123] Dewees, Duff, and Trebilcock, *Exploring the Domain of Accident Law* (Select Bibliography).

[124] Ibid., 12.

6. Economic Analysis in the Context of One Tort Case: The *Norsk* Decision[125]

(A) THE FACTS OF *NORSK*

The New Westminster Railways Bridge, which spans the Fraser River near Vancouver and carries a single railway track, is owned by the Department of Public Works of Canada (PWC). A barge, towed by a tug owned by the defendants (Norsk), and negligently navigated by its captain, damaged the bridge, necessitating its closure for several weeks. As a result, the Canadian National Railway (CNR), who were the plaintiffs in this action, had to re-route traffic over another bridge, incurring considerable additional expense. CNR, who accounted for 86 per cent of the use of the bridge, had a licence contract with PWC which, *inter alia*, obliged them to provide PWC with inspection, consulting, maintenance, and repair services of the bridge as and when requested by PWC and at PWC's expense. Since the marine traffic using the Fraser River was, at the site of the bridge, heavy and had, in the past, occasioned structural damage to the bridge leading to its closure, the licence agreement between CNR and PWC provided that the former could not claim damages from the latter in the event of closure of the bridge in an emergency. CNR owned the land (and tracks) on either side of the bridge (but not the bridge itself or the rails on it). Because they did not own the bridge itself, the loss they suffered was entirely 'economic' or financial. The question, therefore, arose whether they were owed a duty of care in tort in respect of these losses. CNR's tort action for its economic losses was accepted at first instance, by the Court of Appeal, and by four judges out of seven in the Supreme Court of Canada.

(B) THE MAJORITY AND CONCURRING OPINIONS

The majority (McLachlin, L'Heureux-Dubé, and Corry JJ) and minority (La Forest, Sopinka, and Iacobucci JJ) were in agreement on several points. Thus, first, *both* agreed that the 'more flexible approach' to economic loss set out by the House of Lords in *Anns* v. *Merton London Borough Council* was preferable to the reasoning in *Murphy* v. *Brentwood District Council*, in which the approach of *Anns* had been repudiated. *Murphy* was expressly stated as not representing the law in Canada.[126] La Forest J, who delivered the minority judgment, said: 'I fully support this court's rejection of the broad bar on recovery of pure economic loss . . .'.[127] The dispute thus centred around what was termed 'relational economic loss', that is to say economic loss suffered by the plaintiff (CNR) as a result of property damage caused to a third party (here, PWC). Secondly, all the judges agreed that 'the law of tort does not permit recovery for *all* economic loss'.[128] Thirdly, there was full agreement that cases like *Norsk* required a

---

[125] *Norsk Pacific Steamship Co. Ltd.* v. *Canadian National Railway Co.* (1992) 91 DLR (4th) 289 (Supreme Court of Canada).

[126] Ibid., 303 (La Forest J), 367 (McLachlin J), 380 (Stevenson J). The decisions in *Anns* ([1978] 1 AC 728) and *Murphy* ([1991] 1 AC 398) are discussed in Chapter 2, below.

[127] Ibid., 303.   [128] Ibid., 377 (McLachlin J).

discussion of the underlying economic and wider policy considerations.[129] Fourthly, all three judgments implicitly accepted Stevenson J's view that 'the case at bar is a good example of how useful comparative law can be'.[130]

For the majority, McLachlin J essentially adopted the two-pronged test which Lord Wilberforce enunciated in *Anns*.[131] If there were negligence, foreseeable loss, and sufficient proximity between negligent act and the loss, liability should follow *unless* 'pragmatic' considerations dictated the opposite result. 'Proximity may consist of various forms of closeness—physical, circumstantial, causal or assumed—which serve to identify the categories of cases in which liability lies.'[132] Further down she added that:

The meaning of proximity is to be found . . . in viewing the circumstances in which it has been found to exist and determining whether the case at issue is similar enough to justify a similar finding.

The learned judge had no illusions that if this approach is followed 'new categories of case will from time to time arise', and that for a time: 'It will not be certain whether economic loss can be recovered in these categories until the courts have pronounced on them.' But she then continued:

During this period, the law in a small area of negligence may be uncertain. Such uncertainty, however, is inherent in the common law generally. It is the price the common law pays for flexibility.[133]

Moreover, the feared open-endedness of the law, which might result if one were to abandon the rigid exclusionary rule (favoured by the House of Lords in cases such as *Murphy*), had not materialised either in Canada, where the courts had since the mid-1970s moved towards a more liberal rule. (Nor has this occurred in those civil-law systems, which have always opted for a liberal approach to the problem of economic loss.) What then of McLachlin J's pragmatic considerations, notable among which were the insurance and loss-spreading arguments? Did they militate in favour of the non-liability rule?

First, consider the insurance argument that the plaintiff was in a better position to obtain cheaper insurance cover for his loss. McLachlin J thought this was based on 'questionable assumptions'.[134] Quoting Professor Bishop,[135] the learned judge took the view that such an approach reduced the tortfeasor's incentive to take care and thus, in the long run, would result in more accidents and, thereby, eventually increase insurance costs.

The reaction to the 'loss spreading argument' was just as hostile. For, first: 'Where losses are spread by relieving the tortfeasor of liability we can expect more accidents, and so more losses. Secondly, some of the victims must sustain

---

[129] The way the Canadian judges considered insurance arguments must be contrasted with the reference made to this factor by both majority and minority in *Marc Rich & Co. A.G.* v. *Bishop Rock Marine Co. Ltd.* [1996] AC 211. Such a comparison suggests that, at the very least, English students if not English litigants will emerge better informed about the underlying issues if they study carefully the Canadian opinions. This, however, should not be taken as saying that an economic analysis of a case can solve all difficulties; all it is meant to imply is that it can provide yet another tool of analysis and exegesis.

[130] (1992) 91 DLR (4th) 289, 384.
[131] [1978] AC 728, 751–2.
[132] *Norsk*, (1992) 91 DLR (4th) 289, 369.
[133] Ibid., 386.
[134] Ibid., 372.
[135] 'Economic Loss in Tort' (1982) 2 *OJLS* 1.

large losses not small ones . . .' Finally, 'the loss-spreading rationale cannot justify the numerous cases where *there is only one victim*'.

There was a third, pragmatic, argument against the imposition of liability in this case: the law of negligence has no role to play in cases such as the present one where the parties could have made provision in their contract allocating such losses. McLachlin J found this argument, too, unconvincing for three reasons. First, it assumes that all persons organise their affairs in accordance with the laws of economic efficiency. Secondly, it presupposes that the parties to the transaction share an equality of bargaining power which will result in the effective allocation of the risk (but was there not such a balance here?). Finally, it overlooks the significance that personal fault plays in our tort systems and its role in limiting harm to innocent parties.

Stevenson J's concurring judgment is, with respect, the least effective of the three, even though it was the 'swing' judgment that won the case for the plaintiffs. There are two reasons for this harsh characterisation. The first lies at the core of his decision which is, essentially, a variation of the views of Gibbs and Mason JJ of the High Court of Australia in *Caltex Oil (Aust.) Pty. Ltd.* v. *The Dredge Willemstad*.[136] The effect of them was that the plaintiff could recover because the defendant knew or ought to have known that 'a specific individual . . . as opposed to a general or un-ascertained class of the public' was likely in this instance to suffer the foreseeable kind of loss.[137]

The *Caltex* origins of the approach should, it is submitted, have alerted the learned judge to the major weakness of the Australian case that stems from the fact that its judges did not speak with one voice. Stevenson J's proposed solution also suffers from the fact that it 'places [an unwarranted] premium on notoriety'.[138]

But Stevenson J not only advanced a view that has failed to command wider support; he also weakened the overall result of the case by expressly disapproving of McLachlin J's proximity test.[139] The most disturbing aspect of this case as a whole is thus that it has not left us with a clear *ratio decidendi*. For the proximity test advocated by the majority, is espoused only by three justices out of seven. And if one looks at the case purely from the common-law point of view, and removes from the majority camp the vote of the Quebec judge (L'Heureux-Dubé J), one is left with only two justices out of six advocating proximity as the appropriate controlling device.

(c) The Minority

La Forest J's judgment is a veritable *tour de force* which students should read carefully after they have studied the discussion of negligence in Chapter 2. Four areas of his judgment should be singled out for consideration, though, for obvious reasons, the last one will not be reviewed in this book. First, his doubts about the suitability of the proximity test; secondly, his reply to McLachlin J's treatment of the economic considerations; thirdly, his emphasis on the con-

---

[136] (1976) 136 CLR 529.
[138] Ibid., 377; and for more criticism see 339–43.

[137] *Norsk*, (1992) 91 DLR (4th) 289, 387.
[139] Ibid., 387.

tractual relationship between CNR and PWC; and finally his use of comparative law.

La Forest J doubted McLachlin J's view that deciding cases solely on the basis of proximity would lead to the gradual formation of categories of recovery that made sense in policy terms. It is almost impossible to assert which of the two justices is right on this point. But doctrinally La Forest J is on firmer ground when, quoting Professor Feldthusen's work, he insists: 'that different types of factual situations may invite different approaches to economic loss and it seems to . . . be at best unwise to lump them all together for purposes of analysis'.[140] Precedents from the public authorities cases, negligent misstatements, defective rather than dangerous products, and relational economic-loss cases should thus not be used (as they have been by the House of Lords) interchangeably, since they raise different policy issues. The section of the judgment entitled 'The Need to Re-Centre the Analysis on Contractual Relational Economic Loss'[141] thus deserves careful study and may hold the key to the emerging compromise between the 'all' or 'nothing' schools of thought.

La Forest J also countered McLachlin J's economic analysis. The latter's view, that a non-liability rule would encourage risk-takers, cause more accidents, and ultimately raise insurance costs, was countered by the argument that risk-takers would be deterred by the fact that their liability would still be engaged *vis-à-vis* the owners of the damaged property (here the owners of the bridge). This response was also used to counter McLachlin J's rejection of the loss-spreading argument, though no specific reply was given for those accidents that involved only one victim. McLachlin's concern, that plaintiffs in such cases may be unable to obtain insurance, was also doubted. This was largely on the ground that their losses in these instances were more akin to loss of *business* rather than to loss of *profits* (for which business-interruption insurance was widely available and cheaper than liability insurance). One must admit that, in *this type of case*, La Forest J's views seem appealing. However, one must also agree with him when he urges lawyers to 'inform themselves about fundamental matters of insurability'.[142] Yet there are at least two problems with this approach. First, there is inadequate empirical interdisciplinary work to aid judges in this difficult task. Secondly, in England at any rate, there seems to be little inclination on the part of our judges to address these points or to address them openly so that the legal community can engage in a more meaningful discussion of the real issues.

A third and critical difference between majority and minority was the significance the latter attributed to the contractual bond between CNR and PWC. First of all, one should note CNR's 'overwhelming superior risk capacity' since they could protect themselves through contracts both with the property owner (PWC) and their own clients, suppliers, etc., and thus 'combine to minimise the impact of losses once they occur'.[143] Moreover, for reasons which are more fully explained in the judgment, La Forest J argues that if the majority's view prevails, '*both* parties [i.e. CNR and PWC] [will have to] insure at considerable additional social cost. The only gain will be a slight reduction in the plaintiff's

---

[140] *Norsk*, (1992) 91 DLR (4th) 289, 299.   [141] Ibid., 299–301.   [142] Ibid., 350.
[143] Ibid.. 352.

first party insurance costs to take into account the possibility that the insurance company will recover from a tortfeasor under the new doctrine.'[144]

Select Bibliography

CALABRESI, G., *The Costs of Accidents* (1970).

—— and HIRSCHOFF, J. T., 'Toward a Test for Strict Liability in Torts' 81 *Yale LJ* 1055 (1972).

COASE, R., 'The Problem of Social Cost' (1960) 3 *J. Law & Econ.* 1.

COHEN, G. M., 'Posnerian Jurisprudence and the Economic Analysis of Law: The View from the Bench' (1985) 133 *U. Pa. LR* 1117.

DEAKIN, S., 'Law and Economics', ch. 3 in P. A. THOMAS (ed.), *Legal Frontiers* (1996).

DEWEES, D., DUFF, D. and TREBILCOCK, M., *Exploring the Domain of Accident Law: Taking the Facts Seriously* (1996).

LANDES, W. M. and POSNER, R. A., *The Economic Structure of Tort Law* (1987).

OGUS, A. I., 'Economics and Law Reform: Thirty Years of Law Commission Endeavour' (1995) 111 *LQR* 407.

POSNER, R. A., *Law and Economics* (4th. edn., 1993).

—— 'A Theory of Negligence' 1 *Jo. LS* 29 (1972).

WHITE, B., 'Coase and the Courts: Economics for the Common Man' (1987) 72 *Iowa LR* 577.

5. FUNCTIONS OF TORT

The aims of the law of tort have changed throughout its history: appeasement, justice, punishment, deterrence, compensation, and loss spreading can be counted amongst them. None of them has offered a complete justification for the law. Indeed, due to the traditional dualism between law and equity, the 'restitutionary' functions that are (and have for a long time now) been performed by the law of torts, have often been seriously underplayed by academics and confusingly handled by the courts. Overall, however, it can be said with some measure of confidence that at different stages of development of tort law one of its functions may have been more prominent than the rest. Moreover, each in its historical setting reveals something about the socio-economic and philosophical trends of the day.

Appeasement, for example, aims at buying off the victim's vengeance. To the extent that it gives effect to feelings for revenge it now tends to take a backseat, though one still finds some lawyers (e.g. Ehrenzweig) who believe that the 'pay' can be a significant rationale of tort liability; and in so far as appeasement evinces the policy of preventing the prosecution of private feuds its role is in part satisfied by the aim of deterrence discussed below. The idea that 'justice' also requires the tortfeasor to 'pay' has its problems, too. For, to the extent that justice or moral condemnation embodies the idea of 'ethical retribution', it

---

[144] *Norsk*, (1992) 91 DLR (4th), 352.

would also appear to have a small appeal these days. If, on the other hand, just-ice means 'ethical compensation', that is to say the moral need to compensate the victim, then this task seems to be performed by the 'compensation' aim without entering into *moral* arguments, which play little or no role whenever liability is not based on moral guilt (i.e. when it tends to be strict, and even in many cases of negligence). Punishment is also, arguably, an aim which is best left to another branch of the law (criminal law). In Chapter 8, however, we shall note that the English common law has accepted a *limited* number of instances in which penal damages may be awarded to the aggrieved party. In these cases it is thus permissible to look not only at the plaintiff's loss, but also at the defendant's reprehensible behaviour, and increase the damages accordingly. But the 'punitive' element in tort litigation remains minimal. This is partly because modern dogma believes in a (fairly) rigid distinction between crime and tort, but also because it fears that the presence of punitive elements in a civil action, unaccompanied by the evidential and other procedural safeguards of the criminal trial, can be excessively dangerous to any defendant.[145]

Deterrence is another function attributed to tort law. As traditionally under-stood, it plays an interesting but subsidiary part in modern tort law. This is because the deterrent or admonitory effect of money compensation is gener-ally less than that of the corporal punishment of criminal law (e.g. imprison-ment). The lighter consequence of a successful tort action, therefore, blunts its deterrent value. (This is certainly true whenever the defendant is insured; and as we shall note in Chapter 8, courts seem willing to allow, under certain cir-cumstances, even insurance for punitive awards.) Further, as already indicated, tort damages do not, in principle, correspond exactly to the gravity of conduct (as they tend to do in criminal law). The amount of damages is *generally* speak-ing the same whether the tort was committed negligently or intentionally (though some rules, e.g. those concerning 'remoteness of damage', are differ-ent); and the triviality of the fault bears little relation to the possible enormity of its financial consequences.[146] Similarly, deterrence in the form of monetary payment is hardly effective if the tortfeasor is too poor to pay, or is not insured. The greatest objection to the deterrence theory, however, is that it is inapplic-able in those numerous cases where the plaintiff's injury is the result of error rather than blameworthiness. This is particularly true of traffic accidents, the vast majority of which result from regrettable, but statistically inevitable, lapses of attention. It is interesting to note in this respect the empirical studies carried out by the US Department of Transportation in the early 1970s. These suggested that in Washington the average good driver (defined as one who had

---

[145] This objection, however, can be seriously overstated, as Professor Birks, op. cit. (Select Bibliography), 80, has, among others, pointed out. For it ignores the fact that many civil (uninsured or inadequately insured) defendants can be financially ruined by a huge award made against them, given that in tort (unlike crime) the 'punishment' is not always proportionate to the tortfeasor's bad state of mind. This result is, in fact, so unacceptable to some authors that they have tried to explain the non-liability rule in cases of pure economic loss by invoking the injustice of huge liability flowing from a minor inattention (for example, severing an electrical cable while drilling in a street).

[146] That is why it is unconvincing to attribute the non-liability rule in the 'cable cases' to tort law's dis-like of disproportionate consequences.

not been involved in any traffic accident during the preceding four years) commits approximately nine driving errors of four different kinds during every five
minutes of driving![147] In such cases, how can it be said that the threat of a tort
action will deter a potential tortfeasor when it appears humanly unavoidable to
continue making such errors, and when it is clear that even consideration for
the tortfeasor's own safety and the threat of criminal proceedings against him
cannot prevent the harmful results? That such errors are actionable as 'negligence' is not because this will deter others from committing them, but most
likely because, as a result of compulsory insurance, it is the easiest, if not the
only, way of affording the innocent victim compensation without ruining the
defendant or unduly burdening the state with the financial consequences of an
accident. Yet one must also point out that the deterrent element may be important in some torts, such as defamation, deceit, or even negligent statements;
and even in the area of 'accidents', the law can have a deterrent function, for
example, where the tortfeasor is truly negligent or is prone to commit an
unusually large number of errors, for an unusually high incidence of errors
points towards an unusually careless person whose conduct needs to be controlled. This could, for example, happen by increasing his insurance premiums
or even refusing to insure him and thereby, in exceptional cases, even denying
him the right to exercise a particular trade or profession. The admonitory factor may also be significant in those cases (e.g. medical malpractice) where an
adverse judgment can be seen as a negative statement about the tortfeasor's
professional competence or integrity.

Yet the doubts about deterrence persist; and one further reason why it is not
regarded as being very effective is that it is not enough to tell people what not
to do, or simply to tell them that they must behave carefully. One must also
give clear guidance as to the kind of precautions and measures potential tortfeasors should take to avoid the accident; and this, on the whole, the law of
torts does not do. In many instances criminal sanctions, government regulation, and economic incentives can promote accident prevention more effi-
ciently than tort law itself. So, again, deterrence takes second place.

Deterrence could, however, be approached in a different way. This is what
the modern economists/tort lawyers have done; and their views as well as their
significance for modern tort law were summarised in the previous section.

So we come to compensation, which many would regard as a prime function
of modern tort law. The need to compensate victims of modern accidents is
obvious; and throughout this book we shall see how many of the detailed tort
rules have been shaped by this compensatory principle. Yet this approach must
not be overstressed, for two reasons. First, as we shall see in Section 7 of this
chapter, the compensation of accidents is by no means left only to the law of
torts. Other systems of compensation have developed over the years and, in
fact, overall play a more significant role in catering for the needs of accident
victims than does the law of tort. Secondly, and from a theoretical point of view
but just as important, is the fact that the emphasis on compensation has led

---

[147] *Driver Behaviour and Accident Involvement Implications for Tort Liability* (1970), 177–8.

many lawyers (academics and judges) to underplay the importance of 'restitutionary damages' in the law of torts. Thus, it is submitted, one commentator was right in criticising a leading treatise on tort for its 'continuing failure . . . to subject restitutionary damages to coherent and systematic analysis'.[148] If the only consequence of this were doctrinal opaqueness, not all (English) lawyers would complain. But as the same commentator has maintained,[149] and Professor Birks has demonstrated,[150] this (old-fashioned) 'analysis enables courts . . . to conclude (wrongly) that there is something "anomalous" or "exceptional" about restitutionary damages', and even to refuse to grant them on the grounds that they are unknown to tort law.[151] So how important are restitutionary damages to the law of tort?

A number of cases show that such restitutionary damages are, indeed, awarded by our courts. In *Reading* v. *Attorney-General*,[152] for example, Sergeant Reading often travelled in lorries involved in smuggling illicit goods. In all these instances he wore his army uniform, which helped the lorries go through army checkpoints unchecked. When he was eventually arrested and tried, the court held that the proceeds of his wrongdoing should go to the State. The aim of the award in this case was not compensation, since the State had suffered no loss, but recoupment of the unjust enrichment made by the defendant, and this was quantified by reference to the gain made by the defendant.

Other instances can be given. For example, the question of restitutionary damages for trespass to land has caused much discussion in this country,[153] but the colourful American case of *Edwards* v. *Lee's Administrator*[154] shows how just it is to allow an action in equity for an account of profits from trespass to land. In that case, Edwards discovered on his land an entrance to a marvellous underground cave of onyx formations. He built a hotel on his land and turned the cave into a flourishing tourist business. The problem was that the most attractive part of the cave lay under his neighbour's land and, eventually, Lee brought an action claiming a share of these profits, which he obtained from the court.

In his Butterworths Lecture Professor Peter Birks gives many examples of such actions that are not technically torts but are hidden in the interstices of the law of trusts. In his view:

The dominant position of compensation for loss is protected [indeed, preserved in tort books] by banishing the account of profits from the books on damages, by marginalising the wrongs for which an account is most commonly sought, and by the persistence of the old notion of waiver[155] with its implication that the common law gives restitution for a wrong only when the wrong has been transmogrified into something else.[156]

---

[148] McKendrick, 'Review of Clerk and Lindsell on Tort' (16th edn., 1989) in (1991) 54 *MLR* 162.

[149] Ibid., 163.   [150] 'Civil Wrongs: A New World', op. cit. (Select Bibliography).

[151] E.g. *Stoke-on-Trent City Council* v. *W. & J. Wass Ltd.* [1988] 1 WLR 1406, 1415 (per Nourse LJ).

[152] [1951] AC 507.

[153] See e.g. *Phillips* v. *Homfray* (1883) 24 Ch. D 439, and Gummow, 'Unjust Enrichment, Restitution and Proprietory Remedies', in P. Finn (ed.), *Essays on Restitution* (1990), 60–7.

[154] 96 SW (2d) 1025 (1936).

[155] 'When the common law itself allows the victim of a tort to claim the tortfeasor's gain, it traditionally does so by saying that the victim waives the tort. The message is plain. The tort being waived, the restitutionary remedy is given for something that is not a tort at all.' Birks, op. cit. (Select Bibliography), 68.

[156] Ibid., 74.

The result, as the author explained in detail, is an unsatisfactory dichotomy of treatment of the subject of civil wrongs (under at least two courses: tort and equity). If that were all, it would not really matter. But there are more draw-backs. Thus, first, there is uncertainty as to the existence and ambit of new torts (e.g. is breach of confidence a tort?[157] Is 'knowing assistance' in a fraudu-lent misapplication of funds[158] a tort?). Secondly, we have been landed with a theoretically underdeveloped law dealing with the civil liability of accessories. Finally, we are, on occasion, faced with the rejection of the plaintiff's (just) claim because of the difficulties which our courts are faced with when asked to come to terms with a gain-based rather than loss-based action for damages. The case of *Stoke-on-Trent City Council* v. *W. & J. Wass Ltd.*[159] illustrates this last point perfectly.

In *Wass* the eponymous defendants ran an open market without permission, thus infringing the appropriate planning law. Their activity was also a nuisance to the markets held by the plaintiff city which was, by law, entitled to have its monopoly protected within a radius of six and three-quarters of a mile from each of its own markets. The defendants' technique was to run their markets without permission, and when they had exhausted every avenue of appeal against refusal of their application, they would close their 'unlicensed' market and then reopen it nearby and the process would start anew. In Professor Birk's words they were thus 'not so much [set] to defy the law [but] to derive the max-imum advantage from its delays'.[160] The city's application for an injunction and the sum it would have charged for a licence succeeded at first instance. But in the Court of Appeal the money claimed was reduced to a nominal sum since no actual loss could be shown. Nourse LJ's concluding words deserve to be quoted in full:

I rest my decision in this case on the simple ground that where no loss has been suffered no substantial damages of any kind can be recovered . . . It is possible that the English law of tort, more especially the so-called 'proprietary torts', will in due course make a more deliberate move towards recovery based not on loss suffered by the plaintiff but on the unjust enrichment of the defendant . . . But I do not think that the process can begin in this case and I doubt whether it can begin at all at this level of decision.[161]

This statement is indicative of the point made above, namely that the effec-tive concealment of restitutionary damages behind a variety of stratagems or historical accidents can mislead judges and adversely affect deserving plaintiffs, not to mention the danger of hampering the efficient and clear development of its law. As one commentator has observed: 'Can we continue to allow the his-torical division between equity and law to play tricks on us to the extent that it has fooled us into locating equitable wrongs in a course which has nothing to do with wrongs but with the institution of a trust?'[162]

---

[157] Birks, op. cit., 101. Yet note how it was under-used in the *Gordon Kaye* case [1992] FSR 62, discussed in Chapter 7, below.

[158] Cf. *Agip (Africa) Ltd.* v. *Jackson & Co.* [1990] Ch. 265.

[159] [1988] 1 WLR 1406.

[160] Op. cit., 58.

[161] [1988] 1 WLR 1406, 1415.

[162] McKendrick, *Tort Textbook* (5th edn.), 3.

Rhetorical though the question is, it must be emphatically answered in the negative. Tort textbooks must openly admit that compensation has an important role to play in the law of torts. But it is not a monopolistic one. Restitutionary damages are available for many wrongs which can (or should) also be considered as torts. And that their further integration into the subject under review must continue apace, even if considerations of space may mean that (for a time at least) they will not receive in *tort* textbooks the attention that is customarily accorded to some torts, e.g. negligence. In the years to come students should thus expect more developments along these lines.

Select Bibliography

AMES, J. B., 'Law and Morals', 22 *Harv. LR* 97 (1908).

ATIYAH, P., *The Damages Lottery* (1997).

BIRKS, P. B. H., 'Civil Wrongs: A New World', *Butterworth Lectures 1990–91* (1992), 55–112.

CANE, P., *Tort Law and Economic Interests* (2nd edn., 1996).

—— *The Anatomy of Tort Law* (1997).

EHRENZWEIG, A. A., 'Negligence Without Fault', 54 *Cal. LR* 1422 (1966).

—— 'A Psychoanalysis of Negligence', 47 *NWUL Rev.* 855 (1953).

ENGLARD, I., 'The System Builders: A Critical Appraisal of Modern American Tort Theory', 9 *Jo. LS* 27 (1980).

EPSTEIN, R. A., 'A Theory of Strict Liability', 2 *Jo. LS* 151 (1973).

FLEMING, J. G., 'More Thoughts on Loss Distribution', 4 *Osgoode Hall LJ* 161 (1966).

—— 'Is There a Future for Tort?', 58 *Aust. LJ* 131 (1984).

—— *An Introduction to the Law of Torts* (2nd edn., 1985), 1.

FLETCHER, G. P., 'Fairness and Utility in Tort Theory', 85 *Harv. LR* 537 (1972).

McGREGOR, H., 'Compensation versus Punishment in Damages Awards' (1965) 28 *MLR* 629.

MORRIS, C., 'Punitive Damages in Tort Cases', 44 *Harv. LR* 1173 (1931).

WILLIAMS, G. L., 'The Aims of the Law of Tort' [1951] 4 *CLP* 137.

6. FAULT AS THE BASIS OF TORTIOUS LIABILITY

The importance attached to fault largely depends on the functions that a legal system is prepared to assign to its tort law. Since, as we have noted, these have changed over the years, the role of fault as the basis of liability has in turn been ignored, glorified, and questioned. We need not involve ourselves in the problems of whether liability was historically based on fault or simply on damage and causation.[163] The fact remains that by the middle of the nineteenth century it became increasingly accepted that 'sound policy lets losses lie where they fall, except where a special reason can be shown for interference'.[164] Apart from a few exceptional situations such special reason was the tortfeasor's fault

---

[163] For different views see Ames, 22 *Harv. LR* 97 (1908); Fifoot, *History and Sources of the Common Law* (1949), ch. 9; Holmes, *The Common Law* (1923), ch. 1; Wigmore, 7 *Harv. LR* 315 (1894).

[164] Holmes, op. cit., 50 and, in greater detail, 94 ff.

in one or other of the meanings explained earlier. A person at fault was not only guilty of a legal wrong but also of an ethical wrong.[165] As Professor Fleming has put it: '. . . the triumph of fault liability was well-nigh complete and marked a singular judicial triumph in remoulding ancient precedents in the image of a radically different era.'

The moral, social, and economic reasons behind this approach blended so well at that particular historical period that the result appeared attractive. To nineteenth-century moralists the idea that bad people should pay and that very bad people should pay more had obvious appeal. It was thus reflected in a number of rules—intended consequences are never too remote, malice defeats certain defences, a plaintiff is deprived of compensation if he had contributed to his own hurt, etc. Tort law, however, had a deterrent and not only an admonitory function to perform. At a time of a weak or non-existent insurance market the compensation of the victim came out of the tortfeasor's pocket. To quote again from Professor Fleming: 'Personal fortune was regarded as the primary source of compensation, so that the deterrent lash would be at once real and ineluctable.'[166]

Yet there was more in this moralistic movement than one might surmise at first sight. For in logic and law the reverse of a proposition usually commands the same respect as the proposition itself. This meant that persons not at fault could not be liable for the damage they caused. It is here that economic expediency blended in with current morality and created the nineteenth-century legacy of fault,[167] which subsequent generations have found difficult to shake off. For insistence upon fault, and (just as importantly) the need for a plaintiff to prove it, meant that during the period of industrial expansion and increased industrial accidents, an enterprise could be shielded against the costs of accidents. In human terms the result was appalling for the injured workers, who were indirectly called upon to subsidise production at the expense of life and limb. In economic terms any other solution could have ruined enterprises in their infancy. One can find more evidence of this type of economic reasoning in nineteenth-century American cases[168] than in their English counterparts, but it represents part, at least, of the truth for English law as well. Finally, fault had educational and social value in so far as it helped to balance one's freedom of action against the duties and responsibilities arising from such action. People should be allowed some freedom of action and should not be made to pay for the damage they cause if they have not fallen below a certain minimum standard of proper behaviour; nor should they recover if their fault in any way contributed to their own hurt.

Continuing growth of industry, the emergence of modern insurance, and the social effects of two world wars soon encouraged increasing opposition to these arguments. Even moralists were quick to stress that no human being can really

---

[165] Tunc, op. cit. (Select Bibliography), 75.

[166] *Introduction to the Law of Torts* (2nd edn., 1985), 6.

[167] See Woodard, 'Reality and Social Reform: The Transition from Laissez-Faire to Welfare State', 72 *Yale LJ* 286 (1962).

[168] E.g. *Farwell* v. *Boston and Worcester Railroad Corp.* 45 Mass. 4 (Met) 49 (1842).

sit in moral judgement on the acts of another human being; which, in any event, was not the function of a court of law. As votes started to matter as the electorate became politically organised, the social consciousness of the State became increasingly apparent. Indifference to the weak and the needy was something that few politicians could afford to display. Besides, insurance was making the absorption of losses easier than in the past, and the need to protect nascent industrialisation was no longer there. Economic analyses of the law of tort also started to reveal how costly a system based on fault could be, and, above all, the role of fault in imposing liability became increasingly attenuated.

First of all one should note the large number of 'overlooked faults', such as those which are undiscovered or not pursued through lapse of time or expense, as well as social faults, such as pollution, exploitation through tobacco, alcohol, or pornography.[169] In the light of so long a list one is justified in asking what is left of the principle that requires a person to answer for damage caused by his fault.

There is also another reason behind this attenuation of the fault principle, which is simply that a very large number of persons who are actually at fault are never called upon to meet the economic consequences of their wrongdoing. As Professor James has pointed out,[170] those who have to pay are 'innocent absentees', namely, employers and insurance companies; and the ultimate burden of insurance is borne in the end indiscriminately by the just and the unjust.[171]

This allusion to insurance reveals yet another weakness of a fault-based theory of liability. As Professor Tunc has said:[172] 'Liability insurance, apart from automobile insurance and professional insurances, is very cheap . . . If liability for fault is the foundation of society and morality, one must admit that this foundation is strangely cheap.'

The last, but by no means least significant, sign of abandonment of the fault principle that followed the change of emphasis of tort law from loss-shifting to loss-spreading is the transformation of the notion of negligence from a concept with strong moral overtones into a legal notion in which wider policy considerations determine the existence of a duty to take care, its breach, and even the extent of the consequences. The extension of 'negligence' to include cases of unavoidable error has caused a certain amount of conceptual confusion, but it has been prompted by sympathy for the victim and has been facilitated by the availability of insurance. Nevertheless, not all cases lend themselves to this kind of analysis.

In the medical malpractice case of *Whitehouse* v. *Jordan*,[173] an attempt was made to hold an obstetrician liable for allegedly misusing the forceps during delivery and thereby injuring the infant plaintiff. Had the court treated the unfortunate error of the doctor as 'negligence' it would have compensated the plaintiff by holding the doctor liable and so imposed an additional burden on some hospital authority. On the other hand, the actual decision that the doctor

---

[169] Tunc, op. cit. (Select Bibliography), 66.   [170] *Tort Law in Midstream* (Select Bibliography), 331.
[171] 'An Evaluation of the Fault Concept' (Select Bibliography), 398.
[172] Tunc, op. cit. (Select Bibliography), 67.   [173] [1981] 1 WLR 246.

had not been negligent avoided such an outcome, but left the innocent victim without redress. These doubts about fault, however, should not lead us to the opposite extreme of advocating the complete abandonment of fault as a criterion of liability. For truly blameworthy conduct liability should, in principle, be imposed. In these instances fault can be useful. Where, however, one is talking of accidents resulting from statistically inevitable errors, fault is an unsatisfactory criterion of compensation.[174] Fault-orientated liability should here yield to loss-spreading techniques, some of which we have looked at briefly. Only in cases of faults in a narrow sense should civil liability be reintroduced.

Select Bibliography

CANE, P., *The Anatomy of Tort Law* (1997).
FLEMING, J. G., 'The Role of Negligence in Modern Tort Law' 53 *Virginia LR* 815 (1967).
FLETCHER, G. P., 'Fairness and Utility in Tort Theory' 85 *Harv. LR* 537 (1972).
ISON, T. G., *The Forensic Lottery* (1967).
JAMES, FLEMING, 'Tort Law in Midstream: Its Challenge to the Judicial Process' 8 *Buffalo LR* 315 (1959).
—— 'An Evaluation of the Fault Concept' 32 *Tenn. LR* 394 (1965).
—— 'The Future of Negligence in Accident Law' 53 *Virginia LR* 911 (1967).
MALONE, W. S., 'Ruminations on the Role of Fault in the History of the Common Law of Torts' 31 *Louis. LR* 1 (1970).
STOLJAR, S., 'Accidents, Costs and Legal Responsibility' (1973) 36 *MLR* 233.
TUNC, A., in *Int. Encl. Comp. L.* xi. ch. 1, 63–86.

7. ALTERNATIVE SYSTEMS OF COMPENSATION

So far we have talked only incidentally about other methods of compensation, such as social security and private insurance. That the well-established tort books should place emphasis on compensation at law is understandable and in keeping with tradition. On the other hand, an entirely legalistic approach, despite some merits, also has its drawbacks, for it tends to present only one part of the whole picture of the system of compensation for harm and injury. Thus, no lawyer, practising or academic, must be allowed to forget that in the words of the Pearson Committee Report tort law has been reduced to the role of 'junior partner' in the whole compensation system.

Secondly, the attempt to compensate victims through tort, without taking into account other available sources of compensation, may encourage lawyers into making artificial distinctions. For instance, in *Jobling* v. *Associated Dairies Ltd.*,[175] the court had to decide whether damage sustained as a result of a *tort*

---

[174] The diverging cases of *Roberts* v. *Ramsbottom* [1980] 1 WLR 823 and *Mansfield* v. *Weetabix Ltd.* [1998] 1 WLR 1263 offer a good illustration of the point made in the text. Unfortunately, both made little use of insurance arguments and, instead, chose to focus (mainly) on the relevance of some criminal-law cases to tort law.

[175] [1982] AC 794 (mainly a causation case, and this aspect will be discussed in Chapter 2).

should be assessed without regard to a subsequent *non-tortious event*, which supervened and obliterated its effects. In the earlier case of *Baker* v. *Willoughby*,[176] where the *subsequent* event was an independent tort, the House of Lords, applying *causal* language, compensated the victim in respect of the first injury to the full extent as if the subsequent injury had never taken place. In *Jobling*, on the other hand, where the subsequent event was not tortious (supervening illness), the defendant's responsibility for the first injury was limited to the consequences of his prior tort until the moment when the subsequent illness obliterated its effect. This difference between the two cases could explain the different outcome, though it might be possible to sustain a counter argument. Yet, just as noteworthy is the House of Lords' desire to underplay the role of causation and emphasise the role played by the Criminal Injuries Compensation Board, when fixing the compensation payable in tort. The relevant passage from Lord Wilberforce's judgment deserves to be quoted in full.[177]

The fact, however, is that to attempt a solution of these and similar problems, where there are successive causes of incapacity in some degree, upon classical lines ('the object of damages for tort is to place the plaintiff in as good a position as if', etc. '. . . the defendant must compensate for the loss caused by his wrongful act—no more'—'the defendant must take the plaintiff as he finds him', etc.) is, in many cases, no longer possible. We live in a mixed world where a man is protected against injury and misfortune by a whole web of rules and dispositions, with a number of timid legislative interventions. To attempt to compensate him upon the basis of selected rules without regard to the whole must lead either to logical inconsistencies, or to over- or under-compensation. As my noble and learned friend, Lord Edmund-Davies, has pointed out, no account was taken in *Baker* v. *Willoughby* of the very real possibility that the plaintiff might obtain compensation from the Criminal Injuries Compensation Board. If he did in fact obtain this compensation he would, on the ultimate decision, be over-compensated.

In *Hill* v. *Chief Constable of West Yorkshire*[178] we can find an example where the possibility of compensation under the Criminal Injuries Compensation scheme influenced not the element of causation but that of duty of care. *Hill* is one of those cases that was decided during the mid-1980s when legal thinking was increasingly affected by the hostility towards the Wilberforce formula concerning the existence of a duty of care enunciated in *Anns* v. *Merton London Borough Council*.[179] This debate will be discussed more fully in Chapter 2. Here suffice it to say that the argument centred on the stage of the enquiry at which policy considerations would be introduced in order to determine whether there was a duty of care. Thus, should policy be used to negative a prima-facie duty arising whenever there is 'sufficient relationship of proximity or neighbourhood' between the tortfeasor and the victim 'such that, in the reasonable contemplation of the former, carelessness on his part may be likely to cause damage to the latter' (*Anns*)? Or should policy factors be used at the first stage in order to determine whether it was 'just and reasonable' (*Peabody*)[180] to

---

[176] [1970] AC 467. [177] [1982] AC 794, 803–4.
[178] [1988] QB 60 (CA); approved by the House of Lords in [1989] AC 53. [179] [1978] AC 728.
[180] *Governors of the Peabody Donation Fund* v. *Sir Lindsay Parkinson* [1985] AC 210 at 240.

impose such a duty?[181] In *Hill's* case, Lord Justice Fox opted for the second approach and denied that the police were under a duty towards potential victims of a dangerous criminal to apprehend him before he committed a crime. As the learned judge put it: 'If the state [had] made no provision at all for criminal injuries [through the Criminal Injuries Compensation Board], that might be a reason for imposing a legal duty of care upon the police in the conduct of their investigations . . .'[182]

Cases such as the above can be taken to suggest that the courts, when interpreting concepts with a strong normative content,[183] are likely to take into account the availability of, *inter alia*, alternative sources of compensation before deciding whether to impose (or discover) a duty of care. Such an approach is, it is submitted, both illuminating and acceptable *provided* the alternative remedies envisaged by the judges are *genuinely available and effective*. In the *Hill* case, the options available to the plaintiff under the Criminal Injuries Scheme were, if not ideal, good enough. In subsequent cases, however, where much use was made of *Hill*, our courts seemed to have lost sight of the significance of the italicised words and thus, effectively, left very deserving victims uncompensated.[184]

A third and major objection to the complete separation of various available systems of compensation is that this encourages their independent and uncoordinated development. The Pearson Committee recognised this when it said that[185] 'the two systems have for too long been permitted to develop in isolation from each other, with regard to the fact that, between them, they meet many needs twice over and others not at all'. However, its suggestions to overcome this isolationist approach were modest; and even these now look unlikely ever to be implemented.[186] A similar objection could be made to the traditional unwillingness to consider openly and in detail the impact of insurance on the law of torts. We shall return to this point briefly in the next and last section of this Introduction.

In recent times, however, there have been (mainly academic) stirrings against an over-legalistic approach to the law of tort. They owe much to the eco-

---

[181] In the subsequent case of *Stovin* v. *Wise*, [1996] AC 923, 949, Lord Hoffmann suggested that 'provided . . . the considerations of policy etc. are properly analysed, it should not matter whether one starts from one or the other'. A few lines further down, however, the learned judge made clear his own preference for non-liability rules. Though not without much merit, such a starting-point—the Law Lord, using computer language calls it the 'default position'—is not without its difficulties. These are alluded to later on in this chapter but discussed in greater detail in the next.

[182] [1988] QB 60, 73.   [183] Such as legal cause and, even more, duty of care.

[184] Thus in *Elguzouli-Daf and Another* v. *Commissioner of Police of the Metropolis* [1995] QB 355, the plaintiffs were kept in custody for 25 and 85 days respectively and then the Crown Prosecution Service discontinued proceedings against them. The claims for tort damages for malicious prosecution and false imprisonment failed, the Court of Appeal laying great store on the *Hill* judgment. In these cases, however, the remedies left to the plaintiffs, though available on paper, were hardly effective in practice as Lord Justice Steyn appeared to admit in his judgment. As we say in Chapter 3, results such as these may become untenable once the Human Rights Act 1998 comes into force—a point which Lord Justice Steyn, himself, perceptively emphasised in his judgment. The same objections can be raised against a similar argument put forward by Lord Browne-Wilkinson in *X (Minors)* v. *Befordshire County Council* [1995] 2 AC 633. Future plaintiffs and their advisors will thus be well advised to consider raising these points in the future in litigation of this type.

[185] Cmnd. 7054–I, para. 271.   [186] For further details, see Chapter 8, Section 2.

nomic analysis of law which started in the United States and which we described briefly earlier in this chapter. This awareness of the need for a new direction in the teaching of tort law is already reflected in introductory works.[187] And Professor Atiyah's pioneering book on *Accidents, Compensation and the Law* for nearly twenty years now has been both an impetus in this direction as well as a veritable mine of ideas. In this Introduction we shall touch on only some of these wider issues and return to some of them in greater detail in later parts of this work as and when the need arises.

It will be remembered that earlier, in Section 3, we spoke of 'loss distribution' and 'loss allocation' as aims for modern tort law. They are indeed often thought of in such terms. Equally, however, it is obvious that which method of distributing losses or allocating risks is chosen will very largely depend on the kind of political choices one is prepared to make. Broadly speaking, there is a choice between two approaches (which can be ingeniously combined in certain cases). The first is the free-market system, which tends to make people who cause damage pay for it. The other is a more collectivist approach, which lays greater emphasis on equality of treatment and places a greater burden on the State itself. If economic efficiency is something one should aim at, the tort system is expensive, for its administration costs (investigating claims, costs of litigation, etc.—economists usually call them 'transfer payments') represent a very large percentage of the total amounts available for compensation. Thus, the Pearson Committee estimated that it cost 85p to deliver £1 in net benefits to the victim; and, in Professor Fleming's words: 'Studies in the United States raise operating costs to $1.07 for automobile and $1.25 for product liability. In the protracted asbestos litigation it has cost $1.59 in combined litigation expenses to deliver $1 to the average plaintiff.'[188] In that sense tort law could be described as wasteful. On the other hand, the social security system tends to have lower administrative costs, though the wider cost of an ever-growing state and local-authority bureaucracy has not yet been accurately worked out. Though the social security system in many respects is just as complicated as the tort system, it does make its awards reach victims more quickly and often without the uncertainty that accompanies litigation. On the other hand, although social security compensation may be speedier, it also tends to be lower than the amount of a victim's actual loss and less likely to be tailored to his particular injury and needs—especially in the case of serious injuries.[189] Apart from purely economic criteria, ideological and political decisions are also involved in deciding which of these systems should be adopted and to what extent, if any, the one should displace the others. Ours, being a mixed economy, strives for a balance, which of course leaves many unsatisfied.

The structure that has resulted from this compromise may be divided into three levels. (In this chapter we shall merely describe the general outline; but we shall return to the question of tort compensation in Chapter 8, Section 2.) At the first level the State assumes directly a primary if not sole responsibility

---

[187] Williams and Hepple, op. cit. (Select Bibliography); C. Harlow, op. cit. (Select Bibliography).
[188] John Fleming, *The American Tort Process* (1988), 19; Pearson Report, vol. i, para. 261.
[189] See Chapter 8, Section 2.

to provide compensation. At the second level the State role is additional to that played by tort law and/or insurance. Finally, at the third and last level the compensation system—State or private—is at its weakest, leaving potential claimants with few if any rights. We can use this division for the brief remarks that conclude this section.

1. First Level

As stated, at the first level the role of the State is most developed. It provides sickness and unemployment benefits and other compensation for accidents at work, based upon the principle of social insurance that entitlement rests on each individual's contributions while in employment. All these benefits can be accompanied by income support for those in further need. In many cases of personal injury, the State is the only provider of relief. In other cases, however, the state system of benefits may co-exist alongside the tort rules. What form this co-existence takes will be discussed in Chapter 8, below. Here suffice it to say that whereas in the past these awards could (in part or in whole) be cumulated with the tort awards, the current trend is to restrict almost to a vanishing point this right. Though the principle pursued by these (new) rules—the avoidance of double compensation of the plaintiff—is a laudable one, the way it has been implemented in practice has been neither flawless nor notable for its clarity.[190]

2. Second Level

At the second level of the compensation system come those injuries for which the victim has to satisfy himself by prosecuting a tort claim. The money here will come in most cases from insurance of some kind, or from the defendant who, in the case of a corporation, may then pass on the costs of its general overheads. The State's role here is limited to providing *additional* compensation (through what one can broadly describe as the welfare system) as well as the coercive system that helps the victim to obtain his compensation. Additionally, it supplies the kind of regulatory background to ensure that certain potential defendants conduct their business properly, carry insurance, and so on. But in recent times, the State has also come with some additional or supplementary schemes that can be of crucial importance to potential claimants. There are the Criminal Injuries Compensation schemes and the compensation orders that can be made by criminal courts. We shall discuss them in turn.

(A) Criminal Injuries Compensation Schemes

The State's role here can be crucial since it provides direct and, in practice invariably exclusive, assistance to victims of crimes of violence through the Criminal Injuries Compensation Board or, after the Criminal Injuries Compensation Act 1995 came into force,[191] by the Criminal Injuries Compensation Authority. Before describing this regime a few preliminary

---

[190] For further details see Chapter 8, below.
[191] This deals with all complaints received after 1 April 1996.

words are necessary about the vagaries of politics and how they have affected this scheme.

The scheme was originally set up as a result of ideas canvassed in the late 1950s and early 1960s. At that time, support grew for the idea that the 'obligation to the victim of crime rests primarily on the society which has failed to protect him ... and can alone effectively compensate him'. In 1964 the (Labour) government of the day accepted that public sympathy required that such victims should be helped by the State, but rejected the notion of State liability. Payments were thus made *ex gratia*. By the eighties the prevailing opinion in both parties was that such payments should be placed on a statutory basis; and sections 108–17 of the Criminal Justice Act 1988 embodied this new conception of the State's own duties towards victims of crime. But almost immediately fears began to be expressed about the Board being inundated by claims and by huge delays becoming inevitable in the processing of these claims. The operation of the new scheme was thus suspended and an interim (and revised) administrative scheme was brought into application to deal with all claims made after 1 February 1990. This was nowhere near as thorough and well-thought out as the 1988 Act,[192] as the absence of a definition of what amounted to a 'crime of violence' (which triggered off the application of the scheme) showed. Yet such uncertainties were, in a sense, to be expected. For, in addition to the technical worries about the ability of the scheme to cope, the political climate in the government was in a state of flux as differing views about the State's obligations towards its needy members (whether single mothers or victims of violence) began to emerge dividing the 'new right' and the more moderate sections of the Conservative party which was then in office. Nevertheless, the 'interim scheme' was applied with some success (and still regulates the residue of claims made before 1 April 1996) to 'crimes of violence'—which was taken to include arson and poisoning, as well as injuries sustained in the course of apprehending an offender. Excluded from the interim scheme were such matters as acts of domestic violence, injuries arising from the use of motor cars which would be covered by the Motor Insurance Bureau (discussed below) or minor injuries, where compensation would be below a certain level. But the method of calculating the awards remained essentially as it had been since the inception of the scheme. To put it differently, it remained (avowedly) based on the tort method of calculating damages.[193] One stresses the word 'avowedly' for there were some deviations in matters of relevant detail. Thus, for instance, exemplary damages were not payable under these schemes; and, quite consistently with the fact that it was the State that was paying these amounts, the victim could not cumulate them with any other benefits paid by the State in the form of social security benefits. Overall, therefore, the levels of payment made were significantly lower than the normal tort awards even though, as stated, in theory the tort methods were used to calculate the amounts thus paid. Which brings us back to the underlying political debates about the need to cut down

---

[192] The provisions of which were described in the previous edition of the book.

[193] Except that a limit was placed on compensation for lost earnings which equalled one and a half times the gross average industrial earnings.

State expenditure which were raging, at the time, within the ruling party. These led the then Home Secretary to attempt to tinker with the system in an even more radical manner. He thus chose to replace the traditional method of calculation with a tariff method of compensation that, effectively, reduced the levels of compensation even further. His attempt was thrown out by the House of Lords as *ultra vires* in *R* v. *Secretary of State for the Home Department, ex parte Fire Brigade Union.*[194] The reason given was that only Parliament could effect such a radical change of a statute (the Criminal Justice Act 1988, the operation of which, however, had been suspended). Undeterred, the Home Secretary returned to the fray with a new Bill which, eventually, became the new Criminal Injuries Compensation Act 1995 and applies to all claims made after 1 April 1996.

The new statutory scheme follows, in its basics, the interim administrative scheme that it replaces. Some definitional improvements as to what amounts to 'criminal injuries' do exist (though, once again, one feels that the level of precision pursued by the 1988 Act has not been attained). Most significantly, however, the 1995 Act abolishes the tort method of calculation of the award (attempted by ministerial act but declared *ultra vires*) and adopts, instead, a modified tariff-basis that provides for the payment of certain standard[195] amounts for specific types of injury. The only effective concession made to those who complained that behind all the reforming moves of the Home Secretary lay a desire to cut down further[196] on government expenditure was thus a provision that those incapacitated for over twenty-eight weeks would be entitled to an enhanced tariff. Three final points can be mentioned about the new scheme.

First, it does not apply to rescuers claiming for psychiatric injuries nor to members of the emergency services for accidental injuries suffered in the course of their work. Secondly, claims by persons entitled to use the new scheme must be made within two years (instead of the previous three) from the date of the injury. Finally, in fatal accident cases, compensation may include (in addition to lost dependency), funeral expenses and a bereavement sum of £10,000 (which must be shared by all dependants).

---

[194] [1995] 2 WLR 1—a case which attracted at the time much political comment.

[195] The tariffs are adjustable to take into account the severity of the injury: they vary, for instance from £1,000 for temporary partial deafness to £250,000 for permanent serious brain damage. The tariff system ignores other factors such as age, sex, and financial means which, in a tort regime, could have influenced the award. They are also subject to a 'cap' of £500,000.

[196] Yet the complaint that the (original) scheme had been expensive is not borne out by available figures. Thus, since its inception (in the mid 1960s) it has paid out a mere £500 million of public funds. This is because the awards made by the Board were always more modest than those made by the courts in tort cases. Thus, though the average awards made (for example in 1991) were at around £3,000, roughly in tune with net tort damages awarded by the courts, the awards made by the Board at the higher levels involved sums substantially lower than those encountered in contemporaneous serious cases of personal injury compensated through the tort process. Thus, in 1989/90 less than 3 per cent of adjudicated cases (802 to be precise) received £10,000 or more. The nature of the claims made to the Board coupled with the technical rules which apply to the scheme explain this disparity. This statement about the low costs of the scheme is, probably, not affected even if one adds the (admittedly) growing costs of administering the scheme.

One final point remains to be made and it concerns the effect which these developments have had on the law of torts. Since most cases of intentional physical harm result from perpetrators who cannot be tracked down or, more likely, are financially not worth suing, the effect of the schemes has been to reduce significantly the number of cases dealing with trespass to the person which used to figure in tort books. But that should not be taken to mean that the Criminal Injuries schemes have abolished tort law; rather, they have tried to supplement it for the benefit of the victim. Thus, claimants under the schemes may be penalised if, in appropriate cases, they fail to take advantage of the tort rules; and, if they receive any tort award this will be deducted in full from any money paid under the scheme. Last, but by no means least, there are still cases where the use of the action of trespass, for instance against the police for assault or false imprisonment, can yield punitive awards[197] which, as stated, cannot be made under the schemes.

(B) COMPENSATION ORDERS

One of the most interesting and relatively recent ways devised by the State to assist victims of crimes is the power granted to criminal courts to make *compensation* orders for damage resulting from the commission of an offence. This innovation, first introduced by section 1 of the Criminal Justice Act 1972,[198] gives the courts—typically magistrates and Crown Court judges—the power to order *convicted*[199] offenders to pay compensation to their victims. Sadly, however, the criminal courts do not have the power to issue compensation orders against defendants convicted of road-traffic offences. The only (minimal) deviation from this rule can be found in section 104(2) of the Criminal Justice Act 1988. This allows a compensation order to be made in the case of an injury resulting from a road traffic offence whenever the offender is uninsured and the Motor Insurance Bureau will not pay. Such awards can, according to the better view, be combined with custodial orders and/or an order to pay a fine. The idea that compensation (which is typically the remedy of a civil wrong) should not be treated in these cases as merely an appendage of the criminal sanction is reinforced by section 67 of the Criminal Justice Act 1982. This makes it clear that if the offender is incapable of paying both the fine and the compensation, priority should be given to the latter. The compensation order is in respect of 'any personal injury, loss or damage, resulting from [an] *offence*' and in no way depends on the existence of any civil liability (arising from breach of contract or the commission of a tort which are also criminal offences). The amount to be paid is left to the courts' discretion having regard to all the evidence submitted to the court. In theory the Crown Court can, subject to what will be said below, award unlimited compensation. Magistrates' Courts on the other hand have,

[197] For instance *White* v. *Metropolitan Police Commissioner*, *The Times*, 24 Apr. 1982; *Taylor* v. *Metropolitan Police Commissioner*, *The Times*, 6 Dec. 1989.

[198] Which was re-enacted as section 35 of the Powers of Criminal Courts Act 1973 and amended by section 40 of the Magistrates Court Act 1980 and section 67 of the Criminal Justice Act 1982.

[199] A difference here with the Criminal Injury Compensation schemes which never required a criminal conviction before payments could be made under those schemes.

since 1984, been subject to an upper limit of £2,000.[200] In practice, however, the awards seem to be very low. In 1983, for example, 'nearly half of the 122,000 awards in magistrates' courts were for £25 or less; only 18 exceeded £1,000. The pattern was comparable in 1984';[201] and by the end of the 1980s the *average* amount of such orders had gone up only slightly to £134 for Magistrates' Courts and £901 for Crown Courts. In numerical terms most compensation orders are made in cases of theft and handling stolen goods; but the chances of obtaining such an order seems to be at its highest in cases of criminal damage. Section 35 orders, it would appear, have not been used adequately in favour of consumers in the context of violations of the Trade Descriptions Act. Indeed, the number of orders made under this heading seems to be falling. And the average amount awarded in 1981 was £308—a poor record that prompted Sir Gordon (now Lord) Borrie, the Director-General of the Office of Fair Trading at the time, to remark that 'surely it is timely for a little more boldness to be encouraged'.[202]

Michael Ogden QC, the former chairman of the Criminal Injuries Compensation Board, has also expressed the hope that section 67 of the Criminal Justice Act 1982 would prompt the courts to make greater use of this power.[203] The possibility of making such orders, as a convenient and rapid means of avoiding the expense of resort to civil litigation is, in fact, well known and well developed in other systems. This is typically true wherever the device of class actions (enabling one person to bring an action on behalf of a group of injured consumers, each of whom has suffered a relatively small loss that discourages him personally from hazarding litigation) is unknown, or where resort to the usual contractual or tortious remedies is likely to be time-consuming and costly and thus dissuade victims from asserting their rights. In this country, however, the innovation has had only a modest success, with the Magistrates' Courts making the fuller use of these powers (113,000 compensation orders made compared to just under 7,000 ordered by the Crown Court). The relative novelty of the innovation can provide only a very partial answer, even allowing for the fact that sentencing habits may take time to change. Another reason may be the fact that whereas (rightly) the initiative is left to the prosecution, the rights of the injured person to intervene in the proceedings and quantify his loss seem to be too uncertain. Last and by no means least is the effect of dicta in a pre-1982 court decision that courts should refrain from making such orders where there is substantial uncertainty as to the extent of the loss. Decisions of the Court of Appeal in the 1970s also suggested that judges— in practice, as we have seen with magistrates— should be slow in involving themselves in cases where the causation issue was too complicated. The wording of section 67 of the Criminal Justice Act 1982 provides some hope to those who would like to see courts making a more liberal use of their powers; but

---

[200] Criminal Penalties (Increase) Order (SI No. 1984/447).
[201] S. Weatherill, op. cit. (Select Bibliography), 464.
[202] *The Development of Consumer Law and Policy—Bold Spirits and Timorous Souls*, The Hamlyn Lectures (1984), 69.
[203] 'Compensation Orders in Cases of Violence' (1985) *Crim. LR* 500.

legal conservatism may also make courts hesitant to intervene; especially where there is substantial uncertainty over issues of causation and remoteness.

3. Third Level

Finally, at the third level of the compensation system one finds those interferences that the system cannot afford to compensate. Compensation for them through the courts will be denied because in a world of limited resources they come too low in any scale of allocation of resources. Nervous shock cases, for example, have until recently received little attention at law for this reason as well as for their assumed propensity to lead to increased litigation. Put differently (and more bluntly), there is not enough money to go around for every injury, so 'marginal' cases have to be left out. In these the victim is left to bear the loss himself or through his own first-party insurance coverage. As already stated, social security payments and their relationship to tort awards will be considered in Chapter 8. The last part of this section will, thus, briefly touch on the remaining possible source of compensation: insurance.

Insurance presents a number of advantages for all parties concerned. For the victim it represents a considerable guarantee that funds will be available to compensate him if he succeeds in his action. For the party inflicting the injury it means that if his conduct is held to be an actionable wrong, this will not spell economic ruin for him. For the insurers, themselves, there is, of course, the possibility of profitable business—one rarely hears of poor insurers—by means of insurance premiums. Moreover, there is something that appears, at first sight at least, to be very unfair. That is the insurer's rights after he has paid the victim, to take over his rights by way of subrogation. This gives insurers the right to have their cake and eat it (except where it can be shown convincingly that sums recouped through subrogation are used to keep premiums low.) The social interest, too, is served by insurance that enables members of society to obtain compensation through law without thereby ruining others. Further, in certain types of harm the insurance system makes a positive contribution towards accident prevention by inhibiting shortcomings through higher premiums, loss of no-claims bonuses, or, even, by refusing to insure altogether unless certain standards of safety are scrupulously maintained. Indeed, so successful has insurance been that during this century it has been made compulsory in certain areas. Since 1976, for example, any solicitor practising in England or Wales is obliged to take out insurance under a special scheme organised by the Law Society.[204] (Recently the Bar has approved a scheme for compulsory mutual insurance.) Seven years before that the Employers' Liability (Compulsory Insurance) Act 1969 made it obligatory for employers to take out insurance coverage for liability for bodily injury, including death and disease. However, by far the most important instance of compulsory insurance is the earliest of them all, dealing with liability for death or injury arising from the use of a vehicle on a road (introduced in 1930 and now regulated by the Road

---

[204] Solicitors Act 1974, s. 37.

Traffic Act 1972).[205] This is no place to discuss the technical rules on this matter though two points should be noted because of their wider importance.[206]

The first is that, despite the doctrine of privity of contract, any person who is covered by the policy may enforce it against the insurer even though he has supplied no consideration for the coverage.[207] Equally, the victim may, subject to certain formalities, claim from the insurer the amount plus interest and costs for which a court has condemned the tortfeasor.[208]

Secondly, and related to the last point, there is the additional protection given to victims of car accidents where the driver is either uninsured or unknown. Such claims can now be met, subject to certain technical conditions, by the Motor Insurers Bureau, which was set up in 1946 by an Agreement between the Government and insurance companies. The Motor Insurance Bureau is a company limited by guarantee and financed by a levy on member companies in proportion to their motor premium incomes. Under the agreement, the Bureau will meet judgments against uninsured motorists. With regard to the untraced, hit-and-run motorists, the Bureau will give sympathetic consideration to making *ex gratia* payment to victims if it is satisfied that the motorist concerned would have been held liable had he been traced and sued. The scheme was revised in 1972 and now all authorised motor insurers are required to be members of the Bureau.[209] The overall protection thus given to traffic-accident victims is considerable. Certainly, it is greater than that given to employees suing their employers under the 1969 Act, since in this latter case there is no statutory right to claim the amount of an unsatisfied judgment directly from the insurer. Such right of direct access is only provided by section 1 of the Third Parties Against Insurers Act 1930 in the event of a tortfeasor being insolvent. The advantage is that the victim receives the whole of the insurance money and does not have to compete with the other creditors of a bankrupt tortfeasor for a share of his estate.

Non-compulsory insurance can be divided into two broad categories. First-party insurance is taken out by victims to cover themselves against the chance of harm being inflicted on them. Third-party liability insurance, on the other hand, protects tortfeasors against the harm they inflict on others. This latter type can take a number of forms, each with special rules: for example, employers liability insurance, products liability insurance, motor insurance (additional to what is compulsory), libel insurance, etc.

First-party insurance involves two parties, the insurer and the insured whereas third-party liability insurance involves three: the insurer, the insured, and the victim. This difference may have important consequences. For example, in first-party insurance the insured victim will obtain his insurance money once the insured risk materialises without the uncertainty of litigation (subject, of course, to the insurance policy being valid). On the other hand, in third-party

---

[205] Road Traffic Act 1972, ss. 143 ff.
[206] Further details can be found in Williams and Hepple, op. cit. (Select Bibliography).
[207] Road Traffic Act 1972, s. 148(4).   [208] Ibid., s. 149.
[209] Road Traffic Act 1974, s. 20. For further details see Williams, *The Motor Insurance Bureau* (2nd edn., 1972).

liability insurance the insurer will pay the victim only if the insured has been found guilty of a tort. Indeed, insurance companies tend to take over such actions, and by utilising their superior financial resources and expertise they can often drag out, or even frustrate, the compensation process. Another consequence is that, in first-party insurance, premiums are easier to quote, hence lower in some cases. In the 'cable cases', for example, a factory owner who is trying to obtain insurance coverage for the loss that might flow from a power failure should be able to inform the insurer of the precise amount of cover he wishes to purchase. He should also be in a position to tell him what means, if any, he has at his disposal to minimise the effect of a power failure (e.g. an additional electrical generator). A contractor, on the other hand, may find it difficult to name a sum for which he wishes to be covered should he be held liable to the factory owner, especially if he cannot obtain accurate plans of the area in which he is working. Additionally, third-party insurance invariably involves higher transaction costs; for it will be remembered that the insurer in this kind of insurance will not pay unless and until his client (the insured) is found 'guilty' of the tort he is accused of having committed. On the other hand it could be argued that in some cases an extension of liability might help to make such activities safer since insurance companies, which will inevitably be drawn into the picture, are virtually certain to insist on stringent precautions being taken before they extend insurance coverage.[210] This illustration, incidentally, shows not only how insurance actually operates, but also how it could be used[211] to determine the most reasonable and efficient allocation of resources.

Select Bibliography

ALLEN, D. K., BOURN, C. J. and HOLYOAK, J. H. (eds.), *Accident Compensation After Pearson* (1979).

ATIYAH, P., *The Damages Lottery* (1997).

BURN, S., *Injury Tariff*, (1996) 93 (12) *Law Society Gazette*, 22.

CANE, P., *Atiyah's Accidents, Compensation and the Law* (5th edn., 1993), chs. 1, 12–17.

DAVIES, M., 'The End of the Affair: Duty of Care and Liability Insurance' (1989) 9 *Leg. Stud.* 67.

FRANKLIN, M. A., 'Replacing the Negligence Lottery: Compensation and Selective Reimbursement' 53 *Virginia LR* 724 (1967).

GREER, D., *Criminal Injuries Compensation* (1991).

HARLOW, C., *Understanding Tort Law* (1987).

OGUS, A. I. and BARENDT, E. M., *The Law of Social Security* (4th edn., 1995).

Pearson Committee Report, Cmnd. 7054-I, chs. 4–7.

---

[210] This point is made by Kötz, in Zweigert and Kötz, *An Introduction to Comparative Law*, ii, (trans. Weir, 1977), 273. Given that the position in German law presents considerable similarity with ours, the view deserves careful consideration.

[211] Contrast Stapleton, 'Tort Insurance and Ideology' (1995) 55 *MLR* 820, where she doubts whether (a) insurance *is* taken into account by the courts and (b) whether it *should* be taken into account at all. Growing evidence would suggest that the learned author is unconvincing on (a) but may find some support for (b) among those who still believe that tort law performs an important role in corrective justice.

STAPLETON, J., 'Tort, Insurance and Ideolgy', (1995) 58 *MLR* 820.
WEATHERILL, S., 'The Powers of Criminal Courts to Make Compensation Orders' (1986) 136 *New LJ* 459.
WILLIAMS, D. B., *Criminal Injuries Compensation* (2nd edn., 1986).
WILLIAMS, G. L. and HEPPLE, B. A., *Foundations of the Law of Tort* (2nd edn., 1984), chs. 5 and 6.

8. SOME GENERAL WARNINGS TO THE NOVICE TORT LAWYER

Authors of textbooks in general, and on tort law in particular, may inadvertently mislead their readers. We are not talking here of errors and omissions of the type that may creep into any book—often the result of rapid changes in the law. Here, we are referring to a different kind of misdirection. If one single reason had to be found for this phenomenon it might well be the tort syllabus and the way we have been teaching the subject in this country—a way of teaching which has, essentially, remained unaltered since the days of Salmond and Winfield! In broad terms this has meant that, like medieval theologians and lawyers, who attributed equal force to the different passages of the Bible and the Digest, we have—with minor deviations—given roughly equal time and teaching attention to the various topics included in our textbooks. Liability for damage caused by animals and the rule in *Rylands* v. *Fletcher* have thus often received disproportionate attention compared to accidents at work and traffic accidents, both of which have figured only as incidental parts of the tort of negligence. Medical malpractice has also hitherto remained unnoticed by the textbook writers; and the same has been largely true of government liability or, even more recently, what one could call the modern 'Eurotort'. The damages section of tort books has also suffered from this 'equal treatment', even though two-thirds of the nearly 3,000 cases that are actually tried every year by the High Court involve personal injury claims and are mainly concerned with quantum rather than liability issues. Books on tort—understandably but only to a degree—have also neglected or underplayed the compensation that victims of accidents can receive from other—mainly State-funded sources. In this book we have tried to remedy some of these perceived deficiencies. Thus, we have included a longer treatment of some subjects which strike us as particularly important, and abridged the space given to others for reasons which range from lack of space to the feeling that they do not deserve prime space in a student textbook. But trying to rectify some of the perceived defects is not enough; one must also identify and criticise some of the reasons behind this state of affairs.

It seems to us that a need also exists to warn students off some misapprehensions which are common to beginners who tend to assume that tort law in practice is as one finds it in the books: neat, systematic, and legalistic. The following propositions may thus be borne in mind as the reader goes through the pages that follow and encounters criticism of individual rules, decisions, and theories.

(A) What interests academic lawyers is not always of similar importance to practitioners and litigants

Causation is a good example. The Germans and Americans have produced a considerable literature on this subject. Indeed, a well-known French legal writer, paraphrasing Voltaire, once remarked that if the subject did not exist it would have to be invented so as to give the Germans a topic on which to exercise their legal minds. This observation is not meant to belittle the subject. Hart and Honoré's monograph on causation[212] is an example of erudition and style combined in discussing a difficult subject; and cases like *Hotson*[213] and *Wilshire*[214] (discussed below in Chapters 2 and 3) show how complicated this topic can be. Yet it is also worth reminding the reader of what three leading American tort lawyers had to say at the end of the one hundred pages that they devoted to this subject in their best-selling case-book:[215] 'The problem [of legal cause] is a difficult one, but the length of the treatment in this casebook and the time allotted it in most courses may perhaps give an exaggerated impression of its importance. In the great majority of negligence cases, the problem does not arise at all . . .' So, by all means let us study causation cases (and other topics of particular theoretical import) since they can help sharpen the mind; but let us also remember to keep the problem in perspective.

The same point can be made about medical malpractice cases. Few if any of them can escape jurisprudential discussions.[216] These are enriching in the sense that they can encourage lawyers—receiving nowadays more of a black-letter law training than, perhaps, ever before—to look at law, as an eminent American jurist once put it, 'from without' as well as 'from within'.[217] Nevertheless, a note of warning is needed. For when judicial statements in this part of the law are couched in philosophical or even metaphysical terms a strong case could be made for the interpretation that the court is unsure as to what the answer should be and is thus seeking refuge behind jurisprudential or philosophical shibboleths. We shall, for example, see in the so-called 'wrongful-life' cases the judges stating that impaired life is preferable to no life at all.[218] The chances are that statements such as the above will be returned to the domain of philosophers when (rather than if) the courts come to recognise that a claim for damages in such cases is not as inconceivable as they currently seem to think.

The question whether negligently inflicted pure economic loss should be compensated through tort law is another example. The academic literature on

---

[212] *Causation in the Law* (2nd edn., 1985).
[213] *Hotson* v. *East Berkshire Area Health Authority* [1987] AC 750.
[214] *Wilsher* v. *Essex Area Health Authority* [1988] AC 1074.
[215] Prosser, Wade, and Schwartz, *Torts—Cases and Materials* (7th edn., 1982), 364.
[216] See the discussion in Chapter 3, Section 1.
[217] Roscoe Pound, *The Spirit of the Common Law* (1921), 212.
[218] 'Man, who knows nothing of death or nothingness cannot possibly know whether that is so' per Stephenson LJ in *McKay* v. *Essex Health Authority and Another* [1982] QB 1166. A much more meaningful discussion of the real issues behind these cases can be found in the decision of the Supreme Court of New Jersey in *Procanik* v. *Cillo*, 97 NJ 339, 478 A. 2d 755 (1984)—a decision which, incidentally, also reveals how the wider legal background can affect the outcome of the litigation.

the subject is enormous and shows no sign of abatement. This is understand-able since the theoretical importance of the subject is enhanced by the fact that it is in the borderline zone of contract and tort.[219] Yet the pages devoted to this subject are in no way an accurate reflection of the number of times this point comes before the higher courts. Of course, supporters of the present non-liability rule attribute this (comparative) lack of case law to the strictness of the rule itself and talk of an opening of floodgates of litigation should the rule ever be changed. The fact, however, remains that this has not happened in other sys-tems (such as the French or Dutch) where the opposite, liberal, rule prevails. Lawyers in general and judges in particular are conservative by nature; they prefer the devil they know (injustice and artificiality in some cases)[220] to the devil they do not know (uncertainty).

This gap between academic tort law and judges' tort law is also made obvious by the absence of any real dialogue—at any rate until recently—between Bench and universities of the kind which, for historical reasons, we find in other coun-tries.[221] This lack of effective communication is aggravated by three factors.

First, students and academics in this country, unlike the United States, are far too quick to accept without questioning judicial utterances on a particular sub-ject.[222] *Second*, when they so express a view, it is expressed in such muted terms that it has no effect whatsoever on the recipients of the critique;[223] moreover, unless that critique is published in the literally one or two journals most judges read, it is unlikely to come to their attention. And if the objections are voiced strongly, the chances of them being published are rapidly diminished.[224] *Finally*, the insights that judges and academics have of the law are very differ-ent. Thus, Lord Goff—one of the small number of judges who through his own work judicially and extra-judicially has tried hard to bridge this gap—had this to say of this phenomenon:[225]

The judge's vision of the law tends to be fragmented; so far as it extends, his vision is intense; and it is likely to be strongly influenced by the facts of the particular case . . . jurists on the other hand, do not share the fragmented approach of the judges. They

---

[219] See Markesinis in (1987) 103 *LQR* 354. One of the most thoughtful discussions on this topic can be found in Lord Mustill's article cited in the Select Bibliography (see below).

[220] See e.g. Edmund-Davies LJ's dissenting judgment in *Spartan Steel & Alloys* v. *Martin & Co.* [1973] QB 27, and Lord Devlin's views about economic loss in *Hedley Byrne & Co. Ltd.* v. *Heller and Partners Ltd.* [1964] AC 465. Cf. Lord Hoffmann's observations in *White* v. *Chief Constable of South Yorkshire Police* [1998] 3 WLR 1510, 1551.

[221] The best account in English of this fascinating subject can be found in J. P. Dawson's *The Oracles of the Law* (1967).

[222] The point is forcefully made by, among others, Atiyah and Summers, *Form and Substance in Anglo-American Law* (1987), ch. 14.

[223] One (unnamed) Law Lord complained of this very attitude when he said: 'I'd much sooner have a much more detailed criticism than what one gets—the sort of notes which are couched in very respectful language are not particularly helpful, to us at any rate. I would much sooner have a more robust thing of much greater length.' Alan Paterson, *The Law Lords*, 15.

[224] Alan Paterson, op. cit., at 19, observed that academic expectations do not reach the Law Lords in an effective way first because of 'the academic's own reticence at expressing his criticism in a forceful man-ner lest it be perceived as disrespectful; second [because] of the censorship of the editors of the prestigious journals; [and] third [because] of the reluctance of barristers to cite articles which are strongly critical of incumbent Law Lords'.

[225] In his Maccabean Lecture in the British Academy, (see below, Select Bibliography), 183–4.

adopt a much broader approach, concerned not so much with the decision of a particular case, but rather with the place of each decision in the law as a whole. They do not share our intense view of the particular; they have rather a diffused view of the general. This is both their weakness and their strength.

One could interpret this as a plea for greater co-operation; but, as far as the practising Bar is concerned it is, on the whole, still falling on deaf ears. Not so, however, with some of our current judges. This, for example, is what Lord Justice Steyn had to say on the subject when, as a Court of Appeal judge, he had to hear *White* v. *Jones*.[226]

The question decided in *Ross* v. *Caunters* [and which had to be reconsidered in the instant case] was a difficult one. It lies at the interface of what has traditionally been regarded as the separate domains of contract and tort. It is therefore not altogether surprising that the appeal in the present case lasted three days, and that *we were referred to about forty decisions of English and foreign courts*. Pages and pages were read from some of the judgments. But we were not referred to a single piece of academic writing . . . traditionally counsel make very little use of academic materials . . . In a difficult case it is helpful to consider academic comment on the point. Often such writings examine the history of the problem, the framework into which a decision must fit, and countervailing policy considerations in greater depth than is usually possible in judgments prepared by judges who are faced with a remorseless treadmill of cases that cannot wait. And it is arguments that influence decisions rather than the reading of pages upon pages from judgments . . . (Emphasis added.)

The combination of the textbook and the learned article should progressively become an instrument that attempts to combine the vision of the particular and of the general. Lord Goff, again in the Childs Lecture at Oxford University, proclaimed that 'we now live in the age of the legal textbook'.[227] This sounds more like a prophecy than a statement of fact; but, given the form of contemporary legal education, this looks like a prophecy that may well be fulfilled. And if textbooks are to succeed in this mission, they must start by admitting that both in content and style they must be adapted to secure a new and different generation of lawyers.

Yet this plea for greater co-operation between the academic and practising side of the profession cannot be left without an important postscript; and the contents of this postscript are simple. Though, surprisingly, not all academics have been quick to embrace this crusade[228] for a stronger influence on the final direction of a judgment, judges, themselves, are slowly moving in this direction. Thus, one needs no footnotes to show that references to academic literature have increased dramatically during the last ten years or so.

In this context, one should point out another and parallel phenomenon: the modern judge, despite an unprecedented workload, turning to the lecture circuit more than ever before. And this extra-judicial activity is leading to some pieces which are not just analytical essays based on existing case law but are

---

[226] [1995] 2 AC 207, 235 (where the judgments of the Court of Appeal are reproduced before the opinions of the Law Lords).

[227] 'Judge, Jurist and Legislature' (Select Bibliography), 92.

[228] See, for instance, the timid note of Professor Cane in (1997) 113 *LQR* 515, esp. 518–19.

essays with a strong jurisprudential, comparative, and even (thinly veiled) political message. This growing list of lecturing judges now includes (in alphabetical order) Lord Bingham, Lord Browne-Wilkinson, Lord Goff, Lord Hoffmann, Lord Irvine of Lairg, Lord Justice Laws, Lord Mustill, Lord Scarman, Lord Justice Sedley, Lord Steyn, and Lord Woolf. This has been a little-noticed phenomenon but no less important for that. For these examples show, along with many other supporting illustrations from American (Holmes, Cardozo, Traynor, Posner), Canadian (Bora Laskin, Linden, Iacobucci), and Continental European (Josserand, Nipperdey, Zweigert) practice, that when a judge starts writing *and thinking* as an academic some of the academic's ideas, habits, and techniques will also, sooner or later, find their way into his (later) judgments. For a public lecture gives the judge the opportunity to reflect on his chosen subject in an un-rushed manner and from a wider angle than he will normally apply to his judicial work. And once he does that, he may develop a wider and more jurisprudential stance which is bound to affect his position when he later comes to consider a case which, arguably, is a narrow example of his earlier and wider topic.[229]

This is not all that has come out of our judges' recent involvement in academic writing. Some of the most thoughtful are now telling us what we have been suspecting for some time, namely that: 'One cannot always be sure, as regards an individual judge, that the reasons published in a judgment are in fact his reasons for the decision.'[230] Lord Mustill continues as follows:

They [the reasons] may have been constructed after the event to reconcile the decision with legal materials which appeared to stand in its way, and which played no part in his formation of the conclusion, or to call up support from favourable materials for a decision arrived at without recourse to them (for example a decision made intuitively, or on grounds of policy.

And, further down,[231] the learned judge concludes:

Many judges would, I believe, if pressed acknowledge that the outcome of a difficult case may be evolved by an unperceived background working of mechanisms quite different from those employed when he sits down with the rule-book and seeks to apply it to a simple situation.

We believe that the student and, possibly, the practitioner who fully absorbs the novelty and richness of these ideas will be able to see tort law in a very different light than the one it has hitherto been presented in.

(B) IVORY TOWER NEATNESS V. UNTIDINESS AND CONTRADICTION IN THE REAL WORLD

The fact that academics are more listened to by contemporary judges than they were in the past does not mean that the natural predilection for neatness and consistency that characterises their work can be imposed on the real world.

---

[229] On this see Markesinis 'Five Days in the House of Lords: Some Comparative Reflections on *White* v. *Jones*' (1995) 3 *Torts Law Journal* 169.
[230] Lord Mustill, ' What do Judges do?' *Särtryck ur Juridisk Tidskrift*, 1995–96 Nr. 3, 611 at 620.
[231] Ibid., 623.

The point is made here since many an unfortunate student will be pushed in his or her tutorial to fit the decisional law within the particular theory or framework that appeals to their tutor. Such exercises are not devoid of academic merit; but the student should be warned that, in most cases, the effort and the result will bear little resemblance to what happens in the real world. Many academic attempts to bring order to the untidy tort of negligence could be cited to support our provocative statement but, because of lack of space, one alone will suffice.

Professor Stapleton's work seems to fall into this category. For instance, in her feisty 'In Restraint of Tort' she rightly criticises the current trend of our courts to decide cases by first slipping them into a 'relevant pocket of liability'. She then continued: 'Yet for this to produce stability and coherent outcomes two fairly obvious conditions must be satisfied. First, it must be clear what it is about the new case which characterises it and which indicates the relevant earlier case law "pocket" within which it needs to be judged . . . [and secondly] the boundaries of existing pockets must make sense'.[232] The criticism becomes that much more obvious and convincing when, for instance, she forces her readers to ask themselves:

why is it that what is important about the facts of *Smith* v. *Bush* is the form of the defendant's carelessness (negligent professional advice) so that it can be associated with earlier case law allowing a duty of care (*Hedley Byrne*)? Why was not the relevant fact that the plaintiff suffered the economic loss through the acquisition of defective property so that the case would be placed in the *D & F Estates/Murphy* 'pocket' of case law with the result that a duty of care would be denied?[233]

The scholarly ability to criticise then gives way to the professional tendency to become a system builder. Thus Professor Stapleton succumbs to the temptation to erect her own edifice where liability will be imposed if certain positive factors are found to exist and other negative factors are not present. Her 'agenda of countervailing concerns', which militate against the imposition of liability, thus includes assurances on the following points: that the imposition of liability does not produce a 'specific unattractive socio-economic impact'; that the plaintiff has adequate and appropriate alternative means of protection; that the plaintiff is not seeking to use tort to evade an understanding as to where risks should fall; that assisting the plaintiff would not bring the law into disrepute.

In purely doctrinal terms the proposed criteria do not seem to be able to produce the desired results. For instance, Professor Stapleton has not concealed her unhappiness with the decision or the reasoning of the majority in *White* v. *Jones*. Yet would observance of her 'countervailing concerns' lead to a different result? By giving a remedy to the disappointed beneficiary, did *White* v. *Jones* bring the law into disrepute? Or was there an alternative way—*de lege lata*—for the plaintiff to protect himself? Or can one really argue that potential

---

[232] Op. cit. (Select Bibliography), 85–6.

[233] Ibid., 85; references omitted. The complete beginner may wish to return to these comments after he or she has read about these cases in Chapter 2.

beneficiaries are best placed to take out insurance instead of placing this obligation (as so many systems do) on the lawyers who carry out these transactions
(and make much money out of them)? One need not labour the point further.
Any attempt to apply these elaborate criteria to different factual situations
shows that sometimes they work and in others they simply make no sense at
all.[234] Yet even if this critique is unduly harsh, one still has to ask oneself
whether such a highly structured approach will prove more popular to our
courts than their existing (and not always satisfactory) techniques? Time alone
will answer this question. But the history of the tort of Negligence thus far suggests that our courts are likely to continue shifting from one *mutually inconsistent
doctrine* to another as they grapple with the immensely complex problems that
confront them under the heading of the tort of Negligence. The italicised words
are, in fact not ours but Lord Mustill's who, after noting that the House of Lords
has, in the last sixty years, 'embraced six mutually inconsistent doctrines on a
field of great theoretical and practical importance' concluded with the statement:

... it involves no disloyalty on my part to the legal system in which I have spent my
working life, or to past, present and future colleagues to say that the picture thus
painted is not one of unqualified success . . . *The root of the problem is I believe a reluctance on
the part of the judges to accept inwardly, and afterwards to acknowledge outwardly that decisions in
this field are essentially concerned with social engineering.*[235]

Tort lawyers, especially beginners, should thus revert to these points and
reconsider them in the light of the suggested further reading. Above all, however, they should bear all these points in mind when absorbing the more technical arguments which are advanced in the chapters that follow, especially
Chapters 2 and 3 which deal with the most amorphous and most important of
torts: Negligence.

(C) TORT LAW IS USING OLD TOOLS TO MEET SOCIAL NEEDS OF A NEW AND DIFFERENT ERA

The longevity of some tort rules and concepts is as admirable as it is remarkable. Thus, in this country, in many cases much of what we do and how we
think today can be traced back to the Middle Ages. Even the way our books are
divided can, in some respects, be attributed to the forms of action which, as
Maitland put it, we have buried but still rule us from their graves. In the
Continent of Europe one can go back even further to the law of ancient Rome—
parts of the modern French or German law being shaped on the basis of often
erroneous beliefs of what Roman law used to be.

---

[234] This is particularly obvious from Professor Stapleton's latest piece entitled 'Duty of Care Factors: a
Selection from the Judicial Menus', in *The Law of Obligations. Essays in Celebration of John Fleming* (ed. by Peter
Cane and Jane Stapleton, 1998), 59 ff. For here, we find a revamped list of factors which the learned
author feels ought to determine the discovery (or not) of a duty of care. Yet she, herself, admits (at 87) that
these factors may not be applicable to new factual configurations and, more devastatingly for her theory,
may be differently evaluated by different judges. Such exercises, therefore, though highly stimulating for
legal theorists, are not likely to have much effect in the bulk of tort litigation.
[235] Op. cit. (Select Bibliography), 23, 24 (emphasis added).

To a large extent this survival is due to the flexible, if not amorphous, content of some of these concepts. Yet this adaptability cannot conceal the fact that many of these rules were devised for human beings (the plaintiffs and defendants of the past) rather than corporations or legal entities (the typical plaintiffs and defendants of today). They were also developed at a time when risk-spreading techniques (like insurance) were weak or unknown; and had as their prime aim the shifting of losses at a time when a weak social conscience attributed no role to the State in the context of accidents at work and disease. One must also remember that they were built on, or at least flourished around, the idea of fault; and made a crucial distinction (not necessarily supportable in our times) between harm resulting from accident and from disease[236] (e.g. cerebral haemorrhage resulting from cranial injuries or high blood pressure). It is, as stated, a tribute to these concepts' adaptability that they have survived for so long. Indeed, it is almost amazing that the tort of Negligence can be used to tackle the careless manufacturer who allows a snail to slip into a ginger-beer bottle; an obstetrician who makes an error in the process of a complicated delivery of a child by forceps; to the driver who causes multiple injuries as a result of an unexpected brain haemorrhage which causes him to lose control of his faculties. The same could be said of the medieval tort of nuisance and more recent attempts to use it for zoning functions or to combat environmental pollution—a problem certainly not new, but new in its dimensions.

The problem of adapting tort law of the past to a new world has not been unique to this system. A great French jurist—Jean Carbonnier—referring to the ingenious efforts to use an amorphous provision of the Napoleonic Code of 1804 (article 1384 1 CC) to cope with car accidents, has described them as an immense waste of time and intelligence. The French now have a new Act on the subject. It certainly will not solve all the problems; but it does represent a fresh attempt to solve a problem that had hitherto been tackled by provisions devised in the era of horse-and-buggy and no insurance. The reader of tort textbooks should thus not content himself or herself with the criticism of individual decisions but should question constantly the suitability of tort as a means of compensating injuries. This inadequacy is particularly obvious in the case of medical accidents from which both doctors and patients come out as losers. This leads us to the next point.

(D) TORT LAW NEEDS REFORMING BUT REFORM DOES NOT APPEAR TO BE AROUND THE CORNER

The mid-1970s were dominated by the Pearson Committee and its report. It worked hard and in 1978 produced three interesting volumes. They have been gathering dust ever since on some official shelf, confirming A. P. Herbert's cynical remark that Royal Commissions are sometimes set up as lightning-conductors to allay the well-founded suspicion that nothing is actually going to be done about the matter in question.[237] Systematic reform is lacking;

---

[236] The subject of Jane Stapleton's interesting and important work, *Disease and the Compensation Debate* (1986).

[237] *Anything But Action*, Hobart Paper No. 5 (1960).

piecemeal change, on the other hand, is the rule. Sometimes it comes from Parliament on rather narrow topics, for example the Vaccine Damages Scheme. On others, it is prompted by the EC,[238] which speaks from the clouds of Brussels, and then expects its fiats to be painlessly incorporated into the corpus of national law—not always an easy task. On other occasions reform has come from both Parliament and the courts, each ignoring the activities of the other and, in many respects, (inadvertently) creating more problems than they have solved. We shall encounter such examples when we discuss the Misrepresentation Act 1967 and *Hedley Byrne* v. *Heller*,[239] and the Defective Premises Act 1972 and *Dutton* v. *Bognor Regis*[240] and its progenies. Finally, the legislator, himself, keeps fine-tuning his solutions, creating layers of law and much complexity besides.[241]

This way of proceeding does not only encourage confusion; it also raises a wider issue. Since most tort problems do not refer to vote-catching issues, the chances that Parliament will intervene to rectify anomalies must be slim. In fairness, however, one must also admit that (in England but not in the USA) some of the most important tort-law reforms that took place just before and after the Second World War were made by Parliament. If that is the case, should we still adhere to a doctrine—outdated in most respects yet also conveniently kept alive by orthodox academics and timorous judges—that the courts cannot mould the law to meet new circumstances? Tort law has a good number of examples that raise this issue. In *Launchbury* v. *Morgans*,[242] for example (discussed in Chapter 6, Section 3), was the House of Lords right to castigate Lord Denning's attempt in the Court of Appeal[243] to introduce the doctrine of the family car? Was the House of Lords right in *Pirelli*[244] (discussed in Chapter 8, Section 1), to apply a rule which they believed to be patently unjust? In this case the legislature conveniently obliged,[245] but what happened to the Practice Direction of 1966 in which their Lordships gave themselves the right to deviate from some of their earlier opinions? And are the higher courts right in not taking the first available opportunity to alter the English doctrine of privity of contract, which has encouraged the growth of tort law in the late 1970s and early 1980s as the only way of avoiding the undesirable side-effects of our rigid contract law? While studying his tort cases the critically minded student should constantly ask himself if legislation is the only or best way of reform. To quote Lord Goff again:[246]

For all practical purposes, textbooks are as informative as any code could be, indeed more so; and they lack all the defects of codes, since they can be changed without difficulty—as the law develops, and they encourage, rather than inhibit, the gradual

---

[238] For example the Consumer Protection Act. Students of drafting techniques should compare the text of the Act with the EEC Directive that it is meant to implement.

[239] [1964] AC 465.   [240] [1972] 1 QB 373.

[241] See, for instance, our discussion in Chapter 8 about the deductibility of social security benefits from tort awards.

[242] [1973] AC 127.   [243] [1971] 2 QB 245.

[244] *Pirelli General Cable Works Ltd.* v. *Faber (Oscar) and Partners* [1983] 2 AC 1.

[245] By passing the Latent Damage Act 1984.

[246] 'Judge, Jurist and Legislature' (see below, Select Bibliography), 92.

development of the law. To put it shortly; propositions of law in a textbook need not aspire to completeness; they may be changed without legislation; and judges are at liberty to depart from them, if persuaded that it is right to do so.

Once again, therefore, the plea can be made for the exposition and development of tort law through a partnership between case law and academic writing rather than the fossilising and distorting effect that piecemeal legislation can have on the development of the law.[247]

(E) TORT LAW IS, IN PRACTICE, OFTEN INACCESSIBLE TO THE ORDINARY VICTIM

The multitude of cases that a student will encounter in tort textbooks may lead him to believe that victims of accident have easy and frequent recourse to this branch of the law. In reality nothing could be further from the truth; and this misapprehension, as well, is encouraged by the fact that the operation of tort law in practice tends to be ignored by traditional books and cases. The reality is that most victims of accidents do not even go as far as consulting a lawyer as to what their rights are, let alone pursue them to a successful conclusion.

Accidents at home[248] offer an example where legal action is rarely pursued because, quite simply, there is no legal action to pursue (e.g. slipping in the bathtub or scalding in the kitchen). On other occasions, however, no action is sought (though one, for example, might be possible under the Occupiers' Liability Acts) because the victims are unaware of their possible rights or, ignorant of the possible role of insurance, would consider it unsociable to sue the owner/host of the premises.

But even where there are no such inhibiting factors, a large number of victims are left without a remedy either because they never bothered to ascertain their rights or because they were discouraged from doing so by the fear of becoming entangled in a lengthy and costly legal process. The figures are, in fact, quite worrying. The Oxford Socio-Legal Studies Group, in its *Compensation and Support for Illness and Injury*, claims that out of the representative sample of 1,711 victims questioned by them, 444 (26 per cent) considered claiming damages, 392 (23 per cent) thought a claim was possible, 247 (14 per cent) actually consulted a lawyer, and 198 (12 per cent) actually obtained damages.[249] These figures suggest that most potential claims are defeated at the outset: the accident victim does not realise that a legal remedy might be available or, even if he does, other constraining factors prevent him from consulting a solicitor about bringing a claim.[250] Among these constraining factors costs are the most pervasive fear, with the legal-aid scheme being unavailable to all but the poorest and in some cases, such as defamation, not being available at all. The unavailability of the class-action mechanism or the (limited possibility of) undertaking litigation on a contingent-fee system (both possible in the United States) thus enables culpable defendants not only to discourage litigation but also, if one starts, to drag it out so as to force weaker plaintiffs

---

[247] Ibid., 89. [248] On which see Hazel Genn's *Meeting Legal Needs?* (see below, Select Bibliography).
[249] Op. cit., 46. [250] *Compensation and Support for Illness and Injury* (see below, Select Bibliography), 47.

into disadvantageous settlements. Both these weaknesses of the English system are periodically reviewed but it is difficult to predict when and what type of relief will come to this grave problem. The most likely cause of relief for most victims will thus, probably, come when Lord Woolf's monumental review of the civil litigation process is implemented[251] which is likely to reduce litigation costs and speed up the litigation process.

Victims are also discouraged from having recourse to tort law because costs are not only great but also unpredictable (unlike many European systems where, for example, they are fixed in various ways in advance and can be estimated by the prospective litigant). The unpredictability is, of course, also an element of the litigation process that is increased by some of the legal rules that we shall discuss in this book. Prominent among them is the defence of contributory negligence that may lead to the victim's damages being reduced in an often totally unpredictable way. The retention of this defence may appear to be morally sound for, according to this view, why should a victim who has been at fault be in a position to increase through his own fault the extent of the tortfeasor's liability? Yet in reality this argument is considerably weakened where—as in the cases of car-traffic accidents—an insurance company is the ultimate payer and, in many cases, the victim's fault in substance consists of some minor inattention, inevitable in some kinds of claimants, like young children or old people. To this objection the defenders of the *status quo* would counter that the abolition of the defence of contributory negligence would oblige insurers to pay out larger amounts and thus force them to put up the premiums. Even this fear, however, has not been substantiated after the recent reform of the traffic-accident law in France that effectively reduced, and in many cases totally eliminated, this defence. The French innovations are thus worth a closer look, although this is not the right place to discuss them.

The outcome of litigation is further complicated and made uncertain by the necessity for the plaintiff to prove the tortfeasor's fault and/or to establish the causal link between the faulty act or harmful conduct and the damaging result. The system only partially helps the victim through such devices as *res ipsa loquitur*; in many areas, however, the plaintiff's position is unenviable. Actions against the pharmaceutical industry offer a good example. In this country there has not been a single successful action against a drug manufacturer. This bizarre result must surely be as undesirable as the opposite extreme, found in the United States, where many manufacturers—especially of contraceptive devices—have been forced either into bankruptcy or out of the development or distribution of such products.[252]

The overall picture provided by the modern sociological surveys of the operation of the tort system in practice is a grim one. The Oxford Socio-Legal Studies Group[253] likened the position of victims of accident to participants in:

. . . a compulsory, long-distance obstacle race. The victims, without their consent, are placed at the starting line, and told that if they complete the whole course, the umpire

---

[251] See his *Access to Justice* report of 1996.   [252] J. G. Fleming (Select Bibliography, below), 15.
[253] Op. cit. (n. 250 above), 132–3.

at the finishing line will compel the race promoters to give them a prize; the amount of the prize, however, must remain uncertain until the last moment because the umpire has discretion to fix it individually for each finisher. None of the runners is told the distance he must cover to complete the course, nor the time it is likely to take. Some of the obstacles in the race are fixed hurdles (rules of law), while others can, without warning, be thrown into the path of the runner by the race promoters, who obviously have every incentive to restrict the number of runners who can complete the course. As the runners' physical fitness, and their psychological preparedness for the race, varies greatly the relative difficulty of the obstacles also varies from runner to runner. In view of all the uncertainties . . . many runners drop out; others press on . . . After waiting to see how many runners drop out at the early obstacles without any inducement, the promoters begin to tempt the remaining runners with offers of money to retire . . . most runners accept . . . The few hardy ones who actually finish may still be disappointed with the prize money.

(F) MISCELLANEOUS MATTERS

Some of the points we make here are certainly not limited to tort law; though in the course of writing a long, detailed book on this subject we thought they were particularly pronounced in its sphere. Another point that troubled us was: why raise these points here? We came to the conclusion that we should, in the belief that, despite limitations in time and space, the student should not be presented with the rudiments of a particular branch of the law in a compartmentalised way but, every now and then, should be asked to consider the 'details' against the broader fabric of English justice. In one sense this might lead to a more jurisprudential approach to tort law; but then what is wrong with that? All except those following one-year law courses must surely favour a more broadly based instruction of law, even allowing for the fact that most students who are likely to use this book will be in their first or second year of study. So here are some general observations to be tested against the more detailed study of the material provided in this book.

(*i*) Our law of torts is increasingly dominated by statute. An (admittedly) quick study of the laws of Western Europe suggests that we have more and longer statutes on torts than any other system in Western Europe. In itself this may not be a defect; but it becomes a problem given (1) the long-winded nature of English legislative drafting; (2) the lack of proper training in statutory construction; and (3) the lack of co-ordination between the courts and the legislators when dealing with law reform.

(*ii*) Our case law—especially on tort—is the second headache. Judgments are getting longer, to some extent inevitably given the growing complexity of the law. But the length of our judgments compared with the length of judgments from other Commonwealth jurisdictions reveals an excessive use of citation in lieu of substantive reasoning. To give one example: anyone who reads *Murphy* and *Norsk*, two more-or-less contemporaneous decisions of the House of Lords and the Supreme Court of Canada on the question of economic loss, will immediately notice a difference in styles, sources of inspiration, and techniques. For the student at least, *Norsk* provides an excellent functional analysis of an as-yet unresolved problem, whereas *Murphy* seems bogged down in a dry and often not fully thought out consideration of precedents. Anathema though it may seem to some, it is equally true to say that today most of the exciting ideas in tort law are coming from the Supreme Court of Canada and the High Court of Australia and not from the House of Lords.[254]

Select Bibliography

BERLINS, M. and DYER, C., *The Law Machine* (2nd edn., 1986), chs. 1, 6, and 9.

BURMAN, S. and GENN, H. (eds.), *Accidents in the Home* (1977).

CANE, P., *Atiyah's Accidents, Compensation and the Law* (5th edn., 1993), chs. 3–11.

CONAGHAN, J. and MANSELL, W., *The Wrongs of Tort* (1994).

FLEMING, J. G., *The American Tort Process* (1988).

GENN, H., *Hard Bargaining—Out of Court Settlement in Personal Injury Actions* (1987).

—— *Meeting Legal Needs? An Evaluation of a Scheme for Personal Injury Victims* (1982).

GOFF, LORD GOFF OF CHIEVELEY, 'Judge, Jurist and Legislation' (1987) 2 *Denning LJ* 79.

—— 'The Search for Principle', Maccabean Lecture in Jurisprudence (1983) 69 *Proceedings of the British Academy*, 169.

HARLOW, C., *Understanding Tort Law* (1987), ch. 3.

HARRIS, D. et al., *Compensation and Support for Illness and Injury* (1984).

MUSTILL, LORD, 'Negligence in the World of Finance', 5 *The Supreme Court* [Malaysia] *Journal*, 1 (1992).

STAPLETON, J., 'In Restraint of Tort' in *The Frontiers of Liability*, vol. II (ed. by P. B. H. Birks) (1994), 83 ff.

---

[254] In this we agree with Ewan McKendrick, [1992] *LMCLQ* 88, 92: 'The last decade in the House of Lords has generally been witnessed by great conservatism and undue deference to Parliament. It is now rather difficult to maintain that the House of Lords is the most influential court in the common law world.' McKendrick, in his discussion of the House of Lords' decision in *Woolwich Equitable Building Society* v. *IRC* [1993] AC 70, expresses the hope that in that case and others, 'there are now some signs that the House of Lords may rediscover its role'.

2

General Principles of Negligence

1. THE ELEMENTS OF NEGLIGENCE

1. The Conceptual Structure of Negligence

The tort of negligence forms one of the most dynamic and rapidly changing areas of liability in the modern common law. Its expansion since the nineteenth century reflects the pressures which the rise of an industrial and urban society has brought to bear upon the traditional categories of legal redress for interference with protected interests.[1] The growth and increasing sophistication of insurance have also contributed to this expansion.[2] A doctrinal examination of negligence must not lose sight of this wider social and economic context within which the tort has developed, which is reflected in fluidity of the central legal concepts and the courts' ever-increasing recourse to 'policy' as an explanation for their decisions.

The conceptual structure of negligence is highly flexible and capable of general application. These features have allowed the courts to utilise the tort in the context of novel claims for compensation. The evolution of the tort, however, has not all always favoured the expansion of liability, and in recent years courts in most common-law systems have placed restrictions on its scope. It would be wrong to see the tort of negligence as set upon some predetermined path of enlargement.

Duty, breach, causation, and damage are the elements, which together make up any successful negligence claim.[3] Their requirements may be rephrased as a series of questions, each of which must be answered affirmatively if the plaintiff is to win: does the law recognise liability in this type of situation (duty)? Was the defendant careless in the sense of failing to conform to the standard of care set by law (breach)? Has the plaintiff suffered a loss (damage) for which the law regards the defendant as responsible either in whole or in part (causation)? This chapter will address each of these questions in turn. The question of how the court puts a monetary value on the damage suffered by the plaintiff for the

---

[1] See J. G. Fleming, 'Remoteness and Duty: the Control Devices in Liability for Negligence' (1953) 31 *Can. BR* 471, 471–2.

[2] See M. Davies, 'The End of the Affair: Duty of Care and Liability Insurance' (1989) 9 *Leg. Stud.* 967; although a more sceptical view on the role of insurance in the development of the tort is expressed by J. Stapleton, 'Tort, Insurance and Ideology' (1995) 58 *MLR* 820.

[3] See *Lochgelly Iron and Coal Co.* v. *M'Mullan* [1934] AC 1, 25; the tort of negligence 'properly connotes the complex of duty, breach and damage thereby suffered by the person to whom the duty was owing' (Lord Wright); and more recently, *Burton* v. *Islington HA* [1992] 3 WLR 639, 655: 'it is now elementary that the tort of negligence involves three factors: a duty of care, a breach of that duty and consequent damage' (Dillon LJ).

purpose of awarding compensation or *damages* is a separate issue which is considered in Chapter 8.

The courts did not recognise the existence of a general duty in tort imposing liability for careless behaviour across a range of situations and relationships until the 1930s. The turning point was the decision of the House of Lords in *Donoghue* v. *Stevenson*.[4] Prior to this decision, legal liability for carelessness was clearly established only in a number of separate, specified situations, which lacked a unifying principle. A duty to take care was attached by law to certain traditional categories of status, as in the case of the duty owed to a customer by an innkeeper or common carrier, or the duty of an artisan to use the customary degree of skill and care in his work. Other situations, which gave rise to a duty of care without the need for a specific promise or undertaking, included the holding of certain public offices and the bailment of goods.[5] Road and rail accidents and maritime collisions caused by carelessness could also lead to liability in tort, although in many such cases legal responsibility was limited by the operation of the defences of contributory negligence and consent. In the nineteenth century the courts added the category of liability for 'things dangerous in themselves', such as a loaded weapon.[6] In such cases the law recognised 'a peculiar duty to take precaution imposed upon those who send forth or install such articles when it is necessarily the case that other parties will come within their proximity'.[7]

Beyond this the courts declined to go. This was partly on the grounds that duties of care, which originated in *contract*, were confined in their effect to the parties to a particular agreement. To use tort to extend the liability of a landlord, builder, or manufacturer to remote third parties would undermine the strict common-law principle of 'privity of contract'.[8] For example, a landlord who contracted to repair the floor of a house and then failed to do so owed no duty of care to the tenant's wife injured when the floor gave way beneath her since 'there was but one contract, and that was made with the husband. The wife cannot sue upon it.'[9]

This emphasis on privity of contract amounted to a view that in the area of negligence, tort was subordinate to contract as a source of civil liability. However, as we have seen, some exceptions to privity of contract had long been recognised. The restriction of tort claims came to be seen as outmoded because the courts could no longer find a coherent explanation for the admission of some exceptions and the denial of others. The treatment of claims for compensation was perceived as having become arbitrary and unjust.[10]

---

[4] [1932] AC 562.   [5] See Winfield, 'Duty in Tortious Negligence' (1934) 34 *Col. LR* 41, 45.

[6] *Langridge* v. *Levy* (1837) 2 M & W 519; (1838) 4 M & W 337.

[7] *Dominion Natural Gas Co. Ltd.* v. *Collins* [1909] AC 640, 646 (Lord Dunedin).

[8] *Winterbottom* v. *Wright* (1842) 10 M & W 109 is generally taken to be the origin of this strict insistence of privity of contract.

[9] *Cavalier* v. *Pope* [1906] AC 424, 430 (Lord James).

[10] See, in particular, the doubts expressed by Scrutton LJ in *Hodge* v. *Anglo-American Oil Co.* (1922) 12 Ll. L. Rep. 183, 186, and by Greer LJ in *Bottomley* v. *Bannister* [1932] 1 KB 458, 478–9. On the other hand, the early attempt of Brett LJ to formulate a general principle of liability in *Heaven* v. *Pender* (1883) 11 QBD 503, 509, did not meet with general favour: see Cotton and Bowen LJJ in the same case at 516–17; Brett MR himself, Bowen and A. L. Smith LJJ in *Le Lievre* v. *Gould* [1893] 1 QB 491, 497, 502, 504; and Greer and MacKinnon LJJ in *Barnes* v. *Irwell Valley Water Board* [1939] 1 KB 21, 33, 46.

These doubts set the scene for the decision in *Donoghue* v. *Stevenson*,[11] which finally established the duty of a manufacturer to an ultimate consumer to ensure that goods put into circulation are free from defects which he should have foreseen might cause physical injury or damage to property. The appellant alleged that she had been poisoned by drinking the contents of a bottle of ginger beer manufactured by the respondent and purchased for her by a friend from a retailer. The opaque surface of the bottle concealed the remains of a decomposed snail, which the appellant discovered only after she had consumed most of the bottle's contents. She claimed as a result to have contracted gastro-enteritis. By a bare majority, the House of Lords held that there was a duty of care on these facts, overturning the old cases, which had limited the scope of duty in the ways described above.

In his judgment, Lord Atkin addressed the question of how to formulate a 'general conception of relations giving rise to a duty of care, of which the particular cases found in the books are but instances', in the following terms:

> The rule that you are to love your neighbour becomes in law: You must not injure your neighbour and the lawyer's question: Who is my neighbour? receives a restricted reply. You must take reasonable care to avoid acts or omissions which you can reasonably foresee would be likely to injure your neighbour. Who then in law is my neighbour? The answer seems to be persons who are so closely and directly affected by my act that I ought reasonably to have them in contemplation as being so affected when I am directing my mind to the acts or omissions which are called into question.[12]

This statement of the 'neighbour principle' remains controversial, not least because Lord Atkin made no reference to the distinction between physical harm—personal injury or property damage—and pure economic or financial loss, which has since become an important marker of the limits of tort liability. Its status is at best that of a guideline of general principle; in no sense is it a formula that can be mechanically applied to determine the incidence of liability. Nevertheless, in its decisive rejection of the traditional, narrow formulation of duty situations it marks the starting-point for analysis of the modern tort.

According to Lord Atkin, the decision in *Donoghue* v. *Stevenson* supplied a legal remedy to meet an obvious 'social wrong', thereby giving legal expression 'to a general public sentiment of moral wrongdoing'.[13] Fault, in this sense, is at the basis of negligence liability; the plaintiff has to show that the defendant's behaviour was careless. Damage is also an essential requirement. Unlike, for example, the torts of libel, trespass, and false imprisonment, which are said to be actionable *per se*,[14] in negligence the plaintiff must prove that he sustained a loss or injury as a result of the defendant's negligence. Fault, causation, and damage are necessary but not sufficient conditions of liability, however. In the old Roman-law terminology, *damnum sine iniuria* is not enough to justify the imposition of liability. Since the modern expansion of negligence began, the very generality of the notion of liability for fault has made it necessary for the courts to have resort to 'control devices' whose purpose is to confine what

---

[11] [1932] AC 562.   [12] Ibid., 580.   [13] [1932] AC 562, 538, 580, respectively.
[14] See Chapters 4 and 7 below.

would otherwise be an over-extensive legal liability.[15] While to some extent the courts have achieved this by references to causation, including the concept of 'remoteness' or 'legal cause', it is above all the concept of *duty of care* which they have used to shape the tort of negligence.

2. The Duty Concept

The notion of duty of care has been called 'superfluous', the result of an 'historical accident',[16] and the 'fifth wheel on the coach'.[17] In other systems, particularly the civil-law systems of the European mainland, the concept has no precise equivalent, causation or other notions being used to perform the functions duty accomplishes in our law. Thus, though roughly the same process of classifying legal claims as admissible or not inevitably takes place, it is achieved through other notions such as 'fault' (as a legal term of art), causation, and damage (both of the latter being understood in a normative sense).[18] If the concept of duty in the common law serves a useful purpose, this must be found in its capacity to synthesise the numerous different criteria used by the courts to determine the boundaries of negligence liability. Additionally, it also presents a distinct advantage over causative notions in so far as it makes those who are deciding issues of liability fully conscious of the fact that policy determines the final outcome.

The issue of *duty* is thus essentially concerned with whether the law recognises in principle the possibility of liability in a given type of situation. To put it differently, it helps demarcate the range of persons and relationships that receive the protection of the law. Thus, even where the defendant's carelessness can be shown to have caused damage to the plaintiff, the law may nevertheless not acknowledge the existence of a 'duty situation', thereby refusing to impose liability. To put this the other way round, where the law does not acknowledge a duty situation the defendant, effectively, has immunity from liability for damage caused by his negligence.[19] This may happen for a number of reasons, the most important being that the law does not grant equal protection to different *kinds of damage*. Whereas physical injury and damage to tangible property interests are normally within the scope of the duty of care, financial or 'pure economic' losses which are not directly connected to physical damage may not be. The precise extent to which the law recognises liability for economic loss has been one of the most difficult questions to face the courts in the past few years. In its recent decision in *Murphy* v. *Brentwood DC*[20] the House

---

[15] See Fleming, op. cit. (Select Bibliography, below). How arbitrary the 'controlling devices' can be may be seen from the latest decision of the House of Lords in the matter of psychiatric injury. Thus, see *White* v. *Chief Constable of South Yorkshire Police* [1998] 3 WLR 1510, especially Lord Hoffmann's opinion.

[16] Winfield, op. cit. (1932) *Col. LR* 41, 66.

[17] Buckland, 'The Duty to Take Care' (1935) 51 *LQR* 637.

[18] See generally F. H. Lawson, 'Duty of Care: A Comparative Study' (1947) 22 *Tulane LR* 111; B. S. Markesinis, *The German Law of Torts: A Comparative Introduction* (1990), in particular ch. 2. Professor Hepple (see below, Select Bibliography) is the latest writer to express doubts about the continuing need for the notion of duty of care. His proposed solution would bring English law much closer to the French model.

[19] See D. Howarth, 'Negligence after *Murphy*: Time to Rethink' [1991] *CLJ* 58.

[20] [1992] 1 AC 398.

of Lords formulated a narrow rule limiting the scope for recovery in this area, but economic loss remains recoverable in a number of other situations. Another kind of damage which the tort of negligence only partially encompasses is 'nervous shock'—nowadays usually referred to as 'psychiatric injury'. One commonly occurring example of this is the medical condition known as post-traumatic stress disorder which may arise in reaction to the death or injury of a close relative or friend, especially if this occurred in gruesome circumstances. The courts have only slowly, and because of progress in medical science, come to accept that 'nervous shock' constitutes a physical condition for which compensation may be appropriate. Even then, as the House of Lords' decision in *Alcock* v. *Chief Constable of South Yorkshire*[21] indicates, liability will tend to be limited to a small class consisting for the most part of immediate relatives of the victim present at the scene of a particular accident or its immediate aftermath.

The concept of duty is also used to categorise claims for compensation by reference to *classes of plaintiffs and defendants*. For example, the common law at one stage failed to recognise the unborn child or embryo in the womb as a potential plaintiff for these purposes,[22] and statutory intervention was required for this rule to be reversed.[23] The courts have since changed their minds on the question of the availability of an action by a child born alive for injuries sustained in the womb,[24] but for most purposes the (English) common law has now been ousted by the Congenital Disabilities (Civil Liability) Act 1976. Conversely, certain categories of defendants—in particular those involved in the administration of justice[25] and, to a lesser degree, in the public service generally[26]—have what amounts to a qualified immunity from negligence actions. As already stated, these 'blanket' immunities tend to set aside the (English) common law from other legal systems and may well end up being challenged at some future date as being in conflict with some of the basic tenets of human rights legislation (both national and international).

Finally, the concept of duty is concerned with the important distinction between *acts and omissions*.[27] Liability for positive acts of carelessness is well recognised, but liability for failure to act is treated differently, with 'duties of affirmative action' being imposed only in exceptional circumstances. Of these, two of the most important are the duties owed by occupiers of premises to lawful visitors and by employers to their employees. For what are mainly historical

[21] [1992] 1 AC 310. The current trend is, if anything, becoming more restrictive. See *White* v. *Chief Constable of South Yorkshire Police* [1998] 3 WLR 1510 and the more detailed discussion in the text, below.

[22] *Walker* v. *Great Northern Railway* (1891) 28 LR Ir. 69.

[23] In the form of the Congenital Disabilities (Civil Liability) Act 1976. Courts in other common-law jurisdictions took a different view: see in particular the decisions of the Supreme Court of Victoria in *Watt* v. *Rama* [1972] VR 353 and of the Ontario Court of Appeal in *Duval* v. *Séguin* (1973) 40 DLR (3d) 666.

[24] *Burton* v. *Islington HA* [1992] 2 WLR 639.

[25] *Rondel* v. *Worsley* [1969] 1 AC 191; *Sirros* v. *Moore* [1975] QB 118.

[26] The immunity of the Crown is now limited by the Crown Proceedings Act 1947. Local government authorities and similar bodies benefit from a certain degree of immunity in the exercise of their discretionary powers. See *Anns* v. *Merton LBC* [1978] AC 728; *Murphy* v. *Brentwood DC* [1991] 1 AC 398; and Chapter 3, Section 5, below.

[27] Lord Goff extensively discusses this in his judgment in *Smith* v. *Littlewoods Organisation Ltd.* [1987] AC 241.

reasons these areas of law, which have been heavily influenced by statutory intervention, have developed separately from the mainstream of negligence liability and for this reason they are the subject of special treatment in Chapters 3 and 6 respectively. These chapters must thus be read in conjunction with the present one.

3. Duty, Foreseeability, and Fault

The notion of duty is sometimes used in a separate and more specific sense, namely that for there to be a duty of care in a particular case the harm in question must have been foreseeable to the *individual* plaintiff.[28] In *Bourhill* v. *Young* Lord Wright explained that foreseeability 'is always relative to the individual affected. This raises a serious additional difficulty in the cases where it has to be determined not merely whether the act itself is negligent against someone but whether it is negligent *vis-à-vis* the plaintiff.'[29] In this case the House of Lords held that a motorist who was killed in a collision brought about by his own carelessness owed no duty of care to a pedestrian in the vicinity of the accident who suffered nervous shock and a terminated pregnancy as a result of hearing the sound of the crash and witnessing its aftermath. Rather than say that the particular claimant was an 'unforeseeable plaintiff' to whom, as an individual, no duty was owed, this case may now be more accurately explained by saying that she was not within the general class of plaintiffs who were able to recover for damage of this kind, namely nervous shock. In order to keep conceptual confusion to a minimum, it is normally better to regard duty as giving rise to a *general* or '*notional*' question of this kind, and to leave the issue of whether a *particular* plaintiff can recover against a particular defendant to the question of causation or remoteness of damage. This is the approach which will be taken in this book.

This does not mean that the individual relationship between plaintiff and defendant does not matter when it comes to ascertaining whether a duty of care arose between them. In some circumstances the nature of their *pre-tort relationship*—that is to say, the nature of undertakings or assumptions of responsibility made by one party to the other before the damage occurred of which the plaintiff is complaining—may be essential. This is frequently the case, for example, with regard to recovery for financial losses and with regard to liability for pure omissions—two areas in which a duty of care rarely arises between strangers in the same way that it does, for example, in respect of physical damage inflicted by one user of the highway on another.

However, it is important to stress that even where the particular individual circumstances of plaintiff and defendant are significant for establishing the existence and scope of a duty of care, the test is hardly ever concerned with foreseeability as such. Foreseeability alone is, in fact, entirely inadequate as a test for establishing a duty of care. As Lord Goff recently pointed out: 'It is very tempting to try to solve all problems of negligence by reference to an all-

---

[28] See R. W. M. Dias, 'The Breach Problem and the Duty of Care' (1956) 30 *Tulane LR* 376, 380 ff.
[29] [1943] AC 92, 108. See also *Alcock* v. *Chief Constable of South Yorkshire* [1992] 1 AC 310, 319.

embracing criterion of foreseeability, thereby effectively reducing all decisions in this field to questions of fact. But this comfortable option is, alas, not open to us.'[30]

Although Lord Atkin's 'neighbour principle' stresses foreseeability or 'reasonable contemplation' of harm as a preliminary test of duty, the use of this criterion fails to explain why many kinds of non-physical damage[31] which are entirely foreseeable nevertheless lie outside the scope of negligence liability. It may be just as foreseeable, for example, that careless driving on a busy road may result in physical injury and in damage to the property of other road users—both these kinds of damage are in principle recoverable in negligence—as that it will result in financial losses to road-users who are merely delayed following the accident and who, without suffering any injury or damage to property, may as a result forfeit wages or a valuable business opportunity. These financial losses, however, will not normally be recoverable, thanks to the rule limiting liability for what is termed 'pure economic loss'.[32]

Again, foreseeability is only one part of the concept of *breach* of duty. A breach of duty arises where the conduct of the defendant is 'unreasonable' in the sense of failing to reach the appropriate standard of care. This will be the standard of normally careful behaviour in the profession, occupation, or activity in question. In applying this standard in what is sometimes a rough-and-ready way, the courts frequently balance the degree of foreseeability or *risk* of harm against the *costs* to the defendant of avoiding the harm and the wider *benefits* foregone if a certain activity cannot be carried on.[33] The level at which the standard is set is an evaluative question which the courts have acknowledged involves issues of policy and judgment, and not a question which can be addressed solely by asking whether the particular harm was foreseeable in the circumstances. Thus, is a cricket club at fault if a batsman hits a six and the ball lands on and injures a passer-by? The answer may depend on the likelihood of such an injury occurring and the extent of the precautions—which might range from building a higher fence to stopping cricket being played altogether on that site—which could have prevented it.[34]

It can be seen from this discussion that an important distinction exists between *negligence as a state of mind* and the *tort of negligence*. Negligence as a state of mind, distinct from both intention and recklessness, denotes the failure to foresee the consequences of one's actions in terms of the risk of harm they create to others. While negligence in this sense is a necessary condition of liability in tort, it is very far from being sufficient even assuming the existence of a causal link between the defendant's lack of care and the resulting damage. To assess whether the negligence is *tortious* in character one has to know not only whether the damage in question is one which the courts recognise as recoverable in principle (duty), but also whether the defendant could have avoided the

---

[30] *Smith* v. *Littlewoods Organisation Ltd.* [1987] AC 241, 280.
[31] And, as we shall see further down, even some cases of physical injury or property damage.
[32] J. Stapleton, 'Duty of Care and Economic Loss: A Wider Agenda' (1992) 107 *LQR* 249, 254.
[33] *Latimer* v. *AEC Ltd.* [1953] AC 643.   [34] See *Bolton* v. *Stone* [1951] AC 850.

harm by taking precautions which the law regards, in the circumstances, as an acceptable burden (breach).

4. Causation and Damage

Questions of *causation* also require the courts to make value judgments about the ascription of legal responsibility for damage. Where damage results from multiple causes the courts often resort to the test of 'but-for cause'—would the loss have been incurred but for the defendant's negligence?[35] This notion is based on the view that a defendant should only be liable to the extent of his personal responsibility for the loss in question. If a hospital negligently fails to diagnose and treat a patient's condition, following which he dies, the hospital will escape liability if it can show that the patient's condition was untreatable and that he would have died from it no matter how much care had been taken.[36] An employer whose negligence causes an employee to suffer a career-limiting injury will incur only limited liability if he can show that the employee would have retired early anyway, thanks to a quite separate and independent illness which develops after the injury but before the employee's case comes to trial. According to the House of Lords, the employer will only be liable for the *additional* consequences, in terms of premature loss of wages and career, which can be attributed to the injury suffered at work.[37] On the other hand there are cases in which the 'but-for test' tends to break down, in particular where the courts have difficulty distinguishing the causal responsibility of multiple tort-feasors. The test cannot be mechanically applied, as a matter of logic, to every instance.[38]

Another area in which evaluative judgments of this sort are made concerns the question of remoteness: should a defendant be liable for a greater extent of damage than he could reasonably have foreseen would occur as a result of his negligence? The courts have held that the *extent of damage* need not have been foreseeable as long as there was foreseeability of the *kind of damage* sustained by the plaintiff. An illustration is the so-called 'eggshell skull' principle, which grants recovery in full to a plaintiff who is unusually vulnerable or susceptible to the consequences of a particular kind of injury. An employee who sustains a life-threatening disease when an accident at work triggers a condition which would otherwise have lain dormant will recover damages in full for the consequences of the illness, even though the accident itself was comparatively minor and its consequences could not have been predicted.[39] This outcome can be seen as striking a compromise between the idea that the extent of the defendant's legal liability should be strictly limited to his degree of personal responsibility and the idea that he should be made fully liable for the consequences, in terms of the increased risk of harm to others, of his behaviour. It is significant that the courts yet again treat this issue of remoteness differently according to whether injury to the person or interference with economic interests is at stake, with the latter being accorded less extensive protection.[40]

---

[35] *Wilsher* v. *Essex AHA* [1988] AC 1074.   [36] *Barnett* v. *Chelsea and Kensington Hospital* [1969] QB 428.
[37] *Jobling* v. *Associated Dairies Ltd.* [1982] AC 794.   [38] See below, Section 4(3)(e).
[39] *Smith* v. *Leech, Brain & Co. Ltd.* [1962] 2 QB 405.   [40] See below, Section 4(3)(e).

Of the conceptual elements of the tort of negligence the fourth, *damage*, is by far the least developed—perhaps because until recently the use of juries meant that all aspects pertaining to this notion were left for them to determine. Questions of the definition and categorisation of damage, which in other legal systems (because of the absence of the notion of duty of care) are essential determinants of negligence liability, tend to be dealt with in English law under different headings. As we have just seen, the distinction between physical and economic loss is addressed under the headings of duty of care and (to a lesser extent) remoteness of damage. The extent of liability for wrongful death tends to be dealt with as a question of the measurement of compensation. The subsuming of damage questions into other conceptual categories does not end there. As Professor Jane Stapleton has pointed out:

A fundamental question . . . in determining the outer limit of the scope of the tort of negligence is that of what damage is or could be recognised as constituting the minimum for an actionable claim. Is it necessary, for example, to show that palpable and deleterious physical changes have occurred to the person or property of the plaintiff because of the defendant's fault, or is it enough to show the certainty, probability or possibility that such changes will occur in the future? . . . Another major question is this: on the basis of a requirement of actionable damage, how do and how should courts deal with a fact situation where the essence of the plaintiff's complaint (such as defective house foundations) could be formulated in terms either of physical damage or of economic loss? A third important question is this: what is the relationship between the court's formulation of the damage which can form the gist of an action and the level of proof required of the plaintiff in establishing a causal connection between that damage and the defendant's fault? Clearly these sorts of issues are crucial to an understanding of the limits of negligence, yet the courts rarely address them.[41]

To some extent it will not matter under which particular heading the courts address questions of this kind. The point, however, is that a certain lack of conceptual clarity may adversely affect the way in which these questions are formulated and dealt with. The question, for example, of whether a plaintiff should be able to recover for the loss of a chance of avoiding physical injury arose in a case where carelessness by employees of a hospital materially increased the risk that a patient would fail to make a full recovery from a prior accident (which was not itself the responsibility of the hospital). The plaintiff's condition worsened but it could not be shown that his initial injuries would not have led to the same result in any case. By approaching the issue exclusively in terms of whether, on the balance of probabilities, the defendants' carelessness caused the plaintiff's final condition, the House of Lords appeared to sideline the question of whether 'loss of a chance' fell within the definition of compensatable damage.[42]

Another area where conceptual difficulty has arisen concerns the identification, for the purposes of the limitation of actions, of the precise time at which actionable damage occurs. Statutes limit the bringing of actions to a period of a few years after the damage arises,[43] but the period of limitation may start to

---

[41] Stapleton, 'The Gist of Negligence' (1988) 104 *LQR* at 213.
[42] *Hotson* v. *Berkshire AHA* [1987] AC 750.   [43] See generally the Limitation Act 1980.

run before the plaintiff is aware that the loss has been incurred. Suppose, for example, that the plaintiff buys a house which, unknown to him or to the seller, is constructed on defective foundations as a result of the combined negligence of the builder and the local-authority inspector whose job it was to inspect the foundations during construction. At what point does the plaintiff suffer loss?[44] Is it when he pays more for the house than it is truly worth? Or when the foundations begin to cause cracks in the structure of the house? Is it, alternatively, when he has the house valued by a surveyor, perhaps many years later when he wishes to sell it, only to find that it is worth a fraction of what he assumed? These questions, which are of the utmost importance to all the parties concerned and their insurers, continue to receive an uncertain answer from the courts. In part this is because of the lack of a clear conception of what constitutes 'damage' in this instance and where the boundaries lie between 'physical' losses, which are normally recoverable in the tort of negligence, and those which are 'purely economic', and which are much less likely to be recoverable.

5. The Utility of Existing Concepts

The fluidity and equivocation of the basic concepts of negligence make it important to avoid too rigid an insistence on finding the 'correct' technical form in which to phrase an issue. Some questions may equally well be put in terms of either duty or causation (and, in particular, remoteness of damage). In the United States, where most negligence actions are tried with a jury, the labelling of an issue in terms of either duty or remoteness plays an important role in determining the extent of the judge's powers. For, whereas the question of duty is one for him alone to determine, the question of remoteness must, at least in part, go to the jury.[45] This point does not arise in England, where the jury no longer plays a significant part in negligence litigation and both duty and remoteness are questions for the judge. In this regard, Lord Denning once remarked:

The more I think about these cases, the more difficult I find it to put each into its proper pigeon-hole. Sometimes I say: 'There was no duty.' In others I say: 'The damage was too remote.' So much so that I think the time has come to discard these tests which proved so elusive. It seems to me better to consider the particular relationship in hand, and see whether or not, as a matter of policy, economic loss should be recoverable, or not.[46]

Few judges would take *quite* so iconoclastic a view. In recent decisions of the appellate courts there has, if anything, been a reassertion of the need for con-

---

[44] See *Anns* v. *Merton LBC* [1978] AC 728; *Pirelli General Cable Works Ltd.* v. *Oscar Faber & Partners* [1983] 2 AC 1; *Murphy* v. *Brentwood DC* [1991] 1 AC 398; E. McKendrick, '*Pirelli* Reconsidered' (1991) 11 *Leg. Stud.* 326; Chapter 8, Section 1(8) below.

[45] See Professor Robertson's 'American Perspective', Section 5 below. Even in that system, however, leading academics (and some judges) have acknowledged how interchangeable are the basic notions of the tort of Negligence. Thus, see Prosser on *Torts* (3rd edn.).

[46] *Spartan Steel and Alloys Ltd.* v. *Martin & Co. (Contractors) Ltd.* [1973] 1 QB 27, 37.

ceptual precision and an attempt to avoid direct appeals to 'policy'.[47] Unfortunately, this renewed emphasis upon technical rigour has not always led to greater clarity in the use of concepts. This is partly because some of the concepts now in fashion (such as 'proximity' or, the even vaguer 'fair, just and reasonable') are, on closer examination, just as elusive as the ones they are meant to replace (e.g. 'foreseeability'). Lack of clarity may also be the result of a continued attempt by our courts to conflate the phrase 'duty of care' with 'breach of duty', in the sense that the absence of carelessness is sometimes taken to indicate the absence of a duty.[48] The fact that one conceptual basis for a ruling (no duty) can often be exchanged for another (remoteness of damage) without making any difference to the outcome inevitably leads one to question whether the existing conceptual structure of the tort of negligence is serving a useful purpose. Faced with such uncertainties one must ask whether the present preoccupation with formal subdivisions of the duty concept is not obscuring the real issues. Thus, some have argued for the replacement of the duty concept by concepts based on causation, such as the notion of remoteness of damage, as a means of determining the boundaries of liability.[49] Yet these views as well are open to the objection that the causation concepts are not sufficiently clear or robust to subsume all such questions. Causative devices also suffer from the fact that, while pretending to make results appear to flow almost effortlessly from the application of rules of natural science they, too, conceal policy-based value judgments. The courts will thus continue to need to use the duty concept to filter out certain claims before issues of fault, causation, and damage are considered.[50]

The current attitude of the English courts none the less comes close to reviving what an earlier generation of judges and commentators castigated as 'conceptualism'—the tendency for cases to be decided on the basis of verbal formulae without open or considered reference to the policy issues at stake. To reject this kind of 'conceptualism' is not in any sense to imply that the categories used by the courts are irrelevant or could be readily dispensed with. The conceptual structure developed for the tort of negligence since *Donoghue* v. *Stevenson*[51] may be less than perfect in many respects, but it can hardly be replaced by a radically different one short of a programme of statutory codification. Under these circumstances the achievement of conceptual clarity must be acknowledged as a goal in its own right; but it is also necessary for the purpose of enabling policy issues to be properly identified and addressed by the

---

[47] See, in particular, the decisions of the House of Lords which led to the gradual abandonment and final abrogation of the doctrine enunciated in *Anns* v. *Merton LBC* [1978] AC 782, especially *The Mineral Transporter* [1986] AC 1; *The Aliakmon* [1986] AC 785; *Yuen Kun Yeu* v. *Attorney-General of Hong Kong* [1988] AC 175; *Caparo Industries plc* v. *Dickman* [1990] 2 AC 605; and *Murphy* v. *Brentwood DC* [1991] 1 AC 398, discussed by Markesinis and Deakin, 'The Random Element of their Lordships' Infallible Judgment: An Economic and Comparative Analysis of the Tort of Negligence from *Anns* to *Murphy*' (1992) 55 *MLR* 619.

[48] There are many recent examples of this, discussed by D. Howarth, 'Negligence after *Murphy*: Time to Rethink' [1991] *CLJ* 58, 72 ff; and for similar examples in the law of the USA, see Section 5, below at 206.

[49] See W. Tetley, 'Damages and Economic Loss in Marine Collision: Controlling the Floodgates' (1991) 13 *J. Maritime Law & Com.* 539.

[50] *Canada National Railway* v. *Norsk Pacific Steamship Co.* (1991) 91 DLR (4th) 289, 320 (La Forest J).

[51] [1932] AC 562.

courts. What is needed is a frank acknowledgement that policy choices are being made all the time in difficult cases which lie at the boundaries of negligence liability, and that in this area the outcome of decisions cannot be predicted in advance by the mechanical application of verbal formulae. As stated in Chapter 1, Lord Mustill is one of a very small number of judges who have boldly stated extra-judicially that judging involves a considerable degree of 'social engineering' and that judges first decide a case and then find the verbal formulae that express their conclusions on paper. There are signs, however, that other judges are becoming more inclined to admit to exercising such powers.[52]

Select Bibliography

DIAS, R. W. M., 'The Breach Problem and the Duty of Care', 30 *Tulane LR* 377 (1956).
—— 'The Duty Problem in Negligence' [1953] *CLJ* 198.
FLEMING, J. G., 'Remoteness and Duty: The Control Devices in Liability for Negligence' 31 *Can. BR* 471 (1953).
HEPPLE, B., 'Negligence: The Search for Coherence', 50 *Current Legal Problems* (1997) 69.
HOWARTH, D., 'Negligence after *Murphy*: Time to Rethink' [1991] *CLJ* 58.
LAWSON, F. H., 'Duty of Care: A Comparative Study', 22 *Tulane LR* 111 (1947).
STAPLETON, J., 'The Gist of Negligence' (1988) 104 *LQR* 213, 389.
—— 'Tort, Insurance and Ideology' (1995) 58 *MLR* 820.
—— 'Duty of Care Factors; a Selection from the Judicial Menus', ch. 4 in P. Cane and J. Stapleton (eds.) *The Law of Obligations: Essays in Honour of John Fleming* (1998).
WEIR, T., 'The Staggering March of Negligence', ch. 5 in P. Cane and J. Stapleton (eds.) *The Law of Obligations: Essays in Honour of John Fleming* (1998).

2. DUTY OF CARE

1. Formulating the Duty of Care

The question of whether a duty of care exists in a given situation is a question of law upon which the appellate courts are the final arbiters. In *Donoghue* v. *Stevenson* Lord Macmillan asserted that 'the categories of negligence are never closed',[53] in the sense that the courts possess the power to create new duty situations expanding the area of liability. In that case Lord Atkin's formulation of the 'neighbour principle' was not qualified by reference to particular kinds of loss nor to the distinction between acts and omissions. Subsequent courts, however, interpreting the *Donoghue* opinions, soon came to the conclusion that

---

[52] Thus see: 'Negligence in the World of Finance' (1992) 5 *The Supreme Court Journal* 1, at 24. See, also, his remarks in 'What do Judges do?' *Särtryck ur Juridisk Tidskrift*, 1995–96, nr. 3, 611 at 620 and the discussion in Chapter 1, above. See, however, Lord Browne-Wilkinson's comments in 'The Impact on Judicial Reasoning' in *The Impact of the Human Rights Bill on English Law* (ed. Basil S. Markesinis) (1998), 21 ff.: 'The judge looks for what are called "the merits" and having found them seeks to reach a result, consistent with legal reasoning, whereby the deserving win and the undeserving lose.'
[53] [1932] AC 562, 619.

their scope was limited to personal injury and damage to property. The broad 'neighbour principle' was treated as an *obiter dictum*, with the *ratio* limited to the particular case of the duty owed by a manufacturer to an ultimate consumer.[54]

In *Hedley Byrne & Co. Ltd.* v. *Heller and Partners Ltd.*, decided in 1963,[55] the House of Lords recognised for the first time the possibility of an action in the tort of negligence for financial loss suffered through reliance on a misstatement. However, this case was not regarded as giving rise to a general duty of care in relation to pecuniary losses. The misstatement cases were seen as a category on their own, separate from the broad terms of the 'neighbour principle'.[56] Two further judgments of the House of Lords then set the law, for a while, on a more expansive path. In *Dorset Yacht Co.* v. *Home Office* (not an economic loss case) Lord Reid commented of the neighbour principle, 'the time has come when we can and should say that it ought to apply unless there is some justification or valid explanation for its exclusion'.[57] This approach effectively appeared to be shifting onto defendants the onus of justifying the restriction of liability for economic loss and for omissions. It was confirmed by the House of Lords in *Anns* v. *Merton London Borough Council* where Lord Wilberforce said:

The position has now been reached that in order to establish that a duty of care arises in a particular situation, it is not necessary to bring the facts of that situation within those of previous situations in which a duty of care has been held to exist. Rather the question has to be approached in two stages. First one has to ask whether, as between the alleged wrongdoer and the person who has suffered damage there is a sufficient relationship of proximity or neighbourhood such that, in the reasonable contemplation of the former, carelessness on his part may be likely to cause damage to the latter, in which case a prima facie duty of care arises. Secondly, if the first question is answered affirmatively, it is necessary to consider whether there are any considerations which ought to negative, or to reduce or limit the scope of the duty or the class of person to whom it is owed or the damages to which a breach of it may give rise.[58]

Dorset Yacht was concerned with liability for omissions and with responsibility for the acts of third parties, *Anns* with omissions and with the boundary between property damage and pure economic loss. *Anns* established, for a while, that a local authority could be liable in tort for the negligence of its inspectors in failing to exercise with due care the statutory power to check the foundations of houses in the course of construction. The House of Lords held that the duty was owed to occupiers of houses which, as a consequence of such defective construction, had became uninhabitable. The nature of the loss suffered here was ambiguous: the courts classified it as physical, material damage to the house. As Lord Denning later admitted when writing extra-judicially, this was incorrect; the loss suffered should properly have been seen as pecuniary or

---

[54] See *Farr* v. *Butters Bros. & Co.* [1932] 2 KB 606, 613–14 (Scrutton LJ); *Haynes* v. *Harwood* [1935] 1 KB 146, 167–8 (Roche LJ); *Old Gates Estate Ltd.* v. *Toplis & Harding & Russell* [1939] 3 All ER 209, 217 (Greer LJ); *Barnett* v. *Packer* [1940] 3 All ER 575, 577 (Singleton J); *Deyong* v. *Shenburn* [1946] KB 227, 233 (Du Parcq LJ); *Howard* v. *Walker* [1947] KB 680, 683 (Lord Goddard); and see the view of Lord Atkin himself in *East Suffolk Rivers Catchment Board* v. *Kent* [1941] AC 74, 89.

[55] [1964] AC 465.   [56] *Home Office* v. *Dorset Yacht Co.* [1970] AC 1004, 1061 (Lord Diplock).
[57] [1970] AC 1004, 1027.   [58] [1978] AC 728, 751–2.

pure economic loss.[59] Because the house is *built* defectively, the occupier does not suffer property damage as a result of the council's negligence. He takes an interest in property which is *already damaged* and therefore suffers a loss which is purely financial, in the form either of a diminution in the value of the property compared to what he paid for it, or the expenditure required to put it right. This analysis, correctly carried out by the German Supreme Court as early as 1963,[60] was not to become part of the English orthodoxy until the mid to late 1980s.

It is possible that the loss was categorised as property damage in order to make the extension of liability in *Anns* (and in the earlier decision of the Court of Appeal, *Dutton* v. *Bognor Regis Urban District Council*)[61] seem less revolutionary. After all, it must be in the interest of a judge who is conscious of the extent of his innovations to try to disguise them as far as possible in order to ensure their longevity. But in *Junior Books Co. Ltd.* v. *Veitchi Co.*,[62] the House of Lords went one step too far, this time by explicitly allowing in wide dicta a claim in negligence for financial expenditure. In that case, negligence by a building subcontractor led to the instalment of a defective floor in a factory. The floor had to be repaired, at substantial cost to the owner of the factory. For a variety of reasons (not all of which are entirely clear), the owner chose not to sue the main contractor in contract as he might have been expected to do, but instead to pursue the subcontractor in tort. The House of Lords allowed an action in terms that gave substantial encouragement to claims for financial loss. Perhaps because of the explicit nature of the expansion of duty in *Junior Books*, a reaction against it set in almost immediately (though, given the facts of the case, the actual result may not be unjust). Two principal objections to a wide rule of recovery presented themselves. First was the fear of indeterminate liability, or the prospect of releasing a large number of unmeritorious and potentially oppressive claims for compensation. Secondly, there was concern that the traditional relationship between tort and contract was being disrupted, with adverse consequences for legal and commercial certainty.

Criticism of *Junior Books*—which peaked when, only a few years after it was decided, it led a Court of Appeal judge to doubt whether it was worth even citing as authority beyond its own facts[63]—thus began to affect *Anns*, itself. The turning point came with *Murphy* v. *Brentwood District Council* where a seven-judge House of Lords formally overruled *Anns*, invoking the 1966 Practice Statement in order to do so. According to Lord Keith of Kinkel, *Anns* 'did not proceed on any basis of established principle'.[64]

---

[59] *The Discipline of Law* (1979), 255–61.

[60] Markesinis, *The German Law of Obligations*, vol. II, *The Law of Tort* (3rd edn., 1997), 581–5.

[61] [1972] 1 QB 373.   [62] [1983] AC 520.

[63] *Simaan General Contracting Co.* v. *Pilkington Glass Ltd. (No. 2)* [1988] QB 758.

[64] [1991] 1 AC 398, 471. One must not, however, forget that in the *Junior Books* case Lord Keith, unlike Lord Brandon, came very close to the overall position of the majority judgment, which relied heavily on *Anns*. Cf. Lord Hoffmann's opinion in *White* v. *Chief Constable of South Yorkshire Police* [1998] 3 WLR 1510, especially at 1557, where the learned Law Lord seems less concerned with principle and more concerned 'to preserve the general perception of the law as [a] system of rules which is fair between one citizen and another'. Astute students and ingenious practitioners could make much of these real or apparent contradictions in stated philosophy; but a textbook can do no more than note them.

What is left of economic-loss recovery and recovery for omissions after *Murphy* is considered later in our analysis. At this point it is necessary to examine how *Murphy* affects the general formulation of the test of duty of care.

At the basis of the overruling of *Anns* is a rejection of Lord Wilberforce's so-called 'two-stage' test of liability. It is no longer sufficient, if it ever was, to establish a prima-facie duty of care by reference simply to foreseeability of harm. Nor is it enough to prove, as Lord Wilberforce once put it, 'a sufficient relationship of proximity or neighbourhood', leaving it only to considerations of policy to narrow down the prima-facie duty defined in such general terms. This is partly because the courts no longer consider that the reference to 'policy' in Lord Wilberforce's formulation is sufficiently precise; an Australian judge has called the considerations, which would have to come into play here 'indefinable'.[65] Instead, the House of Lords, adopting language used in the High Court of Australia, stated that in 'novel' cases courts should not make a general assumption of prima-facie duty but should, instead, seek to develop the law 'incrementally and by analogy with established categories' of already decided cases. The courts thus turned their back on the broad formulations adopted in *Anns* and *Dorset Yacht* and confined *Donoghue* v. *Stevenson* to cases of physical damage. Incrementalism, however, has come to acquire a much more rigid and narrow form in the English common law than it has in other parts of the Commonwealth where it is seen as a means of preserving flexibility and not as a limiting tool.[66]

In place of the two-stage test some courts have enunciated and applied a new three-stage test through which claims for the extension of duty of care must proceed. In addition to foreseeability, it is now necessary to show that plaintiff and defendant were in a relationship of 'proximity' *and* that it would be 'fair, just and reasonable' to impose a duty on one party for the benefit of the other.[67] A separate and additional requirement of 'policy' has been added in some cases,[68] but in most situations this is indistinguishable from the requirement that imposition of a duty should be 'fair, just and reasonable' which, nowadays, seems to act as the umbrella expression for policy.

The concept of proximity is not new to the law of negligence. The term is mentioned both in late nineteenth-century attempts to formulate the test of duty of care[69] and by Lord Atkin in *Donoghue* v. *Stevenson*[70] and by Lord

[65] Brennan J in *Sutherland Shire Council* v. *Heyman* (1985) 157 CLR 424, 480: 'it is preferable, in my view, that the law should develop categories of negligence incrementally and by analogy with established categories, rather than by a massive extension of a prima facie duty of care restrained only by indefinable "considerations which ought to negative, or to reduce or limit the scope of the duty or the class of person to whom it is owed".'

[66] Thus, see *Bryan* v. *Maloney* (1995) 128 ALR 163 (Australia); *Winnipeg Condominium Corp. No. 36* v. *Bird Construction Co. Ltd.* (1995) 121 DLR (4th) 193 (Canada); *Invercargill* v. *Hamlin* [1994] 3 NZLR 513 (New Zealand).

[67] See, in particular, *Governors of the Peabody Donation Fund* v. *Sir Lindsay Parkinson & Co.* [1985] AC 210, 240–1 and *Yuen Kun Yeu* v. *Attorney-General of Hong Kong* [1988] AC 175, 183 (Lord Keith of Kinkel); *Davies* v. *Radcliffe* [1990] 1 WLR 821, 826 (Lord Goff); *Caparo Industries plc* v. *Dickman* [1990] 2 AC 605, 617–18 (Lord Bridge).

[68] See, in particular, *Hill* v. *Chief Constable of West Yorkshire* [1988] QB 60, [1989] AC 53.

[69] See *Le Lievre* v. *Gould* [1893] 1 QB 491, 497 (Lord Esher MR), 504 (A. L. Smith LJ).

[70] [1932] AC 562, 580–1.

Wilberforce in *Anns* v. *Merton LBC*[71] in their respective formulations of the test. What is new, after the line of cases culminating in *Murphy*, is the emphasis placed on proximity as a central control device within the definition of duty of care. In so far as this rather ambiguous term can be given a general meaning, it normally signifies the presence of a pre-tort relationship of some kind between plaintiff and defendant arising *prior to* the infliction of damage. In *Yuen Kun Yeu* v. *Attorney-General of Hong Kong*[72] Lord Keith of Kinkel referred to two possible meanings of the term 'proximity'. The first sees it as a synonym for foreseeability, or the 'reasonable contemplation of likely harm'. The second and, for his Lordship the preferred meaning, '[imports] the whole concept of the necessary relationship between plaintiff and defendant described by Lord Atkin in *Donoghue* v. *Stevenson*'.

It should not be suggested that in cases of physical damage involving positive acts of commission, this type of proximity is a requirement of a duty of care. Rather, 'a defendant who, by his own positive act, has carelessly caused physical damage to the plaintiff or his property is *always* held to owe a duty of care to the victim.'[73] Hence, where physical damage is concerned, liability typically arises between strangers, such as users of the highway. On the other hand, for economic loss courts have, on occasion, expressed the view that it is necessary to show that the plaintiff and defendant were personally known to each other. Alternatively, it will suffice if the plaintiff formed part of a small class the people, which should have been within the contemplation of the defendant. This, for instance, was the case of *White* v. *Jones*[74] in which the defendant solicitor negligently failed to correct a will as a result of which the plaintiff, the intended beneficiary, failed to receive the intended legacy. By contrast, in *Yuen Kun Yeu* v. *Attorney-General of Hong Kong*[75] a public authority with responsibility for regulating and licensing deposit-taking companies did not owe a duty to safeguard the financial interests of members of the public who invested in the companies to which it granted licences. The authority could not be sued in negligence for the losses of investors when a company, which it had licensed, became insolvent through fraud.

The extent of liability in tort for economic loss caused by negligent misstatements has also been explained using the notion of proximity. After *Murphy*, liability for misstatements is one of the areas in which the possibility of recovery of economic loss is clearly established. In general the plaintiff will succeed only if he can show that he reasonably relied on a statement which the defendant either made to him directly or knew would be immediately passed on to him. In such cases, according to Lord Keith in *Yuen Kun Yeu*, 'the directness and close-

---

[71] [1978] AC 728, 751.   [72] [1988] AC 175, 191.

[73] J. Stapleton, 'Duty of Care Factors' (Select Bibliography, below), 72. In *Marc Rich & Co. A.G.* v. *Bishop Rock Marine Co. Ltd.*, *The Nicholas H* [1996] AC 211, 235, Lord Steyn said that 'the elements of foreseeability and proximity as well as considerations of fairness, justice and reasonableness are relevant to all cases whatever the nature of the harm sustained by the plaintiff'. Not only was there no clear authority for this statement; it contradicts *Donoghue* v. *Stevenson*, as Lord Lloyd pointed out in his dissent in that case. Lord Steyn's dictum can only be regarded as relevant to the special circumstances of *The Nicholas H*, which involved a defendant in a quasi-public position: see below, at 150–151.

[74] [1995] 2 AC 207.   [75] [1988] AC 175.

ness of the relationship between the parties are very apparent'.[76] Where, by contrast, a statement has a potentially wide circulation it is very unlikely that a defendant will be liable to third parties with which he has had no such immediate contact.

The other main area in which proximity, in this specialised sense, is an important component of liability concerns liability for omissions. Here, even liability for physical damage is not, in principle, available in the absence of a pre-tort relationship, giving rise to a duty to act, such as that of parent and child.[77]

In formal (or overt) terms 'policy' thus now seems to play a subsidiary role of limiting duty of care in exceptional circumstances, in contrast to the more wide-ranging function it used to serve in Lord Wilberforce's test. The use of the notion is now reserved to situations where the criterion of proximity is satisfied, but where there is, nevertheless, an overriding public or general interest in granting defendants immunity. The police, for example, appear to have an extensive immunity from liability for negligence arising in the performance of their statutory responsibilities (or their failure to perform them),[78] as do those involved in the administration of justice. However, formal immunities of this kind do not extend to cover all public servants, or to other professions such as the financial or medical professions.[79]

Yet it is difficult to be precise in the application of the so-called three-stage test, and it is far from clear what, if anything, has been achieved by replacing Lord Wilberforce's formulation of the duty question in *Anns* with the present orthodoxy.[80] Proximity, as already stated, is inevitably bound up with issues of policy. In the nervous-shock case of *Alcock* v. *Chief Constable of South Yorkshire*,[81] Lord Oliver thought that ' "policy", or perhaps more properly, the impracticability or unreasonableness of entertaining claims to the ultimate limits of the consequences of human activity, necessarily influences the court's perception of what is sufficiently proximate'. Likewise, in the economic-loss case of *Canadian National Railway* v. *Norsk Pacific Steamship Co.*, McLachlin J remarked that:

Proximity may be usefully viewed, not so much as a test in itself, but as a broad concept which is capable of subsuming different categories of cases involving different factors . . . Viewed thus, the concept of proximity may be seen as an umbrella, covering a number of disparate circumstances in which the relationship between the parties is so close that it is just and reasonable to permit recovery in tort.[82]

[76] Ibid., 192.

[77] *Smith* v. *Littlewoods Organisation Ltd.* [1978] AC 241 (Lord Goff); *Hill* v. *Chief Constable of West Yorkshire* [1989] AC 53.

[78] See *Hill* v. *Chief Constable of West Yorkshire* [1989] AC 53. But in a very recent judgment the European Court of Human Rights in Strasbourg criticised this rule as representing 'a disproportionate restriction on [a citizen's] right of access to a court in breach of article 6.1 of the European Convention on Human Rights': *Osman* v. *United Kingdom*, *The Times*, 5 Nov. 1998. The judgment is potentially far reaching in that its basic reasoning could affect other instances in which English law has used the notion of duty to create immunities which, because of their blanket nature, strike many as being unacceptable to any state that is governed by the rule of law.

[79] See below, Section 4 (discussion of the position of certain classes of parties with regard to duty of care).

[80] Thus, see Lord Hoffmann's observations in *Stovin* v. *Wise* [1996] AC 923, 949.

[81] [1992] 1 AC 310, 410.

[82] *Canadian National Railway* v. *Norsk Pacific Steamship Co.* (1992) 91 DLR (4th) 289, 368–9.

Other judges have been more critical. The majority of the Supreme Court of Canada in *Norsk* rejected the use of proximity as a concept of general applicability. In the words of Stevenson J, 'proximity expresses a conclusion, a judgement, a result, rather than a principle . . . The concept of proximity is incapable of providing a principled basis for drawing the line on the issue of liability.'[83] In *Stovin* v. *Wise*, Lord Nicholls said:

Proximity is a slippery word. Proximity is not legal shorthand for a concept with its own, objectively identifiable characteristics. Proximity is convenient shorthand for a relationship between two parties which makes it fair and reasonable one should owe the other a duty of care. This is only another way of saying that when assessing the requirements of fairness and reasonableness regard must be had to the relationship of the parties.[84]

In general, then, the verbal formulae developed by the House of Lords in the course of the retreat from *Anns* do not, in themselves, provide an adequate basis for drawing the boundaries of negligence liability. Moreover, the present three-stage test tends to obscure the relevant questions of policy by using the apparently value-neutral language of proximity. Thus, as one author put it, the new test is both analytically obscure—'the supposedly separately identifiable second and third limbs of the "new" post-*Anns* duty test are, in truth, one chameleon-like criterion . . . a facet sufficiently malleable to accommodate any desired result'—and liable to confuse. For proximity 'is too impoverished a concept adequately to subsume' the policy issues involved.[85] Proximity thus becomes yet another entry point for policy considerations forcing one to ask oneself why such a repetitive exercise should be deemed to be desirable let alone necessary.

Be that as it may, the picture changes if one looks at what the courts do and not just at what they say. For then it becomes clear that the *approach* to the formulation of the duty of care has changed considerably as a result of the demise of *Anns*. Thus, first, more attention is now paid to the likely impact of any potential extension of the duty concept on other areas of law, such as public law, statutory duties, contract law, and the law of property.[86] Secondly, attempts to formulate a general test for establishing duty of care are now discouraged, in favour of a much closer consideration of what Lord Bridge called 'the more traditional categorisation of distinct and recognisable situations as guides to the existence' of a duty.[87] This means that a the duty concept will

---

[83] (1991) 91 DLR (4th) 289, 387. Stevenson J concurred in the result in favour of allowing economic loss recovery but did not follow the joint opinion of McLachlin, L'Heureux-Dubé, and Cory JJ; La Forest, Lopinka, and Iacobucci JJ dissented.

[84] [1996] AC 923, 932.

[85] N. J. Mullany, 'Proximity, Policy and Procrastination' (1992) 9 *Aust.* Bus. LJ 80, 82.

[86] The existence of possible alternative remedies in the form of statutory actions against the builder under the Defective Premises Act 1972 was a factor in the decision to reject negligence liability in *Murphy* v. *Brentwood DC* [1991] 1 AC 398. So was the concern to avoid a situation in which public authorities could be made liable for the negligent but good faith exercise of their public-law powers. The debate on recovery of economic loss (discussed below) illustrates the general concern that tortious liability might be undermining principles of contract law (*Banque Financière de la Cité SA* v. *Westgate Insurance Co.* [1991] 2 AC 249) and property law (see *Downsview Nomines Ltd.* v. *First City Corp.* [1993] 3 All ER 937). See T. Weir, 'The Staggering March of Negligence' (Select Bibliography).

[87] *Caparo Industries plc* v. *Dickman* [1990] 2 AC 605, 618.

only be applied, or 'extended', to novel or previously unconsidered situations if this can be done by analogy with the existing categories of potential liability. In his judgment in *Stovin* v. *Wise*,[88] Lord Hoffman expressed the contrast between the approaches of the courts pre- and post-*Anns* as follows:

Lord Wilberforce, who gave the leading speech [in *Anns*], first stated the well-known two-stage test for the existence of a duty of care. This involves starting with a prima facie assumption that a duty of care exists if it is reasonably foreseeable that carelessness may cause damage and then asking whether there are any considerations which ought to 'negative, or to reduce or limit the scope of the duty or the class of person to whom it is owed or the damages to which a breach of it may arise'. Subsequent decisions in this House and the Privy Council have preferred to approach the question the other way round, starting with situations in which a duty has been held to exist and then asking whether there are considerations of analogy, policy, fairness and justice for extending it to cover a new situation . . . The trend of authorities has been to discourage the assumption that anyone who suffers loss is prima facie entitled to compensation from a person (preferably insured or a public authority) whose act or omission can be said to have caused it. The default position is that he is not.

In practice, this means that, as Lord Oliver has explained, the discussion of duty of care should be located by reference to those specific areas of liability—such as negligent misstatements, the distinction between acts and omissions, liability for the acts of third parties, and the exercise of statutory duties and powers—which represent the outermost boundaries of liability.[89] Our analysis will follow this general approach by focusing, in turn, on the kind of damage which is suffered; the manner of infliction of harm; and the position of certain special plaintiffs and defendants.

2. Kind of Damage

(A) PHYSICAL (BODILY) HARM AND DAMAGE TO PROPERTY

After *Donoghue* v. *Stevenson* the law recognised a general duty of care protecting the personal safety and health and tangible property interests of the plaintiff. The general duty in relation to physical and property harm is not affected by the overruling of *Anns*. Liability for physical harm caused by negligent misstatements is now well established as part of the *Donoghue* duty.[90] The general duty may, however, be qualified in relation to certain types of plaintiff, such as trespassers, or may be specially extended to cover deserving claims such as those of rescuers; these issues are considered below and in later chapters. Certain defendants, such as public authorities and others serving the collective interest, may benefit from a qualified immunity in respect of physical harm.[91] The limited nature of liability for omissions also affects the protection accorded to physical interests. Finally, it must be remembered that, despite the existence

---

[88] [1996] AC 923, 949.

[89] *Caparo Industries plc v Dickman* [1990] 2 AC 605, 618, 635.

[90] See *Sharp* v. *Avery and Kerwood* [1938] 4 All ER 85; *Dutton* v. *Bognor Regis UDC* [1972] 1 QB 373, 410.

[91] We would suggest that a principle of this kind offers the best explanation for the otherwise puzzling decision of the House of Lords in the property-damage case of *Marc Rich & Co. A.G.* v. *Bishop Rock Marine Co. Ltd.* [1996] 1 AC 211, discussed below at 150–151.

of a general duty of care, claims for compensation for physical loss may be limited by other considerations such as remoteness and causation as well as by the manner in which damages for loss are calculated in different cases.

(B) 'PURE' ECONOMIC LOSS

Personal injury and property damage may both have economic consequences. A person who sustains an injury may lose not simply the use of a limb but also the earning capacity which goes with it. He will receive compensation for loss of future earnings as well as for loss of the limb and facility in question. As far as property damage is concerned, the courts will have primary regard to the market value of the property in question when assessing compensation for its loss. In these cases the law of tort provides compensation for economic losses *arising directly* out of physical loss; this is not controversial.[92] What is disputed is the use of tort law to provide compensation for losses which are merely financial or pecuniary in nature, that is to say, losses which have no connection to personal or physical harm suffered by the plaintiff: these are sometimes termed 'pure' economic losses. Such losses might include financial loss or expenditure incurred as a result of the defendant's negligence, interruption to an expected stream of income such as wages or rents, or failure to make a gain as expected from a valuable contract or from an expected legacy under a will. For the most part an 'exclusionary rule' bars recovery in these cases; liability is the exception.

The logic of this position may not be immediately obvious; nor, indeed, is it shared by many other legal systems.[93] Why should recovery for economic loss be made to depend upon the fortuitous event that it is sustained through the medium of physical or property damage? It is not plausible to say that pure economic losses are, for this purpose, less easily quantified than those flowing from physical damage. The courts compute as a matter of course the future lost earnings of plaintiffs in personal injury cases. These losses are often no easier to estimate accurately than those claimed in cases of pure economic loss, and in some cases they may be more difficult to establish.[94]

On the other hand, few would argue with the proposition that the law should provide greater protection to personal safety and health than to purely economic interests. A general duty of care to avoid causing foreseeable physical injury or disease seems widely accepted. But this does not explain why, *nowadays*, interests in tangible property should be so much better protected than

---

[92] The need to establish a direct causal relationship does not normally give rise to much difficulty in a case where the plaintiff has suffered physical harm, and the extent of compensation will be determined by reference to the principles of computation of damages. An instance of the link being insufficiently direct is *Pritchard* v. *Cobden* [1988] Fam. 22, where an accident victim failed to recover damages for the financial consequences of his divorce which, the court held, was a foreseeable consequence of his injuries. The division of assets between the plaintiff and his wife was too remote from the initial injury to be the subject of compensation. See also *Meah* v. *McCreamer (No. 2)* [1986] 1 All ER 943.

[93] E.g. France, Italy, the Netherlands.

[94] See generally Chapter 8, Section 2, below, and in particular the discussion of how to assess the plaintiff's claim for lost future wages, taking into account the impact of taxation and of collateral benefits such as pensions and insurance.

mere financial interests.[95] Historically, the protection of property rights was one of tort law's principal functions, at least as much as the protection of life and limb.[96] But this historical feature of the law cannot, on its own, provide a satisfactory explanation for the current sharp distinction between physical and economic losses, especially as societies and their hierarchy of values change subtly over the passage of time. So, other explanations must be sought for such *a priori* hostility.

In this context, a factor frequently mentioned by the courts is the fear that without the exclusionary rule the 'floodgates' of liability would open, exposing defendants to an endless series of actions. In itself this is a weak argument, since extensive liabilities are just as likely to arise in certain cases of physical damage such as instances of large-scale pollution and products liability. Hundreds of thousands of claims have thus been made and adjudicated for asbestos-related injuries, dangerous intra-uterine contraceptive devices, or defective heart valves. No one has suggested that in these cases the law should deny the existence of a duty of care simply because of the volume of the losses involved. A (slightly) better argument is that an open-ended duty of care in relation to economic losses creates the danger of indeterminate (not simply extensive) liability, that is to say, liability the extent of which would be unpredictable in terms of both the size of claims and the number of potential plaintiffs.[97] This element of uncertainty would, so the argument runs, have a deterrent effect in relation to activities that are socially necessary or beneficial, which might not be carried on in the light of the risk of 'crushing liability' for economic damage. An example frequently given concerns liability for the consequences of a road accident. If a careless driver were potentially liable not simply to those immediately involved in a collision but to all persons whose businesses or earnings were affected by, for example, a traffic jam resulting from the crash, the costs of motoring (and in particular the cost of liability insurance) would become

---

[95] See *Canadian National Railway* v. *Norsk Pacific Steamship Co.* (1992) 91 DLR (4th) 289, 383 (Stevenson J): 'Some argue that there is a fundamental distinction between physical damage (personal and property damage) and pure economic loss and that the latter is less worthy of protection . . . but I am left unconvinced. Although I am prepared to recognise that a human being is more important than property and lost expectations of profit, I fail to see how property and economic losses can be distinguished.' The same kind of dated 'hierarchy of values' has also been advanced in the akin topic of compensation for psychiatric injury where some have argued against it on the grounds that 'It is widely felt . . . that trauma to the mind is less [serious] than lesion to the body'. (Weir, *A Casebook on Tort*, 7th edn., 88.) Such views are not only debatable; they also show how lawyers and the law fail to adapt to changing social conditions and, in this last example, take note of great progress in medical science which seriously undermines such scientific basis as there ever was in favour of these dated misconceptions.

[96] It may plausibly be argued that the 19th-century common law conferred greater protection upon property (both real and personal) than upon the person. Aside from the well-established liability for trespass, liability for non-trespassory interferences with land was, in many cases, strict, both in nuisance and under the principle of *Rylands* v. *Fletcher* (see below, Chapter 5 and Chapter 6, Section 1), while even negligent harm to the person would quite frequently not give rise to liability as a result both of the limited scope of the duty of care pre-*Donoghue* v. *Stevenson* [1932] AC 562 and of the operation of the defences of contributory negligence, assumption of risk (consent), and common employment (see below, Chapter 8, Section 1).

[97] On the important distinction between liability which is indeterminate and therefore unpredictable, on the one hand, and indefinite (large-scale) liability, see *Canadian National Railway* v. *Norsk Pacific Steamship Co.* (1992) 91 DLR (4th) 289, 338 (La Forest J).

prohibitive for all road-users.[98] Since liability has to stop somewhere, a rule excluding recovery for pure economic loss has the pragmatic benefit of promoting a degree of legal and commercial certainty. 'The solution to cases of this type is necessarily pragmatic and involves drawing a line that will exclude at least some people who have been undeniably injured owing to the [defendant's] admitted failure to meet the requisite standard of care.'[99]

The exclusionary rule has also been based on a preference for contract, rather than tort, as a means of protecting financial interests. Plaintiffs, it is said, should seek to cover economic losses by contracting directly with potential tortfeasors or, if this is not possible, by taking out first-party insurance. Parties may allocate the risk of economic loss between themselves in a number of ways, most importantly by establishing particular standards of contractual performance and by excluding or limiting liability in damages. Where the parties have agreed contractual terms of this kind, there may be little or no justification for the law imposing different standards of performance and liability rules through a general tort duty. Where they have not so contracted, it is said that the law should be prepared to let the loss lie where it falls.[100] These are plausible arguments for restricting liability at least where business entities are concerned although, as we shall note further down, they do not provide satisfactory explanations of all aspects of the case law.

Professor Feldthusen[101] has argued convincingly that it is not possible to discuss all cases of pure economic loss under one heading, and that it is important to distinguish between a number of separate areas, 'the differences among [which] . . . are every bit as significant as the initial distinction from physical damage'. He thus identified the following specific areas: liability of public authorities; responsibility for negligent misstatements; negligence in the performance of a service; recovery of economic loss caused by defective products and buildings; 'relational' economic losses arising from damage to the property of a third party; and negligence in the performance of a service. The question of the overlap between tort and contract as sources of obligation also deserves special treatment. The liability of public bodies is considered in more detail in Chapter 3, Section 5 below. The remaining categories are analysed in what follows.

(i) Liability for Negligent Misstatements Notwithstanding *Murphy* v. *Brentwood DC*, it remains possible to recover financial losses in respect of negligent misstatements, under the principle enunciated by the House of Lords in *Hedley Byrne & Co.* v. *Heller & Partners*.[102] In that case, the plaintiffs were considering supplying advertising services to a potential client, Easipower, and

---

[98] Stapleton, 'Duty of Care and Economic Loss—A Wider Agenda' (1991) 107 *LQR* 249, 254; *Stevenson* v. *East Ohio Gas Co.* (1946) 73 N.E. 2d 400.

[99] *Canadian National Railway* v. *Norsk Pacific Steamship Co.* (1991) 91 DLR (4th) 289, 302 (La Forest J).

[100] This view is expounded by La Forest J in his dissenting judgment in the *Norsk* case (1992) 91 DLR (4th) 289. See also Markesinis and Deakin, op. cit. (1992) 55 *MLR* 619, 625–9.

[101] 'Economic Loss in the Supreme Court of Canada: Yesterday and Tomorrow' (1991) 17 *Can. Bus. LJ* 356. Professor Feldthusen's classification was adopted by La Forest J in his dissenting judgment in the *Norsk* case (1992) 91 DLR (4th) 289.

[102] [1964] AC 465.

through their bank sought a credit reference for Easipower from its bankers, the defendants. The defendants replied 'without responsibility' to the effect that Easipower was financially sound. In fact, Easipower went into liquidation shortly afterwards and the plaintiffs, who had acted on the reference, lost a large amount of money. The House of Lords held that the defendants would have owed a duty of care to the plaintiffs and would have been liable but for a disclaimer that their remarks were made without responsibility.

There is a clear need for a control device to deal with the threat of indeterminate liability, which arises once it is accepted that tort law recognises liability for careless words as well as careless behaviour. Whereas 'it is at least unusual casually to put into circulation negligently made articles which are dangerous . . . words can be broadcast with or without the consent or the foresight of the speaker or writer'.[103] A number of potential tests have been put forward, from time to time, as the basis of negligence liability in this area. Thus the judges speak, in some cases, of the need for a 'voluntary assumption of responsibility' by the person making the statement. In *Hedley Byrne* itself the defendants avoided liability precisely because they told the plaintiffs that their statement was made 'without responsibility'. In other decisions, the 'reasonable reliance' of the plaintiff on the other's advice appears to be of central importance. It has been said that 'these two concepts are, in fact, closely related',[104] a view supported by a dictum of Lord Morris in *Hedley Byrne* to the effect that a duty of care will arise where 'a person takes it upon himself to give information or advice to, or allows his information or advice to be passed on to, another person who, as he knows or should know, will place reliance on it'.[105]

There are nevertheless some serious problems in defining the scope of *Hedley Byrne* liability by reference to the twin concepts of assumption of responsibility and reasonable reliance. A person will rarely be placed under a duty of care for simply 'taking it upon himself' to offer advice (as Lord Morris put it), nor will it necessarily be accurate to term the relevant assumption a 'voluntary' one. The advice may be given voluntarily in the sense that the *plaintiff* will not normally have contracted to receive the information in question.[106] But the defendant will, in many cases of *Hedley Byrne* liability, have a contractual obligation with a *third party* that may require him to take care in divulging the advice or information to the plaintiff. Alternatively, he will have some kind of professional obligation, which similarly places him under a duty to take care. In these circumstances it is entirely unhelpful to refer to there having been a voluntary assumption of responsibility. As Lord Oliver said in *Caparo Industries plc* v. *Dickman*, this phrase: 'was not intended to be a test for the existence of the duty for, on analysis, it means no more than that the act of the defendant in making the statement or tendering the advice was voluntary and that the law attributes

---

[103] Lord Reid in *Hedley Byrne* [1964] AC 465, 483.   [104] McKendrick, *Tort Textbook* (1991 edn.), 52.
[105] [1964] AC 465, 503.
[106] Although it may be the case that there are concurrent duties in contract and tort in a particular situation: see *Pirelli General Cable Works Ltd.* v. *Oscar Faber & Partners* [1983] 2 AC 1.

to it an assumption of responsibility . . . [but] it tells us nothing about the circumstances from which such attribution arises'.[107]

What matters, instead, is that the information or advice in question has been issued in a specific commercial or professional context, and it is this context which often provides the vital clue to the extent of the defendant's liability in tort. This idea is often summed up by saying that the central requirement for a duty of care is the existence of a 'special relationship' between the parties. Prior to *Hedley Byrne* it was understood that, apart from instances of fiduciary duty such as that owed by a solicitor to a client, liability for misstatements could arise only for fraud or for breach of a contractual undertaking. The Court of Appeal had thus ruled against a duty of care arising in negligence on a number of occasions.[108] Considering the earlier judgments, Lord Devlin, however, argued that:

> there is ample authority to justify your Lordships in saying now that the categories of special relationships, which may give rise to a duty to take care in word as well as deed, are not limited to contractual relationships or to relationships of fiduciary duty, but include also relationships which . . . are 'equivalent to contract', that is, where there is an assumption of responsibility in circumstances in which, but for the absence of consideration, there would be a contract.[109]

The duty in this case arose from the purpose for which the information was given out. Although the information was given gratuitously in the sense that the plaintiffs did not pay to receive it, the bank was nevertheless acting in a commercial context and knew that the information would be passed on to the plaintiffs by their bank and relied upon for their business. The defendants would certainly have been expected, as a matter of business practice, to give references of this kind, since without them their own clients might be unable to get business. As Lord Devlin observed, 'it would discourage the customers of the bank if their deals fell through because the bank had refused to testify to their credit when it was good'.[110] On the other hand, the defendants were entitled, in the absence of a contract, to the protection of the disclaimer: 'If the inquirers chose to receive and act upon the reply they cannot disregard the definite terms upon which it was given.'[111] Such a disclaimer would now have to pass a 'reasonableness' test under section 2(2) of the Unfair Contract Terms Act 1977.[112]

Where the context in which advice is given is, by contrast, a casual or social occasion, a duty will not normally arise. An exception, which may have been wrongly decided, is *Chaudhry* v. *Prabhakar*.[113] The Court of Appeal held that advice seriously given between friends might give rise to liability; in this case, the defendant took it upon himself to advise the plaintiff in her purchase of a

---

[107] [1990] 2 AC 605, 607.

[108] Most notably in *Candler* v. *Crane, Christmas & Co.* [1951] 2 KB 164, in which the majority overrode a vigorous dissent from Denning LJ. On fiduciary duty, see *Nocton* v. *Lord Ashburton* [1914] AC 932; on fraud, *Derry* v. *Peek* (1889) 14 App. Cas. 337.

[109] [1964] AC 465, 528–9.   [110] Ibid., 529.   [111] Ibid., 504 (Lord Morris of Borth-y-Gest).

[112] See below, Chapter 8, Section 1, and see *Smith* v. *Eric S. Bush* [1990] 1 AC 829, discussed below.

[113] [1989] 1 WLR 29.

second-hand motor car. He failed to notice that the car he recommended had previously been involved in an accident; a few months after the plaintiff bought the car it was declared unroadworthy and she sued him successfully for the loss of value. It is unlikely that this decision will be extended to produce a general liability for gratuitous advice, though. The existence of a duty was conceded by counsel at first instance and was not the subject of a full argument in the Court of Appeal.

In *Mutual Life & Assurance Co.* v. *Evatt*[114] the Privy Council laid down a further restriction on liability, namely that the duty of a professional adviser was limited to information or advice which he held himself out as qualified to give or which he was in the business of giving. In this case, an assurance company was held not liable for a reply it gave to the plaintiff, a policyholder, concerning the financial soundness of an associated company in which the plaintiff then decided to invest. The Court of Appeal declined to follow this approach in *Esso Petroleum Co.* v. *Mardon*,[115] holding that Esso owed a pre-contractual duty of care to a potential tenant of a petrol station to prepare accurate estimates of the likely business which the station would generate. This decision is perhaps explicable by reference to the difficulty which Mr Mardon would have had in finding out the necessary information from any other source. Normally there will be no duty of care under *Hedley Byrne* between business parties negotiating at arm's length; each side will have to rely on their own judgment or get a third-party opinion. With reason, the courts take the view that parties to pre-contractual negotiations will primarily look to their own interests and not to those of each other. As Glidewell LJ has put it,

liability in tort for economic loss by reliance on a statement which in the event is shown to be wrong arises only within the confines of the *Hedley Byrne* principle. It does not apply in the common situation . . . as between parties negotiating for a prospective contract. They cannot have a right of action in tort if during the course of those negotiations something is said on which they rely and in the event a contract does not result. If, as often happens, one party to negotiations is concerned to protect his or its position but, should the contract in the end not be achieved and, if the passage of time is likely to give rise to damage, then that party must seek to protect its position by obtaining a promise from the other, a promise upon which either a right of action in contract for breach of the promise may be brought or, at the very least, it can be suggested that an estoppel can arise.[116]

---

[114] [1971] AC 793.

[115] [1976] QB 801. In *Howard Marine & Dredging Co.* v. *A. Ogden & Sons (Excavations) Ltd.* [1978] QB 574 a majority of the Court of Appeal (Lord Denning and Shaw LJ) rejected the majority judgment of the Privy Council in *Lovatt*.

[116] *Glen-Mor Fashions Ltd.* v. *Jaeger Company Shops Ltd.* (unreported, transcript on LEXIS) Court of Appeal, 20 Nov. 1991. There are alternatives to *Hedley Byrne* for framing liability for disappointed pre-contractual expectations but these are rarely, if ever, available in English law. As far as estoppel is concerned, there is no equivalent to the wide-ranging Art. 90 of the American Restatement (2d) of Contracts which has been used as a basis for imposing liability for reliance losses: see *Hoffman* v. *Red Owl Stores Inc.* (1965) 133 N.W. 2d 267; cf. *Combe* v. *Combe* [1951] 2 KB 215. The only protection offered by English law is therefore the device of a collateral contract. This will, by its nature, be rare, but see *Blackpool and Fylde Aero Club* v. *Blackpool BC* [1990] 1 WLR 1195; and on 'lock out' agreements, *Walford* v. *Miles* [1992] 2 WLR 174.

In cases where a contract does result from negotiations, it will not normally be necessary to use *Hedley Byrne* to determine liability for pre-contractual mis-statements. Under section 2(1) of the Misrepresentation Act 1967, the victim of a misrepresentation which leads to contractual relations between him and the person making the statement may sue the other party for damages representing his loss, unless the other can show that he took all reasonable care up to the time of contracting to ensure that the information was true. This is, then, a form of statutory tort, which is dependent for its operation on the misstatement inducing a contract. When this condition has been satisfied, section 2(1) provides a superior basis for compensation than *Hedley Byrne* since it does not require the existence of a special relationship and it effectively reverses the burden of proving negligence.[117] Damages under section 2(1) will also be more extensive, being calculated on the basis of the tort of deceit where the rules of remoteness of damage are less restrictive than those which operate in negligence.[118]

Hedley Byrne does not necessarily apply to a failure to speak, at least in cases where a potential tort duty of this kind would overlap with the rules of contract law, which limit liability for non-disclosure. This is the effect of *Banque Financière de la Cité SA* v. *Westgate Insurance Co.*,[119] a case that arose out of a complex insurance fraud. The plaintiff banks were fraudulently misled by the defendant's manager into believing that they were fully covered by an insurance policy negotiated with the defendant. The plaintiffs attempted to make the defendant liable in negligence for the failure of one of the manager's colleagues, who knew about the fraud, to notify them of it. The House of Lords held that there was no liability in tort under these circumstances for a mere failure to speak out as opposed to an active misstatement. The law of contract imposes a duty of disclosure during pre-contract negotiations only under exceptional circumstances, and even then does not grant an action for damages but simply a right to rescind the contract. In the *Banque Financière* case the House of Lords took the view that contract law rules of this kind should not be circumvented by the use of a negligence action; this places a substantial restriction on the potential development of *Hedley Byrne* to cover omissions. But care must be taken to define what is meant by an omission here: there could well be liability in tort, as there is in contract, for a failure to correct a misleading impression created by an ambiguous statement[120] or one which becomes false at a later point in time.[121]

The *Hedley Byrne* principle was re-examined by the House of Lords in *Caparo Industries plc* v. *Dickman*.[122] Caparo made a take-over bid for a company, Fidelity, in which it already had a sizeable shareholding. When the take-over was completed it emerged that Fidelity was effectively worthless and that a false impres-

---

[117] See e.g. *Howard Marine & Dredging Co.* v. *Ogden* [1978] QB 574.

[118] *Royscott Trust Co.* v. *Rogerson* [1991] 3 All ER 294; but cf. the criticism of this decision by R. Hooley (1991) 107 *LQR* 547.

[119] [1991] 2 AC 249.

[120] This is well established in contract cases on misrepresentation: see e.g. *Notts, Patent Brick and Tile Co.* v. *Butler* (1886) 16 QBD 778.

[121] *With* v. *O'Flanagan* [1936] Ch. 75. [122] [1990] 2 AC 605.

sion of its business value had been created. Caparo brought an action against Touche Ross, the company's auditors, claiming that the take-over had been launched in reliance on the accounts prepared by the auditors, which had shown Fidelity making a large profit in the preceding tax year when in fact it had made a loss. The House of Lords held that no duty of care was established on these facts. Lord Bridge held that the central distinction was that between cases in which 'the defendant giving advice or information was fully aware of the nature of the transaction which the plaintiff had in contemplation' and those in which 'a statement is put into more or less general circulation and may foreseeably be relied on by strangers to the maker of the statement for any one of a variety of different purposes which the maker of the statement has no specific reason to contemplate'.[123] Even though a take-over bid was known to be highly probable, to hold the auditors liable for the consequences of an investment decision, which went wrong, would open up the prospect of an open-ended liability. According to Lord Oliver, no logical distinction could be made between existing shareholders such as Caparo who extended their shareholding in reliance on the report, and members of the public who could have read the report and bought shares or lent to the company after having read it.[124]

At the basis of *Caparo* is the House of Lords' view of the purpose of the annual audit of accounts of a publicly listed company. Under the Companies Acts, the auditor, once appointed by the company in general meeting, is required to examine the company accounts to see if they give a 'true and fair view' of the company's finances.[125] The auditor's report must be sent to each one of the shareholders. According to Lord Bridge, the purpose of this is not to protect individual shareholders in their investment decisions, but rather to safeguard the collective interest of the shareholders as a group in ensuring that the company is effectively managed. In the event of a breach of duty by the auditor, any losses would, said Lord Bridge, be recouped by an action brought by the company, thereby making an action in tort by individual shareholders unnecessary and inappropriate.

This last point is open to the objection that it is most unlikely that the company will have an action for contract damages in circumstances such as those in *Caparo*, for the reason that it suffers no loss. The overvaluation in this case harmed only the take-over bidder, who paid too much, and not the company itself, or indeed the other shareholders, who were bought out at a premium. Indeed, once their action in the tort of negligence failed, the new owners of Fidelity started an action in the company's name for breach of contract against the auditors; but this action did not make any progress.[126]

Caparo does not mean that auditors and accountants can never incur liability in tort to those who rely on their statements. In the pre-*Hedley Byrne* decision of *Candler* v. *Crane, Christmas*,[127] a statement of accounts was prepared for the

---

[123] Ibid., 620–1. [124] Ibid., 650–2.
[125] Companies Act 1985, ss. 236 ff. See A. McGee, 'The "True and Fair View" Debate: A Study in the Legal Regulation of Accounting' (1991) 54 *MLR* 874.
[126] See M. Percival, 'After *Caparo*: Liability in Business Transactions Revisited' (1991) 54 *MLR* 739, 743.
[127] [1951] 2 KB 164.

specific purpose of enabling an investor to decide whether or not to put money into the company. The relationship between the parties here was much closer, and the purpose of the advice much more specifically related to a particular transaction, than it was in *Caparo*, and it seems likely that a duty would now arise if similar facts occurred today. In *Morgan Crucible Co. plc* v. *Hill Samuel & Co. Ltd.*,[128] decided after *Caparo*, the Court of Appeal refused to strike out a claim brought by a successful take-over bidder against directors and auditors of the target company which, when he took it over, turned out to be less valuable than he had been led to believe. Here, statements had been made with the avowed purpose of influencing the conduct of an *identified* bidder: the director and auditors could accordingly have owed him a duty of care. At present, however, this appears to be as far as the law will go. If the statement is made to a large class of recipients, or for a number of purposes only one of which is related to the transaction which subsequently goes wrong, a tort claim will not be likely and the plaintiff will be limited to whatever contractual rights he may have.[129]

The House of Lords' view of the limited purpose of the annual audit has been called 'an artificial interpretation, which takes no account of commercial reality'.[130] The annual audit is one of the few reliable means shareholders have of obtaining information concerning the internal operation of a company. The fear of the floodgates also appears to have been misplaced in that instance. If a company's shares are boosted by false information in advance of a take-over bid, any loss will tend to be concentrated on to the successful take-over bidder who ends up with the overvalued shares. Even then, the plaintiff will have to prove that the report was a material factor in his decision to launch the bid. He may be required to show that he would not have bought the shares but for the report, which may be difficult to do in practice. The auditor may also be able to refute allegations of a lack of care in preparing the account. These are illustrations of the point that the imposition of a duty of care does not, by itself, lead inevitably to liability; indeed, Bingham LJ, in the Court of Appeal, thought they might well fail at the full trial of the action on one of these grounds.[131] In relation to policy, the prospects of 'defensive accounting', excessive liability insurance premiums, and accountancy firms going out of business if a duty of care were imposed were all raised in argument in *Caparo*. But the experience of other legal systems—such as Germany, the Netherlands, and certain states of the USA—which have flirted with the imposition of a more extensive liability, suggests that these fears may have been greatly exaggerated. A knowledgeable American judge has thus observed that: 'The sky has not fallen on the account-

---

[128] [1991] Ch. 295; *Galoo Ltd. (in liquidation)* v. *Bright Grahame Murray* [1994] 1 WLR 1360; cf. *James McNaughton Paper Group Ltd.* v. *Hicks Anderson & Co.* [1991] 2 QB 113, where a similar kind of claim failed on the facts.

[129] See in particular the judgment of Neill LJ in *James McNaughton Paper Group Ltd.* v. *Hicks Anderson & Co.* [1991] 2 QB 113; and see M. Percival, 'After *Caparo*', op. cit. (1991) 54 *MLR* 739. It also follows that the director of a company cannot be liable under *Hedley Byrne* for a negligent misstatement made by that company, unless he has assumed a personal responsibility to the recipient of the information in such circumstances as to give rise to a duty of care: *Williams* v. *Natural Life Ltd.* [1998] 1 WLR 830.

[130] Percival, op. cit. (1991) 54 *MLR* 739, 742.   [131] [1989] QB 653, 690.

ing profession'[132] as a result of making auditors potentially liable for their faults. Here, however, as in so many other instances of tort (Negligence) liability, we are faced with statements which are rarely supported by solid empirical evidence available to us all.[133] Such a battle of 'hunches' and 'intuitive guesses' may be useful in the classroom but, it is submitted, forms a very suspicious basis for a court judgment.

In contrast to *Caparo* is another recent decision of the House of Lords in two cases heard together, *Smith* v. *Eric S. Bush* and *Harris* v. *Wyre Forest DC*.[134] These concerned the common situation in which a surveyor prepares a valuation report for a building society (or a local authority) which is considering advancing a loan to a prospective purchaser on the security of the property. Building societies are required by legislation to obtain a valuation report before they make such loans.[135] The report is intended only to establish the value of the house as security; it is not a full structural survey. However, the prospective purchaser effectively pays for the report, by advancing a fee to the building society, which then engages the surveyor, and he normally receives a copy of the report. In *Smith*'s case both the mortgage-application form signed by the plaintiff and the report itself carried a disclaimer of liability by the surveyor, which amongst other things stated that the report 'is not, and should not be taken as, a structural survey'. A similar disclaimer was issued in the *Harris* case; and the report was not even passed on. In both cases the plaintiffs relied on favourable valuations to go ahead with their purchases, only to find that the properties contained defects which required considerable expenditure to put right. In *Smith*'s case the surveyor's report should have identified a structural weakness in the chimney flu; the chimney subsequently collapsed, causing widespread damage to the rest of the house. In *Harris*'s case the report failed to warn of the possibility of settlement of the house. When this was discovered after an interval of a few years, the house was saleable for only a fraction of the price the plaintiffs had paid for it.

Two questions arose: whether, in these circumstances, there was a duty to the purchaser to take care in the preparation of the report; and whether the disclaimer was invalidated by the Unfair Contract Terms Act 1977, which

[132] Judge Richard Posner, writing extra-judicially in *Cardozo—A Study in Reputation* (1990), 112.

[133] For an English example see Lord Hoffmann's point made in *Stovin* v. *Wise* [1996] AC 923, where he said that: 'It would not be surprising if one of the consequences of the *Anns* case . . . was that local council inspectors tended to insist upon *stronger* [our italics] foundations than were necessary.' There are at least two difficulties with such statements. First, if they are based on hearsay evidence or a hunch they may start one thinking along new and original lines; but hunches cannot, by themselves, justify a switch in justifications or legal results. Secondly, why should the potential risk of legal liability lead to excessively strong instead of 'appropriate' foundations being laid? One could thus counter Lord Hoffmann's point by suggesting that while the post-*Anns* regime led to unnecessarily strong and expensive foundations the post-*Murphy* situation may be encouraging the sloppy verification of building calculations. What the law must, surely, be encouraging is neither excessive caution not unnecessary sloppiness; and the latter may well follow a signal from the courts that they favour a non-liability rule just as the former may flow from a rule which seems to invite litigation. Our judges' rejection of a doctrine of 'informed consent' in medical cases is also based on (empirically) unsubstantiated fears about what might follow if patients were given more information than the paternalistic English legal system is at present prepared to grant them. On this see Professor Grubb's comments in Chapter 3, below.

[134] [1990] 1 AC 831. See also *Yianni* v. *Edwin Evans & Sons* [1982] QB 438.

[135] Building Societies Act 1986, s. 13.

regulates exclusion clauses of this kind.[136] The House of Lords unanimously held that a duty of care did arise: the surveyor should have known that a purchaser in this position was unlikely to take out an additional survey, and would instead rely on the valuation report as evidence of the property's structural soundness. Evidence was led to the effect that fewer than 10 per cent of homeowners took out their own surveys prior to the purchase of their property. Like *Hedley Byrne*, this case was close to contract; Lord Templeman thought that 'the relationship between the valuer and the purchaser is "akin to contract". The valuer knows that the consideration he receives derives from the purchaser and is passed on by the mortgagee, and the valuer also knows that the valuation will determine whether or not the purchaser buys the house.'[137] The duty arises, according to Lord Griffiths, notwithstanding the explicit denial of responsibility by the surveyor: his Lordship rejected the use of the phrase 'voluntary assumption of responsibility' as a general test of liability.[138] The fact that the plaintiff was, in effect, paying at least in part for the advice he received makes *Smith* v. *Bush*, if anything, an even stronger case than *Hedley Byrne* itself.[139]

The second question, concerning the scope of the Unfair Contract Terms Act (UCTA), was also answered in favour of the plaintiffs. The defence of exclusion is considered in more detail in Chapter 8; it is sufficient at this stage to note the potential impact of UCTA in misstatement cases. Under section 2(2) of the Act, an exclusion of liability for negligence in relation to property damage or economic loss must be 'reasonable'. This provision applies to all cases of 'business liability' that is to say liability arising out of the course of a business or from the occupation of business premises.[140] Section 2(2) is therefore applicable to the normal range of *Hedley Byrne* cases, arising as they do out of the performance of professional duties. However, the decision on 'reasonableness' in *Smith* v. *Bush* is not necessarily applicable to all disclaimers under *Hedley Byrne*. *Smith* v. *Bush* involved a business–consumer relationship in which the consumer had little or no scope to renegotiate the terms: in Lord Griffiths' words, 'the disclaimer is imposed on the purchaser who has no effective power to object'. The House of Lords also took judicial notice of the fact that the surveyor was likely to be insured against liability. They also noted that the liability in question was unlikely to be extensive, as the duty was limited to those buying 'modest houses' such as 'young first time buyers [who] are likely to be under considerable financial pressure'. Plaintiffs with the capacity for re-negotiation or for

---

[136] UCTA 1977, s. 2(2); see below, Chapter 8.   [137] [1990] 1 AC 831, 846.

[138] Ibid., 864.

[139] The problem with this approach, however, is, why is *Smith* v. *Bush* a *Hedley Byrne* type of case and not a *D & F Estates/Murphy* case, leading to non-liability. As Professor Stapleton has put it convincingly, if 'the boundaries of existing pockets [of liability are to be used, then] they must make sense.' In practice, however, the pockets overlap as *Smith* v. *Bush* clearly shows. For, if one focuses on the negligent professional advice, one then slots the case into the *Hedley Byrne* pocket and liability flows almost automatically. If, however, one looks at the nature of the plaintiff's loss (economic loss resulting from the acquisition of defective property), then one is pushed into the *Murphy* non-liability rule. On all this see Stapleton, 'In Restraint of Tort' in *The Frontiers of Liability*, op. cit., 85–6.

[140] UCTA, s. 1(3).

contracting for the desired service elsewhere are unlikely to benefit from this approach to disclaimers.

Leaving the question of exclusion to one side and focusing simply on duty of care, it is not easy to reconcile *Smith* v. *Bush* with the restrictive approach taken by the House of Lords in the *Caparo* and *Murphy* cases. The most convincing attempt to do so has been that of Hoffman J in his judgment in *Morgan Crucible* v. *Hill Samuel*. According to his Lordship,[141] the different outcomes in *Caparo* and *Smith* 'consist in the different economic relationships between the parties and the nature of the markets in which they were operating'. In *Smith* the mortgagor 'is a person of modest means and making the most expensive investment of his or her life', whereas the take-over bidder in *Caparo* 'is an entrepreneur taking high risks for high rewards'. The prospective home-owner is far more vulnerable to economic risk and more likely, as a result, to act in reliance upon the information he receives, rather than relying upon his own judgment.[142] This explanation is, of course, one based on policy rather than on conceptual grounds; and many commentators remain highly critical of the distinction drawn by the courts in these cases. Thus, not unnaturally, it has left some academic commentators unhappy.[143]

So far we have been considering cases in which the plaintiff incurred economic loss as a result of his own reliance on the defendant's misstatement. There exists a related category of cases in which the courts have imposed liability where the plaintiff's loss has been caused by the reliance of a third party. In *Ministry of Housing and Local Government* v. *Sharp*,[144] a clerk in a local authority registry carelessly stated that certain land was free of charges when answering a request from solicitors acting for a prospective purchaser. In fact a charge had been registered by the Ministry, giving them the right to demand a sum from the owner of the land in return for the granting of planning permission. The land was sold under the assumption that no charge existed; the legal effect of this was to deprive the Ministry of the right to the sum in question. The Court of Appeal held that it was entitled to recover this sum from the local authority. This cannot be regarded as a *Hedley Byrne* case because the statement was not directed to the plaintiff; as such it falls outside the area of misstatement liability and must be judged under the general principles limiting recovery for pure economic loss after *Murphy*. It is possible that the same result would be reached

---

[141] [1991] Ch. 295, 302.

[142] Even then there are doubts that the judgments in *Caparo* paid adequate attention to the 'asymmetry of information' between the company and the shareholders: see Markesinis and Deakin, op. cit. (1992) 55 *MLR* 619, 628–9.

[143] Notably Professor Jane Stapleton, op. cit., who sees them as a good illustration of the deficiencies of the pockets approach taken by our courts. She has thus legitimately asked: Why is it that what is important about the facts of *Smith* v. *Bush* is the form of the defendant's carelessness (negligent professional advice) so that it can be associated with earlier case law allowing a duty of care (*Hedley Byrne*)? Why was not the relevant fact that the plaintiff suffered the economic loss through the acquisition of defective property, so that the case would be placed in the D & F *Estates/Murphy* 'pocket' of case law with the result that a duty of care would be denied? She thus—rightly—concludes that the pre-judged pocket approach is unsatisfactory because in any one case we may find more than one factor which is legally significant.

[144] [1970] 2 QB 223.

today, given that the plaintiff was foreseeable as an individual and that there is no danger of indeterminate liability arising.

In *Spring* v. *Guardian Assurance Ltd*.[145] the House of Lords held that when writing a reference for an existing or former employee, an employer owes a duty to avoid careless misstatements which might result in him being unable to find subsequent employment. This was not an easy case to resolve. For, first, one is faced with pure economic loss in which the role of reliance is at best indirect. Secondly, to impose a duty in these circumstances would be seen as undermining the well-established rule of the law of defamation according to which an employer writing a reference letter is protected by a defence of qualified privilege, and thus should not be liable for untrue statements as long as he acted in good faith (without malice). These grounds led the Court of Appeal to deny liability; as Glidewell LJ put it, in relation to defamation and malicious falsehood 'a substantial section of the law regarding these two associated torts would be emasculated'[146] if a duty of care in negligence were imposed. For similar reasons the Court rejected the implication of a term into the employee's contract of employment which would have placed the employer under a similar duty to take care. However, in the House of Lords, Lord Goff took the view that 'it must often be very difficult for an employee to obtain fresh employment without the benefit of a reference from his present or a previous employer . . . it is plain that the employee relies on him to exercise due skill and care in the preparation of the reference before making it available to the third party'.[147] In other words, it is relevant that the employee has no alternative but to rely on the employer in this situation. The fact that employer and employee are in a pre-tort relationship with implied obligations of mutual trust and confidence is also crucial to the outcome in *Spring*.[148]

Between them, these control factors suggest that the principle in *Spring* can be adequately confined. It certainly does not follow from *Spring* that any inaccurate statement affecting the reputation of an individual or product will give rise to liability if it leads to foreseeable economic loss. In the absence of a close pre-tort relationship between the parties, it highly unlikely that a duty of care in negligence will arise. Fears that *Spring* will fatally undermine the defence of qualified privilege in defamation are also questionable. That defence is as broad as it is partly because defamation is a tort to which strict liability applies; it is not necessary to prove fault. Following *Spring*, the defence of qualified privilege will continue to protect employers who do not act carelessly. Where an action is brought in negligence, proof of carelessness, and the establishment of a causal link between fault and damage, will often be problematic. Where, conversely, fault and causation are established, the case for remedying a clear injustice to the plaintiff will be particularly strong. Thus it is strongly arguable that in *Spring* the right balance was struck between protecting the interests of

---

[145] [1995] 2 AC 296.   [146] [1993] 2 All ER 273, 294.   [147] [1995] 2 AC 296, 319.

[148] *Spring* therefore complements developments in employment law which have seen the expansion of the employer's obligation to act in good faith towards the employee: see Lord Cooke of Thorndon, 'The Right of Spring', in P. Cane and J. Stapleton (eds.) *The Law of Obligations: Essays in Celebration of John Fleming* (1998), and our discussion of *Spring* in the context of employers' liability, Chapter 5, Section 3, below.

the employee in maintaining his reputation and preserving a cost-effective system of employment-based references.

(ii) Negligence in the Performance of a Service In *Henderson* v. *Merrett
Syndicates Ltd.*[149] the House of Lords held that the *Hedley Byrne* principle
extended beyond liability for financial harm caused by misstatements to cover
a wider set of cases of economic loss brought about by negligence in the performance of a service. According to Lord Goff, this wider principle 'rests upon
a relationship between the parties, which may be general or specific to the particular transaction, and which may or may not be contractual in nature';[150] if
the services were performed in a commercial context, 'the concept provides its
own explanation why there is no problem in cases of this kind about liability
for pure economic loss; for if a person assumes responsibility to another in
respect of certain services, there is no reason why he should not be liable in
damages for that other in respect of economic loss which flows from the negligent performance of those services'.[151] For this reason, his Lordship considered
that once the necessary 'special relationship' was established, it was not open
to the defendant to resist the imposition of a duty of care on the 'fair, just and
reasonable' ground. As with *Hedley Byrne* itself, however, the outcome might be
different if services were performed outside a commercial setting, or there was
a disclaimer. In the context of the *Henderson* litigation, Lord Goff's ruling meant
that Lloyd's Names (in effect, investors in the Lloyd's insurance market) were
able to establish that a duty of care was owed to them by the managing agents
who had held themselves out 'as possessing a special expertise to advise the
Names on the suitability of risks to be underwritten'.[152]

   This wider principle of liability was also used in *White* v. *Jones*.[153] In that case
a majority of the House of Lords held that a solicitor could be liable in negligence for failing to prepare timeously a new will, thus thereby depriving the
plaintiffs/intended beneficiaries of the benefits intended by the testator. Lord
Goff, giving again the leading judgment, held that 'the assumption of responsibility by the solicitor towards his client should be held in law to extend to the
intended beneficiary who (as the solicitor can reasonably foresee) may, as a
result of the solicitor's negligence, be deprived of his intended legacy in
circumstances in which neither the testator nor his estate will have a remedy
against the solicitor'.[154] The House of Lords thereby approved the result in
the earlier case of *Ross* v. *Caunters*[155] but rejected the reasoning in that case,
in which Megarry VC based his ruling on the wider neighbour principle
of *Donoghue* v. *Stevenson*.[156] *White* v. *Jones* is, thus, conceptually akin (but not

---

[149] [1995] 2 AC 145.   [150] Ibid., 180.   [151] Ibid., 181.
  [152] Ibid., 182. For subsequent litigation arising out of the losses of Lloyd's Names, see *Brown* v. *KMR
Services Ltd.* [1995] 4 All ER 598; *Aiken* v. *Stewart Wrightson Members Agency Ltd.* [1995] 1 WLR 1281.
  [153] [1995] 2 AC 207. For a full discussion of the case, including its intricate background, see B. S.
Markesinis 'Five Days in the House of Lords: Some Comparative Reflections on *White* v. *Jones*' (1995) 3 *Torts
Law Journal* 169.
  [154] [1995] 2 AC 207, 268.
  [155] [1980] Ch. 297; and see the roughly analogous case of *J'Aire Corp.* v. *Gregory* (1979) 598 P.2d 60
(Supreme Court of California).
  [156] [1932] AC 562.

identical) to the notion of contract in favour of third parties, used in some United States jurisdictions (and Germany) to solve this kind of problem. For in this type of situation, conferring a benefit on the third party is, in Mr Justice Cardozo's words, the 'end and aim' of the entire transaction.[157] Tort law in this case supplies a vital need. If the solicitor negligently breaches the contract with the testator, the estate of the deceased, which inherits his contractual rights, will have no effective action in contract for anything more than nominal damages for the solicitor's negligence, because the estate has suffered no loss. This, it is submitted, unfair result, is a consequence of the rigid privity-of-contract rule, the basis of which is that a party (in this case, the beneficiary) which has not provided consideration (value) for a promise (by the solicitor) cannot sue for its breach.[158] But in the absence of any tort action, the privity rule would in the instant situation have the effect that no person could demand legal sanctions from the negligent solicitor—an outcome which is neither just nor economically efficient.[159] Like *Hedley Byrne*,[160] this is properly understood not as an invitation to the opening of the floodgates, but as a solution to a dilemma. For, if no remedy is granted in this case, the person who has the right to demand a remedy (the testator) has suffered no loss and the person who has suffered the loss (the beneficiary) has no right. Moreover, as Lord Goff was eager to stress, the extent of the tort duty is shaped by the underlying contract (here between the testator and the defendant). Finally, in this particular factual configuration, there is no risk of placing the solicitor in a position of conflict since the interests of his client and of the intended beneficiary overlap completely.[161]

However, it seems that, in part because of these considerations, *White* v. *Jones* will only apply in a narrow range of situations. This is illustrated by decisions in which the intention of the contractor (promisee) to benefit the third party as an individual was less obvious and recovery in tort was denied. In the earlier case of *Clark* v. *Bruce, Lance*,[162] the Court of Appeal concluded that the interests of the client who had contracted for the services potentially conflicted with those of the plaintiff who claimed to have been the intended beneficiary of the contractual performance. This case concerned the granting by a lessor to a lessee of an option to purchase the freehold upon the death of the lessor or of his wife, whichever was later. The terms of the option were not particularly favourable to the lessee and he claimed that the lessor's solicitor had been negligent in not pointing this out to his client. The court, distinguishing *Ross* v.

---

[157] This, and the other reasons given in the text above, explain why the plaintiff's attempt to rely on *White* v. *Jones* in the subsequent case of *Goodwill* v. *British Pregnancy Advisory Service* [1996] 1 WLR 1397 was legally unconvincing. See, on the other hand, *Carr-Glynn* v. *Frearsons (A Firm)*, [1998] 4 All ER 225, and Lord Justice Chadwick's ingenious expansion (at 231–2) of *White* v. *Jones* to cover the facts of that case.

[158] *Tweddle* v. *Atkinson* (1861) 1 B. & S. 393; *Dunlop Pneumatic Tyre Co. Ltd.* v. *Selfridge & Co. Ltd.* [1915] AC 847; *Scruttons Ltd.* v. *Midland Silicones Ltd.* [1962] AC 446; Treitel, *Law of Contract* (8th edn., 1991), ch. 15.

[159] In principle it is inefficient because the party undertaking the obligation is under-deterred from breaching the contract. See Markesinis and Deakin, op. cit. (1992) 55 *MLR* 619, for general discussion.

[160] [1964] AC 465, above.

[161] Cf. the denial of recovery in the Australian case of *Seale* v. *Perry* [1982] VR 193 on the grounds that the interest of the frustrated beneficiary was not substantial enough to merit protection, and the dissent of Lord Mustill in *White* v. *Jones* [1995] 2 AC 207, in particular at 289–91.

[162] [1988] 1 WLR 881.

Caunters, held that the solicitor's principal responsibility lay to his client, and that to impose upon him the suggested duty of care in tort with regard to the plaintiff was not compatible with this responsibility.

Another restriction on *White* v. *Jones* is that it may have no application in a situation where the estate does suffer a loss as a consequence of the solicitor's negligence. In *Carr-Glynn* v. *Frearsons*[163] it was said at first instance that to allow an action under such circumstances would be to expose the solicitor to an unacceptable risk of separate and cumulative claims being brought (one by the personal representatives of the deceased, the other by the frustrated beneficiary) in respect of the same wrong. However, an appeal was allowed on the grounds that the solicitor's duty to the plaintiff was complementary to his duty to the testator.

Nor does *White* v. *Jones* imply that a solicitor will, in general, be liable to third parties for a failure to provide an effective service to his own client. One very obviously different kind of case is that in which a solicitor is sued by his client's opponent in litigation: here, there is normally no duty of care even for situations of loss which is not purely economic.[164] Slightly different is the situation in which the negligence of a solicitor acting for a seller of land causes economic loss to the buyer. In *Gran Gelato Ltd.* v. *Richcliff (Group) Ltd.*,[165] an error by the solicitor led to his own client making an innocent misrepresentation which caused substantial loss to the plaintiff once the transaction was completed. The Vice-Chancellor rejected the plaintiff's claim on the grounds that, in this case, the solicitor's duties were owed only to his own client. The result seems contrary to principle, since there is no danger of indeterminate liability here and a tort claim would avoid the multiplicity of actions. As Professor Tettenborn has explained, the ruling in *Gran Gelato*:

necessitates two actions where one ought to do: Purchaser v. Vendor (for damages) and Vendor v. Solicitor (for an indemnity . . .). Since (i) the vendor is normally not at fault at all, and (ii) everyone accepts that the loss ought ultimately to be borne by the solicitor who is, there seems little point in not allowing this whole long-winded process to be short-circuited by a direct action against the solicitor, saving time and money all round.[166]

A more general difficulty in applying *White* v. *Jones* lies in determining the category of plaintiffs who can be regarded, for this purpose, as the legitimate and intended beneficiaries of the performance of professional services. In the 'wrongful conception' case of *Goodwill* v. *British Pregnancy Advisory Service*[167] the plaintiff sued the defendants in negligence for advising her partner that his vasectomy operation had been successful when this was not the case. In reliance on her partner's assertion[168] that they could not have children, she gave up her own contraception arrangements. She subsequently became pregnant and gave birth to a child. Her claim, which was brought in respect of the

---

[163] [1997] 2 All ER 614 [1998] 4 All ER 225.   [164] See *Al-Kandari* v. *J. R. Brown & Co.* [1988] QB 665.
[165] [1992] Ch. 560.   [166] 'Enquiries Before Contract—The Wrong Answer?' [1992] *CLJ* 415, 417.
[167] [1996] 1 WLR 1397.
[168] The case is strange in more ways than one. Thus, first, the plaintiff also consulted her own doctor about the risk of becoming pregnant. Secondly, it is widely known that vasectomy operations do not produce 100 per cent safe results. The failure of the plaintiff's claim is thus best explained by reference to the reasons given above, n. 157.

costs of raising the child,[169] failed—it is submitted justifiably—largely because her relationship with her partner began some time after the operation had been carried out. Under these circumstances, the Court of Appeal held that the defendant owed her no duty of care. According to Thorpe LJ, 'the plaintiff is no nearer the doctor adviser than one who some three and half years after the operation commenced a sexual relationship with his patient . . . the class to which the plaintiff belongs is in my judgment potentially excessive in size and uncertain in character'.[170] Lord Justice Gibbson, on the other hand, thought that it would not be 'fair, just and reasonable', to impose a duty of care and bring this case under the *White* v. *Jones* heading.[171] As already stated, this is a commendable result. Juristically, however, this result could have been achieved in a more convincing manner if the vague concepts—proximity, fair, just and reasonable—used by the learned judges had been avoided. This could have happened if the learned judges had distinguished *Goodwill* from *White* v. *Jones* by stating that in the former the plaintiff was emphatically not the 'end and aim' of the transaction (the vasectomy operation).[172] To put it differently, if contractual concepts had been available to English law, one would have described the plaintiff in *Goodwill* as an 'incidental' but not the 'intended' beneficiary of the contract and thus easily defeated her claim.

(iii) Economic Loss Arising from Defects in Buildings and Products As we have seen, potential liability for articles which actually cause personal injury or damage to property is not in doubt following *Donoghue* v. *Stevenson*.[173] There is, on the other hand, no liability in tort for producing an article which is found to be merely defective and therefore worth less than the plaintiff paid for it; the plaintiff will have to depend on contract for compensation. After a period of some uncertainty, this rule was clearly reasserted in *Murphy* v. *Brentwood District Council*.[174] An intermediate category arises where an article is both defective and *dangerous*. Can the owner of the article recover from the producer the costs of alleviating the risk of danger or, alternatively, the loss in value as a result of ceasing to use the article? Following *Murphy* the answer is, almost certainly not: these losses are characterised as pure economic loss and therefore as outside the range of recovery, just as much as those which arise where an article is merely defective.[175]

---

[169] It is not clear whether a wrongful conception case of this kind is best regarded as a claim in pure economic loss. In *Walkin* v. *South Manchester HA* [1995] 1 WLR 1543 the Court of Appeal held that claims arising for pre-natal pain and suffering and post-natal economic loss all arose out of a single cause of action for *personal injury*, which accrued at the moment of the unwanted conception. In *Goodwill*, the court appeared to regard the claim as one of economic loss; *Walkin* was not cited. It is unclear whether, in *Goodwill*, the plaintiff's case would, on its merits, have been strengthened had it been classified as one based on physical harm (had it been argued this way it is likely, on the authority of *Walkin*, that it would have been defeated on the grounds of limitation of actions).

[170] [1996] 1 WLR 1397, 1406.

[171] Ibid., 1403.

[172] Cf. *Carr-Glynn* v. *Frearsons* (*A Firm*), [1998] 4 All ER 225.

[173] [1932] AC 562.

[174] [1991] 1 AC 398. See also *Invercargill CC* v. *Hamlin* [1996] AC 624, in which the Privy Council took a somewhat different approach to the issue of relational economic loss in the context of an appeal from New Zealand.

[175] In *East River Steamship Corp.* v. *Transamerica Deleval Inc.* (1986) 476 US 858, the Supreme Court of the United States rejected a claim for pure economic loss arising from a defective product, but this was not viewed as a case of a *dangerously defective* product and may be of doubtful relevance in *Murphy*, despite

English law has reached this position as a result of the overruling, in *Murphy*, of the wide-ranging if rather ambiguous decision of the House of Lords in *Anns* v. *Merton London Borough Council*.[176] A principal difficulty facing the courts after *Anns* was the correct characterisation of the damage in that case. The action was brought against the council by the occupiers of the properties in question who had bought houses on long leases in ignorance of the defective foundations. Lord Wilberforce referred to their loss as 'material, physical damage'.[177] For reasons, which are now generally accepted, however, it cannot be said that they suffered property damage, since at the time they entered into their leases the damage to the structure of the houses had already occurred. As Deane J of the High Court of Australia explained in *Sutherland Shire Council* v. *Heyman*:

The only property, which could be said to have been damaged in such a case, is the building, itself. The building itself could not be said to have been subjected to 'material, physical damage' by reason merely of the inadequacy of its foundations since the building never existed otherwise than with its foundations in that state. Moreover, even if the inadequacy of its foundations could be seen as physical, material damage to the building, it would be damage to property in which a future purchaser or tenant had no interest at all at the time when it occurred.[178]

Lord Keith adopted this passage in *Murphy*.[179] In that case a house was built with a defective concrete raft foundation which began to crack, fracturing a gas pipe and causing other structural faults to occur. The plaintiff, who had bought the house new from the original builders, was unable to carry out the necessary repairs and sold the house for £35,000 less than its market value without the defects. His cause of action, according to the members of the House of Lords, originated in this economic loss, and not in the defects in either the raft or the pipes.

If it could not be accurately characterised as property damage, the loss in *Anns* might nevertheless be described as economic loss consequential upon the threat to health and safety posed by the defective foundations. In *Anns* Lord Wilberforce said, 'what is recoverable is the amount of expenditure necessary to restore the dwelling to a condition in which it is no longer a danger to the health or safety of persons occupying and possibly (depending on the circumstances) expenses arising from the necessary displacement'.[180] Likewise, in *Peabody Donation Fund* v. *Sir Lindsay Parkinson & Co*. Lord Keith spoke of damages 'as representing expenditure necessary to avert injury to safety and health'.[181] This notion of damages as 'preventive' compensation has not, however, survived *Murphy*, and it is arguable, in retrospect, that it did not add much to the clarification of the issues at stake. It allowed a link with physical harm to be maintained without there being a clear acceptance that mitigation or prevention of this kind did not affect the nature of the loss but simply made the recovery of the expenditure more justifiable in policy terms.

being cited by Lord Keith as authority for the general exclusionary rule. On the *East River* case generally see the discussion of Professor Robertson in 'American Perspective', Section 5, below. See also the decision of the Supreme Court of Canada in *Rivtow Marine Ltd.* v. *Washington Iron Works* [1974] SCR 1189, discussed below, Section 5(3).

[176] [1978] AC 728.
[179] [1991] 1 AC 398, 468.
[177] Ibid., 759.
[180] [1978] AC 728, 759.
[178] (1985) 60 ALR 1, 60–1.
[181] [1985] AC 210, 242.

In *Murphy* the correct identification of the loss as 'purely economic', was, for Lord Keith, of itself enough to cast fatal doubt on *Anns*. According to his Lordship, 'It is difficult to draw a distinction in principle between an article which is useless or valueless and one which suffers from a defect which would render it dangerous in use but which is discovered by the purchaser in time to avert any possibility of injury. The purchaser may incur expense in putting right the defect, or, more probably, discard the article. In either case the loss is purely economic.'[182] If an action for 'preventive' economic loss was allowed, there was, according to Lord Keith, nothing to stop courts extending liability to cover merely defective products, and 'that would open on an exceedingly wide range of claims'.[183] In similar vein Lord Oliver described the suggested distinction as 'fallacious'.[184] Although there are strong arguments on the other side,[185] *Murphy* has settled the question at least for the time being.

While the rulings in *Anns* and *Murphy* were immediately concerned with the question of the liability of local authorities for the consequences of failure to inspect building foundations, they also extended to the liability of builders for defective premises and to that of manufacturers for defective products. *Murphy* has been applied to deny a claim in tort for pure economic loss by a commercial owner against the original builder in *Department of the Environment* v. *Thomas Bates & Sons*,[186] and it implicitly confirmed two earlier decisions on manufacturers' liability. In *Muirhead* v. *Industrial Tank Specialities Ltd.*[187] a manufacturer of an electrical pump was liable for property damage incurred by the ultimate user when the pump, which was used to aerate his lobster tanks, failed to work as intended. But the manufacturer was held not liable for loss of profits for the period when the tanks were out of action. In *Simaan General Contracting* v. *Pilkington Glass (No. 2)*[188] the plaintiff had no action for economic losses arising from a defect of quality caused by a subcontractor; he was limited to his rights against the main contractor. To similar effect is the Scottish case of *Scott Lithgow Ltd.* v. *GEC Electrical Projects Ltd.*[189]

The House of Lords in *Murphy* cast doubt on the 'complex structure theory', which had been canvassed in the earlier case of *D. & F. Estates* v. *Church Commissioners of England*[190] as a way out of the difficulties created by *Anns*. In *D. & F. Estates* Lord Bridge maintained that: 'it may well be arguable that in the case of complex structures . . . one element of the structure should be regarded . . . as distinct from another element so that damage to one part of the structure caused by a hidden defect in another may qualify to be treated as damage to "other property" '.[191] If this argument had been accepted, it could have been applied both to chattels (e.g., a car with defective brakes, the failure of which causes the vehicle to crash) and to buildings (e.g., defective foundations, which cause cracks to appear in the roof and walls of the house). In *Murphy*, however, both Lord Bridge and Lord Oliver rejected this theory as 'artificial'.[192]

---

[182] [1991] 1 AC 398, 470.   [183] Ibid., 469.   [184] Ibid., 488.
[185] See Sir Robin Cooke, 'An Impossible Distinction?' (1991) 107 *LQR* 46, and R. O'Dair, 'A House Built on Firm Foundations?' (1991) 54 *MLR* 561, both discussing American law and its use in *Murphy*.
[186] [1991] 1 AC 499.   [187] [1986] QB 507.   [188] [1988] QB 758.
[189] 1992 SLT 244.   [190] [1989] 1 AC 177.   [191] Ibid., 207.
[192] [1991] 1 AC 398, 470 (Lord Keith), 476–9 (Lord Bridge).

Unfortunately the matter does not end there, as the judgments in *Murphy* contain a number of references to 'exceptional' instances of liability which bear a certain resemblance to the complex structure idea. Lord Bridge gave the examples of subcontractors fitting a boiler which subsequently catches fire and burns the building in which it is installed, and of electrical wiring which is defectively installed with the same result. Lords Keith and Jauncey gave similar examples. Lord Oliver, on the other hand, expressed some scepticism about the idea.[193] In the examples given by Lords Keith, Bridge, and Jauncey the existence of an action appears to depend upon the factor that responsibility for the separate parts of the building rests with different persons. It is not clear whether it is also necessary to have regard to the degree of integration of the subcontractor's work into the whole, or the feasibility of physically separating the different components.[194]

Lord Bridge also accepted the possibility of preventive damages being awarded in the following situation:

If a building stands so close to the boundary of the building owner's land that after discovery of the dangerous defect it remains a potential source of injury to persons or property on neighbouring land or on the highway, the building owner ought, in principle, to be entitled to recover in tort from the negligent builder the cost of obviating the danger, whether by repair or by demolition, so far as that cost is necessarily incurred in order to protect himself from potential liability to third parties.[195]

The precise basis for this exception and its potential scope are unclear. Why should expenditure incurred to avoid legal liability to a third party on the highway or on neighbouring land be recoverable when similar expenditure designed to avert physical injury to the occupiers of the property is not? It may be that liability to a third party would, in Lord Bridge's example, lie in the tort of nuisance rather than in negligence; this distinction would limit the scope of the exception, at the expense, it might be said, of doing so in a somewhat arbitrary way. It remains to be seen whether, or how, this apparent exception to the denial of a duty of care will be developed in future.

But the greatest problem to arise from the rejection of liability in *Murphy* is the question of where this leaves the principle enunciated in *Hedley Byrne*. Not only is *Hedley Byrne* still good law, but its *ratio* is apparently capable of being extended to cover cases which, on first sight, seem to have little connection with negligent misstatements. One such case is *Pirelli General Cable Works Ltd.* v. *Oscar Faber & Partners*,[196] in which the owners of a factory site sued consulting engineers who were responsible for the defective design and construction of a chimney on the site. The chimney had to be partially demolished and replaced when the material chosen by the defendants for its inner lining proved to be inappropriate, causing cracks in the chimney's structure. The judges who decided *Pirelli* clearly regarded the damage in question as physical damage to the structure of the chimney; however, according to Lord Keith in *Murphy*, the

---

[193] Ibid., 470 (Lord Keith), 478 (Lord Bridge), 497 (Lord Jauncey), 489 (Lord Oliver).
[194] For discussion, see I. N. Duncan Wallace, '*Anns* Beyond Repair' (1991) 107 *LQR* 228, 235.
[195] [1991] 1 AC 398.   [196] [1983] 2 AC 1.

loss should properly be regarded as economic. Since the defendants had been employed to advise on the choice of the material and design structure of the chimney, *Pirelli* should be seen as coming within the scope of *Hedley Byrne*. Lord Keith also suggested that *Junior Books* v. *Veitchi Co.*[197] could be seen as a *Hedley Byrne* case.[198]

The effect of all this is that while under *Murphy*[199] the careless builder is free of liability for economic loss in tort, consulting engineers, architects, or surveyors, who carelessly give poor advice to site owners or purchasers of property, may face liability under *Hedley Byrne*. This is an odd result for a number of reasons. First, the elements of reliance and proximity are just as likely to be present in the one case as in the other. Secondly, there seems to be no good reason from the point of view of policy for imposing a more extensive duty of care for negligent speech than for negligent conduct or, if there is, this reason has not been stated. Thirdly, the distinction between careless words and careless acts is difficult to draw in practice, as *Pirelli* illustrates. Was that case really about negligent advice, or was it simply an illustration of a service which was negligently performed? Lord Keith's explanation of *Pirelli* as an instance of negligent misstatement seems to be a rather opportunistic, *ex post* rationalisation of the earlier decision. His placing of *Junior Books* in the same category also contradicts his own earlier judgment in *Junior Books* where he had said that *Hedley Byrne* was not in point.[200]

It is doubtful that the notion of reliance, as developed in the *Hedley Byrne* line of cases, can adequately account for these distinctions. Reliance 'is an extremely slippery concept [which] is unlikely to provide a secure foundation for a coherent development of the law'.[201] These difficulties are clearly illustrated by *Nitrigin Eireann Teoranta* v. *Inco Alloys Ltd.*[202] The defendants manufactured and supplied to the plaintiffs some alloy steel tubing which turned out to be defective. The plaintiffs discovered cracking in the structure of which the tubing formed part, but could not identify the cause. The tubing then ruptured, causing an explosion and resulting in damage to the plaintiffs' chemical works. The judge held that this was not a case of liability under *Hedley Byrne*: the cause of action in tort (as opposed to contract) only accrued when the explosion took place and caused physical damage to the plant. This was because the manufacture and supply of the component did not bring the parties into a special pre-tort relationship of the kind required for *Hedley Byrne* liability. Although the defendants were specialist manufacturers who could be taken to have known of the plaintiffs' particular requirements, 'that is neither a professional relationship in the sense in which the law treats professional negligence nor a *Hedley Byrne* relationship'.[203] While this must be correct, it would seem to fol-

---

[197] [1983] AC 520; see above, Section 2(1).

[198] [1991] 1 AC 398, 466. See generally E. McKendrick, '*Pirelli* Re-Examined' (1991) 11 *Leg. Stud.* 326.

[199] And the earlier House of Lords decision of *D. & F. Estates* v. *Church Commissioners for England* [1989] 1 AC 177.

[200] [1980] 1 AC 520, 535. See N. J. Mullany, 'Limitation of Actions—Where are We Now?' [1993] *LMCLQ* 34, 36.

[201] McKendrick, '*Pirelli* Re-Examined', op. cit. (n. 198 above), 332.   [202] [1992] 1 All ER 854.

[203] Ibid., 860.

low that in the absence of liability for pure economic loss caused by dangerously defective products, had the plaintiffs discovered the cause of the cracking before the explosion took place and had then taken steps to remove the danger, they could not have recovered for this expenditure. In this way *Murphy* creates a powerful disincentive to take the necessary precautions to avoid both property damage and potential danger to life and limb. This result may appear to some as 'logical', once the nature of the damage is correctly identified; but it can be reconciled only with difficulty with the important aim of minimising the net costs of accidents and of accident prevention.[204]

It seems unlikely that the House of Lords could reconsider in the near future the sweeping nature of the *Murphy* ruling, and insert into it the important distinction between merely defective products and those which are dangerous. At best it is possible that the apparent exceptions to the rule against recovery mentioned in the judgments of Lords Keith, Bridge, and Jauncey could be developed in favour of a plaintiff who takes steps to mitigate likely future damage. From a doctrinal point of view, however, this would be less than completely satisfactory. In *Rivtow Marine Ltd.* v. *Washington Iron Works*[205] the Supreme Court of Canada, over a strong dissent by Laskin J who would have granted recovery, rejected a claim for expenditure to remedy a dangerous defect in a crane. But it did allow the plaintiff's claim on the more limited ground that the defendants had breached an implied duty to warn the plaintiff of the defect in question. This precise point did not arise in *Murphy* or in *Inco Alloys*, but given some of the broad dicta (examined above) against economic-loss recovery in non-*Hedley Byrne* situations, it may be that even the majority judgment in *Rivtow* would not now be followed in England.

(iv) Relational Economic Loss Arising from Damage to the Property of a Third Party This category of cases concerns the situation in which the plaintiff suffers economic loss by virtue of damage caused by the defendant to the property of a third party with whom the plaintiff is in some kind of relationship, contractual or otherwise. The normal rule is that relational losses of this kind are not recoverable: the plaintiff must show damage to *his* property before he can recover anything. As recently restated by Lord Brandon in *The Aliakmon*,[206]

there is a long line of authority for a principle of law that, in order to enable a person to claim in negligence for loss caused to him by reason of loss of or damage to property, he must have had either the legal ownership or a possessory title to the property concerned at the time when the loss or damage occurred, and it is not enough to have had only contractual rights in relation to such property which have been adversely affected by the loss of or damage to it.

This is the prime example of a 'bright line rule' which aims to place a clear limit to tort recovery in the interests of certainty. As La Forest J of the Supreme Court of Canada has put it, 'since most claims of this nature occur in the

---

[204] See generally A. Grubb and A. Mullis, 'An Unfair Law for Dangerous Products: The Fall of *Anns*' [1991] *Conv.* 225.

[205] [1974] SCR 1189.

[206] [1986] AC 785, 809. For US law, see *Robins Dry Dock & Repair Co.* v. *Flint* (1927) 275 US 303, and Professor Robertson, 'American Perspective', below, Section 5(3).

commercial area, the requisite certainty should exist before the accidents occurs'.[207] The rule is also justified by the argument that those with merely relational interests of this kind should be encouraged to protect themselves by a contract with the property owner (with whom they may be in a pre-existing relationship). They should thus be discouraged from relying on a tort claim, on the basis that allocation of liability and adjustments of risk may most easily take place between parties who are already in a proximate economic relationship.

An example of rights over property falling short of rights of ownership or possession was provided in *The Mineral Transporter*.[208] Time charterers of a ship who suffered economic loss when it was out of action following a collision were unable to recover in tort for their loss since at the time of the collision they had no possessory right in the ship, having merely a right to its use under the terms of the sub-charter. Similarly, in *The Aliakmon* goods being shipped by sea were damaged by the carelessness of the carrier, with the result that the buyer suffered a financial loss equivalent to the difference between the contract price and the value of the goods when he took possession of them. At the time the damage occurred the goods were still owned by the seller but they were at the risk of the buyer—that is to say, he was required by the contract of sale to take the goods and to pay the full price for them regardless of damage. The buyer sued the carrier in tort for the resulting loss but the action failed precisely because he had no possessory right in relation to the goods when the damage occurred.

The facts of *The Aliakmon* were rather unusual: the initial C and F contract[209] for the sale of the goods had been varied to give the buyer more time to pay, with the seller retaining ownership of the goods until he did. The buyer would normally have sued the carrier in contract by virtue of holding the shipping documents, but he had pledged these back to the seller as security for the price. Under these circumstances Lord Brandon considered that the normal exclusionary rule had to apply: the buyer should have protected himself by contracting for the seller to assign to him any rights of action he might have against the carrier for negligence. However, the seller would have had no significant contract action to assign: since he was entitled to full payment of the price from the buyer, he would not have suffered any loss and would therefore have been unable to sue the carrier for contract damages. Lord Brandon's decision effectively means that the carrier was liable to neither the seller nor the

---

[207] La Forest J, in *Canadian National Railway* v. *Norsk Pacific Steamship Co.* (1992) 91 DLR (4th) 289, 337.

[208] [1986] AC 1.

[209] A cost-and-freight contract and (slightly different) a cost-insurance-freight contract are specialised types of contract for the international sale of goods, under which the seller undertakes to transfer certain shipping documents to the buyer while the goods are in transit. Normally the risk passes to the buyer on shipment, but the transfer of documents gives him rights of action against the carrier for any negligence and also the benefit of the insurance policy covering the goods. This correspondence of risk and rights of action broke down in *The Aliakmon* for the reasons explained in the text. On international sales contracts generally see Goode, *Commercial Law* (1982), chs. 22, 23. *The Aliakmon* overruled *The Irene's Success* [1982] QB 481, but cf. *Triangle Steel & Supply Co.* v. *Korean United Lines Ltd.* (1986) 63 BCLR 66 (Supreme Court of British Columbia declining to follow *The Aliakmon*).

buyer for the consequences of his negligence.[210] On this particular point of maritime law the effect of the House of Lords' decision has now been reversed by statute,[211] but the decision remains of importance for the wider issue of tort law which it decided.

The exclusionary rule has been applied in a number of other contexts. Plaintiffs failing to recover have thus included a contractor unable to complete a building job when the defendant flooded the land he was working on,[212] a tug owner who lost a valuable towage contract when the defendant damaged and sank the ship he was towing,[213] and insurers who were required to pay out when the defendant sank and damaged a ship they had insured.[214] These decisions were reaffirmed in *Spartan Steel & Alloys Ltd.* v. *Martin & Co. (Contractors) Ltd.*,[215] where the defendant contractors carelessly cut through a cable supplying electricity to an industrial estate, with the result that the plaintiff steelmakers had to shut down production for a period. The plaintiffs were able to recover for damage actually inflicted to their property, namely to the materials which were being mixed in the furnace at the time of the power-cut and which had to be removed at a loss before the melt could be completed. However, they were unable to recover the net profits from the four further melts, which they would have normally carried out during the period when the electricity was cut off; these losses were purely economic in nature.

A recognised exception to this rule of non-recovery in tort arises out of the maritime-law principle of 'general average contribution'. This is a device for pooling risk, under which owners of goods in a ship's hold undertake in advance to pay a proportion of the costs of any damage caused to the cargo during the voyage, regardless of whether their own share of the cargo is damaged. In *The Greystoke Castle*,[216] the House of Lords held that cargo-owners in this position were engaged in a 'joint venture' which made it appropriate for those whose property was undamaged, and whose loss was therefore merely economic, to recover this amount from the defendant responsible for the collision. However, the notion of a joint venture between the property owner and those with a relational interest in the property has not been extended beyond this specific case.

Although the English courts have consistently rejected attempts to circumvent the exclusionary rule in cases of this kind, a more flexible approach has been adopted elsewhere in the Commonwealth. In *Caltex Oil (Australia) Pty. Ltd.* v. *Dredge Willemstad*,[217] the defendants negligently damaged an oil pipeline belonging to a third party. The plaintiffs, who made use of the pipeline, incurred losses by virtue of the need to make alternative arrangements for transporting their oil. The High Court of Australia allowed an action for damages. A number of potential bases for the decision were advanced in the judgments of the High Court. One of the most important was the 'known plaintiff'

---

[210] See Markesinis, 'An Expanding Tort Law: The Price of a Rigid Contract Law' (1987) 103 *LQR* 359, for extensive discussion.

[211] Carriage of Goods by Sea Act 1992.   [212] *Cattle* v. *Stockton Waterworks* (1875) LR 10 QB 453.

[213] *SA de Rémorquage à Hélice* v. *Bennetts* [1911] 1 KB 243.

[214] *Simpson & Co.* v. *Thomson* (1887) 3 App. Cas. 279.   [215] [1973] 1 QB 27.

[216] [1947] AC 265.   [217] [1976] 136 CLR 529.

principle, to the effect that recovery is permissible where the plaintiff is foreseeable as an *identifiable individual* who would be likely to suffer the loss in question. This deals with the problem of indeterminate liability, and could have led
to a different result in *Spartan Steel*[218] if the plaintiff had been the only user
affected by the rupture of the cable. In general, though, the 'known plaintiff'
exception creates the paradox that the more extensive the harm caused by the
defendant, the less likely he is to be liable, and for this reason it has not been
generally accepted as sufficient basis for determining the existence of a duty of
care.

The relevant policy and doctrinal arguments were fully analysed in the decision of the Canadian Supreme Court in *Canadian National Railway* v. *Norsk Pacific
Steamship Co.*[219] The Supreme Court allowed, by the barest of majorities,[220] an
action where the defendant's steamship negligently collided with a railway
bridge spanning the River Fraser in British Columbia, causing the plaintiff, the
main user of the bridge, expenditure for re-routing its trains while the bridge
was being repaired. The bridge was owned by a public-works commission,
which entered into contracts for its use with several companies of which the
plaintiff was the predominant one, accounting for over 80 per cent of the use
of the bridge. The majority judgment of McLachlin J emphasised the strong
element of proximity in this situation and the absence of dangers associated
with the floodgates argument: the plaintiff's 'position for practical purposes,
vis-à-vis the tortfeasor, is indistinguishable from that of the owner of the damaged property'.[221]

The difficulty with this approach lies in the use made of the concept of proximity, which, according to La Forest J's dissenting opinion in *Norsk*, is too vague
to support a departure from the normal rule of non-liability.[222] Nor is it clear
why liability should rest upon whether the plaintiff is individually ascertainable or one of a very small class, or in some kind of physical propinquity to the
defendant. While these may be relevant factors in rebutting the floodgates
argument, they do not provide in themselves an independent justification for
allowing recovery; something more is needed. On the other hand, if it can be
shown that the plaintiff rather than the defendant was in the best position to
minimise or avert the loss,[223] policy factors could justify rejecting the plaintiff's claim if the case is otherwise evenly balanced. In *Norsk* the plaintiff could
have sought better protection against the risk of damage to the bridge in its
contract with the owner. As it was, this contract specifically provided that the
railway company was to have no right of indemnity from the public-works
commission for the costs of diverting traffic in the event that the bridge was
closed for repairs. There is a strong argument for saying that, in these circumstances, the court should have let the loss lie where it fell, and that a tort action
would upset the allocation of risk which the exemption clauses in the contract

---

[218] [1973] 1 QB 27.   [219] (1991) 91 DLR (4th) 289.
[220] Stevenson J issued an opinion concurring in the result but offering different reasons to those of
McLachlin, L'Heureux-Dubé, and Cory JJ. La Forest, Sopinka, and Iacobucci JJ dissented.
[221] (1992) 91 DLR (4th) 289, 376.   [222] See the discussion above, Section 2(1).
[223] Either by making alternative arrangements in advance or by taking out loss insurance.

between the railway and the public-works commission embodied. As Justice La Forest put it: 'In contracts between sophisticated parties such as those in [*Norsk*], who are well advised by counsel, such exclusions of liability often result from determinations regarding who is in the best position to insure the risk at the lowest cost.'[224]

(v) Overlapping and Concurrent Duties in Contract and Tort   A theme which runs throughout the cases examined so far concerns the difficulties which arise when a given duty situation could be governed by obligations in either contract or tort. The degree to which tort duties should be shaped or perhaps negatived altogether by contract is one with which the courts have had to grapple from the time *Donoghue* v. *Stevenson* began the modern expansion of the tort of negligence. As far as physical injury and damage to property are concerned, the position is now fairly clear: the law imposes a general duty of care in tort based not upon the breach of an undertaking or promise but upon failure to comply with an objective standard of care. In *Donoghue* v. *Stevenson* Lord Macmillan explained this principle in the following important passage:

Where, as in cases like the present, so much depends upon the avenue of approach to the question, it is very easy to take the wrong turning. If you begin with the sale by the manufacturer to the retail dealer, then the consumer who purchases from the retailer is at once seen to be a stranger to the contract between the retailer and manufacturer and so disentitled to sue upon it. There is no contractual relation between the manufacturer and the consumer, and thus the plaintiff if he is to succeed is driven to try to bring himself within one or other of the exceptional cases . . . If, on the other hand, you disregard the fact that the circumstances of the case at one stage include the existence of a contract of sale between the manufacturer and the retailer and approach the question by asking whether there is evidence of carelessness on the part of the manufacturer and whether he owed a duty to be careful in a question with the party who has been injured in consequence of his want of care, the circumstance that the injured party was not a party to the incidental contract of sale becomes irrelevant and his title to sue the manufacturer is unaffected by this circumstance.[225]

This was Lord Macmillan's answer to the dissenting judges, who argued that as the appellant was a stranger to the contracts for the manufacture and sale of the article, she could have no cause of action. If the manufacturer undertook any duties in respect of his products, these were confined to the contracts he had with his distributors. Thus to grant recovery to the ultimate consumer, with whom he had no contractual link, was in Lord Buckmaster's words 'simply to misapply to tort doctrines applicable to sale and purchase'.[226] In rejecting this point the majority effectively reversed the priority of contract over tort: at least where physical loss is concerned, the presence alongside a duty of care of a contract setting a narrower obligation becomes, in Lord Macmillan's word, 'irrelevant' to the tort action. Subsequent cases decided that the defendant can in certain circumstances protect himself against liability in tort by expressly

---

[224] La Forest J at (1991) 91 DLR (4th) 289, 302.
[225] [1932] AC 562, 611. The passage is discussed by Lord Mustill writing extra-judicially, in 'Negligence in the World of Finance', op. cit.
[226] [1932] AC 562, 577 (Lord Buckmaster).

contracting with the plaintiff for the benefit of an exclusion or limitation clause, or, in the case of occupiers' liability, by bringing such a restriction of liability to the plaintiff's notice.[227] Yet even this possibility is now subject to regulation by the Unfair Contract Terms Act 1977.

With pure economic or financial loss it is a different matter; for reasons analysed above it is not possible to place it on a par with physical damage, and there may be good arguments for allowing the rules of contract to prevail over tort in allocating legal responsibility. The first situation to consider here is that in which the parties were brought into a pre-tort relationship of proximity as a result of entering into a contract with each other. If tort is allowed to dictate the outcome of a claim for damages after the event, the parties' capacity to make their own allocation of risk in advance, and set the price accordingly, may be seriously undermined. The contract may indeed have set a different standard of care from that of liability for negligence, or have specified more or less precise obligations from those which tort law would impose upon the parties. Contract damages are calculated on different principles from those applicable to tort, and the limitation periods for bringing an action also differ. The price paid for the service or performance in question is likely to have reflected these factors. Particularly in commercial transactions between business entities, then, the courts should respect the parties' own choice of contractual form. This appears to be what Lord Scarman had in mind in *Tai Hing Cotton Mill Ltd*. v. *Liu Chong Hing Bank Ltd*.[228] In that case, speaking on behalf of the Privy Council, he said that in a case concerning the relationship between banker and customer: 'their Lordships believe it to be correct to adhere to the contractual analysis: on principle because it is a relationship in which the parties have, subject to a few exceptions, the right to determine their obligations to each other, and for the avoidance of confusion because different consequences do follow according to whether liability arises from contract or tort . . .' For these reasons the failure of the parties to agree upon a particular contract term may constitute good grounds for the court to refuse to impose a duty of care where that would have an equivalent effect to the missing term. This would be giving the plaintiff the benefit of a term, which he had been unable to insert into the contract through negotiation. In *Greater Nottingham Co-operative Society* v. *Cementation Piling and Foundation Ltd*.[229] the owner of a site sued a subcontractor for negligence in the course of construction. Although the action was brought in tort, the parties had already agreed a contract for the work in question, which contained undertakings by the subcontractor as to the quality of the basic design and the materials to be used. But no warranty as to the standard of the actual building work had been given. The court refused to imply a duty of care to meet the absence of a contractual remedy.

This principle has also been applied in cases concerning the employment relationship and the relationship between a school and one of its pupils. In *Reid* v. *Rush and Tompkins Ltd*.[230] an employee sued his employer for failing to advise him to take out insurance cover for a period of work overseas. The employee

---

[227] *Ashdown* v. *Samuel Williams* [1957] 1 QB 504.   [228] [1986] AC 80, 107.   [229] [1989] QB 71.
[230] [1990] 1 WLR 212.

had been injured in a car accident in Ethiopia while in the course of his employment. His claim was not for the injuries he suffered but for his economic loss. This resulted from the fact that while overseas he was not covered by the employer's insurance and, in the absence of any scheme of residual liability insurance such as that provided for the United Kingdom by the Motor Insurers' Bureau, was left to bear the financial costs of his injury. Nor was he able to bring an action against the driver whose carelessness was responsible for his injuries. His claim against his employer failed because, according to Ralph Gibson LJ, it was not open to the court to impose a duty of care which was not 'contained in any express or implied term of the contract'. Similarly, in *Scally* v. *Southern Health and Social Services Board*[231] the House of Lords held that an employer's duty to inform his employees about their rights to certain financial benefits under the complex provisions of a pension scheme arose, if at all, in contract. But there was no duty of care in tort. *Van Oppen* v. *Trustees of Bedford School*[232] was another case concerning a failure to extend insurance cover, in this case arising out of a rugby accident which left a school student disabled. It was held that in the absence of any express undertaking, the school owed no duty in tort to extend its insurance to cover students in this way.

These last three decisions are open to the criticism that it may be unrealistic to expect employees, on the one hand, or the parents of school students, on the other, to enter into contractual bargaining on this kind of matter. These are contracts in which the employer or the school frequently imposes the terms but no individual bargaining takes place. The presumption of a rough equilibrium of bargaining power, which the courts are prepared to make in cases involving business entities such as *Tai Hing*, simply does not hold here. The view that contractual allocations of risk will necessarily be efficient has been said by McLachlin J of the Supreme Court of Canada to rest on a series of 'questionable assumptions', including the assumption

that all parties to a transaction share an equality of bargaining power, which will result in the effective allocation of risk. It is not considered that certain parties who control the situation (e.g. the owners of an indispensable bridge) may refuse to indemnify against the negligence of those over whom they have no control, or may demand such an exorbitant premium for this indemnification that it would be more cost effective for the innocent victim to insure itself.[233]

Arguably, similar considerations are relevant in a situation where the plaintiff is relying on the defendant for advice, or is relying on their professional expertise in the performance of a service. In these circumstance, the decision of the House of Lords in *Henderson* v. *Merrett Syndicates Ltd.*[234] shows that a duty of care in respect of pure economic loss can co-exist with a complex matrix of contractual obligations. In that case, relationships between the Lloyd's Names and the managing agents were mediated in some cases by a direct contractual relationship, while in other cases there were a series of intermediary contracts

---

[231] [1991] ICR 771.   [232] [1990] 1 WLR 235.
[233] McLachlin J in *Canadian National Railway* v. *Norsk Pacific Steamship Co.* (1991) 91 DLR (4th) 289, 374.
[234] [1995] 2 AC 145.

between the Names and the managing agents upon whose advice they relied. Lord Goff adopted the reasoning of Oliver J in the earlier case of *Midland Bank Trust Co.* v. *Hett, Stubbs and Kemp.*[235] He thus held that the extended *Hedley Byrne* form of liability for negligence in the performance of a service 'may arise not only in cases where the relevant services are rendered gratuitously, but also where they are rendered under a contract'.[236] At the same time, it was accepted that, in the words of Lord Browne-Wilkinson, 'the agreement of the parties evidenced by the contract can modify and shape the tortious duties which, in the absence of contract, would be applicable'.[237] In particular, the tort duty will not extend to permitting 'the plaintiff to circumvent or escape a contractual exclusion or limitation of liability for the act or omission that would constitute the tort'.[238] A clear exclusion of this kind could only be defeated by the application of the Unfair Contract Terms Act 1977.

The second case to consider is one in which the parties to a tort claim were not in a contractual relationship with each other when the tort took place. Here, the argument made above applies again: if the parties have failed to contract at all, the plaintiff will be getting something for nothing if the court now allows him a negligence claim in essentially the same terms as a contract would have provided for. This is the essential basis of the rule of privity of contract, that only one who is a party to a contract may maintain an action for its breach. In the pre-*Murphy* building case of *Portsea Island Mutual Co-operative Society Ltd.* v. *Michael Brashier Associates Ltd.*, a claim for economic loss caused by negligent design by a firm of architects failed on the grounds that 'Portsea was in effect seeking to recover in negligence sums which they might well have been entitled to claim under a collateral agreement. Portsea could have invited Brashiers to enter into a collateral warranty in respect of the superstore when, for suitable consideration, they might have agreed to do so.'[239]

However, the simple absence of a contract between the parties cannot be decisive reason for a court denying the existence of a duty of care; otherwise the tort of negligence would have no role at all in the compensation of financial loss. As we have seen, one way of explaining cases such as *Hedley Byrne*[240] and *White* v. *Jones*[241] is to view them as legitimate but limited exceptions to the privity rule in contract law. The source of the duty to take care lies in a contract to which the plaintiff is not a party, but of which he is effectively the intended beneficiary. In *Hedley Byrne* the contract between the bank and its customer would probably have contained an implied term to the effect that the bank would avoid carelessly releasing false information about its client. In *Ross* the contract of service between the solicitor and the testator would contain an undertaking by the latter to perform with reasonable care and skill. In the event of breach, however, no contractual action will lie, since the defendant's co-contractor is unlikely to have suffered any loss. Thus in *White* v. *Jones* the loss

---

[235] [1979] Ch. 384.   [236] [1995] 2 AC 145, 193.   [237] Ibid., 206.

[238] This was the formulation of Le Dain J in the Supreme Court of Canada case of *Central Trust Co.* v. *Rafuse* (1986) 31 DLR (4th) 481, 522, which was adopted by Lord Goff in *Henderson* v. *Merrett Syndicates Ltd.* [1995] 2 AC 145, 191.

[239] (1990) 6 *Const. LJ* 63, 70.   [240] [1964] AC 465.   [241] [1995] 2 AC 207.

is suffered not by the estate but by the disappointed beneficiary. In *Caparo Industries* v. *Dickman*[242] the result of the auditor's negligence is not to harm the company, which contracts for their services, but the shareholders who rely on the information contained in the audited accounts. And in *The Aliakmon*[243] breach of contract by the carrier will not harm the seller, who expects to receive payment in full from the buyer in any event, but rather the buyer who takes the goods in a damaged condition. If all other things were equal there would seem to be good reasons for allowing a tort action in this type of case: otherwise the performing party is relieved from the normal legal incentives for the performance of his undertaking.[244]

The Aliakmon illustrates one reason why all other things may not be equal: under the contract the performing party may have been given the benefit of exclusion or limitation clauses which would restrict his liability in the event of his being sued by the defendant. If he cannot take advantage of these clauses in any tort action brought against him by the plaintiff, he may face a much greater liability than he could possibly have contemplated when he entered into the contract. The tort action, then, risks upsetting the allocation of risk between the parties, which would normally have been reflected in the price the defendant charged for his services.[245]

This problem is difficult to deal with if the plaintiff's action is seen as tortious rather than contractual in nature. There are few signs that the English courts are prepared to allow even a narrow departure, here, from the privity rule. In *The Aliakmon* Lord Brandon rejected an argument to the effect that the plaintiff's claim could be viewed as contractual on the basis of the doctrine of 'transferred loss'—a proposal put by Robert Goff LJ in the Court of Appeal.[246] In other cases, however, courts have found ways of effectively extending the benefit of exclusion and limitation clauses to cover actions for negligence brought in tort by third parties. In these cases the presence of exclusion clauses in the underlying contract have been used to deny the existence of a duty of care in tort to the third party.[247] This was done in *Norwich City Council* v. *Harvey*,[248] even though the loss in question was damage to property, and therefore within the scope of the normal duty of care. More generally, the complete denial of a duty of care does not provide an answer to the situation (as in *The Aliakmon*) in which

---

[242] [1990] 2 AC 605.   [243] [1986] AC 785.

[244] One means by which the parties themselves can attempt to ensure that the benefit of any contract claim is passed on from one party to another is through the assignment of the benefit of contract terms. This is plausible in certain situations of building contracts, but it is an extremely complex and even precarious means of achieving the desired result. See J. Cartwright, 'The Assignment of Collateral Warranties' (1990) 6 *Const. LJ* 14; I. N. Duncan Wallace, 'Assignment of Rights to Sue for Breach of Construction Contracts' (1993) 109 *LQR* 82.

[245] It may be noted that this is a completely different situation to that which occurred in the case of the *Nicholas H.* [1996] AC 211. In that case, the plaintiff entered into a contract with a third party, the ship owners, which contained a limitation clause, but this clause did not purport to protect the defendant classification society. See Lord Lloyd's dissent, [1996] AC 211, 223.

[246] [1986] AC AC 785, 819–20, rejecting the approach outlined at [1985] 1 QB 350, 397.

[247] *Southern Water Board* v. *Carey* [1985] 2 All ER 1077; *Norwich City Council* v. *Harvey* [1988] 1 WLR 828; *Pacific Associates Inc.* v. *Baxter* [1990] QB 993; see Markesinis, 'Doctrinal Clarity in Tort Litigation: A Comparative Lawyer's Viewpoint' (1991) 25 *The International Lawyer* 953.

[248] [1989] 1 WLR 828.

a duty is *partially* modified, or a liability *partially* excluded, by the terms of the underlying contract. As the law presently stands the outcome is either all or nothing.

In *White* v. *Jones* the Court of Appeal, in particular, was explicit about the shortcomings of the privity-of-contract rule and of the methods used to limit its effects. Sir Donald Nicholls VC considered 'whether a remedy for breach of contract could be shaped whereby, the client having lost the opportunity to make a gift to the intended beneficiary, (1) his estate should be regarded as having lost a sum equal to the amount of the intended gift, and (2) the executors should hold that sum, when recovered from the solicitor, upon trust for the intended beneficiary'. [249]

In the event he concluded that a solution in tort, which could avoid these complexities, was preferable. Steyn LJ considered the argument that the scope of the duty of care should, in such a case, be largely determined by the nature of the obligations in the underlying contract, including any exclusion and limitation clauses. He concluded that where such clauses were present, 'it seems to me unavoidable that the duty will have to be limited in the way suggested by Robert Goff LJ' in *The Aliakmon*.[250] In the House of Lords in *White* v. *Jones*, Lord Goff considered *obiter* that a contractual solution, however desirable, was impossible to achieve short of parliamentary intervention.[251] But he admitted that the tort action, which he was prepared to fashion in order to avoid injustice, would be shaped by the underlying contractual relationship between testator and solicitor. In its result, therefore, the legal remedy now available to such plaintiffs comes very close to the contractual model discussed above.

(vi) Insurance Considerations and Related Aspects of Policy   Closely allied with the view that contract, rather than tort, should provide the basis for recovery in cases of economic loss, is the argument that the court should let the loss lie where it falls in a situation where the plaintiff has taken out first-party or loss insurance or, alternatively, where he could have done so relatively cheaply. If the court imposes a duty of care in these circumstances it will be effectively forcing the defendant to carry liability insurance, which will increase his costs and perhaps require him to raise his prices. The result will be a potentially wasteful, double insurance. Alternatively, if liability insurance is not available, the defendant may decide to give up the activity in question. Under the law of subrogation the insurance company which has extended loss insurance to the plaintiff is entitled to bring an action in his name to recover the damages in tort

---

[249] [1995] 2 AC 207, 224. One solution to the privity problem is the remedy of a trust of the promise but this has not been widely used in English law since the judgment of Lord Wright in *Vandepitte* v. *Preferred Accident Insurance Co. of New York* [1933] AC 70, while the possibility of the promisee suing for substantial damages on behalf of the third party was limited by *Woodar Investment Development Ltd.* v. *Wimpey Construction (UK) Ltd.* [1980] 1 WLR 227. For a radically different approach (or series of approaches) to the question from that adopted by the House of Lords, see *Trident Insurance Co. Ltd.* v. *MacNiece Bros. Pty. Ltd.* (1988) 165 CLR 107 (High Court of Australia). The reform of the privity doctrine raises wider questions going beyond those with which the law of negligence is concerned. See Law Commission, Consultative Paper No. 121 (1991).

[250] [1995] 2 AC 207, 239.   [251] Ibid., 266.

from the defendant. The consequence of this is that the resulting action may not benefit the plaintiff as an individual one way or the other.

In the past the English courts regarded the availability of insurance as more or less irrelevant to the question of whether a duty of care arises on a given set of facts.[252] In *Murphy* v. *Brentwood District Council*, however, Lord Keith of Kinkel clearly thought it relevant that the plaintiff's loss had been met by his insurance company and that the company was now seeking to recoup this payment by way of the tort action. It is certainly not self-evident why the insurance company, which has been paid to take the risk of the loss occurring, should have a right of action against the council, who will have to bear the loss in some form by passing it on in the form of higher local taxes or a reduction in public services.[253]

Similar considerations influenced the majority of the House of Lords in *Marc Rich & Co. A.G.* v. *Bishops Rock Marine Co. Ltd.*, *The Nicholas H.*[254] The plaintiff was the owner of cargo, which was lost following the sinking of a ship which the employee of the defendant, a shipping classification society, had negligently passed as fit to sail. Although, in this case, the damage was physical harm (damage to property), it was held that the classification society owed no duty of care to the cargo owners. One ground relied on by the majority was the need to avoid upsetting the complex system of loss insurance and liability insurance which operated under arrangements made by cargo owners and ship owners. As Lord Steyn explained:

Cargo owners take out direct insurance in respect of the cargo. Ship owners take out liability risks insurance in respect of breaches of their duties of care in respect of the cargo. The insurance system is structured on the basis that the potential liability of ship owners to cargo owners is limited under Hague Rules and by virtue of tonnage limitation provisions. And insurance premiums payable by owners obviously reflect such limitations on the ship owners' exposure . . . The result of a recognition of a duty of care in this case will be to enable cargo owners, or rather their insurers, to disturb the balance created by the Hague Rules and Hague-Visby Rules as well as by tonnage limitation provisions, by enabling cargo owners to recover in tort against a peripheral party to the prejudice of ship owners under the existing system.[255]

This case illustrates, like so many other recent ones,[256] that insurance factors weigh heavily in the mind of some judges. The case, however, also illustrates the dangers in the courts seeking to make judgments about the insurance implications of their rulings on the basis of limited evidence. As Lord Lloyd pointed out in his powerful dissent, there was no evidence to suggest that

---

[252] See e.g. *Lamb* v. *Camden LBC* [1981] QB 625.

[253] See Lord Keith [1991] 1 AC 358, 458–9, 472; Weir, 'Governmental Liability' [1989] *PL* 40. The subrogation rules which, in practice, often allows insurance companies to have their cake and eat it, may well be one of the reasons that judges are reluctant in many of these cases to allow a cause of action. Thus, see, Lord Hoffmann's views in *Stovin* v. *Wise* [1996] AC 923, 955.

[254] [1996] AC 211.

[255] [1996] AC 211, 239, 240.

[256] For instance, Lord Griffiths in *Smith* v. *Bush* [1990] 1 AC 831, 858–9; Hoffmann J in *Morgan Crucible Co.* v. *Hill Samuel* [1991] Ch. 295, 302–3; Lord Hoffmann in *Stovin* v. *Wise* [1996] 923, 958. Many of Lord Denning's judgments also contain illuminating references to insurance considerations.

classification societies did not already carry liability insurance. Moreover, the imposition of liability might have the effect of raising standards in an area of legitimate concern to the 'shipping community at large'.[257] Such a clash of views does not, it is submitted, reduce either the reality or the utility of insurance reasoning; but it does make one ask for a more substantial discussion of these issues.

Similarly, the cost of liability insurance for professionals and the difficulty of obtaining full cover has been raised in cases concerning accountants and architects. But in *Caparo Industries* v. *Dickman*, Bingham LJ considered, with commendable frankness, that it was impossible to draw any conclusions from such arguments on the grounds that the court did not have before it the relevant information on the state of insurance markets.[258] In practice, courts may well find it difficult to make a definitive judgment on the question of which of the two parties is best placed to take out insurance. At the same time, there is (mainly anecdotal) evidence to suggest that recent large-scale claims arising out of product liability and natural disasters have depleted the spare capacity of insurance markets. An awareness of this growing problem may thus help explain (even when it does not always justify) the increasingly cautious approach of the courts to the development of new duty situations.[259] The plea for increased empirical and inter-disciplinary study of these problems thus remains valid.

On the other hand, the arguments against letting the loss lie where it falls are not all one way. First there is the possibility that denying a duty of care simply on the grounds that the plaintiff is protected by insurance will remove the normal legal incentives on the defendant to avoid causing the loss or damage in question.[260] Secondly, the insurer's rights of subrogation *may* reduce the premiums he charges to potential plaintiffs. Furthermore, insurance may not cover all losses suffered by a plaintiff. Under these circumstances subrogation enables him to share the risk and expense of litigation with the insurance company, which will normally bear the greater part of the costs.[261] This is a relevant factor in cases involving consumers, such as Messrs Anns and Murphy.

Where both plaintiff and defendant are business entities the court would seem to be justified in posing the question of whether the most efficient outcome, in terms of the net costs of the accident, would have been for the plaintiff to have protected himself through either contract or insurance. The importance of this point was stressed by La Forest J in his dissenting judgment in the *Norsk* case. Referring to the need 'to bring insurance considerations into the open', La Forest J argued that of the three parties involved in the accident, the plaintiff was better placed than both the defendant and the owner of the bridge to protect itself against the consequences of an accident. It would have known the value to its own operations of the bridge being open and the likely

---

[257] [1996] AC 211, 228–9.
[258] [1989] QB 653, 688. See also Lord Hoffmann's views in *White* v. *Chief Constable of South Yorkshire Police* [1998] 3 WLR 1510 at 1556.
[259] Davies, 'The End of the Affair?', op. cit.   [260] W. Bishop, 'Economic Loss in Tort' (1982) 2 *OJLS* 1.
[261] O'Dair, 'A House Built on Firm Foundations?', op. cit. (Select Bibliography).

costs of closure. The defendant would have had no means of assessing these costs. More generally, the plaintiff was in a good position to use its expertise, resources, and bargaining power to find a contractual or insurance-based solution; in this regard: 'It is hard to imagine a more sophisticated group of plaintiffs than the users of railway bridges. These parties have access to the full range of protective options: first party commercial insurance or self-insurance, contracts with both the bridge owner and with the railway's customers.'[262]

The situation may well be different where consumer liability is concerned. Here, a realistic approach on the court's part would be to recognise that individual consumers of goods and services are most unlikely to have access to either the resources or the contracting expertise needed effectively to protect themselves against a risk of large scale loss. This is arguably one of the most serious weaknesses of the House of Lords' decision in *Murphy*: for the purposes of denying a duty of care, the position of home-owners and residents was equated with that of sizeable construction companies and property developers. A different approach is evident in *Smith* v. *Bush*,[263] where the House of Lords, in formulating the duty of care, appears to have been influenced by the aims of consumer protection contained in the Unfair Contract Terms Act 1977. Had the plaintiff been acting in a business capacity (as in *Hedley Byrne*) it is most unlikely that a duty of care could have arisen in circumstances where a clear disclaimer of liability was brought to his notice. In such a case, the court would have been justified in asking why he had not sought to contract for the information in question.

(vii) The Respective Roles of Parliament and the Courts In *Murphy* one reason given for denying a duty of care in tort was the availability of a statutory framework for consumer protection, under the Defective Premises Act 1972.[264] This remedy is, however, less than fully effective, thanks to the short limitation period laid down for actions under the Act.[265] At the same time the members of the House of Lords also appear to have been unaware of important changes to the National House Building Council insurance scheme, which have greatly expanded the availability of actions under the Defective Premises Act which were previously barred.[266] If in future the courts are to deny the existence of a duty situation solely on the grounds that Parliament has legislated in the area concerned, the scope of the tort of negligence would be considerably reduced. In the context of claims for negligent construction, the presence of the Defective Premises Act as an alternative to the common law is offset by the Latent Damage Act 1986, the terms of which appear to assume that *Anns* was correctly decided.[267] Indeed, *Murphy* would seem to remove much of the rationale for this Act.[268]

---

[262] (1992) 91 DLR (4th) 289, 349. [263] [1990] 1 AC 831.

[264] See [1991] 1 AC 398, 472 (Lord Keith), 480 (Lord Bridge), and 491 (Lord Oliver).

[265] The limitation period begins to run from the date on which the building is completed or the time at which the relevant work is completed: s. 2(5). The benefits of the extended period allowed for by the Latent Damage Act 1986 do not appear to apply to claims under the Defective Premises Act: see *Warner* v. *Basildon DC* (1991) 7 Const. LJ 146, and on limitation generally see Chapter 8, Section 2, below.

[266] On this, see I. N. Duncan Wallace, '*Anns* Beyond Repair' (1991) 107 *LQR* 228, 243; and see Chapter 3, Section 3(2)(g)(ii).

[267] See below, Chapter 8, Section 1(9). [268] See Stapleton, op. cit. (1991) 107 *LQR* 249.

A more specific argument expressed in recent decisions is that the courts should defer to Parliament in areas where the social and economic effects of a decision extending liability are difficult to assess, or where opposing policy arguments are finely balanced. It is thus true to assert that the courts are immediately concerned with the resolution of the particular dispute before them and with the enunciation of rules which allow as far as possible for doctrinal clarity and ease of application. Parliament, on the other hand, is better equipped to collect evidence on the wider consequences of liability rules and to confront questions of policy head-on. Whatever the merits of this point of view as a general guide, at various times the judges have resisted it on the basis that it would unduly constrain the common law. There are enough previous examples of judicial innovation in areas raising complex questions of policy to suggest that deference to Parliament can easily be overcome in cases seen by the judges as appropriate for this purpose. Moreover, this may also be a desirable course to take if, as has often happened in practice, one is faced with a situation where Parliament is either unable or unwilling to intervene.

(viii) Economic Loss: A Summary and Conclusion   It may be useful to summarise and review this examination of the case law on economic loss. As the law now stands, the situations in which the law recognises a duty of care in relation to 'pure' economic loss are tightly circumscribed. The one area where liability is clearly established concerns negligent misstatements and negligence in the performance of a service, where *Hedley Byrne & Co. Ltd.* v. *Heller & Partners Ltd.*[269] continues to be good law. Indeed, as already stated, it has been extended by the decisions of the House of Lords in *Henderson* v. *Merrett Syndicates Ltd.*[270] and *White* v. *Jones.*[271] As far as the other categories of economic loss are concerned, only in the most exceptional cases will 'relational' loss arising from damage to another's property be compensated, even with the assistance of the proximity test. Economic loss arising from defects in products and buildings is also outside the scope of the tort of negligence. (An exception, perhaps, exists in so far as loss arises from preventive measures taken to avoid legal liability to a third party, or to the degree that the courts continue to apply the 'complex structure' theory in some form or another.)

Murphy v. *Brentwood District Council*[272] has been described as giving rise to a 'negative orthodoxy'.[273] This amounts to denying the existence of a duty of care going beyond the 'traditional categorisations', but offers no set of principles or clear statement to guide the courts in their treatment of situations lying on the boundary of liability. There also remains the difficulty of reconciling *Murphy* with the continuing authority of *Hedley Byrne*, and, within the misstatement cases, of explaining how the restrictive judgment in *Caparo Industries* v. *Dickman*[274] fits together with decisions such as *Smith* v. *Bush.*[275] From this rather unpromising situation there are two possible developments, the beginnings of which may already be discerned. The first is that the courts will begin to distinguish more closely between the types of plaintiffs and defendants involved

---

[269] [1964] AC 465.   [270] [1995] 2 AC 145.   [271] [1995] 2 AC 207.
[272] [1991] 1 AC 398.   [273] Howarth, 'Time to Rethink', op. cit.   [274] [1990] 2 AC 605.
[275] [1990] 1 AC 831.

in economic-loss claims. In particular this could mean acknowledging the different positions of business entities on the one hand, and private consumers of goods and services on the other, when it comes to the capacity to control the risk of economic loss without resort to tort law. The second is that the courts will pay greater regard to the role of contractual standards in this area of the law in shaping the scope and level of tort obligations. Beyond that, it is difficult to predict the future!

(c) Psychiatric Injury and Illness

As with economic loss, the duty concept has been used by the courts to control recovery for various kinds of psychiatric injury and illness. The courts were slow to accept that psychiatric injury or 'nervous shock' could constitute a head of damage for which the tort of negligence provided compensation, in particular where it was caused by harm or the threat of harm to a person other than the plaintiff. It is now generally understood, in the words of Lord Bridge in *McLoughlin* v. *O'Brian*,[276] 'that an acute emotional trauma, like a physical trauma, can well cause a psychiatric illness in a wide range of circumstances and in a wide range of individuals whom it would be wrong to regard as having any abnormal psychological make-up'. But despite the progress which the courts have gradually made over the course of more than a century of litigation towards the recognition of this head of damage, there remain severe restrictions on the scope of recovery. Psychiatric illness is therefore not yet placed on a par with bodily injury or the loss of a limb.

(i) **Defining Psychiatric Injury**   The starting point is to specify what is meant by psychiatric injury. Damages cannot be recovered for mere grief or emotional distress at an injury or death, even of a loved one: 'in English law no damages are awarded for grief or sorrow caused by a person's death'.[277] However, there is in principle a distinction between mere grief and a more serious, prolonged psychiatric condition which may be identified with the help of expert medical testimony. Medical science now recognises a condition known as 'post-traumatic stress disorder', which may occur in reaction to the violent or unexpected death of a close relative or friend.[278] In *Alcock* v. *Chief Constable of South Yorkshire*, relatives and friends of spectators who were crushed to death inside a football stadium as a result of police negligence brought actions for damages based on psychiatric illness suffered in reaction to the event. Some had witnessed the scene at the ground. Others had seen it transmitted live on national television. Yet others had not seen the event but had suffered reactions from, amongst other things: fear that a close friend or relative had been killed or injured; being told that such a person had indeed been killed; and identifying the body at the temporary mortuary set up near the ground. The nature of the condition from which the plaintiffs were suffering was described in court as follows:

---

[276] [1983] 1 AC 410, 433.   [277] *Hinz* v. *Berry* [1970] 2 QB 40, 42 (Lord Denning MR).
[278] Older terms for similar conditions would include neurasthenia, shell shock, and nastalgia: see [1990] 1 AC 310, 317.

It is classified as an anxiety disorder. It follows on a painful event which is outside the normal human experience, the disorder involves preoccupation with the event—that is intrusive memories—with avoidance of reminders of the experience. At the same time there are persistent symptoms of increased arousal—these symptoms may be experienced in the form of sleep difficulty, irritability or outbursts of anger, problems with memory or concentration, startle responses, hyper vigilance and over-reaction to any reminder of the event . . . Many [of the plaintiffs] described an inability or difficulty in carrying out normal life activities such as work, family responsibilities or any activity normally engaged in before the disaster . . . All those in whom post-traumatic stress disorder was identified appear to have undergone a personality change, the significant features of which [included] being moody, irritable, forgetful and withdrawn within themselves, [and] frequent unprovoked outbursts of anger and quarrelsome behaviour were reported.[279]

All of the plaintiffs were suffering from more than one specific and identifiable psychiatric illness, including depression.

The nature of this condition is such that the need to identify an illness of a serious kind would probably, in itself, solve many of the problems associated with the floodgates argument. In *Hevican* v. *Ruane*[280] it was described as 'no more than the most remote of possibilities'; and in *Ravenscroft* v. *Rederiaktebolaget Transatlantic*,[281] in a judgment for the plaintiff which was later overruled as incompatible with *Alcock*,[282] the judge referred to a 'small but significant range of the population' being liable to a reaction of this kind.

For the purposes of determining whether a significant psychiatric injury has been suffered, the Court of Appeal in *Vernon* v. *Boseley (No. 1)*[283] ruled that there was no significant distinction between post-traumatic stress disorder, as just defined, and 'pathological grief disorder' which the court understood to mean an abnormal degree of grief giving rise to a psychological condition. Damages were recoverable for the latter as long as it could be shown that the other conditions for recovery were met.

(ii) Primary Victims   The next step in the analysis involves a fundamental distinction within the law between 'primary' and 'secondary' victims of psychiatric harm. A 'primary victim' is one who suffers psychiatric injury after being directly involved in an accident and is *either* himself physically injured *or* put in fear of injury. A 'secondary victim' suffers psychiatric injury as a consequence of witnessing or being informed about an accident which involves another. As far as primary victims are concerned, it is well established that an accident victim who is physically injured through the negligence of another may, in principle, recover damages for the psychiatric as well as the physical consequences of the accident, subject to the normal rules of causation and remoteness of damage.[284] Equally, if the plaintiff's person is negligently endangered and he is

---

[279] [1992] 1 AC 310, 317.   [280] [1991] 3 All ER 65, 72.   [281] [1991] 3 All ER 73, 79.
[282] [1992] 2 All ER 470.   [283] [1997] 1 All ER 577.

[284] In the unusual case of *Meah* v. *McCreamer (No. 1)*, [1985] 1 All ER 367, the plaintiff recovered damages for the consequences of a car crash which included a personality change and his subsequent imprisonment following conviction of offences of rape and assault. See also the Australian case of *Jaensch* v. *Coffey* (1984) 155 CLR 549, discussed by F. A. Trindade, 'The Principles Governing the Recovery of Damages for Negligently Caused Nervous Shock' [1985] *CLJ* 476, 477.

placed in fear of an injury which does not actually occur, the early cases[285] clearly indicate that there will be liability. These decisions were reaffirmed by the House of Lords in *Page* v. *Smith*.[286] The defendant, driving carelessly, caused a collision between his car and that being driven by the plaintiff. The latter, although receiving no physical injury at the time or later, later suffered a reaction which led to the revival of the condition ME (myalgic encephalomyelitis) which left him chronically ill and unable to work. In his leading judgment, Lord Lloyd said that in the case of a primary victim such as the plaintiff—that is to say, one directly involved in an accident—it was not necessary to consider whether psychiatric injury had been foreseesable. It was enough that injury of some kind—either physical or psychiatric—was foreseeable. Although this ruling has been the subject of some trenchant criticism,[287] it remains good law until such time as the House of Lords chooses to reconsider it.

(iii) Secondary Victims The real difficulties begin when the plaintiff himself was neither physically injured nor threatened with injury. Such plaintiffs were termed 'secondary victims' by Lord Lloyd. The victim may have suffered a psychological reaction after witnessing the scene of an accident where another is killed or injured or through fear of injury to another, which does not then materialise. Witnessing a scene may take the form of being present at the event itself, seeing it relayed through television or hearing about it on the radio, or coming on the scene in its immediate aftermath. Alternatively, the reaction may have been brought about by being informed of another's death or injury in particular circumstances. Psychiatric injury could occur without a 'shock' of any kind being sustained, for example through the burden of caring for an injured relative. The nature of the relationship between the plaintiff and the person suffering the injury in question could range from that of a close family tie to the relations of friendship or employment; the plaintiff could be a rescuer or a mere bystander. At a further extreme, damage to property, such as a house, or to a much-loved pet, could induce a reaction of this kind.

In each of these cases the psychological reaction suffered by the plaintiff may be entirely foreseeable. However, for secondary victims, foreseeability of psychiatric damage being inflicted on the plaintiff is a necessary but not sufficient condition of establishing a duty of care.[288] If, for these purposes, the law regarded psychiatric harm as equivalent to physical harm, there would be no difficulty about a duty of care arising and liability would then depend on questions of fault, causation, and remoteness. Many cases might fail at these later

---

[285] *Bell* v. *Great Northern Railway Co. of Ireland* (1890) 26 LR Ir. 428, not following *Victorian Railway Commissioners* v. *Coultas* (1888) 13 App. Cas. 222; *Dulieu* v. *White* [1901] 2 KB 669.

[286] [1996] 1 AC 155.

[287] See the judgment of Lord Goff of Chieveley in *White* v. *Chief Constable of South Yorkshire* [1998] 3 WLR 1510, 1522–6.

[288] In some early decisions the courts denied recovery to what would now be classified as 'secondary victims' who were not in the likely area of *physical* impact: see *Behrens* v. *Bertram Mills Circus Ltd.* [1957] 2 QB 1 and *King* v. *Phillips* [1953] 1 QB 429, where the judges were divided on the reason for denying recovery. In *Bourhill* v. *Young* [1943] AC 92, Lords Wright and Porter argued for the test of foreseeability of shock or psychiatric damage, and this was accepted by the Privy Council in *The Wagon Mound* (*No. 1*), [1961] AC 388. These dicta should not now be read as referring to primary victims following the judgment of Lord Lloyd in *Page* v. *Smith* [1996] AC 155 (see in particular at 189).

stages, particularly on questions of causation. But the common law does not currently take this view.

The prevailing view instead is that the extent of the duty of care is limited by a number of essentially arbitrary factors. In particular, the plaintiff will have to show, in general, that his illness or condition was caused by a 'shock' of some kind; that he either witnessed the event directly or came upon its immediate aftermath; and that his relationship with the accident victim was sufficiently 'proximate' in the sense defined by the judges. These requirements were reasserted in *Alcock* v. *Chief Constable of South Yorkshire*,[289] where Lord Oliver argued that the policy of the common law was, on the whole, to confine any action in negligence to the 'primary' accident victim. The (inevitable) consequence of this is that any claim for loss by 'secondary' victims is, by its nature, exceptional. He thus maintained that:

The infliction of an injury on an individual, whether through carelessness or deliberation, necessarily produces consequences beyond those to the immediate victim. Inevitably the impact of the event and its aftermath, whether immediate or prolonged, is going to be felt in greater or lesser degree by those with whom the victim is connected whether by ties of affection, of blood relationship, of duty or simply of business. In many cases those persons may suffer not only injured feelings or inconvenience but adverse financial consequences as, for instance, by the need to care for the victim or the interruption or non-performance of his contractual obligations to third parties. Nevertheless, except in those cases which were based upon some ancient and now outmoded concepts of the quasi-proprietorial rights of husbands over their wives, parents over their children or employers over their menial servants, the common law has, in general, declined to entertain claims for such consequential injuries from third parties . . .[290]

Thus statute has abolished the right of a husband to sue for loss of consortium upon the death of his wife or the right of a parent to sue for loss of services of a child.[291] In their stead, a more modern but limited right has emerged; and it is given to a former spouse or a child under the age of majority to sue for bereavement damages.[292] Other examples of the rights of secondary victims to sue, such as the right of dependants of the deceased to sue for financial compensation for the loss of their breadwinner, are supplied by statute[293] and not by the common law. Once this point of view is taken, what is unusual is not that there are arbitrary limits on the right of a victim of psychiatric injury to receive compensation, but that the law permits him an action at all. As Lord Oliver put it:

What is more difficult to account for is why, when the law in general declines to extend the area of compensation to those whose injury arises only from the circumstances of their relationship to the primary victim, an exception has arisen in those cases in which the event of injury to the primary victim has been actually witnessed by the plaintiff and the injury claimed is as stemming from that fact.[294]

---

[289] [1992] 1 AC 310.   [290] Ibid., 409.
[291] Administration of Justice Act 1982; see also *Best* v. *Samuel Fox & Co. Ltd.* [1952] AC 716.
[292] S. 1A Fatal Accidents Act 1976, inserted by Administration of Justice Act 1982, s. 3.
[293] See generally the Fatal Accidents Act 1976.
[294] *Alcock* v. *Chief Constable of South Yorkshire* [1992] 1 AC 310, 410.

An alternative view would be to acknowledge that psychiatric harm is a form of injury in its own right, to cease viewing the sufferer as a 'secondary victim'. In such cases one would then use as limiting devices (a) the requirement that there should be evidence of the seriousness of the psychiatric injury in question and (b) the need for a clear causal connection to be established.[295] Additionally, it would be reasonable to assume that the cost of modern litigation would also act as a *de facto* barrier against the bringing of entirely frivolous claims. The medical understanding of psychiatric illness has arguably reached the stage at which this approach is feasible and therefore preferable to the admittedly arbitrary and illogical distinctions[296] currently operating in this area.

In *White* v. *Chief Constable of South Yorkshire*[297] the House of Lords rejected arguments of the kind just made. Lord Steyn who, with Lord Hoffmann, gave the leading judgments, offered four reasons for treating psychiatric harm as a special area of liability. First, the task of identifying those categories of psychiatric harm which are recognised by law is a highly complex one which involves both sides calling expert medical advice. Secondly, there is the risk that, as his Lordship put it, 'litigation is sometimes an unconscious disincentive to rehabilitation'—in other words, the prospect of recovering damages prevents the plaintiff's condition from improving. We may note before moving on that these factors could also be present in many cases involving purely physical injury, where no question of denying a duty of care arises. Lord Steyn's third reason was the traditional 'floodgates' argument, namely that 'a relaxation of the special rules governing the recoverability of damages for psychiatric harm would greatly increase the class of persons who can recover damages in tort.' His final reason was that potential defendants would be exposed to a risk of liability which would be 'disproportionate to tortious conduct involving perhaps momentary lapses of concentration, e.g. in a motor car accident'.[298] Again, it could be argued that this is not a factor which is unique to cases involving psychiatric harm.

Whatever the merits or demerits of this approach, the effect of *White* v. *Chief Constable of South Yorkshire* is that the House of Lords has set its face against the assimilation of psychiatric harm to other kinds of injury at least as far as secondary victims are concerned. It is therefore necessary to consider the special requirements of recovery for this kind of harm.

1. The plaintiff must not have been abnormally susceptible to psychiatric illness. In order to recover, a secondary victim must show that he was not unusually susceptible to psychiatric harm of the kind in question.[299] The nature of the

---

[295] See generally H. Teff, 'Liability for Psychiatric Illness after Hillsborough' (1992) 12 *OJLS* 440; Mullany and Handford (Select Bibliography, below). For the position in American jurisdictions, see Professor Robertson, 'American Perspective', below at Section 5. Various options for reform of English law are laid out in Law Commission Consultation Paper No. 137, *Liability for Psychiatric Illness* (1995). For a proposal to abolish entirely tortious liability for nervous shock, see J. Stapleton, 'In Restraint of Tort', in P. B. H. Birks (ed.) *The Frontiers of Liability* (1994).

[296] On the lack of logic in these distinctions, see Lord Oliver in *Alcock* [1992] 1 AC 310, 410.

[297] [1998] 3 WLR 1510.   [298] Ibid., 1542.

[299] Lord Wright in *Bourhill* v. *Young* [1943] AC 92, 110.

plaintiff's particular relationship with the accident victim will be taken into account: in one case a test of a 'reasonably strong-willed mother' was adopted.[300] Thus an unduly hypersensitive person will not recover damages, unless a person of normal fortitude would have suffered shock under the same circumstances. But once that requirement is met, the rule that the defendant 'takes the plaintiff as he finds him' applies and the unusually sensitive plaintiff can recover in full.[301]

2. The psychiatric harm must have occurred through 'shock'. Notwithstanding advances in medical understanding, the courts continue to maintain that for recovery under this head to be achieved, the plaintiff must in the first place have suffered a 'shock' of some kind. In *Alcock*,[302] Lord Ackner said that 'psychiatric illnesses caused in other ways, such as by the experience of having to cope with the deprivation consequent upon the death of a loved one, attracts no damages'. It seems, for example, that one who suffers psychiatric damage from caring for a loved one who is seriously injured or mentally impaired by an accident, will have no claim against the person whose negligence caused the initial injury.[303] But why this should be so is far from clear. The question could well be regarded as more suitable for analysis through causation rather than duty. Why should a family member who undertakes to care for the accident victim be unable to recover for an illness triggered by the stress of such a task, in a case where the circumstances were particularly distressing? The range of plaintiffs likely to be able to sue in this kind of action is unlikely to be particularly extensive.

3. The plaintiff must have been in physical proximity to the accident or its aftermath. This requirement is related to the one which we have just considered, and means that he must either have been present at the scene itself or have arrived in the aftermath of the death or injury occurring. In *McLoughlin v. O'Brian*[304] one of the plaintiff's children was killed in a car crash in which two of her other children and her husband were injured. The plaintiff was at home at the time and learned of the crash about an hour after it had happened from a friend who had witnessed it, and who then drove her to a nearby hospital where she saw the surviving members of her family. The scenes at the hospital 'were distressing in the extreme and were capable of producing an effect going well beyond that of grief and sorrow'.[305] The House of Lords held that the plaintiff had a claim for nervous shock. Although it is normally necessary to have been within sight or earshot of the event giving rise to the injury, exceptions do exist. Thus, according to Lord Wilberforce 'an exception from, or I would prefer to call it an extension of, the latter case has been made where the plaintiff does not see or hear the incident but comes on its immediate aftermath'; *McLoughlin*'s case was 'on the margin' of recovery. To similar effect is the decision of the High Court

---

[300] *Kralj v. McGrath* [1986] 1 All ER 54.
[301] *Jaensch v. Coffey* (1984) 54 ALR 417; *Page v. Smith* [1996] AC 155.   [302] Ibid., 403.
[303] See *Jaensch v. Coffey* (1984) 155 CLR 549, 569 (Brennan J), cited with approval by Lord Ackner, [1992] 1 AC 310, 403. See also *Pratt and Goldsmith v. Pratt* [1975] VR 378, discussed by Trindade, op. cit. [1985] *CLJ* 476, 479.
[304] [1983] 2 AC 410.   [305] Lord Wilberforce [1983] AC 410, 417.

of Australia in *Jaensch* v. *Coffee*,[306] another case in which the plaintiff suffered shock after a visit to the hospital where, in this case, her husband had been taken after being involved in an accident.

The law draws a clear dividing-line between witnessing an accident and simply being told about it. According to the Court of Appeal in *Hambrook* v. *Stokes Bros.*[307] and to Lord Wilberforce in *McLoughlin*, there can be no recovery in a case where a third party brought about the shock through communication. By contrast, in *Hevicane* v. *Ruane*[308] liability was established in a case where the father of a boy killed in a car accident was told of his death at a police station and then identified the body at a mortuary. In *Ravenscroft* v. *Rederiaktebolaget Transatlantic*[309] the plaintiff, who suffered a depressive reaction following the death of her son in an industrial accident, and who did not actually see the body, was allowed to recover at first instance. The Court of Appeal, however, reversed this judgment on the grounds that this ruling was incompatible with the House of Lords' ruling in *Alcock*. It seems unlikely that the ruling in *Hevicane*'s case would have gone the same way if it had come after *Alcock*.

In *Alcock*[310] a variety of cases were brought to test the limits of the law. Some plaintiffs witnessed the scene of the disaster from other stands inside the stadium. One of the plaintiffs, sitting in a coach outside the ground, saw the events unfolding on a television in the coach. He then went to find his son, who turned out to have died in the stadium. Yet other plaintiffs, who were at home on the day, heard of the events on the radio or saw television pictures, which were being transmitted live. The television pictures did not pick out individuals; this would have been excluded by broadcasting conventions which, said Lord Keith of Kinkel, would have been known to the defendant, although the relevance of this point is somewhat obscure.[311] The judge excluded claims by those who heard the news on radio but allowed claims by those relatives who had suffered shock after seeing the television reports and later receiving news of the deaths, but on this last point he was reversed by the higher courts. According to Lord Keith:

The viewing of these scenes cannot be equiparated with the viewer being within 'sight or hearing of the event in question' to use the words of Lord Wilberforce [in *McLoughlin* v. *O'Brian*], nor can the scenes reasonably be regarded as giving rise to shock, in the sense of a sudden assault on the nervous system. They were capable of giving rise to anxiety for the safety of relatives known or believed to be present in the area affected by the crush, and undoubtedly did so, but that is very different from seeing the fate of the relative or his condition shortly after the event.[312]

This view is related, then, to the idea that liability arises only where the illness is induced by shock, in the sense of what Lord Ackner called 'the sudden appreciation by sight or sound of a horrifying event, which violently agitates the mind'.[313] But there seems no reason, in principle, why an 'agitation of the mind' cannot come about through witnessing scenes on television or even

---

[306] (1984) 155 CLR 549.   [307] [1925] 1 KB 141.   [308] [1991] 3 All ER 65.
[309] [1991] 3 All ER 73, overruled [1992] 2 All ER 470.   [310] [1992] 1 AC 310.
[311] See ibid., 398.   [312] [1992] 1 AC 310, 398.   [313] Ibid., 401.

through a combination of communications, such as the hypothetical case given by Lord Bridge in *McLoughlin* v. *O'Brian*[314] of a mother who knows that her husband and children are staying in a hotel which, she learns, has burned down. Newspapers show pictures of the victims shouting for help, and she then finds out that all her family died in the fire. She then suffers psychiatric injury as a result of the 'imagination of the agonies of mind and body in which her family died'. As Professor Teff points out, the most important element triggering a psychiatric illness in such a case is not the 'direct perception' of the event but the close relationship between the plaintiff and the accident victim; the precise manner in which the horror of the event is conveyed is irrelevant.[315] In *Alcock* the House of Lords was persuaded to maintain this restriction by fear of the floodgates opening, but this objection could have been dealt with more effectively by insisting on evidence of a serious medical condition.

Another way of looking at the means of communication is to regard the intervention of the broadcast media as a *novus actus interveniens*, or the act of a third party, which breaks the chain of causation. Alternatively,[316] one can treat the damage as being too remote,[317] or treat the television medium as removing the plaintiff from the category of 'proximate' persons:

I do not consider that a claimant who watches a normal television programme which displays events as they happen satisfies the test of proximity. In the first place a defendant could normally anticipate that in accordance with current television broadcasting guidelines shocking pictures of persons suffering and dying would not be transmitted. In the second place, a television programme such as that transmitted from Hillsborough involves cameras at different viewpoints showing scenes all of which no one individual would see, edited pictures and a commentary superimposed.[318]

The notion of the defendant being aware that the television authorities would not show pictures of individuals is, in itself, a somewhat peripheral consideration in the circumstances. It would seem more relevant to point out that the defendant would have been aware of the near certainty that some television pictures showing unspecified dead and dying spectators would be transmitted, and that relatives of those present at the ground would immediately be concerned. Many of the *Alcock* plaintiffs suffered a reaction from a series of events, of which the television pictures formed only part. It is entirely foreseeable that the accumulation of hearing news of the disaster, wondering whether a close relative was involved, and then, in some cases, being required to identify the body of the deceased in the temporary mortuary after nearly an entire day spent searching for him, should have triggered a psychological reaction. Yet the insistence that there should be 'direct, immediate perception' of the event ruled out these claims.[319]

An unresolved question concerns the availability of an action against a defendant whose own negligence is the cause of his injury. In *Bourhill* v. *Young*[320] the plaintiff sued the estate of a motorcyclist who had been killed in an accident.

---

[314] [1983] 1 QC 410, 442.
[315] Op. cit. (1992) 12 *OJLS* 440.
[316] [1992] 1 AC 310, 362 (Parker LJ).
[317] Ibid., 387 (Nolan LJ).
[318] Ibid., 423 (Lord Jauncey of Tullichettle).
[319] See ibid., 387 (Nolan LJ).
[320] [1943] AC 92.

She claimed to have heard the crash and seen blood on the road; she subsequently had a miscarriage. The claim failed, as it clearly should have done since the plaintiff had no relationship of any kind with the dead man and had not even witnessed the accident. A clearer case is the one discussed in *Bourhill*:[321] what would happen if a pregnant woman witnessed a window-cleaner falling to his death on spiked railings, suffered shock and then miscarried? In *Alcock*, Lord Ackner thought that 'there must be a limit at some reasonable point to the extent of the duty of care owed to third parties which rests upon everyone in his actions'.[322]

Other uncertainties arise from the continuing tendency of the courts to view the plaintiff as a 'secondary victim' of the accident. In particular, will the defendant escape on the grounds that the initial victim has been contributorily negligent? The fault of the initial victim cannot be imputed to the plaintiff, and the duty of care is owed to the plaintiff in respect of his 'shock' independently of any duty owed to the initial victim. But the causation aspect of contributory negligence must be considered as well. Normally contributory negligence is not regarded as completely breaking the chain of causation;[323] but it could be open to a court to find that the initial victim's error rendered the loss suffered by the plaintiff too remote.[324]

4. The plaintiff must have had a close personal or familial relationship with the accident victim. Among 'secondary victims', the class of potential plaintiffs is limited, by and large, to those in a close relationship to the accident victim. These will normally be family relatives. Traditionally the category of close relatives clearly included spouses and parents of the accident victim, but excluded those in other relationships such as brothers and sisters. In *McLoughlin* v. *O'Brian* Lord Wilberforce said:[325]

As regards the class of persons, the possible range is between the closest of family ties— of parent and child, or husband and wife—and the ordinary bystander. Existing law recognises the claims of the first; it denies that of the second, either on the basis that such persons must be assumed to be possessed of fortitude sufficient to enable them to endure the calamities of modern life, or that defendants cannot be expected to compensate the world at large . . . other cases involving less close relationships must be very carefully scrutinised. I cannot say that they should never be admitted. The closer the tie (not merely in relationship, but in care) the greater the claim for consideration. The claim, in any case, has to be judged in the light of the other factors, such as proximity to the scene in time and place, and the nature of the accident.

This suggests that if the event is particularly traumatic, there will be a wider range of potential plaintiffs. In *Alcock* v. *Chief Constable of South Yorkshire*[326] the House of Lords rejected claims brought by brothers, brothers-in-law, uncles, grandparents, and friends of the deceased. However, Lord Keith considered that 'reasonable foreseeability should be the guide' to the class of potential

---

[321] In the Court of Session: 1941 SC 395, 399.   [322] [1992] 1 AC 310, 403.

[323] See below, Section 4, and Chapter 8, Section 1.

[324] By extension of *McKew* v. *Holland & Hannen & Cubitts (Scotland) Ltd.* [1969] 3 All ER 1621, discussed below, Section 4(3)(b).

[325] [1983] 1 AC 410, 422.   [326] [1992] 1 AC 310.

plaintiffs. 'The kinds of relationship which may involve close ties of love and affection are numerous, and it is the existence of such ties which leads to mental disturbance when the loved one suffers a catastrophe.'[327] The degree of closeness can therefore be presumed in some cases (the relationship between parent and child and that between fiancés were given by Lord Keith as examples). In others, it is open to being established by the plaintiff through appropriate evidence; while it might also be possible, conversely, to rebut the presumption of proximity between, for example, husband and wife who had been separated for many years. It is doubtful whether this approach opens up the danger of indeterminate liability, since in a peripheral case the burden of proof will be on the plaintiff and this burden may be considerable. The cases of husband and wife and the parents of children remain the 'core' examples of the nature of relationship required, by reference to which other claims will be judged. There seems no reason why the boyfriend or girlfriend of the deceased, or a fiancé, could not recover. One of the *Alcock* plaintiffs, a fiancée of a young man who died in the disaster, almost certainly would have recovered had she been present at the scene; as it was she failed because she had been elsewhere when the disaster took place. Whether a claim by a mistress or paramour of a married victim could be barred by public policy, on the other hand, remains to be seen.

It follows from what has just been said that mere bystanders, who have no ties of love or affection to the main accident victim, will almost certainly have no claim in nervous shock caused by witnessing the event in question. Lord Keith in *Alcock* thought that liability could not be 'entirely excluded' if 'the circumstances of a catastrophe occurring very close to him were particularly horrific',[328] but since this exception was not invoked in the circumstances of the *Alcock* litigation, it is plainly very narrow in scope.

The position of rescuers who suffer nervous shock is more problematic. At one time there seemed to be a judicial policy of accommodating their claims, on the grounds that nothing should be done to discourage rescuers from acting in an emergency. In *Chadwick* v. *British Railways Board*[329] the plaintiff suffered a long-term psychiatric illness after helping out in the aftermath of the 1957 Lewisham railway disaster, which occurred a short distance from where he lived. He was allowed to recover damages for his loss. However, in *White* v. *Chief Constable of South Yorkshire*[330] the House of Lords took a much more restrictive line. In this case, the plaintiffs were police officers who had been closely involved in the events surrounding the Hillsborough stadium disaster. Some of them had been present at the ground and had taken part in attempts to rescue the accident victims; others had witnessed highly distressing scenes in the aftermath of the disaster. The plaintiffs suffered psychiatric harm and brought actions for damages against the Chief Constable (their own employer) on the grounds of his vicarious liability for the conduct of their own fellow officers, whose negligence had caused the deaths and injuries of the spectators concerned.

---

[327] [1992] 1 AC 310, 397.   [328] Ibid., 397.   [329] [1967] 1 WLR 912.   [330] [1998] 3 WLR 1510.

The House of Lords, by a majority, ruled against the plaintiffs on the grounds of the absence of a duty of care. The majority judges were plainly influenced by the injustice of allowing claims by police officers to succeed after many of those brought by relatives of those who died had been rejected in *Alcock*. However, in their concern to avert this injustice, their Lordships introduced a number of new conceptual problems into the law. We consider in Chapter 5 below the problems raised by the fact that the plaintiffs in *White* were suing their own employer. Considered as *secondary* victims, the ruling of the House of Lords was that the plaintiffs were in no better position than bystanders. Plainly they had no close personal or familial ties to the main accident victims; the key to this part of the judgment was the finding that they had no special status as rescuers. According to the judges in the majority, *Chadwick* was a case of a 'primary' victim—the plaintiff had himself been in physical danger when administering help to those injured in the train crash. This was not so in *White*. On this interpretation of *Chadwick*, then, a rescuer can only recover if, as a result of his physical proximity to the scene of the accident, he had been in fear of physical injury.

The reclassification of *Chadwick* as a case of a primary victim makes little sense. The harm he suffered was a result of the distressing scenes he witnessed, not of any fear he might have had for his own safety. The majority ruling in *White* also leads to peculiar results, as Lord Goff pointed out in his dissent in that case.[331] The majority might have distinguished *Chadwick* on a different ground, namely that the rescuers in *White* were professionals who were trained to carry out the tasks in question rather than, as Mr Chadwick was, a concerned member of the public. But this route is not without its difficulties either. To reject claims by professional rescuers *simply* because of their status as fire or police officers—the so-called 'fireman's rule' which is observed in some US jurisdictions—would arguably be too inflexible, as Lord Hoffmann's judgment in *White* recognised.[332] Nor does it follow, once the possibility of liability is admitted, that a claim by professional rescuers must fail on the basis that the training they receive makes it unlikely that they would suffer a pyschiatric injury; in a particularly horrific situation, such an injury is foreseeable. Drawing the line between professionals and volunteers, then, probably leads to more problems than it solves. But the effect of *White* is effectively to end the special protection which rescuers as a class had previously enjoyed in this area of the law; in future, even a volunteer will have to show that he was a 'primary' victim of the accident.

(iv) An 'Assumption of Responsibility' with Regard to Psychiatric Injury   So far we have been considering the cases of 'secondary victims' who were not known to or identifiable by the defendant prior to the accident or event which triggered the condition in question. Different considerations may arise, however, in cases where the plaintiff and defendant are known to each other in advance, and in particular where the defendant can be regarded as having assumed a responsibility to the plaintiff not carelessly to expose him to the risk of psychiatric harm. In other words, just as in the area of recovery for pure economic

---

[331] Ibid., 1535–6.   [332] Ibid., 1557.

loss, the existence of a pre-tort 'special relationship' of this kind may be the basis for a finding of a duty of care when, otherwise, the conditions for the existence of a duty would not be satisfied.

This is, we would suggest, the best explanation for cases which appear to allow recovery for shock induced by damage to the property of the plaintiff which, when considered alongside *Alcock* and other decisions disallowing the claims of relatives of the victims of accidents, are difficult to explain. For example, in *Attia* v. *British Gas*[333] the plaintiff's house was burned down as a result of negligence by the defendants' workmen who were carrying out a job in the house; the defendant sought to have her claim struck out, but it was allowed to stand. In this case there was a high level of proximity between the parties as a result of their already being in a commercial relationship prior to the tort being committed. The possibility of recovery for distress at the death of a favourite pet cat or dog was considered in *Owens* v. *Liverpool Corporation*.[334] This case, in which a tramcar hit a hearse with the result that the coffin it was carrying was overturned, causing distress to the mourners, can be regarded as confined to the particular circumstances of distress arising from injury to a corpse, for which there are also precedents in other common law systems.[335] However, a better view would be that the very thing the undertakers were employed to do was to avoid causing anxiety and upset of this kind to those who attended the funeral. The case is analogous to those decisions in the area of recovery for pure economic loss which enable third parties, external to a contract, to claim compensation for losses, which it was the intention of the contract to avoid.[336]

The same idea seems to be behind a dictum of Nolan LJ in *Alcock* that:

> if a publicity seeking organisation made arrangements for a party of children to go up in a balloon, and for the event to be televised so that their parents could watch, it would be hard to deny that the organisers were under a duty to avoid mental injury to the parents as well as physical injury to the children.[337]

A similar case, from this point of view, is *Al-Kandari* v. *Brown*[338] in which a solicitor acting for the plaintiff's husband in matrimonial proceedings was held responsible for setting in course a chain of events which culminated in the husband arranging the kidnapping and assault of the plaintiff and the abduction of their children. The plaintiff was awarded damages against the solicitor both for her physical injuries and for her psychiatric reaction to these events. In this case there was physical harm, but the psychiatric illness was brought about as much by the abduction of her children as by her own treatment. Had the facts been slightly different and no physical harm had befallen the plaintiff, her claim could have been denied on the authority of *Alcock*, but this result seems entirely artificial.

The potential confusion which is created by the distinction between 'primary' and 'secondary' victims of psychiatric harm is illustrated by *W* v. *Essex County Council*.[339] The council, in breach of a specific undertaking, sent a known

---

[333] [1988] QB 304.   [334] [1939] 1 KB 394.
[335] Cf. *Alcock* [1992] 1 AC 310, 347 (Hidden J); *Christensen* v. *Superior Court* (1991) 820 P.2d 181.
[336] See above.   [337] [1992] 1 AC 310, 386–7.   [338] [1980] QB 665.
[339] [1998] 3 WLR 535, 552 (Stuart Smith LJ).

sexual abuser to live with the plaintiffs as a foster child; he then abused the plaintiffs' children. The Court of Appeal allowed an action by the children but ruled out liability to the parents on the grounds that they were 'secondary victims'. It is strongly arguable, though, that the council assumed a specific responsibility to the parents to avoid the harm which might be expected to befall them—which would inevitably take the form of psychiatric injury—if their own children were abused.

The principle of assumption of responsibility may be taken further to cover cases in which the defendant can be seen as being under a duty of care to transmit distressing information to the plaintiff in a sensitive and careful manner. In *AB* v. *Tameside and Glossop Health Authority*[340] the defendant sent out letters warning former patients that a health worker from whom they had previously received obstetric treatment had been tested positive for HIV, leading to the risk that they would contract the disease. The letters were sent by standard post and no arrangements were made for counselling (although these were later put in place). Claims in respect of psychiatric injury caused by the way in which the news of the possible risk to health was transmitted were rejected by the Court of Appeal, but only after counsel for the defendants had conceded the existence of a duty of care. As Professor Mullany has argued, this concession seems justified: there was a pre-existing relationship and psychiatric harm was foreseeable.[341] The existence of a duty of care should not depend upon the information being false. Nevertheless, it should be borne in mind that even if a duty is established, there may be problems of causation: the plaintiff will have to show that the shock would not have been suffered anyway.

What if *false* information is negligently conveyed to a potential victim of psychiatric harm? The possibility of liability here is indicated by cases in Australia, New Zealand, and the United States concerning false death notices in newspapers.[342] Thus an incorrect report to the effect that persons at the scene of a disaster have been killed or injured could give rise to liability. In *Allin* v. *City and Hackney Health Authority*[343] the defendants were found liable for negligently telling a patient who had just given birth that her baby had died. In this case, the closeness of the pre-tort relationship between the parties was a factor weighing heavily in favour of liability. The responsibility of the broadcast media to remote third parties is much less clear. One possibility is that the visual media could negligently induce shock in viewers, perhaps by focusing on the fate of particular individuals in breach of broadcasting guidelines. Such cases aside, can an organisation be deemed negligent to near relatives of the deceased for showing distressing scenes of a disaster? To hold it liable would raise problems of an infringement of free speech and the need to take into

---

[340] [1997] 8 Med. LR 91.

[341] N. Mullany, 'Liability for Careless Communication of Traumatic Information' (1998) 114 *LQR* 380. Mullany also suggests that even if there is no pre-existing relationship, a duty of care can arise from the assumption of responsibility, which is inherent in the transmission of bad news (see 114 *LQR* 383). This would go further than the proposition outlined in the text.

[342] See Fleming, *Torts* (7th edn., 1987), at 147, and see also Professor Robertson's 'American Perspective', below.

[343] [1996] 7 Med. LR 167; Mullany, op. cit., 114 *LQR* 380.

account the countervailing interest of the public at large in receiving the information in question. These issues have yet to come before the English courts.

(v) Employees   The courts have had considerable difficulty in classifying the claims of employees who witness traumatic deaths or injuries of colleagues. In *Dooley* v. *Cammell Laird & Co. Ltd.*[344] an employee was allowed to recover for the fear that his workmates might have been injured when the crane he was operating, through no fault of his own, dropped a load into the hold of a ship. In *Alcock*,[345] on the other hand, Hidden J considered that it was the nature of the activity or the task undertaken by the employee, and not the relationship he might have with the accident victim, that determined liability. This seems to be the best approach: the liability of the employer in most cases should depend on the duty of care which he owes to employees not to expose them to undue risk of harm, either physical or psychiatric. An employee will only be able to claim as a *secondary* victim if he comes under one of the categories of protected close friends or relatives outlined in *Alcock*.[346]

In the *White* litigation, confusion was caused by the failure of the courts to distinguish clearly between the two very different types of claim being made by the plaintiffs, namely their claims as secondary victims and their claims as employees. The claim of an employee arises from the pre-existing relationship which he has with his employer and is shaped by the nature of that relationship, which, in this case, is one of mutual trust and confidence.[347] This claim is not, therefore, parasitic on witnessing a particular event which causes harm to another. Indeed, for the purposes of this claim (in contrast to an employee's claim as a secondary victim) it is in principle *neither necessary nor sufficient* that the employer's negligence (or that of an employee of the employer) should have led to the accident in question. It is not necessary for the reason that case law suggests that the employer may be responsible for avoiding causing psychiatric harm to his employee in a number of situations. But nor is it sufficient, since an employer may be entitled to expect employees to withstand a certain level of exposure to stress. In particular, an employer is arguably entitled to expect that employees who are trained in rescue services will be able to withstand a greater degree of exposure to shock than ordinary members of the public. Thus, in such situations, police and fire officers may expect to have greater difficulty in showing that their employer has been *in breach* of the personal duty of care which he owes them.

This last point is highly relevant to *White* v. *Chief Constable of South Yorkshire*.[348] It cannot be argued that the Chief Constable was in breach of his duty as employer *simply* for exposing his officers to the harrowing scenes which they witnessed. If the disaster had occurred through the fault of a third party, it seems inconceivable that a reasonable employer would, in the circumstances,

---

[344] [1951] 1 Lloyd's Rep. 271. See also *Galt* v. *British Railways Board* (1983) 133 NLJ 870.
[345] [1992] 1 AC 310, 346–7.
[346] See *Macfarlane* v. *EE Caledonia Ltd.* [1994] 2 All ER 1 and *Robertson and Rough* v. *Forth Bridge Joint Board* [1995] IRLR 251.
[347] See below, Chapter 6, Section 3.   [348] [1998] 3 WLR 1510.

have withdrawn his officers from the scene. Does it make any difference that the employer, in *White*, was responsible for the accident occurring in the first place? At this point, difficult issues of causation arise. It is possible to argue that the plaintiffs in *White* suffered *additional* distress and abuse from the crowd and from relatives during and after the events in the stadium because of the role of their fellow officers in causing the deaths of the victims. More generally, the accumulation of circumstances—the employer's initial responsibility for the disaster together with the highly stressful situation in which the plaintiffs were then placed—could be seen as placing the employer in breach of his duty to have regard to their physical and psychiatric health and safety, as Lord Goff argued in his dissent.

Unfortunately, the approach taken by the majority in *White* was to question whether the employer owed his employees a duty of care at all in the situation which arose in that case. According to Lord Steyn, the liability of the employer to his employees depended on general principles of tort law, which limited the degree to which psychiatric damage was compensable; there was nothing to be gained, then, from formulating the claim as one of employer's liability. If this approach is taken, then a major restriction has been placed on the extent of the employer's personal liability. Lord Hoffmann, on the other hand, seemed to accept that earlier cases, which had held that an employer could be liable for causing certain types of psychiatric harm to an employee, had been correctly decided. However, his Lordship seems to have considered that this line of authority was of no relevance in a case where the psychiatric harm in question was sustained through witnessing the death or injury of another, although why this exception should be carved out of the general law of employer's liability is not clear.

As the law currently stands, then, *White* has cast serious doubt over the principle that an employer can be liable under certain circumstances for psychiatric harm sustained by one of his employees. At the very least, it seems that in cases of nervous shock, where the harm is sustained by witnessing another's death or injury, there is little or nothing to be gained by framing the case as one of employer's liability. Potentially, *White* is a highly restrictive decision for the law of employers' liability.

3. The Manner of Infliction

(A) ACTS AND OMISSIONS

According to Lord Goff in *Smith* v. *Littlewoods Organisation Ltd.*, 'the common law does not impose liability for what are called pure omissions'.[349] This means that there is no general duty of care in tort to prevent harm occurring to another. The normal mechanism for creating such 'affirmative duties of action' is contract (or statute). The hostility of the common law to the concept of affirmative duties in tort is long-standing, the product, it has been said, of 'values of an era in which private selfishness was elevated to the rank of a public

---

[349] [1987] 2 AC 241, 271; see also the judgment of Lord Hoffmann in *Stovin* v. *Wise* [1996] AC 923, 943–4.

virtue'.[350] Though the socio-economic environment is changing, there are few signs that the courts are currently prepared to abandon their unwillingness to treat omissions like acts.

Although the distinction between acting and failing to act—between *misfeasance* and *nonfeasance*—is said to be fundamental to this area of the law, in practice it may be difficult to discern. As two academic lawyers have observed, 'there are many situations in which it is impossible to draw any logical line.'[351] Thus, in *Donoghue* v. *Stevenson*,[352] was it the manufacturer's act of putting a dangerous product into circulation or his failure to check the contents of the bottle which caused the plaintiff's illness? In situations like this the courts normally have little difficulty in establishing a causal link between the positive act of the defendant giving rise to a risk of harm and the damage which subsequently ensued. Potentially much more difficult are situations in which the damage is brought about through the actions either of a third party or of the plaintiff himself. If the defendant could have acted to avert the harm but failed to do so, it is then that the question of legal responsibility for omissions arises in an acute form.

In his speech in *Smith* v. *Littlewoods Organisation Ltd.*,[353] Lord Goff was careful to stress the absence of a *general* duty of affirmative action in tort. For the law does recognise certain *specific* situations in which affirmative duties in tort may arise. Two of the most important concern the duties of occupiers to ensure that their property is safe for lawful visitors and the duties of employers in relation to the health and safety of their employees while at work. These are considered separately in Chapters 3 and 6 of this book. The point about these specific instances is that the duty to act arises from the existence of a pre-tort relationship (and very possibly a contract) between the parties. Other relationships with the potential to give rise to affirmative duties are those between parents and their children;[354] between a school and the children in its care;[355] between a host and his guests;[356] and between prison authorities and similar institutions and those in their charge.[357] In each case the scope of the potential duty imposed on the responsible person is twofold: on the one hand, to see to the safety of the other person in the relationship, and on the other, to see that the other does not cause harm to third parties. These various instances may, no doubt, be drawn together under the general umbrella of 'proximity'. The use of 'proximity' is only the beginning of the analysis, however, since the precise scope and extent of the duty will differ from one situation to another; but without some pre-tort relationship of this kind, it is unlikely that an affirmative duty of any degree can be imposed.

(i) A Duty to Rescue?   This is the main reason for the absence of any general duty to come to the rescue of another who is in a situation of danger. A parent

---

[350] Markesinis, 'Negligence, Nuisance and Affirmative Duties of Action' (1989) 105 *LQR* 104, 112.

[351] Atiyah, *Accidents, Compensation and the Law* (5th edn. by P. Cane), p. 81.

[352] [1932] AC 562.   [353] [1987] AC 241.

[354] This also includes a foster-parent looking after the child: see *Surtees* v. *Kingston-upon-Thames BC* [1992] 2 FLR 559.

[355] *Barnes* v. *Hampshire CC* [1969] 1 WLR 1563.

[356] *The Ogopogo* [1971] 2 Lloyd's Rep. 410.   [357] *Ellis* v. *Home Office* [1953] 2 QB 135.

who sees his child drowning is under an obligation to come to his aid,[358] but no such duty arises between strangers. An illustration of this is the US case of *Osterlind* v. *Hill*,[359] in which the defendant, a strong swimmer who had rented out a canoe to the deceased, sat on the shore and watched him drown when the canoe overturned. He was held to have owed no duty of care. The fact that the deceased rented the canoe from the defendant could be viewed as creating a relationship between them of the kind which would give rise to a duty of affirmative action;[360] but the matter is unclear and it is entirely possible that an English court would follow *Osterlind* v. *Hill* today. In *Barrett* v. *Ministry of Defence*,[361] for example, the Court of Appeal held that there was no duty to rescue in a case where the deceased, a naval airman serving on a remote Norwegian base, drank himself to death. The military authorities were under no duty to ensure that the deceased did not put his own life in danger in this way, even though they were aware that he had a drink problem.

There are suggestions in *Barnett* v. *Chelsea and Kensington Hospital*[362] that a National Health Service casualty department is under a duty to take in a patient who presents himself in an emergency, and NHS general practitioners are placed under a separate statutory duty to provide certain services to local patients.[363] But English law does not in general require specialists such as doctors or ambulance-men and women to come to the aid of stricken accident victims they happen to encounter, unless there is some prior assumption of responsibility. This position has been implicitly confirmed by the recent House of Lords in *X* (*Minors*) v. *Bedfordshire County Council*[364] and *Stovin* v. *Wise*.[365] In the latter case, Lord Hoffmann argued that the failure of a public authority to act under its statutory powers for the benefit of the plaintiff could not give rise to liability unless the statute clearly indicates 'a policy which confers a right to financial compensation if the power has not been exercised'.[366] This approach has been applied to hold that rescue services such as the coastguard[367] and the fire brigade[368] (and, by extension, the providers of health and medical services) are under no duty at common law to come to the rescue of a member of the public. Indeed, if they do so, they can only be liable for making matters worse than they would otherwise had been. In adopting this rather extreme position, the law apparently takes no account either of the magnitude of the danger to be averted or of the potential cost to the rescuer, even though the former may be considerable and the latter relatively insignificant. This is the effect of denying the existence of any duty of care, as opposed to admitting the existence of a duty and then seeking to establish whether in all the circumstances the failure of the defendant to act was reasonable. The latter may well be the case if,

---

[358] *Carmarthenshire CC* v. *Lewis* [1955] AC 549.   [359] (1928) 160 NE 301.

[360] By analogy with *The Ogoqogo* [1970] 1 Lloyd's Rep. 257; [1971] 2 Lloyd's Rep. 410. *Osterlind* v. *Hill* would not now be followed in the majority of US jurisdictions: see 'American Perspective', Section 6 below, p. 224.

[361] [1995] 3 All ER 87.   [362] [1969] 1 QB 428.

[363] National Health Service (General Medical Services) Regulations, SI No. 1992/635, Sch. 3 para. 4(h).

[364] [1995] 2 AC 633.   [365] [1996] AC 923.   [366] Ibid., 955.

[367] *OLL* v. *Secretary of State for Transport* [1997] 3 All ER 897.

[368] *Capital and Counties plc* v. *Hampshire CC* [1997] QB 1004.

for example, he could only have acted at the risk of endangering his own safety or that of a third party. Just as with economic loss, to admit a duty of care merely widens the scope of the court's inquiry to cover questions of fault and causation; it does not, in itself, lead to a finding of liability.

In *Smith* v. *Littlewoods Organisation Ltd.*,[369] the principal speeches, by Lords Goff and Mackay, approached the question of affirmative duties from different angles. The case arose from Littlewoods' failure to protect their property, a large derelict cinema awaiting redevelopment, from the entry of vandals, who caused a fire, which spread to the adjoining properties of the plaintiffs. Lord Goff, as we have seen, formulated his judgment for the defendants in terms of the absence of duty. Lord Mackay, on the other hand, avoided relying on the act–omission dichotomy and argued instead that the defendants had not in the circumstances acted unreasonably, a position which assumes the prior existence of a duty of care. The other members of the House of Lords appear to have taken the same approach as Lord Mackay, although the judgments are not altogether clear on this point. Littlewoods had insufficient knowledge of the presence of trespassers on their property and the threat of a fire was small when set against the enormous cost of averting the danger, which in this case would have required a 24-hour watch on the premises. However, it is clear from Lord Mackay's speech that liability might have been imposed had the risk of fire been clearer in advance. His Lordship's judgment may therefore be read as leaving open the possibility that affirmative duties of action may arise in an appropriate case.

A relationship such as that between a host and his guests may give rise to a duty to rescue, as in the Canadian case of *The Ogopogo*.[370] In the course of a boat party one of the guests fell overboard. The host attempted to reverse the boat back to the spot in question but failed to place the boat in the right position, with the result that a second guest dived in to rescue the first. Both were drowned. The Canadian Supreme Court held that the defendant owed a duty of care as host to do what he could to rescue his guests, but that in the circumstances he had not behaved negligently. In this case there was an additional source of duty in respect of the second guest, namely the failure to achieve an effective rescue of the first: this created the situation of additional danger in which the second guest put his own life at risk. *The Ogopogo* illustrates the effect of a court taking a wide view of duty: the focus of attention shifts to the question of fault, that is, to whether the defendant acted reasonably taking into account the resources at his disposal, and the danger to himself and to the other guests. Taking these factors into account, rescuers will not normally be held to a high *standard* of care. But in a case of an egregious failure to act, the prior existence of a duty leaves open the possibility of a liability.

The Ogopogo raises a further point, namely that a rescuer who is under no duty to begin with may assume a duty of care by starting to come to the victim's aid, and in particular may be under a duty not to make things worse. In *East Suffolk Rivers Catchments Board* v. *Kent*[371] the House of Lords implicitly accepted the prin-

---

[369] [1987] AC 241.   [370] [1970] 1 Lloyd's Rep. 257; [1971] 2 Lloyd's Rep. 410.
[371] [1941] AC 74.

ciple that a defendant exercising his powers in aid of the plaintiff could be made liable for making his predicament worse. As we have just seen, this principle has survived the retrenchment of *Anns* which follows from the more recent decisions of the House of Lords in the *X* (*Minors*) and *Stovin* cases. In this case the defendants avoided liability as they were able to show that their failure to repair the plaintiff's floodwall had left him as badly off as he was before. In *Barrett* v. *Ministry of Defence*[372] the Court of Appeal held that the military authorities were under no initial duty to protect the plaintiff's husband against the consequences of excessive drinking. However, once they began to care for him (after he had collapsed through drunkenness) they were under a duty to exercise due care in doing so. On this basis, damages were awarded to the plaintiff (although reduced for the contributory negligence of the deceased). However, *The Ogopogo* is a signal that rescuers are likely to escape liability on the grounds that only the most serious errors will be deemed to constitute a breach of duty.

(ii) Failure to Warn A failure to warn another of an impending danger is treated in the same way as a failure to come to his rescue. In certain exceptional circumstances a duty to warn may be implied; such a duty normally arises, for example, in the context of products liability, between a manufacturer and ultimate consumers.[373] Otherwise, a close relationship between the parties of the kind already mentioned will be necessary. It is not enough that harm to the defendant is foreseeable; there is no liability in negligence, according to Lord Keith of Kinkel, 'on the part of one who sees another about to walk over a cliff with his head in the air, and forbears to shout a warning'.[374]

A close relationship between the parties is not at first sight so obvious in the American case of *Tarasoff* v. *University of California*,[375] in which a psychiatric patient spoke of his intention to kill his former girlfriend during conversations with his psychiatrist. The psychiatrist failed to pass on any warning, and the patient later murdered the girlfriend. The court found the psychiatrist liable in an action brought by the victim's parents. An English court would have to go well beyond existing authority in order to follow *Tarasoff*. The decision seems supportable when one compares the scale of the threat and the fact that it was taken seriously with the relative ease with which the girlfriend could have been informed. But it also raises difficult problems of confidentiality between doctor and patient and has not been widely followed in the United States, having subsequently been interpreted as a case in which there *was* a close relationship between the psychiatrist and the girlfriend, whose precise identity was known to him.[376]

(iii) Failure to Take Adequate Precautions Persons with responsibility for looking after those in their care may be liable in tort for their failure to do so. In *Kirkham* v. *Chief Constable of Manchester*[377] the police were held responsible for

---

[372] [1995] 3 All ER 87. [373] See below, Chapter 6, Section 4(2)(c)(ii).
[374] *Yuen Kun Yeu* v. *Attorney-General of Hong Kong* [1988] AC 175, 192. [375] (1976) 17 Cal. (3d) 425.
[376] *Thompson* v. *County of Alameda* (1980) 614 P.2d 728. See 'American Perspective', Section 5 below.
[377] [1990] 2 QB 283; *Reeves* v. *Commission of Police of the Metropolis* [1998] 2 WLR 401.

a failure to pass on information to the prison authorities concerning the suicidal tendencies of a prisoner on remand, who subsequently killed himself. An infants' school which let young children out to go home several minutes before the normal time incurred liability to a child who was injured crossing a busy road, on the grounds that her mother would have met her in time had she been released as normal.[378] The same principles appear to apply to parents and their own children. Public policy does not prevent a child suing its own parent in tort, and if the parent is insured there may be a good reason to do so. However, the duty of care does not arise if the parent does not in practice control the child and bear responsibility for its safety and welfare on a day-to-day basis. Nor is the duty one to maintain the 'duties of conscientious parenthood' in terms of general upbringing, but simply to 'protect the child against foreseeable danger' to life and limb.[379]

A duty to safeguard another's property can arise on the basis of an *ad hoc* relationship, as in *Stansbie* v. *Tromans*,[380] in which a decorator failed to safeguard the house he was painting from entry by thieves. The householder with whom he had contracted succeeded in an action against him for the value of the stolen property. Aside from these instances of pre-existing relationships, a duty to act has also been imposed upon defendants who have created a situation of public danger. Such a case was *Haynes* v. *Harwood*,[381] where this took the form of failing to control a horse in a street where children were playing; the plaintiff, a policeman, was injured trying to control the horse.

(B) Liability for the Acts of Third Parties

(i) Parents and Children The intervention of a third party in the chain of events raises particular difficulties in ascribing legal responsibility for damage. The courts could have dealt with these questions through concepts of causation alone; instead, they have consistently applied the concept of duty to exclude liability at the outset.[382] The law was summarised by Dixon J in the Australian case of *Smith* v. *Leurs*:

It is . . . exceptional to find in the law a duty to control another's actions to prevent harm to strangers. The general rule is that one man is under no duty of controlling another to prevent his doing damage to a third. There are, however, special relations, which are the source of a duty of this nature. It appears now to be recognised that it is incumbent upon a parent who maintains control over a young child to take reasonable care so to exercise that control as to avoid conduct on his part exposing the person or property of others to unreasonable danger. Parental control, where it exists, must be exercised with due care to prevent the child inflicting intentional damage on others or causing damage by conduct involving unreasonable risk of injury to others.[383]

The responsibility of parents and teachers for the behaviour of children was confirmed by the House of Lords in *Carmarthenshire County Council* v. *Lewis*.[384] A

---

[378] *Barnes* v. *Hampshire CC* [1969] 1 WLR 1563.   [379] *Hahn* v. *Conley* [1972] ALR 247, 251 (Barwick CJ).
[380] [1948] 2 KB 48.   [381] [1935] 1 KB 146.
[382] See, for a recent example in the Court of Appeal, *Topp* v. *London Country Bus (South West) Ltd.* [1993] 1 WLR 976.
[383] (1945) 70 CLR 256, 261–2.   [384] [1956] AC 549.

child of four years was allowed to wander out of a nursery school on to a busy road. The plaintiff's husband, who happened to be driving by at the time, swerved to miss the child and crashed into a lamppost. He was killed in the collision. The defendant authority was found to be at fault for having failed to install a more effective gate to keep the children inside during school hours. The scope of this duty will clearly vary according to the age of the children in question and to the particular risk which they are likely to pose.

(ii) Custodial Authorities Prison authorities owe a duty of care to safeguard inmates against the foreseeable risk of injury from fellow prisoners. In *Ellis* v. *Home Office*[385] negligence by warders was established, but the standard of care imposed will clearly be limited by the extent to which there was knowledge of the risk of injury and the nature of the precautions taken to avoid it. Custodial authorities may also be liable to third parties for damage caused by escapes. In *Dorset Yacht* v. *Home Office*[386] a number of borstal boys escaped from custody while working on Brownsea Island off the coast of Poole and attempted to make their escape by boarding a yacht for the mainland. They collided with and then boarded the plaintiff's yacht, which was damaged as a consequence. The borstal officers were held to have been in breach of a duty of care in permitting the boys to escape—'the borstal boys were under the control of the Home Office's officers, and control imports responsibility'.[387] The damage suffered by the plaintiff was also held to be within the scope of this duty since it was foreseeable that the boys would seek to escape from the island and that they would attempt to use the yacht to do so.

(iii) Landowners The principles of the tort of nuisance recognise the possibility of liability for omissions in relations between adjoining landowners. In *Sedleigh-Denfield* v. *O'Callaghan*[388] a trespasser laid a pipe in a ditch belonging to the defendants in such a way as to block the drainage of water off the defendants' land. In a subsequent rainstorm the plaintiff's land was flooded. The defendants were liable for their failure to act, since they were aware of the danger of flooding from their own land on to the plaintiff's but did nothing about it. Landowners have also been held liable in nuisance for permitting a fire to catch hold and spread,[389] and for failing to prevent a landslip on to neighbouring land.[390] In these cases the risk of damage to property arose from a combination of natural events, the defendant's failure to act, and, in *Sedleigh-Denfield*, a third party's intervention.

In *Smith* v. *Littlewoods Organisation Ltd.*,[391] on the other hand, no natural event was involved, and the courts treated the issue as whether the defendants could be liable in negligence for the consequences of the fires started by the trespassing vandals. Lord Mackay formulated the relevant test in the following terms: 'What the reasonable man is bound to foresee in a case involving injury or damage by independent human agency, just as in cases where such agency plays no part, is the probable consequences of his own act or omission, but . . .

---

[385] *Ellis* v. *Home Office* [1953] 2 QB 135.
[387] Lord Pearson, ibid., 1055.
[389] *Goldman* v. *Hargrave* [1967] 1 AC 645.
[391] [1987] AC 241.

[386] [1970] AC 1004.
[388] [1940] AC 80.
[390] *Leakey* v. *National Trust* [1980] QB 485.

in such a case, a clear basis will be required on which to assert that the injury or damage is more than a mere possibility.'[392] As we have seen, Lord Mackay's speech assumes the possibility of a duty of care in this case by focusing on the separate and logically dependent question of breach of duty. In the circumstances, Littlewoods had no knowledge of the acts of the trespassers concerned and the risk of fire was slight when set against the considerable cost of mounting a 24-hour security guard. Lord Goff rejected outright the existence of a duty of care. Although he was in a minority of one in this regard, it is not clear from the other judgments quite what is the extent of landowners' affirmative duties to avoid damage to adjoining land. *Smith* confirms a series of authorities in the lower courts suggesting that householders would only in the most extreme circumstances face liability to their neighbours for the acts of third parties, such as thieves and vandals, on their property. Lord Goff justified the outcome in the following terms: 'The practical effect is that it is the owner of the damaged premises (or, in the vast majority of cases, his insurers) who is left with a worthless claim against the vandal, rather than the occupier of the property which the vandal entered (or his insurers), a conclusion which I find less objectionable than one which may throw an unreasonable burden on ordinary households.'[393] The victims of theft and vandalism had not, on the whole, succeeded in obtaining damages from adjoining landowners through whose unoccupied property the thieves gained access to that of the plaintiffs.[394] One factor behind these decisions was the feeling that, since the plaintiff householders were likely to be insured, their loss would be met in full, while to extend liability further would force all householders to carry a new and expensive form of liability insurance. More generally, on the evidence of several recent cases,[395] it seems unlikely that the House of Lords as currently constituted will countenance extensions of the duty concept into novel areas of liability. But the tort of negligence is known for its volatility and this is an issue to which the appellate courts are sure to return.

(iv) The 'Social Host'　　A form of liability which has arisen in several American state jurisdictions is that of the host who serves alcohol to customers or to guests who then drive home drunk. The host owes a duty to road-users injured by the drunk drivers. At first the imposition of a duty of care was limited to the owners of bars and restaurants, 'commercial hosts', but in the New Jersey case of *Kelly* v. *Gwinnell*[396] it was recently extended to cover the 'social host' who plies his party guests with alcohol. Aside from the difficulties of setting the appropriate standard of care for a host who may not know when his guests are over the limit, this form of liability carries the practical difficulty that the host is most unlikely to be insured against the loss in question. This has the unfortunate effect of enabling the insurance companies of both the driver and the

---

[392] [1987] AC 241, 261.　　　　　　　　　　　　　　　　　　　　　　[393] Ibid., 279.

[394] *Lamb* v. *Camden LBC* [1981] 1 QB 625; *Perl* v. *Camden LBC* [1984] 1 QB 342; *King* v. *Liverpool CC* [1986] 1 WLR 890.

[395] In particular *Murphy* v. *Brentwood DC* [1991] 1 AC 398; *Alcock* v. *Chief Constable of South Yorkshire* [1992] 1 AC 310.

[396] (1984) 476 A.2d 1219.

victim to shift some of the loss, which they were paid to bear, on to a party whose responsibility for the accident was at best indirect. It is most unlikely that either commercial or social hosts will be made liable in this way in the English courts. This is because of the clear rejection of foreseeability of harm as the principal criterion of duty coupled with the use by the courts of policy arguments, and in particular arguments concerning insurance, to narrow the scope of duty.[397]

4. Parties

In addition to considering the kind of damage and the manner in which it was inflicted, we now examine the way in which the notion of duty confines liability by reference to the nature of the parties involved. In some cases there exist classes of protected defendants, parties who by virtue of their identity may qualify for a certain degree of immunity from a negligence action: public bodies, those concerned in the administration of justice, and certain professional groups fall into this category. Conversely, in other cases the duty concept has been extended by either legislative or judicial action to include certain groups of plaintiffs within the scope of protection; two such groups requiring particular mention are the children born disabled as the result of pre-natal injuries, and rescuers.

(A) Protected Defendants

(i) Public Bodies The Crown used to enjoy a general immunity from tort action, but this is now subject to the Crown Proceedings Act 1947, under which the Crown can be sued in tort for the actions of its servants and agents.[398] Outside the Act the Crown continues to be immune and the Monarch retains her personal immunity from suit.

Local government authorities and health authorities and certain other bodies with public responsibilities do not enjoy a general immunity from tort action, but as a matter of policy they will be treated differently from private citizens and corporations for the purposes of the duty of care in negligence. The idea is to limit private actions by individuals against bodies with responsibility for looking after the interests of the public as a whole, or of a wide class of persons. Large-scale liabilities in tort, if widely imposed on local authorities for example, will enable a small group of favoured plaintiffs to benefit at the expense of the community as a whole, and may prevent public bodies with regulatory responsibilities from properly striking a balance between the interests of different groups.[399] There is also an argument to the effect that public bodies may be made accountable more effectively through means other than a tort action.

---

[397] J. Horder, 'Tort and the Road to Temperance: A Different Kind of Offensive against the Drinking Driver' (1988) 51 *MLR* 735. On the insurance point raised in the text, see the analysis of Professor Robertson in 'American Perspective', Section 5 below.

[398] See *Pearce* v. *Secretary of State for Defence* [1988] AC 755.

[399] This follows from a number of recent decisions of the House of Lords, in particular *Yuen Kun Yeu* v. *Attorney-General of Hong Kong* [1988] AC 175; *X (Minors)* v. *Bedfordshire CC* [1995] 2 AC 633; and *Stovin* v. *Wise* [1996] AC 923.

This, for instance, could happen either through the ballot box or, in cases of abuse of power, through the public-law doctrine of *ultra vires* and the remedies laid down in public law and statute for the control of administrative action.

None of this necessarily prevents public authorities being liable just like any other body for foreseeable physical harm brought about by their agents and employees. In cases involving economic loss, however, the policy arguments made above increasingly sway the courts against a finding of duty. This can be seen as part of the general retreat from the House of Lords' decision in *Anns* v. *Merton LBC*. Thus, in *Yuen Kun Yeu* v. *Attorney-General of Hong Kong* the Privy Council held that the body in charge of licensing and regulating deposit-taking companies (a variety of bank) was not responsible to deposit-holders of a company which had to be wound up after it had been licensed by the defendant. One of the reasons given by Lord Keith of Kinkel was that 'mere foreseeability of harm does not create a duty, and future would-be depositors cannot be regarded as the only persons whom the commissioner should properly have in contemplation'.[400]

Public authorities may also enjoy some immunity in respect of misstatements committed by their employees, although the precise scope of this principle is open to doubt. In *X (Minors)* v. *Bedfordshire County Council*[401] Lord Browne-Wilkinson held that local authorities, while not otherwise liable for failing to exercise statutory powers aimed at protecting the welfare of children with special educational needs, could nevertheless be liable for negligent diagnoses made by educational psychologists in their employment. However, in other decisions courts have held that employees in this position do not undertake any responsibility to the children in their care, nor to their parents.[402] A remarkable case which largely follows the *X (Minors)* line of reasoning and demonstrates how unconvincingly far the law has gone in protecting public authorities is *W* v. *Essex County Council*.[403] In that case, the defendant local authority sent a foster child, *known to be a sexual abuser*, to live with the plaintiffs, in breach of an undertaking made to the parents that no sexual abuser would be placed with them. The Court of Appeal held that the children who had been physically abused could bring an action for damages against the council for physical and psychiatric injury. But their parents, who had also suffered (one is inclined to add quite understandably) psychiatric harm but no physical injury, could not bring such an action. The majority held that the specific assumption of responsibility by the local authority to the foster parents and their family was sufficient to create a duty of care towards the children. It is surprising that they did not allow a claim by the parents as well in the light of authorities which suggest that they were not 'secondary' victims for the purposes of determining the scope of the duty of care with regard to psychiatric harm.

---

[400] [1988] AC 175, 194–5.

[401] [1995] 2 AC 633, 771; see also *T (A Minor)* v. *Surrey CC* [1994] 4 All ER 577.

[402] See, in particular, *Hillingdon LBC* v. *Phelps* CA, 4.11.98, reversing (1998) 96 LGR 1; also relevant is *Barrett* v. *Enfield LBC* [1997] 3 All ER 171.

[403] [1998] 3 WLR 535.

Anns was based on the premise that a local authority could be liable in tort for the negligent exercise of a statutory power or duty. The relationship between the statutory source of a local authority's power to act and its potential liability in tort is a complex one which is examined in more detail in Chapter 3, below. At this point we may note that the courts are taking an increasingly hostile view of the suggestion that common-law duties of care can, in the words of Lord Keith, be 'superimposed on such a statutory framework'.[404] Even where a common law duty is imposed, the purpose for which the statutory power was granted may restrict the potential class of plaintiffs. Thus, in the pre-*Murphy* case of *Peabody Donation Fund* v. *Sir Lindsay Parkinson & Co.*,[405] the House of Lords held that any duty owed by a local authority under *Anns* to take care in the inspection of foundations of new dwellings was restricted to loss suffered by private individuals and householders. This was because the latter constituted the class for whose protection the Public Health Acts, which were the source of the councils' powers in this instance, had been passed. No action was thus available to a property speculator or construction company.

For similar reasons the courts have placed restrictions on the potential scope of any duty of care owed by the police to members of the public. In *Hill* v. *Chief Constable of West Yorkshire* an action was brought against the police in the name of the last victim of a serial killer for their failure to make an earlier arrest. The claim was struck out on policy grounds, including those elaborated in the following way by Glidewell LJ:

> Investigative police work is a matter of judgement, often no doubt dictated by experience or instinct. The threat that a decision, which in the end proved to be wrong, might result in action for damages would be likely to have an inhibiting effect on the exercise of that judgement . . . While no doubt many such actions would fail, preparing for and taking part in the trial of such an action would inevitably involve considerable work and time for a police force, and thus either reduce the manpower available to detect crime or increase expenditure on police services.[406]

This does not mean that the police or prison officers may not be liable in a case in which there was a close pre-tort relationship with the plaintiff or some form of undertaking of responsibility. The *Dorset Yacht* case is just about at the limit of this version of 'proximity'. A clearer case is *Kirkham* v. *Chief Constable of Manchester*,[407] in which the police failed to pass on to prison authorities information concerning the suicidal tendencies of a remand prisoner who subsequently hanged himself while in custody. Similarly, the police were held to owe a duty to informers not to release their identity in a way which would expose them to threats of violence.[408] On the other hand the police owe no duty of care to a suspect of a crime to avoid negligence in the course of their

---

[404] *Yuen Kun Yen* v. *Attorney-General of Hong Kong* [1988] AC 175, 195.   [405] [1985] AC 210.

[406] [1988] QB 60, 75–6; the decision of the Court of Appeal was confirmed by the House of Lords [1989] AC 53. *Hill* has been applied in a number of cases to deny claims brought in negligence against the police: see in particular *Alexandrou* v. *Oxford* [1993] 4 All ER 328; *Ancell* v. *McDermott* [1993] 4 All ER 355.

[407] [1990] 2 QB 283; to similar effect is *Reeves* v. *Commissioner of Police of the Metropolis* [1998] 2 WLR 401.

[408] *Swinney* v. *Chief Constable of Northumbria* [1997] QB 464; although cf. *Osman* v. *Ferguson* [1993] 4 All ER 344.

investigation, since this would 'prejudice the fearless and efficient discharge of [this] vitally important public duty'.[409]

The decision is cases such as *Hill* may also be explicable by reference to the fact that *Hill* was, arguably, a case of omission and, as we have seen, our law is slow to impose liabilities for non-feasance. Additionally, the existence of the Criminal Injuries Compensation Board may have provided in *Hill* an *effective*[410] alternative remedy. Yet *Hill* proved an important stepping stone in the judgment in the *Elguzouli-Daf* case discussed below even though there some of the features that justified the *Hill* judgment were not as pronounced.

The *Hill* rule, achieving as it does immunity for the police through the use of the notion of duty of care, can effectively be seen as conferring 'a blanket immunity on the police for their acts and omissions during the investigation and suppression of crime.' This, obviously, appeals to the more conservatively-inclined lawyers who see real or imaginary threats to the solvency of any public body if it were ever to be held liable for the consequences of its maladministration. Yet no one in our country has ever paused to ask why the opposite legal result has not led to the financial ruin of public bodies in other systems. Nor have they asked what 'negative' deterrent effect has resulted from our tendency to opt for blanket immunities. Finally, as the Court of European Rights recently held,[410a] such blanket immunities may 'amount to an unjustifiable restriction of an applicant's right to have a determination on the merits of his or her claim against the police in deserving cases'. Thus, the Court ruled that all the considerations that were relevant to the complainant's claim should also 'be examined on the merits and not automatically excluded by the application of a rule which amounted to the grant of an immunity to the police'. This led to a (unanimous) decision that in the instant case the exclusionary rule (in *Hill*) 'constituted a disproportionate restriction on the applicants' right of access to a court and for that reason there had been a violation of article 6.1 of the Convention'. But the significance of the decision just described goes far beyond its immediate facts. For it gives a serious and, arguably, well-deserved blow to the use of the notion of duty of care as a device for stopping all claims of damages directed against public bodies in general (and not just the police) irrespective of any countervailing arguments that may exist in favour of the plaintiff's position. If this leads to an increase in litigation, we hazard the guess that it will only be temporary; frivolous claims will prove confinable through the use of other legal means available to our courts; and in any event this consequence, if it ensues, will be a small price to pay in exchange for ensuring that justice is not only done but also seen to be done. The outrageous facts of the *Osman* case (and, indeed, the *Elguzouli-Daf* case discussed below) suggest that the law, in its current mode, fails to achieve this important result.

(ii) Persons Involved in the Administration of Justice   Judges and arbitrators may not be used in tort for negligence committed in the course of their judicial

---

[409] *Calveley* v. *Chief Constable of Merseyside Police* [1989] 1 All ER 1025, 1030 (Lord Bridge).

[410] Even though, as noted in Chapter 1, the damages awarded under this scheme tend to be lower than those awarded in a tort action.

[410a] *Osman* v. *United Kingdom, The Times*, 5 Nov. 1998.

duties.[411] Nor may a client sue his barrister for negligence in respect of court work and preparatory work closely connected with the court appearance.[412] Reasons given for this immunity include the 'cab rank' principle, whereby the barrister cannot choose his client, and the duty which the barrister owes as an officer of the court. There is also the fear that actions against barristers will result in the costly re-litigation of disputes. The barrister has no immunity when giving general advice out of court. But the scope of this duty does not go very far if *Matthews* v. *Manhshold Life Assurance Co.*[413] is anything to go by: a barrister owes no duty to ensure that the client clearly understands the advice, this being the job of the solicitor. An advocate legally providing court services who is nevertheless not a barrister is extended the same immunity from negligence as one who is by virtue of the Court and Legal Services Act 1990.[414]

As we have seen, as a consequence of decisions including *White* v. *Jones*,[415] solicitors may under certain circumstances be liable to their own clients in both contract and tort and to third parties in tort. However they have an immunity from suit where the litigation against them amounts to an abuse of the process of the court, in the sense of being an attempt to re-litigate or attacking the previous decision of a court on a matter of criminal responsibility.[416] Very occasionally a duty may extend to the adversary of the client, as in *Al-Kandari* v. *J. R. Brown*.[417] This case, however, was unusual in that the solicitor had undertaken a responsibility to his client's opponent—his wife, with whom his client was engaged in matrimonial proceedings—to look after the client's passport. The passport, however, was used by the client to flee the country taking with him the (common) children.[418] Normally, however, there will be no duty towards an adversary to take care in the conduct of litigation, for example by making sure that a winding-up order is sent to the right address.[419]

The potential liability in negligence of the Crown Prosecution Service appears to be heavily qualified both by its involvement in the administration of justice and by its status as a publicly funded body. This, at least, is the impression given by the decision of the Court of Appeal in *Elguzouli-Daf* v. *Commissioner of Police of the Metropolis*[420] to which brief mention has already been made. There, two plaintiffs alleged negligence in the processing of their cases by the CPS, which resulted in their imprisonment on remand being needlessly prolonged. (In one case the incarceration lasted for eighty-five days.) Assuming the allegations to be true for the purposes of a striking-out action, the Court of Appeal held that the CPS owed them no duty of care. According to Steyn LJ, in such a case 'there are compelling considerations, rooted in the welfare of the whole community, which outweigh the dictates of individualised justice'. The considerations to which he referred included the danger of prosecutors taking a

---

[411] *Sirros* v. *Moore* [1975] AC 118; nor may arbitrators, when acting in their arbitral capacity: *Arenson* v. *Arenson* [1977] AC 405.

[412] *Rondel* v. *Worsley* [1969] 1 AC 191; *Saif Ali* v. *Sydney Mitchell & Co.* [1980] AC 198.

[413] *The Times*, 19 Feb. 1988.   [414] S. 62.   [415] [1995] 2 AC 207.

[416] *Smith* v. *Linskills* [1995] 3 All ER 326.   [417] [1987] QB 514.

[418] After arranging for his wife to be kidnapped!

[419] *Business Computers International Ltd.* v. *Registrar of Companies* [1987] 3 All ER 465.

[420] [1995] QB 335; cf. *Welsh* v. *Chief Constable of the Merseyside Police* [1993] 1 All ER 692.

defensive approach to the performance of their duties. Also relevant was the time and energy which would have to be devoted to guarding against the risks of lawsuits. Finally there was the danger of the CPS being enmeshed in continuous litigation—'a spectre that would bode ill for the efficiency of the CPS and the quality of our criminal justice system'.[421] As against these factors, however, one must also mention the fact that this case, unlike *Hill*, was a case of malfeasance not non-feasance. More importantly, the plaintiff's interest that was at stake was his personal freedom. It is submitted that in such circumstances one should be slow in sacrificing such interests to the altar of administrative convenience. In any event, it is very doubtful whether cases like *Elguzouli-Daf* will be able to survive the imminent implementation of the Human Rights Act 1998; and the *Osman* decision discussed briefly above, supports in our view the advisability of some future challenge to these rulings. In other words, here and in other cases such as the *X (Minors)* judgment the new, European-inspired legislation may bring some changes in our law which many might regard as welcome.

(iii) Other Professionals   The decisions in *Hedley Byrne* v. *Heller*, *Henderson* v. *Merrett Syndicates Ltd.* and *White* v. *Jones* opened up the possibility of extensive professional liability for accountants, surveyors, and solicitors. Other groups, including stockbrokers and architects,[422] also once enjoyed immunity in tort, but this cannot survive the expansion of liability for negligence in the performance of a service.

(iv) Regulatory Bodies   Similar considerations apply to regulatory bodies as to other organisations performing public duties; the courts aim to limit the range of matters over which negligence suits may be brought in order not to divert such bodies from the efficient performance of their allotted tasks. This means in practice that regulatory bodies are unlikely to incur liability for omissions and, moreover, that they may escape liability even where they would otherwise be vicariously liable for misstatements made by employees. Thus in *Harris* v. *Evans*[423] the Court of Appeal held that a health and safety inspector owed no duty of care to the plaintiff, the owner of a bungee-jumping business, when he advised a local authority that the crane used by the plaintiff was not safe. Similarly, in *Marc Rich & Co. A.G.* v. *Bishop's Rock Marine Co. Ltd.*, *The Nicholas H.*[424] a shipping classification society was held to have no liability for the decision of one of its surveyors to pass as seaworthy a vessel which was not in a fit condition to sail, with the result that the vessel later sank with the loss of the plaintiff's cargo. Of the various grounds given for this decision, the most convincing (we would suggest) is the suggestion that the defendant was performing a public function which was analogous to that of a public regulatory body: the classification societies, according to Lord Steyn,

act in the public interest . . . [the defendant] is an independent and non-profit-making entity, created and operating for the sole purpose of promoting the collective welfare,

---

[421] [1995] QB 335, 349.   [422] *Jarvis* v. *Moy Davies & Co.* [1936] 1 KB 399.
[423] [1998] 1 WLR 1285; although cf. *Welton* v. *North Cornwall DC* [1997] 1 WLR 570.
[424] [1996] AC 211.

namely the safety of lives and ships at sea. In common with other classification societies, [the defendant] fulfills a role which in its absence would have to be fulfilled by states.[425]

The same principle has been applied to hold that a government department with responsibility for certifying shipping vessels could not be held liable to the owners of a vessel which was negligently classified as meeting minimum safety requirements with the result that the plaintiffs invested in it as a business asset, only for the vessel later to be reclassified as unfit for use, the plaintiffs then losing their investment.[426]

Yet even this type of argument has its flaws. And the *Mark Rich* result underscores these dangers once one recalls that this was a case where policy arguments—important but not, necessarily, overpowering—were used to trump a claim for damage to property and not merely pure economic loss. In the light of the above, it is submitted that the danger that these cases presents is not simply that an inappropriate result may be reached in a given factual situation. By far the greatest danger lies, in our view in the indiscriminate subsequent use of wider dicta and policy arguments which may be compelling for one kind of dispute but considerably weaker for another.

(v) The Armed Forces   The military authorities cannot be made vicariously liable for the harm caused by the negligence of a member of the armed forces under battle conditions. This was the finding of the Court of Appeal in *Mulcahy* v. *Ministry of Defence*.[427] The basis for the court's approach was public policy and, specifically, the perception that 'it would be highly detrimental to the conduct of military operations if each soldier had to be conscious that, even in the heat of battle, he owed such a duty to his comrade'.[428] Under such conditions, no duty is owed either to civilians or their property, or to fellow soldiers. However, this does not rule out the possibility of liability under less abnormal circumstances; the armed forces do not enjoy any blanket immunity from suit.[429]

(B) PROTECTED PLAINTIFFS

We have already encountered a number of situations in which a duty of care is limited by law to a particular class of plaintiffs. Normally only the owner of property has an action in negligence for its damage; only the near relatives of those involved in an accident who are also eyewitnesses of the events surrounding it can sue for psychiatric injury. In this part we are concerned with two further cases in which the status of protected plaintiffs has been clarified.

(i) Injuries Sustained by the Embryo in the Womb   An embryo in the womb or 'unborn child' *en ventre sa mère* may sustain injury as the result of an accident affecting the mother or through other means, such as the negligent

---

[425] [1996] AC 211, 241.   [426] *Reeman* v. *Department of Transport* [1997] 2 Lloyd's Rep. 648.
[427] [1996] QB 732.   [428] [1996] QB 732, 750 (Sir Ian Glidewell).
[429] Under the Crown Immunity Act 1947, s. 10, the armed forces had a blanket immunity in precisely the circumstances which arose in *Mulcahy's* case, namely negligence occurring under battle conditions. The Crown Proceedings (Armed Forces) Act 1987 removed this immunity while giving the Secretary of State the power to reinstate it by order for particular purposes. The immunity was not restored for the purposes of the Gulf War, which makes it surprising that the court in *Mulcahy* should have interpreted the common law the way it did, even though such a route was clearly open to it.

prescription of a course of drugs or a blood transfusion. One objection to any claim brought on the embryo's behalf for compensation is that it was not at the time the injury was sustained a legal person, capable of being owed a duty of care. This was answered in *Burton* v. *Islington Health Authority* by the argument that the duty of care, which is merely 'contingent' or potential at the time of the injury then 'crystallises' upon the birth of the child.[430] In respect of births taking place after 22 July 1976 the matter is now governed by the Congenital Disabilities (Civil Liability) Act. For the child to have an action at all it must be born alive. The Act then provides a 'derivative' action, to the effect that the child has an action against a defendant who owed a duty of care in tort to either one of the parents and would have been liable to them in tort had they suffered actionable injury or damage.[431] If one of the parents was contributorily negligent, this will go to reduce the child's damages.[432] In the case of events which preceded conception (an example might be exposure of one of the parents to a substance which affected their reproductive capacity), the defendant has a defence if either or both of the parents knew at the time of conception that there was a risk of any child they had being born disabled; unless the defendant is the father and he alone knew of the risk.[433]

In the light of the recent *Islington Health Authority* case[434] and Commonwealth authorities, which established the embryo's right of action without recourse to statute, the main effect of the Act is to provide an extensive immunity to the mother of the child. She owes no duty except in the one case of her driving a motor vehicle when she either knew or should reasonably have known that she was pregnant.[435] If she commits a breach of duty by driving carelessly, which results in injury to the embryo, she may then be the subject of an action. This exception indicates the impact of insurance considerations on the extent of negligence liability, since when the mother is driving (as opposed to simply riding in the car as a passenger) she will normally have the benefit of liability insurance.

In a 'wrongful-life' action the child sues for the pain and suffering caused by being born disabled as a consequence, for example, of a doctor's failure to diagnose or to treat a disease or illness of the mother during pregnancy. In *McKay* v. *Essex Health Authority*[436] the Court of Appeal rejected the possibility of a wrongful-life action by the child on the grounds of public policy, both under the common law and (by way of *obiter dicta*) under the Act. In a 'wrongful-birth'[437] action the mother sues for the physical pain and suffering of the birth

---

[430] [1992] 3 WLR 637, following the Australian decision *Watt* v. *Rama* [1972] VR 353 and the Canadian decision *Montreal Tramways* v. *Leveille* [1933] 4 DLR 337. In *Re S* (*Adult: Refusal of Medical Treatment*) [1992] 3 WLR 806, the president of the Family Division held that a doctor had lawful authority to carry out a Caesarean Section operation on a patient who had refused her consent where this was thought to be the only way to save the unborn child; see P. R. Glazebrook, 'What Care Must be Taken of an Unborn Baby?' [1993] *CLJ* 20.

[431] S. 1(3).   [432] S. 2.

[433] S. 1(4). Note also the new s. 1A of the Act, under which a child may have an action against a doctor who caused it to be born disabled through negligent selection of sperm or gametes used to bring about the creation of the embryo; see Chapter 3, Section 1(3)(d)(i).

[434] To which the Act was inapplicable because the plaintiff was born before it came into force.

[435] S. 2.   [436] [1982] QB 1166.   [437] *Rance* v. *Mid-Downs HA* [1991] 1 All ER 801.

and the parents together sue for the expense of rearing the child. Another possibility is an action for 'wrongful conception', where a healthy child is born following the failure of a sterilisation operation or a vasectomy.[438] In *Thake* v. *Maurice*[439] and *Gold* v. *Haringey Health Authority*[440] certain costs of raising the child were recovered. Public-policy objections were overruled in these cases; nor were the losses associated with looking after the child classified as 'pure' economic loss, which they might have been. These were cases in which the pregnancy occurred as the result of failed sterilisation operations. By contrast, in *Rance* v. *Mid-Downs Health Authority*[441] the parents' complaint was to the effect that the hospital failed to discover that the child would be born suffering from a severe handicap. Had the parents known of the embryo's condition, they would have had it aborted. The judge ruled that such an abortion would not have been lawful under the relevant criminal-law provisions, and thereby ruled out a duty of care to the parents on the grounds of policy.

(ii) Rescuers The courts have long ago set aside decisions treating rescuers as a class of parties beyond the contemplation of defendants and have also rejected the application of the defence of *volenti non fit injuria* to defeat their claims. Nor will the rescuer's intervention normally be treated as breaking the chain of causation. The duty is owed to the rescuer as such and is not dependent on the defendant having owed some prior duty of care to the victim. 'Professional rescuers', such as doctors, policeman, and firemen, may fall within the scope of the duty of care just as much as individuals acting out of altruism, and the subject of the rescue can be property as well as people. Thus in *Ogwo* v. *Taylor*[442] the defendant, whose negligence started a blaze on his premises, was liable to a fireman who was injured in the course of attempting to control the fire.

Cardozo CJ's argument in the New York case of *Wagner* v. *International Railway Co.*[443] to the effect that 'danger invites rescue . . . The wrong that imperils life is a wrong to the imperilled victim; it is also a wrong to his rescuer', was followed by the English Court of Appeal in *Baker* v. *T. E. Hopkins.*[444] According to Wilmer LJ, 'assuming the rescuer not to have acted unreasonably . . . it seems to me that he must normally belong to the class of persons who ought to be within the contemplation of the wrongdoer as closely and directly affected by the latter's act'. The duty arises in relation to the rescuer even though the defendant owed no duty of care in relation to the primary accident victim, for example, because the latter was a trespasser. It is unnecessary, moreover, for the precise form of physical harm to the rescuer to be foreseen. On the other hand, it could be that the rescuer suffers an injury entirely through his own fault or otherwise in a way that could not have been foreseen. In *Crossley* v. *Rawlinson*[445] the plaintiff, running with a fire extinguisher to put out a blaze in a lorry, tripped up and fell. The judge held that the manner of his injury was

---

[438] *Thake* v. *Maurice* [1986] QB 644; *Walkin* v. *South Manchester Health Authority* [1995] 1 WLR 1543; *Goodwill* v. *British Pregnancy Advisory Service* [1996] 1 WLR 1397.

[439] [1986] QB 644.   [440] [1988] QB 481.   [441] [1991] 1 All ER 801.
[442] [1988] AC 431.   [443] (1921) 232 NY 176, 180.   [444] [1959] 1 WLR 966.
[445] [1982] 1 WLR 369.

unforeseeable. The case raises a difficult issue of causation; but surely it is entirely foreseeable that, in the heat of the moment, a rescuer who puts himself at risk will suffer an injury which he might otherwise have avoided. For similar reasons, it is unlikely that a defence of contributory negligence will defeat a rescuer. Or if the defence does apply, the reduction in his damages is likely to be small. Finally, there is no reason in principle to deny a duty of care as between the victim of a self-inflicted accident or injury and one who comes to his rescue.[446]

An interesting development in a number of Canadian, American, and German cases concerns the potential liability of a doctor who, through his negligence, endangers a patient with the result that a close relative then agrees to 'donate' an organ, such as a kidney, in a life-saving operation. Can the relative sue the doctor on the basis that he is a rescuer who has, himself, been endangered by the initial act of negligence? An action was allowed in the Canadian case of *Urbanski* v. *Patel*.[447] The requirement of foreseeability is satisfied, given that this is a common type of operation, and an argument from the floodgates seems implausible here as one is not talking about an indeterminate group of potential plaintiffs. In some American cases[448] liability has been denied on the grounds, for example, that the plaintiff has time to reflect on his intervention. But it is arguable that this is a too-literal reading of Cardozo CJ's reference, in *Wagner* v. *International Railway Co.*,[449] to there being no liability where the act of rescue is 'wanton'. Nor should the defence of consent be available here, any more than it is generally as far as rescuers are concerned.[450]

Select Bibliography

AMES, J. B., 'Law and Morals', 22 *Harv. LR* 97 (1908).

ATIYAH, P. S., 'Negligence and Economic Loss' (1967) 83 *LQR* 248.

BINCHY, W., 'The Good Samaritan at the Crossroads: A Canadian Signpost' (1974) 25 *NILQ* 14.

CANE, P., *Tort Law and Economic Interests* (2nd edn., 1997)

COOKE, SIR R., 'An Impossible Distinction?' (1991) 107 *LQR* 46.

FELDTHUSEN, B., 'Economic Loss in the Supreme Court of Canada: Yesterday and Tomorrow' (1991) *Can. Bus. LJ* 356.

FLEMING, J. G. 'Requiem for *Anns*' (1990) 106 *LQR* 525.

—— 'Economic Loss in Canada' (1993) 1 *Tort LR* 68.

GRUBB, A. and MULLIS, A., 'An Unfair Law for Dangerous Products: The Fall of *Anns*' [1991] *Conv.* 225.

HEPPLE, B., 'Negligence: The Search for Coherence', *Current Legal Problems* (1997), 69 ff.

HORDER, J., 'Tort and the Road to Temperance: A Different Kind of Offensive against the Dangerous Driver' (1988) 51 *MLR* 735.

---

[446] *Harrison* v. *BRB* [1981] 3 All ER 650; *Chapman* v. *Hearse* [1961] SASR 51, 106 CLR 112.
[447] (1978) 84 DLR (3d) 650.
[448] See *Moore* v. *Shah* (1982) 458 NYS 33; *Ornelas* v. *Fry* (1986) 727 P.2d 918.
[449] (1921) 232 NY 176, 180.
[450] See generally B. S. Markesinis, *The German Law of Torts* (2nd edn., 1990), 486–8.

LINDEN, A. M., 'Rescuers and Good Samaritans' (1971) 34 *MLR* 241.

MARKESINIS, B. S., 'An Expanding Tort Law—The Price of a Rigid Contract Law' (1987) 103 *LQR* 354.

—— 'Negligence, Nuisance and Affirmative Duties of Action' (1989) 105 *LQR* 104.

—— and DEAKIN, S., 'The Random Element of Their Lordships' Infallible Judgment: An Economic and Comparative Analysis of the Tort of Negligence from *Anns* to *Murphy*' (1992) 55 *MLR* 619.

MULLANY, N. J., 'Proximity, Policy and Procrastination' (1992) 9 *Aust. Bus. LJ* 80.

—— and HANDFORD, P., *Tort Liability for Psychiatric Damage* (1993).

O'DAIR, R., '*Murphy* v. *Brentwood District Council*: A House Built on Firm Foundations?' (1991) 54 *MLR* 561.

RODGER, A., 'Lord Macmillan's Speech in *Donoghue* v. *Stevenson*' (1992) 108 *LQR* 236.

STAPLETON, J., 'Duty of Care and Economic Loss—A Wider Agenda' (1991) 107 *LQR* 249.

—— 'Duty of Care: Peripheral Parties and Alternative Opportunities for Deterrence' (1995) 111 *LQR* 301.

—— 'Duty of Care Factors: a Selection from the Judicial Menus', ch. 4 in P. Cane and J. Stapleton (eds.) *The Law of Obligations: Essays in Honour of John Fleming* (1998).

TEFF, H., 'Liability for Negligently Inflicted Nervous Shock' (1983) 99 *LQR* 100.

—— 'Liability for Psychiatric Illness after Hillsborough' (1992) 12 *OJLS* 440.

WEIR, T., 'Abstraction in the Law of Torts—Economic Loss' (Oct. 1974) *City of London LR* 15.

—— 'Tort—Liability for Defective Foundations' [1991] *CLJ* 24.

3. BREACH OF DUTY

1. Negligence as Fault

The issue of breach of duty is concerned with whether the defendant was careless, in the sense of failing to conform to the standard of care applicable to him. The level at which the standard is set is a question of law, but this question is posed in the most general terms. In *Hazell* v. *British Transport Commission*[451] Pearson J said that 'the basic rule is that negligence consists in doing something which a reasonable man would not have done in that situation or omitting to do something which a reasonable man would have done in that situation, and I approach with scepticism any suggestion that there is any other rule of law, properly so called, in any of these cases'.

The standard of the 'reasonable person'—the man (or, nowadays) woman 'on the Clapham omnibus'[452]—is that of the ordinary citizen. The law expects the defendant to act upon 'those considerations which ordinarily regulate the conduct of human affairs'.[453] On one occasion Lord Radcliffe referred to the notion of the reasonable person as 'the anthropomorphic conception of justice'.[454] Secondly, the test is objective and, with one or two exceptions such as infants, is said to treat all defendants equally, with the effect that an inexperienced defendant will normally be held to the level of skill of one with the normal

---

[451] [1958] 1 WLR 169, 171.   [452] See *Hall* v. *Brooklands Racing Club* [1933] 1 KB 205, 224.
[453] *Blyth* v. *Birmingham Waterworks Co.* (1856) 11 Ex. 781, 784 (Alderson B).
[454] *Davis Contractors Ltd.* v. *Fareham UDC* [1956] AC 686, 728.

level of experience for the job in question.[455] Thirdly, as far as specialist defendants—such as doctors or accountants—are concerned, the standard is that of the reasonably competent person in the profession in question or the particular branch of it. In practice this means that the courts defer very substantially (although not quite completely) to the standards set by and widely observed in the profession itself at any particular time.[456] Fourthly, the standard of care may be varied to meet special circumstances such as situations of rescue or sport.[457]

A more far-reaching effort to inject some substance into the basic negligence standard was made by Judge Learned Hand in a series of American cases. According to the 'Hand formula', the standard of care may be expressed in terms of three variables: the probability that harm will result to the plaintiff from the defendant's act or omission (P); the gravity of the loss or harm (L); and the cost or burden of preventing it (B). A breach occurs where the cost to the defendant of taking the necessary precautions is outweighed by the magnitude of the risk and the gravity of the possible harm to the plaintiff: or where 'B is less than L multiplied by P: i.e., $B < PL$'.[458] In *Conway* v. *O'Brien* Judge Hand described his approach in these terms:

> The degree of care demanded of a person by an occasion is the resultant of three factors: the likelihood that his conduct will injure others, taken with the seriousness of the injury if it happens, and balanced against the interest which he must sacrifice to avoid the risk. All these are practically not susceptible of any quantitative estimate, and the second two are generally not so, even theoretically. For this reason a solution always involves some preference, or choice between incommensurables, and it is thought most likely to accord with commonly accepted standards, real or fancied.[459]

Advocates of the economic analysis of law see the 'Hand formula' as an economically efficient rule, which sets the optimum standard of care for the avoidance of accidents. It suggests that society will tolerate a certain level of accidents, where the costs of avoidance would outweigh the gains in terms of reduced risk. It is also suggested that 'Hand was purporting only to make explicit what had long been the implicit meaning of negligence'.[460] The nature of the risk is certainly a factor taken into account by English and Scottish courts. So, in *Glasgow Corporation* v. *Muir* Lord MacMillan said: 'There is no absolute standard, but it may be said that the degree of care required varies directly with the risk involved.'[461] In *Paris* v. *Stepney Borough Council*[462] an employer was found to be negligent in failing to supply a workman, who was

---

[455] *Nettleship* v. *Weston* [1971] 2 QB 691.

[456] *Bolam* v. *Friern Hospital Management Committee* [1958] 1 WLR 582.

[457] *Wooldridge* v. *Sumner* [1963] 2 QB 43.   [458] *US* v. *Carroll Towing Co.* (1947) 159 F.2d 169.

[459] (1940) 111 F.2d 611, 612.

[460] W. M. Landes and R. A. Posner, *The Economic Structure of Tort Law* (1987), 85.

[461] [1943] AC 448, 456. See also the Scottish case of *Mackintosh* v. *Mackintosh*, 2 M. 1357, 1362–3: 'in all cases the amount of care which a prudent man will take must vary infinitely according to circumstances. No prudent man in carrying a lighted candle through a powder magazine would fail to take more care than if he was going through a damp cellar. The amount of care will be proportionate to the degree of risk run and to the magnitude of the mischief that may be occasioned'; Landes and Posner, *op. cit.*, 87.

[462] [1951] AC 367.

sighted in only one eye, with goggles to protect his remaining eye. As the plaintiff was already partially sighted the consequences of any injury to his remaining eye were sufficiently great to require the employer to take special steps for his protection. The House of Lords, reversing the Court of Appeal on this point, held that both the scale of the potential harm and the magnitude of the risk had to be taken into account. Lord Simonds said: 'I see no valid reason for excluding as irrelevant the gravity of the damage which the employee will suffer if an accident occurs, and . . . I cannot accept the view, neatly summarised by Asquith LJ [in the Court of Appeal], that the greater risk of injury is, but the risk of greater injury is not, a relevant circumstance.'[463] It is not so clear, though, that the English courts specifically have regard to the other aspect of the 'Hand formula', namely the cost of prevention. In *Bolton* v. *Stone*[464] a cricket ball hit for six struck the plaintiff on a street outside the ground. The House of Lords regarded the central question as whether the risk of this happening was sufficiently substantial, and was not so concerned with the costs of prevention. In other decisions, however, the costs of prevention have been more explicitly considered.[465] It is fair to say that the 'Hand formula', loosely conceived, is an approach followed by the English courts in appropriate cases.

In determining for this purpose which issues raise questions of law and which raise questions of fact, the *setting* of the standard needs to be distinguished from its *application* in a particular case. These are logically separate processes although they are sometimes confused in judgments. As we have seen, the law determines the level at which the standard is set—the standard, in most cases, of the reasonably careful person in the situation or occupation in question—but its application in a particular case will be a question of 'fact and degree'.[466] For instance, the question of whether a given form of medical treatment constitutes a lack of due care for the patient is to be judged by reference to the 'standard of the ordinary skilled man exercising and professing to have that special skill'. In applying this standard to a particular defendant the issue may become 'whether he is, in following that practice, doing something which no competent medical practitioner using due care would do, or whether, on the other hand, he is acting in accordance with a perfectly well-recognised school of thought'.[467] Questions of this last kind were traditionally put to the jury. Now that jury trials no longer take place in England and Wales for personal injury and other negligence claims, it is a matter for the trial judge. Decisions on the application of the reasonableness standard do not normally give rise to legal precedents binding courts for the future. However, the appellate courts have the power to overturn the judge on the inferences to be drawn from the facts and to make their own assessment of the various factors to be weighed in the balance. In this context, one should note that decisions which do not create strictly binding precedents may nevertheless indicate in broad terms the kind of approach which courts are likely to take in future.

---

[463] Ibid., 375.   [464] [1951] AC 850.   [465] *Latimer* v. *AEC Ltd.* [1953] AC 643.
[466] *Qualcast (Wolverhampton) Ltd.* v. *Haynes* [1959] AC 743.
[467] *Bolam* v. *Friern Hospital Management Committee* [1957] 1 WLR 582, 585, 592 (McNair J).

The complexity of this balancing process makes the notion of fault underlying negligence liability a highly relative one. If the carelessness of defendants' behaviour is to be judged, at least in part, by undertaking a calculus of the wider social costs and benefits of imposing liability, the result is to dilute the idea of fault based on individual responsibility. In *Nettleship* v. *Weston* Megaw LJ remarked that 'tortious liability has in many cases ceased to be based on moral blameworthiness'.[468] In this case a learner driver was held liable for the consequences of a lack of care in driving which was, in the circumstances, probably all that could have been expected of her; the court was influenced, however, by the fact that she was covered by third-party insurance.[469] A finding of negligence allowed the plaintiff to be compensated and the loss to be spread through the means of insurance. *Nettleship* illustrates the tendency for negligence to verge towards strict liability in areas such as road traffic and employers' liability where the courts see defendants (or their insurers) as better equipped than plaintiffs to absorb or shift the losses in question. Where this is deemed not to be the case the attitude of the courts to liability can be considerably more restrictive, the best example being the cautious attitude to finding carelessness on the part of medical professionals.[470] These points were also considered in Chapter 1 so we shall not return to them again here.

(A) The Objective Standard

(i) The Standard of the Reasonable Person   The standard is that of the 'ordinary citizen' and not that of the defendant himself; an especially careful defendant will not be deemed negligent for merely contravening his own, higher standards. Conversely, one whose personal conception of what is reasonable fails to match up to that of the court will have no defence based on his subjective belief that he acted carefully. As Professors Landes and Posner put it, 'the information cost of determining each injurer's intelligence and ability to make judgments of this sort would be too great to justify departing from the reasonable-man standard'.[471]

The 'ordinary citizen' is not normally required to display the skill or expertise of a professional person in a given area. If he holds himself out to others as possessing a particular skill he would be held to that higher standard, but this does not mean that in every case it is necessary to reach the levels of competence achieved by professionals. In *Wells* v. *Cooper*[472] the plaintiff was injured when a door handle, which had been fitted by the defendant occupier himself, came away from the door. According to Jenkins LJ, 'the degree and skill required of him must be measured not by reference to the degree of competence in such matters which he personally happened to possess, but by reference to the degree of care and skill which a reasonably competent carpenter might be expected to apply to the work in question'.[473] The notion of a 'rea-

---

[468] [1971] 2 QB 691, 709–10.   [469] See ibid., 699 (Lord Denning).
[470] *Bolam* v. *Friern Hospital* [1957] 1 WLR 582; *Whitehouse* v. *Jordan* [1981] 1 WLR 246; *Sidaway* v. *Bethlem Royal Hospital* [1985] AC 871; see below, Section 3(1)(b), and see generally Chapter 3, Section 1.
[471] See *The Economic Structure of Tort Law*, op. cit. (see also Select Bibliography), 127.
[472] [1958] 2 QB 265.   [473] Ibid., 271.

sonably competent carpenter' appears to refer not to the standard set by a professional artisan but to that of a reasonably competent do-it-yourself enthusiast; the court held that the defendant had displayed the necessary skill and the plaintiff's action failed.

(ii) Negligence Distinguished From 'Mere Errors' The standard of the reasonable person is not one of extraordinary care or vigilance. Since most people are susceptible to the occasional error of judgement, mere errors will not necessarily signify negligence, although this will depend on the context. Errors of judgment committed in an emergency will not normally be classified as negligence. Thus in *The Ogopogo*[474] the defendant's decision to reverse the boat back to the point at which the first guest had fallen overboard was a mistake; the court decided that it would have been more effective to have manoeuvred the boat back round in an arc. However, the Supreme Court of Canada also held that in the circumstances of a rescue this was not an error of a sufficiently serious kind to amount to negligence. The courts' attitude to rescuers seems to be to avoid, as far as possible, imposing upon them potential liabilities which will deter assistance or make it more expensive. It seems unlikely, therefore, that a volunteer or non-specialist will be held to a high standard of care. In the case of a qualified rescuer, such as a fireman or police officer, it is more likely that the courts would apply the standard of care of the professional group in question. One who is trained to deal with emergency situations may reasonably be expected to meet a higher standard of care.[475]

Even then, there are cases, not involving rescue as such, in which the courts have judged the actions of the police leniently on the grounds that they cannot be expected, in the heat of the moment, to act with the normal regard for the safety of others. Chasing a suspected criminal may count as an emergency for this purpose. In *Marshall* v. *Osmond*,[476] a suspect was struck by a police car as he got out of his own vehicle to make his escape. The police officer driving the car was held to have committed an error of judgement; but the court refused to say that he had been negligent. The extent to which an emergency justifies taking risks will be one of degree. In *Rigby* v. *Chief Constable of Northamptonshire*[477] the police were held to have acted negligently by firing a CS canister into a shop belonging to the plaintiff, with the aim of flushing out a dangerous psychopath. The police had no fire-fighting equipment at their disposal, and in the resulting fire the plaintiff's shop and stock were damaged.

For the same reasons a misjudgment committed in the course of sporting activity is unlikely to amount to carelessness. In *Wooldridge* v. *Sumner*[478] the plaintiff, who was taking photographs at a horse show, was seriously injured when one of the horses got out of his rider's control and collided with him. The plaintiff alleged that the rider had been negligent in rounding a corner too quickly and in attempting to get back on to the track when he knew spectators were in his path. According to Diplock LJ:

[474] [1971] Lloyd's Rep. 410.

[475] See *Cattley* v. *St John's Ambulance Brigade* (1990, unreported); Weir, *A Casebook on Tort* (7th edn., 1992), 158.

[476] [1983] QB 1034.   [477] [1985] 1 WLR 1242.   [478] [1963] 2 QB 43.

It cannot be suggested that the participant, at any rate if he has some modicum of skill is, by the mere act of participating, in breach of his duty of care to a spectator who is present for the very purpose of watching him do so. If, therefore, in the course of the game or competition, at a moment when he really has no time to think, a participant by mistake takes a wrong measure, he is not, in my view, to be held guilty of any negligence.

The defendant was held not liable. In establishing the standard in this case, Diplock LJ considered that the reasonable spectator would expect the sportsman to 'concentrate his attention on winning'. The reasonable expectations of the *victim* of injury were a relevant factor in determining the standard of care to be imposed upon the defendant.

What is reasonable behaviour between sporting participants will depend in part upon how far the sport has a common understanding of the limits to physical commitment and competition. In *Condon* v. *Basi*[479] an amateur footballer was held liable for breaking an opponent's leg for a tackle which was expressly held not to be malicious, although it was dangerous. This case is perhaps explicable by the fact that the participants were playing in a local league where injuries of this kind are quite rare. In professional soccer and rugby such injuries are common and it is difficult to see how a court could hold a defendant liable for negligence except in extreme circumstances: those who play the sport at this level know that there is a high possibility of serious injury to a limb. The issue cannot turn solely or even principally on whether there was a breach of the game's own rules. A breach of the rules may be minor (a technical foul) or incidental to the injury in question (soccer and rugby players have been known to suffer broken legs in lawful tackles). It is a different matter if the defendant *intended* to injure the plaintiff; except in a sport such as boxing, an action for battery will lie, and consent will not be a defence.[480]

Errors of judgment are routinely classified as negligence in road-traffic accidents. The courts have had regard to the imposition, under successive Road Traffic Acts, of compulsory third-party insurance covering owners and drivers of vehicles against liability for both personal injury and, now, property damage.[481] The intention of this is to ensure that all victims of accidents are, as far as possible, in a position to receive full compensation; in a case where no defendant can be found, compensation is normally available through the Motor Insurers' Bureau. This system of loss-shifting would not work if the courts were not prepared to make findings of liability in the vast majority of cases.

(iii) General or Variable?   It is said that the objective standard applies regardless of the individual abilities or disabilities of defendants. One clear exception to this arises in the case of children. In the Australian case of *McHale* v. *Watson* the principles were stated as follows:[482]

The standard of care being objective, it is no answer for [a child], any more than it is for an adult, to say that the harm he caused was due to his being abnormally slow-witted,

---

[479] [1985] 1 WLR 866.
[480] On the defence of *volenti* in relation to the torts of intentional interference, see Chapter 4, Section 1(3), below.
[481] See below, Chapter 3, Section 2.   [482] (1966) 115 CLR 199.

quick-tempered, absent minded or inexperienced. But it does not follow that he cannot rely in his defence upon a limitation upon the capacity for foresight or prudence, not as being personal to himself, but as being characteristic of humanity at his stage of development and in that sense normal.

In this case a twelve-year-old boy accidentally injured a nine-year-old girl. What happened was that a sharpened steel rod thrown by the boy ricocheted off a post and hit the girl in the eye. The court held that the defendant should be held to the standard of an ordinary boy of twelve, and not to the higher 'degree of sense and circumspection which nature ordinarily withholds till life has become less rosy'. Recovery was denied. The relevant standard here is that of a child of roughly the same age and maturity as the defendant; this last point takes into account the fact that children of the same age are frequently at different stages of development. American decisions also indicate that where children are involved in activities normally undertaken only by adults—such as driving—they will then be held to the normal adult standard of care.[483] English courts have followed the same approach. In *Mullin* v. *Richards*[484] the plaintiff, a fifteen-year-old schoolgirl was injured by a school friend in a mock fight with plastic rulers. It was held that, by the standard of the ordinarily prudent fifteen-year-old schoolgirl, she had not acted carelessly.

Conversely, however, the vulnerability of children means that those responsible for their care will be held to a higher standard than would otherwise be the case: 'A measure of care, appropriate to the inability or disability of those who are immature or feeble in mind or body is due from others, who know of or ought to anticipate the presence of such persons within the scope of hazard of others.'[485] An ice-cream van driver has to take special care of the possible danger to children on the road, although he need not necessarily take extreme precautions, such as driving along at a virtual snail's pace.[486] Parents are responsible for ensuring their children's safety in the home by, for example, keeping dangerous household items such as electrical goods out of their reach or, at an appropriate age, instructing them in their use.[487] In *Surtees* v. *Kingston-upon-Thames BC* the plaintiff sued her foster-parents for injuries she sustained when, at the age of two, she scalded her foot in hot water. The action failed for lack of proof of negligence. Sir Nicolas Browne-Wilkinson VC considered that 'we should be slow to characterise as negligent the care which ordinary loving and careful mothers are able to give to individual children, given the rough-and-tumble of home life'.[488]

The case of infants aside, the English courts have rejected arguments to the effect that inexperienced defendants should be held to a lower standard of care. In *Nettleship* v. *Weston* the Court of Appeal held a learner driver to the same standard of care as an experienced road-user. In the view of Megaw LJ,[489]

[483] See *Terre Haute First National Bank* v. *Stewart* (1984) 455 NE 2d 262; Landes and Posner, op. cit. (Select Bibliography), 128–9.
[484] [1998] 1 WLR 1304.
[485] *Latham* v. *R. Johnson* [1913] 1 KB 398, 416.
[486] *Kite* v. *Nolan* [1982] RTR 253.
[487] *Jauffer* v. *Abkar*, The Times, 10 Feb. 1984.
[488] [1992] 2 FLR 559, 584.
[489] [1971] 2 QB 691, 707.

if this doctrine of varying standards were to be accepted as part of the law on these facts, it could not logically be confined to the duty of care owed by learner drivers . . . The disadvantages of the resulting unpredictability, uncertainty and, indeed, impossibility of arriving at fair and consistent decisions outweigh the advantages. The certainty of a general standard is preferable to the vagaries of a fluctuating standard.

The opposing view was adopted by the High Court of Australia in *Cook* v. *Cook*.[490] As in *Nettleship*, an amateur driving instructor brought the action against the learner driver. The High Court of Australia explained why the standard expected of the defendant would differ as between the plaintiff, who knew of her inexperience, and third parties, who would not:

it is the very absence of skill, which lies at the heart of the special relationship between the driving instructor and his pupil. In such a case, the standard of care, which arises from the relationship of pupil and instructor, is that which is reasonably to be expected of an unqualified and inexperienced driver in the circumstances in which the pupil is placed. The standard of care remains an objective one. It is, however, adjusted to the special relationship under which it arises.[491]

The defendant is not necessarily held to the *same* standard in regard to particular plaintiffs: the normal standard of care may be adjusted where the parties were in a pre-tort relationship within which their particular characteristics were known to each other. This issue is separate from the question of whether defences such as *volenti* or contributory negligence should be available. The outcome in *Nettleship* v. *Weston*[492] is still explicable using this approach: the instructor in that case specifically checked in advance to see if the defendant was covered by liability insurance, and presumably would have refused to go out with her if she had not been. In *Wilsher* v. *Essex AHA*[493] a trainee hospital doctor was held to the same standard in relation to a patient's care as the court would have applied to an experienced doctor. In relation to his colleagues or his supervisors, who would have been more aware of the consequences of his lack of experience, a different standard could plausibly have applied. Similarly, if in *Marshall* v. *Osmond*[494] the police had injured a third party rather than the suspect whom they were chasing, the decision could well have been different. There is no reason why the police should be held to the same standard of care in the case of bystanders as in the case of the suspect. But there is no clear English authority for this approach.

We have already noted the stringent view taken in relation to negligence on the highway. The apparent policy aim of ensuring the maximum coverage of liability would seem to explain decisions such as *Roberts* v. *Ramsbottom*[495] and *Broome* v. *Perkins*[496] in which the drivers concerned could not plausibly be said to have driven carelessly, having suffered respectively a heart attack and a diabetic attack while at the wheel. A different rule is adopted in several American states, which holds the defendant to the standard of a normal person suffering the condition in question. In *Breunig* v. *American Family Insurance Co.*[497] the defen-

---

[490] (1986) 68 ALR 353.   [491] Ibid., 358 (Mason, Wilson, Deane, and Dawson JJ).
[492] [1971] 2 QB 691.   [493] [1987] QB 730.   [494] [1983] QB 1034.
[495] [1980] 1 WLR 823.   [496] [1987] RTR 321.   [497] (1970) 173 NW 2d 619.

dant had a sudden mental blackout and drove her car into the back of another vehicle. She was held to have been careless only because she had received prior warning of the likely effects of her mental illness; her negligence lay in the act of driving itself. Had she not received these warnings, the court would not have made a finding of negligence. Without adopting this rule as such, the Court of Appeal in *Mansfield* v. *Weetabix Ltd.*[498] reiterated that liability in negligence is based on fault, even in road traffic cases. It thus held that a lorry driver who crashed his lorry after losing consciousness at the wheel as a result of a condition (hypoglycaemia) which he was unaware he had, and had no reason to believe he suffered from, was not liable for the damage caused. The relevant standard to apply, in the view of the court, was that of the reasonably careful driver who was unaware that he was suffering from a condition that impaired his ability to drive safely.

(B) Professional Standards

Professional men and women are governed by the standard of care of a normal person of their occupation or specialism: 'the test is the standard of the ordinary skilled man exercising and professing to have that special skill.'[499] An extension of this is the so-called *Bolam* test, by virtue of which a professional person is exonerated if he can show that his practice accorded with a substantial and respectable body of opinion in his field. Thus, 'he is not guilty of negligence if he has acted in accordance with a practice accepted as proper by a responsible body of medical men skilled in that particular art'. Conversely, 'putting it the other way round, a man is not negligent, if he is acting in accordance with such a practice, merely because there is a body of opinion who would take a contrary view'.[500] The facts of *Bolam* illustrate this: medical opinion at the time was divided on the practice of administering electro-convulsive therapy without physically restraining the patient, and evidence suggested that there were risks either way. After hearing McNair J's direction, the jury found for the defendant.

An important aspect of the *Bolam* test is that the court will not expect the defendant to have anticipated future developments in knowledge or practice: he will be judged by the state of knowledge of the normal professional at the time of the alleged tort. This was illustrated in *Roe* v. *Ministry of Health*.[501] Each of the plaintiffs was paralysed when a contaminated anaesthetic was administered to them in the course of an operation. Tiny and undiscoverable cracks in the ampoules in which the liquid anaesthetic was kept were the cause of the contamination. In the view of Lord Denning, the anaesthetist 'did not know that there could be undetectable cracks, but it was not negligent for him not to know it at that time. We must not look at the 1947 accident with 1954 spectacles.'[502] The court dismissed the plaintiffs' appeals.

Where professional opinion is divided, it is not surprising that judges (who have now taken over the jury's function of applying the reasonableness test to the facts) normally consider themselves in no better position than the professionals to resolve the matter. If one body of opinion is against a technique but

[498] [1998] 1 WLR 1263.
[500] [1957] 1 WLR 582, 587.
[499] *Bolam* v. *Friern Hospital* [1957] 1 WLR 582, 586.
[501] [1954] 2 QB 66.
[502] Ibid.

another, which is also sizeable and respectable, is for it, the normal finding is one of no negligence. It is more straightforward when the defendant departed from general practice. Liability was admitted, for example, in *Kralj* v. *McGrath*[503] when a 'horrific' technique was employed to deliver a twin baby. Other factors have led the courts to take a broadly pro-defendant line in medical malpractice cases.[504] One is the argument that the profession itself can bring sanctions to bear against inefficient doctors, and through its own internal procedures can maintain high standards more effectively than the courts can. A second is the fear of 'defensive medicine' and the frequent complaints of medical professionals themselves that the threat of legal liability and the cost of insurance coverage are inhibiting the development of new surgical techniques. The courts have accordingly said that, in the context of medical negligence, a 'mere' error of judgement is unlikely to amount to carelessness, despite the potentially grave consequences of such an error.[505]

The *Bolam* test was considered and broadly confirmed by the House of Lords in *Sidaway* v. *Bethlem Royal Hospital*.[506] This concerned the question of 'informed consent' and the extent of the doctor's obligation to inform the patient of significant risks attached to a particular course of treatment. In this case the defendant's surgeon omitted to tell the plaintiff of a small risk, put by the trial judge at 1–2 per cent, that a back operation could lead to damage to the spinal cord and hence to a degree of paralysis. The operation was performed with full care and skill but as a result of interference with the spinal cord the plaintiff was paralysed. The plaintiff's complaint was that the surgeon had been negligent in not warning her of the risk, and that had she known of it she would not have consented to the operation. In the view of Lord Bridge (with whom Lord Keith of Kinkel agreed), 'the appellant's expert witnesses' agreement that the non-disclosure complained of accorded with a practice accepted as proper by a responsible body of neuro-surgical opinion afforded the respondents with a complete defence to the appellant's claim'. However, Lord Bridge did not accept that the *Bolam* test would apply in every instance:

even in a case where, as here, no expert witness in the relevant medical field condemns the non-disclosure as being in conflict with accepted and responsible medical practice, I am of opinion that the judge might in certain circumstances come to the conclusion that disclosure of a particular risk was so obviously necessary to an informed choice on the part of the patient that no reasonably prudent medical man would fail to make it.[507]

Such a case might be one in which there was 'an operation involving a substantial risk of grave adverse consequences'; the degree of persistence of the patient in seeking information also had to be taken into account. The implication is that in *Sidaway* itself the risk of injury, estimated at around one chance in a hundred, was not great enough. Lord Diplock, likewise, thought that *Bolam*

---

[503] [1986] 1 All ER 54.   [504] See further Chapter 3, Section 1, below.
[505] *Whitehouse* v. *Jordan* [1981] 1 WLR 246.
[506] [1985] AC 871. Cf. the contrary decision of the High Court of Australia in *Rogers* v. *Whittaker* (1992) 67 ALJR 47. See Chapter 3, Section 1, below, for further discussion.
[507] [1985] AC 871.

would normally apply, except in a case where the court was clear that the particular practice was not 'responsible'.

In subsequent cases *Sidaway* has been interpreted as providing general support for the *Bolam* test. However, if this is correct, the degree to which the courts review professional standards objectively is extremely limited; those standards are simply rubber-stamped for the purposes of defining carelessness. Alone of the judges in *Sidaway*, Lord Scarman thought it relevant to ask what the reasonable *patient* would have expected to receive by way of information. As we have seen, there is authority for the view that the plaintiff's reasonable expectations are relevant in setting the standard of care where (as here) the parties in a duty relationship are not strangers, but were in a close pre-tort relationship akin to contract.[508] In the case of many hospital treatments the patient may not know the right question to ask, or may expect to be informed without asking about specific risks. According to Lord Scarman, there might be cases in which fears for the patient's health could justify the doctor's silence; for example, where information concerning a risk of failure could increase stress on the patient. This would be a matter for the court to judge, however, and not solely a question of medical opinion.[509] This approach would no doubt be opposed by those who consider that the courts should not put themselves in such a position, but it does at least have the merit of avoiding the appearance of simply rubber-stamping professional practice. If a doctor is expressly asked about the risks of a particular treatment and still declines to inform the patient, it is more likely that a finding of negligence would be made, although even here some consider that the *Bolam* test alone should apply.

In *Bolitho* v. *City and Hackney Health Authority*[510] the House of Lords confirmed the general position that while the *Bolam* test was still good law, there remained some scope for the judges to depart from the standard set by general professional practice when setting the relevant legal standard. According to Lord Browne-Wilkinson,

the court is not bound to hold that a defendant doctor escapes liability for negligent treatment or diagnosis just because he leads evidence from a number of medical experts who are genuinely of opinion that the defendant's treatment or diagnosis accorded with sound medical practice . . . the court has to be satisfied that the exponents of the body of opinion relied upon can demonstrate that such opinion has a logical basis. In particular in cases involving, as they so often do, the weighing of risks against benefits, the judge before accepting a body of opinion as being responsible, reasonable or respectable, will need to be satisfied that, in forming their views, the experts have directed their minds to the question of comparative risks and benefits and have reached a defensible conclusion on the matter.[511]

This may not advance the law much, however, since his Lordship also remarked that 'it will very seldom be right for a judge to reach the conclusion that views genuinely held by a competent medical expert are unreasonable'.[512]

---

[508] There is normally no contract between the patient and either the hospital or the doctor treating him in the case of NHS treatment, but a contract will normally arise between patient and doctor in private practice: see Chapter 3, Section 1 below.

[509] [1985] AC 871, 889.   [510] [1998] AC 232.   [511] [1998] AC 232, 241–2.   [512] Ibid., 243.

It is important to note that, outside the medical area, the courts have often declined to allow common practice to be a defence. This has happened in cases of employers' liability, although here it is also possible that negligence may consist in failing to take preventive action only once the scale of the threat to occupational health is known and protective equipment has become available, as in *Thompson* v. *Smiths Ship Repairers (North Shields) Ltd.*[513] In *Lloyds Bank* v. *Savory*[514] it was not a defence to show that the defendants had followed general banking practice in their procedures for handling cheques.

(c) Weighing the Risk of Harm Against the Cost of Prevention

As we have seen, the essence of the 'Hand formula' is weighing the magnitude and scale of the risk of harm against the cost of prevention. The approach has been criticised on the grounds that it is both invidious and impractical to compare, for example, the consequences to the plaintiff in terms of the loss of a limb or pain and suffering against what may only be a financial cost to the defendant. Personal injury can never be 'fully compensated' despite the efforts of the tort system to do so, and placing an economic value on the risk of such injury is a process fraught with difficulty. The same objection does not arise with regard to property damage, and here the use of cost–benefit analyses is less contentious.[515] One argument for the use of cost–benefit comparisons even for personal injury is that many socially desirable or necessary activities cannot be carried on without some risk of causing personal injury. Transport is one obvious example. The level of care required in relation to a given activity may be a highly contentious question of policy, and one in which Parliament has stepped in to set standards through statutory regulation for areas such as employers' liability. There will, however, inevitably be cases (including many in the field of employment) to which no statutory standard is relevant, and here the courts cannot avoid the task of weighing the different interests involved.

Assessing the risk of harm has, as we have seen, two related aspects: the court must consider both the *degree of probability* of the risk being realised and the *gravity* of the potential injury itself. If serious injury is a possibility, even a comparatively small risk may weigh heavily in the balance. On the other side, in examining the cost of prevention the court has to consider not simply the potential *expenditure* to the defendant of taking additional steps to prevent the harm. It must also bear in mind the *benefit forgone* if, as may be possible, the activity in question has to be abandoned, as will be the case if the costs to the defendant of carrying on outweigh the gains. Nor is it simply the cost to the defendant which the court has to consider. It may be that the plaintiff is in the best position to take the necessary steps to avert the danger in question. If, in economic terminology, the plaintiff were the 'least cost avoider', social cost as a whole would be minimised by a no-liability rule, which would leave it up to

---

[513] [1960] AC 145.

[514] [1933] AC 201. See also *Edward Wong Finance Co. Ltd.* v. *Johnson Stokes & Master* [1984] AC 296.

[515] For discussion of these and related issues see R. Abel, 'Should Tort Law Protect Property against Accidental Loss?', in M. Furmston (ed.) *The Law of Tort: Policies and Trends in Liability for Damage to Property and Economic Loss* (1985), ch. 8, in particular at n. 182.

the plaintiff to act. An essential qualification to the test adopted by Hand is made by Professors Landes and Posner. According to these authors, what matters in the comparison are not the total or average values but the *marginal* costs and benefits of eliminating a particular risk: 'the court asks, "What additional care inputs should the defendant have used to avoid this accident, given his existing level of care?" '[516] If an incremental gain in safety can only be made at enormous expense, failure to take this precaution is unlikely to amount to negligence in the sense applied by the courts.

These considerations are not always spelled out in the judgments of the English courts. However, they often seem to underlie the judges' apparently intuitive notions of what is reasonable in a particular case, and there are some signs that their use is becoming more explicit.

(i) Risk and Foreseeability of Damage   The relationship between the risk of injury and the degree of foreseeability was considered by the House of Lords in *Bolton* v. *Stone*,[517] the facts of which were described above. The chances of a passer-by being struck by a cricket ball hit out of the ground were found to be very small. Balls had been hit out of the ground only six times in the preceding thirty years, and the street (in which the plaintiff was a resident) was fairly quiet and unfrequented. The House of Lords allowed an appeal by the owners of the ground from findings of liability in the lower courts. Lord Reid approached the case by asking whether the risk was sufficiently substantial and rejected a test based on foreseeability alone: 'on the theory that it is foreseeability alone that matters it would be irrelevant to consider how often a ball might be expected to land in the road and it would not matter whether the road was the busiest street or the quietest country lane. The only difference between these cases is in the degree of risk.' The correct test was: 'what a man must not do, and what I think a careful man tries not to do, is create a risk which is substantial.' In this case the risk was 'extremely small'.[518]

The question in each case, then, is not whether a particular injury was foreseeable, but whether, in the first place, the risk was *sufficiently* substantial, and this is a matter of degree. This is only the first step in the argument, though; the only way to assess whether a risk is sufficiently substantial is to measure it against both the gravity of the resulting injury and the cost of prevention to the defendant. In this regard, Lord Reid said: 'In considering that matter I think that it would be right to take into account, not only how remote is the chance that a person might be struck, but also how serious the consequences are likely to be if a person is struck, but I do not think that it would be right to take into account the difficulty of remedial measures.'[519] This is, in effect, to consider only one half of the equation. In the same case, Lord Radcliffe appeared to take a different view. He thus said: 'It seems to me that a reasonable man, taking account of the chances against an accident happening, would not have felt himself called on either to abandon the use of the ground for cricket or to increase the height of his surrounding fences.'[520] A seven-foot high fence surrounded

---

[516] Op. cit. (Select Bibliography), 87.   [517] [1951] AC 850.   [518] Ibid., 866–7.
[519] Ibid., 867.   [520] Ibid., 869.

the ground, which was itself ten feet above the level of the street outside. One way of explaining the outcome, then, is to say that the costs to the defendants of taking *extra* precautions—of building a higher fence, for example—were considerable in relation to the *extra* degree of safety which would thereby have been achieved. The only way of really being sure that no one could have been hit by a cricket ball would have been to stop playing cricket on the site altogether. This considerable cost to the defendants would have far outweighed the removal of the comparatively small risk of passers-by being struck by a flying cricket ball.

It is not clear, however, that this was the basis for the decision in *Bolton* v. *Stone*. For only Lord Radcliffe's judgment referred, obliquely, to the factor of the cost of prevention, and, as we have just seen, Lord Reid expressly ruled it out as a factor to be taken into account. In *The Wagon Mound (No. 2)*[521] he explained *Bolton* v. *Stone* as a case in which 'the risk was so small that in the circumstances a reasonable man would have been justified in disregarding it and taking no steps to eliminate it'.

On the other hand, Lord Reid's judgment in *The Wagon Mound (No. 2)* explicitly considered the cost of prevention. In this case oil discharged into Sydney harbour from the defendant's vessel was ignited, most probably by a piece of hot metal which fell into the water from welding work going on in one of the wharfs. In the resulting fire the plaintiffs' vessels were damaged. The likelihood of the oil catching fire was very low—oil of the kind in question, on the surface of water, is 'extremely difficult to ignite in the open'—but there was a risk, however small. The gravity of any damage, which would then occur, was enormous, but also relevant was the lack of justification for the initial spillage: to have avoided the risk would have 'presented no difficulty, involved no disadvantage and required no expense'.[522]

The limited relevance of foreseeability of harm as a test is illustrated by the case of *Paris* v. *Stepney Borough Council*, which was analysed above.[523] We also see this in *Haley* v. *London Electricity Board*,[524] where workmen employed by the defendant excavated a hole in a London street and, by way of warning to pedestrians, simply placed a shovel across it. This would have been sufficient, it was said, for sighted pedestrians, but the defendant, who was blind and who frequently walked down that street on his way to a bus stop, missed the shovel with his white stick and fell into the hole. He was seriously injured and lost his hearing. The Electricity Board defended itself on the grounds that this course of events was not reasonably foreseeable; but this was answered by evidence of the large number of blind people who lived in London and who would be used to walking unaccompanied.

Perhaps more to the point in this case was the low cost to the defendants of minimising the risk to the plaintiff: a light fence around the hole could easily have been provided. The defendants possessed such fences and would have used one in this case but for a delay in it being made available. By contrast the cost to the plaintiff would have been considerable: he had taken the normal

---

[521] [1967] 1 AC 617, 642.   [522] [1967] 1 AC 617, 643–4   [523] See above.
[524] [1965] AC 778.

precaution for a blind person of carrying his stick with him, and could have protected himself further only by walking accompanied or by staying at home.

(ii) Assessing the Costs of Prevention A case cited to illustrate the importance of the cost of prevention is the American decision of *Adams* v. *Bullock*.[525] The defendant company ran trolley buses under wires, which were not insulated. Unlike electric wires, the trolley wires could not be protected by insulation. The plaintiff, a young boy, was injured when he dangled a wire on to one of the trolley wires from a bridge several feet above it. According to the court, the only way this injury could have been avoided was to have run the wires underground. The remote possibility of injury occurring in this way did not justify such an expense. Landes and Posner explain the outcome in this way:

This is a clear statement of the proposition that the optimal level of care is a function of its cost, other things being equal. On the one hand, even if the probability of harm is slight, if the cost of avoiding the harm is also slight the failure to avoid may be negligence. On the other hand, even if the probability and magnitude of harm are the same for trolley and electric wires, electric companies may be liable in negligence and trolley companies not, simply because the cost of care is lower for electric companies.[526]

Two decisions in which the House of Lords has had express regard to the costs of prevention are *Latimer* v. *AEC Ltd.*[527] and *Smith* v. *Littlewoods Ltd.*[528] In the *Latimer* case the defendant's factory was flooded by heavy rain. Sawdust was placed on the worst affected areas. However, many areas of the floor remained damp and the plaintiff slipped on one of them, breaking his ankle. The judge found that the employers had done everything necessary short of shutting down the factory for the duration of the shift in question; the House of Lords held that a reasonably prudent employer would not have shut down the works completely in these circumstances. The cost, both to the employer and to the workmen who would have forfeited their wages, outweighed the potential risk: the plaintiff was the only worker to have 'experienced any difficulty'.[529]

The decision seems questionable when it is borne in mind that both tort (through the employer's personal duty of care to his employees)[530] and contract (through the express and implied terms of the contract of employment) place on the employer the principal onus of ensuring that the factory is a safe place in which to work.[531] It is far from clear as a matter of contract law that the employer would not have had to compensate the employees for any closure of the factory, and such an obligation could now arise under statute.[532] *Latimer* illustrates the extent to which these decisions raise difficult questions of degree, in which openly evaluative judgments may have to be made.

Smith v. *Littlewoods*[533] concerned the liability of the owners of a large derelict cinema for the acts of vandals who entered the premises and set fire to it,

---

[525] (1919) 125 NE 93. [526] Op. cit. (Select Bibliography), 87–98.
[527] [1953] AC 634. [528] [1987] AC 241. [529] [1953] AC 643, 659.
[530] See Chapter 6, Section 3, below.
[531] *Johnstone* v. *Bloomsbury HA* [1992] 1 QB 333. In practice this, of course, means the management of the enterprise.
[532] Under the guaranteed pay provisions of the Employment Employment Rights Act 1996.
[533] [1987] AC 241.

causing damage to adjoining properties. Only property damage was in issue here, then. The gravity of the potential harm was substantial in financial terms. Unlike *Latimer*, however, the loss was property damage and not personal injury, and the likelihood of such an event occurring was found to be low: the defendants were not aware of the presence of vandals on the site and had no reason to assume that they constituted a significant threat. Nor, it seemed, were the adjoining owners particularly concerned, since none of them complained to Littlewoods prior to the fire of the potential danger to their own property. Finally, the defendants had taken certain precautions against illicit entry. Short of posting a continuous guard over the property they would not have been in a position to prevent the vandals getting in. Since the plaintiffs were either covered by loss insurance or could easily have been so, they may be regarded as best placed to bear the loss and to shift it.

What is reasonable may depend upon the resources of the defendant. Although, as we have seen, the courts are said to apply a general standard which takes little or no regard of individual disabilities, there may be cases in which it would be pointless to impose too onerous a burden on the defendant. This is particularly so where affirmative duties of action are concerned. In *Goldman* v. *Hargrave*[534] Lord Wilberforce argued that:

the standard ought to be to require of the occupier what it is reasonable to expect of him in his individual circumstances. Thus, less must be expected of the infirm than of the able-bodied: the owner of a small property where a hazard arises which threatens a neighbour with substantial interests should not have to do as much as one with larger interests of his own at stake and greater resources to protect them . . .

This argument may have less force, though, outside the specific context in which Lord Wilberforce was addressing it. Normally the burden of care will not be displaced from one party to the other *simply* because of a disparity of income and resources between them; the relevant question is which of them can act at the least cost. Duties of affirmative action, however, may become unenforceable if the mere ownership of land is taken to carry with it extensive duties to act for the protection of near neighbours.

Another area in which the balancing of costs and benefits gives rise to difficult issues is that of 'negligence in design'. The costs to a company or utility of altering an existing design in order to achieve incremental protection to consumers or users of the service in question may be enormous. In *Wyngrove* v. *Scottish Omnibuses*[535] the complaint concerned the defendants' failure to fit a vertical pillar on the rear platform of their buses. The absence of the pillar allegedly caused the plaintiff to fall out of the bus when attempting to exit from it, as a result of which he sustained serious injuries. Various other handholds had been provided. In the view of Lord Reid, the fact that thousands of journeys had been safely made without a similar accident occurring entitled the bus company to conclude that their system was adequate: the chance of injury occurring in the way alleged was 'very remote'.

[534] [1967] 1 AC 645, 663.

[535] 1966 SC (HL) 47; for helpful discussions see Weir, *A Casebook on Tort* (7th edn., 1992), 142–3; Atiyah, *Accidents, Compensation and the Law* (4th edn. by P. Cane, 1987), 55–9.

Watt v. *Hertfordshire County Council*[536] illustrates the importance of weighing the risk against the benefit, which would be forgone by excessive preventive measures. A fireman sued his employers for negligence when he was injured by heavy lifting gear in the course of a journey by lorry to rescue a woman trapped under a vehicle. The court held that the unusual risk being run by not waiting for a more suitable vehicle in which to carry the lifting gear was justified by the exceptional end in view, namely that of saving the life of the woman; and the plaintiff's action failed.

Can a defendant be made liable for failing to take into account the possibility that another will fail to take due care for his own safety in the sense of being contributorily negligent? The courts have said that this can amount to negligence by the defendant,[537] even though it might seem that the law is thereby requiring the defendant to undertake a degree of prevention which is socially wasteful in the sense that the plaintiff was the 'least cost avoider'. One difficulty in practice, however, is that the court may have insufficient information to make such a categorical judgment about relative fault. Moreover, as far as employer's liability is concerned, the employer's superior resources, his power to direct the pace and form of the work, and his greater loss-shifting capacity, may all point in the direction of imposing on him the responsibility of ensuring that employees are, as far as possible, safeguarded against the consequences of a lack of attention or misjudgment, even if the latter could amount to contributory negligence.

2. Proof of Carelessness

In a civil action the plaintiff is required to prove his case on a balance of probabilities; in so far as proof of carelessness is concerned this means adducing facts from which the courts may make the necessary inference of a lack of care. If the defendant has been convicted of a criminal offence, that may be admitted in evidence in the civil action by virtue of the Civil Evidence Act 1968.[538] This is especially useful in road-traffic cases. Once evidence of a conviction requiring the defendant to have been negligent is admitted, the normal burden of proof is reversed and the defendant has to displace the presumption against him.

More generally the plaintiff may be able to invoke the doctrine known as *res ipsa loquitur* or 'the event speaks for itself'. This means that under certain circumstances the plaintiff may raise a presumption of negligence simply by detailing the manner in which the accident or the loss in question occurred. Negligence will be presumed where the means by which the damage was inflicted were under the defendant's sole control or where, on first sight, no explanation other than carelessness by the defendant is possible. The practical effect is that the plaintiff does not need to 'prove precisely what was the relevant act of omission which set in train the events leading to the accident'.[539]

---

[536] [1954] 1 WLR 835; see also *Daborn* v. *Bath Tramways Motor Co.* [1946] 2 All ER 333.

[537] *Grant* v. *Sun Shipping Co. Ltd.* [1948] AC 549, 567; *London Passenger Transport Board* v. *Upson* [1949] AC 155, 173.

[538] S. 11.   [539] *Lloyde* v. *West Midlands Gas Board* [1971] 1 WLR 749, 755 (Megaw LJ).

According to Lord Griffiths, speaking for the Privy Council in *Ng Chun Pui* v. *Lee Chuen Tat*,[540] this does not mean that the burden of proof is formally reversed. The plaintiff has the burden throughout of establishing his case on the balance of probabilities, and the judge must make an assessment of whether there has been a lack of due care on all the evidence presented to him. Another way of putting this is to say that the defendant does not formally have the burden of *disproving* lack of care on the balance of probabilities simply because *res ipsa loquitur* has been successfully raised against him. All *res ipsa loquitur* does is to assist the plaintiff in establishing his case[541] and to raise a prima-facie finding of lack of care against the defendant. But in practice the application of *res ipsa loquitur* may effectively settle a case where neither side can offer a convincing explanation of the event in question. Here, although the burden of proof is not reversed *as such*, the effect is not dissimilar.[542]

The classic statement of principle is that of Erle CJ in *Scott* v. *London and St Katherine Docks Co*.:[543]

There must be reasonable evidence of negligence. But where the thing is shown to be under the management of the defendant or his servants, and the accident is such as in the ordinary course of things does not happen if those who have the management use proper care, it affords reasonable evidence, in the absence of explanation by the defendants, that the accident arose from want of care.

What amounts to sole control is a question of fact in each case, but some examples may serve to illustrate the scope of the idea. Control of a motor vehicle on the part of the owner or driver is frequently inferred. If a lorry's brakes fail without warning, the owner (but not the driver) has to show that the cause was a hidden defect or some external cause.[544] Thus in *Henderson* v. *Henry E. Jenkins*[545] the defendants failed to show that the cause of the brakes corroding was not their own use of the lorry, and so they were held liable. In *Bennet* v. *Chemical Construction (GB) Ltd*.[546] the doctrine did apply when two panels being worked on by the defendant's employees fell on top of a fellow worker. They must have fallen as a result of the carelessness of those handling them. On the other hand, in *Easson* v. *London & North Eastern Railway Co*.[547] it was decided that *res ipsa loquitur* did not apply in a case where a child fell out of the offside door of an express train. The door could have flown off, but it was equally possible that a passenger could have interfered with or opened it. In *Ng Chun Pui* v. *Lee Chuen Tat*[548] the defendant's coach swerved across the central reservation of a highway and collided with a bus coming in the opposite direction. The defendant escaped liability by showing that an unidentified car had cut across in front of him, causing him to brake and skid. His reaction of braking was not negligent but an understandable response in an emergency.

---

[540] [1988] RTR 298.
[541] Hepple and Matthews, *Tort Cases and Materials* (14th edn., 1992), at 286, helpfully refer to *res ipsa loquitur* as a potential aid to the plaintiff discharging the burden of proof.
[542] A good example of this is *Ward* v. *Tesco Stores Ltd*. [1976] 1 WLR 810.
[543] (1865) 3 H. & C. 596, 601. [544] [1970] AC 282. [545] Ibid.
[546] [1971] 1 WLR 1571. [547] [1944] KB 421. [548] [1988] RTR 298.

In *Ward* v. *Tesco's Stores Ltd.*[549] a shopper slipped on a pool of liquid yoghurt lying on the floor of the defendant's store. The judges of the Court of Appeal disagreed on whether the yoghurt could only have got there as a result of the store's negligence. The only evidence of carelessness led by the plaintiff was to the effect that on another occasion a pool of orange juice had been allowed to stand on the floor for a period of a quarter of an hour. The issue was how long the yoghurt might have been there before the plaintiff slipped on it. Ormrod LJ thought it possible that 'had some customer knocked it off the shelf a few moments before, then no reasonable system which the defendants could be expected to operate would have prevented this accident'.[550] Lawton LJ, with whom Megaw LJ agreed, thought that as the floor was under the defendant's control an explanation as to how the yoghurt got there was required; and none had been forthcoming.

The defendant may rebut the prima-facie finding of fault by showing that he was not in sole control of the means of the accident. In *The Kite*[551] the plaintiff's goods were on a barge being towed by the defendants' tug. The defendants were able to show that those in charge of the barge were also responsible for its steering. Alternatively, the defendant may produce a different explanation for the events, which in no way involves their own carelessness. It is no answer that an explosion in an oxygen pipe could have been caused by the entry of particles into the pipe, if they could have got in there by virtue of the negligence of the defendant's employees.[552]

The effect of *res ipsa loquitur* is to shift the standard of care towards a form of stricter liability, and it is therefore appropriate that its main application lies in areas such as road traffic and employers' liability where a high standard of care has in any case been imposed.[553] In principle, though, it is concerned with inferences from the facts and not with the legal imposition of a stricter standard. In the area of common-law liability for defective products which cause injury or other loss to ultimate consumers, courts from *Donoghue* v. *Stevenson*[554] onwards have rejected the application of *res ipsa loquitur* and required proof of fault by the manufacturer to be established.[555] Statute, in the form of the Consumer Protection Act 1987, has now imposed a form of stricter liability for certain kinds of damage caused by defective products which in many respects is akin to a legal reversal of the burden of proof.[556]

---

[549] [1976] 1 WLR 810.   [550] Ibid.   [551] [1933] P. 154.

[552] *Colvilles Ltd.* v. *Devine* [1969] 1 WLR 475.

[553] Its application to cases of pure economic loss is likely to be highly restricted: see *Stafford* v. *Conti Commodity Services Ltd.* [1981] 1 All ER 691; Hepple and Matthews, op. cit. (n. 541 above), 288.

[554] [1932] AC 562, 622–3 (Lord Macmillan).

[555] Although *Grant* v. *Australian Knitting Mills Ltd.* [1936] AC 85 shows that the courts may be prepared to make certain inferences in the plaintiff's favour, in other cases the need to show fault has led to the rejection of the plaintiff's claim in negligence. See Chapter 6, Section 4(1)(a) below.

[556] See Chapter 6, Section 4, below.

Select Bibliography

EHRENZWEIG, A. A., 'Negligence without Fault' 54 *Cal. LR* 1422 (1966).
JAMES, F., 'Accident Liability Reconsidered: The Impact of Liability Insurance' 57 *Yale LJ* 549 (1948).
LANDES, W. M. and POSNER, R. A., *The Economic Structure of Tort Law* (1987), chs. 3, 4, and 5.
POSNER, R. A., 'A Theory of Negligence' (1972) 1 *Jo. LS* 29.
TUNC, A., 'Tort Law and the Moral Law' [1972] *CLJ* 247.

4. CAUSATION OF DAMAGE

1. The Nature of the Causal Inquiry

The defendant's carelessness must be shown to have caused the loss or damage in question. The finding of a sufficient causal link is an essential ingredient in all forms of tort liability (with the exception of torts actionable without proof of damage).[557] Most of the case law, however, has arisen in connection with the tort of negligence and it is convenient to deal with the issue generally at this point.

It has become customary in the English law of torts to analyse the question of causation in two stages.[558] The first, which is sometimes referred to as 'factual causation', 'cause in fact', or 'but-for cause', is essentially concerned with whether the defendant's fault was a necessary condition of the loss occurring. This 'but-for test' consists of posing the question: would the loss have been sustained but for the relevant act or omission of the defendant? If it would, the defendant is normally (but not always) absolved at this point. If, alternatively, the plaintiff is able to show on the balance of probabilities that he would not have suffered the harm in question, the defendant may still succeed by establishing the absence of what is called a 'legal cause'. At this second stage the courts make an assessment of whether the link between the conduct and the ensuing loss was sufficiently close. To put it differently, judges decide which of the conditions of the plaintiff's harm should also be regarded in a legal sense to be its causes. Judges ask whether a particular event 'broke the chain of causation', and use terms such as 'direct', 'proximate', 'foreseeable', or (alternatively) 'remote' to describe the relation between an act or omission and its consequences. A but-for cause which does not pass one of these tests of (legally relevant) causal proximity may be termed a 'mere condition'. It is, in other words, a factor 'without which' the loss would not have been incurred, but it is a factor to which, for one reason or another, the law attaches no causal responsibility in terms of liability in damages.

---

[557] Even here, causation will have to be established if the plaintiff is claiming to have suffered special damage.

[558] See Honoré, 'Causation and Remoteness of Damage', ch. 7 in Tunc (ed.), *Int. Encl. Comp. L.* (1983), xi., 67, referring to the similar 'bifurcation' of analysis in the American common law and in German law.

The separation of these two stages of inquiry and the use of the terms 'factual' and 'legal' cause to describe them is by no means free of controversy. One may question, for example, whether the issues, which come under the rubric of 'legal cause', really have very much to do with causation in the sense of describing the relations between particular events in time and space.[559] The courts appear to be using (or possibly misusing) the language of cause to decide (yet again) questions of policy, such as which of the parties is best placed to shift the loss in question or which outcome will best promote loss prevention in that context in the future. The issue of insurability is never far away,[560] and conceptual divisions which are familiar from other areas of the law of tort, such as the division between economic loss and other categories of damage, come into play here too.[561]

Certainly the terms used, such as 'direct' or 'proximate', have no precise scientific or logical meaning. As Professor Honoré has said, they 'are not taken literally. They do not refer to what is far or near in space or time. They are simply a short hand used to denote all those considerations, causal or other, which may make the connection between the tortfeasor and the damage legally sufficient.'[562] But this does not necessarily mean that the question of causation could or should be restricted to a basic application of the but-for test, with the rest dismissed as camouflage for policy. Professor Honoré significantly refers to considerations 'causal or other'. In their monograph *Causation and the Law*,[563] Professors Hart and Honoré have argued that, in addition to policy, important notions of personal responsibility for the consequences of one's conduct play a role in this area and that these are to be found underlying many of the judgments of courts. These 'common sense' notions of causation, which are revealed both in everyday and in legal usages of language, are to be found together with more openly policy-based perspectives. What is not acceptable, according to Hart and Honoré, is either the confusing intermingling of the one with the other or the adoption of one of a number of 'reductionist' positions which see the ordinary usages of causation concepts, and the notions of responsibility which they reflect, as largely irrelevant to the question of legal cause. Their own position has itself been criticised as underplaying the importance of policy considerations in this area;[564] but there is no doubt that their work, in addition to sparking off a continuing debate among academic writers, has influenced both directly and indirectly trends in judicial thinking in this area.

One unfortunate consequence of the customary division between 'factual' and 'legal' cause is the misleading impression that the first stage of inquiry is, by and large, a simply technical or evidentiary one, from which policy factors

---

[559] See, for a recent example, the dissenting judgment of McHugh J of the High Court of Australia in *March* v. *E. & M. H. Stamare Pty. Ltd.* (1991) 171 CLR 506, discussed by N. J. Mullany, 'Common Sense Causation—An Australian View' (1992) 12 *OJLS* 431. See also Lord Denning MR in *Lamb* v. *Camden LBC* [1981] QB 625.

[560] See the judgment of Lord Denning in *Lamb* v. *Camden LBC* [1981] QB 625.

[561] See e.g. *The Liesbosch* [1933] AC 449, discussed below at Section 3(e).

[562] 'Causation and Remoteness of Damage', (see below, Select Bibliography), 4.

[563] 1st edn. 1957; 2nd edn. 1985.

[564] For a review of the second edition of *Causation and the Law* which also examines the large critical literature which followed the publication of the first edition, see D. Howarth (1987) 96 *Yale LJ* 1389.

are absent, in contrast to an apparently more evaluative and normative second stage when policy comes to the fore.[565] That this is not the case is amply demonstrated by the numerous significant instances in which the apparent absence of 'factual cause' does not, as predicted, end up absolving the defendant. It may seem obvious that the plaintiff's action must be at least a *conditio sine qua non* of the loss, that is to say an event 'without which' the harm would not have happened. However, there are instances, most notably involving multiple tortfeasors, in which the but-for test breaks down as a guide to liability. If two defendants out hunting, acting negligently, both fire shots which strike the plaintiff in the leg, is he to be denied damages from either defendant on the grounds that his injury would have been sustained in any event by virtue of the negligence of the other? Understandably, perhaps, most courts posed a question of this kind to allow the plaintiff to recover against one or, in an appropriate case both defendants.[566] In the celebrated decision in *Baker* v. *Willoughby*,[567] a literal application of the but-for test would have left the plaintiff recovering for only part of his loss in respect of two independently tortious injuries. The House of Lords carved out an exception to the test to allow the plaintiff more complete recovery of damages. This case suggests that although the but-for test is based on notions of the limits of individual responsibility, and in particular on the precept that the defendant should not be liable for a loss which he personally did not cause, such a principle may come into conflict with the aim of ensuring that the victim of tortious conduct is fully compensated for losses caused by fault.

The courts have also had to deal with the question of the burden of proof and with whether the defendant may be liable, in the absence of conclusive proof under the but-for test, for increasing the risk of particular damage occurring. This possibility has been raised in order to reduce the considerable odds against certain plaintiffs establishing the necessary causal link in industrial-injury and medical-malpractice cases. However, in *Wilsher* v. *Essex Area Health Authority*[568] the House of Lords reaffirmed the strict requirements of the but-for test, while in *Hotson* v. *East Berkshire Health Authority*[569] it cast doubt on the idea that the plaintiff can recover for the diminished prospects or 'loss of a chance' of avoiding harm. Courts in other parts of the common-law world have taken a more flexible view of these questions, albeit with controversial results.[570] Although these decisions make it clear that difficult policy questions are involved in the but-for test, the formal division between 'factual' and 'legal' cause is too well established (and perhaps too convenient from a doctrinal point of view) to be abandoned. However, some confusion might be avoided if the phrase 'but-for cause' were used in preference to 'factual cause' or 'cause in fact', and that will be the approach taken in this book.

---

[565] For refinement of this division see Malone, 'Ruminations on Cause-in-Fact' (1956) 9 *Stan. LR* 60; and see generally Wright, 'Causation in Tort Law' (1985) 73 *Cal. LR* 1735.

[566] This hypothetical case is discussed below, Section 2(c).

[567] [1970] AC 467; see below, Section 2(d).   [568] [1988] AC 1074.   [569] [1989] AC 750.

[570] These are discussed by Professor J. G. Fleming, 'Probabilistic Causation in Tort Law' (1989) 68 *Can. BR* 661.

In *The Wagon Mound* (No. 1)[571] the Privy Council stressed the importance of reasonable foreseeability as opposed to 'directness' as a basis for determining 'remoteness' of damage. This test of legal cause is applicable both to the 'threshold' situation in which the court is trying to establish whether the defendant is liable at all, and in the situation in which it is concerned with establishing the *extent* of liability of one who has caused tortious damage. The test of reasonable foreseeability, like that of but-for cause, is plainly based on the courts' perception that an individual should not be made liable in tort for damage beyond the scope of his personal responsibility. Thus, if damage ensues in an unexpected or unusual way, it may be that the 'chain of causation' has been broken, absolving the defendant from liability for damage occurring after that point.

Since the judgment in *The Wagon Mound* (No. 1), it has become increasingly clear that the test of foreseeability of damage is no more *conclusive* in regard to causation than it is as a test for duty and breach, and that numerous other considerations will come into play, in particular where physical damage, as opposed to economic loss, is the basis of the claim.[572] As far as extent is concerned, *The Wagon Mound* (No. 1) itself established that once the *kind* of damage in question can be seen to have been reasonably foreseeable, its *extent* is then irrelevant: the defendant is liable even though all the consequences could not have been predicted. In this way English law, in common with other systems, favours the plaintiff as against a defendant who is responsible for causing tortious damage of some kind. Once the initial threshold of liability is passed, unless the ensuing damage is of a different 'kind', the risk of greater than expected damage occurring, or of damage occurring in an unexpected way, lies on the defendant.[573] In English law there has been an active debate over what precisely is meant by 'kind of damage' in the context of the rule in *The Wagon Mound* (No. 1). This has largely been resolved in favour of a liberal interpretation, which favours plaintiffs in cases of physical injury or disease, and a more restrictive test for property damage and economic loss.

Notwithstanding the importance of notions of personal responsibility, it is impossible to give an account of this area without returning over and over again to certain central issues of policy which are to be found throughout the tort of negligence and which affect other torts involving damage. These include the search for an economically efficient framework of liability and, in conjunction or sometimes in competition with this, for a system of loss shifting and loss spreading which reflects social values and concerns about the allocation of risks and responsibilities. In a doctrinal sense, it is impossible to write about causation without acknowledging that inherent in the law's account of causation is also a view of what constitutes *fault*.[574] This is clearly so, for example, when the court is considering making an apportionment of legal responsibility

---

[571] [1961] AC 388.

[572] See the judgment of Watkins LJ in *Lamb* v. *Camden LBC* [1982] QB 625; and see below, Section 3(a).

[573] See, in particular, *Hughes* v. *Lord Advocate* [1963] AC 837 and *Smith* v. *Leech, Brain & Co. Ltd.* [1962] 2 QB 405, discussed below.

[574] The converse is true, as David Howarth points out: Book Review, (1987) 96 *Yale LJ* 1389, 1419–20.

between plaintiff and defendant, as in the case of contributory negligence under the Law Reform (Contributory Negligence Act) 1945. More controversially, the same is true of 'loss of a chance' cases such as *Hotson* v. *East Berkshire Area Health Authority*[575] and of cases of probabilistic cause such as *Wilsher* v. *Essex Area Health Authority*.[576] Similarly, in deciding, as in *Smith* v. *Leech, Brain & Co. Ltd.*,[577] that an employer who has negligently put his employees' safety at risk should be liable for the unforeseeable consequence in terms of a life-threatening disease which results in the case of one particular employee whose vulnerability is greater than that of his fellow workers, the court is evidently making a policy judgment based on the importance of the plaintiff's interest and upon the employer's superior capacity to control and minimise the risk in question.

2. But-For Cause

Under the but-for test the plaintiff must prove the existence of a causal link on the balance of probabilities, which is taken to mean a likelihood of more than 50 per cent. If the court finds that it was as likely as not that the injury would have occurred without the defendant's negligence, the action will fail even if there is an admission of carelessness. An illustration of this is *Barnett* v. *Chelsea and Kensington Hospital*.[578] The action was brought by the estate of the plaintiff, who died after doctors at the hospital negligently failed to diagnose that he was suffering from arsenic poisoning. The court held that even with a correct diagnosis the plaintiff's condition was too far advanced for the hospital to have saved him. A gloss on the but-for test was made in *Bolitho* v. *City and Hackney Health Authority*,[579] namely that '[a] defendant cannot escape liability by saying that the damage would have occurred in any event because he would have committed some other breach of duty thereafter'.[580] This is simply saying that the court will seek to establish, as best it can, what would have happened but for negligence *both actual and hypothetical* of the defendant.

(A) Probabilistic Cause: Questions of Risk and Proof

Difficulties arise where there are several alternative explanations of the events leading up to the damage, some innocent and some traceable to the defendant's fault. In *McGhee* v. *National Coal Board*[581] the plaintiff contracted dermatitis after working in a kiln. The immediate cause of the dermatitis was brick dust with which he came into contact while at work. The defendants were not at fault through exposing him to the dust; this was an inevitable feature of the work he was employed to do. However, they were in breach of their common-law duty of care in failing to provide washing facilities at the place of work. The question facing the court was whether the plaintiff had shown that his condition was caused by the absence of washing facilities. Medical evidence could not clearly establish that he would not have contracted it anyway, as a result of the exposure to the dust during working hours. The House of Lords neverthe-

---

[575] [1987] AC 750. [576] [1988] AC 1074. [577] [1962] 2 QB 405, discussed below, Section 3(c).
[578] [1969] 1 QB 428; see also *McWilliams* v. *Sir William Arroll & Co. Ltd.* [1962] 1 WLR 295.
[579] [1998] AC 232. [580] [1998] AC 232, 240 (Lord Browne-Wilkinson).
[581] [1973] 1 WLR 1; E. Weinrib, 'A Step Forward in Factual Causation' (1975) 38 *MLR* 518.

less allowed his appeal from decisions of the lower courts in favour of the defendant. The judgment of Lord Wilberforce appears to accept the possibility that in the absence of conclusive proof of a link between fault and damage, liability may be imposed upon a defendant whose negligence increases the risk of a particular loss occurring, if that risk is subsequently realised. 'It is a sound principle', he said, 'that where a person has, by breach of duty of care, created a risk, and injury occurs within the area of that risk, the loss should be borne by him unless he shows that it had some other cause.'[582] This could be said to shift the burden of proof on to the defendant. The basis for doing so is the inherent difficulty facing the plaintiff in a case where medical opinion cannot establish definitively that the damage is attributable to one potential cause of harm rather than another. In these circumstances 'if one asks which of the parties, the workman or the employers, should suffer from this inherent evidential difficulty, the answer as a matter of policy or justice should be that it is the creator of the risk who, *ex-hypothesi*, must be taken to have foreseen the possibility of damage, who should bear its consequences'.[583]

The superior resources of the defendant in this case and the high standard of care imposed on employers in relation to their employees may help to explain why liability might be shifted in this way. Another, more general rationale for reversing the burden of proof is that the defendant's admitted fault may be the very reason the plaintiff cannot prove his case on the balance of probabilities.[584] But in either case, the defendant is being made liable for damage, which it cannot be proved he personally caused.[585] The mere fact that he was at fault in the sense of breaching a duty of care is not a good reason for imposing liability. To do so may be to impose a powerful incentive for careful behaviour on the part of defendants. But this runs up against the objection that it is not the role of the tort of negligence to penalise careless behaviour *as such*. If this is seen as desirable, there may be an argument for leaving it to Parliament to achieve through statutory regulation of the kind which is widespread in relation to employer's liability.[586]

In the more recent decision of *Wilsher* v. *Essex Area Health Authority*[587] the House of Lords rejected the approach set out by Lord Wilberforce, while leaving intact the authority of *McGhee* and explaining it as a case in which there was sufficient evidence to make the necessary inference of a causal link between fault and damage. In *Wilsher* the plaintiff, who was born three months prematurely, suffered blindness in one eye and near-blindness in the other as a result of a condition known as retrolental fibroplasia. He claimed that this was caused by the carelessness of a hospital doctor who failed to notice that a device for measuring the dosage of oxygen to the blood had been wrongly attached to a vein

---

[582] [1973] 1 WLR 1.

[583] Ibid., 6. In *McGhee* Lord Wilberforce relied on the earlier House of Lords' judgment in *Bonnington Castings Ltd.* v. *Wardlaw* [1956] AC 613, but there are difficulties with this since *Wardlaw*'s case was one of possible cumulative causes, one tortious and one not, whereas the two possible causative factors in *McGhee* were apparently alternative: see Stapleton, 'The Gist of Negligence. Part II' (1988) 104 *LQR* 389, 402.

[584] See Fleming, op. cit. (1989) 68 *Can. BR* 668, 671, discussing the use of this idea in German law.

[585] See Stapleton, 'The Gist of Negligence. Part II' (1988) 104 *LQR* 389, 404.

[586] See generally Chapter 6, Section 3, below.   [587] [1988] AC 1074.

and not, as it should have been, to an artery. As a result the plaintiff had received an excessive dose. Medical evidence established no fewer than six separate potential causes of the plaintiff's blindness, all of which, with the exception of the excessive dose of oxygen, were inherent in his condition as a premature birth. The House of Lords, reversing the Court of Appeal, held that causation had not been adequately established: 'a failure to take preventive measures against one out of five possible causes is not evidence as to which of those five caused the injury.'[588]

In the Court of Appeal in *Wilsher*[589] Mustill LJ had taken the following view of *McGhee*:

> If it is an established fact that conduct of a particular kind creates a risk that injury will ensue; and if two parties stand in such a relationship that the one party owes a duty not to conduct himself in that way; and if the first party does conduct himself in that way; and if the other party does suffer injury of the kind to which the risk related; then the first party is taken to have caused the injury by his breach of duty, even though the existence and extent of the contribution made by the breach cannot be ascertained.

According to Lord Bridge, however, this was a misreading of *McGhee*, the correct rule is that the onus of proof rests on the plaintiff throughout:[590]

> The conclusion I draw is that *McGhee* laid down no new principle of law whatever. On the contrary, it affirmed the principle that the onus of proving causation lies on the pursuer or plaintiff. Adopting a robust and pragmatic approach to undisputed primary facts of the case, the majority concluded that it was a legitimate inference of fact that the defender's negligence had materially contributed to the pursuer's injury. The decision, in my opinion, is of no greater significance than that, and to attempt to draw from it some esoteric principle which in some way modifies, as a matter of law, the nature of the burden of proof of causation, which a plaintiff or pursuer must discharge once he has established a relevant breach of duty is a fruitless one.

If the 'risk principle' enunciated by Lord Wilberforce is clearly rejected, this none the less still leaves open the possibility that a court might take a flexible approach to making the necessary inferences of causation from the evidence. The need to establish a likelihood of greater than 51 per cent has an air of arbitrariness about it. The difference between a likelihood of 50 per cent and one of 75 per cent is ultimately a matter of impression,[591] although it is given an air of scientific precision by the fact that such figures are frequently used by expert witnesses in medical-malpractice and occupational health and safety cases. This has led courts in some jurisdictions to adopt an approach based on 'probabilistic cause'. Statistical evidence based on regression analyses and similar techniques may be led concerning the extent of the defendant's causal contribution to the plaintiff's injury. Evidence of this kind does not conform to the normal requirements of 'particularistic evidence' based on the direct observations of

---

[588] [1987] QB 739, 779 (Sir Nicolas Browne-Wilkinson VC, approved by Lord Bridge at [1988] AC 1074, 1091).

[589] [1987] QB 730, 771–2.   [590] [1988] AC 1074, 1090.

[591] Professor Fleming writes: 'There is no pretence that such a scale is a useful guide', (1989) 68 *Can. BR* 661, 662, and cites hostile judicial comment: *Briginshaw* v. *Briginshaw* (1938) 60 CLR 336, 361 (High Court of Australia). See also the discussion of *McGhee* in *Page* v. *Smith (No. 2)* [1996] 1 WLR 855.

witnesses. However, this may be the only means by which tort liability can be established in cases involving diseases whose origin and precise mode of operation is difficult to identify but which are frequently linked to working conditions, such as asbestosis, or in medical cases where the processes of care are often of a highly technical and specific kind. It might, alternatively, be preferable to search for a solution outside tort law altogether, based on social insurance for certain accidents and diseases, on the basis that the conceptual difficulties facing tort plaintiffs are too great for a reliable and equitable solution to be found.[592]

In *Snell* v. *Farrell*[593] the Supreme Court of Canada chose the same route as the House of Lords in rejecting the interpretation of *McGhee*, which would have formally reversed the burden of proof. However, Sopinka J went on to argue that the normal principles of causation would be sufficient to enable proof on the balance of probabilities to be inferred even where medical opinion was not conclusive. Thus, 'the legal or ultimate burden remains with the plaintiff, but in the absence of evidence to the contrary adduced by the defendant, an inference of causation may be drawn, although positive or scientific evidence of causation has not been adduced.'[594] In this case the plaintiff was blinded in one eye during the course of an operation which was carried out negligently by the defendant. There was a chance that blindness could have resulted however much care was taken. As in *McGhee* the medical evidence was equivocal rather than, as in *Wilsher*, sharply divided, and the Supreme Court decided that there was sufficient evidence to find for the plaintiff. *Snell* v. *Farrell* indicates that the question of causation is ultimately one for the court to determine on its own assessment of the medical evidence, intuitive as this may be. In *Wilsher* Lord Bridge explained *McGhee* as a case in which it was possible to make the necessary inference 'as a matter of common sense'.[595] In practice much will depend on how the medical evidence is presented to the court and to the weight it feels able to give to differing accounts. Commenting on *Snell* v. *Farrell*, Professor Fleming has suggested that Sopinka J's formulation of the question is not 'free from the vice of uncertainty. It sanctions a benign "interference" at least in medical malpractice cases in order to compensate the parties' inequality in access to evidence, in effect (as virtually admitted by the judge) not much different from frank reversal of the burden of proof.'[596]

(B) LOSS OF A CHANCE

The approach in *McGhee* v. *National Coal Board*[597] risks imposing liability for the full extent of the loss on a defendant who cannot be shown to have been personally responsible for the damage under normal principles of causation. An alternative is to hold the defendant liable only for a portion of the loss, based upon the extent of his responsibility for it. The issue arises above all in

---

[592] See generally for discussion of these and related issues, J. Stapleton, *Disease and the Compensation Debate* (1986).

[593] (1990) 72 DLR (4th) 289. [594] Ibid., 301. [595] [1988] AC 1074, 1088.

[596] 'Probabilistic Causation in Tort Law: A Postscript' (1991) 70 *Can. BR* 137, 139.

[597] [1973] 1 WLR 1.

medical malpractice cases where the defendant fails, through negligence, to improve a pre-existing condition of the plaintiff. If losing a less-than 50 per cent chance of recovery is recognised as a form of legal damage in its own right, the plaintiff can recover compensation for this 'loss of a chance'. Causation is established on the balance of probabilities for the loss of the chance even if not for the injury, which the plaintiff actually sustained. The result is similar to the *McGhee* principle in enabling a plaintiff to overcome the formidable difficulties of proof in medical-malpractice and industrial-injury cases, but it differs in offering an alternative to the 'all or nothing' solution of holding the defendant either liable in full or not at all.

The issue came before the English courts in *Hotson* v. *East Berkshire AHA*.[598] The plaintiff, a boy of thirteen, was injured when he fell out of a tree. He was taken to the defendant's hospital, where medical staff failed to make a correct diagnosis of his condition. He was sent home and returned only five days later, in some considerable pain, when a correct diagnosis was made and an operation carried out. The plaintiff was left with necrosis of the hip joint. Medical evidence established that even if the hospital had correctly diagnosed his condition on the first occasion and treated it promptly, there was still a 75 per cent likelihood that the plaintiff would have gone on to develop the necrosis. Another way of putting this is to say that for every one hundred patients admitted in this condition, twenty-five could be expected to make a full recovery. The plaintiff's claim was that he might have been one of these twenty-five, but that the opportunity of recovery was denied him by the defendant's carelessness.

The House of Lords decided for the defendant on the apparently straightforward ground that causation had not been established on the balance of probabilities. Lord Ackner stressed that this 'was a relatively simple case concerned with the proof of causation, on which the plaintiff failed, because he was unable to prove, on the balance of probabilities, that his deformed hip was caused by the authority's breach of duty in delaying over a period of five days a proper diagnosis and treatment'.[599] In the view of Lord Bridge: 'Unless the plaintiff proved on a balance of probabilities that the delayed treatment was at least a material contributory cause of the avascular necrosis he failed on the issue of causation and no question of quantification could arise.'[600]

In taking this line the House of Lords more or less ducked the question of whether the loss of a chance is an appropriate subject-matter for recovery in its own right. Only Lord Mackay gave the question prolonged consideration, and he declined to 'lay it down as a rule that a plaintiff could never succeed by proving loss of a chance in a negligence action'.[601] The tenor of his judgment was, however, against allowing this type of recovery as a matter of course. Lords Bridge and Ackner, by denying that any issue other than causation was involved, would effectively deny any role to loss of a chance of recovery in this context.[602]

The trial judge in *Hotson* argued that in awarding a sum based upon the extent of the injury discounted by the chance that it would have occurred any-

---

[598] [1987] AC 750.   [599] [1987] AC 750, 793.   [600] Ibid., 782.   [601] Ibid. 786.
[602] The other two Law Lords agreed with all three judgments.

way, he was merely following established practice in the quantification of damages. In particular, when the court awards damages for personal injury it reduces the sum representing future loss of earnings by a figure meant to represent the chance or contingency that the plaintiff's working life might have been foreshortened by some other event, for which the defendant cannot be held responsible. There is thus a standard reduction for 'normal vicissitudes' of life and a greater reduction will be made if there is a higher-than-normal chance that the plaintiff would not have carried on working until the standard retirement age.[603] Thus:

in the end the problem comes down to one of classification. Is this on true analysis a case where a plaintiff is concerned to establish causative negligence or is it rather a case where the real question is the proper quantum of damage? Clearly the case hovers near the border. Its proper solution in my judgment depends on categorising it correctly between the two. If the issue is one of causation then the health authority succeeds since the plaintiff will have failed to prove his claim on the balance of probabilities. He will be lacking an essential ingredient of his cause of action. If however, the issue is one of quantification, then the plaintiff succeeds because it is trite law that the quantum of a recognised head of damage must be evaluated according to the chances of the loss occurring.[604]

This argument from quantification can be dealt with, however, by pointing out that when calculating the quantum of damages, the court has already established causation on the balance of probabilities, and is now making the best assessment it can of the present value of the plaintiff's future losses flowing from his injury. It has to make a guess as to what might have happened in the absence of injury, since there is no alternative way of proceeding. But how the court approaches the issue of quantification of damages for the loss of a limb, for example, has no necessary bearing upon the separate question of whether the plaintiff can recover at all for the loss of a chance of keeping that limb. This was the essence of Lord Bridge's judgment in *Hotson*.[605]

A more radical argument, however, is that the strict balance-of-probabilities test is itself inappropriate in a case where the court has to make an estimate of the effect of alternative hypothetical causes. The court has to make a guess, which may be more or less accurate. Under these circumstances the difference between 51 per cent and 49 per cent will be somewhat arbitrary, and the consequences of treating a 51 per cent likelihood as a certainty will be more arbitrary still. This appealed to the High Court of Australia in *Malec* v. *J. C. Hutton Pty. Ltd.*,[606] but was effectively brushed aside by the House of Lords in *Hotson*.

Another argument is that the courts have in some instances awarded compensation for lost expectations of financial gain, even though the plaintiff could only show that he had a chance of making such a gain. In *Kitchen* v. *Royal Air Forces Association*,[607] for example, damages were awarded against a solicitor based on the lost chance of bringing a civil action for damages. Again, in *Allied Maples Group Ltd.* v. *Simmons & Simmons*[608] the plaintiffs won damages against

---

[603] See below, Chapter 8, Section 2(6)(b).   [604] Per Simon Brown J, [1985] 1 WLR 1036, 1044.
[605] [1989] AC 750.   [606] (1990) 64 ALJR 316; discussed further in the following subsection.
[607] [1958] 2 All ER 241; *Chaplin* v. *Hicks* [1911] 2 KB 786.   [608] [1995] 1 WLR 1602.

their solicitors for the loss of an opportunity to bargain over the allocation of rights and liabilities under a lease. These and similar cases do not establish that loss of a chance of *physical recovery* is a form of compensatable damage in its own right; but they do indicate that the courts are capable of providing compensation for a variety of different forms of loss.

The principal argument for loss-of-chance recovery is that the plaintiff has been deprived of something tangible. Prior to the defendant's breach of duty, the plaintiff had a real, if indeterminate, *prospect* of recovery. Professor Joseph King has argued that, 'but for the defendant's tortious conduct, it would not have been necessary to grapple with the imponderables of chance. Fate would have run its course.'[609] Another way of putting it is to say that 'when a defendant's negligent action or inaction has effectively terminated a person's chance of survival, it does not lie in the defendant's mouth to raise conjectures as to the measure of the chances that he has put beyond the possibility of realisation. If there was any substantial possibility of survival and the defendant has destroyed it, he is answerable.'[610] This view, expressed in an *obiter dictum* by the US 4th Circuit Court of Appeals, has been followed in a line of cases allowing lost-chance recovery. However, such recovery has been rejected in a majority of American jurisdictions.[611] The issue has given rise to a lively debate, with opponents arguing that departures from the traditional causation rule 'adversely impact the cost and quality of health care and exacerbate the problems of defensive medicine and cost containment'.[612] A more specific concern is that lost-chance recovery will lead to a multiplicity of new claims, giving rise to fresh evidential difficulties and complicating the relationship between different heads of damage. This version of the familiar 'floodgates' argument appears to have influenced Lord Mackay in *Hotson*.[613] Given the current unwillingness of the House of Lords to countenance the extension of negligence into novel areas of liability, it seems unlikely that the English courts will adopt the theory of lost-chance recovery at any stage in the near future. This is so even though its decision in *Wilsher* v. *Essex Area Health Authority*,[614] rejecting an approach based on probabilistic cause, constitutes a compelling case for them doing so.[615]

(C) MULTIPLE DEFENDANTS: INDETERMINATE AND CUMULATIVE CAUSES

So far we have been considering situations in which the defendant's fault is competing with one or more 'innocent' explanations of the plaintiff's injury. More problematic are cases in which there is no 'innocent' explanation for the injury; the plaintiff's injury could only have occurred through the fault of one

---

[609] 'Causation, Valuation, and Chance in Personal Injury Torts Involving Pre-existing Conditions and Future Consequences' (1981) 90 *Yale LJ* 1353, 1378.

[610] *Hicks* v. *US* 368 F. 2d 626, 632 (4th Circuit Court of Appeals).

[611] For a comprehensive review, see L. Perrochet, S. Smith, and U. Colella, 'Lost Chance Recovery and the Folly of Expanding Medical Malpractice Liability' (1992) 27 *Tort and Insurance Law Journal* 615.

[612] Ibid., 628.

[613] [1987] AC 750, citing doubts expressed in the Supreme Court of Washington in *Herskovitz* v. *Group Health Co-operative of Puget Sound* (1983) 664 P.2d 474 (Brachtenbach J, dissenting).

[614] [1988] AC 1074.   [615] See Stapleton, op. cit. (1988) 104 *LQR* 389, 407.

or more of a number of defendants. In these cases, the strict application of the but-for test has been modified to avoid a result which under-compensates the plaintiff.

A first situation to consider is that in which the plaintiff's injury could only have been caused by the fault of one out of several careless defendants, in circumstances where the individual in question cannot be identified: this may be called the case of 'indeterminate cause'. The best illustration is provided by two similar cases decided in the United States and Canada respectively, *Summers* v. *Tice*[616] and *Cook* v. *Lewis*.[617] In each case the plaintiff was shot by one bullet which was fired by one of two defendants out hunting, each of whom had been careless in aiming his gun in the plaintiff's direction. There was no means of telling from whose gun the shot was fired. The courts adopted the solution of reversing the burden of proof, so that each defendant had to show that he did not cause the injury. In the absence of such proof, both defendants were held liable. Joint tortfeasors are held liable *in solidum*, that is to say each one is potentially responsible for the full amount of the loss. A defendant held liable to the full extent might then seek contribution from the other; but that is a separate matter. The result seems just since it enables the plaintiff to receive full compensation and shifts his loss to the two defendants jointly, but it cannot be reconciled with a strict application of the balance-of-probabilities test. It is likely, notwithstanding *Wilsher* v. *Essex Area Health Authority*,[618] that an English court would take a similar line.

The Supreme Court of California in *Sindell* v. *Abbott Laboratories* adopted a more radical departure from the traditional analysis.[619] The case concerned the liability of manufacturers of a defective pregnancy drug, which induced a cancerous condition in the female children of the mothers taking it. This condition did not appear until the children reached puberty and it was impossible to show which of several hundred manufacturers had produced the particular drug taken by the plaintiffs' mothers. It was known, however, that the defect was inherent in the design of the drug, so that any one of the manufacturers could have been responsible. The court rejected the solution of imposing joint and several liability as in *Summers* v. *Tice*,[620] partly because only a few of the potential defendants were before the court and it was considered unfair to make those who were present responsible to the full extent. Instead, the court held each defendant liable according to the degree of its share of the market for the drug at the relevant time, on the basis that this was the best approximation the court could make of their likely responsibility. Of the many objections to *Sindell*, Professor Fleming suggests, 'by far the most formidable is that it departs from the prior art not merely by lacking all precedent but by being incompatible with the traditional notion of tort as a system of individual responsibility. This was not corrective but distributive justice.'[621] Nor can the economic argument for imposing such liability, on the ground that it increases incentives to take care, be easily justified here. Such a goal is most likely better achieved through general regulation, and only the absence of effective regulation could

---

[616] (1948) 119 P.2d 1.   [617] [1951] SCR 830.   [618] [1988] AC 1074.
[619] 607 P.2d 924 (1980).   [620] (1948) 119 P.2d 924.   [621] Op. cit. (1989) 68 *Can. BR* 661, 668.

justify a common-law court engaging in such a far-reaching form of loss-shifting.

The second type of situation which is relevant here is that in which the plaintiff's loss was caused by cumulative causes attributable to the separate carelessness of multiple defendants. To vary slightly the facts of *Summers* v. *Tice*,[622] this concerns the case which arises when the plaintiff is struck by two bullets, fired by each of the two defendants. If his injuries would have resulted from one bullet only, each defendant is entitled to say that 'but for' his own personal carelessness, the plaintiff would still have sustained his loss. This result would leave the plaintiff 'falling between two stools', and it is therefore likely that were this case to come before an English court it would find the defendants jointly liable, perhaps varying the damages payable by each according to their degree of responsibility.

This is analogous to what happened in *Fitzgerald* v. *Lane*.[623] The plaintiff walked onto a pelican crossing without looking and was struck by a car driven by the first defendant, thrown into the air, and struck again by a car being driven in the opposite direction by the second defendant. Each of the two drivers was driving too quickly and was held to have been in breach of the duty of care they owed to the plaintiff. The plaintiff sustained tetraplegia as a result of the accident, but it could not be established that the second collision contributed to his injury. The second defendant claimed that the first impact alone would have been sufficient, on the balance of probabilities. The Court of Appeal held both of them liable and made an award of damages based on an assessment that they were equally to blame with the plaintiff for the accident. The basis for finding them both liable was the principle, enunciated by Lord Wilberforce in *McGhee* v. *National Coal Board*,[624] namely that each one had materially increased the risk of such injury by his negligence and should, as a consequence, have the burden of disproving a causal link. An appeal was heard in the House of Lords on the question of apportionment only. As the House of Lords later overruled, in *Wilsher* v. *Essex Area Health Authority*,[625] the 'risk principle' on which the Court of Appeal relied in *Fitzgerald*, there might now be a question-mark against the initial finding of liability.

There is, however, a significant difference between *Wilsher* and *Fitzgerald*, namely that in *Wilsher* there was a potentially innocent explanation of the plaintiff's injury. In *Fitzgerald* the collision could only have occurred through the fault of one or both of the defendants. If thus one were to apply the but-for test, this would leave the plaintiff uncompensated for a significant proportion of the damage, which he would not have suffered but for tortious conduct on the part of *someone*. It seems necessary, therefore, to make an exception here to the but-for test, similar to that in *Summers* v. *Tice*.[626]

---

[622] (1948) 119 P.2d 1.
[623] [1987] QB 781; affirmed on different grounds [1989] AC 328. See the similar US case of *Maddux* v. *Donaldson* (1961) 108 NW2d 33, discussed in the 'American Perspective', below.
[624] [1973] 1 WLR 1.   [625] [1988] AC 1074.   [626] (1948) 119 P.2d 1.

(D) SUPERVENING OR OVERTAKING CAUSES

Into this category fall cases in which the causal effect of the defendant's fault is nullified by a later event or by the emergence of a latent condition. In each case the overtaking cause is unrelated to the initial tort. In *Baker* v. *Willoughby*[627] the plaintiff's leg, which was injured in a car accident caused by the negligence of the defendant, was later amputated after a separate and unrelated incident in which he was shot by robbers at the scrap-metal merchants where he worked. The House of Lords held that the defendant was liable for the full consequences of the injury *he* caused regardless of the second incident; he therefore had to pay damages based on the plaintiff's losses *beyond* the point at which the leg was amputated. The causal effect of the accident therefore continued notwithstanding the fact that the use of the leg would have been lost anyway as a result of the amputation. In *Jobling* v. *Associated Dairies*,[628] by contrast, the House of Lords reached what appears at first sight to be a contradictory result. Here, the plaintiff's back was injured as a result of his employer's negligence, but before the trial of the action it became clear that the plaintiff was suffering, quite independently, from a back complaint which would have curtailed his working life in any event. The defendant was held liable for pain and suffering and loss of earnings only up to the time at which the effects of the second cause, the disease, would effectively overtake those of the first, the injury.

Baker v. *Willoughby*[629] has to be seen as an exception to the normal application of the but-for rule, justified by the principle of fully compensating the plaintiff for damage tortiously inflicted. Had the two events—the car accident and the shooting—been related, as they might have been, for example, if the plaintiff's initial incapacity had prevented him from getting away from the robbers, the first defendant (as he may be called for convenience) could have been held responsible for the cumulative consequences of both injuries. As it was, the second injury arose from a wholly unrelated sequence of events. Under these circumstances, it was open to the first defendant to argue that his liability should be confined to the plaintiff's losses up to the point at which the leg was shot. If the court, when applying the but-for test, is required to take into account the possibility that the plaintiff's loss would have occurred regardless of the defendant's fault, then it must also be required to take into account events which have actually taken place before the trial of the action. As Lord Pearson put it, 'the present state of disablement, with the stump and the artificial leg on the left side, was caused wholly by the supervening event and not at all by the original accident. Thus the consequences of the original accident have been submerged and obliterated by the greater consequences of the supervening event.'[630]

This solution would, however, have left the plaintiff significantly undercompensated. If a claim had been made against the robbers as second defendants it would only have covered the *additional* damage they caused, that is to say, the extra loss of facility and the additional lost earnings over and above

---

[627] [1970] AC 467.   [628] [1982] AC 794.   [629] [1970] AC 467, 495.   [630] Ibid.

those caused by the first defendant. The same would have been true of any claim made by the plaintiff before the Criminal Injuries Compensation Board.[631] This point is illustrated by *Performance Cars Ltd.* v. *Abraham*.[632] If a car, which has already been involved in a collision with one defendant and requires a repaint, is involved in a further collision with a second defendant, the second defendant can only be held liable for any additional damage which he has caused. He has damaged a car which is already damaged. The same principle applies to personal injuries: the defendant takes the plaintiff as he finds him, and cannot be liable for greater losses than he has inflicted. If, then, the liability of the first defendant, in *Baker* v. *Willoughby*,[633] had been limited to the period prior to the shooting, a part of the plaintiff's loss—the continuing effect of the initial incapacity—would have remained uncompensated. He would have 'fallen between two defendants'. Because of this 'manifest injustice', there can be no room for the application of the but-for rule in this case. But this is no more than saying that where the initial and supervening causes are both tortious, the but-for test is inapplicable, for the same reasons as it breaks down in *Summers* v. *Tice*[634] and *Fitzgerald* v. *Lane*,[635] where multiple tortfeasors are involved.

Lord Reid offered two different explanations. The first was that the second injury did not diminish any of the consequences, in terms of the loss of facility, of the first one: 'so why should it be regarded as having obliterated or superseded them?' Lord Reid's second argument explained the plaintiff's disability 'as having two causes'.[636] These arguments, however, fail to do justice to the basic point of the but-for test, namely that since the plaintiff lost his leg anyway through an event unconnected with the first accident, the first defendant cannot be held responsible for what happened after that point in time. Nor were the two events concurrent causes of the plaintiff's total disability: the first tort had nothing to do with the complete loss of the leg. In *Jobling* v. *Associated Dairies*[637] Lord Wilberforce suggested that Lord Reid's reasoning was unsustainable, and that Lord Pearson's explanation of the outcome was to be preferred.

Jobling's case was decided on a strict application of the but-for test. Since the plaintiff would have lost the use of his back regardless of the defendant's fault, the latter could only be held responsible for the consequences up to the point when the underlying condition would have made itself felt independently of that fault. Again, it would have been different if the employer's lack of care had triggered or accelerated the underlying back-complaint; but this was not the case. In the words of Lord Bridge,

When the supervening illness or injury, which is the independent cause of the loss of earning capacity, has manifested itself before trial, the event has demonstrated that, even if the plaintiff had never sustained the tortious injury, his earnings would now be reduced or extinguished. To hold the tortfeasor, in this situation, liable to pay damages for a notional continuing loss of earnings attributable to the tortious injury is to put the

---

[631] See McKendrick, *Tort Textbook* (1991 edn.), 94.   [632] [1961] 1 QB 33.   [633] [1970] AC at 467.
[634] (1948) 119 P.2d 1.   [635] [1987] QB 781.   [636] [1970] AC 467, 492.
[637] [1982] AC 794.

plaintiff in a better position than he would be in if he had never suffered the tortious injury.[638]

It is also important to distinguish *Jobling* from *Performance Cars* v. *Abraham*[639] (or, more precisely, from its equivalent in terms of personal injury). *Jobling* was not a case in which the plaintiff was suffering from a *pre-existing* condition or disease; the condition from which the disease sprang was dormant at the time of the injury and the disease did not begin to take effect until after the injury took place. Had the plaintiff's disease already begun to take effect when the injury took place, *Jobling* would not have given rise to the arguments, which it in fact presented. As Lord Wilberforce put it, it was found that 'the myelopathy was not a condition existing, but dormant, at the date of the original injury; it was a disease supervening after that event. If it has been dormant but existing it is not disputed that it would have had to be taken into account in the actual condition found to exist at the trial. But the appellant submits that a different result follows if the origination of the disease takes place after the accident . . .'[640]

Jobling may usefully be compared, in this context, with the American decision of *Dillon* v. *Twin State Gas and Electric Co.*[641] In this case the deceased, a young boy, fell from a bridge and was electrocuted by wires left negligently positioned by the defendant when he was only seconds from hitting the ground. Damages were based on the deceased's limited life expectancy of no more than a few seconds. Here, the threat to the boy was sufficiently serious at the time of the accident for the court to treat it as analogous to a pre-existing medical condition, which was going to lead to loss of life in any event. Similarly, in *Cutler* v. *Vauxhall Motors Ltd.*[642] the plaintiff, who had varicose veins, won damages when he suffered a graze as a result of the defendant's negligence and had to undergo an operation to treat the veins, as a result of which he suffered further complications. But the court reduced his award on the basis that he would have had to undergo this operation in any event at some point in the future.

In *Jobling*, the condition was not pre-existing as such, but there was compelling reasons to treat it as if it were. The outcome, however, might seem unfair to the plaintiff when his position is compared to that of a similar victim of an occupational disease, whose underlying condition does not manifest itself until after the trial. His damages cannot be reduced in the light of later events, although in assessing them in the first place the court will have taken into account the need to make a discount for future contingencies. The answer to this is that the court has to take into account what it knows at the date of the trial, and that as far as the plaintiff whose condition emerges later is concerned, it would be costly and inconvenient to have a rule which permitted the court to re-open damages awards. As Lord Keith of Kinkel put it, 'the court will not speculate when it knows, so that when an event within its scope has

---

[638] Ibid., 820.   [639] [1962] 1 QB 33.   [640] [1982] AC 794, 802.
[641] (1932) 163 A.2d 111; R. Peaslee, 'Multiple Causation and Damage' (1934) 47 *Harv. LR* 1127.
[642] [1971] 1 QB 418.

actually happened prior to the trial date, that event will fall to be taken into account in the assessment of damages'.[643]

In *Jobling* the court was satisfied that the defendant's act and the onset of the plaintiff's condition were wholly unrelated, and that the plaintiff would certainly have suffered the loss in question whether or not the defendant had been negligent: after the relevant date, therefore, his damage was not compensatable. In a case like this the but-for test is applied on the balance of probabilities. A different approach was followed in a decision of the High Court of Australia, *Malec* v. *J. C. Hutton Pty. Ltd.*[644] The High Court essentially took the view that when attempting, under the but-for test, to assess the likelihood that a particular course of events would have ensued in the absence of fault by the defendant, the normal test of the balance of probabilities should be modified. In respect of actual past events, the balance-of-probabilities test would be applied, and an event to which the court allotted a probability of 50 per cent or more would be treated as having occurred. But

in the case of an event which it is alleged would or would not have occurred, or might or might not yet occur, the approach of the court is different. The future may be predicted and the hypothetical may be conjectured. But questions as to the future or hypothetical effect of physical injury or degeneration are not commonly susceptible of scientific demonstration or proof. If the law is to take account of future of hypothetical events in assessing damages, it can only do so in terms of the degree of probability of the events occurring . . . Where proof is necessarily unattainable, it would be unfair to treat as certain a prediction which has a 51 per-cent probability of occurring, but to ignore altogether a prediction which has a 49 per-cent chance of occurring. Thus the court assesses the degree of probability that an event would have occurred, or might occur, and adjusts its award of damages to reflect the degree of probability.[645]

The plaintiff, like *Jobling*, was the victim of an occupational disease for which his employer was responsible but, it was held, was more likely than not to have contracted his depressive condition in any case. Rather than awarding him nothing beyond a certain date, however, the High Court awarded him damages in full for the effects of the disease, subject only to a reduction for the chance (which was less than 100 per cent) that he would have contracted it anyway.

The dictum of Deane, Gaudron, and McHugh JJ cited above accords with the feeling, expressed by many judges and commentators,[646] that leaving aside cases like *Dillon* v. *Twin State Gas and Electric Co.*[647] where the impact of the alternative cause is obvious, it is not appropriate to use a strict balance-of-probabilities test when assessing the effect of hypothetical alternative causes to that of the defendant's fault. If the approach in *Malec* were more widely applied it would open up again the debate about 'loss of a chance'. Although there may be no immediate prospect of the English courts following a similar line, the position taken in *Wilsher* and *Hotson* seems both excessively rigid and heavily

---

[643] [1982] AC 794, 813. See, for further discussion. Professor Robertson, 'American Perspective', below.
[644] (1990) 64 ALJR 316.   [645] Ibid., 318.
[646] See, in particular, Fleming, op. cit. (Select Bibliography).   [647] (1932) 163 A.2d 111.

reliant on what may, in the final analysis, often be a somewhat arbitrary assessment of relative probabilities.

3. Remoteness of Damage

(A) INTERVENING ACTS OF THIRD PARTIES

The question of intervening acts generally arises at the so-called second stage of the causal inquiry, once a but-for relationship has already been established between the plaintiff's loss and the defendant's conduct. Courts speak of the 'chain of causation' between fault and damage being broken by some external event or by the act of a third party, or of a *novus actus interveniens*. Alternatively, an act of the plaintiff himself may suffice; this could either break the chain of causation completely or be regarded instead as contributory negligence in circumstances where the court will then make an apportionment of responsibility under the Law Reform (Contributory Negligence) Act 1945, reducing the plaintiff's damages accordingly. An act of nature, such as a storm, could also be seen as breaking the chain of causation in an appropriate case, as in *Carslogie Steamship Co.* v. *Royal Norwegian Government*.[648]

The degree to which the intervening act is foreseeable is a relevant but not decisive test. In *Dorset Yacht Co.* v. *Home Office*[649] Lord Reid said that an act of a third party 'must have been something very likely to happen if it is not to be regarded as *novus actus interveniens* breaking the chain of causation. I do not think that a mere foreseeable possibility is or should be sufficient.' In this case it was to be expected that the borstal boys would seek to escape from the island and would use a yacht to do so, since there were few other means available; they were the 'very kind of thing' likely to happen. In *Lamb* v. *Camden London Borough Council* Lord Denning criticised both this test and the test of reasonable foreseeability as too wide and liable to 'extend the range of compensation far too widely'. He gave the following example, based on *Dorset Yacht* and the analysis by the Law Lords in that case, to illustrate his point:[650]

Suppose that, by some negligence of the staff, a Borstal boy—or an adult prisoner—escapes over the wall or from a working party. It is not only foreseeable—it is, as we all know, very likely—that he will steal a car in the immediate vicinity. He will then drive many miles, abandon the car, break into a house and steal clothes, get a lift in a lorry, and continue his depredations. On Lord Diplock's test [confining duty to persons in the immediate vicinity of the escape]—and it may be of Lord Morris of Borth-y-Gest and Lord Pearson also—the Home Office would owe a duty to the owner of the stolen car but to none of the others who suffered damage. So the owner of the car could sue but the others could not. But on Lord Reid's test of 'very likely' to happen, the Home Office would be liable not only to the owner of the stolen car, but also to all the others who suffered damage: because it was very likely to happen.

In *Lamb*, contractors working for the defendant council caused the plaintiff's house to be flooded, with the result that her tenant had to move out. The plaintiff, who was living abroad at the time, moved her furniture out of the house and squatters subsequently moved in, causing extensive damage. The plaintiff

---

[648] [1952] AC 292.   [649] [1970] AC 1004, 1030.   [650] [1985] QB, 625, 635.

failed to show that the council was responsible for the damage inflicted by the squatters. According to Lord Denning, this was because the principal responsibility for keeping them out lay with the plaintiff and she had to bear the loss. But this outcome could not be explained by a test of foreseeability, no matter that it might be qualified by requiring a high degree of foreseeability. Policy, and in particular the availability of insurance to the plaintiff, was decisive.[651] Oliver LJ, on the other hand, thought the test was 'not what is foreseeable as a possibility but what would the reasonable man actually foresee if he thought about it', and that in the case of a third-party intervention a 'stringent' test of likelihood would be applied.[652] Watkins LJ regarded evidence of reasonable foreseeability as the minimum the plaintiff had to show, and that the court would take into account a range of features including 'the nature of the event or act, the time it occurred, the place where it occurred, the identity of the perpetrator and his intentions, and responsibility, if any, for taking measures to avoid the occurrence and matters of public policy'. In this case it would be wrong to make the defendants pay for the 'antisocial and criminal' behaviour of the squatters.[653]

These two cases indicate that the relationship between the defendant and the third party may be as important as the nature of the intervening act. In *Dorset Yacht* the borstal boys were in the care of the officers, but there was no such relationship in *Lamb*, no matter how foreseeable it was that squatters might enter an empty house and cause damage to it.[654] Nor was there any such relationship in *Topp* v. *London Country Bus (South West) Ltd.*[655] when, again, it was highly foreseeable that the defendant's bus might be stolen when it was left unattended with the keys in the ignition. The Court of Appeal held that the defendant owed no duty to a remote third party that was killed by the careless driving of the third party that stole the bus.

Equally, the nature of the relationship between the plaintiff and defendant will be important. The defendant may be held to have undertaken a duty of care specifically to the plaintiff as in *Stansbie* v. *Troman*,[656] in which a decorator was liable for allowing thieves into the plaintiff's house which he was painting at the time after he had been warned of this very danger. The intervention of a rescuer will hardly ever be taken to have broken the chain of causation, although if he acts particularly foolishly he could be held to have been contributorily negligent, which will go to reduce his damages.[657]

---

[651] Policy also seems to be the best explanation of *Meah* v. *McCreamer (No. 2)* [1986] 1 All ER 943. The plaintiff, who had been injured in a road accident by the defendant's negligence, recovered damages for a personality disorder brought on by the effects of the accident and which led to him committing a number of vicious criminal assaults, for which he was imprisoned. He was then sued by the victims of his assaults, and brought a further action to recover this sum from the original defendant. Woolf J rejected his claim on the ground of 'remoteness'.

[652] [1981] QB 625, 642.

[653] Ibid. See also *Perl (Exporters) Ltd.* v. *Camden LBC* [1984] QB 342; *Ward* v. *Cannock Chase DC* [1985] 3 All ER 537.

[654] For this reason the question may be better treated as raising a question at the stage of formulating the duty of care, rather than as an aspect of remoteness of damage. See the discussion of *Smith* v. *Littlewoods Organisation Ltd.* [1987] AC 241, above, Section 2(3)(a)(i).

[655] [1993] 1 WLR 976.　　　　　[656] [1948] 2 KB 48.

[657] *Harrison* v. *British Railways Board* [1981] 3 All ER 639.

In cases of rescue and emergency the foreseeability test may be entirely irrelevant. In *The Oropesa*[658] the defendant's ship of that name collided with the *Manchester Regiment*, causing it serious damage. The captain of the *Manchester Regiment* set out in a lifeboat to consult the captain of the *Oropesa* on the means of saving his crew; the lifeboat capsized and many lives were lost. Although this sequence of events was not easily foreseeable, the action of the captain was reasonable in the circumstances and did not break the chain of causation. A contrasting case is *Knightley* v. *Johns*,[659] in which the defendant negligently overturned his car in a tunnel. A police officer ordered a police motorcyclist to close the tunnel and the latter drove against the traffic in order to do so. He was involved in a collision with another motorist. The defendant was not held liable, as the behaviour of the police officers was, in the circumstances, entirely unreasonable.

Where the defendant has, through his fault, created an unjustifiable and unusual risk of danger, the fact that the precise chain of events by which that danger is realised is unpredictable may not absolve him of legal responsibility. This may explain *Philco Radio and Television Corp.* v. *Spurling*,[660] in which the defendant mistakenly delivered some highly inflammable film material to the plaintiff's premises, where it was left lying around. It was then ignited by one of the plaintiff's employees 'as a lark'. The defendants were held liable for the damage to the plaintiff's premises in the ensuing explosion and fire.

(B) ACT OF THE PLAINTIFF

An act of the plaintiff may be classified as a *novus actus* without necessarily amounting to contributory negligence, which implies a failure to take due care for one's own safety. Paradoxically, while contributory negligence is only a partial defence under the Law Reform (Contributory Negligence) Act 1945, a complete defence will be made out if the plaintiff's own act is shown to have broken the chain of causation. In *McKew* v. *Holland and Hannen and Cubitts (Scotland) Ltd.*[661] the plaintiff, who had temporarily lost the full use of his leg following an injury caused by the negligence of the defendants, sustained further injury when his leg gave way on a steep flight of stairs which had no handrail. He was held to have been the sole cause of this additional injury, by placing himself in a position where he might be in danger. The similar case of *Wieland* v. *Cyril Lord Carpets*[662] was decided the other way, on the grounds that the plaintiff in that case had taken sufficient regard for her own safety. In other cases positive acts of the plaintiff have been held not to break the chain of causation; in *Pigney* v. *Pointer's Services*[663] an accident left the plaintiff suffering from a form of neurosis, as a result of which he took his own life. The defendants were held liable for his death.

In *Emeh* v. *Kensington, Chelsea and Fulham AHA*[664] the plaintiff underwent a sterilisation operation which, thanks to the negligence of the surgeon who carried it out, reversed itself with the result that she became pregnant again. In an

---

[658] [1943] P. 32.
[659] [1982] 1 WLR 349.
[660] [1949] 2 All ER 882.
[661] [1969] 3 All ER 1621.
[662] [1969] 3 All ER 1006.
[663] [1957] 1 WLR 1121.
[664] [1985] QB 1012.

action to recover damages for the pain and suffering of the birth and for the costs of raising the child, the defendant argued that the plaintiff could have avoided these costs by having the child aborted. The court held that in this case, where there was no medical reason for the pregnancy to be terminated, the plaintiff's decision not to have an abortion could not be regarded as a *novus actus*.

The defence of contributory negligence, which is considered in greater detail in Chapter 8 below,[665] depends to a certain extent on the specialised application of the principles of causation, although it was clear before the Law Reform (Contributory Negligence) Act 1945 that contributory negligence was a defence in its own right. Since the Act transformed the defence from a total bar into a partial defence only, going to the reduction of damages, the approach to cause has been closely bound up with the court's task of adjusting the loss between the parties according to their relative fault. Contributory negligence operates to reduce the plaintiff's damages in a case where his lack of care for his own safety contributed to his loss. The plaintiff is held to the standard of a reasonably careful person in his position, but he does not have to owe a duty of care to the defendant; the duty issue is irrelevant since the defendant is not claiming that he has suffered loss but rather that the plaintiff is the victim of his own carelessness. A causal link between the plaintiff's lack of self-care and the damage he suffers is therefore required. Prior to the Act of 1945 a complex case law developed on the precise circumstances under which the plaintiff's own fault was deemed to be a relevant causal factor. Now, under the Contributory Negligence Act, the plaintiff's claim is not to be defeated only 'by reason of the fault of the person suffering the damage, but the damages recoverable in respect thereof shall be reduced to such extent as the court thinks just and equitable having regard to the defendant's share in the responsibility for the damage'.[666] The courts have interpreted this as meaning not simply that they may now adjust the plaintiff's damages award to take into account the degree to which he was at fault, where before it was all or nothing, but that much of the old case law on the particular meaning given to contributory negligence as cause is no longer applicable. In particular, the old doctrine of 'last opportunity', under which the party who had the last chance to avoid the accident was deemed to be entirely responsible for it, has apparently disappeared from the law.[667]

Thus, while it remains possible for a court to hold that a plaintiff's lack of care for himself was the sole cause of his loss, or, on the other hand, that it was causally insignificant, the tendency now is to use the Act to apportion responsibility between the parties according to their degree of fault. In the words of Lord Porter in *Stapley* v. *Gypsum Mines Ltd.*,[668] the Act 'enables the court . . . to seek less strenuously to find some ground for holding the plaintiff free from blame or for reaching the conclusion that his negligence played no part in the ensuing accident in as much as owing to the change in the law the blame can now be apportioned equitably between the two parties'. Causation is still a

---

[665] See Section 1(2).
[667] See e.g. *Cakebread* v. *Hopping Brothers (Whetstone) Ltd.* [1947] KB 641.
[666] S. 1(1).
[668] [1953] AC 663, 677.

requirement of the defence's application, as the wording of section 1(1) indicates. This means, in the first place, that the plaintiff's act must be shown to have been one of the operative causes of the damage in the sense of being a but-for cause, and, secondly, that it must also be a 'proximate' or legal cause. In *Jones* v. *Livox Quarries Ltd.*[669] the plaintiff, a worker on a construction site, rode on the back of a vehicle contrary to instructions and was injured when it was involved in a collision. He was held to have been contributorily negligent and a reduction of one-fifth was made to his damages award. According to Lord Denning,

> if the plaintiff while he was riding on the tow bar, had been hit in the eye by a shot from a negligent sportsman, I should have thought that the plaintiff's negligence would in no way be a cause of his injury. It would only be a circumstance in which the cause operated. It would only be a part of the history. But I cannot say that in the present case. The man's negligence here was so much mixed up with the injury that it cannot be dismissed as mere history. His dangerous position on the vehicle was one of the causes of his damage.[670]

As in the case of intervening acts of third parties, in determining what is an 'operative cause' of damage a number of policy factors may come into play. In the context of contributory negligence the court's power to apportion blame has clearly influenced its approach to the issue of weighing causal responsibility. Prior to the Act, in Lord Denning's view, the negligence of the driver in *Jones* would have been regarded as the 'predominant cause' and the plaintiff would have recovered in full, but now 'we have regard to all the causes, and one of them undoubtedly was the plaintiff's negligence in riding on the tow bar'.[671]

The power to make an apportionment between plaintiff and defendant could not, it seems, have been derived from the common law with its all-or-nothing approach, but had to be provided by statute. Once the Act was passed the courts were quick to give it a wide interpretation which provided them with a broad discretion to adjust damages awards to take into account the relative fault of the parties. When they do this, the courts perform the same kind of balancing act with which the debate over 'loss of a chance' and probabilistic cause are concerned. As we have seen, in these two areas the English courts have retained the all-or-nothing approach, in part out of fear of introducing uncertainties into the law and its application. Yet a similar modification of the common law in the area of contributory negligence has become a fully accepted part of the judicial function. In this respect, the decision in *McKew*—where the Contributory Negligence Act was ignored and the claim rejected completely on the grounds of causation—seems contrary not simply to recent practice but also, on one interpretation, to the Act itself, which in section 1(1) appears to bar the total exclusion of damages and to insist upon apportionment in circumstances where the damage caused is partly the result of the fault of the plaintiff and partly of the defendant.[672] On the other hand, there is the view of Watkins LJ in *Lamb* v. *Camden London Borough Council:*[673]

---

[669] [1952] 2 QB 608.   [670] Ibid.   [671] Ibid.
[672] See *Pitts* v. *Hunt* [1991] QB 24 for this view of s. 1(1) of the Act.   [673] [1981] QB 625, 646.

I prefer to regard *McKew* as a good example of a determination to bring realistic consideration to bear upon the question of fresh damage arising from an event or act occurring subsequently to the initial negligent act in the context of remoteness of damage. The plaintiff *McKew* had caused fresh damage to himself as a result of taking an unreasonable risk. That he would be likely or quite likely to do this was said to have been reasonably foreseeable. Yet because he had behaved unreasonably in the doing of it, his act was found to be a *novus actus interveniens* which freed the defendants from all liability for it.

(c) FORESEEABILITY OF THE KIND OF DAMAGE

We now turn to the question of the extent of legal liability of a defendant who has caused tortious damage to the plaintiff. A major limitation on recovery following the decision of the Privy Council in *The Wagon Mound (No. 1)*[674] is the principle that the defendant will not be liable for a *kind of damage* which he could not reasonably have foreseen. However, once foreseeability of the kind of damage is established, the *extent* of loss is irrelevant and the defendant will be liable in full. Where this is the case, it is said that the defendant 'must take the plaintiff as he finds him', with all his particular susceptibilities. The difficulty here lies in knowing what is meant by the 'kind of damage' which the defendant should have foreseen.

In *The Wagon Mound (No. 1)*[675] an engineer on the defendant's ship negligently discharged a quantity of furnace oil into Sydney harbour, fouling the wharf owned by the plaintiffs and halting repair-work on two other ships, the *Corrimal* and the *Aubrey D*. After they were advised that the oil could not be ignited, the plaintiffs resumed welding work, but the oil was ignited by a piece of molten metal and the wharf and the two ships were consumed in the resulting fire. The plaintiff's action for the damage to the wharf failed on the grounds that while damage by pollution was reasonably foreseeable, damage by fire was not. The Privy Council rejected the test apparently laid down by the Court of Appeal in the earlier case of *Re Polemis* under which the defendant was liable if there was a direct link between his carelessness and the resulting damage. Viscount Simonds said:

It does not seem consonant with current ideas of justice or morality that, for an act of negligence, however slight or venial, which results in some trivial foreseeable damage, the actor should be liable for all consequences, however unforeseeable and however grave, so long as they can be said to be 'direct'. It is a principle of civil liability, subject only to qualifications which have not present relevance, that a man must be considered to be responsible for the probable consequences of his act. To demand more of him is too harsh a rule, to demand less is to ignore that civilised order requires the observance of a minimum standard of behaviour.[676]

As this dictum indicates, the decision in *The Wagon Mound* was based on a strong assertion that the extent of the defendant's liability should be proportionate to his fault. In elevating foreseeability to be a main test of remoteness, Viscount Simonds was influenced by *Donoghue v. Stevenson* and in particular by Lord Atkin's expressed view that liability should be modelled upon a 'general public sentiment of moral wrongdoing for which the offender must pay'.[677] Yet this is

---

[674] [1961] AC 388.   [675] Ibid.   [676] Ibid., 422–3.   [677] [1932] AC 562, 580.

only one of a number of possible ways of looking at negligence liability; it takes a wholly exaggerated view of the degree to which the legal concept of carelessness is based on moral fault and pays no regard at all to the aims of loss-shifting and accident-prevention. These considerations, almost completely absent from Viscount Simonds's judgment, have nevertheless influenced other courts in their treatment of *The Wagon Mound (No. 1)*, and account to a large degree for a steady decline in its influence over the past thirty years.

In *Re Polemis and Furness, Withy & Co.*,[678] a stevedore employed by the defendant charterers carelessly dropped a plank into the hold of the plaintiff's ship while it was being unloaded. The hold contained petrol vapour, which was ignited by a spark struck by the falling plank; in the ensuing fire the ship was completely destroyed. The arbitrators found that 'the causing of the spark could not have been anticipated from the falling of the board, though some damage to the ship might reasonably have been anticipated'. The defendants were held liable for the full loss, the Court of Appeal rejecting an argument that they should not have to pay for damage of a kind they could not have foreseen:

if the act would or might probably cause damage, the fact that the damage it in fact causes is not the exact kind of damage one would expect is immaterial, so long as the damage is in fact caused sufficiently directly by the negligent act and not by the operation of independent causes having no connection with the negligent act, except that they could not avoid its results. Once the act is negligent, the fact that its operation was not foreseen is immaterial.[679]

These wide dicta of Scrutton LJ were rejected in *The Wagon Mound (No. 1)* in favour of the test of foreseeability of the kind of damage. The difference between the cases is based, then, upon their respective approaches to the definition of 'kind of damage'. In *The Wagon Mound* damage by pollution was deemed to be a different 'kind' of damage from damage by fire. On this basis the outcome in *Re Polemis* would presumably now be reversed. *Polemis* could be reconciled with *The Wagon Mound* only if 'kind of damage' were construed sufficiently widely to cover any form of property damage.

This is broadly what has happened to *The Wagon Mound (No. 1)* as far as *physical injury* to the person is concerned: the courts have reached a position where, as long as some kind of injury or harm to the person was foreseeable, its extent does not matter. Nor is any distinction drawn for this purpose between physical injury and psychiatric harm; these are not separate 'kinds of damage'.[680] Possibly this approach does less than full justice to the *Wagon Mound* principle but it conforms to long-standing precedents and also has the advantage of respecting the principle of fully compensating the victim of tortious damage. In *Smith* v. *Leech Brain & Co. Ltd.*[681] the plaintiff was burned on the lip by hot molten metal. The burn induced a cancer from which he died. The defendants, who were in breach of duty by not providing him with a protective shield, were held liable for his death. This case exemplifies the 'eggshell skull' principle, which is to the effect that the defendant takes the victim as he finds him. The defendant

---

[678] [1921] 3 KB 560.   [679] Ibid.   [680] *Page* v. *Smith* [1996] 1 AC 955.   [681] [1962] QB 405.

cannot deny liability for the full extent of the plaintiff's loss on the grounds that he was unusually vulnerable to a particular disease or condition.

Smith v. *Leech Brain & Co. Ltd.*[682] has since been followed in other cases of physical injury, both in England and in other Commonwealth jurisdictions. A rare exception is the first-instance decision in *Tremain* v. *Pike.*[683] A farm worker contracted a rare disease, Weil's disease, after coming into contact with rats on his employer's farm. The defendant was held to be in breach of the employer's duty to provide his employee with safe working conditions, but the extent of his liability was limited on the grounds that injury through rat-bites was foreseeable, but contracting Weil's disease was not. The decision seems anomalous and unsatisfactory given the high *standard* of care, verging on strict liability, to which employers are held. The Court of Appeal implicitly rejected *Tremain* v. *Pike* in *Parsons* v. *Uttley Ingham*,[684] in which the plaintiff recovered for the consequences of an unusual illness contracted by his pigs after they were fed mouldy nuts from a hopper installed by the defendant. As this decision concerned damage to property (the pigs) there would be a compelling case for it to be followed where personal safety and health were the interests affected, since by general consent the protection of life and limb ranks above that of tangible and intangible property.

In the case of property damage generally the trend is less clear, but there are signs that the courts will take a flexible view of what is meant by 'kind of damage'. In *The Wagon Mound (No. 2)*[685] the owners of the two ships damaged in the fire sued the owners of the *Wagon Mound*. This time the judge found as a fact that there was a small but significant risk of damage by fire, and the Privy Council held that this was sufficient for them to hold the defendants liable for the full amount of the loss. It might appear that the second *Wagon Mound* case reversed the first.[686] Yet the decisions are probably compatible since in *The Wagon Mound (No. 1)* it was found that damage by fire was not foreseeable; in each case the premise was that a *specific* kind of property damage had to be foreseeable, and not just property damage of *any* kind.[687] In *Vacwell Engineering Co.* v. *BDH Chemicals Ltd.*[688] the defendants supplied a chemical to the plaintiffs without warning that it was liable to explode in water. An employee of the plaintiffs placed a consignment of the chemical in a sink; this set off a chemical reaction, which caused a huge explosion. The judge held that the magnitude and extent of the explosion were irrelevant, as long as the explosion itself and the type of damage to property, which it could cause, were foreseeable.

There is no clear authority indicating that for the purpose of *The Wagon Mound (No. 1)* test, all kinds of property damage are deemed to be as good as each other. On the contrary, it would appear that the test of remoteness for property damage (and, by extension, for pure economic loss) is more strict than for interferences with physical safety and health. The precise limits to recovery

---

[682] See in particular *Bradford* v. *Robinson Rentals* [1967] 1 WLR 337; *Robinson* v. *Post Office* [1974] 1 WLR 1176.

[683] [1969] 3 WLR 1556.   [684] [1978] QB 791.   [685] [1967] 1 AC 617.

[686] See generally the important discussion of Dias, 'Trouble on Oiled Waters: Problems of the *Wagon Mound (No. 2)*' [1967] *CLJ* 62.

[687] McKendrick, *Tort Textbook* (1991 edn.), 101.   [688] [1971] 1 QB 88.

can probably only be established on a case-by-case basis. But in general, the restrictive approach to property and economic loss may be justified both by the higher priority accorded to protecting bodily integrity and by the widespread availability of loss insurance for property damage.

(D) FORESEEABILITY OF THE CAUSAL SEQUENCE

A further qualification to the test in *The Wagon Mound (No. 1)* is that if the type of damage suffered was foreseeable, the precise sequence of events by which the injury was brought about need not have been. In *Hughes* v. *Lord Advocate*[689] the defendants left a manhole uncovered and protected only by a tent and paraffin lamp. A child climbed down into the hole and, as he was re-ascending, kicked over one of the lamps, which fell into the hole, causing an explosion in which he was burned. The Court of Session denied liability on the grounds that although injury by burning was foreseeable as the boy might have come into contact with one of the lamps, burning by means of this sequence of events was not. The House of Lords reversed on the grounds that the precise chain of events was immaterial. In contrast is the decision of the Court of Appeal in *Doughty* v. *Turner Manufacturing Co. Ltd.*[690] Here the court drew a distinction between burning caused by a splash of hot liquid, which was deemed to be foreseeable, and burning caused by an explosion, which was not. An employee of the defendants carelessly tipped the asbestos cover of a molten metal container into the metal, setting off a chain reaction which caused an explosion in which the plaintiff, who was standing nearby, was injured, suffering bad burns. The court held that the manner and extent of his injuries were not foreseeable. The case is hard to reconcile with *Hughes*.[691]

The celebrated American case of *Palsgraf* v. *Long Island Railroad Co.*,[692] which is frequently (but mistakenly) thought to turn on the absence of any duty of care to an unforeseeable plaintiff, is better regarded as raising an issue which an English court would today treat as one of remoteness. Nor is it obvious that Cardozo J's judgment would be followed, bearing in mind the decision of the House of Lords in *Hughes* v. *Lord Advocate*.[693] In *Palsgraf* the plaintiff was standing on the defendant's railway platform, waiting for a train, when another train stopped to collect passengers. As it was about to pull out again a passenger tried to climb on board; he was assisted by two guards who dislodged a package he was carrying. Unknown to them it contained fireworks, which ignited on contact with the tracks, setting off an explosion which tipped over a set of scales on to the plaintiff. Her action for damages failed on appeal in the New York Court of Appeals.

A first point to note is that whatever was intended by Cardozo J and other judges of the majority, the case does not turn on the absence of a duty of care as that term is now understood.[694] The plaintiff was within the class of persons

---

[689] [1963] AC 837.
[690] [1964] 1 QB 518.
[691] McKendrick, *Tort Textbook* (1991 edn.), argues that the remarks of the Court of Appeal concerning remoteness were *obiter*, since it was not in fact foreseeable that any injury could have occurred from the employee's initial act.
[692] (1928) 162 NE 99.
[693] [1963] AC 837.
[694] W. Prosser, '*Palsgraf* Revisited' (1953) 52 *Mich. LR* 1.

to whom the railway owed a general duty of care to avoid exposure to physical harm. Moreover, the standard of care imposed was a high one since the plaintiff was not a stranger but a passenger who had purchased a railway ticket. The case is properly classified as turning on causation rather than the anterior question of duty, and the relevant question is whether injury of the kind in question was too remote. Since it was conceivably foreseeable that the scales might cause physical injury if they fell over, the issue resolves itself into the foreseeability of the precise sequence of events through which this took place. Following *Hughes*, the unforeseeability of this precise sequence would not matter and the defendants would be held liable.

(E) Remoteness and Economic Loss

An exception to the 'eggshell skull' rule apparently operates in relation to certain economic losses. In *The Liesbosch*[695] the plaintiffs' dredger was sunk outside Patras harbour by the defendants' ship. All the plaintiffs' capital was tied up in the contract it had to dredge the harbour and in order to complete this work it had to hire another dredger. This turned out to be more expensive than buying a substitute. The House of Lords denied a claim for this additional expense on the grounds (as expressed by Lord Wright) that 'the appellants' actual loss in so far as it was due to their impecuniosity arose from that impecuniosity as a separate and concurrent cause, extraneous to and distinct in character from the tort'.[696]

It is not clear why this form of economic vulnerability—in the sense that impecuniosity here is the equivalent of the 'eggshell skull' principle—should be analysed differently from physical vulnerability. The only plausible explanation is the argument of policy to the effect that the law places a higher value on physical interests and in particular on personal health and safety. However, it should be borne in mind that the issue in *The Liesbosch* did not concern pure economic loss as such, but economic loss flowing from property damage. Lord Wright's reference to causation is unconvincing in itself since it does not explain the different outcome in a case of physical injury such as *Smith* v. *Leech Brain & Co. Ltd.*[697] Nor does the policy argument explain everything. If the plaintiff's economic losses in the sense of lost earning capacity are unusually extensive—if, for example, he is a particularly highly-paid earner—the defendant will, nevertheless, be required to meet his loss in full. Why then must a tortfeasor 'take his victim as he finds him in terms of exceptionally high or low profit earning capacity, but not in terms of pecuniosity or impecuniosity which may be their manifestations'?[698] Doubts such as these have confined *The Liesbosch* to cases where the plaintiff was unable to mitigate his losses when it would have been reasonable to do so, as opposed to cases where he could have done so but chose, for good reasons, not to.[699]

---

[695] *Liesbosch Dredger* v. *SS Edison* [1933] AC 449.   [696] Ibid., 460.   [697] [1962] 2 QB 405.
[698] *Dodd Properties (Kent) Ltd.* v. *Canterbury CC* [1980] 1 All ER 928, 940 (Donaldson LJ).
[699] See, in particular, *Dodd Properties (Kent) Ltd.* v. *Canterbury CC*, ibid.

(F) REMOTENESS OF DAMAGE IN CONTRACT AND TORT

In principle the rules of remoteness are more generous in tort than in contract. The tort test, even after *The Wagon Mound (No. 1)*,[700] holds that if the kind of damage suffered was foreseeable, the extent need not be. In contract those losses arising 'naturally . . . according to the usual course of things' are recoverable, subject to a more extensive liability arising if the plaintiff made the defendant aware of special circumstances before entering into the agreement.[701] According to Lord Reid in *The Heron II*,[702] a higher degree of foreseeability is required for recovery of consequential damage flowing from breach of contract than is the case in tort; moreover, the relevant point at which foreseeability is judged is the time at which the contract was made and not the point at which, as in tort, the relevant duty is breached. The basis for this more restrictive rule may be that in contract the parties are brought together by their own agreement, and should be able to rely upon their own allocation of risk or that which would implicitly attach to a contract of that kind. However, in *H. Parsons (Livestock) Ltd.* v. *Uttley, Ingham & Co. Ltd.*[703] Lord Denning suggested that, regardless of the origin of a particular obligation in contract or tort, the tort rule should apply in cases of physical injury or property damage. This would leave the contract rule to apply only in cases of pure economic loss. There is much to be said for this, at least as far injury to the person is concerned. In relation to the contract of employment, for example, it would be unusual if the employer's general duty of care in tort to his employees could be implicitly cut down by the existence of a contract term setting a lower standard of care and, according to one reading of the broad dicta of *The Heron II*, a more restrictive conception of remoteness of damage.[704] In relation to property damage, Lord Denning's dicta in *Parsons* were rejected by the majority of the Court of Appeal, although they reached the same result in that case, holding the defendant liable for the full extent of the harm caused to the pigs.

As far as pure economic loss is concerned, the *Hadley* v. *Baxendale* rule in contract clearly places limits on recoverability which would involve the drawing of distinctions within the general category of 'economic loss' as a kind of damage. In *Wroth* v. *Tyler*[705] an unexpectedly large loss suffered following the collapse of a house-sale was recovered on the grounds that the *type* of loss had been foreseeable; this seems hard to reconcile with the normal contract rule, and may have been a misapplication of the normal tort rule. One area where the different contract and tort rules on remoteness may make a substantial impact concerns liability for misrepresentation. The normal foreseeability principle applies for liability in negligence under *Hedley Byrne & Co. Ltd.* v. *Heller & Partners Ltd.*[706] But in the tort of deceit the 'directness' test of *Re Polemis*[707] applies on the grounds of the greater fault of the defendant. This more extensive basis

[700] [1961] AC 388.
[701] *Hadley* v. *Baxendale* (1854) 9 Exch. 341.
[702] [1969] 1 AC 350, 385.
[703] [1978] QB 791.
[704] See the discussion of this point in the context of *Johnstone* v. *Bloomsbury HA* [1992] QB 333; see Chapter 6, Section 3, below.
[705] [1974] Ch. 30.
[706] [1964] AC 465.
[707] [1921] 3 KB 560.

for recovery also applies to claims brought under section 2(1) of the Misrepresentation Act 1967,[708] thanks to the reading of section 2(1) adopted by the Court of Appeal in *Royscott Trust Co.* v. *Rogerson*.[709]

Select Bibliography

DIAS, R. M. W., 'Trouble on Oiled Waters: Problems of the *Wagon Mound (No. 2)* [1967] *CLJ* 62.

EPSTEIN, R. A., 'A Theory of Strict Liability' (1973) 2 *Jo. LS* 151.

FLEMING, J. G., 'Probabilistic Causation in Tort Law' (1989) 68 *Can. BR* 661.

—— 'Probabilistic Causation in Tort Law: A Postscript' (1991) 70 *Can. BR* 137.

FRASER, J., and HOWARTH, D., 'More Concern for Cause' (1984) 4 *Leg. Stud.* 131.

HART, H. L. A. and HONORÉ, A. M., *Causation and the Law* (2nd edn., 1985).

HONORÉ, A. M., 'Causation and Remoteness of Damage', in A. Tunc (ed.), *Int. Encl. Comp. L.* (1983), xi. ch. 7.

KING, J., 'Causation, Valuation, and Chance in Personal Injury Torts Involving Pre-existing Conditions and Future Consequences' (1981) 90 *Yale LJ* 1358.

MULLANY, N. J., 'Common Sense Causation—An Australian View' (1992) 12 *OJLS* 431.

PROSSER, W., '*Palsgraf* Revisited' (1953) *Mich. LR* 1.

STAPLETON, J., 'Law, Causation and Common Sense' (1988) 8 *OJLS* 111.

—— 'The Gist of Negligence, Part II' (1988) 104 *LQR* 389.

WEINRIB, E., 'A Step Forward in Factual Causation' (1975) 38 *MLR* 518.

5. NEGLIGENCE: A SUMMARY AND CONCLUSION

The evolution of the tort of negligence since it was synthesised in *Donoghue* v. *Stevenson* has consisted of a search for 'control devices', mechanisms which could set limits to the scope of the tort and prevent it encroaching on other areas of civil obligation.[710] At various times, both duty and causation have served this need,[711] with the former gradually becoming the focus of attention. Within the case law on duty there has been a gradual move away from general conceptual formulae, and the adoption instead of more specific criteria, many of them explicitly policy-orientated, to guide the courts. Thus, as we have seen, the courts have come to make increasing reference to arguments based on insurability, the deterrent effects of liability, the possibilities of loss shifting, and the dangers of unwelcome or 'defensive' reactions to extensions of the duty concept. Notions of fault have also been affected by the concern to ensure that the perceived goals of tort law, in particular ensuring effective compensation, have been met.

In general, this tendency should be welcomed. The issues involved in setting the boundaries to liability in negligence are too complex to be adequately cap-

---

[708] *Doyle* v. *Olby Ironmongers* [1969] 2 QB 158; *East* v. *Maurer* [1990] 2 All ER 737.

[709] [1991] 3 All ER 294; R. Hooley (1991) 107 *LQR* 547.

[710] Whether they have been successful is open to debate. See T. Weir, 'The Staggering March of Negligence', ch. 5 in P. Cane and J. Stapleton (eds.), *The Law of Obligations: Essays in Honour of John Fleming* (1998).

[711] See D. Howarth, *Textbook on Tort* (1995), 114–18.

tured by such open-ended terms as 'proximity', or the 'fair, just and reasonable' test. At the same time, there is legitimate concern that negligence lacks an adequate conceptual structure, a framework of principle within which the complex balancing of different factors can be placed. Unadorned references to 'policy' are unappealing; so is the judicial tendency to make assumptions concerning the possible consequences of decisions which are based on little or no evidence. But while a degree of conceptual fluidity, and perhaps some confusion, seem unavoidable, both these are preferable to the solution of freezing the law in its present state, leaving the existing categories of recovery as they are and refusing to add to them. We may leave the last word to McLachlin J, speaking on behalf of the majority of the Canadian Supreme Court in the *Norsk* case, in terms which describe a particular attitude both to the specific question of economic loss but also to the tort of negligence as a whole:

The fact is that situations arise, other than those falling within the old exclusionary rule, where it is manifestly fair and just that recovery of economic loss be permitted. Faced with these situations, courts will strain to allow recovery, provided they are satisfied that the case will not open the door to a plethora of undeserving claims. They will refuse to accept injustice merely for the sake of the doctrinal tidiness, which is the motivating spirit of *Murphy*. This is in the best tradition of the law of negligence, the history of which exhibits a sturdy refusal to be confined by arbitrary forms and rules where justice indicates otherwise.[712]

6. AN AMERICAN PERSPECTIVE
by
Professor D. W. Robertson[*]

1. Fundamental Differences in Legal Culture

English readers of decisions by courts in the United States need to consider at least three major differences between the legal cultures of the two countries before drawing any conclusions based on the American picture. These differences combine to make it greatly more important in the United States than in England that the law of negligence—its conceptual and doctrinal apparatus and its essential vocabulary—be firm, clear, and simple.[713] In fact American law rarely achieves those virtues. Nevertheless, one cannot fully understand and evaluate American judicial products without reflecting on the continuing quest and yearning for them.

First, it is a well-known but frequently forgotten fact that the United States has no unified law of negligence, but rather at least fifty-two discrete and autonomous systems. Each of the fifty states has its own tort law. The legislature and highest court in each state constitute the supreme authority as to that state's

---

[*] A. W. Walker Centennial Chair in Law, University of Texas

[712] (1991) 91 DLR (4th) 289, 365.

[713] For in-depth treatment of the conceptual structure of negligence law, see D. Robertson, 'The Vocabulary of Negligence Law' (1997) 58 *La. LR* 1; D. Robertson, 'Allocating Authority Among Institutional Decision Makers' (1997) 57 *La. LR* 1079.

private law. The decisions of the federal courts, including the United States Supreme Court, are not authoritative on issues of private state law, but merely persuasive.[714] The federal maritime law is a distinct fifty-first system; here the United States Supreme Court and the Congress constitute the supreme authority.[715] The fifty-second system is a federal common law of torts that supplements national legislation on matters such as antitrust.[716] In addition some commentators view 'a conglomerate of statutory and common law dealing with the tort liability of the federal government' as a fifty-third discrete system.[717]

It follows from what has just been said that a decision of the United States Supreme Court on a point of maritime law is no more (and no less) representative of the American law of negligence than a decision on a similar point of New York law by that state's highest court. It thus counts as an analytical mistake to say that a United States Supreme Court maritime decision has 'destroyed the authority'[718] of an earlier New York state law decision on a similar point. New York's law remains that reflected in the decisions of its own courts unless and until those courts are persuaded by the United States Supreme Court's reasoning—or by the reasoning in some persuasive decision from the House of Lords or a court in another of the American states—to change it.

The fifty-plus American negligence systems are independent of one another. Moreover, they are operated by judges and lawyers whose educational backgrounds—even within a single jurisdiction—are often significantly divergent from one another's in content and sometimes in quality. Nevertheless, these disparate negligence systems share common policy goals and generally strive for common outcomes. Thus, authorities from one system are routinely cited as persuasive in another. If a court in Florida is to understand and evaluate the decision and reasoning of a court in Montana, the conceptual structure of negligence law needs to be as uniform as we can make it. From this point of view the American law of negligence is intranational comparative law, and the conceptual apparatus of negligence law is its essential vocabulary. Americans are reconciled to never achieving a uniform national law of torts; indeed, some analysts have perceived a 'growing divergence'[719] among the American states' tort laws. That is all the more reason to try especially hard to speak a uniform national language of torts.

The second fundamental difference between England's and America's legal cultures is America's pervasive use of juries in negligence cases. In a bench-trial system like England's, where experienced judges determine issues of fact and issues of law, the law of negligence can be fairly subtle and fairly flexible and still serve its functions of forecasting outcomes and guiding the judges and

---

[714] See, e.g., *State v. Perry* (1992) 610 So.2d 746 (Louisiana) (stating that 'this court is the final arbiter of the meaning of the state constitution and laws').

[715] See, e.g., *East River Steamship Corp.* v. *Transamerica Delaval Inc.* (1986) 476 US 858, 106 S.Ct. 2295.

[716] See, e.g., *Texas Industries Inc.* v. *Radcliff Materials Inc.* (1981) 451 US 630, 101 S.Ct. 2061.

[717] M. S. Shapo, *Towards a Jurisprudence of Injury: The Continuing Creation of a System of Substantive Justice in American Tort Law: Report to the American Bar Association* (1984), 2–21.

[718] *Murphy* v. *Brentwood DC* [1991] AC 398, 469 (Lord Keith of Kinkel), 496 (Lord Jauncey of Tullichettle).

[719] T. Reavley and J. Wesevich, 'An Old Rule for New Reasons: Place of Injury as a Federal Solution to Choice of Law in Single-Accident Mass-Tort Cases' (1992) 71 *Texas LR* 1, 3 n. 4.

lawyers in their handling of disputed cases. In jury-trial systems, like those of forty-nine[720] of the American states, the situation is far different. The American trial judge's major tasks are determining which issues are for the jury and how to instruct the jury on those issues. If there is to be any consistency and predictability in the way those tasks are performed by the huge number of trial judges who perform them on a daily basis throughout the United States, the governing negligence law needs to be as clear, firm, and simple as can be achieved. Probably no one would claim that any American state actually has a body of negligence law that is in any sense more solid or simple than England's. The claim is rather that we have a much greater need for such features in our law. An approach to a particular legal problem that an English jurist might properly decry as 'conceptualism' might in America be regarded as necessary and welcome guidance for the everyday participants in a naturally unrulier legal market-place.

The third difference stems from the American system of compensating plaintiffs' lawyers. Almost invariably the American tort plaintiff pays his lawyer nothing out of pocket. Instead the client and lawyer agree that the lawyer will take a percentage of whatever can be recovered from the defendant. Such a 'contingency fee agreement' would be illegal in England and most other countries. It is quite legal and proper throughout the United States. The chief virtue of the contingency fee system is enabling the downtrodden to approach the halls of justice. This is a considerable virtue. But it may be outweighed by the flood of silly, vindictive, or purely mercenary litigation that could ensue if plaintiffs' lawyers do not exercise rigorous discipline as to the kinds of cases they will accept. There are many thousands of plaintiffs' lawyers in America, and not all of them have as much work as they would like. In such a country a major goal of the law of negligence must be furnishing clear guidance to lawyers as to which cases are *not* worth pursuing. Again this difference argues for a firmer, clearer, and simpler doctrinal apparatus than may be appropriate in England.

2. The Quest for Conceptual Clarity: The Traditional Model

On the conceptual outlines of the cause of action in negligence there has been broad general agreement: The plaintiff in a negligence action cannot succeed without satisfying the five elements of duty, breach of duty, factual causation, legal causation, and damages.[721] The *duty* inquiry is a matter for the judge's determination. It asks whether there is a rule of law that shields the defendant from liability even when it is apparent that unacceptable conduct on the part of the defendant has been a factual and a legal cause of cognisable harm.

---

[720] Louisiana is the exception. Litigants in that state have a right to jury trial, but a jury's findings of fact—including even its assessment of damages—are exposed to fairly sweeping appellate review. Thus, many litigants determine that there is no advantage in jury trial and elect to try their cases to the bench.

[721] See, e.g., D. W. Robertson *et al.*, *Cases and Materials on Torts* (2nd edn., 1998) 83–4; W. P. Keeton *et al.*, *Prosser and Keeton On Torts* (5th edn., 1984) 164–5. The legal causation issue is often termed the 'proximate cause' issue. Because the latter term carries a great deal of confusing historical baggage, legal causation is emerging as the preferred term.

The other four elements present jury questions—matters for the jury's determination under limiting instructions given by the judge—unless reasonable minds could not differ. In its typical operation the *breach* issue addresses whether the defendant's conduct was unacceptable, viz., unreasonable under the circumstances. Other names for the breach issue are the substandard conduct issue and the negligence issue.[722] The *factual causation* issue is normally confined to inquiring whether the harmful event of which the plaintiff complains would probably have been avoided if the defendant's conduct had been reasonable under the circumstances. If the harmful event would probably have occurred regardless of defendant's wrongful conduct, then such conduct was not a cause-in-fact of any injury. The *legal causation* inquiry is difficult to encapsulate; in general terms it addresses whether the injury the plaintiff suffered was so remote or attenuated a consequence of the defendant's wrongful conduct that imposing liability seems unfair or otherwise inappropriate. One recurrent approach to legal causation seeks 'to confine the liability of a negligent actor to those harmful consequences which result from the operation of the risk, or of a risk, the foreseeability of which rendered the defendant's conduct negligent.'[723] The *damages* issue addresses whether the particular consequences for which the plaintiff seeks compensation are attributable to the harmful event for which the defendant is responsible; it also seeks to set an appropriate monetary equivalent for such injurious consequences.

The broad agreement on the conceptual model entails recognition that the five elements are best defined with care and kept separate. But in practice several varieties of confusion or conceptual mistakes have sometimes occurred.[724] *First*, judges and lawyers often say 'no duty' when a more careful articulation would be 'no breach'.[725] This confusion is frequently harmless, but it can have the unintended or unjustified effect of awarding the trial judge additional power over an issue that is normally assigned to the jury.[726] *Second*, the vocabulary of duty is sometimes used to address the problem of legal causation.[727] Again the effect is an artificial accretion of power to the judge and a corresponding inroad into the normal province of the jury.[728] *Third*, courts often

---

[722] It would be conducive to better understanding of the terminology if the word 'negligence' took a capital 'N' when referring to the law of negligence or to the cause of action in negligence and a lower-case 'n' when referring to the substandard conduct element of such a cause of action.

[723] *Socony-Vacuum Oil. Co.* v. *Marshall* (1955) 222 F.2d 604, 610.

[724] The remainder of this subsection deals with seemingly random conceptual mistakes. The immediately following subsection addresses an arguably purposive pattern whereby some courts have seemingly set out to alter the traditional model.

[725] See, e.g., *Clinton* v. *Commonwealth Edison Co.* (1976) 36 Ill.App.3d 1064, 344 NE2d 509, 514–15, upholding a trial judge's decision that the defendant power company 'had to duty' to insulate a high-voltage transmission line near the plaintiff's house. This is the American version of 'conflat[ing] the phrase "duty of care" with "breach of duty", in the sense that absence or carelessness is sometimes taken to indicate the absence of a duty.' See text above at p. 79.

[726] See D. W. Robertson *et al.*, *Cases and Materials on Torts* (2nd edn., 1998) 186–8.

[727] See, e.g., *Palsgraf* v. *Long Island R. Co.* (1928) 248 NY 339, 162 NE 99, 100, concluding that a railroad had 'no duty' to use reasonable care to prevent its employees' dangerous activities at one end of the station platform from causing unforeseeable injury to a passenger at the other end.

[728] See D. W. Robertson *et al.*, *Cases and Materials on Torts* (2nd edn., 1998) 186–7, 205–19.

conflate the issues of factual causation and legal causation.[729] This third type of confusion always entails muddled analysis and the use of inappropriate precedents. Usually it also suppresses any discussion of the policy considerations that actually influence judges' answers to difficult legal causation questions. *Fourth*, courts sometimes transfer the issue of the victim's fault from the realm of affirmative defences where it belongs into the legal cause issue, for example stating that the plaintiff's 'extraordinary negligence was the superseding and sole proximate [legal] cause' of the injuries in suit.[730] *Finally*, certain problems that are normally treated under the issue of damages are sometimes mistakenly lumped into the factual causation inquiry. The effect of this last type of confusion is to hold the plaintiff to a much higher standard of proof than is normally thought to be appropriate.[731]

The antidote to the first two types of confusion—using 'no duty' to mean 'no breach' or 'no legal causation'—is confining the vocabulary of duty to its proper place. The traditional hallmarks of a true issue of duty involve *categories* of defendants (e.g., land occupier), of plaintiffs (e.g., trespasser), of conduct (e.g., nonfeasance), or of types of harm (e.g., pure economic damage or purely psychic harm). If the asserted impediment to plaintiff's recovery—the particular defensive argument under consideration—is not a categorical claim but instead depends upon factual details or nuances, the problem is not generally to be regarded as one of duty but rather as one of breach of duty or legal causation. (Whether the alleged impediment goes to breach of duty or to legal causation does not matter very much, as both are defined as jury issues unless reasonable minds could not differ. Generally speaking, if at its core the defensive argument asserts that defendant's behaviour was acceptable under the circumstances, it is a breach argument. If it implicitly concedes unacceptable behaviour but insists that the injury was too remote a consequence thereof, it is a legal causation argument.)

The antidote to the third type of confusion—the conflation of the factual causation and legal causation elements—is careful delimitation of the factual causation inquiry.[732] The plaintiff satisfies the law's factual causation requirement by producing evidence from which a reasonable person could conclude that the harmful event forming the basis for the lawsuit probably would not have happened in the absence of the defendant's wrongful conduct. On the basis of such evidence the jury is free to determine that the defendant's wrongful conduct was a factual cause of the harm. Obviously other forces, often including the negligent conduct of tortfeasors other than the defendant, will also compete for attention as putative causes of the harm. The existence of such other forces

[729] See, e.g., *Novak v. Rathman* (1987) 153 Ill.App.3d 408, 505 NE2d 773, 776, finding 'no causal connection' between the defendant's conduct in releasing a dangerous psychotic from incarceration and a murder later committed by the psychotic.

[730] *Exxon Co. v. Sofec, Inc.* (1996) 517 US 830, 835. In this case the victim's fault was seen as so egregious that the court approved a trial in which only that issue was presented; the plaintiff was not even permitted to put on evidence of the defendant's fault.

[731] See *DePass v. United States* (1983) 721 F.2d 203, 208-9 (Posner J, dissenting, taking his colleagues to task for forgetting the factual-causation/damages distinction and for holding the plaintiff to an inappropriately heavy burden of proof respecting the extent of his injuries).

[732] See generally D. Robertson, 'The Common Sense of Cause In Fact' (1997) 75 *Texas LR* 1765.

may present difficulties to be dealt with under the duty, breach, or legal causation inquiries, but these form no proper part of the factual causation issue. The plaintiff's factual causation burden is satisfied by showing that the defendant's wrongful conduct was probably *a* cause of the harmful event; requiring proof that it was *the* cause would burden the plaintiff's case far too greatly.

The antidote to the fourth type of confusion—attempting to treat the issue of victim fault under the rubric of the legal causation issue—is the realisation that in a system that has made the general determination to use the fault of the victim to reduce rather than to bar recovery—viz., a 'comparative fault' or 'comparative responsibility' system—it will always be inappropriate to conclude in a particular case that the victim's negligent conduct is so egregious that it prevents the defendant's negligent conduct from being a legal cause of the harm. If the defendant was guilty of negligent conduct which was a factual cause of the harm and which (putting the victim's fault to one side) would be regarded as a legal cause of the harm, then the defendant should pay something, no matter how negligent the victim may have been.

Dealing with the final type of confusion—intermingling of factual causation and damages considerations—once again entails careful delimitation of the factual causation inquiry. As was observed above, the factual causation issue asks whether the defendant's wrongful conduct was among the causes of the harmful even on which the lawsuit is based. Once that element is satisfied, whether particular injurious consequences are attributable to that event is properly approached under the damages inquiry, where the plaintiff's burden of proof has traditionally been less demanding than at the factual causation stage. In traditional judicial thinking we must guard against holding a defendant responsible when he has caused no harm; this is the appropriate province of the factual causation issue. But once we know that the defendant has caused some legally cognisable harm, we need not worry overmuch about making him pay too much. '[T]he extent of [the plaintiff's] injury [is] an issue on which courts traditionally do not impose a heavy burden of proof on plaintiffs. . . . Doubts are resolved against the tortfeasor.'[733]

Once the five elements of the negligence cause of action are properly delimited and the recurrent confusions sorted out and put to one side, the resultant model—the traditional model—works well to direct the trial judge's attention to the right questions and to provide a workable indication of which issues should be decided by the judge and which, if any, left to the jury. It works equally well to focus the attention of an appellate court on the asserted or actual flaws in a lower court's determination of the case. And it is a very useful tool for scholars and others charged with the task of rationalising and explaining a system's negligence jurisprudence. In the following subsections we will first look at recent (and to this author regrettable) efforts by some courts to radically revise the traditional model. We will then use the traditional model to analyse American decisions in certain developing areas of negligence law that are proving troublesome in both England and the United States.

---

[733] *DePass* v. *United States* (1983) 721 P.2d 203, 208–9 (Posner J, dissenting).

3. Recent Efforts Toward Radical Revision of the Traditional Model

Judge Guido Calabresi, who was a stellar torts teacher and scholar before he ascended to the federal bench, has recently provided us with a powerful demonstration of the traditional model's intended function in delimiting the roles of trial judge and jury. In *Stagl* v. *Delta Airlines*,[734] the plaintiff was a 77-year-old woman who was injured while trying to reclaim her luggage after a Delta flight from Florida to New York. The flight was late in arriving, and the passengers were consequently hurried and impatient. At the luggage-retrieval area provided by Delta at LaGuardia Airport, the plaintiff suffered a broken hip when an unidentified man caused suitcases to fall from the baggage carousel onto her. She sued Delta for negligence in failing to take any crowd-control measures or to provide a safe method whereby elderly and disabled people could retrieve their luggage. The district (i.e., trial) judge granted Delta's motion for summary judgment, holding that Delta had 'no duty' to control the crowd at the luggage retrieval area or to designate a separate area for elderly passengers. Reversing and remanding the case for trial, Judge Calabresi's opinion for the United States Court of Appeals for the Second Circuit explained that the trial judge had made a negligence-law mistake by transmogrifying a breach issue into a duty issue:

There is no question that Delta, as an owner or occupier of the premises, owed a duty to take reasonable steps in maintaining the safety of its baggage retrieval area. . . . [Yet the district judge decided] that 'Delta was under no duty to protect against or warn of potential negligent conduct of third persons within the terminal building'. . . . [T]he district judge refused to impose an obligation upon Delta to safeguard passengers against the foreseeable risks caused by its concentration of allegedly unruly travellers around a congested baggage carousel. In the district [judge's] opinion, such a duty would 'offer little if any real public benefit, and yet would impose upon the airline burdensome and costly obligations.' Although we appreciate that . . . the existence and scope of an alleged tortfeasor's duty is usually a policy-laden declaration reserved for judges . . . we also note that . . . *courts do not exercise this authority on an ad hoc basis.*

To the contrary, the judicial power to modify the general rule that 'whenever one person is by circumstances placed in such a position with regard to another that every one of ordinary sense who did think would at once recognise that if he did not use ordinary care and skill in his own conduct with regard to the circumstances he would cause danger of injury to the person or property of the other, a duty arises to use ordinary care and skill to avoid such danger' . . . is reserved for very limited situations. [It is true that courts have occasionally] conducted *fact-specific duty analyses.* But where, as here, the applicable duty relationship [the premises owner–invitee relationship] is well established, we do not . . . condone the limitation of a familiar liability rule simply to avoid placing a disproportionate burden on a defendant in a particular case. The law deals with that problem *not by redefining the defendant's duties in each case, but by asking whether—considering all the circumstances of the particular case—the defendant breached its duty of care.*[735]

[734] (1995) 52 F.3d 463.
[735] 52 F.3d at 467–9 (emphasis supplied). The internal quotations in the first paragraph are from the district judge's opinion. The internal quotation in the second paragraph is from *Heaven* v. *Pender* [1883] 11 QBD 503, 509.

Despite Judge Calabresi's warnings, some courts seem to be increasingly attracted to 'fact-specific' or 'ad hoc' duty analyses whereby the jury's traditional role is effectively absorbed by the trial judge. For example, in *McCarthy* v. *Olin Corporation* Judge Calabresi's own court upheld the dismissal of a complaint against the manufacturer of 'Black Talon' bullets—bullets that are 'designed to bend upon impact into six ninety-degree angle razor-sharp petals or "talons" that increase the wounding power of the bullet by stretching, cutting and tearing tissue and bone as it travels through the victim'—that were used by a deranged person named Colin Ferguson to commit a massacre aboard a Long Island Railroad commuter train.[736] The complaint alleged defendant's negligence in advertising the bullets in such a way as to make them attractive to dangerous and deranged persons and in failing to restrict the marketing of the bullets to law-enforcement agencies. The trial judge dismissed the complaint on 'no duty' grounds. Affirming over Judge Calabresi's dissent, the appellate court stated that:

[t]o impose a duty on ammunition manufacturers to protect against criminal misuse of its product would likely force ammunition products—which legislatures have not proscribed, and which concededly are not defectively designed or manufactured and have some socially valuable uses—off the market due to the threat of limitless liability. Because Olin did not owe a legal duty to plaintiffs to protect against Colin Ferguson's horrible action, appellants' complaint does not state a cause of action for negligence and the claim was properly dismissed.[737]

Judge Richard Posner—who, like Judge Calabresi, had a brilliant academic career in the torts field before becoming a federal appellate judge—has cogently explained that ad-hoc or fact-specific duty doctrines (like those rejected in *Stagl* and accepted in *McCarthy*) are attractive to judges who feel it necessary 'to rein in juries'.[738] But the price is arguably high: the jury's traditional role is being usurped on a selective and seemingly ad-hoc basis and without principled explanation, and the law of negligence is in danger of becoming rigidified in the areas in which courts have uttered their authoritative 'no duty' declarations. For example, recent decisions of the California Supreme Court have held that the manufacturer of an over-the-counter medication marketed for children had no duty to label the product with Spanish-language warnings of serious risks;[739] that a rubbage-disposal operator had no duty to design or operate its machine so as to minimise noises calculated to frighten horses on nearby bridle paths;[740] and that the operator of a business had no duty to open the cash register to an armed robber who was threatening to shoot a customer unless the robber's demands were complied with.[741] As a dissenting California justice has noted, no matter how desirable may be the public policy effectuated by these judicial determinations, they are subject to criticism on two fundamental fronts: (*a*) 'By framing [these issues] as [questions] of duty, the majority usurps the jury's historic function in a negligence case to determine the rea-

---

[736] (1997) 1129 F.3d 148, 152.　　　　　　　[737] Ibid., 157.

[738] *Edwards* v. *Honeywell, Inc.* (1995) 50 F.3d 484, 488.　　[739] *Ramirez* v. *Plough, Inc.* (1993) 863 P.2d 167.

[740] *Parsons* v. *Crown Disposal Co.* (1997) 936 P.2d 70.

[741] *Kentucky Fried Chicken* v. *Superior Court* (1997) 927 P.2d 1260.

sonableness of defendant's conduct under the surrounding circumstances.'[742] (b) 'It is always possible to recast any question of whether the standard of care has been breached as a question of "duty". . . . If a court does so, however, it abandons the flexibility inherent in the application of the reasonable person standard and instead dictates a rigid, inflexible rule of conduct that applies not only to the defendant in the case before it but also to all defendants in future cases who are confronted by a risk of the same type of harm to another, regardless of differences in the surrounding circumstances.'[743]

4. Duty Frontiers: Pure Economic Damage

All legal systems necessarily impose some 'limits on tort actions for intangible injuries'.[744] One recurrent type of intangible injury is 'pure economic loss', defined as financial loss that is not produced by a physical injury to the plaintiff's person or tangible property. Courts in the United States approach the issue of imposing negligence liability for such intangible economic losses under the influence of two broad policy concerns: proper maintenance of the tort/contract boundary and avoiding the floodgates problem. Courts feel that the tort/contract boundary should be policed because tort law's central concern is human safety whereas contract law is often better designed to control the shifting of financial losses.[745] One cogent evocation of the particular floodgates concerns that arise in economic loss cases runs as follows:

In cases of physical injury to persons or property, the task of defining liability limits is eased, but not eliminated, by the operation of the laws of physics. Friction and gravity dictate that physical objects eventually come to rest. The amount of physical damage that can be inflicted by a speeding automobile or a thrown fist has a self-defining limit. Even in chain reaction cases, intervening forces generally are necessary to restore the velocity of the harm-creating object. These intervening forces offer a natural limit to liability.

The laws of physics do not provide the same restraint for economic loss. Economic relationships are intertwined so intimately that disruption of one may have far-reaching consequences. Furthermore, the chain reaction of economic harm flows from one person to another without the intervention of other forces. Courts facing a case of pure economic loss thus confront the potential for liability of enormous scope, with no easily marked intermediate points and no ready recourse to traditional liability-limiting devices such as intervening cause.[746]

The tort/contract problem and the floodgates problem combine to instil caution in the American courts' approach to economic-loss cases, but certainly do not foreclose all such liability. Liability for negligent misstatements (more often called 'misrepresentation') is reasonably well entrenched in most of the American systems.[747] Much of the current ferment involves the other types of

---

[742] Ibid. at 1272 (Kennard J, dissenting). [743] Ibid. at 1276 (Kennard J, dissenting).

[744] *Christensen* v. *Superior Court* (1991) 54 Cal.3d 868, 820 P.2d 181, 206 (Kennard J, concurring and dissenting).

[745] See generally *East River S.S. Corp.* v. *Transamerica Delaval, Inc.* (1986) 476 US 858, 106 S.Ct. 2295.

[746] H. Perlman, 'Interference With Contract and Other Economic Expectancies: A Clash of Tort and Contract Doctrine' (1982) 49 *UCLR* 61, 71–2.

[747] See, e.g., *Gulf Contracting* v. *Bibb County* (1986) 795 F.2d 980 (Georgia). See also *Restatement (Second) of Torts* (1977) ss. 552, 552A, 552B (hereinafter cited as 'Restatement').

pure economic loss cases. There is no clear consensus, not even on an organisational framework within which to classify these other types. The following subsections reflect one of many possible organisational schemes.[748]

(A) THE PURE ECONOMIC LOSS PROBLEM VIEWED GENERALLY[749]

A few courts have approached the problem of economic loss in a global fashion and attempted to devise principles that can be applied without particular reference to whether the loss arose from physical harm negligently inflicted on the person or property of someone other than the plaintiff, from negligence in the defendant's performance of a service, or from a defect in a building or product. The two leading cases of this type are probably the decision of the United States Court of Appeals for the Fifth Circuit in the maritime case of *State of Louisiana ex rel. Guste* v. *M/V Testbank*[750] and the New Jersey Supreme Court's decision in *People Express Airlines Inc.* v. *Consolidated Rail Corporation.*[751]

These two well-reasoned decisions point in opposite directions. In the *Testbank* decision ten members of the fifteen-judge court held that a vessel whose negligent navigation spilled a chemical into the lower Mississippi River, causing great disruption to shipping, fishing, and other activities in a huge surrounding area, had no duty to anyone (perhaps other than commercial fishermen)[752] whose losses did not stem from physical damage to tangible property. The key to the majority's reasoning was the view that a 'bright line rule'[753] denying all liability for economic loss not caused by physical harm to the plaintiff's person or tangible property best serves the law's administrative and economic concerns. The five dissenters urged that in the *Testbank* context such a bright-line rule of no duty was too clumsy, too arbitrary, and too unfair; they would have sorted among the interests damaged by the defendant's negligence by using familiar principles of legal causation with the modification that losses must be foreseeable in a 'particular' sense in order to be recoverable.[754]

In *People Express* the unanimous New Jersey Supreme Court took an approach virtually identical to the *Testbank* dissenters' in upholding a negligence cause of action of behalf of an airline forced to suspend operations at its main terminal

---

[748] A completely different concept of how to organise the area is reflected in Restatement, s. 766C, which combines cases of negligent harm to the person and property of others and cases of negligence in the performance of a service under the general rubric 'Negligent Interference with Contract or Prospective Contractual Relation'. See also W. P. Keeton *et al.*, *Prosser and Keeton on Torts* (5th edn., 1984) 962–1031, where chapter 24 on 'Economic Relations' is broken down into subsections on 'injurious falsehood', 'interference with contractual relations', and 'interference with prospective advantage'.

[749] Whether the area can usefully be viewed generally is subject to vigorous debate. See *Canadian National Railway Co.* v. *Norsk Pacific Steamship Co.* (1992) 11 CCLT (2d) 1, 58: 'To phrase the key issue in this case as a simple one of "is pure economic loss recoverable in tort" is misleading. I do not doubt that pure economic loss is recoverable in some cases. It does not follow, however, that all economic loss cases are susceptible to the same analysis, or that cases of one type are necessarily relevant to cases of another. . . . The fact is that different types of factual situations may invite different approaches to economic loss, and it seems to me at best unwise to lump them all together for purposes of analysis.' (La Forest J, dissenting).

[750] (1985) 752 F.2d 1019, *cert. denied* (1986) 477 US 903, 106 S.Ct. 3271.

[751] (1985) 100 NJ 246, 495 A.2d 107.

[752] Some courts have held that commercial fishermen are entitled to an exception to the 'pure economic loss' rule on historical grounds. See, e.g., *Union Oil Co.* v. *Oppen* (1974) 501 F.2d 558 (9th Cir.). No claims by commercial fishermen were before the Fifth Circuit in *Testbank*.

[753] 752 F.2d at 1029.   [754] Ibid. at 1049.

because of the threat of an explosion at the defendant's nearby rail yard. The *People Express* court was sharply critical of the physical injury requirement, stating that it 'capriciously showers compensation along the path of physical destruction, regardless of the status or circumstances of the individual claimants.'[755] A better limiting principle, the court said, would allow recovery to '[a]n identifiable class of plaintiffs [that is] particularly foreseeable in terms of the types of persons or entities comprising the class, the certainty or predictability of their presence, the approximate numbers of those in the class, as well as the type of economic expectations disrupted'.[756]

(B) Economic Loss Caused by Negligent Injury to the Person or Tangible Property of Another

Under the influence of a maritime decision authored by Justice Oliver Wendell Holmes,[757] most courts in the United States have denied recovery for economic loss flowing from negligent injury to the person or property of someone other than the plaintiff.[758] This is the area within the economic-loss field where the American courts have been the most conservative.[759] An interesting deviation was *Mattingly* v. *Sheldon Jackson College*,[760] in which the court recognised a cause of action on behalf of an employer who suffered 'losses of business income and profit and increases in expenses'[761] as a result of defendant's negligent injury to three of the plaintiff's employees (one of whom was the plaintiff's son). In this portion of the opinion the *Mattingly* court relied extensively on the reasoning in *People Express*.[762] However, in a separate section of the opinion the *Mattingly* court then stated: 'We now adopt the modern rule that employers may not recover simply for the loss of their employees' services or for loss of profits arising from the negligent injury of their employees by a third person.'[763] The court did not explain the inconsistency between its two announced holdings. *Mattingly* thus stands as a kind of monument to the general confusion that seems to pervade the economic-loss field.

---

[755] 495 A.2d at 111. [756] Ibid. at 116.

[757] See *Robins Dry Dock & Repair Co.* v. *Flint* (1927) 275 US 303, 48 S.Ct. 134 (holding that a vessel's time charterer—a type of lessee—could not recover from the dry dock whose negligence damaged the vessel and caused the charterer to lose the use of it).

[758] See, e.g., *Louisville & N. R. Co.* v. *M/V Bayou Lacombe* (1979) 597 F.2d 469 (5th Cir.); *PPG Industries, Inc.* v. *Bean Dredging* (1984) 447 So.2d 1058; *Fifield Manor* v. *Finston* (1960) 54 Cal.2d 632, 354 P.2d 1073; *Stevenson* v. *East Ohio Gas Co.* (1946) 73 NE2d 200 (Ohio App.).

[759] See *Christensen* v. *Superior Court* (1991) 54 Cal.3d 868, 820 P.2d 181, 189 (listing as two factors explaining the conservatism: (*a*) the fact that in these cases 'the plaintiff had no pre-existing relationship' with the defendant and (*b*) 'the defendant had not previously assumed a duty of care beyond that owed to the public in general'); *J'Aire Corp.* v. *Gregory* (1979) 24 Cal.3d 799, 598 P.2d 60, 65 (allowing recovery for economic loss caused by the negligent performance of a service and distinguishing the cases involving negligent harms to the person or property of others); D. Robertson, 'Recovery in Louisiana Tort Law for Intangible Economic Loss' (1986) 46 *Louis. LR* 737, 753 (stating that courts are 'more reluctant to award recovery' in cases involving harms to the person or property of others than in other types of economic-loss cases).

[760] (1987) 743 P.2d 356 (Alaska). [761] Ibid. at 361.

[762] See ibid. at 359: 'We are persuaded by the approach of the New Jersey Supreme Court and set forth its analysis in some detail.'

[763] Ibid. at 363.

(c) Economic Loss Caused by Negligence in the Performance of a Service

Two of the leading American treatises describe a consensus that recovery in tort should generally be denied for economic losses caused by the defendant's negligence in the performance of a service or undertaking.[764] This viewpoint is offset to a very considerable degree by the fact that American contract law often allows the injured party to bring a successful action either as a party to the contract whereby the defendant agreed to perform the service or as a third-party beneficiary of that contract.[765] Furthermore, there are a significant number of decisions allowing recovery for negligently inflicted economic loss without regard to the requirements of contract law when 'a benefit to the plaintiff was the purpose of the contract [whereby defendant undertook to perform the service] and the damage was foreseeable.'[766]

Some authorities suggest that the conceptual thread uniting these successful negligence claims is that the defendant 'renders a service or has some other contractual relationship in which he owes a duty to use reasonable care to avoid a risk of pecuniary loss to the person with whom he is directly dealing, and that same duty is held to extend to another person whom he knows to be pecuniarily affected by the service rendered'.[767] Others believe that the only unifying principle is a 'limitation to specifically foreseeable plaintiffs'.[768]

In truth the decisional law is uncertain to a highly unsatisfactory degree. When the defendant's negligent performance happens to consist of a misstatement, liability is reasonably likely.[769] When it consists in some other kind of conduct, the recognition of a duty of care will turn on 'various factors, among which are the extent to which the transaction was intended to affect the plaintiff, the foreseeability of harm to him, the degree of certainty that the plaintiff suffered injury, the closeness of the connection between the defendant's conduct and the injury suffered, the moral blame attached to the defendant's conduct, and the policy of preventing future harm'.[770] Factors of such generality and elasticity do not furnish much predictive or resolving power.

(d) Economic Loss Caused by Defects in Buildings and Products

On the problem of economic loss caused by defects in buildings the American courts are sharply divided. In some states recovery of economic losses from negligent builders seems to be freely allowed.[771] Other states take the opposite

---

[764] See W. P. Keeton *et al.*, *Prosser and Keeton on Torts* (5th edn., 1984), s. 129; *Restatement*, s. 766C.

[765] See *Prosser and Keeton*, s. 129 at 1000. See also *Hale* v. *Groce* (1987) 304 Or. 281, 744 P.2d 1289 (holding that intended beneficiary of will negligently prepared by defendant attorney has both a third-party-beneficiary cause of action and a negligence cause of action).

[766] *Christensen* v. *Superior Court* (1991) 54 Cal.3d 868, 820 P.2d 181, 194. See also *J'Aire Corp.* v. *Gregory* (1979) 24 Cal.3d 799, 598 P.2d 60, 65 (allowing recovery under negligence law where there is 'a special relationship' between the plaintiff and defendant, where 'the risk of harm is foreseeable and is closely connected with the defendant's conduct, where damages are not wholly speculative and the injury is not part of the plaintiff's ordinary business risk').

[767] *Restatement*, s. 766C at 26.   [768] *Prosser and Keeton*, s. 129 at 1001.

[769] See *Restatement*, s. 766C at 26. See also text and [DWR note 35] above.

[770] *Biakanja* v. *Irving* (1958) 49 Cal.2d 647, 320 P.2d 16, 19.

[771] See, e.g., *Sewell* v. *Gregory* (1988) 371 SE2d 82, 84–5 (West Virginia).

view and deny a negligence remedy to disappointed home-buyers who have not sustained personal injury or physical damage to other property than the defective structure.[772] A third group of states have found a middle ground that allows recovery against a negligent builder for the costs of remedying building defects that threaten personal injury.[773] Other permutations and compromise positions can also be found in the jurisprudence and literature.

The leading American decision on the problem of economic loss caused by defects in products is probably that of the United States Supreme Court in the maritime case of *East River Steamship Corporation* v. *Transamerica Delaval Inc.*,[774] in which the charterers (lessees) of ships whose engines failed were denied recovery against the manufacturer of the defective engines for the monetary losses caused by the ships' unfitness for service. The court held that 'a manufacturer in a commercial relationship has no duty under either a negligence or strict products liability theory to prevent a product from injuring itself'.[775] The court noted a wide divergence among the American courts that had considered the point and justified its resolution in three ways. First, the paramount concern of the law of negligence, human safety, is not centrally implicated when a product injures only itself.

The tort concern with safety is reduced when an injury is only to the product itself. When a person is injured, the 'cost of an injury and the loss of time or health may be an overwhelming misfortune', and one the person is not prepared to meet. In contrast, when a product injures itself, the commercial user stands to lose the value of the product, risks the displeasure of its customers who find that the product does not meet their needs, or, as in this case, experiences increased costs in performing a service. Losses like these can be insured. Society need not presume that a customer needs special protection. The increased cost to the public that would result from holding a manufacturer liable in tort for injury to the product itself is not justified.[776]

Second, if tort liability were extended too far, 'contract law would drown in a sea of tort'.[777]

Contract law, and the law of warranty in particular, is well suited to commercial controversies of the sort involved in this case because the parties may set the terms of their own agreements. The manufacturer can restrict its liability, within limits, by disclaiming warranties or limiting remedies. In exchange, the purchaser pays less for the product. Since a commercial situation generally does not involve large disparities in bargaining power, we see no reason to intrude into the parties' allocation of the risk.[778]

Third, the court discussed the floodgates problem:

In products liability law, where there is a duty to the public generally, foreseeability is an inadequate brake. Permitting recovery for all foreseeable claims for purely economic

---

[772] See, e.g., *Casa Clara Condominium Ass'n* v. *Charley Toppino & Sons* (1993) 620 So.2d 1244 (Florida).

[773] See, e.g., *Council of Co-Owners* v. *Whiting-Turner Contracting Co.* (1986) 308 Md. 18, 517 A.2d 336, 344–5.

[774] (1986) 476 US 858, 106 S.Ct. 2295.

[775] 106 S.Ct. at 2302. The *East River* rule contemplates tort recovery when the defective product injuries other property but not when the damage is confined to the 'product itself'. Distinguishing between 'the product itself' and 'other property' can be extremely tricky. See, e.g., *Saratoga Fishing Co.* v. *J. M. Martinec & Co.* (1997) 520 US 875, 117 S.Ct. 1783.

[776] 106 S.Ct. at 2302 (citations omitted). [777] Ibid. at 2300.

[778] Ibid. at 2303 (citations omitted).

loss could make a manufacturer liable for vast sums. It would be difficult for a manufacturer to take into account the expectations of persons downstream who may
encounter its product. In this case, for example, if the charterers—already one step
removed from the transaction—were permitted to recover their economic losses, then
the companies that subchartered the ships might claim their economic losses from the
delays, and the charterers' customers also might claim their economic losses, and so on.
'The law does not spread its protection so far.'[779]

5. Duty Frontiers: Nervous Shock

In the United States nervous shock is more often called mental or emotional
distress. A leading treatise announces: 'No general agreement has yet been
reached on many of the issues involving liability for negligence resulting in
fright, shock, or other mental or emotional harm, and any resulting physical
consequences.'[780] Such statements should not lead the reader to conclude that
chaos reigns. While confusion may be found in the language and reasoning of
some of the judicial opinions in the area, when one considers the actual results
of the reported cases there seems to be broad agreement among the American
states on the general outlines of this body of law.[781] The law in virtually all
states reflects the view that the policies of the law of negligence would be ill
served by allowing recovery for all emotional harms that foreseeably result
from negligent conduct. It is common ground that the floodgates problem, the
problem of easily fabricated and easily exaggerated injuries, and the need to
avoid encouraging or validating undue sensitivity[782] all point in the direction of
retaining special duty limitations on recovery for emotional harm.

In broad outline, the salient features of this body of American law are as follows. All states have long allowed recovery for negligently inflicted emotional
harm when it is 'parasitic to' (caused by) a compensable physical injury. For
example, a negligent injury to the hand of an amateur violinist will lead to liability for the emotional harm stemming from the plaintiff's inability to pursue
his avocation.

When one moves away from this classic case of 'parasitic' emotional harm,
the courts' reasoning and rhetoric begin to develop divergent tendencies.
However, common policies and themes are visible. On two preliminary matters
there seems to be complete agreement. All courts try to restrict recovery to serious emotional distress; pursuit of claims for transient or slight distress is
actively discouraged.[783] Moreover, the precipitating event must have been one

---

[779] 106 S.Ct. at 2304 (citations omitted). The internal quotation is from the Holmes opinion in *Robins Dry Dock*, treated above at p. 213, 275 US at 309, 48 S.Ct. at 135.

[780] W. P. Keeton *et al.*, *Prosser and Keeton on Torts* (5th edn., 1984), s. 54 at 359–60.

[781] See generally *Consolidated Rail Corp.* v. *Gottshall* (1994) 512 US 532, 114 S.Ct. 2396; D. W. Robertson *et al.*, *Cases and Materials on Torts* (2nd edn., 1998) 241–63.

[782] See *Bosley* v. *Andrews* (1958) 393 Pa. 161, 142 A.2d 263, 266–7: 'Such an event, if compensable, may cause normal people, as well as nervous persons and persons who are mentally disturbed or mentally ill, to honestly believe that the sudden and unexpected event caused them fright or nervous shock or nervous tension with subsequent emotional distress or suffering or pain or miscarriage or heart attack, or some kind of disease.'

[783] See, e.g , *Rodrigues* v. *State* (1970) 472 P.2d 509, 520 (Hawaii): 'It is universally agreed that there are compelling reasons for limiting the recovery of the plaintiff to claims of *serious* mental distress.' Emphasis in original.

that would produce serious emotional distress in what Lord Ackner has called 'a reasonably strong-nerved person'.[784]

With those two background requirements in mind, we can see that the reported cases in which plaintiffs have been successful in recovering for negligently inflicted emotional distress that is not parasitic to a physical injury fall into the following four categories. *First*, the great majority of the states will allow recovery for emotional injury incurred in an accident in which the plaintiff suffered an impact with his person[785] or sustained a compensable physical harm.[786] For example, when the defendant allowed a large sheet of glass to fall off its lorry on an interstate highway and smash into the windscreen of a following car, the following driver, though physically unhurt, was allowed to recover for the serious emotional distress that he suffered as a result of having his windscreen shattered and being showered with glass fragments.[787]

Second, most of the states will also allow recovery for emotional trauma produced by the plaintiff's fear for her or his own physical safety, provided the plaintiff suffered such fright while in a zone of physical danger created by the defendant's negligent conduct.[788] Along with the requirements that the emotional harm should flow from the plaintiff's fear for her own physical safety and should be incurred in the zone of danger created by the defendant's negligent conduct, many of the states require in addition that the emotional harm for which recovery is sought should have manifested itself in physical symptoms or illness.[789] In states where this 'physical manifestation' requirement obtains and is taken seriously, it is seen as a useful guarantee that the emotional distress was genuine and serious. For example, in one recent case it precluded recovery on behalf of an otherwise deserving victim who could allege nothing more in the way of physical symptoms of her distress than frequent 'crying, sleeplessness, increased migraine headaches, and becoming upset when she viewed pregnant women'.[790] In other states little more than lip-service is paid to the physical manifestation requirement; in those jurisdictions allegations of sleeplessness and migraine headaches would suffice to meet the requirement. In recognition that the requirement has a tendency to become trivialised under the pressure of plaintiffs' counsels' ingenuity, a number of states have jettisoned it altogether.[791]

Third, many states will also allow recovery for emotional injury produced by the plaintiff's having witnessed injury or death to a loved one, provided the

---

[784] *Alcock* v. *Chief Constable of South Yorkshire* [1991] 3 WLR 1057, 1106.

[785] See, e.g., *Stoddard* v. *Davidson* (1986) 355 Pa.Super. 262, 513 A.2d 419 (jostling of occupants of vehicle as it ran over a corpse in the roadway sufficed for impact).

[786] See, e.g., *Potere* v. *City of Philadelphia* (1955) 380 Pa. 581, 112 A.2d 100 (fall of plaintiff's lorry into deep hole in street produced minor physical injuries and an 'anxiety neurosis' that was not caused by the minor physical injuries but rather by the fall; recovery for the anxiety neurosis allowed).

[787] See *Schultz* v. *Barberton Glass Co.* (1983) 4 Ohio St.3d 131, 447 NE2d 109.

[788] See, e.g., *Niederman* v. *Brodsky* (1970) 463 Pa. 401, 261 A.2d 84.

[789] For discussion of the 'requirement that the emotional distress result in (although it need not be caused by) physical injury', see *Bass* v. *Nooney Co.* (1983) 646 SW2d 765, 771 (Missouri).

[790] *Robbins* v. *Kaas* (1987) 163 Ill.App.3d 927, 516 NE2d 1023, 1027.

[791] See, e.g., *St. Elizabeth Hospital* v. *Garrard* (1987) 730 SW2d 649, 652–3 (Texas); *Molien* v. *Kaiser Foundation Hospitals* (1980) 27 Cal.3d 916, 616 P.2d 813, 819–21.

plaintiff can satisfy three criteria of having been at or near the scene, sustaining the emotional distress through direct and contemporaneous perception of the harm to the loved one, and having a close relationship with the loved one. (Here, too, many states add a physical manifestation requirement.) For a time after the landmark California decision[792] allowing emotional suffering recovery in this situation, some courts treated the three criteria as mere guidelines to be used in deciding whether the emotional distress was a foreseeable enough consequence of defendant's negligent conduct for recovery to be appropriate.[793] More recently the three criteria have been regarded as doctrinal requirements[794]—part of the duty rule whose ingredients the plaintiff must satisfy—such that failing to satisfy any one of them is fatal to recovery.

Fourth, two early exceptions to the normal rule denying recovery for negligently inflicted emotional distress allowed such recovery to persons aggrieved by negligence in the transmission of a telegram or similar message regarding a serious illness or death in the family[795] or by being a witness to or otherwise directly affected by the defendant's negligent handling of the corpse of a loved one.[796] Not many courts require physical manifestation of these types of emotional distress.[797] Perhaps the ease with which all of us can imagine the horror of the situations is thought to provide a sufficient guarantee that the distress was genuine.

Aside from the foregoing four categories, virtually all of the states deny recovery for negligently inflicted emotional suffering except when it is parasitic to a compensable physical injury. For the most part, the results of the reported cases are harmonious. But there is one important qualification, necessitated by the presence of isolated decisions throughout the country that seem to ignore the normal impediments to recovery for emotional harm. For example, scattered decisions can be found allowing recovery for emotional suffering incident to negligence in the disposal of body parts,[798] in the handling of pets,[799] and in the destruction or damage of property.[800]

In summary, even though there may be persuasive policy arguments in favour of more generous treatment of emotional injuries,[801] the simple truth is that no jurisdiction could afford to treat emotional injuries on the same basis as physical injuries. In reality there are bound to be duty limits, and the courts

---

[792] *Dillon v. Legg* (1968) 68 Cal.2d 728, 441 P.2d 912.

[793] See, e.g., *Haught v. Maceluch* (1982) 681 F.2d 291 (Texas law).

[794] See *Thing v. LaChusa* (1989) 48 Cal.3d 644, 771 P.2d 814.

[795] See, e.g., *Johnson v. State of New York* (1975) 37 NY2d 378, 334 NE2d 590; *Young v. Telegraph Co.* (1890) 107 NC 370, 11 SE 1044.

[796] See, e.g., *Christensen v. Superior Court* (1991) 54 Cal.3d 868, 820 P.2d 181; *Gammon v. Osteopathic Hospital of Maine, Inc.* (1987) 534 A.2d 1282.

[797] See W. P. Keeton *et al.*, *Prosser and Keeton on Torts* (5th edn., 1984), s. 54 at 361–2.

[798] See *Mokry v. University of Texas Health Science Center* (1975) 529 SW2d 802 (Tex.App.) (defendant negligently lost plaintiff's diseased eyeball entrusted to it for testing).

[799] See *Campbell v. Animal Quarantine Station* (1981) 63 Haw. 557, 632 P.2d 1066 (dog).

[800] See *Rodrigues v. State* (1970) 472 P.2d 509 (Hawaii) (flooded home); *Adams v. State* (1978) 357 So.2d 1239 (La.App.) (pecan tree with sentimental value).

[801] For an array of such arguments, see N. J. Mullany and P. R. Handford, *Tort Liability for Psychiatric Damage* (1993). For an assessment of their persuasiveness, see D. Robertson, 'Review Article: Liability in Negligence for Nervous Shock' (1994) 57 MLR 649.

are not doing their job if they do not articulate those limits in a clear enough fashion to inform counsel for potential plaintiffs that only limited types of emotional claims can be allowed. In this area many scholars feel that bright-line rules would be very welcome. For example, 'no pets'.

6. Duty and Legal Causation Frontiers: Liability for Others' Crimes and Intentional Harms[802]

The English cases of *Dorset Yacht*[803] and *Smith* v. *Littlewoods*[804] treat a social and legal problem that arises in America in a wide variety of contexts:[805] the victim of a crime or intentional tort (such as vandalism or theft), on finding that the immediate perpetrator is uninsured and impecunious and therefore useless as a potential source of compensation, seeks to attribute responsibility to some other person or entity whose negligence arguably set the stage for the injuries or in some other fashion contributed to them. It will facilitate discussion if we think of these as cases in which the plaintiff seeks to hold the defendant liable for negligent conduct that permitted or facilitated the commission of a crime or intentional tort by X, a third person who is not in such a relationship with the defendant that defendant can be made vicariously liable for X's conduct. All of these cases present legal causation issues. In addition, many (though by no means all) of them implicate the settled common-law reluctance to 'impose liability for what are called pure omissions'[806] or 'nonfeasance'.[807] Because of the way in which legal causation arguments and arguments over the no-duty-to-act issue tend to become intertwined and to dominate discussion in them, cases of negligence liability for the crimes and intentional harms of others constitute a discrete area within the law of negligence.

(A) The Legal Causation Issue

The legal causation issue leaps to the forefront in many of these decisions because it is so obvious that the most immediate and direct cause of the harm was the bad conduct of X rather than the (by comparison) more 'background' or 'remote' contribution of the defendant. However, when courts use a causation doctrine to resolve liability questions in this area it usually has the effect of obscuring the true policy grounds of the decision. For example, one court found

---

[802] For a fuller treatment see D. Robertson, 'Negligence Liability for Crimes and Intentional Torts Committed by Others' (1992) 67 *Tulane LR* 135 (hereinafter cited as 'Others' Crimes').

[803] *Dorset Yacht Co. Ltd.* v. *Home Office* [1970] AC 1004.   [804] *Smith* v. *Littlewoods Ltd.* [1987] 1 AC 241.

[805] Dramatic examples include *McCarthy* v. *Olin Corp.* (1997) 119 F.3d 148 (New York) (upholding dismissal on 'no duty' grounds of complaint against manufacturer of 'Black Talon' ammunition for negligent marketing leading to massacre aboard commuter train); *Kitchen* v. *K-Mart Corp.* (1997) 697 So.2d 1200 (Florida) (holding that department store could be liable for selling a rifle to a drunken man who then used the weapon to intentionally shoot the plaintiff); *Buczkowski* v. *McKay* (1992) 490 NW2d 330 (Michigan) (holding that department store had no duty to avoid selling shotgun shells to a drunken man who then used the shells to intentionally shoot the plaintiff); *Taco Bell* v. *Lennon* (1987) 744 P.2d 43 (Colorado) (upholding recovery against restaurant by customer who was shot by a gunman during the course of an armed robbery).

[806] See text at p. 137 above, quoting Lord Goff's judgment in *Smith* v. *Littlewoods Organisation Ltd.* [1987] 1 AC 241.

[807] W. P. Keeton *et al.*, *Prosser and Keeton on Torts* (5th edn., 1984), s. 56 at 373.

'no causal connection' between an Illinois mental institution's negligent release of a dangerous schizophrenic from custody and a murder committed by the schizophrenic in Florida fourteen months later.[808] But obviously there *was* a causal connection; if the schizophrenic had remained locked up in Illinois he would not have been able to get to Florida to kill the plaintiffs' decedent. The court's choice of a causation basis for deciding the case provided no useful information beyond the boundaries of that single case. Similarly obscurant is an oft-repeated shibboleth that the provider of liquor is not liable for harms caused by an intoxicated consumer 'because the law deem[s] the consumption rather than the serving of liquor as the proximate cause of an accident'.[809] This liquor-provider causation shibboleth is a no-duty rule disguised in the raiment of legal causation. If the disguise were removed the rule could not so easily be set forth as somehow self-justifying. No-duty rules traditionally have called for policy justifications.

The standard view of the operation of the legal-causation issue in the present context is set forth as follows in a leading treatise:

> An act or an omission may be negligent if the actor realises or should realise that it involves an unreasonable risk of harm to another through the negligent or reckless conduct of . . . a third person. . . . An act or an omission may [also] be negligent if the actor realizes or should realize that it involves an unreasonable risk of harm to another through the conduct of . . . a third person which is intended to cause harm, even though such conduct is criminal. . . . The act of a third person in committing an intentional tort or crime is a superseding cause of harm to another resulting therefrom, although the actor's negligent conduct created a situation which afforded an opportunity to the third person to commit such a tort or crime, unless the actor at the time of his negligent conduct realized or should have realized the likelihood that such a situation might be created, and that a third person might avail himself of the opportunity to commit such a tort or crime.[810]

The inquiry described boils down to whether the risk that X would harm the plaintiff in some fashion broadly similar to that which occurred was a foreseeable enough risk of the defendant's conduct to call for reasonable precautions on the defendant's part. This is obviously a highly flexible inquiry to which judicial responses will differ depending on factual nuances. Predicting courts' responses to it in particular cases is assisted to a modest degree by realising that 'legal causation tends to become more inclusive as the degree of defendant's fault increases. Legal causation also tends to be more inclusive in cases of physical harm to human beings than in cases involving other types of damage.'[811] It will be remembered that *Dorset Yacht* and *Smith* v. *Littlewoods* were property-damage cases.

Almost always there will be a large overlap between the legal causation and negligence (breach-of-duty) issues in these cases, and sometimes the two issues will virtually coalesce. Suppose a citizen sees that his automobile is being

---

[808] *Novak* v. *Rathnam* (1987) 153 Ill.App.3d 408, 505 NE2d 773, 776.
[809] *Otis Engineering Corp.* v. *Clark* (1983) 668 SW2d 307, 318 n. 3 (Texas; McGee J dissenting). See also La.R.S. 9:2800.1(A).
[810] Restatement, ss. 302A, 302B, 448.   [811] 'Others' Crimes', cited above at p. 219, at 139.

driven away by a thief and commandeers another vehicle to engage in high-speed pursuit through a densely populated area. During the chase the thief runs down a pedestrian. Should the citizen be liable to the pedestrian?[812] The duty and factual causation issues are not problematic in this case. Obviously the citizen owes a duty to use reasonable care in all respects in operating a vehicle on a public roadway. Equally obviously the citizen's conduct in pursuing the thief was a factual cause of the pedestrian's injuries. The pivotal issue in this case is the breach-of-duty issue. Was it unreasonable for the citizen to chase the thief? Given the obvious risks of high-speed pursuit to other roadway users, would a reasonable person have sought police assistance, thereby taking the substantial risk that he would never see his car again, in lieu of high-speed pursuit through crowds of his neighbours? The answer to this question depends in substantial part on the degree of foreseeability that the chase would lead to a traffic accident. Once this risk is seen to be high enough to lead to the conclusion that the citizen was guilty of negligence, there is little remaining work to be done on the issue of legal cause.[813] Similarly, suppose that an abandoned building—one that presents no appreciable risk of fire or tumbling-down damage to persons in the vicinity—is used by a sociopath as a hiding place for molesting children. Whether the building owner is negligent for failing to lock up or otherwise secure the building against intruders depends in major part on the degree of foreseeable risk that the building will be used for such purposes.[814] If the owner is found guilty of negligence, there is really nothing further to be said about legal causation.

It follows from the foregoing discussion that legal causation is seldom a legitimately dispositive issue in the present context. In most of these cases 'tortious or criminal action by a third party is . . . the "very kind of thing" '[815] that made it arguably negligent for defendant to act or fail to act as it did. Legal causation defences are routinely invoked in these cases but usually turn out to be a poor way of saying something about duty or breach of duty. If the risk that X will commit a crime or intentional tort is one of the reasons defendant's conduct appears negligent, then X's fault cannot sensibly be regarded as an intervening or superseding cause that insulates defendant from liability. If defendant is to be absolved in this situation, some other reason must be found.

(B) THE NO-DUTY-TO-ACT ISSUE

The common-law precept that excludes liability for what is variously called 'nonfeasance' or 'pure omissions'[816] is firm but quite narrow. How narrow

---

[812] See *Smith* v. *English* (1991) 586 So.2d 583 (La.App.), *cert. denied*, 590 So.2d 80 (Louisiana) (imposing liability).

[813] The negligence and legal cause issues overlap but do not fully coalesce in this case. The foreseeable risks that may lead to the conclusion that the citizen's conduct was negligent included not only the risk that the thief would run down someone but also the risk that the citizen himself would.

[814] Cf. *Nixon* v. *Mr. Property Management Co.* (1985) 690 SW2d 546 (Texas) (liability based on violation of city ordinance).

[815] *Dorset Yacht Co. Ltd.* v. *Home Office* [1970] AC 1004, 1030 (Lord Reid).

[816] See text at p. 219 above. See also Restatement, s. 314: 'The fact that the actor realises or should realise that action on his part is necessary for another's aid or protection does not of itself impose upon him a duty to take such action.

depends in the first place on what is regarded as a 'pure' omission and in the second place on the exceptions that courts are willing to devise to the basic no-duty-to-act rule. Judicial and societal views have changed on these matters over the years. 'Merely' owning real estate was at one time regarded as bearing such a close resemblance to doing nothing whatever that the landowner could rarely be held liable for injuries caused by conditions on the land. From this point of view the modern law of landowners' and land occupiers' liability began with the law's willingness to recognise something that laymen had known all along, viz., that owning land is itself an activity that has societal implications.[817]

Analysis of the cases in which the defendant is sought to be held liable for the intentional or criminal actions of X is facilitated by separating out the ones that do not involve any significant nonfeasance issue and further by grouping those that do involve nonfeasance issues into the categories suggested by the exceptions to the basic no-duty-to-act rule that may be coming to be recognised in the modern cases. This technique yields the categories embodied in the following subsections.

(i) Liability Based on Affirmative Negligent Conduct ('Misfeasance')   When the defendant contributes to the injuries caused by X in some active way, such as chasing a fleeing automobile thief under circumstances likely to cause the thief to injure others, liability for negligence may readily be imposed.[818] Such cases present no nonfeasance problem; liability flows from 'misfeasance',[819] defined as affirmative conduct that is negligent under the circumstances. The same can be said of cases in which an employer negligently hires or retains an unsuitable person for a job presenting unusual opportunities or temptations to commit crimes. Here again the basis of liability is affirmative negligent conduct, viz., putting the unsuitable person into contact with the foreseeable victim.[820]

One large group of misfeasance cases involve what is sometimes called 'negligent entrustment'.[821] When the defendant entrusts X with a dangerous instrumentality such as a pistol[822] or a belly-full of whisky[823] under circumstances when a reasonable person would have refrained from doing so, the defendant can be liable for injuries X causes by reason of having been provided with the dangerous instrument or substance.

Liquor-provider or 'dram shop' liability raises special problems, but not because there is any conceptual difficulty in classifying the defendant's conduct as misfeasance and not because of any legitimate legal causation difficulties.

---

[817] See the discussion in *Sprecher* v. *Adamson Companies* (1981) 30 Cal.3d 358, 636 P.2d 1121, 1125–8.

[818] See text at p. 221 above.

[819] W. P. Keeton *et al.*, *Prosser and Keeton on Torts* (5th edn., 1984), s. 56 at 373.

[820] See, e.g., *Bonsignore* v. *City of New York* (1982) 683 F.2d 635 (New York) (police department was liable to the victim of a shooting by a disturbed policeman who should not have been assigned to street duty); *Becken* v. *Manpower, Inc.* (1976) 532 F.2d 56 (Illinois) (furniture-moving company was liable for thefts from customers by temporary employees who should not have been hired because they had arrest records for theft); *Ponticas* v. *KMS Investments* (1983) 331 NW2d 907 (Minnesota) (apartment complex liable for rape of tenant by apartment manager).

[821] W. P. Keeton *et al.*, *Prosser and Keeton on Torts* (5th edn., 1984), s. 33 at 197.

[822] See, e.g., *Phillips ex rel. Phillips* v. *Roy* (1983) 431 So.2d 849 (La.App.) (liability for selling pistol to deranged man).

[823] See, e.g., *El Chico Corp.* v. *Poole* (1987) 732 SW2d 306 (Texas) (liquor-seller liability for traffic accident).

Liquor-provider liability is a special problem because of societal factors. Injuries caused by intoxicated persons are prevalent. Many of the intoxicated persons who cause these injuries turn out to be impecunious and uninsured. Taverns, other sellers, and social hosts of all kinds often dispense alcoholic beverages under circumstances that a moment's reflection would reveal as endangering highway users and others. Yet vast numbers of people do not regard such conduct as wrongful, at least not unless the circumstances are highly egregious. Furthermore, liquor, beer, and wine are major American industries with considerable financial and political power.

As a result of this complex of factors and many others, all of the states are struggling with the liquor-provider problem. Some have 'dram shop' statutes that impose liability on liquor sellers under certain circumstances.[824] Others recognise a common-law duty of reasonable care that can hold both liquor sellers and social providers of alcohol liable for alcohol-induced injuries.[825] Quite a few have recently gone in the other direction by enacting statutes precluding liquor-provider liability in most circumstances.[826]

Various middle grounds seem to be emerging. In a few states liquor-provider liability is limited to grossly negligent[827] conduct on the part of the provider. In several others a rule has developed as follows: One can be liable for injuries that result from having provided liquor to a minor, because doing so is a misdemeanour in most states and is in any event generally regarded as wrongful.[828] In the cases of injuries to or by an adult drunk, one cannot be liable for having provided the liquor, but there remains the possibility of liability for affirmative acts over and above providing the liquor, such as ejecting a helplessly intoxicated customer from a tavern[829] or 'jump-starting' the automobile of an obviously liquor-impaired man to enable him to try to drive home.[830] One frequent type of argument against liquor-provider liability should be identified so as to explore and question its premises. This is the view that holding the liquor provider liable will somehow 'erode . . . the concept that an individual is responsible for his or her own actions'[831] by shifting responsibility away from the drunken immediate perpetrator of the harm onto the more indirectly responsible liquor provider. A partial answer to this argument is the tort doctrine of indemnity; in some American states a liquor provider who was held liable to the victim of a drunk driver could get a judgment against the drunk for

---

[824] See, e.g., Tex. Alco. Bev. Code Ann., ss. 2.02, 2.03.

[825] See, e.g., *Kelly* v. *Gwinell* (1984) 96 NJ 538, 476 A.2d 1219 (social host); *Alumni Ass'n* v. *Sullivan* (1987) 369 Pa.Super. 596, 535 A.2d 1095 (college fraternity).

[826] See, e.g., La. R.S. 9:2800.1.

[827] See, e.g., Tex. Alco. Bev. Code Ann., s. 2.02 (liquor seller liable only if 'it was *apparent* [that the customer] was *obviously* intoxicated to the extent that he presented a *clear* danger to himself and others') (emphasis added).

[828] See, e.g., *St. Hill* v. *Tabor* (1989) 542 So.2d 499 (Louisiana) (social host who provided liquor to minors held liable as a matter of common law); *Edson* v. *Walker* (1991) 573 So.2d 545, cert. denied, 573 So.2d 34 (Louisiana) (liability imposed on violator of statute prohibiting sale of alcohol to minors).

[829] See *Pence* v. *Ketchum* (1976) 326 So.2d 831, overruled in part by *Thrasher* v. *Leggett* (1979) 373 So.2d 494 (Louisiana).

[830] See *Leppke* v. *Segura* 632 P.2d 1057 (Colo. App.).

[831] *Otis Engineering Corp.* v. *Clark* (1983) 668 SW2d 307, 319 (Texas; McGee J, dissenting).

full indemnity[832] and would therefore be in a position to claim the proceeds of whatever liability insurance policy the drunk driver had. In fact, drunk drivers in America often have little or no insurance, so the real choice is between saddling the injured person with the loss or placing it on the liquor provider and hence ultimately on the cost of liquor.

(ii) Liability Based on Defendant's Failure to Take Reasonable Steps to Alleviate Dangers Created by Defendant's Prior 'Innocent' Conduct The immediately preceding subsection discusses cases that base liability on affirmative negligent conduct and thus fall outside the no-duty-to-act rule. We now turn to the first of the settled exceptions to that rule. In a leading decision from the state of Nebraska the court refused to find an automobile driver negligent when his vehicle struck a trolley pole and knocked it across the roadway, but held him liable for thereafter failing to take steps to protect other motorists from hitting the downed pole.[833] A very similar decision from the state of Georgia held that a motorist who was 'innocent' in striking a cow in the roadway nevertheless could be held liable for failing to use reasonable care to warn other motorists of the danger created by the cow's body.[834] The principle of these decisions has come to be widely recognised. A leading treatise offers the following summary:

(1) If an actor does an act, and subsequently realises or should realise that it has created an unreasonable risk of causing physical harm to another, he is under a duty to exercise reasonable care to prevent the risk from taking effect.
(2) The rule stated in Subsection (1) applied even though at the time of the act the actor has no reason to believe that it will involve such a risk.[835]

The principle is often called the 'prior innocent conduct' exception to the no-duty-to-act rule. It is simple and easy to accept; certainly if the defendant's previous activities, albeit without fault, have contributed to the dangerous situation in which the plaintiff is found, the defendant should have a duty of reasonable care to alleviate the danger. Few if any American courts would follow *Osterlind* v. *Hill*[836] today. The conduct of renting a canoe would be regarded as prior innocent conduct that generates a duty to take reasonable steps once the renter knew or should have known that the customer was in danger.

Many of the situations in which defendants have been held liable for failing to guard against the risk that X will commit an intentional tort or a crime fall into the prior-innocent-conduct category. *Dorset Yacht* is a good example. If the borstal boys had never been incarcerated the defendant would have had no duty to guard against the risk that they might steal or damage the plaintiff's boat. But incarcerating the boys and putting them to work off the coast of Poole was prior innocent conduct that created new dangers by putting the boys together in a kind of critical mass and in the plaintiff's vicinity under circumstances in which an escape attempt was a distinct possibility. When the boys

---

[832] See W. P. Keeton *et al.*, *Prosser and Keeton on Torts* (5th edn., 1984), s. 51; Restatement, s. 886B.
[833] *Simonsen* v. *Thorin* (1931) 234 NW 628 (Nebraska).
[834] *Hardy* v. *Brooks* (1961) 103 Ga.App. 124, 118 SE2d 492.   [835] Restatement, s. 321.
[836] (1928) 263 Mass. 73, 160 NE 301. See the discussion above at p. 139.

escaped and damaged the boat, the defendant was liable for having failed to take reasonable steps to guard against dangers that defendant's own conduct had created. On the other hand, if the plaintiff's boat had been stolen or damaged by bad boys who needed to be but never had been locked up, no basis for liability would have been found.[837]

The American cases involving harms done by escaped prisoners reflect the same analysis. The opinions often indicate that liability turns on whether the injury occurred 'during, or as an integral part of, the process of escaping'.[838] The quoted phrase is a cryptic way of saying that in order to fall within the scope of the prior-innocent-conduct exception to the no-duty-to-act rule, the harm must have been among the risks created by the incarceration situation—as opposed to the general risks that result from the existence of criminally-inclined persons in society.

The prior-innocent-conduct principle may also be used to clarify the different approaches taken in the judgments of Lord Mackay and Lord Goff in *Smith* v. *Littlewoods Ltd.*,[839] in which the defendants were charged with failing to take reasonable steps to guard against the risk that vandals would start a fire in defendants' abandoned cinema and thereby damage neighbouring property. The House of Lords concluded that the defendants should not be held liable. Lord Mackay's judgment seemed to recognise that the defendants owed a duty of reasonable care but concluded that under the circumstances shown the duty had not been breached. Lord Goff, on the other hand, appeared to conclude that no duty of care was owed. The difference between the two approaches can usefully be viewed as stemming from differences over the scope of the prior-innocent-conduct exception to the no-duty-to-act rule. When *Smith* v. *Littlewoods* is viewed in that light it will be seen that Lord Mackay was willing to recognise the ownership or occupancy 'of property, particularly property of the tenement type'[840] as itself sufficient prior conduct to give rise to a duty of care to guard against foreseeable risks that vandals would use the property to harm others. Lord Goff, on the other hand, viewed the case as one in which the plaintiffs were seeking to 'impose liability for pure omissions'.[841] For Lord Goff, the ownership of 'property of the tenement type' did not constitute prior innocent conduct that was itself sufficient to generate a duty of reasonable care. In his view only when the owner of such property 'has knowledge or means of knowledge that a third party has created or is creating a risk of fire, or indeed has started

---

[837] See *Green* v. *State* (1956) 91 So.2d 153, 155 (La. App.): 'An institution's duty to restrain a convicted criminal is not based upon the purpose of protecting the general public from all harms that the prisoner might inflict if he were allowed to escape. A convicted person may be as dangerous on the day of his legal release as he was on the first day that he was confined. . . . There is no more reason for the State to be civilly responsible for the convict's general misconduct during the period of his escape than for the same misconduct after a legal release, unless there is some further causal relationship than the release or escape to the injuries received.'

[838] *Wilson* v. *Department of Public Safety* (1991) 576 So.2d 490, 493 (Louisiana).

[839] [1987] 1 AC 241 (HL).

[840] Ibid. at 262 (Lord Mackay of Clashfern, quoting with approval the judgment of Lord Wylie in *Evans* v. *Glasgow District Council*, 1978 SLT 17, 19).

[841] Ibid. at 270.

a fire, on his premises'[842] would a duty of reasonable care to alleviate such risks arise.[843]

The American decisions that are analogous to *Smith* v. *Littlewoods* are divided in their results. Far too frequently the courts discuss the issue of liability *vel non* under the rubric of legal causation formulas that obscure the true policy grounds of the decision.[844] Breach and duty considerations also tend to become commingled in ways that obfuscate. However, one thing at least emerges with reasonable clarity: in the modern American cases the ownership of real estate counts as an activity[845] that is itself sufficient under the prior-innocent-conduct rule to give rise to a duty of care under appropriate circumstances to alleviate dangers created by vandals and similar trespassers on the premises.[846]

(iii) Liability Based on Defendant's Failure to Carry Through after Volunteering Assistance The second settled exception to the no-duty-to-act rule holds one who undertakes or volunteers to provide safety precautions or assistance to persons in peril to a duty of reasonable care in carrying out the undertaking.[847] This principle is quite broad in its application to landlords and other businesses who may have no initial duty to guard against the risk of crime associated with their operations but who can become liable for holding out an assurance of security measures that are then not properly carried out. For example, one recent decision held a restaurant that had an armed security guard on the premises liable for a criminal's acts in shooting patrons during a robbery on the basis that '[a] duty of protection which has been voluntarily assumed must be performed with due care.'[848]

Many of the cases that base liability upon the volunteer principle state that the defendant's duty is limited to using reasonable care not to worsen the situation.[849] Other cases ignore that limitation entirely.[850] In any event it is a limitation that usually seems quite easy to meet. If the other requisites for liability are in place, usually the court will be persuaded by an argument that the victim could have made other provisions for avoiding or alleviating the danger, such as by looking to others for help, had the defendant not purported to provide it.[851]

---

[842] [1987] 1 AC 241 (HL) at 274.

[843] For further discussion of the possible reasons for Lord Goff's refusal to recognise the ownership of real property as itself sufficient to amount to 'prior innocent conduct'; see text surrounding pp. 227–8, below.

[844] See e.g. *Brown* v. *Tesack* (1989) 556 So.2d 84, 87, rev'd (1990) 566 So.2d 955 (Louisiana).

[845] See text at p. 225, above.

[846] See e.g. *Nixon* v. *Mr. Property Management Co.* (1985) 690 SW2d 546 (Texas) (abandoned apartment used as refuge by rapist); *Torrack* v. *Corpamerica* (1958) 51 Del. 254, 144 A.2d 703 (arsonist set fire to abandoned building).

[847] See generally W. P. Keeton *et al.*, *Prosser and Keeton on Torts* (5th edn., 1984), s. 56 at 378–82; Restatement, ss. 323 and 324.

[848] *Harris* v. *Pizza Hut* (1984) 455 So.2d 1364, 1369 (Louisiana).

[849] See e.g. *Farwell* v. *Keeton* (1976) 396 Mich. 281, 240 NW2d 217, 220: 'Without regard to whether there is a general duty to aid a person in distress, there is a clearly recognised legal duty of every person to avoid any affirmative acts which may make a situation worse.'

[850] See W. P. Keeton *et al.*, *Prosser and Keeton on Torts* (5th edn., 1984), 381–2.

[851] See D. W. Robertson *et al.*, *Cases and Materials on Torts* (2nd edn., 1998), 226–7.

(iv) Liability Based on a Pre-existing Relationship Between Defendant and X[852]

A leading treatise states that a *pre-existing* relationship between the immediate perpetrator of the harm and the defendant whose negligence allegedly contributed to the injuries may itself be sufficient to count as an independent exception to the no-duty-to-act rule.[853] However, the decisional law supporting that proposition is exceedingly thin.[854] For a time the California Supreme Court's decision in *Tarasoff* v. *Regents of University of California*[855] was the leading authority for the proposition. When handed down, *Tarasoff* seemed to stand for the proposition that the relationship between a psychotherapist and a mental patient could generate a duty of reasonable care on the part of the therapist to take steps to guard against foreseeable harms the patient might do to a third person with whom the therapist had no relationship. But the California Supreme Court later seemed to retreat from that proposition. In *Thompson* v. *County of Alameda*[856] the court refused to hold a detention facility liable for failing to warn potential victims against the risk of foreseeable harms by a dangerous inmate who was released on furlough. The *Thompson* court reinterpreted *Tarasoff* as having rested liability on the therapist's relationships with *both* the patient and the potential victim.[857]

With the authority of *Tarasoff* thus weakened, few cases can be found supporting the view that a relationship between defendant and X is alone sufficient to constitute an exception to the no-duty-to-act rule. Asking about the relationship between defendant and X can sometimes be a useful way of asking whether defendant has engaged in affirmative negligent conduct that was a legal cause of the harm and, if not, whether defendant has engaged in prior innocent conduct contributing to the situation in a way that obligates defendant to take reasonable steps to alleviate the danger. If neither question can be answered affirmatively, the existence of some kind of prior relationship between defendant and X seems unlikely in itself to persuade the court that defendant should have taken steps to guard against X's torts.

Obviously there is a large element of arbitrariness to any particular method of organising the decisions in which defendant is sought to be held liable for the results of a crime or intentional tort committed by X. The lines between the

---

[852] It will be remembered that we are ruling out of the discussion relationships between defendant and X that would suffice to make defendant vicariously liable for X's torts. See text at p. 219, above.

[853] See Restatement, s. 315: There is no duty so to control the conduct of a third person as to prevent him from causing physical harm to another unless (a) a special relation exists between the actor and the third person which imposes a duty upon the actor to control the third person's conduct, or (b) a special relation exists between the actor and the other which gives the other a right to protection'.

[854] For one of the relatively rare cases supporting it, see *Greenberg* v. *Barbour* (1971) 322 F.Supp. 745 (Pennsylvania), where, without even acknowledging the no-duty-to-act issue, the court imposed a duty on a hospital staff doctor whose failure to admit a mental patient into the hospital for treatment resulted in the patient's attacking the plaintiff.

[855] (1976) 17 Cal.3d 425, 551 P.2d 334.   [856] (1980) 27 Cal.3d 741, 614 P.2d 728.

[857] The 'relationship' that the *Thompson* court discovered between the therapist and the victim in *Tarasoff* was that the therapist knew the victim's exact identity ahead of time; the patient had told him whom he meant to kill. See the discussion and explanation in *Brady* v. *Hopper* (1983) 751 F.2d 329, 331 (Colorado) (citing *Thompson* as persuasive authority for refusing to hold that the psychiatrist of the man who wounded the plaintiffs during an attempt to assassinate President Reagan had a duty to the plaintiffs).

various exceptions to the no-duty-to-act rule are frequently blurred. For example, *Dorset Yacht* could with approximately equal facility be explained (as suggested above) as resting liability on defendant's failure to take reasonable steps to guard against dangers created by its prior innocent conduct, or as resting liability on a special relationship between defendant and X, the borstal boys. In *Smith* v. *Littlewoods* Lord Goff took the latter view.[858] This led him to reject the persuasiveness of *Dorset Yacht* in the *Smith* v. *Littlewoods* situation; the *Smith* defendants had no relationship at all with the vandals who started the fire in the abandoned cinema. Had Lord Goff viewed *Dorset* as falling under the prior-innocent-conduct exception as opposed to the supposed 'relationship with X' exception, he might then have been led to examine his unstated premise that owning property is not itself an activity.

The 'relationship with X' explanation of cases like *Dorset Yacht* seems inferior to the prior-innocent-conduct explanation in two senses. In the sense just indicated, the 'relationship with X' explanation is too narrow; it directs one's attention away from a useful comparison of the amount of actual involvement of the defendant in the circumstances leading up to the harm. In another sense it is too broad; it fails to provide a basis for explaining why the *Dorset Yacht* defendant should not be liable for all of the crimes and torts done by the boys after their escape, even when they have left the immediate area of the prison and been absorbed back into society. Yet we all know intuitively and without a moment's hesitation that the *Dorset Yacht* defendant would not have been found liable had the boys made good their escape, gone home, and then set forth a week later to steal a boat. The 'relationship with X' concept does not afford a felicitous explanation for that intuition, but the prior-innocent-conduct concept does. As indicated above, the prior-innocent-conduct principle carries with it the explanation that liability is limited to the risks that were created by the defendant's having incarcerated the boys.

(v) Liability Based on a Pre-Existing Relationship Between Defendant and Plaintiff   In all of the American states certain relationships (between the victim and the eventual defendant) are viewed as sufficient to give rise to a general duty of protection that is broad enough to include protection against foreseeable risks of injury through the crimes and intentional torts of others. This is probably the most frequently invoked of the exceptions to the no-duty-to-act rule. A mother must take reasonable care to protect her children; a school, its pupils; a jail, its prisoners; a hospital, its patients; an employer, its employees; a common carrier, its passengers; an innkeeper, his guests; and a business, its invitees. This listing is by no means exhaustive; the details of the putative *pre-existing* relationship will always be important. Thus, while most states would probably hold as a general matter that the relationship between a host and a social guest does not itself suffice to call upon the host to take affirmative steps to protect his guest, one of the leading cases held that two friends out for an

---

[858] [1987] 1 AC at 272: '[A] duty may arise from a special relationship between the defender and the third party, by virtue of which the defender is responsible for controlling the third party: see, for example, *Dorset Yacht* . . .'

evening of carousing owed each other a duty of reasonable care to guard against foreseeable risks of injury from others' intentional torts.[859]

There is a split of authority on the extent of the duty that an ordinary business owes to protect its customers against the risks of crimes and intentional torts. Some states recognise a fully-blown duty of reasonable care that is sufficient to require the business to provide security precautions against generally foreseeable risks of crimes.[860] Others limit the duty to situations in which 'the business has actual or imputed knowledge of an *impending* assault and the opportunity to prevent it'.[861] On the latter view, while a hotel in a high-crime area would owe a duty to protect its guests against the risks of injury from generally foreseeable crimes and intentional torts,[862] an ordinary business in the same area would have no responsibility to a customer until seeing a specific criminal threat in the process of developing. 'The distinction [between hotels and ordinary businesses] is no doubt rooted in the belief that business patrons of innkeepers, like those of common carriers and unlike those of other businesses, have entrusted their personal security to the innkeeper.'[863]

7. Recurrent Problems of Factual Causation and Damages[864]

(A) FACTUAL CAUSATION IN GENERAL

Usually the factual causation issue is solved by application of the but-for test, under which the defendant is not responsible for an injury that would have occurred regardless of whether the defendant had engaged in the wrongful conduct with which he is charged. For example, a product manufacturer whose only wrongful conduct was failing to place on the product's label a warning of a particular danger was not liable to a consumer injured by that danger who testified that he did not read the label provided and would not have read any label.[865]

When *Baker* v. *Willoughby* came before the House of Lords, Lord Pearson responded to a defensive argument based on the but-for test by stating: '[I]t is formidable. But it must not be allowed to succeed, because it produces manifest injustice.'[866] He was reminding us that occasionally the courts must relax the but-for test in plaintiffs' favour. This happens when that test would exonerate a defendant as to whom our sense of justice cries out that his causal contribution was sufficient to impose responsibility. In these situations the courts have at their disposal at least three familiar techniques for relaxing the but-for test. The relaxation may take the form of shifting to a 'substantial factor' test.[867] It may take the form of 'unitising' two or more tortfeasors by treating each as vicariously responsible—for cause-in-fact purposes only—for the others'

---

[859] *Farwell* v. *Keeton* (1976) 396 Mich. 281, 240 NW2d 217. [860] See Restatement, s. 344.

[861] *Banks* v. *Hyatt Corporation* (1984) 722 F.2d 214, 220 (discussing Florida and Louisiana law) (emphasis added).

[862] See *Wassell* v. *Adams* (1989) 865 F.2d 849 (Illinois). [863] 722 F.2d at 221.

[864] See generally D. Robertson, 'The Common Sense of Cause In Fact' (1997) 75 *Texas LR* 1765.

[865] See *Technical Chemical Company* v. *Jacobs* (1972) 480 SW2d 602 (Texas).

[866] [1970] AC 467, 495 (HL).

[867] See, e.g., *Northington* v. *Marin* (1996) 102 F.3d 1564 (Colorado).

contribution to the injury as well as directly responsible for his own.[868] Or it
may take the form of shifting the burden of proof on the issue of factual causation to the defendant.[869] Each of these techniques for relaxing the but-for test
is well settled in the decisional law. But each is narrowly limited to a specific
range of situations; in almost all cases the normal operation of the but-for test
is deemed perfectly satisfactory, and whatever answer it yields is controlling on
the issue of factual causation.

Occasionally the but-for test will produce a strong sense of 'manifest injustice' by exonerating a defendant under circumstances where none of the familiar relaxation techniques seems to work. American judicial responses to such
situations have varied. Often the sense of 'manifest injustice' will be suppressed
and the defendant exonerated.[870] But a number of courts have been attracted
to creative new approaches to the factual causation issue. For example, a recurrent problem in the product liability context has involved the plaintiff who can
show that she was injured by using a particular drug or other product; that the
product was unreasonably dangerous and has caused injuries to hundreds or
thousands of consumers; and that the product was manufactured and distributed by a number of different companies whose identities are known. But the
plaintiff has no way of showing which of these companies actually supplied the
particular product that caused her individual injuries. In this situation an application of the but-for test in the normal way would exonerate any of the companies the plaintiff chooses to sue. To meet this 'manifest injustice', several
states have adopted a 'market-share' causation theory whereby a manufacturer
can be held liable based on its proportional share of the overall distribution of
the product.[871]

(B) 'Probabilistic Causation' and 'Lost Opportunity' Theories

Another situation in which some courts perceive 'manifest injustice' in the normal operation of the but-for test involves victims of medical malpractice who
are unable to produce expert testimony that the wrongful conduct of the defendant probably caused the injury in question. Often the medical experts whose
opinion testimony is necessary to establish causation in malpractice and similar cases will insist on expressing their opinion in the form of percentages. For
example, rather than saying that the malpractice probably caused the victim's
death, the expert may prefer to state that the malpractice deprived the victim
of a 75 per cent chance of surviving.[872] When the medical opinion testimony is
to the effect that the malpractice deprived the victim of a chance of surviving
(or of avoiding whatever other undesirable consequences form the basis of the
lawsuit) that was greater than 50 per cent, most courts are willing to 'translate'

---

[868] See, e.g., *Oliver* v. *Miles* (1927) 144 Miss. 852, 110 So. 666.

[869] See, e.g., *Summers* v. *Tice* (1948) 33 Cal.2d 80, 199 P.2d 1.

[870] See, e.g., *Kurczi* v. *Eli Lilly & Co.* (1997) 113 F.3d 1426 (Ohio) (rejecting the 'market share' causation theory).

[871] See, e.g., *Hamilton* v. *Accu-Tek* (1996) 935 F.Supp. 1307 (New York); *Sindell* v. *Abbott Laboratories* (1980) 26 Cal.3d 588, 607 P.2d 924, cert. denied (1980) 449 US 912.

[872] See *Hamil* v. *Bashline* (1978) 481 Pa. 256, 396 A.2d 1280.

that into an opinion that the malpractice probably caused the death (or other undesirable consequence).[873]

The real difficulty arises when the most the expert will say is that the malpractice made a less-than-50-per-cent chance still lower. Most courts will conclude against causation in such cases, on the view that the expert's statement amounts to an opinion that the malpractice probably did not cause the injury. But many judges and commentators have perceived 'manifest injustice' in this situation. Two techniques have been proposed for dealing with it. The first, called 'probabilistic causation', is radical; it would hold the defendant whose wrongful conduct is shown to have cost the victim an appreciable but lower-than-50-per-cent chance of avoiding the injury in question liable for full damages.[874] Only a small minority of analysts think this approach has much promise. The second approach is called the 'lost chance' or 'lost opportunity' theory. It would allow partial recovery against a defendant who probably did not cause a physical injury but whose wrongful conduct can be shown to have damaged the victim's chances of avoiding the injury by treating the 'lost opportunity' as itself a valuable interest that is redressible under the law of negligence.[875]

Courts in the United States are divided as to the validity of the 'lost opportunity' theory.[876] The arguments over its desirability are fairly evenly balanced.[877] Many observers believe that a fairness argument weighs rather heavily in favour of accepting the theory. Economic and administrative concerns may count against it. In the United States medical-malpractice liability is widely viewed as having helped to drive up health-care costs to an unacceptable level; adopting the 'lost opportunity' theory would add to that burden. And the 'lost opportunity' theory is potentially very complex. Its effect is to translate doubts about factual causation into a damages-reduction technique. Once that begins to be done, the courts may find it very hard to find a stopping-place.[878]

(c) MULTIPLE TORTFEASORS GENERALLY

The presence of multiple tortfeasors often makes it easier for courts to solve problems of 'manifest injustice' that are perceived to follow from the normal operation of the but-for test. For example, the technique of treating each tortfeasor as vicariously responsible (for causation purposes) for the other's

---

[873] See D. W. Robertson *et al.*, *Cases and Materials on Torts* (2nd edn., 1998), 150–1.

[874] In *Herskovits* v. *Group Health Co-op.* (1983) 99 Wash.2d 609, 664 P.2d 474, the expert testified that the malpractice reduced the victim's chances of survival from 39% to 25%. Two of the justices would have allowed full wrongful death damages in this situation.

[875] Four members of the *Herskovits* court adopted this theory, whereby the defendant's liability would be calculated at 14% of wrongful-death damages.

[876] See *Smith* v. *State Dep't of Health* (1996) 676 So.2d 543, 547 (Louisiana) (stating that the lost opportunity theory 'has been recognised by a majority of the states'); *Kramer* v. *Lewisville Mem'l Hosp.* (1993) 858 SW2d 397, 400 (Texas) (stating that 17 states had accepted the lost opportunity theory while 8 had rejected it).

[877] See the majority and dissenting opinions in *Weymers* v. *Khera* (1997) 563 NW2d 647 (Michigan) (in which the majority disapproved the theory) and in *Falcon* v. *Memorial Hospital* (1990) 462 NW2d 44 (Michigan) (in which the majority adopted the theory).

[878] See, e.g., *Hardy* v. *Southwestern Bell Telephone Co.* (1996) 910 P.2d 1024 (Oklahoma) (holding that the theory can apply only in medical malpractice actions).

wrongful conduct[879] is obviously confined to multiple-tortfeasor situations. For another example, consider a hypothetical case that is famous in academic circles. A negligently failed to repair the brakes on a car it had leased to B; B failed to apply the brake pedal and ran down the plaintiff.[880] If the two cases are viewed entirely separately, the but-for test will exonerate each tortfeasor. But for A's wrongful failure to repair the brakes, the plaintiff would still have been run down; B did not try to use the brakes. But for B's wrongful conduct in not using the brakes, the plaintiff would still have been run down; the brakes would not have worked even if B had tried to use them. The solution to this situation is the insight that each tortfeasor's wrongful conduct has deprived the plaintiff of viable cause of action against the other.[881] If A had properly repaired the brakes, B's failure to apply the brake pedal would then have been a clear factual cause of the injuries. Similarly, if B had applied the brake pedal, A's failure to repair the brakes would then have been a clear factual cause of the injuries. Each tortfeasor's wrongful conduct has therefore damaged or defeated the plaintiff's cause of action against the other tortfeasor; each should therefore be liable for the plaintiff's loss.[882]

The technique just described helps to explain the House of Lords' decision in *Baker* v. *Willoughby*.[883] First the defendant hurt Mr Baker's leg. Later the robber shot that same leg, necessitating its amputation. Visualise each of Mr Baker's potential lawsuits separately. Had the plaintiff sued the robber who shot his leg, the robber would have defended by saying that the leg was already damaged and virtually useless when he shot it. When he sued the defendant who initially hurt his leg, the defendant responded by saying that we now know that the leg was soon to be lost in any event. Each of these defensive arguments, taken by itself, is valid.[884] But when they are viewed together, each of the two tortfeasors is seen to have greatly damaged the victim's potential cause of action against the other; each should therefore be liable for the full value of the leg.[885]

The situation of the plaintiff in *Jobling* v. *Associated Dairies Ltd.*[886] was very similar to Mr Baker's, except that the second injury in *Jobling* did not emanate from a second tortfeasor but from implacable nature. That difference was crucial.

---

[879] See text and at pp. 229–30, above.

[880] The hypothetical is based on *Saunders Sys. Birmingham Co.* v. *Adams* (1928) 117 So. 72 (Alabama). See D. W. Robertson, 'The Common Sense of Cause in Fact' (1997) 75 *Texas LR* 1765, 1798, and n. 97.

[881] Some commentators see the deprivation-of-cause-of-action approach as too contrived or clever to be useful. See e.g. R. Wright, 'Causation in Tort Law' (1985) 73 *Cal. LR* 1735, 1787, 1801. But the approach is in fact familiar thinking in many analogous areas. See generally R. Peaslee, 'Multiple Causation and Damage' (1934) 47 *Harv. LR* 1127.

[882] An alternative way to express the theory is that a tortfeasor whose wrongful conduct has created a serious defect in the plaintiff's potential case against another tortfeasor should be estopped from asserting the same defect in the case against himself.

[883] [1970] AC 467.

[884] The robber's is a standard 'pre-existing condition' argument of the sort that is typically accepted. The defendant's is the 'looming threat' variation of that argument. For further discussion of these two types of defensive arguments see text at pp. 235–7, below.

[885] For a similar explanation of *Baker*, see Lord Keith's speech in *Jobling* v. *Associated Dairies Ltd.* [1982] AC 794, 815.

[886] [1982] AC 794.

The *Jobling* defendant negligently hurt the plaintiff in 1973. The injury disabled the plaintiff from working. Then in 1976 the plaintiff was overwhelmed by a new illness, unrelated to the injury caused by the defendant, that would have prevented his working regardless of the defendant's injury. The trial occurred in 1979. In the House of Lords no respectable technique for avoiding the normal operation of the but-for test could be found. Inasmuch as it was known at the trial of the case that the plaintiff would have been disabled from working regardless of the injury inflicted by the defendant, the defendant could not be said to be a factual cause of the lost earnings except for the interval between the 1973 injury and the manifestation of the 1976 illness. Had the 1976 illness resulted from the negligence of a second tortfeasor, the *Baker* technique would have been available as a way of awarding full compensation.

(D) Joint and Several Liability

Another approach to the factual-causation issue that is confined to multiple-tortfeasor situations is provided by the doctrine of joint and several liability. In its standard operation this doctrine does not address the issue of factual causation. The standard operation of the joint-and-several-liability doctrine is illustrated by a case in which a passenger on a coach is hurt in a collision between the coach and a railway train.[887] Neither the coach operator nor the locomotive engineer is keeping a proper look-out. Both are liable to the plaintiff, because each is guilty of negligent conduct that was a but-for cause of the plaintiff's harm, viz., each could have avoided the collision by using reasonable care. There is no need for resort to any causation test other than the but-for test in standard form. Once factual causation (and the other elements of negligence liability) are seen to be established against each of the defendants, the 'joint and several liability' doctrine then steps in to provide that, while plaintiff is entitled to recover no more than his total assessed damages, each of the defendants is jointly and severally liable for that total. This means that the plaintiff can collect the total from either of them or from the two of them in any combination. (They may then be able to adjust the loss as between themselves through actions for contribution.)

The coach-passenger case is the easy, standard case for joint and several liability. In that standard operation, the joint-and-several-liability doctrine is not affecting the cause-in-fact issue. It is simply providing that the risk of insolvency of one of the judgment debtors rests on the other judgment debtor and not on the plaintiff. In recent times many states have altered the law of joint and several liability by using comparative-fault principles in various ways to limit the ultimate exposure of each tortfeasor.[888] These changes do not affect the analysis of factual causation in multiple-tortfeasor cases and are not of immediate relevance to the present discussion.

The coach-passenger case shows that in its standard operation the joint-and-several-liability doctrine does not address the plaintiff's burden of establishing

---

[887] See *Baylor University* v. *Bradshaw* (1932) 52 SW2d 1094 (Tex. App.), *Aff'd* 84 SW2d 703 (Texas), overruled in part on other grounds in *Duncan* v. *Cessna Aircraft Co.* (1984) 605 SW3d 414 (Texas).

[888] See D. W. Robertson *et al.*, *Cases and Materials on Torts* (2nd edn., 1998), 634–46.

cause in fact. But occasionally the joint-and-several-liability doctrine does help the plaintiff with the issue of factual causation. In the coach-passenger case, the plaintiff sustained a single indivisible injury. But cases often arise in which the conduct of several tortfeasors has combined to cause injuries that are divisible in nature. When the facts provide a basis whereby the injuries can be divided and causally apportioned among the defendants, this will be done. But when the injuries are theoretically apportionable among the defendants but not so as a practical matter—when the facts provide no basis whereby causal apportionment can occur—application of the joint-and-several-liability doctrine provides a way whereby plaintiff can meet an otherwise insuperable factual-causation burden. For example, when pollution from two negligent sources drained into the plaintiff's lake, rendering it useless for watering cattle and killing the fish,[889] it seemed clear that each tortfeasor was a but-for cause of part but not all of the damage. But requiring the plaintiff to prove how much of the damage was caused by each tortfeasor would have resulted in exonerating the defendants, because as a practical matter the evidence necessary to apportion was simply not available. In such cases most American courts will agree that while the trier of fact should apportion the separate damages between or among the tortfeasors when that is feasible, when apportionment is not feasible the tortfeasors should be held jointly and severally liable for the entire damage.[890]

Note that the effect of using the joint-and-several-liability doctrine against the tortfeasors in the polluted lake case is to hold each of them liable for damages that we know the tortfeasor did not cause. If we were talking about tortfeasors who had somehow acted in concert in causing the pollution, the factual-causation problem would be readily solvable by 'unitising' them, that is, by holding each tortfeasor as liable for his own pollution and at the same time vicariously responsible (for cause-in-fact purposes) for the other's pollution.[891] But in the case under discussion the tortfeasors are strangers to one another, and there is no honest way to construct a concert-of-action or other vicarious-liability treatment of them. Nevertheless, by treating the cluster of theoretically apportionable injuries that cannot as a practical matter be apportioned as though they constituted a single indivisible injury, the law of joint and several liability means that each tortfeasor can be made to pay for more harm than he actually caused.

A leading American case showing the reach of the joint-and-several-liability doctrine to impose liability upon a tortfeasor for such a cluster of injuries is *Maddux* v. *Donaldson*.[892] Mrs Maddux suffered multiple injuries when the automobile was struck by Donaldson's vehicle and knocked into the path of Byrie's vehicle; the impact with Byrie's vehicle occurred almost immediately after the original collision. Mrs Maddux sued both Donaldson and Byrie but then discontinued the suit against Donaldson. The trial court dismissed the suit against

---

[889] See *Landers* v. *East Texas Salt Water Disposal Co.* (1952) 248 SW2d 731 (Texas).

[890] See *Loui* v. *Oakley* (1968) 438 P.2d 393, 396–7 (Hawaii); *Maddux* v. *Donaldson* (1961) 108 NW2d 33, 36–8 (Michigan). Cf. *Lamoureaux* v. *Totem Ocean Trailer Express, Inc.* (1981) 632 P.2d 539, 544–5 (Alaska) (requiring plaintiff to apportion as between the effects of a pre-existing injury and the effects of a collision with the defendant, but stating that the trier should be allowed to make its 'best guess' at apportionment).

[891] See text at pp. 229–30, above.   [892] (1961) 108 NW2d 33 (Michigan).

Byrie because of the lack of evidence showing which of the injuries were caused by the impact with Byrie.[893] Reversing, the Michigan Supreme Court held that joint and several liability should be imposed, stating:

[I]f there is competent testimony, adduced either by plaintiff or defendant, that the injuries are factually and medically separable, and that the liability for all such injuries and damages, or parts thereof, may be allocated with reasonable certainty to the impacts in turn, the jury will be instructed accordingly and mere difficulty in doing so will not relieve the triers of the facts of this responsibility [of apportionment]. . . . But if, on the other hand, the triers of the facts conclude that they cannot reasonably make the division of liability between the tortfeasors . . . we have, by their own finding, nothing more than an indivisible injury [for which the tortfeasors are jointly and severally liable].[894]

In other words, if it is impossible as a practical matter to apportion the various parts of a cluster of theoretically separable injuries, the cluster will be treated as though it were a single indivisible injury.

Viewed through American eyes, *Fitzgerald* v. *Lane*[895] appears to be functionally indistinguishable from *Maddux*. The House of Lords' determination to hold each of the two motorists liable for Mr Fitzgerald's full damages (less a reduction to reflect his own contributory fault) would not strike most American judges or commentators as in any way problematic. The law of negligence strives with some diligence to avoid extracting damages from a tortfeasor whose conduct has probably caused *no* harm, no matter how faulty the conduct. But a defendant whose tortious conduct is known to have caused some significant harm to the plaintiff can often be held liable for additional harm without offending judicial sensibilities.

(E) Pre-Existing Conditions and Looming Threats

Every victim of tortious conduct inevitably brings to the transaction 'a tangle of pre-existing conditions.'[896] It is common ground in England and the United States that the tortfeasor should not be held liable for the effects of the pre-existing conditions. Thus in a typical American case in which a roadway accident injured the shoulder of a man who already had shoulder problems, the court stressed that the damages assessed against the defendant should not include the original condition but only the new effects of the accident for which the defendant was responsible; 'courts recognise that a defendant whose acts aggravate a plaintiff's pre-existing condition is liable only for the amount of harm actually caused by the negligence.'[897] Thus also, in *Jobling* v. *Associated Dairies*, Lord Wilberforce began his analysis of the issue presented in that case by stating that if the 1976 illness had been the result of a dormant condition

---

[893] In a suit against Donaldson this problem would not have arisen. Donaldson's negligent conduct was a but-for cause of both the original impact with his vehicle and of the subsequent impact with the Byrie vehicle. Byrie, of course, made no causal contribution to the original impact.

[894] 108 NW2d at 36–8.   [895] [1989] 1 AC 328 (HL).

[896] J. King, 'Causation Valuation, and Chance in Personal Injury Torts Involving Pre-existing Conditions and Future Consequences' (1981) 90 *Yale LJ* 1352, 1354.

[897] *Lamoureaux* v. *Totem Ocean Trailer Express, Inc.* (1981) 632 P.2d 539, 544 (Alaska).

that pre-existed the injury brought about by the defendant in 1973, 'it is not disputed that it would have had to be taken into account'.[898]

The problem in *Jobling* was that the 1976 illness was *not* the result of a condition that pre-existed the original injury 'but a [new] disease supervening after that event'.[899] In other words, at the point in time at which the defendant's negligent conduct hurt the plaintiff, the 1976 illness was not a pre-existing condition but merely a future contingency or threat. In both England and the United States the judicial treatment of such contingencies or threats has been somewhat less clear than the firm rule that holds that the defendant should not be made to pay for the effects of pre-existing conditions. But the following discussion will show that the two problems raise identical policy issues and should take the same treatment.

If an innocent pedestrian is killed by a negligent driver as the pedestrian is walking to board an airplane flight that later takes off on time and crashes, killing all aboard, traditional judicial attitudes will be quite impatient with the negligent driver's argument that the life he took was essentially worthless because his victim was only a short airplane ride away from dying in any event. On the other hand, if a skydiver whose parachute has failed to open should happen to be shot by a negligent sportsman just seconds before hitting the ground, the sportsman will probably end up owing no tort damages.[900] The difference between the two situations is easy to grasp intuitively;[901] some threats are far enough advanced at the time the defendant's wrongful conduct harms the plaintiff to demand to be taken into account, and others are not. 'The operative line—roughly speaking, the line between future contingencies and imminent threats—cannot be described with precision, but the rule is roughly this: We will take into account only those threats that are so far advanced and so nearly certain at the time of the accident that any attempt to ignore their functional identity with pre-existing conditions would seem dishonest.'[902] With relief, we ignore other contingencies. 'The retrospective conjuring up of events contingent at the time of injury would open the door to absurd results. Allowing such contingencies to affect valuation would create a rule that could not be administered.'[903]

In 1973, when the defendant's negligent conduct injured the victim in *Jobling* v. *Associated Dairies*, the 1976 illness was far in the unknowable future and hence wholly contingent. Had the trial occurred in 1975, no court would have

---

[898] [1982] AC at 802.   [899] Ibid.

[900] The leading case in America is *Dillon* v. *Twin State Gas & Electric Co.* (1932) 163 A. 111 (New Hampshire), in which (on one view of the facts) the defendant's negligent conduct electrocuted a boy after he was already in the process of falling from a high bridge. The court reasoned that on that factual scenario the defendant's conduct had not deprived the boy of anything of value. A member of the court that decided *Dillon* later wrote a celebrated law review article based on the case. See R. Peaslee, 'Multiple Causation and Damage' (1934) 47 *Harv. LR* 1127.

[901] See W. P. Keeton *et al.*, *Prosser and Keeton on Torts* (5th edn., 1984), s. 52 at 353: 'There is a clear distinction between a person who is standing in the path of an avalanche when the defendant shoots to kill, and one who is about to embark on a steamship doomed later to strike an iceberg and sink. The life of the latter has value at the time, as any insurance company would agree, but that of the former has none.'

[902] D. Robertson, 'The Common Sense of Cause In Fact' (1997) 75 *Texas LR* 1765, 1798.

[903] J. King, 'Causation, Valuation, and Chance in Personal Injury Torts Involving Pre-existing Conditions and Future Consequences' (1981) 90 *Yale LJ* 1353, 1358.

regarded the possibility that some other illness than the one the defendant caused might soon disable the plaintiff in any event as calling for any significant limitation of the plaintiff's damages. But at the time of trial, in 1979, the 1976 illness could no longer be regarded as a contingency because 'a court must not speculate when it knows the facts, and must therefore have regard to relevant events which have occurred before trial'.[904] That principle was also recognised in *Baker* v. *Willoughby*: 'There is no doubt that it is proper to lead evidence at the trial as to any events or developments between the date of the accident and the date of the trial which are relevant for the proper assessment of damages.'[905]

The *Jobling* victim's later illness and the *Baker* victim's later shooting injuries, each highly contingent at the time of the injury, was each fully certain by the time of the trial. This certainty meant that the effects of the later event were indistinguishable in principle from the effects of a medical condition that pre-existed the events in which the defendant injured the victim. The now-known-to-be-certain future events had to be taken into account, just as pre-existing conditions (and imminent threats) have to be taken into account, in order to avoid offending the principle that a tortfeasor should not be made to pay for something that we know he had nothing to do with. It was only because the future event in *Baker* emanated from a potential tortfeasor that the court was able to perceive it as fair and find a way to make the defendant pay for the effects of that event.

---

[904] [1982] AC at 807 (Lord Edmund-Davies). See also ibid. at 813: '[T]he court will not speculate when it knows, so that when an event within its scope has actually happened prior to the trial date, that event will fall to be taken into account in the assessment of damages' (Lord Keith of Kinkel).

[905] [1970] AC at 490 (Lord Reid).

3

Special Forms of Negligence

1. PROBLEMS OF MEDICAL LAW
by
Professor Andrew Grubb*

1. Medical Malpractice and Medical Law

(A) MEDICAL LAW AND TORT

Medical malpractice is a species of professional malpractice and, as such, forms part of the law of tort. Medical malpractice is, of course, concerned with claims for damages for injuries suffered by patients (and others) at the hands of doctors and other health care professionals. Unlike other professional contexts, the law of contract plays little or no part in medical law. Other than in situations where the patient seeks treatment privately, patients do not enter into contracts with their doctors.[1] Even where they do, the courts have been most reluctant to impose greater obligations on the doctor than are imposed in tort.[2] Hence, exceptional circumstances apart, a doctor will only be held to contract to exercise reasonable care and skill (the tortious duty) rather than warranting a particular outcome from the treatment (a usual contractual duty elsewhere).[3] Thus, for the vast majority of patients in England and Wales, it is the law of tort which provides the only basis, if any, for a claim for damages.

Both negligence and, most recently, the law of battery have played important roles in the legal regulation of the relationship between health care provider and patient. Also, the tort of false imprisonment should not be forgotten since it is particularly important in the context of detention of mentally disordered patients. Such a patient's detention in hospital (or elsewhere) will amount to false imprisonment unless justified under the Mental Health Act 1983 or the common law.[4] The law of negligence imposes a duty of care not to unreasonably injure the patient or, possibly, another when diagnosing, giving advice and undertaking the treatment of a patient. Battery has, arguably, found its most important modern manifestation in medical cases.[5] As we shall see, it is this

---

* Professor of Medical Law, Cardiff Law School, Cardiff University.

[1] *Pfizer Corp* v. *Ministry of Health* [1965] AC 512.
[2] Discussed, Kennedy and Grubb (eds.), *Principles of Medical Law* (Select Bibliography) paras. 5.06–5.20.
[3] *Thake* v. *Maurice* [1986] QB 644 (CA) and *Eyre* v. *Measday* [1986] 1 All ER 488 (CA).
[4] See *R* v. *Bournewood Community and Mental Health NHS Trust, ex parte L* [1998] 3 All ER 289 (HL).
[5] See J. Munby, 'Rhetoric and Reality: The Limitations of Patient Self-Determination in Contemporary English Law' (1998) 14 *J. of Contemporary Health Law and Policy* 315 and R. Francis, 'Compulsory Caesarean Sections: An English Perspective' (1998) 14 *J. of Contemporary Health Law and Policy* 365.

medieval tort that the courts have used to allow them to recognise a patient's so-called 'right of self-determination'. This, in turn, gave the patient a legally enforceable right to decide about medical treatment (including the right to refuse it) however much others might consider it desirable for him.

(B) BEYOND TORT

It is, of course, the law of tort and its application in the medical context that is the concern of this section on medical malpractice. However, it would be short-sighted in any overview of medical law to confine oneself merely to this subset of civil law or, indeed, the law in general.

Whilst the law of tort is a central part of the emergent discipline of medical law, it is only part of the subject. Medical law is much broader and looks to both civil and public law for its principles. It encompasses, for example, family law, criminal law, public law and even principles of personal property law and equity, although the latter remain controversial. Its sources range across statute law (e.g., Abortion Act 1967, Human Tissue Act 1961), delegated legislation (e.g., the NHS (General Medical Services) Regulations 1992[6]) and case law.

It would also be wrong to see medical *law* as being confined to the discrete and conventional categories of law with which we are familiar. It is more than law as found in statutes or judgments of the courts. Obviously, these form a consider-able corpus of the body of medical law but there are other parts that are just as important. There are thus many other regulatory schemes both statutory and non-statutory which pervade the provision of health care in this country.

There is, for instance, disciplinary regulation of the health care professions through, for example, the General Medical Council (for doctors)[7] and the United Kingdom Central Council for Nursing, Midwifery and Health Visiting (for nurses and others).[8] To these we must add the General Dental Council (for dentists)[9] and other bodies that regulate such practitioners as opticians,[10] osteopaths[11] and chiropractors.[12] The list is, in fact, considerable. In perform-ing what is sometimes called their self-regulatory function, these bodies are actually operating within the broad field of public law.[13]

There are other regulatory bodies which police, monitor, and set standards in particular areas of medical practice. Some are statutory, such as the Human Fertilisation and Embryology Authority (HFEA) created in 1990.[14] This regulates most (but not all) forms of assisted conception and research on human embryos. Others are non-statutory. Among them we can mention the Local Research Ethics Committees (LRECs)[15] and Multi-Centre Research Ethics Committees (MRECs),[16] which control research on humans, the United

---

[6] SI 1992/635 (as amended).
[7] Medical Act 1983.
[8] Nurses, Midwives and Health Visitors Act 1979.
[9] Dentists Act 1984
[10] Opticians Act 1989.
[11] Osteopaths Act 1993.
[12] Chiropractors Act 1994.
[13] For a discussion see Montgomery, *Healthcare Law* (Select Bibliography), ch. 6.
[14] Human Fertilisation and Embryology Act 1990.
[15] *Local Research Ethics Committees* (DoH 1991), HSG(91)5.
[16] *Ethics Committee Review of Multi-Centre Research: Establishment of Multi-Centre Research Ethics Committees* (DoH 1997), HSG(97)23.

Kingdom Xeno-Transplanation Interim Regulatory Authority (UKXIRA), dealing with trans-genic tissue transplants, the Human Genetic Advisory Commission (HGAC), the Gene Therapy Advisory Committee (GTAC), and Advisory Committee on Genetic Testing (ACGT), which deal with various aspects of genetic developments and technology. The list can easily be made much longer. These bodies—and one must note that there is no overarching national regulatory or advisory body—operate with or without legal 'teeth'; but in each instance they effectively control the area of medical practice within their remit. Their function and performance is very much part of the regulation of medical practice and as such part of medical law.

Beyond these, there are quasi-legislative mechanisms that regulate the delivery of health care to patients and are properly seen as *law* and thus part of medical law. Some examples would include the complaints procedures, which exist for patients who are dissatisfied with the care they have received from a doctor, a hospital or elsewhere in the National Health Service.[17] Equally, there is a plethora of 'dictats' issued by the Department of Health and NHS Executive, which operate, effectively, as law—certainly regulation—within the NHS system. Some of these are actually binding. For instance, Directions issued under the National Health Service Act 1977[18] and the National Health Service and Community Care Act 1990.[19] Others, such as Health Service Guidance (HSGs), Circulars (HSCs) and Executive Letters (ELs),[20] are merely 'directory'. In practice, however, they act as strong indicators of what should be done or not done at a policy or, indeed, individual level, with internal and external legal consequences if they are not considered and acted upon, only to be departed from on a reasoned and rational basis.[21]

Certainly, it can be confidently predicted that in the future the importance of public law regulation of health care provisions is going to come to the fore. Increasingly, the structural changes to the NHS have brought with them a managerial bureaucracy. Whatever one may think of the merits of this change, it has brought greater transparency to decision-making at both a macro- and micro-provision level. Decisions have more and more fallen within the purview of discretionary decision-making by a public body. The latter is 'grist to the mill' for public law and, as a result, has created opportunities for patients to challenge decision-making within the NHS that was previously unavailable or, at least, not realised by those acting for patients.[22] One particular development calls for mention. The new clinical standards body, the National Institute for Clinical Excellence (NICE) and its remit to produce 'clinical guidelines' will be important.[23] For example, the latter will have a direct impact upon the standard of care expected of a doctor; they will in effect come to be seen as setting the 'bench-mark' of care for individual patients. Departure will require expla-

---

[17] See Montgomery, op. cit. (Select Bibliography), ch. 5.   [18] Ss. 13–17.   [19] Sch. 2, para. 6.
[20] Recently the Department of Health has sought to rationalise the almost random nature of which measure is used—HSG, HSC or EL—so that all are now designated *Circulars*.
[21] See Newdick, *Who Shall We Treat?* (Select Bibliography) at 190–3; and Montgomery, op. cit., (Select Bibliography) at 12–14.
[22] See generally, Newdick, op. cit. (Select Bibliography).
[23] *The New NHS—Modern, Dependable* (DoH 1997).

nation and justification and not mere 'whim', ignorance or prejudice. The standard of care expected will be transparent and a patient will have an opportunity to challenge any departure in advance by judicial review or subsequently in a negligence action if injury results.[24]

Regarding the latter, there are already unmistakable signs that the courts will deploy the public law principles of 'legality', 'rationality' and 'fairness' in the health care context so as to give both content and procedural rigour to decision-making that affects patients. The two cases of *R* v. *Cambridge HA, ex parte B*[25] in 1995 *and R* v. *North Derbyshire HA, ex parte Fisher*[26] in 1997 illustrate this, though, in the first, the patient's victory at first instance was short lived as the Court of Appeal reversed the trial judge on the day he gave judgment.

In *Ex parte B*, a young girl suffered from non-Hodgkins lymphoma. Following chemotherapy she relapsed and developed acute myeloid leukaemia. She unsuccessfully underwent a bone marrow transplant from her younger sister. Her doctors thought no further treatment would be beneficial. Her health authority refused to fund any further treatment. Her father obtained a more favourable second opinion. The evidence was that each of the two stages of treatment had a success rate of between 10 and 20 per cent. He brought a judicial review action. Laws J quashed the health authority's decision. He concluded that its discretion had been unlawfully exercised. The patient's 'right to life' was implicated by the decision and its interference could only be justified on 'substantial public interest' grounds. That would be so if the treatment was not in her 'best interests' but that was primarily a question for her father; and the authority had not considered the father's view of her best interests. Finally, the authority could not, where a patient's life was at stake, simply 'toll the bell of scarce resources' to justify its non-funding decision; it must explain its priorities.

The Court of Appeal reversed the decision. The authority had not failed to consider the views of the patient's father. It was for the authority to decide how best to spend its limited budget to provide the maximum advantage to the maximum patients. The court could not require an account and could not interfere unless the authority behaved irrationally. In this case, it had not.

In *ex parte Fisher*, the applicant suffered from multiple sclerosis. He was assessed as suitable for treatment with a new drug, beta-interferon. However, the health authority refused to pay for it. It had, in effect, a blanket ban on funding it. In an application for judicial review, Dyson J quashed the decision on a number of grounds. First, the decision was not in accordance with, nor had taken into account, the factors stated in a circular issue by the NHS Executive on the effective introduction of the drug into the NHS. Secondly, the authority's reasons for not funding the treatment were that the funding could only be done on a 'first come, first served basis' but believed this was inequitable for other patients. This reasoning process did not justify not funding the patient's treatment because it was irrational.

---

[24] See B. Hurwitz, *Clinical Guidelines and the Law* (1988).
[25] (1995) 25 BMLR 5 (Laws J) and (1995) 23 BMLR 1 (CA).   [26] (1997) 38 BMLR 76.

2. Medical Law and Ethics

Medicine is about life, quality of life, and death. Ethics is about how we as human beings should live together and what obligations we have to each other: what is 'right'. The stock in trade of ethics is founded in the notions of such things as 'personhood', 'human dignity', 'autonomy' and the 'intrinsic value of human life'. Who counts morally and how much do they count if they do?[27] But not all people share the same views about these basic notions. There is also much disagreement about the correct approach to moral reasoning: is its concern with certain moral fundamentals—the prohibition on killing innocent human life—as in traditional Judaeo-Christian ethics? Or, is it concerned with attributing 'rights' to rational autonomous persons and, if so, what rights do these rights-bearers possess? How do we resolve situations where the rights of individuals come into conflict? Or is it solely concerned with the consequences of an individual's action—in particular, seeking to achieve the greater good of the utilitarian calculus? How can the interests of different individuals be measured and weighed against one another as part of this calculation? Even if the approach is agreed, its application in particular circumstances may not be. All of these are 'big' questions; questions which philosophers have mused over since the time of Aristotle. The body of philosophical literature is enormous. For every argument or claim, there is a different view or counter claim.

Human life is, of course, greatly valued and effectively protected by all civilised societies—secular or religious. But to some people—devout Catholics and certain Protestant fundamentalists—life is more than valuable: it is a gift from God and hence sacred. Such beliefs, when taken to their logical extremes, can have serious implications for the law. Moreover, the nature of the beliefs is such that those who hold them are unwilling to compromise. Those who are pro-life, for example, are unlikely to make any significant concessions on issues such as abortion, embryo experiments, or neonaticide. Termination of pregnancy, to take the abortion example, is unlikely to appeal to them even during the very early stages of the life of the foetus.

It is obvious that medical law and ethics exist in a close relationship. The latter lies at the heart, or if not is very close to the surface, of many of the issues faced by the law. Yet, courts are courts of law, not morals. Their function is to determine and apply the law to the instant case. Often, however, they and others who determine questions of medical law cannot altogether avoid the fact that their decision involves questions of medical ethics. The legal outcome may not always be the same as some would suggest it should be from a philosophical perspective. This may well be because the law, as an instrument of social regulation, has a more limited (more permissive) role to play or, conversely, it may be because it has a more intrusive (or coercive) function: the moral outcome might be otherwise. An example of the former might be the law's defence of a competent woman's right to refuse medical treatment when she is pregnant even if this will have deleterious consequences for her foetus.

[27] For an interesting discussion of some of the main issues see J. Harris, *The Value of Life: An Introduction to Medical Ethics* (1985).

An example of the latter may be the law relating to euthanasia and assisted-suicide where, for some, such acts could be morally acceptable in certain compelling circumstances. The law, however, may not be able to contemplate for public policy reasons any relaxation of an absolute prohibition against killing or aiding death for 'good reasons'.

Philosophy and law are distinct disciplines and ethics (or medical ethics) as an intellectual pursuit is the territory of philosophers. This section is not, however, the place to investigate the very rich and complex sub-discipline of philosophy which is (medical) ethics. The reader must look elsewhere to specialist philosophical works for that. Instead, here, it is intended to identify, by way of example, a number of areas where law and philosophy intermingle but the law must take a view. Unashamedly these examples go well beyond the remit of tort. They will demonstrate the collage of legal areas—criminal law, family law, property law, etc.—that makes up medical law.

(A) THE BEGINNING OF LIFE

Human life begins at conception; that is a biological fact. It does not tell us, necessarily, whether that life counts legally and, if it does, whether to the same extent as a born person such as a child or adult. The law takes a middle course. The foetus is neither a 'legal person' nor is it 'nothing'. It occupies an intermediate space entitling it to 'special status'. The issue recently arose before the House of Lords in *Attorney-General's Reference (No. 3 of 1994)*.[28] The issue to be decided was whether a conviction for murder or manslaughter could be sustained where the defendant had injured a pregnant woman so that she had later given birth prematurely and her child had died. The House of Lords held that manslaughter but not murder could be committed.[29] Of interest here is the view taken by the judges of the status (and hence legal protection) afforded a foetus *prior* to birth by the common law. Killing *in utero* could not be murder or manslaughter because the foetus was not a legal person.[30] (As we shall see, this position is reflected in the civil law as well.)[31] But both Lords Mustill and Hope (speaking for the court) held that this did not mean that the law ignored the existence of the foetus when *in utero*. They rejected the view taken in the Court of Appeal that the foetus was part of the woman; a kind of organ or limb of the woman. Lord Mustill acknowledged that there was an 'intimate bond' between mother and unborn child 'created by the total dependence of the foetus on the protective physical environment furnished by the mother'. They were, however, genetically different and their relationship was 'one of bond, not of identity'. He concluded:[32]

The mother and foetus were two distinct organisms living symbiotically, not a single organism with two aspects. The mother's leg was part of the mother; the foetus was not.

[28] [1997] 3 All ER 936 (HL).

[29] The issues are discussed in the context of the Court of Appeal's decision in Grubb (1995) 3 *Med. L. Rev.* 302.

[30] *R* v. *Tait* [1989] 3 All ER 682 (CA). Ibid., discussing the case law.

[31] *Re F (In Utero)* [1988] 2 All ER 193 (CA). See also, *Winnipeg Child and Family Services* v. *DFG* (1997) 152 DLR (4th) 193 (Can. Sup. Ct.).

[32] N. 28 above, at 943.

Whilst not a legal person, the unborn child was not nothing either. It was, in the words of Lord Mustill,[33]

an organism *sui generis* lacking at this stage the entire range of characteristics both of the mother to which it is physically linked and of the complete human being which it will later become.

Lord Hope added:[34]

An embryo is in reality a separate organism from the mother from the moment of conception . . . [T]he foetus cannot be regarded as an integral part of the mother . . . notwithstanding its dependence upon the mother for its survival until birth.

In line with this approach, English law protects the foetus even at the very early stages of pregnancy. Even experimental research for the purposes of detecting or curing genetic abnormality of an extra-corporeal embryo is seen as an unacceptable interference except at the very earliest stages of its development (up to 14 days).[35]

There are two areas where it is of interest to see how the law has dealt with early human life and what, if any, protections it has been afforded: abortion and assisted conception.

(i) Abortion   For those who believe that a human person is created at conception, abortion is immoral; and, according to this viewpoint, it is also a crime indistinguishable from murder. As Heilbron J said in *C* v. *S*:[36] 'Abortion . . . is a very controversial subject . . . It involves sociological, moral and profound religious aspects, which arouse anxieties.' For those with strong religious views, abortion is thus unacceptable except, *perhaps*, where the killing of the foetus is the secondary consequence, the prime and sole aim being to save the mother's life. For others—arguably the majority—such an approach is unduly restrictive, especially during the early stages of pregnancy; it also fails to acknowledge a woman's right to determine the fate of her own body. Protecting the rights of a living organism, which, however, is not yet a human being, must thus be balanced against the rights of a fully developed human being—the mother. The law, partly statutory and partly found in decisions, has tried to achieve a balance between these conflicting positions. The amendment of the Abortion Act 1967 in 1991 has done much, though not everything, to clarify the ambiguities of the law.[37]

Originally, the Offences Against the Person Act 1861 outlawed all abortions.[38] The Abortion Act of 1967 was passed to modify this rigid attitude of the law in the light of altered socio-economic circumstances, and an undesirable

---

[33] N. 28 above, at 943.   [34] Ibid., at 954.

[35] Human Fertilisation and Embryology Act 1990, s. 3.

[36] [1987] 1 All ER 1230, 1238 discussed by A. Grubb and D. Pearl in 'Protecting the Life of the Unborn Child' (1987) 103 LQR 340.

[37] By s. 37 of the Human Fertilisation and Embryology Act 1990 (coming into force on 1 April 1991). See A. Grubb, 'The New Law of Abortion: Ambiguity or Clarification?' [1991] *Crim. LR* 659.

[38] Some therapeutic abortions, performed in the interests of the life or health (including mental health) of the mother, were accepted as lawful by Macnaughten J in *R* v. *Bourne* [1939] 1 KB 687. See the discussion in J. Keown, *Abortion, Doctors and the Law* (1988) and A. Grubb, 'Abortion Law in England: the Medicalization of a Crime' (1990) 18 *Law, Medicine & Health Care* 146.

increase in illegal abortions that flourished under the old regime. The 1967 Act did not, however, abolish or interfere with the provisions of the Infant Life (Preservation) Act 1929. The aim of section 1(1) of this latter Act was to create the (separate) offence of 'child destruction', punishable with a maximum penalty of life imprisonment. This occurs where 'any person who, with intent to destroy the life of a child *capable of being born alive*, by any wilful act causes a child to die before it has an existence independent of its mother' (emphasis added). While the Act certainly prohibited the killing of such a child in the process of being born, it also had important implications for the medical termination of pregnancies, since to terminate a 'child capable of being born' was an offence under the 1929 Act. Consequently, it was the 1929 Act (and not the Abortion Act 1967) which set the upper time limit for abortions. It was essential, therefore, to understand the meaning of the phrase 'capable of being born alive'. The Act was singularly unhelpful. Although it made clear that a foetus over twenty-eight weeks old was presumed to be 'capable of being born alive', before that stage of development the Act provided no guidance. Certainly, it seemed that with the progress made in medical science making it possible to keep alive a foetus between the twenty-fourth and twenty-eighth month of pregnancy, the upper time-limit for abortion was being progressively pushed back.[39] In practical terms, the legal difficulties were thus likely to arise during this period (twenty-four to twenty-eight weeks). In purely legal terms, the meaning of the statutory phrase was largely a mystery. Did it require a child to have the capacity to survive on birth or merely not to be dead? If the former, how long did the child have to be able to survive? Would any time suffice or did it have to be for a reasonable time? If the latter, did survival have to be by natural means or should account be taken of technological intervention? These issues were never satisfactorily resolved, though the subject of much academic[40] and judicial[41] discussion. The uncertainty was wholly unsatisfactory, not least since it exposed doctors to potential criminal liability under the 1929 Act. Hence, in 1990 Parliament decided to legislate to remove any ambiguities. During the passage of the Human Fertilisation and Embryology Bill, the Abortion Act 1967 was amended so as to disentangle the law of abortion from the provisions of the 1929 Act. Accordingly, section 5(1) now provides that an abortion is lawful if carried out in accordance with the 1967 Act. In such a case no offence of 'child destruction' is committed under the 1929 Act even if the child is 'capable of being born alive'. At the same time Parliament amended the 1967 Act so as to ensure that the upper time-limits under the various grounds for abortion were clear.

The Abortion Act 1967 creates four grounds for terminating a pregnancy. In each case two registered medical practitioners must form the opinion in good faith that the ground exists.

---

[39] According to expert evidence given in *C* v. *S*, above, in the UK no foetus less than 23 weeks old has survived after delivery.

[40] See G. Williams, *Textbook of Criminal Law* (2nd edn., 1983), 303–4; J. Keown, 'The Scope of the Offence of Child Destruction' (1988) 104 LQR 120.

[41] *C* v. *S* [1987] 1 All ER 1230; *Rance* v. *Mid-Downs HA* [1991] 1 All ER 801.

First, a pregnancy may be terminated if its continuation involves: (*a*) a risk of injury to the woman's physical or mental health (the maternal health ground); or (*b*) a risk of injury to the physical or mental health of any existing children of her family (the so-called 'social clause').[42] In both instances the risk in question must be greater than if the pregnancy were terminated and, importantly, *the pregnancy must not have exceeded its twenty-fourth week*. Here, Parliament has expressly limited terminations on the most common grounds to the first twenty-four weeks of pregnancy.[43]

Secondly, a pregnancy may be terminated in order to prevent grave permanent injury to the mother's physical or mental health (section 1(1)(b)).

Thirdly, a pregnancy may be terminated if its continuation involves a risk to the mother's life greater than if it were terminated (section 1(1)(c)).

Fourthly, a pregnancy may be terminated if there is a substantial risk that the child—if born—would suffer from such physical or mental abnormalities as to be seriously handicapped (section 1(1)(d)).

Significantly, these last three grounds are not subject to any upper time-limit. While the 1929 Act would, in any event, have permitted terminations where the mother's life was threatened (and possibly to avoid serious injury), Parliament has widened the availability of terminations where foetal abnormality is the ground. At least in theory, though perhaps not in practice, all these grounds permit a termination at any time before the foetus is born. It is not clear, however, the extent to which the grounds based upon a serious danger to the mother's health or life would be relied upon late in pregnancy when the child could, quite consistently with protecting the mother's life or health, be delivered alive. Is this a termination of pregnancy within the 1967 Act or merely induced labour leading to a live delivery?

Another and no less important issue that arises with abortions concerns the father's 'interests' or 'rights' in this matter. Two English decisions have dealt with this problem: *Paton* v. *British Pregnancy Advisory Service*[44] and *C* v. *S*.[45] In both cases, however, it was held that the father had no right to seek an injunction (either in his own right or acting on behalf of the foetus) to prevent the abortion or to prevent the commission of a *crime* (i.e. if (then) the 1929 Act was not complied with, and (now) that the 1967 Act is not complied with). To like effect, courts throughout the world have refused to grant paternal injunctions to prevent a termination.[46] It is equally likely that the courts would not recognise a father's legal right to be consulted before a termination since this might be no less intrusive on the mother–doctor relationship and does not seem to be contemplated by the framework of the 1967 Act.[47]

---

[42] Section 1(1)(a).

[43] For the uncertainty surrounding the calculation of the twenty-four weeks, see Grubb, op. cit., n. 37 above, at 665–6.

[44] [1979] QB 276 involving the husband of the women seeking an abortion.

[45] [1987] 1 All ER 1230 involving the boyfriend of the woman in question.

[46] *Kelly* v. *Kelly*, 1997 SLT 896 (Scot. Ct. of Sess.); *Attorney-General* (*ex rel Kerr*) v. *T* (1983) 46 ALR 275 (Australian High Ct.); *Tremblay* v. *Daiglé* [1989] 2 SCR 530 (Canadian Sup. Ct.).

[47] See *Planned Parenthood of South-Eastern Pennsylvania* v. *Casey* (1992) 120 L Ed 2d 674 (US Sup. Ct.) (striking down legislation requiring consultation with the father prior to a termination).

It would thus appear that the courts seem to be reluctant to challenge a medical decision, honestly reached, about an abortion. In general, they prefer to leave any challenge to the legality of such a decision to the criminal courts, where a jury would make the decision and not a judge sitting alone. As Sir George Baker P said in *Paton v. Trustees of BPAS*:[48]

Not only would it be a bold and brave judge . . . who would seek to interfere with the discretion of doctors acting under the Abortion Act 1967, but I think he would really be a foolish judge who would try to do any such thing, unless possibly, there is clear bad faith and an obvious attempt to perpetrate a criminal offence. *Even then, of course, the question is whether that is a matter which should be left to the Director of Public Prosecutions and the Attorney General.* (Italics supplied.)

(ii) Assisted Conception Perhaps more than any other, the modern developments in reproductive technology have generated great controversy. Taken together with advances in genetic science, they continue to produce dilemmas for the philosophical and legal community.[49] The advances are so fast and unpredictable that policy-makers are almost always playing 'catch-up regulation'; constantly engaging in public consultation or review, and taking a view of the proper scope of the law as a matter of public policy. There are many instances of this in the area of genetics and assisted conception.

For example, a recent debate has questioned the techniques of cloning humans using embryos or the so-called 'Dolly technique' of transferring a nucleus from an egg into an adult human cell. Are such procedures lawful and, if not, should they be permitted?[50] In 1990, Parliament believed it had outlawed cloning of human beings on the advice of the Warnock Committee.[51] It now turns out that this was not so, since the legislation is narrowly drawn so as not to prohibit the 'Dolly technique'.[52] Indeed, it is arguable that this technique is not even regulated by the Human Fertilisation and Embryology Authority and so can be carried out without a licence.[53] The Authority takes a different view of its powers and currently will not license any activity involving cloning of human beings.[54]

Is there any moral difference between *'non-reproductive' cloning*, i.e., the creation of cloned embryos as part of genetic research, and *'reproductive' cloning* where genetically identical individuals are created, for example, to replace dead children or relatives or to provide suitable donors of tissue and organs for existing people? Some would see moral obstacles to all these possibilities. Such practices could be seen as 'unnatural' or an affront to human dignity. Others would see a clear difference between research that might benefit others and

---

[48] [1979] QB 276, 252; approved by Sir John Donaldson MR in *C v. S* [1987] 1 All ER 1230, 1243.

[49] See Harris, *Clones, Genes, and Immorality* (below, Select Bibliography).

[50] See P. Walsh and A. Grubb, 'I Want To Be Alone' (1997) 7(2) *Dispatches* 1.

[51] S. 3(3)(d), Human Fertilisation and Embryology Act 1990.

[52] See House of Commons Science and Technology Committee Fifth Report (Session 1996–7) *The Cloning of Animals From Adult Cells* (HC 373), 2 vols.

[53] Walsh and Grubb, op. cit., n. 50 above.

[54] *Cloning Issues in Reproduction, Science and Medicine* (HGAC/HFEA 1998).

the creation of clones, which could be said to infringe the Kantian edict that persons should not be used merely as a means to an end.[55]

More commonplace, however, is the use and/or storage of human embryos for the purpose of treating infertility which involves the creation of an embryo in a laboratory, its subsequent freezing, and eventual implantation in a woman. This procedure, and others deployed in infertility clinics, raise a host of legal issues.

If the fertilised egg is a living organism, who determines its fate? Can a woman ask for the embryo to be implanted after she has divorced the father or after the father's death? What happens if both parents die? Can their existing children or other relatives request the destruction of the embryos, thus frustrating possible claims on the parents' estate once these embryos develop (through the use of a surrogate mother) into children? Finally, to give one last example, if an embryo is donated and implanted in a woman other than its genetic mother, can it (eventually) lay claim to the latter's estate? Does genetics or gestation dictate parentage?

The unease felt by many at the developments in modern reproductive technology and embryology led the government to set up the Committee of Inquiry into Human Fertilisation and Embryology (known as the Warnock Committee) which reported in 1984.[56] Parliament responded by enacting the Human Fertilisation and Embryology Act 1990, which seeks to provide solutions to these difficult problems.[57] At the centre of the legislative framework is a statutory licensing authority known as the Human Fertilisation and Embryology Authority. In a number of instances the moral quagmire has resulted in the imposition of solutions, in large part, as a matter of expediency. A number of examples include the following.

Embryos may not be used for research once they have reached fourteen days' development.[58] A man whose sperm is used after his death will not be the father of any resulting child, thereby avoiding legal problems of delayed posthumous births.[59] Finally, the Act vests control over gametes (sperm or eggs) in the 'gamete provider', and in the case of embryos in the 'gamete providers' jointly.[60] English law may thus avoid the legal problems faced in other countries where disputes over the fate of embryos (between 'gamete providers' and the doctor[61] or between the 'gamete providers' themselves[62]) have forced courts to analyse these novel problems within the strait-jacket of the tradi-

---

[55] See Walsh and Grubb, op. cit., n. 50 above and J. Harris, ' "Goodbye Dolly?" The Ethics of Human Cloning' (1997) 23 *J. of Medical Ethics* 353. See the papers in the special issue of (1998) 7(2) *Cambridge Quarterly of Healthcare Ethics*.

[56] Cmnd. 9314 (1984). For a discussion of some of these issues see A. Grubb and D. Pearl, 'Medicine, Health, the Family and the Law' [1986] *Family Law* 227. See also the DHSS Consultation Paper, Legislation on Human Infertility Services and Embryo Research (Cmnd. 46) published in Dec. 1986 and the subsequent White Paper published in Nov. 1987 (Cmnd. 259) entitled Human Fertilisation and Embryology: A Framework for Legislation.

[57] See Morgan and Lee, (Select Bibliography, below) and Douglas, (Select Bibliography, below).

[58] Ss. 3(3)(a) and 3(4).   [59] S. 28(6)(b).   [60] Sch. 3.

[61] *York* v. *Jones* (1989) F. Supp 421 (E. D. Va.).

[62] *Davis* v. *Davis* (1992) 842 S.W. 2d 605 (Tenn. Sup. Ct.).

tional principles of property and family law.[63] However, even the comprehensive and tightly drafted 1990 Act cannot wholly avoid litigation. Thus, in a case that attracted considerable public attention in 1997, a widow (Diane Blood) sought to obtain sperm taken from her comatose husband shortly before his death.[64] This had been done without his consent and he had never specifically agreed to its use posthumously. The taking of the deceased's sperm was illegal under the common law (not being in his 'best interests'); and use of the sperm in the UK was not permitted under the 1990 Act without his written consent. None the less, Diane Blood was allowed to take the sperm to another European Union country, where less strict requirements for its use pertained, in order to be inseminated. Her claim was successful because her lawyers made skilful use of European Union law. The case created considerable public sympathy and prompted calls for changes in the law, which have, so far, been resisted.

Other legal problems exist. Can the child born as a result of a donated egg, sperm, or embryo, upon reaching majority, demand to know who his genetic mother and father are? A child adopted after birth is entitled to do so. Is there really any difference where the child is, in a sense, 'adopted' before birth? Apparently there is, since at present a child may not obtain such information under the 1990 Act, although this may change in the future.[65] And what is the doctor's and the donor's potential liability if the latter, through his sperm, transmits some genetic defect or infection to the child? In theory, the donor must exercise reasonable care in disclosing any facts that might alert the doctor to the danger. However, in practice it will be very difficult to establish that the donor is liable and, in any event, he is unlikely to have a 'deep pocket' worth pursuing through the courts.[66] Instead, it is against the doctor (or clinic or hospital) that such claims will most profitably be directed. Of course, the doctor must act with reasonable care in screening and selecting the donor or the donated material. He must also carry out any appropriate tests for genetic defects or infection such as HIV. No doubt he could be liable *to the mother* if he acts negligently. Whether a duty is owed to the child and whether he can bring an action depends, as we shall see later, on the claim falling within the Congenital Disabilities (Civil Liability) Act 1976. Although as originally drafted no liability was likely to be incurred, it is now beyond doubt.[67]

(B) THE END OF LIFE

(i) Treatment Decisions
When, if ever, is it lawful to bring about the death of a patient? Is there any difference between actively killing a patient and

---

[63] See A. Grubb, 'The Legal Status of the Frozen Human Embryo', in A. Grubb (ed.), *Challenges in Medical Care*, 69–91.

[64] *R v. Human Fertilisation and Embryology Authority, ex parte Blood* [1997] 2 All ER 687 (CA). Discussed in Grubb (1996) 4 *Med. L. Rev.* 329.

[65] S. 31(4) states that a child on reaching 18 may obtain such information as is permitted by Regulation. None currently exists (and identifying information cannot be included in Regulations with retrospective effect).

[66] See Grubb and Pearl, op. cit. (Select Bibliography), 117–21 (discussing a blood-donor's liability).

[67] S. 1A(1)(b) (added by the 1990 Act) includes within the 1976 Act claims where 'the disability results from an act or omission in the course of the selection, or the keeping or use outside the body, of the embryo . . . or of the gametes used to bring about the creation of the embryo'.

allowing them to die? Does the sanctity of human life mean that any intentional causing of death is illegal?[68] As a starting point, English law does not see
the sanctity of human life as constituting an absolute principle. Let us look at
these situations separately.

(1) Refusal of Treatment. A patient's right to determine what happens to his
body is a basic and inviolable human right.[69] English law recognises the
patient's right of self-determination and the autonomy of the patient and gives
effect to it through the law of consent. Any treatment of a competent adult
patient will be unlawful (being the crime or tort of battery) unless the patient
has consented to the treatment.[70] The right to choose whether to undergo
treatment includes the right to refuse treatment, including life-sustaining treatment. For example, in *Re T (Adult: refusal of treatment)*[71] the court accepted that a
competent adult Jehovah's Witness has the right to refuse a blood transfusion
even though this would lead to death. In such a situation there is no question
of the patient having committed suicide. Consequently a doctor is not assisting suicide,[72] he is merely respecting the patient's wishes in accordance with
his legal duty.[73] Subsequently, courts have accepted a patient's refusal of a
Caesarean section,[74] renal dialysis[75] and artificial feeding.[76]

In *Re T*, the court further held that this right could be exercised where the
patient's refusal was expressed at an earlier time prior to the patient becoming
unconscious or otherwise incompetent to make a decision.[77] In other words, a
patient may validly make what is called an advance directive (or 'living will')
refusing medical treatment. Three conditions have to be satisfied. *First*, the
patient must be competent at the time the refusal is made (i.e. understood what
was involved). *Secondly*, the patient must have intended the refusal to cover the
situation that subsequently arose (e.g. that her life might be threatened).
Thirdly, the refusal must not have been made under the undue influence of
another. On the facts, the court held that T's refusal of a blood transfusion
made before she became unconscious was invalid because the last two conditions were not satisfied. T had not realised that she might die without a transfusion because she had been misled that there were medical alternatives. In
any event, her refusal was the product of pressure from her mother (who was
an active Jehovah's Witness) who had visited her in hospital.

The approach in *Re T* was subsequently applied in the case of *Re C*[78] in 1994.

---

[68] For a discussion from moral perspectives, see J. Glover, *Causing Death and Saving Lives* (1977) and
B. Steinbock and A. Norcross (eds.), *Killing and Letting Die* (2nd edn., 1994).
[69] *Sidaway* v. *Governors of Bethlem Royal Hospital* [1985] 1 All ER 634 at 649 per Lord Scarman.
[70] *Re F (A Mental Patient: Sterilisation)* [1990] 2 AC 1 at 72–3 per Lord Goff.
[71] [1992] 4 All ER 649.
[72] See D. P. T. Price, 'Assisted Suicide and Refusing Medical Treatment: Linguistics, Morals and Legal
Contortions' (1996) 4 *Med. L. Rev.* 270.
[73] *Airedale NHS Trust* v. *Bland* [1993] 1 All ER 821 at 866 per Lord Goff.
[74] *St George's Healthcare NHS Trust* v. *S* [1998] 3 All ER 673.
[75] *Re JT (Adult: Refusal of Medical Treatment)* [1998] 1 FLR 48.
[76] *Secretary of State for the Home Department* v. *Robb* [1995] 1 All ER 677.
[77] Approving *Malette* v. *Shulman* (1990) 67 DLR (4th) 321 (Ontario CA) ($20,000 awarded when a blood
transfusion was administered to an unconscious Jehovah's Witness who carried a card refusing even a life-
sustaining blood transfusion).
[78] [1994] 1 All ER 819. Discussed in Grubb (1994) 2 *Med. L. Rev.* 92.

The decision removes any doubt that advance directives can be valid in English law. The patient suffered from paranoid schizophrenia and was detained in Broadmoor. He developed gangrene in his foot. He was advised he would die without surgery to remove it but he refused it. Thorpe J granted the patient an injunction preventing the removal of his foot now or in the future without his express consent. Despite his psychiatric condition, which included delusions, the judge held that the patient was able to comprehend and retain the information given to him about his condition and treatment; he was able to *believe* it and *weigh* it up so as to *arrive at a choice*. Hence, in law he was competent to refuse treatment now or, in anticipation, for the future.[79]

Who has the right to refuse treatment? The situation contemplated in *Re T* was that of the competent adult patient. What if the decision of the competent adult would harm 'another'? For example, could a pregnant woman refuse medical intervention, such as a blood transfusion or Caesarean section, if this would lead to the death of her unborn child? In *Re T* Lord Donaldson[80] left open the possibility that the law might ignore the woman's refusal in such a case. Faced with the formidable arguments against forcing treatment upon an adult in a liberal society, one might expect the courts to stay their hand, leaving it to Parliament to create a framework for making such decisions if it thought that was the appropriate response. After all, it must in practice be rare that a pregnant woman would refuse treatment that would save her unborn child.[81] Yet this was not their first reaction. In the first case of its kind in this country, a court declared that it would be lawful to carry out a Caesarean section upon a competent pregnant woman whose refusal was based upon her religious beliefs.[82]

Subsequently, however, in *Re MB*[83] and *St George's Healthcare NHS Trust* v. *S*,[84] the Court of Appeal has emphatically rejected any suggestion that a competent woman's right to refuse treatment is modified by the fact that she is pregnant. In the latter case, the court was faced with a pregnant woman (carrying a 36-week-old foetus) who was refusing medical treatment for the life threatening condition of pre-eclampsia. The Court of Appeal stated that the 'autonomy of each individual requires continuing protection' and there were dangers in making even 'minor concessions'. The court recognised that the foetus was 'not nothing . . . it is not lifeless and it is certainly human'.[85] Nevertheless, a woman's right to decide prevailed. The court indicated that the law and morality might part company on the proper solution to the issue. Judge LJ stated:[86]

[W]hile pregnancy increases the personal responsibilities of a woman it does not diminish her entitlement to decide whether or not to undergo medical treatment. Although human . . . an unborn child is not a separate person from its mother. Its need for

---

[79] The three-stage test in *Re C* is the accepted test of legal competence: *Re MB* [1997] 2 FLR 426 (CA) and *St George's Healthcare NHS Trust* v. *S* [1998] 3 All ER 673 (CA). The test is equally applicable to children who suffer from mental disability: *Re C (Detention: Medical Treatment)* [1997] 2 FLR 180; discussed in Grubb (1997) 5 *Med. L. Rev.* 227.

[80] Op. cit., n. 71 above, at 653.

[81] See e.g. *Re F (In Utero)* [1988] Fam. 122 (CA).

[82] *Re S (Adult: Refusal of Treatment)* [1992] 4 All ER 671.

[83] [1997] 2 FLR 426 (CA).

[84] [1998] 3 All ER 673 (CA).

[85] Ibid. per Judge LJ at 688, 688 and 687 respectively.

[86] Ibid. per Judge LJ at 693.

medical assistance does not prevail over her rights. She is entitled not to be forced to submit to an invasion of her body against her will, whether her own life or that of her unborn child depends on it. Her right is not reduced or diminished merely because her decision to exercise it may appear morally repugnant.

What of children? Can they refuse medical treatment, including life-saving treatment? By statute a child between the ages of 16 and 18 may consent to 'medical, surgical and dental' treatment to the same extent as an adult.[87] In *Gillick* v. *West Norfolk and Wisbech AHA*,[88] the House of Lords held that a competent child under the age of 16 could, under the common law, also give a valid consent to medical treatment if it was sufficiently mature to understand what was involved in the treatment.[89] Though that case involved contraceptive advice and treatment, the decision is one of general application allowing children to consent to all medical treatment providing they are mature enough to appreciate fully the physical and emotional implications of the particular decision.[90] Where a child is not sufficiently mature to be competent in law, a doctor must rely upon the parents' decision acting in the child's 'best interests'. But if there is any doubt, he should ask the court (under the Children Act or the court's inherent jurisdiction) to decide, especially if the girl and her parents have conflicting views.[91]

But is a competent child able legally to refuse treatment? In English law the answer, for the time being, is 'no'.[92] In *Re W (A Minor) (Medical Treatment)*[93] a 16-year-old girl suffering from the eating disorder anorexia nervosa was forced to undergo a regime of treatment which she refused. The Court of Appeal held that the court under its inherent jurisdiction could consent to medical treatment which it considered objectively to be in a child's 'best interests' even if the child was competent to make the decision for herself. Approving its earlier decision in *Re R (A Minor) (Wardship: Medical Treatment)*,[94] the court held that it had a duty to protect her, in effect, from herself. But both Lord Donaldson MR and Balcombe LJ, also concluded that the parents of a child could consent to medical treatment even if the child refused. The third judge, Nolan LJ concluded that such conflicts should come before the court to determine the child's 'best interests'.[95] Is it a real limitation on the court's (or parents') power

---

[87] Family Law Reform Act 1969, s. 8(1).   [88] [1985] 3 All ER 402 (HL).

[89] *Gillick* v. *West Norfolk and Wisbech AHA* [1986] AC 112. From the rich literature on this case, see G. Williams, 'The Gillick Saga' (1985) 135 *New LJ* 1156; I. Kennedy, *Treat Me Right*, (below, Select Bibliography), ch. 5; B. Hoggett, in P. Byrne (ed.), *Rights and Wrongs in Medicine* (1982), 158.

[90] See *C* v. *Wren* (1986) 35 DLR (4th) 419 (Alberta CA) (girl aged 16 had capacity to consent to an abortion). See also *Ney* v. *Attorney-General of Canada* (1993) 102 DLR (4th) 136 (B.C. Sup. Ct.).

[91] The courts have required a high level of understanding (and appreciation) from children such that they are usually found to be incompetent to refuse life-sustaining treatment which may then be administered if in their 'best interests': see, e.g., *Re E (A Minor)* (1990) 9 BMLR 1 and *Re S (A Minor) (Consent to Medical Treatment)* [1994] 2 FLR 1065; discussed in Grubb (1995) 3 *Med. L. Rev.* 84.

[92] See M. Brazier and C. Bridge, 'Coercion or Caring: Analysing Adolescent Autonomy' (1996) 16 LS 84 and A. Grubb, 'Treatment Decisions: Keeping it in the Family' in A. Grubb (ed.), *Choice and Decisions in Health Care* (1993), 37.

[93] [1992] 4 All ER 627.

[94] [1991] 4 All ER 177 (where the mentally ill girl was aged 15 and on the facts held to be incompetent to make a decision to refuse medication for her illness).

[95] Op. cit. 648–9.

to override the child's refusal that it is limited (at least by Balcombe and Nolan LJJ) to situations where the child's life is threatened or grave permanent harm will result from the refusal?[96] Where else will conflict between the child and others really matter?

(2) Active Killing.[97]   The law does, however, prohibit the active (intentional) killing of a patient, for example, by administering a lethal injection. 'Mercy-killing' is not accepted in English law.[98] It is either murder (where death is caused by the doctor) or assisted suicide[99] (where the doctor helps the patient take her own life). By contrast, English law seems to accept the medical practice of giving a patient increasing levels of pain-killing drugs which ultimately (and to the knowledge of the doctor) lead to the death of the patient.[100] The practice was recently highlighted by the case of a terminally-ill patient who suffered from motor-neurone disease (which renders the patient eventually 'locked in' her body with a fully functioning brain). She applied to the court for a declaration that it would be legal for her doctor to provide pain-killing drugs when her suffering became unbearable even if this killed her. The court did not grant the declaration but only because it was accepted—by all parties and the court—that such an accepted medical practice was obviously lawful.[101]

There are considerable analytical difficulties with the law's position.[102] Why, if the doctor knows death will result, is this not murder? The doctor intends (on these facts) to cause the patient's death even though he may not desire it.[103] It is pure sophistry to say he does not cause death but that death results from natural causes. He accelerates the patient's death albeit by a short time, perhaps weeks, perhaps even hours. Yet, accelerating death is *causing* death since, after all, that is the only thing anyone can do since death is inevitable for everyone.

Mercy killing is not illegal everywhere.[104] In Oregon, physician-assisted suicide is legal in particular, well defined circumstances although active killing remains illegal.[105] Both practices, however, are lawful in the Netherlands where the patient is terminally ill, their condition is hopeless, and their suffering unbearable provided the doctor complies with the requirements of 'careful practice'.[106] The current law is seen as inhumane and requiring doctors to 'bend the rules' and fudge the way in which the patient dies by relying on the 'pain-killing' exception. There have been many calls, over many years, for changes in English law. None has, as yet, been heeded and there seems to be a

---

[96] Op. cit., at 643 and 648 respectively.

[97] See Otlowski, *Voluntary Euthanasia and the Common Law*, (Select Bibliography).

[98] *R* v. *Cox* (1992) 12 BMLR 38 and *Airedale NHS Trust* v. *Bland* [1993] AC 789 (HL).

[99] Under s. 2(1), Suicide Act 1961.

[100] See *Airedale NHS Trust* v. *Bland*, op. cit., per Lord Goff at 867 and *Re J* (*Wardship: Medical Treatment*) [1991] 2 WLR 140 per Sir John Donaldson MR at 149. See generally, Otlowski, (below, Select Bibliography) at 170–84.

[101] See *Hansard*, HL, cols. 720–44, November 1997 (debate following the case of Annie Lindsell).

[102] See Otlowski, op. cit. and D. P. T. Price, 'Euthanasia, Pain Relief and Double Effect' (1997) 17 LS 323.

[103] *R* v. *Woolin* [1998] 3 All ER 103 (HL).

[104] For a short while it was lawful in the Northern Territory in Australia under the Rights of the Terminally Ill Act 1995. It has since been repealed by the federal legislature.

[105] Death with Dignity Act 1994.

[106] See J. Griffiths, A. Bood and H. Weyers, *Euthanasia and Law in the Netherlands* (1998).

political consensus that any change to the law would not be beneficial.[107] With an ever-increasing ageing population, calls for law reform to allow 'help in dying' are, however, likely to continue undeterred by the legislators' current reticence.

(3) *Withholding and Withdrawing Treatment.* If intentionally causing a patient's death by active means is illegal, what of the situation where treatment is withheld or withdrawn? We have already seen the legal position where this is done at the request of a competent patient. His right to self-determination trumps the principle of the sanctity of human life.

What, however, if the patient is incompetent: an immature child or an adult who is suffering from mental disability or disorder, or who is unconscious? As regards children, those with parental responsibility (usually the parents), have a legal duty to take decisions whether to consent or not to treatment in the child's 'best interests'. But what of incompetent adults?

At one time it was frequently stated (and assumed) that a spouse or parent of an adult offspring or the next of kin could give a valid consent if the patient was incompetent, for example, unconscious.[108] This is not the law in England and it never has been. No one may consent to medical treatment where the patient is an adult and incompetent.[109] Yet, it would be absurd if a doctor could not treat a patient in an emergency in a casualty department, for example, just because the patient was unconscious. Equally, it would be a strange state of affairs if a doctor could not carry out a medical procedure on an intellectually disabled (and permanently incompetent) adult if it was not an emergency but the treatment was desirable in the interests of such a patient, for example, filling a decayed tooth. In *Re F (A Mental Patient: Sterilisation)*[110] the House of Lords accepted that the principle of necessity justified treatment in the 'best interests' of the patient. This was to be determined by applying the *Bolam* test used in medical negligence cases.[111] *Re F* concerned a *permanently incompetent* patient, but it is clear that the principle of necessity would also justify treatment that was 'reasonably required' when the patient is *temporarily incompetent*, for example, is unconscious after an accident.[112] Of course, less treatment may be 'reasonably required' in the latter case because the patient will 'regain consciousness and can then be consulted about longer term measures'.[113]

Could an incompetent patient's 'best interest' include the withholding or withdrawal of life-sustaining treatment? The issue arose in *Airedale NHS Trust* v.

---

[107] See *Report of the Select Committee on Medical Ethics* (Session 1993–4) (HL Paper 21). Successive Governments have indicated that they have no intention of changing the law on voluntary euthanasia.

[108] See *Wilson* v. *Pringle* [1986] 2 All ER 440 at 447 per Croom-Johnson LJ.

[109] *T* v. *T* [1988] 1 All ER 613. See also *Re F*, op. cit.

[110] [1990] 2 AC 1 (HL). The case concerned the sterilisation of a 36-year-old woman with the mental capacity of a 5-year-old. For a discussion of the case in this context see Kennedy, *Treat Me Right* (Select Bibliography), ch. 20.

[111] For a criticism of this aspect of the case see Grubb [1989] All ER Rev. 200.

[112] See Lord Goff, supra at 76–7.

[113] Ibid. See the factually contrasting Canadian cases of *Marshall* v. *Curry* [1933] 3 DLR 260 (removal of diseased testicle during hernia operation justified) and *Murray* v. *McMurchy* [1949] 2 DLR 442 (sterilisation during operation to remove fibroid tissue from uterus not justified).

Bland.[114] There the patient was in a persistent vegetative state (PVS) which meant that he was permanently unconscious. He had been in this state for over three years and the medical evidence was that he would never recover. He was kept alive by tube-feeding and hydration. His doctor and parents all agreed that it would be best for the patient if his tubes were withdrawn and he was allowed to die. The House of Lords granted a declaration that it would be lawful to do so. Applying *Re F*, the judges reasoned that the doctor had a duty to care for the patient that required him to act in the patient's 'best interests'. However, it was futile to continue his treatment since he had no hope of recovery. It could not, therefore, be in his 'best interests' to continue and thus it would be lawful to withdraw the life-support (indeed it might be unlawful to continue).[115]

The judges distinguished this situation from one where a doctor actively and intentionally brought about the death of a patient, which was murder. Even though the doctors intended the patient's death, even though the withdrawal would cause the patient's death, it would not be murder. The law drew a distinction between acts and omissions. Withdrawal of treatment fell within the latter category, unlike the provision of a lethal injection, and could only be unlawful if the omission amounted to a breach of the doctor's duty to the patient which, of course, the judges held it did not.

While acknowledging the legal situation, one judge (Lord Mustill) considered the law to be morally and intellectually 'misshapen'[116] in making this distinction; the implication being that even 'mercy-killing' is morally defensible in some situations. It may also be legally defensible as a matter of principle as the Dutch courts have shown by their extension of the defence of 'necessity' under Article 40 of the Dutch Criminal Code to euthanasia.[117] English law rejects the defence of necessity (or duress) to the crime of murder.[118] But a significant rationale for doing so, namely it is better to sacrifice oneself rather than kill,[119] may have little or no application where only the patient's life is in issue and the doctor is driven by his 'duty' to relieve a patient's suffering.[120]

In *Bland* the judges said nothing about the legality of withdrawing treatment where a patient was not permanently unconscious; where, in the words of Lord Mustill, he had the 'glimmerings of awareness'.[121] In other cases concerned mainly with disabled babies (but also adults), however, the courts have concerned themselves with the underlying philosophical dispute as to whether 'sanctity of life' may depend on the 'quality' of the life concerned. A series of decisions in the Court of Appeal has accepted that the decision-maker, acting in

[114] [1993] AC 789. Discussed in I. Kennedy and A. Grubb (1993) 1 *Med. L. Rev.* 359.

[115] See A. Grubb, 'The Persistent Vegetative State: A Duty (Not) To Treat and Conscientious Objection' (1997) 4 *European J. of Health Law* 39.

[116] N. 114 above, 887.

[117] See J. Griffiths, A. Bood and H. Weyers, op. cit., ch. 2 (development), ch. 3 (current position).

[118] *R* v. *Howe* [1987] 1 All ER 771 (HL) (duress) approving *R* v. *Dudley and Stephens* (1884) 14 QBD 273 (necessity) and *R* v. *Pommell* [1995] 2 Cr App Rep 607 (CA).

[119] *Dudley and Stephens*, ibid., per Lord Coleridge CJ at 286–8; *Howe*, ibid., per Lord Hailsham at 779–80.

[120] But note *R* v. *Rodger* [1998] 1 Cr App Rep 143 (CA) (necessity only available where the crime committed resulted from causative element extraneous to the defendant: suicidal thought processess and emotions of defendant insufficient to ground defence).

[121] Supra, n. 114, at 899.

the child's 'best interests', must assess the child's quality of life but with this proviso: treatment may only be withheld if the child's life will be intolerable.

The leading case is *Re J (A Minor) (Wardship: Medical Treatment)*.[122] Baby J suffered severe and irreparable brain damage at birth. He suffered horrendous mental and physical disabilities. However, he had a normal capacity to suffer pain, which would continue during his shortened lifetime into perhaps his late teens. The Court of Appeal agreed that the baby need not be reventilated if he required it. The judges emphasised the strong legal policy in preserving life: there is 'a strong presumption in favour of taking all steps capable of preserving [human life], save in exceptional circumstances'.[123] The court held that the correct approach in determining whether treatment could be withheld or withdrawn was to balance the benefits of treatment against the burdens of the treatment to the baby. For 'to preserve life at all costs, whatever the quality of life to be preserved, and however distressing to the ward . . . may not be in the interests of the ward'.[124] In determining the baby's quality of life, the Court of Appeal was influenced by the fact that the baby's existence would be painful and the benefits of the treatment continuing this painful existence would be minimal.[125] On the facts the burdens of treatment outweighed the benefits. One judge stated that 'the quality of life the child would endure if given the treatment . . . would be intolerable to that child'.[126]

The court contrasted the case of *Re B (A Minor) (Wardship: Medical Treatment)*[127] where the court had authorised a duodenal operation upon a newly born baby with Down's Syndrome. In that case, the court had held that the baby's quality of life after the operation to remove an intestinal blockage was not such that non-treatment was in its 'best interests'. In *Re B* the child had a prospect of a life-expectancy of between twenty and thirty years. The precise extent of its physical and mental disabilities would be unclear for some time. However, it was not in any pain and its life could not, on the evidence before the court, be described as 'intolerable'. In *Re J*, the court pointed out that the only reason why a dispute arose in *Re B* was because both the doctors and the judge at first instance had been influenced by the parents' objection to the treatment. Medically, all the evidence was in favour of the operation, and the Court of Appeal had rightly treated the parents' wishes as 'irrelevant, since the duty of decision had passed from them to the court'.[128]

Most cases that have followed *Re J* have concerned very severely disabled patients with a short life-expectancy, little or no cognitive ability, and whose life was full of pain and suffering.[129] In one case, the court seems to have gone further. In *Re R*,[130] the patient was twenty-three and suffered profound learning and physical disability. He was described in the evidence as having a 'low state

---

[122] [1990] 3 All ER 930.   [123] Per Taylor LJ at 943.   [124] Per Balcombe LJ at 942.

[125] See also *Re C (A Minor) (Wardship: Medical Treatment)* [1989] 2 All ER 782 (CA) which concerned a 'dying' neonate for whom medical treatment was futile. In such a case death is inevitable and the court is not balancing life against death other than 'a marginally longer life with pain against a marginally shorter life free from pain and ending in death with dignity'.

[126] Per Taylor LJ at 945.   [127] [1990] 3 All ER 927.   [128] Ibid., at 937.

[129] E.g., *Re C (A Baby)* [1996] 2 FLR 43; *Re C (A Minor)* (1997) 40 BMLR 31.

[130] [1996] 2 FLR 99. Discussed, Kennedy (1997) 5 *Med. L. Rev.* 104.

of awareness'. He was also in poor physical health. The court was asked to grant a declaration that it would be lawful not to resuscitate him if he suffered a cardiac arrest and not to treat infections with antibiotics. The court agreed as regards resuscitation, accepting the medical evidence that, given his physical condition, it was unlikely to be successful: it was practically futile. As regards the withholding of antibiotics, the court held that this was a clinical decision to be taken after consultation between the patient's doctors and with the agreement of his parents. Whilst the court did not say this would be in his 'best interests', the implication was that it could well be, even in his present condition. Yet, on the face of it, the patient was not nearly so disabled or suffering to the same degree as those in the earlier cases.

(ii) **Alive or Dead?**   At one time, when a person was dead could not be disputed: cessation of heartbeat and circulation clearly led to a diagnosis of death. Today, however, matters may not be so clear. Artificial life-support may maintain the basic life functions of a patient beyond the time when he can do so himself. No longer can death be equated with irreversible cessation of breathing and circulating. What, then, amounts in law to death? Doctors have developed the concept of 'brain death'.[131] When the brain ceases to function, then the essence of the individual ceases and death has ensued. Doctors determine the destruction of the brain stem—which maintains basic vegetative responses—as the sign that brain function no longer exists. Philosophers have been inclined to the concept of 'brain-stem death'.

Does the law also recognise it? The question is important for a number of reasons beyond the fact that it is vital that society set the outer limits of its citizens' existence—the space between life and death. It is important because *first*, treatment may be withdrawn from a dead person as being futile. *Secondly*, organs may be lawfully removed (providing the Human Tissue Act 1961 is otherwise complied with) from a so-called 'beating-heart cadaver' on a life-support machine if death has occurred. *Thirdly*, for the purposes of the law of murder and manslaughter, the withdrawal of life-support from such a 'person' will not break the chain of causation between the death and a violent attack.[132] What little case law exists suggests that 'brain-stem death' is accepted in English law.[133]

But what of the patient whose brain stem is still functioning although the higher parts of the 'thinking brain' are totally destroyed? Is such a patient dead or merely comatose? For the present, English law considers such a patient, for example, in a persistent vegetative state, to be alive.[134] While the judges in the *Bland* case[135] were prepared (albeit reluctantly for some of them) to permit the withdrawal of hydration and nutrition from PVS patients leading to their deaths, only Parliament can make the policy decision that such patients are already dead.

---

[131] Most recently, *A Code of Practice for the Diagnosis of Brain Stem Death* (DoH 1998), HSC 1998/999.

[132] *R* v. *Malcherek and Steel* [1981] 1 WLR 422 (CA).

[133] *Re A (A Minor)* [1992] 3 Med. LR 303 and in Northern Ireland: *Re TC (A Minor)* (1994) 2 *Med. L. Rev.* 376.

[134] *Airedale NHS Trust* v. *Bland* [1993] 1 All ER 821.   [135] Ibid.

(iii) The Human Body and Donation   The value that we place on human life
and the sanctity of the human body provokes a dilemma when use of parts of
the human body or tissue is contemplated. Modern medicine and developments in medical research and genetics are forcing societies throughout the
world to consider to what extent we are prepared to see the human body and
its parts as *property*. Perhaps the vision is that the individual 'owns' his own
body or that others may 'own' it (or them) after death.[136]

It is a rule of some antiquity, but probably little pedigree, that at common
law a human corpse or its parts are not 'property'.[137] In the case of a corpse,
this applies before and after burial or cremation.[138] As a result, an individual
cannot give his body away in his will as part of his estate;[139] and proprietary
claims cannot be made by others in relation to the body.[140] There are, however,
exceptions. Those who have a duty to dispose of the body have a right to possess the body for that purpose.[141] Equally, anyone possessing the body for the
purposes of donation (under the Human Tissue Act 1961) or for anatomical
examination (under the Anatomy Act 1984), will most probably have a possessory right over it against others who might interfere with the body.[142] As
regards parts of the body, the common-law rule is also subject to exceptions. In
addition to situations where the parts are possessed under the 1961 and 1984
Acts, where a body part has work or skill expended upon it, which makes the
part different or distinct from what it was,[143] the artificer will acquire a property right in the part which will allow him to prevent unlawful taking by
others.[144] Such takings will amount to conversion and theft of the individual's
property.

But what of parts of a living person?[145] It does not follow that the law's reluctance to see dead bodies (or their parts) as property is carried over where parts
are removed from a living person. Here are a few examples of where the legal
characterisation of the nature of human tissue arises. Is it permissible for a person to sell an organ, for example, a kidney to be transplanted into a patient
who may well die without it? Does it matter whether the donor and the
patient/recipient are related to one another or are total strangers? Is it relevant
that the donated material will regenerate in the donor (e.g. bone marrow)?
Even though there are strong arguments for permitting competent adults to do
as they wish with their bodies unless they are exploited or coerced, it is well

---

[136] For an early account, see R. Scott, *The Body as Property* (1981). See also, P. Matthews, 'Whose Body?
People As Property' (1983) 36 CLP 193 and P. D. G. Skegg, 'Human Corpses, Medical Specimens and the
Law of Property' (1975) 4 *Anglo-American LR* 412.

[137] Recently acknowledged in *R* v. *Kelly* (1998) May 14 (CA). Discussed, Grubb (1998) 6 *Med. L. Rev.*

[138] In England, ibid. But not in Scotland: *Dewar v H.M. Advocate* 1945 JC 5 (High Ct. Just.) (no property rule
limited to corpses buried or interred).

[139] *Williams* v. *Williams* (1882) 20 Ch D 659.

[140] *R* v. *Lynn* (1788) 100 ER 394; *R* v. *Sharpe* (1856–1857) 169 ER 959.

[141] *R* v. *Fox* (1841) 2 QB 246; *Williams* v. *Williams*, supra and *Dobson* v. *North Tyneside HA* [1996] 4 All ER 474
(CA), discussed in Grubb (1997) 5 *Med. L. Rev.* 110.

[142] P. D. G. Skegg, 'Medical Uses of Corpses and the "No Property" Rule' (1992) 32 *Med. Sci. Law* 311.

[143] As in the case of anatomical specimens held in medical schools or museums.

[144] *Doodeward* v. *Spence* (1908) 6 CLR 406 per Griffiths CJ at 414. Approved in *R* v. *Kelly*, supra.

[145] G. Dworkin and I. Kennedy, 'Human Tissue: Rights in the Body and Its Parts' (1993) 1 *Med. L. Rev.* 291
and P. Matthews, 'The Man of Property' (1995) 3 *Med. L. Rev.* 251.

recognised that English law does prohibit some consensual touching.[146] The English courts never considered these issues in the context of donation, but the spectre of 'commodification' of the human body might well have led the courts to hold that such donations were contrary to public policy and a valid consent could not be given by the donor. In the result, Parliament acted through the Human Organ Transplants Act 1989 to prohibit commercial dealings in organs and to prohibit even altruistic donation (at least of non-regenerative organs) between unrelated individuals unless the approval of a statutory authority (Unrelated Live Transplant Regulatory Authority) was first obtained.[147] This requirement is to ensure, *inter alia*, that the donor fully understands what is involved, has consented, and that there is no coercion or undue influence. Donation between genetically related individuals (as defined in section 2(2) of the Act) is not regulated even though the presence of familial pressure and emotional coercion may be only too apparent, particularly in a case of a parent agreeing to a donation between siblings.[148]

Finally, one should consider the American case of *Moore* v. *Regents of University of California*.[149] Moore was treated for hairy-cell leukaemia. During the course of the treatment it was discovered that Moore's cells had remarkable therapeutic qualities. As a result, subsequently a therapeutic cell-line was developed from his blood and other body fluids and tissue which had enormous financial potential. These were removed without telling him why it was being done. Moore brought an action claiming an account of the profits to be made from the Mo-cell line (named after him). The California Court of Appeal (by a majority) held that Moore had a property interest in his body parts and hence he could bring a claim for conversion. The California Supreme Court (again by a majority) reversed. The majority of the court held that an individual did not have a property right over parts of his body once separated. Instead, the court held that Moore's claim could proceed to trial on the basis that the doctor owed Moore a duty to disclose his potential financial interest when obtaining consent from Moore to the extraction of blood, etc. In a strong dissent, Mosk J recognised an individual's right to control severed body parts, arguing that this was the only way that the law could adequately protect a patient from exploitation in the new world of scientific research. It is far from clear how such a claim would fare in the English courts. Certainly there are significant implications for research if individuals have a claim for any resulting profits (even if they would only be entitled to a small share) derived from the research.

---

[146] *R* v. *Brown & Others* [1993] 2 All ER 75 (HL); *Airedale NHS Trust* v. *Bland* [1993] 1 All ER 821, 889 (Lord Mustill).

[147] S. 2(1) and the Human Organ Transplants (Unrelated Persons) Regulations 1989 (SI No. 1989/2107).

[148] It is unclear whether a parent could consent to such a donation since it is difficult to see how it is in the 'best interests' of the donor/child: see *Curran* v. *Bosze* (1990) 566 N.E.2d 1319 (Ill. Sup. Ct.) (bone-marrow harvesting between half-siblings). However, see *Re Y (Mental Patient: Bone Marrow Donation)* [1997] Fam 110 (incompetent adult permitted to donate bone marrow to her sister in her 'best interests'): discussed, Grubb (1996) 4 *Med. L. Rev.* 204.

[149] (1990) 793 P.2d 479 (Cal. Sup. Ct.). See B. Dickens, 'Living Tissue and Organ Donors and Property Law: More on *Moore*' (1992) 8 *J. of Contemporary Health Law and Policy* 73 and Dworkin and Kennedy, op. cit., n. 145 above.

3. The Doctor–Patient Relationship and Civil Actions

(A) INTRODUCTION

Britain has a mixed system of private and state funded health care provision. Although the incidence of private medical insurance has increased in recent years, the vast majority of patients are treated with the National Health Service (NHS). The statutory duty to provide an NHS is imposed upon the Secretary of State for Health by the National Health Service Act 1977.[150] In fact, the duty to ensure provision of health services is that of local health authorities with oversight from the Department of Health and NHS Executive. Hence, the NHS consists of many parts, for example, general practitioners, dentists, etc., providing primary care and NHS Trusts providing community health and secondary care.[151] By virtue of the National Health Service and Community Care Act 1990, there is an 'internal market' within the NHS. This enables 'purchasers' of health care, such as local Health Authorities and 'GP fund-holders', to bargain for and buy health services from 'providers' such as self-governing NHS Trusts which operate the facilities for the public.[152] Contracts and agreements between purchasers and providers specify the level and quality of service that is to be provided to the public.

The system for the provision of health care in Britain raises many legal issues.[153] Here, in summary, are some:

(i) A patient who is treated by the NHS has no contractual relationship with the treating doctor.[154] The doctor's duty to the patient is in tort—not contract. A private patient, by contrast, may have an action for breach of contract. As we shall see later, the standard of care expected from a doctor is that of the reasonably skilled and experienced doctor of the same speciality. This is the tort standard of care owed to NHS patients and no account is taken of inexperience.[155] The contractual duty owed to private patients can, at least in theory, be higher.[156]

(ii) An NHS patient has no right to demand that a particular doctor perform the required surgery.[157] A private patient may well have such a contractual right and can expect his private doctor to perform the agreed services.[158]

---

[150] Ss. 1, 3 and 5.

[151] See Montgomery, (below, Select Biography), ch. 3.

[152] From 1 April 1999 the system will change. GP fundholders (who will cease to exist) and Health Authorities will lose their purchasing role. The latter will take on a supervisory and strategic planning function, and purchasing will be the function of newly created 'primary care groups' based upon primary health practitioners in a particular area: see *The New NHS—Modern Dependable* (DoH 1997).

[153] C. Newdick, 'Rights to NHS Resources After the 1990 Act' (1993) 1 *Med. L. Rev.* 53.

[154] *Pfizer Corp.* v. *Ministry of Health* [1965] AC 512.

[155] See *Wilsher* v. *Essex AHA* [1986] 3 All ER 801 (CA).

[156] See *La Fleur* v. *Cornelis* (1979) 28 NBR (2d) 569 (guarantee of success of cosmetic surgery). See Kennedy and Grubb (eds.), *Principles of Medical Law*, (below, Select Bibliography), ch. 5.

[157] This is made explicit in the standard consent form recommended by the Department of Health: *A Guide to Consent for Examination or Treatment* (1990), App. A(1) (as updated by HSG (92)32).

[158] *Michael* v. *Molesworth* (1950) 2 *BMJ* 171 and *Perna* v. *Pirozzi* (1983) 457 A.2d 431 (NJ Sup. Ct.).

(iii) An NHS patient will normally sue the treating doctor and his employer (on grounds of vicarious liability).[159] This will, typically, be the NHS Trust (or occasionally the local health authority). Primary liability[160] of the latter may also be found where, for example, it can be shown that there was insufficient, inadequate, or unsupervised staff dealing with the plaintiff in one of its hospitals[161] or where the system for the provision of health care has broken down or failed.[162] A further possibility arises under the arrangements of the 'internal market'. A health authority or 'GP fund-holder' may (*qua* purchaser of services) owe a duty to a patient who is injured if this is due to the purchaser's failure to make adequate provision of services through the contract/agreement with the NHS Trust where the patient is treated.[163] Of course, this would not arise where the patient's lack of care arises from an error by the provider/NHS Trust, for example, due to a doctor's negligence.

Actions based upon a breach of primary duty will undoubtedly give rise to difficult issues of the allocation of limited resources within the NHS.[164] To what extent can an NHS Trust argue that they did the best they could, given their limited resources? In a series of cases patients on waiting lists have brought judicial review proceedings against health service institutions for failure to provide intensive-care facilities or an orthopaedic ward.[165] In these cases, in dismissing the actions, the courts have been extremely reluctant to inquire into questions of resource allocation.[166] The courts view resource allocation as a political rather than a judicial issue best left to Parliament and the government.[167] However, it would be remarkable if the courts did permit NHS Trusts to, in effect, lower the standard of care owed to patients on the basis of their limited resources. Generally, the standard of care in tort is an objective one with no regard paid to the defendant's financial position.[168] One judge has commented that it should not be assumed that the courts would accept a defence of limited resources.[169] Surely the courts should set the minimum standard of care required of an NHS Trust in respect of the medical services offered,

---

[159] For a detailed discussion, see Kennedy and Grubb (eds.), *Principles of Medical Law*, op. cit. (Select Bibliography), ch. 8.

[160] See ibid.

[161] See *Wilsher* v. *Essex AHA* [1986] 3 All ER 801 at 831, per Glidewell LJ, and at 833, per Browne-Wilkinson VC. See also *Bull* v. *Devon AHA* [1993] 4 Med. LR 117 (CA); *Blyth* v. *Bloomsbury HA* [1993] 4 Med. LR 151 (CA).

[162] See *Robertson* v. *Nottingham HA* [1997] 8 Med. LR 1.

[163] See C. Newdick, op. cit., n. 158 above at 56–70.

[164] For a detailed discussion, see Kennedy and Grubb (eds.), *Principles of Medical Law*, op. cit. (Select Bibliography), ch. 8.

[165] For breach of his statutory duty under the National Health Service Act 1977, ss. 1 and 3.

[166] *See R* v. *Secretary of State for Social Services, ex p Hincks* (1992) 1 BMLR 93 (CA); *R* v. *SOS for Social Services, ex p Walker* (1992) 3 BMLR 32 (CA); *R* v. *Central Birmingham HA, ex p Collier* (unreported, 6 Jan. 1988) (CA).

[167] See also *Wilsher* v. *Essex AHA*, op. cit., per Browne-Wilkinson VC at 834 *and R* v. *Cambridge HA, ex p B* [1995] 6 Med. LR 250.

[168] For exceptional cases see *Goldman* v. *Hargreave* [1967] 1 AC 645; *Leakey* v. *National Trust* [1980] QB 485; *British Rail Board* v. *Herrington* [1972] AC 877.

[169] *Bull* v. *Devon AHA*, op. cit., per Mustill LJ.

even if this might mean that (indirectly) resources will have to be diverted from elsewhere if the particular service is to continue to be provided?[170]

Unlike the NHS patient, the fee-paying patient will, on the other hand, sue his own surgeon or anaesthetist, but not the private hospital (the latter's liability will be restricted to negligence in the nursing or ancillary care).[171] Vicarious liability of the NHS Trust will not in such cases be possible for conduct of the treating doctors, even if employed by the NHS, for in such cases they are acting privately and not in the course of their NHS employment.

This could have two serious and adverse implications for the private patient. *First*, the private patient will not be able to have the security of suing the financially sound (and probably insured)[172] NHS Trust unless he can show that somehow they are in breach of their own, primary duty.[173] The private practitioner may, of course, be insured through a defence organisation. *Secondly*, (and in practice perhaps more importantly) the private patient may be faced with considerable problems of proof when it is difficult to identify the individual who caused him the injury. The NHS patient who is faced with such problems will be in a better position to rely on the doctrine of *res ipsa loquitur* (and make the NHS Trust liable vicariously for the fault of whichever of its employees committed the fault). As stated, the private patient will be more hard-pressed to invoke this evidentiary inference whenever he cannot identify the tortfeasor.

(B) TORT, FIDUCIARY, AND EQUITABLE DUTIES

In the sections which follow we are concerned with the civil (private) law obligations of a doctor to his patient: (i) to obtain a valid consent (battery) and (ii) to exercise reasonable care (negligence). These obligations derive from the law of tort. There are, of course, others. For instance, a doctor must not falsely imprison a patient. This latter obligation is particularly important, as was noted before, in relation to the detention of mentally disabled and disordered patients. Restraint and detention of a patient requires legal justification, otherwise it will amount to the tort of false imprisonment. That justification may be the patient's consent if he or she is competent to give it and agrees to the restriction on their liberty. Otherwise, it must be found in the Mental Health Act 1983 whenever the patient is involuntarily detained or under the common-law principle of necessity if the patient it informally admitted and restrained.[174]

---

[170] See further some of the remarks of Pill J in *Knight* v. *Home Office* [1990] 3 All ER 237.

[171] Unless, exceptionally, the private hospital or clinic itself owes a primary duty to take care of the patient where, for example, the patient approaches the clinic directly and not through a consultant who then introduces the patient to the clinic: *Ellis* v. *Wallsend District Hospital* [1990] 2 Med. LR 103 at 130 per Samuels JA. An example of this might arise in the context of privately-sought infertility treatment.

[172] Under the Clinical Negligence Scheme for Trusts, see the National Health Service (Clinical Negligence Scheme) Regulations 1996, SI No. 1996/251. Discussed, Kennedy and Grubb (eds.), *Principles of Medical Law*, op. cit. (Select Bibliography), ch. 8.

[173] See *Cassidy* v. *Ministry of Health* [1951] 2 KB 343, 359–60; *Roe* v. *Ministry of Health* [1954] 2 QB 66, 82 (per Denning LJ) suggesting an onerous *duty to ensure that care is taken* of a patient in an NHS hospital. See also *Ellis* v. *Wallsend District Hospital*, op. cit., per Kirby P at 112. For a recent case imposing such a duty within the NHS, see *M* v. *Calderdale & Kirkless HA* [1998] Lloyd's Rep. Med. 157.

[174] *R* v. *Bournewood Community and Mental Health NHS Trust, ex p L* [1998] 3 All ER 289 (HL).

Further, not all the doctor's civil obligations derive from the law of tort (or contract). The doctor–patient relationship is one in which the one partner commands a pre-eminent position partly due to his superior knowledge, and partly as a result of the feeling of 'dependency' that sick people have on their healers. Moreover, it is a relationship of trust and confidence. It has been suggested that, as a result of this, the relationship manifests aspects of a fiduciary nature giving rise to a duty of loyalty to a patient.[175] This duty could create negative obligations, for example, not to create a conflict of interest as well as positive obligations, for example, to provide information to a patient (before and after treatment) including access to medical records.[176] In England, this proposal has not found favour with academics[177] or the courts.[178] Canadian courts, however, have embraced the notion,[179] whilst Australian courts have not.[180] Whilst English law has, for the present, rejected claims that the doctor–patient relationship is fiduciary in nature, the courts have found ways of giving effect, without any discernible conceptual basis, to one of the principal components of a fiduciary duty. This is the duty to give a patient access to his or her medical records.[181] Even more prominent, however, would be the doctor's duty to respect a patient's confidences.[182]

The ethical obligation to respect a patient's confidences has long been recognised. Thus, it finds expression in the well-known Hippocratic Oath. Likewise, without recourse to notions of a fiduciary law, English law recognises the confidential nature of the relationship. It thus imposes an equitable obligation upon a doctor not to disclose any confidential information he receives from the patient or from others in respect of the patient, or which he discovers by examining the patient. In short, anything of a personal nature relating to the patient's health that he obtains *qua* doctor must be treated in confidence. Is a doctor always legally obliged to abstain from disclosing information confidentially imparted to him?

The legal obligation is not absolute. In one case[183] the court was prepared to allow disclosure 'in very exceptional circumstances'. Subsequently, the courts

---

[175] A. Grubb, 'The Doctor as Fiduciary' (1994) 47 *CLP* 311. See also, P. Bartlett, 'Doctors as Fiduciaries: Equitable Regulation of the Doctor–Patient Relationship' (1997) 5 *Med. L. Rev.* 193.

[176] Contrast, *Attorney-General* v. *Blake* [1998] 1 All ER 833 per Lord Woolf MR at 843: 'equity is proscriptive, not prescriptive . . . It tells the fiduciary what he must not do. It does not tell him what he ought to do.'

[177] See I. Kennedy, 'The Fiduciary Relationship and its Application to Doctors and Patients' in P. Birks (ed.), *Wrongs and Remedies in the Twenty-First Century* (1996), 111.

[178] See *Sidaway* v. *Governors of Bethlem Royal Hospital* [1984] 1 All ER 1018 (CA) per Browne-Wilkinson LJ at 1031–2; [1985] 1 All ER 643 per Lord Scarman at 650–1 and *R* v. *Mid-Glamorgan FHSA, ex p Martin* (1993) 16 BMLR 81 (Popplewell J) and (1994) 21 BMLR 1 (CA).

[179] *McInerney* v. *MacDonald* (1992) 93 DLR (4th) 415 (patient entitled to access to her medical records); *Norberg* v. *Wynrib* (1992) 92 DLR (4th) 449 per McLachlin J (L'Heureux-Dubé J concurring) (doctor liable for sexual assault on patient in return for prescribing her drugs).

[180] *Breen* v. *Williams* (1996) 70 ALJR 772 (Aust. H. Ct.). Discussed in Kennedy (1997) 5 *Med. L. Rev.* 115. Cf. Grubb (1995) 3 *Med. L. Rev.* 102 (discussing the decision of the New South Wales Court of Appeal).

[181] *R* v. *Mid-Glamorgan FHSA, ex p Martin* (1994) 21 BMLR 1 (CA). Discussed in Grubb (1994) 2 *Med. L. Rev.* 353.

[182] See discussion in Kennedy and Grubb (eds.), *Principle of Medical Law*, op. cit. (Select Bibliography), ch. 9.

[183] See *Hunter* v. *Mann* [1974] QB 767, 772. For further details see Mason and McCall Smith, (below, Select Bibliography), ch. 8.

have recognised that a breach of confidence will be lawful where the public interest in disclosure outweighs the public interest in respecting confidences.[184] In *W* v. *Egdell*[185] a psychiatrist disclosed a medical report on W, his patient, who had been convicted of killing five people and who was detained in a secure hospital. The psychiatrist's report indicated that W was still dangerous as evidenced by his fascination with fireworks and explosives. Dismissing an action for breach of confidence, the Court of Appeal held that the public interest in protecting the public from a potentially dangerous prisoner who might be released outweighed the public interest in preserving confidentiality. Consequently, disclosure to the hospital, the Home Office, and a Mental Health Review Tribunal (which was considering whether he should be moved to a less-secure prison with a view to release) was lawful.

The difficulty here lies in deciding when the public interest is sufficiently compelling to justify disclosure. Where the law obliges the doctor to make such disclosures—e.g., to inform the public-health authorities of certain infectious diseases—then no problem arises. By contrast, where the disclosure did little more than satisfy public curiosity, even the public interest in preserving the freedom of the press did not justify publishing in a newspaper the identity of two doctors who were carrying the HIV (Human Immune-Deficiency Virus) infection.[186] In striking the balance between competing public interests the court will, undoubtedly, have regard to a number of factors, for example, the magnitude (how great?) and kind (how serious?) of the risk created by the patient and the extent of the disclosure (did the recipient 'need to know'?).[187]

(c) CONSENT[188]

We have already seen that any intentional interference with the body of another person without lawful excuse constitutes the tort of battery (and it is also a crime). In the medical context this is very important. Medical treatment requires the consent of a competent patient and will be unlawful without it.[189] The patient's legal right to self-determination has already been discussed in the context of the right to *refuse* treatment. Here we are concerned with the converse—the patient's consent to treatment. As a Canadian judge once remarked:[190]

Consent is not a mere formality; it is an important individual right to have control over one's own body, even where medical treatment is involved. It is the patient, not the doctor, who decides whether surgery will be performed, where it will be done, when it will be done and by whom it will be done.

---

[184] *Attorney-General* v. *Guardian Newspapers Ltd.* (*No. 2*) [1989] 1 All ER 1089, 1102 per Lord Goff.

[185] [1990] 1 All ER 835. See also *R* v. *Crozier* (1990) 8 BMLR 128 (CA).

[186] *X* v. *Y* [1988] 2 All ER 648.

[187] *W* v. *Egdell*, above, per Stephen Brown P at 845–5 and per Bingham LJ at 848 and 852–3.

[188] For a full discussion, see Kennedy and Grubb (eds.), *Principles of Medical Law*, op. cit. (Select Bibliography), ch. 3.

[189] If the patient is incompetent or a child, treatment may be justified under the principle of necessity or with the consent of the child's parents, the court or, in exceptional circumstances, under the common-law principle of necessity: see above.

[190] *Allan* v. *New Mount Sinai Hospital* [1980] 28 Ont (2d) 356, 364 per Linden J.

A consent once given may be withdrawn by the patient at any time whilst still competent to do so.[191] Thereafter, the effect is as if the patient had refused the treatment.

Consent may be oral or in writing. In English law there is no general requirement that it be in writing.[192] A consent form may be helpful evidentially to establish the patient's consent but it is no more than that.[193] Consent may also be express or implied. Implied consent may be discovered by the court where the patient's conduct or the circumstances reasonably lead to the inference that the patient was agreeing to the procedure.[194] It may also be held to exist where the procedure is necessarily incidental to the main operation consented to. This, for example, will be the case for anaesthesia;[195] but doctors should be wary of 'omnibus consent forms' which have typically authorised them to do 'such further or alternative measures or treatment as may be found necessary'. Courts are more than likely to take a hostile view of such clauses.[196] The Department of Health's model consent form contains a modified version pointing out to the patient that only procedures that are 'necessary' and in his 'best interests' will be carried out. It also allows the patient, unlike its predecessor, to indicate which procedures he would not wish to have without being consulted. Regardless of what the forms say, in the end, as one judge put it, what matters is the 'reality' of consent and not the mere 'appearance' of it.[197]

A valid consent in law requires that the patient be *competent*,[198] the consent should be *real* and the patient's agreement should be *voluntary* and not reached as a result *of undue influence*.[199] Here, we shall concentrate on the requirement that the consent should be *real*.

(i) Battery A patient's consent will be real if he is adequately informed about what he is agreeing to. Unlike the doctor's duty in the tort of negligence, it is not, here, wholly accurate to speak in terms of the doctor's duty to provide information. The crucial question is what information does the patient know when agreeing to the treatment since consent is a state of mind of the patient. That information may be derived from sources other than the doctor. Because of the technical nature of medicine, however, it is usually the doctor who is the source of the information.

How much information does a patient need to have in order for consent to be real so that a battery action will not lie? On the whole, the courts allow an

---

[191] *Ciarlariello* v. *Schacter* (1993) 100 DLR (4th) 609 (Can. Sup. Ct.). Discussed in Kennedy (1994) 2 *Med. L. Rev.* 117.

[192] For a statutory example where consent must be in writing, see Human Fertilisation and Embryology Act 1990, Sch. 3.

[193] *Chatterton* v. *Gerson* [1981] 1 QB 432, 443 per Bristow J.

[194] E.g., *O'Brien* v. *Cunard SS Co.* (1891) 28 NE 266 (Mass. Sup. Jud. Ct.) (plaintiff held out her arm and was vaccinated: held she had impliedly consented).

[195] *Villeneuve* v. *Sisters of St Joseph* (1971) 18 DLR 3d. 537, 552. The matter is expressly dealt with in the DoH's standard consent form: *A Guide to Consent to Medical Examination or Treatment* (1990), App. A(1).

[196] See *Brushnett* v. *Cowan* (1990) 69 DLR (4th) 743 and *Pridham* v. *Nash* (1986) 33 DLR (4th) 304.

[197] *Chatterton* v. *Gerson* [1981] 1 QB 432, 443 per Bristow J.

[198] See above.

[199] On which, see *Freeman* v. *Home Office (No. 2)* [1984] 2 WLR 130 (CA) and *Re T (Adult: Refusal of Medical Treatment)* [1992] 4 All ER 649 (CA) and Kennedy and Grubb (eds.), *Principles of Medical Law*, op. cit. (Select Bibliography), ch. 3 and Jones, op. cit. (Select Bibliography), paras. 6-020–6-022.

action in battery on the grounds of lack of consent in very limited instances. As Bristow J put it in *Chatterton* v. *Gerson*:[200]

In my judgment once the patient is informed in *broad terms* of the nature of the procedure which is intended, and gives his consent, that consent is real, and the cause on which to base a claim for failure to go into risks and implications is negligence, not trespass.

In 1984 the Court of Appeal again echoed what was by then the orthodox view. In *Sidaway* v. *Board of Governors of the Bethlem Royal Hospital* Sir John Donaldson MR said[201] that: 'It is only if the consent is obtained by fraud or misrepresentation of the nature of what is to be done that it can be said that an apparent consent is not a true consent.' Thus, where no consent has been given, or the patient's consent was obtained by fraud,[202] an action in battery will lie. So, for example, battery actions have succeeded where a wholly unauthorised operation takes place[203] or where the procedure has been expressly prohibited by the patient.[204] Rarely, however, have actions succeeded where the *quality* of the information is the issue. One such case is *Appleton* v. *Garrett*.[205] The plaintiff underwent unnecessary dental work. The defendant carried out the expensive treatment on the patient's healthy teeth purely for financial gain. Dyson J held that the plaintiff's claim in battery succeeded. The patient was not aware of the nature of what was being done and thus her consent was not 'real'.

There is no doubt that the courts have restricted the availability of battery actions for patients, leaving patients to claims in negligence unless the procedure can really be said to be unauthorised. Two questions remain to be answered. Why and how have the courts approached claims in negligence based upon non-disclosure of information to a patient?

First, the 'why?' The reasons are undoubtedly reasons of policy.[206]

Battery is an intentional tort, related closely to the crime of assault, and as a result seen as inappropriate as a cause of action where the doctor has acted bona fide in the patient's 'best interests'. It does not capture the essence of non-disclosure of information such as the risks inherent in, and alternatives to, a particular medical procedure. The tort of battery is restricted to the most opprobrious interference with the patient's body.

---

[200] *Chatterton* v. *Gerson* [1981] 1 QB 432, 443 (italics supplied).

[201] [1984] 1 All ER 1018 at 1026. For a case where a claim for battery succeeded because the doctor had (in good faith) misled his patient, see *Potts* v. *North West RHA*, Guardian, 23 July 1983, 24 (discussed by Brazier (Select Bibliography), at 380–1).

[202] *R* v. *Flattery* (1877) 2 QBD 410. Quaere whether the fraud can relate not only to the broad terms of the nature of the procedure but also to other co-lateral matters? Cf. Bristow J in *Chatterton* v. *Gerson* [1981] 1 QB 432, and Sir John Donaldson MR in *Freeman* above. See now, *R* v. *Richardson* (1998) *The Times*, 6 April (consent vitiated when fraud or mistake as to the nature of the procedure or identity of the person: consent valid even though dentist was disqualified).

[203] *Cull* v. *Royal Surrey County Hospital* [1932] 1 *BMJ* 1195 (hysterectomy in addition to an authorised abortion); *Devi* v. *West Midlands AHA* [1980] 7 CL 44 (sterilisation during repair of uterus).

[204] *Allan* v. *New Mount Sinai Hospital* (1980) 109 DLR (3d) 634 (anaesthetic administered to left arm despite prior express objection); *Mulloy* v. *Hop Sang* [1935] 1 WWR 714 (amputation of hand despite prohibition).

[205] [1997] 8 Med. LR 75. Discussed in Kennedy (1996) 4 *Med. L. Rev.* 311.

[206] See Robertson, 'Informed Consent to Medical Treatment' (1981) 97 LQR 102.

Also, there are procedural and substantive differences between actions in negligence and battery, which might point the court towards an action in negligence as the more appropriate.[207] *First*, battery is a tort actionable *per se*, so the plaintiff need not prove that he suffered any harm. In negligence, by contrast, damage is an element of the tort and without it the action will fail. This difference, however, is, in most cases, a theoretical one since in the absence of any harm few people would contemplate bringing an expensive lawsuit. *Secondly*, the burden of proof might be different in the two torts. In the case of battery some Commonwealth cases suggest that it is for the defendant, the doctor, to prove consent.[208] The most recent English decision, however, has placed the onus of proof on the patient, so it is for him to prove that he did *not* consent to the treatment.[209] If this view (which, incidentally, favours the doctor) prevails, then the evidentiary burden of proof in battery and negligence will be on the plaintiff. More significant is the *third* difference, which comes under the general heading of causation. Establishing cause-in-fact will, invariably, be easier in cases of intentional interference than in cases when the harm is linked to negligent conduct. The test of remoteness is also different in these two torts. For battery is an intentional tort and intended consequences are never too remote. In negligence, on the other hand, the test of foreseeability, as explained in Chapter 2, will determine the extent of liability. So an action in battery could lead to more extended liability for the doctor/defendant.

Finally, the payment of damages may be affected depending upon whether the action was framed in negligence or battery. Under the NHS Indemnity Scheme, which came into effect on 1 January 1990,[210] health authorities (and Trusts) were required to take responsibility for claims against their employees/doctors. However, that scheme was probably limited to claims for 'medical negligence' and excluded claims for battery. The same appears to be true for the Clinical Negligence Scheme for Trusts introduced on 1 March 1996, since it is restricted to 'clinical negligence' claims which arise from 'breach of a duty of care'.[211] It seems that this phrase bears its 'legal meaning'[212] and hence excludes battery.[213] The solution may be that even a claim framed in battery may additionally satisfy all the elements of negligence and so be treated as falling within the scheme.[214]

---

[207] Sometimes patients choose to sue in negligence even though the substance of their claim is that they did not consent to the procedure: see *Abbass* v. *Kenney* (1995) 31 BMLR 157 and *Williamson* v. *East London and City HA* [1998] Lloyd's Rep. Med. 6.

[208] See the cases collected in the judgment of McHugh J in *Department of Health & Community Services (NT)* v. *JWB and SMB* (1992) 66 ALJR 300 at 337 (Aust. High Ct.).

[209] *Freeman* v. *Home Office (No. 2)* [1984] 1 QB 524, 537–9, 557 per McCowan J and Sir John Donaldson MR respectively.

[210] HC (89) 34.

[211] The National Health Service (Clinical Negligence Scheme) Regulations 1996, SI No. 1996/251, Reg. 4.

[212] *Arrangements for Clinical Negligence Claims in the NHS* (DoH 1996), HSG(96)48.

[213] See *Stubbings* v. *Webb* [1993] 1 All ER 322 (HL) interpreting the phrase 'breach of duty' in s. 11(1), Limitation Act 1980.

[214] This could explain why is some recent cases the plaintiff has chosen to sue in negligence when the claim was, essentially, that no valid consent had been given: *Williamson* v. *East London and City HA* [1998] Lloyd's Rep. Med. 6.

(ii) Negligence   Turning now to the second question, how have the courts approached the issue of consent—more particularly the duty to disclose information—in the tort of negligence? [215]

The idea that the patient would understand, let alone question, the doctor's views about their ailment and the proposed treatment was unthought-of during an era when doctors adopted an authoritarian if not an autocratic posture towards their patients. The absence of litigated cases is supported by the classic, if now outdated, treatise on medical negligence by Lord Nathan.[216] Indeed, the bulk of litigation concerning doctors throughout the nineteenth century seemed to have been related to defamation, not malpractice.[217]

The view that 'doctor knows best' predominated until well into the middle of this century. As late as 1954 Lord Denning was happy to leave it to the individual doctor to decide how much he told his patient.[218] In the leading case of *Bolam* v. *Friern Hospital Management Committee*[219] in 1957 McNair J made it clear that 'generally accepted medical practice' was the yardstick in determining whether a doctor was in breach of his duty to a patient. The case was essentially one concerned with diagnosis and treatment; but it also contained explicit and important dicta determining the standard of disclosure of risks required of the doctor. The judge had no doubt that if the doctor had complied with established practice he would not be liable. And even if established practice required the giving of some warning, the outcome might still not be against the doctor unless the giving of a warning would have convinced the patient not to go ahead with the treatment.[220] This approach remained unchallenged for a long time; and it was only recently that it was pointed out that: 'In the context of the disclosure of information, the very notion of a professional standard is something of a nonsense. *There simply is no such standard*, if only because the profession has not got together to establish which risks should be disclosed, to which patients, in which circumstances.'[221] The case that provoked a reconsideration of the standard of disclosure to make consent valid was *Sidaway* v. *Board of Governors of the Bethlem Royal and the Maudsley Hospital*.[222] The facts of that case were as follows.

Mrs Sidaway agreed to have an operation to relieve some pain in her arm and shoulder. The operation was carried out competently by an eminent neurosurgeon and Mrs Sidaway did not allege otherwise. But the operation carried with

---

[215] From the extensive literature see Skegg, op. cit. (Select Bibliography), ch. 4; Kennedy, *Treat Me Right* (Select Bibliography), ch. 9; Brazier (1987) 7 *Leg. Stud.* 169; Teff, *Reasonable Care* (Select Bibliography): Kennedy and Grubb (eds.), *Principles of Medical Law* (Select Bibliography), ch. 3.

[216] Nathan, *Medical Negligence* (1957).

[217] Hawkins, *Mishap or Malpractice* (1985), 43.   [218] *Hatcher* v. *Black*, The Times, 2 July 1954.

[219] [1957] 1 WLR 502, 567. See also *Gold* v. *Haringey Health Authority* [1987] 2 All ER 888, where it was repeated in the context of advice on sterilisation that the advice was not negligent if a responsible body of medical opinion would have acted as the defendant did.

[220] The test of causation is a *subjective* one—would the patient have consented to the procedure had he known of the risk? *Chatterton* v. *Gerson* [1981] QB 432 and *Ellis* v. *Wallsend District Hospital* [1990] 2 Med. LR 103 (NSW CA). Contrast the rule in Canada: *Arndt* v. *Smith* [1997] 2 SCR 980 (Can. Sup. Ct.) (adopting a 'modified objective test'—what would a reasonable person with the patient's attributes and characteristics have decided?).

[221] I. Kennedy, *Treat Me Right* (Select Bibliography), 189.

[222] [1984] 1 QB 493 (CA); [1985] AC 871 (HL).

it a 1 per cent risk of damage to her spinal cord which, if realised, could lead to partial paralysis. This, in fact, is what occurred and an expensive and prolonged action began against the surgeon. (The case was actually heard by the House of Lords ten years after the unfortunate operation, a not unusual delay, but one which, nevertheless, underlines one of the main weaknesses of the tort system as a method of compensating this type of misadventure.) Mrs Sidaway's complaint was that the surgeon did not disclose to her the said risk. By the time the case came to court the surgeon had died, so there was some uncertainty as to what exactly she had been told.

The courts, however, approached the case, in Lord Diplock's words, as one raising 'a naked question of legal principle' and dismissed Mrs Sidaway's claim. Refusing to espouse the doctrine of informed consent, adopted with (at times confusing) variations in the United States,[223] they affirmed the traditional English view that the legal standard of disclosure was that of a 'reasonable doctor' and not that of the 'prudent' or 'reasonable' patient.[224] There is little doubt that policy reasons—the perceived situation in the United States—had a general influence on the mind of the judges. Dunn LJ's judgment in the Court of Appeal provides clear evidence of this, for in reaching his (negative) conclusion he said:[225]

I confess that I reach this conclusion with no regret. The evidence in this case showed that a contrary result would be damaging to the relationship of trust and confidence between doctor and patient, and might well have an adverse effect on the practice of medicine. It is doubtful whether it would be of any significant benefit to patients, most of whom prefer to put themselves unreservedly in the hands of their doctors. This is not in my view 'paternalism' . . . it is simply an acceptance of the doctor/patient relationship as it has developed in this country. The principal effect of adopting the [prudent patient test enunciated in *Canterbury* v. *Spence*] would be likely to be an increase in the number of claims for professional negligence against doctors. This would be likely to have an adverse effect on the general standard of medical care, since doctors would inevitably be concerned to safeguard themselves against such claims, rather than to concentrate on their primary duty of treating their patients.

The House of Lords, with the exception of Lord Scarman, was no more sympathetic towards the more pro-patient test of North American courts than the Court of Appeal. There were, however, rumblings that the judges were not content with a legal standard set exclusively by the medical profession.

The four speeches delivered in the House of Lords are by no means easy to synthesise, with each judge stating the legal standard somewhat differently.[226] Lord Scarman applied the 'prudent patient' or 'reasonable patient' test. His was, however, a minority judgment. The remaining judges all affirmed the

---

[223] *Canterbury* v. *Spence* 464 F.2d. 772 (1972) is a leading American decision but the picture in the USA is confusing due to many variations among the different state jurisdictions.

[224] *Bolam* v. *Friern Hospital Management Committee* [1957] 1 WLR 582; *Chatterton* v. *Gerson* [1981] 1 QB 432; *Hills* v. *Potter* [1984] 1 WLR 641.

[225] [1984] 1 QB 493, 517.

[226] For attempts, see Kennedy, *Treat Me Right* (Select Bibliography), ch. 9 and A. Grubb, 'A Survey of Medical Malpractice Law in England: Crisis? What Crisis?' (1985) 1 *J. of Contemporary Health Law & Policy* 75 at 93–111.

'reasonable doctor' standard. Lord Diplock (perhaps the most conservative) stated that the court has to determine its application on the basis of evidence of accepted professional practice as in *Bolam*. Lord Bridge (with whom Lord Keith agreed) likewise said the *Bolam* test applied but he reserved for the court the final word. He stated:

I am of the opinion that the judge might in certain circumstances come to the conclusion that disclosure of a particular risk was so obviously necessary to an informed choice on the part of the patient that no reasonably prudent medical man would fail to make it.

By way of illustration, he instanced 'a substantial risk of grave adverse consequences, for example a ten percent risk of a stroke from the operation'.[227] There is no doubt that Lord Bridge (unlike, on the face of it, Lord Diplock) looked beyond *Bolam* and its deference to professional standards and evidence to set the legal standard. This test may well be invoked rarely in practice if it means that both the chances of the risk materialising are substantial *and* the resultant injury grave. If this view were to prevail then the concession will, indeed, be virtually meaningless.

Lord Templeman's speech is, to say the least, idiosyncratic. He does not refer to the *Bolam* test or, indeed, the 'prudent patient' tests at all. Instead, he begins as if the legal canvas is empty and then seeks to paint a new picture. Unfortunately, the result is more in the style of a Picasso than a Monet in its construction! It requires considerable imagination and interpretation to see his design. Four key features of his speech are as follows. *First*, a doctor is not entitled to determine absolutely what information a patient should be provided but, equally, a patient is not entitled to know everything. *Secondly*, a patient is entitled to such information as is necessary for him to make a 'balanced judgment' whether or not to consent to the treatment. *Thirdly*, a doctor has a clinical discretion in determining what information should be given and in what terms it should be couched. *Finally*, in fulfilling his duty a doctor should provide information sufficient to alert the patient to the general dangers in the procedure and must draw to the patient's attention any dangers which are 'special in kind or magnitude or special to the patient'. As regards the latter he too instanced the 10 per cent risk of stroke and also the 4 per cent risk of death in the case of *Reibl* v. *Hughes*.

So there we have it: as 'clear as mud'. One interpretation of Lord Templeman's speech is that it cannot be understood and is riddled with internal inconsistencies and contradictions.[228] Another, less nihilist, interpretation is remarkably conventional and has much to be said for it. Starting with the 'reasonable doctor' standard of care Lord Templeman sought to give legal content (or at least guidance) as to how a doctor should approach his duty to provide information and the kinds of risks a reasonable doctor would disclose. This is as if he were saying 'a reasonable driver must balance the risks of driving'. But 'driving on the wrong side of the road? No; reasonable drivers don't do this.' For doctors, then, medical opinion whilst relevant, was not conclusive, as

---

[227] Per Lord Bridge at 663.   [228] See Kennedy, *Treat Me Right* (Select Bibliography), 205–9.

in other areas of life; the courts ultimately set the standard. In this, he has much in common with Lord Bridge.

The only matter on which a majority of the judges definitely agreed was in relation to an inquiring and persistent patient who asked questions. In this case the doctor will have a duty to answer the questions 'both truthfully and as fully as the questioner requires.'[229]

Despite the fact that the Australian High Court in *Rogers* v. *Whittaker*[230] has recently rejected *Bolam* and adopted the 'prudent patient' or 'reasonable patient' standard, it seems most unlikely that the English courts will explicitly follow suit. The Court of Appeal in *Gold* v. *Haringey HA*,[231] in the context of contraceptive advice, applied the *Bolam* test relying on the speech of Lord Diplock in *Sidaway* which is, on any view, the most restrictive view expressed by any of the Law Lords.

There are a number of signs of what the future may hold out for doctors. These suggest an expansion of the doctor's duty to disclose information. *First*, it may well be that the courts will expand the doctor's duty to answer questions. The initial response of the courts in such a case was not encouraging, the Court of Appeal relying upon *Bolam* to determine the standard of disclosure notwithstanding the dicta in *Sidaway*.[232] In a recent decision of the court, however, Lord Woolf MR stated '[counsel for the plaintiff] correctly submitted that it is clear that if a patient asks a doctor about the risk, then the doctor is required to give an honest answer.'[233] If he did not, the implication is clear.

Secondly, some judges have interpreted the *Sidaway* decision more creatively than did the Court of Appeal in *Gold*. By synthesising the speeches of Lord Bridge and Lord Templeman (in particular), the courts have concluded that the doctor's duty to volunteer information is not solely a matter for professional practice. In 1994 in *Smith* v. *Tunbridge Wells HA*,[234] the judge held a doctor negligent in failing to disclose the risk of impotence inherent in an operation even though that was accepted as proper practice at the time.[235]

The third development is linked to the previous one and may have been part of the judge's reasoning in *Smith* itself. The House of Lords in *Bolitho* v. *City and Hackney HA*,[236] re-interpreted the so-called '*Bolam* test'. Following the approach developed in the Court of Appeal,[237] the Law Lords held that *Bolam* itself left room for judicial examination of medical practice and medical evidence. Neither was conclusive of the standard of care expected of a doctor. A court always had the final say of whether a breach of duty had occurred. The *Bolam* test required that the accepted practice of the medical profession (or proposed by the medical evidence) should be 'responsible, reasonable and respectable'. It

---

[229] N. 225 above, per Lord Bridge at 661. See also Lord Diplock at 659 and Lord Templeman at 664.

[230] (1992) 67 ALJR 47. Discussed in Chalmers and Schwartz, 'Rogers v. Whittaker and Informed Consent in Australia: A Fair Dinkum Duty of Disclosure' (1993) 1 *Med. L. Rev.* 139.

[231] [1987] 2 All ER 888. Discussed in Grubb [1988] *CLJ* 12.

[232] *Blyth* v. *Bloomsbury HA* [1993] 4 Med. LR. See discussion in Grubb (1993) 1 *Med. L. Rev.* 115.

[233] *Pearce* v. *United Bristol Healthcare NHS Trust* (1998) 20 May (CA)(unreported).

[234] [1994] 5 Med. LR 334 (Moreland J).   [235] Discussed in Grubb (1995) 3 *Med. L. Rev.* 198.

[236] (1997) 39 BMLR 1.

[237] *Bolitho* v. *City and Hackney HA* (1992) 13 BMLR 111 (discussed in Grubb (1993) 1 *Med. L. Rev.* 241) and *Joyce* v. *Merton, Sutton and Wandsworth HA* [1996] 7 Med. LR 1 (discussed in Grubb (1996) 4 *Med. L. Rev.* 86).

must have a 'logical basis'.[238] The experts must direct their minds to all the relevant factors and reach a defensible conclusion. In *Bolitho*, the House of Lords was only concerned with cases of medical negligence arising out of diagnosis and treatment. Lord Browne-Wilkinson specifically excluded information cases.[239] Perhaps, he did so because of *Sidaway* which, in any event, appears to look beyond *Bolam* as the standard of disclosure. In hindsight, however, a synthesis of *Bolitho* with *Sidaway* now seems wholly plausible.[240] Lord Bridge (with whom Lord Keith agreed) took a step beyond *Bolam*: where disclosure of the risk was 'so obviously necessary to an informed choice on the part of the patient that no reasonably prudent medical man would fail to [disclose] it'.[241] There is even common ground here with Lord Templeman who requires the doctor to provide information (particularly about 'special risks') in order to allow the patient to make a 'balanced judgment'.[242] Lord Diplock also, in applying *Bolam*, refers to the need for the practice to be 'responsible'.[243] Here, then, we have the 'reasonable', 'responsible' oversight demanded in *Bolitho*. Also, it should not be forgotten that in the Court of Appeal in *Sidaway*, Sir John Donaldson MR spoke of a practice 'rightly' accepted by the medical profession.[244] The vigour with which the judges will scrutinise non-disclosure on the basis of the 'new *Bolam*' approach after *Bolitho* is unclear. In one recent case, the Court of Appeal showed a renewed appetite to set the standard of disclosure. Having referred to both *Sidaway* and *Bolitho*, Lord Woolf MR stated:

Obviously the doctor, in determining what to tell a patient, has to take into account all the relevant considerations, which include the ability of the patient to comprehend what he has to say to him or her and the state of the patient at the particular time, both from the physical point of view and an emotional point of view . . . where there is what can realistically be called a 'significant risk', then, in the ordinary event . . . the patient is entitled to be informed of that risk.

On the facts, the court concluded that an increased risk of 1–2 in 1,000 that a child might be stillborn if not delivered was not 'significant'. Despite the actual outcome, the approach is encouraging. Perhaps the judges will take the lead from the medical profession itself, which, in recent times, has been much more aware of the need to provide patients with as much information as possible prior to treatment.[245]

(D) NEGLIGENCE

Medical negligence, as has been said before, is merely a species of the tort of negligence. As a consequence, the usual elements of the tort apply—duty, breach, causation, remoteness and damage—which has been discussed in Chapter 2 in more general terms. In this section, we will consider some issues that are particularly interesting in the medical context.

---

[238] N. 237 above, at 9 and 10.　　　　　　[239] Ibid., at 10.
[240] A synthesis of the speeches in *Sidaway* itself is a 'Herculean' task: see Kennedy, *Treat Me Right* (Select Bibliography), ch. 9.
[241] [1985] 1 All ER 643 at 663.　　　　　[242] Ibid., at 666.　　　　　[243] Ibid., at 657.
[244] [1984] 1 All ER 1018 at 1028.
[245] See e.g., GMC Guidance: *Consent. The Ethical Considerations* (1998).

(i) Duty of Care[246]   As we have seen, the doctor's duty to an NHS patient is in tort; towards a private patient it also derives from contract. In practice, in most cases the duty is the same irrespective of its origins. When does the duty come into being? The answer may seem obvious—when the individual is the doctor's (or hospital's) patient. This may be an adequate description; but it is less than helpful in many instances since it does not tell us when the doctor–patient relationship comes into being. The answer was given some forty years ago by Lord Nathan:[247]

The medical man's duty of care . . . is based simply upon the fact that the medical man undertakes the care and treatment of the patient.

In other words, a doctor who holds himself out as possessing special skill and assumes responsibility for an individual, thereby undertakes a duty of care.[248] The duty is to exercise reasonable care in diagnosis and treatment of the individual. Generally, this will present no difficulties: it will be obvious that in the 'undertaking' and thereafter, the duty exists between patient and GP, hospital doctor, institution or health care professional.

If no such relationship exists, the general law on omissions prevails and no doctor is obliged to act as the good Samaritan.[249] Even if he does, it has recently been suggested that his legal duty is limited to not 'make the victim's condition worse'.[250] The reasoning (such that there is) is not convincing. Surely the issue is really relevant in determining whether the doctor has acted reasonably or is in breach of his duty of care: less, perhaps, being expected in an emergency situation.

Possible exceptions to the 'no-duty to act' rule can be found in the case of hospitals running casualty departments[251] and GP's treatment of visitors in their practice area who require emergency treatment at an accident.[252] But it is far from clear, in England, that there is any more pervasive obligation to provide aid. One case has, however, gone considerably further. It was held in a recent Australian case that a doctor who was requested 'in a professional context' to provide assistance in an emergency owed a duty to the victim. In *Lowns* v. *Woods*[253] the defendant, a general practitioner was requested, while at his

---

[246] See for a full discussion: Kennedy and Grubb (eds.) *Principles of Medical Law* (Select Bibliography), ch. 5 and Jones, *Medical Negligence* (Select Bibliography), ch. 2.

[247] Nathan, *Medical Negligence* (1957) at 8.

[248] See *R* v. *Bateman* (1925) 94 LJKB 791 per Hewart LCJ at 794 and *Cassidy* v. *Ministry of Health* [1951] 2 KB 343 per Denning LJ at 360.

[249] See *Re F (Mental Patient: Sterilisation)* [1990] 2 AC 1 per Lord Goff at 77–8. Generally, B. S. Markesinis, 'Negligence, Nuisance and Affirmative Duties of Action' (1989) 105 *LQR* 104.

[250] *Capital and Counties plc* v. *Hampshire CC* [1997] 2 All ER 865 per Stuart-Smith LJ at 883. See also *Powell* v. *Boldaz* (1997) 39 BMLR 35 per Stuart-Smith LJ at 45.

[251] E.g. *Barnett* v. *Chelsea & Kensington HMC* [1969] 1 QB 428 (the duty is probably that of the institution unless a doctor or nurse comes to the individual's aid). It probably does not exist with a hospital, let alone an individual doctor, where the patient has merely made an out-patient's appointment: see *Clunis* v. *Camden and Islington HA* (1997) 40 BMLR 181 (CA).

[252] The National Health Service (General Medical Services) Regulations 1992 (SI No. 1992/635), Sch. 2, para. 4(h).

[253] (1995) 36 NSWLR 344 (NSW Sup. Ct.) and (1996) Aust Torts Reports ¶ 81–376 (NSW CA). Discussed in Grubb (1998) 6 *Med. L. Rev.* 121 ff.

surgery, to come and provide help to the plaintiff a short distance away who was undergoing an epileptic seizure. He refused and the plaintiff suffered profound brain damage. A majority of the New South Wales Court of Appeal held that the defendant owed a duty of care to the plaintiff: injury to the plaintiff was foreseeable, there was 'physical' and 'circumstantial proximity', and there was no reasonable impediment upon the defendant providing help.

(1) *Psychiatric Injury and Financial Loss.* As we have seen, the doctor's duty of care to his patients relates to their care (diagnosis, advice and treatment). A patient may, therefore, claim for injury negligently caused by the treatment (iatrogenic injury) or where the doctor negligently fails to improve or cure the patient's condition. Such actions may include damages for physical injury and financial loss and mental distress and suffering arising from the injury.

In appropriate circumstances, a patient may also claim for psychiatric injury caused by the doctor's negligent treatment. Because there is a pre-existing duty of care, the patient's claim will be governed by the decision of the House of Lords in *Page* v. *Smith*.[254] As a 'participant' or 'primary victim', the patient will not be required to satisfy the restrictive *McLoughlin/Alcock* rules applied to 'secondary victims'[255] (discussed in Chapter 2, above). Provided the circumstances justify a finding that injury was foreseeable, for example during a horrendous obstetric procedure, damages for psychiatric injury can be recovered.[256] The duty may also extend to cases where the doctor communicates false information or accurate information carelessly after the treatment is completed.[257]

Similarly, a patient may be able to claim economic loss caused by the doctor's advice or report. The patient will have to satisfy the current restrictive rules imposed by English law for recovery of such loss discussed earlier in Chapter 2, above. Thus, it is unlikely that a sufficiently close relationship of 'proximity' will exist unless the doctor knows the patient will rely upon his advice or report for financial purposes. For example, where the patient consults a doctor specifically for the purpose of providing a report to settle a road accident claim the proximity test will be satisfied.[258]

(2) *Pre-natal Injury and Birth.*[259] Does a doctor owe a duty of care to an unborn child such that an action may be brought for pre-natal injury? The common law struggled with this issue for a long time and, until comparatively recently, a negative answer was given.[260] In a number of cases, however, Commonwealth courts allowed such actions.[261] Finally, in 1992 the English Court of Appeal in

---

[254] [1996] AC 155.
[255] See for a full discussion, Kennedy and Grubb (eds.) *Principles of Medical Law* (Select Bibliography), ch. 5.
[256] *Tredgett and Tredgett* v. *Bexley HA* [1994] 5 Med. LR 178.
[257] *AB* v. *Tameside and Glossop HA* [1997] 8 Med. LR 92 (CA) (duty of care assumed). Discussed in Kennedy (1997) 5 *Med. L. Rev.* 338.
[258] See *Hughes* v. *Lloyds Bank plc* [1998] PIQR P38 (CA). Cf., *Stevens* v. *Bermondsey and Southwark Group HMC* (1963) 107 SJ 478 (general consultation: no liability).
[259] See for a full discussion: Kennedy and Grubb (eds.) *Principles of Medical Law* (Select Bibliography), ch. 12.
[260] *Walker* v. *Great Northern Rly. Co. of Ireland* (1891) 28 LR Ir 69.
[261] In Canada—*Duval* v. *Seguin* (1973) 40 DLR (3d) 666, and Australia—*Watt* v. *Rama* [1972] VR 353; *X and Y* v. *Pal* [1992] 3 Med. LR 195.

Burton v. *Islington HA*[262] also recognised that a child (once born) could bring an action for pre-natal injury. The reasoning of the courts, and of *Burton* in particular, is not without difficulty.[263]

The common law is of lesser significance today because in any event in England[264] Parliament intervened in the Congenital Disabilities (Civil Liability) Act 1976 to create liability for pre-natal injuries. Section 4(5) of the Act makes it clear that it has replaced the common law for births that occurred after 22 July 1976. The Act, described by one commentator as 'ambitious', 'complex', and 'largely irrelevant',[265] affords the mother (but not the father) of the child extensive immunity. With one exception,[266] the child cannot sue its mother, for example, for excessive drinking, smoking, or even drug abuse during pregnancy that results in its injuries.[267]

Under the 1976 Act a child will have an action only if it is born alive. Viability at the time of the injury (and death) is thus not enough (as it is in some states of the United States).[268] As in any other medical negligence actions, the child will face the formidable difficulties of establishing breach of duty and causation that plague all medical-malpractice actions but which, as far as causation is concerned, may be particularly acute in this situation.

For an injured child to succeed it must be shown that its disabilities resulted from an 'occurrence' which (a) 'affected either parent of the child in his or her ability to have a normal, healthy child' or (b) 'affected the mother during her pregnancy, or affected her or the child in the course of its birth, so that the child is born with disabilities which would not otherwise have been present'.[269] Thus, three situations are contemplated.

First, a negligent pre-conception event may affect one parent's ability to have a healthy child, for example, where the defendant gives an infected blood

---

[262] [1992] 3 All ER 833.

[263] See Grubb (1993) 1 *Med. L. Rev.* 103 and (1993) 1 *Med. L. Rev.* 119.

[264] In Scotland liability is still based upon the common law: see *Hamilton* v. *Fife Health Board* (1993) 13 BMLR 156 (Ct. Sess. Inn. H.).

[265] Brazier, op. cit. (Select Bibliography), 235.

[266] Section 2 renders a mother who drives a motor vehicle carelessly liable to her child provided she knew or ought to have known herself to be pregnant. If, as a result of such negligent driving, the child is born with disabilities which would not otherwise have been present, then it will be able to bring an action in tort. This provision can be seen as representing an acknowledgement of the role of the insurance factor in 'discovering' liability where otherwise, for different policy reasons, there would be none. A further explanation might be that there is no difficulty in setting the standard of care in a driving case involving a pregnant woman while this would be more problematic if other maternal conduct were questioned (for similar reasoning see *Pitts* v. *Hunt* [1990] 3 All ER 344).

[267] It is not clear whether such a claim could have been brought at common law. In *Lynch* v. *Lynch* [1992] 3 Med. LR 62 the New South Wales Court of Appeal permitted a child to sue its mother for damage caused *in utero* during a driving accident. The court treated this situation as a special one, as indeed it is under the 1976 Act, and left open whether the claim could have been brought if it raised questions about other maternal conduct during pregnancy. In *Burton*, Dillon LJ (at 843–4) assumed that such a claim would lie and that it would be a matter for Parliament to limit the common law.

[268] S. 4(2)(a). The vast majority of States (37) in the USA have adopted a rule permitting an action by a stillborn child: see e.g. *Johnson* v. *Ruark Obstetrics* (1990) 395 S.E. 2d 85 (NC Sup. Ct.) (action by stillborn child after doctor failed to treat mother's diabetes). Contrast *Smith* v. *Columbus Community Hospital* (1986) 387 N.W. 2d 490 (Neb. Sup. Ct.). Only six states allow the claim where the foetus is not 'viable', e.g., *Farley* v. *Sartin* (1995) 466 S.E. 2d 522 (W. Va. Sup. CA). See D. Meade, 'Wrongful Death and the Unborn Child: Should Viability Be a Prerequisite for a Cause of Action?' (1998) 14 *J. of Contemporary Health Law & Policy* 421.

[269] S. 1(2)(a) and (b).

transfusion to the mother prior to conception.[270] In this situation the foetus is damaged *in utero*.[271] Another situation where a pre-conception event affects a parent and leads to the birth of a disabled child would be where the doctor's negligence causes the child to be conceived in a damaged condition, for example, where a male patient is exposed to excessive X-rays which damage his sperm. However, it is clear that a claim could not be brought under the Act by the grandchildren of the original 'victim' who subsequently inherited damaged genetic material.[272]

Secondly, the negligent event may occur during pregnancy and damage the foetus *in utero*, for example, during an operation that goes wrong.[273]

Thirdly, the negligent event may occur during birth.[274]

A *fourth* situation was introduced by the Human Fertilisation and Embryology Act 1990 which brings within the 1976 Act claims for disabilities arising from the selection, storage or use of embryos or gametes during infertility treatment.[275]

In all these claims under the 1976 Act, the nature of the child's action is derivative in that the child will have to prove that there was, or could have been had the parent suffered injury,[276] liability to the affected parent before the child can recover. The derivative nature of the child's action is illustrated by section 1(4) of the Act which provides that in the case of a pre-conception occurrence, the person responsible for the occurrence will not be answerable to the child 'if at that time either or both of the parents knew the risk of their child being born disabled (that is to say, the particular risk created by the occurrence)'.[277] However, the section continues: 'but should it be the child's father who is the defendant, this subsection does not apply if he knew of the risk and the mother did not.'

Different from pre-natal injuries (now covered by the Act) and raising infinitely more complicated issues are the so-called 'wrongful conception', 'wrongful birth', and 'wrongful life' actions.[278] The first two claims are brought by parents for the physical harm and financial cost associated with the birth of a child.

---

[270] *Renslow* v. *Mennonite Hospital* (1977) 367 N.E. 2d 1250. See also *Bergstresser* v. *Mitchell* (1978) 577 F.2d 22 (8th Cir.); *Yeager* v. *Bloomington Obstetrics and Gynaecology Inc.* (1992) 585 N.E. 2d 696 (Ind. CA). Contrast *Albala* v. *City of New York* (1981) 429 N.E. 2d 786 (NY CA).

[271] The situation may also fall within s. 1(2)(b) on the basis that the 'occurrence' (i.e. the negligent act) continues to 'affect . . . the mother during pregnancy'.

[272] S. 5.4(5) Such actions have not been permitted in America: *Enright* v. *Eli Lilly & Co.* (1991) 570 N.E. 2d 198 (NY CA) (action by plaintiffs, whose grandmother took diethylsilboestrol (DES), who subsequently developed cancer).

[273] As in the *Burton* case.

[274] As in the well-known case of *Whitehouse* v. *Jordan* [1981] 1 WLR 246 where, although a case at common law, this point was not taken.

[275] S. 1A.   [276] S. 1(3).

[277] See also s. 1A(3) in relation to claims under s. 1A. See further, s. 1(6) dealing with exclusions and limitations by contract with a parent, and s. 1(7) attributing the contributory negligence of a parent to the child.

[278] On which see: G. Tedeschi, 'On Tort Liability for "Wrongful Life"' (1966) 1 *Israel L. Rev.* 513; A. M. Capron, 'Tort Liability for Genetic Counselling', 79 *Col. LR* 618 (1979); H. Teff, 'The Action for "Wrongful Life" in England and the United States' (1985) 34 *ICLQ* 423.

A '*wrongful conception*' action arises where a doctor fails to carry out successfully a sterilisation operation, with the result that a child is subsequently conceived and born healthy.[279] There are, of course, legal difficulties of this action associated with any medical-negligence claim, such as establishing breach of duty and causation.[280] In addition, the claim is problematic because the action is for the costs of rearing a healthy child.[281] There are policy arguments which suggest that the 'joy' or 'benefit' of having a healthy (albeit unwanted) child—which cannot be an injury—means that rearing costs should not be recovered.[282] The majority of American states do not allow recovery of rearing costs in such claims; most limit the parents' action to damage and losses associated with the pregnancy alone.[283] While recovery of rearing costs was not initially accepted in England,[284] the current trend is to allow recovery of these (ever-increasing) costs.[285] But the House of Lords has yet to consider a 'wrongful conception' case.

A '*wrongful birth*' action could arise in two ways. First, the doctor may negligently carry out pre-conception genetic testing and counselling so that the parents, relying on his advice, conceive a child that is subsequently afflicted with a genetic disability.[286] Alternatively, the doctor may fail to diagnose that a pregnant woman is infected by rubella[287] or is carrying a child suffering from Down's Syndrome,[288] and thus fail to give her the chance to abort the

---

[279] Discussed in A. Grubb, 'Conceiving—A New Cause of Action?' in Freeman (ed.), *Medicine, Ethics and Law* (1988) 121, W. V. Horton Rogers, 'Legal Implications of Ineffective Sterilisation' (1985) 5 *LS* 296 and A. Mullis, 'Wrongful Conception Unravelled' (1993) 1 *Med. L. Rev.* 320.

[280] In some jurisdictions in the USA it is argued that the parents must 'mitigate' their loss by putting the child up for adoption. This horrific suggestion has not yet been made in this country. Another possibility is to argue that the mother should, where medically possible, seek an abortion. These possibilities have not found favour in the US courts: *Custodio* v. *Bauer* (1967) 59 Cal. Rptr. 463 (Cal. Sup. Ct.); *Burke* v. *Rivo* (1990) 555 N.E. 2d 1 at 4 (Mass. Sup. Jud. Ct.). In *Emeh* v. *Kensington, Chelsea and Westminster AHA* [1984] 3 All ER 1044, the latter argument was rejected where the mother was nearly 20 weeks pregnant when she discovered her condition. The court left little room for the argument that failure to undergo an abortion could be a *novus actus interveniens* (but note Waller LJ discussing an 8-week pregnancy). But it is extremely unlikely that a court will view a refusal in any circumstances as excusing the defendant, especially if it is based upon a religious or moral objection to abortion.

[281] But, see *Walkin* v. *South Manchester HA* [1995] 4 All ER 132 (claim is for 'personal injury'). Discussed in Grubb (1996) 4 *Med. L. Rev.* 94.

[282] See discussion in Symmons, 'Policy Factors in Actions for Wrongful Birth' (1987) 50 *MLR* 269.

[283] See e.g. *Cockrum* v. *Baumgartner* (1983) 447 N.E. 2d 385 (Ill. Sup. Ct.) and *Boone* v. *Mullendore* (1982) 416 So 2d 718 (Ala. Sup. Ct.). Some courts only permit the claim where the parents' decision to seek a sterilisation was based upon economic grounds: *Burke* v. *Rivo*, op. cit., *Hartke* v. *McKelway* (1983) 707 F 2d 1544 (DC Cir.); other courts permit the claim but require that the 'benefits' accruing from the birth should be offset against the damages: *Lovelace Medical Center* v. *Mendez* (1991) 805 P.2d 603 (N.M. Sup. Ct.) and cases cited therein.

[284] *Udale* v. *Bloomsbury AHA* [1983] 2 All ER 522.

[285] *Emeh* v. *Kensington, Chelsea and Westminster AHA* [1984] 3 All ER 1044 and *Thake* v. *Maurice* [1986] 1 All ER 479. See also in Scotland: *McFarlane* v. *Tayside Health Board*, 1998 SLT 307 (Ct. Sess. Inn. Hs.). The Court of Appeal in *Thake* refused to require the set-off of the intangible benefits of having the child against the upkeep costs limiting this, instead, to offset the intangible burdens of bringing up the child. See also *Lovelace Medical Center* v. *Mendez*, op. cit.

[286] E.g. *Viccaro* v. *Milunsky* (1990) 551 N.E. 2d 8 (Mass. Sup. Jud. Ct.) (failure to detect genetic disorder in mother that was subsequently inherited by child).

[287] *Salih* v. *Enfield HA* [1991] 3 All ER 400.

[288] *Rance* v. *Mid-Downs HA* [1991] 1 All ER 801 (failure to carry out ultra-scan to detect if the child was suffering from spina bifida): *Gregory* v. *Pembrokeshire HA* [1989] 1 Med. LR 81 (failure in testing for Down's Syndrome).

(potentially disabled) child in accordance with the Abortion Act. The action will only succeed if the plaintiff proves that an abortion would have been legally available and that she would have agreed to undergo it.[289] In such cases, the parents' claim is for damages for pain and suffering and costs for rearing the disabled child, including extra medical costs associated with its disability.[290]

In the factual situations giving rise to a 'wrongful birth' claim by the parents, a child, too, may seek to bring a *'wrongful life'* action, claiming medical and other expenses arising from its disability in addition to general damages for having been born at all. The attitude of the courts to such claims by disabled children is, in all systems, hostile. The majority of courts in the United States have rejected the child's claim.[291] Only three courts have allowed the plaintiff/child its *special* or *extraordinary* costs associated with its disability while rejecting the wider claims for pain, suffering, and emotional distress for having come into this world disabled.[292]

In English law *McKay* v. *Essex Area Health Authority*,[293] decided on facts occurring before the 1976 Act had come into force and dealing with a negligent failure to diagnose rubella in a pregnant mother, rejected the child's 'wrongful life' action under the common law. A number of reasons lie behind this attitude and, although not without much force, are not, it is submitted, conclusive. A strong case could be made in the future for a limited recognition of the 'wrongful life' action.[294] What then are the prime reasons advanced against recognition of such an action?

First of all it must be remembered that in the *McKay* case the doctor caused no damage. 'To damage is to make worse, not to make *simpliciter*.' It will be remembered 'the child was deformed *ab initio*, just like Mr Anns' house.[295] And just as the Merton Borough Council did not damage Mr Anns' house (though they damaged him, financially), so the defendants (in the *McKay* case) did not damage the child . . . (though they damaged the mother both financially and emotionally).'[296] While in *Anns* the House of Lords was not impressed by this view, the subsequent decisions of the House of Lords in *The Aliakmon* and *Murphy* have accepted it. The argument is logically appealing but it is excessively legalistic. The parallel with the defective house shows how the 'human factor' is com-

---

[289] See *Rance*, above, (plaintiff lost because by the time ultra-scan should have been carried out an abortion would have been illegal because the child was 'capable of being born alive' under the Infant Life (Preservation) Act 1929. The abortion would now be lawful under s. 1(1)(d) of the Abortion Act 1967).

[290] Some American courts have restricted the 'rearing costs' claim to the extraordinary expenses associated with the child's condition: *Smith* v. *Cote* (1986) 513 A.2d 341 (NH Sup. Ct.); and see cases cited in *Viccaro* v. *Milunsky*, op. cit., at 10–11.

[291] See e.g. *Siemieniec* v. *Lutheran General Hospital* (1987) 512 N.E. 2d 691 (Ill. Sup. Ct.). The courts have also rejected claims by children for 'impaired life' where they have, through negligence, been born into socially imperfect circumstances: *Williams* v. *State* (1966) N.E. 2d 343 (NY CA) (illegitimate and mentally ill mother); *Zepeda* v. *Zepeda* (1963) 190 N.E. 2d 849 (Ill. App. Ct.) (illegitimate); *Cowe* v. *Forum Group Inc.* (1991) 575 N.E. 2d 630 (Ind. Sup. Ct.) (mentally disabled mother). No such claim could lie under the 1976 Act in England (s. 4(1) defining 'child born disabled').

[292] *Turpin* v. *Sortini* (1978) 643 P.2d. 954 (Cal. Sup. Ct.); *Procanik* v. *Cillo* (1984) 478 A 2d. 755 (NJ Sup. Ct.); *Harbeson* v. *Parke-Davis Inc.* (1983) 656 P.2d 483 (Wash. Sup. Ct.).

[293] [1982] QB 1166.

[294] See Whitfield, 'Common Law Duties to Unborn Children' (1993) 1 *Med. L. Rev.* 28 at 46–9 and Fortin, 'Is the "Wrongful Life" Action Really Dead?' [1987] *JSWL* 306.

[295] In *Anns* v. *Merton Borough Council* [1978] AC 728.   [296] Weir [1982] *CLJ* 227.

pletely ignored for the sake of conceptual consistency. As some American courts have shown,[297] there is every reason why the courts should recognise the child's claim for economic loss here.[298]

Secondly, a 'wrongful life' action suggests that life, even disabled life, is an injury. For the religious purist this cannot be so; and even judges have held that impaired life can be better than no life. The problem once again is that such abstract dicta are hardly likely to appeal to the majority of the population, let alone to the parents of a severely disabled child who will have to cope with it for the rest of their lives. Philosophically, the decision whether disabled life is better than no life may be a question that is incapable of a 'right' answer. Pragmatically, it should be left to the individual concerned. Of course, the disabled child will—initially at any rate—be incapable of taking any decision. And, if in later life it wishes to be allowed to die, it will still be denied such a request since active euthanasia is prohibited by our law, as is the assistance of others in the individual's suicide. In effect, therefore, the *status quo* gives the courts the right to decide these issues and ignores the contrary wishes of the parents who will be called upon to cope with the consequences of such a decision. It is submitted therefore, that in such cases the decision is best left with the parents, acting closely with the doctor and hospital.

Not unrelated to this argument is a *third* argument, namely that to recognise the child's 'wrongful life' claim would be to impose a duty on the doctor to facilitate an abortion. On closer analysis this argument is not convincing. The law would not be imposing a duty upon a doctor to bring about an abortion but rather to advise the mother of the child's condition and leave her the choice of whether to seek a termination.[299] Providing the termination would fall within the foetal abnormality ground in section 1(1)(d) of the Abortion Act, how can it be contrary to public policy to impose a duty upon a doctor to appraise the mother of her right to seek an abortion? Indeed, how is this duty any different from the one utilised to give the mother a 'wrongful birth' claim in exactly the same circumstances?

The *fourth* argument advanced by proponents of the *McKay* view is that it is impossible for the court to assess damages—to assess the value of life as it occurs against non-existence. It is trite law that the difficulty in assessing damages is never a good reason for not awarding them. Also, for many years the English courts indulged in the equally fruitless exercise of evaluating the 'loss of expectation of life'; if they managed the task in that case, why cannot they manage it in the case of 'wrongful life' actions? There is no reason to believe that, at any rate where *disabled* life is concerned, the courts cannot compare this against a normal one and arrive at a sum which is only partially an arbitrary one.[300] Finally, surely this argument only relates to a claim for general damages

---

[297] See n. 292, above.   [298] See Grubb (1993) 1 *Med. L. Rev.* 119.

[299] *A fortiori* if the doctor's negligence arises before conception, for example, in genetic counselling and the child's claim is that it would not have been conceived if there had been no negligence: see *Turpin* v. *Sortini*, above, and Whitfield, op. cit., n. 294 above, at 47–9.

[300] A claim under s. 1A of the Act brought by a disabled child claiming that a doctor negligently selected 'him' as a damaged embryo is a 'wrongful life' claim (since he could never have existed other than in a disabled condition) and will require the courts to award damages presumably both general and special.

for pain and suffering, etc? Why should this argument, even if correct, prevent the recovery of the extraordinary costs associated with the disability?

Two final comments should be made on the state of English law. *First*, all the judges in *McKay* stated *obiter* that 'wrongful life' claims could not be brought under the 1976 Act because of the wording of section 1(2)(b),[301] which requires that when the negligence arises after conception that 'the child is born with disabilities *which would not otherwise have been present*' (emphasis added). In a 'wrongful life' case, of course, the child's claim is that it should not have been born at all. The assumption under the Act, it seems, is that for the child's claim to succeed it must show that it would have been born healthy.[302] However, the Act only abolishes the common law for claims by 'a child in respect of disabilities' (s. 4(5)). Could it not be argued that the child's claim is for its financial losses caused by, and hence not for, the disabilities? Further, section 1(2)(a) which deals with pre-conception events may bring within the Act certain 'wrongful life' situations. Consider the case where a doctor negligently advises parents about the risk of a future child inheriting a genetic disorder and on the strength of that a child is conceived and born disabled. Has the doctor 'affected [the parents'] *ability* to have a normal, healthy child' within section 1(1)(a) of the 1976 Act? (Emphasis added.) The answer turns on the meaning of 'ability' and whether it includes situations where the parents' *opportunity* to have a normal child is affected as well as cases where their *physical capacity* is affected. Arguably, if the parents could have avoided the conception of this disabled child and conceived a different healthy child, the claim would fall within the Act. But, of course, this would be a 'wrongful life' claim because this child would never have been born if the doctor had not negligently advised the parents.[303]

Secondly, if a 'wrongful life' claim cannot be brought by the child, there will be little disadvantage to the child and his family if the parents are able to bring a 'wrongful birth' claim to recover the financial burden of the disabled child. A problem will only arise if the parents' claim is restricted to expenses up to the age of the child's majority. It would, however, be reasonable for the common law to accept the legal obligation of the parents to care for their disabled (adult) child. If the evidence establishes that the child will be cared for by the parents after majority they should also be able to claim the costs associated with this period.[304]

(3) *Duties to Third Parties*.[305]   Can a doctor ever owe a duty of care to a third party who is not his patient, for example, to protect that third party from his dangerous patient? A number of examples come to mind: the psychiatric patient who threatens to injure or kill another;[306] the patient who suffers from

---

[301] Per Stephenson LJ at 779; per Ackner LJ at 785–6; per Griffiths LJ at 789.

[302] See Law Commission's Report No. 60 on Injuries to Unborn Children (1974, Cmnd. 5709), at 60.

[303] As would be the case of a claim under s. 1A where a disabled child alleges that a doctor negligently selected 'him' as a damaged embryo during infertility treatment.

[304] See *Viccaro* v. *Milunsky* (1990) 551 N.E. 2d 8 (Mass. Sup. Jud. Ct.).

[305] See, for a full discussion, Kennedy and Grubb (eds.) *Principles of Medical Law* (Select Bibliography), ch. 5.

[306] See *Tarasoff* v. *Regents of the University of California* (1976) 551 P. 2d. 334.

an infectious disease and is likely to transmit it to his or her partner;[307] or, the epileptic patient who refuses to give up driving.[308] In America such actions have been successful but not universally.[309]

In English law, actions of this nature are fraught with difficulties because they involve potential liability for an omission (to warn or prevent conduct) and the voluntary act of an intermediary. It has even been suggested that a doctor can never owe a duty of care to someone who is not his patient.[310] This is an untenable proposition and it is clear that, in principle, a doctor may be liable to relatives of a patient for psychiatric injury and, even, economic loss if the particular requirements of 'proximity' and policy are met.[311] It is the need to satisfy these latter requirements of the 'three-stage' test in *Caparo Industries plc* v. *Dickman*[312] which will prove difficult.

It is likely that English law will look for a number of factors (alone or in combination). These would include that the doctor had 'control' over the patient, that the doctor increased the risk of harm to the patient, that the third party was identifiable to a high degree of specificity and that no breach of confidence would be involved. Two recent cases illustrate the difficulties.

In *Goodwill* v. *BPAS*,[313] the defendant performed a vasectomy on his patient and subsequently advised him that the operation had been successful and that he need take no further precautions. Three years later he met the plaintiff, he told her about his vasectomy but she became pregnant because it had failed. She unsuccessfully sued her partner's doctor. The Court of Appeal held that she was not owed a duty of care. Applying the test adopted in negligent advice cases where loss is caused to a third party (*Caparo*), the court concluded that there was no special relationship between the doctor and plaintiff. The doctor did not know (nor could he have known) that his advice would be passed on to the plaintiff and relied upon by her. The court was clearly concerned about the breadth of the defendant's potential liability: she belonged to a class 'excessive in size and uncertain in character'.[314] Rather more bluntly, Peter Gibson LJ remarked that the plaintiff 'was merely, like any other woman in the world, a potential future partner [of the patient], that is to say a member of an indeterminately large class of females who might have sexual relations with [the patient] during is lifetime'.[315] It would have been different if she had been the patient's partner at the time of the procedure and had been involved in the consultations.[316]

Goodwill is a curious case. It was argued as an economic loss case but according to an earlier decision of the Court of Appeal, the plaintiff's claim was for 'physical injuries'. Even if this does not make the specific requirements of

---

[307] See *Pittman Estate* v. *Bain* (1994) 112 DLR (4th) 257.   [308] *Spillane* v. *Wasserman* (1992) 13 CCLT 267.
[309] See Kennedy and Grubb (eds.) *Principles of Medical Law* (Select Bibliography), ch. 5 at paras. 5.49–5.59.
[310] *Powell* v. *Boldaz* (1997) 39 BMLR 35 (CA) per Stuart-Smith LJ at 45.
[311] *Sion* v. *Hampstead HA* [1994] 5 Med. LR 170 (CA) (psychiatric injury): discussed in Grubb (1994) 2 *Med. L. Rev.* 365; *Goodwill* v. *BPAS* [1996] 2 All ER 161 (CA) (economic loss arising out of a failed sterilisation).
[312] [1990] 2 AC 605 (HL). According to certain dicta, this test is applicable whether the claim is one for economic loss, property damage or physical injury: *Marc Rich & Co. A.G.* v. *Bishop Rock Marine Co. Ltd.* [1996] 1 AC 211 (HL) (see, however, a different view expressed at p. 84, above).
[313] [1996] 2 All ER 161 (CA).   [314] Ibid., per Thorpe LJ at 170.   [315] Ibid., at 169.
[316] As in *Thake* v. *Maurice* [1986] QB 644 (CA).

'proximity' in *Caparo* irrelevant, it is not at all clear why those requirements are relevant in the quite different context of failed sterilisations. Perhaps the crux of the case which explains the outcome, is that the plaintiff should (and actually did) obtain independent advice about contraception; she saw her own GP. Thorpe LJ said: '[h]er responsibility is to protect herself against unwanted conception and to take independent advice.'[317] The expectation of self-reliance may be reasonable where the plaintiff and third party have a relationship but, to that extent, it will be atypical of the usual 'dangerous' patient cases.

While *Goodwill* is a duty to a third-party case, it does not manifest the usual problems inherent in such actions: deliberate wrong of a patient, possible breach of confidence. In *Palmer* v. *Tees HA*,[317a] the court dealt with a legally (if thankfully not factually) more typical situation. The plaintiff was the mother of a four-year-old girl who was abducted, sexually abused and murdered by a psychiatric patient who had been cared for over time by the defendant. The plaintiff suffered psychiatric injury as a result of discovering her daughter had been abducted, what she feared had happened and what she learned had actually happened to her daughter. She sued the defendant alleging they had negligently failed to discover the killer's propensities and to treat him or otherwise prevent him from killing her daughter.

The judge struck out the plaintiff's claim on the basis that no duty of care was owed.[318] First, he held that there was no 'proximity' between the plaintiff and defendant. Following *Hill* v. *Chief Constable of West Yorkshire*, Gage J held that a defendant could only be liable for the actions of a third party if the victim was someone 'who came into a special or exceptional or distinctive category of risk from the activities of the third party'. It was not sufficient to show that the victim was merely at risk as a member of the general public. On the facts, the judge concluded that while the dangerous patient was known to the defendant the victim was not and she was not at a special risk from him greater than all young girls given his propensities. He remarked, however, that if she had been, he would have held there to be a 'proximate' relationship. In any event, the judge went on to state that it was not 'fair, just and reasonable' to impose a duty of care on the defendants. For this he relied upon the following factors: the danger that doctors might engage in 'defensive medicine', the burden of increased claims upon the health authority, the diversion of resources that defending and dealing with such claims would entail, the limited control the defendant had over the patient, that the defendant might be required to breach the patient's confidence in order to warn others and, finally, the fact that plaintiff had a claim for compensation from the Criminal Injuries Compensation Board.

Palmer will not be the final word on a doctor's liability to third parties. Future cases will present factual situations where some, or many, of the problems of 'proximity' will be absent. The plaintiff may be specifically at risk and known

---

[317] As in *Thake* v. *Maurice* [1986] QB 644 (CA), at 170.
[317a] [1998] Lloyd's Rep. Med. 447.
[318] He did so also on the basis that the plaintiff's claim for psychiatric injury did not fall within the *McLoughlin/Alcock* rules since she had not witnessed the event or its immediate aftermath.

to the defendant.[319] Breach of confidence will not always be a problem since the content of the defendant's duty will not require him to warn another, for example, where to warn the patient would provide reasonable protection of the plaintiff.[320] There will be no question of the defendant having to control or restrain another.[321] In any event, given the type of situations contemplated, any breach of confidence would be legally justified in the public interest because of the danger to the plaintiff. Where is the problem in imposing a duty of care if that is so? Finally, the policy arguments relied upon by the judge in *Palmer* under the third limb of the *Caparo* test were unsubstantiated—and in the case of the danger of 'defensive medicine' may simply be false and *in terrorem*. They simply may not appeal to a future appellate court for this reason alone but also because if taken seriously they would strike at the heart of medical negligence litigation in general. Is it really being suggested that otherwise justified actions against doctors and NHS Trusts should fail because they are expensive? Leaving aside the political rhetoric, the answer must surely be negative.

(4) *Doctors Engaged by Others*.[322] In a number of situations a doctor may be requested to examine and provide a report on an individual's health, for example, by an insurance company or (prospective) employer. Clearly, the doctor will owe the person who engaged him a duty of care. Usually, of course, there will be a contract between the parties also. The doctor will know the identity of the recipient, the purpose for which they require it and that they will rely upon it. Liability follows on ordinary *Hedley Byrne* principles.[323] What, if any, duty will the doctor owe the examinee? It could be argued that the doctor's duties must be owed to the person who engaged him, otherwise a conflict of interest might arise. Thus, the doctor will not owe the examinee a duty to make a careful report to the insurance company or employer: that duty will be owed exclusively to the person who engaged him. But what if he discovers that the examinee may (or does) have a health problem? Will he have a duty to advise the examinee of it, or more likely to seek dedicated medical care? Or, can he instead turn his back on his examinee and leave him to take his chances?

English law seems, for the time being at least, reluctant to impose any duties upon the doctor beyond one not to injure the patient in the course of the examination. In *X (Minors)* v. *Bedfordshire CC*,[324] a child was examined by a psychiatrist engaged by a local authority social services for suspected sexual abuse. Following a mistaken diagnosis that the partner of the child's mother was the culprit, the child was unnecessarily taken into care and suffered psychiatric

---

[319] As in *Tarasoff*, above. See also, *Osman* v. *Ferguson* [1993] 4 All ER 344 (CA).

[320] See e.g., *Reisner* v. *Regents of the University of California* (1995) 37 Cal Rptr 2d 518 (Cal. CA) (duty to advise patient that she is infected with HIV so as to allow for practice of 'safe sex'). Discussed in Grubb (1997) 5 *Med. L. Rev.* 250.

[321] For example, in actions where a relative claims a doctor should have disclosed the risk of harm based upon genetic inheritance from the patient: *Pate* v. *Threlkel* (1995) 661 So 2d 278 (Fla. Sup. Ct.) and *Safer* v. *Pack* (1996) 677 A 2d 1188 (N.J. Sup. Ct. App. Div.).

[322] See Kennedy and Grubb (eds.) *Principles of Medical Law* (Select Bibliography) at paras. 5.88–5.104 and Jones, *Medical Negligence* (Select Bibliography) at paras. 2-031–2-036.

[323] Following the reasoning in *Spring* v. *Guardian Assurance plc* [1994] 3 All ER 129 (HL); but note the reservation of Lord Goff at 147.

[324] [1995] 3 All ER 353 (HL).

injury. The House of Lords held that the psychiatrist's duties were owed to the local authority. Lord Browne-Wilkinson drew an analogy with the situation where a doctor is retained by an insurance company to examine an applicant for the purposes of life insurance. He said:[325]

The doctor does not, by examining the applicant, come under any general duty of medical care to the applicant. He is under a duty not to damage the applicant in the course of the examination: but beyond that his duties are owed to the insurance company and not to the applicant.

No authority was offered for this analysis of the relationship in the insurance context and it is not abundantly clear that it is convincingly analogous to the statutory framework of welfare law raised in the *Bedfordshire* case. This, it is suggested, is the real point in the latter case, which was fatal to the plaintiff's action.[326]

Despite this rather discouraging start in *Baker* v. *Kaye*[327] the court took a different view. The plaintiff was denied a job because of an adverse medical report made by the defendant at the behest of the plaintiff's prospective employer. The plaintiff sued for the economic loss he had suffered. The court held that the defendant owed him a duty of care. The judge concluded such loss was foreseeable if the report was made carelessly. Further, there was a 'proximate' relationship between the parties: the defendant knew that the plaintiff's employment depended upon his medical advice, the plaintiff had entrusted himself and information to the defendant, and the defendant regarded himself as under a duty to report anything untoward he discovered to the plaintiff. Finally, it was 'fair, just and reasonable' to impose a duty of care; in particular, there was no conflict between the duty owed by the defendant to the plaintiff and to the company who engaged him. In the result, however, the judge denied the plaintiff's claim, holding that the defendant had not been careless in his assessment of the plaintiff.

The U-turn of the courts was short-lived. In *Kapfunde* v. *Abbey National*,[328] the Court of Appeal disapproved the decision in *Baker* v. *Kaye*. The plaintiff applied for a job and completed a confidential medical questionnaire in which she indicated she had previously been absent from work due to sickle-cell anaemia. The defendant/doctor, engaged by the prospective employer, advised on the strength of this that the plaintiff would have a higher than average absentee record. As a result, the plaintiff was not given the job. She sued for the economic loss she suffered. The Court of Appeal, relying on the *Bedfordshire* case, held that no duty was owed. The court relied upon a number of factors: there was no doctor–patient relationship, in fact the parties had never met; the claim was for economic loss; the plaintiff had not entrusted the doctor with the conduct of her affairs. In the end, like in *Baker* v. *Kaye*, the court also concluded that the doctor had not been careless.

---

[325] [1995] 3 All ER 353 (HL), at 383. Lord Nolan disagreed on this point, at 400.
[326] See also *Clunis* v. *Camden and Islington HA* (1997) 40 BMLR 181 (CA) (no duty owed where the defendant purporting to act under s. 117, Mental Health Act 1983).
[327] (1996) 39 BMLR 12.   [328] (1998) 25 March (CA) (unreported).

Whether *Kapfunde* limits the doctor's duty not to injure the examinee is not clear. The court did not consider what would have been the position if he had discovered that the plaintiff was ill or that further medical consultation was called for. There are indicators in the judgments that the court might contemplate a duty in this situation. For example, both Kennedy and Millett LJJ emphasised that the case concerned a claim for economic loss—notoriously difficult to win in England—and not one for personal injury. Further, Kennedy LJ seemed to consider it important that the doctor had never actually seen, let alone examined, the plaintiff.

It is the situation where there is a failure to advise the examinee of his potential or actual deleterious health condition which calls out for the courts to impose a duty of care. As one American court persuasively put it:[329]

When a doctor conducts a physical examination, the examinee generally assumes that 'no news is good news' and relies on the assumption that any serious condition will be revealed.

In other situations, professionals (such as solicitors) may owe duties to individuals other than their clients,[330] providing this does not conflict with their duties to their client.[331] Always bearing this caveat in mind, there is room for this development in English law in the case of doctors engaged by third parties.

(ii) Breach of Duty and the Standard of Care   In many cases the plaintiff's difficulties will lie not with the duty of care but with the (possible) breach of that duty. For the action will succeed only if the defendant/doctor has not attained the requisite standard of care and the plaintiff proves this. There are thus two points that have to be discussed under this heading: (1) what is the appropriate standard; and (2) who bears the burden of proof?

(1) The Standard of the Reasonable Doctor.   The standard of care in medical negligence actions is the standard of the reasonable professional, namely the 'reasonable doctor' and it is the same in both diagnosis and treatment.[332] The standard will be determined at the time of the treatment and not at the later time of the trial.[333] In *Bolam* v. *Friern HMC*[334] the judge said that:

the appropriate test is the standard of the ordinary skilled man exercising and professing to have that special skill. A man need not possess the highest expert skill; it is well established now that it is sufficient if he exercised the ordinary skill of an ordinary competent man exercising that particular art.

This means that a GP has to be tested against the competence of another GP and not of a specialist of any sort. Conversely, the standard that a specialist has

---

[329] *Betesh* v. *United States* (1974) 400 F. Supp 238 (DC Dist Ct.) per Bryant J at 246 (liability for failing to advise examinee during military pre-induction physical examination of abnormality on X-ray indicating cancer). See also, *Green* v. *Walker* (1990) F 2d 291 (5th Cir.) and *Webb* v. *T D* (1997) 951 P 2d 1008 (Mont. Sup. Ct.).

[330] *White* v. *Jones* [1995] 2 AC 207 (HL) (solicitor). See also, *Smith* v. *Eric S Bush* [1991] AC 831 (HL) (surveyor).

[331] See *Al-Kandari* v. *J.R. Brown & Co* [1988] 1 All ER 665.

[332] *Whitehouse* v. *Jordan* [1981] 1 WLR 246 (HL) (treatment); *Maynard* v. *West Midland Regional Health Authority* [1984] 1 WLR 634 (HL) (diagnosis).

[333] *Roe* v. *Minister of Health* [1954] 2 QB 66.

[334] [1957] 1 WLR 582.

to attain is that of the ordinary competent practitioner of his speciality. In the words of Lord Scarman, a doctor who professes to exercise a special skill must exercise 'the ordinary skill of his speciality'.[335]

The rules of liability for medical malpractice thus follow the general law of negligence. So, for example, just as a learner-driver will be judged by reference to the standard of care and skill displayed by an experienced driver,[336] so it will be no defence for a doctor to attribute the plaintiff's hurt to his (the doctor's) inexperience.[337] In this case, however, a strong case could be made against the health authority for using inexperienced staff for tasks that required prior experience or allowing them to practise without adequate supervision. The same could be said for over-stretched or overworked doctors. Courts, conscious of the long hours some doctors have to work in some hospitals, may feel some sympathy with such defendants;[338] but they are unlikely to exonerate them solely on such a ground. On the whole it would, again, be preferable to impose liability in such cases directly on the health authority or Trust responsible for the hospital, not least since being found liable in negligence may well carry with it a stigma.[339]

(2) *Proving the Standard.* Proving carelessness can be a considerable task in a medical negligence action. It almost always involves adducing expert evidence. Occasionally, the use of the maxim, *res ipsa loquitur* may raise an inference of carelessness against the doctor. In practice, however, this tends to be so in the most obvious cases, for example, where forceps are left inside the plaintiff's body,[340] where the surgeon cuts off the wrong foot or the plaintiff wakes up in the course of a surgical procedure having been given a general anaesthetic.[341] But in difficult, complex or technical cases it has been less effective for the plaintiff.[342] Where the plaintiff and/or defendant call expert evidence, *res ipsa loquitur* is unlikely to apply since the court will be called on to reach a conclusion on the basis of all the evidence.[343]

What then is the effect of expert evidence in a medical negligence case? As Lord President Clyde said in *Hunter* v. *Hanley*:[344] 'In the realm of diagnosis . . . there is ample scope for a genuine difference.' The same could, equally, be said of treatment in many situations. This has led the courts to display great deference to medical evidence. In *Bolam*, McNair J stated:[345]

A doctor is not guilty of negligence if he has acted in accordance with a practice accepted as proper by a responsible body of medical men skilled in that art.

This is the so-called '*Bolam* test'. It is unlikely that McNair J intended to hand over to the medical profession the standard of care expected of a doctor by the law. His use of the word 'responsible' and statements he made elsewhere in his

---

[335] *Maynard* v. *West Midlands RHA* [1984] 1 WLR 634, 638.   [336] *Nettleship* v. *Weston* [1971] 2 QB 691.
[337] *Wilsher* v. *Essex AHA* [1986] 3 All ER 801 (CA).
[338] See e.g., *Johnstone* v. *Bloomsbury HA* [1992] 1 QB 333 (CA).
[339] Above, per Browne-Wilkinson VC at 834.   [340] E.g. *Mahon* v. *Osborne* [1939] 2 KB 14.
[341] See the cases collected in *Ratcliffe* v. *Plymouth and Torbay HA* [1998] Lloyd's Rep. Med. 162 (CA).
[342] In *Bull* v. *Devon AHA* [1993] 4 Med LR 117 Mustill LJ went so far as to doubt whether *res ipsa loquitur* could assist in a medical negligence case where 'all the facts are before the court'.
[343] *Ratcliffe* v. *Plymouth and Torbay HA*, above, per Brooke LJ at 173.
[344] 1955 SC 200, 204.   [345] [1957] 2 All ER 118 at 122.

summing-up to the jury, suggest otherwise.[346] This was, however, how it came to be interpreted. *First*, the courts—with one exception[347]—treated compliance with *accepted* professional practice as conclusive evidence that the defendant was not negligent.[348] In the *Sidaway* case,[349] Lord Scarman famously said:

In short, the law imposes the duty of care; but the standard of care is a matter of medical judgment.

Secondly, it did not matter if there were more than one practice accepted within the profession as long as the defendant adhered to one. In *Maynard* v. *West Midlands RHA*,[350] the House of Lords held that the court's preference of one body of opinion to another was no basis for a conclusion of negligence. *Thirdly*, the courts applied the *Bolam* test not just to accepted *practices* but also to situations where there was no practice as such. Instead, the defendant was backed by expert evidence given at the trial which supported the defendant's conduct. This resembles a kind of *ex post facto* approval-rating from his peers ('Yes, I would have done as the defendant did' or 'No, I wouldn't have done that but it was reasonable for the defendant to do it').[351] Here, arguably, the *Bolam* test had less importance—at least in its most virulent form. Clearly, English courts did not relish the thought of having to choose between competing and diverging medical views or second-guessing the medical experts. In that regard, the courts went further in medical cases than in negligence cases involving other professions, where expert evidence of practice is only *some evidence*, perhaps even strong evidence, that the defendant was not careless: but is not conclusive.[352] The final word is always for the courts.

However, the English courts were out of line with a wealth of Commonwealth authority.[353] Thus in 1993 the Court of Appeal reinterpreted *Bolam*, leaving the courts with the final say on whether a doctor had been careless.[354] Subsequently, the Court of Appeal approved the 'new *Bolam*' approach;[355] and a series of first instance decisions adopted it.[356] The stage was set[357] for the

---

[346] Ibid., at 122, 124 and 127. [347] *Hucks* v. *Cole* (1968) [1993] 4 Med. LR 393 (CA).

[348] The converse, however, is not always necessarily true. A doctor who departs from established practice may yet not be guilty of negligence if he succeeds in convincing the court that his methods in the particular case were suitable: *Clark* v. *MacLennan* [1983] 1 All ER 416 (the doctor failed to discharge this (reversed) burden of proof; but the ruling that in theory he should be given the chance of showing the suitability of his treatment is to be applauded, for otherwise novel methods of treatment would never be tried out). In *Wilsher* v. *Essex AHA* [1986] 3 All ER 801, Mustill LJ was of the view that this case went too far in reversing the burden of proof, though it might be correct on its own facts.

[349] *Sidaway* v. *Bethlem Royal Hospital Governors* [1985] 1 All ER 643 at 649.

[350] [1984] 1 WLR 634. [351] E.g., *Hughes* v. *Waltham Forest HA* [1991] 2 Med. LR 155 (CA).

[352] E.g., *Edward Wong Finance Co. Ltd.* v. *Johnson, Stokes & Master (A Firm)* [1984] AC 296 (PC) (lawyers).

[353] E.g., *F* v. *R* (1983) 33 SASR 189 ('The ultimate question, however, is not whether the defendant's conduct accords with the practices of his profession or some part of it, but whether it conforms to the standards of reasonable care demanded by the law.' Per King CJ); and the very powerful rejection of *Bolam* by the High Court in *Rogers* v. *Whittaker* (1992) 67 ALJR 47, especially Gaudron J.

[354] See *Bolitho* v. *City and Hackney HA* (1992) 13 BMLR 111 (CA).

[355] *Joyce* v. *Merton, Sutton and Wandsworth HA* (1995) 27 BMLR 124 (CA); *De Freitas* v. *O'Brien* [1995] 6 Med. LR 108.

[356] E.g., *Gascoine* v. *Ian Sheridan & Co. (A Firm)* [1994] 5 Med. LR 437; *Bowers* v. *Harrow HA* [1995] 6 Med. LR 16; *Wiszniewski* v. *Central Manchester HA* [1996] 7 Med. LR 248; *Dowdie* v. *Camberwell HA* [1997] 8 Med. LR 368.

[357] The developing law of 'new *Bolam*' is analysed and discussed in Grubb (1993) 1 *Med. L. Rev.* 241; (1995) 3 *Med. L. Rev.* 198; (1996) 4 *Med. L. Rev.* 86 and Kennedy (1995) 3 *Med. L. Rev.* 195.

House of Lords to make a conclusive shift away from the conventional understanding of *Bolam* in *Bolitho* v. *City and Hackney HA*[358]—and the Law Lords did just
that.

The plaintiff, a two-year-old boy, suffered brain damage following cardiac
arrest caused by obstruction of his bronchial passages whilst he was in hospital.
It was accepted that the failure of a doctor to attend when summoned was negligent. The issue for the House of Lords was whether the defendant had caused
the plaintiff's injuries. It was argued by the defendants that even if a doctor had
attended he or she would not have intubated the plaintiff and thereby avoided
his injury—in other words, there was no 'but-for' causation. The House of Lords
accepted the trial judge's finding that the doctor would not have intubated the
patient had she attended him. However, that was not the only relevant question. Causation could also be established by proving that she ought to have
intubated, that is, her failure would, itself, have been negligent.[359] Expert evidence was given that supported two practices: one that would have intubated
the patient and another that would not have. Was this conclusive against the
plaintiff on the conventional understanding of *Bolam*? The House of Lords held
that it was not: the court could inquire whether the body of professional opinion was 'reasonable' or 'responsible'. Lord Browne-Wilkinson said, having
referred to some earlier cases:[360]

These decisions demonstrate that in cases of diagnosis and treatment there are cases
where, despite a body of professional opinion sanctioning the defendant's conduct, the
defendant can properly be held liable for negligence . . . In my judgment that is because,
in some cases, it cannot be demonstrated to the judge's satisfaction that the body of
opinion relied upon is reasonable or responsible.

Lord Browne-Wilkinson then went on to explain when such a case would
arise:[361]

In the vast majority of cases the fact that distinguished experts in the field are of a particular opinion will demonstrate the reasonableness of that opinion. In particular,
where there are questions of assessment of the relative risk and benefits of adopting a
particular medical practice, a reasonable view necessarily presupposes that the relative
risks and benefits have been weighed by the experts in forming their opinions. But if, in
a rare case, it can be demonstrated that the professional opinion is not capable of with-
standing logical analysis, the judge is entitled to hold that the body of opinion is not reasonable or responsible.

His use of the term 'logical' is problematic since many medical decisions will
not be based upon logic but rather judgment. What he thus appears to be contemplating is a three-fold review of the expert evidence. First, have the experts
directed their mind to all the relevant matter and facts. Secondly, have they
applied a sensible, coherent and, if appropriate, logical reasoning process to
this material to reach a conclusion. Finally, is their decision defensible as a
rational and reasonable one. The first two look towards the decision-making
process and the latter to the decision reached itself. On the facts, it was held

---

[358] (1997) 39 BMLR 1 (HL).   [359] On this aspect of causation, see Grubb (1996) 4 *Med. L. Rev.* 86.
[360] Above, at 10.   [361] Ibid.

that neither school of thought was 'illogical'—really they were both defensible in the sense of being properly reached and rational and reasonable in their conclusions.

Lord Browne-Wilkinson acknowledged that it will be a 'rare' or 'exceptional' case where judicial intervention will be justified: 'it will seldom be right for a judge to reach the conclusion that views genuinely held by a competent medical expert are unreasonable'.[362] Nevertheless, the law has been put back on its proper course. Clinical judgments will, in all probability, remain untouched by the court's reviewing eye, as *Bolitho* and a subsequent decision[363] show; but they will be subject to it and that is a very important reaffirmation of the court's role.

(iii) Causation and Remoteness[364] Proving that the defendant is responsible for any injury raises the usual questions of whether the defendant caused the injury (in fact and in law) and whether that injury was too remote. The general requirements of these are discussed in Chapter 2, above. It is unusual, but not unheard of, for it to be argued in a medical negligence case that the plaintiff or some other person's conduct amounts to a *novus actus interveniens*[365] or that his injury is too remote.[366] By contrast factual causation is often an issue.

Proving that the negligence caused the plaintiff's hurt is another formidable task that the latter has to overcome. In medical negligence cases these difficulties are often amplified for two reasons. First, the aetiology of disease and injury is frequently difficult to establish even for experts. Secondly, patients are, by definition, usually ill and the doctor's negligence will usually relate to a failure to cure or alleviate their existing condition requiring the court to ask the hypothetical question: 'What would have happened if there had been no negligence?'[367] The starting-point involves the application of the 'but-for' test and is well illustrated by the case of *Barnett* v. *Chelsea and Kensington Hospital Management Committee*.[368]

In that case the plaintiff presented himself to the casualty unit of a hospital early one morning complaining of abdominal pains. The casualty officer, without examining him, told him to go home, have some tea, and return later the next day if the pain had not subsided. In fact, five hours later the plaintiff died from arsenic poisoning. The trial judge held that the defendant had been negligent. Nevertheless, he found for the defendant on the ground that the plaintiff had failed to show that on the balance of probabilities the defendant's negligence was the cause of the death. This was because the judge accepted expert evidence that at the time when the plaintiff first appeared at the

---

[362] Ibid.   [363] *Wisniewski* v. *Central Manchester HA* [1998] Lloyd's Rep. Med. 223 (CA).

[364] For a full discussion see, Kennedy and Grubb (eds.), *Principles of Medical Law* (Select Bibliography), ch. 7 and Jones, *Medical Negligence* (Select Bibliography), ch. 5.

[365] *Emeh* v. *Kensington and Chelsea AHA* [1984] 3 All ER 1044 (action for failed sterilisation: refusal to undergo an abortion not a *novus actus interveniens*).

[366] *R* v. *Croydon HA* (1997) 40 BMLR 40 (CA) (damages for birth of healthy baby (her 'private life') too remote from defendant's negligence in failing to disclose in a pre-employment examination that she suffered from hypertension which would have caused her to avoid pregnancy).

[367] For an alternative where further conduct of the defendant (or someone else) would have been necessary to complete the causal chain, see *Bolitho* v. *City and Hackney HA* (1997) 39 BMLR 1 (HL).

[368] [1969] 1 QB 428.

hospital his poisoning was at such an advanced stage that even if tests had been carried out immediately his life would probably not have been saved.

There have been a number of court attempts to overcome these difficulties of causation (which are aggravated in cases involving drug-induced injuries[369] or actions under the Congenital Disabilities (Civil Liability) Act 1976). The first attempt was made in *McGhee* v. *National Coal Board*,[370] but this decision has been shrouded by much controversy and its exact ambit and future prospects were a matter of some speculation. The second attempt came with *Hotson* v. *East Berkshire Area Health Authority*,[371] though the decision of the House of Lords on this matter does not seem to indicate that much life, if any, has been left in this experiment.[372]

In *McGhee* the plaintiff contracted dermatitis while employed by the defendants to clean kilns at the latter's brick works. Due to lack of adequate washing facilities the plaintiff had to wait until he reached his home before he could wash. To do this he had to cycle back home, perspiring and covered in dust, and this, he argued, 'materially increased the risk' of contracting the disease. The plaintiff, however, was unable to prove that on the balance of probabilities the supply of washing facilities would have prevented the development of dermatitis. The 'but-for' test was thus not satisfied. Yet the House of Lords accepted his claim since they felt it was sufficient that he had shown that the defendant's breach of duty had 'materially increased the risk of his injury', which could not be differentiated from the view that it had contributed towards the injury itself.

The five speeches delivered in the House of Lords have caused much uncertainty as to what exactly *McGhee* decided. The better view is, perhaps, that where the plaintiff can show that the defendant's negligence made the risk of injury more probable, then the plaintiff will win even if it remains uncertain whether it was the actual cause.[373] As Mustill J put it in the subsequent case of *Thompson* v. *Smiths Ship-Repairers* (*North Shields*) *Ltd.*:[374]

Where *McGhee* did break new grounds was in the situation to the plaintiff's . . . problem [of establishing] causation. The 'evidential gap' created by the absence of proof that the breach was at the very least a *causa sine qua non* was bridged by treating the proof that the breach had increased risk of the disease as if it were proof that the breach had actually caused the disease. This device was a fiction . . . but it was one which had to be adopted in the interest of justice, to prevent the plaintiff from losing his claim through failure to prove that which in the current state of medical knowledge, he had no means of proving.

McGhee's effect was extended by the Court of Appeal in *Wilsher* v. *Essex AHA*[375] to cases where the hurt complained of could have been occasioned by any one of

---

[369] Here it may be difficult to establish that the drug does, in principle, cause the kind of damage suffered by the plaintiff: see *Loveday* v. *Renton* [1990] 1 Med. LR 117 (held whooping-cough vaccine cannot cause brain damage in young children). See also *Kay* v. *Ayrshire and Arran Health Board* [1987] 2 All ER 417 (held overdose of penicillin cannot cause deafness).

[370] [1973] 1 WLR 1.

[371] [1987] 2 All ER 909 (CA) reversed by the House of Lords in *Wilsher* [1987] AC 750.

[372] See *Tahir* v. *Haringey HA* [1998] Lloyd's Rep. Med. 104 (CA).

[373] See Grubb, 'A Survey of Medical Malpractice Law in England: Crisis? What Crisis?', op. cit., at 85–9.

[374] [1984] 1 All ER 881, 909.   [375] [1986] 3 All ER 416.

a series of consecutive factors but only one of which was attributable to the defendant's negligence. But in the House of Lords, Lord Bridge of Harwich agreed with Sir Nicolas Browne-Wilkinson VC (who had been in a minority in the Court of Appeal in *Wilsher*). In his view, *McGhee* was distinguishable and the Court of Appeal (in *Wilsher*) was wrong to have tried to resolve the conflict between the experts by applying the *McGhee* rule. *McGhee* was not—as some lawyers had anticipated—subjected to a frontal attack but, through interpretation, reduced in significance as a case turning on its own facts.[376] It should certainly not be treated as having disturbed 'the principle that the onus of proving causation lies on the . . . plaintiff . . . [and any] attempt to extract from it some esoteric principle . . . is a fruitless one'.[377] Further, *McGhee* was merely a case where the court took 'a robust and pragmatic approach to the undisputed primary facts'.[378] The court was able to infer that the defendant's negligence (lack of washing facilities) was a/the cause of the plaintiff's injuries (dermatitis), even though none of the experts in the case were prepared to say so. In *Wilsher* five possible causes of the plaintiff's injuries were present. The House held that to show that the defendant's negligence materially increased the risk of the plaintiff's injuries did nothing to exclude the other causes; therefore, it was impossible for the court to infer that the defendant was the cause of the injuries. The extent to which the *McGhee* approach may assist a plaintiff in a medical-negligence case in the future remains unclear, although it has been applied subsequently (in the light of *Wilsher*) by the Canadian Supreme Court in a plaintiff's favour where there was no positive evidence of causation.[379]

Hotson v. *East Berkshire AHA*[380] was a more controversial case. In that case the young plaintiff fell and was taken to hospital where his knee was X-rayed, but a hip injury was not diagnosed. Five days later the boy returned to hospital, at which time the hip injury was discovered. However, by this time the hip injury had also resulted in a deformity of the hip joint—or so the plaintiff contended. The defendants argued that the deformity would have occurred whether or not a timely diagnosis had been made during the first visit at the hospital. The trial judge found that the health authority's delay in diagnosis denied the plaintiff a 25 per cent chance of avoiding the hip deformity. He thus gave the plaintiff 25 per cent of the amount of damages he would have received had the injury been solely caused by the delayed diagnosis. The Court of Appeal agreed, with the Master of Rolls saying that: 'As a matter of common-sense, it is unjust that there should be no liability for failure to treat a patient, simply because the chances of a successful cure by that treatment were less than 50 per cent . . .'.[381] The House of Lords took a different view. Lord Bridge first quoted from the judgment of Simon Brown J at first instance where the judge had said.[382]

In the end the problem comes down to one of classification. Is this on true analysis a case where the plaintiff is concerned to establish causative negligence, or is it rather a case where the real question is the proper quantum of damage? . . . If the issue is one of

---

376 See Grubb [1988] *CLJ* 350.
377 [1988] 1 All ER 871 at 882.
378 Ibid., per Lord Bridge at 881.
379 *Snell* v. *Farrell* (1990) 72 DLR (4th) 289 (Can. Sup. Ct.).
380 [1987] 1 All ER 210 (CA) [1987] 2 All ER 909 (HL).
381 Above, at 215.
382 [1985] 1 WLR 1036, 1043–4.

causation then the health authority succeeds since the plaintiff will have failed to prove his claim on the balance of probabilities . . . If, however, the issue is one of qualification then the plaintiff succeeds because it is trite law that the quantum of a recognised head of damage must be evaluated according to the chances of the loss occurring.

His Lordship, unlike the judge at first instance, took the view that the problem was one of causation and that the plaintiff had failed to prove on the balance of probabilities that the delayed treatment had at least been a material contributory cause of the deformity. And he concluded:[383] 'Unless the plaintiff proved on a balance of probabilities that the delayed treatment was at least a material contributory cause of the avascular necrosis he failed on the issue of causation and no question of quantification could arise.'

The original decision, favouring plaintiffs in medical negligence actions, was thus overturned. Their Lordships also refused to consider the wider question put to them. Put simply, this was the following. In a claim for damages for personal injury, would it ever be appropriate to award the plaintiff a proportionate fraction of the full damages where the cause of the injury was unascertainable and all that the plaintiff could show was a statistical chance that was less than even that, but for the defendant's breach of duty, he would not have suffered the injury? The House of Lords' opinion in *Wilsher* would appear to suggest a negative answer. Indeed, Lord Mackay in *Hotson* suggests a negative answer.[384] Whether the law should allow recovery for a statistical chance of injury or avoiding injury undoubtedly involves policy arguments on both sides.[385] These arguments have led courts in America to reach diverging decisions,[386] although an increasing number of jurisdictions are allowing recovery where the plaintiff claims a 'loss of (or reduction in) chance' of survival usually where the defendant has failed to diagnose the plaintiff's terminal condition, for example, cancer.[387]

(E) A COMPARATIVE EPILOGUE

Medical law inclines towards foreign law and the comparative method. On many occasions our courts and, on even more occasions, our academic writers have shown in this subject a keen interest in how matters are resolved elsewhere: indeed, that is the approach that was adopted in this section. There are a number of reasons why this should be so. Sometimes reference to a foreign system is made in order to make sure that English law does not commit the 'mistakes' that others have made. On other occasions the foreign law is presented as an example worthy of consideration if not imitation. There is no

---

[383] Above, at 913.

[384] Above, at 918–19 referring to the judgment of Brachtenbach J in *Herskovits* v. *Group Health Cooperative of Puget Sound* (1983) 664 P. 2d 474 at 491.

[385] For a discussion, see Hill (1991) 45 *MLR* 511, and Stapleton (1988) 104 *LQR* 389.

[386] See e.g. the various positions taken in the Washington case of *Herskovits* (above): Dore J (*Wilsher* approach); Pearson J (recovery for the 'chance'); and Brachtenbach J (no recovery).

[387] For examples, see *Perez* v. *Las Vegas Medical Center* (1991) 805 P.2d 589 (Nev. Sup. Ct.) (where there was a dissent) and *Wollen* v. *DePaul Health Center* (1992) 828 S.W. 2d 681 (Missouri Sup. Ct.) and cases cited at 683–4. But the claim is not recognised in Canada: *Lawson* v. *LaFerrière* (1991) 78 DLR (4th) 609 and Grubb (1993) 1 *Med. L. Rev.* 124.

objection to such comparative exercises so long as they do not merely scratch the surface of foreign law, drawing conclusions that deeper knowledge of that other system does not really support.

An example of the first type of comparative exercise (that we should treat with caution) can be found in the area of consent. Our courts have, as we noted when we discussed the *Sidaway* case, looked at the American doctrine of 'informed consent'. This, it will be remembered, requires the doctor to tell the patient all that a *prudent* patient would require to know in order to make up his mind. They rejected it as unworkable and dangerous. Policy reasons for such an approach were given by almost all the judges that were involved in that case. One of the most crucial was the belief that the adoption of the American ideas would lead to unlimited claims and defensive medicine (which is both costly and time-consuming) and, one could add, demoralises the medical profession. That medical malpractice law in the United States is in a state of near-crisis, few would dispute.[388] There seems, however, to be little evidence to support the view that in the area of informed consent the more pro-patient attitude adopted by the American courts has contributed to this crisis. Quoting from the three-volume report of the President's Commission published in 1982, Professor Ian Kennedy stated[389] that: 'A national survey of claims in 1975–76 showed that informed consent was *raised* as an issue in only 3 per cent of cases.' This is also the experience in Canada where the 'prudent patient' test was adopted by the Supreme Court in the 1980 case of *Reibl* v. *Hughes*.[390] Moreover, some of the important factors that contribute to the crisis of modern tort law in the United States have nothing to do with the doctrine of informed consent, but with other features of the tort trial which are not present in the United Kingdom. These include jury trials, huge contingent fees, absence of a developed social-welfare system, and a greater availability of punitive damages.[391] In Germany the law on this subject has, *inter alia*, for historical reasons gone even further. German law thus accepts that, barring instances of therapeutic privilege (where the doctor has to prove that he did not disclose information because it would have harmed the patient), the medical practitioner must disclose all the information that the *individual patient* needs in order to give his consent.[392] But the apocalyptic picture painted by those who oppose any change in our law never materialised. Should not our courts at least take some note of these developments and quiz counsel when they next urge them not to depart from our existing, pro-doctor practice?

The comparative method can also be used in order to encourage improvement and reform. That the English law is bad, in the sense that no one who

[388] See the Harvard Medical Practice Study to the State of New York: (1991) 324 *NEJM* 370 and 377 and (1991) *NEJM* 245.

[389] *Treat Me Right* (Select Bibliography), 108, n. 67.

[390] (1981) 144 DLR (3d) 1 and Robertson, 'Informed Consent Ten Years Later: The Impact of *Reibl* v. *Hughes*' (1991) 70 *Can. BR* 423.

[391] Markesinis, 'Litigation-mania in England, Germany and the USA: Are We So Very Different?' [1990] *CLJ* 233.

[392] For a comparative account of English and German law on this point, see J. Shaw, 'Informed Consent: A German Lesson' (1986) 35 *ICLQ* 864.

comes into contact with it in the context of a medical dispute stands to gain, can also not be seriously doubted.

The position of patients is, as indicated time and again, unenviable. Litigation is costly and the legal hurdles often insurmountable. Procedural changes have helped, and the Woolf Reforms will further improve the system, but the basic difficulties remain. The law protects English doctors more than other systems do. Yet the medical profession seems just as unhappy with it as potential claimants. The concern is not only with the slowly growing tendency to sue doctors rather than to thank them; it is primarily directed at the gladiatorial nature of our law, which seeks to attribute blame and destroy reputations. For unfortunately a finding of negligence is often felt by doctors to carry with it an imputation of professional incompetence which, of course, it need not do. The confrontational nature of the law often encourages doctors and their insurers (or employers) to resist claims to the bitter end. Rising costs and mental anguish thus, once again, seem to be the only consequence of using tort law as the way of distributing the cost of medical accidents.

It is this situation that has prompted interest in no-fault schemes of compensation of the type that we find, *inter alia*, in New Zealand (until recently) and in Sweden. This is no place to describe such schemes; the interested reader must look up details in the specialised literature.[393] However, one must note, albeit briefly, the main common advantage that they share. This is a speedy determination by non-lawyers[394] in a non-confrontational atmosphere of the question whether compensation is to be paid to those suffering 'personal injury by accident',[395] or persons suffering injury or illness as a result of a procedure related to health-care.[396] The weakness of these systems—and one cannot deny their existence—should be obvious from the way they designate those who can claim. In New Zealand, for example, only the victims of 'medical, surgical, dental or first aid *misadventure*' can claim. That excludes injuries resulting from infection, disease, and the ageing process—a dividing-line which is not always easy to draw.[397] The definition of 'misadventure' has also caused difficulties.[398] After considerable judicial disagreement, in 1989 the New Zealand Court of Appeal in *Green* v. *Matheson*[399] adopted an expansive definition. Cooke P stated that it:

---

[393] For a detailed account, see K. Oliphant, 'Defining 'Medical Misadventure': Lessons from New Zealand' (1996) 4 *Med. L. Rev.* 1. A good brief account of the New Zealand scheme (now substantially modified by the Accident Rehabilitation and Compensation Insurance Act 1992) is given by R. Smith in (1982) 284 *BMJ* 1243–5; 1323–5; 1457–9. See also, G. Palmer, *Compensation for Incapacity: A Study of Law and Social Change in New Zealand and Australia* (1979). For the Swedish system see C. Oldertz, 'The Swedish Patient Insurance Scheme: Eight Years of Experience' (1984) 52 *Medico-Legal Journal*, 43–59.

[394] The right to sue is removed while the right to appeal to a court of law is acknowledged but rarely exercised.

[395] The New Zealand scheme—dating from 1974; consolidated in the Accident Compensation Act 1982.

[396] The Swedish approach.

[397] In *ACC* v. *Mitchell* [1992] 2 NZLR 436 the Court of Appeal greatly narrowed the 'disease' exclusion to the Act where there is an 'internal accident', e.g., a sudden cessation of breathing leading to brain damage.

[398] See Mahoney, 'New Zealand's Accident Compensation Scheme: A Reassessment' (1992) 40 *Amer. J. of Comparative Law* 159.

[399] [1989] 3 NZLR 564. See also, decided on the same day, *Willis* v. *AG* [1989] 3 NZLR 574. Discussed in D. Collins, *Medical Law in New Zealand* (1992), ch. 5.

applies naturally . . . whether the failure alleged be insufficient or wrong treatment, failure to inform, misdiagnosis, misrepresentation (innocent or fraudulent) or administrative shortcomings. It all arose from the way in which she was dealt with as a medical case.[400] If her case was mishandled, it was her misfortune or ill-luck; this falls squarely within the idea of misadventure.

No longer would it be necessary to show that the injury was the result of an 'unexpected' and 'undesigned' error or mishap for it to qualify as a misadventure. Also compensation could be paid to the patient even though the doctor was not found guilty of negligence.[401]

However, no-fault schemes of the New Zealand type are expensive; and, in the light of the court's approach in the *Green* case, the scheme was substantially amended (restrictively) by the Accident Rehabilitation and Compensation Insurance Act 1992 with effect from 1 July 1992. Importantly, it now limits claims for 'medical misadventure' by narrowing its definition. The Act specifically excludes claims for 'medical errors', that is, failure to obtain consent, to provide treatment, or to make a correct diagnosis unless such failures are shown to be negligent.[402] Beyond this, adverse consequences of treatment will only fall within the Act (as 'medical mishaps') if they are 'rare' (i.e. occur in less than 1 per cent of cases) and 'severe' (i.e. cause death or require, for example, hospitalisation for more than fourteen days or significant disability for more than twenty-eight days).[403] Cases like *Whitehouse* v. *Jordan*[404] or *Sidaway*[405] would thus probably receive no different an answer in New Zealand.[406]

The New Zealand experience thus raises a serious doubt as to whether no-fault schemes really are the solution to the compensation problems faced by the victims of medical accidents.

The Swedish system also has its drawbacks. Like the New Zealand scheme it attempts to exclude compensation for injury which is traceable to an original disease and is not the result of a medical procedure; but it does make provision for compensation for injury resulting from medically unjustified inaction. Compensation is made to depend on the all-important determination that the medical procedure that led to the injury was 'not medically justified'—a test that can often reintroduce the issue of negligence in this debate.

Finally, there is a question of size of awards under these schemes and of costing them in a manner that would be realistic for the English scene. Until that is done it is unlikely that there is going to be any radical change in our system of compensation. Instead, we are likely to concentrate on piecemeal reforms which introduce strict liability in selected areas of tort law (e.g. products liability) or no-fault schemes providing limited compensation (e.g. the Vaccine Damage Payments Act 1979) and co-exist alongside the traditional tort rules. For this reason as well, the law of medical malpractice is thus destined to

---

[400] The plaintiff had, without her consent, been used as a guinea-pig in a study of women diagnosed with pre-malignant cervical disease. As a result she received unconventional treatment which, it was claimed, advanced her development of malignant cervical cancer.

[401] See *Polansky* v. *ACC* [1990] NZAR 481.   [402] S. 5.   [403] S. 5.

[404] [1981] 1 WLR 246.   [405] [1984] 1 QB 493; [1985] AC 871.

[406] If the claim is not accepted by the Accident Compensation Corporation a tort action is possible.

remain a controversial topic of modern tort law. For the law student (and practitioner) this is a plus; but for the victim of medical errors it may be a disaster. The need to balance the competing interests must, therefore, never be let out of mind.

Select Bibliography

MEDICAL NEGLIGENCE

DUGDALE, A. and STANTON, K., *Professional Negligence* (3rd edn., 1998).
JACKSON, R. M. and POWELL, J. L., *Professional Negligence* (4th edn., 1996, ch. 6).
JONES, M., *Medical Negligence* (2nd edn., 1996).
TEFF, H., *Reasonable Care: Legal Perspectives on the Doctor/Patient Relationship* (1994).

Medical Law

BRAZIER, M., *Medicine, Patients and the Law* (2nd edn., 1992).
DOUGLAS, G., *Law, Fertility and Reproduction* (1991).
GRUBB, A., 'The Emergence and Rise of Medical Law and Ethics' (1987) 50 *MLR* 241.
—— (ed.), *Challenges in Medical Care* (1992).
—— *Choices and Decisions in Health Care* (1993).
—— *Decision-Making and Problems of Incompetence* (1994).
—— and PEARL, D. S., *Bloodtesting, AIDS and DNA Profiling* (1990).
HARRIS, J., *Clones, Genes and Immortality* (2nd edn., 1998).
HOGGETT, B., *Mental Health Law* (4th edn., 1996).
KENNEDY, I., *Treat me Right: Essays in Medical Law and Ethics* (1991, paperback edn.).
—— and GRUBB, A., *Medical Law: Text with Materials* (2nd edn., 1994).
—— (eds.), *Principles of Medical Law* (1998).
KEOWN, J., (ed.), *Euthanasia Examined: Ethical, Clinical and Legal Perspectives* (1996).
LEE, R. and MORGAN, D. (eds.), *Birth Rites: Law and Ethics at the Beginnings of Life* (1990, paperback edn.).
—— *Death Rites: Law and Ethics at the End of Life* (1994).
LOCKWOOD, M. (ed.), *Moral Dilemmas in Modern Medicine* (1986).
McHALE, J., FOX, M. and MURPHY, J., *Health Care Law: Text and Materials* (1997).
MASON, J. K. and McCALL SMITH, R. A., *Law and Medical Ethics* (4th edn., 1994).
MONTGOMERY, J., *Health Care Law* (1997).
MORGAN, D. and LEE, R., *Blackstone's Guide to the Human Fertilisation and Embryology Act 1990* (1991).
NEWDICK, C., *Who Should We Treat?: Law, Patients and Resources in the NHS* (1995).
OTLOWSKI, M., *Voluntary Euthanasia and the Common Law* (1997).
SKEGG, P. D. G., *Law, Ethics and Medicine* (1988, paperback edn.).

Comparative Material

COLLINS, D. B., *Medical Law in New Zealand* (1992).
FURROW, B. R., GREANEY, T. L., JOHNSON, S. H., JOST, T. S. and SCHWARTZ, R. L., *Health Law* (2 vols.) (1995).
GIESEN, D., *International Medical Malpractice Law* (1988).
International Encyclopaedia of Laws (ed.) Blanpain, R.; *Medical Law* (2 vols.), (ed.) Nys, H. (1993).
OLIPHANT, K., 'Defining "Medical Misadventure": Lessons from New Zealand' (1996) 4 *Med. L. Rev.* 1.

PICARD, E. and ROBERTSON, G., *Legal Liability of Doctors and Hospitals in Canada* (3rd edn., 1996).

SKENE, L., *Law and Medical Practice* (1998).

2 ROAD-TRAFFIC ACCIDENTS

Liability for road-traffic accidents is at present governed by the principles of negligence. For reasons that will appear, negligence in fact works much more strictly here than in other areas, so much so that in many instances it has become artificial to continue calling it by that name. The historical development of liability for road-traffic accidents has moved from an early regime of (probably) strict liability to one based on fault, and is now swinging back, *de facto* if not *de iure*, towards increasing strictness. The way ahead points in a new direction, namely some form of automatic compensation through a system of social or private insurance, with the law of tort playing at most a subordinate role. Such a move should be doubly welcomed. For not only would it benefit many innocent victims of contemporary technology, it would also free our overworked courts of a substantial number of disputes which depend on them for their resolution.

Until the last century actions in respect of road injuries, which in the nature of things were nearly always directly inflicted, lay in trespass. Liability was strict *in the sense that plaintiffs were not required to establish fault as an ingredient of a prima-facie case*; and, probably, juries acquitted defendants whom they did not regard as negligent. Then, in the course of the nineteenth century, there grew up a rule, at first confined to highway accidents, that even if a plaintiff sued in trespass he had to prove fault.[407] There may have been two reasons for this development. One could have been the increase in road accidents, which were reaching the courts in the form of suits for compensation. Proof of fault may thus have been demanded as a part of a prima-facie case in trespass in order to stem litigation by discouraging plaintiffs from bringing suits in view of the heavier burden of proof. A more philosophical reason was, perhaps, the general swing towards fault, which some judges saw as being in keeping with the individualism of that era: no one should be deprived of his wealth and substance unless he had been to blame. That this trend ran counter to another trend found at the same time in other areas of tort law (e.g. nuisance, *Rylands* v. *Fletcher*) does not seem to have been noticed or, at least, to have concerned unduly the lawyers of the time.

Then a new development began to alter the position radically. The severity of a good many injuries sustained by victims of road accidents called in some instances for heavy damages if they were to be in any sense commensurate with the harm caused; but not every defendant was financially in a position to pay them. The solution lay in insurance. For plaintiffs thus received their

---

[407] E.g. *Holmes* v. *Mather* (1875) 33 LT 361, 363. This version of Bramwell B's judgment confines the need to prove fault to highway cases. Cf. (1875) LR 10 Ex. 261, 268, where his remarks as reported apply generally to trespass to the person. See Landon in *Pollock on Torts* (15th edn.), 132.

compensation while the financial burden was taken off the shoulders of defendants by insurance companies whose resources, coming as they did from a large section of the community, ensured that the cost of damages was spread as painlessly as possible throughout society. Motor insurance eventually became commonplace, and insurance by motorists against third-party liability was finally made compulsory by the Road Traffic Act 1930.[408] One result of the growth of insurance was the removal of any inhibition that might have existed against awarding damages that, if they had to be borne by impecunious defendants, might prove crushing to them. Another result was that it gave an indirect boost to other endeavours to try to improve standards of careful behaviour on the roads so as to reduce, if not halt, the mounting toll of deaths and injuries each year. For it is obvious that insurance companies, in their own interest, like to ensure that care will be taken by motorists and will not grant insurance cover unless there is some assurance of this. Further, the possible loss of no-claim bonuses and increased premiums provide, to some extent, an inducement to motorists to take care. Insurance companies have also played a prominent part in promoting and supporting safety schemes. Despite the above, the 'deterrence' value of insurance has overall been low in this part of the law of torts; and despite fluctuations in the figures, the accident rate remains depressingly high. The Report of the Royal Commission, *On Civil Liability and Compensation for Personal Injury* (the Pearson Report), stated that in the mid-1970s 'each year about 7,600 people [were] killed and some 400,000 [were] injured in road accidents in the United Kingdom'.[409]

Leaving aside a certain toughening in the criminal law and regulations relevant to the circulation of motor vehicles, the law's reaction to this problem has hitherto been twofold. On the one hand, there has been a tendency to tighten up the principles of common law in certain respects and, on the other, to impose strict liability. Yet, as Professor Spencer (and others) have shown, repeated 'opportunities' to move away from the notion of fault were sadly lost. Our law of traffic accidents is thus still nominally based on negligence, though in practice it often comes very close to strict liability. A notable sign of this trend can be found in the fact that observance of, or failure to observe, the Highway Code is only evidence tending to establish or negative liability.[410] But—and this is the significant point—compliance with the Code does not *per se* absolve a person from negligence.[411]

The objective approach of the courts is also evident in the fact that no account is taken of the 'personal equation' in respect of the weaknesses of particular individuals, except where these were known or should have been

[408] Extended to cover liability towards voluntary passengers in 1971; Motor Vehicles (Passenger Insurance) Act 1971, s. 1, and in 1988 to cover liability in respect to a third party's property. All the relevant provisions can be found in Part 4 of the Road Traffic Act 1988. Exempt from the requirement to insure are the Crown, local, and police authorities.

[409] Cmnd. 7054–1, p. 205. The number of deaths has fallen since the 1970s to 5,400 killed (in 1989) and some 340,000 injured. Of those killed and injured 32% were car drivers, 22% were pedestrians. The decrease in numbers is more attributable to the combined effect of criminal law and regulations (e.g. seat-belts, etc.) than to the effectiveness of tort law.

[410] Road Traffic Act 1972, s. 37(5); *Hoadley* v. *Dartford District Council* [1979] RTR 359.

[411] *White* v. *Broadbent and British Road Services* [1958] Crim. LR 129.

known. Indeed, in road-traffic cases the law appears to go further: not only does it take no account of individual frailty, but it also takes no account of human frailty generally. Modern road conditions add to the problems besetting motorists. For instance, driving at night in town confronts them with an unending kaleidoscope of flashing lights from shops, advertisements, and road signs that is bewildering and makes it difficult if not impossible to distinguish quickly between beacons and road signs and others. Route signs are now complex and tend to be overloaded so that, in trying to pick out the route he wants, the driver's concentration is taken away from driving, which can be highly dangerous on fast roads. Should an error, often unavoidable and induced by circumstances such as these, result in disaster, it will be accounted negligent. For, once the error has been isolated for legal purposes as being 'the cause', the objective approach requires us to say that the mythical 'reasonable man' would not have made that particular error. Momentary inattention and distractions are not morally blameworthy, but the point is that in this area the law has chosen not to distinguish between 'error' and 'fault'. To err is certainly human, but traffic law is far from divine, and it makes little sense to ask it to forgive.

Examples were given in the last chapter of the stern attitude now taken by the common law. Thus, no concession was made to the motorist whose reactions had become clouded after an unsuspected cerebral haemorrhage,[412] nor to the omnibus driver who had to adhere to a time schedule along the route as well as take heed of the congested state of the traffic,[413] nor to an inexperienced learner-driver.[414] A van, which was waiting to emerge from a drive, was signalled on by a lorry driver who had halted for him. The van driver emerged slowly and collided with a motor cyclist, who was overtaking the lorry. Both were held to have been negligent.[415] In another case the onus of rebutting a presumption of negligence was viewed so stringently as to impose liability on the owners of a lorry, who did not know and, indeed, could not reasonably have known, of the defect that led to the collision.[416] The doctrine of the vicarious liability of an employer for the tort of his employee has been stretched to impose liability on one who lent his car to another, who was not an employee, to use for some purpose of the lender.[417] Vicarious liability was itself bypassed in a case where the owner, in breach of his statutory duty, did not have third-party insurance cover, and he was held liable to a person injured by a third party who was driving the car.[418] The court did not argue on the principles of vicarious liability, but based liability instead on breach of statutory duty in that the purpose of the third-party insurance was the protection of the public. The case is significant in that it marks one of the earliest manifestations of the

---

[412] *Roberts* v. *Ramsbottom* [1980] 1 WLR 823; *Broom* v. *Perkins* [1988] RTR 321.

[413] *Daly* v. *Liverpool Corporation* [1939] 2 All ER 142.   [414] *Nettleship* v. *Weston* [1971] 2 QB 691.

[415] *Lesson* v. *Bevis & Tolchard Ltd. and Another* [1972] RTR 373. See also *Clarke* v. *Winchurch* [1969] 1 WLR 69; *Garstang Warehousing Co. Ltd.* v. *O. F. Smart (Liverpool) Ltd.* [1973] RTR 377; *Worsfold* v. *Howe* [1980] 1 WLR 1175.

[416] *Henderson* v. *H. E. Jenkins & Sons* [1970] AC 282.

[417] *Morgans* v. *Launchbury* [1973] AC 127 (on the facts there was no liability since the driver was not using the car for the owner's purposes). Of greater interest is the conclusion of the Court of Appeal [1971] 2 QB 245, in which Lord Denning MR sought to impose liability on the party insured.

[418] *Monk* v. *Warbey* [1935] 1 KB 75; and see Goddard LJ in *Tattersall* v. *Drysdale* [1935] 2 KB 174, 181.

'purpose of the rule' basis of liability. In all the above examples it is obvious that insurance cushioned the effect of the decisions against defendants, and it is tempting to suppose that the fact of insurance may have unobtrusively influenced the interpretation of the law and helped to move it towards something akin to strict liability.

Collisions between motor vehicles involve their respective insurance companies. A considerable number of traffic accidents, however, involve pedestrians, who are not as a rule insured. The usual danger-point of contact between them and vehicles is at pedestrian crossings, which are now governed by special regulations.[419] Liability for breach of these has been interpreted more severely against motorists.[420] For example, in one case the Court of Appeal refused to treat a breach of the Highway Code by a pedestrian as creating a presumption of negligence on his part.[421] In another case the same court held that a pedestrian was not obliged to cross a road only at pedestrian crossings, but may cross at whatever point he chooses provided he takes reasonable care.[422]

Despite the tightening of the principles of common-law negligence, the entire fault basis of liability in this area is open to criticism.[423] If a motorist is not at fault, there is no remedy against him or his insurance company. In a case where a motorist, through no fault of his, ran down a child cyclist, the House of Lords was compelled to refuse damages to the plaintiff, but Lord Wilberforce uttered a call for some scheme of compensation not based on proof of fault in such cases.[424] Process by way of action at law is itself open to serious objections on the grounds that it is slow, costly, and capricious. As for slowness, the congestion of work in courts leads to inordinate delay, while even settlements out of court take considerable time. It is estimated that barely half the number of claimants are paid within the first year and some 5–10 per cent of such claimants will still not have been compensated five years after the accident. It is costly, since litigation costs and insurance overheads represent a substantial percentage of the total sums available for compensation. The system also works capriciously, so that some have referred to it as the forensic lottery. Proof of fault depends on evidence, and when this has to rest on the testimony of witnesses it is often hard to procure. Human memory becomes blurred especially when the trial comes on long after the event. Of the parties involved, a victim who has been seriously hurt is probably not in a condition to remember much, especially if he was concussed. The evidence of the party inflicting the injury, even if he remembers, is likely to be self-serving. In addition to the difficulty of establishing the facts, there is the uncertainty surrounding the interpretation and application of the law. With regard to the compensation awarded to vic-

---

[419] 'Zebra' Pedestrian Crossing Regulations 1971.

[420] *Kozimore* v. *Adey* (1962) 106 SJ 431; *LPTB* v. *Upson* [1949] AC 155.

[421] *Powell* v. *Phillips* (1972) 3 All ER 864. See also the earlier cases *Knight* v. *Sampson* [1938] 3 All ER 309; *Chisholm* v. *LPTB* [1939] 1 KB 426; *Wilkinson* v. *Chetham-Strode* [1940] 2 KB 310; *Sparks* v. *Ash* [1943] KB 223; *LPTB* v. *Upson*, preceding note.

[422] *Tremayne* v. *Hill* [1987] RTR 131.

[423] Part II of the Report of the Lord Chancellor's Department mentioned in the Select Bibliography contains an excellent summary of the shortfalls of the current tort system.

[424] *Snelling* v. *Whitehead*, *The Times*, 31 July 1975. See also Atiyah et al., (below, Select Bibliography).

tims, there is a great deal to be desired. For not only are substantial numbers of persons injured without tort rights, but also those who do have rights will often see their awards reduced, sometimes considerably, so as to take into account contributory negligence. Moreover, it has to be remembered that courts are called upon to do the impossible, namely to estimate in money what crippling injuries with all their attendant consequences are worth. Some measure of uniformity in the amounts awarded is secured by the evolution of 'conventional sums' for certain types of injuries, but these are wholly arbitrary.

An argument in favour of retaining the fault basis of liability is that if people are found liable on proof of carelessness, this acts as an inducement to act carefully; in other words, that the fault principle helps to maintain, and, if possible, improve standards. This argument loses force when it is realised that the vast majority of accidents are not due to 'fault', but to errors, which fallible human beings cannot avoid however carefully they may be temperamentally. For example, a study conducted by the World Health Organization in 1962 revealed that on average even a good driver makes a mistake every two miles of driving, while a comparable American study commissioned by the Department of Transportation and published in 1970 showed that in the United States the average good driver commits about nine violations (of the criminal law concerning traffic circulation) for every five minutes of driving. Further, the existence of insurance undermines the basis of the argument, for even if a party is proved to have been at fault, it is not he who pays but his insurance company. The resulting position is somewhat paradoxical. Drivers of vehicles, whose activities are more likely to do damage because of the lethal propensities of the machines they operate, suffer less personal-liability loss through their lapses. Pedestrians, on the other hand, who are more likely to suffer injury,[425] tend to be under-protected in respect of their lapses unless they happen to be insured, which is unusual; and as stated, contributory negligence may further reduce their damages. It may well be that the only effective deterrence on motorists is likely to be fear of injury to themselves, coupled with the fear of criminal sanctions, and to a much lesser extent, the fear that they may lose their no-claim bonuses.

Empirical research on the effects of introducing no-fault compensation systems for road traffic accidents has not been able to show conclusively whether the abolition of fault has any impact on accident levels. In part this is because it is difficult if not impossible to disentangle the effects of changes in the law from the impact of insurance. Nevertheless, a number of studies suggest that the introduction of no-fault schemes in Australia, New Zealand and certain North American jurisdictions was accompanied by increases in road traffic fatalities. The impact of no-fault compensation may therefore depend upon whether the insurance system offers effective financial penalties for careless driving: 'the empirical evidence does indicate that without added financial

---

[425] Child pedestrians, for example (aged 10–14) are more than twice as likely to be killed or injured as adults. The law may be adding insult to injury whenever in such cases it allows such a child's contributory negligence to reduce the insurer's liability.

deterrence incentives, no-fault schemes are likely to lead to increased accident rates, injuries and fatalities'.[426]

Another objection to the use of traditional concepts in this area is the legal approach to causation.[427] Traffic accidents are the result of a multiplicity of causes rather than one person's fault. There are, for instance, skid-prone roads, and others have defects of various kinds not detectable by approaching motorists; there are faults in vehicle design, for example protruding wing-mirrors. Many cars have the controls for indicator lights, headlights, and wind-screen-wipers set close together on the steering column. In switching on the windscreen wiper, for instance, drivers occasionally knock the indicator lights at the same time, thus conveying a dangerously misleading idea of their intentions to other road-users.

The scale of traffic accidents is now more or less a fact of social life and this is shown by innumerable statistical surveys. Given that motor vehicles have come to stay, putting these far-from-perfect and potentially lethal machines in the hands of fallible handlers gives rise to a fairly predictable accident rate, which has to be accepted as unavoidable. That being the case, it appears artificial and inappropriate to continue trying to dig out means of redress from the ragbag of negligence. It is time that alternative methods were evolved.

1. Motor Insurers Bureau

One difficulty, which cannot be met by the law of negligence or through normal insurance, is how to compensate victims of uninsured drivers, or drivers who are insured but whose insurers are not liable for some reason, or untraceable drivers. Some remedy for such victims has been found through the Motor Insurers Bureau, which was set up originally by an agreement between the Minister of Transport and the motor industry on 17 June 1946. It is a limited liability company, whose members are all insurance companies engaged in road-traffic insurance in Great Britain. Section 20 of the Road Traffic Act 1974 requires all authorised insurers to become members of the MIB. The current position is regulated by three agreements with the Minister of State, the Untraced Drivers' Agreements of 1972 and 1977 and the Uninsured Drivers' Agreement 1988, by which the Bureau agrees to meet any unsatisfied judgment with regard to liability requiring insurance under the Road Traffic Act.

The basis of a claim by the victim of a road accident against the Bureau is not based on any specific statute. The Bureau's liability arises out of its agreements with the minister, and the principle of privity of contract prevents the victim, who is a third party, from enforcing it. The minister could presumably get an order for specific performance against the Bureau to force it to fulfil its undertaking; or even a declaration might be obtained from the court; but the theoretical difficulty is unreal, since it is unthinkable that the Bureau would ever repudiate its undertaking.[428]

---

[426] D. Dewees, D. Duff and M. Trebilock, *Exploring the Domain of Accident Law* (1996) (Select Bibliography), 26.

[427] See above.

[428] Just as the Crown, prior to 1947, never refused to pay if a Crown servant was held liable. The Crown Proceedings Act 1947 has made the Crown liable (subject to a few exceptions). In 1989 the MIB received some 15,000 applications and paid out over £28 million in compensation.

There are different situations in which the MIB can be called upon to pay.

There is, *first*, the case of an identified, but uninsured, motorist, who is legally responsible for the injury. The MIB acts like an ordinary insurance company. It has to be informed of proceedings within seven days of their commencement, and it will then negotiate with the victim just as an ordinary insurance company would. Failing settlement, the Bureau will defend the action on behalf of the uninsured defendant.

Secondly, there is the identified, insured motorist, whose insurance company is not liable for some reason, for example because the policy had been obtained by fraud or misrepresentation, or where there has been a breach of a condition by the insured. Under a 'Domestic Agreement' between the MIB and its members, the Bureau will proceed to deal with the matter as though the policy were valid; which makes the invalidation of the policy through fraud, misrepresentation, or breach of condition irrelevant as far as the victim is concerned. An interesting case is *Gurtner* v. *Circuit and Another*[429] where the plaintiff was injured by an insured motorist, who subsequently emigrated and could not be discovered. The police had no record of his insurer, who could not be discovered either. The MIB applied to court to be joined as a party to the action, and the Court of Appeal allowed this to be done because the Bureau was regarded as having a sufficient interest in the case to be made a party by virtue of its agreement with the minister.

Thirdly, there is the unidentified motorist, the commonest example being the hit-and-run motorist. At first the Bureau used to make *ex gratia* payments, but such a position was clearly unsatisfactory.[430] Now, however, as the result of a further agreement with the minister, the Bureau has undertaken liability and acts like an ordinary insurer. It will accordingly inquire into a claim by a victim, and, if satisfied that the circumstances of the case are those in which insurance is compulsory under the Road Traffic Act, it will offer compensation. If the victim considers the offer to be inadequate, he may appeal to an arbitrator appointed by the Bureau from a panel of Queen's Counsel, whose fee will be paid by the Bureau. But the victim is required to authorise the arbitrator to order him to pay all or part of the fee if there is no ground for appealing. Since the 1977 Un-traced Drivers' Agreement, a simpler and less formal procedure has been introduced for applications estimated as being less than £50,000.

There are several limits to the liability of the Bureau. It is not liable if the circumstances of the case do not require compulsory insurance. Nor is it liable if the victim was not injured through negligence. A modification of this, however, is to be found in *Gardner* v. *Moore and Another*,[431] where the first defendant deliberately drove his car at the plaintiff and inflicted criminal injury on him. He was uninsured at the time. The House of Lords held the MIB liable to the plaintiff, since the first defendant's liability would have been for injury 'caused by, or arising out of, the use of his car', even though such use had been to inflict wilful injury. Also, the rule that a person cannot benefit from his own

---

[429] [1968] 2 QB 587.
[430] Criticized in *Adams* v. *Andrews* [1964] 2 Lloyd's Rep. 347, and the Justice Report 1966, App. 3.
[431] [1984] AC 548.

wrongdoing does not avail against an innocent third party. There is no liability in respect of damage to property, and no liability even for personal injury if this does not occur on a public road. In *Randall* v. *MIB*[432] the plaintiff was injured by a lorry at a moment when only the front of it was on a public road, and it was held that he could recover from the Bureau. The Bureau is also not liable for injury to a person who is not the owner of the vehicle involved but who happens to be driving it, even though his injury is attributable to the fault of the owner. In *Cooper* v. *MIB*[433] the owner of a motor cycle did not have an insurance policy covering 'third-party risks' as required by section 143(1) of the Road Traffic Act 1972. He asked the plaintiff to test the vehicle for him, but failed to warn that the brakes were defective. The plaintiff was injured because of the faulty brakes and obtained judgment for negligence against the owner, who was unable to satisfy it. The Court of Appeal held that the Bureau was not liable here because section 143(1) obliges an owner to insure against the risk of death or injury to third parties from the use of a vehicle by himself or anyone else. But 'third-party risks' does not cover injury to the driver of the vehicle.

2. Alternatives to Fault-Based Liability

Apart from the above, the unsatisfactory results of applying the ordinary law of negligence to traffic accidents have led to experiments in various countries to find workable alternatives. Since the present work deals mainly with the law as it exists in this country, it is not proposed to discuss these others in detail, but only to outline the developments in order to indicate possible lines of future reform.[434]

One line of development is the imposition of a regime of strict liability (coupled with compulsory insurance) as adopted in various forms in several Continental countries. This gets rid of the difficulties and vagaries of proving fault, but is attended by problems of its own. One is the question of on whom such liability is to be imposed: should it be the driver, or the 'controller' of the vehicle? Further questions then arise as to who is to be regarded as a 'controller', whether this is the owner, possessor, or custodian, and in what way vicarious liability fits into all this. Again, there is the question of what 'strict liability' means in this context, which is another way of asking what escapes from liability are available and to what extent these are to be allowed. Liability may be strict in the sense of the reversal of the onus of proof, that is, it is for the defendant to show absence of fault in himself. Alternatively, liability may be truly strict and subject only to the defences of act of God, act of plaintiff, or act of third party.

Different systems have admitted some of these excuses, but not others. How far any excuse should be admitted depends on the philosophy underlying liability. On the 'creation of risk' theory, for example, which regards motoring as creating a risk against which the public needs to be protected, it is arguable that act of third party should not be a defence. Perhaps the same should be said

---

[432] [1968] 1 WLR 1900.   [433] [1985] QB 575.

[434] For a comparative survey, see A. Tunc, (below, Select Bibliography), ch. 14. Current proposals about the future of English law will be discussed in the next subsection.

of certain forms of act of God, for example, ice on roads. A fairly common defence is that the owner or person on whom liability is cast is not liable for damage done by a person who steals his vehicle, or drives it against his will, save where he was negligent in allowing either situation to occur. Difficulties will always remain in interpreting the facts in all these cases. Some countries distinguish between vehicles driven by unauthorised drivers, in which case the owners remain liable, as distinct from stolen vehicles, in which case they are exempt. There is yet a further modification of strict liability in cases of collision between vehicles. Each party has created a risk by the mere fact of driving. Practice varies, but the favoured situation, which is also the simplest, seems to be to make each owner or driver liable for the damage inflicted by his vehicle. Apart from possible modifications of the strict principle, there is the wholly different question of the persons for whose benefit such liability exists. For instance, should all passengers be treated alike, or should gratuitous passengers be placed in a less favourable position than those who are in public vehicles? In between these categories there is the passenger in a private vehicle who, for example, contributes towards the cost of petrol. There are further questions as to the kind of damage that is to be covered by strict liability. On the whole, the position seems to be that damage to property is compensated less well than personal injuries and, with regard to the latter, pain and suffering is compensated to a lesser extent than physical injuries.

The most important development and the one that has attracted wide attention is a system of automatic compensation. This kind of proposal is by no means new, and can come in various forms. Of these the less radical, and the one generally favoured by the legal profession (which makes its living largely out of this type of litigation), preserves the tort system intact and merely aims at remedying the financial losses of victims of minor injuries on a no-fault basis. The satisfaction of such victims in practice discourages them from facing the vagaries of litigation. Since these minor-injury claims are a significant percentage of the total number of traffic accidents, the saving achieved from non-litigation may thus offset the cost of this automatic coverage. These 'add-on' plans, as they are known in the United States, were first pioneered in Canada and require special agencies to administer the funds raised by the usual third-party insurance premiums.

A more radical method of compensation is to provide for automatic payment of certain benefits up to a specified amount and to exclude tort remedies for that amount against the insurers of the car that caused the accident. At the same time, however, one would preserve tort remedies in respect of claims exceeding the threshold. Steps in this latter direction were taken in Great Britain in the sphere of industrial injuries by the old Workmen's Compensation Acts. These have been widened by later legislation, which provides automatic benefit up to specified *maxima* in respect of injury, disablement, or death.[435] The ordinary law of torts remains available to a person who seeks damages over and above the statutory compensation. Similar schemes for compensating

---

[435] National Insurance (Industrial Injuries) Acts 1946–65; Social Security Act 1975 and Social Security (Consequential Provisions) Act 1975; Social Security Benefits and Contributions Act 1992, Part V.

victims of traffic accidents have been put forward in other countries,[436] but the most far-reaching practical implementation of such a scheme came in New Zealand in 1972. Under this, the compensation for traffic victims figures as part of a comprehensive scheme of social insurance in cases of personal injuries and death. Significantly, actions in tort for these were abolished.[437] However, this system was substantially modified, and the tort system largely restored, by the Accident Rehabilitation and Compensation Insurance Act 1992.

Following this example and in response to considerable pressure,[438] a Royal Commission was set up in 1974 under the chairmanship of Lord Pearson to report on the feasibility of introducing a comparable scheme in Britain. The terms of reference were confined to death or personal injury (not damage to property) suffered by a person through, *inter alia*, 'the use of a motor vehicle or other means of transport'. The report, entitled *On Civil Liability and Compensation for Personal Injury*, was published in April 1978. An overall feature of it was that, unlike the New Zealand scheme, it did not recommend the abolition of the law of tort. Naturally, the Report contained a section on road-traffic accidents; and a summary of the type of 'no-fault' scheme it proposed was described in the second edition of this book. Those proposals, however (as, indeed, with most of the recommendations contained in the Report), have been ignored and now seem unlikely to be implemented. In any event, as far as traffic accidents are concerned, the current official thinking is more accurately reflected in a report prepared by an *ad hoc* Committee set up by the Lord Chancellor's Department. Its report, published in 1991, repays careful reading. What follows is, inevitably, merely a summary of some of its ideas, provided simply in order to make law students aware of the type of problems encountered by reforms in this area of the law.

3. Recent Thinking on Law Reform

The immediate reasons for the current proposals contained in the 1991 Report are as much concerned with the improvement of the position of victims of traffic accidents as they are with the decrease of the number of cases that have to be tried by our overworked judges. In this sense the 1988 Civil Justice Review provided a much-needed impetus to do something about our current law on the subject.

The new proposals differ from the Pearson proposals in two key respects: first in their financing (the scheme would be financed by private insurers), and secondly, in their ambit (the proposed no-fault scheme would be limited to the

[436] See particularly Keeton and O'Connell, (below, Select Bibliography); Report by the Committee to Study Compensation for Automobile Accidents to the Columbia University Council for Research in the Social Sciences (the Columbia Plan, 1932); Ehrenzweig, (below, Select Bibliography). The Columbia Plan inspired the Automobile Act 1946 of Saskatchewan, which provides (a) loss insurance for personal injuries and damage to vehicle, and (b) liability insurance to cover liability at common law for damages paid over and above what a plaintiff recovers under (a).

[437] Accident Compensation Act 1972 and Accident Compensation Amendment (No. 2) Act 1973, consolidated in the Accident Compensation Act 1982. These were the result of the Report of the Royal Commission, Compensation for Personal Injury in New Zealand, under the chairmanship of Arthur Owen Woodhouse (the Woodhouse Report, 1967).

[438] Especially Atiyah et al., op. cit. (Select Bibliography).

less serious traffic injuries—claims of less than £2,500). The reason behind this limitation was to avoid a sudden and substantial increase in premiums that might follow if the scheme were to be applied to all accidents. It was estimated that the proposed changes might provoke a modest increase in insurance premiums (about 5–7 per cent); but they would also 'take out' of the courts a substantial number of all claims that are currently litigated before judges.

The proposed scheme would cover personal injury leading to claims of over £250 but below £2,500 and arising from accidents involving motor vehicles. Not covered by the scheme would be injured cyclists and injured pedestrians where no motor vehicle was involved. The scheme would cover accidents occurring on 'any highway or any other road to which the public had access'. By recommending this phraseology (which, in fact, is the one adopted by the Road Traffic Act 1985) instead of a wider one (e.g. accidents on 'roads or other public places') the scheme would thus *not* cover accidents occurring, for example, on public car-parks or private land to which the public has no right of access.

A difficult question that had to be addressed by the Lord Chancellor's Committee was the following. What connection should there be between the harm suffered for which compensation is to be paid and the motor vehicle in question? Two tests had to be considered. The first would make liability depend on injury caused by, or arising out of the *use* of the vehicle; the second would link the claim of compensation to the 'presence' or 'involvement' of a vehicle. The Committee preferred the first test (use of a vehicle); and this would cover the vast majority of cases (and such less usual cases as a cyclist running into a 'negligently' parked car or swerving to avoid a moving car and injuring himself *without making contact with the said car*). But the (narrower) proposed test would not cover the case of the cyclist who ran into a *properly* parked car or swerved to avoid such a *properly* parked car. The rejection of the second (wider) test (or tests) must be explained partly because of the definitional difficulties that might accompany the words 'presence' or 'involvement' of a vehicle, but mainly because of the wish to keep the new scheme under control and avoid the excessive increase of premiums. Similar considerations led the Committee to propose that the new scheme be limited to cases of personal injury and *not* to cover property damage.

Financial considerations also led the Committee to leave 'open' the question 'who might be allowed to claim from whom?' Once again, there existed two possibilities. The most comprehensive and expensive one would involve introducing a 'first-party' scheme. This would mean that every car policy would provide compulsory first-party insurance for the owner of the vehicle, any authorised driver, any passenger travelling in the car, and any other person who suffers an injury caused by or arising out of the use of the vehicle. It would *not* cover drivers of other vehicles. The less radical and less costly alternative would be to opt for a 'third-party scheme' which would extend the present third-party liability to cover the risk of causing injury to third parties injured by the use of the vehicle regardless of the driver's fault. Such a scheme would not cover drivers injured in an accident in which no other vehicle was involved (e.g.

the case of a car that runs into a brick wall and injures the driver/passengers). As stated, the Committee refused to take a stand on this point; but if 'economy' is an important factor in making this scheme acceptable to the government, the general public, and insurers, the chances are that the first option will be taken.

Two further issues considered by the Committee must be mentioned, albeit briefly.

First, what relationship should there be between awards made under the scheme and claims for civil damages? Again various possibilities were considered. The more sensible situation, however, would seem to be the following. In serious-injury cases (involving claims in excess of £2,500) the idea is that the claimant should be allowed to make his full no-fault claim and then pursue, if he so wishes, an additional civil claim in negligence. In less serious cases (i.e. involving claims below the £2,500 upper limit) the claimant's *tort* claim ought to be effectively restricted or removed so as to 'force' claimants to use the new scheme and avoid court congestion.

The last major point that confronted the Committee was whether certain types of conduct on the part of the plaintiff/claimant should deprive him of the chance of making a claim under the scheme. What type of conduct should entail such consequences? Criminal misconduct? Drink-drive offences? Self-inflicted injuries? Contributory negligence on the part of the claimant? How many of these types of conduct should justify exclusion from the scheme depends on a combination of 'moral' and 'economic' considerations. All that can be said here is that if the wish to take most of these cases out of the courts is real, then the list of 'excluding types of conduct' should be kept to a minimum or, arguably, even totally omitted. But like so many other areas of traffic-accident law this is an area on which there seems to be little agreement.

Select Bibliography

ATIYAH, P. S., *Accidents, Compensation and the Law* (5th edn. by P. Cane, 1993).

—— et al., 'Compensation for Personal Injuries' (1969) 119 *New LJ* 653.

BLUM, W. J. and KALVEN, H., *Public Law Perspective on a Private Law Problem—Auto Compensation Plans* (1965).

—— —— 'The Empty Cabinet of Dr. Calabresi, Auto Accidents and General Deterrence' 34 *UCLR* 239 (1967).

CALABRESI, G., 'The Decision for Accidents: An Approach to Non-fault Allocation of Costs', 78 *Harv. LR* 713 (1965).

—— 'Fault, Accidents and the Wonderful World of Blum and Kalven' 75 *Yale LJ* 216 (1965).

CONRAD, A. F., et al. *Automobile Accident Costs and Payments* (1964).

DEWEES, D., DUFF, D. and TREBILCOCK, M. *Exploring the Domain of Accident Law* (1996), ch. 2.

EHRENZWEIG, A. A. ' "Full Aid" Insurance for the Traffic Victim—A Voluntary Compensation Plan', 43 *Cal. LR* 1 (1955).

ELLIOTT, D. W. and STREET, H. *Road Accidents, Law and Society* (1968).

KEETON, R. E. and O'CONNELL J., *Basic Protection for the Traffic Victim: A Blueprint for Reforming Automobile Insurance* (1965).

Lord Chancellor's Department, *Compensation for Road Accidents: A Consultation Paper* (1991).

Report of the Royal Commission, *Compensation for Personal Injury in New Zealand* (Woodhouse Report 1967).

—— *On Civil Liability and Compensation for Personal Injury* (Pearson Committee Report) (Cmnd. 7504–1, 1978), ch. 18.

SPENCER, J. R., 'Motor-cars and the Rule in *Rylands* v. *Fletcher*. A Chapter of Accidents in the History of Law and Motoring' [1983] *CLJ* 65.

TUNC, A., 'Traffic Accident Compensation: Law and Proposals', in *Int. Encl. Comp. L.*, Vol. xi. ch. 14.

3. LIABILITY OF OCCUPIERS AND BUILDERS

1. Introductory Remarks

Until fairly recently the liability of occupiers towards persons injured whilst on premises was subject to a special regime. Today the occupier's liability is, essentially, the law of negligence in statutory form that has materialised in the shape of successive legislative accretions. This means that prime importance must be attached to the wording of the statutes; and in some respects their interrelationship must also be considered. But the common law has not entirely disappeared. On the contrary, its continued vitality is assumed by the Acts. The diversity of the sources of this part of the law, as much as custom and convenience, may thus still justify its treatment under a separate heading.

The law discussed in this subsection regulates the liability of an occupier of *premises*[439] towards persons *on* the premises and not to those outside them. Liability to the latter is often based on the common-law rules of negligence, but may also overlap with nuisance (private or public), which will be dealt with in Chapter 6.

The Occupiers' Liability Acts of 1957 and 1984 are at present the governing statutes though, as will be seen, the protection they afford is by no means identical. The philosophy of the common law, before it was reformed and (largely) rendered in statutory form, was the preservation of the freest use and enjoyment of land by the occupier—a cherished idea to the land-owning class in England during the period when these ideas were being developed.[440] This led to a gradation of standards of care varying with the status of a person coming on to the land (which depended upon the purpose of the visit) rather than with the nature of the land, the risks encountered on it, or the occupier's ability to obviate them. Thus, the occupier's standard of care was at its highest towards *contractors*, that is, those who entered under a contract. Liability was based on an implied warranty that the premises were fit for the purpose contemplated

---

[439] The word is given a very special and broad meaning by s. 1(3)(a) of the Occupiers' Liability Act 1957 so that it applies also to ladders, electricity pylons, grandstands or diving boards, lifts, aeroplanes, and so on.

[440] See F. Bohlen, *Studies in the Law of Torts* (1926), 46.

by the contract. The standard was less onerous towards *invitees*, that is, those who shared with the occupier a mutual interest of a business or material nature, for example, customers in a shop. Towards them an occupier had to 'use reasonable care to prevent damage from unusual danger, which he knew *or ought to have known'*.[441] Towards *licensees*—a misleading term since a friend *invited* to a meal is not an invitee but a licensee—the standard was lower still. These were persons with permission to enter premises for some purpose of their own, as distinct from a mutual interest, or, where there was a mutual interest, one which was not of a business or material nature. The occupier was only obliged to warn them of any concealed danger or trap of which he actually knew. Obviously the dividing line between liability to invitees and licensees was far from easy to draw. For the twin requirements of mutuality of interest and its business or material nature created permutations which tended to be ignored, while the distinction between 'unusual dangers' and 'traps' defied elucidation. Also, 'actual knowledge' of traps was often stretched to mean 'ought to have known', thus blurring still further the distinction between invitees and licensees.[442] Towards 'uninvited' persons (not covered by these three categories) the occupier used to owe no duty in negligence. Later developments in the common law[443] and the passing of the Occupiers' Liability Act 1984 have considerably improved the position of such 'uninvited' entrants.

These capricious distinctions, which produced unnecessary litigation, became increasingly untenable as the socio-economic environment changed. With the passage of time they became virtually meaningless as a result of fictions invented by the courts in order to bypass them, so in 1957 the legislature stepped in and removed many of the peculiarities of the old law. The 1984 Act has nearly completed this process. As stated, however, the changes have come in the form of successive waves and this accounts for a degree of complexity in the law which is unknown to systems that are outside the sphere of the common law.

2. The Occupiers' Liability Acts 1957 and 1984

(A) THE SCOPE OF THE ACTS

The drawback of the common law was that it fixed different standards of care *vis-à-vis* different types of visitors. With the passage of time and in order to avoid some of the unfairness thus created, judges began to distinguish between

---

[441] Per Willes J in *Indermaur* v. *Dames* (1866) LR 1 CP 274, 288. This increased protection is really the result of the mid-19th-century idea that only 'bargains' could give rise to duties of affirmative action. But Willes made it clear that the 'protection does not depend upon the fact of a contract being entered into . . .' (ibid., at 287–8); and Canadian cases have extended this higher protection to a young child accompanying its mother on a shopping expedition. *Kaplan* v. *Canada Safeway* (1968) 68 DLR (2d) 627.

[442] See e.g. Asquith LJ's interpretation of 'actual knowledge' in *Pearson* v. *Lambeth BC* [1950] 2 KB 353, 364. *Stowell* v. *The Railway Executive* [1949] 2 KB 519 shows how licensees were sometimes turned into invitees, and *Fairman* v. *Perpetual Investment Building Society* [1923] AC 74 illustrates the strange results that were created by these distinctions.

[443] *British Railways Board* v. *Herrington* [1972] AC 877. In the past uninvited entrants were frequently and indiscriminately referred to as trespassers but the implication that they were 'wrongdoers', undeserving of legal protection, was frequently not justified by the facts.

'occupancy duties' and 'activity duties'. The former, which concerned the state of the premises, were indeed graded in the way described above; but the latter were concerned with what an occupier did on his premises rather than their state or condition, and here the ordinary rules of negligence applied uniformly to entrants regardless of categories.[444] This distinction did not go far enough, so the first Occupiers' Liability Act 1957 (which according to section 1(3)(a) applies to premises and movable structures) rolled contractors, invitees, and licensees into a single category of 'lawful visitors' to whom an occupier now owes 'the common duty of care'.[445] Subsequently the 1984 Act provided further protection to entrants other than those covered by the 1957 Act.

One final point is that, in the words of Lord Gardiner LC in *Commissioner for Railways* v. *McDermott*,[446] 'occupation of premises is a ground of liability and is not a ground of exemption from liability'. This implies that there may be situations in which a plaintiff, suffering injury through the defective condition of premises controlled by the defendant, might recover for breach of a duty imposed on him in some capacity other than that of occupier.[447]

(B) OCCUPIER

There is no definition in either Act of who is an 'occupier'. As one learned judge put it, the word is only a convenient label for the kind of relationship which gives rise to a duty of care.[448] Like all labels, however, it must be treated with

---

[444] *Dunster* v. *Abbott* [1954] 1 WLR 58. See also *Riden* v. *A. C. Billings & Son Ltd.* [1957] 1 QB 46; affirmed [1958] AC 240. As some distinguished American tort lawyers have observed: 'Throughout the judicial consideration of these duties to trespassers, licensees, and invitees, the distinction between misfeasance and nonfeasance is recurrently drawn, and a duty of care is more readily found where defendant's conduct is viewed as involving dangerous activity than where it is looked on as a mere failure to take affirmative steps for plaintiff's protection.' Harper, James and Gray, *The Law of Torts* (2nd edn., 1986), v. 131.

[445] There has been some doubt whether this common duty of care replaced only the 'occupancy duty', or the 'activity duty' as well. The wording of s. 1(1) of the Act suggests the latter, whereas s. 1(2) suggests the former. The interpretation based on s. 1(2) (i.e. abolition of 'occupancy duty') should be preferred, for the Act was clearly meant to remove the subtle distinctions of the common law and it is clear that it deals with liability for dangers arising from the state of the premises, i.e. the occupancy duty. Activities remain unaffected, since in this instance there was no need for statutory intervention as the gradation between contractors, invitees, and licensees was never relevant. Dicta by Brown LJ in *Ogwo* v. *Taylor* [1988] 1 AC 431, 438, support this interpretation. So does the judgment of Lord Goff in *Ferguson* v. *Welsh* [1987] 1 WLR 1553, 1563 (though he reached this conclusion by interpreting the wording of s. 2(2) of the 1957 Act). In the same case, however, Lord Keith, relying on the same section, took the view that: 'The safety referred to [in this section] is safety not only from dangers due to the state of the premises but also known dangers due to things *done or omitted to be done* on them' (ibid. 1559, italics supplied). Despite this divergence of opinion, the difference between the two views may, in practice, not be that important since the standard of care at common law and under the Act is the same. The view propounded in the text was recently re-affirmed by Neill LJ in *Revill* v. *Newberry* [1996] 1 All ER 291, at 297–8, (though the pronouncements of the learned judge were in the context of the 1984 Act, discussed below) and *Fowles* v. *Bedfordshire CC* [1995] PIQR P380.

[446] [1967] 1 AC 169, 186.

[447] E.g. occupiers carrying out structural alterations to buildings may be additionally liable for failure to comply with s. 38 of the Building Act 1984 (not yet in force). Sometimes these statutory duties may be strict duties. See e.g. the Education Act 1944, s. 10 (as amended by Education (Miscellaneous Provisions) Act 1948, s. 7 and Education Act 1968, s. 3(3)) imposing on those in charge of schools a duty to keep them in good repair. *Reffell* v. *Surrey County Council* [1964] 1 WLR 358 held this to be an 'absolute' duty.

[448] *Wheat* v. *Lacon & Co. Ltd.* [1966] 1 QB 335, 366 per Diplock LJ (affirmed [1966] AC 552). The existing case law understandably refers to the 1957 Act. In this context, however, there is no difference between the 1957 and 1984 Acts.

caution. For example, a person may not be in 'occupation' as the word is understood in the law of property or landlord or tenant, but he may none the less be an 'occupier' for the purposes of one of the Acts. Nor is the owner of premises necessarily its 'occupier' under the Act. What is decisive is *control*, which can exist with or without complete physical possession of the premises. The absence of sufficient 'control' thus explains why a landlord is not liable under the Occupiers' Liability Act (though he may, as we shall note further down) be liable under the Defective Premises Act 1972. The same is true of a time charter[449] and, apparently, the chairman and secretary of a club.[450]

A detailed discussion of who is an occupier in this branch of the law can be found in *Wheat* v. *Lacon & Co. Ltd.*[451] The defendants, who owned a public house, entrusted it to a manager under a service agreement that required him, *inter alia*, to sell their drinks on the ground floor. The manager was granted a licence to live on the first floor and to take in paying guests. There was no direct access between the ground floor and the accommodation on the first floor and there were separate entrances to the two parts of the building. A paying guest of the manager was fatally injured while descending an unlit and defective staircase on the first floor. His widow sued and the main issue was who was in occupation of that part of the premises. On the construction of the agreement, the House of Lords held that there was nothing to prevent two or more persons from being occupiers of the same premises if they shared control. In such a case, each would come under the duty to lawful visitors depending on his degree of control.[452] In *Ferguson* v. *Welsh*[453] Lord Goff further suggested that if land is in the occupation of two (or more) persons, then an entrant could, in appropriate circumstances, be regarded as a lawful visitor *vis-à-vis* one occupier but not with regard to the other.

The possibility of joint occupation is well illustrated in *AMF International* v. *Magnet Bowling Ltd. and Another.*[454] Magnet Bowling, the first defendants, decided to build a number of bowling alleys. This was an expensive operation and it was agreed, *inter alia*, that AMF would retain property in all equipment and raw materials brought into any of these centres until the installation was completed. Magnet Bowling also instructed a firm of architects, the second defendants, to erect the buildings and agreed to send for AMF to build the alleys 'when the centre shall be ready to accept delivery of the said goods'. Following such notice AMF moved in, but its equipment was damaged by rainwater, which entered the building through an imperfectly completed doorway. Claims were made in contract (which is not relevant) and in tort. One issue was who should be treated as occupier of the premises. The court took the view that both defendants were occupiers, and that the standard of care owed by each depended on their respective degrees of control. The point that there can be

---

449 *Ellis* v. *Scruttons Maltby Ltd. and Cunard Steamship Co.* [1975] 1 Lloyd's Rep. 564.

450 *Robertson* v. *Ridley* [1989] 2 All ER 474. This case, however, poses a question which does not arise in the preceeding two illustrations, namely, if the 'officers' of a club are not 'in control' of its premises, who is?

451 [1966] AC 552, especially in Lord Denning's speech.

452 *Fisher* v. *CHT Ltd. (No. 2)* [1966] 2 QB 475 is a good illustration.   453 [1987] 1 WLR 1553, 1562–3.

454 [1968] 1 WLR 1028.

more than one occupier of premises is well settled, as is the rule that the degree of control will determine the level of care that will have to be attained by each occupier before the duty is deemed to have been discharged.[455]

Absentee ownership may not deprive the owner of 'control'. In *Harris* v. *Birkenhead Corporation*[456] the first defendants were a local authority carrying out a slum-clearance programme. Their practice was to brick up the ground-floor openings in all the houses they acquired so as to prevent vandals from entering and damaging the property. The house in question had been owned by the second defendant, managed for her by a reputable firm of estate agents, and occupied by a tenant, who kept it in a first-class condition. In July 1967 the local authority served on the second defendant a notice to treat and a notice of entry, but agreed to allow the tenant to remain until 23 December. The tenant left on the agreed date and within a few days the house became a prey to vandals. Before the local authority's employees entered the property the infant plaintiff entered through a smashed door, went to the top floor, and fell out of a broken window, sustaining brain injuries. The court distinguished *Wheat* v. *Lacon*[457] on the ground that in the present case no one was in physical occupation of the premises after the tenant's departure and refused to hold the first and second defendants as joint occupiers. Since the immediate supervision and control and the power to permit or prohibit entry had passed to the local authority, it alone was deemed to be the occupier even though it had not actually or symbolically taken possession of the house.[458]

One may summarise the law by saying that the decision in each case, therefore, as to who is an occupier depends on the particular facts, the nature and extent of the occupation, and the control exercised by the defendants over the premises in question.[459] Actual physical possession of the premises, however, may not always be necessary even though its presence tends to reinforce the existence of control.

(c) LAWFUL VISITOR UNDER THE 1957 ACT

According to section 1(2) of the Act the common duty of care is owed to 'lawful visitors' and also in respect of their property (s. 1(3)(b)). This section merely defines the *extent* of the occupier's duty, so one has to see if a particular entrant exercising a right would have been a 'contractor',[460] invitee, or licensee at

---

[455] For a more recent confirmation of the rule, see *Collier* v. *Anglian Water Authority, The Times*, 26 Mar. 1983. But a self-employed painter who, while employed by a contractor, fell off the roof of the building he was meant to paint could not sue the contractor *inter alia* under the 1957 Act since the latter did not 'occupy' the roof: *Page* v. *Read* (1984) 134 *New LJ* 723.

[456] [1975] 1 WLR 379. See also *Hawkins* v. *Coulsdon and Purley UDC* [1954] 1 QB 319 (requisitioning authority).

[457] [1966] AC 552. [458] For another example see *Clare* v. *L. Whittaker & Son (London) Ltd.* [1976] ICR 1.

[459] See also *Bunker* v. *Charles Brand & Sons Ltd.* [1969] 2 QB 480. This case, involving a tunnel-boring machine, illustrates the wide definition of 'premises' given by s. 1(3)(a) of the 1957 Act.

[460] A visitor entering premises pursuant to a contract is entitled to claim any higher protection that the contract may confer upon him. It is submitted, however, that the occupier's duty is, essentially, a tort duty and, therefore, the occupier should be allowed the defence of contributory negligence. This is certainly the case where the plaintiff pleads his case in tort: *Sole* v. *Hallt* [1973] QB 574; and, arguably, should be so irrespective of how the action is pleaded: *Sayers* v. *Harlow UDC* [1958] 1 WLR 623 and *Forsikringsaktieselskapet Vesta* v. *Butcher* [1989] AC 852 (affirmed by the House of Lords, ibid. 890 ff.).

common law and hence a lawful visitor. Persons entering, *as of right* are also lawful visitors even though the occupier may object to their presence (s. 2(6)). Examples include policemen entering premises in execution of a search warrant, firemen attending a fire, employees of public utilities (gas and electricity-board men entering to read meters), etc., properly pursuing their lawful duties.

Where entry is the result of an invitation or express provision, the question concerning the entrant's status is simple and the main problem is usually whether the requisite standard of care has been satisfied. However, an entrant may be a lawful visitor even if he has entered the premises on an implied permission, and this can present considerable difficulties. The implied licence test is not easy to apply in practice. In *Lowery* v. *Walker*[461] the defendant owned a plot of unfenced land, which members of the public, including the plaintiff, used as a short cut. Although the defendant had often protested, he had never taken any serious action because most of the people involved were customers for his milk. The plaintiff was attacked by a wild horse, which had been let loose in the field without notice. It was held that he was a licensee, not a trespasser, by virtue of implied permission to be there, and so entitled to recover. On the other hand, in *Great Central Railway Co.* v. *Bates*[462] a policeman on duty saw the door of X's warehouse open and a bicycle inside the premises. He went in with a view to removing the bicycle to safer quarters and fell into an uncovered hold. The court refused to entertain the idea of implied permission on the facts and hence he was not entitled to recover. The harshness of the decision can be explained, if at all, only by reference to the importance that the law attaches to the privacy of one's premises and the wish to discourage entries without properly executed warrants. Only in exceptional circumstances, for example a crime actually taking place, is even a policeman allowed to enter the premises. Atkin LJ's judgment[463] implies that the result *might* have been different had this been the case.

The willingness of courts, as in *Lowery* v. *Walker*,[464] to imply permission was often due to the severity of the common law towards trespassers prior to *Herrington* v. *British Railways Board*.[465] Along with the tendency to ascribe liability to an 'activity' of the occupier rather than to the 'state' of his premises, which made the status of an entrant irrelevant, they created a fictitious permission so that they could treat an entrant as a licensee rather than as a trespasser.[466] Now that trespassers, too, can recover in negligence, it may well be that implied permission will no longer be inferred so readily. However, even before the position of trespassers was improved, judges had begun to voice anxiety against undue eagerness to infer permission. In *Edwards* v. *Railway Executive*,[467] for example, Lord Goddard stressed that 'repeated trespass itself confers no licence', and a few years later Devlin J repeated the idea in *Phipps* v. *Rochester Corporation*.[468] 'Knowledge', he said, 'is not of itself enough to constitute a licence; there is a distinction between toleration and permission.'

[461] [1911] AC 10.   [462] [1921] 3 KB 578.   [463] Ibid., at 581–2.
[464] [1911] AC 10.   [465] [1972] AC 877.
[466] *Pannett* v. *P. McGuiness & Co. Ltd.* [1972] 2 QB 599, 605–6.   [467] [1952] AC 737.
[468] [1955] 1 QB 450, 455.

Difficulties arise when the plaintiff enters with the permission not of the occupier but of one of his employees. What kind of protection will the entrant receive if the employee acted contrary to instructions in giving permission? Suppose, for example, that an au pair girl, contrary to her employer's instructions, lets her boyfriend into the house one night. While going upstairs, he is injured through a defective tread. His rights might be affected by his status as lawful visitor or as a trespasser, which will turn on the employer's 'right' to invite him to enter the premises. Thus in the analogous context of *Stone* v. *Taffe*[469] the entrant was treated as a lawful visitor and allowed to recover from the occupier. The Court of Appeal took the view that in such circumstances, provided the entrant was bona fide, he should be treated as a visitor rather than a trespasser since the employee, though breaking his employer's instructions, was 'still in the course of his employment' according to the rules of vicarious liability. So long as the plaintiff bona fide believes that he is entitled to be on the premises, it might be more appropriate to use the terminology found in the law of agency. It might thus be more appropriate to say that he relied on the employee's *apparent authority* to invite him on the premises, rather than to put the emphasis on 'course of employment', which can be a vaguer concept. This, in fact, was the approach taken by the House of Lords in *Ferguson* v. *Welsh*. In that case an occupier A contracted with B to demolish property and to allow subcontractors on to the land *only* with A's consent. Acting *without* A's consent, B employed a subcontractor whose employee (the plaintiff) was injured while on the site. It was held that A had clothed B with ostensible authority to 'invite' the plaintiff. As a result, the plaintiff was the lawful visitor of A.[470] But if the plaintiff was aware, or ought to have been aware, of a prohibition, and entered or remained on the premises despite this, he would become a trespasser.

Related to this problem is that of permissions limited by space (or area), time, or purpose of entry. A person who has permission only to enter a certain part of premises has no permission to go to another part. In Scrutton LJ's words: 'When you invite a person into your house to use the stairs, you do not invite him to slide down the banisters.'[471] The question, as always, must be approached with common sense. For example, a customer of a public house may use its lavatory and remains a lawful visitor while making a reasonable search for it.[472] Common sense should also be shown with regard to limitations in time. An example of a limitation on the purpose of entry is *R* v. *Jones and Smith*,[473] where a son entered his father's premises and stole some goods. He was charged with burglary and the question concerned the application of section 9(1)(b) of the Theft Act 1968, which states that 'a person is guilty of burglary if having entered any building as a trespasser he steals or attempts to steal anything in it'. Given that the son had a general permission to enter his father's home, the question was whether he was a trespasser for the purposes of section

---

[469] [1974] 1 WLR 1575.
[470] *Ferguson* v. *Welsh* [1987] 1 WLR 1553. In the event, however, the plaintiff's claim failed since the court took the view that the common duty of care had not been breached.
[471] *The Carlgarth* [1927] P. 83, 110.   [472] *Gould* v. *McAuliffe* [1941] 2 All ER 527.
[473] [1976] 1 WLR 672.

9(1)(b). The court held that he was, since he entered the premises knowing or being reckless as to whether his entry was in excess of any permission given to him. Occupiers of dwellings, for example, are usually taken to give implied licence to members of the public pursuing their lawful business to walk up the drive, for example, to sell goods.[474] If a licence is revoked the entrant must be given reasonable time to leave;[475] and, in any event, the revocation of the licence must be clear and unambiguous. Thus, in *Snook* v. *Mannion*[476] a policeman followed a motorist up the driveway of his house and asked to breathalyse him. The occupier turned and said 'fuck off'. The Divisional Court took the view that the words that were uttered—which must be taken to have referred to the policeman's presence on the motorist's premises rather than merely to the attempt to breathalyse him—were *not* sufficiently clear to amount to a revocation of the licence usually implied allowing members of the public (including the police) to proceed from the (outer) gate to the door of a house on legitimate business. The existence of such a licence, however, may be in doubt if entry is expressly forbidden; notices like 'private' or 'keep out' may not be sufficient.[477]

The status of children gives rise to special difficulties. Infancy raises two problems: first, when does it convert a child into a licensee where an adult would be a trespasser? Secondly, assuming that the child is a lawful visitor, does infancy affect the standard of duty owed to him? The latter point is more appropriately discussed under the next heading, so here we shall discuss only the former.

In *Glasgow Corporation* v. *Taylor*[478] Lord Sumner said that 'infancy as such is no more a status conferring rights, or a root of title imposing obligations on others to respect it, than infirmity or imbecility'. The mere fact that the occupier has on his premises a dangerous object attractive to children does not make him liable to a trespassing child who meddles with it and gets injured. Yet the presence of such an object in a place accessible to children may aid the inference of an implied licence.[479] Prior to *British Railways Board* v. *Herrington*,[480] which recognized that trespassers, too, were entitled to some protection by the law of negligence, the courts often relied on this 'allurement doctrine' in order to imply licences. This enabled them to circumvent the old rule refusing a remedy to trespassers, and enabled them to compensate injured children. However, now that trespassers can recover in negligence, the 'allurement' doctrine is likely to be absorbed into the general consideration of what is reasonable in the circumstances (which will include the foreseeability of children) in the light of any attraction presented to them.[481]

---

[474] *Dunster* v. *Abbot* [1954] 1 WLR 58.   [475] *Robson* v. *Hallett* [1967] 2 QB 939.

[476] [1982] *Crim. LR* 601.

[477] *Christian* v. *Johannesson* [1956] NZLR 664, 666. Cf. *Snook* v. *Manion* [1982] *Crim. LR* 601.

[478] [1922] 1 AC 44, 67.   [479] See Cmnd. 9305, para. 301.   [480] [1972] AC 877.

[481] This is not to say that the 'allurement' doctrine is now completely irrelevant. For a recent application of the doctrine, see *Jolley* v. *Sutton London Borough Council* [1998] 1 Lloyd's Rep. 433.

(D) COMMON DUTY OF CARE

Section 2 of the Occupiers' Liability Act provides:[482]

(1) An occupier of premises owes the same duty, the 'common duty of care', to all his *visitors*, except in so far as he is free to and does extend, restrict, modify, or exclude his duty to any *visitor* or *visitors* by agreement or otherwise.
(2) The common duty of care is a duty to take such care as in all the circumstances of the case is reasonable to see that the visitor *will be reasonably safe* in using the premises for the purposes for which he is invited or permitted by the occupier to be there.

The duty imposed by subsection (2) was described by Lord Denning in *Wheat* v. *Lacon*[483] as 'simply a particular instance of the general duty of care which each man owes to his "neighbour"'.

Whether the duty, which covers acts and omissions, has been fulfilled is a matter of fact to be decided according to the circumstances. What was said about this in Chapter 2 applies here too. The magnitude of the risk, the likelihood of injury, the cost of avoiding it, etc., will be taken into account.[484] But however widely defined, the duty cannot be expected to cover all possible 'defects' in the premises.[485]

In *appropriate* circumstances an occupier may also be liable to one of his visitors for harm caused to him by another visitor. This is particularly likely to happen where the conduct of the wrong-doing visitor can be seen as a foreseeable consequence[486] of a breach of duty by the occupier himself. So, for example, in *Cunningham* v. *Reading Football Club Ltd.*[487] the defendants were held liable to police officers injured by hooligans who broke off loose pieces of concrete from the football ground and (as had happened in the past) hurled them at the police.

Section 2(3) specifically mentions two special factors: (*a*) an occupier must be prepared for children to be less careful than adults; and (*b*) an occupier is entitled to expect that a person exercising his calling will appreciate and guard against special risks 'ordinarily incident to it'.

---

[482] The italicised words make it clear that it is the visitor (not the premises) that must be reasonably safe.

[483] [1966] AC 552, 578. For litigated illustrations see Clerk and Lindsell, *On Torts* (17th edn.) ss. 10–30 to 10–32.

[484] For a recent illustration see *Murphy* v. *Bradford Metropolitan Council*, *The Times*, 11 Feb. 1991. Whether lighting has been adequate gives rise to certain problems. The cases do not support a general rule putting an occupier of land under a duty to provide lighting at all times of darkness. The answer depends on the circumstances and, in particular, upon whether the visitor was invited to use the premises in the dark or not. So, a hotel visitor who was injured while searching in the dark for the lavatory was held entitled to recover: *Cabell* v. *Shelborne Hotel* [1939] 2 KB 534. But the plaintiff may have his damages reduced if wandering in the dark amounts to contributory negligence: see *Ghannan* v. *Glasgow Corporation*, 1950 SLT 2.

[485] *Berryman* v. *Hounslow LBC* (unreported CA), 20 Nov. 1996: broken lift in premises forced resident to walk up stairs carrying his shopping and thereby injure his back. Held: absence of a working lift was not a breach of s. 2 of the 1957 Act.

[486] This is why the court in *Skusa* v. *Commonwealth of Australia* (1985) 62 ALR 108, was right in refusing to hold the defendants liable as occupiers of a court room when a disgruntled litigant decided to shoot one of the lawyers in that case.

[487] [1992] PIQR P.141.

With regard to (a), if a child is a lawful visitor he is owed the common duty of care, but reasonable care requires the occupier to take the characteristics of children into account. In the words of Hamilton LJ in *Latham* v. *R. Johnson & Nephew Ltd.*,[488] he should appreciate 'that in the case of an infant, there are moral as well as physical traps. There may accordingly be a duty towards infants not merely not to dig pitfalls for them, but not to lead them into temptation.'

In *Glasgow Corporation* v. *Taylor*[489] a 7-year-old boy died as a result of eating poisonous berries off a shrub in a public park. It was alleged that the local authority knew that the berries were poisonous and presented a temptation to young children. The corporation was held liable. As one would expect, every case turns on its own facts.[490] What is not a danger to an adult may well be one to a child. In *McGinlay or Titchener* v. *BR Board*[491] Lord Fraser said that 'the duty will tend to be higher in a question with a very young or very old person than in the question with a normally active and intelligent adult or adolescent'. For example, in *Moloney* v. *Lambeth London Borough Council*[492] an occupier was held liable to a 4-year-old boy who fell through the bars of a balustrade. Since a person of the plaintiff's size was liable to go through the gaps, the staircase was held not to comply with the occupier's duty of care to a child of that age.

In the case of children another relevant circumstance is the degree of care which the occupier may assume will be exercised by parents. In *Phipps* v. *Rochester Corporation*[493] the plaintiff, aged five, was walking across a piece of land which was being developed by the defendants. He fell into a trench, which was obvious enough to an adult. Evidence was adduced to the effect that children frequently played there and that the defendants had done nothing to prevent it. Devlin J held that the plaintiff was a licensee, but refused to hold the defendants liable since he took the view that in measuring the care taken by the occupiers the habits of prudent parents should also be taken into account[494] along with all other relevant circumstances. The *Phipps* reasoning was applied more recently in *Simkiss* v. *Rhondda Borough Council*,[495] a case that shows that plaintiffs may sometimes find themselves in a no-win situation. The action in *Simkiss* was brought by a 7-year-old girl who fell off a steep slope of land that lay opposite the block of flats where she lived with her family. In fact her father had left her there to picnic with a friend since, according to his evidence, he had described the slope as not dangerous, adding that many children used to picnic on the spot. The plaintiff and her friend sat on a blanket they had with them and, apparently, were trying to slide down the slope when the accident occurred. The action against the local authority (occupiers of the land), for alleged negligence in failing to fence the area and to warn off the plaintiff, was dismissed. The Court of Appeal took the view that this was not a concealed trap.

---

[488] [1913] 1 KB 398, 415.   [489] [1922] 1 AC 44.

[490] For illustration, see Clerk and Lindsell, *On Torts* (17th edn.), 12 ss. 12–16.

[491] [1983] 1 WLR 1427, 1432–3.

[492] (1966) 198 EG 895. Cf. the Building Regulations 1976 (SI No. 1976/1676), which impose strict liability under s. 71 of the Health and Safety at Work Act 1974 (an enactment which imposes stringent requirements in this respect).

[493] [1955] 1 QB 450.   [494] Ibid., at 472.   [495] (1983) 81 LGR 461.

If the plaintiff's father did not consider the area dangerous, the defendants could not be asked to achieve a higher standard of care. As stated the plaintiff's position under the *Phipps* test is that he should carry the prime responsibility for leaving his child there without warning and adequate protection. On the other hand, if he states that the area is safe, then the implication is that in failing to take precautions to avoid the accident he cannot complain that the occupier was negligent.

This unfortunate predicament can and should be avoided if we accept that the father's assessment of the possible dangers is one but not the only crucial factor. The fact that the father may be unduly casual in assessing the degree of danger should not be sufficient to absolve the occupier. The dangerous state of his premises, and the degree of care required to make them safe, must be assessed objectively. But if the father's carelessness or indifference was a factor in the realisation of the child's harm, then the occupier's liability should be reduced rather than completely avoided, so as to avoid leaving the hapless child without any compensation whatsoever. When one considers how generous courts are these days towards *trespassing* children, the *Simkiss* judgment stands out as a rather harsh decision.

Section 2(3)(b) mentions the second consideration which is relevant when determining the occupier's standard of care: the occupier is entitled to assume that persons exercising a particular calling, trade, or profession will guard against risks ordinarily incidental to it. For example, in *General Cleaning Contractors Ltd.* v. *Christmas*,[496] the plaintiff, a window-cleaner, was employed to clean windows. While he was standing on the outside of the wall and holding on to one sash of a window for support, the other sash came down on his fingers, causing him to let go and fall to the ground. He failed in his action against the occupiers. The decision might have been different had he been injured through some defect of the staircase when going upstairs in the ordinary way to reach the upper windows, for this would not be regarded as a risk ordinarily incident to his job. Similarly, in *Roles* v. *Nathan*[497] two chimney sweeps were killed by carbon monoxide fumes while sealing up a sweephole in a vertical shaft on the defendant's premises. Lord Denning said that:[498]

The occupier here was under no duty of care to these sweeps, at any rate in regard to the dangers that caused their deaths. If it had been a different danger, as for instance if the stairs leading to the cellar gave way, the occupier might no doubt be responsible, but not for these dangers which were special risks ordinarily incidental to their calling.

Special skills possessed by the entrant will not, however, automatically absolve the occupier of all liability. Indeed, a number of recent decisions dealing with injured firemen could be taken to suggest a certain judicial reluctance to utilise section 2(3)(b) and absolve too quickly, as some American courts do,

---

[496] [1953] AC 180. Note the words 'ordinarily incidental'. Thus, in *Bird* v. *King Line* [1970] 2 Lloyds Rep. 349, a foreman scaler who tripped over empty bottles on the deck of a ship was allowed to recover for his injuries since the risk that had caused his injuries could not be described as ordinarily incidental to his job.

[497] [1963] 1 WLR 1117. See also *Phillips* v. *Perry & Dalgety Agriculture Ltd.*, (unreported CA), 6 March 1997.

[498] At 1123–4.

the negligent occupier of all liability towards, for example, the injured fireman. Thus, in *Salmon* v. *Seafarer Restaurants Ltd.*[499] a fireman entered a fish-and-chip shop to extinguish a fire. He was injured as a result of an explosion caused by leaking gas which, in turn, was the result of the heat generated by the fire melting seals on gas meters, leading to an escape of gas. The defendant/occupier attempted to argue that towards an entering fireman his duty was to protect him against some 'special, exceptional or additional risk' and not the ordinary risks that are a necessary part of his job. The court refused to accept this argument. Instead, it took the view that, though the fireman's special skills and training were relevant in determining liability, where it was foreseeable that (though exercising these skills) he would be injured through the negligence of the occupier, the latter was in breach of his duty of care. In such cases, the occupier should thus be liable to the plaintiff.

Among the various defences open to an occupier, section 2(5) of the Act expressly preserves consent (*volenti non fit injuria*)[500] and section 2(3) implies the defence of contributory negligence. Since both these are generally available in other torts, they will not be discussed here. But mention must be made of two defences peculiar to this branch of the law, namely warning and exclusion of liability.

Due warning may in appropriate circumstances discharge the occupier's duty of care; in others, it may raise the defence of *volenti* or contributory negligence.[501] In all instances it must be adequate in order to have the desired effect and this is obviously a matter of fact. In *London Graving Dock Co.* v. *Horton*[502] the House of Lords had given the impression that if a visitor recognised the significance of a warning, the occupier would be absolved altogether. Section 2(4)(a) of the Act, however, negatives so wide a proposition by providing that regard must be had to all the circumstances in each case and a warning should not be treated as automatically absolving the occupier from liability.[503]

The presence of an adequate warning is thus one of many circumstances in determining whether the occupier has discharged his duty of care. Therefore a warning in an unusual language,[504] or in an unsuitable place,[505] or one not given in a serious manner,[506] will not suffice. Likewise, in circumstances of excessive danger the presence of a warning—however appropriately phrased—

---

[499] [1983] 1 WLR 1264 applied in *Ogwo* v. *Taylor* [1988] 1 AC 431 and approved by the House of Lords [1988] 1 AC 443 (another fireman's case).

[500] Invoked against a 15–year-old boy in *McGinlay* v. *British Railways Board* [1983] 1 WLR 1427.

[501] *Slater* v. *Clay Cross Co. Ltd.* [1956] 2 QB 264, 271 (per Denning LJ).

[502] [1951] AC 737.

[503] For illustration see *Stone* v. *Taffe* [1974] 1 WLR 1575. In *Bunker* v. *Brand (Charles) & Sons Ltd.* [1969] 2 QB 480, the plaintiff's damages were reduced by one half, and in *Bird* v. *King Line Ltd.* [1970] 2 Lloyd's Rep. 349, by two-thirds.

[504] *Geier* v. *Kujawa, Weston and Warne Bros., Transport* [1970] 1 Lloyd's Rep. 364 suggests that a notice to be valid may have to be translated to a party who is known not to comprehend the language in which it is expressed. Probably, the same is true of a notice erected in a public place—e.g. a beach—known to be frequented by foreigners (e.g. tourists). On the other hand, the notice in *Geier's* case would, nowadays, be invalidated by s. 148(3) of the Road Traffic Act 1972.

[505] *Coupland* v. *Eagle Bros. Ltd.* (1969) 210 EG 581.

[506] *Bishop* v. *J. A. Starnes & Sons Ltd.* [1971] 1 Lloyd's Rep. 162. Cf. *White* v. *Blackmore* [1972] 2 QB 651, where the warning was held to be adequate.

may not be sufficient, the occupier being expected to take additional precautions to avoid injury to the plaintiff.[507] At the other end of the spectrum we find cases where the risk is obvious to the visitor. In such cases, the need of a warning may be dispensed with altogether. Thus, in *Staples* v. *West Dorset District Council*[508] the court took the view that the defendants/occupiers of a famous sea wall in Lyme Regis known as 'the Cobb', which was covered in algae and seaweed and obviously very slippery, were under no duty to warn users of its inherent dangers.

What about a notice which is appropriate to an ordinary adult but unintelligible to the particular plaintiff because he is, for example, a very young child? Older cases seemed to take the view that in these instances permission to be on the premises depended on the plaintiff being accompanied by a competent guardian. This notion of conditional licence was rejected as unduly complicated by Devlin J in *Phipps* v. *Rochester Corporation*,[509] and perhaps the answer here, too, is that one has to consider all relevant factors (including parental responsibilities towards children) before deciding whether or not the warning was adequate. However, in view of the generous attitude towards child trespassers the importance of the problem can be exaggerated.

The second defence, found in section 2(1), concerns the possibility of excluding liability, and this remains open to some extent even after the Unfair Contract Terms Act 1977. Exclusion can apply to liability arising from the occupation of premises that are *not* used as business premises and thus fall outside the 1977 Act. But the same can be true of business premises, provided the exclusion term satisfies the requirement of the reasonableness laid down in section 2(2) of the 1977 Act and the action does not relate to personal injury or death. For simplicity's sake we can describe the occupier that is subject to the 1957 Act as the *private* occupier and use the words *business occupiers* for those subject to the 1977 Act.

In *Ashdown* v. *Samuel Williams and Sons, Ltd.*[510] the second defendants occupied industrial premises surrounded by land owned by the first defendants. Access to the second defendants' land was by two roads, one of which was safe while the other, a short cut, could be used at the user's risk. There were notices to that effect, which an employee of the second defendants saw when using the short cut. She was injured by railway trucks being negligently shunted along the line and claimed damages. It was held that the second defendants were not liable, since they had provided the plaintiff with a reasonably safe way of reaching her work in so far as it was necessary for her to traverse the premises of the first defendant. It was held further that the first defendants were not liable, since they could exclude their liability by a properly phrased notice.

Now, there is nothing illogical in saying that if I can exclude you from my property altogether, I can permit you to enter upon my terms.[511] This

---

[507] *Rae* v. *Mars (UK) Ltd.* [1990] 3 EG 80 at 84.

[508] (1995) 93 LGR 536. See also, *Cotton* v. *Derbyshire Dales District Council*, *The Times*, 20 June 1994 (danger of walking at the edge of a steep cliff).

[509] [1955] 1 QB 450.   [510] [1957] 1 QB 409.

[511] It would follow that if the occupier cannot exclude entry—e.g. to visitors covered by s. 2(6) of the 1957 Act—he should not be able to exclude his liability either.

proposition, though logical, was seriously curtailed by the Unfair Contract Terms Act 1977, which refers to 'business occupiers' and which will be considered presently. Further, it is clear from *Ashdown* and *White* v. *Blackmore*[512] that what matters is not whether the entrant knew of the risk, but whether the occupier had made all reasonable effort to inform him of it.[513]

Following *Ashdown*[514] and section 2 of the Occupiers' Liability Act, the occupier's liability can still be excluded by contract, by an adequate notice, or 'otherwise'. This refers, for example, to rules and regulations made and published under bye-laws or other statutory authority, which are binding whether they are 'agreed to' by the visitor or not. An example could be found in a condition limiting the liability of the British Railways Board towards holders of railway platform tickets set out in section 43(7) of the Transport Act 1962.

Finally, an occupier's duty may be limited, excluded, etc., 'in so far as he is free' to do so. Until recently the only limitation on his power to restrict or exclude his duty altogether was in section 3(1) of the Occupiers' Liability Act. This states that an occupier cannot by contract with one person (X) *reduce* the common duty of care he owes to third parties (e.g. X's employees), though he may *extend* it for their benefit. This includes situations where the occupier is bound to let third parties enter his premises. Since he cannot prevent them from entering in the first place, it would be inconsistent if he were able to restrict his duty towards them.

Such is the regime that governs the position of private occupiers subject to the Occupiers' Liability Act 1957. Today, however, most important cases are likely to be concerned with *business occupiers* and thus affected by the Unfair Contract Terms Act 1977 which, in one deep scoop, undermined the *laissez-faire* thinking which had dominated the law until its coming into force. If the old law attached undue importance and protection to land-ownership, the new law may have gone too far the other way.

The relevant provisions of this Act, which in some respects appear to be inadequately thought out and ill drafted, apply only to cases of 'business liability'. According to section 1(3) this means liability for breach of obligations or duties arising *either* from things done by a person 'in the course of business' *or* 'from the occupation of premises used for business purposes of the occupier'. This last part is crucial but vague, and a number of questions are likely to arise. Should the Act apply only to premises which are 'mainly used' for business purposes by their occupier, or only 'exclusively' used for such purposes? Where the use of premises for business is only minor or incidental the application of the Act should, arguably, be excluded. What if a doctor uses his sitting room as an overflow waiting room? And what if the entire premises are used for private purposes except for one hour every morning? Would the Act apply for that hour, and for the rest of the day would we revert to the old law? Other problems will no doubt arise. While the *Ashdown* situation would now call for a different solution, what answer should be given if the facts were similar to those in *White* v.

---

[512] [1972] 2 QB 651.
[513] Ibid., 674. This may cause undue hardship, however, to infants, blind persons, and illiterate persons.
[514] [1957] 1 QB 409.

Blackmore,[515] where a fee was charged for entrance on land, the proceeds going to a charitable purpose? What if a student or employee of a college (which is a charity) is injured on its premises? (Section 2 of the Occupiers' Liability Act 1984, amending section 1 of the 1977 Act, may provide an answer to this last hypothetical case.) If the scope of the 1977 Act turns out to be too wide, it would not be surprising to see courts placing a narrow interpretation on this section.

Once it has been decided that the premises are business premises, attention focuses on section 2, which states unequivocally that in cases of personal injury or death it is not possible to exclude liability resulting from the negligence of the occupier (s. 2(1)). The important point to note is that for this purpose negligence is defined in section 1(1)(c) as including, *inter alia*, the breach of the common duty of care imposed by the Occupiers' Liability Act 1957 (s. 1(1)(c)). As for other kinds of loss, for example, damage to property, exclusion is possible only if it is reasonable in view of all the circumstances obtaining when the liability arose (s. 11(3)).

The effect of all this is that liability for breach of the common duty of care under the Occupiers' Liability Act 1957 can no longer be excluded, *vis-à-vis* lawful visitors at any rate. What about trespassers? Liability to them does not arise under this Act, but initially arose at common law (and subsequently under the Occupiers' Liability Act 1984) when there has been a breach of the 'duty of common humanity'. As we shall see, the difference between these two notions—common duty of care, duty of common humanity—is not one of law but one of fact, depending on the factual situation of each case. Yet differences may remain in practice. For example, it would appear that due to defective drafting of the 1984 Occupiers' Liability Act the occupier can exclude his liability towards persons covered by that Act whereas the 1977 Unfair Contract Terms Act makes such an exclusion impossible towards the type of lawful entrants covered by the 1957 Occupiers' Liability Act. One hopes, however, that such a solution would not prevail and the courts, if the opportunity arose, would hold that the duty owed under the 1984 Act is non-excludable. Two arguments might support such a construction. The 1984 Act, unlike the 1957 Act, makes no provision for 'contracting out'; and the omission must have been intentional since it was provided for in the Law Commission's Draft Bill on which the 1984 Act was based. Secondly, duties owed to trespassers are really minimal duties and, therefore, as a matter of public policy they should not be excludable.

An interesting point arises out of the definition of 'negligence' in section 1(1)(c) as including the breach of common duty of care imposed by the 1957 Act. Once this has been breached, liability for it cannot be excluded according to the Unfair Contract Terms Act. If, of course, the duty has been fulfilled and has not been breached, there is no liability to be excluded. Now, we have seen that according to the Occupiers' Liability Act warning notices may, in certain circumstances, prevent the duty from arising altogether (s. 2(1)), or discharge the occupier's duty towards his visitor (s. 2(4)(a)). For a time, one could have argued that such notices do not offend against the Unfair Contract Terms Act

---

[515] [1972] 2 QB 651.

1977, since section 2 of this Act refers to notices excluding or limiting *liability for breach*, as distinct from notices which show that there has been no breach in the first place. If this way of looking at section 2 of the 1977 Act had prevailed,[516] it would have limited the application of the Act considerably, and in that sense it could be seen as being contrary to the intentions of the legislator. However, in the light of the recent decision of the House of Lords in *Smith* v. *Bush*,[517] this view no longer seems tenable. This means that a disclaimer of liability would be ineffective under section 2(2) of the 1977 Act unless it satisfied the requirement of reasonableness provided by section 1(3) of the same statute.

(E) LIABILITY FOR INDEPENDENT CONTRACTORS

An occupier will, of course, be vicariously liable for torts committed by his servants in the course of their employment, whatever it may be. What if work is performed by an independent contractor? On principle the employer of an independent contractor is not vicariously liable so that an occupier would not be answerable for his independent contractor. Yet in *Thomson* v. *Cremin*[518] the House of Lords appeared to say that the occupier owed his invitees a personal, non-delegable duty to see that care was taken, which he could not avoid by entrusting its performance to an independent contractor. His liability was not vicarious, but personal. This has now been altered by section 2(4)(b) of the Occupiers' Liability Act, which states that:

Where damage is caused to a visitor by a danger due to the faulty execution of any work of construction, maintenance or repair by an independent contractor employed by the occupier, the occupier is not to be treated without more as answerable for the danger if in all the circumstances he had acted reasonably in entrusting the work to an independent contractor and had taken such steps (if any) as he reasonably ought in order to satisfy himself that the contractor was competent and that the work had been properly done.

Three points should be noted about this section: first, it is a particular application of the general rule set out in section 2(4) according to which the standard of care owed by an occupier towards lawful visitors is determined after all surrounding circumstances are taken into account.

It follows, secondly, that in the case of work done by an independent contractor the questions to be answered before an occupier is deemed to have attained the requisite standard include, in appropriate circumstances, the following: (*a*) did the occupier act reasonably in entrusting the work to an independent contractor? (*b*) did he select him with reasonable care? (*c*) circumstances permitting, did he supervise him properly while the work was being

---

[516] As suggested by *Harris* v. *Wyre Forest DC* [1988] QB 835 (reversed by the House of Lords in *Smith* v. *Bush* [1990] 1 AC 831).

[517] [1990] 1 AC 831, especially at 848 (per Lord Templeman), 857 (per Lord Griffiths). The factual context of *Smith* v. *Bush* is different to that discussed in the text above but, it is submitted, the reasoning of the House of Lords is applicable to both situations. For further discussion of this case, see below, Chapter 8, at p. 702 ff.

[518] [1956] 1 WLR 103.

done? and (*d*) did he check its completion? In this last context the words of Mocatta J in *AMF International* v. *Magnet Bowling*[519] are important:[520]

In the case of the *construction of a substantial building* or of a ship . . . the building owner, if he is to escape subsequent tortious liability for faulty construction should not only take care to contract with a competent contractor or shipbuilder, but also to cause that work to be supervised by a properly qualified professional man such as an architect surveyor, or a naval architect or Lloyd's surveyor. Such cases are different in fact and in everyday practice from having a flat rewired.

The concluding words distinguish cases such as *Green* v. *Fibreglass Ltd.*[521] where an occupier, who employed an independent contractor to rewire his office, was held not liable to a charwoman who received severe electrical burns as a result of faulty rewiring. In *Woodward* v. *Mayor of Hastings*,[522] on the other hand, a pupil at a school injured himself on an icy step left in a dangerous condition by a negligent cleaner. Even on the assumption that the cleaner was an independent contractor of the corporation, the latter was liable as its officers could have inspected the way she had done the job. 'The craft of the charwoman may have its mysteries,' said du Parcq LJ,[523] 'but there is no esoteric quality in the nature of the work which the cleaning of a snow-covered step demands.' The occupier in this case was therefore under a duty to select a competent person and to inspect the work. On the other hand, in *Haseldine* v. *Daw*[524] the plaintiff was injured when the lift that he was wiring collapsed to the bottom of its shaft as a result of negligent repairs by a firm of independent contractors. The occupier was not liable, for 'to hold him responsible for the misdeeds of his independent contractor would be to make him insure the safety of his lift. That duty can only arise out of contract . . .'

Finally, one should draw attention to the vagueness of section 2(4)(b). Is work not involving 'work of construction, maintenance or repair' excluded from it? What comes under these words? In *AMF International* v. *Magnet Bowling Ltd.*[525] it was held that a builder's failure to take adequate precautions against flooding should come under this section even though it was strenuously argued that at most he was guilty of non-feasance rather than misfeasance. Mocatta J said:[526]

---

[519] [1968] 1 WLR 1028.

[520] At 1044. It is submitted that the italicised words must be read with caution and that everything must in the end depend on the nature and complexity of the work that is undertaken and the other surrounding circumstances. Thus in *Ferguson* v. *Welsh* [1987] 1 WLR 1553 (another construction/demolition case), Lord Keith observed, at 1560: 'It would not ordinarily be reasonable to expect an occupier of premises having engaged a contractor, to supervise the contractor's activities in order to ensure that he was discharging his duty to his employees to observe a safe system of work. In special circumstances, on the other hand, when the occupier knows or has reason to suspect that the contractor is using an unsafe system of work, it might well be reasonable for the occupier to take steps to see that the system was made safe.' Lord Keith here is, of course, speaking of injury to the contractor's employees given the facts of that case; naturally, however, the same applies towards all third parties.

[521] [1958] 2 QB 245. [522] [1945] KB 174. [523] At 183.

[524] [1941] 2 KB 343. [525] [1968] 1 WLR 1028.

[526] At 1043. In *Ferguson* v. *Welsh* [1987] 1 WLR 1553, 1560 Lord Keith thought that s. 2(4)(c) required 'a broad and purposive interpretation' which led him to the conclusion that the word 'construction' embraces also the word 'demolition'. With the greatest respect this seems a strained interpretation, at any rate in cases when pure demolition work is involved. By contrast, a stronger case can be made for applying s. 2(4)(b) in those instances where demolition has to procede construction.

It seems to be that if a builder in the course of constructing a building fails to take adequate precautions against flooding and that causes damage to the property of a visitor, it would be altogether too technical to hold this not within the true construction of the words 'a danger due to the faulty execution of any work of construction, maintenance or repair'.

(F) PROTECTED ENTRANTS UNDER THE 1984 ACT

(i) The Development of the Common Law   The common law and the 1957 Act had little time for persons who were not included in any of the three types of entrants which together made up the category of 'lawful visitor', namely, contractors, invitees, and licensees. If they were injured while on other persons' premises due to the defective state of these premises they had only themselves to blame. This group of persons, who were beyond the pale of the law of negligence, came under four sub-categories. First were persons exercising *private* rights of way. Then we had entrants under section 60 of the National Parks and Access to the Countryside Act 1949—sometimes referred to as 'authorised ramblers'. A third category included persons exercising *public* rights of way. Finally we had trespassers. It was, in fact, this last category that attracted the full wrath of the traditional common law and led to most of the litigation.

A trespasser is a person who has no permission, express or implied, to be where he is. The common law's traditional severity towards trespassers was exemplified by *Robert Addie & Sons (Collieries)* v. *Dumbreck*.[527] In that case it was held that an occupier was not liable for injury to trespassers unless he had acted intentionally[528] or recklessly. As late as 1964 the Privy Council found occasion to reaffirm this rule in *Commissioner for Railways* v. *F. J. Quinlan*.[529]

The policy reasons behind such a harsh rule may have been a desire to leave owners of land free to use it as they wished, especially at a time when freedom of property was as sacrosanct as freedom of the person. American authors and courts have, on the whole, been more forthright than their English counterparts in acknowledging the importance attached traditionally to land, the dominance of landowners, and the heritage of feudalism.[530] Such considerations progressively lost their appeal. The Supreme Court of California was thus surely right to argue that the classifications into trespassers, licensees, and invitees bore no relation 'to the factors which ought to determine the liability of an occupier. These should include the connection between the injury and the occupier's conduct, his moral blameworthiness, the need to prevent future harm, and the prevalence and availability of insurance'.[531]

---

[527] [1929] AC 358.

[528] In *Revill* v. *Newberry* [1996] 2 WLR 239—a case much discussed in the popular press of the time—the defendant was thus held liable to the plaintiff/burglar whom he shot while he was trespassing on his grounds. The latter's damages were, however, reduced by two-thirds to account for his own crime.

[529] [1964] AC 1054. The *Quinlan* case even rejected an attempt made a year earlier in *Videan* v. *British Transport Commission* [1963] 2 QB 650, to limit the *Addie* ruling to breaches of the 'occupancy duties'.

[530] *Rowland* v. *Christian*, 443 P.2d 561, 564–5 (1968) decided by the Supreme Court of California. The conclusion was that an occupier owed the common duty of care towards all persons—including trespassers—who came on to his land. One of the latest converts to this rule is New York: see *Basso* v. *Miller* 386 NYS 2d 564, 352 NE2d 868 (1976); and some authors have already argued that occupiers of business premises should be under strict liability towards those on their premises. Thus, Ursin, 22 *UCLA L. Rev.* 820 (1975).

[531] *Rowland* v. *Christian* (preceding note), at 567.

Another argument in favour of the old harsher treatment of trespassers derived from the nineteenth-century moral judgment that a trespasser was a wrongdoer deserving of his plight. This argument, however, is no more convincing than the previous one, as Lord Dunedin himself admitted in the *Addie* case.[532] 'The term trespasser', he said, 'is a comprehensive one; it covers the wicked and the innocent; the burglar, the arrogant invader of another's land, the walker blithely unaware that he is stepping where he has no right to walk, or the wandering child—all may be dubbed as trespasser.'

In this country, however, the injustice of the Victorian attitudes was only gradually appreciated. Thus, in the beginning only indirect attempts were made to avoid the harshness of the old rule, for example, by resorting to the implied permission and the allurement doctrines.[533] Powerful doubts as to the correctness of the law were, however, voiced by the Court of Appeal in *British Railways Board* v. *Herrington*, and on appeal the House of Lords[534] heeded them by making it possible for occupiers to be liable in negligence to trespassers. It said that the *Addie* case would be decided differently today and that it was no longer an exclusive statement of the law. The facts in that case were that the plaintiff, aged six, was electrocuted by the defendant's railway line after crossing a gap in the fence bordering it. The fencing had been in a dilapidated condition for some time. The local stationmaster was aware of this and of the fact that children were in the habit of passing through, but he took no steps. The House of Lords held that, although the plaintiff was a trespasser, he could recover in negligence.

Lord Pearson drew attention to the changes that have taken place in the socio-economic conditions and said that the time had come to abandon the old rule and to mitigate the plight of trespassers.[535] Accordingly, by applying the 'neighbour' principle, a new duty-situation was created with regard to them. However, although they deserved more compassionate treatment than hitherto, the House of Lords was unable to extend its compassion as far as to abandon the interests of occupiers. Concern for the former is essential; but it was felt that this should not result in an unbearable burden being placed on the latter. A fair balance was sought by saying that the new duty—dubbed the duty 'of common humanity'—was less onerous than the common duty of care in (possibly) two respects. First, that the presence of a trespasser in most cases will not be reasonably foreseeable.[536] Secondly, the standard of care required of the occupier would, in such cases, be less exacting than that towards a lawful visitor.[537]

Herrington was a turning point in the law; but the way the humanitarian duty was described gave rise to considerable discussions in the 1970s as to how this differed from the common duty of care. But while the battle of semantics

---

[532] [1929] AC 358, 371.

[533] Similar methods were adopted in the USA. See *Kermarec* v. *Compagnie Générale Transatlantique*, 358 US 625, 630–1, 79 S. Ct. 406, 3 L. Ed. 2d 550 (1959) (refusing to accept the common-law rules for the law of admiralty); *Rowland* v. *Christian*, 443, P.2d 561, 565–7 (1968). The Victorian attitudes towards trespassers, however, still retain some support. See for instance, Weir, *Casebook on Tort* (2nd edn.), 68–99.

[534] [1971] 2 QB 107; [1972] AC 877.   [535] At 929.   [536] At 941 (per Lord Diplock).

[537] At 898–9 (per Lord Reid).

raged, the courts in England and in other common law jurisdictions made it increasingly clear that at least child trespassers were not to be left without protection.[538] Only in exceptional situations, where the cost of keeping the young trespasser out of the potentially dangerous premises was exorbitant, would the courts deny liability.[539] As for the totally unmeritorious trespasser—e.g. the thief—the courts felt confident that an impressive array of concepts and maxims—foreseeability, *volenti*, *ex turpi causa non oritur actio*—still enabled them to exclude recovery where justice so demanded.

(ii) The Intervention of the Legislator: The 1984 Act[540]   The Act, though mainly concerned with ameliorating the protection afforded to trespassers has, in fact, achieved the same result for two of the three other categories of entrants who were not lawful visitors under the 1957 Act. These are the persons exercising private rights of way and the 'authorised ramblers'. On the other hand, those using public rights of way have not been included in the Act and do not enjoy the rights given by it.[541] Their exclusion was prompted by the fear that any contrary decision would have resulted in large expenditure being incurred by the owners of the servient land. Users of those public highways *adopted* by local authorities do, however, enjoy the protection afforded to them by the Highways (Miscellaneous Provisions) Act 1961 (now the Highways Act 1980) discussed briefly towards the end of Chapter 5, Section 3.

The existence of a duty under the Act is covered by section 1(3). According to this section a duty will arise if three requirements are satisfied. First, the defendant must be '*aware* of the danger' or 'have reasonable grounds to believe that it exists' (s. 1(3)(a)). Secondly, he must '*know*' or have 'reasonable grounds to believe that the entrant is in the vicinity of the danger . . . or that he may come into the vicinity of the danger' (s. 1(3)(b)). Finally, 'the risk is one against which, in all the circumstances of the case, he may reasonably be expected to offer the other some protection'.

The criteria mentioned by the Act are ambiguous in that whereas the last of the three is, clearly, objective, the first two (contained in ss. 1(3)(a) and (b)) could be seen as being subjective (note the italicised words) *or* objective (reasonable awareness, etc.). This lack of clarity, particularly annoying given the difficulties experienced by the courts (and scholars) during the post-*Herrington* years, is unfortunate; and it has hardly been rectified by *White* v. *St Albans City and District Council*,[542] one of the few cases decided so far under the 1984 Act. In that case the Court of Appeal held that an occupier who had taken measures to keep the public off his dangerous premises should not, by that reason alone, be deemed to have reason to believe that persons were likely to be in the vicinity of the danger for the purposes of section 1(3)(b). Rather, the answer should be made to depend on all the facts of the case, including the state of the land. This

---

[538] Thus, see *Pannett* v. *McGuiness* [1972] 2 QB 599; *South Portland Cement* v. *Cooper* [1974] AC 623.

[539] *Penny* v. *Northampton BC* (1974) 72 LGR 733.

[540] For a discussion of the Act, see Buckley [1984] *Conv.* 413.

[541] Nor are they regarded as 'visitors' of the owner of the subsoil: *McGeown* v. *N.I. Housing Executive* [1995] 1 AC 233; *Campbell* v. *N.I. Hosuing Executive* [1996] 1 BNIL 99. But other avenues of redress may be open to them. Thus, see, *Thomas* v. *British Rail Board* [1976] QB 912.

[542] *The Times*, 12 Mar. 1990.

would appear to suggest that knowledge that the entrant is in the vicinity of the danger will be more readily imputed where the fencing around the occupier's land was defective and evidence could be adduced to show that persons used the land, for example, as a short cut to their work. If, on the other hand, the occupier's land was properly fenced, it would be wrong to impute to the occupier any knowledge that the plaintiff may have entered the danger zone. This 'objective' formulation—liability depends on constructive knowledge— seems to have been replaced by a more 'subjective' test. Thus, according to the more recent (but unreported) decision of the Court of Appeal in *Swain* v. *Buri*, the words 'has reasonable grounds to believe', found in section 1(3)(b) of the 1984 Act, must be taken to refer to 'actual knowledge of the facts that would lead a reasonable man to expect the presence of a trespasser; mere culpable ignorance, or constructive knowledge, [will] not do.'[543]

In that case an owner of an empty warehouse abutting on a council estate was thus absolved from all liability towards an agile but mischievous small boy who climbed on the roof and then fell through a skylight.

When one turns to the *contents* of the duty (discovered only once the preceding requirements have been satisfied), matters are more straightforward. Thus, section 1(4) of the 1984 Act, adopting the familiar negligence standard, expects the occupier 'to take such care as is reasonable in all the circumstances'. Section 1(6), essentially, requires the courts to consider the defence of *volenti non fit iniuria* at the same time as they consider whether a duty arises under the 1984 Act. For, if the trespasser willingly accepted the risk, no duty of care will arise. Thus, as a result of such reasoning, the Court of Appeal recently held[543a] that the occupiers of a college open-air swimming pool owed no duty of care under section 1 to a student trespasser who was seriously injured after climbing over a locked gate one night and then diving head on into the school pool knowing that it was closed for the winter and its water levels kept low. The decision, though unfortunate for the plaintiff, shows that the fears expressed in the 1960s and 1970s that the recognition of a duty of care towards trespassers would bring indeterminate liability have proved unfounded. More generally, one might thus argue that this case law provides an illustration of the ability of the courts to keep liability within reasonable bounds and avoid the apocalyptic consequences that conservative lawyers fear every time liberalisation of our tort rules is mentioned through the abandonment of the device of duty of care. Finally, to return to the 1984 Act, section 1(8) limits the duty of the occupier to personal injury suffered by the entrant. Property damage is thus excluded *under the 1984 Act*. But the wording of sections 1(1) and 1(8) of the Act *may* not have excluded any residual liability the occupier may have towards a trespasser's property under the rule in *Herrington*'s case.[544]

---

[543] Clerk and Lindsell, *On Torts* (17th edn., 2nd supplement), s. 10–74.
[543a] *Ratcliffe* v. *McConnell*, *The Times*, 3 Dec. 1998.
[544] See the quaint case of *Tutton* v. *A. D. Walter* [1986] QB 61. On the other hand, McKendrick, *Tort Textbook* (5th edn.), (1991), 150, argues that the *Herrington* test was designed to deal with personal injuries and not property damage.

(G) Liability of Non-Occupiers: Vendors, Landlords, Builders, Local Authorities

Any of the above *may* be occupiers in the sense described in the previous paragraphs, in which case their liability could be engaged under the Occupiers' Liability Act(s). Where, however, this is not the case, their liability may arise under statute, the evolving common law, or both. We shall discuss the liability of these potential defendants in turns.

(i) Vendors and Landlords Purchasers or lessees of premises might first consider suing vendors or landlords in contract. However, the rule of *caveat emptor* ('buyer beware', arguably eroded in recent times),[545] makes it unlikely that such actions will succeed. In the case of land, therefore, implied obligations about the quality of the premises are considerably narrower than those found in the case of sale of chattels.

At common law, tort rules were equally unfavourable to plaintiffs. *Cavalier* v. *Pope*[546] established precisely such an immunity for landlords as far back as 1906; and less than thirty years later, the same immunity was conclusively given to vendors.[547] In the years that followed, various attempts were made to restrict these immunities but, subject to what will be said in the next paragraphs, their success was only marginal.[548]

The immunity of landlords and vendors for acts or omissions before letting or selling the premises thus persisted until the 1970s when it was frontally assaulted by *Dutton* v. *Bognor Regis UDC*.[549] The best interpretation of this decision is that it abolished the immunity of landlords and vendors for dangers *positively* created *before* the sale or demise of the premises, thus extending the ruling in *Billings* but not totally avoiding (as it could not) the effect of *Cavalier* v. *Pope*. As noted in Chapter 2, *Dutton* was subsequently approved (in most respects) by *Anns* v. *Merton London Borough Council*.[550] The case law of the House of Lords subsequent to *Anns* has, however, cast so much uncertainty on the *Dutton* type of reasoning that it is doubtful whether this line of attack will offer great chances to future plaintiffs. Happily for them, legislative intervention in the form of section 3 of the Defective Premises Act 1972 has reached results very similar (though not identical)[551] to those foreshadowed by *Dutton*, so the old-fashioned immunities of landlords and vendors has, for most intents and purposes, been interred by statute.

Section 3(1) provides that 'where work of construction, repair, maintenance or demolition or any other work is done on or in relation to premises, any duty of care owed, because of the doing of the work, to persons who might reason-

---

[545] See Gleeson and McKendrick, 'The Rotting Away of Caveat Emptor?' [1987] *Conv.* 121.
[546] [1906] AC 428. [547] *Bottomley* v. *Bannister* [1932] 1 KB 458.
[548] Thus, in *A. C. Billings & Son* v. *Riden* [1958] AC 240 the House of Lords abolished the landlord's immunity for dangers positively created after the demise of the premises; and in *Rimmer* v. *Liverpool City Council* [1985] QB 1 it was held that a landlord, who designed or built premises, owed a duty of care to persons who might reasonably be expected to be affected by the condition of the premises.
[549] [1972] 1 QB 373. [550] [1978] AC 728.
[551] For further details on the changes brought about by case law and statute, see Spencer in works cited in Select Bibliography.

ably be expected to be affected by defects in the state of the premises created by the doing of the work shall not be abated by the subsequent disposal of the premises by the person who owed the duty.' (Section 3(2) goes on to specify the situations when the section does *not* apply.) The main effect of the section is to abolish the common-law immunity of a vendor or lessor in negligence in respect of damage caused by the dangerous state of the premises sold or let by him. The way this section was designed to operate was explained by the Law Commission:[552]

Any person who does work on land is under a duty of care at the time when he does the work, but if he subsequently sells or lets the premises on which he did the work, his potential liability for breach of that duty comes to an end. The transaction of sales or letting alone confers this immunity. It is only, therefore, necessary to provide that a sale or letting shall have no effect upon a pre-existing duty arising from the doing of the work and the general principles of negligence will apply.

The Act achieves this result in a cumbersome and ambiguous way; and it also raises two further points.

First, unlike *Dutton*, section 3(1) does not impose liability for misfeasance generally, but only for misfeasance by 'work of construction, repair, maintenance or demolition or *any other work*' (emphasis added). The italicised words may provide a way to widen the application of the Act if they are not construed as being limited to works of construction, repair, and maintenance; and in the context of occupiers' liability Mocatta J attempted a broad definition of similar terms.[553] Even a wide interpretation might still leave outside the scope of the section some activities, such as spraying a field with poisonous fertiliser. If this is so, then a vendor or lessor who did the spraying would not be liable to the purchaser. Secondly, the section appears to restrict the landlord's immunity to damage created 'on or in relation to premises', which could limit its applicability to buildings unless the term 'premises' is understood in a broad sense.

It will be clear from what has been said so far that neither *Dutton* nor section 3 renders a landlord liable for careless omissions, in particular an omission to carry out necessary repairs. This has been achieved (at any rate as far as omitted repairs are concerned, for there is still no liability for failing to warn of existing dangers not created by himself) by section 4, which states:

Where premises are let under a tenancy which puts on the landlord an obligation to the tenant for the maintenance or repair of the premises, the landlord owes to all persons who might reasonably be expected to be affected by defects in the state of the premises a duty to take such care as is reasonable in all the circumstances to see that they are reasonably safe from personal injury or from damage to their property caused by a relevant defect.

First, the landlord's duty is additional to any other duty imposed on him by contract or statute, and it cannot be excluded or restricted in any way.[554]

---

[552] Law Commission No. 40, s. 46.

[553] *AMF International Ltd.* v. *Magnet Bowling Ltd.* [1968] 1 WLR 1028. In *Andrews* v. *Schooling* [1991] 1 WLR 783 the Court of Appeal held that the words 'taking on work' of s. 1(1) of the Act (which deals with the liability of builders discussed later) also extends to non-feasance.

[554] S. 6(3) of the 1972 Act. This must now be read in conjunction with the Unfair Contract Terms Act 1977.

Secondly, the duty is owed to all those 'who might reasonably be expected to be affected'[555] by the defects in the premises, and they include not only 'visitors' but also neighbours, users of the highway, and even trespassers. Nowadays this protection must be analogous to that offered by the *Herrington* rule and the Occupiers' Liability Act 1984. Thirdly, liability is imposed only for damage due to 'a relevant defect', which section 4(3) defines as:

a defect in the state of the premises existing at or after the material time and arising from, or continuing because of, an act or omission by the landlord which constitutes or would, if he had had notice of the defect, have constituted a failure by him to carry out his obligation to the tenant for the maintenance or repair of the premises . . .

It will be noticed that a 'relevant defect' exists only if the landlord is in breach of his express or implied obligation to repair: express if it derives from an express undertaking to repair, implied if it derives, for example, from statute.[556] As to the latter, sections 11 and 12 of the Landlord and Tenant Act 1985 provide for implied covenants by a lessor to *repair* the structure and exterior of dwelling-houses (and certain installations in them) where the lease is for less than seven years.[557] Further, section 4(4) of the 1972 Act in effect provides that, save in one exceptional circumstance, whenever a landlord has a right to 'enter the premises to carry out any description of maintenance or repair', that is, has a power to repair, he will be deemed to be under an obligation to do so. This last sentence of section 4(4) makes clear that for the purposes of section 4 the landlord's power to effect repairs is transformed into a *sui generis obligation* to repair. We say *sui generis* for a tenant cannot force a landlord to exercise this power, but he can sue him for damage resulting from the failure to exercise it. This represents a potential widening of a landlord's obligations, especially since the Court of Appeal decided in *Mint* v. *Good*[558] that such an implied power exists in any situation in which a landlord may reasonably be expected to enter and carry out repair. This is now the rule as far as weekly tenancies are concerned.

(ii) Builders   At common law, builders who built on *other* persons' land would be held liable in negligence. However, if they built on their *own* land they were treated as vendors and thus enjoyed the immunity of the latter.[559] This immunity was undermined[560] by *Dutton* (where two members of the Court of Appeal proceeded to hold a *local authority* liable for negligent inspection of the foundations of a house); and it was definitely withdrawn by subsequent cases.[561] But an unfortunate 'coupling' of the two liabilities (i.e. that of builders and local authorities) had been made;[562] and when, in more recent times, the House of

---

[555] S. 4(1).   [556] S. 4(5).

[557] But this duty does not require the landlord to correct defects that existed from the time the building was put up, let alone to make the house fit for human habitation: *Quick* v. *Taff Ely BC* [1986] QB 809.

[558] [1951] 1 KB 517.

[559] *Bottomley* v. *Bannister* [1932] 1 KB 458; *Otto* v. *Bolton & Norris* [1936] 2 KB 46.

[560] *Dutton* v. *Bognor Regis* [1972] 1 QB 373. It was subsequently argued that since the builder was not a party to the action, the removal of his immunity was only contained in dicta. The acceptance of *Dutton* by later cases such as *Anns* and *Batty* made this debate an academic one. See next note for references.

[561] *Anns* v. *Merton London Borough Council* [1978] AC 728; *Batty* v. *Metropolitan Properties Ltd.* [1978] QB 554.

[562] Cane, *Tort Law and Economic Interests* (1991), 513, also doubts the wisdom of making the liabilities of builders and local authorities 'co-extensive'. Contrast Lord Oliver's views in *Murphy* [1991] 1 AC 398, 483.

Lords overruled *Anns* in a case involving a local authority,[563] the liability of builders was further redefined in a restrictive way following the trend set by the slightly earlier decision in *D. & F. Estates* v. *Church Commissioners for England*.[564] The end result would thus seem to be that a builder may be liable to a third party (be he the owner, occupier, visitor, or passer-by) on the principle of *Donoghue* v. *Stevenson* but only if (i) a *latent* defect causes the plaintiff to suffer (ii) *physical* injury.[565] To put it differently, the builder will not be liable if: (a) the harm suffered by the plaintiff is purely economic loss (e.g. expenditure to prevent a collapse of the roof) or (b) if the occupier becomes aware of the defect before further damage occurs, for at that stage it ceases to be latent and, according to Lord Keith again, it is 'the latency of the defect which constitutes the mischief'.[566] On this kind of reasoning, therefore, it is the occupier of the premises who must be sued.

Taking conclusions to their logical extremes may not, however, always make practical sense. Thus in *Targett* v. *Torfaen BC*[567] Sir Donald Nicholls VC (as he then was) rightly pointed out that:

... knowledge of the existence of a danger does not always enable a person to avoid the danger. In simple cases it does. In other cases, especially where buildings are concerned, it would be absolutely unrealistic to suggest that a person can always take steps to avoid a danger once he knows of its existence, and that if he does not do so he is the author of his own misfortune.

The *Targett* judgment thus proposes an attenuation of the *Murphy* ruling as far as personal injury or damage to other property is concerned. It would thus seem sensible to suggest that the builder remains liable for the harm (as defined above) suffered by the plaintiff (be he the occupier or visitor of the premises) when it would be unreasonable to expect the occupier to remove the patently obvious defect but not unreasonable for the plaintiff to run the risk of harm through that danger.[568]

A second way one might attempt to make a builder liable would be to argue that the builder was in breach of one of the many statutory duties contained, for example, in section 38 of the Building Act 1984. This could open new vistas to disappointed plaintiffs. However, at the time of writing this section has not yet been brought into force and there is, therefore, no case law to enable one to predict how such actions might fare in practice.

The third and final way for rendering builders liable to third parties may be found in the Defective Premises Act 1972. Section 3 of that statute has already been discussed when the liability of builders/vendors was being considered, so little need be added here. However, section 1 of the same enactment has recently acquired enhanced significance and, despite its limitations, may yet

---

[563] *Murphy* v. *Brentwood DC* [1991] 1 AC 398. See Chapter 2, above, for extensive discussion.
[564] [1989] AC 177.
[565] See e.g. the observations in *Murphy* of Lord Keith at [1991] 1 AC 398, 462 and Lord Bridge at 475.
[566] [1991] 1 AC 398, 464.   [567] [1992] 3 All ER 27 at 37.
[568] In *Targett* the plaintiff, a tenant of a council house, successfully sued the designer/builder of the premises when he fell down some external steps which were unlit and had no handrail to make them safe. A 25% reduction in the amount of damages was, however, made on the grounds of contributory negligence.

offer the best chance of making builders liable to persons affected by their negligent work. Section 1(1) of the 1972 Act provides that:

A person taking on work or in connection with the provision of a dwelling . . . owes a duty: (*a*) if the dwelling is provided to the order of any person, to that person; and (*b*) without prejudice to paragraph (*a*) above, to every person who acquires an interest (whether legal or equitable) in the dwelling, to see that the work which he takes on is done in a workmanlike or, as the case may be, professional manner, with proper materials and so that as regards that work the dwelling will be fit for habitation when completed.

A number of points should be made about this section (in conjunction with section 1(2) and section 2 of the same Act).

First, by person 'taking on work . . .' one understands—and, in the absence of case law on the Act, this and the points that follow can only represent academic speculation—builders, architects, engineers, surveyors, and all kinds of subcontractors. Local authorities and their subcontractors and surveyors are, most likely, excluded from this section (see subsection (*iii*), below).

Secondly, the duty is owed to those commissioning the work and anyone who subsequently acquires a legal or equitable interest in the land.

Thirdly, the duty is higher than the ordinary duty in negligence; one knowledgeable commentator has thus described it as 'a wide-ranging "due care" tortious warranty of suitability in favour of purchasers and their successors'.[569]

Fourthly, the duty applies only to dwellings and, debatably, excludes other types of buildings such as factories, shops, etc. Further, it covers misfeasance as well as non-feasance;[570] and, arguably, allows compensation for pure economic loss,[571] which is, however, excluded by the common law.

Fifthly, the person who takes on work in accordance with section 1(1) may enjoy the defence given him in section 1(2) of the Act. In effect this excuses him from liability if he agreed to do the work in accordance with instructions given by the other party (for whom he is doing the work). The defence does not apply if he owes a duty to warn the other party of any defects in the instructions.

Sixthly, actions under the Act are subject to an arguably very brief limitation period of six years. Moreover, this limitation period in effect runs from the date of completion of the work. Surprisingly, the alternative discoverability periods provided by the Latent Damage Act 1986 do not seem to apply.[572]

Finally, and most importantly, in the early years of the Act, dwellings covered by an 'approved scheme'—typically by the National House Builders Protection Scheme—were excluded from the purview of section 1. Surprisingly, at some unspecified date prior to 1988 an agreement was reached between the government and the NHBC that made it possible to utilise the section 1 remedy

---

[569] Duncan-Wallace, '*Anns* Beyond Repair' (1991) 107 *LQR* 228, 242.

[570] *Andrews* v. *Schooling* [1991] 1 WLR 783. In *Jacobs* v. *Morton* (1994) 72 BLR 92 at 105, the court took the view that this statutory duty did not apply to the rectification of an existing building.

[571] *Andrews* v. *Schooling*, previous note. Contrast *Murphy* v. *Brentwood DC* [1991] 1 AC 398. It is submitted that if the text, above, is correct, it leads to diverging results depending upon whether a cause of action can be framed under the Act or the common law which may not be very logical.

[572] *Warner* v. *Basildon DC* (1991) Const. LJ 146, 154; and see the discussion of the Latent Damage Act 1986 in Chapter 8, below.

against builders. This agreement, however, was never publicised; and apparently both our courts and the practitioners in the field remained unaware of it, at least until late in 1990.[573] Two points would follow from this. First, this ignorance did not really matter to plaintiffs while their *Anns* rights remained alive; but now that they have been taken away by *Murphy*, the 1972 Act acquires much greater significance. Secondly, if the courts (including the House of Lords) were indeed unaware of the 1988 change of practice (which made it possible to use section 1 of the 1972 Act against builders), how could they have been reassuring litigants (and themselves) that the 'abolition' of the common-law remedies did not really matter given the existence of the statutory remedies? In this context, therefore, the most that one can say of *Murphy* is that it is consistent with the current mode of their Lordships to leave 'consumer protection' to statute law and not undertake this task themselves. This attitude may satisfy those who believe in the separation of powers; but, in practice, it allows powerful pressure groups to intervene in the legislative process and dilute consumers' rights.

(iii) Local Authorities The liability of local authorities is discussed later in this chapter (Section 5). Here, suffice it to say that after *Murphy* they are not liable for any economic harm (e.g. repair costs) suffered by owners of premises. Surprisingly, their Lordships were also eager to stress that they were also leaving open the question of liability for physical injury to persons (or damage to other property) under the usual *Donoghue* v. *Stevenson* principle. As for damage to other property, the High Court[574] recently refused to hold a local authority liable for damages caused by its failure to detect a defect in the property which was the result of the builder's plans to comply with building regulations. The result was largely achieved by invoking the elusive device of 'fair, just and reasonable'; and it may even be regarded as dubious in so far as it introduces a distinction—unknown to the common law—between personal injuries and physical damage to property. As stated, the recoverability of the former has yet to be determined whenever compensation for the latter seems to have been excluded.

Select Bibliography

BOWETT, D. W., 'Law Reform and Occupier's Liability' (1956) 19 *MLR* 172.

DUNCAN-WALLACE, I., 'Anns Beyond Repair' (1991) 107 *LQR* 228.

GRAVELLS, N., 'Defective Premises: Negligence Liability of Builders' (1979) *Conv.* (NS) 97.

JAMES, FLEMING, 'Tort Liability of Occupiers of Land: Duties Owed to Licensees and Invitees' 63 *Yale LJ* 605 (1954).

Law Commission Report, *Liability for Damage or Injury to Trespassers and Related Questions of Occupier's Liability* (No. 75, Cmnd. 6428).

---

[573] Thus in *Warner* v. *Basildon DC* [1991] 7 Const. LJ 146 at 154, Gibson LJ believed that 97% of houses built in any year were covered by the NHBC scheme 'and, in consequence, the section 1 remedy [of the 1972 Act] is excluded'. There is little concrete evidence that in *Murphy* their Lordships were better informed.

[574] In *Tesco Stores Ltd.* v. *Wards Construction (Investment) Ltd.* (1995) 76 BLR 94.

Law Reform Committee's Third Report, *Occupier's Liability to Invitees, Licensees and Trespassers* (Cmnd. 9306, 1954).

McMAHON, B. M. E., 'Conclusions on Judicial Behaviour from a Comparative Study of Occupiers' Liability' (1975) 38 *MLR* 39.

MESHER, J., 'Occupiers, Trespassers and the Unfair Contract Terms Act 1977' (1979) *Conv.* (NS) 58–65.

NEWARK, F. H., 'The Occupiers' Liability Act (Northern Ireland) 1957' (1958) 12 *NILQ* 203.

NORTH, P. M., *Occupiers' Liability* (1971).

PAYNE, D., 'The Occupiers' Liability Act' (1958) 21 *MLR* 359.

Report of the Royal Commission, *On Civil Liability and Compensation for Personal Injury* (Pearson Committee Report) (Cmnd. 7054–1, 1978), ch. 28.

ROGERS, W. V. H. and CLARKE, M. G., *The Unfair Contract Terms Act 1977* (1978).

SPENCER, J., 'The Defective Premises Act 1972: Defective Law and Defective Law Reform' [1974] *CLJ* 307; [1975] *CLJ* 48.

4. Breach of Statutory Duty

1. The Nature of the Action

The action for breach of statutory duty enables the plaintiff to recover compensation for losses brought about by the defendant's failure to comply with a statutory obligation. Increasing areas of commercial and business activity are regulated by legislation designed to protect the health and safety of employees, consumers, and road-users; regulation may also have the aim of protecting certain property and financial interests. It is unusual for a regulatory statute explicitly to create a private, civil right of action; more frequently, they simply create criminal offences that are sanctioned by fine or imprisonment. It is also possible for a statute to be entirely silent on the question of remedies, making no reference to either civil or criminal sanctions. Unless the statute is explicit on the presence or absence of a private action, it is the task of the court to determine whether, on its proper construction, a civil action arises by implication.[575] A common instance of such an action is the claim of an employee who has been injured at work as a result of the employer's failure to comply with the provisions of health and safety legislation, such as that which requires machinery to be securely fenced. However, a private action for damages will not be inferred automatically. On the contrary, the rules of construction are strict and normally require the plaintiff to show that he belongs to a class of persons whom the statute was passed to protect. Together with other presumptions of statutory interpretation, this has the effect of substantially restricting the availability of the action for breach of statute.

The action for breach of statutory duty is conceptually separate from the general tort of negligence. The modern view was expressed by Lord Wright in *London Passenger Transport Board* v. *Upson*,[576] where he said that the action for breach of statute was

---

[575] *Cutler* v. *Wandsworth Stadium Ltd.* [1949] AC 398.
[576] [1949] AC 155, 168; *Caswell* v. *Powell Duffryn Associated Collieries Ltd.* [1940] AC 152, 177–8.

a special common law right which is not to be confused in essence with a claim for negligence. The statutory right has its origin in the statute, but the particular remedy of an action for damages is given by the common law in order to make effective for the benefit of the injured party his right to the performance by the defendant of the defendant's statutory duty. It is not a claim in negligence in the strict or ordinary sense.

It follows that the availability and scope of the private action for breach of statute are, in each case, a matter for the construction of the relevant legislation.[577]

It is vital, as a consequence, to distinguish between the action for breach of statute and the action sometimes known as negligence in the exercise of a statutory power.[578] The latter is an instance of negligence at common law, and while the statutory origin of the power in question may help to shape the common-law duty, the statute is not, in principle, the *origin* of the action. Thus the celebrated case of *Anns* v. *Merton London Borough Council*[579] was not an action for breach of statutory duty even though the Public Health Acts were used in that case to set the limits to the duty owed by the council; it was an action at common law. Although *Anns* has now been overruled on the precise point of negligence law which it decided,[580] the principle that statutory bodies may be liable for the negligent exercise of their powers remains good law and will be considered later in this chapter.[581]

Although the view expressed by Lord Wright represents the modern consensus, there is some authority for a contrary position according to which the true basis for the action is the idea of 'statutory negligence'. According to this view, the action for statutory breach retains the essential features of the general negligence action. There is, however, one exception. The *standard* of care is no longer set by the common law through the notion of the 'reasonable man' but by the particular statute which 'concretises', or makes more specific, the standard of behaviour required.[582] For example, while an employer is under a general duty of care at common law to have regard to the health and safety of his employees, a provision such as section 14 of the Factories Act 1961 would specify more precisely the content of this obligation by requiring him to fence dangerous machinery.

The question is of more than just theoretical interest. Under the statutory negligence approach, the court is relieved of the need to look for what is almost certainly a fictitious Parliamentary intent to grant a private cause of action. There is also a clear acknowledgement that the general law on the scope of the duty of care is relevant to the existence of a statutory claim. The general law on causation and defences (such as consent and contributory negligence) also comes into play. Finally the question of fault is affected and it might become possible, under certain circumstances, for a defendant to avoid liability if he

---

[577] *Lonrho Ltd.* v. *Shell Petroleum Co. Ltd.* (*No. 2*) [1982] AC 173, 185 (Lord Diplock).

[578] See P. P. Craig, 'Negligence in the Exercise of a Statutory Power' (1978) 94 *LQR* 240; S. Arrowsmith, *Civil Liability and Public Authorities* (1992), ch. 6.

[579] [1978] AC 728.   [580] *Murphy* v. *Brentwood DC* [1991] 1 AC 398.

[581] Section 5, below.

[582] Glanville Williams, 'The Effect of Penal Legislation in the Law of Tort' (1960) 23 *MLR* 233.

can show that his breach of the statute was not due to fault (either intention or carelessness) on his part.[583]

The incorporation of breach of statutory duty actions into the general law of negligence is accepted in numerous jurisdictions in the United States, where two theories have developed. Thus, one argues that a breach of statute is *evidence* of negligence on the part of the defendant, whereas the other suggests that such a breach is negligence *per se*. In each case the scope of the private action is limited to a situation where the common law already recognises a duty of care between the parties. This would, for example, happen in a case of physical injury sustained by an employee as a result of his employer's negligence but would not, necessarily, be the case if the damage fell into the category of pure economic loss. In his classic article on the subject, Thayer suggested that breach of the statute might be negligence *per se* for the reason that no reasonable person commits a crime.[584] This could, on the other hand, lead to a situation in which a minor breach of a criminal regulation, punishable perhaps by a small fine, gives rise to a much more extensive liability to pay tort compensation, which could ruin the defendant financially. The extent of liability might be out of all proportion to the degree of fault involved, in particular if the plaintiff would not otherwise have incurred a duty of care towards the defendant.[585] The view that the statute provides evidence of negligence in a situation where a general duty of care is already imposed by virtue of the common law received the support of Professor Glanville Williams. This great scholar argued persuasively for the adoption of the statutory negligence theory in English law, finding support for this position in a number of nineteenth-century cases.[586]

As the law currently stands the action for breach of statutory duty is closer to strict liability than to liability for negligence. In particular, in the context of accidents at work the employer's fault is normally irrelevant if there has been a breach of a statutory health and safety regulation for which he is responsible. This approach could be justified by the policy of providing employers with strong incentives to perform these particular duties. In other cases, as we shall see, the courts have given statutes a reading that implies the need to show fault. Though it has been suggested that 'the language used in legislation seems to be largely haphazard . . . it is upon the accident of language that the issue is made to turn'.[587]

Numerous decisions ostensibly applying the test of 'legislative intention' for deciding the presence of an action could be just as well and perhaps better explained using the statutory negligence approach. In the leading case of *Cutler*

---

[583] German law adopts an essentially similar position under Art. 828–II BGB: if liability under the statute could arise without fault, civil liability will none the less be imposed only if the defendant was at fault. See B. S. Markesinis, *The German Law of Torts* (2nd edn., 1990), at 10, 653–7, and 692–705.

[584] 'Public Wrong and Private Action' (1914) 27 *Harv. LR* 317.

[585] See C. Morris, 'The Role of Criminal Statutes in Negligence Actions' (1949) 49 *Col. LR* 21; G. Fricke, 'The Juridical Nature of the Action on the Statute' (1960) 76 *LQR* 241.

[586] Williams, op. cit.; see *Blamires* v. *Lancashire & Yorkshire Railway* (1873) LR 8 Ex. 283; *Cayzer, Irvine & Co.* v. *Carran Co.* (1884) LR 9 App. Cas. 873.

[587] Williams, op. cit. (1960) 23 *MLR* 232, 243.

v. *Wandsworth Stadium*[588] the plaintiff, a bookmaker, sued the occupier of the stadium for breach of section 11(2) of the Betting and Lotteries Act 1934. This made it an offence for the occupier of a licensed dog-racing track to exclude any bookmaker if a lawful totalisator was being operated on the track. The House of Lords held that the purpose of the statute was to protect the public by preventing the tote having a monopoly, and not to protect the livelihood of the bookmakers. Another way of looking at the case would be to point out that the plaintiff's claim was for financial or pure economic loss, and as a result outside the normal scope of the duty of care in negligence. A similar case is the recent decision of the House of Lords in *Scally* v. *Southern Health and Social Services Board*.[589] Here, several junior doctors sued for financial losses suffered as a result of their employers' failure to notify them of options available under the complex terms of an occupational pension scheme. By the time the doctors found out about these rights, their opportunity to exercise them had expired. This was a breach by the employer of the obligation under employment-protection legislation to provide full information concerning terms and conditions of employment.[590] In rejecting a claim for damages in tort for breach of statutory duty the courts pointed to the existence of an alternative remedy under the Act itself, namely an application to an Industrial (now Employment) Tribunal for rectification of the written statement of contract terms.[591] Yet this judgment also reflects the current preference of the courts for a contractual rather than a tort-based remedy for pure economic losses.[592]

To similar effect is *Pickering* v. *Liverpool Daily Post*,[593] which concerned an action for damages brought by a mental patient for the release, contrary to regulations, of information concerning his application for discharge before a mental health tribunal. This was, in essence, a claim for damages for a breach of privacy, and as such outside the normal range of interests protected by tort law. The Court of Appeal allowed the claim for damages on the ground that the regulations were designed to protect applicants from unwelcome publicity, but the House of Lords reversed their decision on the basis that there is

no authority where a statute has been held . . . to give a cause of action for breach of statutory duty when the nature of the statutory obligation or prohibition was not such that a breach of it would be likely to cause to a member of the class for whose benefit or protection it was imposed either personal injury, injury to property or economic loss. But publication of unauthorised information about proceedings on a patient's application for discharge to a mental health review tribunal, though it may in one sense be adverse to the patient's interest, is incapable of causing him loss or injury of a kind for which the law awards damages.[594]

The view that the law of tort is inherently incapable of providing damages for breach of privacy is questionable.[595] But the *Pickering* decision nevertheless

---

[588] [1949] AC 398.   [589] [1991] 4 All ER 563, noted by M. R. Freedland (1992) 21 *ILJ* 135.
[590] See Employment Protection (Consolidation) Act 1978, s. 1 ff. (now contained in the Employment Rights Act 1996, s. 1 ff.), and the equivalent provision for Northern Ireland which was considered in *Scally*, Contracts of Employment and Redundancy Payments Act (Northern Ireland) 1965, s. 4(1)(d).
[591] See the judgment of Kelly LJ in the Northern Ireland Court of Appeal [1991] 4 All ER 563.
[592] Freedland, op. cit.   [593] [1991] 4 All ER 622.   [594] Ibid., at 632.
[595] See Chapter 7 below.

illustrates an increasing tendency for the courts to deny actions for statutory breach if the effect would be a significant widening of the scope of civil liability in a particular context.

Appeals to precedent aside, the principal argument against the 'statutory negligence' theory is that confining liability to cases where the common law has already recognised the existence of a duty situation and where the defendant can be shown to have been at fault, would unduly restrict the development of the law of tort. The courts, it is said, should be able to grant a private action for damages going beyond the existing common law in areas where Parliament has recognised the importance of the interests at stake.[596] Recovery for financial loss developed in this way, through actions for breach of statutory duty, before the decision in *Hedley Byrne & Co. Ltd.* v. *Heller & Partners Ltd.*[597] which established a non-contractual duty of care at common law in respect of economic loss caused by financial misstatements. The most striking decision is *Monk* v. *Warbey*,[598] in which the Court of Appeal allowed the victim of a road accident an action for damages against the owner of the car who had permitted another to drive it uninsured, contrary to section 35 of the Road Traffic Act 1930. This was a claim for financial losses flowing from the inability of the plaintiff to claim on the defendant's insurance; it was not a claim to the effect that the plaintiff had caused the physical injuries himself.

In reality, the growth of a nominate tort separate from the general tort of negligence can only be accounted for by an historical rather than a conceptual perspective. The action for breach of statutory duty developed as it did in the final quarter of the nineteenth century precisely in order to avoid the restrictiveness of the then common law in the area of employers' liability. As we shall note in Chapter 6, for most of the nineteenth century it had been possible to defeat common law claims for personal injury through one or more of the three defences of consent, contributory negligence, and common employment.[599] The action for breach of statutory duty was a means of overcoming these defences. In *Groves* v. *Lord Wimborne*[600] the Court of Appeal held that common employment was no defence to a claim based on the employer's failure to fence dangerous machinery under the Factory and Workshop Act 1878. It was later held that consent could be no defence to a claim based on statute either.[601] The rationale for this was that no one could effectively grant his consent to the breach of an obligation imposed by Parliament. But the defences could not have been side-stepped in this way had the courts perceived the action as originating in the common law. But for *Groves* v. *Wimborne*,[602] the action for breach of the statute would most likely have been consigned to a 'history of total obscurity' and 'haphazard applications'.[603]

---

[596] R. A. Buckley, 'Liability in Tort for Breach of Statutory Duty' (1984) 100 *LQR* 204, 208.
[597] [1964] AC 465; see *Woods* v. *Winskill* [1913] 2 Ch. 303.   [598] [1935] 1 KB 75.
[599] Which barred any action against the employer where the plaintiff was injured through the negligence of a fellow worker.
[600] [1898] 2 QB 402.   [601] *Wheeler* v. *New Merton Board Mills Ltd.* [1933] 2 KB 669.
[602] [1898] 2 QB 402.
[603] K. M. Stanton, *Breach of Statutory Duty in Tort*, Modern Legal Studies Series (1986), 3.

The scope of these defences is, today, substantially reduced (common employment was abolished altogether in 1948),[604] largely removing the rationale for treating the action for breach of statutory duty any differently from common-law negligence. It should be stressed that the action for breach of statute, if not part of the tort of negligence, is nevertheless 'tortious in character'.[605] Principles of causation apply in the normal way[606] and there is modern authority to suggest that consent and contributory negligence may be partially applicable as well.[607] But if the separation of the statutory action from general principles of negligence is, more than anything else, an historical accident, a strong case for its reintegration exists in terms of doctrinal clarity and predictability of application. Nor has its separation from the tort of negligence allowed the action for breach of statute to develop into new areas of liability. On the contrary, the action for breach of statute has declined to the point where the courts scarcely recognise the possibility of an Act or regulation creating a new private action unless it does so explicitly. This is partly because, when the courts are seeking the necessary Parliamentary intention, they are 'looking for what is not there'.[608] The fiction of legislative intention, which formerly made the law of statutory breach unpredictable, now simply tends to make it restrictive, as the recent decisions in *Scally* v. *Southern Health and Social Service Board*[609] and *Pickering* v. *Liverpool Daily Post*[610] only too clearly illustrate. As a consequence the modern action for statutory breach is really of much significance only in the area of industrial health and safety, where the courts have freely inferred its existence in a range of situations. Outside this area the instances of civil liability for statutory breach are few and far between.

When the Canadian Supreme Court recently had the chance to reconsider the nature of breach of statutory duty in *R in the Right of Canada* v. *Saskatchewan Wheat Pool*[611] it decisively rejected the current position of English law. Reviewing the authorities, Dixon J contrasted American developments assimilating the tort of statutory breach into general negligence with the 'painful emergence' in England of the separate nominate tort. He also rejected Thayer's view that breach of statutory duty should amount to negligence *per se* in favour of the more flexible view that it was only evidence of negligence, at least in cases not involving industrial health and safety. In this case, the breach by the defendants of a regulation prohibiting the discharge of infected grain from an elevator did not, in the absence of proof of a lack of care, give the plaintiff authority for an action for damages for the costs of fumigating the two ships which had been loaded with the grain.

---

[604] Law Reform (Personal Injuries) Act 1948, s. 1.

[605] *American Express Co.* v. *British Airways Board* [1983] 1 WLR 701, 709 (Lloyd J).

[606] See e.g. *McWilliams* v. *Sir William Arrol* [1962] 1 WLR 295; below, Section 2(c).

[607] See respectively, *Imperial Chemical Industries* v. *Shatwell* [1965] AC 656 and *Caswell* v. *Powell Duffryn Associated Collieries Ltd.* [1940] AC 152.

[608] Glanville Williams, op. cit. (1960) 23 *MLR* 233, 244.

[609] [1991] 4 All ER 563, above.

[610] [1991] 4 All ER 622.

[611] (1983) 143 DLR (3d) 9.

2. The Components of Liability

It is necessary, in the first place, to determine whether a private action arises under a particular statute, and then secondly to see whether the plaintiff's claim falls under the scope of the action in question.

(A) THE AVAILABILITY OF A CIVIL REMEDY

In some cases a statute will state explicitly whether or not a private action lies for its breach. Private actions of any kind may be completely excluded.[612] Alternatively, as in the Nuclear Installations Act 1965, the scheme of compensation provided by the Act may be stated to be exhaustive. Section 12(1)(b) states that compensation for breach of the Act's provisions is payable only in accordance with the terms of the Act itself, and that 'no other liability shall be incurred by any person in respect of that injury or damage'. The Sex Discrimination Act 1975 sets up a scheme of remedies, including damages, administered by Employment Tribunals. The regular courts are excluded by a provision to the effect that 'no proceedings, whether civil or criminal, shall lie against any person in respect of an act by reason that the act is unlawful by virtue of a provision of this Act'.[613]

A third possibility is to provide for enforcement through a specially created action for breach of statutory duty. The Health and Safety at Work Act 1974 provides that 'breach of a duty imposed by health and safety regulations . . . shall, so far as it causes damage, be actionable except in so far as the regulations provide otherwise'.[614] Regulations made under the Act are gradually modernising and in some cases replacing regulations under the Factories Act 1961 and Offices, Shops and Railway Premises Act 1963, although many of the latter remain in force. However, it should be noted that the *general* duty of an employer 'to ensure, so far as is reasonably practicable, the health, safety and welfare of his employees' under section 2(1) of the Health and Safety at Work Act does not give rise to a private action for damages.[615] Had it done so it could have rendered obsolete most of the employer's general duty of care at common law and pushed employers' civil responsibility farther in the direction of stricter liability.[616]

A variety of statutory formulae may be used explicitly to create a private action. For example, section 145 of the Trade Union and Labour Relations (Consolidation) Act 1992, which prohibits a refusal to deal with a prospective supplier of goods and services on the grounds related to his employment of trade unionists, is enforced as follows.

'The obligation to comply with this section is a duty owed to the person with whom there is a refusal to deal and to any other person who may be adversely affected by its contravention; and a breach of the duty is actionable accordingly (subject to the defences and other incidents applying to actions for breach of statutory duty).'

---

[612] See e.g. Safety of Sports Grounds Act 1975, s. 13; Guard Dogs Act 1975, s. 5(2).

[613] S. 62; on remedies more generally see ss. 63–6. See also the parallel provisions of the Race Relations Act 1976, ss. 53–7.

[614] S. 47(1)(a).   [615] Health and Safety at Work Act 1974, s. 47(1)(a).

[616] On employer's liability in general, see Chapter 6, Section 3, below.

Yet another model is provided by the Local Government Act 1988, section 17 of which governs the terms of commercial contracts agreed by local authorities with commercial suppliers. Failure to comply with section 17 is stated not to be a criminal offence, but it is 'actionable by any person who, in consequence, suffers loss or damage'.[617]

The difficulties begin when the statute is silent on the question of civil liability. The Law Commission has proposed the enactment of a general presumption to the effect that in these circumstances a breach of statutory duty will be actionable in damages,[618] but this has not been taken up. In the absence of such a measure, the courts' approach is that expressed by Viscount Simonds in *Cutler* v. *Wandsworth Stadium*. There, the learned judge stated that 'the only rule, which in all the circumstances is valid, is that the answer must depend on a consideration of the whole Act and the circumstances, including the pre-existing law, in which it was enacted'.[619]

In *Cutler*'s case the House of Lords rejected the notion of a general presumption of civil liability for statutory breach which was raised by Greer LJ in *Monk* v. *Warbey*.[620] In the latter case, Greer LJ had said that:

prima facie a person who has been injured by breach of a statute has a right to recover damages from the person committing it, unless it can be established by considering the whole of the Act that no such right was intended to be given.

Although there are nineteenth-century precedents for the view that the common law provides 'an action on the case for special damage sustained by the breach of a public duty',[621] this approach is not generally followed today.

The law was restated by Lord Diplock in *Lonrho Ltd.* v. *Shell Petroleum Co. Ltd.* (*No. 2*).[622] The normal rule, according to his Lordship, was to the effect that a civil action was excluded in any case where the statute provided for a criminal sanction as the means of enforcing the relevant duty. To this there were two exceptions:

the first is where on the true construction of the Act it is apparent that the obligation or prohibition was imposed for the benefit or protection of a particular class of individuals . . . The second exception is where the statute creates a public right (i.e. a right to be enjoyed by all those of Her Majesty's subjects who wish to avail themselves of it) and a particular member of the public suffers what Brett J in *Benjamin* v. *Storr*[623] described as 'particular, direct and substantial' damage 'other and different from that which was common to all the rest of the public'.

If anything, Lord Diplock's second exception states the law rather broadly; there are very few examples of such a wide principle being invoked to grant a civil action for breach of statutory duty other than in the context of public

---

[617] S. 19(7).   [618] Law Com. No. 21, 1969.

[619] [1949] AC 398, 407.   [620] [1935] 1 KB 75, 81.

[621] *Couch* v. *Steel* (1854) 3 E. & N. 402, 415 (Lord Campbell CJ), in which a merchant seaman who fell ill at sea successfully sued his employer for damages arising from breach of legislation requiring ships to carry medicines on board. This case would now quite easily be interpreted as a case of a statute designed for the protection of a particular group.

[622] [1982] AC 173, 182.   [623] (1874) LR 9 CP 400, 407.

nuisance.[624] In this case, Lonrho complained that the defendants' alleged supply of oil and gas in breach of sanctions orders made under the Southern Rhodesia Act 1965 had caused it a loss of business. For it had maintained the illegal Rhodesian regime in power and postponed the resumption of normal oil supplies through the plaintiff's pipeline. The action was misconceived, said Lord Diplock, because the orders were neither passed for the protection of a group of which the plaintiffs formed part nor did they confer a benefit on the public generally: they simply imposed a prohibition on activity which had previously been lawful. The implication is that a measure passed for the protection of the public as a whole may give rise to a private action for damages by a person who suffers special damage. This second category is wider, however, than any envisaged by the House of Lords in *Cutler* v. *Wandsworth Stadium Ltd.*,[625] and it is difficult to reconcile with the approach taken in other leading authorities.[626] It also rests on the difficult distinction between an Act that is read as conferring a public benefit, on the one hand, and one that is read as simply prohibiting an activity, on the other.

It must normally be shown, then, that the statutory duty was imposed for the benefit of a particular class of persons separate from the public at large. In *Cutler* v. *Wandsworth Stadium Ltd.*[627] the House of Lords, as we have seen, decided that regulations providing for bookmakers' access to licensed racing tracks were imposed in the interests of ensuring choice for the public and not to protect the bookmakers' economic interests. More recently, in *R* v. *Deputy Governor of Parkhurst Prison, ex parte Hague*[628] the House of Lords held that the Prison Rules 1964 were essentially regulatory in character. Thus, they did not give rise to a private right of action on the part of a prisoner who was confined in breach of the Rules. Conversely, the initial expansion of employers' civil liability for statutory breach took place because the courts saw the Factory and Workshop Acts as clearly passed for the benefit of the industrial workforce. In *Groves* v. *Lord Wimborne*[629] A. L. Smith LJ had this to say of the Factory and Workshop Act 1878:

The Act . . . is not in the nature of a private legislative bargain between employers and workmen as the learned judge seemed to think, but is a public Act passed in favour of the workers in factories and workshops to compel their employers to do certain things for their protection and benefit.

As a guide to construction, however, the 'recognisable class of plaintiffs' test has not always proved easy to apply consistently. In *Phillips* v. *Britannia Hygienic Laundry Co.*[630] the Court of Appeal held that no right of action arose out of

---

[624] As Lord Diplock put it ([1982] AC 173, 182), 'most of the authorities about this second exception deal not with public rights created by statute but with public rights existing at common law, particularly in respect of use of highways'. *Boyce* v. *Paddington BC* [1903] 1 Ch. 109 is 'one of the comparatively few cases about a right conferred on the general public by statute' (ibid.).

[625] [1949] AC 398.

[626] *Atkinson* v. *Newcastle Waterworks Co.* (1877) 2 Ex. D. 441; *Phillips* v. *Britannia Hygienic Laundry Co.* [1923] 2 KB 832.

[627] [1949] AC 498.

[628] [1992] 1 AC 58, 159–61 (Lord Bridge of Harwich), 178–9 (Lord Jauncy of Tullichettle). See also *Calveley* v. *Chief Constable of Merseyside* [1989] AC 1228, 1237 (Lord Bridge of Harwich).

[629] [1898] 2 QB 402, 406.

[630] [1923] 2 KB 832, 840.

breach of a vehicle-use and construction order which produced a defective condition in the defendant's van. The defect led to an accident in which the plaintiff's van was damaged. According to Bankes LJ, 'the public using the highway is not a class; it is the public itself and not a class of the public'.[631] The decision cannot be reconciled with *Monk* v. *Warbey*,[632] in which breach of a vehicle owner's obligation to take out appropriate liability insurance under the Road Traffic Act 1930 was held to create a right of private action on the part of an accident victim. Of the two decisions *Monk* v. *Warbey* now seems anomalous, given the restrictive modern approach to allowing statutory actions. The courts' protective attitude towards victims of industrial accidents is at odds, however, with the approach taken with regard to those injured on the highway.

Another restrictive decision is *McCall* v. *Abelesz*,[633] in which the Court of Appeal denied a private action to residential tenants in a case where the breach of statutory duty amounted to the crime of harassment. It is not clear why this group could not have constituted a relevant class for whose protection the regulations were passed. More recently the courts have had to consider claims for damages for breach of legislation prohibiting the unauthorised recording and distribution of musical performances by 'bootleggers'. After some debate, it was held that actions for damages could be brought by the performers and musicians affected but not by their record companies. Yet the latter would undoubtedly suffer loss, as contracts with the artists for their exclusive recording rights would be made less valuable as a result of the illegitimate competition of the bootleggers.[634]

The provision by the Act of a criminal penalty or other remedy for its breach has been seen in numerous cases as having some bearing on the availability of the civil remedy, but it is difficult to draw any clear conclusion either way as to the effect it might have. The presence of criminal penalties under the nineteenth-century Factory and Workshop Acts did not stop the courts from developing employers' liability for statutory breach. Divergent conclusions, however, have been reached in cases concerning utilities and public authorities. *Atkinson* v. *Newcastle and Gateshead Waterworks Co.*[635] was an early decision restricting liability.

In that case a waterworks company had failed to maintain the necessary water pressure, in contravention of legislation,[636] with the result that firemen were unable to put out a fire which then damaged the plaintiff's house. The court held that the £10 fine prescribed by the Act was meant to be an exclusive

---

[631] Ibid.

[632] [1935] 1 KB 75; the relevant provision is now contained in the Road Traffic Act 1988, ss. 143 ff. See Hepple and Matthews, *Tort Cases and Materials* (4th edn., 1991), 885–90.

[633] [1976] QB 585.

[634] *RCA Corporation* v. *Pollard* [1983] Ch. 135; *Rickless* v. *United Artists Corporation* [1988] QB 40; see also *Ex parte Island Records* [1978] Ch. 122 and *Lonrho Ltd.* v. *Shell Petroleum Co. Ltd.* [1982] AC 175, discussed further below. The relevant legislation, the Dramatic and Musical Performers' Protection Act 1958, has now been replaced by the Copyright, Designs and Patents Act 1988, ss. 180 ff., which provides protection for both performers and those with exclusive recording rights.

[635] (1877) LR 2 Ex. D. 441.

[636] The Waterworks Clauses Act 1847, s. 47.

remedy. In *Dawson & Co.* v. *Bingley UDC*,[637] on the other hand, the defendant council was held liable in a civil action for the consequences of placing an inaccurate direction to a fire plug in breach of the Public Health Act 1875. For, as a result of this misdirection, the fire brigade had been delayed in putting out a fire on the plaintiff's premises. *Atkinson* was distinguished on the unconvincing grounds that the Act of 1875 provided for no separate penalty, and that the defendant in *Atkinson* was a private company. The decision in *Atkinson* is more easily explicable as a justified attempt to avoid the imposition of 'floodgates' liability on utilities, and to shift the burden of fire insurance on to householders.[638] Legislation regulating the privatised utilities now provides for them to compensate consumers affected by the interruption to supplies of gas, water, and electricity.[639]

Atkinson was, again, distinguished in *Read* v. *Croydon Corporation*,[640] a case involving the same Act, the Waterworks Clauses Act 1847, but a different section which placed the defendants under a duty to supply clean water.[641] As a result of their breach, the plaintiff's infant daughter contracted typhoid. The case was not, as it might appear, one of damages for injury and disease. The action was, instead, brought by the father in his capacity as a ratepayer and therefore a member of a protected class, and compensation was awarded for pure economic loss, namely his expenses incurred as a result of the child's illness.

A potentially significant extension of the liability of local authorities for statutory breaches was made in *Thornton* v. *Kirklees MBC*,[642] in which the Court of Appeal held that a person wrongfully denied relief under the Housing (Homeless Persons) Act 1977 could sue the authority in damages. The court was influenced by the absence of any specified penalty for breach of the Act. Where, by contrast, the statute provides for a distinct adjudicative procedure for determining eligibility for a public benefit, as it does for social-security payments, a separate civil action for damages will normally be excluded.[643]

Thornton was criticised as 'quite out of line with other cases regarding civil liability for breach of statutory duty'[644] and as a 'puzzling' decision which 'may have to be reconsidered at some future date'.[645] Decisions since *Thornton* suggest that even in a case where there is a recognisable class of plaintiffs, the courts will lean against finding a private cause of action where the statutory provisions in question confer broad discretionary powers on public bodies. In *X*

---

[637] [1911] 2 KB 149.

[638] Buckley, op. cit.; see also *Clegg, Parkinson & Co.* v. *Earby Gas Co.* [1896] 1 QB 592.

[639] Both the utility itself and third persons who induce a breach of its statutory duty may be liable in tort. See generally the discussion of G. S. Morris, 'Industrial Action in Essential Services: The New Law' (1991) 20 *ILJ* 89.

[640] [1938] 4 All ER 631.   [641] S. 35.

[642] [1979] 1 WLR 637. See also *West Wiltshire DC* v. *Garland* [1995] Ch. 297, in which the same factor led the Court of Appeal to hold that a local council had a cause of action against district auditors for their failure to fulfil their statutory obligation to audit the council's accounts.

[643] See *Jones* v. *Department of Employment* [1989] QB 1.

[644] Weir, 'Governmental Liability' [1988] *PL* 40, 52. Cf. *Wyatt* v. *Hillingdon LBC* (1978) 76 LGR 727, 723: 'a statute . . . which is dealing with the distribution of benefits . . . does not in its very nature give rise to an action by the disappointed . . . person' (Geoffrey Lane LJ).

[645] *X (Minors)* v. *Bedfordshire CC* [1995] 2 AC 633, 748 (Lord Browne-Wilkinson).

(*Minors*) v. *Bedfordshire CC*[646] the House of Lords ruled out claims for breach of statutory duty brought by victims of child abuse against local authorities who, it was alleged, had failed to take adequate steps to protect them. In particular, it was argued that the defendants had failed to act in accordance with their statutory duties to initiate proceedings to take them into care. Lord Browne-Wilkinson concluded, on the basis of a close reading of the relevant legislation, that:

> the section itself points out the basic tension which lies at the root of so much child protection work: the decision whether to split the family in order to protect the child. I find it impossible to construe such a statutory provision as demonstrating an intention that even where there is no carelessness by the authority it should be liable in damages if a court subsequently decided with hindsight that the removal, or failure to remove, the child from the family either was or was not 'consistent with' the duty to safeguard the child.[647]

This approach was applied in *O'Rourke* v. *Camden London Borough Council*,[648] in which *Thornton* was finally overruled. According to Lord Hoffmann, it was inappropriate to infer the existence of a private cause of action given the wide discretion which the Act conferred upon the council when making decisions on the allocation of resources to deal with homelessness.

(B) THE SCOPE OF THE CIVIL REMEDY

Once the existence of the action is established, it remains to see whether the plaintiff's claim falls within its scope. Here, three issues are relevant: whether the defendant's conduct infringed the standard set by the Act; whether the plaintiff was a member of the class protected by the Act; and whether the damage occurred in the manner the Act was meant to guard against. These requirements are strictly enforced and frequently result in the failure of actions for breach of statutory duty.

It is axiomatic, first of all, that the terms of the relevant provision must have been broken. Criminal statutes are strictly construed. In *Chipchase* v. *British Titan Products Co. Ltd.*[649] a regulation required a platform more than 6 feet 6 inches from the ground to be at least 34 inches wide if there was a danger of a workman falling from it. The plaintiff fell from a platform that was 9 inches wide but only 6 feet above the ground. On this basis no claim could arise under the statute, although a claim in general negligence could be argued.

In conformity with the view that the right to bring the action derives from the particular statute which creates the obligation and not from the general law of negligence, the appropriate standard for judging the defendant's behaviour can only be arrived at by a process of statutory construction. Certain provisions have been interpreted as giving rise to strict liability, such as the requirement in section 14(1) of the Factories Act 1961 that 'every dangerous part of any machinery . . . shall be securely fenced'. Thus, in *John Summers & Sons Ltd.* v. *Frost*[650] this provision was used to impose liability for an injury caused by

---

[646] [1995] 2 AC 633; see also *Clunis* v. *Camden and Islington HA* [1998] 2 WLR 902.
[647] [1995] 2 AC 633, 747–8.   [648] [1998] AC 189.   [649] [1956] 1 QB 545.
[650] [1955] AC 740.

the unfenced part of a grinding-wheel, even though the machine could not have been used at all if completely fenced in. In effect, it was impossible to comply with the statute except by removing the machine from service, which was unlikely to have been the aim of the Act. The effect of the decision had to be reversed by statutory order.[651]

In other cases the otherwise unconditional words of the statute are qualified by the use of a phrase requiring the employer to maintain a safe workplace 'as far as reasonably practicable', a standard which comes close to that of negligence liability.[652] In *Nimmo* v. *Alexander Cowan & Sons*[653] a bare majority of the House of Lords held that the use of this phrase in section 29 of the Factories Act 1961 placed the onus on the employer of showing that he had taken all reasonable precautions. Sometimes the word 'practicable' appears on its own, which may be taken as indicating a standard midway between negligence and strict liability; thus section 157 of the Mines and Quarries Act 1957 enables the employer to avoid liability where 'it was impracticable to avoid or prevent the contravention'. There is little consistency in the way provisions such as these are drafted, and 'often it is difficult to find any reason' for one formulation being preferred over another.[654]

The very strict interpretation given to section 14 of the Factories Act is something of an exception, explicable perhaps by the historical importance of that section in the development of the statutory action and its practical importance for workplace safety. In interpreting other provisions the courts normally manage to avoid finding an employer or occupier strictly liable if he has been wholly blameless. In *Scott* v. *Green & Sons*[655] the plaintiff, who was injured when a cellar flap on the pavement gave way beneath him, failed in an action against the owner for breach of section 154 of the Highways Act 1959. The flap had been damaged shortly before when an unidentified lorry driver had driven his vehicle on to it; the defendants had not had time to become aware of the damage let alone to have done anything about it. To similar effect is *Whitfield* v. *H. & R. Johnson (Tiles) Ltd.*[656] There, the plaintiff sued her employer for breach of section 72 of the Factories Act, which provides that 'a person shall not be employed to lift, carry or move any load so heavy as to be likely to cause injury to him'. Unknown to either party the plaintiff was suffering from a latent back condition which was triggered when she lifted a load which would normally have given her no difficulty. In rejecting the claim, the Court of Appeal held that section 72 did not require the employer to take the plaintiff as he found her. The section, according to the court, was 'intended to make sure that the weight of the load was appropriate to the sex, build and physique, or other obvious characteristic, of the employee in question'.[657] The employer was protected against liability for a concealed risk of injury without the court finding, as such, that the standard was less than strict. But the decision can be ques-

---

[651] Abrasive Wheels Regulations 1970, reg. 3.

[652] See e.g. ss. 28 and 29 of the Factories Act 1961 (obligation to keep floors, etc. and means of access free of obstruction).

[653] [1968] AC 107.   [654] *Nimmo* v. *Cowan* [1968] AC 107 (Lord Reid).

[655] [1969] 1 WLR 301.   [656] [1990] 3 All ER 426.   [657] Ibid., 434–5 (Beldam LJ).

tioned since had it been a negligence action the 'eggshell skull' principle—that the defendant takes the plaintiff as he finds her—would most likely have resulted in a finding for the plaintiff in this case.

The second issue to consider is whether the plaintiff falls into the class of persons protected by the Act. In *Knapp* v. *Railway Executive*[658] an accident occurred when a level-crossing gate that had been insecurely locked swung back across the railway line when a train was approaching, as a result of which its driver was injured. This was a breach of a regulation requiring gates to be kept closed to the road when a train was approaching and closed to the railway at all other times. The driver's claim for damages for breach of statutory duty failed. The Court of Appeal found that the purpose of the regulation was the protection of the road-using public and not the employees of the railway. 'The conflict of interest' said the court, 'with which the legislature is here dealing is clearly a conflict between the road-using public . . . and the railway company . . . and the whole purport of the section is to protect the road-using public against the railway company, it being assumed that the railway company, having got its power of running over the railway, will so manage its affairs that its traffic can proceed in safety.'[659]

If the principle is clear, however, its application here is open to question. There is no reason why the regulation should not have sought to protect the safety of those on the train, both employees and passengers, as well as those using the highway. Also open to question is *Hartley* v. *Mayoh & Co.*[660] A fireman was electrocuted in the course of fighting a blaze at the defendant's factory. His injury was brought about by a breach of electricity regulations passed for the protection of 'persons employed' in factories and workshops. It was held that a fireman was not a person employed in a factory, and so an action for damages for statutory breach failed. The result is the consequence of seeing the statutory breach in isolation from any wider tort duty. It also stems directly from the 'statutory interpretation' approach, which as explained above, ascribes the existence of the damages claim to a fictitious Parliamentary intent as opposed to a pre-existing duty of care at common law.

The most severe limitation of the action for statutory breach is the principle, laid down in *Gorris* v. *Scott*,[661] that the loss or damage must have been of the kind which the statute was passed to prevent and must have occurred in the manner the statute contemplated. An order made under the Contagious Diseases (Animals) Act 1869 required cattle to be placed in separate pens of a certain size when being transported by ship. The plaintiff's cattle were carried on board a ship without pens of any kind, as a result of which they were washed overboard in heavy seas. An action on the statute failed as the court found that its purpose was to control the spread of disease and not to prevent the cattle from being washed away. While breach and damage were undoubtedly linked in the sense of *but-for cause*, the damage here could not be said to be within the scope of the risk envisaged by the statute. Hence, to use the

---

[658] [1949] 2 All ER 508. [659] Ibid., 515 (Jenkins LJ). [660] [1954] 1 QB 383.
[661] (1874) LR 9 Exch. 125.

language of negligence liability, it was *too remote* as far as the statutory action was concerned.

While *Gorris* v. *Scott* is undoubtedly correct in principle, its application in industrial injury cases has been controversial. In particular, the courts have interpreted the duty to fence machinery in section 14 of the Factories Act 1961 and its predecessors as intended to cover a situation in which an employee puts his hand into a moving machine, and not one in which an employee is injured by a part of an unfenced machine flying out and hitting him.[662] It is not obvious that this interpretation of section 14 is the correct one.[663] But assuming that it is correct, the strictness with which the 'risk principle' is applied in statutory cases of personal injury contrasts with the much looser approach we find in the general law of negligence. For in the latter case, it is not open to a defendant to claim that injury of a foreseeable kind occurred in a *manner* which was not foreseeable.[664] If *Gorris* v. *Scott* is essentially the application of remoteness rules in the context of statutory actions, there is something to be said for adopting the approach of the common law and drawing a distinction between property damage, where liability is narrowly confined to the envisaged risk, and personal injury cases, where a far more flexible approach is taken.

(c) Causation and Defences

'But-for' or 'factual' causation must be established in the normal way. Thus in *McWilliams* v. *Sir William Arrol & Co. Ltd*.[665] the employer successfully defended a claim for damages brought by the widow of the deceased employee, who had fallen from a platform 70 feet above ground while not wearing a safety harness as required by legislation.[666] The defendant's defence succeeded because he was able to show that the employee would not have worn a harness even if one had been provided. The plaintiff's claim will thus fail if the only reason for the employer's breach of the statutory duty was the plaintiff's own act of carelessness. To put it differently: the plaintiff can have no claim if he was the sole cause of his own loss.[667] For the same reason, contributory negligence used to be a total defence before the law was modified by the Law Reform (Contributory Negligence) Act 1945. The position was summarised by Lord Atkin in *Caswell* v. *Powell Duffryn Associated Collieries*.

The person who is injured, as in all cases where the damage is the gist of the action, must show not only a breach of duty but that his hurt was due to the breach. If his damage is due entirely to his own wilful act no cause of action arises as, for instance, if out of bravado he puts his hand into moving machinery or attempts to leap over an unguarded cavity. The injury has not been caused by the defendants' omission but by the plaintiff's own act.[668]

---

[662] See in particular, the decision of the House of Lords in *Close* v. *Steel Company of Wales Ltd*. [1962] AC 367, and the authorities cited there.

[663] See the vigorous dissent of Lord Denning in *Close* v. *Steel Company of Wales Ltd*. [1962] AC 367.

[664] *Hughes* v. *Lord Advocate* [1963] AC 837.   [665] [1962] 1 WLR 295.

[666] Factories Act 1937, s. 61: 'Where any person is to work at a place from which he is liable to fall a distance more than ten feet, then . . . means shall be provided, so far as is reasonably practicable, by fencing or otherwise for ensuring his safety.'

[667] *Ginty* v. *Belmont Building Supplies Ltd*. [1959] 1 All ER 414; *Boyle* v. *Kodak Ltd*. [1969] 1 WLR 661.

[668] [1940] AC 152, 164.

Lord Atkin went on to say that where the employers' breach and the plaintiff's lack of care for himself combine to cause the injury, the defence of contributory negligence would apply to defeat the plaintiff's claim. This, however, must now be read subject to the 1945 Act and the interpretation subsequently placed upon it, namely that in such a case of concurrent causes the court will apportion the responsibility of the two parties and award the plaintiff a reduced measure of damages.[669] For the employee's own breach of statutory duty constitutes 'fault' for the purposes of the Act of 1945.[670]

Many statutes that have given rise to the possibility of a private action expressly prevent the application of exclusion and limitation clauses.[671] Rather more uncertainty surrounds the defence of consent. It was suggested earlier that this defence should apply to a statutory claim as to any other claim in tort. But since the action for breach of statutory duty was separated from the common law of negligence in large part because of the need to limit the scope of the defence of consent,[672] its application remains in some doubt.[673] As the defence has been narrowed considerably since the 1890s there is probably now no good reason to exclude it. Nevertheless, the House of Lords was appropriately cautious in allowing a partial application of the defence in *ICI Ltd.* v. *Shatwell.*[674] Lords Reid and Pearce both suggested that the defence would be inapplicable if the employer either in person or, if a corporation, through its managerial or supervisory employees, was directly implicated in the breach of statutory duty. However, the defence of *volenti* could apply where the employer was liable for breach of statutory duty solely by virtue of his vicarious liability for a breach committed by the plaintiff. This was the case in *Shatwell*, where the plaintiff clearly consented to running the risk of the danger in question. According to Lord Pearce:

the defence should be available where the employer was not himself in breach of statutory duty and was not vicariously in breach of any statutory duty through the neglect of some person who was of superior rank and whose commands the plaintiff was bound to obey (or who had some different and special duty of care . . .).[675]

This creates an area of difficulty since it may be far from clear what, in any given case, the phrase 'employee of superior rank' really means.

(D) A WIDER PRINCIPLE OF CIVIL LIABILITY?

The feeling has persisted that in *Cutler* v. *Wandsworth Stadium*[676] the House of Lords clarified the law of liability for statutory breach in an unduly restrictive way. None the less, no clear agreement has emerged on the possibility of a wider principle of liability. In *Lonrho Ltd.* v. *Shell Petroleum Co.* (*No. 2*)[677] the House of Lords rejected the so-called *Beaudesert* principle announced by the High Court of Australia, to the effect that 'a person who suffers harm or loss as the

---

[669] *Jones* v. *Livox Quarries Ltd.* [1952] 2 QB 608.
[670] See the judgment of Lord Diplock in *Boyle* v. *Kodak Ltd.* [1969] 1 WLR 661.
[671] See Stanton, *Breach of Statutory Duty in Tort*, op. cit., 123–4.
[672] *Baddeley* v. *Earl Granville* (1887) 19 QBD 423.
[673] *Wheeler* v. *New Merton Board Mills Ltd.* [1933] 2 KB 669. [674] [1965] AC 656.
[675] Ibid., 687.   [676] [1949] AC 398, discussed above.   [677] [1982] AC 173, 188 (Lord Diplock).

inevitable consequence of the unlawful, intentional and positive act of another is entitled to recover damages from that other'.[678] This goes too far in two ways. First, as we have seen, it is not the case that every breach of a statute must give rise to civil liability. Secondly, liability for the economic tort of causing loss by unlawful means normally requires the defendant's illegal act to have been directed at the plaintiff.[679]

A more likely candidate is the equitable principle that an injunction (and possibly damages) will be available in respect of a breach of a penal statute that infringes a substantial economic or 'property' interest of the plaintiff. The leading modern case is *Ex parte Island Records*,[680] in which performers and recording companies won injunctions to restrain the sale and distribution by 'bootleggers' of unauthorised concert recordings, made contrary to the Dramatic and Musical Performers' Protection Act 1958. Lord Denning rejected the normal analysis in terms of the action for breach of statutory duty—'the dividing line between the pro-cases and contra-cases is so blurred and so ill-defined that you might as well toss a coin to decide it.' Instead, equity would intervene 'to protect a private individual in his rights of property, and in aid of this would grant an injunction to restrain a defendant from committing an unlawful act, even though it was a crime punishable by the criminal courts, and would supplement its jurisdiction in this regard by its power under Lord Cairns' Act to award damages in lieu of or in addition to an injunction'.[681] The basis of the action was interference with a private right, over and above injury to the public as a whole.[682] Waller LJ agreed with grant of an injunction but did not support Lord Denning's view as to the availability of damages; Shaw LJ dissented on the grounds that the statute provided no private cause of action.[683]

In *Lonrho Ltd.* v. *Shell Petroleum Co. Ltd.* (*No. 2*)[684] Lord Diplock rejected any 'wider general rule, which does not depend on the scope and language of the statute by which a criminal offence is committed'. This amounts to a reassertion of what many now regard as the fiction of Parliamentary intent as the crucial test. The difficulty with Lord Diplock's approach is that it fails to deal with some far-from-insignificant nineteenth-century authorities in which the availability of equitable relief to restrain breaches of the criminal law threatening property and commercial interests was clearly recognised.[685] At the same time, it would be anomalous if breach of a criminal statute could be restrained by way of injunction as to the future, while no action for damages for past losses could be brought in respect of the same legal wrong. In the different context of

---

[678] *Beaudesert Shire Council* v. *Smith* (1966) 120 CLR 145, 160.

[679] P. Elias and A. Tettenborn, 'Crime, Tort and Compensation in Private and Public Law' [1981] *CLJ* 230.

[680] [1978] Ch. 122.   [681] Ibid., 135.

[682] Where the applicant for an injunction does not suffer special damage, the action may only be brought with the consent of the Attorney-General through his relator action: *Gouriet* v. *Union of Post Office Workers* [1978] AC 435.

[683] In the later case of *Rickless* v. *United Artists Corporation* [1988] QB 40, a different Court of Appeal held that the statute did confer an action for breach of statutory duty on the performers, although not on the record companies (see above).

[684] [1982] AC 173, 188.

[685] See in particular, *Springhead Spinning* v. *Riley* (1868) LR 6 Eq. 551; Wedderburn, 'Rocking the Torts' (1983) 46 *MLR* 224.

civil liability for breach of Community law Lord Diplock, himself, has said that if an injunction lies in equity to restrain an unlawful act threatening economic loss to the plaintiff, a damages action must follow in respect of the same breach 'at any rate since 1875 when the jurisdiction conferred upon the Court of Chancery . . . passed to the High Court'.[686] Statute has now intervened to deal with the specific situation of 'boot-legging' by granting an action for statutory damages both to performers and those to whom they grant exclusive recording rights.[687] But until the House of Lords has a further opportunity to reconsider it, the general status of the *Island Records* principle is likely to remain somewhat confused.

(E) LIABILITY FOR BREACH OF EUROPEAN COMMUNITY LAW

The possibility of liability in damages for breach of an obligation arising by virtue of European Community law was recognised by the House of Lords in *Garden Cottage Foods Ltd.* v. *Milk Marketing Board*.[688] This cause of action is limited to measures which have direct effect in national law and, so far at least, has only been applied to certain of the more important measures under the EC Treaty itself as opposed to the provisions of Directives or Regulations made under the Treaty. *Garden Cottage Foods* concerned a breach of Article 86 of the then EEC Treaty which is concerned with trading arrangements amounting to abuse of a dominant market position. Lord Diplock, with whom three other Lords agreed, held that since Article 86 had direct effect in national law its breach could 'be categorised in English law as a breach of statutory duty, that is, imposed not only for the purpose of promoting the general economic prosperity of the common market but also for the benefit of private individuals to whom loss or damage is caused by a breach of that duty'.[689] Lord Wilberforce dissented on the basis that the direct effect of a provision was not sufficient to give rise to tortious liability, in particular in a situation where the Treaty itself made no provision for damages for breach of the relevant Article.

In *Garden Cottage Foods* the primary issue was not damages but the availability of an interlocutory injunction.[690] But Lord Diplock's judgment was subsequently applied to enable damages to be claimed in another breach of Article 86 case.[691] However, in *Bourgoin SA* v. *Ministry of Agriculture, Fisheries and Food*[692] the Court of Appeal ruled out an action for damages for breach of Article 30 of the Treaty of Rome. In this last case, however, the main reason given for this result was the absence of a clear abuse of power by the Ministry. In such circumstances, the administrative law remedy of judicial review was deemed sufficient. The questions raised by this decision are considered in greater detail later in this chapter, in the discussion of governmental liability.[693]

---

[686] *Garden Cottage Foods Ltd.* v. *Milk Marketing Board* [1984] AC 130, 144.

[687] Copyright, Designs and Patents Act 1988, ss. 180 ff.; s. 194 creates a private right of action for breach of this Part of the Act.

[688] [1984] AC 130.   [689] Ibid., 141.

[690] The question of whether damages might be available had a bearing on the court's discretion to grant an interlocutory injunction under the test in *American Cyanamid Co.* v. *Ethicon Ltd.* [1975] AC 396.

[691] *An Bord Bainne Co-operative Ltd.* v. *Milk Marketing Board* [1984] 2 CMLR 584; Shaw [1984] *CLJ* 255.

[692] [1986] QB 716.   [693] See Section 5, below.

Select Bibliography

BUCKLEY, R. A, 'Liability in Tort for Breach of Statutory Duty' (1984) 100 *LQR* 204.

FRICKE, G. L., 'The Juridical Nature of the Action upon the Statute' (1960) 76 *LQR* 240.

Law Commission, *The Interpretation of Statutes* (Law Com. No. 21).

MORRIS, C., 'The Role of Criminal Statutes in Negligence Actions', 49 *Col. LR* 21 (1949).

STANTON, K., *Breach of Statutory Duty in Tort*, Modern Legal Studies Series (1986).

THAYER, E. R., 'Public Wrong and Private Action' (1914) 27 *Harv. LR* 317.

WILLIAMS, G. L., 'The Effect of Penal Legislation in the Law of Tort' (1960) 23 *MLR* 233.

5. Liability of Public and Statutory Bodies

1. The Distinctive Nature of Governmental Liability

In principle, liability in tort may attach to the acts or omissions of a statutory utility, local authority, or government department in just the same way as it would to those of a private person. Public authorities, their agents, and employees enjoy no general immunity from civil liability. The Victorian constitutional theorist A. V. Dicey noted that: 'the Reports abound with cases in which officials have been brought before the courts, and made, in their personal capacity, liable to punishment, or to the payment of damages, for acts done in their official character but in excess of their lawful authority'.[694] He regarded this general application of the 'ordinary' principles of civil liability as a fundamental aspect of the rule of law. Many of the important cases in the torts of trespass to the person, false imprisonment, and trespass to property, which are considered in later chapters, have been actions brought to attack the abuse of governmental authority.[695] In the field of negligence, the liability of public bodies was clearly established in the middle of the nineteenth century,[696] and then consolidated in a series of actions brought against utilities and other statutory undertakings for negligent interference with property.[697] These cases are normally considered under the rubric of 'negligence in the exercise of a statutory power'. In relation to liability for personal injury, it has long been clearly established that both the general duty of care arising under *Donoghue* v. *Stevenson*[698] and the more specific duties imposed, for example, on occupiers and employers, apply without distinction to public authorities.

In certain other respects, however, this picture of the general application of the principles of tortious liability has to be qualified. Immunities for both central and local government have operated at various times. Historically the Crown was immune from both civil and criminal liability, with the effect (amongst others) that central government bodies could not be sued directly in tort. A way round this was found in the form of actions brought against state

---

[694] *An Introduction to the Study of the Law of the Constitution* (1885), 1979 reprint, 193.

[695] See below, Chapter 4, Section 1; Chapter 5, Section 1.

[696] *Mersey Docks & Harbour Board* v. *Gibbs* (1866) LR 1 HL 93.

[697] Most notably, *Geddis* v. *Proprietors of the Bann Reservoir* (1878) 3 App. Cas. 430.　　　[698] [1932] AC 562.

officials, but the government departments and offices of state for which they worked were not, strictly speaking, vicariously liable for the torts committed by their servants and agents. It was normal, however, for any damages awarded by a court against such officials to be paid by the Crown and for cases to be settled when it was thought that a private employer would have been vicariously liable. But these practices did not rest upon any legal principle and some considered them to be illegal.[699] The Crown Proceedings Act 1947 formally removed this immunity and made the Crown liable for the torts of its servants and agents as 'if it were a person of full age and capacity'.[700] Since then it has become also common practice for legislation extending or clarifying tort duties (such as the Occupiers Liability Acts of 1957 and 1984), or altering the scope of defences (such as the Law Reform (Personal Injuries) Act 1948), to bind the Crown formally. There are thus few if any areas in which a significant immunity remains.[701] The liability of local authorities was limited for a time by statute, in the form of the Public Authorities Protection Act 1893. This imposed time limits of six months or, in some cases, a year, on any actions against public bodies acting by way of the exercise of statutory duties or powers. The origins of this Act are obscure and it was repealed, without great objection, in 1954.[702]

More recently, the decision of the House of Lords in *Anns* v. *Merton London Borough Council*[703] appeared to herald a significant expansion of governmental liability justified, it seemed, by the 'deep pockets' theory of public defendants. *Anns* implied that local authorities could be liable, amongst other things, for negligent failure to ensure compliance with bye-laws, and for causing pure economic loss to remote parties.[704] The House of Lords attempted to preserve an area of immunity in relation to decisions of 'policy' involving the balancing of competing interests, in contrast to 'operational' negligence occurring in the course of day-to-day administration, for which the council could be liable. This distinction was, however, criticised as unclear and difficult to apply in practice. In the event, *Anns* has turned out to be a false dawn for those who would have welcomed an expansion of liability. Its formal demise came with *Murphy* v. *Brentwood District Council*[705] after a series of earlier decisions had substantially restricted its application to statutory bodies.[706] Since *Murphy*, two further decisions of the House of Lords have restricted further the scope for negligence claims against public bodies.

In *X (Minors)* v. *Bedfordshire County Council*[707] their Lordships struck out as disclosing no cause of action a number of claims brought against local authorities

---

[699] See C. Harlow, *Compensation and Government Torts* (1982), ch. 2.   [700] S. 2(1).

[701] The Crown Proceedings Act 1947 preserves the immunity in a small number of areas. See below.

[702] The Law Reform (Limitation of Actions etc.) Act 1954. See Weir, 'Governmental Liability' [1989] *PL* 40, 48.

[703] [1978] AC 728; see above, Chapter 2.

[704] In this case, home owners who bought properties which had been constructed on defective foundations after the council had failed to carry out an adequate inspection of them.

[705] [1991] 1 AC 398.

[706] See in particular, the judgments of Lord Keith in *Peabody Donation Fund* v. *Sir Lindsay Parkinson & Co.* [1985] AC 210, *Yuen Kun Yeu* v. *Attorney-General of Hong Kong* [1988] AC 175, and *Rowling* v. *Takaro Properties* [1988] AC 473, discussed below.

[707] [1995] 2 AC 633.

in respect of alleged failures to perform statutory duties relating to the care, protection and education of children. In *Stovin* v. *Wise* (*Norfolk County Council, third party*)[708] they ruled (by a bare majority) that a highway authority did not owe a duty of care to a road user to exercise its statutory powers in such a way as to maintain the highway in a safe condition. Two guiding principles emerge from these decisions. First, statutory policy plays a major role in 'framing' any potential common-law duty of care. Secondly, the courts should seek to avoid second-guessing decisions of public bodies on questions which are 'non-justiciable'.

There are several reasons of policy for treating governmental liability as a special case, at least as far as liability for omissions and economic loss is concerned. If substantial claims for economic protection are made by a particular group of plaintiffs, the cost has to be met either by a diversion of resources away from general expenditure or by an increase in taxation. It is not obvious that the loss is better borne by the local authority (or by the taxpayers or community at large) than by the plaintiffs. Indeed, the latter may be in a better position to cover the risk in question through additional precautions or through insurance. This seems to have been the case in *Anns*[709] and *Murphy*,[710] where actions nominally brought in the names of the occupiers and owners of the properties were, in essence, actions brought by their insurers by virtue of the doctrine of subrogation. This enables the liability insurer, after having indemnified his insured, to step into his shoes and sue the tortfeasor for the initial loss caused to the plaintiff. Tony Weir has summed up the issues in the following way:

Now it hardly needs saying (any more) that a local authority does not normally have to pay companies which suffer merely pecuniary loss as a result of their carelessness, as the Norwich Union did in this case, and it is hard to imagine anybody less deserving of a dip in the public trough than the insurer who profits from taking the risk that houses may collapse . . . But our absurd law on subrogation to tort claims means that the public must bail out private insurers.[711]

Similarly, in *Stovin* v. *Wise*[712] Lord Hoffman noted that: 'denial of liability [in that case] does not leave the road user unprotected' since not only do drivers of vehicles owe each other a duty of care, but 'if, as in the case of [the defendant], they do not, there is compulsory insurance to provide compensation to victims'.

A second reason for granting some kind of immunity is the wish to avoid the situation in which public authorities become inundated with frivolous and unmeritorious claims. This is a real possibility because, unlike commercial entities or individual defendants, local authorities cannot (normally) become insolvent or bankrupt. An important practical bar to speculative litigation therefore does not apply. *Anns*[713] illustrates the risks of making local authorities 'defendants of last resort': the most obvious action, by the householder against the builder whose negligence the local authority failed to correct, is frequently

---

[708] [1996] AC 923.
[711] Weir, op. cit. [1989] *PL* 40, 43.
[709] [1978] AC 728.
[712] [1996] AC 923, 958.
[710] [1991] 1 AC 398.
[713] [1978] AC 728.

ruled out by insolvency of the firm in question. Under *Anns* the local authority and the builder were joint tortfeasors, with the builder being assessed for the predominant part of liability; but the difficulty, in practice, of getting the builder to pay anything would normally lead to the local authority paying everything. In this context the argument that, given the difficulties of proving carelessness, few claims will actually succeed in practice, has little force. For, as Lord Browne-Wilkinson noted in *X (Minors)* v. *Bedfordshire County Council*,[714]

if a common law duty of care is held to exist, there is a very real risk that many hopeless (and possibly vexatious) cases will be brought, thereby exposing the authority to great expenditure of time and money in their defence.

A third factor is the fear of courts unduly restricting the policy-making functions of the body in question and interfering with decisions that are not susceptible to judicial control. As Lord Keith of Kinkel recognised in his judgment in *Yuen Kun Yeu* v. *Attorney-General of Hong Kong*,[715] many decisions taken by regulatory bodies may end up favouring one group against another or elevating the public interest above that of a particular interest group. If that group is able to demand automatic compensation for its losses, the regulatory body may be unable to act in the general interest. Nor will the court have the expertise or the information to judge whether one group should be favoured over another. For instance, if a regulatory authority shuts down a bank that has been involved in fraud it thereby protects future, would-be investors at the possible expense of those who have already made deposits. This latter group, who may well lose all or most of their savings, may feel particularly aggrieved since they can claim that the reason they kept their money in the bank was the re-assurance they felt they had from the regulatory authority that all was well with the bank.[716] Since, in these circumstances, the court is said to lack the criteria by which to assess negligence, it should deny a duty of care altogether.

Related to this is a fourth consideration, the fear that the threat of legal liability will give rise to 'defensive' or wasteful practices by potential defendants. This has to be weighed against any 'deterrent' effect or raising of standards of performance which judicial intervention may bring in its wake. In *Stovin* v. *Wise*,[717] Lord Hoffman said that 'it was important to consider, before extending the duty of care owed by public authorities, the cost to the community of the defensive measures which they are likely to take in order to avoid liability'. The existence of a duty of care would, he thought,

distort the priorities of local authorities, which would be bound to play safe by increasing their spending on road improvements rather than risk enormous liabilities for personal injury accidents. They will spend less on education or social services.

In addition to these considerations of policy, there are specific legal reasons for recognising the distinctive nature of governmental liability. The analysis of

---

[714] [1995] 2 AC 633, 762. [715] [1988] AC 175.

[716] This is one of the issues to arise out of the Bank of England's closure of the London arm of the Bank of Commerce and Credit International in 1990.

[717] [1996] AC 923, 958. See also *X (Minors)* v. *Bedfordshire CC* [1995] 2 AC 633, 748 (Lord Browne-Wilkinson).

the common-law duty of care is complicated by the presence of statutory powers and duties. With the exception of the Crown, which possesses various
inherent prerogative powers,[718] most of the activities of public bodies are
underpinned by statute in this way. The presence of statute means, in the first
place, that an alternative ground of liability may arise, namely a liability for
breach of statutory duty. As we have seen,[719] the action for breach of statutory
duty is conceptually separate from negligence liability. But it is also normally
harder to establish, in the sense that the plaintiff must show that the statute
was meant to create a private cause of action for a particular group, of which
he is part. The relationship between the action for breach of statutory duty and
the separate, common-law liability for negligence in the exercise of a statutory
power is far from clear. In particular, it is uncertain how far the absence of any
private action for statutory breach should prevent the court imposing a parallel duty of care at common law. Recent decisions suggest that the fit between
these two separate areas of liability is increasingly close.[720]

In the second place, it is possible for a statute to create a specific immunity
from common-law liability in tort. This may be the case where liability in
nuisance or under the tort of *Rylands* v. *Fletcher*[721] is concerned. The principles
governing statutory immunity for these torts of interference with property are
considered separately in a later chapter.[722] It is rare, however, if not completely
unknown, for a statute to grant immunity for *negligence*; and there is a
presumption that liability for negligence will arise if an authorised activity is
carried on in a negligent manner.[723]

In addition it is necessary to consider the overlap between the liability of public bodies to pay damages for tortious injury, and the separate question of the
validity of their acts under administrative law. Thus, a person affected by an
administrative decision can challenge it on the grounds that it was taken in
excess of the relevant statutory powers, that is to say, was *ultra vires*.[724] The
decision can be quashed (or nullified) by an order of *certiorari*. Alternatively, an
action may lie to compel a public body to perform a statutory duty (mandamus)
or to prevent it from acting in breach of such a duty (prohibition). These remedies, called the prerogative writs, must now be sought under a specially designated procedure known as the application for judicial review, under Order 53
of the Rules of the Supreme Court.[725] It is vital to stress, however, that no
action for damages lies either in tort law or in administrative law on the
grounds simply that a statutory authority has acted *ultra vires*. The relevant principles of administrative law are concerned solely with the question of the validity of the act in question and not with liability to pay damages to one who is
affected by it. Conversely, however, it may be that an authority cannot be liable

---

[718] See Wade and Forsyth, *Administrative Law* (7th edn., 1994), 53 ff.

[719] Section 4 of this chapter, above.

[720] See in particular, the decision of the Court of Appeal in *Clunis* v. *Camden and Islington HA* [1998] 2 WLR
903, applying *X (Minors)* v. *Bedfordshire CC* [1995] 2 AC 623.

[721] (1866) LR 1 Ex. 265 (1868) LR 3 HL 330.   [722] See Chapter 5, Section 3.

[723] *Geddis* v. *Proprietors of the Bann Reservoir* (1878) 3 App. Cas. 430.

[724] For an introduction to the *ultra vires* principle see Wade, *Administrative Law* (6th edn., 1988), 39–48.

[725] As amended by the Supreme Court Act 1981, s. 32.

in the tort of negligence unless the act or omission in question was *ultra vires*.[726] In this sense, the scope of the *vires* principle in administrative law is important for the scope of common law liability in negligence.

In addition, there is a significant procedural point concerning the form of damages actions brought against public bodies. As a result of the House of Lords' decision in *O'Reilly* v. *Mackman*,[727] actions of a 'public law' nature may only be brought by way of the application for judicial review under Order 53 of the Rules of the Supreme Court. To proceed by way of a writ in the High Court is an abuse of process. This means that where an action for damages is bound up with a challenge to the validity of an administrative act, it may have to be brought as a public-law action under Order 53.[728] While Order 53 permits damages claims to be combined with a claim for one or more of the prerogative writs, the limitation period is extremely short (three months) and the procedure is not entirely suitable for the argument of a claim for compensation as opposed to a challenge to validity. For this reason, the procedural separation of public-law and private-law issues may have resulted in the grant to statutory bodies of a kind of limited immunity, similar to that of the old Public Authorities Protection Act, from certain kinds of claims for damages. However, the extent of any such immunity has been considerably narrowed as a result of the more recent decision of the House of Lords in *Roy* v. *Kensington and Chelsea and Westminster Family Practitioner Committee*. For in that case the court reasserted the importance of private-law claims proceeding in the normal way by writ.[729]

A further point should be borne in mind. That is that where negligence, in the sense of maladministration by central-government departments or local government is concerned, there is an alternative remedy to civil litigation. This can take the form of a complaint to the parliamentary Ombudsman.[730] The Ombudsman can sometimes make a substantial impact on the availability of compensation in circumstances where a negligence claim, although possible, would face considerable difficulties in terms both of establishing a duty of care and in proving causation. A good illustration of this can be found in the Ombudsman's report on the Barlow Clowes affair. In that case a large number of investors lost their savings following the collapse of a fraudulent investment company which had been licensed to trade by the Department of Trade and Industry. The Report led to the government paying out to the investors around £16 million in *ex gratia* sums.[731] In this case, a claim in negligence would have been difficult and time-consuming, not least in the light of the ruling of the Privy Council in *Yuen Kun Yeu* v. *Attorney-General of Hong Kong*.[732]

We now turn to a more detailed consideration of governmental liability in negligence. We shall examine in turn the extent of common law liability in negligence; liability for breach of statutory duty; public law as a source of liability and, alternatively, of immunity; and Crown proceedings. We then

---

[726] See in particular, Lord Diplock's judgment in *Dorset Yacht Co.* v. *Home Office* [1970] AC 1004, 1068.
[727] [1983] 2 AC 237.   [728] *Cocks* v. *Thanet DC* [1984] 2 AC 286.   [729] [1992] 1 AC 625.
[730] The powers of the parliamentary Ombudsman derive from the Parliamentary Commissioner Act 1967. Several ombudsman schemes now operate in the private sector too, some of them with statutory backing. See generally P. Cane, *Tort Law and Economic Interests* (1996), 2nd. edn., at 366 ff.
[731] Ibid., 389.   [732] [1988] AC 475.

consider the possible impact on this area of law of two developments of increasing but as yet unclear significance. The first is the principle of state liability under European Community law, stemming from the decisions of the European Court of Justice in the *Francovich*[733] line of cases. The second is the obligation upon public authorities to observe the provisions of the European Convention on Human Rights and of a number of its Protocols, which are derived from the Human Rights Act 1998.

2. Negligence in the Exercise of a Statutory Power

(A) The Recognition of a Common Law Action

Two decisions in the middle of the nineteenth century clearly established that public bodies could be liable in tort for negligence occurring in the performance of activities authorised by statute. In *Mersey Docks and Harbour Board Trustees* v. *Gibbs*[734] the dock trustees were held liable for their failure to maintain a clear passage into a harbour, with the result that the ship carrying the plaintiff's cargo ran aground. The House of Lords, adopting an opinion of Blackburn J, rejected an argument to the effect that the trustees were covered by Crown immunity. Such bodies, which performed commercial and related activities for profit, should be subject to a liability 'co-extensive with that imposed by the general law on the owners of similar works'.[735] In *Geddis* v. *Proprietors of the Bann Reservoir*[736] Lord Blackburn confirmed this result. He said:

It is now thoroughly well established that no action will lie for doing that which the legislature has authorised, if it be done without negligence, although it does occasion damage to anyone; but an action does lie for doing that which the legislature has authorised, if it be done negligently.

In this case the defendants, who had statutory authority to undertake public works for the supply of water, in diverting various rivers failed to clear one of them of obstructions, with the result that it overflowed and flooded the plaintiff's land. His action for damages was successful.

Lord Blackburn's approach was thus to treat statutory bodies like any others for the purposes of negligence. Only if the statute clearly specified a defence would a negligence action be defeated. Similarly, the fact that the negligence was that of a statutory body was not, in itself, an additional ground of liability. The action originated at common law, and was governed by the rules normally applicable to a negligence claim; it was not a special form of liability in the same sense as the (entirely separate) action for breach of statutory duty.

The prospect of a limited immunity for statutory bodies was raised again, however, by the later judgment of the House of Lords in *East Suffolk Rivers*

---

[733] Joined Cases C-60/90 and C-9/90 *Francovich and Bonifaci* v. *Italian Republic* [1991] ECR I-6911; see below, Section 7.

[734] (1866) LR 1 HL 93.

[735] Ibid., 107 (Blackburn J). See Harlow, *Compensation and Government Torts*, (below, Select Bibliography), 23–4.

[736] (1878) 3 App. Cas. 430, 455–6.

Catchment Board v. *Kent*.[737] In that case the plaintiff's land was flooded following a high tide and a breach in a floodwall. The defendants, acting under statutory powers, attempted to mend the breach in the wall but negligently failed to do so, with the result that the plaintiff's land remained flooded far longer than it would otherwise have done. Viscount Simon LC, noting that the defendants were under no statutory duty to act, held that they could not be liable for merely failing to improve the situation. He thus adopted the view of du Parcq LJ in the Court of Appeal that the Rivers Catchment Board could not be held liable

for damage suffered through failure to exercise its powers adequately, or at all, even though the damage might have been averted or lessened by the exercise of reasonable care and skill.[738]

Similarly Lord Romer held that:

Where a statutory authority is entrusted with a mere power, it cannot be made liable for any damage sustained by a member of the public by reason of a failure to exercise that power. If, in the exercise of their discretion, they embark upon an execution of that power, the only duty they owe to any member of the public is not thereby to add to the damage which he would have suffered had they done nothing.[739]

Since some of the judges in the majority appeared to decide the case on the grounds of causation as much as on the nature of the duty of care, the *ratio* of *East Suffolk* has not been entirely clear. But Lord Romer's formulation enjoyed general support at least until the decision of the House of Lords in *Anns* v. *Merton London Borough Council*[740] was handed down.

In the *East Suffolk* case Lord Atkin gave a dissenting judgment.[741] In it he argued that the central question was not whether the board was under a pre-existing statutory duty to act but whether the relationship between the two parties was sufficiently close to give rise to a duty of care at common law. In his view, once the board had gone on to the plaintiff's land and undertaken the responsibility of closing the breach in the floodwall, they came under a duty to take care in the way the work was executed. This was an application of the general principle laid down in *Donoghue* v. *Stevenson*[742] in the formulation of which he had, a few years earlier, played such a vital part.

(B) A LIMITED IMMUNITY

The apparent *ratio* of the *East Suffolk* case has been criticised as resting on a *non sequitur*. It does not necessarily follow from the fact that a public body has been granted a statutory discretion (as opposed to a duty) to act that it may not be liable for common-law negligence if it decides to do so and then goes on to execute its powers carelessly. The correct distinction, from this point of view, is between, on the one hand negligence in the formulation of general policy or

---

[737] [1941] AC 74. See also the earlier case of *Sheppard* v. *Glossop Corp.* [1921] 3 KB 132, discussed by Craig, op. cit. (1978) 94 *LQR* 428, 431–2.

[738] [1940] 1 KB 319, 337.

[739] [1941] AC 74, 102. Lords Porter and Thankerton also held in favour of the Rivers Catchment Board.

[740] [1978] AC 728.   [741] [1941] AC 74, 88–94.   [742] [1932] AC 562.

planning[743] and, on the other, negligence in the operation or implementation of the policy decision.[744] As Professor Craig has explained,

The . . . dichotomy between planning and operation can be applied to the *East Suffolk* case. On the facts it appeared that the catchment board could not afford the most sophisticated machinery (or the most skilled labourers) but that the greater part of the damage resulted from using the wrong technique to repair the wall. The best approach to the case would, it is submitted, have been to ask 'given the limited resources possessed by the board (the planning decision) did the workmen use reasonable dispatch'. The answer would appear to be that on the facts they did not. Even taking account of the limited resources, the work took far too long due to administrative inefficiency and use of the wrong technique.[745]

The distinction between 'policy' and 'operational' decisions originates in the Federal law of the United States, where legislation of 1946 abolishing sovereign immunity substituted a more limited immunity for negligence committed by agencies or officials in the exercise of a discretionary function.[746] Examples of policy decisions include the decision of the federal government to export a highly dangerous fertiliser which exploded when it was being shipped,[747] and the maintenance by a state government of 'open house' in a reform school for young offenders, from which an inmate escaped to burn down the plaintiff's property.[748] By contrast, where the federal government allocated resources to provide a lighthouse and a lifeguard service it was liable to the owners of a vessel which sank as a result of the failure of the lifeguards to ensure that the lighthouse was working properly.[749] And in another case, a state that placed a youth with foster-parents was liable for failing to warn them of his violent tendencies with the result that he assaulted the mother.[750]

In *Anns* v. *Merton London Borough Council*[751] the policy–operation distinction won the approval of Lord Wilberforce, with whose judgment three of the other Law Lords agreed. The apparent *ratio* of the *East Suffolk* case, to the effect that a statutory body may only be liable for additional damage caused by its negligence as opposed to a failure to prevent harm, was rejected. Lord Wilberforce recognised that the liability of public bodies had to be formulated with regard both to the statutory origin of their powers and to the discretion with regard to policy that these powers conferred. The court could not neglect the 'essential factor' that the 'local authority is a public body, discharging functions under statute; its powers and duties are definable in terms of public not private law. The problem which this type of action creates, is to define the circumstances in which the law should impose over and above, or perhaps alongside, these

[743] When the body is called upon to make decisions concerning the distribution of resources which the court is ill-equipped to second-guess.

[744] When adequate criteria for judging negligence are much more likely to exist.

[745] Craig, 'Negligence in the Exercise of a Statutory Power', op. cit., 94 *LQR* 428, 434–5.

[746] The Federal Tort Claims Act 1946. See Craig, op. cit., 94 *LQR* 438, 442 ff. Subsequently the distinction found its way into the laws of several states, which either adopted this provision in legislation or had it read in by decision of courts.

[747] *Dalehite* v. *US* (1953) 346 US 15.

[748] *Evangelical United Brethren Church of Adna* v. *State of Washington* (1965) 407 P.2d 440.

[749] *Indian Towing Co.* v. *US* (1955) 350 US 61.

[750] *Johnson* v. *State of California* (1968) 447 P.2d 352.   [751] [1978] AC 728.

public-law powers and duties, a duty in private law towards individuals so that they may sue for damages in a civil court.'[752] Lord Wilberforce's judgment in effect fused the argument from policy (to the effect that the courts should not interfere with planning decisions) with the more conceptual point concerning the statutory origins of the council's powers and the need to ensure that private and public law remedies should not come into conflict. He thus said:

Most, probably all, statutes relating to public authorities or public bodies, contain in them a large area of policy. The courts call this 'discretion', meaning that the decision is one for the authority or body to make, and not for the courts. Many statutes, also, pre-scribe or at least presuppose the practical execution of policy decisions: a convenient description of this is to say that in addition to the area of policy or discretion, there is an operational area. Although this distinction between the policy area and the operational area is convenient, and illuminating, it is probably a distinction of degree; many 'opera-tional' powers or duties have in them some element of 'discretion'. It can safely be said that the more 'operational' a power or duty may be, the easier it is to superimpose on it a common law duty of care.[753]

The House of Lords' earlier decision in *Home Office* v. *Dorset Yacht Co.*[754] had already recognised this distinction implicitly. Lord Reid had argued that the prison officers had not been granted any discretion in relation to the borstal boys who were under their care; they had simply failed to carry out their instructions, with the consequence that the boys escaped. There was no ques-tion, on the other hand, of making the Home Office liable for the consequences of adopting a policy of allowing borstal boys to be given work experience out-side the detention centre, or for setting up an 'open borstal'.[755]

In *Anns* Lord Wilberforce paid considerable attention to the form and aims of the particular statute under which the council's powers arose. The Public Health Act 1936 was intended 'to provide for the health and safety of owners and occu-piers of buildings, including dwelling-houses, by, *inter alia*, setting standards to be complied with in construction, and by enabling local authorities, through build-ing bye-laws, to supervise and control the operations of builders'.[756] The Act con-sisted mainly of powers and imposed few statutory duties on authorities; the manner in which they carried out building inspections, the number of inspectors employed, and the manner in which tests were to be carried out were matters for the councils themselves to decide. However, the mere fact that the Act created a power to inspect, rather than a duty to do so, was not, according to Lord Wilberforce, relevant because 'they were under a duty to give proper considera-tion to the question whether they should or not'.[757] As far as the actual inspec-tion was concerned, this was 'heavily operational' and the inspector, once appointed, was under a duty to take care to ensure that the bye-laws were com-plied with. Even this, however, being a duty originating under statute, carried with it a small element of discretion, and a corresponding area of immunity for the purposes of any private law action for negligence.

[752] Ibid., 754. [753] Ibid. [754] [1970] AC 1004.
[755] Ibid., 1031, discussing *Greenwell* v. *Prison Commissioners* (1951) 101 LJ 486; see also Lord Diplock at [1970] AC 1004, 1069.
[756] [1978] AC 728, 753. [757] Ibid., 755.

The notion of the council's 'duty to give consideration' was arguably unnecessary here. Even in the absence of such a duty, it could be said that once the decisions to make bye-laws and to enforce them through the appointment of inspectors had been taken it was irrelevant that there was no pre-existing statutory duty requiring the council to do so. A common law duty could arise from the expectation of potential occupiers that the foundations of the houses they bought had been checked by the inspectors at an early stage of construction. The only relevant question then would be whether the negligence of the inspectors was 'operational' in the sense described above. If the action is clearly seen as arising at common law, subject only to a limited immunity for policy decisions, there is no need to search for a pre-existing statutory duty as opposed to a power. Lord Wilberforce seemed to recognise this when he said, in relation to the *East Suffolk* case, that:

quite apart from such consequences as may flow from an examination of the duties laid down by the particular statute, there may be room, once one is outside the area of legitimate discretion or policy, for a duty of care at common law. It is irrelevant to the existence of this duty of care whether what is created by the statute is a duty or a power: the duty of care may exist in either case.[758]

This also follows from Lord Wilberforce's explanation of *East Suffolk*,[759] namely that the judges in that case, with the exception of Lord Atkin, had not fully recognised the potential scope of the 'neighbour principle' as a basis for common law liability across a range of situations.

The effect of *Anns* may therefore be summarised as follows: the issue of whether the defendant was acting under a statutory duty or by way of a mere power is irrelevant to liability, once a common law duty of care has been established on the basis of general principles. However, the common law recognises a limited immunity for public bodies based on the distinction between decisions of policy, which are non-justiciable, and operational negligence; and in determining the scope of the immunity for policy, the aims and form of the relevant statute are factors to be taken into account.

The principal effect of the House of Lords' more recent decision in *Murphy* v. *Brentwood District Council*,[760] overruling *Anns*, is to restrict the class of situations in which a general common-law duty of care will arise. In particular, the House of Lords held that *Anns* had gone too far in recognising a potentially open-ended liability for pure economic loss and for omissions. Following *Murphy* these categories of liability are much more tightly drawn up, and will certainly not extend to the case of a council compensating occupiers for pure economic loss caused by its failure to inspect building foundations.[761]

The later decisions of the House of Lords in the *X* (*Minors*) and *Stovin* cases go further still in casting doubt on the principles enunciated in *Anns* for determining the liability of public bodies. It is thus no longer clear that much turns on the policy–operation dichotomy. In *Stovin*[762] Lord Hoffman said that 'the distinction between policy and operations is an inadequate tool with which to

---

[758] [1978] AC 728, 758.   [759] [1941] AC 74.   [760] [1991] 1 AC 398.
[761] See above, Chapter 2.   [762] [1996] AC 923, 951.

discover whether it is inappropriate to impose a duty of care or not'. This was because, in practice, the distinction is 'often elusive'. Lord Hoffman, however, went further. He suggested that even in a case where the distinction could be clearly applied, the mere fact that the performance of the duty or, as the case might be, the exercise of the power in question fell under the category of 'operations' did not suffice to establish liability. In the same vein, Lord Browne-Wilkinson in *X (Minors)*[763] held that, separately from the policy–operation dichotomy, it was not permissible for a court to impose a common-law duty of care. This would be the case if its observance 'would be inconsistent with, or have a tendency to discourage, the due performance by the local authority of its statutory duties'.

Emerging from these two decisions is a two-pronged test for the existence of a common-law duty which focuses, first, on the *statutory context* of the power or duty in question and, secondly, on the issue of *justiciability*. We must look at these two points in turn.

(i) The Statutory Context   A statute will normally now be read as impliedly excluding a private law action in tort if it makes separate provision for the adjudication or resolution of disputes arising out of administrative action. Claimants for social-security benefits, for example, will have to pursue appeals through the adjudicative procedure laid down by the Social Security Acts, and will not have a separate common-law claim for compensation for negligence.[764]

It is possible to go further and argue that the aims and contents of the statute are relevant in determining the scope of any common-law duty of care that would otherwise arise. The statutory context is important, according to Lord Browne-Wilkinson in *X (Minors)* v. *Bedfordshire County Council*, because:

[w]here Parliament has conferred a statutory discretion on a public authority, it is for that authority, not for the courts, to exercise the discretion: nothing which the authority does within the ambit of the discretion can be actionable at common law.[765]

In *Stovin* v. *Wise* Lord Hoffman expressed the view that in order for a common-law duty to exist, there has to be a 'public law duty to act' in the sense that the failure to do so would amount to irrationality.[766] Although it is not necessary, then, to find a statutory duty as opposed to a power, in the case of a mere power it must be shown that the actions (or omissions) of the authority constituted an abuse of that power from a public law point of view.[767]

The importance of the statutory context has been stressed in numerous cases since *Anns*. In *Governors of the Peabody Donation Fund* v. *Sir Lindsay Parkinson & Co.*[768] the council failed to exercise a statutory power to halt work for the installation

---

[763] [1995] 2 AC 633, 739.

[764] *Jones* v. *Department of Employment* [1989] QB 1; see also the use of a separate right of appeal to defeat a negligence claim in *Mills* v. *Winchester Diocesan Board of Finance* [1989] Ch. 428.

[765] [1995] 2 AC 633, 738.   [766] *Stovin* v. *Wise* [1996] AC 923, 953.

[767] This is not quite the same as saying that an *ultra vires* act is either a necessary (or sufficient) condition for the existence of a common-law duty; it is enough that the public body has failed properly to exercise its discretion. See Lord Browne-Wilkinson in *X (Minors)* v. *Bedfordshire CC* [1995] 2 AC 633, 736.

[768] [1985] AC 210. See also *Curran* v. *Northern Ireland Co-Ownership Housing Assocation Ltd.* [1987] AC 718.

of an unauthorised drainage system on land that the plaintiff/company was developing. Two years later the plaintiff had to reconstruct the system at a considerable financial loss. It brought an *Anns*-style action against the council. But it failed in the House of Lords on the grounds that the statutory power in question had been conferred for the purposes of protecting the health and safety of future occupiers and their families, and not the financial interests of companies involved in the construction work. The decision, which would now follow from the simple application of *Murphy*, seems right in any event. For the alternative, of turning the council into a defendant of last resort to business parties engaged in activities for commercial profit, can hardly have been contemplated when the particular statutory power was conferred. Not only was the plaintiff capable, on the advice of his architects and other advisers, of making his own judgment on the question of whether the bye-laws had been complied with; he, himself, as well as the council, was under a duty to comply with them.[769] However, there is no doubt that there had been 'operational' carelessness in the sense used in *Anns*. The decision, therefore, rests on a restriction of duty by reference to the purpose of the statute and not upon the application of the policy–operation distinction.

Considerations such as these led the High Court of Australia to reject an *Anns*-style action altogether in a decision anticipating *Murphy* by several years. The case was *Sutherland Shire Council* v. *Heyman*[770] but its *ratio* is not, alas, all that clear. The minority (Gibbs CJ and Wilson J) held that the council owed a duty of care but that there was no evidence of negligence in its exercise of the discretionary power to inspect. The majority denied the existence of a duty of care, but gave different reasons for that conclusion. The plaintiffs, as in *Anns*, bought property containing a hidden defect that the council had failed to discover through inspection when the house was being constructed. However, they failed to make inquiries of the council or seek from it a compliance order giving details of the property and of its inspection, as they could have done. Under these circumstances Mason J held that they could not show that they had relied on the council's power to inspect, and on this basis he concluded that the council owed no duty of care to the plaintiffs. The judgments of Brennan and Deane JJ, on the other hand, constitute a much more direct assault on *Anns*. This assault was, in part, related to the general question of whether recovery for pure economic loss should be the norm or whether, instead, it should be regarded as exceptional. This point was considered in Chapter 2, above, so we shall not return to it here. For present purposes it is more important to focus on the critique that Lord Wilberforce formulated in *Anns* of the relationship between the private tort action in negligence and the statutory origin of the council's discretionary powers.

In Brennan J's view it was not open to a court to impose a common law duty of care in relation to the exercise of a statutory power, in a case where the

---

[769] See the discussion of the Court of Appeal in *Investors in Industry Commercial Properties Ltd.* v. *South Bedfordshire District Council* [1986] QB 1034, another case restricting *Anns* which has now been overtaken by *Murphy*.

[770] (1985) 157 CLR 424.

statute in question could not be read as impliedly imposing a duty which sounded in private damages by an injured party. He said:

Before the repository of a statutory power can be liable in negligence for a failure to exercise it, the statute, must (either expressly or by implication) impose a duty to exercise the power and confer a private right of action in damages for a breach of the duty so imposed. The question whether Parliament has conferred a private right of action depends upon the interpretation of the statute.[771]

Having decided that the relevant legislation was not intended to create a private cause of action for breach of statutory duty, Brennan J went on to say that:

If the court ascertains from the Act and Ordinance that Parliament did not intend to impose on the council any other duty to future purchasers of property, it is not open to the court to remedy a supposed deficiency by superimposing a general common law duty on the council to prevent any damage that future purchasers of property might suffer in the event of a non-exercise or a careless exercise of their statutory powers. To superimpose such a general common law duty on a statutory power would be to 'conjure up' the duty in order to give effect to judicial ideas of policy. The common law does not superimpose such a duty on a mere statutory power.[772]

Similarly, Deane J argued against liability on the grounds that:

protection of the owner of land from the mere economic loss which might be sustained by reason of a defect in a building erected upon his or her land is not part of the purpose for which the relevant legislative powers and functions were conferred upon the Council.[773]

These opinions go even further than the House of Lords did in *Peabody*[774] in using the statute to limit a common-law duty of care. *Peabody* held that the purposes for which the statutory power is conferred should limit the common law duty. In *Sutherland* Brennan J's judgment suggests that the court should adopt a self-denying ordinance against imposing any common law duty in a case where no *statutory* action for breach of duty can be implied using the (highly restrictive) test of legislative intent.[775]

In contrast to the decision in *Sutherland*, the Canadian Supreme Court decided, in *City of Kamloops* v. *Nielsen*,[776] to allow an *Anns*-style action for negligence against a local authority. By a bare majority, it rejected an argument to the effect that the relevant legislation must be found to impose a private-law duty on the defendant. The case was a slightly unusual one in that the council's inspector had found evidence of defective foundations and had ordered construction work to stop. The house was being built for the father of the builder and he used his position as a councillor to make a 'plea to his fellow council members [to the effect that] this was his retirement home. . . . Since he was

---

[771] (1985) 157 CLR 424, 482.   [772] Ibid., 483.   [773] Ibid., 511.

[774] [1985] AC 210, discussed above.   [775] See above, Section 4 of this Chapter.

[776] [1984] 2 SCR 2. See also the decision of the Privy Council in the New Zealand appeal of *Invercargill CC* v. *Hamlin* [1996] AC 624, in which, perhaps surprisingly, their Lordships declined to follow *Murphy* on the grounds that different policy considerations were relevant to the determination of the duty of care in the context of a claim from New Zealand.

going to live in it, any problems that arose would be his and his alone.'[777] Quite independently there then began a strike of council employees, and the inspection process lapsed with nothing more being done to enforce the inspector's recommendation. In due course the house was sold, without notice of the defect, to the plaintiff who sued both the vendors and the council. The majority of the Supreme Court applied *Anns* and argued with reference to the policy–operation distinction that the council's failure to act had been grounded on an improper motive and that it could not, therefore, invoke the immunity for discretionary exercises of power.[778] The minority argued that the council's only fault lay in its failure to enforce the stop-work order, and that this had to be regarded as a discretionary statutory power.[779]

The result in *Kamloops* may offer some support for *Anns*. However, the approach of the majority does not appear to have been based on the notion of an extensive common-law duty that is 'superimposed' on the statutory powers in question. On the contrary, Wilson J took a view more consonant with *Peabody* when she suggested that the private-law remedy must be 'impliedly sanctioned' by the legislature:

In order to obtain recovery for economic loss the statute has to create a private law duty to the plaintiff alongside the public law duty. The plaintiff has to belong to the limited class of owners or occupiers of the property at the time the damage manifests itself . . . Finally, and perhaps this merits some emphasis, economic loss will only be recoverable if as a matter of statutory interpretation it is a type of loss the statute intended to guard against.[780]

More recently the *Kamloops* decision was described by the Canadian Supreme Court as based on the principle that 'the statute has to create a private law duty to the plaintiff alongside the public law duty. . . . Economic loss will only be recoverable if *as a matter of statutory interpretation* it is a type of loss the statute was intended to guard against.'[781]

Similar arguments have won favour with the House of Lords. As Lord Keith of Kinkel put it in *Yuen Kun Yeu* v. *Attorney-General of Hong Kong*,[782] 'it would be strange that a common law duty of care should be superimposed on such a statutory framework'. In *Murphy* v. *Brentwood District Council* Lord Mackay LC, noting that in *Anns* Lord Wilberforce had not suggested that the Public Health Act manifested any intention to create a private right of action, said:

While of course I accept that duties at common law may arise in respect of the exercise of statutory powers or the discharge of statutory duties I find difficulty in reconciling a common law duty to take reasonable care that plans should conform with bye laws or regulations with the statute which has imposed on the local authority the duty not to pass plans unless they comply with the bye laws or regulations and to pass them if they do.[783]

Murphy, unlike *Anns*, was a case where the council had a duty and not merely the power to withhold approval of the defectively designed building. However, according to Lord Oliver,

---

[777] [1984] 2 SCR 2, 6–7.   [778] Ibid., 24 (Wilson J).   [779] Ibid., 48 (McIntyre J).
[780] [1984] 2 SCR 35.
[781] *Canadian National Railway* v. *Norsk Pacific Steamship Co.* (1992) 91 DLR (4th) 289, 314 (La Forest J).
[782] [1988] AC 175, 195.   [783] [1991] 1 AC 398, 457.

there is nothing in the terms or purpose of the statutory provisions which support the creation of a private law right of action for breach of statutory duty. There is equally nothing in the statutory provisions, which even suggests that the purpose of the statute was to protect owners of buildings from economic loss. Nor is there any easily discernible reason why the existence of the statutory duties, in contradistinction to those existing in the case of other regulatory agencies, should be held in the case of a local authority to create a special relationship imposing a private law duty to members of the public . . .[784]

Some other decisions have practically equated the action for negligence in the exercise of a statutory power with the action for breach of statutory duty.[785] To similar effect are the observations of O'Connor LJ and Lord Oliver in *Caparo Industries plc* v. *Dickman* concerning the relationship between the auditor's statutory duty under the Companies Acts and the plaintiff's common-law claim for negligent misstatement.[786]

(ii) Justiciability and Public Policy The question of justiciability goes to the inability of the courts to assess complex policy issues of the kind which public bodies are required to make. This idea overlaps to a certain extent with the 'policy' element of the policy–operation dichotomy, and with the concept of 'policy' as one of the factors to be weighed in the balance in determining the existence of a duty of care.[787] According to Lord Browne-Wilkinson:

Since what are under consideration are discretionary powers conferred on public bodies for public purposes the relevant factors will often include policy matters, for example social policy, the allocation of finite financial resources between the different calls made upon them or (as in *Dorset Yacht*) the balance between pursuing desirable social aims as against the risk to the public inherent in so doing. It is established that the courts cannot enter upon the assessment of such 'policy' matters.

However, the application of the 'policy' test has gone far beyond what was said in *Anns*, as justiciability has become entwined with a separate line of authority associated with the decision of the House of Lords in *Hill* v. *Chief Constable of West Yorkshire*.[788] These cases suggest that certain categories of *operational* negligence cannot be the subject of common-law claims for damages, where the effect would be to distort decisions on the distribution of resources by public bodies.

In *Hill* the estate of the last victim of a serial killer brought an action against the police for negligence in failing to identify and apprehend the murderer at an earlier date. The action was struck out. According to Lord Keith:

The manner of conduct of such an investigation must necessarily involve a variety of decisions to be made on matters of policy and discretion, for example as to which particular line of inquiry is most advantageously to be pursued and what is the most advantageous way to deploy the available resources. Many such decisions would not be regarded as appropriate by the court to be called into question.[789]

---

[784] Ibid., 490

[785] See also C. Harlow, *Understanding Tort Law* (1988), 132: 'today the cases of statutory power and statutory duty are as far as possible being aligned'; for criticism of this trend, see S. Todd, 'The Negligence Liability of Public Authorities: Divergence in the Common Law' (1986) 102 *LQR* 370, 396–7.

[786] [1989] QB 653, 714 and [1990] 2 AC 605, 653–4 respectively.

[787] See Chapter 2, above.   [788] [1989] AC 53.

[789] [1989] AC 53, 63. See also *Rowling* v. *Takaro Properties* [1988] AC 473.

In contrast stands *Lonrho plc* v. *Tebbit*.[790] There, Sir Nicolas Browne-Wilkinson VC declined to strike out an action for damages brought by Lonrho in respect of alleged negligence by the Secretary of State for Trade and Industry in the exercise of powers under the Fair Trading Act 1973 governing take-overs and mergers. The alleged negligence lay in failing to release Lonrho from an undertaking not to mount a take-over bid for the House of Fraser until after the point at which another bid had been made, successfully, by the Fayed brothers. According to Lonrho, there was no reason to delay the release of the undertaking once the Monopolies and Mergers Commission had reported that a take-over by Lonrho would not be contrary to the public interest. Sir Nicolas held that no issue of policy arose, since 'the timing of the release did not involve the allocation of resources or the distribution of risks'; nor were there any other obvious public policy considerations. Accordingly the matter was justiciable.[791]

The *Lonrho* case is one of the few decisions in which the justiciability issue has been decided in favour of the plaintiff. By contrast, in the leading case of *X (Minors)* v. *Bedfordshire County Council*[792] Lord Browne-Wilkinson regarded the complexity of decisions relating to child protection orders as one reason for denying the existence of a duty of care. He cited similar factors in ruling that local authorities could not be sued for alleged breaches of duty under legislation governing the provision of services for children with special educational needs. Public bodies exercising regulatory and prosecutorial functions have also escaped liability in this way. Thus, in *Elguzouli-Daf* v. *Commissioner of Police of the Metropolis and Another*[793] the plaintiffs sued the Crown Prosecution Service for negligently processing their prosecutions, with the result that they were detained in custody (on remand) for lengthy periods. The actions were struck out, on the grounds that 'there are compelling considerations, rooted in the welfare of the whole community, which outweigh the dictates of individualised justice'. These included the risk of 'defensive' action by CPS prosecutors and the diversion of resources away from their principal functions. In this context, according to Steyn LJ, the application of the policy–operation distinction would be 'impractical, unworkable and not capable of avoiding . . . adverse consequences for the CPS'.[794] In *Harris* v. *Evans*[795] the plaintiff's business was temporarily shut down when a Health and Safety inspector decided (allegedly on the basis of a mistaken understanding of HSE policy) that the mobile crane which he used to provide bungee jumping was unsafe. His action for damages for lost profits was struck out. Said the Vice Chancellor:

it would be seriously detrimental to the proper discharge by enforcing authorities of their responsibilities in respect of public health and safety if they were to be exposed to

---

[790] [1991] 4 All ER 973; [1992] 4 All ER 280.
[791] [1991] 4 All ER 973, 980. The Vice Chancellor's judgment was upheld in the Court of Appeal: [1992] 4 All ER 280.
[792] [1995] 2 AC 633. See also *Barrett* v. *Enfield London Borough Council* [1997] 3 All ER 171.
[793] [1995] QB 335. Cf. *Welsh* v. *Chief Constable of the Merseyside Police* [1993] 1 All ER 692.
[794] [1995] QB 335, 349–50.
[795] [1998] 1 WLR 1285. Cf. *Welton* v. *North Cornwall DC* [1997] 1 WLR 570.

potential liability in negligence at the suit of the owners of the businesses adversely affected by their decisions.[796]

In related contexts, *Hill* has been cited in a string of cases to deny liability on the part of the police to the victims of crimes and accidents. Hence the owner of a shop could not sue the police for losses allegedly caused by their negligent failure to catch a burglar.[797] Nor has the estate of a victim of a road-traffic accident a cause of action against the police for failing to alert road users to the presence of slippery diesel oil left on the highway by a third party.[798] The same principle has been applied to public rescue services, such as the fire service and the coastal rescue. Thus, such bodies are under no private-law duty to respond to emergency calls, and cannot be liable for an omission to act when carrying out a rescue.[799]

If the courts are prepared to go this far, a return to a version of the *East Suffolk*[800] principle seems likely. This would mean that statutory bodies would, in effect, enjoy a wide immunity from liability for omissions under the general common law of negligence, unless it could be shown that the statute under which they operate creates a private cause of action for breach of statutory duty. The one remaining possibility, however, is that a public authority could be liable for *making things worse*, as discussed in *East Suffolk*. Thus, in *Capital and Counties plc* v. *Hampshire County Council*,[801] the defendant fire authority was held to be liable for the carelessness of fire officers in switching off the automatic sprinkler system in the plaintiff's factory as part of a failed attempt to keep it from going up in flames. The intervention of the fire service, in this instance, had actively exacerbated the situation.

A related idea is that liability may be based on an assumption of responsibility by the defendant authority to a particular person or group of persons. It seems to be generally agreed that the police owe a duty of care to take steps to ensure the safety of arrested persons who are known to be at risk of committing suicide.[802] Similarly, the police may owe a duty of care to conceal the identity of their informants and to protect the confidentiality of the information that they provide, so as to minimise the risk of retaliation against them.[803] A regulatory authority, which would not otherwise be liable for failing to have regard to the economic interests or more general welfare of the plaintiff, may incur liability for negligent misstatements. This would be the case if the existence of a pre-tort relationship, based on reliance by or an assumption of responsibility to a particular individual, can be established.[804] But even here, it is possible that the plaintiff's claim will be defeated by policy considerations.

---

[796] [1998] 1 WLR 1285, 1301 (Sir Richard Scott VC).

[797] *Alexandrou* v. *Oxford* [1993] 4 All ER 328.

[798] *Ancell* v. *McDermott* [1993] 4 All ER 355.

[799] *Capital and Counties plc* v. *Hampshire CC* [1997] QB 1004; *OLL Ltd.* v. *Secretary of State for Transport* [1997] 3 All ER 897.

[800] [1941] AC 74. [801] [1997] QB 1004.

[802] *Reeves* v. *Commissioner of Police of the Metropolis* [1998] 2 WLR 401.

[803] *Swinney* v. *Chief Constable of Northumbria Police Force* [1997] QB 464.

[804] *T* v. *Surrey CC* [1994] 4 All ER 577; *Welton* v. *North Cornwall DC* [1997] 1 WLR 570; *X (Minors)* v. *Bedfordshire CC* [1995] 2 AC 633, 763–4.

In *Osman* v. *Ferguson*[805] the relationship between the police and the family of the murder victim was, prior to the killing, sufficiently close for the Court of Appeal to consider that there might have been a special pre-tort relationship sufficient to give rise to a duty of care. However, the court decided that even if this had been the case, it would be against public policy for a duty of care to be imposed on the police with regard to the safety of a particular individual or group of individuals.

However, in *Osman* v. *United Kingdom*[806] the European Court of Human Rights ruled that as a consequence of the Court of Appeal's ruling, there had been a breach of Article 6 of the European Convention on Human Rights, which guarantees a person's right to have a claim relating to his civil rights and obligations brought before a court or tribunal. The Court ruled that although the principle of protecting the police from litigation which would encourage defensive and wasteful practices was a potentially legitimate one under the Convention, the Court of Appeal's ruling resulted in a 'blanket immunity' which could not be regarded as proportionate to this objective. In the Court's view, it should have been open to a court to weigh other public interest considerations in the balance, and to have taken account of the proximity of the parties and of the seriousness of the harm which occurred in that case. This decision of the Court of Human Rights is likely to prove highly significant not just for the extent of the 'immunity' provided to the police by the *Hill* line of cases, but also for the use, more generally, of the duty concept to limit the potential liability of public bodies. *Osman* therefore calls into question the entire approach of the court to the use of the duty concept in cases of public authorities. In particular, it suggests that although some degree of protection for public bodies can be regarded as compatible with the protection of individuals' human rights, a much more flexible approach to the formulation of the duty question is called for. As we shall see shortly, under the Human Rights Act 1998 the UK courts will be required to take the provisions of the Convention into account under domestic law, and for this purpose a decision such as *Osman* is likely to be regarded as highly persuasive.

3. Liability for Breach of Statutory Duty

The general principles concerning the action for breach of statutory duty have already been considered.[807] Conceptually, the action is seen as arising under the statute by virtue of an implied legislative intent. It is, therefore, distinct from the common-law action for negligence in the exercise of a statutory power, even if the recent tendency of the courts in cases such as *Peabody*[808] has been, as Professor Harlow puts it, to 'align' the two.[809]

---

[805] [1993] 4 All ER 344. See also, in a different context, *Harris* v. *Evans* [1998] 1 WLR 1285, in which the Court of Appeal questioned whether a health and safety inspector could come under a duty of care to avoid causing economic loss to a business whose safety he was investigating, even if there was an element of reliance by the latter on the information provided by the former. Also relevant in this context is the decision of the Court of Appeal in *W* v. *Essex CC* [1998] 3 WLR 535, discussed in Chapter 2 above.

[806] *The Times*, 5 Nov. 1988.   [807] In Section 4 of this chapter.

[808] [1985] AC 210.   [809] See n. 785 above.

The tests for identifying the necessary statutory intent are restrictive. It will normally be necessary for the plaintiff to show that he fell within a particular class of persons that the statute was passed to protect. The effect of the decision in *Atkinson* v. *Newcastle Waterworks*[810] was felt for a long time to restrict the potential liability of utilities and statutory bodies under this head of liability. To some extent this assumption was challenged by the much-criticised[811] decision in *Thornton* v. *Kirklees Metropolitan Borough Council*,[812] in which the Court of Appeal accepted the possibility of statutory action for damages arising under the Housing (Homeless Persons) Act 1977. However, the *Thornton* case did not give rise to a spate of statutory actions against public bodies, in part because of the procedural changes introduced into public law which limited the availability of private law actions for administrative negligence and it was formally overturned in 1998.[813]

The principal significance of the statutory action in the present law seems to be to restrict the potential scope of negligence liability. As we have just seen, the House of Lords increasingly takes the view that no common law duty may be imposed in a case where it is not possible to imply an intention to create a statutory action. As the statutory action is only rarely available, this has created a certain presumption against liability.

4. Public Law as a Source of Liability

(A) DAMAGES FOR *ULTRA VIRES* ACTS?

Judicial review may be available to challenge an administrative act that is *ultra vires*. This could be on the grounds that the authority in question failed to take into account relevant considerations, failed to direct itself correctly on the law, or did not observe the requirements of natural justice (or 'due process'). As we have already noted, however, a finding of *ultra vires* does not necessarily entail liability for damages in negligence.[814] It is one thing to have an act declared invalid thereby restoring the *status quo*, but quite another for the authority to find itself indemnifying a potentially wide range of persons for various losses. In the former case the plaintiff or applicant is required to show only that he has a sufficient interest to challenge an excess of authority by the relevant body; in the latter, he must show that that a private-law right of his had been infringed.[815]

The relationship between *vires* and claims for damages was considered by Lord Keith of Kinkel in *Rowling* v. *Takaro Properties Ltd*.[816] A minister exercised powers under statute to prevent the issue of shares in Takaro to a foreign company, with the result that a rescue plan for Takaro failed. The minister's action

---

[810] (1877) LR 2 Ex D. 441.   [811] See in particular, Weir, 'Governmental Liability' [1988] *PL* 40, 52.
[812] [1979] 1 WLR 637.   [813] *O'Rourke* v. *Camden LBC* [1998] AC 189.
[814] 'The improper exercise of statutory powers does not, by itself, give rise to any civil liability in English law.' *Lonrho plc* v. *Tebbit* [1991] 4 All ER 973, 978 (Sir Nicolas Browne-Wilkinson VC). See also, *Bourgoin SA* v. *Ministry of Agriculture* [1986] 1 QB 785, per Parker LJ. For further discussion of damages for invalid acts, see P. P. Craig, 'Compensation and Public Law' (1980) 96 *LQR* 413, 435–43.
[815] See J. Beatson, '"Public" and "Private" in English Administrative Law' (1987) 103 *LQR* 34. Professor Beatson refers to a 'Hohfeldian' right, meaning one which is the corollary of an obligation owed in private law by the authority to the plaintiff or applicant individually.
[816] [1988] AC 473.

was later held to be *ultra vires* and an action was brought against him for compensation for the economic losses arising from the failure of the share deal. The Privy Council, overruling the New Zealand courts, found for the minister. Lord Keith noted that the normal consequence of an *ultra vires* act will simply be delay, as the act or decision can be nullified by proceedings for judicial review or its equivalent. In itself this is not much of an argument against granting damages for *ultra vires* acts, since in commercial matters even a short delay may cause considerable loss; and this was precisely the case in *Takaro*. Lord Keith went on, however, to argue that 'in the nature of things, it is likely to be very rare indeed that an error of law of this kind by a minister or other public authority can properly be categorised as negligent'.[817] A misinterpretation of powers, on its own, is unlikely to be actionable in damages; there must be something more such as the elements of knowledge or malice required for the tort of misfeasance in a public office.[818]

It is possible, alternatively, that a public body may undertake a specific duty of care under *Hedley Byrne & Co. Ltd.* v. *Heller & Partners Ltd.*[819] to avoid causing loss to the plaintiff through a negligent misstatement. For this to happen, however, there must be a pre-tort 'special relationship' between the parties and, in most cases, some element of reasonable reliance. General announcements and statements made to the public at large are unlikely to be enough. The Australian case of *Shaddock and Associates Pty. Ltd.* v. *Paramatta City Council (No. 1)*,[820] in which the council was held liable for giving misleading information concerning planning proposals to a potential buyer of property, lies at the furthest extreme of what would now be acceptable to the English courts. In *Davy* v. *Spelthorne Borough Council*[821] the House of Lords refused to strike out a claim for damages based on negligent advice given to the plaintiff in respect of his right to appeal against an enforcement notice placed on his property. A public body may also incur liability for economic loss outside the strict confines of *Hedley Byrne* in cases of specific relationships. *Ministry of Housing and Local Government* v. *Sharp*,[822] where a mistake by a clerk in a land registry led to the Ministry losing the right to recover statutory compensation, would probably be decided the same way today. In these cases it is largely beside the point that the administrative action was *ultra vires*; the central question was whether the requirements for a duty of care at common law were satisfied.

(B) THE TORT OF MISFEASANCE IN A PUBLIC OFFICE

Damages may none the less be available for an *ultra vires* act if an official *knowingly* acts in excess of his powers or acts with *malice* towards the plaintiff. This is the tort of misfeasance in a public office. Lord Diplock described the tort as

---

[817] [1988] AC 502.   [818] See below, Section 4(b).   [819] [1965] AC 465.
[820] (1981) 150 CLR 225.

[821] [1984] AC 262: the principal issue here was whether an action brought by writ was an abuse of process under the doctrine enunciated in *O'Reilly* v. *Mackman* [1983] 2 AC 237.

[822] [1970] QB 223. See the discussion of this case by Lord Oliver of Aylmerton in *Murphy* v. *Brentwood DC* [1991] 1 AC 398. See also *Lonrho plc* v. *Tebbit* [1991] 4 All ER 975, [1992] 4 All ER 280 (courts refusing to strike out action for compensation for pure economic loss arising out of a minister's exercise of powers in respect of mergers and take-overs).

'well established'[823] and it has been frequently and recently applied in England and other Commonwealth jurisdictions.

The essence of liability is the abuse of public office, leading to damage to the plaintiff. It is said that the power alleged to have been abused must have a statutory or public origin,[824] but this requirement is loosely interpreted. A public body exercising a private-law power will not escape the application of the tort. In *Jones* v. *Swansea City Council*[825] the plaintiff alleged that a council resolution turning down her application to amend the terms of a lease between herself and the council was actuated by malice. The ruling party on the council appeared to be opposed to the change of user because the plaintiff's husband had previously been a councillor for an opposing party. The council attempted to argue that the power in question arose under private law as part of the council's general contractual capacity. This was rejected on the grounds that a power exercised by a public officer or by a statutory body collectively should only be exercised for the public good: 'it is not the juridical nature of the relevant power but the nature of the council's office which is the important consideration.'[826]

It is now clearly established that either knowledge that the relevant act was taken in excess of powers or malice towards the plaintiff will suffice to establish the necessary element of abuse of office. 'Malice' refers here to an intention to injure the plaintiff. The authorities were carefully reviewed by Mann J in *Bourgoin SA* v. *Ministry of Agriculture*.[827] The action concerned the decision by the minister to ban the import of French turkeys into the United Kingdom, contrary to Article 30 of the Treaty of Rome which prohibits such restrictions on free trade within the European Community. It was alleged that the minister's motive was to protect British turkey farmers from competition. The plaintiff, whose business was affected by the ban, brought an action for damages. His claim for breach of statutory duty failed but both Mann J and the Court of Appeal held that an action for misfeasance would lie if it could be shown that the minister had knowingly acted in excess of his powers. According to the judge:

There is no sensible distinction between the case where an officer performs an act which he has no power to perform with the object of injuring A . . . and the case where an officer performs an act which he knows he has no power to perform with the object of conferring a benefit on B but which has the foreseeable and actual consequence of injury to A.[828]

---

[823] *Dunlop* v. *Woollahra Municipal Council* [1982] AC 158, 172; see Craig, 'Compensation in Public Law', op. cit. (1980) 96 *LQR* 413, 426–8.

[824] *Jones* v. *Swansea City Council* [1990] 1 WLR 54, 71 (Slade LJ).   [825] [1990] 1 WLR 54, 1453.

[826] Ibid., 71 (Slade LJ).

[827] [1986] 1 QB 716. Cf. *Bennett* v. *Commissioner of Police of the Metropolis* [1995] 1 WLR 488, 501 in which Rattee J held that recklessness is insufficient for this tort. A better formulation is that of Clark J in *Three Rivers DC* v. *Bank of England (No. 3)* [1996] 3 All ER 558, namely that malice in the sense of an intention to injure, and knowledge by the defendant that the act in question was unauthorised and was likely to injure the plaintiff, are *alternative*, and not *cumulative*, grounds of liability.

[828] [1986] 1 QB 716, 740. See also *Cullen* v. *Morris* (1819) 2 Stark. 577; *Tozer* v. *Child* (1857) 7 El. & Bl. 377; *Farrington* v. *Thomson and Bridgland* [1959] VR 286; *David* v. *Abdul Cader* [1963] 1 WLR 834, 839–40 (Viscount Radcliffe).

The Ministry settled the case and so it is not known if the tort could actually have been established. In practice, plaintiffs are likely to face considerable difficulties of proof. The action succeeded before the Supreme Court of Canada in *Roncarelli* v. *Duplessis*,[829] in which the prime minister of Quebec had ordered a liquor licence to be withdrawn from a restaurant apparently as punishment for its owner's support for the Jehovah's Witnesses. This clear case may be contrasted with *Jones* v. *Swansea City Council*,[830] in which the plaintiff failed to show that a vote of councillors on a planning matter had been actuated by malice. The Court of Appeal and the House of Lords agreed that an action would lie if it could be shown that a majority of councillors, voting at a particular meeting, did so when motivated by malice. The Court of Appeal ordered a retrial of the action but the House of Lords overturned this decision. The burden on the plaintiff in such a case will be extremely difficult to overcome.

5. Public Law as a Source of Immunity

(A) VALIDITY OF ADMINISTRATIVE ACTION AS A PRIVATE-LAW DEFENCE

It will almost certainly be a defence to a claim in negligence to show that the relevant act or omission was taken within the relevant statutory powers. The reason was explained by Lord Diplock in *Dorset Yacht Co.* v. *Home Office.*[831] The *ultra vires* principle was one means by which the courts were kept out of areas which were non-justiciable in the sense of providing 'no criterion by which a court can assess where the balance lies between the weight to be given to one interest and that to be given to another'. To cross the boundary of *ultra vires* and allow a negligence action for acts within the authority's statutory discretion would undermine its policy-making function:

It is, I apprehend, for practical reasons of this kind that over the past century the public law concept of *ultra vires* has replaced the civil law concept of negligence as the test of the legality, and consequently of the actionability, of acts or omissions of government departments or public authorities done in the exercise of a discretion conferred upon them by Parliament. According to this concept Parliament has entrusted to the department or authority charged with the administration of the statute the exclusive right to determine the particular means within the limits laid down by the statute by which its purpose can best be fulfilled. It is not the function of the court, for which it would be ill-suited, to substitute its own view of the appropriate means for that of the department or authority by granting a remedy by way of a civil action at law to a private citizen adversely affected by the way in which the discretion has been exercised. Its function is confined in the first instance to deciding whether the act or omission complained of fell within the statutory limits imposed upon the department's or authority's decision. Only if it did not would the court have jurisdiction to determine whether or not the act or omission, not being justified by the statute, constituted an actionable infringement of the plaintiff's rights in civil law.[832]

---

[829] [1959] SCR 121; see also *Gershman* v. *Manitoba Vegetable Producers' Marketing Board* (1976) 69 DLR (3d) 114.

[830] [1990] 1 WLR 54, 1453.   [831] [1970] AC 1004, 1068.

[832] Ibid. See also to the same effect, *Fellowes* v. *Rother District Council* [1983] 1 All ER 513 (Robert Goff J); *Lonrho plc* v. *Tebbit* [1991] 4 All ER 973, 980 (Sir Nicolas Browne-Wilkinson VC).

To a large extent this immunity for *intra vires* acts has now been subsumed into the policy–operation dichotomy and into the courts' reluctance to adjudicate on 'non-justiciable' matters of discretionary judgment. Where a policy decision is taken *ultra vires*, it is still up to the plaintiff to establish a breach of a duty of care: as we just saw, damages are not automatically available for an *ultra vires* act. Even if both fault and invalidity are established it is highly likely that the courts will still decline to intervene in the policy-making area.[833] Where, on the other hand, negligence is operational in character—such as a failure to carry out an inspection with due care—the carelessness of the employee concerned will almost certainly amount to an *ultra vires* act. As far as validity is concerned, most statutory powers must be exercised with due care: where a body exercises powers negligently it will almost certainly have exceeded its powers.[834]

(B) Procedural Immunity Under Order 53, RSC

Where a claim for damages in tort (either in negligence or for breach of statutory duty) directly raises the question of the validity of an act or omission in administrative law under the *ultra vires* rule, it may be necessary for the damages claim to be brought by way of proceedings for judicial review under Order 53 of the Rules of the Supreme Court rather than through the normal method of a writ issued in the High Court. This has a number of important procedural consequences, not least that the action must be begun within a short limitation of three months, in contrast with the normal six-year limitation period for civil claims in tort.[835] It is also necessary to seek the leave of the court to proceed with an application for judicial review. The application is likely to be decided on the basis of affidavit evidence with limited opportunity for cross-examination. These restrictions, designed to protect public bodies from harassment, make sense when the *validity* of an act is under challenge and there is a need for a speedy decision which avoids delay and the consequent harmful effects on public administration. What is less obvious is whether they serve any purpose when a claim for damages is being brought after the event, unless it is the aim, which has some support,[836] of returning to the days of the Public Authorities Protection Acts when local authorities enjoyed a similar kind of procedural immunity from suit.

The requirement that questions of public law should be raised exclusively by means of an application for judicial review originates in the judgment of the House of Lords in *O'Reilly* v. *Mackman*.[837] If a 'public law' action is begun by writ, it will be struck out as an abuse of process. The implication for tort claims was made clear at once in the twin decision of *Cocks* v. *Thanet District Council*.[838] The plaintiff sued in the county court for a mandatory injunction requiring the council to grant him permanent accommodation under the Housing (Homeless

---

[833] Craig, 'Negligence in the Exercise of a Statutory Power', op. cit., considers various circumstances in which a finding of *ultra vires* might be of assistance in overcoming the policy immunity: (1978) 94 *LQR* 428, 447–52.

[834] Ibid., 453.   [835] On limitation generally, see Chapter 8, Section 1, below.

[836] See generally Weir, op. cit. (Select Bibliography).   [837] [1983] 2 AC 237.

[838] [1983] 2 AC 286.

Persons) Act 1977, and coupled this with a claim for damages for breach of statutory duty under *Thornton* v. *Kirklees Metropolitan Borough Council*.[839] The action was struck out on the grounds that an essential step or 'necessary condition precedent' in establishing the private-law claim for damages was a public law finding that the council had acted in excess of its powers under the Act.[840] It was therefore appropriate for the council to invoke the procedural protections of Order 53 and to require the plaintiff to bring his claim as an application for judicial review.

Later decisions have, however, substantially qualified the potential scope of this ruling. In *Davy* v. *Spelthorne Borough Council*[841] the plaintiff sued for damages for allegedly negligent advice given to him by the council's officers concerning an enforcement order restricting the use of his premises. The advice was to the effect that the plaintiff should not appeal against the order; as a result he failed to lodge a protest in time. The House of Lords allowed the action for damages to proceed by way of writ on the grounds that the claim of negligence did not involve a challenge to the validity of the enforcement order or to any other determination. This decision seems correct in terms both of principle and of policy. As we have seen, the question of validity is generally irrelevant to the availability of a private-law claim in negligence. It is only necessary to show *ultra vires* in the negative sense that if an act is *intra vires*, the statutory body may have a defence. In *Davy* the plaintiff was essentially making an allegation of operational negligence against the council's officers which necessarily carries with it the implication that they had acted in excess of their powers. However, he was not seeking to *challenge* their advice—such an action would have been meaningless—but to claim compensation for the damage it caused. Under these circumstances there is no merit in blocking the claim on the grounds that to allow it to proceed will cause undue delays to the administrative process.

In *Wandsworth London Borough Council* v. *Winder*[842] the defendant attempted to defend a claim for the repossession of his flat and arrears of rent on the grounds that a council resolution increasing his rent had been *ultra vires*. The council attempted to have this defence struck out on the grounds that he should have raised it at the time of the resolution, several years earlier, by judicial review. The House of Lords allowed the defence to stand even though it clearly entailed a challenge to the validity of the resolution. According to Lord Fraser, in *Cocks* the 'impugned decision of the local authority did not deprive the plaintiff of a pre-existing private law right; it prevented him from establishing a new private law right'. In *Winder*, on the other hand, the defendant was seeking to defend a private law right to the possession of his flat which pre-existed the alleged *ultra vires* act.[843] This could, however, be seen as a distinction without a difference. In *Winder* the defendant was making a private law claim to the effect that the council had no right to demand the higher rent, and this arose directly out of the public law claim that it had acted *ultra vires* at the time of the rent increase. It might be preferable to see *Winder* as a decision which goes a long way

---

[839] [1979] QB 626, now overruled by the House of Lords in *O'Rourke* v. *Camden LBC* [1998] AC 189.
[840] [1983] 2 AC 286, 294 (Lord Bridge).　　　　[841] [1984] AC 262.　　　　[842] [1985] AC 461.
[843] [1985] 1 AC 461, 508.

towards confining the effects of *O'Reilly* v. *Mackman* to cases involving no private law issues of any kind. In the Court of Appeal Parker LJ said that:

a public policy which had the result contended for [by the council] and interfered with the rights of the subject to defend himself when sued by any defence open to him or to bring an action for private law relief save in the one case exemplified in *Cocks* v. *Thanet District Council* would, in my view be more than unruly: it would have bolted and both outrun the legislature and overturned long-standing principles laid down by the House of Lords.[844]

The relationship between validity and claims for damages received further consideration in *Lonrho plc* v. *Tebbit*.[845] Sir Nicolas Browne-Wilkinson accepted that for the purposes of a claim in negligence, it would be necessary for Lonrho to show that the Secretary of State had acted *ultra vires*, for the reasons given by Lord Diplock in *Dorset Yacht* v. *Home Office*.[846] The issue of *vires* was, therefore, not simply collateral to the private-law claim, but was one ingredient in the establishment of that claim. However, this was not a case in which it was intended to challenge the validity of the decision in order to have it reversed; the only remaining action was for damages. The facts upon which Lonrho's action was based did not come to its attention until some time after the events in question. Under these circumstances, 'to strike out the claim on this ground and require the case to be brought by way of judicial review would in all probability lock out Lonrho from the remedy in damages it seeks'.[847] Lonrho would be out of time and would have to seek leave to proceed under Order 53, which might not be forthcoming. As a result, the action was allowed to proceed. This judgment is a strong indication of the courts' reluctance to use Order 53 as the basis for giving public bodies a procedural immunity from private law claims.

This tendency was further confirmed by the decision of the House of Lords in *Roy* v. *Kensington and Chelsea and Westminster Family Practitioner Committee*.[848] This was concerned with a claim by a general practitioner in the National Health Service that the Committee (a statutory body with responsibilities in relation to local health-care services) had wrongfully withheld part of his salary. He began an action by writ for payment of the sum in question only to be met by a defence that he should first have to bring proceedings for judicial review to establish the impropriety of the Committee's decision. Rejecting the defence, Lord Lowry described the plaintiff as having 'a bundle of rights, which should be regarded as his individual private law rights against the committee, arising from the statute and regulations and including the very important private law right to be paid for the work which he has done'.[849] Lord Lowry distinguished *Cocks* v. *Thanet District Council*[850] on the ground that 'Mr. Cocks was simply a homeless member of the public . . . whereas Dr. Roy had already an established

---

[844] [1985] AC 461, 492. See also the judgment of Lord Wilberforce in *Davy* v. *Spelthorne Borough Council* [1984] AC 262, 267: 'We have not yet reached the point at which mere characterization of a claim as a claim in public law is sufficient to exclude it from consideration by the ordinary courts: to permit this would be to create a dual system of law with the rigidity and procedural hardship for plaintiffs which it was the purpose of [Order 53] to remove.'

[845] [1991] 4 All ER 973.   [846] [1970] AC 1004, 1068.   [847] [1991] 4 All ER 973, 987.

[848] [1992] 1 AC 625.   [849] Ibid., 647–8.   [850] [1983] 2 AC 286.

relationship with the committee' when the dispute arose. This is unconvincing: Mr Cocks was seeking to establish a private law right to damages which would have been just as much a 'right' as that asserted by Dr Roy. Nevertheless, the impression is given that *Cocks* will not be followed in decisions which do not relate to claims of the kind that arose in that case.

Because the issue of *ultra vires* is not central to most negligence claims, few such claims will have to be litigated via Order 53. It could be a different matter with actions for breach of statutory duty such as *Cocks* v. *Thanet District Council*[851] which are directly concerned with whether a particular act or omission fell within the scope of the statute. There would seem, however, to be a fundamental distinction between a damages action, which is concerned with damage already inflicted by a statutory breach, and an application for judicial review to have a decision set aside. There is no rationale, other than the formalist one that negligence and breach of statutory duty are separate nominate torts, for the different outcomes in *Cocks* v. *Thanet District Council*[852] and *Davy* v. *Spelthorne Borough Council*.[853] Nor does it appear to have been suggested that actions for misfeasance in a public office should have to be brought under Order 53, even though such actions must establish that an *ultra vires* act took place. The best prospect for a return to doctrinal clarity in this area would be for the House of Lords formally to overrule *Cocks* v. *Thanet District Council*.[854]

In *Roy*[855] Lord Lowry distinguished between two possible approaches to the relationship between private rights and the principle laid down by the House of Lords in *O'Reilly* v. *Mackman*.[856] First, a broad approach, according to which *O'Reilly* 'did not apply generally against bringing actions to vindicate private rights in all circumstances in which those actions involved a challenge to a public law act or decision, but . . . merely required the aggrieved person to proceed by judicial review only when private law rights were not at stake'. Second, a narrow approach which 'assumed that the rule applied generally to *all* proceedings in which public law acts or decisions were challenged, subject to some exceptions when private law rights were involved'. His Lordship expressed a preference for the broad view as being consonant with principle and having the 'practical merit of getting rid of a procedural minefield', but did not feel compelled formally to adopt it as the basis for the rejection of the Committee's defence. Nevertheless, a clear enough signal has been given for future courts in this area.[857]

6. Crown Proceedings in Tort

Central-government departments and certain other bodies exercising state functions, such as the armed forces, are viewed for the purposes of liability in contract and tort as exercising the powers of the Crown. Until the Crown

---

[851] [1983] 2 AC 286.   [852] Ibid.   [853] [1984] AC 262.   [854] [1983] 2 AC 286.
[856] [1992] 1 AC 625, 651.

[857] See S. Arrowsmith, *Civil Liability and Public Authorities* (1992), 25–6. *Roy* has since been followed in a number of cases involving claims in tort, contract and restitution. See *Woolwich Equitable Building Society* v. *IRC* [1993] AC 70; *Mercury Communications Ltd.* v. *Director-General of Telecommunications* [1996] 1 WLR 48; *British Steel plc* v. *Customs and Excise Commissioners* [1997] 2 All ER 366; *Trustees of the Dennis Rye Pension Fund* v. *Sheffield CC* [1997] 4 All ER 747; *Andreou* v. *Institute of Chartered Accountants of England and Wales* [1998] 1 All ER 14.

Proceedings Act 1947 this meant that they could take advantage of the Crown's general immunity from suit. In practice, actions in tort would be brought against an individual civil servant. While the Crown was, in theory, not responsible for the torts committed by its agents and employees, it was the practice for it to pay any damages awarded against those acting on its behalf. The anomaly of immunity in tort was formally removed by section 2(1) of the 1947 Act. This provides that the Crown shall be subject to the normal liability in tort in three cases. First, where torts are committed by its servants or agents.[858] Secondly, in respect of a breach of the employer's personal common-law duty of care to his employees. Finally, in respect of a breach of common-law duties attaching to the ownership, occupation, possession, or control of property. Section 2(2) provides that the Crown shall be liable for breach of statutory duty in a case where the duty in question does not bind the Crown alone. This means that the Crown is caught by the most common kind of statutory action, namely for breach of employers' duties under the Factory Acts.[859] In addition, a number of specific statutes providing for particular duty situations and particular defences have specifically included the Crown in their scope. These include the Occupiers' Liability Acts 1957[860] and 1984,[861] the Defective Premises Act 1972,[862] the Latent Damage Act 1986,[863] and the Consumer Protection Act 1987.[864] The 1947 Act makes provision for statutory provisions concerning contributory negligence, joint liability, and contribution and indemnity to apply to the Crown.[865] Immunities retained by the 1947 Act in respect of activities of the armed forces were repealed in 1987, subject to a power on the part of the Secretary of State to revive them in the event of war or national emergency.[866] The Crown retains immunity in respect of the discharge of judicial responsibilities.[867]

7. Liability for Breaches of European Community Law

As we have seen,[868] one of the few areas of growth for the action for breach of statutory duty in recent years concerns liability in damages for breach of a directly effective provision of European Community law. Even here, however, there are policy arguments for restricting the potential liability of governmental bodies. As Nourse LJ put it in *Bourgoin SA* v. *Ministry of Agriculture, Fisheries and Food*:[869]

In this country the law never allowed that a private individual should recover damages against the Crown for an injury caused him by an *ultra vires* order made in good faith.

---

[858] On the relevant definition of a Crown servant, see s. 2(6).

[859] See *Nicholls* v. *Austin (Leyton) Ltd.* [1946] AC 493; *Sparrow* v. *Fairey Aviation Co. Ltd.* [1964] AC 1019. See also the discussion of s. 2(2) of the 1947 Act in the context of liability for breach of European Community law in Oliver LJ's dissenting judgment in *Bourgoin SA* v. *Ministry of Agriculture, Fisheries and Food* [1986] 1 QB 716.

[860] S. 6.   [861] S. 3.   [862] S. 5.   [863] S. 3(7).   [864] S. 9(2).   [865] S. 4.

[866] Crown Proceedings (Armed Forces) Act 1987.

[867] Crown Proceedings Act 1947, s. 2(5). For further detail on Crown proceedings see H. W. R. Wade and C. F. Forsyth, *Administrative Law* (7th edn., 1994), ch. 21; see also ibid., ch. 6 for details of certain specific statutory immunities conferred on public corporations such as the Post Office.

[868] See Section 4, above.   [869] [1986] 1 QB 716, 790.

Nowadays this rule is grounded not in procedural theory but on the sound acknowledgement that a minister of the Crown should be able to discharge the duties of his office expeditiously and fearlessly, a state of affairs which could hardly be achieved if acts done in good faith, but beyond his powers, were to be actionable in damages.

Nourse and Parker LJJ held that Community law did not require the fashioning of a new remedy which would effectively extend potential liability for breach of statutory duty to the point where an *ultra vires* act of an official or statutory body would automatically give rise to a damages claim. By contrast, Oliver LJ argued that a remedy of this kind was necessary to protect the plaintiff's European law rights under Article 30 and that there was no basis consonant with European law for protecting the minister's discretion as a matter of domestic public policy.

Doubt has been cast on *Bourgoin* by the judgment of the European Court of Justice in *Francovich* v. *Republic of Italy*.[870] For according to this decision the government of a Member State could be held liable in damages to one of its citizens for loss caused by its failure, in breach of Community law, to implement a Directive. For this to happen, three conditions must be satisfied. First, the provision in question must be designed to confer individual rights. Secondly, the content of the rights in question must be capable of being determined from an examination of the Directive and its aims. Finally, there must be a sufficient causal link between the breach of Community law and the loss suffered by the individual. The liability thereby created appears to be strict. It also appears to be free of the limitations imposed on governmental liability in English law and, in particular, by the restrictions placed on liability for breach of statutory duty by *Bourgoin*. For example, the distinction drawn by the English case law between measures passed in the interests of a particular group,[871] and those passed in the interests of the public,[872] could cease to be tenable with respect to this particular area of liability for breach of a Community law obligation.

The basis of *Francovich* is the principle that effective judicial remedies should be made available within national legal systems for the protection of rights established by Community law. The *Francovich* judgment itself concerned the defective implementation of a Directive. But the terms in which the judgment was made, together with subsequent decisions of the European Court of Justice, indicate that the principle is not confined to acts of a legislature, but can also extend to breaches of Community law committed by public authorities.[873] It is also possible (although not yet clearly established) that Community law rights can give rise to liabilities on the part of individuals and entities in the private

---

[870] Cases C-6/90 and C-9/90 *Francovich and Bonifaci* v. *Italian Republic* [1991] ECR I-5357; Case C-46/93 *Brasserie du Pecheur* v. *Federal Republic of Germany* and Case C-48/93 R v. *Secretary of State for Trade and Industry, ex parte Factortame Ltd.* [1996] ECR I-1029; Cases C-178/94, C-179/94, C-188/94, C-189/94 and C-190/94 *Dillenkofer* v. *Federal Republic of Germany* [1996] All ER (EC) 917. Lord Goff has suggested that *Francovich* may have effectively reversed *Bourgoin*: see *Kirklees MBC* v. *Wickes* [1992] 3 WLR 170, 188; and see generally R. Caranta, 'Governmental Liability after Francovich' [1993] *CLJ* 272; S. Arrowsmith, *Civil Liability and Public Authorities* (1992), 254–7.

[871] Which may give rise to a private tort action.   [872] Which may not give rise to such an action.

[873] See W. Van Gerven, 'Bridging the unbridgeable: Community and national tort laws after *Francovich* and *Brasserie*' (1996) 45 *ICLQ* 507.

sector.[874] Leaving aside this unresolved question of liability between private persons, the *Francovich* principle might, in practice, have the following meaning. This is that the constraints currently placed by the English common law on the tort liability of public authorities would no longer hold, at least in so far as the enforcement of rights under European Community law was concerned. This would have important implications for those substantive areas where rights are well established under European Community law. These include not just competition law and the law of the single market, but also, for example, health and safety law and areas of environmental law. Within these areas, national courts could be seen as coming under a duty to develop existing causes of action so as to ensure the effectiveness of Community law. This could imply changes to, for example, the components of the tort of breach of statutory duty or, as the case may be, the tort of misfeasance in a public office. It could also be argued that if extensions to these torts take place within the context of Community law, it would be anomalous (and unjust) not to make parallel extensions in areas of common law liability not touched on by Community law. Finally, one should bear in mind one further point. Given the principle of the supremacy of Community law over domestic law, the scope of the changes needed to bring the common law into line with the EC Treaty would be an issue that would, ultimately, have to be decided by the European Court of Justice and not the domestic courts alone.[875]

8. Liability under the Human Rights Act 1998

Under the Human Rights Act 1998, it is 'unlawful for a public authority to act in a way which is incompatible with a Convention right',[876] that is, with one of the specified rights identified by the 1998 Act from among those contained in the European Convention and various of its Protocols.[877] These consist of Articles 2–12 and 14 of the Convention, which concern the right to life, the prohibition of torture, the prohibition of slavery and forced labour, the right to liberty and security, the right to a fair trial, no punishment without law, the right to respect for private and family life, freedom of thought, religion and conscience, freedom of expression, freedom of assembly and association, the right to marry, and the prohibition of discrimination. Also included are Articles 1–3 of the First Protocol (the right to protection of property, the right to education, and the right to free elections) and Articles 1–2 of the Sixth Protocol (these concern the death penalty). The Act requires courts and tribunals to interpret and give effect to both primary and subordinate legislation, as far as possible, 'in a way which is compatible with the Convention rights'. This measure, however, does not affect the validity or effect of any primary legislation that is incompatible with Convention rights.[878] A public authority is relieved of the obligation to act in accordance with the Convention rights if, as a result of primary legislation, it could not have acted differently. Likewise, if it was acting in order

---

[874] See ibid., 530 ff., discussing Case 128/92 *Banks* v. *British Coal Corporation* [1994] ECR I-1209.
[875] See generally the full discussion of Van Gerven, op. cit., n. 873 above.
[876] Human Rights Act 1998, s. 6(1). [877] Ibid, s. 1. [878] Ibid., s. 3.

to give effect to primary legislation which cannot be read or given effect to in such a way as to be compatible with Community rights.[879]

At the time of writing, the Human Rights Act has not yet come into force and the exercise of evaluating its possible impact on the law of tort is, inevitably, somewhat speculative. The Act nevertheless seems likely to have a particular impact in the field of governmental liability, if only because it is public authorities, in the first instance, which are required to respect Convention rights. In principle, these rights only have 'vertical effect'—in other words, they do not give rise to obligations that are binding on private individuals or entities. It should, however, be borne in mind that the influence of the Convention on the law of tort is already obvious in certain areas, such as privacy[880] and freedom of expression.[881] This process seems likely to continue and, indeed, intensify once the Act comes into force, not least because of the requirement that the courts should interpret legislation, wherever possible, so as to comply with the Convention. Moreover, the courts themselves are public authorities for the purposes of the Act.[882] This means that they, too, must act in accordance with the Convention. How, precisely, this will affect future the future development of the common law remains to be seen. But it implies that even when interpreting and applying an area of judge-made law with no statutory content, the judges may have to pay some regard to the Convention.

The definition of 'public authority' under the Act also deserves close attention, in particular since it differs from the notion of an organ of the state which has been adopted in European Community law for the purposes of determining the extent of state liability. Under section 6 of the Act, a public authority includes 'any person certain of whose functions are functions of a public nature'. This definition may not include, for example, privatised corporations in the regulated utilities that tend to fall within the public sector for the purposes of determining the vertical direct effect of European Community Directives.[883]

Moreover, the Act states that 'in relation to a particular act, a person is not a public authority . . . if the nature of the act is private'. A public body, such as a local authority, could therefore have mixed public and private functions; the precise boundary between them is not clear.

While it remains for case law to begin addressing these problems, the potential for the Act to reshape aspects of governmental liability in tort is also apparent. As we have seen in this chapter, courts since the early 1980s have gradually expanded the immunity of public bodies from liability in negligence. With the advent of the Human Rights Act 1998, our courts will be forced to undertake more balancing. In particular, they will have to weigh human rights against instrumental considerations of the kind which have provided the rationale for restrictions on the scope of the duty of care, such as the dangers of 'defensive' practices and of opportunistic litigation. This development is particularly significant since, until now, the case law on governmental liability has made very

---

[879] Human Rights Act 1998, s. 6(2).   [880] See below, Chapter 7, Section 3.
[881] See *Middlebrook Mushrooms Ltd.* v. *Transport and General Workers' Union* [1993] IRLR 232.
[882] Human Rights Act 1998, s. 6(3)(a).   [883] See *Griffin* v. *South West Water Services Ltd.* [1995] IRLR 15.

little mention of rights-based considerations. Thus, in *Elguzouli-Daf* v. *Commissioner of Police of the Metropolis*,[884] no account appears to have been taken of the extended and, in the event, unnecessary infringement of the personal liberty of the plaintiffs. Article 5 of the European Convention, which must now be observed by a prosecuting authority, states that 'no-one shall be deprived of his liberty' save in a number of specified cases, one of which is 'the lawful arrest or detention of a person effected for the purpose of bringing him before the competent legal authority on reasonable suspicion of having committed an offence . . .'.[885] But in relation to such arrest or detention, the person arrested 'shall be brought promptly before a judge or other officer authorised by law to exercise judicial power and shall be entitled to trial within a reasonable time or to release pending trial'.[886] Persons who are detained in contravention of this provision 'shall have an enforceable right to compensation'.[887] It is arguable that *Elgozouli-Daf* could not now be decided the same way. In that case, the effect of the Court of Appeal's decision was that the substance of the plaintiffs' claims could not even be addressed. To rule out a duty of care was to prevent the plaintiffs from making their respective cases on the merits, and to deny them compensation even on the assumption that their allegations of negligence were true. This seems incompatible with the requirements of Article 5 of the Convention.

Also highly relevant in this context is the decision of the European Court of Human Rights in *Osman* v. *United Kingdom*,[888] which throws into question the extent of the apparently 'blanket immunity' enjoyed by the police from liability in negligence in the course of operational decisions'.

9. Towards a Synthesis of the Law Relating to Governmental Liability?

The law relating to governmental liability has, in recent years, been subject to conflicting pressures. On the one hand, we have attempts made by the courts to contain the consequences of *Anns* by providing a qualified immunity for public bodies from liability for omissions. On the other, we are (or will be faced) with developments in European Community law and in human rights law which promise to open up new areas of liability. Under these circumstances it would be premature to speak of an emerging synthesis of the principles of liability. However, we can identify the questions around which the legal debates seem likely to coalesce.

First, what precisely is the rationale for treating public authorities as a special case? The courts have identified several factors in the course of the long retreat from *Anns*, most notably the danger of opportunistic litigation against defendants of last resort and the diversion of resources into wasteful 'defensive' practices aimed at warding off litigation. Whether these factors, and their tendency to produce blanket exclusions of liability, will withstand the onslaught of the Human Rights legislation is another matter. We may also legitimately ask whether these are factors which are unique to the public sector and, indeed,

---

[884] [1995] QB 335.   [885] European Convention on Human Rights, Art. 5(1)(c).
[886] Ibid., Art. 5(3).   [887] Ibid., Art. 5(5).   [888] *The Times*, 5 Nov. 1998.

whether it makes any sense for this purpose to classify all public bodies (police, rescue services, regulators, local councils, government departments) in the same way for this purpose.

Secondly, if there is a case for treating public bodies in a distinct way, where is the boundary to be drawn between the public and the private? This is a particular problem given the current lack of a legal common definition of the public sector across the different areas of tort law, European Community law and human rights law. The possibility of, eventually, giving a horizontal effect to the new Human Rights legislation must also not be excluded; and if or when this occurs, it could affect large areas of the law of obligations. Thirdly, how are the courts to resolve clashes between the instrumental or efficiency-based considerations which have dominated recent decisions limiting the scope of the duty of care, and the jurisprudence of human rights which derives from the European Convention on Human Rights and the Human Rights Act 1998? The cross-fertilisation of tort law with emerging concepts of citizenship may yet prove to be one of the most productive areas for doctrinal development in the years to come. In all this, we may well see more and interesting examples of a phenomenon of recent vintage: the constitutionalisation of private law. But this is not the place, and certainly not the time, to go into this fascinating subject in any further detail.

Select Bibliography

ARROWSMITH, S., *Civil Liability and Public Authorities* (1992).
BEATSON, J., ' "Public" and "Private" in English Administrative Law' (1987) 103 *LQR* 34.
CRAIG, P. P., 'Negligence in the Exercise of a Statutory Power' (1978) 94 *LQR* 428.
—— 'Compensation and Public Law' (1980) 96 *LQR* 413.
HARLOW, C., *Compensation and Government Torts* (1982).
—— *Understanding Tort Law* (1988), ch. 7.
TODD, S., 'The Negligence Liability of Public Authorities: Divergence in the Common Law' (1986) 102 *LQR* 370.
WADE, H. W. R. and FORSYTH, C. F., *Administrative Law* (7th edn., 1994), chs. 20, 21.
WEIR, J. A., 'Governmental Liability' [1989] *PL* 40.

4

*Interference with the Person**

1. Intentional Physical Interference

1. Introduction: The Meaning of Intentional Interference

English law does not acknowledge a single tort of intention in the same sense that it acknowledges the existence of the tort of negligence. One reason for this is historical. Until the middle of the nineteenth century and before the forms of action were abolished, wrongdoing was remedied by variants of trespass or case. Liability for intentional conduct was distributed among these two and over the years some forms of liability for intention acquired particular names, such as assault, battery, and so on. This did not happen with careless conduct, which fell under trespass or case depending on whether the resulting harm was direct or consequential. After the forms of action disappeared it became possible gradually to collate the nameless instances of liability for carelessness under the rubric 'negligence'. In this way the new tort of negligence made its appearance. This was not possible with intention, however, since liability for intentional harm had already crystallised into the specific nominate torts which still exist today.

Intentional physical interference with the person may occur by way of an act that threatens violence (assault), amounts to unlawful contact (battery), or constitutes the deprivation of liberty (false imprisonment). There is, in addition, a residuary and uncertain form of liability for the intentional infliction of physical harm, known as the rule in *Wilkinson* v. *Downton*.[1] These torts are normally actionable without proof of damage and they also involve a sharp distinction being drawn between an act and an omission: the latter will not normally suffice to ground liability. Malice is not a necessary ingredient of liability, but the defendant must have had the relevant intention. Although there are some equivocal dicta,[2] modern case law takes the view on the whole that the defendant must not simply intend to commit the act in question; he must also intend the consequence, that is to say, the interference in question. This represents a change from the traditional point of view which effectively imposed *strict* liability once it had been shown that the interference derived directly from a

---

* This chapter draws on material prepared by R. W. M. Dias for the second edition of this book.

[1] [1897] 2 QB 57.

[2] E.g. *Wilson* v. *Pringle* [1987] QB 237, 249: 'it is the act and not the injury that must be intentional. An intention to injure is not essential to an action for trespass to the person. It is the mere trespass itself which is the offence' (Croom-Johnson LJ). This statement is ambiguous in that it refers to 'injury' rather than 'interference'. It is clear that intention to injure is not necessary since injury itself is not necessary, trespass being actionable *per se*. 'Interference' in the sense of unlawful contact is the gist of the tort of battery, with or without damage, and it would seem in the light of other authorities (cited in the text) that the defendant must have intended the interference, in this sense.

positive act of the defendant, leaving the defendant to show that his case fell under one of a number of defences.[3] The need to show fault was first clearly articulated in nineteenth-century decisions concerning accidents on the highway, and it has since been normal to analyse collision cases in terms of negligence and not in terms of trespass.[4] Since then the extension of negligence liability following *Donoghue* v. *Stevenson*[5] has reinforced this tendency. In *Fowler* v. *Lanning*[6] the plaintiff simply alleged that the defendant had shot him, without alleging either intention or negligence. Diplock J held that this did not constitute a cause of action, on the basis that 'trespass to the person does not lie if the injury to the plaintiff, although the direct consequence of the act of the defendant, was caused unintentionally and without negligence on the defendant's part'. Diplock J would have preserved a category of negligent trespass to the person; Lord Denning MR went one step further in *Letang* v. *Cooper*[7] by suggesting that: 'when the injury is not inflicted intentionally, but negligently, I would say that the only cause of action is negligence and not trespass. If it were trespass, it would be actionable without proof of damage; and that is not the law today.' Certain questions of limitation of actions aside,[8] the practical consequences of *Fowler* v. *Lanning* and *Letang* v. *Cooper* may not be all that great, since few actions are started where no damage has been sustained. However, these two decisions significantly narrow the scope of the 'interference' torts in comparison to negligence. The preponderance of the tort of negligence in the modern law of torts is a reflection of the tendency to focus on loss-spreading and to use the 'fault principle' as a basis for judging activity that causes damage. It should be stressed, however, that the function of the interference torts is not to engage in loss-spreading as such but to affirm the fundamental importance of certain interests, such as personal bodily integrity and freedom of movement, *in their own right*. In this sense the torts of trespass to the person are similar in nature to the torts of interference with land and with chattels, which still bear clear signs of their origins as torts of strict liability.[9]

2. Assault

The conduct forbidden by this tort is an intentional act that threatens violence, or in other words one that produces in the plaintiff a reasonable expectation of immediate, unlawful force.[10] The tort is actionable *per se*. Assault is both a tort

---

[3] See Winfield, 'The Myth of Absolute Liability' (1926) 42 *LQR* 37; Goodhart and Winfield, 'Trespass and Negligence' (1933) 49 *LQR* 37; Prichard, 'The Rule in *Williams* v. *Holland*' [1964] *CLJ* 237.

[4] See *Fletcher* v. *Rylands* (1866) LR 1 Ex.1 265, 268 (Blackburn J); *River Wear Commissioners* v. *Adamson* (1977) 2 App. Cas. 743 (Lord Blackburn); *Holmes* v. *Mather* (1875) LR 10 Ex. 261 (Bramwell LJ); see generally Fleming, *Torts* (7th edn.), 18 ff.

[5] [1932] AC 562.   [6] [1959] 1 QB 426, following *Stanley* v. *Powell* [1891] 1 QB 86.

[7] [1965] 1 QB 232, 240, applied by the Court of Appeal in *Wilson* v. *Pringle* [1987] QB 237.

[8] *Letang* v. *Cooper* was argued in the tort of battery in order to take advantage of the longer limitation period of 6 years, as opposed to 3 years for negligence, in force at that time. On the present law of limitation, see Chapter 8, Section 1(9) below.

[9] See below, Chapter 5, Sections 1 and 2, and see generally P. Cane, *The Morality of Tort Law* (1997), in particular chs. 2 and 3. See also U. Burnham, 'Negligent false imprisonment – scope for re-emergence' (1998) 61 *MLR* 573, discussing *W.* v. *Home Office*, The Times, 14 Mar. 1997.

[10] *R* v. *Beasley* (1981) 73 Cr. App. R. 44.

and a crime; the relevant principles of law apply to both. The actual application of force is known as the tort of 'battery' and the term 'assault' is used in both ordinary and (sometimes) in legal speech to refer to both the threat and the application. The two torts are distinct, however, in that there may be an assault without an actual blow[11] and a battery without an assault where, for example, a sleeping person is hit or there is a blow from behind.

The threat must relate to *immediate* force; a threat of more remote future force is not enough. The reaction induced in the plaintiff need not be fright as such, merely the apprehension of force.[12] As long as the plaintiff reasonably expects immediate force, the defendant's ability actually to apply it is not essential. It follows that the necessary intention is the intention to produce an expectation that force is about to be used, or recklessness as to this consequence.[13] Pointing an unloaded gun at the plaintiff is common-law assault provided he does not know it is unloaded;[14] and it is still assault even though the plaintiff manages to escape in time,[15] or if the defendant is restrained before actually hitting him.[16] Words by themselves do not constitute an assault.[17] They could be used, however, to invest an otherwise innocuous act with menace, as when a person strolls up to another uttering threats; conversely words may negative the threat which would otherwise have arisen. In *Tuberville* v. *Savage*[18] the defendant laid his hand on his sword, saying as he did so: 'if it were not assize time, I would not take such language from you.' Since the words made it clear that the threat would not be carried out, this was held not to be an assault. On the other hand, words which do not negative a threat as such but which make it conditional in some way will not prevent there being an assault. In *Read* v. *Coker*[19] the menacing gesture was accompanied by a threat to break the plaintiff's neck unless he 'got out', and the defendant was held liable for assault. The need for a threat of force means that mere passive obstruction is not assault, as when a person simply stands in front of another in order to obstruct him, but without touching or threatening him.[20]

3. Battery

(A) Unlawful Contact

The tort of battery consists of a direct act of the defendant resulting in an unlawful and undesired contact with the person of the plaintiff. The contact must be intentional. At the same time, though, it need only be nominal: 'the least touching of another in anger is a battery.'[21] For example, in *Ashton* v. *Jennings*[22] an act of placing a hand on another to assert social precedence was held to be a battery. In *Wilson* v. *Pringle*[23] the Court of Appeal held that the touching has to be 'hostile', but this seems contrary to authority and is probably incorrect. The need to find some element of hostility was thought to arise

[11] *Jones* v. *Sherwood* [1942] 1 KB 127.
[12] *R* v. *Norden* (1755) Fost. 129.
[13] See *R* v. *Venna* [1976] QB 421.
[14] *R* v. *St George* (1840) 9 C. & P. 483, 493.
[15] *Mortin* v. *Shoppee* (1828) 3 C. & P. 373.
[16] *Stephens* v. *Myers* (1830) 4 C. & P. 349.
[17] *Mead's* v. *Belt's Case* (1823) 1 Lew. CC 184.
[18] (1669) 1 Mod. Rep. 3.
[19] (1853) 13 CB 850.
[20] *Innes* v. *Wylie* (1844) 1 C. & K. 257.
[21] *Cole* v. *Turner* (1704) 6 Mod. Rep. 149.
[22] (1674) 2 Lev. 133.
[23] [1987] QB 237.

in order to avoid the conclusion that incidental contact on the street or in a crowd can constitute battery. However, in *Re F*[24] Lord Goff, invoking an earlier judgment of his own in *Collins* v. *Wilcock*,[25] argued that an

exception has been created to allow for the exigencies of everyday life: jostling in a street or some other crowded place, social contact at parties and such like. This exception has been said to be founded on implied consent, since those who go about in public places, or go to parties, may be taken to have impliedly consented to bodily contact of this kind. Today this rationalization can be regarded as artificial: and, in particular, it is difficult to impute consent to those who, by reason of their youth or mental disorder, are unable to give their consent. For this reason I consider it more appropriate to regard such cases as falling within a general exception embracing all physical contact which is generally acceptable in the ordinary conduct of everyday life.

The requirement that a touching be 'hostile' was incompatible, according to Lord Goff, with the basic principle that 'any touching of another's body is, in the absence of lawful excuse, capable of amounting to a battery and a trespass'. Other authorities suggest that what Holt CJ called 'anger' should not be taken literally. Stealing a kiss is a battery even though the intention may be far from 'hostile'.[26] Lord Goff's test of what is acceptable in everyday life would cover the case of a person touching another in the course of conversation or slapping a person on the back by way of congratulation.

The contact must be direct. In *Dodwell* v. *Burford*[27] the defendant struck the horse on which the plaintiff was riding and he was thrown off; the court held that there had been a battery. It is arguable, however, that the plaintiff's fall was consequential, for which the appropriate action at that time would have been in case and not in trespass. With the abolition of the forms of action it no longer matters how the claim is framed, although there is some difficulty over the precise scope of the modern tort of battery. It seems that there should be liability where the harm is inflicted intentionally but indirectly, as, for example, by daubing the inside of the plaintiff's hat with filth as a joke so that he dirties his hair. Winfield referred to this category as 'intentional physical harm other than trespasses to the person', but the American Restatement of Torts[28] includes it within the scope of battery; this would extend the tort to cover willful acts of the kind which may lie within the rule in *Wilkinson* v. *Downton*.

The need for the contact to be intentional has already been noted. It has been held that the intention need not be present at the commencement of the relevant act, provided it is formed while the act is still continuing. In *Fagan* v. *Metropolitan Police Commissioner*[29] the defendant unintentionally stopped his car on a policeman's foot. When told to get off he deliberately delayed doing so. He was held guilty of criminal assault because his later intention to inflict an unlawful contact was directed to a continuing act.

Since assault and battery are crimes as well as torts, statute has made provision for avoiding unnecessary double process. Criminal proceedings will be a bar to

---

[24] [1990] 2 AC 1.   [25] [1984] 1 WLR 1172, 1177.
[26] *R* v. *Chief Constable of Devon and Cornwall, ex p. CEGB* [1982] QB 458, 471 (Lord Denning MR, citing Salmond and Heuston, *Law of Torts* (19th edn.), 133).
[27] (1670) 1 Mod. Rep. 24.   [28] S. 18.   [29] [1969] 1 QB 439; see also *R* v. *Miller* [1983] 2 AC 161.

further civil proceedings where the hearing was a summary one and ended, after a hearing on the merits, either with a certificate of dismissal or with the accused being convicted and either being imprisoned or paying the fine levied on him.[30] However, these provisions do not prevent civil actions being brought in respect of more serious crimes tried on indictment; nor do they prevent action being brought against those who, for one reason or another, are not prosecuted.[31]

(B) DEFENCES

Consent operates as a defence to the tort of battery. This is particularly important in cases of medical treatment. As Lord Browne-Wilkinson put it in *Airedale NHS Trust* v. *Bland*,[32] in general 'any treatment given by a doctor to a patient which is invasive (i.e. involves any interference with the physical integrity of the patient) is unlawful unless done with the consent of the patient: it constitutes the crime of battery and the tort of trespass to the person.' Consent must be 'real' in the sense of not being induced by fraud or misrepresentation. This does not mean that a doctor who fails to give a patient full information prior to an operation will necessarily be liable in trespass. His liability in negligence will depend on the so-called *Bolam*[33] test, which asks whether his practice conformed with that of a respectable body of opinion within the relevant part of the medical profession, with the rider, added by the House of Lords in *Sidaway* v. *Bethlem Royal Hospital*,[34] that there might be circumstances in which the nature of the risks in question would dictate disclosure regardless of the normal practice. However, the question of whether the defendant conformed to the necessary standard of care in advising the patient is separate from the question of whether the patient has given his consent to surgery: 'justice requires that in order to vitiate the reality of consent there must be a greater failure of communication between doctor and patient than that involved in a breach of duty' in negligence.[35] In *Chatterton* v. *Gerson* Bristow J thought that 'once the patient is informed in broad terms of the nature of the procedure which is intended, and gives her consent, that consent is real, and the cause of action on which to base a claim for failure to go into the risks and implications is negligence, not trespass'.[36] It might be different, perhaps, if a surgeon, through error, carried out a circumcision on a patient when he was meant to undertake a tonsillectomy.[37] The point is that the patient's consent to being operated on is broadly effective to protect the surgeon in respect of that type of operation. If the surgeon makes an error leading to the failure of the operation, the plaintiff's complaint is not that he was operated on against his will but that the outcome of the operation was detrimental to him.[38] Additional protection for the

---

[30] See Offences Against the Person Act 1861, ss. 42–5; *Ellis* v. *Burton* [1975] 1 WLR 386.

[31] As in *Halford* v. *Brookes* [1991] 1 WLR 428.

[32] [1993] 1 All ER 821, 881. See also *Secretary of State for the Home Department* v. *Robb* [1995] 1 All ER 677; *Re JT (Adult: Refusal of Medical Treatment)* [1998] 1 FLR 48; *St. George's Healthcare NHS Trust* v. *S* [1998] 3 All ER 673, and the discussion in Chapter 3, Section 1, above.

[33] *Bolam* v. *Friern Hospital* [1957] 1 WLR 582; Chapter 2, above.   [34] [1985] AC 871.

[35] *Chatterton* v. *Gerson* [1981] QB 432 (Bristow J).   [36] [1981] QB 432, 443.   [37] Ibid.

[38] See *Hills* v. *Potter* [1984] 1 WLR 641; *Sidaway* v. *Bethlem Royal Hospital* [1985] AC 871; *Freeman* v. *Home Office (No. 2)* [1984] QB 524; *F* v. *R* (1984) SASR 189.

surgeon derives from the ruling in *Freeman* v. *Home Office (No. 2)*[39] to the effect that the burden of proving that consent to treatment was not given lies on the plaintiff or patient.

An adult of sound mind is entitled to refuse to consent to medical treatment. A doctor who respects this wish does not commit the crime of aiding and abetting a suicide;[40] indeed, he would normally be liable in trespass if he continued the treatment against the patient's wishes. This means, for example, that a patient on a life-support system can, if in full possession of his faculties and if properly informed, insist that the life-support system be switched off.[41] It is also possible that a patient might indicate his wishes in advance of falling unconscious or being unable to express his will clearly, although the court would have to be sure that the conditions for the removal of medical treatment had been met and that the prior expression of will remained fully effective.[42]

As far as medical treatment of children is concerned, much depends on whether the child is old enough to appreciate the significance of what is being proposed, but this is subject to the court's inherent power to make a child a ward of court and to take decisions on his or her behalf in what are deemed the child's best interests. The starting point is section 8 of the Family Law Reform Act 1969 which provides that a child over the age of 16 may consent to medical treatment without seeking the consent of his parent or guardian. In *Gillick* v. *West Norfolk Area Health Authority*[43] the House of Lords held that a child under the age of 16 who possessed 'sufficient understanding and intelligence'[44] could consent to the receipt of contraceptive advice and treatment without the consent of her parents. For young children the consent of the parents is usually necessary and sufficient. Where there is doubt or the views of the parents are in conflict, the child can be made a ward of court and the doctor can then seek the court's permission to carry out the operation. In *Re P (A Minor)*[45] a child's father objected to the termination of her pregnancy. Her local authority made her a ward of court and the court's consent to the operation was granted. In *Re B (A Minor)*[46] a child of 17 with a mental age of five or six was made a ward of court, following which the court gave leave for her to be sterilized with the agreement of her mother and of the local authority. In some cases, however, the courts have gone further and used their inherent jurisdiction to consent to medical treatment on a child's behalf, even though the child was of an age where she was competent to refuse consent.[47] Once the child is a ward of court, the court will, in effect, decide what is in 'his best interests', having regard to

---

[39] [1984] 1 QB 524, 537–9 (McCowan J), 557 (Sir John Donaldson MR).

[40] For this crime, see Suicide Act 1961, s. 2(1).

[41] *Airedale NHS Trust* v. *Bland* [1993] 1 All ER 821, 866 (Lord Goff of Chieveley), approving the Canadian decision in *Nancy B* v. *Hôtel-Dieu de Québec* (1992) 86 DLR (4th) 385.

[42] As in the case of the Jehovah's Witness, *Re T (Adult: Refusal of Medical Treatment)* [1992] 3 WLR 782, discussed in Chapter 3, Section 1, above.

[43] [1986] AC 112.

[44] On this see P. M. Bromley and N. V. Lowe, *Bromley's Family Law* (8th edn., 1992), 305 ff.

[45] (1981) 80 LGR 301.   [46] [1988] AC 199.

[47] *Re W (A Minor) (Wardship: Medical Treatment)* [1991] 4 All ER 177; *Re W (A Minor) (Wardship: Medical Treatment)* [1991] 4 All ER 627.

appropriate medical opinion and, it would seem, to the views of parents even though they may be in conflict with those of the child.[48]

The court has no such power in relation to an adult, who cannot be made a ward of court.[49] None the less, it may be that medical treatment can be justified, in the absence of the patient's consent, on the grounds of necessity. 'It very commonly occurs that a person, due to accident or some other cause, becomes unconscious and is thus not able to give or withhold consent to medical treatment. In that situation it is lawful, under the principle of necessity, for medical men to apply such treatment as in their informed opinion is in the best interests of the unconscious patient.'[50] The defence may also apply to other cases. In *Re F* the House of Lords invoked the principle of necessity to authorise a sterilisation operation to be carried out on a woman of 36 whose mental age was such that she could not give her consent to the operation. According to Lord Brandon, 'a doctor can lawfully operate on, or give other treatment to, adult patients who are incapable, for one reason or another, of consenting to his doing so, provided that the operation or other treatment concerned is in the best interests of such patients',[51] the notion of 'best interests' being decided according to the *Bolam* test of respectable medical practice. The House of Lords also decided that in such cases, in the absence of any wardship jurisdiction, the doctors should seek a declaration from the court stating the legal position in the case in question.

In *Airedale NHS Trust* v. *Bland*[52] the courts were faced with a different question again, whether to authorise the withholding of medical treatment from an adult patient in a 'persistent vegetative state' (PVS). The patient sustained injuries that caused him to suffer brain damage, as a result of which he was unable to respond to any external stimuli. He had to be fed by a tube inserted into his nose and stomach, and medical staff were required to take steps to ensure that he remained free of infections which would otherwise have been fatal to him. In the words of the President of the Family Division,[53] 'there is simply no possibility whatsoever that he has any appreciation of anything that takes place around him'. Doctors treating him, who were unanimously of the opinion that he had no prospect of recovery, made an application for a declaration that medical treatment could lawfully be withdrawn notwithstanding the patient's inability to give his consent; the application was supported by the patient's parents.

There was no question in this case of applying the wardship jurisdiction; the patient, who was 17 when he sustained his injuries, was aged 21 at the time the case was brought to court. Lord Goff, giving the leading judgment in the

---

[48] See the discussion in Chapter 3, Section 1, above; and see *Re B (A Minor) (Wardship; Sterilization)* [1988] AC 199; *Re C (A Minor) (Wardship; Medical Treatment)* [1990] Fam. 26; *Re J (A Minor) (Wardship, Medical Treatment)* [1991] Fam. 33; *Airedale NHS Trust* v. *Bland* [1993] 1 All ER 821, 836 (Sir Thomas Bingham MR).

[49] The *parens patriae* jurisdiction formerly exercised by the courts in the case of adults, such as mental patients, unable effectively to express their will or consent to medical treatment, has been repealed by statute: *Re F* [1990] 2 AC 1; *Airedale NHS Trust* v. *Bland* [1993] 1 All ER 821, 860 (Lord Keith of Kinkel).

[50] *Airedale NHS Trust* v. *Bland* [1993] 1 All ER 821, 860 (Lord Keith of Kinkel).

[51] [1990] 2 AC 1, 55.   [52] [1993] 1 All ER 821.   [53] Ibid., 825 (Sir Stephen Brown P).

House of Lords,[54] said that there was no absolute rule that a patient's life had to be prolonged by treatment or care regardless of all the circumstances; the patient's 'right of self-determination', which meant that he could withhold consent for medical treatment, qualified the principle of the 'sanctity of life'. It was, moreover, inconsistent with the principle of self-determination that the law should provide no means of enabling treatment to be lawfully withheld in a case where the patient was in no condition to indicate whether or not he consented to treatment being continued. The difficulty was whether the doctor could be held civilly or criminally liable for his failure to treat the patient. In this regard, Lord Goff considered that there was a fundamental difference between a case in which a doctor sought to bring life to an end by a positive act of commission—by, for example, administering a fatal overdose—and one in which he discontinued life-saving treatment. The latter could be accurately characterised as an omission, and could only give rise to liability in circumstances where the doctor was under an affirmative duty of action. The central question, then, concerned the precise extent and scope of the doctor's duty to his patient in these circumstances. This was to act according to the 'patient's best interests' in accordance with the *Bolam* test, subject to the need to seek the court's opinion by obtaining a declaration on an originating summons, the procedure laid down for such cases in *Re F*.

The House of Lords unanimously agreed that the declarations sought should be granted on the basis that it was in the patient's best interests that the treatment should be discontinued. There was no support for the approach taken in certain American cases, namely to seek a 'substituted view' of the patient's wishes based on evidence either of his own personal attitude, in the past, to the question of termination of life in the event of incurable illness, or on a number of different factors such as his former character and feelings. As Lord Mustill said, such an approach to fictive consent 'is surely meaningless'.[55] On the other hand, the view that it was in the patient's best interests for the treatment to be terminated was based on the difficult distinction, in this context, between acts and omissions, which seems less than convincing as a basis for granting the declarations requested. Lord Mustill also cast doubt on the appropriateness of using the *Bolam* test of medical practice in this context: 'I accept without difficulty that this principle applies to the ascertainment of the medical raw material such as diagnosis, prognosis and appraisal of the patient's cognitive functions. Beyond this point, however, it may be said that the decision is ethical, not medical, and that there is no reason in logic why on such a decision the opinions of doctors should be decisive.'[56]

Consent and necessity may arise as defences to trespass to the person in other contexts. Consent may be a defence to a criminal conviction for assault, but this is subject, at least in the criminal law, to the possibility that consent will be negatived by public policy. In *Re F* Lord Griffiths said that 'although the general rule is that the individual is the master of his own fate the judges through the common law have, in the public interest, imposed certain

---

[54] Lords Keith and Lowry expressed their broad concurrence with the reasoning adopted by Lord Goff.
[55] [1993] 1 All ER 821, 892.   [56] Ibid., 895.

constraints on the harm that people may consent to being inflicted on their bodies'. Examples include participation in a prize-fight, fighting in circumstances likely to give rise to actual bodily harm, and serious bodily injury inflicted as part of sexual practices.[57] In *Bland* Lord Mustill referred to consent being a defence both to criminal assault and to a claim in tort 'at the bottom end of the scale'. He then suggested that 'whatever the scope of the civil defence of *volenti non fit injuria* there is a point higher up the scale than common assault at which consent in general ceases to form a defence to a criminal charge . . . If one person cuts off the hand of another it is no answer to say that the amputee consented to what was done.'[58]

Necessity may be a defence to the torts of trespass to the person in the absence of consent, one example being an emergency that compels a rescuer to act. In *Re F* Lord Goff said: 'to fall within the principle, not only (1) must there be a necessity to act when it is not practicable to communicate with the assisted person, but also (2) the action taken must be such as a reasonable person would in all the circumstances take, citing in the best interests of the assisted person. 'Officious' intervention would not therefore be protected, but action taken by rescuers or carers in an emergency would be. Where, following a railway accident, passengers are trapped in the wreckage, 'it is this principle which may render lawful the actions of other citizens, railway staff, passengers or outsiders, who rush to give aid and comfort to the victims: the surgeon who amputates the limb of an unconscious passenger to free him from the wreckage; the ambulance man who conveys him to hospital; the doctors and nurses who treat him and care for him while he is unconscious.'[59]

In general, however, necessity is much less likely to apply as a defence to the torts of trespass to the person than it is to the torts of trespass to property. This is because 'the necessity for saving life has at all times been considered a proper grounds for inflicting such damage as may be necessary upon another's property'.[60]

It is also doubtful if lawful authority will amount to a defence beyond the clear cases in which specific statutory authority is provided, for example, for the exercise of police powers.[61] In *Leigh* v. *Gladstone*[62] force-feeding a prisoner was held to be justified; but since then the practice has not been carried on by the prison authorities and this first instance judgment would probably not be followed.

The defendant may also invoke self-defence. The force used by the defendant to defend himself must not be out of proportion to the force exerted against him, as it was in *Lane* v. *Holloway* where a provocative blow by the plaintiff did not excuse a savage retaliation;[63] nor will the defence avail one who, in seeking to defend himself, strikes an innocent bystander.[64] In this regard it is relevant

---

[57] [1990] 2 AC 1, 70, citing, respectively, *R* v. *Coney* (1882) 8 QBD 534, *Attorney-General's Reference (No. 6 of 1980)* [1981] QB 715 and *R* v. *Donovan* [1934] 2 KB 498; and see also *R* v. *Brown and Others* [1993] 2 All ER 75.

[58] [1993] 1 All ER 821, 889.   [59] [1990] 2 AC 1, 76.

[60] *Southport Corp.* v. *Esso Petroleum Co.* [1954] 2 QB 182 (Devlin J).

[61] The question of police powers under the Police and Criminal Evidence Act 1984 lies outside the scope of this book.

[62] (1909) 26 TLR 169.   [63] [1968] 1 QB 379.

[64] *The Case of Thorns* (1466) YB 6 Ed. fo. 7 pl. 18; *Lambert* v. *Bessey* (1681) T. Ray 421.

to note section 3 of the Criminal Law Act 1967, which provides that a person has the right to use 'such force as is reasonable in the prevention of crime'.

The relevance of contributory negligence is not clear. It had no application in *Lane* v. *Holloway*,[65] but in *Murphy* v. *Culhane*[66] it was suggested that the defence would have applied in circumstances where the plaintiff initiated a criminal affray in the course of which he was killed, had not total defences been available in the form of consent and illegality. It is doubtful that the defence will have much of a role in relation to the intentional torts, where the process of shifting loss through apportionment is not so much to the point as it is in negligence.

4. False Imprisonment

The tort of false imprisonment consists of the complete restriction of the plaintiff's freedom of movement without lawful excuse or justification. The tort is actionable *per se*. The restriction need not be in a room or a prison cell: according to the *Terms de la Ley*, 'imprisonment is the restraint of a man's liberty, whether it be in the open field, or in the stocks, or in the cage in the streets or in a man's own house, as well as in the common gaole'.[67] The wrongful continuation of an original lawful imprisonment is actionable.[68] Old authorities also suggest that holding a person in a place that is unauthorised is actionable, although this may have limited relevance for modern-day inmates whose prison regime is laid down by the Prison Rules.[69] Imprisonment need not involve seizure of the plaintiff; touching and informing him that he is under arrest are sufficient.[70]

It is not necessary that the plaintiff should have been aware of his imprisonment at the time of confinement. This point has given rise to some difficulty in the case law. In *Herring* v. *Boyle*[71] a mother went to fetch her son from a private school, but was not allowed to remove him until she paid the bill. The court held that the boy had not been falsely imprisoned because there was nothing to show that 'the plaintiff was at all cognisant of any restraint'. What is not clear from the report is whether the boy was imprisoned at all, quite apart from the question of his knowledge. In *Meering* v. *Graham-White Aviation Co. Ltd.*[72] the Court of Appeal held that knowledge was not necessary, but the authority is impaired by the failure of the court to cite *Herring* v. *Boyle*. *Meering* is preferable on the grounds of policy, however: not only is there a general interest in upholding individual liberty which goes above and beyond individual circumstances, but the individual concerned may feel equally aggrieved to find out after the event that he was the subject of an unjustified confinement. This view was endorsed by the House of Lords in *Murray* v. *Ministry of Defence*.[73] The plaintiff was detained in her house for half an hour by soldiers, who were searching

---

[65] [1968] 1 QB 379.   [66] [1977] QB 94.   [67] S. v. 'Imprisonment'.
[68] *Withers* v. *Henley* (1614) Cro. Jac. 379; *Mee* v. *Cruikshank* (1902) 86 LT 708; although cf. *Olutu* v. *Home Office* [1997] 1 All ER 385, 391–2.
[69] Thus *Cobbett* v. *Gray* (1850) 4 Ex. 729 must now be read subject to *R* v. *Governor of Parkhurst Prison, ex p. Hague* [1992] 1 AC 58 (and see in particular Lord Jauncey at 175), discussed below.
[70] *Hart* v. *Chief Constable of Kent* [1983] RTR 484.   [71] (1834) 1 C.M. & R. 377.
[72] (1919) 122 LT 44.   [73] [1988] 1 WLR 692.

for terrorist suspects, without being told that she was under arrest, following which she was further detained at a screening centre. She failed in her action for false imprisonment because the defendants had lawful authority to act as they did under section 14 of the Northern Ireland (Emergency Provisions) Act 1978. On the point of knowledge, Lord Griffiths stated *obiter* that: 'if a person is unaware that he has been falsely imprisoned and has suffered no harm, he can normally expect to recover no more than nominal damages . . . [but] the law attaches supreme importance to the liberty of the individual and if he suffers a wrongful interference with that liberty it should remain actionable even without proof of special damage.'

The restraint must be complete; that is to say, the plaintiff's freedom of movement has to be impeded in every direction. It is not sufficient to prevent a person from going forward if he is free to go back, or vice versa. In *Bird* v. *Jones*[74] a section of Hammersmith Bridge was temporarily fenced off. The plaintiff, who insisted on climbing over the fence to go forward, was prevented from doing so, but was told he could go back instead. The court held that he had not been falsely imprisoned and held that his attempt to go forward was a breach of the peace for which he had been lawfully arrested. It must be the case, on the other hand, that the avenues of escape are reasonably accessible and safe. It would not normally be false imprisonment to turn the key on a person in a room on the ground floor from which he could easily escape by stepping out of a window, but it would be a different matter if the room were several storeys up in a block of flats.

A person may be restrained either by the defendant acting personally or through someone else, usually an official. In the latter case a distinction was drawn in a number of nineteenth-century cases between a 'ministerial act' and a 'judicial' act.[75] A 'ministerial' act, in this sense, consists of an act of the official where he is merely the instrument or agent of the defendant, so that it is the latter who will be liable for the imprisonment.[76] A 'judicial' act is one where the official exercises his own judgment:[77] in this case the person who initiated the process is not normally liable for false imprisonment although he may be liable for malicious prosecution or for malicious abuse of process.[78]

The basic distinction between these categories of cases was recently reaffirmed by the Court of Appeal in *Davidson* v. *Chief Constable of North Wales and Another*.[79] The second defendant, a store detective, gave information to the police that led to the arrest of the plaintiff on suspicion of shoplifting. She and a friend were detained by the police for two hours until they were released when it became clear that the store detective's suspicions had been unfounded. The plaintiff's claim against the store detective for false imprisonment was struck out as disclosing no cause of action, a ruling which was upheld on appeal: according to Sir Thomas Bingham MR, 'what distinguishes the case in which a defendant is liable from a case in which he is not is whether he has

---

[74] (1845) 7 QB 742.
[75] See *Austin* v. *Dowling* (1870) LR 5 CP 543, 540.
[76] *Hopkins* v. *Crowe* (1836) 4 A. & E. 774.
[77] *Brown* v. *Chapman* (1848) 6 CB 365.
[78] See below, Section 2; *Lock* v. *Ashton* (1842) 12 QB 871; *Lea* v. *Carrington* (1889) 23 QBD 45.
[79] [1994] 2 All ER 597.

merely given information to a properly constituted authority on which that authority may act or not as it decides or whether he has himself been the instigator, promoter and active inciter of the action that follows'.[80]

It is not altogether clear whether 'intention' in false imprisonment refers to an intention to confine the plaintiff or an intention to perform the act that results in imprisonment. If the defendant commits an act resulting in imprisonment without realising what he is doing, but in circumstances where he could be described as negligent, is he liable for the tort of false imprisonment that, in contrast to negligence, is actionable *per se*? Although the point remains open, there is a case for saying that the need to uphold personal liberty requires the broadest possible interpretation to be given to false imprisonment. On the other hand, modern decisions on the mental element in the tort of battery, while not strictly in point, suggest that there is no trespass in a case where the defendant neither intended the consequences of his act nor was reckless or negligent with regard to them.[81]

Consent is a defence to false imprisonment, but the problem lies in determining when the plaintiff's consent may be inferred. *Sunbolf* v. *Alford*[82] held that there can be no private power of arrest for debt or breach of contract, but later cases have appeared to erode the effects of this rule. One such case is *Robinson* v. *Balmain New Ferry Co. Ltd*.[83] in which the plaintiff paid one penny to enter a wharf in order to board a ferry. He then decided not to wait for the ferry and sought to go back through the turnstile. Above the turnstile on both sides of the barrier was a notice requiring payment of a penny by any person entering or leaving the wharf. The plaintiff refused to pay and was prevented from leaving. The Privy Council held that he had no claim in false imprisonment. Lord Loreburn argued that the plaintiff had contracted to leave the wharf via the ferry and that the defendants were under no obligation to let him leave by any other way. In effect, this was imprisonment for breach of contract; *Sunbolf* v. *Alford* was not cited. A better explanation for the outcome may be that Robinson could have escaped his confinement by taking the ferry: assuming that this means of exit was a reasonable one, he was not subject to the requisite degree of confinement.

A second difficult case is *Herd* v. *Weardale Steel, Coal and Coke Co. Ltd*.[84] The plaintiff, a miner, descended a mine at the usual time but when he got to the pit bottom he declined to carry on working and asked to be returned to the surface in the cage. The defendants refused to let him take an empty cage that was available and he had to wait a further twenty minutes until the end of the shift before he was allowed to return. The House of Lords held that the employer had the defence of consent, but this is extremely dubious as not only was there no express agreement to this effect but the judgment again goes against *Sunbolf* v. *Alford*. However, the outcome may be explained by the distinction between acts and omissions: it could be argued that the defendants had simply failed to take

---

[80] [1994] 2 All ER 597, 602.
[81] *Fowler* v. *Lanning* [1959] 1 QB 426; *Letang* v. *Cooper* [1965] 1 QB 232; see above, Section 1(1).
[82] (1838) 3 M. & W. 248.   [83] [1910] AC 295.   [84] [1915] AC 67.

steps to release the plaintiff in a situation where there was no affirmative duty upon them to do so.

Imprisonment is authorised by statute in circumstances of lawful arrest and the confinement of persons remanded in custody pending the hearing of a criminal charge and of those convicted and sentenced to a term of imprisonment. The extent of powers of arrest of the police and of private citizens is outside the scope of this book.[85] The basic authorisation for the imprisonment of persons convicted of offences is found in section 12(1) of the Prison Act 1952;[86] the Prison Rules, which are made pursuant to statutory powers, lay down in greater detail the manner in which the prison regime is to be arranged. The tort of false imprisonment has practically no role to play in this area following the decision of the House of Lords in two joined cases, *R* v. *Deputy Governor of Parkhurst Prison, ex p. Hague* and *Weldon* v. *Home Office*.[87] In each case prisoners who had been lawfully detained following conviction complained of mistreatment alleged to be contrary to the Prison Rules; in the *Hague* case this consisted of segregation, in *Weldon*, of confinement in a 'strip cell'. In *Weldon* in the Court of Appeal Ralph Gibson LJ accepted that 'there is no reason . . . why the nature of the tort, evolved by the common law for the protection of personal liberty, should be held to be such as to deny its availability to a convicted prisoner, whose residual liberty should, in my judgment, be protected so far as the law can properly achieve unless statute requires otherwise'.[88] However, the notion that a convicted prisoner has a 'residual liberty' in this sense was rejected by the House of Lords.[89] In the view of Lord Bridge,

the concept of the prisoner's 'residual liberty' as a species of freedom of movement within the prison enjoyed as a legal right which the prison authorities cannot lawfully restrain seems to me quite illusory. The prisoner is at all times lawfully restrained within closely defined bounds and if he is kept in a segregated cell, at a time when, if the rules had not been misapplied, he would be in the company of other prisoners in the workshop, at the dinner table or elsewhere, this is not the deprivation of his liberty of movement, which is the essence of the tort of false imprisonment, it is the substitution of one form of restraint for another.[90]

According to Lord Jauncey, the prisoner

is lawfully committed to a prison and while there is subject to the Prison Act 1952 and the Prison Rules 1964. His whole life is regulated by the regime. He has no freedom to

---

[85] The reader is referred to specialist texts on constitutional law and the law of civil liberties. The principal legislation in this area is the Police and Criminal Evidence Act 1984; other legislation, such as the Theft Act 1978, s. 3(4), is also relevant, as is the common-law power to arrest for a breach of the peace. On the information which must be given to a person upon his arrest or as soon as practicable thereafter, see *Christie* v. *Leachinsky* [1947] AC 573, *John Lewis & Co.* v. *Tims* [1952] AC 676 and Police and Criminal Evidence Act 1984, s. 28. The fact that an arrested person later pleads guilty to a charge is not conclusive evidence that his initial confinement by the police was lawful, according to the Court of Appeal in *Hill* v. *Chief Constable of South Yorkshire* [1990] 1 All ER 1046.

[86] 'A prisoner, whether sentenced to imprisonment or committed to prison on remand or pending trial or otherwise, may be lawfully confined in any prison.'

[87] [1992] 1 AC 59.   [88] [1992] 1 AC 58, 139.

[89] The House of Lords thereby repudiated dicta to the contrary of Ackner LJ in *Middleweek* v. *Chief Constable of Merseyside* (1985) [1992] 1 AC 179, 186 (Note).

[90] [1992] 1 AC 58, 163.

do what he wants, when he wants. His liberty to do anything is governed by the prison regime. Placing Weldon in a strip cell and segregating Hague altered the conditions under which they were detained but did not deprive them of any liberty that they had not already lost when initially confined.[91]

Any action for mistreatment has to be brought instead in negligence (which requires proof of fault) or via a public-law remedy; alternatively, the House of Lords accepted that a personal action for false imprisonment would lie against a prison officer who acted in abuse of his powers or against a fellow prisoner. However, Lord Bridge thought that the prison authorities would not be vicariously liable for any such abuse of power by an officer.[92]

There are several difficult aspects to this decision. The notion that the prisoner has no 'residual liberty' within the terms set down by the Prison Rules is disturbing enough, according as it does a narrow and formal meaning to the concept of imprisonment and unduly widening the scope of the lawful-authority defence, which effectively now applies even when the Prison Rules have been breached. It is also the case that few of the arguments put forward for restricting the tort in this context are particularly compelling. It cannot be the case, for example, that the tort of false imprisonment should be narrowed down on the grounds, suggested by Lords Bridge and Jauncey, that a contravention of the Prison Rules cannot be construed as giving rise to a private action for breach of the statutory duty. The question of the availability of a private action for breach of the statute is a logically separate matter with no bearing on the scope of the false imprisonment tort. The suggestion that the prison authorities would not be liable for an officer acting in abuse of his powers is a contentious reading of the difficult concept of an employer's vicarious liability for torts committed by an employer in the 'course of his employment'.[93] Nor is it the case that a prisoner able to show that his confinement had passed the bounds of legality would be able, in the event of there being false imprisonment, to walk out of the prison, as Lord Bridge suggested; it would simply be the case that the additional and unlawful confinement to which he had been subjected would have to be discontinued.

5. Residuary Trespass: The Rule in *Wilkinson* v. *Downton*

The boundaries of liability under this rule are not clear. Broadly speaking it can be said to cover the intentional and indirect infliction of injury to another. In the case itself a practical joker falsely told the plaintiff that her husband had broken both his legs. She suffered nervous shock and fell ill. The court allowed her claim for damages. She could not sue in trespass because the damage to her was inflicted indirectly through words, and at that time the courts were not prepared to award damages for nervous shock as such. Wright J nevertheless held the defendant liable on the basis that he had 'wilfully done an act calculated to cause physical harm to the plaintiff—that is to say, to infringe her legal right to personal safety, and has in fact thereby caused physical harm to her. That proposition without more appears to me to state a good cause of action,

---

[91] [1992] 1 AC 58, 176.   [92] Ibid., 164.   [93] See below, Chapter 6, Section 3(c).

there being no justification alleged for the act.'[94] Although the injury resulted from a false statement, there is no reason why it should be so limited. A true statement could be sufficient as long as the intention to harm the plaintiff was present. Acts generally should be included, as should other kinds of physical injury; the plaintiff would surely have recovered damages if, on hearing the news, she had fainted and injured herself.

Wilkinson v. *Downton* has only been followed twice in England. In *Janvier* v. *Sweeney*[95] the defendants, private detectives, were held liable to the plaintiff for threatening, without any justification, to denounce her fiancé, a German internee, to the authorities as a spy. This was done in order to get her to obtain some letters of her mistress.

In the second English authority, *Khorasandjian* v. *Bush*,[96] the defendant repeatedly made unwanted and harassing phone calls to the plaintiff, placing her under considerable stress but not inflicting any physical injury as such. The Court of Appeal, upholding the judgment of Judge Stockdale QC, decided that it was appropriate to grant an injunction against the defendant under the rule in *Wilkinson* v. *Downton*.[97] According to Dillon LJ, although there was no evidence of the plaintiff having suffered any physical or psychiatric condition, 'there is . . . an obvious risk that the cumulative effect of continued and unrestrained further harassment such as she has undergone would cause such an illness';[98] on this basis, a *quia timet* injunction could be issued. It is important that the defendant was taken to have intended the plaintiff to have suffered the harm in question; had he merely been negligent, he presumably could not have been held liable under *Wilkinson* v. *Downton*. The question of his possible liability in the tort of negligence was not considered by the court.[99]

Wilkinson v. *Downton* was approved in Australia in *Bunyan* v. *Jordan*[100] although it was distinguished on the facts, since the words in question were not uttered in the defendant's presence. According to Latham CJ, 'none of the cases has gone so far as to suggest that a man owes a duty to a person who merely happens to overhear statements that are not addressed to them'. Where the defendant knows, however, that it is almost certain that the plaintiff will overhear a statement addressed to a third party, and intends her to be harmed as a consequence of doing so, there would seem to be no reason why he should not be held liable.[101]

The widest rule that can be gleaned from *Wilkinson* v. *Downton* is that of a general principle of residuary liability outside the nominate torts of intentional interference. It is unlikely that it could be used as a basis for creating a generalised tort of intentional interference of a physical or economic kind. Despite

---

[94] [1897] 2 QB 57.   [95] [1919] 2 KB 316.   [96] [1993] QB 727.
[97] The Court of Appeal also held that an injunction could lie on the basis of a cause of action in private nuisance, but this is no longer good law following the decision of the House of Lords in *Hunter* v. *Canary Wharf* [1997] 2 WLR 684 (see below, Chapter 5, Section 3).
[98] [1993] QB 727, 736.
[99] On liability in negligence for physical harm resulting from statements (both true and false), see Chapter 2, above.
[100] (1937) 57 CLR 1.
[101] As in the Canadian case of *Bielitski* v. *Obadiak* (1922) 65 DLR 627.

some wide dicta in *Rookes* v. *Barnard*,[102] the courts have preserved the separate heads of liability in this area.[103] However, the law in relation to vexations and disturbing behaviour has been strengthened by the Protection from Harassment Act 1997. This makes it a tort (as well as a crime) for a person to pursue a course of conduct which he knows or ought to know amounts to harassment of another.[104] 'Conduct' here includes speech. The victim has the right to seek damages for anxiety.[105]

Select Bibliography

HANDFORD, P. R., 'Tort Liability for Threatening or Insulting Words', 54 *Can. BR* 563 (1976).

KODILINYE, G., 'False Imprisonment through Ministerial Officers: The Commonwealth Experience' (1979) 28 *ICLQ* 766.

NORTH, P. M., 'Civil and Criminal Proceedings for Assault' (1966) 29 *MLR* 16.

PROSSER, W. L., 'False Imprisonment: Consciousness of Confinement' 55 *Col. LR* 847 (1955).

TRINDADE, F. A., 'Some Curiosities of Negligent Trespass to the Person: A Comparative Study' (1971) 20 *ICLQ* 706.

—— 'Intentional Torts: Some Thoughts on Assault and Battery' (1982) 2 *OJLS* 211.

TURNER, J. W. C., 'Assault at Common Law', in L. Radzinowicz and J. W. C. Turner (eds.), *The Modern Approach to Criminal Law* (1945), ch. xviii.

WILLIAMS, G. L., 'Two Cases on False Imprisonment', in *Law, Justice and Equity: Essays in Tribute to G. W. Keeton* (1967), ch. 5.

2. MALICIOUS PROSECUTION AND ABUSE OF PROCESS

1. Malicious Prosecution

To succeed in an action of malicious prosecution the plaintiff must show: (1) that the defendant prosecuted him; (2) that the prosecution ended in the defendant's favour; (3) that there was no reasonable and probable cause for the prosecution; and (4) that the defendant was actuated by 'malice'. Damage is also a necessary ingredient. The interests protected by the tort were described by Holt CJ in *Savill* v. *Roberts*:[106] 'there are three sorts of damages, any one of which is sufficient to support this action. First, damage to [the plaintiff's] fame, if the matter whereof he be accused be scandalous. Secondly, to his person, whereby he is imprisoned. Thirdly, to his property, whereby he is put to charges and expenses.' A further possibility is damage sustained through the seizure of the plaintiff's property. Damage to 'fame' appears to mean the harm done to reputation by charging a person with a crime of a dishonourable nature.[107] Damage

---

[102] [1964] AC 1129.   [103] *Lonrho* v. *Shell Petroleum Co. Ltd.* [1982] AC 173.
[104] Protection from Harassment Act 1997, 5.1(1), (2).
[105] Ibid., 5.3.
[106] (1698) 12 Mod. 208; see *Berry* v. *BTC* [1962] 1 QB 306.
[107] *Rayson* v. *South London Tramways Co.* [1893] 2 QB 324; *Wiffen* v. *Bailey* [1915] 1 KB 600.

to the person has been held to include the threat of imprisonment and not just actual imprisonment.[108]

(A) THE DEFENDANT INITIATED THE PROSECUTION

In false imprisonment the defendant acts directly to restrain the plaintiff; in malicious prosecution he does this indirectly by setting the official process in motion. Therefore the distinction between ministerial and judicial acts of officials, which is relevant to false imprisonment, is also relevant here.[109] That apart, the wrongful continuation of a prosecution after the defendant comes to know that it is baseless is sufficient, unless he informs the court of the facts which have come to his attention.[110]

For the purposes of this tort a criminal charge includes 'all indictments involving either scandal to reputation or the possible loss of liberty to the person'.[111] Preferring a complaint is not sufficient by itself: the test is whether proceedings have reached a stage at which they damage the plaintiff.[112] Signing a charge sheet is not necessarily the start of a prosecution;[113] but in *Malz* v. *Rosen*[114] signing the charge sheet and being prepared to give evidence were held to be sufficient. The fact that the defendant was bound over to attend does not of itself indicate that he was the prosecutor.[115] Similarly, the preparation of a medical report at the behest of the police has been held not to amount to setting the legal process in motion.[116]

Normally, merely providing information to the prosecuting authorities would not be enough to give rise to liability. However, in circumstances where the facts in question could only be known to the defendant, and raise a matter of such seriousness that the prosecutor has no effective discretion, it is possible for the tort to be committed if the information was provided falsely and maliciously. This was the case in *Martin* v. *Watson*,[117] where the defendant maliciously made a groundless accusation of indecent exposure against the plaintiff who was subsequently prosecuted. Lord Keith of Kinkel, delivering the single judgment of the House of Lords, ruled that:

Where an individual falsely and maliciously gives a police officer information indicating that some person is guilty of a criminal offence and states that he is willing to give evidence in court of the matters in question, it is properly to be inferred that he desires and intends that the person he names should be prosecuted. Where the circumstances are such that the facts relating to the alleged offence can be within the knowledge only of the complainant, as was the position here, then it becomes virtually impossible for the police officer to exercise any independent discretion or judgment, and if a prosecution is instituted by the police officer the proper view of the matter is that the prosecution has been procured by the complainant.[118]

---

[108] *Wiffen* v. *Bailey* [1915] 1 KB 600.   [109] See above, Section 1(4).
[110] *Tims* v. *John Lewis & Co. Ltd.* [1951] 2 KB 459, 472 (reversed on other grounds [1952] AC 676).
[111] *Quartz Hill Consolidated Gold Mining Co.* v. *Eyre* (1883) 11 QBD 674, 691 (Bowen LJ).
[112] *Mohammed Amin* v. *Bannerjee* [1947] AC 322.   [113] *Austin* v. *Dowling* (1870) LR 5 CP 534.
[114] [1966] 1 WLR 1008, 1012–13.
[115] *Brown* v. *Stradling* (1836) LJPC 295; cf. *Fitzjohn* v. *Mackinder* (1861) 9 CB (NS) 505.
[116] *Evans* v. *London Hospital Medical College* [1981] 1 WLR 184.
[117] [1996] 1 AC 74.   [118] [1996] 1 AC 74, 86–7.

It should also be noted that notwithstanding the introduction in 1985 of the Crown Prosecution Service[119] it is still possible for the police to be the prosecutors for the purposes of this tort, since they continue to have a role in determining the stage at which the proceedings may be said to cause damage to the plaintiff.

(B) THE PROSECUTION FAILED

The prosecution must end in the plaintiff succeeding. This is a fundamental rule that is designed to avoid the retrial, by civil means, of the criminal action.[120] It does not matter how the proceedings ended in the plaintiff's favour. The magistrate's refusal to commit for trial will suffice, even if a new charge may then be brought.[121] Nor does it matter what the ground of acquittal was: it could be a 'technicality' not related to innocence or guilt on the merits[122] or it could be the discontinuance of the prosecution[123] or the quashing of the conviction on appeal. On the other hand, once there is no further appeal the fact of conviction will defeat the plaintiff, even if it is clear that the conviction was obtained by fraud.[124]

(C) ABSENCE OF REASONABLE AND PROBABLE CAUSE

This is a formidable obstacle for the plaintiff to surmount; in effect he has to prove a negative. The following definition of reasonable and probable cause, given by Hawkins J in *Hicks* v. *Faulkner*,[125] was quoted by approval by Lord Atkin in *Herniman* v. *Smith*:[126] 'an honest belief in the guilt of the accused based upon a full conviction, founded upon reasonable grounds, of the existence of a state of circumstances, which, assuming them to be true, would reasonably lead any ordinarily prudent and cautious man, placed in the position of the accuser, to the conclusion that the person charged was probably guilty of the crime imputed.' In other words, there must be both an honest belief and objective facts on which to base it. As far as the defendant's belief is concerned, the question is 'did he honestly believe in the plaintiff's guilt?', not 'did he honestly believe that there was reasonable and probable cause?'[127] The defendant's knowledge of facts negating the plaintiff's guilt is relevant to the honesty of his belief,[128] as is taking legal advice, which may be evidence of an honest belief if all the relevant facts are made known to the legal adviser.[129] The same applies if the true facts were stated to the police, who then advised that an offence had been committed.[130] On the other hand, the mere fact that a prosecution has been initiated by the Director of Public Prosecutions does not of itself preclude

---

[119] By virtue of the Prosecution of Offences Act 1985.

[120] *Gilding* v. *Eyre* (1861) 10 CB (NS) 592.   [121] *Delegal* v. *Highley* (1861) 3 Bing. NC 950.

[122] *Wicks* v. *Fentham* (1791) 4 TR 247, 248.

[123] See the Canadian case of *Casey* v. *Automobiles Renault of Canada* (1965) 54 DLR (2d) 600.

[124] *Basébé* v. *Matthews* (1867) LR 2 CP 684.   [125] (1878) 8 QBD 167, 171.

[126] [1938] AC 305, 316.

[127] *Tempest* v. *Snowdon* [1952] 1 KB 130, 137. The question of whether reasonable and probable cause is shown is, in the end, a question of law for the judge: see *Herniman* v. *Smith* [1938] AC 305, 315 (Lord Atkin); *Glinski* v. *McIver* [1962] AC 726.

[128] *James* v. *Phelps* (1840) 11 A. & E. 483.   [129] *Hewlett* v. *Crutchley* (1813) 5 Taunt. 277.

[130] *Malz* v. *Rosen* [1966] 1 WLR 1008.

an action for malicious prosecution: 'there may be cases where there has been, even by a responsible authority, the suppression of evidence which has led to a false view being taken by those who carried on a prosecution and by those who ultimately convicted.'[131] Nor is the conviction of the plaintiff at first instance—then quashed on appeal—necessarily evidence of reasonable and probable cause, since it could, for example, have been procured by perjured evidence which comes to light later.[132]

(D) MALICE

Malice here refers to the defendant's motive, and includes any motive other than the desire to secure the ends of justice. The requirement is separate from the requirement of reasonable and probable cause; even though lack of a reasonable cause may be *evidence* of malice it is not conclusive.[133] The onus of proof of malice is on the plaintiff and it is a matter for the jury,[134] although if there is no evidence of a motive that is potentially malicious the judge will not permit the matter to go to the jury.[135]

2. Malicious Abuse of Process

Malicious prosecution concerns criminal charges; if civil proceedings are used maliciously, the tort of malicious abuse of process may arise. Special damage is required for liability. Forms of this tort include the malicious presentation of a winding-up order or petition in bankruptcy;[136] malicious execution against property;[137] malicious arrest, based on evidence in other proceedings;[138] and malicious procurement of a search-warrant.[139] This tort is closely aligned with the tort of misfeasance in a public office.[140]

Select Bibliography

HARPER, F. W., 'Malicious Prosecution, False Imprisonment and Defamation', 15 *Texas LR* 157 (1937).

SHELBOURN, C., 'Compensation for Detention' [1978] *Crim. LR* 22.

WINFIELD, P. H., *The History of Conspiracy and Abuse of Legal Procedure* (1921).

—— *The Present Law of Abuse of Legal Procedure* (1921).

---

[131] *Riches* v. *Director of Public Prosecutions* [1973] 1 WLR 1019, 1026 (Stephenson LJ).

[132] *Herniman* v. *Smith* [1938] AC 305 has impliedly overruled the old case of *Reynolds* v. *Kennedy* (1784) 1 Wils. KB 232 on this point.

[133] See *Wershof* v. *Metropolitan Police Commissioner* [1978] 3 All ER 540.

[134] *Mitchell* v. *Jenkins* (1835) 5 B. & Ad. 588, 595.   [135] *Brown* v. *Hawkes* [1891] 2 QB 718.

[136] *Chapmam* v. *Pickersgill* (1762) 2 Wils. KB 145; *Johnson* v. *Emerson & Sparrow* (1872) LR 6 Ex. Ch. 329; *Quartz Hill Consolidated Gold Mining Co.* v. *Eyre* (1883) 11 QBD 674.

[137] *Clissold* v. *Cratchley* [1910] 2 KB 244.   [138] *Roy* v. *Prior* [1971] AC 470.

[139] *Elsee* v. *Smith* (1822) 1 D. & R. 97; *Everett* v. *Ribbands* [1952] 2 QB 191, 205; *Reynolds* v. *Commissioner of Police of the Metropolis* [1985] QB 881, 885; *Gibbs* v. *Rea* [1998] 3 WLR 73.

[140] On this tort, see Chapter 3, Section 5(4)(b) above.

5

*Interference with Property and Economic Interests**

1. CHATTELS

1. Introduction

The present law of trespass to chattels is governed by the Torts (Interference with Goods) Act 1977, which introduces a collective term 'wrongful interference with goods' to cover trespass, conversion, negligence, and any other tort resulting in damage to goods or to an interest in goods.[1] The Act abolishes the tort of detinue,[2] but otherwise has little or no impact on the principles of liability developed by the common law.

2. Trespass to Goods

Any direct interference with possession of goods amounts to a trespass. It appears that liability is strict but there is some uncertainty over this. In the case of collisions on the highway the rule has long since evolved that even if the plaintiff sues in trespass, he has to prove negligence.[3] The same is true of trespass to the person, where it has even been suggested that the trespass will not lie for a non-intentional interference, with the result that the plaintiff must bring the action in negligence and prove both fault and damage.[4] In cases not involving collisions there is authority to suggest that as long as there is voluntary conduct directed at the thing in question, that is to say an intention in relation to the goods, the defendant is liable even though he thought the thing was his or did not realise that he was committing a trespass.[5] To this extent liability is strict in the sense that absence of fault is no defence. Where, on the other hand, the defendant interferes unintentionally with the plaintiff's thing without being aware of its presence, he may escape liability altogether if he has not been negligent. In *National Coal Board* v. *J. E. Evans & Co. (Cardiff) Ltd.*[6] the defendants, without negligence on their part, damaged a cable belonging to the plaintiff which ran beneath land owned by a local authority. The presence of the cable was unknowable since it had been laid by the plaintiff's predecessors

---

* Sections 1, 2, and 4 of this chapter draw on parts of the text prepared by R. W. M. Dias for the second edition of this book.

[1] S. 1

[2] S. 2(1). Except for one case, the scope of detinue had already been taken over by conversion, and that one case has now been made into a case of conversion: see below, Section 1(3).

[3] *Holmes* v. *Mather* (1875) 133 LT 361.

[4] *Letang* v. *Cooper* [1965] 1 QB 232; see above, Chapter 4, Section 1(1).

[5] *Wilson* v. *Lombank Ltd.* [1963] 1 WLR 1294.

[6] [1951] 2 KB 861.

without notifying the landowner. The defendants consciously performed the act of digging a trench, but the court found in their favour on the basis of their lack of knowledge of the cable. This case appears to decide that liability is strict when the defendant knows of the presence of the thing, but based on fault if he neither knows nor could be expected to know.

It is not altogether clear whether liability is based on damage or whether the tort is actionable *per se*. It may be possible to distinguish between deliberate touchings, which are actionable *per se*,[7] and unintended or careless acts of touching, which require damage.[8] If no damage is suffered damages will only be nominal,[9] unless the interference is carried out by agents of government in which case there is constitutional justification for awarding aggravated damages.[10]

The interference must be direct. Looking at a letter or listening-in to a private conversation does not amount to a trespass.[11] On the other hand, it is not necessary to show that the thing was physically moved or transported; deliberate damage, if inflicted directly, will be a trespass.[12]

Since trespass is an invasion of possession, the possessor of the goods at the time is the person who has the right to sue. It is not easy to generalise from the numerous particular instances of possession. A bailee always has possession. When the bailment is terminable at will the bailor who can terminate the bailment at any time has an immediate right to possession; this right to immediate possession is treated as being the same thing as possession itself.[13] In this situation the bailee at will can also sue.[14] If the bailee sues for the whole loss, the bailor is precluded from bringing an action.[15] Where, on the other hand, the bailment is for a period of time, the bailor has no immediate right of possession and only the bailee has the right to sue for trespass to the goods. The right to possess is also treated as possession in the case of trustees, executors, and administrators and owners of franchises. As far as the employment relationship is concerned, the employee is normally said only to have 'custody' of the thing so that the employer retains possession, but there is some authority to suggest that the employee may also have the right to sue in trespass in certain instances.[16] Things attached to or beneath land are possessed by the landowner,[17] but things left lying loose on land fall into the possession of the person who picks them up.[18] Things lost continue for this purpose to be possessed by the loser.[19]

---

[7] *Leitch & Co.* v. *Leydon* [1931] AC 90, 106.   [8] *Everitt* v. *Martin* [1953] NZLR 298.

[9] *Kirk* v. *Gregory* (1876) 1 Ex. D. 55 (one shilling).   [10] *Entick* v. *Carrington* (1765) 19 St. Tr. 1030.

[11] See *Malone* v. *Metropolitan Police Commissioner* [1979] Ch. 344, 374–6.

[12] *Fouldes* v. *Willoughby* (1841) 8 M. & W. 540.

[13] See *United States of America and Republic of France* v. *Dolfus Mieg et Cie SA and Bank of England* [1952] AC 582, 605 (Viscount Jowitt); *Towers & Co. Ltd.* v. *Gray* [1961] 2 QB 351, 361 (Lord Parker CJ).

[14] *Burton* v. *Hughes* (1824) 2 Bing. 173, 175.

[15] *The Winkfield* [1902] P. 42, as modified by the 1977 Act, s. 8.

[16] See generally *Meux* v. *Great Eastern Railway Co.* [1895] 2 QB 387.

[17] *Elwes* v. *Brigg Gas Co.* (1886) 33 Ch. D. 562; *South Staffordshire Water Co.* v. *Sharman* [1896] 2 QB 44; *City of London Corp.* v. *Appleyard* [1963] 1 WLR 982.

[18] *Bridges* v. *Harkesworth* (1851) 15 Jur. 1079; *Parker* v. *British Railways Board* [1982] QB 1004; cf. the different approach of criminal law: *R* v. *Foley* (1889) 17 Cox 142 (Ir.).

[19] *R* v. *Thurborn* (1849) 1 Den. 387.

Interference with possession being the gist of trespass, a defence of *jus tertii*—to the effect that a third party has a better right than the plaintiff (except in a case where the defendant acts on behalf of, or with the authority of, that party)—was not available. The 1977 Act, section 8, now provides that in any action for wrongful interference with goods a defendant may show, in accordance with rule of court, that a named third party has a better right than the plaintiff. This is designed to prevent a defendant being doubly liable.[20] Rules of Court made under the Act[21] generally oblige a plaintiff to furnish particulars of his title and to identify any other person who, to his knowledge, has or claims an interest in the thing. The defendant may apply for directions as to whether the third party so named should be joined to the action. The Act states that contributory negligence is no defence to proceedings based on *intentional* trespass to goods,[22] leaving open the possibility of the defence applying in cases of negligent interference.

Sections 8–22 of the Police and Criminal Evidence Act 1984 govern the powers of the police to search for and seize property. A consideration of these provisions, however, lies outside the scope of this book.

3. Conversion

The gist of conversion (known originally as trover) is any dealing with another's property in a way which amounts to a denial of his right over it, or an assertion of a right inconsistent with his right, by wrongfully taking, detaining, or disposing of it. The defendant does not have to assert ownership as such or intend to acquire the thing for himself. For example, in *Tear* v. *Freebody*[23] the defendant took certain goods of the plaintiff with the intention of taking a lien over them; this was held to be conversion. On the other hand, a case where there was trespass but no conversion was *Fouldes* v. *Willoughby*:[24] the defendant wrongfully refused to carry two horses of the plaintiff after the defendant had boarded his ferry and proceeded to take the horses ashore when the plaintiff refused to do so. This amounted to an unjustified interference with the plaintiff's property but not a denial of his right of ownership.

In order to be able to sue, the plaintiff must have the right to any one of ownership, possession, or the immediate right to possess,[25] or a lien or equitable title; however, a mere contractual right will not suffice.[26] A reversionary interest may become a right to immediate possession if the act of conversion by the possessor is inconsistent with the terms on which he holds the possession.[27]

The finder of a chattel gets possession of it by taking it and retaining it; the question is whether he has a better right than anyone else. A person with a prior right to possession will defeat one whose right is acquired later in time. The finder therefore has a better right than total strangers and those whose

---

[20] S. 7(2). It will also normally restrict the damages payable to plaintiffs with a limited interest in the goods to the value of that interest.

[21] RSC Ord. 15, R 10A (SI No. 1978/579).   [22] S. 11(1).

[23] (1858) 4 CB (NS) 228.   [24] (1841) 8 M. & W. 540.   [25] *The Winkfield* [1902] AC 42.

[26] *Rogers* v. *Kennay* (1846) 9 QB 592; *International Factors Ltd.* v. *Rodriguez* [1979] QB 35.

[27] *Union Transport Finance Ltd.* v. *British Car Auctions Ltd.* [1978] 2 All ER 385, 389.

rights are derived from him. In *Armory* v. *Delamirie*[28] a chimney-sweep's boy who found a jewel (possibly in a chimney) succeeded in an action for conversion against a jeweller to whom he had handed the jewel for valuation, and who refused to return it to him. The owner could not be found.[29]

Liability in conversion is strict, in the sense that all that is needed is an intention to do the act in question and not an intention to bring about the consequences, namely the interference with the plaintiff's title. Ignorance or mistake is no defence, as the numerous cases involving sales by rogues and others who have obtained the goods by deception indicate: the original owner can always sue the third party in conversion as long as title has not passed to the rogue.[30] Similarly, an auctioneer who sells and delivers an article on behalf of a client who has no title will be liable to the owner.[31]

There must be an act of some kind; an omission will not suffice. The act need not be a sale as such. In *Ashby* v. *Tolhurst*[32] the attendant at a car park allowed a stranger to take away the plaintiff's car. His employers were held not liable for conversion, for although the attendant had been negligent, he had not done any act.[33] Similarly, a mere contract of sale of a third person's property, without delivery having taken place, does not constitute conversion either by the buyer or by the seller:[34] section 11(3) of the Act now declares that 'denial of title is not of itself conversion'. An exception to the requirement for an act as well as a denial of title is in the case of a bailee who in breach of his duty to the bailor allows the thing to be lost or destroyed. This used to give rise to liability in detinue as opposed to conversion, but section 2 of the Act abolishes detinue and subsumes this case into conversion. It would now seem to be the case that if there is neither loss nor destruction of a thing but merely detention, there is no liability as there was previously in detinue. But this would only be so where possession was obtained without some wrong being committed, and would not apply in the case of a bailee who does not have a right to possess as against the bailor once the latter demands the return of the goods.[35]

Acts denying title may assume many forms, the most obvious being a taking of the thing. Although taking possession is not essential, should this occur then conversion could overlap with trespass: 'the distinction between the actions of trespass and trover [or conversion] is well settled: the former is founded on possession; the latter on property.'[36] Thus a mere taking, which does not amount to a denial of the plaintiff's title, is a trespass not conversion; so is mere possession.[37] This may matter, as the means of computing damages will differ

---

[28] (1721) 1 Stra. 505.

[29] The position of a finder against the owner or occupier of land will depend on the latter's implied or express intention to retain a better right than those who come on to his land: see *Bridges* v. *Hawkesworth* (1851) 15 Jur. 1079; *Parker* v. *BRB* [1982] QB 1004.

[30] E.g. *Hollins* v. *Fowler* (1875) LR 7 HL 757. The doctrine of fundamental mistake in contract law may frequently operate to prevent the rogue taking good title: *Cundy* v. *Lindsay* (1878) 3 App. Cas. 459; cf. *Lewis* v. *Averay* [1982] 1 QB 198.

[31] *Consolidated Co.* v. *Curtis* [1892] 1 QB 495.   [32] [1937] 2 KB 242.

[33] There might, instead, have been liability for breach of contract or breach of occupier's duty.

[34] *Douglas Valley Finance Co. Ltd.* v. *S. Hughes (Hirers) Ltd.* [1969] 1 QB 738.

[35] See below.   [36] *Ward* v. *Macauley* (1791) 4 Term Rep. 489, 490 (Lord Kenyon CJ).

[37] *Caxton Publishing Co.* v. *Sutherland* [1939] AC 178, 202.

according to which tort is committed. Despite the abolition of detinue, however, detention could amount to conversion if it is adverse to the plaintiff. In *Howard E. Perry & Co. Ltd.* v. *British Railways Board*[38] the defendant carrier held the plaintiffs' steel in depots. During a strike by steelworkers the defendants, fearing sympathy-strike action by their own employees if the plaintiffs were allowed to remove the steel, refused to let them do so. This was held to be conversion: once a bailee refuses to restore goods on the bailor's demand he commits conversion,[39] even though without such a demand he would only be liable for breach of the contract of bailment.

Mere reception of the thing may amount to conversion. With regard to pledge, section 11(2) states that 'receipt of goods by way of pledge is conversion if the delivery of the goods is conversion'. Apart from pledge, the case of the 'involuntary bailee' deserves attention. No person can be regarded as a bailee, involuntary or otherwise, if he is unaware that he has the thing.[40] An involuntary bailee is not liable for the loss for the thing through mere negligence, nor for making a reasonable attempt to return it to its owner.[41] He is only liable if he intentionally damages or destroys it, although even here he will not be liable for disposing of perishable goods.[42]

Conversion can also consist of wrongful delivery of possession of a thing to a third party. In *Hollins* v. *Fowler*[43] a broker who had received goods obtained fraudulently without notice of the fraud was liable in conversion to the owner even though he acted in good faith. *A fortiori* a person is liable if he confers a good title on the third party, for example by a sale in market overt or by sale or delivery by a seller in possession.[44] However, a distinction has to be drawn between these cases and those in which the defendant acts purely in an instrumental capacity innocently and without notice of the plaintiff's right. For example, an innocent depositee of the plaintiff's article will not be liable simply because he restores it to the depositor.[45] Nor in all probability will an innocent holder of a thing be liable for delivering the thing to a third party at the order of the person from whom he received it, provided he is unaware that such delivery is in pursuance of a transaction that could affect title and he acts purely in an instrumental capacity. As Blackburn J said in *Hollins* v. *Fowler*:[46]

On principle, one who deals with goods at the request of the person who has actual custody of them in the bona fide belief that the custodian is the true owner, or has the authority of the true owner, should be excused for what he does if the act is of such nature as would be excused if done by the authority of the person in possession, if he was the finder of the goods or entrusted with their custody.

---

[38] [1980] 1 WLR 1375.   [39] *Clayton* v. *Le Roy* [1911] 2 KB 1031.

[40] *Lethbridge* v. *Phillips* (1819) 2 Stark. 544.

[41] *Elvin and Powell Ltd.* v. *Pummer Roddis Ltd.* (1933) 50 TLR 158.

[42] Under the Unsolicited Goods and Services Act 1971 the recipient may, in certain circumstances, treat unsolicited goods as unconditional gifts after 6 months or 30 days from notice to the sender, so long as the sender does not take possession in the meantime and recipient does not unreasonably refuse him permission to do so.

[43] (1875) LR 7 HL 757.   [44] Sale of Goods Act 1979, ss. 22, 24.

[45] *Hollins* v. *Fowler* (1875) LR 7 HL 757, 767 (Blackburn J).

[46] (1875) LR 7 HL 757, 766. See also 18th Report of the Law Reform Committee (Cmnd. 4774, 1971), paras. 46–50.

Apart from taking or delivering possession unlawfully, the abuse of possession could also be conversion. For this reason a carrier (bailee) who goes against instructions (for example, by delivering to the consignee after notice of stoppage *in transitu*) commits conversion.[47] In *Moorgate Mercantile Co. Ltd.* v. *Finch and Read*[48] F hired a car under a hire-purchase agreement and lent it to R, who transported goods in it which had not cleared customs. The customs authorities forfeited and sold the car. F having disappeared, the hire-purchase company recovered damages for conversion from R, who was deemed to have realised that forfeiture was likely to result from his conduct. If a thing is destroyed, that could amount to conversion, but if it is simply damaged it is possible that the action must lie in trespass. Changing a thing's character, for example, making wine out of grapes (as in the Roman *specificatio*) would amount to conversion.

As between co-owners, each owns the whole so that one co-owner is guilty of conversion if he destroys the goods or disposes of them in a way that gives good title to the entire property, or destroys the other's interest.[49] This includes anything that is equivalent to destruction, including forceful exclusion of the other from the enjoyment of possession or of the fruits of the property.

Defences include the exercise of a right of distress, which is discussed below,[50] and *jus tertii* under section 8 of the Act. A bailee is estopped from denying his bailor's lack of title on the grounds that he either never had it or has lost it.[51] But under section 8 the bailee may seek to join to the action a third party who he believes has better title than the bailor, in order that the third party may assert this superior right. Consent is a defence but contributory negligence is not, by virtue of section 11(1) of the Act. Prior to the 1977 Act the House of Lords appeared to suggest in *Moorgate Mercantile Co. Ltd.* v. *Twitchings*[52] that there could be, in principle, a duty of care on the part of the plaintiff owner to the defendant third party to register the hire-purchase agreement, and would be estopped from asserting his title if he negligently failed to do so. It is unclear whether the possibility of estoppel survives as a means of outflanking section 11(1). The possibility of contributory negligence is retained in the specific case of actions against banks.[53]

The traditional remedy for conversion is an action for damages in which the plaintiff recovers the market value of the thing and any special loss that has resulted.[54] There is a special rule that where a document such as a cheque or other negotiable instrument represents a sum of money, the measure of damages will be that sum and not the value of the piece of paper.[55] Where damages paid represent the whole of the plaintiff's interest, or such sum as has been agreed in settlement, payment extinguishes his title which then vests in the defendant.[56] Because of the open-ended nature of the conversion and the

---

[47] *The Tigress* (1863) 32 LJ Adm. 97; *Booth Steamship Co. Ltd.* v. *Cargo Fleet Iron Co. Ltd.* [1916] 2 KB 570.
[48] [1961] 1 QB 701.   [49] S. 10 of the Act.   [50] See below, Section 2(1).
[51] See *Biddle* v. *Bond* (1865) 6 B. & S. 225; *Rogers, Sons & Co.* v. *Lambert & Co.* [1891] 1 QB 318.
[52] [1977] AC 890.   [53] By virtue of the Banking Act 1979, s. 47.
[54] *BBMB Finance (Hong Kong) Ltd.* v. *Eda Holdings Ltd.* [1991] 2 All ER 129; see also *IBL Ltd.* v. *Coussens* [1991] 2 All ER 133.
[55] See *Lloyds Bank Ltd.* v. *The Chartered Bank of India, Australia and China* [1929] 1 KB 40, 55–6 (Scrutton LJ).
[56] S. 5.

multiple interests that may operate in respect of a particular article, statute seeks to protect a defendant against double liability by requiring the plaintiff to identify any other person who, to his knowledge, has an interest in the goods.[57] The Act also apportions damages between the different claimants, with provision for restitution to the defendant in the event of unjust enrichment,[58] and also requires the plaintiff to make an allowance to an innocent improver or to a subsequent transferee from such a person.[59]

Self-help is permissible as long as it is peaceful and involves no more force than is reasonable in the event of opposition. The common law did not possess a real action for the recovery of chattels to correspond to the Roman law *vindicatio*, but specific restitution could be provided for in equity. Sections 3(2)–(3) now provide for the court to grant specific delivery and damages at its discretion, with the possibility also of an interlocutory order for delivery pending the full trial.[60] If the court does not order this, the plaintiff can choose whether to claim damages only (including consequential damages) or to ask for specific delivery, in which case the defendant has the alternative of paying the value of the goods and any consequential damages.

The common law had a remedy known as *replevin* in a case where an article was taken out of another's possession by a trespassory act for the purpose of distraining it for rent, rates, damage feasant, or some other similar reason. *Replevin* allowed the latter to regain provisional possession pending a decision on title. Section 4 of the Act, by providing for interim possession pending a decision as to title, would appear to have left little scope for the common-law *replevin* action whose scope is, as a result, unclear.

4. Negligence

Wrongful interference overlaps with the tort of negligence. Section 1(a) of the Act extends its scope to 'negligence in so far as that results in damage to goods or to an interest in goods'. This implies that the procedural and remedial provisions of the Act could apply in cases of carelessly inflicted damage. In practice there is unlikely to be much overlap, as the court is unlikely to exercise its discretion in favour of an order for specific delivery in a case of mere negligence.

Select Bibliography

BURNETT, H. W., 'Conversion by an Involuntary Bailee' (1960) 76 *LQR* 364.

DERHAM, D. P., 'Conversion by Wrongful Disposal as Between Co-owners' (1952) 68 *LQR* 507.

ELLIOTT, J. H. S., 'Damages in Detinue and Conversion' (1951) 9 *NILQ* 157.

FLEMING, J. G., 'Tort Liability for Damage to Hire Purchase Goods', 32 *Aust. LJ* 267 (1958).

GOLDRING, J., 'The Negligence of the Plaintiff in Conversion' (1977) 11 *MULR* 91.

GOODHART, A. L., 'Three Cases on Possession', in *Essays in Jurisprudence and the Common Law* (1937), ch. 4.

---

[57] S. 8.   [58] S. 7.   [59] S. 6.   [60] S. 4.

GORDON, D. M., 'Anomalies in the Law of Conversion' (1955) 71 *LQR* 346.

GUEST, A. G., 'Accession and Confusion in the Law of Hire-Purchase' (1964) 27 *MLR* 505.

LAW REFORM COMMITTEE, *Conversion and Detinue* (18th Report, Cmnd. 4774, 1971).

MARSHALL, O. R., 'The Problem of Finding' (1949) 2 *CLP* 68.

MILSOM, S. F. C., 'Not Doing is No Trespass' [1954] *CLJ* 105.

PALMER, N. E., 'The Abolition of Detinue' [1981] *Conv.* (NS) 62.

—— 'The Application of the Torts (Interference with Goods) Act 1977 to Actions in Bailment' (1978) 41 *MLR* 629.

PATON, G. W., *Bailment in the Common Law* (1952).

PEDEN, J. R., 'Measure of Damages in Conversion and Detinue', 44 *Aust. LJ* 65 (1970).

PROSSER, W. L., 'The Nature of Conversion', 42 *Cornell LQ* 168 (1957).

SIMPSON, A. W. B., 'The Introduction of the Action on the Case for Conversion' (1959) 74 *LQR* 364.

SLATER, R. B., 'Accessio, Specificatio and Confusio: Three Skeletons in the Closet', 37 *Can. BR* 597 (1959).

TAY, A. E. S., 'Possession and the Modern Law of Finding', 4 *Syd. LR* 383 (1964).

TETTENBORN, A. M., 'Damages in Conversion—The Exception or the Anomaly?' [1993] *CLJ* 128.

THORNLEY, J. W. A., 'New Torts for Old or Old Torts Refurbished?' [1977] *CLJ* 248.

—— 'Transfer of Title to Chattels by Non-owners' [1966] *CLJ* 186.

WARREN, E. H., 'Qualifying as a Plaintiff in an Action for Conversion', 49 *Harv. LR* 1084 (1936).

2. LAND

1. Trespass to Land *Quaere Clausum Fregit*

Any direct interference with land in the possession of another is trespass, and is actionable *per se*.[61] It is not a crime except where statute has made it so.[62] 'Interference' may take the form of entering land or part of it, or of remaining there after the withdrawal of permission, or of dispossessing the occupant. It also implies that the defendant acted without the permission of the occupier; permission is therefore a defence and is considered below.

The distinction between direct and indirect or consequential interference is a legacy of the old distinction between trespass and case: direct intrusion constituted trespass, consequential interference with the occupier's use and enjoyment amounted at best to nuisance. In a Canadian case, *Mann* v. *Saulnier*,[63] a fence properly constructed by the defendant, and which when constructed did not intrude into the plaintiff's land, began to lean over it after a while. This was held to be a nuisance, not trespass, since it was the consequence of erecting the fence. What is 'direct' and 'consequential' is no more clear-cut here than it is with trespass to the person, however. In *Gregory* v. *Piper*[64] a quantity of rubbish was dumped near the plaintiff's wall without touching it. When it dried out, some of it rolled up against the wall, and this was held to be trespass. In

---

[61] *Entick* v. *Carrington* (1765) 19 St. Tr. 1029, 1066.   [62] See the Criminal Law Act 1977.
[63] (1959) 19 DLR (2d) 130.   [64] (1829) 9 B. & C. 591.

contrast to this is *Southport Corporation* v. *Esso Petroleum Co. Ltd.*[65] The master of an oil-tanker, which had been stranded in an estuary, jettisoned a quantity of oil to lighten the vessel. This drifted ashore and polluted the foreshore of the plaintiff. Denning LJ in the Court of Appeal and Lords Radcliffe and Tucker in the House of Lords treated the damage as consequential;[66] Morris LJ in the Court of Appeal treated it as direct.[67]

Trespass can be committed in various ways. Entry on to land is simply the most obvious example; placing things on land or inducing animals[68] to enter are also potentially trespassory. As was stated in *Gregory* v. *Piper*,[69] 'if a single stone had been put against the wall it would have been sufficient'. With regard to entry into the airspace, a distinction has to be drawn between entry within the area of ordinary user and outside it. An illustration of the former is *Kelsen* v. *Imperial Tobacco Co. (of Great Britain and Ireland) Ltd.*,[70] in which an advertisement sign projected into the airspace above the plaintiff's shop; this was held to be a trespass. A trespass is also committed when the jib of a crane swings over the plaintiff's airspace, even though it causes no damage of either a physical or economic kind. An injunction will normally be available to protect the plaintiff's rights in his property.[71] By contrast, in *Bernstein of Leigh* v. *Skyviews & General Ltd.*[72] the defendant's activity took place above the area of ordinary user and was held not to be a trespass. Here, an aircraft flew hundreds of feet above the plaintiff's property in order to take photographs of it. In connection with aircraft, the provisions of the Civil Aviation Act 1982 should be noted. Section 76(1) states that it is not a trespass for aircraft to fly at a reasonable height having regard to wind, weather, and all the circumstances prevailing at the time. Section 76(2) states that loss or damage caused by civil (not military) aircraft, or by a person or article carried on one, while in flight or landing or taking off, is to be compensatable without proof of fault.

Continuing trespass, usually by things placed on land, is actionable from day to day;[73] and this is so even if the original plaintiff transfers the land to a third party, who is then entitled to sue for the continuation.[74] If a thing is lawfully on land to begin with, but then the permission to keep it there has been withdrawn, continuation of its presence thereafter is a trespass.[75] The position is the same if a person's permission to be on land is withdrawn, and if he fails to leave within a reasonable time he then becomes a trespasser.

Trespass can be committed to the subsoil. Normally, possession of the surface carries with it the subsoil and the things embedded in it.[76] It is possible, however, for one person to possess the surface and another to possess the min-

---

[65] [1954] 2 QB 182; [1956] AC 218.   [66] [1954] 2 QB 182, 196; [1956] AC 218, 242, 244.
[67] [1954] 2 QB 182, 204.   [68] But not bees, according to *Tuton* v. *A. D. Walter Ltd.* [1986] QB 61.
[69] (1829) 9 B. & C. 591, 594; see also *Westripp* v. *Baldock* [1939] 1 All ER 279.   [70] [1957] 2 QB 334.
[71] *Woollerton & Wilson Ltd.* v. *Richard Costain Ltd.* [1970] 1 WLR 411; *Anchor Brewhouse Developments Ltd.* v. *Berkly House (Docklands Developments) Ltd.* [1987] 2 EGLR 187; Cane, *Tort Law and Economic Interests* (1991), 54.
[72] [1978] QB 479.
[73] *Holmes* v. *Wilson* (1839) 10 A. & E. 503.   [74] *Hudson* v. *Nicholson* (1839) 5 M. & W. 437.
[75] *Lonskier* v. *B. Goodman Ltd.* [1928] 1 KB 421.   [76] *Elwes* v. *Brigg Gas Co.* (1886) 33 Ch.D. 562.

erals beneath, so that there could be trespass to both or to the owner of the minerals alone.[77]

With regard to the highway, it is not trespass against the owner of the sub-soil for persons to pass along the highway in the course of ordinary passage and take part in activities incidental to that, but it is trespass if that purpose is exceeded. In *Hickman* v. *Maisey*[78] the defendant committed trespass by using the highway for the purpose of spying on the performance of racehorses on the plaintiff's land. So, too, although there is a right to navigate in tidal waters and anchor temporarily, there is no right to establish permanent moorings if the soil is privately owned.[79] Picketing may amount to trespass of the highway sub-soil if it falls outside the right to take part in peaceful picketing at one's own place of work under section 220 of the Trade Union and Labour Relations (Consolidation) Act 1992.

Finally there is trespass *ab initio*. Where a person enters land under the authority of law and abuses that authority by a positive act of misfeasance, he is deemed to become a trespasser *ab initio*, that is, from the moment of his orig-inal, authorised entry. In *The Six Carpenters' Case* the defendants entered a tavern and, having consumed food and drink, refused to pay. Mere failure to pay being an omission as opposed to an act they were held not liable of trespass *ab initio*. If the abuse is independent of the authority under which a person enters, it does not constitute trespass *ab initio*.[80] This antiquated doctrine has been criti-cised by Lord Denning amongst others,[81] but he made use of it in *Cinnamond* v. *British Airways Authority*[82] to hold that minicab drivers unlawfully touting for business had abused the authority given them by law and were therefore tres-passers *ab initio*.

Trespass requires voluntary conduct. The necessary intention is the intention to perform the act that amounts to interference, and it is immaterial that the defendant was unaware that he was trespassing or that he was genuinely mis-taken. In *Smith* v. *Stone*[83] the defendant, who had been deposited on the plain-tiff's land by a gang of men, was held not liable in trespass since he had committed no voluntary act. In *Gilbert* v. *Stone*,[84] on the other hand, where the defendant had been forced by threats to enter the plaintiff's land, he was held liable since his presence there was the result of his conscious act. This indicates that once an act of this kind can be identified, liability in trespass to land is strict in the sense that it does not depend upon intention or negligence as to the consequences of the act. Whether the complete absence of fault could be a defence, as it appears to be in the case of interference with chattels,[85] is unclear.

---

[77] See *Cox* v. *Glue* (1848) 5 CB 533. Petroleum is vested in the Crown by virtue of the Petroleum (Production) Act 1934 and coal in the British Coal Corporation by virtue of the Coal Industry (Nationalisation) Act 1946. The Crown also has prerogative rights in gold and silver.

[78] [1900] 1 QB 752.   [79] *Fowley Marine (Emsworth) Ltd.* v. *Gafford* [1967] 2 QB 808, 823.

[80] *Ellis* v. *Pasmore* [1934] 2 KB 164.

[81] See his judgment in *Chic Fashions (West Wales) Ltd.* v. *Jones* [1967] 2 QB 299, 313, 317, 320.

[82] [1980] 1 WLR 582, 588.   [83] (1647) Style 65.   [84] (1647) Style 72.

[85] As in *National Coal Board* v. *J. E. Evans & Co. (Cardiff) Ltd.* [1951] 2 KB 861, discussed above, Section 1(2).

As with trespass to goods, it is the possessor who is entitled to sue. This includes a person with the immediate right to possess. Just as possession is prima-facie evidence of ownership, it appears that the converse is true.[86] Acts of enjoyment of land, for example, the cultivation of crops or building on the land, constitute evidence of possession.[87] Occupation of buildings is also evidence and simply having means of access, such as a key, may also be sufficient.[88] By virtue of the doctrine of 'trespass by relation', when a person with a right to possess enters the land his possession is 'related back' to the time when his right accrued so that he can sue for trespass between such accrual and his entry. A trespasser has no right to possess and cannot acquire one simply by entry; at best he can do so only after acquiescence by the owner, for example, by delay. A tenant or subtenant, as distinct from a lodger or licensee,[89] does have possession. A reversioner can sue in respect of permanent damage to the reversion. As between co-owners, each possesses the whole,[90] so it is only in a case of total exclusion of one by the other that the former can sue.

A party in possession can sue in trespass for damages, and *jus tertii* in a third person is no defence.[91] The plaintiff's possession will only yield to ownership in the defendant himself or if the latter acted on the authority of the owner.[92] On the other hand, an owner who has been dispossessed has to recover his land by an action for recovery. This used to be known as the action for ejectment. It finds a place in a work on torts by virtue of the fact that this proprietary action evolved out of the law of trespass with the aid of one of the most famous fictions of English law. Questions of title used to be decided by ancient real actions beside which the action by way of trespass was speedy. To enable these questions to be decided under the guise of trespass a fictitious ploy was used. This involved the pretence, which a defendant was not allowed to challenge, that the plaintiff had demised or leased the land to an imaginary character, John Doe, who had been ejected by another imaginary character, Richard Roe. The plaintiff brought his action with John Doe as nominal plaintiff against Richard Roe, who disclaimed any interest in the land and advised the real defendant to defend it himself. The action took the name of *Doe d. A. v. B.* The principle on which the issue was decided has remained more or less the same. This is that a plaintiff out of possession has to establish a better right to possess than the defendant, and he has to win by the strength of his own title and not by the weakness of that of the defendant.[93] It is here that the vexed question arises whether, in an action for recovery of land, a defendant can set up the defence of *jus tertii*, even though he is unable to do so in the ordinary case of trespass to land. It would seem that if a plaintiff has to win by virtue of the strength of his own title, then evidence that someone else has a better title should prevail, so that the defence of *jus tertii* would indeed be available. This

---

[86] *Hebbert* v. *Thomas* (1835) 1 Cr. M. & R. 861, 864 (Parke B).
[87] *Jones* v. *Williams* (1837) 2 M. & W. 326.
[88] *Jewish Maternity Home Trustees* v. *Garfinkle* (1926) 95 LJKB 766.
[89] *Hill* v. *Tapper* (1863) 2 H. & C. 121.   [90] *Murray, Ash and Kennedy* v. *Hall* (1849) 7 CB 441.
[91] *Nicholls* v. *Ely Beet Sugar Factory Ltd.* [1931] 2 Ch. 84.
[92] *Delaney* v. *T. P. Smith Ltd.* [1946] KB 393, 397.
[93] *Martin d. Tregonwell* v. *Strachan* (1744) 5 Term Rep. 107 n.

was the view of the court in *Doe d. Carter* v. *Barnard*,[94] but there are strong authorities the other way.[95] Even so, if the defendant acquired possession from a person with defective title he cannot seek to establish a better title in someone else as against the person from whom he acquired or his successors.[96] Nor may he do so if his acquisition of possession was wrongful as against the plaintiff.[97]

In addition to the action for recovery of land, a plaintiff also has an action for mesne profits in respect of the loss he has suffered through being kept out of possession.[98] Mesne profits include not just rents and gains from possession and exploitation of the land but also damage caused by deterioration of the land and the costs of regaining possession. The basis for calculating damages is know as the 'user principle'. In *Inverugie Investments Ltd.* v. *Hackett*[99] Lord Lloyd stated this as follows:

The plaintiff may not have suffered any *actual* loss by being deprived of his use of the property. But under the user principle he is entitled to recover a reasonable rent for the wrongful use of his property by the trespasser. Similarly, the trespasser may not have derived any *actual* benefit from the use of the property. But under the user principle he is obliged to pay a reasonable rent for the use that he has enjoyed. The principle need not be characterised as exclusively compensatory, or exclusively restitutionary; it combines elements of both.[100]

In this case, the defendants, who held the freehold of a hotel complex, had unlawfully ejected the plaintiff, the tenant, and run the hotel for a period of years at an average occupancy rate of between 35 and 40 per cent. The House of Lords held that for the period in question, the plaintiff was entitled to compensation based on a reasonable rent for the continuous use of all the apartments in the complex, and not just for those apartments actually used by the defendant, nor even for those which the plaintiff was likely to have been able to fill.

It used to be the case that before he could bring this action the plaintiff first had to regain possession and then use the doctrine of trespass by relation to backdate his possession to cover the period during which he was excluded. This is now largely unnecessary, after an amendment to the Rules of the Supreme Court that allows the plaintiff to join his claim for mesne profits to the action for recovery.[101] If the plaintiff's interest in the land has come to an end, he can still sue for mesne profits.[102]

Self-help may be used in certain circumstances but the law does not encourage resort to self-help and so these are hedged about with restrictions. A party actually in possession may use reasonable force to resist wrongful entry, or attempted entry, by a trespasser. His possession must be legal. In *Holmes* v.

---

[94] (1849) 13 QB 945.

[95] *Asher* v. *Whitlock* (1865) LR 1 QB 1, 6; *Perry* v. *Clissold* [1907] AC 73, 79–80; *Allen* v. *Roughley* (1955) 94 CLR 98. See Wiren, Hargreave and Holdsworth, op. cit. (Select Bibliography).

[96] *Doe d. Johnson* v. *Baytup* (1835) 3 A. & E. 188.   [97] *Davison* v. *Gent* (1857) 1 H. & N. 744.

[98] On the availability of injunctions, see Chapter 8, Section 3, below.   [99] [1995] 1 WLR 713.

[100] Ibid., 718.   [101] RSC Ord. 15, r. 1.

[102] *Mount Carmel Investments Ltd.* v. *Peter Thurlow Ltd.* [1988] 1 WLR 1978; see also *Southport Tramways Co.* v. *Ganey* [1897] 2 QB 66.

Bagge[103] it was held that cricketers were not in possession of the playing area and were thus not entitled to eject the plaintiff, a substitute player, who had refused to leave when ordered to do so by the captain. Secondly, the force used must be reasonable. In *Collins* v. *Renison*[104] the defendant found a trespasser up a ladder placed on his land and, according to his plea, 'gently shook the ladder, which was a low ladder, and gently overturned it and gently threw the plaintiff from it upon the ground'. The force used was held to be unreasonable. If trespass is peaceful, the trespasser must be asked to leave before force is used, unless he turns violent. Thirdly, a person ousted by a trespasser may regain possession by using reasonable force.[105] Subject to this requirement, an owner can expel squatters or demonstrators taking part in a 'sit-in'. If he re-enters peacefully, he should first request the trespasser to leave, and on refusal, use reasonable force.[106] However, against one who has possession, an owner out of possession commits a criminal offence if he uses force to re-enter. The old Statutes of Forcible Entry and Detainer have been replaced by the Criminal Law Act 1977, which makes it a criminal offence to resort to force, however reasonable, except in the case of a 'displaced residential occupier' or 'protected intending occupier'.[107] The criminal law goes further than the civil law, since an owner who uses reasonable force to re-enter will not commit a tort and yet might be liable to conviction under legislation.[108] Entry on to the land of another may be lawful for other purposes: a person may enter the land of a neighbour to abate a nuisance[109] or, in some cases, to retake a chattel, at least where it was wrongfully taken by the landowner.[110]

Another form of self-help is distress damage feasant. If a chattel is unlawfully on land and is doing damage, the landowner may impound it until the owner pays, or offers to pay, compensation for the damage done. At common law this power applied to trespassing things and to animals. Distrained animals had to be fed and watered and cows milked; the distrainor was liable for any damage resulting from his failure to do this. Section 7 of the Animals Act 1971 abolishes the common-law power in relation to 'livestock' in favour of a more-or-less equivalent statutory power that includes a power of sale. The Act may have inadvertently abolished the common-law power of distraint in respect of 'any animal' unless this phrase in section 7(1) can be read as confined to livestock.

A modern application of the law relating to distress damage feasant occurred in *Arthur* v. *Anker*.[111] The lessees of a private car park employed the defendants to clamp the wheels of vehicles that were parked there without permission. The defendants refused to release vehicles except on payment of a fee. Notices on the land indicated that unauthorised vehicles would be clamped and that a specified release fee would be charged. The Court of Appeal, Hirst LJ dissenting, held that in a case such as this a landowner could only invoke distress damage

---

[103] (1853) 1 E. & B. 782; *Dean* v. *Hogg* (1834) 10 Bing. 345. [104] (1754) 1 Sayer 138.

[105] *McPhail* v. *Persons, Names Unknown* [1973] Ch. 447, 465–7 (Lord Denning MR).

[106] *Green* v. *Goddard* (1704) 2 Salk. 641. [107] S. 12(3).

[108] See *Hemmings* v. *Stoke Poges Golf Club* [1920] 1 KB 720. [109] See below, Section 3(6)(b).

[110] See *Anthony* v. *Haney and Harding* (1832) 8 Bing. 186, and the 18th Report of the Law Reform Committee, Cmnd. 4774, paras. 116–26.

[111] [1996] 2 WLR 602.

feasant to clamp unauthorised vehicles if they were causing damage. According to Sir Thomas Bingham MR:

It is plain that physical damage to the land or anything on it is not necessary to found a claim to distress damage feasant. But I do not think a mere technical trespass, mere unlawful presence on the land, is enough. Actual damage would be shown if the party entitled to the use of the land were denied, or obstructed in, the use of it . . . Thus if any of the leaseholders, or any of the leaseholders' licensees (including suppliers seeking to make deliveries), were unable to use the car park, or prevented from unloading, by a trespassing car, that would amount to actual damage. But there is no evidence and no finding of any such evidence in the present case.[112]

His Lordship rejected the proposition that the cost of towing away the car could, in itself, constitute 'damage' for this purpose. He also cast doubt on the use of flat-rate fines for the release of vehicles. Even if damage is suffered—and the landowner thereupon becomes entitled to retain the chattel as security for a claim for compensation—the flat-rate charge levied by the wheel clamper is paid to augment the latter's profits, and not to compensate the landowner.

Neill LJ gave a concurring judgment; Hirst LJ, however, dissented on the basis that since the tort of trespass itself is actionable *per se*, damage should be presumed for the purposes of the remedy. While there is much to be said for this view, the policy factors referred to by Neill LJ in his judgment should also be borne in mind. As he stated, the remedy of distress damage feasant 'had its origins in medieval times and provided a convenient form of self-help in agricultural communities', but in the context of motor vehicles,

the courts should do nothing to encourage the use of clamping without notice. One can anticipate that many disputes would be likely to arise if clamps were applied to motor vehicles without any prior warning . . . Pending some control by Parliament it seems to me that the matter can be satisfactorily dealt with by means of clearly worded notices and by the application of the doctrine of *volenti*.[113]

The *volenti* defence was, then, the route adopted by the majority to finding in the defendants' favour: the plaintiffs were taken to have consented to the clamping of their vehicles and to the payment of a fee in return for their release.

In general, a trespasser's liability is clear; as far as licensees are concerned, a bare licensee comes under a duty to leave as soon as his licence is revoked, and if he refuses or fails to leave within a reasonable time he becomes a trespasser. Depending on the terms of the contract, a contractual licence may be revocable in which case the licensee becomes a trespasser even if the revocation is actionable as a breach of contract.[114] This is subject, however, to an exception where a contract is specifically enforceable and the licensee has conducted himself properly.[115] Nor can a licence be revoked if it is coupled with an interest, whether in land or in chattels.[116]

---

[112] [1996] 2 WLR 602, 610.   [113] Ibid., 615.   [114] *Kerrison v. Smith* [1897] 2 QB 445.
[115] *Hurst v. Picture Theatres Corp.* [1915] 1 KB 1; *Winter Garden Theatre (London) Ltd.* v. *Millenium Productions Ltd.* [1948] AC 173, 189 (Viscount Simon); cf. *Thompson v. Park* [1944] KB 408.
[116] *Wood v. Manley* (1839) 11 A. & E. 34.

2. Defences

The Limitation Act 1623, section 5, which is the oldest surviving tort-law statute, provides that if the defendant pleads disclaimer of title to the land and if 'the trespass was by negligence or involuntary' and he makes a tender of sufficient amends, action against him shall be barred. 'Involuntary' here should be taken to mean 'unintentional', since if there is no act the tort of trespass is not made out in any event; however, the effect of the statute was nullified by interpreting it narrowly to mean 'no act' in *Basley* v. *Clarkson* in 1681.[117] The defence of *jus tertii* has already been touched upon, as has that of mistake and the defence of one's own property.

The plaintiff's consent is always a defence in the sense that it constitutes 'leave and licence'.[118] It is, however, a trespass to exceed the terms of a licence: 'where you invite a person into your house to use the stairs you do not invite him in to slide down the bannisters.'[119] Certain licences, such as the licence of traders and canvassers to walk up a garden path to call on the occupier, may be implied subject to the landowner's power to exclude them by advanced notice, while others are regulated by law such as the powers of entry of the police. Rights of entry are also affected by rights of way, easements, and immemorial customary rights, as well as by numerous statutes. These matters are outside the scope of this book and the reader is referred to texts on civil liberties and on land law for the details.

The defence of necessity may also be available under certain limited circumstances. In *Re F*[120] Lord Goff identified three situations in which the defence might apply. First, there are cases of public necessity such as the destruction of property to prevent the spread of fire, as in the Great Fire of London of 1666 or the case of *Dewey* v. *White*,[121] in which firemen threw down a chimney stack which was threatening to fall damaging the plaintiff's house; secondly, cases of private necessity, as in *Cope* v. *Sharpe* (*No. 2*)[122] where the defendant went on to the plaintiff's land to prevent a fire spreading to neighbouring land over which his employer had shooting rights; and thirdly, a category of cases in which action is taken as a matter of necessity to come to the aid of another whose person or property is in imminent danger. In this last category, 'to fall within the principle not only (1) must there be a necessity to act when it is not practicable to communicate with the assisted person, but also (2) the action taken must be such as a reasonable person would in all the circumstances take, acting in the best interests of the assisted person'.[123] If anything the modern tendency is to restrict the scope of this defence. In *Southwark London Borough Council* v. *Williams*,[124] a case in which squatters attempted to argue that their unlawful occupation of an empty house was justified by their need to find shelter for

---

[117] 3 Lev. 37.
[118] *Thomas* v. *Sorrell* (1674) Vaughan 330.
[119] *The Carlgarth* [1927] P. 93, 110.
[120] [1990] 2 AC 1, 74.
[121] (1827) M. & M. 56.
[122] [1912] 1 KB 496.
[123] *Re F* [1990] 2 AC 1, 75 (Lord Goff). See also the Criminal Law Act 1967, s. 3, which enables a member of the public to use 'such force as is reasonable in the prevention of crime', a provision which draws no distinction between defence of oneself or of another.
[124] [1971] 1 Ch. 734, 744.

homeless families, Lord Denning MR had this to say about the matter. 'Necessity would open a door which no man could shut . . . The plea would be an excuse for all sorts of wrongdoing. So the courts must, for the sake of law and order, take a firm stand. They must refuse to admit the plea of necessity to the hungry and the homeless; and trust that their distress will be relieved by the charitable and the good.'

Where necessity is a defence to trespass there may remain the possibility that it will not cover liability in another tort, such as negligence. In *Rigby* v. *Chief Constable of Northamptonshire*[125] the police fired a CS-gas canister into the plaintiff's shop in order to flush out a dangerous psychopath who had taken refuge in the shop. The shop was burned out. The court held that necessity was a good defence to the plaintiff's claim of trespass, but that the police were none the less liable in negligence for firing the canister into the shop without arranging for any fire-fighting equipment to be present.

A final possibility open to the defendant is to plead 'inevitable accident'. This is tantamount to a denial of fault and its scope is limited given that the tort of trespass to land is essentially based on strict liability.[126]

Select Bibliography

DENNING, A. T., 'Re-entry for Forfeiture: The Case of *Elliott* v. *Boynton*' (1927) 43 *LQR* 53.

HARGREAVES, A. D., 'Terminology and Title in Ejectment' (1940) 56 *LQR* 376.

HOLDSWORTH, W. S., 'Terminology and Title in Ejectment: a Reply' (1940) 56 *LQR* 479.

MITCHELL, J. D. B., 'Learner's Licence' (1954) 17 *MLR* 211.

RICHARDSON, J. E., 'Private Property Rights in the Air Space at Common Law' 31 *Can. BR* 116 (1953).

SHAWCROSS, C. N. and BEAUMONT, K. M., *Air Law* (3rd edn., 1966), ch. 25.

SMITH, J., 'Liability for Substantial Physical Damage to Land by Blasting—The Rule of the Future' 33 *Harv. LR* 542, 667 (1920).

WADE, H. W. R., 'What is a Licence?' (1948) 64 *LQR* 57.

WILLIAMS, G. L., 'A Strange Offspring of Trespass *Ab Initio*' (1936) 52 *LQR* 106.

WIREN, S. A., 'The Plea of *Jus Tertii* in Ejectment' (1925) 41 *LQR* 139.

3. NUISANCE

1. Definition

'There is perhaps no more impenetrable jungle in the entire law', wrote Dean Prosser, 'than that which surrounds the word nuisance.'[127] Nuisances may be private or public. Because of the vagaries of history,[128] and the connection

---

[125] [1985] 1 WLR 1242.

[126] See *Southport Corp.* v. *Esso Petroleum Co. Ltd.* [1953] 2 All ER 1204, 1212 (Devlin J).

[127] Prosser and Keeton on *Torts* (5th edn.), 616.

[128] The early history of the tort is traced by Winfield and Newark, (below, Select Bibliography) and McRae, 'Development of Nuisance in the Early Common Law', 1 *U. Fla. LR* 27 (1948). For the 19th-century developments see Brenner, 'Nuisance Law and the Industrial Revolution', 3 *Jo. LS* 403 (1974) and, more recently, John McLaren's excellent article on nuisance law, (below, Select Bibliography).

between the two forms, private nuisance has come to cover different types of conduct on the part of defendants.[129] Indeed, beyond saying that all these instances are actionable because they are intolerable inconveniences, the only other common element is that they affect the plaintiffs' use or enjoyment of their land. Private nuisance is therefore commonly defined as any substantial and unreasonable interference with the plaintiff's land or any right over or in connection with its enjoyment.

2. Basis of Liability

The gist of liability is unreasonable interference with the plaintiff's interest. This is sometimes referred to as the 'principle of reasonable user' which is (rightly) seen as the main controlling mechanism of this tort. But the words 'reasonable' and 'reasonableness' must be used with some caution in order to avoid confusion with the tort of negligence where they can also be found. Thus, in nuisance the law does not concentrate so much on the quality of the 'doing' (unreasonableness of the defendant's conduct) as on the quality of the 'deed' (unreasonableness of the result to the plaintiff). The two considerations are by no means mutually exclusive (for the unreasonableness of the defendant's conduct is often a factor which makes the resulting interference unreasonable);[130] but the different optic adopted in the two torts can produce different results.

The defendant may interfere with the plaintiff's interests by (a) affecting materially his land, or (b) affecting his use or enjoyment of it, or (c) interfering with servitudes and similar rights over the land. The second type can pose interesting problems of delimitation, while the last is more the concern of books on property than on tort,[131] so it will be omitted from this account.

The distinction between material interference with property and interference with use or enjoyment was sanctioned by the House of Lords in *St Helens Smelting Co.* v. *Tipping*[132] in 1865. The plaintiff bought an estate near a smelting factory and later complained that noxious fumes from it were damaging his trees and crops. The defendants contended that the whole neighbourhood was devoted to similar manufacturing purposes and that, therefore, the smelting operations should be allowed to continue with impunity. Dismissing this argument, the Lord Chancellor, Lord Westbury, pointed out that when interference with a plaintiff's enjoyment is alleged, the surrounding circumstances are relevant, but that different considerations apply when the alleged interference is with material injury to property.

In descending order of significance, three reasons could be advanced for this distinction (which appears to be restricted to the common-law systems). The

---

[129] *Goldman* v. *Hargrave* [1967] 1 AC 645, 657 per Lord Wilberforce.

[130] We shall return to this point below, Section 3(b)(iv).

[131] *Gale on Easements* (14th edn.); Jackson, *Law of Easements and Profits* (1978), Megarry and Wade, *The Law of Real Property* (5th edn.), 834 ff. Some of these nuisances are actionable *per se*. See *Nicholls* v. *Ely Beet Sugar Factory Ltd.* [1936] Ch. 343. The deviation from the rule (which requires damage as an element of nuisance) may be due to the close analogy with trespass and the fact that both actions are, in such circumstances, aiming at vindicating rights and not necessarily compensating the plaintiff. Thus, Buckley, op. cit. (Select Bibliography), 105.

[132] (1865) 11 HLC 642, 650; 11 ER 1483, 1486, per Lord Westbury, LC.

first is that property and, in particular, tangible, material interference with it, generally receives greater protection than the enjoyment derived from it.[133] This argument would certainly have commended itself to earlier generations. Nowadays, however, it may appear less attractive, especially since a clear-cut distinction between property damage and mere interference with enjoyment is not always easy to make. Secondly, it might be said that property damage is more easily assessable and quantifiable than mere interference with enjoyment.[134] The answer to this is that difficulty in quantifying damages has not prevented courts from awarding them in personal-injury cases, so there is no reason why it should justify a rigid distinction here between two types of interference. Thirdly, the distinction may represent an attempt by the House of Lords to reconcile two conflicting earlier decisions. In *Hole* v. *Barlow*[135] the Court of Common Pleas had held that a defendant would not be liable if he carried on his activity in a 'convenient and proper' location. In *Bamford* v. *Turnley*[136] the Court of Exchequer Chamber disapproved of this decision on the ground that it was too favourable to defendants. The suggested reconciliation is that the relevance of locality should be confined to cases of discomfort (*Hole*) as distinct from property damage (*Bamford*).[137]

All three arguments may partially explain the distinction between the two kinds of interferences, though it would be a mistake to accept Lord Westbury's opinion as creating a *sharp* legal dichotomy between them. Indeed, in the *Hunter* case,[138] the House of Lords and, especially, Lord Hoffmann, were keen to dispel the impression that Lord Westbury's distinction created two separate torts.[139] Three reasons could be given why Lord Westbury's dichotomy should not be overstressed.

The first has already been mentioned: the difference between material damage and discomfort is not always easy to draw. Thus, noise and smells may (*a*) inconvenience the plaintiff, (*b*) affect his business, and (*c*) even reduce the value of his property. While (*a*) would not qualify as material damage to property, (*b*) and (*c*) pose greater difficulty. It is by no means clear that (*c*), for example, could be included in Lord Westbury's definition and the absence of conclusive authority leaves the point open to argument.[140]

---

[133] On this idea of hierarchy of values in the law of torts, see Markesinis, 'Policy Factors and the Law of Torts', *The Cambridge Lectures* (1981) 199, 204 ff. For an economic explanation and criticism (with further references), see Ogus and Richardson, (below, Select Bibliography), 299 ff.

[134] An illustration on this can be found in *Bone* v. *Seale* [1975] 1 WLR 797, where, in a nuisance action provoked by smells emanating from a nearby pig farm, the court held that the damages should be fixed by analogy with damages for loss of amenity in personal injury actions. This approach was convincingly criticised by Lord Hoffmann in his opinion in *Hunter* v. *Canary Wharf Ltd.* [1997] 2 WLR 684 at 708, where he argued that the damages in such cases should be calculated either by reference to the diminished capital value of the land (which could not be proved in the *Bone* case), or by calculating the 'diminution in the amenity value of the property during the period for which the nuisance persisted.' That this (second) instance involved 'placing a value on intangibles' did not worry his Lordship, especially in the light of what was said in *Ruxley Electronics and Construction Ltd.* v. *Forsyth* [1996] AC 344.

[135] (1858) 4 CBNS 334; 140 ER 1113. [136] (1860) 3 B. & S. 62; 122 ER 25.

[137] For the suggestion of a *via media*, see Buckley, (below, Select Bibliography), 7–8.

[138] *Hunter* v. *Canary Wharf Ltd.* [1997] 2 WLR 684. [139] Ibid., 709.

[140] For the difficulties generally, see Ogus and Richardson, op. cit. (Select Bibliography), 229; McLaren, op. cit. (Select Bibliography), 534.

The second reason was forcefully advanced by Lord Hoffmann in his pene-
trating opinion in the *Hunter* case.[141] In his view the Westbury dichotomy
resulted in a tendency to regard cases falling in the second category as being
'actions in respect of the discomfort or even personal injury which the plaintiff
has suffered . . .' This was an intended and unacceptable side effect of the
dichotomy. For even in cases ' "productive of sensible personal discomfort" the
action is not for causing discomfort to the person but, as in the case of the first
category, for causing injury to the land. True it is that the land has not suffered
"sensible" injury, but its utility has been diminished by the existence of the nuisance.' A correct appreciation of this fact thus has important consequences on
two further issues: (*a*) the rule that plaintiffs in nuisance must have an interest
in the land in question and (*b*) the way that damages should be calculated in
nuisances of this second kind.

The final reason why a rigid distinction should be avoided is that it could convey the belief that it would suffice to prove any material injury to property in
order to establish an actionable nuisance, which would be wrong. For not every
'fleeting or evanescent'[142] interference will be an actionable nuisance, but only
one which is substantial and unreasonable. Thus, when water flowed over the
plaintiff's land but caused only 'trivial injury', the claim in nuisance was
rejected.[143] The same conclusion was reached when the defendant's land was
subject to minor subsidence causing the plaintiff no 'appreciable harm'.[144]
There is also some authority to suggest that the pervading notion of 'reasonableness' is not restricted to nuisances resulting from discomfort, but is also relevant in cases of material damage to the plaintiff's property. So, in *Watt* v.
Jamieson,[145] where the defendant's vent-pipe discharged vapour on the plaintiff's land and thereby caused, *inter alia*, dry rot (material damage to property),
Lord President Cooper took the view that 'the critical question is whether what
he (the plaintiff) was exposed to was *plus quam tolerabile* when due weight has
been given to *all the surrounding* circumstances of the offensive conduct and its
effects'. The plaintiff's action was dismissed. Similarly, in *Stearn* v. *Prentice
Brothers*[146] the defendants collected manure on their land, thereby attracting
rats that attacked the plaintiff's crops. The plaintiff's action was again dismissed since it was held that what the defendants had done was, in the circumstances of that case, neither excessive nor unusual.

Despite these arguments the distinction between property damage and interference with enjoyment or use cannot be totally ignored. For the requirement
of substantial and unreasonable interference is more easily satisfied in cases of
material interference with property and, as one leading tort lawyer put it,
'English courts (remain) . . . chary of protecting personal discomforts falling
short of physical injury to property'.[147] Further, the nature of the locality is a
factor seriously taken into account when nuisance takes the form of interference with enjoyment of the land, but it is ignored when the nuisance materi-

---

[141] [1997] 684, 708.   [142] *Benjamin* v. *Storr* (1874) LR 9 CP 400, 407 per Brett J.
[143] *Nobilo* v. *Waitemata County* [1961] NZLR 1064, 1067.
[144] *Mitchell* v. *Darley Main Colliery Co.* (1884) 14 QBD 125, 137; affd. (1886) 11 App. Cas. 127.
[145] 1954 SC 56.   [146] [1919] 1 KB 394.   [147] Street, *Torts* (7th edn.), 243.

ally affects the plaintiff's land. Finally, the availability of injunctive relief and the rules for calculating damages may not be the same in both instances. So, despite the fact that no clear-cut distinction between the two types of interference is possible, the distinction between material damage to property and interference with use and enjoyment is still of some importance in English law.

3. Unreasonable Interference

(A) MATERIAL DAMAGE TO PROPERTY

In addition to what has been said so far it should be noted that even material interference can take different forms, for example, a lightning strike not properly dealt with by the defendant,[148] flooding,[149] encroachment by roots,[150] contamination by sewage,[151] and so on. What is interesting about all these are the reasons which have led to the gradual imposition of affirmative duties of action on the landowners from whose land danger emanates, and the devices adopted by courts towards this end. Three cases call for comment: *Sedleigh-Denfield* v. *O'Callaghan*,[152] *Goldman* v. *Hargrave*,[153] and *Leakey* v. *National Trust*.[154]

In the first, the plaintiff's land was flooded because the drainage system in the defendant's land became blocked through the act of a trespasser; the defendants were held liable because they were aware of the cause of the flooding, but had failed to take reasonable steps to abate it.

In the second case a tree on the defendant's land was struck by lightning. Though the defendant felled it, he did not extinguish the fire after doing so in the belief that the fire would eventually burn itself out. It kept smouldering, however, and, fanned by a sudden gust of wind, spread to the plaintiff's land. The Privy Council held that the rule in *Sedleigh-Denfield* v. *O'Callaghan* applied to cases such as this where the danger arose not from the act of a trespasser, but from an operation of nature on something on the defendant's land.

In the third case the defendants, the National Trust, owned and occupied land on which there was a large mound known as 'Burrow Mump'. Because of its geological structure, known by the defendants, this was prone to subsidence. After an unusually dry summer followed by a very wet autumn, the mound developed cracks, which eventually caused a substantial earth-slip on to the plaintiff's adjoining property. The defendants, though warned by the plaintiff of the possibility of an impending collapse, refused to do anything about it and merely gave the plaintiff permission to abate the cause of the nuisance at his own expense. Nor were they willing to remove the fallen debris after the subsidence or to compensate the plaintiff, arguing that there was no liability in law for an occurrence of this sort. O'Connor J at first instance and a unanimous Court of Appeal held otherwise.

---

[148] *Goldman* v. *Hargrave* [1967] 1 AC 645.

[149] *Fletcher* v. *Smith* (1877) 2 App. Cas. 781. But not if the flooding occurs because water is diverted before it reaches the defendant's land: *Home Brewery plc* v. *William Davis & Co. (Loughborough) Ltd.* [1987] 1 All ER 637.

[150] *Davey* v. *Harrow Corp.* [1958] 1 QB 60; *Masters* v. *Brent LBC* [1978] QB 841; *Solloway* v. *Hampshire CC* (1981) 79 LGR 449.

[151] *Humphries* v. *Cousins* (1877) 2 CPD 239.   [152] [1940] AC 880.   [153] [1967] 1 AC 645.

[154] [1980] QB 485.

In the light of *Sedleigh-Denfield* v. *O'Callaghan* and *Goldman* v. *Hargrave*, the extension in *Leakey* was as inevitable as it was just. *Sedleigh-Denfield* had held a landowner liable, in certain circumstances, for the act of a trespasser. *Goldman* v. *Hargrave* extended that rule to dangers arising by operations of nature affecting something on the land. Finally, *Leakey* completed the process by including dangers arising out of operations of nature on the land itself. Ingenious distinctions, which in the past stood in the way of enlarging the duty of occupiers of land, had been criticised by judges and writers for something like fifty years before being abandoned.[155] But such criticisms used to be brushed aside as being only *obiter dicta* or the product of academic thinking. *Leaky* put an end to all this and in so doing cast upon occupiers of land a general, though measured, duty to take care in relation to hazards on their land, whether natural or artificial.

The technique of imposing liability in *Leakey* is also known. In substance this was a case of non-feasance, so a duty to act had to be 'discovered' by the court. Subsuming omissions under the bad performance of activities and thereby imposing liability where previously there would be none, is not new.[156] Such duties to take positive action, though on the increase, have not developed into a general duty to act in favour of another. Yet in this limited area of the law we do appear to be moving towards such a general duty.

More noteworthy than the reasoning techniques is the reason behind the extension of liability. *Leakey* reveals in part the policy factors that determine the final result but which are often concealed behind the legal jargon. For in this, as in so many other cases, the court was faced with a clash of interests. For, on the one hand we have the interest of occupier to protect himself against liability resulting from the natural use of his land. On the other hand, however, there is also the neighbour to be protected against potential dangers arising from the land of the other occupier. For a long time the law was satisfied with the conception of separate and autonomous proprietors, each of whom was entitled to exploit his territory in a natural manner and none of whom was obliged to restrain or direct the operations of nature in the interest of avoiding harm to his neighbour. In that era, which elevated the pursuit of private interest to the level of a public virtue, the emphasis was on the landowner's right to use or not use his land as he chose and to avoid making him liable if at all possible.

Today, however, the emphasis is more on accident prevention and loss distribution, and both these policy arguments may be seen in play here. For accident prevention suggests that the owner of land on which a cause of interference arises will usually be in a better position to prevent or control it. In *Leakey*'s case this may not have been entirely true, since the National Trust was prepared to allow the plaintiff to enter on their land and abate the danger, so they were not the only entity that could have prevented the harm. Arguably, however, they were best placed to bear the cost of such preventive action. This

---

[155] E.g. Wright J in *Noble* v. *Harrison* [1926] 2 KB 332; Lord Wright in *Sedleigh-Denfield* [1940] AC 880 at 910; Goodhart [1930] 4 *CLJ* 13.
[156] Above, Chapter 2, Section 2(3)(a).

leads to the second policy argument that focuses on a benefit–burden analysis. The occupier of land on which the nuisance arises no doubt derives benefit from its use and, so runs the argument, he should also shoulder the corresponding burden, especially if this is likely to be modest. This is particularly true in this type of situation since what we are ultimately talking about is the (modest) cost of insurance against such risks, as against the cost of cure of the resulting harm, which may run into thousands of pounds.

The extension of the duty of positive action is, however, accompanied by the rider that the standard of care to be shown by a landowner is not the objective standard of the 'reasonable man', but a more subjective one. For the standard is tailored to the abilities and resources of the particular defendant who has a hazard thrust upon him through no seeking or fault of his own. This probably is right (though if the policy reasons given in the previous paragraph are convincing, then they could be taken to justify the imposition of the usual, objectively determined, duty of care). Interestingly, however, in *Leakey* the defendants attempted to exploit quite subtly this requirement that the standard of care should take into account the financial position of the defendant (and, perhaps, by implication of the plaintiff as well). For they argued that in this case it should determine not merely the standard of duty, but also its very existence. They argued, in other words, that this kind of balancing operation was almost bound to lead to such delays and complexities that it would be better if the court refused to discover a duty altogether. The Court of Appeal, however, remained unimpressed. A lighter, subjective standard of care did not appear to create problems when it was applied to liability towards trespassers in the post-*British Railways Board* v. *Herrington* era.[157] And it has caused no difficulties after *Goldman* v. *Hargrave*; so there was little reason to suppose that it might do so if adopted in this instance. Policy thus favoured the imposition of liability; and there was no contrary reason why this should not be so. Though the court held that it mattered not whether the case was pleaded in negligence or nuisance, we see here a certain similarity to the method of approach advocated by the leading negligence cases in the 1970s (though under attack since the mid-1980s). For, if harm is foreseeable, there will be liability so long as there is no special policy reason why there should be none.

The trilogy of cases discussed in the previous paragraphs could have further and, it is submitted, unexplored implications for the law of negligence. For, as we have noted already, in nuisance the courts have shown a greater willingness to impose liability for omissions than they have done in the law of negligence. This becomes particularly obvious if one compares the nuisance trilogy of cases just discussed with another set of cases, this time pleaded in negligence: *Lamb* v. *Camden London Borough Council*,[158] *P. Perl (Exporters) Ltd.* v. *Camden London Borough Council*,[159] and *Smith* v. *Littlewoods Organisation Ltd.*[160] For in these negligence cases the defendants, occupiers of empty premises, were held *not* liable to their neighbours (plaintiffs) for harm caused by third parties/strangers who entered the plaintiff's premises after having obtained easy access into the

---

[157] [1972] AC 877.   [158] [1981] QB 625.   [159] [1984] QB 342.   [160] [1987] 2 WLR 480.

defendant's (occupier's) premises. Originally the justification given for this result was that A could not be made liable to C for the acts of B who was neither A's servant, child, nor other person for whom A had to answer. Eventually, however, it became clear that the real reason was the reluctance of our law to impose liability for pure omissions in the context of the tort of negligence. Yet such a liability could be imposed if the action could be brought under the heading of *Sedleigh-Denfield* v. *O'Callaghan*—something that in the *Smith* case was considered theoretically possible by both Lords Mackay and Goff.[161] This could be taken to suggest that the newly-found liability for non-feasance in pure nuisance situations could, with a minimum of ingenuity, spread to nuisance-negligence cases once the courts work out the necessary safeguards for such an extension of the law.[162] But our courts have not, thus far, taken this step; and until that happens, nuisance may offer plaintiffs opportunities for compensation that negligence still does not.

(B) INTERFERENCE WITH USE OR ENJOYMENT OF LAND

The plaintiff's enjoyment of land may be affected in various ways. Most typically this is done through noise, smell, or interference with his rights to light, air, and uninterrupted view. However, while 'English law had long recognized the duty of occupiers of land not to offend their neighbour's sense of smell or hearing, it has left them lamentably free to offend their neighbour's sense of sight'.[163] To the extent that this statement refers to a right of uninterrupted view, it is correct, since no such right has ever been recognised. But a plaintiff's right to the free passage of light (for purposes of illumination and heating)[164] can be protected according to the usual rules of nuisance[165] so long as it exists as an easement. The right to the free access of air will be protected in an even more limited way, the main requirement being that it is flowing from defined or limited openings.[166] The same (non-liability) rule was recently held to apply to interferences with television reception caused by the defendant erecting on his land a huge tower block. As Lord Hoffman put it: 'The general principle is that at common law anyone may build whatever he likes upon his land. If the effect is to interfere with the light, air or view of his neighbour, that is his misfortune. The owner's right to build can be restrained only by covenant or the acquisition (by grant or prescription) of an easement of light or air . . . for the benefit of windows or apertures on adjoining land.'[167] The plaintiff's main protection thus lies in the observance of the planning system.[168] Any detailed discussion of interference with light and air would require an extended excursion into the law of servitudes and this lies outside the scope of this book.

---

[161] [1987] 2 WLR 480, 497. See also Lord Goff's speech at 510.
[162] On this see Markesinis, 'Negligence, Nuisance and Affirmative Duties of Action', 105 *LQR* 104 (1989).
[163] *McVittie* v. *Bolton Corp.* [1945] KB 281, 283 (per Scott LJ).   [164] *Allen* v. *Greenwood* [1980] Ch. 119.
[165] *Colls* v. *Home and Colonial Stores Ltd.* [1904] AC 179 (the deprivation of light must not be trivial).
[166] *Bass* v. *Gregory* (1890) 25 QBD 481.   [167] *Hunter* v. *Canary Wharf Ltd.* [1997] 2 WLR 684, 711.
[168] Which in this case, however, was for business and economic reasons seriously truncated—an element which exarcebates the, arguably, unfair result. Contrast *Nor-Video Services Ltd.* v. *Ontario Hydro* (1978) 84 DLR (3rd) 221.

Not every interference with enjoyment of property will be actionable. The following statement from the Vice-Chancellor's judgment in *Walter* v. *Selfe*[169] conveys in substance (if not in modern language) the kind of standard courts are likely to apply. The inconvenience must thus be 'considered in fact as more than fanciful, more than one of mere delicacy or fastidiousness, as an inconvenience materially interfering with the ordinary comfort . . . of human existence, not merely according to elegant or dainty modes and habits of living, but according to plain and sober and simple notions among the English people'. In order to determine this in practice, the courts often find themselves weighing more openly a variety of factors in the process of determining the 'unreasonableness' of the situation. As always, the basic requirement is that the interference must be objectively unreasonable and, if it is not, the plaintiff's claim will fail however opprobrious the defendant's conduct may be. As Knight-Bruce VC's statement implies, people must learn to put up with the 'give and take' which is part of social coexistence, and only to this extent will the law protect interferences. Protection ceases when this limit is exceeded and interferences beyond it become actionable as nuisances.[170] So judges have here to strike a balance, so far as possible, between the conflicting interests of the occupier of land and his neighbour.[171]

Paradoxically, it would seem that the more 'advanced' a society becomes the more likely it is that a growing number of interfering activities may be regarded as reasonable. So, what is reasonable depends on the facts of each case and the tests that have been periodically suggested are, inevitably, flexible. As Lord Wright put it in *Sedleigh-Denfield* v. *O'Callaghan*,[172] echoing in less flowery language the above-quoted statement of Knight-Bruce VC:

A balance has to be maintained between the right of the occupier to do what he likes with his own, and the right of his neighbour not to be interfered with. It is impossible to give any precise or universal formula. Broadly speaking it may be said that a useful test is perhaps what is reasonable according to the ordinary usages of mankind living in society, or, more correctly, in a particular society.

'Reasonableness', therefore, has come to depend on a variety of factors of which the most important are the duration of the interference, the sensitivity of the plaintiff, the character of the neighbourhood, and the fault of the defendant.

(i) Duration of Interference   The general rule is that for an interference to be thought unreasonable it has to be of appreciable duration. As Talbot J put it in *Cunard* v. *Antifyre Ltd*:[173] 'Private nuisances, at least in the vast majority of cases, are interferences for a substantial length of time by owners or occupiers of property with the use or enjoyment of neighbouring property.' What amounts to 'substantial length' is a matter of fact, though in *Crown River Crusies Ltd.* v.

---

[169] (1851) 4 De G. & Sm. 315; 64 ER 849 (per Knight-Bruce VC).

[170] Succinctly explained in the *American Restatement (Second) Torts*, para. 822, note g.

[171] Expressed e.g. by Veale J in *Halsey* v. *Esso Petroleum Co. Ltd.* [1961] 1 WLR 683, 698, echoing Knight-Bruce VC in *Walter* v. *Selfe* (1851), 4 De G. & Sm. 315, 322; 64 ER 849, 852.

[172] [1940] AC 880, 903.

[173] [1933] 1 KB 551, 557. See also *AG* v. *PYA Quarries Ltd.* [1957] 2 QB 169, 192 (per Denning LJ).

Kimbolton Fireworks Ltd.[174] a firework display on a moored vessel which lasted for about a quarter of an hour and caused a fire to another vessel moored nearby was deemed capable of giving rise to liability in nuisance. *Harrison* v. *Southwark and Vauxhall Water Co.*[175] shows that an activity which could otherwise be characterised as a nuisance may be excused because of its temporary and useful nature. The defendants, in the exercise of their statutory powers, sank a shaft in land adjoining the plaintiff's house. The operation entailed a certain amount of noise and vibration in respect of which the plaintiff brought an action in nuisance. It was held that, as the disturbance was only temporary and for a lawful object, it was not a nuisance. These dicta, however, seem more relevant to nuisance involving interference with the use and enjoyment of land rather than with occurrences leading to physical injury where isolated events have resulted in liability. A long line of cases involving personal injury caused by falling masonry or other projections supports this view. And the same scepticism about 'continuity' or 'recurrence' as an essential element of nuisance liability is also appropriate in cases involving property damage, at any rate where there exists a dangerous state of affairs.

This is supported by *Midwood & Co. Ltd.* v. *Manchester Corporation*[176] where the electric mains installed by the defendants fused. For three hours inflammable gas had accumulated and an explosion occurred, setting fire to the plaintiff's adjoining premises. The defendants were held liable on account of the dangerous state of affairs. The event itself was serious, and the fact that it was isolated did not matter. The need for a potentially dangerous state of affairs was also stressed in *Spicer* v. *Smee*,[177] where on facts similar to those in the *Midwood* case, the court held that it was the defective wiring, rather than the resulting fire, that rendered the defendant liable. By contrast, in *Bolton* v. *Stone*[178] both the trial court and the Court of Appeal held that the isolated escape of a ball from a cricket field was not a nuisance because the evidence showed that there was no dangerous state of affairs. As Jenkins LJ said:[179] 'The gist of such a nuisance . . . is the causing or permitting of a state of affairs from which damage is likely to result.'

Perhaps, therefore, the position is that an isolated interference, unlikely to be repeated in the future, will not amount to a nuisance.[180] For if there were no physical interference there will be no question of damages under *St Helens Smelting Co.* v. *Tipping*,[181] and there will also be no point in seeking an injunction.[182] But if there is a state of affairs suggesting that the interference may not

---

[174] *The Times*, 6 Mar. 1996.   [175] [1891] 2 Ch. 409, esp. 413–14.

[176] [1905] 2 KB 597. See also Lawton J in *British Celanese* v. *A. J. Hunt Ltd.* [1969] 1 WLR 959, 969. According to Professor Fleming, *The Law of Torts* (8th edn., 1992), 420, n. 93: 'The origin of the idea that nuisance must be continuous or recurring apparently lay in the assize of nuisance, the object of which was abatement. This led the courts to regard nuisance as a condition capable of abatement after it was known to be injurious, but the modern trend is away from this requirement.'

[177] [1946] 1 All ER 489.   [178] [1951] AC 850.

[179] [1950] 1 KB 201, 208. The House of Lords eventually decided the case on negligence, nuisance having been dropped by the plaintiff.

[180] But it may give rise to liability in negligence under the rule of *Rylands* v. *Fletcher*.

[181] (1865) 11 HLC 642; 11 ER 1483.

[182] And if one is sought the court will be slow in granting it. *Swaine* v. *Great Northern Ry. Co.* (1846), 4 De G.J. & S. 211; 46 ER 899.

remain an isolated event, then an action in nuisance (and probably in negligence) may lie. Indeed, in the *Bolton* v. *Stone* situation the fact that the cricket balls had reached the public road only very exceptionally in the past indicated that there was no dangerous state of affairs to justify an action in nuisance.[183]

(ii) Sensitivity In determining whether an interference is reasonable or not the courts will refuse to take account of any abnormal sensitivity of the plaintiff himself or his property which renders an otherwise innocuous activity of the defendant harmful to him. As Lord Robertson said in *Eastern and South African Telegraph Co. Ltd.* v. *Cape Town Cos. Ltd*:[184] 'A man cannot increase the liabilities of his neighbour by applying his own property to special uses, whether for business or pleasure.'

In *Robinson* v. *Kilvert*[185] the landlord of certain premises let a floor to the plaintiff to be used as a paper warehouse, but retained the cellar immediately below. He himself manufactured products in the cellar that required the air to be hot and dry and this was achieved by means of special apparatus. The plaintiff sought an injunction to restrain the landlord from producing these conditions on the ground that the heat damaged his own paper. At the time of the contract the landlord did not know that the plaintiff intended to store a very sensitive kind of paper. The injunction was refused; and the result would, probably, accord with common sense given the facts of the case. In other instances, however, the balancing of competing interests may make it difficult to decide how to evaluate the plaintiff's particular sensitivity. Thus, in the American case of *Amphitheatres* v. *Portland Meadows*[186] the court refused to grant an injunction to the owners of an open-air cinema affected by the floodlights of their neighbours who operated a race track. Though the case cannot be taken as stating categorically that shedding light on the plaintiff's land can never be a nuisance, it does suggest that in that instance the court felt that the exceptionally sensitive use to which the plaintiff had put his land did not entitle him to protection against his neighbour putting his land to an equally legitimate use.

The sensitivity rule in these cases must not be misinterpreted so as to extend to the remoteness-of-damage phase of the inquiry. If a plaintiff succeeds, on grounds other than special sensitivity, in establishing an actionable nuisance, he will then be compensated even for damage that was the result of the particular sensitivity of his property. Thus, in *McKinnon Industries Ltd.* v. *Walker*[187] sulphur dioxide emitted from the defendant's factory damaged the plaintiff's commercially grown orchids. His claim for his damage was successful even though the defendants argued that the growing of these plants was a particularly sensitive horticultural activity.

---

[183] Contrast this case with the later and, in this respect, different cricket case of *Miller* v. *Jackson* [1977] QB 966, where the balls landed regularly like 'thunderbolts from the heavens' (per Cumming-Bruce LJ at 988).

[184] [1902] AC 381, 393. See also *Heath* v. *Brighton Corporation* (1908) 98 LT 718, 721.

[185] (1889) 41 Ch.D. 88, esp. at 97, per Lopes LJ.

[186] 198 P.2d 847.

[187] [1951] 3 DLR 577. The case is pre-*Wagon Mound*, but it is unlikely that a different result would be reached today.

(iii) Character of the Neighbourhood   In *St Helens*[188] it was held that the character of the neighbourhood was not to be taken into account in cases of physical damage to property, but might be a relevant factor in cases of interference with enjoyment or use. In *Sturges* v. *Bridgman*[189] Thesiger LJ said:

Whether anything is a nuisance or not is a question to be determined, not merely by an abstract consideration of the thing itself, but in reference to its circumstances; what would be a nuisance in *Belgrave Square* would not necessarily be so in *Bermondsey*; and where a locality is devoted to a particular trade or manufacture carried on by the traders and manufacturers in a particular established manner not constituting a public nuisance, Judges and juries would be justified in finding, and may be trusted to find, that the trade or manufacture so carried on in that locality is not a private or actionable wrong.

This 'locality' principle, however, should not be taken to mean that courts will automatically sanction an interference merely because it is typical in a particular area. *Rushmer* v. *Polsue & Alfieri Ltd.*[190] in fact shows that the locality principle will rarely be applied against a meritorious plaintiff. For in that case both the Court of Appeal and the House of Lords accepted the plaintiff's claim for an injunction to restrain the use of the defendant's printing-presses at night, even though the premises were in the printing area of London.

(iv) Fault   Is a defendant liable only if he knew or ought to have known of the cause of a nuisance; or could he be liable irrespective of the fault? This may well be the most vexed question in the tort of nuisance. Unfortunately, even though it appears to have attracted much academic attention it still appears to be an unresolved question, largely because one can cite judicial dicta which support both strict and fault liability. Thus, in *Goldman* v. *Hargrave* Lord Wilberforce said[191] that 'the tort of nuisance, uncertain in its boundary, may comprise a wide variety of situations, in some of which negligence plays no part, in others of which it is decisive'. The dictum would appear to confirm the view that some forms of nuisance are strict[192] while others are fault-based; but it does not clarify the *standard* of duty that is appropriate to the different kinds of situations.[193]

   To decide this important issue the traditional view favoured a distinction between the creator of a nuisance and one who continued or adopted an existing nuisance. In the first case the liability was said to be strict, while in the second it depended upon whether the defendant knew or ought to have known of the nuisance in the first place.

---

   [188] (1865) 11 HLC 642; 11 ER 1483.   [189] (1879) 11 Ch.D. 852, 865.
   [190] [1906] 1 Ch. 234, esp. Cozens-Hardy LJ at 250–7; affd. [1907] AC 121. The decision is criticised by Ogus and Richardson, op. cit. (Select Bibliography), 298, as economically inefficient.
   [191] *Goldman* v. *Hargrave* [1967] 1 AC 645, 657.
   [192] See the differing views of the Court of Appeal and House of Lords on this point in *Cambridge Water Co.* v. *Eastern Counties Leather plc,* [1994] 2 WLR 53. see Weir, 'The Polluter Must Pay—Regardless' [1993] *CLJ* 17.
   [193] Indeed the case adds, as already noted, a further dimension of uncertainty. For where the nuisance is the result of an act of nature (or, possibly, of a third party) the defendant's standard of care will be fixed by reference to his particular circumstances, i.e. it will be 'subjective'. On the other hand, where the nuisance develops out of a prima-facie lawful activity of the defendant's, then he will be liable only if he failed to foresee what the reasonable man would have foreseen in his position. Here, in other words, we are back to the 'objective' standard which normally prevails in negligence.

The idea that the liability of the creator of a nuisance was strict was encouraged by older dicta to the effect that carelessness was not necessary for liability. Many of these cases, however, were decided before the modern development of liability for negligence and should therefore be treated with caution.[194] Other dicta come from cases primarily concerned with availability of an injunction where considerations as to the nature of the defendant's duty are irrelevant. For example, in *Rapier* v. *London Tramways Co.*[195] Lindley LJ said: 'If I am sued for nuisance and nuisance is proved it is no defence to say and to prove that I have taken all reasonable care to prevent it.' The action was for an injunction for excessive noise and smell coming from the defendant's large and overcrowded stables. This dictum should be understood in context as suggesting that evidence that the defendant had done all he could was no reason for denying the plaintiff his injunction for an activity which did amount to a nuisance. But depriving the defendant of this defence does not imply that he was not aware of the likely consequences of the state of affairs existing on his land. As one writer has put it:[196] 'It is quite consistent to deny a defendant the defence that he has taken every precaution against an invasion yet insist that his liability depends on actual or presumed knowledge of its likelihood and indeed to hold him liable if he has such knowledge. Prevention must not be confused with detection.' A defendant who has to have actual or presumed knowledge of the likely consequences of his activity can hardly be said to be liable strictly. The important point is that it is unsafe to make the 'fault/strict liability' question depend on the 'creating/continuing a nuisance' dichotomy. For, as we said, it is *implicit* in most cases where the creator of the nuisance was held liable that he knew of the invasion. Only where it cannot be assumed that the creator of nuisance was aware of the consequences of his activity will the state of his knowledge be relevant. But this is equally true for him who creates the nuisance as it is for him who continues it.

The above position was recently reaffirmed by Lord Goff in the *Cambridge Water*[197] case. He there said: '. . . that in this field we must be on our guard, when considering liability for damages in nuisance, not to draw inappropriate conclusions from cases concerned only with a claim for an injunction. This is because, where an injunction is claimed, its purpose is to restrain further action by the defendant which may interfere with the plaintiff's enjoyment of his land, and *ex hypothesi* the defendant must be aware, if and when the injunction is granted, that such interference may be caused by the act which he is restrained from continuing. It follows that these cases provide no guidance on the question whether foreseeability of harm of the relevant type is a prerequisite of the recovery of damages for causing such harm to the plaintiff.'

---

[194] Eekelaar, op. cit. (Select Bibliography), regards *Humphries* v. *Cousins* (1877) 2 CPD 239 as a good example of this group of cases. Clerk and Lindsell on *Torts* (15th edn.), ch. 23, no. 18 thus warn that: 'It [is] important . . . to be guided by the more recent cases and to treat with caution statements concerning the standard of duty to be found in the older cases.'

[195] [1893] 2 Ch. 588, 600. Similar dicta can be found in *Midwood* v. *Manchester Corporation* [1905] 2 KB 597; *Charing Cross Electricity Supply Co.* v. *Hydraulic Power Co.* [1914] 3 KB 772.

[196] Eekelaar, op. cit., 197.

[197] *Cambridge Water Co.* v. *Eastern Leather plc* [1994] 2 WLR 53, 75.

In attempting to resolve the role that fault (and, more precisely, foreseeability) play in the tort of nuisance we must, nowadays, look at the wider picture of modern tort law. Thus, in our analysis we must include not only the tendency of the tort of negligence to encroach upon the domain of other torts but also the possibility of intermediate positions between the possible 'extremes' of strict and negligence liability. The current judicial tendency to treat the principle of 'reasonable user' as the main controlling mechanism for the tort of nuisance must also be born in mind. The combination of these considerations thus leads us easily into Lord Goff's most recent pronouncement on the subject that can be found in the *Cambridge Water* case.[198] There he said:

> . . . it is still the law that the fact that the defendant has taken all reasonable care will not of itself exonerate him from liability, the relevant control mechanism being found within the principle of reasonable user. But it by no means follows that the defendant should be held liable for damage of a type which he could not reasonably foresee. The development of the law of negligence in the past 60 years points strongly towards a requirement that such foreseeability should be a prerequisite of liability in damages for nuisance, as it is of liability in negligence.

Lord Goff was speaking here of cases where the nuisance was created by the defendant, himself, or by a person for whose actions he is responsible. When the nuisance is caused by natural causes or by the act of persons for whom the defendant is *not* responsible, the liability of the latter will be determined by cases such as *Sedleigh Denfield* v. *O'Callaghan* and *Goldman* v. *Hargraves*. The forward march of the tort of negligence (and its individual criteria) is thus discernable, making it increasingly difficult to deny that strict liability is, in this area of the law as well, in retreat.

(v) Malice   Another form of fault is malicious behaviour, and here the question is whether a lawful act becomes unlawful if done maliciously. In *Bradford Corporation* v. *Pickles*[199] the defendant, annoyed by the plaintiff's refusal to buy his land at the inflated price he demanded, maliciously prevented water percolating in unknown and undefined channels under his land from reaching the plaintiff's adjoining land. The abstraction of water as such was lawful and the House of Lords refused to hold that the defendant's act became unlawful because of his bad motive. This case has traditionally[200] been taken to give a negative answer to the question 'does a lawful act become unlawful because it is done with malice?' For, although it concerns water rights with regard to which special rules apply, it contains dicta of wider import that, with other subsequent and equally wide pronouncements, influenced the development of English law on this subject. On the other hand, it could be argued that the water which Pickles abstracted was only a *prospective* amenity as far as the plaintiffs were concerned; from which it might follow that a malicious interference with a *present* amenity could be actionable. Two cases lend some support to this contention.

---

[198] *Cambridge Water Co* v. *Eastern Leather plc* [1994] 2 WLR at 75.   [199] [1895] AC 587.

[200] But see Buckley, (below, Select Bibliography), 16. It must be remembered, of course, that the defendant in that case was not motivated by any spite against the people of Bradford, but was merely trying to obtain the highest possible price for his land. See also Fridman, (below, Select Bibliography).

In *Christie* v. *Davey*[201] the plaintiff, a music teacher, lived in a semi-detached house next to the defendant. The latter, annoyed by the plaintiff's piano lessons, started to produce loud noises designed to make life intolerable for the plaintiff. An injunction was granted. *Christie* v. *Davey* was followed in *Hollywood Silver Fox Farm Ltd.* v. *Emmett*[202] where the defendant, whose premises adjoined the plaintiff's silver-fox farm, maliciously procured his son to discharge guns on his own land as near as possible to the breeding pens so as to prevent the silver foxes from breeding and thus cause damage to the plaintiffs. He, too, was held liable.[203] This shows how the defendant's malice may characterise the interference with the plaintiff as unreasonable. For in the absence of malice this could well have been treated as a case of undue sensitivity.

These cases, however, do not establish any broad proposition that a plaintiff is entitled to success whenever a defendant maliciously interferes with an existing amenity of his.[204] For, as far as water rights are concerned at any rate, there is authority[205] to the effect that abstraction of water, even in the plaintiff's land (a present amenity), is still not actionable (though the particular case does not deal specifically with malicious abstraction). These unsatisfactory distinctions are the result of the piecemeal approach of the common law as well as the absence of a general and coherent theory of abuse of rights.

4. Who Can Sue and Who Can be Sued?

(A) Who Can Sue

The traditional position of English law has been that only those who have a legal interest in the land affected can sue in private nuisance.[206] An alternative way to put this is to say that only those with an exclusive possession of the land can bring an action in nuisance. In practice this means freehold owners,[207] but it also includes tenants in occupation,[208] licensees with exclusive possession,[209]

---

[201] [1893] 1 Ch. 316, esp. at 326–7, per North J.

[202] [1936] 2 KB 468, noted in 52 *LQR* 461, and 53 *LQR* 1–3. Another possible way of reconciling *Pickles'* case with *Christie's* and *Silver Fox* is to say that in the latter two cases the interference was capable of being regarded as a nuisance (even absent of malice) but that this was not so in *Pickles*. A slightly different explanation is offered by *Salmond and Heuston on the Law of Torts* (20th edn., 1992), 66.

[203] In *Hunter* v. *Canary Wharf Ltd.* [1997] 2 WLR 684 at 722, Lord Cooke said (obiter) that he did 'not think . . . that the view that malice is irrelevant would have wide acceptance today.'

[204] Lord Denning is one of the few judges who has consistently tried to build a more generalised theory of abuse of rights. For example, in *Secretary of State for Employment* v. *ASLEF (No. 2)* [1972] 2 All ER 949, 967, he said: 'There are many branches of our law when an act which would otherwise be lawful is rendered unlawful by the motive or object with which it is done.' This bold approach goes back to his dissenting judgment in *Chapman* v. *Honig* [1963] 2 QB 502, 510. Malice, of course, plays an important part in the law of defamation in the sense that when proved it can destroy certain defences.

[205] *Popplewell* v. *Hodkinson* (1869) LR 4 Exch. 248. For a discussion of the 'water cases' see Fleming, *The Law of Torts* (7th edn.), 400–1. See also *Stephens* v. *Anglian Water Authority* [1987] 3 All ER 379 (no action in negligence either).

[206] *Malone* v. *Laskey* [1907] 2 KB 141 is the decision most influential for this point of view; and it has been followed by *Nunn* v. *Parkes & Co.* (1924) 59 LJ 806; *Cunard* v. *Antifyre* [1933] 1 KB 551 (esp. at 557 per Talbot J); *Metropolitan Properties Ltd.* v. *Jones* [1939] 2 All ER 202 (esp. 205 per Goddard LJ).

[207] Co-owners can sue each other: *Hooper* v. *Rogers* [1975] Ch. 43, 51.

[208] *Jones* v. *Chappell* (1875) LR 20 Eq 539 (weekly tenant); *Burgess* v. *Woodstock* [1955] 4 DLR 615, at 619 (tenant at will). The same applies to tenants wishing to sue their landlord: *Vaughan* v. *Halifax Dartmouth Bridge Commission* (1961) 29 DLR (2d) 523.

[209] *Newcastle-under-Lyme* v. *Wolstanton Ltd.* [1947] Ch. 92, at 106–8.

reversioners if they can prove permanent injury to their interests,[210] and even a person who has no title to the land but has exclusive possession of it.[211] Mere visitors, on the other hand, cannot bring an action. At common law the same was true of the tenant's wife. So, when in *Malone* v. *Laskey*[212] vibrations on the defendant's premises caused the collapse of a cistern and consequent injury to the wife of the occupier of the adjoining premises, she was denied an action in nuisance because she had no proprietary or possessory interest in the land.[213] This rule has, nowadays, been modified by the Matrimonial Homes Act 1967 (consolidated by amendments in the Matrimonial Homes Act 1983) and the Family Law Act 1996, which give *spouses* a statutory right of occupation which, if properly registered, is enforceable against all the world.[214] But cohabiting partners, children, other relatives and guests cannot, in English law, bring an action for nuisance in the absence of exclusive possession as defined above.[215]

By re-confirming the validity of the above restrictive interpretation of the list of possible claimants, the majority decision of the House of Lords in *Hunter* v. *Canary Wharf Ltd.*[216] has gone against a number of Commonwealth judgments[217] as well as a bold attempt by a majority of our own Court of Appeal[218] to liberate our law from its past. None the less, the majority decisions embody a rigorous analysis of the existing case law (as well as the history of the tort) and in this sense provide interesting (for students if not for practitioners) insights into how differing judicial philosophies and techniques can affect the outcome of a dispute.

The examination—necessarily brief—of this aspect of this case must start by quoting an interesting observation by Lord Cooke. The learned Lord thus stressed, it is submitted correctly, that:

> . . . in logic more than one answer can be given [to this problem]. Logically it is possible to say that the right to sue for interference with the amenities of a home should be confined to those with propriatory interests . . . No less logically the right can be accorded to all who live in the home. *Which test should be adopted . . . is a question of the policy of the law. It is a question not capable of being answered by analysis alone. All that analysis can do is to explore the alternatives . . .* The reasons why I prefer the alternative [to the position adopted by the majority] . . . is that it gives better effect to widespread conceptions concerning the house and family.[219]

Lord Cooke would thus have been willing to respond to the appeal of textbook writers[220] to attempt 'a degree of modernasiation' in the law 'while freeing it

---

[210] *Colwell* v. *St. Pancras Borough Council* [1904] 1 Ch. 707, 713, per Joyce J. What if the nuisance merely interferes with use or enjoyment but does not affect the property? Older cases, e.g. *Simpson* v. *Savage* (1856) 1 CB NS 347; 140 ER 143, seemed to deny the reversioner any right of action, but *Hampstead & Suburban Properties Ltd.* v. *Diomedous* [1969] 1 Ch. 248 seemed to find this distinction unattractive.

[211] *Foster* v. *Warblington UDC* [1906] 1 KB 648.

[212] [1907] 2 KB 141 (not overruled on this point by *Billings AC & Sons* v. *Riden* [1958] AC 240, 254, 264).

[213] Her action in negligence also failed though, nowadays, it would succeed.

[214] For fuller details, Kodilinye, op. cit. (Select Bibliography). See, also, *Hunter* v. *Canary Wharf Ltd.* [1997] 2 WLR 684 at 696 (per Lord Goff) and at 710 (per Lord Hoffmann).

[215] This is now beyond dispute as a result of the *Hunter* decision.   [216] [1997] 2 WLR 684.

[217] E.g. *Motherwell* v. *Motherwell* (1976) 73 DLR 3rd 62; *Devon Lumber Co. Ltd.* v. *MacNeil* (1987) 45 DLR 4th, 300.

[218] In *Khorasandjian* v. *Bush* [1993] QB 727.   [219] Ibid., 719. Emphasis added.

[220] Led by Clerk and Lindsell, *On Torts*, (17th edn., 1995), ss. 910 and 911.

from undue reliance upon the technicalities of land law.' One suspects that such an approach to case-law development would have appealed to judges such as Lord Denning or pioneering jurists such as Professor John Fleming of the Berkeley Law School. But it was doomed to failure in the current climate that prevails in our highest court where, for instance, Lord Hoffmann boldly stated that 'the development of the common law should be rational and coherent. It should not distort its principles and create anomalies merely as an expedient to fill a gap.'[221] Once this is accepted as the cornerstone of the philosophy of the majority, the resolution of the dispute acquires a certain legalistic tone. Thus, the question (implicitly) becomes what technical arguments can be found in favour of the status quo. Between them, the majority had little difficulty in finding three; and one cannot deny their force (once one accepts the basic premise that one is not free to break free from the existing technicalities of land law). Thus, Lord Goff argued that the current state of the law could claim 'certainty' and 'efficiency' on its side.[222] To these two points one must add Lord Hoffmann's analysis of Lord Westbury's views discussed above. For once one accepts the view that in his *St Helen's* judgment Lord Westbury did not intend to create two separate torts (one dealing with material interference and one with interference with enjoyment), it follows logically and inexorably that only those with an interest in land can sue. The decision in *Hunter* thus does more than tackle, for the time being at least, a particular problem area of the law in nuisance: it gives us some revealing insights into the views our judges have about the interplay of interpretation and development of the law.

To return to more prosaic matters. What is the legal position if the damage occurred before the plaintiff acquired an interest in the property? Prima facie, the answer should be that the plaintiff would have no remedy unless he proved that the damage resulted from a continuing nuisance; in which case he could recover whether the loss began before or after his acquisition of the premises. This proposition is supported and illustrated by *Masters* v. *Brent London Borough Council*,[223] where the plaintiff's father was the leasehold owner of premises which developed cracks because of the encroaching roots of a line of trees planted by the defendant local council in the vicinity of his house. Unable to meet the cost of repairs, the plaintiff's father sold the premises to him in order to enable him to raise a mortgage and, *inter alia*, meet the repair costs with the mortgage money. This, the plaintiff did and then sued the local authority, which unsuccessfully argued that since the damage had occurred before the plaintiff had acquired an interest in the premises, it should not be compensated.

As stated, nuisance liability primarily protects interests in land, though damages in respect of chattels on the land can also be recovered.[224] Until not long ago it would have also been possible to argue that personal injury, incidentally

---

[221] Ibid., 709. Echoes, here, of Lord Mustill's dissent in *White* v. *Jones* [1995] 2 AC 207.   [222] Ibid., 696.
[223] [1978] QB 841. The case, however, has atypical facts in so far as it involved a sale by one member of a family to another, which may have been accompanied by a discount in the purchase price. For without such a discount the hazards of litigation would make such a transaction dubious, to say the least.
[224] *Halsey* v. *Esso Petroleum Co. Ltd.* [1961] 1 WLR 683.

suffered by the occupier, might also be compensatable.[225] But the current trend of House of Lords decisions suggest that such claims should be entertained under our 'fully developed law of negligence'[226] and are thus unlikely to fair well if pleaded in nuisance. Disturbance of health, comfort, and enjoyment might, likewise, be actionable in those nuisances that come under the heading of 'interferences with enjoyment and use'. As Professor Fleming has remarked,[227] '. . . certain sophisticated interests of personality which, standing alone, receive only limited protection by our law, are most amply vindicated if asserted in the title of the free use and enjoyment of land, where such factors as personal taste and sensibilities are accorded fuller protection'. Yet, once again, one must remind the reader of the current hostile climate towards such expanding views. This may explain the disapproval shown towards the majority view in *Khorasandjian* v. *Bush*[228] which had enabled a plaintiff to rely on the tort of nuisance in order to obtain redress for persistent telephone harassment by the defendant.[229]

(B) Who Can be Sued

In most private nuisances the activity complained of will emanate from the defendant's land and the person who will be sued is its owner or occupier. We have seen that in rare cases the cause of the interference may be a floating barge,[230] could occur on the public highway,[231] or could emanate from the sea,[232] neither of the last two being in private ownership. That an action will lie in such cases is not in dispute; but whether it is to be dubbed private or public nuisance seems to be less settled.[233] One commentator has argued that it would be 'unduly restrictive and illogical to limit the scope of private nuisance to disputes between neighbouring landowners'.[234] In such cases, however, the person sued is clearly the *creator* of the nuisance, and that seems sufficient to establish his liability subject, of course, to the other requirements of liability being satisfied.

[225] There was no English case that had allowed recovery of damages for personal injuries in an action of *private* nuisance, though the Canadian case of *Devon Lumber Co. Ltd.* v. *MacNeill* (1988) 45 DLR 4th 300 did. The recovery of pure economic loss by means of an action in *private* nuisance also seems uncertain, especially in these days when this kind of loss receives short shrift in the context of the tort of negligence. Yet there was some (slender) authority to support recovery. See *British Celanese Ltd.* v. *A. H. Hunt Ltd.* [1969] 1 WLR 959; *Ryeford Homes Ltd.* v. *Sevenoaks District Council* (1989) 16 Con. LR 75.

[226] *Hunter* v. *Canary Wharf Ltd.* [1997] 2 WLR 684, 695.   [227] *Torts* (8th edn., 1992), 417.

[228] [1993] QB 727.

[229] That defect in our law has now been cured by the enactment of the Protection from Harassment Act 1997 (see Chapter 4, above). The potential of the *Khorasandjian* judgment goes beyond what is now covered by the 1977 Act but its continued vitality must be in doubt even though in *Hunter* Lord Hoffmann was careful not to say that the case was 'wrongly decided' (n. 226 above, at 709); and Lord Cooke was not against it at all: ibid., at 719.

[230] *Crown River Cruises Ltd.* v. *Kimbolton Fireworks Ltd.*, *The Times*, 6 Mar. 1996.

[231] E.g. *Midwood & Co. Ltd.* v. *Manchester Corporation* [1905] 2 KB 597. For Canadian authorities, see McLaren, 'The Common Law Nuisance Actions' (Select Bibliography), 505, 519, n. 64.

[232] *Southport Corp.* v. *Esso Petroleum Co. Ltd.* [1953] 3 WLR 773 (affd. in the House of Lords [1956] AC 218).

[233] Cf. Devlin J's views in the *Southport* case [1953] 3 WLR 773, 776, with Denning LJ in the Court of Appeal [1954] 2 QB 182, 196–7. See also *Hubbard* v. *Pitt* [1976] QB 142.

[234] Buckley, op. cit. (Select Bibliography), 5.

Where the occupier of the land is held liable for his own conduct, the situation is straightforward. But liability may also attach to the occupier for his failure to rectify the unreasonable conduct or state of affairs created by his predecessor, or even a trespasser, provided that he knew or ought to have known of it; provided, in other words, he knowingly or negligently *continued* the nuisance. In *Sedleigh-Denfield* v. *O'Callaghan*,[235] for example, the plaintiff's field was flooded as a result of the blockage of the drainage system in the defendant's land by a trespasser. The defendants were liable, for they were aware, or ought to have become aware through one of their servants, of the possibility of flooding, and had done nothing to prevent it. Similarly, with regard to nuisance created by third parties after the defendant's occupation has begun, he will be liable if he knew or ought to have known of it, or if he adopted it, for example, by making use of it. Generally speaking, however, failure to remedy an inherited state of affairs tends to be judged more leniently and the occupier's circumstances and resources may be taken into account. As Lord Wilberforce said in *Goldman* v. *Hargrave*:[236]

the law must take account of the fact that the occupier on whom the duty is cast has, ex hypothesi, had this hazard thrust upon him through no seeking or fault of his own. His interest and his resources, whether physical or material, may be of very modest character either in relation to the magnitude of the hazard, or as compared with those of his threatened neighbour. A rule that required of him in such unsought circumstances in his neighbour's interest a physical effort of which he is not capable, or an excessive expenditure of money, would be unenforceable or unjust.

An occupier is, of course, liable for nuisance caused by his servants committed in the course of their employment; but his possible liability for independent contractors requires separate consideration. The general rule is that in the absence of carelessness in choosing a competent independent contractor, the employer is not liable for a contractor. Yet in nuisance there seems to be a number of exceptions,[237] which is not surprising, since occupiers may be liable even for the acts of strangers. The precise extent of this wider liability is not clear. In *Bower* v. *Peate*[238] Cockburn LJ proclaimed that anyone who orders work to be done, the natural consequences of which are likely to be injurious, cannot escape liability by relying on someone else to do what is necessary to avoid harm. *Bower* v. *Peate* was a case of withdrawal of support from the plaintiff's adjoining premises. It could thus be argued[239] that Cockburn LJ's dictum is too wide and should be restricted to withdrawal of support or, at least, to nuisance which produces dangers to property rather than occasional discomfort and annoyance to the plaintiff. Withdrawal of support cases, however, are not the only instances of the liability of occupier for the torts of independent contractors. Moreover, any restriction of this wider liability to nuisances affecting materially the plaintiff's property would be incompatible with *Matania* v.

---

[235] [1940] AC 880.   [236] [1967] 1 AC 645, 663.
[237] *Spicer* v. *Smee* [1946] 1 All ER 489, 495, per Atkinson LJ 2.
[238] (1876) 1 QBD 321, 326.
[239] See e.g. *Hughes* v. *Percival* (1883) 8 App. Cas. 443, 447 (per Lord Blackburn).

National Provincial Bank Ltd.,[240] where the defendants were held liable for the discomfort and annoyance caused to the plaintiff as a result of dust and noise being produced by independent contractors working in the defendants' flat. The better view may be that an occupier of land is under a so-called non-delegable duty, which perhaps also gives the clue to the possible escape from liability. For a non-delegable duty does not impose strict liability, but merely a duty to ensure that care is taken.[241] So, if the occupier can show that neither he nor his independent contractor was at fault, he is not liable. There is also Scottish authority[242] to support the view that an occupier may also avoid liability if he can show that his independent contractor had exclusive control of the premises at the time of the occurrence of the nuisance.

Finally, the liability in nuisance of landlords and tenants towards (a) neighbours and (b) passers-by creates difficulties. Generally it is the occupier (invariably the tenant[243]) who is liable in nuisance—in public nuisance, if injury or damage is sustained by a passer-by on the street (discussed in Section 7); and in private nuisance, if injury is sustained by a neighbouring occupier. But to this rule there are exceptions that render the landlord liable, even though he is not the occupier. This happens if (a) he had authorised the nuisance;[244] (b) he had let the premises knowing of the nuisance;[245] (c) he ought to have known of the nuisance before he let the premises;[246] (d) he is under a duty to repair;[247] (e) though not bound to repair, he has expressly reserved the right to enter and inspect the premises;[248] and (f) he has an implied right to enter and inspect.[249] It should be noted, however, that before the enactment of section 4(1) of the Defective Premises Act 1972 the landlord's liability in nuisance extended only to occupiers of adjoining premises and not to members of their families and/or their lawful visitors.[250] These persons, however, now receive the same protection as the occupier and, indeed, any other reasonably foreseeable plaintiff.

5. Defences

The following are good defences:

(i) Inevitable accident is a defence in cases where negligence is essential to liability. Where negligence is not essential, only act of God or secret opera-

---

[240] [1936] 2 All ER 633.

[241] See *The Pass of Ballater* [1942] P. 112, 117 (per Langton J); *Morris* v. *C. W. Martin & Sons Ltd.* [1966] 1 QB 716, 725 (per Lord Denning MR).

[242] *Gourock Ropework Co.* v. *Greenock Corp.*, 1966 SLT 125, where it is said that there was no difference in this respect with English law.

[243] Lack of effective control is, invariably, the reason why landlords are not held liable. Thus, in *Habinteg Housing Association* v. *James* (1995) 27 H.L.R. 299, the landlord—a housing association—were not held liable to one of their tenants for a cockroach infestation which may have started in another part of the estate owned by the association.

[244] *Harris* v. *James* (1876) 45 LJQB 545; *Sampson* v. *Hodson-Pressinger* [1981] 3 All ER 710, noted by M. Owen in [1982] *CLJ* 38.

[245] *Roswell* v. *Prior* (1701), 12 Mod. Rep. 635; 88 ER 1570. This includes where it is the *ordinary and necessary consequences* of the permitted act or perhaps even where the nuisance is the foreseeable consequence: *Tetley* v. *Chitty* [1986] 1 All ER 663 (noise from go-karting track leased by local authority) for this purpose.

[246] *Brew Bros. Ltd.* v. *Snax (Ross) Ltd.* [1970] 1 QB 612, 636, per Sachs LJ; 644, per Phillimore LJ.

[247] *Payne* v. *Rogers* (1749) 2 H.BL. 350; 126 ER 590.   [248] *Wilchick* v. *Marks and Silverstone* [1934] 2 KB 56.

[249] *Mint* v. *Good* [1951] 1 KB 517.   [250] E.g. *Malone* v. *Laskey* [1907] 2 KB 141.

tions of nature will suffice. The practical significance of this defence is minimal.[251]

(*ii*) Act of trespasser will not, as already stated, be a defence. The occupier will only be liable if he knowingly or negligently continued the nuisance.[252]

(*iii*) Ignorance of the state of affairs will be a defence unless it is due to a failure to use reasonable diligence to know of it. In *Ilford Urban District Council* v. *Beal*[253] the defendant built a wall on her land eight or nine feet above a sewer belonging to the plaintiff, which cracked as a result. She was held not liable in negligence or even in nuisance, because she was unaware of the existence of the sewer and could not reasonably have been expected to know of it.

(*iv*) Prescription applies to (private) nuisances which, if legalised, could be the subject of servitudes. Time starts to run not when the defendant begins his activity, but when it begins to interfere with the plaintiff. This follows from the fact that the gist of nuisance is the result to the plaintiff not the activity of the defendant. Thus, in *Sturges* v. *Bridgman*[254] the defendant's premises adjoined those of the plaintiff, a medical practitioner. For over twenty years the defendant had been using noisy machinery, which had not interfered with the plaintiff's use of his land until the latter built a consulting room at the bottom of his garden near the defendant's machinery and then complained of the noise. Prescription was pleaded as a defence but failed, since the nuisance commenced only when the new building was erected, since before then there was no right of action. This defence rarely succeeds in practice.

(*v*) Contributory negligence could be a defence except, possibly, when the consequence was intended by the defendant. Dicta in *Trevett* v. *Lee*[255] (a case of public nuisance) appear to support this. However, authority is scanty, which seems to suggest that the practical significance of this defence is minimal,[256] even though section 14(5) of the Contributory Negligence Act 1945 seems to be clear about the availability of the defence.

---

[251] In *Lord Chesham* v. *Chesham UDC* (1935) 79 SJ 453, the defence was pleaded but rejected. Where the activity is actionable both as a nuisance and under *Rylands* v. *Fletcher* the defence may succeed, e.g. *Nichols* v. *Marsland* (1876) 2 Ex. D. 1.

[252] *Sedleigh-Denfield* v. *O'Callaghan* [1940] AC 880, 897; *Page Motors Ltd.* v. *Epsom and Ewell Borough Council* (1982) 80 LGR 337.

[253] [1925] 1 KB 671. Cf. *Humphries* v. *Cousins* (1877) 2 CPD 239; *National Coal Board* v. *Evans* (*J. E.*) & *Co.* (*Cardiff*) *Ltd.* [1951] 2 KB 861.

[254] (1879) 11 Ch. D. 852. Cf. *Harvey* v. *Walters* (1873) L.R. 8 C.P. 162 (right to discharge water from eaves on adjoining land); *Hulley* v. *Silversprings Bleaching Co.* [1922] 2 Ch. 268 (acquired right to pollute watercourse); *Jones* v. *Pritchard* [1908] 1 Ch. 630 (emission of smoke). Prescriptive rights cannot, apparently, be acquired for the creation of noise, smell, or for the encroachment of branches and roots: *Lemmon* v. *Webb* [1894] 3 Ch. 1; [1895] AC 1.

[255] [1955] 1 WLR 113. See also *Caswell* v. *Powell Duffryn Associated Collieries Ltd.* [1940] AC 152, 165 (per Lord Atkin).

[256] Winfield in [1930–2] *CLJ* 189, 200, maintained that the defence is never available in nuisance; Williams, *Joint Torts* (1951), 203–5, believes the opposite; *Salmond and Heuston on the Law of Torts* (20th edn.), 75, states that it would be unlikely for the defence to succeed while Fleming, *The Law of Torts* (8th edn., 1992), 442–3, adopts a more subtle approach.

(vi) Statutory authority.[257] The general principles of this defence will be discussed later. For the present, suffice it to say that in an action for nuisance statutory authorisation will be a defence only if it can be shown that the interference with the plaintiff's rights was permitted by express wording in the statute or by necessary implication. It was held in *Metropolitan Asylum District Managers* v. *Hill*[258] that authority to purchase land and erect buildings for the poor and sick could not be regarded as authorisation to site a smallpox hospital in an area so as to interfere with adjoining landowners. The argument that, because there was authority to erect a smallpox hospital, it could be erected anywhere was tantamount to saying that the statute gave a licence to commit any nuisance by means of the hospital, which was clearly unacceptable.

The whole question of statutory authorisation as a defence to nuisance was considered by the House of Lords in *Allen* v. *Gulf Oil Refining Ltd.*,[259] the facts of which were as follows. In 1965 Gulf Oil secured a private Act of Parliament, which stated in its preamble that 'because of increasing public demand for the company's products in the UK . . . it was essential that further facilities for the importation of crude oil and petroleum products and for their refinement should be made available'. Strangely, though the Act contained specific provisions relating to the acquisition of the necessary land by Gulf Oil, and the construction of a refinery and certain subsidiary works, it contained no express authority for the use and operation of the refinery once it had been built. Their Lordships unanimously took the view that the essential problem was one of statutory construction. They also agreed with Lord Dunedin in *Corporation of Manchester* v. *Farnworth*,[260] where he said: 'When Parliament has authorised a certain thing to be made or done in a certain place, there can be no action for nuisance caused by the making or doing of that thing if the nuisance is the inevitable result of the making or doing so authorised. The onus of proving that the result is inevitable is on those who wish to escape liability for nuisance . . .' Agreement, however, ended here. Lord Keith was inclined to construe the Act in accordance with the *contra proferentum* rule, i.e. against the party offering a document in support of his case,[261] and took the view that the purpose of the Act was merely to confer powers of compulsory purchase of land and not to authorise the operation of a refinery. The rest thought otherwise. True, the Act touched but lightly on the matter of operation and use of the refinery; but they felt that it was unlikely that Parliament merely intended to authorise the acquisition of land and the construction of certain works and not their operation as well. As Lord Diplock put it:[262] 'Parliament can hardly be supposed to have intended the refinery to be nothing more than a visual adornment to the land-

---

[257] Linden, 'Strict Liability, Nuisance and Legislative Authorization', 4 *Osgoode Hall LJ* 196 (1966). See, generally, Chapter 3, Section 5(5) above.

[258] (1881) 6 App. Cas. 193.

[259] [1981] AC 1001. But if a nuisance is created through the exercise of statutory powers the creator will be liable if he exercised the powers in a negligent manner: see *Tate and Lyle* v. *Greater London Council* [1983] 2 AC 509. Useful guidelines can be found in *Fellowes* v. *Rother District Council* [1983] 1 All ER 513 895. These points are also discussed below in Chapter 8, Section 1.

[260] [1930] AC 171, 183.   [261] [1981] AC 1001, 1020.   [262] Ibid., at 1014.

scape in an area of natural beauty. Clearly the intention of Parliament was that the refinery was to be operated as such . . .' Lord Wilberforce took a similar view. If the plaintiff was granted an injunction, he reasoned, this would mean that the refinery could not be operated, thereby leaving Gulf Oil as owners of land that they had compulsorily acquired but could not use.[263]

Such a result seemed so absurd that the majority felt they had to accept (a) that the Act, by necessary implication, not only authorised the building of the refinery, but also its operation and use, and (b) that it thereby bestowed immunity on Gulf Oil from any 'non-negligent' interferences. Point (a) is an understandable and desirable reading of the wording of the enabling Act, but (b) is more open to doubt, especially if it leads to a large number of innocent and detrimentally affected citizens being left without legal redress. The difficulty which prevented the majority from separating (a) and (b) was the belief that if liability for a 'non-negligent' interference were accepted, a plaintiff would then be more or less 'entitled' to an injunction. This would lead to the closing of the refinery—a result that their Lordships considered to be undesirable. The reasons for this reluctance of the courts to rely on the power given by Lord Cairns's Act (now section 50 of the Supreme Court Act 1981) and to 'downgrade the plaintiff's remedy from an injunction to mere damages'[264] will be discussed presently. Here suffice it to stress the fear of English courts that such a solution might amount to buying a licence to continue with an interfering activity. Quite apart from the fact that 'interference' in the context of nuisance is a relative concept, the point is whether English law should be more willing, in appropriate circumstances, to award compensation for damage caused even by a lawful activity. As things stand at the moment this can, apparently, only be done by express statutory authority. The Land Compensation Act 1973, section 1, offers an apt example. It provides *inter alia* for compensation to be paid for the depreciation in the value of land by physical factors caused by 'public works'.[265] Gulf Oil's works could not be described as 'public works', though they indirectly benefited the public. Would it not be possible, therefore, to use such enactments by way of analogy so as to provide compensation for deserving plaintiffs without jeopardising the useful activities of certain defendants? If English law wishes to remain committed to the principle that, in the absence of express authorisation, compensation for damage caused through lawful conduct cannot be paid, then it should be prepared to find some way in which to widen the ambit of existing enactments to cover cases such as this.

The following are ineffectual as defences:

(i) It is no defence that the plaintiff came to the nuisance.[266] This has been recently confirmed by a majority of the Court of Appeal in *Miller* v. *Jackson*,[267] when Geoffrey Lane LJ stated: 'It is no answer to a claim in nuisance for the defendant to show that the plaintiff brought the trouble on his own head by building or coming to live in a house so close to the

---

[263] Ibid., at 1013.
[264] Jolowicz [1981] *CLJ* 226, 228–9.
[265] On this, and related matters, see Craig, 'Compensation in Public Law' (1980) 96 *LQR* 413.
[266] *Bliss* v. *Hall* (1838) 4 Bing. NC 183; 132 ER 758; *Sturges* v. *Bridgman* (1879), 11 Ch. D. 852.
[267] [1977] QB 966, 987.

defendant's premises that he would inevitably be affected by the defendant's activities where no one had been affected previously.' Lord Denning MR, however, remained unimpressed. The Millers, he felt, came to the nuisance with their eyes open, they had bought a house with a pleasant view of a green and the accompanying disadvantage of being hit occasionally by a cricket ball. There are echoes here of the defence of *volenti* (consent), which the courts have recently resurrected from the quiescence into which the defence of contributory negligence had reduced it.[268] However, this kind of reasoning runs counter to the decision in *Sturges* v. *Bridgman*, which Lord Denning regarded as no longer binding. But authority cannot just be ignored, and some explanation as to why it is not binding should be forthcoming. So the position is that *Sturges* v. *Bridgman* is by no means dead and Lord Denning's view must remain, at the very least, debatable.

(ii) It is also no defence that the defendant's activity is a useful one. In *Adams* v. *Ursell*[269] the defendant was prevented from maintaining a fried-fish shop in a fashionable neighbourhood, even though it was argued on his behalf that to do so would cause hardship both to him and to the poorer inhabitants.

(iii) It is not a valid defence to allege and prove that the nuisance resulted from the *combined acts* of different persons, and that the act of the defendant alone was not a nuisance.[270]

(iv) Planning permission. Unlike statutory authorisation, the granting of planning permission does not provide a defence to committing a nuisance—hence the inclusion of this topic in this section. But in *Gillingham Borough Council* v. *Medway (Chatham) Dock Company Ltd.* a local authority was denied an injunction that it sought against an operator of a large port to which they had previously granted planning permission. In that case, Buckley J stated that '. . . where planning consent is given for a development or change of use, the question of nuisance will thereafter fall to be decided by reference to a neighbourhood with that development or use *and not as it was previously*.'[271] The italicised words give the impression that the implementation of planning permission could affect the standard of what would be a nuisance by changing the nature of the locality. In the subsequent case of *Wheeler* v. *J. J. Saunders*[272] the court reaffirmed the general view about planning permission *not* amounting to a defence in nuisance. But the court also doubted whether the *Gillingham* view (about the effect that the granting of consent could have on the neighbourhood) could apply to planning permissions that, as in the instant case, merely involved an intensification of an existing use.[273] This (real or apparent) back-peddling from the *Gillingham* position has had the unfortunate effect of establishing two types of planning permission—those which can effect the locality and those which cannot—without providing clear criteria for distinguishing the one type from

---

[268] E.g. *Cummings* v. *Granger* [1977] QB 397; *Murphy* v. *Culbane* [1977] QB 94.
[269] [1913] 1 Ch. 269.
[270] *Thorpe* v. *Brumfit* (1873) LR 8 Ch 650, 656 (per James LJ); *Blair and Sumner* v. *Deakin* (1887) 57 LT 522.
[271] [1993] QB 343 at 361. Emphasis added.   [272] [1995] 2 All ER 697.
[273] In *Wheeler* the planning permission had enabled the defendant to increase the number of pigs which he held on his farm.

the other. The confusing case law can be explained (if not justified) by dis-covering the policy concerns that lie behind these decisions. Thus, as a lead-ing environmental practitioner has observed, there is an unexpressed public policy behind these disputes: 'If we have a complete system of plan-ning law, under which decisions are taken to allow or promote develop-ments which will have an important regenerative effect, ought a limited number of affected people be able to stop them by claiming injunctions for nuisance?'[274] If our courts had a more flexible approach towards nuisance, and were more readily willing to grant damages in lieu of injunctions in cases of proven nuisances, these dilemmas might be reduced if not totally avoided. But, as will be stated in the next section, our courts have not yet taken this bull by the horns.

6. Remedies

A plaintiff in a nuisance action has a choice between three remedies: damages, injunction, and a limited form of self-help known as 'abatement'. Damages are discussed in Chapter 8. The general requirements for an injunction will also be discussed there, but it is necessary to make a few remarks here concerning injunctions in the context of nuisance.

(A) INJUNCTION[275]

More often than not a plaintiff will be anxious to stop a defendant from con-tinuing his activity. This interest of the plaintiff will generally be matched by a corresponding willingness on the part of the defendant to pay damages (if found guilty of nuisance) rather than give up his activity. Injunctions, being dis-cretionary remedies, are well suited to balance these conflicting interests. This balancing operation, however, gives rise in practice to considerable difficulties and uncertainties. The availability of an injunction in the case of an established nuisance was discussed in *Miller* v. *Jackson*[276] and *Kennaway* v. *Thompson*,[277] to which we now turn.

Assuming that the majority in *Miller* v. *Jackson* was right on the issue of liabil-ity, the question that then had to be determined was whether the plaintiff should be granted an injunction. For an affirmative answer to the issue of lia-bility does not automatically decide the question of whether or not to grant an injunction. Leaving aside Geoffrey Lane LJ's judgment as being in this respect a dissenting judgment, Cumming-Bruce LJ thought an injunction should be refused despite the defendant's liability, and Lord Denning MR would have thought likewise had he held the defendants liable, which he did not. Two fac-tors influenced them: first, the defendants' actions were reasonable and even beneficial; and secondly the plaintiff had bought her house with her eyes open and had 'come to' the nuisance. Though Cumming-Bruce LJ was not prepared

---

[274] Tromans [1995] *CLJ* 494, at 496.
[275] For further details see Buckley, op. cit. (Select Bibliography), 118 ff.; Jolowicz, 'Damages in Equity—A Study of Lord Cairns' Act' [1975] *CLJ* 224; Markesinis and Tettenborn, and Tromans, (below, Select Bibliography).
[276] [1977] QB 966.   [277] [1981] 1 QB 88.

to go along with Lord Denning in saying that this negated liability altogether, he was nevertheless prepared to let it militate against the grant of an injunction.[278]

In *Kennaway* v. *Thompson*[279] the plaintiff, who did not come to the nuisance, was disturbed in her lakeside home by powerboat racing organised by the defendants. The defendants rightly admitted liability in nuisance, but contested the plaintiff's claim to an injunction, saying that the activities were just as beneficial as in *Miller* v. *Jackson* and therefore ought not to be restrained. This time Lawton LJ for the Court of Appeal discounted the idea of allowing the merits, social or otherwise, of the defendants' conduct to stand in the way of the plaintiff's right to an injunction. Even meritorious defendants, he argued, could be restrained from carrying on activities that substantially invaded other people's right to peace and quiet.

Three points arise out of these two cases. First, the plaintiff's case in *Kennaway* was, it could be argued, weaker than in *Miller* because she had suffered no 'sensible material injury' to her property; only her enjoyment of it had been interfered with. That the plaintiff succeeded in *Kennaway* but not in *Miller* is thus all the more remarkable.

Secondly, Lawton LJ in *Kennaway* did not actually say that the court in *Miller* had been wrong to refuse the plaintiff his injunction. Yet his decision is not easily reconcilable with the first ground in *Miller* v. *Jackson* that the playing of cricket is a good thing and ought not to be stopped. Does this mean that the other ground, namely that plaintiffs who come to nuisances should be refused injunctions at the court's discretion, is sound and justifies that decision on its facts?[280] It is submitted that, although *Sturges* v. *Bridgman*[281] may be hard to justify today, courts should not mitigate, or even subvert entirely, the effects of established cases which they dislike by way of equitable discretion: which was the effect of *Miller* v. *Jackson*. If such cases are no longer to be followed, this should be done by forthright judicial reversal or by legislation.[282]

Thirdly, a more serious point about *Kennaway* is that behind the statement that the grant of an injunction is at the discretion of the court there lurk some fairly rigid rules governing even the exercise of discretion. Thus, in *Shelfer* v. *City of London Electric Lighting Co.*[283] A. L. Smith LJ, at the instance of a publican, restrained the defendant company from causing excessive vibration, even though the result was to deprive many Londoners of a desirable service, namely the provision of electricity. To a claim by the defendant that the plaintiff should be limited to damages in lieu of an injunction under Lord Cairns's Act, his Lordship stated that only in exceptional circumstances should a plaintiff who

---

[278] Another possibility considered was granting an injunction but postponing its operation for a year to give the defendants time to rectify the situation.

[279] [1981] QB 88.

[280] In granting an injunction in *Tetley* v. *Chitty* [1986] 1 All ER 663, 675 McNeill J took account of the fact that the plaintiff had lived there for some time before the nuisance began.

[281] (1879) 11 Ch. D. 852.

[282] Stamp J has expressed doubts on just this use of equitable discretion: see his comments in *Woollerton & Wilson Ltd.* v. *Costain Ltd.* [1970] 1 WLR 411, 413, and Russell LJ in *Charrington* v. *Simons & Co. Ltd.* [1971] 1 WLR 598, 602.

[283] [1895] 1 Ch. 287.

proved a tangible invasion of his rights be deprived of an injunction to protect them. However beneficial a defendant's activity, if it were a nuisance, courts would not let him 'buy the right to commit it'. Later decisions confirmed this attitude. In *Cowper* v. *Laidler*,[284] for instance, a plaintiff who bought property with its appurtenant right to light as a pure speculation in order to extract as much money as possible from the defendant for the release of his rights when the latter wanted to redevelop his own neighbouring land, was held entitled to an injunction to prevent the redevelopment. Similarly, the plaintiff in *Marriott* v. *East Grinstead Gas and Water Co.*[285] was able to restrain the defendants from passing their pipes under his land, even though the general gain from doing so was considerable and the plaintiff's resulting prejudice nil. The principle was further emphasised by the Court of Appeal in *Pride of Derby and Derbyshire Angling Association Ltd.* v. *British Celanese Ltd.*,[286] where the court granted an injunction that interfered drastically with the defendant's disposal of municipal sewage by preventing its discharge directly into the River Derwent.

On the other hand, the courts have at times departed from this attitude, especially where adherence to it would benefit unreasonable and unmeritorious plaintiffs. Thus, in *Llandudno Urban District Council* v. *Woods*[287] a local authority failed to restrain an undoubted, though technical, trespass on its land; and in a similar case, *Behrens* v. *Richards*,[288] the owner of a Cornwall cliff-top was denied an injunction to prevent its long-standing use by walkers.

Admittedly, when confronted with *Shelfer*'s case, a court can generally find special circumstances to justify departing from it; as, indeed, Cumming-Bruce LJ did in *Miller* v. *Jackson*. But it could be argued that that kind of development is undesirable. The point about *Shelfer* is that a court's discretion to refuse an injunction is highly circumscribed, and is not to be exercised merely because of the merits of a case. The importance of *Kennaway* is that it reiterated the *Shelfer* principle in the face of recent tendencies to undermine it in favour of greater discretion. Of course, there are cases where the effects of granting an injunction would be so extreme or catastrophic that no one would advocate it, for instance, closing a major industry. So far such situations have been relatively few, and courts have developed various means to avoid such results. Thus, the operation of the injunction may be suspended for a period of time (and even extended further) in order to give the defendant the chance of avoiding or minimising the effects of the nuisance.[289] Another way is to qualify the injunction, for example, by limiting its operation to a certain time.[290] Such solutions may not go far enough; but arguably they do make the present law less unacceptable than some critics try to make out.

It could be said, therefore, that English courts more or less take the view that in the case of a proven nuisance an injunction should issue as of course, though not as of right, but that the desirability of such an approach is increasingly in

---

[284] [1903] 2 Ch. 337.   [285] [1909] 1 Ch. 70.   [286] [1953] Ch. 149.   [287] [1899] 2 Ch. 705.
[288] [1905] 2 Ch. 614.

[289] E.g. *Pennington* v. *Brinsop Hall Coal Co.* (1877) 5 Ch. D. 769; *Shoreham UDC* v. *Dolphin Canadian Proteins Ltd.* (1972) 71 LGR 261.

[290] E.g. *Kennaway* v. *Thompson* [1981] QB 88. Contrast *Tetley* v. *Chitty* [1986] 1 All ER 663 (a blanket ban on go-karting).

doubt. The point is that in determining the availability of injunctive relief one should not balance the plaintiff's interest only against that of the defendant, but also weigh his interest in obtaining an injunction against the wider implications of such a course of action (e.g. closure of a major industry). The law of nuisance, in other words, could be used as a kind of compulsory purchase of private enterprise, by awarding damages generously but injunctions sparingly where the activity sought to be restrained has some wider social value. The net result, so it could be argued, would be to allow a valuable enterprise to flourish while making sure that it pays the costs in terms of loss of amenity.[291] In the light of contemporary social and economic conditions this view may gain wider acceptance, but so far it does not represent the prevailing English practice[292] and, indeed, may present certain problems of its own.

In the first place, control of development in this way through private law (as is often the case in the United States) would appear to be needed less urgently in this country. For we are more accustomed to a system of development control which takes place in advance through the use of administrative procedures than a system of *ex post facto* control by a judiciary which, one would have thought, is not the best body to resolve zoning issues.

Secondly, even apart from this, there is still something to be said for a social philosophy that allows (in some instances at least) the interests of even an eccentric or over-sensitive individual to prevail over public interest, which is often rather nebulous. In some ways this is a mark of a liberal society, and the law of nuisance in particular exists, *inter alia*, in the interest of minorities.[293] Nor is this entirely an individualistic view. For not only are the 'social costs' of pollution or other interferences with amenity notoriously difficult to compute (thus making an analysis of economic efficiency rather impracticable), but also any price put on the deprivation of amenity is bound to be artificial. Many people would not agree to be deprived of the peace and quiet of their home at any price; hence a person whose house is rendered uninhabitable by the act of another may have a justifiable complaint, whatever compensation he is offered. Further, despite the theory that everything has its value, a house subject to some serious disadvantage may turn out to be unsaleable in fact; so an award of damages reflecting the supposed reduction in the value of a house due to a nuisance may prove to be inadequate in practice.

---

[291] See Fleming, *Introduction to the Law of Torts* (2nd edn., 1985), 188–9. This view, which is gaining ground in the USA, is epitomised by *Boomer* v. *Atlantic Cement Co.*, 257 NE2d 870 (1970). On these environmental aspects of the problems in nuisance, see the articles by McLaren, Ogus and Richardson, and Tromans (Select Bibliography).

[292] Thus, in *Shelfer* v. *City of London Electric Lighting Co.* [1895] 1 Ch. 287, 316, Lindley LJ said: 'Neither has the circumstance that the wrongdoer is in some sense a public benefactor (e.g. a gas or water company or a sewer authority) ever been considered a sufficient reason for refusing to protect by injunction an individual whose rights are being persistently infringed. Expropriation, even for a money consideration, is only justifiable when Parliament has sanctioned it. Courts of Justice are not like Parliament, which considers whether proposed works will be so beneficial to the public as to justify exceptional legislation, and the deprivation of people of their rights with or without compensation.' This approach has, apparently, been accepted by Canadian judges; McLaren, op. cit., 552 ff.

[293] See Buckley in (1978) 41 *MLR* 334, 337.

Thirdly, *Kennaway* v. *Thompson* shows that certainty may well be no less desirable even in the context of 'discretionary' remedies than elsewhere in the law. There is no reason why such relief should be regarded as less important in this respect than an award of damages, and hence to be granted or refused according to a court's perception of the merits of the individual case. Indeed, in a tort like nuisance, whose effectiveness depends largely on the availability of injunctive relief, some certainty in the principles on which injunctions are granted is more important than elsewhere.

(B) ABATEMENT

Abating a nuisance is a form of self-help and as such not favoured as a remedy.[294] This attitude underlies three rules. The first is that while abatement may take the form of removing an obstruction or other nuisance emanating from the neighbour's land (e.g. cutting off intruding roots, etc.), it cannot normally take the form of other positive acts, such as erecting structures on the latter's land. This, at any rate, appears to be established in public nuisance affecting, for example, the right of access to the highway. In *Campbell Davys* v. *Lloyd*[295] there was a public right of way over the plaintiff's land and a decrepit bridge, which spanned a nearby river. While rebuilding the bridge, the defendant was forced to place piles on the plaintiff's land and, when sued in trespass, replied that he was abating a nuisance (interference with the right of way as a result of the state of the bridge). The defence was rejected, *inter alia*, for the reason stated. However, this reluctance to sanction positive acts of repair and maintenance does not apply quite so clearly in private nuisance. For example, the owner of a dominant tenement has the right to maintain and improve the surface of a road on which he has a private right of way; and the same is true if he is seeking to preserve an easement of support.[296] The precise ambit of these rights, however, is uncertain and it is unlikely that it extends to major works on servient property.

The second limitation can be seen in the exhortation of Eyre CJ in *Kirby* v. *Sadgrove*,[297] where he said: 'Abatement ought only to be allowed in clear cases of nuisance where the injury is apparent at the first view of the matter, the abator makes himself his own judge and proceeds at his own hazard to destroy the thing which he considers as an infringement of his right.' In other words, where the existence of a nuisance rests on a delicate balance between competing interests, this type of self-help is inappropriate.

---

[294] *Lagan Navigation Co.* v. *Lambeg Bleaching, Dyeing and Finishing Co. Ltd.* [1927] AC 226, 242 per Lord Atkinson. For the abator, however, it may present three distinct advantages: first, it may offer a cheap way of eliminating a cause of interference without going to court, secondly, in cases of emergency it may be the most efficient remedy, and thirdly, it may be available in cases where no actionable nuisance exists. Thus, encroaching roots and branches which cause no damage are not actionable, but may nevertheless be severed by the abator. *Lemmon* v. *Webb* [1894] 3 Ch. 1; [1895] AC 1. See *Clerk & Lindsell on Torts* (15th edn.), 304–7.

[295] [1901] 2 Ch. 518, 523.

[296] *Newcomen* v. *Coulson* (1877) 5 Ch. D. 133; *Jones* v. *Pritchard* [1908] 1 Ch. 630, 638 (per Parker J). For further details, see Jackson, *The Law of Easements and Profits* (1978).

[297] (1797), 3 Anst. 892, 896; 145 ER 1073, 1074.

Finally, if abatement requires, as it may often do, the abator to enter another person's land, he must generally give notice to that person.[298] However, when precisely notice has to be given is not clear. In *Jones* v. *Williams*[299] Parke B suggested that notice to the plaintiff is necessary if the nuisance was caused by his predecessor in title and he only continued it. In that case, the abator's claim that he had lawfully entered the plaintiff's land in order to remove a heap of manure, which constituted a nuisance by smell, was rejected because he did not state that notice was given, or that the plaintiff was himself the wrongdoer. Notice is also unnecessary in cases of 'emergency',[300] but when this exists has not been clearly defined.

Whether notice is necessary or not, the abator must in all cases ensure that his action does not affect the property of the other in excess of what is absolutely necessary in the circumstances.[301] So, if branches from a tree on A's land overlap B's land, B may be allowed to enter A's land and cut them back to the point of encroachment. B will not be allowed to keep the severed branches nor to break down A's fence, for example, in order to get on his land and cut the branches; nor will he be permitted to cut down the whole tree.

7. Public Nuisance

So far we have spoken of private nuisance. But there is the other type of nuisance, known as public nuisance, which is an amorphous and unsatisfactory area of the law covering an ill-assorted collection of wrongs, some of which have little or no association with tort and only appear to fill a gap in the criminal law. The definition of public nuisance given by the classic book *Archbold's Criminal Pleading and Practice* confirms this. This runs as follows:[302] 'Every person is guilty of an offence at common law, known as public nuisance, who does an act *not warranted by law*, or *omits to discharge a legal duty*, if the effect of the act or omission is to endanger life, health, property, morals, or comfort of the public, or to obstruct the public in the exercise or employment of rights common to all Her Majesty's subjects.' As one commentator put it: 'With such a broad concept in existence, backed with such broad remedies, what need have we of any other criminal offence?—or torts?—or remedies in administrative law?'[303] The mess that public nuisance is in is partly due to the haphazard and piecemeal growth of a legal system developed solely by practitioners without the kind of doctrinal backing that universities provided to the law of the Continent of Europe. Unfortunately, the result is not just an intellectual mess; it also offends all contemporary notions of certainty and precedent in criminal law and must thus be

---

[298] No notice is required for a man to cut off branches overhanging his own land: *Lemmon* v. *Webb* [1895] AC 1, 5, per Lord Herschell. The abator, however, cannot retain the branches for that would be to convert them: *Mills* v. *Brooker* [1919] 1 KB 555.

[299] (1843) 11 M. & W. 176, 181–2; 152 ER 764, 766–7.

[300] *Earl of Lonsdale* v. *Nelson* (1823), 2 B. & C. 302, 311–12; 107 ER 396, 400, per Best J. Immediate danger to life or health is an emergency: *Lemmon* v. *Webb* [1895] AC 1.

[301] *Roberts* v. *Rose* (1865) LR 1 Ex. 82.

[302] 42nd edn. (1985), paras. 27–44. See also *R* v. *Soul* (1980) 70 Cr. App. R. 295; *R* v. *Madden* [1975] 1 WLR 1379.

[303] Spencer, (below, Select Bibliography).

regarded as dangerous. In this subsection we shall focus on one particular category of public-nuisance cases which we could generically describe as 'abuses of the highway'.

Public nuisance in this sense refers to interference with members of the public in the exercise of their common rights on the highway. For example, in *Hubbard* v. *Pitt*[304] the defendants were picketing on the road outside the plaintiffs' offices. An interlocutory injunction was granted to the plaintiffs on the ground that picketing on the highway, other than in pursuance of a trade dispute, was unlawful and a public nuisance. In the Court of Appeal the plaintiffs laid more emphasis on their allegation that the defendants' conduct constituted a private nuisance, and there was some doubt as to whether the facts supported the existence of either a private or a public nuisance.[305] But the Court of Appeal, by a majority, felt that they should apply the test laid down by the House of Lords in the *American Cyanamid* case[306] and decided on a balance of convenience. In the majority's view this required that the injunction be maintained. In another case, *Attorney-General* v. *Gastonia Coaches Ltd.*,[307] coach operators parked sixteen coaches outside their offices and these inevitably interfered with the passage of traffic. Gastonia was guilty of public nuisance and were restrained from parking their coaches on the highway. They were also made to pay damages to private litigants who had suffered particular harm from the emission of exhaust gases.

Public and private nuisance, apart from the name, have not much else in common. Public nuisance is a crime triable summarily or on an indictment, which can also give rise to civil liability towards anyone suffering special damage. Private nuisance, on the other hand, is only a tort. Public nuisance affords protection to persons other than those with an interest in land. Private nuisance is concerned with interferences with the use and enjoyment of land. In public nuisance, damages for personal injury and even economic loss can be recovered, while in private nuisance it is primarily damage to land which is compensated and, perhaps, damage to goods. Finally, prescription is a defence to an action in *private nuisance* but it is not in the case of public nuisance.[308]

As stated, the same activity may constitute both forms of nuisance and, despite the differences, their overlap and the terminological similarity have led many to discuss these two types of liability together, with resulting confusion to both.[309] The connection with negligence might also be mentioned at this stage. Public nuisance differs from negligence in two respects. First, though the point is not free of doubt, the better view would seem to be that fault is an ingredient in actions of public nuisance, but, even so, its presence is presumed and it is for the defendant to excuse himself. In negligence, on the other hand,

---

[304] [1976] QB 142.

[305] There is no reason in principle why it cannot be both: *Halsey* v. *Esso Petroleum Co. Ltd.* [1961] 1 WLR 683 at 699 ff.

[306] *American Cyanamid Co.* v. *Ethicon Ltd.* [1975] AC 396.　　　　[307] [1977] RTR 219.

[308] The reason is that 'it cannot have a lawful beginning by licence or otherwise, being an offence against the common law'. *Dewell* v. *Sanders* (1618) Cro. Jac. 490; 79 ER 419; *R* v. *Cross* (1812) 3 Camp. 224; 170 ER 1362.

[309] *Hubbard* v. *Pitt* [1976] QB 142.

the burden of proof lies squarely on the plaintiff's shoulders.[310] Secondly, the tort of negligence remedies primarily physical damage, but public nuisance, which includes dangers on the highway, also extends to mere obstruction.

Public nuisance is first and foremost a crime because, as Denning LJ put it:[311] 'a public nuisance is a nuisance which is so widespread in its range or so indiscriminate in its effect that it would not be reasonable to expect one person to take proceedings on his own responsibility to put a stop to it, but that it should be taken on the responsibility of the community at large.' The prosecution must prove that the acts complained of affected a considerable number of persons or a section of the public. So a person who makes a bogus telephone-call falsely giving information as to the presence of explosives may have committed this offence. This requires that 'the public, which means a considerable number of persons or a section of the public, was affected, as distinct from individual persons'. In *R* v. *Madden*[312] the appellant's conviction for committing public nuisance in the above manner was quashed, *inter alia*, on the ground that his hoax message had reached only the telephonist who received it and eight policemen who were involved in searching for the bomb.

It would be unreasonable if in such circumstances, without more ado, the law allowed every person who was inconvenienced to bring an action. But, as already indicated, the crime may become a tort as well if the complainant can prove special loss over and above the inconvenience suffered by the public in general. So, in order to sue in tort the plaintiff has to prove special (or, perhaps more accurately, particular) damage which is 'particular, direct and substantial' to himself.[313] What this means exactly remains obscure.[314] One line of thought insists that the plaintiff must prove damage that is not merely different in degree from that suffered by the general public, but also different in kind. A different and more liberal approach, which probably prevails nowadays, is to allow the action whenever the plaintiff can show that the right he shares with others has been appreciably more affected by the defendant's behaviour. So a barge-owner, navigating a creek obstructed by the defendant's barges, could successfully claim from the latter his extra costs for unloading his cargo off his barges and transporting them by land to the place of ultimate destination, for in Lord Ellenborough's view he had suffered further damage than other members of the public who might have been contemplating using the creek.[315] The

---

[310] This solution is appropriate if the plaintiff is seeking damages for personal injury. Where an injunction is sought, the position is likely to be analogous to that of private nuisance where a fault-based approach seems to be irrelevant.   [311] *A-G* v. *PYA Quarries* [1957] 2 QB 169, 191.

[312] [1975] 1 WLR 1379. In *A–G* v. *PYA Quarries* [1957] 2 QB 169 the Court of Appeal refused to state how many people were needed to constitute a 'class of Her Majesty's subjects'. The question was one of fact with the result that the Court of Appeal would rarely interfere with the findings of the trial judge.

[313] 'The requirement of particular damage was strictly insisted on in the mid-nineteenth century, lest the construction of railways, which was necessarily disruptive, became too expensive' (*Ricket* v. *Metropolitan Ry. Co.* (1867) LR 2 HL 175; Weir, *A Casebook on Tort* (7th edn., 1992), 197).

[314] This issue is examined by Fridman, 'The Definition of Particular Damage in Nuisance', 2 *UWALR* 490–503 (1953).

[315] *Rose* v. *Miles* (1815) 4 M. and S. 101, 103; 105 ER 773. The decision which, it will be noticed, allows recovery for pure economic loss, has impeccable origins that can be traced back to *Iveson* v. *Moore* (1699) 1 Ld. Raym. 486; 91 ER 1224 (another case allowing recovery for pure economic loss resulting from highway obstructions).

most obscure point, however, is the requirement that special damage has to be 'direct'. Apparently, the test of this is narrower than that for damage elsewhere. Thus, Lord Reid said that in public nuisance the question is 'whether the damage caused to the plaintiff by the nuisance was other and different from the damage caused by the nuisance to the rest of the public. When the word "direct" is used in determining that question, its meaning or connotation appears to be narrower than when it is used in determining whether damage is too remote.'[316] In what sense it is 'narrower' or 'different' is left unexplained and the matter must be left open.

In *Jacobs* v. *London County Council*[317] Lord Simonds accepted the definition of nuisance on the highway 'as any wrongful act or omission upon or near a highway, whereby the public are prevented from freely, safely, and conveniently passing along the highway'. Generally speaking, nuisance on the highway can be produced either by the condition of the highway itself, or by obstructions thereon. As to the first, at common law highway authorities were not liable for non-feasance—failure to keep the highway in repair—though they could be liable for misfeasance—damage caused by some wrongful action. The Highways Act 1980 (re-enacting the provisions of the Highways (Miscellaneous Provisions) Act 1961) abolishes this distinction and makes highway authorities liable for damage resulting from failure to maintain (adopted) highways. But section 58(1) of the 1980 Act gives them a defence if they prove that they have taken such care as is reasonable in the circumstances. In order to assist the courts, section 58(2) of the 1980 Act has specified a number of factors to be taken into account in deciding the issue. 'The character of the highway', 'the standard of maintenance appropriate for a highway of that character', 'the state of repair in which a reasonable person would have expected to find that highway', and the highway authority's knowledge (actual or presumed) will be among the circumstances which will be weighed by the courts in deciding whether the authority is in breach of its duty. Parenthetically, it might be noted that the Act provides an example of statutory liability for the acts of independent contractors.

With regard to obstruction on the highway, not every obstacle will be a nuisance and the all-important test of reasonableness has to be applied. Obviously, whether an obstruction is unreasonable will be a matter of opinion based on fact.[318] Obstruction or injury caused by *projections* into the highway form a particularly unsatisfactory and unsettled part of the law. A distinction between *natural* and *artificial* projections is invariably adopted, the latter being more severely treated than the former. The distinction is not easy to explain or justify. One commentator has asked:[319] '. . . what are the grounds for distinction between a tree and a bit of a house? Is it that a house is used and a tree is not? . . . Is it because a house is always built and a tree is not always planted? . . . Is it because people are supposed to know about houses and not about trees, trees

---

[316] *Wagon Mound (No. 2)* [1967] 1 AC 617, 636.

[317] [1950] AC 361, 375, quoting Pratt and Mackenzie, *Law of Highways* (18th edn.), 107.

[318] Thus, see *Trevett* v. *Lee* [1955] 1 WLR 113.   [319] Weir, *A Casebook on Tort* (7th edn.), 199.

being subject, as houses are usually not, to secret unobservable processes of nature?' Whatever the reason for the distinction, the fact is that it is made.

With regard to *natural* projections, the rule is that damage caused by the collapse of branches protruding from land adjacent to the highway will be actionable only if the occupier was negligent, that is, he knew or should have known of the defect that caused the collapse. In *Noble* v. *Harrison*[320] a branch of a tree growing on the defendant's land and overhanging a highway suddenly broke and damaged the plaintiff's vehicle. It was found that the fracture occurred owing to a latent defect not discoverable by a reasonable and careful inspection. It was held that the mere fact that the branch overhung the highway did not make it a nuisance since it did not obstruct free passage along the highway. Although, in the event, the branch proved to be a danger, the defendant was not liable since he had not created the danger and had no knowledge, actual or implied, of its presence.

With regard to *artificial* projections, for example a protruding lamp-bracket, the authorities are in confusion. According to one view, liability is based on negligence as with natural projections. A contrary view imposes on the defendant a stricter form of liability, except where the collapse occurred through the act of a trespasser or by a secret and unobservable operation of nature, such as a subsidence under or near the foundations of the premises. In *Wringe* v. *Cohen*[321] a part of the defendant's premises collapsed because of want of repair. The plaintiff was held entitled to damages. Atkinson J formulated the rule in the terms stated above. It should be noted that the exceptions formulated by the Court of Appeal deprive the rule of much of its significance. For, to quote Friedman,[322] 'it can hardly be imagined that any damage caused neither by the act of a third person nor by a latent defect could be due to anything but knowledge or negligence of the occupier'.

Though the effect of the exceptions is probably that the rule in *Wringe* v. *Cohen* has been substantially assimilated to ordinary fault liability, it remains true to say that the onus of proof has been reversed. Once the plaintiff proves that the defendant was in control of the premises and that he suffered injury because of their dangerous condition, it will be for the defendant to prove, for example, that this resulted from a secret and unobservable operation of nature.

As already stated, a public nuisance becomes actionable as a tort if the plaintiff proves special damage to himself. In cases like those discussed above this poses few difficulties. Problems do, however, arise in cases where custom is lost as a result of an unlawful obstruction of the highway, for example, by theatre queues preventing access to nearby shops. In *Lyons, Sons & Co.* v. *Gulliver*[323] the plaintiff's shop was obstructed by crowds, at times five deep, queuing daily from 2.30 p.m. to 6.20 p.m. to enter the defendant's variety theatre. It was held that the obstruction amounted to an actionable public nuisance and an injunction was granted.

---

[320] [1926] 2 KB 332. On similar facts the House of Lords reached the same conclusion in *Caminer* v. *Northern and London Investment Trust Ltd.* [1951] AC 88.
[321] [1940] 1 KB 229, 233.   [322] (1940) 3 *MLR* 305.   [323] [1914] 1 Ch. 631.

8. Nuisance and Other Forms of Liability

Nuisance liability overlaps with trespass, negligence, and the rule in *Rylands* v. *Fletcher*.[324] It may be helpful to consider its relationship to trespass and negligence, leaving *Rylands* v. *Fletcher* until the next chapter.

The main difference from trespass is the historical distinction between actions in trespass and in case.[325] As indicated in the last chapter, trespass lay where the invasion was a *direct* interference, an action on the case lay where the interference was *consequential*. So, in *Mann* v. *Saulnier*[326] a fence, which had been properly constructed by the defendant, began to lean over towards the plaintiff's land after a period of time. This was treated as a nuisance, since the leaning was only a consequence of the act of erecting the fence. However elusive and unattractive to the modern mind this distinction may be, it 'is still attended with practical significance. For the one [trespass] there is liability without actual harm, for the other [nuisance] damage is essential; [moreover] every trespassory intrusion is tortious unless privileged, while a nuisance is never actionable unless it is unreasonable.'[327] By far the most significant and obscure relationship, however, is that between negligence and nuisance. The issue is not thereby clearly formulated for, as indicated previously, the term negligence refers either to the defendant's careless conduct, or to the independent tort of negligence in which carelessness is but one element of liability. The role played in nuisance by carelessness, which is an aspect of fault, has already been dealt with,[328] but something has still to be said of the overlap with the tort of negligence. If, as discussed earlier on, nuisance is not, or at least not always, a form of strict liability, then there is a tendency to assimilate those nuisances that are not intentional with the tort of negligence. This view has, indeed, been advanced on the ground that in both cases 'reasonableness' is the standard by which the defendant's behaviour is tested, and it deserves careful consideration, not least because of the reputation of its advocates.[329]

Yet at present it is difficult to identify the two torts for the following reasons. *First*, as regards reasonableness, it must be stressed that the gist of nuisance is the 'deed' not the 'doing', i.e. it is primarily the result suffered by the plaintiff rather than the defendant's activity that is scrutinised by the courts.[330] This

[324] (1866) LR 1 Ex. 265; (1868) LR 3 HL 330.

[325] Another difference is that trespass applies to 'things'; nuisance also covers intangible interferences, e.g. fumes, vibrations, noise, etc. See further Keeton and Winfield, (below, Select Bibliography).

[326] (1959) 19 DLR (2d.) 130.

[327] Fleming, *The Law of Torts* (8th edn.), 417. Proof of damage in nuisance is *generally* essential since without it there is only a potential nuisance. However, whenever damage is inevitable the courts will presume it: *Fay* v. *Prentice* (1845) 1 CB 828; 135 ER 769 (rain-water dripping over the plaintiff's garden from a projecting cornice). In cases of discomfort, the inconvenience *is* the damage and there must be evidence of this.

[328] Above, Section 3(a)(iv).

[329] Thus Williams and Hepple, *Foundations of the Law of Torts* (2nd edn., 1984), 127 state: 'Whether the tort is called nuisance or negligence, the question is whether the defendant has acted "reasonably".' See also Lord Denning MR in *Miller* v. *Jackson* [1977] QB 966, 980.

[330] This test was adopted by Geoffrey Lane LJ in *Miller* v. *Jackson* [1977] QB 966, 985, where he asked: 'Was there here a use by the defendants of their land involving an unreasonable interference with the plaintiffs' enjoyment of *their* land?' Academic writers have taken a similar view.

result is the unreasonable interference with the plaintiff's land or his use and enjoyment of it, and the defendant's wrongdoing may be one factor along with others which, in certain circumstances, can make an interference unreasonable. By contrast, the gist of negligence lies in the unreasonableness of the defendant's conduct, i.e. his wrongdoing. Unreasonableness, therefore, is viewed differently in these two torts. In negligence, the issue whether the defendant's conduct is unreasonable will be judged by its foreseeable consequences; in nuisance it is primarily the unreasonableness of what has happened to the plaintiff which is in issue. In these cases 'a negligent interference with the use and enjoyment of land is private nuisance in respect to the *interest invaded*, and negligence in respect to the type of *conduct* that causes the invasion'.[331]

There is never any talk of intentional interferences falling under a form of liability called 'intention'; instead, with reference to the interest invaded they are often called private nuisances. The same goes for those instances of nuisance, if any, where liability may be truly strict. Thus Prosser has argued that 'nuisance is not a separate tort . . . subject to rules of its own. Nuisances are types of damage—the invasion of two quite unrelated kinds of interests, by conduct that is tortious because it falls into the usual categories of tort liability.'[332] This is why he describes nuisance as 'a field of tortious liability rather than *a type* of tortious conduct'. It may be that much of our own confusion on the subject has been generated by our failure to appreciate this fact and to look upon nuisance as a type of liability independent of other torts.

A *second* reason why nuisance cannot be assimilated with the tort of negligence is that the two torts afford protection to different interests. The difference is due to history since they represent different stages in the development of the law of civil responsibility. Nuisance, the earlier of the two, protected interests in land and only a person with an interest in the affected land could succeed in this tort. Negligence, on the other hand, is the more modern and, in some respects, the wider of the two torts.

Thirdly, in cases involving neighbouring landowners English law has shown greater willingness to impose liability in negligence for omissions than it has in other areas of the tort of negligence.[333] Cases like *Goldman* v. *Hargrave*[334] and *Leakey* v. *National Trust*[335] show that for a variety of reasons courts are willing to acknowledge the special relationship between neighbouring landowners and to impose a general, though measured, duty of care in order to ensure that landowners are protected by the law of negligence from dangers emanating from their neighbour's land. *Smith* v. *Littlewoods Organisation Ltd.* has blurred further the borderline between nuisance and negligence; and the Lord

---

[331] *Restatement (Second) Torts*, para. 833(*c*) (italics supplied). Lord Denning in *Miller* v. *Jackson* [1977] QB 966, 980, said: 'It is the very essence of a private nuisance that it is the unreasonable use *by a man of his land* [italics supplied] to the detriment of his neighbour.' To place emphasis on the 'doing' rather than on the 'deed' is, at the very least, unorthodox. Cf. Geoffrey Lane LJ, dictum at 985, quoted in preceding note.

[332] *Torts* (4th edn.), 577. Prosser talks of 'two unrelated interests', referring thereby to the interests protected by public and private nuisance. This point is made clear in his *Selected Essays on the Law of Torts*, 164.

[333] On this see Markesinis in [1980] *CLJ* 259 ff.   [334] [1967] 1 AC 645.

[335] [1980] QB 485.

Chancellor's judgment certainly does not appear to be rigidly opposed to liability for omissions.[336]

Even if the above arguments are unconvincing, it still remains to be shown what advantage, conceptual or otherwise, would be gained by treating those nuisances in which fault is relevant as a sub-category of the tort of negligence. As Shaw LJ said in *Leakey* v. *National Trust*:[337] 'I do not for myself . . . see how the difficulty [of resolving nuisance cases] is disposed of by transmuting a liability in nuisance (however occasioned) into a duty to do what can reasonably be done in the circumstances of a particular case to prevent or to diminish the consequence of a nuisance. This formulation may, so it seems to me, create fresh problems and the derivative problems may defy resolution.'

At present, therefore, the identification of the torts of nuisance and negligence thus seems wrong, or at least premature for, of course, one should never forget the tendency of the tort of negligence to absorb older torts. *Smith* v. *Littlewoods Organisation Ltd.*[338] suggests that this may well come about; but this has not yet occurred.

9. Nuisance and Protection of the Environment

Nuisance is an old tort; environmental pollution, though an old concern,[339] has only recently been appreciated as a real problem. As reliance on fuels like oil and coal is threatened or diminishes, new sources of energy are brought into use carrying with them hitherto unthought-of hazards. But this is not the only risk to the environment. Massive and often ill-planned industrialisation and new methods of bulk transportation of goods like crude oil have meant that land, air, and sea can be seriously affected, often through the activity of one polluter only.[340] Concern about destruction of the environment is a product of the material rise in standards of living. Clearly, such problems can be resolved by concerted action by politicians, lawyers, economists, and other experts. Unfortunately, such co-operation is not always forthcoming. For a solution commending itself to an expert may be unattractive to vote-seeking politicians, and solutions offered by lawyers have often failed to take account of the ideas of economists. These dimensions are not within the purview of this book, but the student should at least be made aware of their connection with the tort of nuisance. We shall, therefore, discuss briefly two related problems: the economic efficiency of the action in nuisance in achieving pollution control, and measures taken by the State to combat this problem.

---

[336] [1987] AC 241 discussed by Markesinis, 'Negligence, Nuisance and Affirmative Duties of Action' (1989) 105 *LQR* 104.

[337] [1980] QB 485, 529. In a similar vein, Geoffrey Lane LJ in *Miller* v. *Jackson* [1977] QB 966, 985.

[338] [1987] AC 241.

[339] It seems that the first Act on this matter was passed in the reign of Edward I, banning, in certain circumstances, the use of coal as being detrimental to health matters. Not until Victorian times did systematic legislation start to appear, e.g. Nuisance Removal Act 1846, Alkali Act 1863, Public Health Act 1875, and Rivers Pollution Act 1876. For a review of these developments, see Brenner, 'Nuisance Law and the Industrial Revolution' 3 *Jo. LS* 403 (1974).

[340] E.g. the extensive destruction caused by the grounding of one oil-tanker, *Amoco Cadiz*, near the north coast of France.

(A) EFFICIENCY OF THE ACTION IN NUISANCE

Protection of the environment suggests that our first reaction should be to consider the possibility of public rather than private nuisance. This, however, is rather limited for a number of reasons. The first is the requirement of special damage which, as we have seen, has to be proved before an individual can sue in respect of public nuisance. Absence of 'special damage', however, is not fatal to proceedings, since a private citizen could always try a 'relator action', that is, obtain the permission of the Attorney-General to lend his name to the suit. This is straightforward from a purely legal point of view, and many of these cases, especially the older ones, were cases where the Attorney-General appears as the nominal plaintiff. Though this procedure overcomes the requirement of 'special damage', it presents another drawback: would a private citizen, who has not suffered 'special damage', hazard the risk and cost of modern litigation for the benefit of the general public? A private person is unlikely to do so, though some pressure group (e.g. for preserving the environment) might well be willing to do so. Here again there are doubts and difficulties. Doubts, because some statutory nuisances (discussed below) offer a speedier method of solving these problems. Difficulties, because many modern activities which are great polluters (building refineries, factory zones, railway depots, etc.) are increasingly sanctioned by private Acts of Parliament which, as in the *Gulf Oil* case, tend to be construed so as to confer immunity for non-negligent interferences. For these reasons, the action for public nuisance has not played a dominant role in the battle against environmental pollution.

What of private nuisance? It would certainly be intriguing if a tort which evolved out of the problems of neighbourhood in the later Middle Ages could be assigned such a modern function, but then tort concepts are remarkably pliable and have adapted to changes in the socio-economic environment. There are indeed lawyers[341] who argue that private nuisance has considerable potential in this respect,[342] because, first, 'the conceptual framework of nuisance is sufficiently malleable to allow the injection of the environmental perspective'. Secondly, 'judges who have been faced with private nuisance litigation which involved pollution problems have been prepared to recognize that fact'. Thirdly, and related to the above, in their selection of remedies courts have often shown willingness to 'use the law of nuisance to make polluters change their ways'.[343] Though there is force in, and some support for, these arguments, it is undeniable that the English law of nuisance has not played a primary role in pollution control. Indeed, it has been seriously doubted whether the tort of nuisance is economically the most efficient way to achieve this goal. For Ogus and Richardson, who have done the most detailed study of this type in this country, the reasons are three:[344]

---

[341] McLaren, 'The Common Law Nuisance Actions' (Select Bibliography); Katz, 'The Function of Tort Liability in Technology Development', 38 *U. Cin. LR* 587 (1969).

[342] McLaren, op. cit., 560.

[343] See e.g. Denning LJ in *Pride of Derby and Derbyshire Angling Association Ltd.* v. *British Celanese Ltd.* [1953] Ch. 149, 192: 'The power of the courts to issue an injunction for nuisance has proved itself to be the best method so far devised of securing the cleanliness of our rivers.'

[344] Op. cit. (Select Bibliography), 324.

The first is the principle of justice which postulates that existing property rights must be protected even where the result will impose greater costs on society at large. The second is the private law's limited ability to deal with generally inferior environmental conditions, both because it can intervene only where there has been a perceptible change (damage) and because the system of control presupposes an interest in neighbouring land. Finally, enforcement of standards created by private law is only to be selective.

This statement and the account preceding it suggest that the requirements and characteristics of private nuisance make it a clumsy device for controlling pollution. For example, the requirement that plaintiffs must have an interest in land is difficult to rationalise in terms of efficiency. Thus *Malone* v. *Laskey*,[345] which denied the tenant's wife a right of action, left the loss on the person who was clearly less able to bear it and totally incapable of preventing it. The distinctions between interferences with property and amenity, which were criticised earlier, are also dubious, if not indefensible, on any economic ground.[346] The use of the locality principle in *Rushmer* v. *Polsue and Alfieri*[347] can also be doubted on economic grounds. Commenting on the decision in this case to order the printers to cease their night operations for the sake of the *only* resident in that part of Fleet Street, Ogus and Richardson suggest that 'the decision may accord with the justice notion that the plaintiff should be protected against adverse changes in the environment but on pure efficiency criteria it probably resulted in the printer subsidising the milkman's [plaintiff's] use of his land'.[348]

The *Cambridge Water*[349] case also illustrates the severe limitations on the use of nuisance actions to secure an efficient level of environmental protection. The defendants ran a tanning business that involved the use of certain chemicals. These chemicals entered the water supply and contaminated a bore-hole that was purchased by the plaintiffs, a statutory water company, in 1976. The contamination was not thought to be serious in nature and the plaintiffs were satisfied, before they bought the bore-hole, that the water was 'wholesome' in the sense of conforming to the legislative standards which applied at that time. However, in 1980 an EC Directive (80/778) laid down a higher standard, with the result that the plaintiffs could no longer use the bore-hole to supply water for human consumption. They thus had to shut down their operations and purchase another well, at a cost of around £1 million which they then claimed from the defendants. The judge rejected their claim on two grounds. First, liability under *Rylands* v. *Fletcher* was excluded, since the defendants' use had been natural (the location, Sawston, having been an 'industrial village' since at least the nineteenth century). Secondly, there could be no liability in nuisance or negligence since the defendants had not been in any way at fault. The loss suffered by the plaintiffs was not foreseeable at the time the spillages occurred. Indeed, the defendants had taken steps to reduce the spillages in the 1970s and

---

[345] [1907] 2 KB 141.
[346] Ogus and Richardson, op. cit., 299.
[347] [1906] 1 Ch. 234; affd. [1907] AC 121.
[348] Op. cit., 298.
[349] *Cambridge Water Co.* v. *Eastern Counties Leather plc* [1994] 2 WLR 53 Weir [1993] *CLJ* 17. See also the report of the judgment of Ian Kennedy J in (1992) 4 *Journal of Environmental Law* 81, and the note by N. Atkinson.

had even been praised for achieving a good environmental record. All of this was of no avail in the Court of Appeal, which allowed an appeal on the basis that liability in nuisance was strict in the case of interference with a 'natural' incident of ownership, such as the right of a landowner to naturally occurring water which comes underneath his land through underground channels. The decision is both unjust and inefficient, since it imposes upon potential defendants a degree of responsibility that is out of all proportion to the level of care which they could reasonably be expected to take with regard to the environment. In this case, not only was liability strict, but it extended many years beyond the initial spillage. This type of potential liability cannot be effectively insured against; and the consequences for the defendants in *Cambridge Water* were that they were in danger of being put out of business until the Court of Appeal's ruling was reversed by the House of Lords.

Finally, the dicta of Lindley LJ in the *Shelfer*[350] case, which has so influenced the English law on injunctions in this context, may accord with the prevailing philosophy of the time and even of today that in such matters the courts should not usurp the role of the legislature. But this attitude also shows how the choice of remedy is determined by preferring individual rights to general social welfare. All this suggests that nuisance has been either too capricious in its application, or too insensitive towards wider economic considerations, to serve as the main weapon in protecting the environment and achieving the economically optimum result for society in general.

However, though these considerations cast doubts on the usefulness of nuisance in protecting the environment, they do not impair its value in other respects. For, not only in some cases may it provide the only method of compensation for pollution victims, but it may also afford those individuals an opportunity to air legitimate grievances and even succeed in condemning wrongful activities which affect others as well.[351]

(B) STATUTORY NUISANCES

Where the common law proved to be ineffective or slow, the legislator has intervened in two ways: either by controlling the activity in advance, or by providing expeditious methods of dealing with some of their obnoxious side-effects. The first method is to require certain trades (referred to as 'offensive trades' and described in Acts of Parliament or local bye-laws)[352] to be licensed in advance by the local authority. These requirements will often be related to planning regulations to be found in the Town and Country (Use Classes) Order 1972 and, alone or together with other rules, they may go a long way towards preventive control. The second method is to describe certain unacceptable

---

[350] [1895] 1 Ch. 287, 317.

[351] The importance of not underestimating this consideration was stressed by Sax, *Defending the Environment—A Strategy for Citizen Action* (1970), 112.

[352] Section 107(1) of the Public Health Act 1936 provides a list of such trades (e.g. fat-extractor, fat- or glue-maker, soap- or tallow- or tripe-boiler), all of which are likely to cause obnoxious fumes, or smells, while other provisions of the Act (as well as the Local Government Act 1972, s. 235) enable local authorities to extend the scope of the legislation to other trades or business, subject to confirmation by the Secretary of State.

states of affairs as statutory nuisances and to provide summary remedies for them. For instance, section 92(1) of the Public Health Act 1936 describes certain matters as 'statutory nuisances' if they are nuisances at common law, *or* are 'prejudicial to health' (described by section 343(1) as 'injurious or likely to cause injury to health'). Run-down or defective premises, whether an actionable nuisance or not, may come under statutory nuisance prejudicial to health; and the same qualification may apply to the keeping of animals and to accumulations or deposits, such as manure or refuse. The Clean Air Act of 1956, section 16, also provides that the emission of smoke may, in certain circumstances, be treated as a statutory nuisance for the purposes of the Public Health Act 1936. The Control of Pollution Act 1974, in effect incorporating section 1 of the older Noise Abatement Act of 1960, also provides for summary proceedings in addition to any common-law remedy for noises amounting to a nuisance. Incidentally, turning certain 'noisome trades' into statutory nuisances may mean removing them from the cumbersome area of public nuisance to which they traditionally belonged.

Where a statutory nuisance has been committed, it will be usual for the local authority to serve an abatement notice which, if not complied with, will result in proceedings before magistrates. If nuisance is proved, they will make such order as they think fit and failure to comply with it will be an offence. In other circumstances, however, for example in noise nuisance, the procedure may be even simpler in that failure to comply with the original abatement notice may itself be an offence without the need for a nuisance order. These nuisance orders or notices will be directed to the person whose act or default causes the nuisance, although in certain circumstances the local authority will itself be empowered to abate the nuisance. It will be clear, however, that all such technical matters are matters of administrative law and this is no place to enter into their detail.[353]

Select Bibliography

BUCKLEY, R. A., *The Law of Nuisance* (1981).

BURROWS, P., 'Nuisance, Legal Rules and Decentralised Decisions: A Different View of the Cathedral Crypt', in P. Burrows and C. G. Velijanovski (eds.), *Economic Approach to Law* (1981).

BUXTON, R. J., 'The Negligent Nuisance' 8 *Malaya LR* 1 (1966).

—— 'Nuisance and Negligence Again' (1966) 29 *MLR* 676.

CALABRESI, G. and MELAMED, A. D., 'Property Rules, Liability Rules and Inalienability: One View of the Cathedral' 85 *Harv. LR* 1089 (1972).

CANE, P. 'Justice and Justification for Tort Liability' (1982) 2 *OJLS* 30, 51–61.

DIAS, R. W. M., 'Trouble on Oiled Waters. Problems of the *Wagon Mound* (*No. 2*)' [1967] *CLJ* 62.

EEKELAAR, J. M., 'Nuisance and Strict Liability' (1973) 8 *Ir. Jur.* 191.

FRIDMAN, G. H. L., 'Motive in the English Law of Nuisance' 40 *Virginia LR* 583 (1954).

---

[353] A brief account can be found in Buckley, op. cit. (Select Bibliography), 151–72.

GEARTY, C., 'The Place of Private Nuisance in a Modern Law of Torts' [1989] *CLJ* 214.

GOODHART, A. L., 'Liability for Things Naturally on the Land' [1930–2] 4 *CLJ* 13.

KEETON, P., 'Trespass, Nuisance and Strict Liability' 59 *Col. LR* 457 (1959).

KIDNER, R., 'Television Reception and the Tort of Nuisance' [1989] *Conv.* 279.

KODILINYE, 'Public Nuisance and Particular Damage in Modern Law' 6 *Leg. Stud.* 182 (1986).

—— 'Standing to Sue in Private Nuisance', 9 *Leg. Stud.* 284 (1989).

MCLAREN, J. P. S., 'The Common Law Nuisance Actions and the Environmental Battle—Well-tempered Swords or Broken Reeds?' 10 *Osgoode Hall LJ* 505 (1972).

—— 'Nuisance Law and the Industrial Revolution—Some Lessons from Social History' (1983) 3 *OJLS* 155.

MARKESINIS, B. S. and TETTENBORN, A. M., 'Cricket, Power Boat Racing and Nuisance' (1981) 131 *New LJ* 108.

NEWARK, F. H., 'The Boundaries of Nuisance' (1949) 65 *LQR* 480.

OGUS, A. I. and RICHARDSON, G. M., 'Economics and the Environment—A Study of Private Nuisance' [1977] *CLJ* 284.

SPENCER, J., 'Public Nuisance—A Critical Examination' [1989] *CLJ* 55.

STEELE, J., 'Private Law and the Environment: Nuisance in Context' (1995) 15 *Leg. Stud.* 236.

TROMANS, 'Nuisance—Prevention or Payment' [1982] *CLJ* 87.

WINFIELD, P. H., 'Nuisance as a Tort' [1930–2] *CLJ* 189.

4. DECEIT

The common law rules concerning liability for dishonesty were synthesized to create the tort of deceit at the end of the eighteenth century in *Pasley* v. *Freeman*,[354] and the tort takes its modern form from the decision of the House of Lords in *Derry* v. *Peek*[355] in 1889. Most of the cases concern non-physical damage, that is to say, financial or pure economic loss, although the tort can also extend to cover personal injuries[356] and damage to property.

The requirements of liability are as follows: the defendant must make (1) a false statement (2) of existing fact (3) with knowledge of its falsity and with the intention that the plaintiff should act on it, with the result (4) that the plaintiff does act on it to his detriment.[357]

1. A False Statement

A false statement may be made orally or in writing or by conduct. In *R* v. *Bernard*,[358] the accused entered a shop in Oxford wearing academic dress to which he was not entitled, thereby representing himself as a member of the university. He was held to be guilty of obtaining goods by false pretences. If a statement is ambiguous the plaintiff has to show that the false sense was the

---

[354] (1789) 3 Term Rep. 51.

[355] 14 App. Cas. 337.

[356] See *Langridge* v. *Levy* (1837) 2 M. & W. 519.

[357] For a judicial summary of these requirements see *Bradford Third Equitable Benefit Building Society* v. *Borders* [1941] 2 All ER 205, 211.

[358] (1837) 7 C. & P. 784.

one which the defendant wished him to understand.[359] Silence can only render a person liable if he was under a duty to speak or to correct a misleading impression.[360] Sometimes the defendant may be held liable for stating a half-truth: if what was left unsaid would have negated what was said, there may be liability.[361] In some cases statute has created a special duty of disclosure, as in the provisions of the Companies Acts which place companies under certain duties of disclosure in respect of company prospectuses.[362] The statement must normally be made by the defendant himself but there is some authority for the suggestion that one who uses a false impression created in the plaintiff's mind by a third party in order to profit by it can then be made liable.[363]

A statement of fact that was true when made but which becomes untrue later will ground liability provided the defendant learned of the falsity and then chose not to warn the plaintiff.[364] Equally, if the statement was false when made but the defendant believed it to be true at the time and later discovered that it was false, it would seem that he would be liable in deceit if he failed to notify the plaintiff.[365] What happens if a false statement was made fraudulently but, before the plaintiff can act upon it, it becomes true? Here there is no liability.[366] On the other hand, if the statement becomes true only after the plaintiff has acted on it—by, for example, entering into a contract in reliance on the statement—there will be liability since the statement was still false when the cause of action accrued.

2. A Statement of Existing Fact

The statement has to be of existing fact. Promises and declarations of future purpose are not, generally speaking, actionable unless they are contained in a contract supported by consideration. Sometimes it is difficult, however, to distinguish between a statement of fact and a promise. A declaration of future intention may be treated as a representation of a present state of mind. In *Edgington* v. *Fitzmaurice*[367] a misstatement concerning the objects for which debentures were issued was held sufficient to give rise to liability; Bowen LJ said that 'the state of man's mind is as much a fact as the state of his digestion'.[368] Thus a false opinion made deliberately will be actionable since it is a misrepresentation of the mind of the person giving it.[369] By contrast, in *Wales* v. *Wadham*[370] a wife's statement that she intended not to remarry following the

---

[359] *Gross* v. *Lewis Hillman Ltd.* [1970] Ch. 445; see also *Smith* v. *Chadwick* (1884) 9 App. Cas. 187; *Woodhouse AC Israel Cocoa Ltd.* v. *Nigerian Produce Marketing Co. Ltd.* [1972] AC 741.

[360] *Schneider* v. *Heath* (1813) 3 Camp. 506; *Arkwright* v. *Newbold* (1881) 17 Ch. D. 301, 318.

[361] *Peek* v. *Gurney* (1873) LR 6 HL 377.

[362] Financial Services Act 1986, ss. 150–2, 166–8. These provisions, and their predecessors, effectively reverse the House of Lords' judgment in *Derry* v. *Peek* (1889) 14 App. Cas. 337 on the narrow point of company law with which it was concerned.

[363] *Bradford Building Society* v. *Borders* [1941] 2 All ER 205, 208.

[364] *Incledon* v. *Watson* (1862) 2 F. & F. 841.

[365] This seems to follow from *Briess* v. *Woolley* [1954] AC 333.

[366] *Ship* v. *Croskill* (1870) LR 10 Eq. 73.　　　　　　　　[367] (1885) 29 Ch. D. 459.

[368] 29 Ch. D. 459, 483.

[369] *Anderson* v. *Pacific Insurance Co.* (1872) LR 7 CP 65, 69; *Bissett* v. *Wilkinson* [1927] AC 177, 182.

[370] [1977] 1 WLR 199.

divorce was held to be an opinion as to the future and not a representation of fact. Statements of law may be statements either of opinion or of fact. A statement of what a legal rule might be, based on ambiguous words in a statute or on a difficult matter of interpretation, will be a statement of opinion, but a deliberate misstatement of a statutory provision's meaning will be treated as a statement of fact. In *West London Commercial Bank Ltd.* v. *Kitson*[371] a false statement to the effect that the defendants had power to accept bills of exchange was held to give rise to liability.

There is a special rule concerning representations about the creditworthiness of third parties. Section 6 of the Statute of Frauds (Amendment) Act 1828 (Lord Tenterden's Act) provides that a fraudulent misrepresentation as to 'the character, conduct, credit, ability, trade or dealings of any other persons, to the intent or purpose that such other person may obtain credit, money, or goods upon' has to be made in writing and signed by the defendant for any action to lie. A company can make a written representation through a duly authorised agent acting within the scope of his authority or through an employee acting in the course of his duties.[372] The Statute only applies to actions in deceit and not to negligence;[373] this creates the odd situation, following the expansion of negligence liability,[374] that in the absence of writing there might be liability in negligence even though there would be none if the misstatement had been made intentionally.[375] Another difficulty is that the Act only affects actionability and not liability. This has repercussions for the principle of the employer's vicarious liability for the torts of his employee: the employee might, in a case of an unwritten misstatement, invoke the Act to avoid being sued, but since he is still *liable* an action could conceivably lie against his employer.[376]

3. The Defendant's State of Mind

The relevant mental state is that the defendant must either have known that the statement was false or must have been reckless as to its truth or falsity. Recklessness here includes indifference as to whether a statement is true or false, but if the defendant *carelessly but honestly* makes a false statement he will not be liable for deceit.

In the leading case of *Derry* v. *Peek*[377] an Act of Parliament incorporating a tramway company provided that it could operate steam-driven carriages with the consent of the Board of Trade. The directors issued a prospectus declaring that they had the right to use steam, on the faith of which the plaintiff bought shares in the company. The Board of Trade subsequently refused the necessary permission. The House of Lords held that there was no action in deceit since the defendants had honestly believed that permission was a formality; they had merely been careless. This principle still holds. In *Thomas Witter Ltd.* v. *TBP*

---

[371] (1884) 13 QBD 360, 363 (Bowen LJ).

[372] *UBAF Ltd.* v. *European American Banking Corp.* [1984] QB 713.

[373] *Banbury* v. *Bank of Montreal* [1918] AC 626.

[374] In *Hedley Byrne & Co. Ltd.* v. *Heller & Partners Ltd.* [1964] AC 465.

[375] See *W. B. Anderson & Sons Ltd.* v. *Rhodes (Liverpool) Ltd.* [1967] 2 All ER 850; *Diamond* v. *Bank of London and Montreal Ltd.* [1979] QB 333.

[376] See *Brown* v. *Morgan* [1953] 1 QB 397.   [377] (1889) 14 App. Cas. 337.

Properties Ltd.[378] the vendor of a business was alleged to have failed to check whether a profit forecast was accurately based. Jacob J held that in the absence of evidence of dishonesty, the defendant could not be liable in deceit.

Derry v. *Peek* established that carelessness was not sufficient for the action of deceit; later, in *Hedley Byrne & Co. Ltd.* v. *Heller & Partners Ltd.*,[379] the House of Lords held that carelessness might, in certain circumstances, give rise to liability for breach of a duty of care in negligence. Section 2(1) of the Misrepresentation Act 1967 also provides for damages for the victim of reliance on a misstatement that induces a contract with the representor. The representor has the duty of, in effect, disproving negligence. Much of the significance of the distinction between liability for deceit and the near-strict liability provided for by section 2(1) has been effaced by the decision of the Court of Appeal in *Royscott Trust Ltd.* v. *Rogerson*[380] to the effect that the measure of damages under section 2(1) is the same as it is for deceit.[381]

The defendant must also intend the plaintiff to act on the statement. In *Peek* v. *Gurney*[382] the plaintiff, who bought shares in the open market in reliance on fraudulent misstatements in a company prospectus, was held to have no action since the intention behind the prospectus was to induce persons to apply for shares, not to buy them in the market. As long as the defendant intends the plaintiff to act on his statement, it does not matter that it is made to a third party. In *Langridge* v. *Levy*[383] the defendant sold a gun to a father for use by him and his son, having knowingly made a false statement about its manufacture. When the son used the gun, it burst and injured him. He was able to maintain an action against the defendant for fraud.

4. Reliance

The plaintiff must act on the statement. If the plaintiff took independent advice or if it can be shown that he would have acted as he did despite the defendant's statement, the latter is not liable.[384]

5. Damage and Damages

Loss is an essential element of the tort. Damages are calculated not on the basis of foreseeability and the *Wagon Mound (No. 1)*[385] test in negligence but, instead, on the basis of a test of directness. The defendant will thus be liable for all damage directly flowing from the misstatement, even if certain losses and certain kinds of damage were not foreseeable.[386] One consequence is that the defendant takes the risk of the plaintiff's loss being augmented by events occurring after the fraud took place that were outside the control of either party, such as a fall in the market which further devalues the property which was the subject

---

[378] [1996] 2 All ER 573. [379] [1964] AC 465. [380] [1991] 3 All ER 294.
[381] See generally the discussion in Chapter 2, Section 2(2)(b)(i) above. [382] (1873) LR 6 HL 377.
[383] (1837) 2 M. & W. 519. [384] *Central Railway of Venezuela* v. *Kisch* (1867) LR 2 HL 99.
[385] [1961] AC 388.
[386] *Doyle* v. *Olby (Ironmongers) Ltd.* [1969] 2 QB 158; *Downs* v. *Chappell* [1996] 3 All ER 344; *Smith New Court Securities Ltd.* v. *Scrimgeour Vickers (Asset Management) Ltd.* [1996] 4 All ER 769.

of the transaction between them. The basis for taking this approach to intentional wrongdoing is, as Lord Steyn has explained, twofold:

First it serves a deterrent purpose in discouraging fraud . . . in the battle against fraud civil remedies can play a useful and beneficial role. Secondly, as between fraudster and the innocent party, moral considerations militate in favour of requiring the fraudster to bear the risk of misfortunes directly caused by his fraud.[387]

Select Bibliography

FULLAGAR, W. K., 'Liability for Representations at Common Law', 25 *Aust. LJ* 278 (1951).
KEETON, R. E., 'Fraud—Misrepresentations of Law', 15 *Texas LR* 409 (1937).

5. THE ECONOMIC TORTS

1. The Framework of the Economic Torts

The purpose of the economic torts is to protect a person in relation to his trade, business, or livelihood. However, he will only be protected from certain kinds of interference, principally those inflicted intentionally or deliberately. Nor will an intention to harm suffice, on its own, to ground liability. For the interference to be actionable some additional element of unlawfulness must normally be present. Most of the cases fall into one of two categories: those involving wrongful interference with a *pre-existing legal right* of the plaintiff, and those involving the use of *independently unlawful means*. The only exception to the principle just stated arises in the tort of conspiracy to injure, where the act of combination or association between the defendants, when coupled with an intention to harm the plaintiff, is sufficient for liability even though lawful means are used.

The fact that the economic torts are restricted in this way illustrates the lower priority which the law of tort accords to the protection of 'pure economic' or financial interests, as opposed to the protection of physical integrity and of property rights.[388] The torts of trespass to the person and trespass to goods and to land are actionable *per se*, that is to say without proof of damage, upon evidence of an intentional act of interference. With the economic torts, by contrast, not only is damage or the threat of damage a necessary ingredient of liability, but the mere intention to harm another's economic interests cannot give rise to liability if the losses were inflicted through lawful means. Conversely, the defendant will not be liable for foreseeably but unintentionally causing economic loss, even where unlawful means are used.[389]

---

[387] *Smith New Court Securities Ltd.* v. *Scrimgeour Vickers (Asset Management) Ltd.* [1996] 4 All ER 769, 790. The result in *Smith New Court* may be contrasted with the decision of the House of Lords in the *Banques Bruxelles Lambert* case (sub. nom. *South Australia Asset Management Corp.* v. *York Montague Ltd.* [1997] AC 191) which concerned *negligent* misrepresentation.

[388] See T. Weir, *Economic Torts*, 8–13, for a restatement of this distinction.   [389] Ibid., 14–20.

These basic principles were laid down in a series of decisions dating from the turn of the present century, in which the English courts rejected the notion of a prima-facie liability in tort for the infliction of economic losses through 'unfair competition'. In *Mogul Steamship Co. Ltd.* v. *McGregor, Gow & Co.*[390] the plaintiffs complained that they had been driven out of the market for the shipping of tea from the Chinese ports by the concerted acts of the defendants acting as a 'shipping conference'. The defendants had sought to monopolise the trade by, amongst other things, offering uneconomic rates to the local shippers and giving local agents special rebates in return for an agreement to deal exclusively with the defendants. The plaintiffs' claim failed on the grounds that no unlawful act had been committed and that the defendants had simply been acting in pursuit of their own economic self-interest through collective action. The distinction between means and ends emerged clearly in the speech of Bowen LJ in the Court of Appeal:

[A trader's] right to trade freely is a right that the law recognises and encourages but it is one which places him at no special advantage as compared with others. No man, whether trader or not, can, however, justify damaging another in his commercial business by fraud or misrepresentation. Intimidation, obstruction and molestation are forbidden; so is the intentional procurement or violation of individual rights, contractual or other, assuming always that there is no just cause for it . . . [but] the defendants have been guilty of none of these acts. They have done nothing more against the plaintiffs than pursue to the bitter end a war of competition waged in the interest of their own trade.[391]

The same principle was applied to labour disputes in the great case of *Allen* v. *Flood*.[392] Boilermakers employed at a shipbuilding yard discovered that the plaintiffs, who were working in the yard as shipwrights, had previously worked as boilermakers at another yard without being members of the boilermakers' trade union. An official of the union, Allen, indicated to the employers that the boilermakers would go on strike in protest at the employment of the plaintiffs unless they were dismissed, and they were duly dismissed later the same day. The House of Lords allowed Allen's appeal from the findings of liability of the lower courts. The case turned on the absence of any unlawful means. The contracts of employment of the men working at the yard were effectively 'contracts at will', that is to say, they could be terminated on notice of an hour or so. This meant that Allen's threat of a strike did not amount to a threat to induce a breach of the men's contracts with their employer; had the strike gone ahead, they would have given lawful notice to walk off the job. Equally, Flood's dismissal was not a breach of contract: the employers were not required to give him any more notice than he in fact received. Although Allen intended to inflict economic harm on Flood, he did so without upsetting any pre-existing right of Flood to continuing employment and without threatening independently unlawful means. The House of Lords held this distinction between lawful and unlawful means to be vital. Lord Davey said:

[390] (1889) 23 QBD 598, [1892] AC 25. [391] (1889) 23 QBD. [392] [1898] AC 1.

The right which a man has to pursue his trade or calling is qualified by an equal right of others to do the same and compete with him, though to his damage. And it is obvious that a general abstract right of this character stands on a different footing from such a private particular right as the right to performance of a contract into which one has entered. A man has no right to be employed by any particular employer, and no right to any particular employment if it depends on the will of the employer.[393]

Lord Shand saw the case as 'one of competition in labour, which . . . is in all essentials analogous to competition in trade, and to which the same principles apply'.[394]

The majority therefore rejected the view that 'malice' against the plaintiff was a sufficient basis for liability. They did so largely through concern that the notion of 'malice' was too vague to be applied consistently by courts and in particular (at that time) by juries. The meaning of malice in the law of torts is not always clear. It denotes something more than an intention to hurt the plaintiff but it is not necessarily synonymous with an illegitimate motive. The absence of any factor justifying the defendant's behaviour, when coupled with the intention to harm the plaintiff, comes close to capturing the essence of the concept. Professor Richard Epstein has suggested the following definition in the context of the economic torts: 'Malice in its pure form means more than an intention to inflict some injury. All competition, and most economic activity, will do that. Instead, it refers to actions done out of spite or ill will, whereby someone is prepared to impose costs upon himself solely to make someone else worse off.'[395] An example of this concept of malice is the American case of *Tuttle* v. *Buck*,[396] in which liability was imposed upon the defendant, a wealthy industrialist, who drove the plaintiff out of business by setting up a rival barber to him in his home town, for reasons related entirely to a personal grudge. This case would not be followed in England because the means used were lawful and the defendant acted alone. In some American jurisdictions the requirement that the defendant should disprove an implication of malice by showing that he acted out of economic self-interest has given rise to the notion of a 'prima-facie tort liability'. English law recognises a form of this only in the isolated case of conspiracy to injure. In *Quinn* v. *Leathem*,[397] decided three years after *Allen* v. *Flood*, the House of Lords held that acts carried out by a combination of workers with the aim of driving out of business an employer who took on non-union labour could be tortious, if the actions were motivated by ill will against the plaintiff personally as opposed to the economic self-protection of the defendants. For some time it was not clear whether this decision had implicitly qualified *Allen* v. *Flood*, but in due course it was decided that the principle of *Quinn* v. *Leathem* was confined to cases of combination and, moreover, that the defence of justification would normally be available to trade unionists acting, for example, to defend their trade against non-union competition.[398]

---

[393] [1898] AC 1, 173.   [394] Ibid., 164.

[395] R. A. Epstein, 'A Common Law for Labour Relations: A Critique of the New Deal Legislation' (1983) 92 *Yale LJ* 1357, 1368.

[396] (1909) 119 NW 946.   [397] [1901] AC 495.

[398] See *Sorrell* v. *Smith* [1925] AC 700; *Crofter Hand Woven Harris Tweed Co.* v. *Veitch* [1942] AC 435; *Lonrho Ltd.* v. *Shell Petroleum Co. Ltd.* [1982] AC 173.

Conspiracy aside, then, the English common law has adopted a *formal* criterion—the presence of an element of unlawfulness, in the sense of a crime or a civil wrong such as a breach of contract or possibly breach of a statutory obligation—as opposed to *substantive* criteria for identifying illegitimate or unfair competition. Writing extra-judicially,[399] Lord Devlin complained that *Allen* v. *Flood* had thereby dammed up a stream of liability which could have developed within the common law, although he warned that 'only a tenuous barrier' held it back. As it is, *Allen* v. *Flood* remains (just) good law, and with the common law abandoning the task of working out the limits of legitimate competition the responsibility has gradually been assumed by Parliament. In the commercial sphere, matters such as predatory pricing, retail-price maintenance, and exclusive dealing are dealt with by legislation that includes the Competition Act 1998. This legislation has largely displaced the common law of tort in favour of a number of administrative and judicial procedures for regulating anti-competitive arrangements; it is underwritten, in its turn, by European Community legislation deriving from Articles 85 and 86 of the Treaty of Rome. A consideration of this body of law lies outside the scope of this book.[400] The common law of tort retains its importance in employment cases, however, where it operates in conjunction with legislation concerning the scope of lawful trade disputes now to be found in Part V of the Trade Union and Labour Relations (Consolidation) Act 1992, and as a residual form of redress in cases of competition between businesses.[401]

The absence of any unifying principle drawing together the different heads of economic tort liability has often been remarked upon. There is no equivalent in this area of law to the role played by *Donoghue* v. *Stevenson* in the tort of negligence.[402] Attempts to provide a general theory have tended to break down against the reluctance of the courts to engage in the kind of synthesis needed.[403] It is probably futile to expect such a synthesis to emerge in the near future. This is because of the context in which most of the modern case law arises, that is to say, industrial disputes involving trade unions and employers. Since the Trade Disputes Act 1906 Parliament has conferred extensive immunities on trade unions, their members, and others involved in the organisation of strike action which would otherwise be tortious. This immunity was felt to be necessary if the purposes of trade unionism were to be rendered lawful and

---

[399] *Samples of Lawmaking* (1962).

[400] See R. Whish, *Competition Law* (3rd edn., 1993) for a systematic treatment of the principles of both UK and EC competition law.

[401] Recent non-labour cases include *CBS Songs Ltd.* v. *Amstrad Consumer Electronics plc* [1988] AC 1013 and *Lonrho plc* v. *Fayed* [1992] 1 AC 448.

[402] See Wedderburn, 'Rocking the Torts' (1983) 46 *MLR* 223, 229.

[403] An important article which provides perhaps the best attempt at a general explanation is Weir, 'Chaos or Cosmos? *Rookes, Stratford* and the Economic Torts' [1964] *CLJ* 225. See also P. Elias and K. Ewing, 'Economic Torts and Labour Law: Old Principles and New Liabilities' [1982] *CLJ* 321; and H. Carty, 'Intentional Violation of Economic Interests: The Limits of Common Law Liability' (1988) 104 *LQR* 250. P. J. Sales, 'The Tort of Conspiracy and Civil Secondary Liability' [1990] *CLJ* 491 offers an altogether different perspective, suggesting that many of the cases are best explained in terms of a principle of secondary liability for aiding or assisting a civil law wrong.

an equilibrium established in industrial relations.[404] However, since the decision of the House of Lords in *Rookes* v. *Barnard* in 1964[405] the courts have embarked on an expansion of economic tort liability which has had the effect of 'outflanking' the immunities provided by statute through the creation of new, nominate torts. In particular, this period has seen: the development of the general tort of interference with trade by unlawful means; the extension of the tort of inducing breach of contract to cover a wider category of acts of interference with contractual performance; the acceptance of the tort of inducing breach of statutory duty as a new head of liability; and the evolution of economic duress as a grounds for recovery of money and, in the view of some, as a tort in its own right. At times it has seemed that the courts (and the Bar) were engaged in a battle of wits with the Parliamentary drafter, to see which side could develop the optimal formula for widening or for narrowing liability respectively. To some extent this tension (or the potential for it) still exists, despite a change in labour-law policy since 1979 which has seen Parliament, rather than the courts, take the lead in the narrowing down of the immunities.[406] This change of policy notwithstanding, courts are likely to continue the process of developing the common law in novel directions to meet what they clearly see as the needs of plaintiffs for protection. The dynamic quality of the economic torts, which makes them so resistant to synthesis, is undoubtedly a reaction to Parliament's attempts since 1906 to neutralise this area of common-law liability.

As we have seen, some degree of classification is nevertheless possible. There are three broad sub-categories of liability: those torts based on the defendant's wrongful interference with the plaintiff's pre-existing legal rights (inducing breach of contract and inducing breach of statutory duty, in particular); the tort of interference with trade or business by unlawful means; and the tort of conspiracy. These will now be considered in turn, to be followed by an outline of the statutory immunities in relation to trade disputes.

2. Wrongful Interference with the Plaintiff's Pre-Existing Rights

Where the defendant intentionally and knowingly interferes with a pre-existing right of the plaintiff to receive income, goods, or services with the result that the plaintiff suffers economic damage, liability in tort may arise. The right in question may exist under a contract or by virtue of a fiduciary relationship, or it may, more exceptionally, arise under a statutory obligation. The classic instance is the tort of inducing breach of contract; since that tort was given its modern form in the nineteenth century, various additions have been made by the courts.

---

[404] Numerous labour-law texts provide an account of the background to the enactment of the immunities and their relationship to the industrial-relations system. See, in particular, O. Kahn-Freund, *Labour and the Law* (3rd edn., by P. Davies and M. Freedland, 1983), ch. 1, and Lord Wedderburn, *The Worker and the Law* (3rd edn., 1986), ch. 1.

[405] [1964] AC 1129.

[406] See generally S. Deakin and G. Morris, *Labour Law* (2nd edn., 1998), ch. 11.

(A) INDUCING BREACH OF CONTRACT

It is a tort for the defendant (A) knowingly to persuade a third party (B) to break his contract with the plaintiff (C), to the damage of C. This tort was established in *Lumley* v. *Gye*[407] and confirmed by the House of Lords in *Allen* v. *Flood*.[408] In *Lumley* v. *Gye* the plaintiff had a contract for the exclusive services of the opera singer Johanna Wagner, who was then lured away by the defendant to sing at his theatre for a higher fee. The defendant was aware of the terms of the contract between Lumley and Wagner. The plaintiff sued for damages and the Court of Queen's Bench decided by a majority that he had a good cause of action.[409] It was irrelevant, according to Erle J, that the plaintiff could also sue Miss Wagner for damages for breach of contract (in fact this action was brought separately).[410] The remedy on the contract might be inadequate, in the sense that damages might be restricted by the duty to mitigate or by the rule of remoteness in contract law. Under these circumstances, 'he who procures the damage maliciously might justly be made responsible beyond the liability of the contractor'. The essence of the tort, then, lies in what Erle J called malice but which is now thought of, more precisely, as the knowing or deliberate procurement of the breach. The status of the tort was unclear for a long period until *Allen* v. *Flood* was decided. It was made clear in that case that there could be no liability for persuading someone not to enter into a contract.[411] The crucial dividing line was between the case in which the plaintiff had a legal right to performance, protected by contract, and the case in which he merely had a moral or commercial expectation of some kind which was not embodied in contractual form.

Lumley v. *Gye* concerned an employment contract, and the authorities relied on by the majority as precedents were mainly cases arising out of actions by masters for the enticement away of their servants, an area heavily regulated at that time by statute. However, the modern tort has been extended beyond employment contracts, and the original statutory context in which the action for enticement arose has also been forgotten. The tort has been applied to contracts for the commercial supply of goods,[412] contracts of hire,[413] and exclusive dealing contracts.[414] The contract in question must be a valid one: it must not be illegal or in restraint of trade,[415] nor, it would seem, capable of being rescinded.[416] Damage is necessary, but business losses of some kind flowing from a breach of contract are frequently assumed.[417]

The relevant mental state is that of intention: the defendant must intend to interfere with the plaintiff's contractual rights, in the sense of doing so

---

[407] (1853) 2 E. & B. 216.
[408] [1898] AC 1.
[409] The judgment of the dissenting judge, Coleridge J, is perhaps the most convincing of the four.
[410] *Lumley* v. *Wagner* (1852) 1 De G. M. & G. 604.
[411] [1898] AC 1, 121 (Lord Herschell).
[412] *Temperton* v. *Russell* [1893] 1 QB 715.
[413] *J. T. Stratford & Son Ltd.* v. *Lindley* [1965] AC 269.
[414] *Jasperson* v. *Dominion Tobacco Co.* [1923] AC 709.
[415] *Joe Lee Ltd.* v. *Damleny* [1927] 1 Ch. 300; *De Francesco* v. *Burnum* (1890) 43 Ch. D. 165; *Greig* v. *Insole* [1978] 1 WLR 302.
[416] *Greig* v. *Insole* [1978] 1 WLR 302, 341.
[417] See *Exchange Telegraph Co.* v. *Gregory & Co.* [1896] 1 QB 147; *Goldsoll* v. *Goldman* [1914] 2 Ch. 603.

knowingly. Malice in the separate sense of a personal animus against the defendant or an illegitimate motive is not part of the modern tort;[418] on the other hand, mere carelessness is evidently not sufficient.[419] The defendant must either know of the contract[420] in question, or turn a blind eye to its existence. It will, however, suffice if he is reckless as to the consequences of his actions, in the sense of knowingly creating a risk of breach and being indifferent whether or not it happens.[421]

However, it seems that it is not necessary that the defendant should have been aiming to hurt the plaintiff *as such*. This is a requirement of the separate tort of interference with trade or business by unlawful means; but here what matters is the intention to interfere with the plaintiff's contractual right and not the desire to cause him loss.[422] The normal form of the tort involves direct persuasion being brought to bear on the contract-breaker. According to some authorities, it is possible to commit it where A and B enter into a contract which, to A's knowledge, is incompatible with B's contract with C.[423] The passing-on of information, for example to the effect that a given company is being 'blacked' or boycotted by the union, may also be sufficient.[424] It may also be possible to induce breach by 'direct prevention' of performance, as in *GWK Ltd.* v. *Dunlop Rubber Co. Ltd.*[425] where A clandestinely arranged for tyres manufactured by C to be removed from B's vehicles, leaving B in breach of his contract with C. In the same way, hiding an employee's tools may be inducing breach of his contract with his employer.[426]

At the same time, many commentators insist that a firm line should, in principle, be drawn between cases in which the defendant intends to interfere with the contractual rights of the plaintiff, and those situations in which he merely prevents the performance of the contract in question.[427] According to this point of view, *merely* assisting in or facilitating a breach of contract should not, in itself, give rise to tortious liability. However, in *Millar* v. *Bassey*[428] the Court of Appeal came close to holding otherwise. The singer Shirley Bassey was sued by the plaintiffs on the grounds that by deliberately refusing to perform a contract which she had made with a record production company, Dreampeace, she made it impossible for Dreampeace to perform the contracts which it had made with the plaintiffs, who were sessions musicians hired to work on that recording. It was alleged that Ms Bassey knew about the contracts made with the plaintiffs and was aware that they would be broken by Dreampeace as a conse-

---

[418] *Quinn* v. *Leathem* [1901] AC 495, 510 (Lord Macnaghten).

[419] E.g. *Cattle* v. *Stockton Waterworks Co.* (1875) LR 10 QB 453.

[420] As in *Stratford* v. *Lindley* [1965] AC 269.

[421] *Torquay Hotel Co. Ltd.* v. *Cousins* [1969] 2 Ch. 106, 138 (Lord Denning); *Emerald Construction Co. Ltd.* v. *Lowthian* [1966] 1 WLR 691.

[422] See *Smithies* v. *NATSOPA* [1909] 1 KB 310, 316; *D. C. Thomson Ltd.* v. *Deakin* [1952] Ch. 646, 696–7 (Jenkins LJ), 702 (Morris LJ); *Edwin Hill & Partners* v. *First National Finance Corp.* [1989] 1 WLR 225, 234 (Stuart-Smith LJ).

[423] *British Motor Trade Association* v. *Salvadori* [1949] Ch. 556.

[424] As in *Stratford* v. *Lindley* [1965] AC 269; *Torquay Hotel* v. *Cousins* [1969] 2 Ch. 106; but cf. *Thomson* v. *Deakin* [1952] Ch. 646.

[425] (1926) 42 TLR 376.   [426] *Thomson* v. *Deakin* [1952] Ch. 646, 686 (Evershed MR).

[427] See Howarth, *Textbook on Tort* (1995), 479–84; Weir, *Economic Torts*, 35–42.

[428] [1994] EMLR 44.

quence of her own breach. At first instance the claim was struck out as disclosing no cause of action, but the Court of Appeal, Peter Gibson LJ dissenting, reversed this decision and allowed the claim to proceed. The judgment which most clearly supports the view that the law should be clarified in favour of liability in such a case was that of Beldam LJ, who said:

If it is actionable to cause loss to the plaintiff by enticing or persuading another to break his contract with the plaintiff, can it be said to be unarguable that it is actionable to cause such loss by voluntarily and deliberately refusing to perform a contract knowing that such refusal will make it impossible for the other party to fulfil his obligations to the plaintiff? I do not think so.[429]

Peter Gibson LJ, by contrast, maintained that it was a requirement of the tort that the defendant should have intended to interfere with the contract in question. Ralph Gibson LJ agreed and said that '[i]n a case where the defendant has done nothing more than refuse to perform her positive obligations under the contract with the co-defendant, the requirement as to intention may indeed be more than mere knowledge that her refusal will render her co-defendant incapable of performing its contract with the plaintiffs'.[430] Nevertheless, his Lordship went on to hold that the case should proceed to trial so that the principle of law involved could be properly tested. Thus only one judge, Beldam LJ, clearly decided in favour of the extension of liability argued for by the plaintiffs; however, the failure of the Court of Appeal to uphold the judgment of first instance has left the scope of the tort even more unclear than it was before.

In the context of industrial action, the union official who organises the strike action will almost certainly commit the tort of inducing breach of the employment contracts of his members (and will therefore have to show that he has the protection of the trade-dispute immunity, considered below). In part this is because, contrary to what happened in *Allen* v. *Flood*,[431] contracts of employment now normally require notice of several weeks to be given for the contract to be terminated lawfully.[432] Even if the union gives the employer extensive strike notice (and in practice this is unusual), this is most unlikely to amount to notice on behalf of the members lawfully to terminate their contracts. The union is not normally authorised to act as agent of the members for this purpose.[433] It is theoretically possible that the members could give the union the necessary authority, but the practical difficulties of proceeding in this way are probably too great to make it worthwhile. Another point to bear in mind is that employees who go on strike rarely intend to put an end to the employment relationship: almost invariably, they intend to return to work once the dispute is settled. This makes it unrealistic to regard strike notice as evidence of an intention to terminate the employment relationship as opposed to suspending it. However, the common law does not recognise the possibility that the contract of employment could be lawfully suspended for the duration of the

---

[429] [1994] EMLR 44, 55.   [430] Ibid., 72.   [431] [1898] AC 1.
[432] See, in this regard, Employment Rights Act 1996, s. 86 ff.
[433] See *Boxfoldia Ltd.* v. *NGA* [1988] IRLR 383.

dispute: going on strike will almost certainly amount to a repudiatory breach of the contract of employment by the striker.[434]

The common law does recognise a limited justification defence to this tort, but its scope is so limited as to be practically meaningless, at least in cases of labour disputes. In *South Wales Miners' Federation* v. *Glamorgan Coal Co. Ltd.*[435] the House of Lords rejected an argument to the effect that a union could be justified in organising strike action where it was in the economic interests of its members, although a similar defence was later to prove acceptable in the context of conspiracy to injure. The difference lies, perhaps, in that conspiracy to injure does not involve the use of unlawful means. Something exceptional is required to invoke the defence, such as the argument, accepted by the court in *Brimelow* v. *Casson*,[436] that industrial action taken to raise the wages of chorus girls was the only means available to save them from resort to prostitution. It may be easier to establish justification in non-labour cases. In *Edwin Hill & Partners* v. *First National Finance Corp.*[437] the Court of Appeal accepted that justification would be made out in a case where the defendant had an equal or superior right to that of the plaintiff. In this case the defendant had rights as a secured creditor over certain land, having lent money to the developer. The plaintiffs, a firm of architects, had a contract with the developer. The defendant could have called in its loan with the result that the plaintiff would immediately have lost any right it had to insist on its contract with the developer. Instead, the defendant arranged a re-financing deal as part of which the developer had to agree to appoint new architects and dismiss the plaintiffs. The Court of Appeal held that the defendant had been acting in pursuance of its own rights over the property and therefore had a defence to an action of inducing breach of the plaintiff's contract.

(B) OTHER FORMS OF INTERFERENCE WITH CONTRACT

In the classic tort exemplified by *Lumley* v. *Gye*, it was essential that the inducement be *direct* and that it should lead to a *breach* of the relevant contractual obligation. These requirements have been watered down in a number of recent, controversial decisions.

(i) 'Indirect' Interference with Contract   This occurs when, in the course of a strike, the organisers of the strike put the employer in a position where he cannot perform commercial contracts with third parties. No direct inducement to the breach of these contracts has taken place; breach comes about indirectly, because the employer's workforce is temporarily unavailable to him. Although it is not possible to talk about direct inducement, the courts

---

[434] *Simmons* v. *Hoover Ltd.* [1977] QB 284; the attempt of Lord Denning to argue the contrary in *Morgan* v. *Fry* [1968] QB 710 has not found favour.

[435] [1905] AC 239. See also *Smithies* v. *NATSOPA* [1909] 1 KB 310; *Pratt* v. *British Medical Association* [1919] 1 KB 244; *De Jetley Marks* v. *Lord Greenwood* [1936] 1 All ER 863; *Camden Nominees* v. *Forcey* [1940] Ch. 352.

[436] [1924] 1 Ch. 302.

[437] [1989] 1 WLR 225. See also *SOS Kinderdorf International* v. *Bittaye* [1996] 1 WLR 987, 993–4: 'circumstances such as to justify an employer in dismissing an employee cannot, except perhaps in exceptional circumstances, constitute justification for a third party interfering with the contract' (Lord Keith of Kinkel).

have held that the third-party employer may complain about indirect induce-ment to breach of the commercial contract in question. This tort first made its appearance in *D. C. Thomson & Co. Ltd.* v. *Deakin*.[438] The union NATSOPA was conducting a boycott of Thomsons, which did not permit union members to be among its workforce. In sympathy with NATSOPA, members of the Transport and General Workers' Union (TGWU) who were employees of Bowaters, a firm which supplied printing material under contract to Thomsons, told their employer that they would not be willing to supply mat-erial to Thomsons in pursuance of this contract. Subsequently Bowaters failed to supply the material and Thomsons sued officials of the TGWU for an injunction. The Court of Appeal held that liability in tort could arise where the interference, although indirect, came about through unlawful means. The requirements, according to Jenkins LJ, were as follows. The defendant must have known of the existence of the commercial contract and must have intended to procure its breach; he must have induced breach of the employ-ment contracts of the relevant work-force; and there must have been, as a necessary consequence of this, a breach of the commercial contract. Jenkins LJ thought that the withdrawal of labour had to be 'comparable, for practical purposes, to a direct invasion of the contractual rights' of the plaintiff. On the facts found by the court, Thomsons' action failed because Bowaters' employ-ees did not break their contracts of employment: Bowaters did not actually require its employees to undertake the necessary deliveries. This was a rather exceptional case. By contrast, in *J. T. Stratford & Son Ltd.* v. *Lindley*[439] the union action in question was unlawful, in the sense that an instruction issued by the union amounted to inducing breach of the employment contracts of its mem-bers. This was enough to establish the tort of indirect interference.

The tort of 'indirect interference' is, in truth, a hybrid of the tort of induc-ing breach of contract and the tort of interference with business by unlawful means (considered below). Because the interference is not direct, it cannot be regarded as a straightforward application of *Lumley* v. *Gye* and so it is necessary to find some other element of unlawful means: 'indirect interference is only unlawful if unlawful means are used.'[440] However, the tort also differs from the normal situation of interference by unlawful means. It is an element of that tort that the defendant should have been 'aiming at' the plaintiff, in the sense of intending to cause him economic damage;[441] but this does not appear to be an element of the tort of 'indirect interference'. With indirect interfer-ence, it is sufficient that the defendant should have intended to procure the relevant breach of contract; the plaintiff can sue if he is denied performance even if he is not the person against whom the defendant was aiming. In addi-tion to being unsatisfactory from a doctrinal point of view, this is a potentially considerable extension of liability since it opens a wider range of potential plaintiffs who may well be the incidental and unintended victims of industrial action.

[438] [1952] Ch. 646. [439] [1965] AC 269.
[440] *Torquay Hotel* v. *Cousins* [1969] 2 Ch. 106, 138 (Lord Denning MR).
[441] *Hadmor Productions Ltd.* v. *Hamilton* [1983] 1 AC 191.

The problems inherent in extending tortious liability in this way were evident in *Middlebrook Mushrooms Ltd.* v. *Transport and General Workers' Union*.[442] Members of the trade union distributed leaflets outside supermarkets with the aim of persuading members of the public not to buy mushrooms produced by the plaintiff (which was in dispute with a number of its employees who were members of the union). The Court of Appeal lifted an injunction that had been granted at first instance on the grounds, among others, that there was no clear intention to induce breach of the contracts that the supermarkets might have had with the plaintiffs. Although such a breach *might* have been a consequence of the defendant's conduct, this was not a case of direct inducement, since at no stage did the defendant approach the supermarket managers with the aim of persuading them to break an existing contract. Nor, in the context of indirect interference, were unlawful means used in seeking to convince members of the public not to buy the plaintiff's products. However, the issues at stake were sufficiently unclear for the judge hearing the case to have granted an injunction that severely disrupted the defendant's efforts to organise industrial action in defence of its members' interests.

(ii) 'Bare' Interference with Contractual Performance   It appears to be the case that the plaintiff does not have to show that the contractual obligation in question was actually broken. It is enough to show that there was an interference with performance, falling short of breach but causing loss to *either party* (B or C) to the contract in question.

This notion of liability for 'bare' interference falling short of inducing breach started life in *Torquay Hotel Co. Ltd.* v. *Cousins*.[443] The defendants succeeded in interrupting supplies of fuel to the hotel, with whom their members were in dispute. The contract for the supply of the fuel contained a *force majeure* clause according to which neither side was to be liable if performance was prevented by factors outside their control, such as industrial action. The owners of the hotel nevertheless succeeded in getting an injunction on the basis that their right to receive contractual performance had been interfered with, even though they could not themselves have brought an action against the supplier for damages for breach of contract. Lord Denning said: 'There must be *interference* in the execution of a contract. The interference is not confined to the procurement of a *breach* of contract. It extends to a case where a third person *prevents* or *hinders* one party from performing his contract, even though it be not a breach.[444]

This decision has been criticised as going against *Allen* v. *Flood*, since that case decided that some element of independent unlawfulness is a precondition of economic tort liability (conspiracy aside).[445] *Torquay Hotel* was nevertheless confirmed by the House of Lords in *Merkur Island Shipping Corp.* v. *Laughton*,[446] in which the relevant commercial contract contained a similar *force majeure* clause. Lord Diplock cited the judgment of Jenkins LJ in *Thomson* v. *Deakin* (discussed above), but omitted to say that Jenkins LJ spoke at each relevant point about the

---

[442] [1993] IRLR 232.   [443] [1969] 2 Ch. 106.   [444] Ibid., 138.
[445] See in particular Weir, *Economic Torts*, 36–8.   [446] [1983] 2 AC 570.

inducement of a *breach* of contract and not of mere interference with contract *falling short of breach*. Lord Diplock also said that since Parliament, in the relevant legislation at that time,[447] had granted immunity in certain circumstances (of which this was not one) from liability for the tort of interference with contract, this was some evidence that the tort did indeed exist at common law. Since it is clear that the draughtsman included this provision just in case the tort invented by Lord Denning in *Torquay Hotel* might, in the future, be seen as legitimate, in order that it should then be immunised, Lord Diplock's interpretation can only be regarded as perverse. His approach could conceivably be justified on the basis that the exclusion clause does not prevent there being a breach of the *primary* contractual obligation to perform; its effect is confined to excluding the *secondary* liability to pay damages arising out of breach. This distinction is developed in Lord Diplock's own judgment in *Photo Production Ltd.* v. *Securicor Transport Ltd.*[448]

The House of Lords relied on the tort of interference in slightly different circumstances in *Dimbleby & Sons Ltd.* v. *National Union of Journalists*.[449] The union was conducting a boycott of a third-party company, TBF Ltd., in pursuance of a trade dispute. Dimbleby had a contract for some printing to be carried out by another company in the TBF group. The union called on its members employed at Dimbleby to 'black' the TBF contract. It was held that the union had thereby committed the tort of interfering with the commercial contract between Dimbleby and the TBF company, and Dimbleby was granted an injunction.[450] This is not as straightforward as it might seem, since Dimbleby was the party whose performance was being interfered with (B), not the party to whom performance was owed (C). Moreover, Dimbleby did actually perform its contract, but at greater expense to itself.

It seems that once the tort is extended from inducement of breach to interference with contractual performance, either party to the contract can sue without necessarily being the person against whom the defendant was 'aiming'. The potential range of the tort is indicated by the county court judgment *Falconer* v. *Aslef*.[451] Because of a rail-strike called by the defendant unions in pursuance of a trade dispute, the plaintiff was unable to make a return journey from London to the North of England as he had planned and had to stay in a hotel in London for a further two days. He successfully sued the unions for damages representing his expenses. His return ticket incorporated an exclusion clause exempting British Rail from liability but this did not prevent him from suing for interference. The case is also distinctive in that the plaintiff was not

---

[447] Trade Union and Labour Relations Act 1974, s. 13(1); now Trade Union and Labour Relations (Consolidation) Act 1992, s. 219(1).

[448] [1980] AC 827.   [449] [1984] 1 WLR 427.

[450] There was no immunity on account of the secondary action provisions of s. 17 of the 1980 Employment Act: see Simpson, op. cit.

[451] [1986] IRLR 331. See also *SOS Kinderdorf International* v. *Bittaye* [1996] 1 WLR 987 in which the Privy Council, on appeal from the Court of Appeal of The Gambia, held, rather surprisingly, that the first defendant's act of cutting off the power to the plaintiff's residence and depriving him of the use of his car amounted to the tort of interference with his contract of employment with the second defendant. Somewhat unsatisfactorily, the interference point receives only the briefest of consideration by Lord Keith ([1996] 1 WLR 987, 993).

being 'aimed at' by the defendant: his loss was foreseeable but he was not the intended victim of pressure.

(iii) Making a Contract Less Valuable   This is *not* a tort, nor does it constitute unlawful means, in the absence of interference with a contractual obligation. The point was discussed in *RCA Corp.* v. *Pollard*,[452] one of the 'bootlegger' cases concerning claims brought by performers and record companies against distributors of recordings of concert performances made illegally. The illegal activities of the bootleggers undoubtedly diminished the value to the record companies of their exclusive recording contracts with the performers, but this was held to be insufficient on its own to form the basis for a cause of action: a person cannot be held liable in tort for knowingly making certain contractual rights less valuable, without actually interfering with the performance of the contractual obligations in question.

(c) Inducing Breach of Fiduciary Duty

In principle, contractual rights are not the only rights which may be protected from interference by an action in tort. Inducing breach of a fiduciary duty was found to be tortious in *Prudential Assurance Co.* v. *Lorenz*,[453] a case of a strike of insurance agents. However, there may be a limit to how far tortious liability may be incurred through inducing or assisting in a breach of an equitable obligation, not least because the intervention of tort could upset rules of equity in this area. For this reason the Court of Appeal in *Metall und Rohstoff AG* v. *Donaldson Lufkin Jenrette Inc.*[454] held that assisting in the breach of a constructive trust did not give rise to liability in tort (although it may be noted that the *Prudential Assurance* case was not cited to the court). As a result of these contradictory decisions, the precise scope of tortious liability for interference with equitable obligations is unclear.[455]

(d) Inducing Breach of Statutory Duty

In *Meade* v. *Haringey London Borough Council*[456] the Court of Appeal held that, in principle, a person affected by the failure of an employer to maintain a service which he was required to maintain by virtue of a statutory obligation could bring an action against the employer for breach of statutory duty and also against the union which had *induced* the breach of statute. In this case a trade union had called a strike of caretakers and others employed in the council's schools. The council ordered the schools to close on the day of the strike. Lord Denning suggested that the council was in breach of its statutory duty to parents under the Education Acts and that the union could have been liable for inducing this breach. In the event no injunction was issued, since the strike had come to an end by the time the case reached the Court of Appeal. However, the principle

---

[452] [1983] 1 Ch. 135.

[453] (1971) 1 KIR 78. In this case, the tort was committed when a strike of insurance agents was called.

[454] [1990] 1 QB 391. See also *Law Debenture Trust Ltd.* v. *Ural Caspian Oil Corp.* [1995] 1 All ER 157, 167 (no liability in tort for interference with a contingent equitable right to the return of property), discussed by Weir, *Economic Torts*, 30.

[455] For discussion, see Weir, *Economic Torts*, 31–2, in particular fn. 29.   [456] [1979] ICR 494.

established in *Meade* has since gained more general acceptance.[457] This is particularly significant for labour-dispute cases, since unlike the torts of interference with contract there is no statutory immunity for this particular tort.[458]

The development of the principle of liability for a breach of an obligation imposed by European Community law[459] has also increased the scope of liability. In *Barretts & Baird (Wholesale) Ltd.* v. *Institution of Professional Civil Servants*[460] there was a strike by civil servants employed by the Meat and Livestock Commission, a body with a statutory duty to operate a guaranteed price system both under the Agriculture Act 1967 and under European Community law. The judge found that on the facts the employer had not been placed in breach of the relevant obligation, but had it been he was prepared to grant an injunction to meat producers who would have been affected by the strike. It is possible that 'bare interference' with a statutory duty will suffice to establish liability, by analogy with the *Torquay Hotel* principle.[461]

At one stage it was thought that the statutory duty in question had to be independently actionable at the suit of the plaintiff, in the sense of satisfying the test laid down in *Cutler* v. *Wandsworth Stadium Ltd.*[462] In *Associated British Ports* v. *Transport and General Workers Union* the Court of Appeal ruled that a non-actionable breach of statutory duty could constitute unlawful means for the purpose of the general tort of interference with business by unlawful means.[463] Although in this case it will be necessary to show that the defendant intended to injure the plaintiff in the sense of aiming at him, the scope of potential tort liability is once again greatly increased by this possibility.

An area particularly affected by the growth of the tort of inducing breach of statute concerns public-sector workers whose employers are responsible by statute for the maintenance of certain services. In some cases the relevant Act of Parliament makes specific provision both for the initial statutory duty to be actionable and for any party inducing a breach to be held responsible. For example, the Telecommunications Act 1984 contains a provision for the Director-General of Telecommunications to impose an enforcement order on a licensed operator under certain circumstances. Any person affected by subsequent non-compliance with the order can bring an action for damages for breach of statutory duty and, in the event of the failure being due to industrial action, may bring an action against the organiser of that action for loss suffered.[464]

---

[457] In particular in *Associated British Ports* v. *TGWU* [1989] IRLR 305 (CA), discussed below.

[458] Cf. Trade Union and Labour Relations (Consolidation) Act 1992, s. 219.

[459] *Garden Cottage Foods Ltd.* v. *Milk Marketing Board* [1984] AC 130.

[460] [1987] IRLR 3; noted by Napier [1987] *CLJ* 222.

[461] See *Associated British Ports* v. *TGWU* [1989] IRLR 305 (CA).

[462] [1949] AC 398. See above, Chapter 3, Section 4(1). The view that the economic tort of inducing breach of statutory duty would be limited in this way was based on *Lonrho Ltd.* v. *Shell Petroleum Co. Ltd.* [1983] AC 173 and *Barretts & Baird* v. *IPCS* [1987] IRLR 3. See also *Wilson* v. *Housing Corp.* [1998] ICR 151, in which Dyson J held that there was no cause of action for inducing another to commit an unfair dismissal of an employee.

[463] [1989] IRLR 305. The House of Lords allowed an appeal on the narrower ground that no statutory duty of any kind arose on the particular facts: [1989] IRLR 399.

[464] Telecommunications Act 1984, s. 18. Actions may also be possible under the slightly different provisions of the Gas Act 1986, s. 30; the Water Industry Act 1991, s. 22; and the Electricity Act 1989, s. 27. See G. S. Morris, 'Industrial Action in Essential Services' (1991) 20 *Industrial Law Journal* 89, 96.

3. Interference with the Plaintiff's Trade or Business by Unlawful Means

The 'genus' tort of causing loss by unlawful means has expanded considerably since the decision of the House of Lords in *Rookes* v. *Barnard*.[465] The categories of unlawful means are now very wide. The term 'unlawful means' signifies *acts which the defendant was not at liberty to commit* or, by virtue of the tort sometimes called 'intimidation', *threats* to commit such acts. The notion of 'not being at liberty'[466] to commit a given act covers restraints imposed by the law of tort (including fraud and misrepresentation) and by contract; more uncertainly, it appears, at least according to some authorities, to extend to obligations derived from the criminal law and from statutory duties.[467] The wrong in question does not need to be independently actionable, as it normally does for the torts considered in the previous section. In this sense, the tort of causing loss by unlawful means has a much broader scope than torts based on interference with the plaintiff's pre-existing rights. However, there is another sense in which the tort of causing loss by unlawful means is narrower. It is necessary to show that the defendant had an 'intent to injure' the plaintiff, or that he was 'aiming at him' as the object of the economic pressure he was seeking to exert or the damage he was seeking to inflict. It has to be borne in mind both that the economic torts are torts of intention and that the focus of intention differs from one tort to another. With inducing breach of contract and related torts, the plaintiff must intend to interfere with the performance of the obligation in question; with causing loss by unlawful means, he must intend to inflict economic damage on the plaintiff as such.

(A) CATEGORIES OF UNLAWFUL MEANS

(i) Physical Threats   The application of physical force or violence, or the threat of such violence, is the classic case of unlawful means.[468] A threat of violence made by a striker to a worker crossing a picket line would constitute the tort of intimidation, for example.[469]

(ii) Fraud and Misrepresentation   The use of fraud or misrepresentation will also constitute unlawful means. The tort was used to enforce a price-maintenance agreement in *National Phonograph Co. Ltd.* v. *Edison Bell Co. Ltd.*[470] The defendants had been placed by the plaintiffs on the 'suspended list' for failure to sell at the set price of the plaintiffs' products, with the result that they

---

[465] [1964] AC 1129.

[466] This is the phrase used by Lord Denning in numerous cases: e.g. *Torquay Hotel Co.* v. *Cousins* [1969] 2 Ch. 106, 139.

[467] See generally H. Carty, 'Intentional Violation of Economic Interests: The Limits of Common Law Liability' (1988) *LQR* 250, 265 ff., for a discussion of the concept of unlawful means and of possible alternatives to the test of the defendant 'not being at liberty' to commit a particular act. An argument exists to the effect that only breaches of the civil law should constitute unlawful means: this is related to the idea that many (although not all) of the economic torts cases can be explained in terms of a more general theory of secondary civil liability: P. Sales, 'The Tort of Conspiracy and Civil Secondary Liability' [1990] *CLJ* 491.

[468] As in the old case of *Tarleton* v. *McGawley* (1793) Peake NP 270.

[469] See *Messenger Group Newspapers* v. *NGA* [1984] ICR 397.   [470] [1908] 1 Ch. 335.

could not buy from the plaintiff or its agents. The defendants none the less obtained the plaintiff's products by deception, by having their employees act as independent dealers. This placed the plaintiffs' dealers, unknowingly, in breach of their contracts with the plaintiffs. The plaintiffs succeeded in their action against the defendants on the grounds that the latter had used unlawful means, namely a fraudulent misrepresentation, to impose a loss on them.

The point arose more recently in *Lonrho plc* v. *Fayed*.[471] Lonrho argued that it had incurred damage as a result of an alleged fraud perpetrated on the Secretary of State for Industry by Fayed, which led to the Secretary of State permitting them to make a bid for the department store Harrods when Lonrho had previously been prevented from doing so. Lonrho's claim under the tort of interference with trade was struck out as disclosing no cause of action, but the Court of Appeal, affirmed by the House of Lords on this point, reinstated the claim. The Court of Appeal accepted that 'the unlawful act was in some sense directed against the plaintiff or intended to harm the plaintiff', but rejected a proposition that it was necessary, in addition, to show that the 'predominant purpose' of the defendant was to injure the plaintiff. They also rejected an argument that the unlawful means—here, the alleged fraud—had to be independently actionable.

(iii) Breach of Contract and Inducing Breach of Contract   The central issue decided by *Rookes* v. *Barnard* was that a threat of breach of contract or of inducement to breach of contract could constitute unlawful means and, therefore, that the scope of unlawful means was not confined to physical threats and fraud. Prior to *Rookes* there was clear authority only for the proposition that certain criminal or tortious acts and threats of physical violence or coercion could constitute unlawful means,[472] although the notion that a threatened breach of contract would suffice is implicit in several of the judgments in *Allen* v. *Flood*.[473] In *Rookes* the plaintiff, a draughtsman employed by BOAC, left the draughtmen's union after a dispute. His colleagues threatened to strike unless he was dismissed, and the employer duly suspended and then dismissed him by giving him the necessary notice under his contract of employment. Because he received notice of his dismissal, he could not take advantage of the tort of inducing breach of contract: BOAC had not committed a breach. However, the threat made by his colleagues had been unlawful, in the sense that a strike would have involved them in a breach of their contracts of employment. This was the crucial difference between *Rookes* and *Allen* v. *Flood*. In *Allen*, the threat to strike had been lawful: the notice required to quit was so short that no breach of contract would have been involved. In *Rookes*, by contrast, not only was the notice required to be given to terminate the contracts of employment much longer (several weeks) but, on one reading of the case, the contracts had incorporated a 'no-strike' clause which bound the individual employees.

It was the case, of course, that Rookes himself could not have sued BOAC for breach of contract; but this was not fatal to his claim. Because BOAC had

---

[471] [1990] 2 QB 479 (CA); [1992] 1 AC 448 (HL).
[472] Hence the judgment of the Court of Appeal which found for the defendants: [1963] 1 QB 623.
[473] [1898] AC 1.

responded immediately to pressure of an unlawful kind from the defendants, and because the defendants were intending to injure Rookes in the case of aiming their pressure at him as a non-union member, the tort of intimidation was established. What Rookes was suing for was, as Lord Reid put it, 'loss caused to him by the use of an unlawful weapon against him—intimidation of another person by unlawful means'. In this respect, a breach of contract was as much unlawful means as a threat of physical harm. Lord Reid said:

I agree with Lord Herschell [in *Allen* v. *Flood*] that there is a chasm between doing what you have a legal right to do and doing what you have no legal right to do, and there seems to me to be the same chasm between threatening to do what you have a legal right to do and threatening to do what you have no legal right to do. It must follow from *Allen* v. *Flood* that to intimidate by threatening to do what you have a legal right to do is to intimidate by lawful means. But I see no good reason for extending that doctrine. Threatening a breach of contract may be a much more coercive weapon than threatening a tort, particularly when the threat is directed against a company or corporation, and, if there is no technical reason requiring a distinction between different kinds of threats, I can see no other ground for making such a distinction.[474]

The House of Lords has since confirmed the nature of this tort. In *Stratford* v. *Lindley*[475] the defendants committed the tort of interference with business by the unlawful means of inducing breach of the employment contracts of their members, thereby placing the plaintiff in breach of numerous commercial contracts and causing him loss. In *Hadmor Productions Ltd.* v. *Hamilton*[476] action taken to 'black' the plaintiff's business by inducing the union's members not to deal with it, in breach of their contracts of employment, amounted to interference by unlawful means.

There are, nevertheless, some unexpected consequences of treating a breach of contract as unlawful means. This is the case in so-called two-party intimidation where the plaintiff and defendant are parties to the same contract. If one threatens the other with breach of contract, it might seem odd to allow the victim to sue in tort rather than in contract, thereby permitting him to avoid rules of contract law (such as the mitigation and remoteness rules) which limit the extent of contract damages in comparison with tort. For this reason it has been suggested that breach of contract should only be treated as unlawful means for the purposes of three-party intimidation, that is to say the position in *Rookes* v. *Barnard* and in most labour dispute cases, and that for two-party intimidation the plaintiff should have to show a physical threat of some kind.[477]

(iv) Crime The extent to which non-violent activity that involves a breach of a regulatory statute providing for criminal sanctions constitutes unlawful means is not altogether clear. In principle it appears that it may, but for the plaintiff to have an action in tort he must show not simply that the activity in question has caused him harm; he must also show that he was the intended as opposed to the incidental victim. In *Lonrho Ltd.* v. *Shell Petroleum Co. Ltd.*[478]

---

[474] [1964] AC 1129, 1168–9.   [475] [1965] AC 269.   [476] [1983] 1 AC 191.
[477] See Carty, op. cit. (Select Bibliography), 260–2.   [478] [1982] AC 173.

Lonrho sued the oil companies Shell and BP for losses it had occurred as a consequence of alleged sanctions-busting by the defendants, consisting of the supply of oil to the illegal Rhodesian regime contrary to orders made under legislation. Sanctions-busting was said to have maintained the illegal regime in power, thereby preventing Lonrho making profits from its own legitimate activities in that part of Africa. The action was struck out on the basis that even if the allegation were true, no cause of action arose since it had not been shown that Shell and BP had any intention to injure Lonrho.

Had Lonrho been able to show that the statute in question created an implied action for breach of statutory duty on its part, it could have brought an action under this head of liability. However, the House of Lords found that, under the established tests, no implied action for breach of statute arose in this case. Lonrho also argued that the principle enunciated in *Gouriet* v. *Union of Post Office Workers*[479] could form the basis for a claim in damages. In this case the plaintiff sued for an injunction to prevent the union carrying out a boycott of post destined for South Africa, which would have been in breach of various criminal statutes. The House of Lords held that a statutory obligation which confers an interest on the public as a whole (as opposed to one conferring protection upon a particular group, in the sense used in *Cutler* v. *Wandsworth Stadium Ltd.*)[480] could be enforced by a plaintiff who by virtue of the breach had suffered special damage over and above that of the general public. In *Gouriet* itself the plaintiff failed since he had not attempted to post a letter to South Africa; he was simply a concerned member of the public.[481] However, the principle laid down in *Gouriet* was then taken up by Lord Denning in *Ex parte Island Records Ltd.*,[482] in which the Court of Appeal granted an injunction to performers and record companies for the enforcement of legislation prohibiting the unauthorised recording of dramatic performances by 'bootleggers'.

However, in *Lonrho* v. *Shell* Lord Diplock cast doubt on the existence of any such principle, at least in so far as it could be said to extend to grant a plaintiff a right to damages as opposed to an injunction. He also formally rejected the proposition advanced by the High Court of Australia in *Beaudesert Shire Council* v. *Smith*[483] that an action for damages may be brought by one who suffers damage 'as the inevitable consequence of the unlawful, intentional and positive act of another'. This proposition, it is true, has no authority of any substance in its favour and has not been followed.[484] In particular, it is deficient in failing to consider whether the statute in question was meant to confer a civil action on the plaintiff or whether the plaintiff was the intended victim of the defendant's acts. However, Lord Diplock's broad dicta go much further than a rejection of *Beaudesert*. If *Gouriet* is correct (and there is no reason to assume it is not) the odd situation arises of an injunction being made available to an individual damaged

---

[479] [1978] AC 435.　　　　　　　　　　　　　　[480] [1949] AC 398.

[481] He was a member of a group known as the National Association for Freedom.

[482] [1978] Ch. 122.

[483] (1966) 120 CLR 145. On the status of *Beaudesert* in Australian law, see *Northern Territory* v. *Mengel* (1995) 185 CLR 307; N. Mullany, 'Beaudesert buried' (1995) 111 *LQR* 583; Weir, *Economic Torts*, 13.

[484] See *Kitano* v. *Commonwealth of Australia* (1974) 129 CLR 151; *Dunlop* v. *Woollahra MC* [1982] AC 158.

by unlawful action, but damages nevertheless being unavailable in respect of the same wrong.[485]

In *RCA Corporation* v. *Pollard*[486] the Court of Appeal found a solution in the context of the 'bootlegging' statutes by reinterpreting the relevant legislation to give performers (but not their record companies) an action for breach of statutory duty under the principles in *Cutler* v. *Wandsworth Stadium*. But *Cutler* remains authority, in general, for the courts taking a restrictive approach to the discovery of the implied action for breach of statute.[487]

(v) Interference with Statutory Obligations   A related question is how far interference with the performance of an obligation imposed by statute, which might have nothing to do with any criminal offence, can constitute unlawful means. We have already seen that inducing breach of a statutory duty owed to a third party is almost certainly actionable by that person; by analogy with breach of contract, there is no reason why a breach of statute (or, by extension, mere interference) should not also be unlawful means. It has also been suggested that for the purposes of the tort of causing loss by unlawful means, it does not matter whether the breach of statute is independently actionable as a tort. Again, *Rookes* v. *Barnard*[488] can be invoked as authority for this proposition. The unlawful means in that case (the threatened breach of contract by Rookes's colleagues) was certainly not actionable by Rookes himself and was probably not actionable by BOAC either, in the sense of being only a threatened breach. Lord Reid's notion of unlawful means as an act that the defendant was 'not at liberty to commit' could certainly cover a breach of statute *as such* whether or not a third party could bring an action in respect of the loss. This reasoning persuaded the Court of Appeal to grant an injunction in *Associated British Ports* v. *Transport & General Workers' Union*,[489] a case in which a threatened strike would have involved the workers concerned acting in breach of an obligation to work normally which was contained in regulations incorporating the National Dock Labour Scheme. The House of Lords reversed on the narrow ground that the regulations in question did no more than repeat the *contractual* duty of the workers under their contracts of employment; since the unlawful means of inducing breach of the contract of employment was covered by the relevant statutory immunity, the injunction was lifted.[490]

It is possible that the person upon whom a statutory duty is placed could also seek an injunction to prevent interference with its performance. Quite apart from the specific statutory provisions (mentioned above) governing the position of certain utilities, this may be the case wherever an employer is placed under a statutory obligation to ensure the continuity of a particular service.[491] By analogy with the tort found in *Dimbleby & Sons* v. *NUJ*,[492] an employer subjected to a strike of his own employees could argue that unlawful means—

---

[485] There is important 19th-century authority supporting the principle invoked in *Gouriet*: see *Springhead Spinning Co.* v. *Riley* (1868) LR 6 E1. 551. See also *Department of Transport* v. *Williams* [1993] Times LR 367, discussed by Weir, *Economic Torts*, 19.

[486] [1983] Ch. 135.   [487] See above, Chapter 3, Section 4(1).

[488] [1964] AC 1129.   [489] [1989] IRLR 305.   [490] [1989] IRLR 399.

[491] See above.   [492] [1984] 1 WLR 427; discussed above, Section 2(b)(ii).

interference with the statutory duty imposed upon him—were being used to cause him loss. As the unlawful means in this case would not be covered by any statutory immunity, the point—although still undecided—is of considerable practical significance for the scope of the freedom to strike.

(vi) Other Categories   Other categories of unlawful means have been invoked from time to time. One possibility is contempt of court, although the authorities here are equivocal.[493] In *Associated Newspaper Group* v. *Wade*[494] Lord Denning thought that 'interference with the freedom of the press' might qualify, but this is thought to be incorrect: the defendant's freedom of action must be restrained by a specific legal obligation. It would appear to follow from *Mogul Steamship* v. *McGregor, Gow*[495] that restraint of trade is not unlawful means for this purpose.

(B) Economic Duress

Economic duress is another area in which the boundaries of liability are being tested. In *The Universe Sentinel*[496] the House of Lords allowed the plaintiff to recover money which it had paid over to the union under duress, in order to free its ship from blacking. To establish economic duress, it must be shown firstly that the defendant brought pressure to bear on the plaintiff in such a way as to vitiate his will or consent, and secondly that the pressure was of a kind 'which the law does not regard as legitimate'.[497] It is not necessary to find independently unlawful means. In commercial cases, even where duress involves a threat to break a pre-existing contractual obligation, the courts have sometimes been reluctant to apply the doctrine if that would mean invalidating arms-length commercial transactions.[498] In cases of labour disputes, the House of Lords held in *The Universe Sentinel* that what counts as 'legitimate' is to be decided by reference to the statutory trade-dispute immunities, a rare and controversial example of the common law borrowing from legislation. 'This was judicial legislation, for there was no immunity in [the Trade Union and Labour Relations Act 1974] for economic duress (for the good reason that Parliament in 1974 had no idea that any such liability could possibly arise in trade disputes).'[499] In general, economic duress acts as a basis for a restitutionary action for the return of money or for rescission of a contract at the option of the victim of the pressure. In *The Universe Sentinel*, however, Lord Scarman expressed the view that it could be 'actionable as a tort'.[500] If this view is adopted, *Allen* v. *Flood* will be further undermined.

---

[493] In *Acrow (Automation) Ltd.* v. *Rex Chainbelt Inc.* [1971] 3 All ER 1175 Lord Denning MR thought that it could be unlawful means on the grounds that contempt of court involved acts which the defendant was not at liberty to commit, but cf. *Chapman* v. *Honig* [1963] 2 QB 502 (in which Lord Denning MR dissented).

[494] [1979] ICR 664.   [495] [1892] AC 25.

[496] *Universe Tankships Inc. of Monrovia* v. *International Transport Workers' Federation* [1983] 1 AC 366; see also *Dimskal Shipping Co.* v. *International Transport Workers' Federation, The Evia Luck* [1991] 4 All ER 871.

[497] *The Universe Sentinel* [1983] 1 AC 366, 384 (Lord Diplock).

[498] See *Pao On* v. *Lau Yiu Long* [1980] AC 614 (PC); *The Atlantic Baron* [1979] QB 705.

[499] Lord Wedderburn, *The Worker and the Law* (3rd edn., 1986), 653.   [500] [1983] 1 AC 366, 400.

(C) Defences

In *Rookes* v. *Barnard*[501] the House of Lords rejected any possibility of a justification defence. This follows from the use of unlawful means: pressure intentionally exercised through unlawfulness is not capable of being justified by any superior motive of the defendant. However, it may be that there is a limited justification defence by way of analogy with the defence which is available in cases of inducing breach of contract, namely that the defendant was asserting a pre-existing legal right which was at least the equal of the right he was interfering with.[502]

4. Conspiracy

It is necessary to distinguish two senses of the tort of conspiracy: conspiracy to injure, which does not require an element of independent unlawfulness, and conspiracy to use unlawful means.

(A) Conspiracy to Injure

This tort is based on an agreement amongst several persons to combine together with the aim of injuring the plaintiff, with resulting damage. No unlawful means are required but there is a wide justification defence: the defendants will avoid liability if they can show that their purpose in combining together was legitimately to advance their own self-interests.

In *Quinn* v. *Leathem*[503] the jury found that the motive of the defendants in boycotting the plaintiff's business was 'to injure the plaintiff in his trade as distinguished from the intention of legitimately advancing their own interests'. On its facts the decision to award the plaintiff damages was problematical, since it could have been argued that the defendants, by placing pressure on the business of a non-union employer, were seeking to advance their own economic self-interest at the expense of non-union competitors. Parliament was sufficiently concerned to enact the wide-ranging 'second limb' of section 3 of the Trade Disputes Act 1906, according to which, within the scope of the trade-dispute formula, a simple act of interference with the trade or business of another was not to be actionable in tort. This turned out be unnecessary when the House of Lords confined *Quinn* v. *Leathem* to a case in which the defendants had exhibited malice towards the plaintiff, that is to say, their interest in doing him down outweighed their own interest in preserving their share of the trade.[504]

The tort of conspiracy to injure received a further narrowing in *Crofter Hand Woven Harris Tweed Co.* v. *Veitch*.[505] This concerned an agreement between officials of a trade union and a group of employers, with whom it operated a closed

---

[501] [1964] AC 1129.   [502] See *Rookes* v. *Barnard* [1964] AC 1129, 1206, 1209 (Lord Devlin).
[503] [1901] AC 495.
[504] *Sorrell* v. *Smith* [1925] AC 700. The successor provision to the 'second limb', s. 13(2) of the Trade Union and Labour Relations Act 1974, was repealed in 1982, but the best view is that this makes no difference in practice to the scope of the immunities.
[505] [1942] AC 435.

shop, to 'black' the supplies of the plaintiff and other employers on the island of Harris who were outside the closed-shop agreement. The union in question (the Transport and General Workers' Union) had members both in the mills and in the docks at Stornoway, the island's main port. The plaintiff's claim in conspiracy was rejected on the grounds that the predominant purpose of the defendants was to protect their own economic interests. Lord Wright said: 'The true contrast is between the case where the object is the legitimate benefit of the combiners and the case where the object is deliberate damage without any such just cause. The courts have repudiated the idea that it is for them to determine whether the object of the combiners is reasonably calculated to achieve that benefit.'[506] *Crofter*, decided in 1942, represents the high-water mark of judicial abstention in industrial disputes and of the courts' acceptance of the essential legitimacy of trade-union organisation. The test of whether the action is intended to further the defendants' self-interest is a *subjective* one: the court does not make its own assessment of whether the action was, from an *objective* point of view, proportional to the end in question. It is also necessary for the aim in question to be an economic one. Malice of a personal kind will give rise to liability;[507] but the notion of an economic motive is sufficiently broad to include action against a discriminatory 'colour bar' operated by certain employers, which harmed the members of the union who were thereby excluded from employment.[508]

In *Lonrho Ltd.* v. *Shell Petroleum Co.*[509] and again in *Lonrho plc* v. *Fayed*[510] the House of Lords has confirmed the existence of the tort, but on each occasion doubts were expressed as to its rationale. Why should two persons be made liable for doing together what each one would have had a lawful right to do if he had done it separately? The answer to this undoubtedly is that the act of combination with the purpose of inflicting unjustified harm on a third party amounts to an abuse of the right in question.[511] The extensive scope of the justification defence will tend to limit the practical significance of this tort.

(B) Conspiracy Using Unlawful Means

Where the combiners intend to use unlawful means as the mechanism for inflicting harm, there can be no defence of justification. It is therefore unnecessary to show that the combiners had the 'predominant purpose' of harming the plaintiff as opposed to benefiting themselves. It is enough that they intended to hurt the plaintiff in the sense generally used in the economic torts, that it to say of directing or aiming their pressure at him.[512] The existence of the tort of conspiracy using unlawful means may, in a given case, provide a basis for significantly widening the category of defendants. In *Rookes* v. *Barnard*[513] a trade-union official (Silverthorne) who participated in the threat of

---

[506] [1942] AC 435, 469.
[507] *Huntley* v. *Thornton* [1957] 1 WLR 321.
[508] *Scala Ballroom (Wolverhampton) Ltd.* v. *Ratcliffe* [1958] 1 WLR 1057.
[509] [1982] AC 173.
[510] [1992] 1 AC 448.
[511] Weir, *A Casebook on Tort* (7th edn., 1992), 601.
[512] *Lonrho plc* v. *Fayed* [1992] 1 AC 448, overruling on this point *Metall und Rohstoff AG* v. *Donaldson Lufkin & Jenrette Inc.* [1990] 1 QB 391. See generally P. J. Sales, 'The Tort of Conspiracy and Civil Secondary Liability' [1990] *CLJ* 491.
[513] [1964] AC 1129.

the strike was not employed by BOAC and could not therefore have threatened to break his contract of employment; he was nevertheless held liable in conspiracy.[514]

5. The Trade Dispute Immunity

A full account of the law relating to the trade dispute immunity must be left to texts on labour law.[515] Here the main outlines of the immunity will be noted. The organisation of strike action will almost certainly involve the commission of one or more of the economic torts. Parliament's response to this has been to enact a statutory *immunity* from liability in tort for industrial action which falls within the *trade-dispute formula*. The precise terms of this formula and its scope have varied considerably since it was first introduced, in the context of criminal conspiracy, in the Conspiracy and Protection of Property Act 1875. The rapid expansion of economic-tort liability in the last quarter of the nineteenth century, coupled with the decision of the House of Lords in *Taff Vale Railway Co. v. Amalgamated Society of Railway Servants*[516] which allowed an action in damages to be brought against the trade union in its registered name,[517] led to the passage of the Trade Disputes Act 1906. This gave trade unions a *complete* immunity from liability in tort (s. 4) and gave individual organisers of strikes a more limited immunity in respect of the tort of inducing breach of the contract of employment, where the act was done 'in contemplation or furtherance of a trade-dispute' (s. 3). Section 5 defined a trade dispute as 'any dispute between employers and workmen, or between workmen and workmen, which is connected with the employment or non-employment, or the terms of the employment, or with the conditions of labour, of any person', while 'workmen' meant 'all persons employed in trade or industry, whether or not in the employment of the employer with whom a trade-dispute arises'. Section 2 enacted a right to take part in peaceful picketing 'merely for the purpose of peacefully persuading or communicating information, or of peacefully persuading any person to work or abstain from working'. Finally the protection contained in the Conspiracy and Protection of Property Act was extended to cover both criminal and tortious conspiracy.

These immunities were meant to establish an equilibrium in labour relations by allowing trade unions to organise and to mobilise their members in support of collective bargaining over pay and conditions without the constant threat of illegality.[518] In the *Crofter* case the House of Lords essentially accepted the legitimacy of this aim—the right to strike, said Lord Wright, was 'an essential element in the principle of collective bargaining'[519]—and were undoubtedly

---

[514] He could of course have been held liable for the tort of inducing breach of the employment contracts of others, but this was immunised by s. 3 of the Trade Disputes Act 1906.

[515] See Deakin and Morris, op. cit, ch 11.6–11.7.

[516] [1901] AC 426.

[517] That is to say, the name under which the union was registered under the Trade Union Act 1871. Strictly speaking the trade union did not acquire legal personality by virtue of such registration. See generally Wedderburn, *The Worker and the Law* (1986), 526 ff.

[518] See generally O. Kahn-Freund, *Labour and the Law* (3rd edn., 1983) and in particular ch. 1.

[519] [1942] AC 435.

influenced by it in placing a narrow interpretation on the tort of conspiracy to injure. However, for most of its history the trade-dispute immunity has been regarded with hostility by the courts, according to a principle that legislation affecting to oust the common law should be construed strictly.[520] In *Rookes* v. *Barnard*[521] judicial acquiescence in the application of the trade-dispute formula effectively came to an end. That decision turned not so much on the extension of economic-tort liability as on an exceptionally narrow reading of the immunity contained in the 1906 Act, which admittedly extended to a case of inducing breach of contract but which the House of Lords held did not cover a *threatened breach of contract*. After *Rookes* the second great expansion of economic-tort liability, comparable to that of the 1890s and 1900s, got under way. In the Trade Union and Labour Relations Act 1974[522] Parliament, under a Labour government, re-enacted the immunities in what was meant to be a stronger and clearer form. However, there followed several years of uncertainty until the House of Lords clarified their meaning in *Duport Steels Ltd.* v. *Sirs* in 1980.[523] By this stage a Conservative government had taken office, and Parliament began a gradual process of rolling back the extensive immunities granted in 1906 and reaffirmed in 1974. The major landmarks in this process were the abolition of the 'blanket' immunity of the trade union (1982) and the placing of restrictions on the remaining trade dispute immunity, including bans on 'secondary' or solidarity strikes (1980, 1982, and 1990), the restriction of issues coming within the definition of a trade dispute (1982), the outlawing of strike action in support of the closed shop (1988), and the introduction of trade union ballots and majority support for strike action as preconditions of obtaining immunity (1984, 1988, 1990, and 1993).

The relevant statutory provisions are now contained in the Trade Union and Labour Relations (Consolidation) Act 1992 (as amended by the Trade Union Reform and Employment Rights Act 1993). Section 219 re-enacts the trade-dispute formula protecting action in contemplation or furtherance of a trade dispute; however, the only torts covered by this are conspiracy,[524] inducing breach of contract, and interference with contract (as well as threats of inducement or interference).[525] The tort of interference with business by unlawful means is not mentioned as such; however, it is almost certainly the case that any tortious act that is immunised by section 219(1)–(2) cannot be unlawful means for the purpose of the 'genus' tort.[526] The most important omission concerns breach of statutory duty and interference with statute. The failure of Parliament to extend the scope of the provisions now consolidated in section 219 after the courts began to develop this novel head of tort liability means that once this tort is established (whether independently or as part of the tort of

---

[520] *Valentine* v. *Hyde* [1919] 2 Ch. 129, 153 (Astbury J).   [521] [1964] AC 1129.

[522] As amended in the Trade Union and Labour Relations (Amendment) Act 1976.

[523] [1980] 1 WLR 142.   [524] S. 219(2).   [525] S. 219(1).

[526] This was the view of Lord Diplock in *Hadmor Productions Ltd.* v. *Hamilton* [1982] IRLR 102; hence it is probably irrelevant that Parliament has repealed (in the Employment Act 1982) s. 13(2) of the Trade Union and Labour Relations Act 1974, which sought to make a declaration to this effect 'for the avoidance of doubt'. It was also specified that breach of contract could not be unlawful means either. On the effects of this repeal see *Barretts & Baird (Wholesale) Ltd.* v. *IPCS* [1987] IRLR 3.

interference with business by unlawful means) the immunity is inevitably lost. Nor is there any mention of economic duress in section 219.

The requirement of 'contemplation or furtherance' essentially means that the dispute, if not actually going on, must be reasonably imminent and not far off in the future.[527] The concept of trade dispute is contained in section 244(1) of the Act. A dispute must be between workers and *their own employer*[528] and must be related *wholly or mainly* to one of the following:

(a) terms and conditions of employment, or the physical conditions in which any workers are required to work;

(b) engagement or non-engagement, or termination or suspension of employment or the duties of employment, of one or more workers;

(c) allocation of work or the duties of employment between workers or groups of workers;

(d) matters of discipline;

(e) a worker's membership or non-membership of a trade union;

(f) facilities for officials of trade unions; and

(g) machinery for negotiation or consultation, and other procedures, relating to any of the above matters, including the recognition by employer or employers' associations of the right of a trade union to represent workers in such negotiation or consultation or in the carrying out of such procedures.

It can be seen from this that strikes of a purely political nature are not (and never have been) protected. Where there is a great deal of uncertainty, on the other hand, is in the application of the 'wholly or mainly' test to a case where there are mixed motives. In *Mercury Communications Ltd.* v. *Scott-Garner*[529] the Court of Appeal held that a dispute in which British Telecom workers sought to 'black' British Telecom's non-unionised competitor, Mercury, was a politically motivated dispute concerning the union's campaign of privatisation and not, as the union suggested, a dispute over possible future redundancies. On the other hand, the 1989 docks strike was found to be based on a dispute over the form of collective bargaining following the abolition of the statutory National Dock Labour Scheme, and not a political strike aimed at halting the Scheme's demise.[530]

The great General Strike of 1926 was almost certainly based on a trade dispute since it involved workers striking in sympathy with the mineworkers who were then in dispute with their employers over pay.[531] This type of 'secondary' action has now been made unlawful by the withdrawal of immunity. Secondary action means action taken which involves an interference with the contracts of employment of workers who are not employed by the employer in the trade dispute.[532] Other cases of exceptions to the trade dispute immunity include

---

[527] *Bent's Brewery Co. Ltd.* v. *Hogan* [1945] 2 All ER 570.

[528] This is a change from the 1906 formula which means that workers cannot lawfully be in dispute with *another* employer over the terms and conditions of *his* workers (as they might well be if he is a non-union employer).

[529] [1974] ICR 74.   [530] *Associated British Ports* v. *Transport and General Workers Union* [1989] IRLR 291.

[531] See A. L. Goodhart (1926) 36 *Yale LJ* 464; cf. the view of Astbury J in *National Sailors' and Fireman's Union* v. *Reed* [1926] Ch. 539–40.   [532] S. 224.

action taken to enforce trade-union membership;[533] action taken because of the dismissal of a worker following his participation in unofficial industrial action;[534] and pressure to impose union recognition.[535] The effect of a failure of the union to ballot its members in accordance with the requirements of the Act[536] will also be to remove the statutory immunity.

The right to picket has also been confined by recent legislation. Section 220 of the Act now limits protection to peaceful picketing at the worker's own place of work, thereby opening up the likelihood of liability for 'secondary picketing'.[537]

An employer or worker who suffers damage as a result of tortious industrial action may bring an action for an injunction or for damages against the individual or union concerned. The circumstances under which the union will be liable for the acts of officials and members are laid down in the Act, as are upper limits to the damages which may be awarded against a trade union in tort in respect of each plaintiff's claim.[538] The principles governing the grant of an injunction are laid down in section 221: amongst other things, the court is required, in exercising its discretion,[539] to take into account the likelihood of a trade-dispute defence succeeding at a full trial of the action.[540]

6. The Future of the Economic Torts

The removal of large parts of the statutory immunity for industrial action in the 1980s and 1990s has given new life to the common-law heads of liability. A greater role has been accorded to the courts in protecting the interests of employers, consumers, and workers affected by trade disputes. They have responded by introducing the notion of liability for economic duress and by expanding the tort of interference with business by unlawful means, in particular in cases involving interference with statutory obligations. Partly as a consequence of these trends, the treatment of the economic torts in labour or industrial cases is diverging from their treatment in commercial cases. In industrial cases it seems that the courts are far more willing to protect 'bare' expectations and intangible economic interests. In commercial cases, on the other hand, they have insisted on the traditional need to show independently unlawful means, refusing to supply a remedy for bare interference with contractual expectations[541] and restricting the application of economic duress.[542]

The restriction of the immunities in the 1980s and 1990s might have led the courts to take a more limited view of the scope for expansion of the economic torts, on the grounds that innovation in the common law is no longer needed

---

[533] S. 222.   [534] S. 223.   [535] S. 225.   [536] Ss. 226–34.

[537] On picketing generally see the recent cases of *Thomas* v. *NUM (South Wales Area)* [1985] IRLR 136; *News Group Newspapers Ltd.* v. *Sogat (82)* [1986] IRLR 336; *Rayware Ltd.* v. *TGWU* [1989] IRLR 134; *Union Traffic Ltd.* v. *TGWU* [1989] IRLR 127.

[538] Ss. 20–3.

[539] Under *American Cyanamid Co.* v. *Ethicon Ltd.* [1975] AC 396; see below, Chapter 8, Section 3(1).

[540] S. 221(2); *NWL* v. *Woods* [1979] ICR 867; *Associated British Ports* v. *TGWU* [1989] IRLR 291, 305, 399.

[541] As in *Lonrho Ltd.* v. *Shell Petroleum Co.* [1982] AC 173 and *RCA Corp.* v. *Pollard* [1983] Ch. 135.

[542] *Pao On* v. *Lau Yiu Long* [1980] AC 614.

to outflank the much broader Parliamentary immunity of the 1970s. There is little evidence, as yet, that they see it this way.[543] Nor have they come close to evolving a synthesis of the different heads of economic-tort liability. The preservation of separate heads of nominate torts and separate categories of unlawful means is likely for the immediate future.

From time to time proposals are put forward for the replacement of the system of common-law liabilities and statutory immunities by a framework of 'positive' rights to engage in industrial action.[544] Such a framework would no doubt have to specify in some detail the circumstances in which these rights could be exercised, and the limitations upon them. This would mean moving closer towards the type of labour law regulation found in some mainland European systems, in which the correlative rights and obligations of employers and trade unions have been systematically developed over time by courts and by legislatures. Whether assimilation of this kind will gradually take place, perhaps as part of the United Kingdom's membership of the European Community, remains to be seen.

The role of the economic torts in regulating competition in commercial relations seems likely to remain a marginal one. With the passage of the Competition Act 1998, the United Kingdom has the makings of a systematic and integrated approach to competition law. The 1998 Act, rather than taking its inspiration from the common law, effectively extends into domestic law the principles laid down in Articles 85 and 86 of the EC Treaty. These principles recognise substantive grounds for legal intervention going far beyond those acknowledged by the law of tort. The impact of this legislation on the law of tort itself, however, is unlikely to be at all substantial, because of the insulation of the common law from statutory influences which has been a feature of the approach of the courts in this area.[545]

Select Bibliography

CARTY, H., 'Intentional Violation of Economic Interests: The Limits of Common Law Liability' (1988) 104 *LQR* 250.

CLERK, J. F. and LINDSELL, W. H. B., *On Torts* (17th edn., 1996), ch. 17.

ELIAS, P. and EWING, K., 'Economic Torts and Labour Law: Old Principles and New Liabilities' [1982] *CLJ* 321.

HEYDON, J. D., *Economic Torts* (2nd edn., 1978).

WEDDERBURN, K. W., 'The Right to Threaten Strikes' (1961) 24 *MLR* 572.

—— *The Worker and the Law* (3rd edn., 1986), chs. 7 and 8.

Weir, J. A., 'Chaos or Cosmos: *Rookes, Stratford* and the Economic Torts' [1964] *CLJ* 225.

—— *Economic Torts* (1997).

---

[543] Although a straw in the wind might be the decision of the House of Lords in *Associated British Ports* v. *TGWU* [1989] IRLR 399. Even then, the union won on the interpretation of the relevant statutory obligation without being able to get the House of Lords to consider the wider dicta laid down in the Court of Appeal on the scope of the tort of interference with business by unlawful means, with the result that these dicta still stand.

[544] See generally K. D. Ewing, *The Right to Strike* (1990).   [545] See Weir, *Economic Torts*, 27 (esp. fn. 19).

6

Stricter Forms of Liability

1. THE RULE IN *RYLANDS* V. *FLETCHER*

1. General Observations

Anyone who in the course of 'non-natural' use of his land 'accumulates' thereon for his own purposes anything likely to do mischief if it escapes, is answerable for all direct damage thereby caused. This is the rule in *Rylands* v. *Fletcher*[1] the facts of which were as follows. The defendants employed independent contractors to construct a reservoir on their land, which was separated from the plaintiff's colliery by intervening land. Unknown to them, beneath the site of the reservoir there were some disused shafts connecting their land with the plaintiff's mine. The independent contractors were negligent in failing to discover this. Water from the reservoir burst through the shafts and flooded the plaintiff's mine. The defendants were held personally liable, despite the absence of blame in themselves.

This liability could not have been based on any of the then-existing torts. Since the flooding was not direct and immediate, trespass could not lie,[2] and since the activity was not continuous or recurring[3] it could not have been, as the law then stood,[4] an actionable nuisance. Nor at that time was any liability for the negligence of an independent contractor accepted.[5] The existing law was extended to cover the situation by means of analogies. Blackburn J in the Court of Exchequer Chamber said:

We think that the true rule of law is, that the person who for his own purposes brings on his lands and collects and keeps there anything likely to do mischief if it escapes, must keep it in at his peril, and, if he does not do so, is *prima facie* answerable for all the damage which is the natural consequence of its escape . . . The general rule, as above stated, seems on principle just. The person whose grass or corn is eaten down by the escaping cattle of his neighbour, or whose mine is flooded by the water from his neighbour's reservoir, or whose cellar is invaded by the filth of his neighbour's privy, or whose habitation is made unhealthy by the fumes and noisome vapours of his neighbour's alkali works, is damnified without any fault of his own; and it seems but

---

[1] (1865) 3 H. & C. 774; 159 ER 737 (Court of Exchequer); (1866) LR 1 Ex. 265 (Court of Exchequer Chamber); (1868) LR 3 HL 330 (House of Lords).

[2] See Martin B in *Fletcher* v. *Rylands* (1865), 3 H. & C. 774, 796; 159 ER 737, 746.

[3] Which was then regarded as essential to a nuisance action. For another reason why it could not be treated as a nuisance, see Martin B, ibid. Cf., however, the more recent case of *British Celanese* v. *A. H. Hunt* [1969] 1 WLR 959 where the judge, following *Midwood & Co. Ltd.* v. *Manchester Corp.* [1905] 2 KB 597, said, probably *obiter*, that 'an isolated happening by itself can create an actionable nuisance' (ibid., 969).

[4] It is implicit in Professor Newark's thesis, (below, Select Bibliography), that one of the reasons behind the *Rylands* rule was the need to deal with isolated escapes, a view endorsed most recently by Lord Goff in *Cambridge Water Co.* v. *Eastern Leather plc* [1994] 2 WLR 53, 74, 80.

[5] *Bower* v. *Peate* (1876) 1 QBD 321, was the first inroad into this principle.

reasonable and just that the neighbour, who has brought something on his own property which was not naturally there, harmless to others so long as it is confined to his own property, but which he knows to be mischievous if it gets on his neighbour's, should be obliged to make good the damage which ensues if he does not succeed in confining it to his own property.[6]

The judgment is noteworthy, because it is an outstanding example of a creative generalisation.[7] As Wigmore wrote, this epoch-making judgment owes much of its success to 'the broad scope of the principle announced, the strength of conviction of its expounder, and the clearness of his exposition'.[8]

The simplicity and lucidity of Blackburn J's statement is the second noteworthy feature of this judgment, for not only is it virtually impossible to improve on its careful phraseology, but it also conceals the fact that the foundations of new law were being created behind a screen of not-always-convincing analogies.[9] In any event, *Rylands* v. *Fletcher* undoubtedly opened a new chapter in the law of torts, and one which could have evolved into a comprehensive theory of strict liability for escaping things and also for independent contractors. That this did not happen is largely due to the fact that there was, almost from the outset, and certainly during the turn of the last century and the first half of ours, a concomitant desire to restrict, for ideological reasons,[10] the ambit of the rule. So it was that, on appeal to the House of Lords, Lord Cairns adopted Blackburn J's formulation with a limitation to 'non-natural users' of land, a point which will be considered later.

Thirdly, Blackburn's judgment conceals whatever policy reasons may lie behind it. Indeed, Prosser has suggested that it is futile to search for them.[11] There is certainly nothing in the judgments to suggest any specific policy aims; and a consideration of the background of the judges[12] makes it unlikely that they were favouring, as some have suggested, the dominant landed gentry at

---

[6] (1866) LR 1 Ex. 265, 279–80.

[7] Such generalisations, however, are rare. Another famous example is Lord Atkin's speech in *Donoghue* v. *Stevenson* [1932] AC 562. A 'negative' generalisation occurs in *Bradford Corp.* v. *Pickles* [1895] AC 587, 594, 598–9, per Lords Halsbury, Watson, and Ashbourne. The style of the Blackburn judgments, short and uncluttered by citations, should be compared with contemporary judgments in the House of Lords; and more advanced students should ask themselves why a long string of citations is used to replace cogent legal reasoning. For further thoughts on this topic (in the context of negligence litigation) see Markesinis and Deakin (1992) 55 *MLR* 619, 642.

[8] Op. cit. (Select Bibliography), 78.

[9] Some contemporary authors have argued that Blackburn was not 'aware . . . that he was extending the law in any singificant way' (McKendrick, *Tort Textbook*, 5th edn., 1991) thus, essentially, repeating Professor Newark's view (op. cit., Select Bibliography) and, indeed, Balckburn himself in *Ross* v. *Fedden* (1872) 26 LT 966, 968. Yet, as Professor Simpson has remarked (below, Select Bibliography at 199) '[this explanation] signally fails to make sense of the case's status as a leading case.' This, in turn, raises a wider (and fascinating) point namely, what matters most: the judge's original understanding or the way his judgment has been interpreted by subsequent generations of judges, including himself? We shall return to this point briefly in the last part of Section 1 of this chapter. A further point which students may wish to ponder is this: does a judge who makes new law admit this openly? Or has he, effectively, made new law then try to cover up the tracks?

[10] This may explain, in part at least, the fact that such fervent supporters of the fault principle as Pollock (*The Law of Torts*, 1887, 398) and Holmes (*The Common Law*, 1881, lectures 3 and 4) experienced such difficulty with this decision. See, also, Ames, 'Law and Morals' (1908) 22 *Harv. L. Rev.* 97.

[11] Op. cit. (Select Bibliography), 139.

[12] Thus Molloy and Pound, (below, Select Bibliography).

the expense of the middle-class-based developing industry.[13] On the other hand, there is little doubt that the case is best understood if seen in its proper historical and socio-economic context and this, perhaps, explains why there have been so many theories to explain the case and to promote (or prevent) its subsequent adoption in various parts of the United States. Thus, Roscoe Pound's explanation of the case, that it was an attempt to subject 'the landowner to a liability at his peril, in the interest of the general security',[14] shows greater concern for public welfare than might have existed in the mid-nineteenth century. Leon Green's view,[15] that in deciding that the surface industrialist should be saddled with the loss since he, rather than the subterranean land owner, was better able to prevent the risk, could also be accused of ascribing to the nineteenth century an accident prevention approach more typical of our times. Whether any theory represents the truth, or even part of it, must remain unsolved. Their study, however, certainly adds perspective to the decision and may possibly explain its subsequent fate. It also raises the possibility that some (leading) Victorian judges (and, besides Blackburn, himself, one counts among them Willes) were coming to view that strict liability was the rule rather than the exception.[16] This last point may be a crucial one. For, if correct, it undermines the most recent attempts of the House of Lords to buttress their preference for fault (and the tort of Negligence) with arguments which ascribe to Blackburn, himself, such a predilection. More about this point, however, at the end of this section.

The rule in *Rylands* v. *Fletcher* has been interpreted to cover a variety of things 'likely to do mischief' on escape irrespective of whether they are dangerous *per se*. These include, *inter alia*, water,[17] electricity,[18] explosions,[19] oil,[20] vibrations,[21] and at one time even gypsies.[22] Dr Stallybrass reviewed the older cases and suggested that the common thread running through them is the question:[23]

Was the risk one which the defendant was entitled to take only on condition of paying compensation to those injured thereby irrespective of negligence on his part? And the answer to that question will not depend upon whether the thing in question was dangerous *per se*, but upon whether it was dangerous in the circumstances of the particular case.

---

[13] So Bohlen, whose interpretation (below, Select Bibliography) is accepted by Harper and James, *The Law of Torts*, ii. 793.

[14] *Interpretations of Legal History* (1923), 109.

[15] See below (Select Bibliography), 5. Green also argues that any contrary decision would have hurt the mining industry which at that time was more important to the English economy than the surface-based milling industry which required the storage of extra quantities of water. In support of this he recites the hostile reception of *Rylands* v. *Fletcher* in the US eastern seaboard, where the milling industry was clearly more important than mining. This last point, however, has been doubted by others, e.g. Pound and Prosser.

[16] See Simpson, op. cit. (Select Bibliography), 198.   [17] *Rylands* v. *Fletcher* (1868) LR 3 HL 330.

[18] *National Telephone Co.* v. *Baker* [1893] 2 Ch. 186.14.222.

[19] *Rainbam Chemical Works* v. *Belvedere Fish Guano Co.* [1921] 2 AC 465.

[20] *Mulholland & Tedd Ltd.* v. *Baker* [1939] 3 All ER 253.

[21] *Hoare & Co.* v. *McAlpine* [1923] 1 Ch. 167; but cf. *Barrette* v. *Franki Compressed Pile Co. of Canada Ltd.* (1955) 2 DLR 665.

[22] *A.-G.* v. *Corke* [1933] Ch. 89; but cf. *Smith* v. *Scott* [1973] Ch. 314. The last two are questionable.

[23] [1929] *CLJ* 387.

2. The Requirements of Liability

(A) The Thing Must be Brought on to the Defendant's Land (i.e. 'accumulated')

Such accumulation must be voluntary so that an occupier will not be liable for things naturally on his land[24]—spontaneous accumulations, for example, rainwater flowing by gravity on to the plaintiff's land.[25] Nor will he be liable for the side-effects of normal operations on his land. In *Smith* v. *Kenrick*,[26] rainwater accumulated naturally in a subterranean lake surrounded by a bar of coal. It was obvious that if the coal were mined the water would be released and would flow into the plaintiff's mine; which indeed occurred. Cresswell J, delivering the judgment of the court, refused to hold the defendant liable, on the ground that: 'It would seem to be the natural right of each of the owners of two adjoining mines . . . to work his own in the manner most convenient and beneficial to himself, although the natural consequence may be, that some prejudice will accrue to the owner of the adjoining mine . . . '

But what if something naturally on the defendant's land is deliberately released by him on the plaintiff's land? If the release is deliberately aimed at the plaintiff, the best cause of action may well be trespass;[27] but the *Rylands* rule may be relevant where the release is intentional though not deliberately aimed at the plaintiff.[28]

(B) Escape

There is a distinction between an escape of a thing already *on* the land and the diversion of a thing or substance *away from* the land. There is no liability for the latter, even though this inflicts damage on a neighbour. In *Gerrard* v. *Crowe*,[29] in order to prevent water from a boundary river from flooding his land, the defendant erected a wall on his own land, thereby diverting the water and increasing the flow over the plaintiff's land. The House of Lords held that no action lay. In *Read* v. *J. Lyons & Co. Ltd.*[30] Viscount Simon said that: ' "Escape" . . . means escape from a place where the defendant has occupation of or control over land to a

---

[24] Such as self-sown weeds on the defendant's land blowing onto the plaintiff's land: *Giles* v. *Walker* (1890) 24 QBD 656. *Goldman* v. *Hargrave* [1967] 1 AC 645, and *Leakey* v. *National Trust* [1980] QB 485, may now suggest that an occupier of land may be under a measured duty of care to protect his neighbours from harm arising naturally from his own land. In such cases, however, liability would not be based on the *Rylands* rule.

[25] *Pontardawe RDC* v. *Moore-Guyn* [1929] 1 Ch. 656; *Neath RDC* v. *Williams* [1951] 1 KB 115; cf. Goodhart [1930] CLJ 27–8.

[26] (1849) 7 CB 515; 137 ER 205. The case was extensively considered in *Rylands* v. *Fletcher* where it was obvious that the plaintiff could only succeed by distinguishing *Smith* v. *Kenrick*. Hence his insistence on artificial accumulation. In all these cases, however, liability may be arguable on some other ground, e.g. negligence or nuisance. See *Leakey* v. *National Trust* [1980] QB 485.

[27] *Rigby* v. *Chief Constable of Northamptonshire* [1985] 1 WLR 1242.

[28] *Crown River Cruises* v. *Kimbolton Fireworks Ltd.* [1996] 2 Lloyd's Rep. 533 (*obiter* of Potter J).

[29] [1921] 1 AC 395.

[30] [1947] AC 156, 168. Lord Macmillan defined it in even narrower terms: 'there must be the escape of something from one man's close to another man's close' (at 181). The escape will usually be unintentional and involuntary. Arguably, *Rylands* v. *Fletcher* cannot apply to a deliberate and voluntary escape: *Rigby* v. *Chief Constable of Northamptonshire* [1985] 2 All ER 983, 996 per Taylor J (but cf. the *Crown River Cruises* case).

place which is outside his occupation or control.' In that case while an employee of the Ministry of Supply was performing her duties in a munitions factory managed by the defendants on behalf of the Ministry, a shell exploded and injured her. The House of Lords refused to hold the defendants liable since she was inside the premises at the time, which meant that her injury had not resulted from any 'escape' therefrom. As to this, it should be noticed, *first*, that though there are in this decision dicta on many aspects of the rule in *Rylands* v. *Fletcher* (liability for personal injuries, non-natural user, etc.), the main issue was that of escape. *Secondly*, the House of Lords had no doubt that there is no special rule about 'dangerous' things and the only thing that can be said these days about this is that the more dangerous a substance or thing is the more likely it is to help characterise the use of the land as 'non-natural'. *Thirdly*, counsel's argument that 'escape' could also mean escape from control and not only escape 'out' of the defendant's land was rejected, thus preventing any further extension of the rule to other cases. *Fourthly*, the case was argued exclusively on *Rylands* v. *Fletcher*, i.e. strict liability. Nowadays a negligence argument might, in some circumstances, succeed, aided by the doctrine of *res ipsa loquitur*. But in *Read* negligence was not argued. The reason why this tort was not argued may be related to the fact that the injurious event was caused by the fault of a co-employee and this, according to the then-prevailing doctrine of common employment, would have prevented the employer being vicariously liable to one employee for the fault of another employee.[31]

In most cases the thing which by escaping causes harm is situated on land which belongs to the defendant. There do exist, however, some rather isolated exceptions to this statement. Thus, cases like *Midwood* v. *Manchester Corporation*[32] suggest that where a dangerous thing is brought on the highway, or interferes with any dangerous thing already there, and causes damage to adjoining property (but not to other users of the highway), he who introduced it there will be liable without proof of negligence, unless he can prove that the accident was due to the act of a stranger or to the act of God. In that case the defendants had laid a defective electrical cable, which fused and caused inflammable gas to escape from the highway into the plaintiff's house, resulting in an explosion and fire. For this they were held liable in damages. Nearly ten years later the Court of Appeal extended this in *Charing Cross Electricity Supply Co.* v. *Hydraulic Power Co.*[33] by holding that *Rylands* v. *Fletcher* applied as between two companies using the same highway. The defendant water company was held liable for damage to the electrical cables of the plaintiff company caused by water escaping from broken mains.

[31] It is equally unclear why the employer's non-delegable duty to provide a safe place of work, invented precisely in order to circumvent the inconvenience of common employment, was not invoked. However, it must be remembered that this duty was not expressly mentioned in Lord Wright's speech in *Wilsons'* case [1938] AC 57, and it took courts some time to give it more precise content. See below, Section 3.

[32] [1905] 2 KB 597. See also *Powell* v. *Fall* (1880) 5 QBD 597. In *Rigby* v. *Chief Constable of Northamptonshire* [1985] 2 All ER 983, 995–6, Taylor J expressed the view (*obiter*) that *Rylands* v. *Fletcher* could apply to unintentional escapes from the highway as well as from private land. On this see the cases discussed by J. Spencer [1983] *CLJ* 65.

[33] [1914] 3 KB 772.

3. Controlling Mechanisms

Providing workable limits to tort liability has been a concern of tort law from Roman times to this day. The reason for this is obvious: the spectrum of open-ended and uncontrolled liability is not one that any society can tolerate. This policy attitude is reflected in every tort where we find appropriately crafted concepts and mechanisms that perform such limiting functions. Since their common aim is to control liability, we call them here 'controlling mechanisms'. In the tort of Negligence, for instance, the concept of duty of care performs this task, though the bounds of liability are also kept in check through the notions of causation, remoteness, and, of course, through a fluctuating standard of care which defendants are excepted to display in their daily life. In the tort of nuisance the controlling function is, primarily, performed through the notion of 'reasonableness' (which, as we have noted in the previous chapter, is understood differently in nuisance than it is in the tort of Negligence); and in *Rylands* v. *Fletcher* we find three controlling mechanisms: 'non-natural user', foreseeability (as has now been interpreted by the House of Lords in the *Cambridge Water* case) and a special list of defences. Each of these three mechanisms must now be looked at in turn.

(A) 'Non-Natural Use' of Land

This is the most flexible and elusive[34] of the ingredients of liability. Blackburn J most probably understood 'natural' to refer to things 'naturally on the land and not artificially created'.[35] In the House of Lords, however, uncertainty crept in for the first time as a result of Lord Cairn's paraphrase of Blackburn J's formulation. It is, again, a matter of some dispute whether he intentionally or inadvertently introduced the additional requirement of 'non-natural user'. Indeed, Professor Newark believes that Lord Cairns did not introduce any additional requirement at all since, according to him, 'Lord Cairns' non-natural user is ... merely an expression of the fact that the defendant has artificially introduced on to the land a new and dangerous agent'.[36]

Through a series of subsequent historical accidents the courts took a different view and have come to look upon 'natural' as signifying something that is ordinary and usual even though it may be artificial, instead of non-artificial. Thus, what to Blackburn would be non-natural simply because it was artificial, would now be regarded as non-natural if it were abnormal, excessive, or inappropriate to its location. As Lord Moulton put it in *Rickards* v. *Lothian*:[37] 'It is not every use to which land is put that brings into play that principle [i.e. of *Rylands* v. *Fletcher*]. It must be *some special use bringing with it increased danger to others*, and must not merely be the ordinary use of land or such a use as is proper for the

---

[34] In the *Cambridge Water* case Lord Goff thought the expression to be 'lacking in precision' but did not feel that the facts of the case before him called for 'any redefinition': [1994] 2 WLR 53, 82–3.

[35] According to Newark, op. cit. (Select Bibliography), 560, he was contrasting 'the immunity from liability in the case of natural accumulations, such as a water pond with the *Rylands* v. *Fletcher* liability in the case of artificial accumulations, such as constructed reservoirs'. In the judgment itself, as Newark points out, the words 'natural' and 'naturally' are not used consistently.

[36] Ibid., 561.   [37] [1913] AC 263, 280.

general benefit of the community.' The italicised words may amount to an 'alternative criterion' for deciding what is non-natural. Thus, something that benefits the community might not easily be regarded as non-natural. Indeed, in the *Cambridge Water* case the judge at First Instance took the view that the activity in question could not be characterised as non-natural. In the House of Lords, however, Lord Goff was, it is submitted correctly, hesitant about the value of the criterion. But neither was he willing to accept the argument that 'the creation of employment as such . . . is sufficient of itself to establish a particular use as constituting a natural and ordinary use of land.'[38]

What is 'natural' is thus viewed differently in different cases. In the words of Lord Porter, whether use is 'natural' or 'non-natural' is 'a question of fact subject to a ruling of the judge as to whether the particular object can be dangerous or the particular use can be non-natural, and in deciding this question I think that all the circumstances of the time and place and practice of mankind must be taken into consideration so that what might be regarded as dangerous or non-natural may vary according to those circumstances'.[39] The latter part of his dictum indicates that there is no objective test for determining what is 'non-natural'. This varies from place to place and time to time, which may explain why an explosives factory was considered to be a non-natural use of land in 1921, but natural in 1946.[40] All this means that the requirement of non-natural use embodies an evaluation of risk along lines similar to those in negligence where, *inter alia*, the gravity of the harm threatened is weighed against the utility of the defendant's conduct, etc.[41] This merger of notions has, indeed, been advocated by some lawyers; and first-instance judgments such as that of Mr Justice Mackenna's in *Mason* v. *Levy Auto Parts of England Ltd.*[42] can, arguably, be seen in this light, since the kinds of factors that led the judge to find that there had been a non-natural use of the land (and thus impose liability under the *Rylands* rule) were precisely the kind of factors that would also have to be considered to find negligence liability. Yet not all judgments support such an approach;[43] and it is thus best to regard the requirement that the land is not put to a non-natural use as one of the controlling mechanisms of this 'strict' liability tort. Having said this, however, one must also note that now that the House of Lords has accepted that foreseeability of harm of the relevant type is a prerequisite of liability in damages under the *Rylands* v. *Fletcher* rule, our courts may be less tempted to extend the use of the concept of natural user in order to avoid imposing liability. Thus, in the *Cambridge Water* case the defendants' storage of substantial quantities of chemicals for their business was characterised as 'almost a classical case of non-natural use'.[44] Nevertheless, because the plaintiff's harm was unforeseeable no liability was imposed.

---

[38] [1994] 2 WLR 53, 83. [39] *Read* v. *J. Lyons & Co. Ltd.* [1947] AC 156, 176.
[40] Compare *Rainbam Chemical Works* with *Read* v. *Lyons*.
[41] Prosser, below (Select Bibliography), 179, 185; and see above, Chapter 2, Section 3(1)(c).
[42] [1967] 2 QB 530. [43] See e.g. *British Celanese* v. *A. H. Hunt* [1969] 1 WLR 959.
[44] [1994] 2 WLR 53, 83 per Lord Goff.

(b) Foreseeability

We know, both from *Rylands* v. *Fletcher*, itself, and the *Cambridge Water* decision that liability in this tort is strict in the sense that, where the requirements of the tort are satisfied (accumulation, escape, etc.), the defendant will be liable even if he exercised all reasonable care to prevent the escape from taking place.[45] To put it differently, the strictness here is complete if we look at it from the point of view of level of care. But if we look at things from the angle of extent of damage, the strictness may depend upon the exact meaning we attribute to the notion of foreseeability.[46] The question which thus arises at this stage is the following: should we say that the defendant is liable only for foreseeable damage *provided the escape, itself, was also foreseeable by the reasonable person*? Or is it better to say that the escape, itself, is taken for granted (i.e. we do not inquire whether it was foreseeable) and limit our inquiry to the question whether the damage in suit was foreseeable? In *Cambridge Water* Lord Goff seemed to place considerable emphasis on the fact that the seepage that occurred in that case was not foreseeable;[47] and that could suggest that he was opting for the first of the two possibilities given above—namely, that there could be no liability if the escape was not also foreseeable. This approach, however, does not square easily with either the dicta of Blackburn J in *Rylands* v. *Fletcher* or the result itself, since it will be remembered that in that leading case liability was imposed even though the escape was not foreseeable.[48] Not surprisingly, therefore, the preponderance of academic opinion has thus come down in favour of the view that what needs to be foreseen is the harm in suit but not the escape itself.[49]

(c) Defences

Whenever liability can be easily incurred, its *extent* tends to be limited in various ways. One way of achieving this is by increasing the number of exceptions and defences applicable to the rule. To put that proposition in a slightly different form, we may say that where there are few restrictions at the point of 'duty', there tend to be many more at the point of 'causation'.[50] Thus it is a matter of no surprise, though arguably one of regret, to see that a number of defences have sapped the rule of *Rylands* v. *Fletcher* of much of its vitality. We shall here briefly describe five.

---

[45] [1994] 2 WLR 53, 83 per Lord Goff.

[46] On which see Wilkinson, '*Cambridge Water Company* v. *Eastern Counties plc*: Diluting Liability for Continuing Escapes', (1994) 57 *MLR* 799 at 893 ff.

[47] [1994] 2 WLR 53, 67, 69, 81.

[48] As Professor Fleming was quick to point out in his note on the *Cambridge Water* case in (1995) *Tort Law Rev.* 56.

[49] Thus, for instance, Salmond and Heuston, on *The Law of Torts* (21st edn., by R.A. Buckley), 314; Winfield and Jolowicz on *Torts* (15th edn., 1998, by W. V. H. Rogers), 541.

[50] This can be seen most clearly in other legal systems (e.g. French) where one finds more instances of strict liability than one does in the English common law.

(i) Statutory Authority   Statute may exclude liability that would otherwise arise.[51] In *Smeaton* v. *Ilford Corporation*[52] the court interpreted section 31 of the Public Health Act 1936 as affording the defendants a complete defence to liability under *Rylands* v. *Fletcher* for the escape of sewage, which they had accumulated under the Act.

As one might expect, the question whether the rule in *Rylands* v. *Fletcher* has been excluded is largely one of construction of the statute in question.[53] In *Green* v. *The Chelsea Waterworks Co.*[54] for example, Parliament authorised the defendants to lay a water pipe, which burst without the defendant's negligence and flooded the plaintiff's premises. Since the defendants were under a statutory duty to maintain a continuous supply of water through the pipes, it was held that by necessary implication they were exempt from all liability where the damage was not due to their negligence. But in *Charing Cross Electricity Co.* v. *Hydraulic Co.*,[55] where the facts were similar, the plaintiff succeeded in his claim. The difference can be explained on the grounds that in the second case the defendant had only the *power* to supply water and keep pumping it through the mains, but no duty to do so.

The rules that apply to Nuisance are also relevant here.

(ii) Consent of the Plaintiff[56]   This is a specific application of the defence of *volenti non fit injuria* and need not be discussed in detail. In practice it has been often invoked when water from a top floor of a building affects the occupants of lower floors (e.g. overflowing cisterns, bathtubs, etc.). In many cases, however, it may not really be necessary to fall back on this defence, for the defendant can always argue that the existence of normal amounts of water is not a 'non-natural use'. An extension of the idea of consent is that it is a defence that the course of danger is maintained for the common benefit of both defendant and plaintiff. In *Carstairs* v. *Taylor*,[57] for example, the plaintiff occupied the ground floor of a building, the top floor of which was occupied by the defendant. Rainwater from the roof was collected in a specially constructed box from which it was discharged into the drains. A rat gnawed a hole in the box and water drained into the plaintiff's premises and damaged his goods. The defendant, not being negligent in any way, was held not liable.[58]

(iii) Act of Third Party   In *Rickards* v. *Lothian*[59] property on the second floor of a building was damaged by an overflow of water from a basin on the top floor because the tap had been turned on and the waste pipe plugged by some third

---

[51] E.g. Nuclear Installations Act 1965. Statutes may also restrict the extent of the defence. See, for instance, the Reservoirs Act 1975, s. 28 and Sch. 2.

[52] [1954] Ch. 450. The position *vis-à-vis* local authorities, however, has not been clarified. Compare Lord Evershed MR's views with those of Denning LJ in *Pride of Derby etc.* v. *British Celanese Ltd.* [1953] Ch. 149, 172–7, 189–90.

[53] On this point see now *Allen* v. *Gulf Oil Refining Ltd.* [1981] AC 1001 (a nuisance action); above, Chapter 5, Section 3(5).

[54] (1894), 70 LT 547; *Geddis* v. *Proprietors of Bann Reservoir* (1878) 3 App. Cas. 430.

[55] [1914] 3 KB 772.   [56] *A.-G.* v. *Cory Brothers & Co. Ltd.* [1921] 1 AC 521, 539.

[57] (1871) LR 6 Ex. 217.

[58] See also *Anderson* v. *Oppenheimer* (1880) 5 QBD 602. The collection of water in a cistern has been considered as a natural use of land: *Rickards* v. *Lothian* [1913] AC 263. *Contra* industrial water under pressure: *Charing Cross Electricity Supply Co.* v. *Hydraulic Power Co.* [1914] 3 KB 772.   [59] [1913] AC 263.

person. It was held that, by having on his premises a reasonable supply of water, the defendant was only making an ordinary and proper use of his house, and that he was not responsible for the wrongful act of a third party.

It has been suggested[60] that the defence should be limited to the 'mischievous, deliberate and conscious act of a stranger', as in *Rickards* v. *Lothian*. Such a restrictive view has little to commend it, for, as Jenkins LJ pointed out in *Perry* v. *Kendricks*,[61] the basis of the defence is the absence of any control by the defendant over the acts of a stranger on his land and therefore the nature of the stranger's conduct is irrelevant. It is for the defendant to satisfy the court that on a balance of probabilities the escape was caused by the *unforeseeable*[62] act of a stranger.

Who is a stranger in this context is not always easy to determine. A trespasser clearly is. A servant, acting in the course of his employment will, however, render his master liable and cannot be treated as a stranger. But *Stevens* v. *Woodward*[63] shows that a servant, when acting outside the course of his employment, may be a stranger. Likewise, the occupier will be liable for the negligence of his independent contractors and perhaps of lawful visitors, provided he has some control over their acts. Finally, no uniform answer is possible as far as members of the defendant's family are concerned. The degree of control over such persons may hold the key to discovering the right answer.

(iv) Act of God   This ill-defined defence is, probably, available whenever an escape is caused by the operation of natural forces beyond human anticipation or avoidance. Despite its name, it is a defence destitute of any theological connotation and the term *vis major* is preferable. An illustration is *Nichols* v. *Marsland*,[64] where the defendant created some artificial ornamental lakes by damming up a natural stream. He was held not liable when rainfall 'greater and more violent than any within the memory of witnesses' caused the embankments to collapse and the escaping water destroyed four nearby bridges. Nowadays, however, there is a tendency to restrict the ambit of this defence, not least because of the increased ability to predict such occurrences.[65] The enhanced degree of foreseeability may have also contributed to the decline of this defence.

(v) Default of the Plaintiff   This defence, recognised by Blackburn J himself in his judgment in *Rylands* v. *Fletcher*, is applicable if the damage to the plaintiff is due entirely to his act or default.[66] Where this amounts to his own contributory

---

[60] Per Singleton LJ in *Perry* v. *Kendricks* [1956] 1 WLR 85, 87.   [61] Ibid., 90.

[62] If the act of the third party is foreseeable then the defendant will, probably, be liable in negligence. Contrast *Greenock Corporation* v. *Caledonian Railways Co.* [1917] AC 556.

[63] (1881) 6 QBD 318: a servant used a private lavatory against instructions and did not turn off the tap; it was held that the master was not liable for the flooding.

[64] (1876) 2 Ex. D. 1. cf. *Greenock Corp.* v. *Caledonia Railways Co.* [1917] AC 556.

[65] See the criticism in *Greenock Corp.* v. *Caledonia Railways Co.* (previous note), where it was held that the 'criterion is no longer whether the event can reasonably be anticipated, but whether or not human foresight and prudence can reasonably recognise the possibility of such an event'.

[66] *Dunn* v. *Birmingham Land Co.* (1872) LR 7 QB 244, 246. If the plaintiff's conduct merely contributed to his harm then this damage may be reduced accordingly under s. 1 of the Law Reform (Contributory Negligence) Act 1945.

negligence, then his damages will be reduced in accordance with general principles.[67]

4. Who is Protected and For What?

What interests does the rule protect? Can a plaintiff, whose interests in land have been violated, recover in respect of consequential damage to chattels or to his person? In 1868 Blackburn J allowed a claim for damage to chattels,[68] and subsequent judges have followed his example. With regard to personal injury the position is less clear. In *Read* v. *J. Lyons*[69] Lord Macmillan denied liability *obiter*; but he failed to refer to the earlier decision in *Hale* v. *Jennings Bros.*,[70] where an *occupier* of land was awarded damages for personal injuries under this rule. So Lord Macmillan may only have been condemning an extension of *Rylands* v. *Fletcher* to injury suffered by *non-occupiers. Shiffman* v. *Order of St John*,[71] was such a case. The plaintiff there was awarded damages for injury suffered by a falling flagpole in Hyde Park. This liability followed a finding of negligence, but the court stated *obiter* that the defendants would have been liable under *Rylands* v. *Fletcher* even if negligence had not been proved. Arguably, it was this extension of the rule that was being attacked and not the application of the rule to cases of personal injury suffered by occupiers of land. Until recently, therefore, one could plausibly argue that Lord MacMillan's view was an isolated one, having not found favour either with his fellow Law Lords in *Read* v. *Lyons*[72] nor with the subsequent decision of the Court of Appeal in *Perry* v. *Kendricks Transport Ltd.*[73] In English law, even more doubtful was (and is) the position of a non-occupier and this despite favourable dicta in some English cases[74] and even more encouraging authority from Canada.[75]

These expansive interpretations, using *Rylands* v. *Fletcher* as a possible cause of action for personal injuries (suffered by an occupier or non-occupier of land) must now be re-considered and regarded as being less persuasive in the light of the recent decisions of the House of Lords in the *Cambridge Water* case[76] and the *Hunter* v. *Canary Wharf* decision.[77] For both decisions, adopting a distinctly historical approach, see a closer relationship between these two torts and place them unequivocally within the context of measures which are meant to vindicate violations of interests in land. This optic, coupled with the equally undoubted contemporary tendency to restrict the field of application of *Rylands* v. *Fletcher*, must make reliance on the above-mentioned case law of doubtful wisdom. The fact that the wisdom of the identical dicta mentioned above has not been expressly challenged allows little room for optimism for any

---

[67] But contrast *Martins* v. *Hotel Mayfair* [1976] 2 NSWLR 15, 67.

[68] *Jones* v. *The Festiniog Ry. Co.* (1868) LR 3 QB 733; see now *Halsey* v. *Esso Petroleum Co. Ltd.* [1961] 1 WLR 683; but a non-occupier cannot: *Cattle* v. *Stockton Waterworks Co.* (1875) LR 10 QB 453.

[69] [1947] AC 156, 170–1.

[70] [1938] 1 All ER 579. Likewise in *Miles* v. *Forest Rock Granite Co.* (1918) 34 TLR 500.

[71] [1936] 1 All ER 557.   [72] [1947] AC 156.   [73] [1956] 1 WLR 85.

[74] *Miles* v. *Forest Rock Granite Co. (Leicestershire) Ltd.* (1918) 34 TLR 500 and *Perry* v. *Kendricks Transport Ltd.* [1956] 1 WLR 85.

[75] *Aldridge* v. *Van Patter* [1952] 4 DLR 93.   [76] A *Rylands* v. *Fletcher* case.

[77] A private nuisance case.

practitioner who would wish to go against this modern trend (as exemplified by *Hunter* and *Cambridge Water*). Academics, however, are entitled to doubt the wisdom of this judicial retreat from strict liability—hence the concluding paragraph of this first section of Chapter 6. Before we come to this, however, a few words must be said about the relationship of the *Rylands* rule to the tort of nuisance.

5. *Rylands* v. *Fletcher* and Nuisance

The distinction between the two is not easy to draw and in practice it is not uncommon for the two torts to be pleaded together.[78] Yet differences do exist, at least at the conceptual level. Thus, first, *Rylands* v. *Fletcher* is a tort of strict liability (in the sense described in the previous paragraphs) whereas the meaning of 'strictness' in nuisance is, as we have seen, far less clear. Secondly, in *Rylands* v. *Fletcher* liability depends on 'non-natural use' of land by the defendant; in nuisance even 'natural use' may give rise to liability. Thirdly, nuisance, unlike *Rylands* v. *Fletcher*, does not require 'accumulation' and 'escape'. Fourthly, some nuisances, for example obstruction of light or noise, are not covered by *Rylands* v. *Fletcher*. Fifthly, prescription may legalise certain types of *private* nuisance. Finally, in *Rylands* v. *Fletcher* the defendant is strictly liable for his independent contractors; in nuisance the position is not clear.

6. *Rylands* v. *Fletcher* and the Future of Strict Liability in General

Rylands v. *Fletcher* gave the common law one of its most widely discussed and, arguably, most influential generalisations. Not for the first time, an English seed was borrowed by America, combined with indigenous elements, and brought to full bloom under the doctrine of liability for extra-hazardous activities. On the other hand, in its country of origin the idea had a mixed reception almost from the very beginning. Originally, it looked as if it had the kind of future ahead of it which was, subsequently, destined for another bold judicial generalisation: that found in Lord Atkin's opinion in *Donoghue* v. *Stevenson*. Yet after a moderately welcoming start, given to it by some Victorian judges, the rule was progressively emasculated of all its potential as it struck at the heart of another Victorian favourite: fault. For the Victorian era became (progressively) moralistic and thus any legal rule that encouraged tort to depart from this favoured shibboleth was suspicious to say the least. In fact it was both suspicious and dangerous in so far as it also challenged the hypocrisy of the age. This is because the fault rule—as it came to be applied by the end of the nineteenth century—served this hypocrisy as well, since it protected nascent industries at a time of weak if not non-existent insurance practices. For by this time the fault rule had acquired a double aspect: not only did it mean that if you are at fault you must pay; it was also (less convincingly) understood to require that

---

[78] See Newark, op. cit. (Select Bibliography) and also West, 'Nuisance or *Rylands* v. *Fletcher*', 30 Conv. [NS] (1966) 95.

if you are not at fault, you need not pay.[79] This clash of philosophies, evident in a number of traffic-accident cases decided during the first twenty-odd years of our century,[80] came to a head with the decision of *Read* v. *Lyons & Co. Ltd.*[81] where the adherents of the fault principle won their most decisive battle. In the words of Professor John Fleming: '. . . The most damaging effect of [that] decision [was] that it prematurely stunted the development of a general theory of strict liability . . .'[82]

Yet the retreat back into fault has had more casualties than the lost opportunity for our law to formulate a generalised principle of strict liability. Most notable among them was, as we noted in Chapter 3, our law of traffic accidents which became firmly embedded in fault and missed the opportunity of being based on some strict or no-fault liability scheme (as so many other European systems are) and thereby sparing our courts of a large chunk of their daily (and unnecessary) workload.[83] But it also led our judges to attempt a bold reinterpretation of the notion of fault in a way which has not only stripped it of most if not all of its moral content but has also led it to be understood (as noted in Chapter 1, above) in different ways in different factual situations.

So how have our courts (and our legal system as a whole) achieved the demolition of the *Rylands* rule given that they are loath to give us openly their policy and philosophical objections? Three avenues of thought were followed.

First, the Pearson Committee, objecting to the American developments, argued that general pronouncements (of the kind found in paragraph 519 of the *American Restatement (Second) on Torts*[84]), entail '. . . important change[s] in the substance of liability [by means of] . . . a long drawn-out process of judicial legislation.'[85]

At least three possible objections could be advanced against this argument.

First, is not the common law accustomed and well attuned to growth through well-understood judicial incrementalism that is, inevitably, the result of disputes being litigated before some tribunal?[86] Secondly, has our tendency to push cases (which could be handled more easily through strict liability regimes) into the tort of Negligence, avoided the feared increase in litigation?

[79] In practice this, of course, also included cases where the plaintiff could not prove the defendant's fault, something which happened frequently as growing industrialisation increased the number of what the French at the time aptly called 'anonymous accidents'—often exploding boilers in various industrial settings.

[80] And beautifully described by Professor John Spencer in 'Motor Cars and the Rule in *Rylands* v. *Fletcher*: A Chapter of Accidents in the History of Law and Motoring' [1983] *CLJ* 65.

[81] [1947] AC 156.   [82] *On Torts* (8th edn.), 341.

[83] This is ironic, of course, since those who opposed the *Rylands* rule believed that its adoption would increase the volume of litigation.

[84] This reads as follows: '(1) One who carries on an abnormally dangerous activity is subject to liability for harm to the person, land or chattels of another resulting from the activity, although he has exercised the utmost care to prevent the harm. (2) This strict liability is limited to the kind of harm, the possibility of which makes the activity abnormally dnagerous.' This principle is severely qualified by numerous exceptions found in §§ 520–4A.

[85] Cmnd 7054-I, § 647. It is submitted that the use of the word 'legislation' instead of (the more obvious) 'decision', itself, betrays the hostility towards the idea of allowing the rule to develop through case law.

[86] McLachlin J. observations in *Norsk Pacific Steamship* v. *Canadian National Railway Co.* [1992] 91 DLR (4th) 289, make the same point in the context of the tort of Negligence.

And, thirdly (and in a related way) does not a properly conceived regime of strict liability (unencumbered by multiple layers of defences and exceptions) lead to speedy compensation and avoid excessive recourse to our courts?

The second line of reasoning pursued by our courts (in refusing to develop a generalised rule of strict liability) stresses the fact that a decision to go down that route would entail unfathomed economic consequences for our society. More precisely, it would mean that 'the cost of damage resulting from such operations would have to be absorbed as part of the overheads of the relevant business rather than be borne (where there is no negligence) by the injured person or his insurance, or even by the community at large.'[87] The fact that attempts such as the one favoured by the authors of this book have, in fact, taken place in other countries (USA and Commonwealth), and have also been advocated by experienced tort experts such as Professor Fleming, has not carried much weight in our country since our judges are, undeniably, uncomfortable when asked to employ economic reasoning to tort disputes. Thus, from a practitioner's point of view an economic/insurance approach seems to hold out little promise of appeal. In the classroom, however, such an analysis of the underlying problems holds out rich rewards as well as the opportunity to experience the refreshing effect of other common-law judgments which have shown less attachment to our more legalistic and avowedly historical judicial reasoning.[88]

Indeed, this avowedly historical approach of the recent decisions of the House of Lords is the third and last feature of this current trend to merge the *Rylands* rule with the tort of Nuisance (and, perhaps also Negligence).[89] In two recent decisions of the House of Lords[90] we thus saw Lord Goff relying heavily on an article which, though obviously learned, was written sixty years ago and was based on (mainly) nineteenth and early twentieth-century cases, in order to forestall attempts to make old torts serve modern environmental concerns.

In this struggle to minimise the effect of the *Rylands* rule courts and academics that oppose its survival have not hesitated even to imply that its creator, one of the common law's greatest judges, was 'unconscious' of its import. Indeed, they have shrewdly used (misused?) his own subsequent dicta to suggest that he had never intended to bring about any legal revolution. The fact that he may have deliberately attempted to minimise the full effect of his innovation, precisely in order to give it a good start in life, has thus not even been considered by academic or practising lawyers, even though nowadays we have increasing evidence that 'creative' judges are not averse to such tech-

[87] Per Lord Goff in the *Cambridge Water* case [1994] 2 WLR, 53 at 79.

[88] Thus in *Benning* v. *Wong* (1969) CLR 249, Windeyer J said: '. . . to regard negligence as the normal requirment of responsibility in tort, and to look upon strict liability as anomalous and unjust, seems to me to mistake present values as well as past history. In an age when insurance against all forms of liability is commonplace, it is surely not surprising or unjust if the law makes persons who carry on some kind of hazardous undertaking liable for the harm they do, unless they can excuse or justify it on some recognised grounds.'

[89] Something which the High Court of Australia had the courage to do more openly than our House of Lords. See, *Burnie Port Authority* v. *General Jones Pty* (1994) 68 ALJR 331.

[90] The *Cambridge Water* case and the *Canary Wharf* case.

niques.[91] Nor has it been widely noticed that in *Rylands* v. *Fletcher* Willes J—the outstanding common lawyer of his time—(as well as Keating and Montague Smith JJ) came round to Blackburn's view of strict liability even though they had, three months earlier, taken a leading hand in deciding in *Indermauer* v. *Dames*[92] that the negligence principle should apply to an accident which occurred on private premises.[93] Nor, finally, have any of the modern commentators paid sufficient attention to another reality—namely, that whatever Blackburn's real views about strict liability, subsequent judges (and legal historians) in this country and abroad saw his judgment as one which contained a great potential for growth. The demolition of the strict liability rule may thus be neither as (historically) obvious nor as desirable as the House of Lords has recently made it out to be. About this, history as much as modern realities allows plenty of room for doubt.

Yet notwithstanding the intellectual appeal which the historical analysis holds out to anyone who uses it, it is unlikely to be able to displace the modern court-room trend to subsume *Rylands* under the tort of Negligence. So, if the history of *Rylands* v. *Fletcher* holds any lessons for us today it must be a different one. In our view it must surely be that we cannot go on using torts devised hundreds of years ago to meet the more complex problems which confront our modern society. For tackling these problems we need new approaches, new ideas, and new techniques. Thus, it may well be that in these days of 'common law fatigue' the initiative must pass on to the legislator. Indeed, this is Lord Goff's final conclusion in the *Cambridge Water* case though unfortunately it, too, is not without serious problems. Here are two.

First, at what level of generality should this legislation be pitched? The Pearson proposal[94] was, probably, narrower than that found in the American Restatement; yet it, too, was subject to the same objections that were levelled against the American document. Moreover, many academics argued at the time that the Commission's proposals would, in practice, lead to many irrational distinctions being drawn. This is even more likely to happen if we were to opt for the kind of approach which one finds in Germany and which, in Lord Goff's words enables each, specific statute to 'lay down precise criteria and the incidence and scope of such liability'.[95] All these points are, of course, worthy of further discussion but this book is not the place to attempt it.

Secondly, even if specific statutory intervention holds the answers for the future, the question is will it come about and when? To this question the answer must be pessimistic in tone since, invariably, tort reform holds out no

---

[91] Cf. Lord Denning's judgment in *Dutton* v. *Bognor Regis Urban District Council* [1972] 1 QB 373 at 396, with the views he subsequently expressed in one of his books—*The Discipline of the Law* (1979) at 264—about the nature of the harm suffered by Mrs Dutton. See, also, Lord Mustill's observations on this point in his recent lecture 'What do Judges Do?' Särtryck ur Juridisk Tidskrift, 1995 96 Nr. 3, 611.

[92] (1866) LR 1 CP 274; affirmed (1867) LR 2 CP 311.

[93] A point stressed by Professor Simpson (Select Bibliography).

[94] Its main thrust was for a statutory scheme which would impose strict liability on the 'controllers of things or operations . . . which by their unusually hazardous nature require close, careful and skilled supervision', or on controllers of things or operations 'which, although normally by their nature perfectly safe, are likely, if they go wrong, to cause serious and extensive casualties.' Cmnd. 7054-I, § 1643.

[95] *Cambridge Water* [1994] 2 WLR 53, 80.

prospect of votes for busy politicians; and, if it does—as problems with environmental connotations do—it is likely to run into considerable difficulties with vested interests and the currently prevailing philosophy which is ideologically opposed to government regulation and intervention. Such intervention as we may get is thus likely to be sporadic and limited to high-visibility cases; and its patchy nature will, inevitably, also reveal un-principled differences and verbal ambiguities that run the risk of creating more litigation. Sooner or later, our law is also likely to come into conflict with international treaties that are increasingly regulating matters that affect the environment and consumer expectations. Once again, we may thus be faced with the task of importing foreign regimes instead of being able to show that our indigenous ones are just as good or better than the foreign models. For modern plaintiffs, the recent decisions of the House of Lords thus hold out little hope. It is from the European scene that the next boost to their rights will have to come; and faint traces of this prospect can even be found in the *Cambridge Water* case.

Select Bibliography

BOHLEN, F. H., 'The Rule in *Rylands* v. *Fletcher*', 59 *U. Pa. LR* 423 (1911) (repr. in *Studies in the Law of Torts* (1926), ch. 7).

FRIDMAN, G. H. L., 'The Rise and Fall of *Rylands* v. *Fletcher*' 34 *Can. BR* 810 (1956).

GREEN, L., 'Tort Law Public Law in Disguise' 38 *Texas LR* 257 (1959).

HEUSTON, R. F. V., 'Judges and Judgments' 20 *UBCLR* 33 (1986).

LAW COMMISSION REPORT No. 32 on *Civil Liability for Dangerous Things and Activities* (1970).

LINDEN, A. M., 'Whatever Happened to *Rylands* v. *Fletcher*', in L. Klaz (ed.), *Studies in Canadian Tort Law* (1977), 325 ff.

MOLLOY, R. T., '*Fletcher* v. *Rylands*: A Re-examination of Juristic Origins' 9 *UCLR* 266 (1942).

MORRIS, C., 'Hazardous Enterprises and Risk Bearing Capacity' 61 *Yale LJ* 1172 (1952).

NEWARK, F. H., 'Non-natural User and *Rylands* v. *Fletcher*' (1961) 24 *MLR* 557.

POUND, R., 'The Economic Interpretation and the Law of Torts' 53 *Harv. LR* 365 (1940).

PROSSER, W. L., 'The Principle of *Rylands* v. *Fletcher*', in *Selected Topics on the Law of Torts* (1953), ch. 3.

SIMPSON, B., 'Legal Liability for Bursting Reservoirs: The Historical Context of *Rylands* v. *Fletcher*' (1984) 13 *Jo. LS* 209, reprinted (in a slightly different form) in ch. 8 of *Leading Cases in the Common Law* (1995).

STALLYBRASS, W. T. S., 'Dangerous Things and the Non-natural User of Land' [1929] *CLJ* 376.

WIGMORE, J. H., *Selected Essays in the Law of Torts* (1924), 78 ff.

WILLIAMS, D. W., 'Non-Natural Use of Land' [1973] *CLJ* 310.

2. LIABILITY FOR ANIMALS

1. Application of the General Law

Damage by animals is a familiar mischief in agricultural communities and, not surprisingly, it attracted the attention of the law from very early times. Even today a large number of injuries (in the late 1970s the Pearson Committee Report estimated 50,000 a year), together with a very small number of deaths, are attributable to animals, mainly dogs or horses.[96] These figures, however, give a distorted idea of the importance of this part of law. Since the 1971 Animals Act, the wording of which has been judicially described as 'cumbersome', 'inept', and 'difficult to construe',[97] a small number of cases[98] have been decided under it, a fact which would indicate that in the numerically frequent, but relatively trivial, cases no litigation follows, while the more serious injuries tend to be litigated, if at all, under the rules of negligence.[99]

Although the subject has reduced significance today, at any rate when compared with the tort of negligence, this was not always so. The richness of the common law, which is still sometimes relevant for the understanding of the modern law, testifies to the old ancestry of the subject. For characteristic of primitive systems is the tendency to identify the owner with his animals, and even inanimate property,[100] and to hold him liable irrespective of fault. This has now changed, but it explains why strict liability has remained acceptable in this field of law. One could argue, of course, that with the growth of law of negligence since the middle of last century, the old rules of strict liability could have been abandoned. However, this did not happen since modern views of policy came to their aid. For, notwithstanding the usefulness of animals, their ability for independent locomotion, coupled with their propensity for harm, justifies the imposition upon the owner of a duty to protect the public at least against the typical risks involved in keeping animals for his own benefit. Cattle-trespass and liability for dangerous animals is thus but an instance, indeed historically the earliest, of wider principles of strict liability.

Though every legal system has developed special rules of liability for animals, this has nowhere resulted in the exclusion of the ordinary law. A host of ordinary torts, therefore, can be committed through animals. If I choose to teach my parrot to utter defamatory words and it does so in the presence of a third person, I shall be responsible for the defamation as if I had spoken it myself. More realistically, if I drive livestock on the highway and cause an obstruction, I am liable in public nuisance.[101] In *Pitcher* v. *Martin*[102] the defendant, who was walking with a dog on a long lead, carelessly let it escape from control. The lead became entangled with the plaintiff's legs and tripped her up. It was held that a dog with a long lead loose upon the road was a nuisance, and

[96] There are about six million dogs and half-a-million horses in the UK: Cmnd. 7054-1, para. 1597. Very few injuries appear to be caused by wild animals.

[97] Sections 2(2)(a) and 2(2)(b) have given rise to particular problems. Thus, see: *Smith* v. *Ainger*, *The Times* 5 June 1990; *Curtis* v. *Betts* [1990] 1 All ER 769; *Jaundrill* v. *Gillett*, *The Times* 30 Jan. 1996.

[98] Of which the most important is probably *Cummings* v. *Granger* [1977] QB 397.

[99] In some cases (e.g. Dangerous Wild Animals Act 1976, Riding Establishments Acts 1964 and 1970) there are provisions for compulsory insurance against liability for damage caused, and here the compensation of victims tends to come through insurance companies, not the courts. There has been some doubt as to whether these Acts are meant to provide unlimited insurance cover: see Cmnd. 7054-1, paras. 1627, 1628.

[100] See *R* v. *The Eastern Counties Ry. Co.* (1842) 10 M. & W. 58; 152 ER 380.

[101] *Cunningham* v. *Whelan* (1917) 521 LT 67. In *Leeman* v. *Montagu* [1936] 2 All ER 1677, the noise made by cockerels from about two o'clock every morning was held to be a private nuisance.

[102] [1937] 3 All ER 918.

she also succeeded in negligence. Again, anyone who incites an animal to attack will be liable in assault and battery as if he had assaulted the plaintiff, himself. And in *League Against Cruel Sports* v. *Scott*[103] the court took the view that a master of hounds would be held liable in trespass if he knew that there was a real danger of his hounds entering prohibited land, provided he intended this to happen or negligently failed to prevent it. In the instant case such an intention could be inferred from the fact that in the circumstances it was effectively impossible to prevent entry by the hounds. Thus, in all these cases the ordinary tort rules may apply concurrently with the provisions of the 1972 Act.

With regard to liability in negligence, the special rules concerning liability for animals in no way affect the ordinary duty to take care,[104] not only when doing something with an animal, but also by allowing it to be in such a place as to give rise to a foreseeable risk. Thus, in *Draper* v. *Hodder*[105] the infant plaintiff was savaged by a pack of Jack Russell terrier puppies that suddenly dashed from the defendant's premises next door. The dogs had not previously misbehaved apart from frequently raiding the adjoining premises in scavenging expeditions. It was impossible to prove knowledge of a dangerous propensity in any of the animals, not only because none of them had done such a thing before, but also because it was impossible to show which dog or dogs actually took part in the attack. The strict liability claim for damage inflicted by dangerous animals, which will be dealt with shortly, was therefore rejected. However, the owner was held responsible in negligence for allowing the dogs to escape. As an experienced dog-breeder, he should have known the propensity of Jack Russells, when in a pack, to attack moving persons or objects; and though aware of their habit to dash next door, he had neither kept them in a compound nor maintained a fence. Once some kind of damage was foreseeable, then according to the ordinary rules of negligence neither its extent nor precise method of infliction needed to be foreseeable.[106] In the present case it was enough that some kind of injury to the toddler next door was foreseeable, for example, by being bowled over and scratched rather than being bitten all over his body.

There was, however, one example of a common-law refusal to extend to animals the principles of negligence: an owner or occupier used to owe no duty to users of the highway to prevent livestock from straying from his land *on to* the highway and causing damage to its users. This rule, which originated before the great enclosure movement of two centuries ago and before the advent of fast-moving vehicles, may have been reasonable in those times, because in view of the prevailing traffic conditions it was deemed not to be unreasonable to let livestock stray upon the road. However this gradually hardened into an arbitrary rule and was reaffirmed in 1946 by the House of Lords in *Searle* v. *Wallbank*.[107] This decision meant that, irrespective of the type of road and the volume of traffic on it, adjoining landowners could not be liable to injured

---

[103] [1985] 2 All ER 489.

[104] *Fardon* v. *Harcourt-Rivington* (1932) 146 LTR 391, 392, per Lord Atkin. In *Smith* v. *Prendergast, The Times*, 18 Oct. 1984 the Court of Appeal held the defendant liable for negligently failing to discover the vicious propensities of an Alsation which he had decided to keep as a guard dog when it strayed on to his land a mere 3 weeks before it attacked the plaintiff.

[105] [1972] 2 QB 556.   [106] Above Chapter 2.   [107] [1947] AC 341.

users of the highway; it amounted to a kind of subsidy to farmers at the expense of road-users. This immunity has now happily been abolished by section 8(1) of the Animals Act (the only section of the Act which, according to Lord Hailsham, was really worth enacting).[108] So now, when damage is caused by animals straying on the highway, liability will be decided in accordance with the ordinary rules of negligence.[109] Section 8(2), however, goes on to provide that:

where damage is caused by animals straying from unfenced land to a highway a person who placed them in the land shall not be regarded as having committed a breach of the duty to take care by reason only of placing them there if: (a) the land is common land, or is land situated in an area where fencing is not customary, or is a town or a village green; and (b) he had a right to place the animals on that land.

The Act thus does not require landowners to fence in against the highway. In *Davies* v. *Davies*[110] it was held that the defendant, who had a licence to graze sheep on a certain piece of land, could avail himself of this defence and thus avoid liability to the owner of a car who collided with some of his animals on the highway.

We move next to the special rules of strict liability under the Act which we shall examine under three headings: liability for straying livestock, liability for 'dangerous animals', and liability for dogs.

2. Liability for Straying Livestock

This is one of the oldest forms of strict liability and the most important progenitor of the *Rylands* v. *Fletcher*[111] rule. It is now regulated by section 4 of the 1971 Act. 'Livestock' is defined in section 11 to include cattle, horses, asses, mules, hinnies, sheep, pigs, goats, and poultry, as well as deer not in a wild state. Dogs and cats, however, were never included under this heading and remain excluded from this part of the Act, probably on the grounds that it is impossible to control them to the same degree as one can control cattle, but also because their propensity for damage during transient intrusions is negligible.

According to section 4(1), the livestock must 'stray' (a word that awaits authoritative definition) 'on to land' in the ownership or occupation of another, and under the common law, which still remains valid, this includes even the 'slightest degree of entry', such as reaching over a fence or putting a hoof through a hedge.[112] The fact that entry could have been prevented if the plaintiff had fenced his own land and so stopped animals from straying in will not be a defence, for in general there is no duty to fence out. But if a duty to fence

---

[108] *Hansard*, HL, vol. 312, cols. 887–8.

[109] If the defendant's negligence enabled third parties to release horses from his field on to the highway and while there cause danger on the highway, the defendant may be liable to the injured user of the highway. See: *Jaundrick* v. *Gillett*, *The Times*, 30 Jan. 1996.

[110] [1975] QB 172; but cf. *Rees* v. *Morgan* [1976] CL para. 245: cow straying on the highway.

[111] (1868) LR 3 HL 330.

[112] *Ellis* v. *The Loftus Iron Co.* (1874) LR 10 CP 10.

out livestock is indeed imposed upon the plaintiff occupier,[113] by way of contract or easement or ancient custom,[114] but is ignored and, as a result, animals
stray into his land, he will not be allowed to complain (s. 5(6) of the 1971 Act).
As already noted, this strict rule of liability cannot be invoked by travellers on
the highway who are injured by livestock straying *from adjoining land* on to the
highway; liability here is based in negligence.

It is still not entirely clear whether the liability is strict or is based on negligence when livestock escapes from land on to the highway and thence on to
adjacent property. An Australian court has favoured strict liability[115] whereas
our Court of Appeal touched upon (but, it is submitted, did not entirely solve)
this problem not that long ago in its decision in *Matthews* v. *Wicks*.[116] In that
case the plaintiff's sheep, while lawfully grazing on common land strayed on to
the highway where they were left to wander freely before moving on to the
defendant's land causing damage to his plants. The defendant, relying on section 7 of the 1971 Act, retained the sheep until proper compensation was paid
to him.[117] The plaintiff, regarding the defendant's request for monetary compensation as exorbitant, began proceedings for the return of the sheep. The
defendant counter-claimed damages relying on section 4 of the 1971 Act. To
this point the plaintiff's answer was section 5(5) of the 1971 Act, which
excludes liability under section 4 whenever the livestock strays from a highway
'and its presence there was a lawful use of the highway'. In the opinion of the
Court of Appeal the presence of the sheep on the highway was not, in those
circumstances, lawful so the defence of section 5(5) was not available to the
plaintiff's case.

It would *appear* that English law has, in effect, now opted for the view taken
by the Australian Court. For, since the defendant has based his counter-claim
on section 4, and the plaintiff had lost his argument on section 5(5), it could be
said that an action under section 4 can be maintained in cases where animals
stray from land on to the highway and from there on to someone else's land.
But the only published report of this case does not suggest that the court was
asked to decide this wider question but only to consider the availability in such
circumstances of the defence of section 5(5). If that is so, then the main point
remains undecided; and one hopes that if the point ever arises again, strict liability under section 4 will not be available for this type of cattle trespass. For if
it is, it will result in 'the anomaly that the travelling public must accept the risk

---

[113] But the duty need not be owed to the defendant whose livestock strays on to the plaintiff occupier's
land; it may, for instance, be owed by the plaintiff occupier to his landlord (e.g. a duty to maintain the
fences of the leased land). At common law the defendant could not take advantage of such breach, since
no duty to fence was owed to him. The wording of the 1971 Act now suggests a different solution, with
the result that the defendant may be absolved. On this see North (Select Bibliography, below), 136 ff.

[114] As was the case in *Egerton* v. *Harding* [1975] QB 62.

[115] *D'Agruima* v. *Seymour* (1951) 69 WN (NSW) 15.   [116] *The Times*, 25 May 1987.

[117] The old remedy, known as distress damage feasant, is now limited to cases where the detention of
the trespassing chattel is needed to secure compensation for damage actually caused. Thus, according to
the majority of the Court of Appeal in *Arthur* v. *Anker* [1996] 2 WLR 602, wheel-clamping of cars unlawfully
parked on private property cannot normally be justified by recourse to this defence. The restriction of the
ambit of the medieval remedy seems in keeping with the tendency of modern courts to look with disfavour upon most forms of self-redress.

of such strays'[118] while abutting landowners need not; and that an owner of stock trespassing from the highway is liable only for negligence if he put them on the road, yet strictly liable if they strayed thither to start with. None of this makes a great deal of sense.'[119]

The defence of section 5(5), mentioned in the preceding paragraphs, is justified by the belief that the escapes it refers to (i.e. of animals lawfully on the highway) should be treated as normal hazards incident to the use of the highway and should be repressible only on proof of negligence. It thus only codifies the common-law rule exemplified by *Tillet* v. *Ward*,[120] which defeated the claim of an ironmonger into whose shop an ox strayed from the highway, causing a fair amount of damage before getting out.

Originally, cattle-trespass supported only claims for damage to the surface of the land and depasturing of crops. The range of protection gradually widened to include injury to the plaintiff's livestock through the spread of disease carried by strays,[121] and misbreeding resulting from a trespassing 'scrub' bull serving a thoroughbred heifer.[122] Even bodily injury was included at common law.[123] Section 4(1)(a) abolishes this last extension (i.e. bodily injury), so the kind of damage recoverable under the section is limited to damage to land or property on it. This restriction is welcome since it is consonant with the nature of the action to confine redress to those consequences which are typical of the tasks involved in trespass, rather than to extend its range to situations which are adequately covered by the rules of negligence or liability for dangerous animals.[124]

The defences available to a defendant are the following:

(*i*) under section 5(1) he will not be liable if the damage is due wholly to the fault of the person suffering it; lack of adequate fencing, however, may be evidence of fault in the plaintiff but will not, in the absence of a duty to fence, amount to fault in itself (s. 5(6));

(*ii*) contributory negligence (s. 10, applying the Law Reform (Contributory Negligence) Act 1945);

(*iii*) under section 5(5) there will be no liability for livestock straying from a highway so long as its presence on the highway was lawful—a point already noted when *Matthews* v. *Wicks*[125] was discussed above;

(*iv*) finally, on the analogy of *Rylands* v. *Fletcher*, it could be argued that the defendant is not responsible for the act of a stranger (e.g. leaving a gate open).[126] But the authority, such as it is, is not convincing; given the wording of sections 4(1) (liability arises 'except as otherwise provided by *this Act*') and 5 of the Act, the better view would be not to recognise this defence.

---

[118] For in such cases it is for the injured plaintiff to prove negligence under s. 8(1) of the Act.

[119] Fleming, *The Law of Tort*, (8th edn., 1992), 354.

[120] (1882) 10 QBD 17. A person who has animals on the highway will be liable in negligence if they stray off it due to his carelessness: *Gaylor* v. *Davies* [1924] 2 KB 75.

[121] *Theyer* v. *Purnell* [1918] 2 KB 333.   [122] *McLean* v. *Brett* (1919) 49 DLR 162.

[123] *Wormald* v. *Cole* [1954] 1 QB 614.

[124] The wider definition of damage contained in s. 11 should, for present purposes, thus be ignored.

[125] *The Times*, 25 May 1987.   [126] *M'Gibbon* v. *M'Curry* (1909) 43 ILT 132.

3. Liability for 'Dangerous Animals'

The common law distinguished between animals *ferae naturae* (wild by nature) and animals *mansuetae naturae* (tame animals), but the distinction is more appropriate to describe who owns the animal than who should be made liable for the damage it causes, so it might be preferable to distinguish between dangerous and harmless animals. Rabbits and pigeons, for example, are classed as 'wild' but they are not dangerous. Though the Act adopts the latter distinction, it does not introduce in practice any *significant* deviation from the old common law. The older cases are thus still relevant, though in the last resort it is the wording of the Act that must prevail.[127]

Liability for dangerous species is governed by section 2(1) of the Act and is strict. According to section 6(1), a dangerous species is a species which is (a) not commonly domesticated in the British Isles *and* (b) whose fully grown animals normally have such characteristics that they are likely, unless restrained, to cause damage, or that any damage they may cause is likely to be severe.

The use of the words 'not commonly domesticated' in Britain makes it clear that dangerous species include not only animals such as bears, tigers, and lions, which are not indigenous, but also animals such as foxes, which can be found in the British Isles but not in captivity and mostly in a wild state. The definition of dangerous animals, it will be noted, can be wider than the old common-law definition of animals *ferae naturae*. For camels, though clearly not *ferae naturae*,[128] will be regarded as dangerous, and the fact that they are domesticated elsewhere in the world (e.g. in Arabia) will not affect the question in English law.[129] Secondly, according to section 11, no distinction is made between subspecies or individual animals within a species. In *Behrens* v. *Bertram Mills Circus Ltd.*[130] it was held that since an Indian elephant belongs to a species which is *ferae naturae* (dangerous), it was of no avail to the defendant to show that the particular elephant was docile. Finally, it should be noted that whether or not an animal is dangerous is a matter of law. In most cases the common-law characterisation will be followed. In some instances there is now also statutory guidance: for example, animals included in the Schedule to the Dangerous Wild Animals Act 1976[131] will almost certainly be regarded as dangerous for the purposes of the 1971 Act.[132] Omission, however, from the Schedule to the 1976 Act is not conclusive.

It is not enough that an animal is not domesticated in this country; there must also be a likelihood of severe injury or damage either because of the mis-

---

[127] Though the Act defines dangerous and non-dangerous animals, nowhere does it define 'animals'. The term should undoubtedly be taken to include birds and reptiles. Insects should also be included, but not, it is submitted, bacteria. See North, op. cit., 22.

[128] *McQuaker* v. *Goddard* [1940] 1 KB 697.

[129] *Tutin* v. *Mary Chipperfield Promotions Ltd.* (1980) 130 NLJ 807.   [130] [1957] 2 QB 1.

[131] An interesting feature of this enactment is that it lays down the rule that a licence to possess an animal to which that Act applies will be granted only on condition that the licensee is insured against liability for any damage caused by the animal in question. The quantum of the available insurance, however, has not been defined.

[132] *Quaere* whether 'vipers and adders' listed in the schedule are 'not commonly domesticated'? (See 305 HL deb. c. 1433 Lord Wilberforce.)

chievous or dangerous nature of the particular species, or because any injury or damage which this species is likely to cause will be severe. In other words, the characterisation of 'dangerous' turns either on the 'great risk of harm' or 'the risk of great harm'. An elephant, for example, is not particularly likely to cause harm, but if it does, the harm is likely to be great. In the main the test appears to be special danger to mankind. But the wording of section 6(2) is neutral and, therefore, despite the customary emphasis on the risk of personal injury, there is no reason to believe that liability under section 2 would not extend to property damage.

4. Liability for Non-Dangerous Animals

Liability for non-dangerous animals is regulated by section 2(2). It provides that liability will be incurred provided that the plaintiff can show that *each* of these three requirements is satisfied in turn:

1. the damage is of a kind which either
   (a) 'the [particular] animal, unless restrained, was *likely*[133] to cause'; or
   (b) 'if caused by [that] animal, was likely to be severe';[134] and
2. the likelihood of the damage or its severity was because the particular animal had characteristics which are either
   (a) not normally found in members of its species;[135] or
   (b) not normally so found except at particular times, or in particular circumstances (for example, the vicious disposition of cats which have just given birth);[136] and
3. these characteristics were known to the 'keeper', or
   (a) to a person under 16, who has the animal and is a member of the keeper's household; or
   (b) to anyone employed by the keeper who is in charge of the animal.

From reading this section, one thing seems reasonably clear: in cases of a non-dangerous animal, the keeper will not be held strictly liable unless he was actually aware of its dangerous characteristics.[137] Beyond that, much uncertainty

---

[133] In *Smith* v. *Ainger*, *The Times* 5 June 1990, the Court of Appeal suggested that this word should not, necessarily, be taken to refer to 'high probability' of the harmful event happening; it was sufficient that 'there [was] a material risk that it [would] happen'.

[134] Notice that the likelihood of damage being caused or of its being severe refers to the tendency of this particular animal in s. 2(2) and not 'fully grown' examples of the species generally as in s. 2(1).

[135] E.g. a dog which attacks people carrying handbags: *Kite* v. *Napp*, *The Times*, 1 June 1982.

[136] See the examples given by the Court of Appeal in *Cummings* v. *Grainger* [1977] QB 397, per Ormrod LJ: held that an Alsatian dog which barked and ran around guarding its territory and then bit the plaintiff was exhibiting characteristics not normally found except in particular circumstances such as this and was therefore within s. 2(2). See, also, *Jaundrill* v. *Gillett*, *The Times*, 30 Jan. 1996: horses released from the defendant's land through the intervention of third parties and bolting towards the planitff's oncoming car in the dark could not be brought under s. 2(2)(b). Additionally, the harm in that case was held to have been caused by the release of the horses on to the highway and not their alleged abnormal characteristics.

[137] In *Wallace* v. *Newton* [1982] 1 WLR 375 at 381. Park J held that s. 2(2)(b) of the 1971 Act did not require the plaintiff to prove that the animal was vicious, the words were to be given their ordinary natural meaning so that the animal had particular characteristics not normally found in animals of the same species. Park J held that a horse called 'Lord Justice', which was unpredictable and unreliable in its behaviour, fell within s. 2(2) when it injured the plaintiff's arm when being loaded into a horse-box.

exists and several judges have condemned the phrasing of the Act as either 'cumbrously worded'[138] or 'inept'.[139]

The difficulties caused by the wording of this section became obvious in *Curtis* v. *Betts*[140] when a bull mastiff (usually lazy and docile) attacked the young plaintiff (who had been friendly with him all his life) while the latter went up to talk to the dog as it was being loaded into the rear of a Land Rover in order to be taken for a walk. The Court of Appeal took the view that paragraph 2(2)(*a*) was satisfied since the harm caused by the mastiff was 'likely to be severe'. The court further held that the opening words of the subsection ('the likelihood of the damage or of its being severe') were awkward and, probably, included by mistake. In the view of the court the words 'the damage' should replace the existing, inept phrase and, if this were done, it would be clear that this subsection merely required that a causal link be established between the characteristic of the animal and the damage. In the instant case the crucial characteristic was the animal's known tendency to act in a menacing and aggressive manner when protecting its territory (which, here, included the rear of the Land Rover). The keepers of the dog were thus held liable.

The requisite knowledge that the keeper of the animal must have must relate to the particular propensity that caused the damage. Thus, it was held in *Glanville* v. *Sutton*,[141] where a horse bit a man, that it was not sufficient to prove that it was known to have bitten other horses. But it is not necessary to prove that the animal has actually done the particular kind of harm on a previous occasion; it is sufficient if, to the defendant's knowledge, it has manifested a tendency to do that kind of harm.[142] A mere propensity to cause mischief through playfulness or the display of some other non-aggressive characteristic shared by the rest of its species will not be sufficient, though it may attract a duty to take care in negligence.[143] *Hunt* v. *Wallis*[144] has made it clear that when deciding whether the dog had characteristics not normally found in animals of the same species comparisons should be made with the same breed and not with dogs in general.

Liability under the Act attaches to the '*keeper*' of the animal, or who is defined in section 6(3) as the person who owns the animal, or has it in his or her possession, or who is the head of a household of which a member under the age of sixteen owns the animal or has it in his possession. A person remains the keeper, even if he has lost control over it, until another person becomes its keeper in accordance with the rules given above. But section 6(4) provides that where the animal is taken into and kept in possession for the purpose of preventing it from causing damage or of restoring it to its owner, a person is not a keeper by virtue only of that possession.

---

[138] *Cummings* v. *Granger* [1977] QB 397, 404 (per Lord Denning MR).
[139] *Curtis* v. *Betts* [1990] 1 WLR 459, 468 (per Nourse LJ).   [140] [1990] 1 All ER 769.
[141] [1928] 1 KB 571.
[142] Thus, see *Kite* v. *Napp, The Times*, 1 June 1982 (owner of a dog which had a known propensity to bite people carrying bags held liable to plaintiff who was carrying a bag when attacked by said dog).
[143] *Draper* v. *Hodder* [1972] 2 QB 556.   [144] *The Times*, 10 May 1991.

5. Defences

The defences under section 5(1) and (2), which have been mentioned in connection with straying livestock, apply here too. Thus, assumption of risk is a defence, and so is proof that the damage suffered by the plaintiff was wholly due to his own fault. Contributory negligence is also a defence in the sense that it will reduce the plaintiff's damages.

The defence under section 5(3), however, needs closer attention. This reads:

A person is not liable under section 2 of this Act for any damage caused by an animal kept on any premises or structure to a person trespassing there, if it is proved either:
  (*a*) that the animal was not kept there for the protection of persons or property; or
  (*b*) (if the animal was kept there for the protection of persons or property) that keeping it there for that purpose was not unreasonable.

Keeping a lion for the purpose of protection would thus certainly be characterised as 'unreasonable', whereas keeping a dog, even a fierce one, may be considered reasonable in the circumstances. Moreover, though section 5(3) may provide a defence to an action under section 2 in strict liability, it does not affect any liability that may be imposed upon the defendant as *occupier* of the premises in accordance with the ordinary rules of negligence.

In *Cummings* v. *Granger*[145] the defendant was the occupier of a breaker's yard, which was locked at night, and his untrained Alsatian dog was turned loose inside it to deter intruders. One night an associate of the defendant, who had the key, unlocked a side gate and entered the gate accompanied by his girlfriend. The dog attacked her and caused serious injuries. In her action under section 2 the main issue was whether the defendant could rely on any of the defences in section 5. The court of first instance and the Court of Appeal thought that the case came under section 2(2), since (*a*) the damage likely to be caused was severe; (*b*) the dog would run around and bark guarding its territory, and this was not characteristic of Alsatians except in circumstances where they are used as guard dogs, which constituted 'particular circumstances' within the meaning of the subsection; and (*c*) these characteristics were known to the defendant. As for possible defences, the Court of Appeal took a different view from that of the High Court. Section 5(1) was inapplicable since the attack was not wholly, but only partly, due to the plaintiff's fault. Section 5(2), however, could apply, for the plaintiff knew of the risk and had decided to take it.[146]

The Court of Appeal also felt that even the defence under section 5(3) could apply since keeping a dog as a means of protecting the premises was, in the circumstances, a reasonable way of preserving one's property. In this context mention must now be made of section 1 of the Guard Dogs Act 1975, which provides that a guard dog cannot be allowed to roam about in premises unless it is under the control of its handler.[147] In *Cummings* v. *Granger* the Guard Dogs

---

[145] [1977] QB 397.

[146] On which see *Ilott* v. *Wilkes* (1820) 3B. & Ald. 304, 313; 106 ER 674, 678 per Bayley J.

[147] If not it must be chained up: see *Hobson* v. *Gledhill* [1978] 1 All ER 945. The court held that it would depend upon all the circumstances (including the purpose of having a guard dog) whether a 12-foot chain prevented a dog being at liberty so as to 'go freely about the premises' which the Act prohibits.

Act did not apply since the incident had occurred before this Act came into force. Contravention of the Guard Dogs Act only entails criminal liability to a fine up to £400, but the Act does not confer a right of civil action. It could, however, indirectly affect the civil action because such contravention may show that this was an unreasonable method of protecting persons or property.[148] If this were so, the defence of section 5(3) would disappear in the case of guard dogs, though in the present case the defendant would still have escaped liability under section 5(2) by virtue of the plaintiff's voluntary acceptance of the risk.

6. Remoteness of Damage and Strict Liability

There is nothing in the Act concerning remoteness and the position at common law is not clear. Both the *scienter* as well as the cattle-trespass rule have a strong affinity with *Rylands* v. *Fletcher*,[149] which was expressly excluded from the foreseeability test in the *Wagon Mound (No. 1)*.[150] One might infer, therefore, that directness, not foreseeability, is the test in such cases. Assuming that this is so, does it mean that the keeper's liability extends to all injury resulting from the animal's vicious propensity? We have already noted *Granville* v. *Sutton*[151] and the rule that in the case of non-dangerous animals the keeper will only be liable if an animal causes harm of the kind that is expected from its known vicious characteristics. The owner of a biting dog will not, therefore, be liable for every harm it causes although he will be liable for such harm that flows from the expected harm. Is the rule the same in the case of dangerous animals and is recovery limited to typical injury? American courts have, on the whole, taken the view that here, too, responsibility should be confined to such consequences as lie within the special risk warranting strict liability. English courts, on the other hand, appear to have adopted the more stringent position that liability is not limited to savage acts but applies equally to all acts. Thus liability was imposed when a scared elephant ran after a barking dog;[152] and according to Devlin J (as he then was) the same would apply where a person suffered a heart attack on seeing an escaped tiger, however amiable, sitting on his bed. *Brook* v. *Cook*[153] offers a contrary example. The plaintiff aged sixty-one, saw her neighbour's pet monkey, twelve inches high, suddenly jump on to the wall dividing their gardens. She took fright and while rushing indoors slipped and broke her wrist. She claimed that the monkey was an animal *ferae naturae*, and that its owner was therefore under a strict duty for any damage suffered through its activity. After deciding that it was an animal *ferae naturae*, Lord Evershed MR, held that there was no liability because this was not a case of an injury resulting from an attack of any sort of animal. Unfortunately, the judgment is not fully reported so the wider rule of remoteness probably prevails.[154]

---

[148] *Quaere* where the dog is both a pet and a guard dog? E.g. an Alsatian kept by an old lady.
[149] (1868) LR 3 HL 330.   [150] [1961] AC 388, 426–7.
[151] [1928] 1 KB 571. Except if one takes the view that foreseeability is not necessary for the imposition of liability, but is still the test of remoteness once liability has attached.
[152] *Behrens* v. *Bertram Mills Circus Ltd.* [1957] 2 QB 1.   [153] (1961) 105, SJ 684.
[154] There is little convincing authority. In *Eustace* v. *Eyre* [1947] LJNCCR 106, a county court held the owner of a cow which strayed into the plaintiff's field liable for injury to the latter's bull, which broke its leg trying to mate with her.

7. Liability for Dogs

Section 3 of the Act states that 'where a dog causes damage by killing or injuring livestock,[155] any person who is a keeper of the dog is liable for the damage, except as otherwise provided by this Act'. The defences are assumption of risk, fault of the plaintiff, and contributory negligence; the latter, of course, only reduces the amount of the damages awarded to the plaintiff. Section 5(4) provides an additional defence, namely that 'a person is not liable under section 3 of this Act if the livestock was killed or injured on land on to which it had strayed and either the dog belonged to the occupier or its presence on the land was authorised by the occupier'.

There is also the provision of section 9 of the Act, which entitles a person to kill a dog if this is necessary to protect his livestock or crops.[156] The defence is available if:

(a) . . . the defendant acted for the protection of any livestock and was a person entitled to act for the protection of that livestock; and
(b) . . . within forty-eight hours of killing or injury notice thereof was given by the defendant to the officer in charge of a police station.

A person is entitled to act for the protection of livestock if either the livestock, or the land in which it is, belongs to him or to any person under whose express or implied authority he is acting, and it is not a case covered by section 5(4) of the 1971 Act. Such authority is deemed to exist whenever the defendant believes or has reasonable ground to believe that the dog is worrying or is about to worry the livestock and there are no other reasonable means of ending or preventing the worrying; or when the dog has been worrying livestock, has not left the vicinity, and is not under the control of any person and there are no means of ascertaining to whom it belongs.

Select Bibliography

NORTH, P. M., *The Modern Law of Animals* (1972).
WILLIAMS, G. L., *Liability for Animals* (1939).

3. EMPLOYERS' LIABILITY

1. Introduction

The term 'employment' is ambiguous; a person can be said to be 'employed' either as an employee or as an independent contractor, and the law is very different in the two cases. For a long time it has been customary to use the term 'servant' rather than 'employee', and some judges continue to do so to this day.

---

[155] Which here, by contrast with s. 4, includes pheasants, partridges, and grouse, while in captivity.
[156] The common-law rule is crystallised in *Creswell* v. *Sirl* [1948] 1 KB 241.

This use, however, has become incorrect and anachronistic. The term 'servant' denoted, in the nineteenth century, a particular status for workers, which was derived from certain statutes, the last of which was repealed in 1875. Then the practice changed and, for a time, statutes used the term 'workman'. The modern expression is 'employee'; and this term will be used here since it signifies that the employment relationship originates in contract and is no longer based principally on forms of status derived from statute.[157]

The liability of an employer to an employee has two aspects. There is his liability to employees for harm *suffered by them*, and his liability for harm *caused by them* in the course of their employment (vicarious liability). Both represent forms of stricter liability. This is true of the first aspect, where an employer owes a 'non-delegable' duty to his employees; and is certainly true of most statutory duties imposed in the interests of safety of workmen. It is also true of the second aspect (vicarious liability) in that an innocent employer can in certain instances be made to pay for the torts of his employees. Yet in all these instances (save perhaps in the case of statutory duties which can be truly strict) the term *stricter* (rather than strict) form of liability has been chosen because negligence is not altogether irrelevant. Thus, as previously explained, a non-delegable duty is not strict or absolute, but is a duty to see that care is taken, so that if there is no want of care by anyone, the employer is not liable. In the case of vicarious liability one must never forget that a tort of the employee (be it negligence or any other) is the basis of action, so that if the employee is not liable, neither is the employer; and if the employee has a good defence the employer will enjoy the vicarious benefit of it.[158]

2. Employer's Liability to his Employees

According to statistics supplied by the Pearson Committee Report,[159] in the United Kingdom every year some 1,300 people are killed and over 700,000 are injured at work. The practical significance of this topic is considerable. Since it tends to be dealt with by specialised works, here we shall deal with it only in outline. Before we do so, however, we should stress the complexity of the subject. This is largely (but not exclusively) due to the fact that the injured employee's rights to compensation may derive from many sources that are not mutually exclusive. Diagrammatically this can be depicted as in Fig. 6.1.

(A) SOCIAL SECURITY

Injured workmen have enjoyed limited no-fault benefits since the first Workmen's Compensation Act of 1897. Most of these rights can now be found integrated and, at times, enlarged in the Social Security Contributions and Benefits Act 1992 and the Social Security Administration Act of the same year. These enactments have created a national-insurance system that provides benefits for injuries arising out of and in the course of insurable employment. Both

---

[157] See S. Deakin, 'L'évolution des Statuts des Travailleurs en Grande Bretagne' (1988) 38 *Travail et Emploi* 38.

[158] *ICI Ltd.* v. *Shatwell* [1965] AC 656.

[159] Vol. i. para. 958; for further details, see vol. ii. paras. 154 ff.

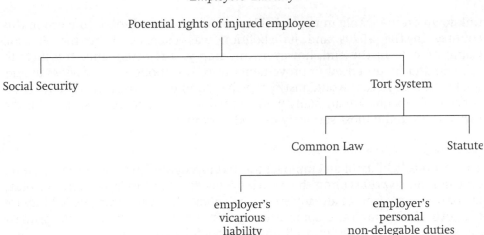

Fig. 6.1 Employee's rights to compensation

employers and employees contribute to a common fund and claims are made against the State, not the employer. Since entitlement to payment in no way depends upon proof of fault or breach of duty by the employer, the system substantially favours the victim for obvious reasons. Though persons injured at work fare, on the whole, better than other accident victims (with the possible exception of victims of traffic accidents in those cases in which they succeed), their damages, in most cases, do not amount to full compensation.[160] As a result, approximately 12 per cent of those injured at work turn to the law of tort for additional compensation despite the risks, costs, and delays that accompany tort litigation. This resort to tort law was particularly strengthened by the (gradual) weakening of the so-called 'unholy Trinity', namely, (*a*) the doctrine of common employment, (*b*) the abandonment of the rule that contributory negligence is a *complete defence*, and (*c*) the weakening of the defence of *volenti non fit injuria*. The trend towards tort litigation was also strengthened by the Employers' Liability (Compulsory Insurance) Act 1969, which made liability insurance compulsory for all employers[161] (except for nationalised industries, local authorities, and the police). This system of automatic compensation, combined with the possibility of extra tort damages (which, incidentally, is

---

[160] Yet, as the Pearson Committee noted (vol. i. para. 182), one should not underestimate the possible value of social-security benefits which, in the case of severe disablement of a young worker, could produce inflation-proofed payment exceeding the damages in a suit against his master.

[161] Failure to insure is a criminal offence. But in *Richardson* v. *Pitt-Stanley* [1995] ICR 303 the Court of Appeal (by majority) refused to entertain a *civil* action by the plaintiff (an injured employee) who sued the directors and secretary of the company for their failure to take out insurance, thus frustrating his efforts to claim damages from the uninsured company which, because of its subsequent liquidation, had no assets to satisfy the judgment which he had obtained against it. The diverging judgments are interesting as much for their rigour as for revealing the haphazard nature of trying to discover the legislator's intent concerning the availability of a civil remedy in addition to the expressly provided criminal sanction. The provision of the German Civil Code—§ 823 II BGB—that a culpable violation of a criminal statute also provides a civil remedy for those whom it intended to protect against the damage in suit, thus seems to avoid both the unnecessary complexity and unfairness of the English decision.

unknown on the whole in most civil-law systems), caused some concern in this country in the 1970s and its abolition was considered by the Pearson Committee.[162] In the end, however, this step was rejected since the no-fault scheme and its proposed improvements were not thought to provide an adequate alternative that would justify the abandonment of the tort remedy. Thus, considerable sums are annually paid and will continue to be paid through the tort system to the most seriously injured workmen.

(B) TORT LAW SYSTEMS

The tortious liability of an employer for his employee's hurt can be based either on common-law rules or on the breach of specific statutory provisions. Liability at common law can, as already stated, be subdivided into vicarious liability for the tort of one employee committed against a fellow worker,[163] and primary liability of the employer himself under a non-delegable duty.

Various explanations have been put forward for their distinction. Professor Atiyah, for example, believes that the distinction between primary and vicarious liability may have something to do with the much older distinction between misfeasance and non-feasance (traditionally 'condemned' less frequently by the law of torts).[164] Others[165] feel that the distinction may be linked to some failure of the managerial system on the one hand (for which primary liability is appropriate) and casual acts of negligence on the other (where vicarious liability is applicable). A third explanation (which, incidentally, also finds some support from the study of other legal systems) may be historical: primary liability rules may have been multiplied where vicarious liability proper was either non-existent (see, for example, § 831 of the German Civil Code) or seriously affected by doctrines (such as that of 'common employment') developed to shield modern industry (at its formative stage) from excessive claims. At the end of the day, however, the search for a theoretical explanation may be unnecessary and all that a contemporary lawyer should remember is that different rules apply to cases of primary and vicarious liability.

Since the doctrine of 'common employment' is still (occasionally) mentioned in decisions and the literature, the student should be told briefly of the reasons which led to its rise and fall. Thus in the mid-nineteenth century, for reasons connected with the need to protect nascent industries (at a time of weak or non-existent insurance markets) the rule developed that masters would not be vicariously liable for the harm caused by one of their servants to another.[166] As stated, this doctrine was abolished by section 1 of the Law Reform (Personal

---

[162] Vol. i. ch. 17.

[163] Such actions were made possible by the abolition of the doctrine of common employment (referred to above) by s. 1 of the Law Reform (Personal Injuries) Act 1948. But there may still be instances where an injured employee cannot succeed, e.g. where the tortfeasor was not acting within the course of his employment. In such cases, the employer's personal, 'non-delegable duty' (discussed below) may provide a remedy to the injured co-employee.

[164] *Vicarious Liability in the Law of Torts* (1967), 217.   [165] Jones, *Textbooks on Torts* (5th edn., 1996), 218.

[166] The socio-economic conditions are discussed by Friedman and Ladinsky, (Select Bibliography, below). *Priestley* v. *Fowler* (1837) 3 M. & W. 1; 150 ER 1030, is the *fons et origo* of the doctrine in England. Its American counterpart, more explicit in its invocation of policy, is *Fazwell* v. *Boston and Worcester Ry. Corp.* 45 Mass. (4 Met.) 49 (1842). See the discussion in Chapter 8, below, Section 1(3)(a).

Injuries) Act 1948 and an employer's liability for the tort of one employee against another of his employees is now part of the ordinary law of vicarious liability, discussed in subsection 3 below. The belated abolition of the doctrine is largely due to the fact that the courts in England (and in the United States) had already found ways of circumventing its application once industry was firmly on its feet and modern insurance had enabled such losses to be easily absorbed by liability insurance. The chief way[167] for avoiding the harshness of the doctrine of 'common employment' was by developing the notion of non-delegable duty so that an employer could delegate the performance of his own duty to another, but he could not rid himself of the answerability for its bad performance. The responsibility is personal to him, that is to say non-delegable.

The classic exposition of the non-delegable duty principle is in *Wilsons and Clyde Coal Ltd.* v. *English*,[168] where the estate of a miner sued his employers, the question being whether they were liable for his death since they had entrusted to a competent servant the task of providing a reasonably safe system of working in the mine, which he had failed to do. The House of Lords held them liable, not vicariously, but for breach of their non-delegable duty, the exposition of which is to be found in the speech of Lord Wright.[169] This duty, he said, is threefold: to see that reasonable care is taken to provide competent staff, adequate material, and a proper system, including effective supervision. To these a fourth should be added: a safe place of work.

Convenient as these categories are, they are only aspects of the broad duty to see that reasonable care is taken. Moreover, as in all cases where the imposition of a duty is being considered by a court, wider policy considerations may militate against such a result. Thus, in *Mulcahy* v. *Ministry of Defence*[170] the Court of Appeal held that it would not be 'fair, just and reasonable' to impose a duty of care 'on one soldier in his conduct towards another when engaging the enemy during hostilities'. Nor were the defendants under any duty in such circumstances to maintain a 'safe system of work'. Their liability on vicarious primary liability grounds was denied.

Traditionally, the employer's duty was one to protect, so far as it is reasonable in the circumstances, the employee's *physical* safety. Recent decisions have however recognised the employer's responsibility to safeguard the employee against certain kinds of psychiatric harm as part of a growing recognition that the employment relationship is one of mutual trust and confidence between the parties.[171] In *Walker* v. *Northumberland County Council*[172] it was held that the defendant employer could be liable for exposing the plaintiff, who had been

---

[167] But not the only one. A second inroad was made fairly early in the day by excluding the application of the doctrine of common employment in cases of breach of statutory duties. *Groves* v. *Lord Wimborne* [1898] 2 QB 402. Just as important was the insistence of the House of Lords that the doctrine of *volenti non fit injuria* would only be considered where the employee has truly consented to running the risk (that injured him) and was not merely aware of it: *Smith* v. *C. Baker & Sons* [1891] AC 325; see Chapter 8, below, Section 1(3)(a).

[168] [1938] AC 57.   [169] Ibid., 78; see too Lord Maugham at 86.

[170] [1996] 2 All ER 758.

[171] See Dolding and Mullender, 'Law, Labour and Mental Health' (1996) 59 *MLR* 296: Deakin and Morris, *Labour Law* (2nd edn., 1998), 330–6.

[172] [1995] 1 All ER 737.

the manager of a social-work department, to a nervous breakdown caused by overwork. It was relevant here that the plaintiff had, to the employer's knowledge, suffered a previous breakdown because of overwork; hence the risk of him suffering significant work-related stress a second time was a foreseeable one. The employer will not be liable where the employee's adverse reaction was not foreseeable;[173] in the case of a managerial or professional employee, in particular, the employer may be able to argue that it was entitled to expect the employee to be able to withstand a certain level of occupational pressure. The defence of *volenti non fit injuria* may also be available to the employer if, for example, the employee agrees to undertake a job that requires long hours and/or heavy responsibilities,[174] although the precise scope of the defence, in this context, is unclear.[175]

The question of whether the employer has a duty to protect its employees against psychiatric harm has also arisen in the context of claims brought by employees suffering from post-traumatic stress disorder after having witnessed or participated in traumatic or catastrophic events. If the principle in *Walker* v. *Northumberland County Council* accurately states the law, an action may lie *whether or not the employer was responsible for the accident* if the employee can show that the employer unreasonably exposed him to the risk of post-traumatic stress disorder. Unfortunately, the decided cases have tended to confuse these two bases of liability, which conceptually are quite separate, with the result that the law in this area lacks clarity. In *Macfarlane* v. *E.E. Caledonia*[176] the plaintiff, who witnessed at close hand the aftermath of the explosion on the oil rig Piper Alpha, which led to very heavy loss of life, failed in a claim for negligence against his employer, in part because he was off duty at the time the explosion occurred; he was in no better position than a bystander who happened to be on the scene at the time. By contrast, in *Frost* v. *Chief Constable of South Yorkshire* the Court of Appeal allowed a number of claims by policemen and women who had been present during and immediately after the Hillsborough stadium disaster, when, as a result of negligence on the part of senior police officers who were responsible for crowd control, ninety-six football spectators were crushed to death. According to Rose LJ:

Once it is accepted that there is no justification for regarding physical and psychiatric injuries as different kinds of injury, when an employer negligently causes physical injury to one employee, it seems to me to be impossible to contend that he is not equally liable to a fellow employee of normal fortitude working on the same task who sustains psychiatric injury, whether through fear for himself or through witnessing what happens to his fellow workmen . . . whereas in cases outwith the master and servant relationship [sic] the courts have found it necessary, in identifying those to whom a duty of care is owed, to draw a distinction between primary and secondary victims and to impose limiting criteria to determine those within the second category who can recover, in the master and servant context a duty of care exists by reason of that relationship.[177]

---

[173] *Petch* v. *Customs and Excise Commissioners* [1993] ICR 789.
[174] See *Johnstone* v. *Bloomsbury Area Health Authority* [1991] 1 WLR 1314, [1992] 1 QB 333.
[175] See our discussion of the *volenti* defence below, Chapter 8, Section 1.
[176] [1994] 2 All ER 1. See also *Robertson and Rough* v. *Forth Bridge Joint Board* [1995] IRLR 251.
[177] [1997] IRLR 171, 177.

However, when the case reached the House of Lords under the name *White* v. *Chief Constable of South Yorkshire*,[178] the Court of Appeal's ruling was overturned, and liability to the plaintiffs denied. The essence of the House of Lords' decision was that employees were owed no special duties as secondary victims of accidents, even if they were acting as rescuers. Unfortunately, the leading judgments of Lords Steyn and Hoffmann do not deal fully with the point that the cause of action for breach of the employer's personal duty of care is conceptually distinct from any claim which the employee might have as a secondary victim. Lord Steyn appears to have thought that the same principles which limit recovery for nervous shock in cases involving secondary victims should also limit the scope of the employer's personal duty of care[179]. If this is so, it seems doubtful that *Walker* v. *Northumberland County Council* can remain good law. More cautiously, Lord Hoffmann thought that *Walker* had no application in a case where the employee's psychiatric harm was caused by witnessing physical harm to another. The reason for this was the need to avoid causing an anomaly in the treatment of employees and relatives in nervous shock cases.[180] However, the result is a highly anomalous exception to the scope of the employer's personal duty to have regard to the health and safety of his employees. It is to be hoped that this matter can be clarified by the higher courts in the near future.

The scope of the employer's duty with regard to pure economic loss has also been expanded by recent decisions. In *Reid* v. *Rush & Tompkins Group plc*[181] the Court of Appeal refused to hold that an employer was under a duty to warn an employee posted overseas to take out personal accident insurance. In the event, the employee was involved in a hit-and-run traffic accident while working for his employer in Ethiopia and was left uncompensated, since that country has nothing equivalent to the UK Motor Insurers' Bureau. This decision must now be seen in the light of two House of Lords' decisions, *Spring* v. *Guardian Assurance Ltd.*[182] and *Scally* v. *Southern Health and Social Services Board*.[183] In *Spring* it was held that an employer could be liable to an employee (or ex-employee) in respect of economic losses caused by a negligently prepared reference, while in *Scally* the employer was held liable for loss caused by its failure to provide employees with information concerning valuable occupational pension rights. It is not clear how far these cases can be used as the basis for a widening of the employer's personal duty of care to its employees. *Spring* can be seen as an extension of the principle of *Hedley Byrne* v. *Heller*,[184] since it involves the voluntary assumption by the employer of a particular responsibility to the employee; but it is not a conventional *Hedley Byrne* case, since it was not the employee but rather the third-party employer who relied on the false information provided by the defendant. *Scally* was argued on the basis of an implied-term contract rather than the employer's duty of care in tort; however, in this

---

[178] [1998] 3 WLR 1510.   [179] Ibid., 1545.   [180] Ibid., 1553.

[181] *Reid* v. *Rush & Tompkins Group plc* [1990] 1 WLR 212. It might be different if it could be shown that the employer voluntarily assumed responsibility (in the sense of *Hedley Byrne*) for the employee's economic welfare.

[182] [1994] 3 All ER 129.   [183] [1992] 1 AC 294.   [184] [1964] AC 465; see above, Chapter 2.

context there may be little merit in distinguishing between obligations taking the form of implied terms in the contract of employment and those deriving from the employer's tortious duty. According to Lord Woolf in *Spring*,[185] 'just as in the earlier authorities the courts were prepared to imply by necessary implication a term imposing a duty on an employer to exercise due care for the physical well-being of his employees, so in the appropriate circumstances would the court imply a like duty as to his economic well being'.

The responsibility, as already noted, is personal to the employer in the sense that he is not relieved of it even though he delegates performance to a third party, however competent, including an independent contractor. What is personal, therefore, is not performance of the obligation, but responsibility for *bad* performance, so that the employer remains liable for the breach of the obligation.[186] Thus, it is not enough to show that the employer has personally taken care, for example, by engaging a competent third party; he has to ensure that care is taken by that party.[187] All the same, though this duty requires more than simply taking reasonable care oneself, it is not strict.[188] For in most cases it is a defence to show that proper care has been taken by everyone, the employer and the person engaged by him.

Apart from the provision of adequate materials, an employer is only liable for the defaults of persons actually engaged by him. With regard to defective materials, however, the Employers' Liability (Defective Equipment) Act 1969 makes him answerable for the default of anyone (i.e. manufacturer, supplier, etc.), whether engaged by him or not, which renders equipment defective. *Davie* v. *New Merton Board Mills Ltd.*[189] had held that an employer who bought a badly manufactured tool in open market was not liable to his employee because neither the manufacturer nor the seller had been 'engaged' by him to make or supply the tool. This case was overruled by the Act of 1969 so that, with regard to equipment, liability became (in theory) wider than it used to be in that an employer became answerable even for the default of persons not engaged by him. On the other hand the Act preserves the employer's right to recover a more-or-less complete indemnity from the party actually to blame.

Despite fears expressed at the time of the passing of the Act that it would cast a great burden on employers, this has not in fact occurred. Indeed, the rather limited case law, most of it interestingly enough unreported,[190] revealed the

---

[185] [1994] 3 All ER 129, 178.

[186] For the distinction, see McNair J in *The Brabant* [1967] 3 QB 588, 603–4. A recent case is *McDermid* v. *Nash Dredging and Reclamation Co. Ltd.* [1987] AC 906. (Unsafe system on a tug: defendants held liable even though duty delegated to skipper of tug employed by third party; skipper negligently caused the plaintiff's injuries.) Lord Hailsham explained the duty as follows: '[a non-delegable duty] does not involve the proposition that the duty cannot be delegated . . . but only that the employer cannot escape liability if the duty has been delegated and then not properly performed.' Ibid., 910.

[187] Cf. Langton J in *The Pass of Ballater* [1942] P. 112, 117: 'The point may perhaps be crystallized by saying that he has not merely a duty to take care but a duty to provide that care is taken.'

[188] Note, however, Viscount Simond's opinion in *Davie* v. *New Merton Board Mills Ltd.* [1959] AC 604, 620 that at times 'the subject-matter may be such that the taking of reasonable care may fall little short of absolute obligation.'

[189] [1959] AC 604.

[190] Which is discussed and criticised by Lang, (Select Bibliography, below).

two main weaknesses of the Act:[191] (a) the difficulties encountered by employees to prove that the third party had been at *fault*, and (b) the difficulty of proving that the accident was *caused* by the third party's fault. As a result of the Consumer Protection Act 1987, giving effect to the European Commission's Directive on Products Liability,[192] the employee/plaintiff's first burden may have now been considerably eased. But the second hurdle (connected with causation) remains and will continue to prejudice injured workers until such time as the courts reverse the onus of proof and oblige the employer to show, on the balance of probabilities, that the defective equipment was *not* the cause of the injury. This result would appear particularly sensible in this situation since it would facilitate the compensation of the injured employee without placing the financial burden on his employer, who would be insured and who, in any event, would be able in most cases to reclaim his costs from the guilty third party.

The non-delegable duty applies when the relationship of employer and employee exists. An independent contractor employed to do a piece of work cannot rely on such a duty and sue his employer. Furthermore, the duty is owed to each workman individually and, therefore, each employee's particular circumstances, which are known or ought to be known to the employer, will determine the degree of precaution required. Thus, in *Paris* v. *Stepney Borough Council*[193] an employer was held liable to his employee for not having provided him with goggles when he knew that that employee had only one eye and was running a risk of greater injury in consequence. But although the employer is required to show a high standard of care, there are limits. As *Withers* v. *Perry Chain Co. Ltd.*[194] shows, the law does not require an employer to dismiss the employee even if this might be the only way of avoiding the risk of harm. Finally, it is not entirely clear to what extent these common-law duties may be modified (in favour of the employer) through the *express* terms of the contract of employment. In *Johnstone* v. *Bloomsbury Health Authority*[195] the plaintiff, a junior doctor, was employed by the defendants and undertook to work forty hours a week in addition to making himself available for a further forty-eight hours on average a week over a specified period. For this he now sued the defendants, in essence claiming that this express duty under the contract violated the employer's common-law duty to take care for his safety and well-being. In the light of the facts of that particular case the plaintiff, by a majority, succeeded in his action. However, on the important *legal* issue involved, the Court of Appeal was divided in a different way. For the dissenting judge (Leggatt LJ) and one of the majority judges (Sir Nicolas Browne-Wilkinson) thought that the common-law duty to take care of the employee would have to cede

---

[191] Other weaknesses are: (a) that it does not apply to borrowed employees (s. 1(1)(a) combined with s. 1(3)); (b) that the word 'defect' used in s. 1(1) probably does not include design faults.

[192] Discussed below, Section 5.

[193] [1951] AC 367, followed in Scotland in *Porteous* v. *NCB*, 1967 SLT 117 (Ct. of Sess.).

[194] [1961] 1 WLR 1314, 1320.

[195] [1991] 2 WLR 1362. The court felt that it was immaterial to decide whether the duty to take care of the employee's health derived from tort or arose by implication of law into the contract of employment. See also Chapter 8, below, Section 1(4)(b).

precedence to a clearly defined express term that gave the employer a right (and not just a discretion) to call upon the plaintiff (employee) to provide up to an additional forty-eight hours per week. To the other (majority) justice (Stuart Smith LJ), however, the answer depended on the interaction of the two sets of rules (the tort rules and the terms of the contract), and this meant that the defendant could only exercise his discretion to ask the plaintiff to do the additional hours if this could be done without breaching the common-law duty to take care of the employee's health. This last view seems preferable, for otherwise the entire law of negligence, dealing with the employer's liability to his employees, could be swallowed up (and thus avoided) by carefully drafted contracts of employment which would be seriously disadvantageous to employees.

As already stated, the employer's duty to see that reasonable care is taken falls into four categories.

(i) Competent Staff   In *Hudson* v. *Ridge Manufacturing Co. Ltd.*[196] an employee was injured as a result of a foolish prank practised upon him by a fellow employee, whose propensity for mischief had been known to the employers for a long time. The latter were held liable for a breach of their *personal* duty[197] to see that safe fellow employees were provided. Streatfield J said:[198]

Here is a case where there existed, as it were in the system of work a source of danger, through the conduct of one of the defendants' employees, of which they knew, repeated conduct which went on over a long period of time, and which they did nothing whatever to remove, except to reprimand and go on reprimanding to no effect. In my judgment, therefore, the injury was sustained as a result of the defendants' failure to take proper steps to put an end to that conduct.

(ii) Adequate Materials   The Employers' Liability (Defective Equipment) Act 1969 puts this aspect of the duty into statutory form. Section 1 says that if the employee suffers personal injury in the course of his employment as a result of a defect in equipment provided by his employer for the purposes of the latter's business, and he, the employee, can prove that it is attributable wholly or partly to the fault of a third party, then the employee's injury will also be attributable to the negligence of the employer without prejudice to the latter's right to contribution or a complete indemnity from the party at fault. But the employer's obligation is not absolute. Reasonable care is taken if the appliances are of the type usual for the work in question,[199] but this does not imply that the employer must always adopt the latest improvements available in the mar-

---

[196] [1957] 2 QB 348. Cf. *Smith* v. *Crossley Bros. Ltd.* (1971), 95 SJ 655; and see also next footnote.

[197] The importance of stressing the employer's personal liability is because a practical joke by one employee against another was rarely considered to fall within the course of the former's employment so as to render the employer vicariously liable. See *O'Reilly* v. *National Rail and Tramway Appliances Ltd.* [1966] 1 All ER 499; *Coddington* v. *International Harvester Co. of Great Britain* (1969) 6 KIR 146. *Chapman* v. *Oakleigh Animal Products* (1970) 8 KIR 1063 appeared an exception to this tendency. *Harrison* v. *Michelin Tyre Co. Ltd.* [1985] 1 All ER 918 may be signalling a willingness to render employers vicariously liable for the horseplay of their employees where the incident is 'part and parcel of the employment'. The test for determining that question was said to be 'a reasonable approach' (ibid., at 920) which is sufficiently amorphous to enable future judges to extend vicarious liability for practical jokes in their (presumed) desire to aid victims.

[198] [1957] 2 QB 348 at 351.   [199] *Roberts* v. *Alfred Holt & Co.* (1945) 61 TLR 289.

ket. Nor will he be liable if the employee fails to make proper use of the equipment. In *Parkinson* v. *Lyle Shipping Co. Ltd.*[200] the plaintiff was injured while attempting to re-light a boiler. His action in negligence failed because the court took the view that the injury was not the result of defective equipment, but of the manner in which the plaintiff used it. The weaknesses of this enactment have already been mentioned; so has the possible relief that may come in the guise of the Consumer Protection Act 1987.[201]

From the above, it will have been noticed that the Act obliges the employer to supply his employees with safe 'equipment'. Somewhat surprisingly section 1(3) of the Act defines equipment to include 'any plant and machinery, vehicle, aircraft and clothing'. The extent of this wide definition was, however, tested in the case of *Coltman* v. *Bibby Tankers Ltd.*[202] when the Court of Appeal had to decide whether a ship could be included in the above definition of equipment. The House of Lords, giving the lie to the widely held view that English courts invariably give effect to the clear wording of statutes, adopted a purposive interpretation of the Act and, contrary to the view of the Court of Appeal, held that there was no reason to exclude vessels from the ambit of the 1969 statute.

(iii) Safe Place of Work   Whether the place of work is safe or not depends on the circumstances and the nature of the place. The requisite standard is that of the reasonably prudent employer. A place originally safe may subsequently become unsafe because of some new factor. It was held in *Latimer* v. *AEC Ltd.*[203] that the defendants' liability depended on whether they had taken the appropriate steps which a reasonably prudent employer would have taken. In the circumstances they had done so, and the fact that the floor of the factory had become slippery did not warrant the closure of the factory.

Not only the premises where the work takes place must be safe but also the access to them.[204] Moreover, the duty is not discharged by the mere issuing of warnings to the employees. Finally, one cannot generalise on the effect, if any, that the plaintiff/employee's knowledge of the danger will have on his claims. The answer must, overall, depend on all the circumstances of each case, though the protective philosophy that the courts have adopted towards employees may well work in his favour.[205]

The duty with regard to a safe place of work applies even when the employee is not working on his employer's premises, although, as a matter of common sense, the requisite standard may vary and the discharge of the duty may be easier. In *Wilson* v. *Tyneside Window Cleaning Co.*[206] the defendants sent their employee to clean windows of a client. Owing to their dangerous condition he fell and injured himself. It was alleged on his behalf that the defendants had failed to take reasonable care not to expose him to unnecessary risk. It was held

---

[200] [1964] 2 Lloyd's Rep. 79.   [201] Discussed below, Section 5.

[202] [1988] AC 276. The same broad approach to the Act was adopted by the Court of Appeal in *Knowles* v. *The Liverpool City Council, The Times*, 2 July 1992, when it held that equipment included a flagstone on which the employee was working.

[203] [1953] AC 634.   [204] *Ashdown* v. *Samuel Williams & Sons Ltd.* [1957] 1 QB 409.

[205] *McCafferty* v. *Metropolitan Police District Receiver* [1977] 1 WLR 1073.

[206] [1958] 2 QB 110. For variations in the standard of care, see the dictum by Pearce LJ at 121–2. See also *Smith* v. *Austin Lifts Ltd.* [1959] 1 WLR 100.

that though an employer owes his employees a duty even in respect of work done outside his premises, in the present case it had been fulfilled. If, however, the risk that exists at the place where the work has to be done has been encountered on previous occasions, then the employer may be under a duty to devise a safe system of work and may be liable if he does not.[207]

Although an employer is, in most cases, under no duty to inspect the premises where his employee will have to work, he is still under a duty to provide proper instructions and the necessary implements;[208] nor will he be necessarily absolved of liability if he proves that the employee was aware of the danger and had not objected to it.[209]

(iv) Proper System   This is probably the most important, but ill-defined, aspect of the employer's duty. It includes special instructions and reasonably effective supervision to ensure that the system and instructions are adhered to. In the words of Lord Reid:[210]

It is the duty of the employer to consider the situation, to devise a suitable system, to instruct his men what they must do and supply any implements that may be required . . . No doubt he cannot be certain that his men will do as they are told when they are working alone. But if he does all that is reasonable to ensure that his safety system is operated he will have done what he is bound to do.

This, too, was a case where a window-cleaner sued his employers in respect of injuries sustained while cleaning a window. The House of Lords held them liable because they had failed to devise a safe system of work providing for an obvious danger. In leaving it to the initiative of individual workmen to take appropriate precautions, the defendants had failed in their duty. But,

where there is a recognised and general practice which has been followed for a substantial period in similar circumstances without mishap [the employer] is entitled to follow it, unless in the light of common sense or newer knowledge, it is clearly bad: but, where there is developing knowledge, he must keep reasonably abreast of it and not be too slow to apply it; and where he has in fact greater than average knowledge of the risks, he may be thereby obliged to take more than the average or standard precautions.[211]

It is a question of fact whether: (*a*) a system should be devised (a recurring danger will, for instance, be a strong reason for devising a system to deal with it) and (*b*) whether the one devised is effective. An employer will not necessarily be relieved of liability merely by issuing orders not to do certain things;[212]

---

[207] Cf. *General Cleaning Contractors* v. *Christmas* [1953] AC 180.   [208] Ibid.

[209] *McCafferty* v. *Metropolitan Police District Receiver* [1977] 1 WLR 1073. See also, *McDermid* v. *Nash Dredging and Reclamation Co. Ltd.* [1987] AC 906. Lord Brandon (esp. at 919) held the defendants liable for the negligence of the tug skipper in operating the system for casting off. He required no more than this for the defendants to be in breach of their non-delegable duty. Is this consistent with a notion that an employer's duty is to take reasonable care that care is taken? If not, then the employer's liability seems strict. See the explanation of Mason J in the Australian High Court case *Kondis* v. *State Transport Authority* (1984) 55 ALR 225.

[210] *General Cleaning Contractors Ltd.* v. *Christmas* [1953] AC 180, 194.

[211] *Stokes* v. *GKN* [1968] 1 WLR 1776, 1783 (per Swanwick J) followed by Mustill J in *Thompson* v. *Smiths Ship Repairers (North Shields) Ltd.* [1984] QB 405, 1 All ER 881, 889.

[212] E.g. *Baker* v. *T. E. Hopkins & Son Ltd.* [1959] 1 WLR 966.

indeed, in cases of extreme risk he will be expected to issue absolute and explicit instructions against doing a particular job in a certain manner and will be saddled with part (at least) of the consequences if he does not.[213] Finally, although the discharge of the duty may involve a measure of supervision, this does not imply that 'an employer is bound, through his foreman, to stand over workmen of age and experience every moment they are working and every time that they cease work, in order to see that they do what they are supposed to do'.[214]

(C) STATUTORY DUTIES

The various statutory duties of an employer towards his employees need only be discussed in the form of a few general points. The first is that in theory the common-law duty of the employer, emanating as it does from the employment relationship, is of a general nature, whereas statutory duties depend on the specific statute creating them.[215] In practice employers are subjected to an ever-growing number of duties designed to improve the health and safety at work.

Secondly, liability in these instances is often absolute and, therefore, a statutory duty facilitates the employee's task of establishing his employer's liability. So, for example, in *John Summers and Sons Ltd.* v. *Frost*[216] the House of Lords interpreted section 14(1) of the Factories Act 1937 (providing for the fencing of every dangerous part of machinery) as giving rise to an absolute liability even where it could be shown that fencing would render the machine inoperable. Even when phrases such as 'so far as reasonably practicable' appear in a statute (e.g. s. 28(1) of the Factories Act 1961), it is for the employer[217] to prove that it was not reasonably practicable, to avoid the results.[218]

Thirdly, the various enactments tend, as a rule, to amplify and give effect to one or other aspect of the *Wilsons* case, namely, safe equipment, safe place of work, or safe system. The Factories Act 1961, the Mines and Quarries Act 1954, the Offices, Shops and Railway Premises Act 1963, and the Health and Safety at Work Act 1974 are examples of statutory intervention in this area. The Acts of 1954, 1961, and 1963 are gradually being replaced by regulations which, among other things, implement the EC Framework Directive on Health and Safety[219] and various 'daughter directives'.[220] The reader is referred to specialist works on health and safety for a more detailed treatment of this legislation.

---

[213] *King* v. *Smith* [1995] ICR 339.

[214] *Woods* v. *Durable Suites Ltd.* [1953] 1 WLR 857, 862, per Singleton LJ.

[215] S. 2 of the Health and Safety at Work Act 1974, however, casts upon employers a general duty to ensure, as far as possible, the health, safety, and welfare at work of all their employees. Breach of this duty entails only penal, not civil, sanctions.

[216] [1955] AC 740.   [217] *Nimmo* v. *Alexander Cowan and Sons Ltd.* [1968] AC 107.

[218] It is not clear whether 'reasonably practicable' introduces the test of 'reasonable care' of negligence. In yet other instances the term 'practicable' (rather than 'reasonably practicable') is used; see, for example, s. 157 of the Mines and Quarries Act 1954. Since everything ultimately depends on the construction of the wording of the relevant statute it is to be regretted that the relevant language appears often to have been chosen haphazardly.

[219] Directive 89/391.

[220] The most important provision is the Workplace (Health, Safety and Welfare) Regulations, SI No. 1992/3004, which has replaced many of the provisions of the Factories Act 1961 and the Office, Shops and Railway Premises Act 1963 relating to the provision of a safe workplace and system of work.

Select Bibliography

FLEMING, J. G., 'Tort Liability for Work Injury', in *Int. Encl. Comp. L.* xv. (1975), ch. 9.

FRIEDMAN, L. M. and LADINSKY, J., 'Social Change and the Law of Industrial Accidents' 67 *Col. LR* 50 (1967).

LANG, B., 'The Employer's Liability (Defective Equipment) Act—Lion or Mouse?' (1984) 47 *MLR* 48.

McKENDRICK, E., 'Vicarious Liability and Independent Contractors—A Re-examination' (1990) 53 *MLR* 770.

MUNKMAN, J. H., *Employers' Liability at Common Law* (10th edn., 1985).

NEWARK, F. H., 'Bad Law' (1966) 17 *NILQ* 469.

WILLIAMS, G., 'The Effect of Penal Legislation in the Law of Tort' (1960) 23 *MLR* 233.

4. VICARIOUS LIABILITY

Vicarious liability is liability imposed on an employer to a third party for the tort of his employee committed in the course of employment. This means that a relationship of employer and employee, as distinct from employer and independent contractor, has to exist. A few apparent exceptions to this rule are not really such. First, however, it needs to be pointed out that vicarious liability is another instance of stricter liability in the sense that the employer who is not at fault is made responsible for the employee's default. It thereby gives the injured party compensation from the person who is better able to pay and spread the cost of the injury, namely the employer.

Some justification for this departure from the fault principle was needed and many reasons have in fact been offered. Some have an air of fiction about them, such as the 'control' test, which attributes to the employer the ability to control the behaviour of his employee. Others base liability on an analogy with causation in that the employer set the whole thing in motion[221] and that, therefore, he should bear the consequences if a third party suffers through the employee's wrongful conduct. The 'deeper pocket' justification has economic overtones: the employer is richer so he should pay; which also suits the victim since the employer is invariably in a better position to pay than his employee.[222] Economic and moral considerations also seem to be satisfied by those who advocate that the person who derives a benefit from the activity of another should also bear the risk of damage inflicted by those acts.[223] Yet another economic variant is that the employer is in a better position to spread the loss through insurance or the price of his products. Though the theoretical justifications of vicarious liability vary, it is not a problem that worries the courts. Lord Pearce's remark that the doctrine of vicarious liability has not grown from any clear logical or legal principle but from social convenience and

---

[221] *Hutchinson* v. *The York, Newcastle and Berwick Ry. Co.* (1850) 5 Exch. 343, 350; 155 ER 150, 153, per Alderson B.

[222] Inference from Alderson B in *Hutchinson's* case (1850) 5 Exch. at 350; 155 ER at 153.

[223] Would this not be a good reason for making parents liable vicariously for the torts of their minor children as in French law?

rough justice[224] is typical of their pragmatic approach to the question. Perhaps it should also be taken to suggest that, although no single theory can explain the rule, its basis cannot be dismissed entirely. As Professor Glanville Williams wrote:[225]

Vicarious liability is the creation of many judges who have had different ideas of its justification or social policy, or no idea at all. Some judges may have extended the rule more widely or confined it more narrowly than its true rationale would allow; yet the rationale, if we can discover it, will remain valid so far as it extends.

Anyone who wishes to hold an employer vicariously liable must prove: (*a*) that the offender was his employee; (*b*) that he committed a tort; and (*c*) that he committed it in the course of his employment.

1. Who is an 'Employee'?

The determination of the nature of the work relationship (employee/ independent contractor) is normally said to be a question of mixed fact and law, although where the discovery of the correct status depends on the construction of written documents it may be a pure question of law.[226] It has been said that 'the . . . evaluation of the factual circumstances in which the work is performed . . . is a question of fact to be determined by the trial court'.[227] The construction of the relevant document must thus be undertaken 'in its contractual matrix',[228] something which gives the trial court considerable power in weighing the plethora of (usually) conflicting elements but also gives the process a certain impressionistic character.[229] But let us now move to specifics.

It is sometimes said that where there is a contract of service or of employment, there is necessarily an employer–employee relationship and the employer will be liable for the employee's tort; where the contract is for services, this is an employer–independent contractor relationship and the employer is not vicariously liable for the torts of the other. This criterion, however, like so many others, only restates the problem rather than solves it. What one has to do is to marshal various tests, which cumulatively point either towards an employer–employee relationship, or away from one.

Before discussing the various criteria used by the courts to decide whether there is an employer–employee relationship a note of warning about the rich case law may not be out of place.

[224] *ICI Ltd.* v. *Shatwell* [1965] AC 656, 685. See also *Duncan* v. *Findlater* (1839) 6 Cl. & F. 894, 910; 7 ER 934, 940, per Lord Brougham. In the same sense Slade J in *Longdon-Griffiths* v. *Smith* [1950] 2 All ER 662, 667, and Denning LJ in *Broom* v. *Morgan* [1953] 1 QB 597, 608.

[225] 'Vicarious Liability and the Master's Indemnity' (1957) 20 *MLR* 220, 231. See also Seavey and Fleming James, (Select Bibliography, below).

[226] *Davies* v. *Presbyterian Church* [1986] 1 WLR 323.

[227] *Lee Tin Sang* v. *Chung Chi-Keung* [1990] 2 AC 374, 414 (per Lord Griffiths).

[228] *McMeechan* v. *Secretary of State for Employment* [1995] IRLR 461, 463. See also the judgment of the Court of Appeal in this case at [1997] IRLR 353.

[229] These factors are sometimes so evenly divided between them that the trial court's power to assess them *qualitatively* may, in the end, be influenced by the wider policy desire to afford greater protection to the victim. This can be achieved by granting the plaintiff the status of emloyee and thus according him the benefits invariably reserved by special statutes to employees but not independent contractors. See, for instance, *Lane* v. *Shire Roofing Company (Oxford) Ltd.* [1995] IRLR 493.

It will be noticed that the cases that follow do not always deal with the existence of an employer–employee relationship, in the context of the *potential liability* of the employer for his employees' torts. Many of them, on the contrary, are concerned to discover the true nature of the relationship for the purposes of tax obligations and duties and, as already alluded to, the applicability of employment-protection laws. An employee, for example, enjoys greater employment security than an independent contractor. Are the courts likely to draw the distinction between employees and independent contractors in the same way, irrespective of the wider context of the dispute? Some commentators think so,[230] whereas others[231] warn against a mechanical use of decisions rendered in one context (i.e. employment-protection laws) in the very different situation where the liability of the employer might be at issue. The case of *O'Kelly* v. *Trusthouse Forte plc*[232] offers a good illustration of the attractiveness of the second view. In that case the defendants, owners of the Grosvenor House Hotel, operated a hotel and restaurant business for which they employed permanent staff. Additionally, they also hired out rooms for private functions for which they provided catering facilities. This part of the business was in need of casual staff some of whom were known as 'regulars' and who were rostered in preference to other casual staff (though they were free to refuse these more-frequently offered jobs). When the plaintiff (and two other regulars) were 'dismissed', allegedly for belonging to a trade union, they brought an action for unfair dismissal under section 58 of the Employment Protection Consolidation Act 1978 (now s. 152 of the Trade Union and Labour Relations (Consolidation) Act 1992). The court held that they were not employees for the purposes of the employment-protection legislation, because the necessary element of mutuality of obligation was absent from their relationship with the employer.[233] As Professor McKendrick points out, however,[234] the result would surely have been different if one of them had spilt wine over a hotel customer and the employer–employee relationship was being investigated for the purposes of rendering the hotel (employers) liable to the customers.

The traditional criterion for distinguishing employees from independent contractors is the degree and right of control.[235] Bramwell LJ regarded a servant as anyone who was subject to the command of the employer as to the manner in which he shall do his work.[236] On the other hand, if the employer only determined 'what' was to be done rather than 'how' it was to be done, then the person working for him would be an independent contractor. In *Honeywill and Stein Ltd.* v. *Larkin Brothers Ltd.*[237] Slesser LJ expressed this idea as follows:

---

[230] Winfield and Jolowicz on *Tort* (15th edn., 1998), 696.

[231] McKendrick, *Tort Textbook* (5th edn.), 18.   [232] [1984] QB 90.

[233] On the mutuality test, which has been significant mainly in the context of employment protection legislation and which has given rise to an extensive case law, see S. Deakin and G. Morris, *Labour Law* (2nd edn., 1998), at para. 3.4.8.

[234] Op. cit. (Select Bibliography).

[235] For an oft-quoted statement, see *Short* v. *J. & W. Henderson Ltd.* (1946) 62 TLR 427, 429, per Lord Thankerton. For an elaborate examination of the employment relationship, see Atiyah, (Select Bibliography, below), 31 ff.

[236] *Yewens* v. *Noakes* (1880) 6 QBD 530, 532–3.   [237] [1934] 1 KB 191, 196.

The determination whether the actual wrongdoer is a servant or agent on the one hand or an independent contractor on the other depends on whether or not the employer not only determines what is to be done, but retains the control of the actual performance, in which case the doer is a servant or agent; but if the employer while prescribing the work to be done, leaves the manner of doing it to the control of the doer, the latter is an independent contractor.

In *Performing Rights Society Ltd.* v. *Mitchell and Booker (Palais de Danse) Ltd.*[238] the defendants engaged a band for their dance hall. The agreement stipulated that the musicians should not infringe the plaintiff's copyright, which they did. The liability of the defendants depended on whether the musicians were their servants and it was held that they were.

The control test was more appropriate to the social conditions of an earlier age. For, as Professor Kahn-Freund put it, the distinction between servant and independent contractor on the basis of the control test 'reflects a state of society in which the ownership of the means of production coincided with the possession of technical knowledge and skill and in which that knowledge and skill was largely acquired by being handed down from one generation to the next by oral tradition and not by being systematically imparted in institutions of learning . . .'[239]

As specialist skills of employees increased, the unskilled employer was less and less able to control their work, and it might be thought that the control test might be preserved by saying that the employer would have the right to control their work if he possessed the necessary skill. This, however, begs the question, since saying that the defendant has the right to control work results from the decision *already* made that he is an employer. Moreover, the term 'servant', as it was used in the nineteenth-century cases, does not necessarily correspond to the modern term 'employee'. The term 'servant' denoted, on the whole, manual workers as opposed to clerical and professional employees. This distinction is of practically no relevance in the modern law.[240]

The increasing subtlety of the employment relationship makes the control test, however modified, inadequate. As Lord Parker CJ put it:[241]

Superintendence and control cannot be the decisive test when one is dealing with a professional man, or a man of some particular skill and experience. Instances of that have been given in the form of the master of a ship, an engine driver, or a professional architect . . . In such cases, there can be no question of the employer telling him how to do work, therefore the absence of control and direction in that sense can be of little, if any, use as a test.

To this list one should add doctors. Indeed, it was in this context that the courts experienced their earliest difficulties with the control test. This implied that hospitals could not be liable for the torts of medical experts, who could hardly be dictated to by hospital authorities as to how they should exercise

---

[238] [1924] 1 KB 762.   [239] Below (Select Bibliography), 505.
[240] See A. Merritt, 'Control v. Economic Reality: Defining the Contract of Employment' [1982] *Aust Bus. LR* 105.
[241] *Morren* v. *Swinton and Pendlebury BC* [1965] 1 WLR 576, 582.

their calling.[242] A change in attitude appeared in the early 1940s. In *Gold* v. *Essex County Council*[243] the Court of Appeal held that a radiographer was a servant of the hospital that employed him and thus rendered it vicariously liable for his negligence in the course of his duty, even though the hospital authorities were not competent to dictate to him how he should exercise his skill. In *Cassidy* v. *Ministry of Health*[244] a hospital's liability for the professional negligence of its permanent medical staff was unequivocally established. In that case it was unclear whether the negligence that resulted in the plaintiff's injury was that of the whole-time assistant medical officer, the house surgeon, or one of the nurses. The Court of Appeal was not deterred by this in holding the hospital liable to the plaintiff. All three judges felt that it was unnecessary to pinpoint whose negligence had caused the harm; the hospital was vicariously liable for the professional negligence of its staff.

In addition to the shortcomings of the control test, another factor behind the change that came about was the change in the social and economic environment. In the past, when hospitals were supported by voluntary contributions, it was essential to preserve their valuable services as much as possible by avoiding liability so as to safeguard their slender resources from being depleted by payment of heavy damages. Accordingly, courts distinguished between torts committed by doctors and nurses in the course of routine and administrative functions, for which hospitals were vicariously liable, and in the course of exercising professional skill, for which they were not liable. However, once hospitals came to rest on a more secure financial basis, especially after the introduction of the National Health Service, courts became more willing to hold them liable. So today a hospital authority would be liable except in cases where a surgeon or consultant treats a patient under private contract.

The emphasis placed on control has thus been reduced, but not abandoned. It has become a kind of residuary test in the sense that it can be outweighed by other considerations; but these being equal or inconclusive, the control test will decide the issue. *Argent* v. *Minister of Social Security and Another*[245] offers a good example. In that case the applicant worked as a part-time teacher in a drama school but he combined this with work as a full-time actor with various theatre companies. The school did not prescribe a syllabus and in no way interfered with his teaching. On being classified as a self-employed person within section 1(2)(b) of the National Insurance Act 1965, he appealed, alleging that he was a servant, not an independent contractor, and that consequently he should be regarded as an employed person. His contention was rejected. Roskill J said:

If one studies the cases . . . a number of tests have been propounded over the years for resolving the problem that I have to solve. For example, in the earlier cases it seems to have been suggested that the most important test, if not the all-important test, was the

[242] *Hilyer* v. *St Bartholomew's Hospital* [1909] 2 KB 820.

[243] [1942] 2 KB 293. The judgments also indicate reliance on a breach of the hospital's 'non-delegable' duty to ensure that care is taken of the patient.

[244] [1951] 2 KB 343. *Roe* v. *Minister of Health* [1954] 2 QB 66 has probably added staff anaesthetists. See further Hamson, op. cit. in *Law in Action* (Select Bibliography).

[245] [1968] 1 WLR 1749, 1758–9. To similar effect McCardie J in *Performing Rights Society* v. *Mitchell and Booker (Palais de Danse) Ltd.* [1924] 1 KB 762, 767.

extent of the control exercised by the employer over the servant . . . But it is also clear that as one watches the development of the law in the first 60 years of this century and particularly the development of the law in the last 15 or 20 years in this field, the emphasis has shifted and no longer rests so strongly upon the question of control. Control is obviously an important factor. In some cases it may still be the decisive factor, but it is wrong to say that in every case it is the decisive factor. It is now, as I venture to think, no more than a factor, albeit a very important one.

More recent decisions continue to show the secondary role attached by some judges to the control test. In *WHPT Housing Association Ltd.* v. *Secretary of State for Social Services*[246] an architect worked on a freelance basis for the plaintiff's association and eventually sought to be included as a member of its permanent staff for the purposes of the Social Security Act 1975. Despite a considerable degree of integration in the business and the fact that his work was subject to fairly close and regular control by the association's chief architect, he was found to be self-employed because he had retained control over the issue of how many hours of service he would offer his employer. Webster J put it in this way: 'In a contract of service . . . the principal obligation undertaken by the employee is *to provide himself to serve*: whereas in a contract for services the principal obligation is not to provide himself to serve the employer *but his services for the use of the employer*.'[247]

The difficulties that accompany the control test have led other judges to propose a more impressionistic approach. One is the integration test of Denning LJ in *Stevenson Jordon and Harrison Ltd.* v. *MacDonald and Evans*,[248] where he said that 'under a contract of service, a man is employed as part of the business, and his work is done as an integral part of the business; whereas, under a contract for services, his work, although done for the business, is not integrated into it but is only accessory to it.'

The idea was extended in *Market Investigations Ltd.* v. *Minister of Social Security*,[249] where an appellant company was engaged in market research employing a few full-time workers and many part-time interviewers selected from a panel of nearly 500 persons. In 1966 the company asked the minister to decide whether a part-time interviewer was employed for the purposes of the National Insurance Acts 1946 and 1965. The minister's conclusion was that the particular interviewer worked under a contract of service (or contract of employment) and not, as the company contended, a contract for services; and his decision was upheld on appeal. In the opinion of Cooke J, control, though relevant, was not decisive. What mattered more was whether the interviewer could be said to be in business on her own account, or as an employee working for an agreed wage whose employer took the risk of loss and the chance of profit. This 'economic reality' test has since been approved by the Privy Council.[250]

---

[246] [1981] ICR 737.   [247] Ibid., 748.

[248] [1952] 1 TLR 101, 111. Also Denning LJ in *Bank voor Handel en Scheepvaart NV* v. *Slatford* [1953] 1 QB 248, 295: 'whether the person is part and parcel of the organization'.

[249] [1969] 2 QB 173, esp. at 184.

[250] *Lee Ting Sang* v. *Chung Chi-Keung* [1990] 2 AC 374.

The common-sense basis for this approach, however, and its advantage of avoiding the artificiality of the control test, should not obscure the fact that it does not solve all problems. Not surprisingly, therefore, parallel attempts have been made to provide more elaborate criteria. A full discussion of this topic can be found in *Ready Mixed Concrete (South East) Ltd.* v. *Minister of Pensions and National Insurance*,[251] where a concrete-manufacturing company agreed with the owner of a lorry to pay him a fixed mileage rate for transporting concrete. The contract described him as an independent contractor, and he was obliged to maintain his vehicle in good order and at his own expense. He was also free to employ a competent driver whenever necessary. He, on the other hand, undertook to make his lorry available whenever the company wanted it, to have it painted in the company's colours, and to wear the company's uniform. The company also prescribed a special way in which he should present the accounts. The question whether he was an employed person within the National Insurance Act 1965 turned on whether or not he was under a contract of service. MacKenna J, after a lengthy review of the authorities, decided that he was an independent contractor. He laid down the conditions of a contract of service as follows:

(i) The servant agrees that, in consideration of a wage or other remuneration, he will provide his own work and skill in the performance of some service for his master. (ii) He agrees, expressly or impliedly, that in the performance of that service he will be subject to the other's control in a sufficient degree to make that other master. (iii) The other provisions of the contract are consistent with its being a contract of service.

In this case, the driver owned the lorry and bore the financial risk, and 'he who owns the assets and bears the risk is unlikely to be acting as an agent or servant. If the man performing the service must provide the means of performance at his own expense and accept payment by results, he will own the assets, bear the risk, and be to that extent unlike a servant.'[252] The lorry-owner's contract was thus one of services, not of service.

MacKenna J's conditions must not be applied rigidly—successive judges have warned against the risks of doing so. In *Market Investigations Ltd.* v. *Minister of Social Security* Cooke J said:[253] 'No exhaustive list has been compiled and perhaps no exhaustive list can be compiled of the considerations which are relevant in determining that question, nor can strict rules be laid down as to the relative weight which the various considerations should carry in particular cases.'

What emerges from all this is that courts will take into account a variety of tests to determine the nature of the relationship between the tortfeasor and his employer. How much weight will attach to each test depends on each case; and, as already stated, the determination may vary depending upon whether the court is ultimately deciding the issue in a, say, tax or liability situation.[254]

---

[251] [1968] 2 QB 497, 515, 525.

[252] In the United States this is sometimes referred to as the 'economic reality' argument. See: *United States of America* v. *Silk* 331 US 704 (1946) referred to by our Court of Appeal in *Lane* v. *Shire Roofing* [1995] IRLR 493.

[253] [1969] 2 QB 173, 184–5; approved by McNeill J in *Warner Holidays Ltd.* v. *Secretary of State for Social Services* [1983] ICR 440, 453–4 and by Nolan J in *Wickens* v. *Champion Employment* [1984] ICR 365, 369.

[254] Describing the 'worker' as an independent contractor may confer upon him tax benefits; but it may also decrease his protection if his claim for compensation for personal injury is at stake. See, for instance, *Lane* v. *Shire Roofing* [1995] IRLR 493 (CA). But, it seems, the courts will rarely admit this in open.

If on balance the multiple factors point towards one type of relationship, then the courts will accept it even if the parties themselves have given a different label to their relationship. So, in *Ferguson* v. *John Dawson & Partners (Contractors) Ltd.*[255] the plaintiff worked on the defendant's building site and was described as a subcontractor working as part of the 'lump' labour force.[256] He was injured, and argued that he was an employee for the purposes of statutory safety duties owed by employers to their employees. The defendant's contention, that the parties had characterised their relationship as that of employer–independent contractor and that the statutory duties were thus not owed to the plaintiff, was rejected, since in the court's view all the other circumstances pointed towards a relationship of employer and employee. Where, however, the surrounding circumstances point towards a relation of either employer–employee or employer–independent contractor and there is no underlying illegality, there is no reason why the courts should not strive to give effect to the label that the parties have attached to their relationship.[257]

The preceding paragraph may be an over-simplification of the law in so far as it implied that in the absence of any illegality the will of the parties—as manifested in the negotiated terms—may be paramount. In reality, however, it would appear that the courts go beyond the declared will of the parties and take into account wider societal interests whenever they conclude that the label chosen by the parties, however honestly chosen, must give way to the true realities of each situation.[258] So, in *Warner Holidays Ltd.* v. *Secretary of State for Social Services*[259] McNeil J said:

When the community has an interest . . . in the collection of contributions for social security purposes, while the intention of the parties as to the nature of the contract they intend is itself important, it is not necessarily conclusive. The parties to a contract of employment cannot, by private arrangement, exclude from the arrangement public and community obligations.

---

[255] [1976] 1 WLR 1213. To similar effect, see the recent decision of the Privy Council in *Lee Ting Sang* v. *Chung Chi-Keung* [1990] 2 AC 374.

[256] Such characterisation can bring legal and illegal advantages to both contracting parties. In the case of a self-employed person, for example, the employer is spared the trouble of making deductions in respect of income tax and paying National Health Insurance contributions. It can also mean that in a case like *Ferguson* v. *Dawson* the employer will not be liable for breach of certain statutory duties, which are meant to ensure the safety of employees. For a worker, his description as a self-employed person may enable him to deduct certain expenses from his pay-packet and generally place him in a better tax position, and it may also give him the opportunity to evade tax obligations, since as a self-employed person he is resonsible for his own tax declarations.

[257] *Massey* v. *Crown Life Insurance Co.* [1978] 1 WLR 676. It will be noted that in this case there was no suspicion of tax impropriety. The status of home-workers, part-time workers, etc. can also have important consequences as far as payment of social-security contributions, withholding of taxes, and the law of unfair dismissal is concerned. The case law gives no unequivocal guidance on this. See *Wickens* v. *Champion Employment* [1984] ICR 365, 368; *Nethermere (St Neots) Ltd.* v. *Gardiner* [1984] ICR 612; *O'Kelly* v. *Trusthouse Forte plc* [1984] 1 QB 90.

[258] 'The question [whether the plaintiff is an employee or an independant contractor] is not determined by the label which the parties themsleves put on the relationship'. Per Mummery J in *McMeechan* v. *Secretary of State for Employment* [1995] IRLR 461, 463.

[259] [1983] ICR 440, 454; although cf. *Calder* v. *H. Kitson Vickers (& Sons) Engineers Ltd.* [1988] ICR 232, 250 (Ralph Gibson LJ).

It may be reasonable, therefore, to assume that in that case the state's interest to collect secondary contributions from the employer may have influenced the court's decision to hold that the contractual terms of entertainers engaged at a holiday camp for a summer season should be interpreted as making the entertainers 'employed earners'. In other instances, however, the courts may have been influenced in its characterisation of the relationship by other factors such as the desire to protect employees from contracting out of the advantages given to them by employment legislation. So, in *Young and Woods* v. *West*[260] a skilled metal-worker who had clearly opted in favour of being described as 'self-employed' (since this gave him a legitimate tax advantage) was, nevertheless, held to be an employee when he was dismissed and then (successfully) blew 'hot and cold' and invoked statutory employment rights. Thus the dividing-line between all these cases is often a fine one; and the partial concealment by the courts of the true reasons that motivate their decisions make it difficult to state the law with any greater degree of authority.

Before leaving this topic some mention should be made of borrowed employees, which is best illustrated by *Mersey Docks and Harbour Board* v. *Coggins and Griffith (Liverpool) Ltd.*[261] A harbour authority hired out to X, a firm of stevedores, a mobile crane with its operator. The contract expressly provided that the operator was to work for the time being as the employee of X, although the harbour authority retained the power of dismissal. The question was whether it or X was vicariously liable to the plaintiff, who was injured by the negligence of the operator. It was held that the harbour authority was liable as it still controlled the manner in which the crane was worked. This case is one of a number dealing with the same problem, but it probably contains the clearest enunciation of the applicable principles. Though obviously a number of factors have to be considered in deciding which of the two masters will be liable, the courts still attach significance to the control test as an ultimate resort. Other factors include the type of machinery that has been loaned (the more complicated it is, the more likely the permanent employer will remain liable), the duration of the service under the temporary employer, and such general matters as who pays, who stamps his national-insurance card, who retains the power of dismissal, and whether the two employers, themselves, have attempted to regulate this matter.

The general employer's ability to shift liability on to the shoulders of the temporary employer may, however, be seriously restricted by the Unfair Contract Terms Act 1977 as two interesting and, apparently, contradictory cases suggest: *Phillips Products* v. *Hyland*[262] and *Thompson* v. *T. Lohan (Plant Hire) Ltd.*[263]

Phillips and *Thompson* had, for all intents and purposes, similar facts. They both involved owners hiring out JCBs along with their operators. Both contracts

---

[260] [1980] IRLR 201.

[261] [1947] AC 1, 61. It was further said, at 13–14, that the question which of the two employers would be liable for the tort of the borrowed servant was not determined by any agreement between them.

[262] [1987] 1 WLR 659. Despite the year of publication this decision was, in fact, decided two-and-a-half years earlier than *Thompson*.

[263] [1987] 1 WLR 649.

of hire made, according to their clauses 8, the hirers (temporary employers) and not the owners of the machinery (permanent employers) liable for the negligent conduct of the machine operators. In both cases the operators' negligence caused harm—in *Phillips* it damaged the hirer's property; in *Thompson*'s case it killed the plaintiff's husband who was also employed by the owner of the machinery. In *Phillips* the plaintiffs (hirers) sued the owners of the machinery for the damage to their property. The owners relied on clause 8 of the contract (with the hirers) and attempted to deny liability for the operator's negligence. The Court of Appeal took the view that clause 8 was caught by section 2(2) of UCTA and would protect the owners if the clause satisfied the requirement of reasonableness as set out in section 13 of UCTA. In the court's view it did not and hence the clause transferring liability to the hirers (and, in effect, exonerating the owners) was held to be void. In *Thompson*, by contrast, the plaintiff's widow sued the owner of the machinery (permanent employer of the negligent operator) and recovered damages. In third-party proceedings the owner then tried to shift the loss on to the hirer (temporary employer of the negligent operator). Not unnaturally the defendants (hirers) tried to invoke UCTA in order to avoid the application of clause 8 which, if valid, would transfer liability to them. This move, though—as we have seen, successful in *Phillips*—failed in *Thompson*.

The different treatment of clause 8 by the two courts raises a number of questions. Arguably, however, the different treatment of the same clause can be explained by the fact that if it had been validated in *Phillips* it would, in effect, have denied a remedy to the victims of the negligent act whereas in *Thompson* the validation of clause 8 did not deny the victim (Mrs Thompson) any remedy but merely stopped the owner of the machinery (first defendant) from shifting the loss to the hirer (second defendant). Such an interpretation (and reconciliation of the two cases)[264] thus makes the validity of such indemnity clauses depend on how they affect the primary victim. 'If the victim's claim is prejudiced by an indemnity clause, then section 2 [of the UCTA] applies (as in *Phillips*) [and makes the transfer of liability to the temporary employer void]; if the victim's claim is not prejudiced, then section 2 [of the UCTA] does not apply [and the clause is valid, transferring ultimate liability on to the shoulders of the temporary employer].'[265]

In view of the above it is, therefore, safe to assert that, overall, the courts place a heavy burden of proof on the permanent employer before they will allow him to shift responsibility on to the shoulders of the temporary employer.[266] There may, however, be much to be said for the view taken by some American courts which allow the plaintiff to sue *both* employers and have

---

[264] This is the explanation offered by Adams and Brownsword, (see below, Select Bibliography), and it seems convincing, not least since it derives some support from Fox LJ's judgment in *Thompson* v. *T. Lohan (Plant Hire) Ltd.* [1987] 1 WLR 649, 657.

[265] Adams and Brownsword [1988] *JBL* 146, 149.

[266] This is certainly true where skilled workers are left with complicated machinery. In theory, however, it should be different where unskilled labour is hired out. See *Bhoomidas* v. *Port of Singapore Authority* [1978] 1 All ER 956, 960.

them subsequently sort out among themselves which of them should bear the cost.[267]

Another special case of vicarious liability is 'casual delegation', where, for example, one person drives another's car with his permission and, partly at least, in his interest. In these cases there is no employment relationship and the courts use the terms 'principal' and 'agent' rather loosely. Whatever the terminology, the fact is that the courts are prepared to hold the owner of a vehicle liable for the negligence of its driver when the latter is driving with the owner's permission and, partly at least, in the latter's interests. In *Ormrod* v. *Crosville Motor Services Ltd.*,[268] A asked B to drive his (A's) car from England to the South of France where eventually they were to have a joint holiday. While still in England B negligently caused an accident for which A was held vicariously liable, even though B was not A's employee, because B was pursuing not only his own interests but A's as well. Subsequently, the Court of Appeal in *Morgans* v. *Launchbury*[269] attempted, largely out of insurance considerations, to widen this type of vicarious liability by applying it to the authorised use of cars even where the owner had no interest or concern in the use; but the House of Lords[270] reversed the decision and reinstated the traditional rule. In that case the defendant wife owned a car, which was treated as a 'family' car. Her husband promised her that he would get a friend to drive should he ever have too much to drink. One day the husband got drunk and asked C, a friend, to drive him and the plaintiffs back home. Owing to C's negligence a collision occurred in which the husband was killed and the plaintiffs were injured. The Court of Appeal by a majority held that the defendant should be vicariously liable since she had allowed the use of her car. The House of Lords unanimously reversed the decision on the ground that mere permission to drive without the owner having some concern or interest in the use of the car was insufficient to render her vicariously liable. But the defendant/owner of the loaned car (or other chattel) must have a specific and identifiable interest in the use of the car.[271]

2. The Employee Must Commit a Tort

This requirement seems obvious since vicarious liability is, by definition, liability imposed on one person for the wrongdoing of another. It has been challenged by the so-called 'employer's tort' theory according to which an employer is liable because the employee's wrongdoing is the employer's own tort, i.e. liability is primary, not vicarious.[272] Whatever its merits, this theory was repudiated by the House of Lords in *Staveley Iron and Chemical Co. Ltd.* v. *Jones*,[273] which restored the traditional view, namely that vicarious liability is indeed vicarious and an employer can only be liable provided his employee

---

[267] *Strait* v. *Hale Constr. Co.*, 26 Cal. Ap. 3d. 941, 103 Cal. Rptr. 487 (1972) and for further references to US views Henderson and Pearson, *The Torts Process* (1981), 177–9.

[268] [1953] 1 WLR 1120. Cf. *Hewitt* v. *Bonvin* [1940] 1 KB 188, where the defendant, who lent his car to his son entirely for the latter's use, was not held responsible for damage negligently caused by him.

[269] [1971] 2 QB 245.   [270] [1973] AC 127.   [271] *Norwood* v. *Navan* [1981] RTR 457.

[272] Williams (1956) 72 LQR 522; cf. the language of Denning LJ in e.g. *Cassidy* v. *Ministry of Health* [1951] 2 KB 343, 361.

[273] [1956] AC 627.

commits a tort. A mere procedural bar, however, preventing action against the employee does not relieve the employer, because the employee remains guilty of a tort, albeit one for which *he* cannot be sued. So, in *Broom* v. *Morgan*[274] the plaintiff and her husband were employed by the defendant. The plaintiff was injured through her husband's negligence and she sued the defendant who disputed vicarious liability, contending that, as the law then stood, husbands and wives could not sue each other in tort, and that if the husband was not liable to his wife, he could not be liable either.[275] The Court of Appeal, however, held him liable, since the husband's immunity was only from suit, not from responsibility for a tort. This was also the *ratio* of *Smith* v. *Moss*,[276] where the plaintiff recovered damages from her mother-in-law, who was held vicariously liable for the negligent driving of her son, the husband of the plaintiff, since on the facts he was acting as her agent *ad hoc*.

The traditional theory received further support in *Imperial Chemical Industries Ltd.* v. *Shatwell*.[277] Two brothers, George and James, were employed as shot firers. Safety regulations, imposed on them personally, required that tests of electrical circuits for shot firing should only be conducted from behind cover, but rather than inconvenience themselves by having to comply with regulations, they agreed to test a circuit in the open. An explosion followed, injuring both of them. George sued the company, alleging that it was vicariously liable for the negligence and breach of regulations by his brother James. The House of Lords held the company not liable on the ground of consent. Since James himself would not have been liable to George for this reason, the employers were entitled to the vicarious benefit of that defence just as they would have had to carry the vicarious liability in its absence. Lord Pearce put the point succinctly:[278] 'Unless the servant is liable the master is not liable for his acts; subject only to this, that the master cannot take advantage of an immunity from suit conferred on the servant.'

3. Course of Employment[279]

The most vexed requirement is that an employee has to commit his tort 'in the course of his employment'. The problem is to devise suitable criteria for determining this, and to apply these to particular situations. Unfortunately, the plethora of often irreconcilable authorities does not make the task of exposition easy. As Comyn J said in a recent case:[280] 'the large body of case law . . . is notable for one thing, its inconsistency very often with an immediately preceding case.' However, without detracting from the wisdom of that warning,

---

[274] [1953] 1 QB 597.
[275] The husband-and-wife rule has since been abolished by the Law Reform (Husband and Wife) Act 1962.
[276] [1940] 1 KB 424.
[277] [1965] AC 656. The regulations have since been altered so as to impose the obligation on the master.
[278] Ibid., at 686.
[279] For a thorough discussion, see Atiyah, op. cit. (Select Bibliography), 171–285. See also Fleming James, op. cit. (Select Bibliography), 173 ff.
[280] *Harrison* v. *Michelin Tyre Co. Ltd.* [1985] 1 All ER 918, 920.

one is tempted to suggest that the courts tend to expand the notion of 'course of employment' if by doing so they are serving better an 'important purpose'. One such important purpose, for which admittedly there seems to be little express textual support, can be found in the courts' desire to secure greater protection for the victim of the tort.[281] A wider understanding of the notion of course of employment has this effect since it provides the victim of the tort with a credit-worthy person (the employer) to sue. Another 'important purpose'—more 'modern' and, this time, more openly admitted by the courts—may be related with the attainment of racial and sex equality in our society. Thus, in *Jones* v. *Tower Boot Co. Ltd.*[282] the Court of Appeal, after stating that the meaning of 'course of employment' should be given a wider meaning whenever the Race Relations Act 1976 was involved, proceeded to hold an employer liable for the actions of his employees which violated section 32(1) of the 1976 Act.[283]

Let us return to the main point discussed in this subsection. That an employer is liable for acts that he expressly authorises is obvious; but this is primary, not vicarious liability. Clearly, it is impracticable to require that an employer should specifically authorise each and every action of his employee. So from early times it was sought to justify the employer's vicarious liability on the hypothesis of implied authority. The difficulty was to fix the limits of this, and the solution was to say that authority is deemed to extend only so far as the scope of the employment. Was implied authority, then, the test of the scope of employment, or vice versa. It was neither; and it only helped to confuse matters, for in reality it was little more than a justification for the decision to make employers liable for the torts of employees. None the less, the language of implied authority as the test of scope of employment has been used. In *Poland* v. *Parr & Sons*[284] the employee of a company reasonably believed that some children were stealing a company's property and he struck one of them, who was seriously injured. It was held that although his act was unreasonable it was still within the course of his employment, because, in the words of Bankes LJ: 'As a general rule a servant has an implied authority upon an emergency to endeavour to protect his master's property if he sees it in danger or has reasonable ground for thinking that he sees it in danger.' The case involved assault and battery by the servant, and the difficulty of holding such acts as being in the course of his employment is obvious. The notion of implied authority was here clearly of some use, for if the act complained of could be regarded as one which the employee has discretion to do, then the employer can be held liable even for the wrongful exercise of that discretion. In *Poland* v. *Parr* such discretion to pro-

---

[281] One could further refine this *speculation* by saying that the courts will enlarge the course of employment if they are anxious to secure compensation for physical injuries suffered by the victim; but they will be less likely to do the same thing if he has suffered only pure economic loss. Cf., for instance, two decisions: *Vasey* v. *Surrey Free Inns* [1995] 10 CL 641 (employer liable for assault committed by his employee) with *Generale Bank Nederland NV* v. *Export Credits Guarantee Department*, *The Times*, 4 Aug. 1997 (employer not liable for employee's fraudulant acts which were not within his ostensible authority).

[282] [1997] ICR 254.

[283] One is inclined to think that the same would apply to the corresponding s. 41 of the Sex Discrimination Act 1975.

[284] [1927] 1 KB 236, 240.

tect the employer's property was readily applied, but Atkin LJ was also eager to state its limits:[285]

where the servant does more than the emergency requires, the excess may be so great as to take the act out of the class. For example, if Hall [the servant] had fired a shot at the boy, the act might have been in the interest of his employers, but that is not the test.

Thus an employee who wrongly arrests someone after a supposed attempt at theft has ceased is not regarded as acting within the limits of implied authority because his motive is no longer protection of property but vindication of justice.[286] In another case[287] the employer of a garage attendant, who out of personal vengeance attacked one of the customers, was not liable. Similarly, a bus passenger who complained of a bus conductor's language and found himself assaulted by the conductor as a result cannot render the latter's employer liable.[288] However, the employer of a person put in charge of premises (e.g. a public house) or of a vehicle (or vessel) will be liable for the reasonable force used by such a person to maintain order on the premises, car, or vessel, and may even be liable (though, it is submitted less justifiably so) where the wrongful act was primarily motivated by malice or spite.[289] Such extensions of liability, however, though explicable, perhaps, by reference to 'deep pocket' theories, must not be undertaken lightly if the doctrine of vicarious liability is not to be totally distorted. On the whole, therefore, in such cases it is better to try to base liability on the employer's own fault in selecting an aggressive or irresponsible employee or some other grounds of liability.

The employee's tort must have been committed in the course of his employment and it is not enough that the employment merely gave him the opportunity to commit the wrong. That is why a firm of cleaners will not be liable if one of its employees uses the plaintiff's telephone while cleaning the latter's premises and runs up high bills as a result of making unauthorised calls.[290] In *General Engineering Services Ltd.* v. *Kingston and Saint Andrew Corp.*[291] the plaintiff's house was burnt down because the local firemen had an industrial dispute with their employers (defendants) and operated a 'go slow' policy as a result of which it took them seventeen minutes (instead of three) to cover the distance from the fire brigade's offices to the plaintiff's home. The Privy Council refused to hold the employers vicariously liable. It is unclear whether this ruling would also cover the situation in which the employees were involved in an all-out

---

[285] Ibid., at 245. Does an employee have a discretion to protect the property of a third party entrusted to the care of his master? Liability for an employee's assault is discussed by F. D. Rose in (1977) 40 *MLR* 420.

[286] *Hanson* v. *Waller* [1901] 1 QB 390.

[287] *Warren* v. *Henlys Ltd.* [1948] 2 All ER 935.

[288] *Keppel Bus Co. Ltd.* v. *Sa'ad bin Ahmad* [1974] 1 WLR 1082. In an earlier case, however, a tram company was held liable when one of the conductors pushed a passenger off the tram: *Smith* v. *North Metropolitan Tramways Co.* (1891) 55 JP 630. For a more recent decision (imposing liability) see *Vasey* v. *Surrey Free Inns* [1995] 10 CL 641.

[289] *Petterson* v. *Royal Oak Hotel Ltd.* [1948] NZLR 136. This and other related cases are discussed by Rose, op. cit. (Select Bibliography).

[290] *Heasmans* v. *Clarity Cleaning Co. Ltd.* [1987] ICR 949. *Jones* v. *Tower Boot Co. Ltd.* [1997] ICR 254: one employee burning the arm of another with a hot screwdriver as part of a series of acts of racial harrassement; employee not in the course of his employment.

[291] [1989] 1 WLR 69.

strike rather than performing their work badly in pursuance of an industrial dispute.

It is significant, in this context that tests of the employer's vicarious liability under statutes such as the Race Relations Act 1976, which are meant to have an educative or exemplary effect upon employers, are beginning to diverge from the common-law test. In *Irving* v. *The Post Office*[292] the Court of Appeal held that the Post Office was not vicariously liable under the Race Relations Act for racially abusive words written on an envelope by one of their employees who bore a grudge against the plaintiffs (who were his neighbours) and who were of Jamaican origin. However, in the later case of *Jones* v. *Tower Boot Co. Ltd.*,[293] the Court of Appeal, as we have seen, took a broader view of the 1976 Act. Here, an employer took no action to prevent racial taunts and assaults that were directed by his employees against one of their fellow workers. The Employment Appeal Tribunal held that the employer was not vicariously liable for the actions of his employees, but the court of Appeal reversed on the grounds that this would produce the perverse result that 'the more heinous the act of discrimination, the less likely it will be that the employer would be liable'.[294] In this case, the court took the view that the statutory background to the act of discrimination justified it taking a view of the employer's vicarious liability that went beyond the common-law approach. However, it is not inconceivable that innovations in statutory interpretation, such as this, can also have an influence on the development of the common law, just as the common law plainly influences to some degree the interpretation of the statute.[295]

At common law it nevertheless remains the case that the definition of 'scope of employment' is crucial though, unfortunately, numerous decided cases show it cannot be reduced to a concise and workable formula. As Finnemore J remarked:[296] 'I think the answer to much of the argument on both sides is that there is no one test which is exhaustive by which this particular problem can be solved.'

Notwithstanding the above statement, courts often appear to find less difficulty with this issue than writers who keep striving to reconcile the irreconcilable. There seems to be only one simple rule: if an employee committed his tort within the scope of his employment, the employer is liable; if he acted outside it, the employer is not liable. The question whether an act was within or outside the scope of employment is one of fact. As the Lord President put it in the leading Scottish case of *Kirby* v. *National Coal Board*:[297] 'It is probably not possible, and it is certainly inadvisable, to endeavour to lay down an exhaustive

---

[292] [1987] IRLR 289. See also *Deaton's Property Ltd* v. *Flew* (1949) 79 CLR 370: the employers of a barmaid were not held responsible when she threw a glass of beer at a customer.

[293] [1997] IRLR 168. See also the Race Relations Act case of *Burton* v. *De Vere Hotels Ltd.* [1996] IRLR 596, dealing with the statutory equivalent to the employer's personal duty of care.

[294] [1997] IRLR 168, 172.

[295] For a development of this argument see S. Deakin, 'Private Law, Economic Rationality and the Regulatory State' in P. Birks (ed.) *The Classification of Obligations* (1997).

[296] *Staton* v. *NCB* [1957] 1 WLR 893, 895.

[297] 1958 SC 514, 532 quoted with approval by the House of Lords in *Williams* v. *A. & W. Hemphill Ltd.*, 1966 SLT 259, 260. (Another deviation case containing interesting dicta.)

definition of what falls within the scope of the employment. Each case must depend to a considerable extent on its particular facts.'

So how do the courts approach this task? It would appear that the position is analogous to that in negligence where likewise there is a simple rule; if a person has behaved carelessly, he is liable (subject to certain other conditions being fulfilled); if he was not careless, he is not liable. The question whether his behaviour was careless or not is one of fact. Just as there are guidelines (not rules) to help in determining carelessness, so too there are only guidelines that help in determining scope of employment. The decision is ultimately impressionistic. Leaving aside the 'implied authority' fiction, the test is simply: was this what the employee was employed to do? was it a bad way of doing it? The courts have in fact frequently used as a starting-point Salmond's formulation[298] according to which a wrongful act is deemed to be in the course of employment 'if it is either (1) a wrongful act authorised by the master, or (2) a wrongful and unauthorised mode of doing some act authorised by the master'. From there on, the process is one of applying these guidelines to the facts in a way that conforms with the judge's overall appreciation of the merits of the case and without attaching too much importance to available precedents.

On that approach an employer may sometimes be liable even for an act which he has forbidden. An obvious reason for this harsh possibility is that if the law were otherwise, an employer need only issue appropriate instructions to evade liability. There are, however, different kinds of prohibitions. One kind may delimit the scope of employment so that if the employee disobeys he acts outside it. Another kind may only limit the manner in which a job is to be done without limiting the job itself. The distinction is easier to grasp than apply. A general statement of it was made by Lord Dunedin in *Plumb* v. *Cobden Flour Mills Co. Ltd.*[299]

There are prohibitions which limit the sphere of employment, and prohibitions which only deal with conduct within the sphere of employment. A transgression of a prohibition of the latter class leaves the sphere of employment where it was, and consequently will not prevent recovery of compensation. A transgression of the former class carries with it the result that the man has gone outside the sphere.

Two cases illustrate the point. In *Limpus* v. *London General Omnibus Co.*[300] the defendants forbade drivers of buses to race on the road. One driver disobeyed instructions and caused a collision. The defendants were held liable as he was still acting within the scope of his employment. On the other hand, in *Conway* v. *George Wimpey & Co. Ltd.*[301] the defendants provided transport for their workmen to distant parts of a construction site. As other firms were also working there, the defendants gave specific directions to the drivers of their lorries not to transport any workmen employed by other firms. One driver gave a lift to

---

[298] *Torts* (19th edn.), 521. In *Harrison* v. *Michelin Tyre Co. Ltd.* [1985] 1 All ER 918, 920, Comyn J suggested a paraphrase which, in some cases, might prove more helpful: 'was the incident [complained of] part and parcel of the employment in the sense of being incidental to it although and albeit unauthorized or prohibited? . . . or was it so divergent from the employment as to be plainly alien to and wholly distinguishable from the employment? A "reasonable approach" must be adopted in answering these questions.'

[299] [1914] AC 62, 67.   [300] (1862) 1 H. & C. 526; 158 ER 993.   [301] [1951] 2 KB 266.

the plaintiff, who was employed by another firm, but the driver was not aware of this. The plaintiff was injured by the driver's negligence, but the Court of Appeal held the defendants not liable, one reason being that the driver was acting outside the scope of his employment. The distinction between these two is that in *Limpus* the driver was doing the job he was employed to do, namely to drive a bus for public transport; disobeying the instructions not to race only made it a bad way of doing that job. In *Conway*, on the other hand, the driver was employed to transport only the defendants' workmen; when he gave a lift to a workman employed by another firm, he was not doing that job. But Asquith LJ did not even attempt to distinguish; he simply brushed *Limpus* aside with the remark:[302] 'I am not unaware that a prohibition has been held in some cases not to curtail the scope of employment, as in *Limpus* v. *London General Omnibus Co.*, but I think it does so in this case.'

The statement is revealing in that it shows that judges appear to treat this matter as a question of fact and are not disposed to worry over-much about nice distinctions. But though judges treat these matters as ultimately questions of fact, they have on several occasions tried to formulate general guidelines and have warned against the risk of applying too narrow a test in deciding whether the act complained of is a different act or a bad way of performing an authorised act. Thus in *Ilkiw* v. *Samuels*[303] Diplock LJ argued that:

. . . where there is an express prohibition, the decision into which of these two classes the prohibition falls seems to me to involve first determining what would have been the sphere, scope, course . . . of the servant's employment if the prohibition had not been imposed. As each of these nouns implies, the matter must be looked at broadly, not dissecting the servant's task into its component activities . . . by asking, what was the job on which he was engaged for his employer? and answering that question as a jury would.

In *Rose* v. *Plenty*[304] a milkman, contrary to an express prohibition, took a young boy with him on his milk round. Partly owing to the boy's own carelessness, but mainly owing to the milkman's negligent driving, the boy was injured. Despite the express prohibition, the majority of the Court of Appeal had no doubt about holding the employer vicariously liable; the employee was still performing the duty he had been employed to perform, even though he was carrying it out in a bad way. The decision is in tune with the prevailing tendency to give a generous interpretation to course of employment; but, despite Scarman LJ's efforts, it is not easily reconcilable with earlier cases. In both *Twine* v. *Bean's Express Ltd.*[305] and *Conway* v. *Wimpey*[306] the employers were not held liable when their employees, through their negligent driving, injured passen-

---

[302] [1951] 2 KB at 276. See also *Ricketts* v. *Thomas Tilling Ltd.* [1915] 1 KB 644, where a retrial was ordered as there was evidence that the bus-driver was negligent in letting the conductor turn it round—i.e. that it was a bad way of doing his job of driving a bus. Cf. *Beard* v. *London General Omnibus Co.* [1900] 2 QB 530, where a conductor, who decided to drive the bus himself, was acting outside the course of his employment. This was not his job.

[303] [1963] 1 WLR 991, 1004.   [304] [1976] 1 WLR 141.

[305] (1946) 62 TLR 458, an ambiguously phrased judgment, especially at first instance, scrutinised by Newark, op. cit. (Select Bibliography).

[306] [1951] 2 KB 266.

gers whom they should not have allowed into the vehicles. Perhaps, in view of what we have said, such a reconciliation is neither always possible nor even desirable, since decisions in this area of the law should not be used like tin-tacks with which to nail down particular solutions, but simply as starting-points in a process of reasoning by analogy, by the use of contrasting examples, guided by common sense. Nevertheless, one possible reconciliation can be found in Lord Denning's judgment, which stressed that in *Rose* v. *Plenty*, by contrast with *Twine* and *Conway*, the unauthorised passenger was furthering the purposes of the employer (i.e. by helping to distribute the milk).[307]

Considerable difficulty has also arisen in cases where drivers of vehicles depart from the authorised routes. The question whether they are still within the scope of employment while on detour is again not easily answered. The classical formulation is that of Parke B in *Joel* v. *Morrison*:[308] 'If he [the driver] was going out of his way, against his master's implied commands, when driving on his master's business, he will make his master liable; but if he was going on a frolic of his own, without being at all on his master's business, the master will not be liable.'

This test is devoid of guidance since it begs the question. To call an action a 'frolic' is not to give a reason why it is outside the course of employment; it only expresses a decision already made that it is outside. The real question is, why is it a 'frolic'? The answer is purely a matter of impression, and much depends on the way in which the factual statement is phrased. Often a decision turns on which of two alternative ways of stating the same activity is more plausible, one form of words making it fall within the course of employment, the other making it fall outside. For instance, in *Storey* v. *Ashton*[309] Cockburn CJ said:

I am very far from saying, if a servant when going on his master's business took a some-what longer road, that owing to this deviation he would cease to be in the employment of the master, so as to divest the latter of all liability; in such cases, it is a question of degree as to how far the deviation could be considered a separate journey. Such a consideration is applicable to the present case, because here the cabman started on an entirely new and independent journey which has nothing at all to do with his employment.

The reasoning in the concluding sentence again begs the question. Similarly, in *Hilton* v. *Thomas Burton (Rhodes) Ltd.*[310] the plaintiff's husband was killed while being driven in the defendant's car by a fellow employee. They were returning after having refreshment in a coffee shop. Diplock J held that although the driver was using the car with the defendant's permission, he was doing something he was not employed to do and, therefore, the defendants were not vicariously liable. This is simply an opinion on those facts.

---

[307] A presumed benefit which the master obviously did not desire if it were accompanied by corresponding liability.

[308] (1834) 6 C. & P. 501, 503; 172 ER 1338, 1339. '[A] memorable phrase [that] has been the subject-matter of innumerable questions in Law examinations for the last 150 years.' Per Comyn J in *Harrison* v. *Michelin Tyre Co. Ltd.* [1985] 1 All ER 918, 919. For further details, see Smith, op. cit. (Select Bibliography).

[309] (1869) LR 4 QB 476, 479–80.   [310] [1961] 1 WLR 705.

Detour cases are inconclusive; so are cases involving travel by car to and from work. In this last context, however, the case of *Smith* v. *Stages*[311] contains some interesting guidelines. Lord Lowry's summary, in particular, deserves to be quoted in full. He thus said:[312]

The paramount rule is that an employee travelling on the highway will be acting in the course of his employment if, and only if, he is at the material time going about his employer's business. One must not confuse the duty to turn up for one's work with the concept of already being 'on duty' while travelling to it.

It is impossible to provide for every eventually and foolish, without the benefit of argument, to make the attempt, but some prima facie propositions may be stated with reasonable confidence.

1. An employee travelling from his ordinary residence to his regular place of work, whatever the means of transport and even if it is provided by the employer, is not on duty and is not acting in the course of his employment, but, if he is obliged by his contract of service to use the employer's transport, he will normally, in the absence of an express condition to the contrary, be regarded as acting in the course of his employment while doing so.

2. Travelling in the employer's time between workplaces (one of which may be the regular workplace) or in the course of a peripatetic occupation, whether accompanied by goods or tools or simply in order to reach a succession of workplaces (as an inspector of gas meters might do), will be in the course of the employment.

3. Receipt of wages (though not receipt of a travelling allowance, will indicate that the employee is travelling in the employer's time and for his benefit and is acting in the course of his employment, and in such a case the fact that the employee may have discretion as to the mode and time of travelling will not take the journey out of the course of his employment.

4. An employee travelling *in the employer's time* from his ordinary residence to a workplace other than his regular workplace or in the course of a peripatetic occupation or to the scene of an emergency (such as a fire, an accident or a mechanical breakdown of plant) will be acting in the course of his employment.

5. A deviation from or interruption of a journey undertaken in the course of employment (unless the deviation or interruption is merely incidental to the journey) will for the time being (which may include an overnight interruption) take the employee out of the course of his employment.

6. Return journeys are to be treated on the same footing as outward journeys.

All the foregoing propositions are subject to any express arrangements between the employer and the employee or those representing his interests. They are not, I would add, intended to define the position of salaried employees, with regard to whom the touchstone of payment made in the employer's time is not generally significant.

Determining the 'scope of employment' is no easier in other cases where the liability of master depends on such a definition. This, of course, should come as no surprise since the various ways in which an employee can be said to perform his duty wrongfully, and so make his employer liable, are truly infinite. For instance, in *Century Insurance Co. Ltd.* v. *Northern Ireland Road Transport Board*,[313] the driver of a petrol lorry negligently threw down a lighted match while petrol

---

[311] [1989] AC 928. The Court of Appeal's decision, especially Glidewell LJ's judgment, printed in [1988] ICR 201, also deserves careful reading.

[312] Ibid., 955–6.   [313] [1942] AC 509.

was being transferred from the lorry to a tank. An explosion and fire ensued. Viscount Simon had no doubt that his act was in the course of employment; and the way he stated it was that 'negligence in starting smoking and throwing away a lighted match in that moment is plainly negligence in the discharge of the duties upon which he was employed'.[314] In *Bayley* v. *The Manchester, Sheffield and Lincolnshire Railway Co.*[315] a porter in the company's service forcibly removed the plaintiff from the train, erroneously believing that he was in the wrong carriage. It was the duty of porters to ensure that passengers were in their right carriages. The company was held liable. The porter's tort was held to have been committed within the scope of his employment, since he was doing clumsily what he was employed to do, namely to see that passengers were in the right carriages. Kelly CB said: 'It is obviously very likely that the servant may, while acting in the performance of the general duty cast upon him, neglect any particular direction as to the mode of doing it. But it appears to me that he will be none the less acting within the scope of his employment.' One cannot, therefore, generalise, nor should one dissect the servant's task into its component activities. In Diplock LJ's words, 'the matter must be looked at broadly'[316] and all the surrounding circumstances carefully taken into account.

Theft and fraud by employees raise nice problems, for it might be thought that in this case the employee is surely acting outside the course of his employment.[317] Earlier cases in fact took this view, but the modern approach is much more *nuancé*. In *Morris* v. *C. W. Martin & Sons Ltd.*[318] the plaintiff took her fur coat to a furrier to be cleaned. The furrier did not undertake this type of work, so with the plaintiff's consent, but without acting as her agent, he subcontracted the work to a firm of cleaners, who handed it to one of their employees to clean. The employee stole it and the firm was held liable to the plaintiff. The firm's liability was not for any carelessness in the choice of employee, for there was no reason to suspect his honesty. Instead, its liability was based on the breach of its non-delegable duty as bailee for reward. This duty, as we have said, is not strict or absolute; it is simply a duty to see that care is taken. Lord Denning pointed out[319] that if the firm could show that it had taken care and that its employees had also exercised due diligence and, despite this, the coat had been stolen, it would have been absolved from liability. In the event, however, the firm could not establish the second part of the proposition so it was held liable for breach of its own duty and not vicariously. The same, *primary*, liability would, probably, arise if it could be shown that the employer had negligently employed the employee who stole the plaintiff's property. In *Nahhas Pier House (Cheyne Walk) Management Ltd.*[320] the defendant negligently hired an ex-'professional thief' to work as a porter in a block of flats. The porter, using the

---

[314] Ibid., at 514.

[315] (1873) LR 8 CP 148, esp. at 153, per Kelly CB. Blackburn J seemed to hint that the company was liable for its own negligence in failing to select a good servant.

[316] *Ilkiw* v. *Samuels* [1963] 1 WLR 991, 1004. See also *Duffy* v. *Thanet District Council* (1984) 134 NLJ 680; *Harrison* v. *Michelin Tyre Co. Ltd.* [1985] 1 All ER 918.

[317] *Cheshire* v. *Bailey* [1905] 1 KB 237.

[318] [1966] 1 QB 716, approved in *Port Swettenham Authority* v. *T. W. Wu & Co.* [1979] AC 580.

[319] Ibid., at 726.   [320] (1984) 270 EG 328.

key entrusted to him by one of the tenants, entered the latter's flat and stole some jewellery. The employer was held primarily liable for the theft. The same would probably be true if, for instance, a security company employed an ex-thief to patrol and guard premises and the guard used his position to commit a new theft. But it would be extending liability too far if such a rule were applied indiscriminately whenever an ex-criminal was hired by an employer to do some work, for the adoption of such a wide rule of (potential) liability would defeat the general and, it is submitted, justifiable interest that society has to assist the rehabilitation of offenders.

If we return to *Morris*, however, we notice that the same result could have been achieved equally well through the doctrine of vicarious liability. For in that case the employee who stole the coat was in fact the employee who had been asked to look after it, so he did badly what he had been asked to do properly, thereby acting in the course of his employment and rendering his employer vicariously liable. On the other hand, if the coat had been stolen by some other employee (e.g. the night porter or a guardsman) who had not been entrusted with its care, then the employer's vicarious liability would have been excluded, though his primary liability under the non-delegable duty would still have been possible.

There used to be a similar judicial reluctance towards making employers liable for the fraud of their employees. It was not until the middle of the last century[321] that vicarious liability was accepted here too, though for many years it seemed that this would only have been where an employer benefited from the fraud. This qualification was laid to rest by the House of Lords in *Lloyd* v. *Grace, Smith & Co.*,[322] where a solicitor was held liable for the fraud of his managing clerk who, having fraudulently persuaded a client to hand over some title-deeds, disposed of the property for his own benefit. The decision is important not only for its ruling, but also for its terminology. Fraud in cases such as this involves a deception of the victim by the employee, and it is impossible to say whether this deception was in the employee's course of employment before one determines the extent of his authority, whether actual or apparent, to do such acts. In *Lloyd* v. *Grace, Smith & Co.* there was such apparent authority, for the solicitor, who took little interest in his firm's affairs, had allowed the clerk to deal with such matters and thereby represented that he had authority to do what he actually did. The conclusion, therefore, seems to be that in some cases at least—notably fraud—the employer will be vicariously liable for the employee's fraud only when the latter has acted within his ostensible authority. For, in reality, in such cases, a decision whether the employee committed a fraud 'in the course of his employment' can be made only after it has been ascertained with what authority, actual or apparent, the employee is clothed. But in torts which involve no *reliance* by the plaintiff upon representation by the employee, but involve other wrongs (e.g. intentional or negligent physical acts by the employee), the ostensible authority of the employee does not pro-

---

[321] *Barwick* v. *English Joint Stock Bank* (1867) LR 2 Ex. 259.   [322] [1912] AC 716.

vide the criterion for his employer's possible vicarious liability.[323] It follows from the above that the plaintiff must prove that he relied on this ostensible authority and, therefore, his action will fail if he was not aware that the fraudulent employee did not work for the defendants.[324]

4. Contribution

There has been little doubt that employers and employees are to be treated as joint tortfeasors. It follows from this that if the employer is held liable for the tort of his employee in the course of employment, he would have a right to recover a complete indemnity.[325] The proposition was, indeed, asserted on a number of occasions, yet never actually tested until the Law Reform (Married Women and Tortfeasors) Act 1935 created a new statutory right.[326] This right is now to be found in section 1(1) of the Civil Liability (Contribution) Act 1978, which allows any person who is liable for damages suffered by another to recover a contribution from any other person liable in respect of the same damage (the contribution between the joint tortfeasors being determined by the court, taking into account both the relative blameworthiness of the parties and the causative potency of their respective conducts in producing the harm in suit). In the typical vicarious liability case this would mean the employer (or rather his insurers) claiming a complete indemnity from the culpable employee. Apart from this statutory right, however, the House of Lords held in *Lister* v. *Romford Ice and Cold Storage Co.*[327] that an employer was entitled to an indemnity from his wrongdoing employee on the ground that the latter impliedly undertook in his contract of employment to perform his contractual duties with due care. This common-law (as distinct from the statutory) right to an indemnity is lost (*a*) where the employee, though acting in the course of his employment, was actually carrying out a task other than the specific task for which he was employed,[328] or (*b*) where the employer was personally liable, or liable through other employees.[329]

The right to an indemnity, whether statutory or common-law, has had supporters, especially in the past, on the basis that 'the person who caused the damage is the person who must in law be called on to pay damages arising therefrom'.[330] Retribution apart, the rule also seemed to be supported by policy considerations. It was argued, for example, that any contrary ruling would involve the creation of a special class of person to whom the ordinary rules of

---

[323] *Armagas Ltd.* v. *Mundagas SA, The Ocean Frost* [1985] 3 WLR 640 (with a most illuminating judgment by Lord Justice Goff). For a more recent illustration see: *Generale Bank Nederland NV* v. *Export Credits Guarantee Department, The Times*, 4 Aug. 1997.

[324] *Kooragang Investments Property Ltd.* v. *Richardson and Wrench Ltd.* [1982] AC 462. Apparent authority can result only from a representation made by the principal and not the agent. For details see Markesinis and Munday, *An Outline of the Law of Agency* (3rd edn., 1994).

[325] The rule of *Merryweather* v. *Nixan* (1799) 8 TR 186; 101 ER 1337, prohibiting contribution or indemnity between joint tortfeasors, does not apply to cases where one of them was completely innocent.

[326] See Denning LJ's remarks in *Jones* v. *Manchester Corp.* [1952] 2 QB 852, 870.

[327] [1957] AC 555.   [328] *Harvey* v. *O'Dell Ltd.* [1958] 2 QB 78.

[329] *Jones* v. *Manchester Corp.* [1952] 2 QB 852.

[330] *Semtex Ltd.* v. *Gladstone* [1954] 1 WLR 945, 953, per Finnemore J; similarly Jolowicz [1956] *CLJ* 101 ('reason and justice alike seem to call for the liability').

liability for negligence do not apply;[331] and perhaps, even make employees more slap-happy in the execution of their work. Yet this rule, which is not shared by most civil-law systems, may have more disadvantages than advantages. On moral grounds the prevailing view is unacceptable when severe consequences flow from minor lapses.[332] On economic grounds it makes little sense to shift the loss from the person who can best bear it and place it on the person who cannot bear it and is, in practice, unlikely to be insured. On pragmatic grounds the existing rule can only contribute to bad industrial relations.[333] Finally, on theoretical grounds the right of subrogation or indemnity should not be a concern of the law of torts, which exhausts its function once the victim has been compensated.[334] That these objections do have force is evident from the aftermath of *Lister* v. *Romford Ice*.[335] For it became clear that in practice a person suing for the indemnity was not really the employer but his insurance company; and if it is wrong for the reasons suggested to allow an employer to sue his employees, it must be more objectionable to allow his insurers to take over his rights. Insurance companies are paid to cover risks, and if they were allowed to claim damages through subrogation when those risks materialised, they would, in effect, be having their cake and eating it.[336] The upshot of this storm was a 'gentleman's agreement' by which liability insurers agreed not to exercise their subrogation rights in such circumstances unless there was evidence of collusion or wilful misconduct. The 'gentleman's agreement', however, does not cover all eventualities, and the ruling in *Lister* is still, technically, the law. This means that, on occasion, it has to be evaded by means that add little to the clarity and simplicity of the legal system.[337] Since legislative intervention appears unlikely in the foreseeable future, one must hope that the House of Lords will, on the first available opportunity, remedy this defect. *De lege ferenda*, therefore, it would be best to limit such a right to an indemnity to cases where the employee intentionally inflicted the loss on the victim.

5. Liability for the Torts of Independent Contractors

We have noted that an employer is not vicariously liable for the torts of his independent contractors. He may, however, be primarily liable if he is in breach of his own duty, and this may happen in one of two ways:

(i) He may authorise the commission of a tort, in which case he is liable as a joint tortfeasor along with the independent contractor. This is not vicarious

---

[331] Jolowicz, ibid., 107.   [332] Which, of course, is a general criticism of the fault system.

[333] See Lord Denning's remarks in *Morris* v. *Ford Motor Co. Ltd.* [1973] QB 792, 801.

[334] Weir, 'Subrogation and Indemnity—A Note on *Morris* v. *Ford Motor Co. Ltd.* [1973] QB 792' (a privately published case-note).

[335] [1957] AC 555.

[336] Insurance companies might counter this by saying that by exercising such subrogation rights they can keep premiums at affordable levels. There seems to be no published empirical evidence to support this; and the premiums do not appear to have gone up as a result of giving up the right to exercise the subrogation claims following the 'gentleman's agreement'.

[337] See the tortuous ways employed by the majority in *Morris* v. *Ford Motor Co. Ltd.* [1973] QB 792, to deny the plaintiffs, who were not insurers, their right of subrogation.

liability. The main problem in such cases lies in deciding what constitutes authorisation.

(ii) He will be liable for a breach of his own non-delegable duty, which requires him to see that care is taken. This, as already indicated, goes further than personally taking care, for however carefully he may have selected and instructed the contractor, he will remain answerable for the latter's default. Unfortunately, it is not at all clear when and why[338] the law determines that such non-delegable duties will arise.

Very often non-delegable duties are created by statutes and whether this is so will depend on the construction of the statute in question. For example, section 1(1) of the Employers' Liability (Defective Equipment) Act 1969 renders an innocent employer liable for injury suffered by his employee as a result of supplying him with equipment in a defective state 'attributable wholly or partly to the fault of a third person'.[339] Section 2(4)(b) of the Occupiers' Liability Act 1957 also shows that in certain circumstances an occupier may be liable for dangers due to the faulty execution of any work of construction, maintenance, or repair, even when this has been done by an independent contractor. Little difficulty also arises in cases of strict, or near strict, liability where non-delegable duties are generally discovered without much difficulty. It has been noted, for example, that possibly in all cases of nuisance the duty is non-delegable;[340] and in *Rylands* v. *Fletcher*,[341] where liability is truly strict, the defendant did not escape liability for the negligence of his independent contractors. But these are not the only instances where the common law has imposed non-delegable duties. *Bower* v. *Peate*[342] suggests that such a duty arises in cases of withdrawal of support from neighbouring land. Other cases are operations involving extra-hazardous acts,[343] and the liability of bailees for reward.[344] It should, however,

---

[338] Jolowicz, 9 *Stan. LR* 690 (1957), has suggested that the value of the interest protected and the 'character of the risk' created may be significant factors. He thus concludes that, whereas the considerations which led the courts to introduce vicarious liability 'are founded upon the assured social desirability of giving an injured plaintiff a defendant worth powder and shot and do not depend in any way upon the degree of protection ordinarily afforded by the law to the particular interest affected, or upon the magnitude of the risk involved, the considerations leading to the imposition of liability for independent contractors are essentially legalistic. They are founded not upon any assumed social policy, but upon the preconceived ideas of value to which familiarity with the law gives rise.' See also the discussion of the situation when such duties arise by Mason J in *Kondis* v. *State Transport Authority* (1984) 154 CLR 672 (employer/employee; adjoining landowners; hospital/patient; school authority/pupil; occupier of land/visitor). Mason J thought a common thread was the undertaking of responsibility by one party over the person or property of another. Why should this give rise to a duty not only to take care but also to ensure that care is taken? Is this really no more than an attempted *ex post facto* rationalisation of a random group of cases?

[339] What if the defect is attributable wholly to ordinary wear and tear (i.e. no one's fault), but the third party's fault lies in failing to put it right? The answer requires a creative interpretation of the words of the Act for it to apply.

[340] Certainly public nuisance on or adjoining the highway (e.g. *Tarry* v. *Ashton* (1876) 1 QBD 314 but not work *near* the highway: *Salsbury* v. *Woodland* [1970] 1 QB 324). *Matania* v. *National Provincial Bank Ltd.* [1936] 2 All ER 633 suggests that the same rule may apply to private nuisance as well.

[341] (1866) LR 1 Exch. 265: (1868) LR 3 HL 330.

[342] (1876) 1 QBD 321, 326. The dicta are of wider import than withdrawal of support and are generally held to be too wide: *Hughes* v. *Percival* (1883) 8 App. Cas. 443, 447.

[343] *Honeywill & Stein Ltd.* v. *Larkin Bros. Ltd.* [1934] 1 KB 191; *Balfour* v. *Barty-King* [1957] 1 QB 496.

[344] *Morris* v. *C. W. Martin & Sons Ltd.* [1966] 1 QB 716. *British Road Services Ltd.* v. *Arthur Crutchley & Co. Ltd.* [1968] 1 All ER 811, suggests that a bailee for reward will even be liable for the torts of the servants of his independent contractor. Similarly *Riverstone Meat Co. Ltd.* v. *Lancashire Shipping Co. Ltd.* [1961] AC 807.

be stressed that even in non-delegable duty situations the employer's liability does not extend to the independent contractor's 'collateral negligence'. This is negligence unconnected with the job that the independent contractor was engaged to perform; but its application is not easier than the application of 'course of employment'.[345]

6. Non-Delegable Duties/Vicarious Liability: An Epilogue

We have noted that the two doctrines are intertwined, only partially capable of being subject to a coherent justification, and constantly witnessing an expansion of the scope of their application. This latter characteristic is in tune with the current trend, prevalent in modern tort law, to compensate liberally physical injuries. It should not, however, be taken as axiomatic that all injuries should be compensated in all circumstances; nor that employers are in *all* cases economically in the best position to shoulder such losses. Equally, one cannot assume that the wrongs committed by those who belong to atypical forms of contemporary employment,[346] involving flexible terms and patterns of work, will attract the liability of those who derive some benefit from their work. This latter phenomenon, daily growing in importance, has presented the courts with some important challenges that have, briefly, led to the following responses.

(i) The Gradual and Unsystematic Expansion of the Non-Delegable Duties   In *McDermid* v. *Nash Dredging and Reclamation Co. Ltd.*[347] the plaintiff was an inexperienced deck hand employed by the company of the defendants. While working on a tug (owned by the parent company of the defendants) he was injured as a result of the negligence of the master of the tug. Since the master of the tug was not an employee of the defendants, the latter could not (according to traditional doctrine) be held liable vicariously for his wrongs. They were, however, held liable on non-delegable grounds. The House of Lords (unlike the Court of Appeal) appeared to think that the ruling involved no real extension of the law. Yet, in reality, the effect of the case is that the employer's duties to *provide* competent staff, a safe place of work, safe equipment, and a safe system of work (discussed earlier on) were extended to include a non-delegable duty to ensure the proper *operation* of the devised system of work.[348] It is easy to treat this as yet another common-law extension of the list of non-delegable duties. Yet this new non-delegable duty—unlike the traditional four that have followed *Wilsons and Clyde Coal Ltd.* v. *English*[349]—was hardly within the defendant's (employer's)

---

[345] *Padbury* v. *Holliday & Greenwood Ltd.* (1912) 28 TLR 494.

[346] A growing percentage of the work-force belongs to this category, which includes casual workers, part-time workers, agency workers, home-workers, temps, and those working on government training schemes. If these workers are not deemed in law to be employees, they cannot—subject to what will be said in the text, above—bring into play the rules of vicarious liability. The most recent decision to discuss their status is *McMeecham* v. *Secretary of State for Employment* [1997] IRLR 353 where the Court of Appeal proposed that a temporary worker could be treated as an employee for 'specific assignments' even if he did not have that status under the general terms of his agreement.

[347] [1987] AC 906.

[348] In this case the courts felt that the system of work devised was safe but its operation had not been adequate.

[349] [1938] AC 906.

control, so 'the effect was as if vicarious liability had been imposed for the tort of an independent contractor',[350] even though the language used by the House of Lords was that of non-delegable duties. Notwithstanding this point, however, the ruling marks an extension of the protection afforded to the injured party even though subsequent case law has limited the applicability of the *McDermid* rule to cases where the victim/plaintiff is an employee of the defendants.[351]

(ii) Imposing Affirmative Duties on Employers This can be seen happening in some foreign systems;[352] and there may even be some scattered dicta in our case law supporting, in some instances, primary duties of supervision,[353] co-ordination,[354] and even control of the activities of third parties.[355]

(iii) Assumption of Responsibility Though this principle cannot yet be claimed to be part of English law it has found a clear exposition in the Australian case of *Kondis* v. *State Transport Authority*[356] where Mason J said:

It appears that there is some element in the relationship between the parties that makes it appropriate to impose on the defendant a duty to ensure that reasonable care and skill is taken for the safety of the persons to whom the duty is owed . . . [I]n these situations the special duty arises because the person on whom it is imposed has undertaken the case, supervision or control of the person or property of another or is so placed in relation to that person or his property as to assume a particular responsibility for his or its safety, in circumstances where the person affected might reasonably expect that due care will be exercised.

(iv) The Extension of the Vicarious Liability Rules Solely for the Purposes of Imposition of Liability We have already noted that, in principle, there is nothing illogical in saying that a person might be treated as an employee of another person for one purpose (e.g. liability) but not for another (e.g. for tax or social-security reasons). If this view were to gain wider acceptance than it currently enjoys, it could well be used to justify the liability of the 'employer' of the atypical work-force described at the beginning of this section. This view would, *de lege lata*, find some support in the judgment of Staughton J in his *McDermid*[357] decision and, as stated, in the result (but *not* the judgments) of the House of Lords in the same case. The point, however, is not yet finally resolved; and, as stated, the legitimate wish to compensate the victims should not hurry lawyers into imposing unlimited liability on employers who should not always be assumed to have deeper pockets or, necessarily, be in a better position to obtain effective insurance cover.

---

[350] McKendrick, op. cit. (Select Bibliography), at 773–4, where one can find an excellent discussion of this emerging topic.

[351] Thus, see *Watts* v. *Lowcur Ltd.*, quoted and discussed by McKendrick, op. cit.

[352] E.g. the German, the reason being that in that system the rules of vicarious liability are weak.

[353] See e.g. Lord Bridge in *D. & F. Estates Ltd.* v. *Church Commissioners for England* [1989] AC 177, 209.

[354] See *Stevens* v. *Brodribb Sawmilling Co. Pty. Ltd.* (1986) 160 CLR 16 (but not yet accepted by English law).

[355] *Smith* v. *Littlewoods Organisation Ltd.* [1987] AC 241 provides the best starting-point but, it must be admitted, this development is still in an embryonic stage.

[356] (1984) 154 CLR 672, 687.

[357] *The Times*, 31 July 1984, noted by Murdoch in (1985) 1 *Professional Negligence* 119.

Select Bibliography

ADAMS, J. N. and BROWNSWORD, R., 'Double Indemnity—Contractual Indemnity Clauses Revisited' [1988] *JBL* 146.

ATIYAH, P. S., *Vicarious Liability in the Law of Torts* (1967).

BARAK, A., 'Mixed and Vicarious Liability—A Suggested Distinction' (1966) 29 *MLR* 160.

BRILL, R. L., 'The Liability of an Employer for the Wilful Torts of his Servants' 45 *Chicago-Kent LR* 1 (1968).

HAMSON, C. J., 'Master and Servant—Duty of Master—Defective Tool' [1959] *CLJ* 157.

—— 'Liability of Hospitals for Negligence', in *The Law in Action* (1954), 19.

JAMES, FLEMING, Jr., Vicarious Liability' 28 *Tulane LR* 161 (1954).

JOLOWICZ, J. A., 'The Right to Indemnity between Master and Servant' [1956] *CLJ* 101.

—— 'Liability for Independent Contractors in the English Common Law—A Suggestion' 9 *Stan. LR* 690 (1957).

KAHN-FREUND, O., 'Servants and Independent Contractors' (1951) 14 *MLR* 504.

McKENDRICK, E., 'Vicarious Liability and Independent Contractors—A Re-Examination' (1990) 53 *MLR* 770.

—— 'Vicarious Liability and Industrial Action' (1989) 18 *ILJ* 161.

MORRIS, C. ROBERT, Jr., 'Enterprise Liability and the Actuarial Process—the Insignificance of Foresight' 70 *Yale LJ* 554 (1961).

NEWARK, F. H., '*Twine* v. *Bean's Express Ltd.*' (1954) 17 *MLR* 102.

ROSE, F. D., 'Liability for an Employee's Assault' (1977) 40 *MLR* 420.

SEAVEY, W. A., 'Speculations as to "Respondeat Superior" ', in *Harvard Legal Essays* (1934), 433.

WILLIAMS, G. L., 'Vicarious Liability: Tort of the Master or of the Servant?' (1956) 72 *LQR* 522.

—— 'Vicarious Liability and the Master's Indemnity' (1957) 20 *MLR* 220.

5. PRODUCT LIABILITY

Introduction

The emergence in England of a body of 'product liability law' is comparatively recent. Its development can be traced to EC Directive 85/374 and to the Consumer Protection Act 1987 that aimed to implement the principles contained in the Directive. Before this it was not possible to speak of 'product liability law' as such, but only of various laws relating to liability for defective products.[358] A consumer who was injured or whose property was damaged by a product that he had bought could bring an action against the retailer for damages for breach of contract. The standard here was and is strict: where goods are sold in the course of a business the Sale of Goods Act implies into the contract of sale a term (amongst others) to the effect that the goods will be fit for the purpose intended.[359] The doctrine of privity of contract, however, prevents an action for contract damages being brought by a third party even though it might be entirely foreseeable that a defective product would cause harm, for

---

[358] Lord Griffiths *et al.*, (see below, Select Bibliography), 355.　　[359] Sale of Goods Act 1979, s. 14(3).

example, to a member of the purchaser's family or to an employee. Nor can the person who has bought the goods sue for the losses sustained by that other person unless they in turn cause loss to him.[360] Contract actions are also limited in the sense that they normally lie only against the retailer who sold the product and not against the manufacturer whose default was most likely responsible for its defective state. In *Donoghue* v. *Stevenson*[361] the House of Lords cut through these limitations by acknowledging the possibility of an action in negligence by the ultimate consumer against the manufacturer. There remained the difficulty, however, of proving negligence. The EC Directive and Consumer Protection Act 1987 address this by imposing a form of strict liability not just upon manufacturers but upon all those, including distributors and retailers, in the supply chain. In doing so they have incorporated into English law a model of extended liability borrowed largely from the law of the United States.

A number of justifications have been offered for the imposition of strict liability on manufacturers and other producers. One is that producers are best able to *spread* the risk of damage through the adoption of insurance or through pricing of products; another is that producers are in the best position to *minimise* the risks of damage by taking precautions at the design and manufacturing stages of production. These efficiency-based considerations rest upon insights of economic analysis which have themselves been challenged by critics of the strict liability principle, who argue that it loads excessive costs of precaution upon manufacturers, stifles innovation, and threatens to lead to an 'insurance crisis'. An alternative, non-consequentialist rationale for strict liability has been proposed by Professor Jane Stapleton, namely 'a moral argument that if, in seeking to secure financial profit, an enterprise causes certain types of loss, it should be legally obliged to pay compensation to the victim';[362] this idea, she suggests, links together most of the areas of strict liability in tort (such as the employer's vicarious liability for the torts of employees) although she also accepts that it does not explain all aspects of modern product liability law.[363]

In this area, then, the principles of the common law tort of negligence overlap with stricter forms of liability derived from contract law and from legislation. These different sources of civil liability have not as yet been synthesised into a single, coherent body of doctrine. They provide alternative and possibly cumulative bases for a cause of action in damages. The Consumer Protection Act 1987 has provided rights to consumers over and above those provided by the common law of tort and contract, without in any way removing the protection which the common law already conferred. Because of the limited scope of the Act, however, the plaintiff may, in certain circumstances, have to frame the cause of action in negligence or breach of contract. To gain a full view of this field, therefore, it will be necessary to examine and compare the separate bases for civil liability and to see how they differ in regard to such questions as: who are the potential plaintiffs and defendants to the action? What degree of fault is required for liability? What kinds of loss can be compensated? Which

[360] *Priest* v. *Last* [1903] 2 KB 148.   [361] [1932] AC 562.   [362] *Product Liability* (1994), 186.
[363] Ibid., 204.

defences are available? And how are damages to be computed? A detailed examination of these questions will be preceded by an overview of the law's historical development in England and America. The American law is important to an understanding of the strict liability principle that underlies the 1985 Directive and the Consumer Protection Act.

1. The Evolution of Product Liability Law in England and America

(A) THE REJECTION OF THE 'PRIVITY OF CONTRACT FALLACY'

As an earlier chapter has already explained,[364] the scope of liability for negligence was limited in the nineteenth century by the idea that obligations that originated in contract could not be extended beyond the scope of a particular agreement. The attitude of the courts was epitomised by *Winterbottom* v. *Wright* in which Lord Abinger complained that any other rule would produce 'the most absurd and outrageous consequences, to which I can see no limit'.[365] The plaintiff was the driver of a horse-drawn coach who was injured in an accident brought about, it was alleged, by the failure of the defendant to maintain the coach in a good state of repair as required by a contract with the coach's owner. The case was not much of an authority in itself, being an instance of an omission to take due care rather than one of active misfeasance;[366] none the less it was widely relied on as a basis of a rule of non-liability for manufacturers. Two exceptions were however recognised in the case of 'things inherently dangerous', such as a bottle of poison[367] or an explosive device, and fraudulent misrepresentation made directly to the plaintiff. *Langridge* v. *Levy*,[368] in which a gun which was falsely represented to be safe went off in the plaintiff's hand and injured him, illustrates both lines of authority. The wider privity rule was first abandoned in the United States where the overwhelming majority of state jurisdictions adopted the rule formulated by Justice Cardozo for the New York Court of Appeals in *MacPherson* v. *Buick Motor Co.* in 1916.[369] In this case the plaintiff was injured when a wheel on the car he was driving, and which he had bought from a retailer, fell to pieces, causing the car to crash. He brought an action for negligence against the manufacturer. The court upheld the plaintiff's claim on the grounds that liability 'is not limited to poisons, explosives, and things of like nature, to things which in their normal operation are implements of destruction. If the nature of a thing is such that it is reasonably certain to place life and limb in peril when negligently made, it is then a thing of danger. Its nature gives warning of the consequences to be expected.'[370] The court found 'nothing anomalous in a rule which imposes upon A, who has contracted with B, a duty to C and D and others according as he knows or does not know that the subject-matter of the contract is intended for their use'.

The equivalent decision for English and Scottish law was that of the House of Lords in *Donoghue* v. *Stevenson*[371] where the plaintiff was poisoned by the con-

---

[364] See above, Chapter 2.
[366] See Bohlen, *Studies in the Law of Torts* (1926), 236–7.
[368] (1837) 2 M. & W. 519.
[370] 217 NY 382, 389; 111 NE 1050, 1053.

[365] (1842) 10 M. & W. 109, 114.
[367] *Thomas* v. *Winchester* (1852) 6 NY 397.
[369] 217 NY 382, 111 NE 1050.
[371] [1932] AC 562; see above, Chapter 2.

tents of a ginger beer bottle bought for her by a friend. By a bare majority the House of Lords allowed an action in negligence direct against the manufacturer. Lord Buckmaster's vigorous dissent would have confined any liability to the immediate contracting parties. Lord Atkin, by contrast, focused on the manufacturers' knowledge and intention that the goods would eventually reach consumers beyond the end of the contract chain: 'I confine myself to articles of common household use, where everyone, including the manufacturer, knows that the articles will be used by persons other than the actual ultimate purchaser—namely, by members of his family and his servants, and, in some cases, his guests.'[372] Lord Macmillan asserted the priority of negligence over the privity rule and expressed the manufacturer's duty in similar terms:

. . . a person who for gain engages in the business of manufacturing articles of food and drink intended for consumption by members of the public in the form in which he issues them is under a duty to take care in the manufacture of those articles. That duty, in my opinion, he owes to those whom he intends to consume his products. He manufactures his commodities for human consumption; he intends and contemplates that they shall be consumed. By reason of that very fact he places himself in a relationship with all the potential customers of his commodities, and that relationship, which he assumes and desires for his own ends, imposes upon him a duty to take care to avoid injuring them. He owes them a duty not to convert by his own carelessness an article which he issues to them as wholesome and innocent into an article which is dangerous to life and health.[373]

In the United States the *MacPherson* judgment became the basis for 'a general rule imposing negligence liability upon any supplier, for remuneration, of any chattel';[374] English law has broadly followed the same route. Liability has been extended to products and articles of all kinds, ranging from tombstones[375] to defective hair-dyes[376] and contaminated underwear.[377] The scope of the duty has been extended beyond manufacturers *qua* producers to embrace all those who handle the goods in a business capacity along the chain of supply; those potentially liable include makers of component parts, assemblers, distributors, retail sellers, as well as those doing installation work, repairs, and contract work of various kinds.[378] Potential plaintiffs include all those coming into contact with the goods either as ultimate consumers or users; employees of the purchaser, members of his family, subsequent purchasers, and even 'bystanders' exposed to danger may sue.[379] The one general restriction on the scope of liability is that it remains confined to physical injury or property damage caused by contact with the goods; 'pure economic' loss is not normally recoverable either in England or in most US jurisdictions.[380]

---

[372] Ibid., 583.　　　　　　　　　　　　　　[373] Ibid., 620.

[374] W. Prosser, 'The Assault upon the Citadel (Strict Liability to the Consumer)', (1960) 69 *Yale LJ* 1099, 1102.

[375] *Brown* v. *Cotterill* (1934) 51 TLR 21.　　　[376] *Parker* v. *Oloxo Ltd.* [1937] 3 All ER 524.

[377] *Grant* v. *Australian Knitting Mills Ltd.* [1936] AC 85.

[378] See the cases cited below, Section 2(A).　　　[379] See below, ibid.

[380] *Murphy* v. *Brentwood District Council* [1991] 1 AC 398; *East River Steamship Corp.* v. *Transamerica Delaval Inc.* (1986) 476 US 858. It should be noted, however, that some American jurisdictions do allow limited recovery for pure economic loss caused by defective chattels, on a theory of liability for breach of

The most serious restriction on the use of the tort of negligence for consumer protection, however, is the need to show fault. This could be overcome,
in an appropriate case, by an inference of negligence in the plaintiff's favour.
In *Grant* v. *Australian Knitting Mills Ltd.*[381] the plaintiff caught dermatitis from a
suit of underwear manufactured by the defendants. The underwear had been
infected with an 'irritant chemical' at some stage in the manufacturing process.
The Privy Council, allowing an appeal, held the manufacturers liable in negligence:

According to the evidence, the method of manufacture was correct; the danger of excess
sulphites being left was recognised and was guarded against; the process was intended
to be foolproof. If excess sulphites were left in the garment, that could only be because
someone was at fault. The appellant is not required to lay his finger on the exact person
in all the chain who was responsible or to specify what he did wrong. Negligence is
found as a matter of inference from the existence of the defects taken in connection
with all the known circumstances; even if the manufacturers could by apt evidence have
rebutted that inference they have not done so.[382]

In numerous American decisions, courts have taken the view that product liability is an appropriate area for the application of the doctrine of *res ipsa
loquitur*, effectively reversing the burden of proof. *Res ipsa loquitur* applies where
it can be shown that the defendant had exclusive control of the thing which
caused the accident and where no explanation other than the defendant's negligence is forthcoming.[383] While 'control' is normally taken in English law to
refer to control at the time the accident occurred, American courts have been
prepared to extend the relevant time back to the process of manufacture itself.
In *Escola* v. *Coca-Cola Bottling Co. of Fresno*[384] the defendants were held liable on
the assumption that for a cola bottle to explode in the hands of a waitress, it
must have been defectively manufactured and inadequately inspected. The
defendants were in control of the manufacturing and inspection of the bottles
and there was no evidence that the bottle had been interfered with or mishandled after leaving the factory. Although *res ipsa* can be answered by a defendant
showing that the defect could not have been avoided by reasonable care, the
leading commentator on the American case law wrote in 1960 that 'such cases
are so extremely rare as to be almost negligible'.[385]

The English courts have not allowed the formal use of *res ipsa loquitur* in
claims for product liability based on negligence, instead insisting upon the
plaintiff's obligation to prove fault.[386] In practice they have achieved much the
same result by making an 'inference of negligence' of the kind used by Lord
Wright to decide *Grant* v. *Australian Knitting Mills Ltd.*[387] However, this is not an
automatic aid to the plaintiff, and courts have from time to time declined to

---

warranty: see *Seely* v. *White Motor Co.* (1965) 403 P.2d 145; J. Phillips, 'Misrepresentation and Products
Liability' (1991) 20 *Anglo-Am. LR* 327; see also the discussion in the text, below.

[381] [1936] AC 85.   [382] Ibid., 101 (Lord Wright).
[383] See above, Chapter 2, Section 3(2).   [384] (1944) 150 P.2d 436.
[385] Prosser, 'The Assault upon the Citadel', op. cit. (Select Bibliography), 1115.
[386] Finnemore J, *Mason* v. *Williams and Williams Ltd.* [1955] 1 All ER 808, relying on *Donoghue* v. *Stevenson*
[1932] AC 562.
[387] [1936] AC 85.

make the inference in his favour. In *Evans* v. *Triplex Safety Glass Co. Ltd.*[388] a manufacturer of 'toughened safety glass' fitted into the windscreen of a car avoided liability for injuries suffered by the drivers and passengers when the glass shattered without warning. The court held that the fault might have occurred when the glass was fitted, and that suppliers had had sufficient time to check the glass. The possibility of intermediate examination and the length of time between the manufacturing process and the accident prevented an inference of negligence being drawn. The English courts have also taken conflicting views on the question of whether a manufacturer can escape liability by showing that he had a rigorous manufacturing and inspection process.[389]

Even in the United States, where as we have seen *res ipsa* was flexibly applied to assist the plaintiff, dissatisfaction with the negligence remedy led courts to develop forms of strict liability. The central point was that only strict liability would allow the plaintiff to sue all those who had handled the goods down the length of the supply chain. As Dean Prosser explained,

It is here that negligence liability breaks down. The wholesaler, the jobber and the retailer are simply not negligent. They are under no duty to test or inspect the chattel, and they do not do so; and when, as is usually the case today, it comes to them in a sealed container, examination becomes impossible without destroying marketability. No inference of negligence can arise against these sellers, and res ipsa loquitur is of no use at all.[390]

As a result there began a movement towards strict liability along two routes: initially through the concept of a transmissible warranty or representation that the goods were free of any hidden defects, and then increasingly through the imposition of a strict tort duty. In England, by contrast, the courts rejected such far-reaching conceptual solutions within the common law, leaving it to statute to introduce a measure of stricter liability in the form of the 1987 Act.

(B) FROM NEGLIGENCE TO STRICT LIABILITY

(i) Liability for Breach of Warranty After the destruction of the 'privity of contract fallacy' broadly two types of action were available to the consumer: an action in negligence against the manufacturer and an action for breach of contract against the retailer. Sales law implied into contracts for the sale of goods terms or warranties to the effect that the goods complied with the contract description, were fit for the purpose intended, and were of merchantable quality.[391] If a defective product injured a consumer, the seller would be held liable for breach of one of these contract terms. Moreover, the courts awarded the injured consumer damages according to the foreseeable extent of his injuries; he was not limited to claiming the difference between the contract price of the goods and their real value.[392] These actions for breach of warranty have been

---

[388] [1938] 1 All ER 283.

[389] Cf. *Daniels and Daniels* v. *R. White & Sons* [1938] 4 All ER 258; *Hill* v. *James Crowe (Cases) Ltd.* [1978] ICR 298; see below, Section 2(c).

[390] Prosser, 'The Assault upon the Citadel', op. cit., 1117.

[391] In England, ss. 12 and 14 of the Sale of Goods Act 1893, which codified the common law (now ss. 12 and 14 of the Sale of Goods Act 1979).

[392] *Brown* v. *Edgington* (1841) 2 Man. & G. 279.

described by Professor Waddams as essentially tortious in nature. Certainly, in the nineteenth century it was not obvious that liability depended on breach of promise or that the warranty in question had to be contained in a contract between the manufacturer and the consumer.[393] It was only in the course of the nineteenth century that the action for warranty came to be regarded as exclusively contractual in nature, with the result that (in the absence of fraud) representations made outside a contract would not give rise to an action for damages.[394]

Whereas the English courts stuck rigidly to the idea that representations and warranties could only give rise to liability where the parties were in privity of contract,[395] in the United States courts began to impose strict liability upon manufacturers according to various notions of extended liability for breach of warranty. The imposition of strict liability began with cases of contaminated food and drink and developed from there to include products of all kinds.[396] One idea was that the manufacturer's warranty to the initial purchaser ran with the goods in a manner similar to restrictive covenants over land.[397] In other cases the courts brought the manufacturer and the consumer into privity by (somewhat fictitiously) regarding the retailer as the agent of one or the other. Alternatively, as in the famous English contract case of *Carlill* v. *Carbolic Smoke Ball Co.*,[398] they deemed the manufacturer to have made an implied unilateral offer to the consumer that the latter accepted by purchasing the goods from the retailer.[399]

In due course the notion of an extended liability for breach of warranty came to be embodied in section 2–318 of the Uniform Commercial Code, which was adopted by all the state jurisdictions with the exception of Louisiana. This provides that: 'A seller's warranty whether express or implied extends to any natural person who is in the family or household of the buyer or who is a guest in his home if it is reasonable to expect that such person may use, consume or be affected by the goods and who is injured in person by breach of the warranty. A seller may not exclude or limit the operation of this section.' A comment to the section provided that 'the section is neutral and not intended to enlarge or restrict the developing case law on whether the seller's warranties, given to his buyer who resells, extend to other persons in the distributive chain'. This limitation on the potential doctrinal significance of the section, and the apparently illogical restriction of the right of action to members of the purchaser's household,[400] operated as substantial constraint on the scope of the provision. There were, however, other difficulties with using warranty as the basis of liability. Thus contract damages might be more limited than those available in tort, in

---

[393] S. J. Waddams, 'The Strict Liability of Suppliers of Goods' (1974) 37 *MLR* 154, 155–7.

[394] *Heilbut, Symons* v. *Buckleton* [1913] AC 30.

[395] English law currently takes a broader view of potential liability for negligent misrepresentation, under the principle enunciated in *Hedley Byrne & Co. Ltd.* v. *Heller & Partners Ltd.* [1964] AC 465, while as between contracting parties there are increased opportunities to sue for damages for a non-contractual representation under the Misrepresentation Act 1967, s. 2: see below, Section 2(c).

[396] Prosser, 'The Assault upon the Citadel', op. cit., 1103 ff.

[397] *Coca-Cola Bottling Works* v. *Lyons* (1927) 111 So. 305.   [398] [1893] 1 QB 256.

[399] See generally C. W. Gillam, 'Products Liability in a Nutshell' (1957) 37 *Oregon LR* 119.

[400] Waddams, op. cit. (Select Bibliography), 159.

particular in a case of wrongful death. Warranty law also required the consumer to show that he had relied on the representation, which might be problematic in a case where the goods were purchased by someone else and the ultimate consumer was ignorant of or indifferent to their precise origin.[401] Then, the warranties in question might be excluded or limited by a clause in one or more of the contracts in the supply chain. Finally, at least in cases where the warranty was regarded as running with the goods, one who did not actually gain title to them at any point, such as an employee or guest of the purchaser, could not recover. Some of these difficulties could be avoided in a case where a manufacturer's promotional literature or advertising could be construed as a set of representations made direct to the final consumer. If a product advertised as safe turned out to be dangerously defective an action either for deceit or for negligent misrepresentation might lie, as in a case where glass fitted into a car windscreen was described by the manufacturer as 'shatterproof'.[402] Unless deceit was proved or assumed, however, this action was subject to some of the difficulties already mentioned. As Prosser noted at the time, 'what all this adds up to is that "warranty" as a device for the justification of strict liability to the consumer, carries far too much luggage in the way of undesirable complications, and is leading us down a very thorny path'.[403]

(ii) Strict Liability in Tort The restrictions on the warranty action were confronted in a series of judgments in America in the early 1960s, from which there emerged the principle of strict liability in tort for harm caused by a defective product. In *Henningsen* v. *Bloomfield Motors Inc.*[404] the Supreme Court of New Jersey enlarged the scope of the transmissible warranty of quality by reference to general considerations of public policy. The action, against both the manufacturer and the retailer, was initiated by the wife of the purchaser of a Chrysler Plymouth car who was injured while driving it. There was no evidence of any negligence. The court offered the following justification for the imposition of strict liability without regard to privity:

where the commodities sold are such that if defectively manufactured they will be dangerous to life and limb, then society's interests can only be protected by eliminating the requirement of privity between the maker and his dealers and the reasonably expected ultimate consumer. In that way the burden of losses consequent upon use of defective articles is borne by those who are in a position to either control the danger or make an equitable distribution of the losses when they do occur . . . Accordingly, we hold that under modern marketing conditions, when a manufacturer puts a new automobile in the stream of trade and promotes its purchase by the public, an implied warranty that it is reasonably suitable for use as such accompanies it into the hands of the ultimate purchaser. Absence of agency between the manufacturer and the dealer who makes the ultimate sale is immaterial.[405]

---

[401] Prosser gave the following example: 'The husband or guest who eats a plate of beans seldom asks the housewife whose product they are, and still less often at what store she bought them': 'The Assault upon the Citadel', op. cit., 1128.

[402] *Baxter* v. *Ford Motor Co.* (1932) 12 P.2d 409; cf. the similar English law case of *Evans* v. *Triplex Safety Glass Co. Ltd.* [1938] 4 All ER 283, in which the action was brought in negligence under *Donoghue* v. *Stevenson* [1932] AC 562 and the action failed for lack of proof of fault in the process of manufacture.

[403] Prosser, 'The Assault upon the Citadel', op. cit., 1133.   [404] (1960) 161 A.2d 69.

[405] (1960) 161 A.2d 69, 81, 84.

The scope of this principle, the setting-aside of the technical limitations of sales law, and the court's insistence that exclusion or limitation of liability by contract would not be permitted had important consequences. Notably, it led to the belief that the basis of liability should lie not in contract, as the *Henningsen* court had suggested, but in terms of strict liability in tort. This view was, indeed, subsequently articulated by the Supreme Court of California in *Greenman* v. *Yuba Power Products Inc.*[406] In that case the defendant raised a defence available under sales law, namely that the plaintiff had failed to give prompt notice of the breach of warranty and therefore forfeited any contract action. The court excluded the defence of lack of notice as far as the warranty action was concerned and then went on to impose a more general strict liability upon the manufacturer in tort:

A manufacturer is strictly liable in tort when an article he places on the market, knowing that it is to be used without inspection for defects, proves to have a defect that causes injury to a human being. Recognised first in the case of unwholesome food products, such liability has now been extended to a variety of other products that create as great or greater hazards if defective. Although in these cases strict liability has usually been based on the theory of an express or implied warranty running from the manufacturer to the plaintiff, the abandonment of the requirement of a contract between them, the recognition that the liability is not assumed by agreement but imposed by law, and the refusal to permit the manufacturer to define the scope of its own responsibility for defective products make clear that the liability is not one governed by the law of contract warranties but by the law of strict liability in tort. Accordingly, rules defining and governing warranties that were developed to meet the needs of commercial transactions cannot be invoked to govern the manufacturer's liability to those injured by their defective products unless those rules also serve the purposes for which such liability is imposed.[407]

At this time the courts put forward a number of justifications for moving towards strict liability in tort. One, emphasised by Traynor J in *Yuba*[408] and in his earlier concurring opinion in *Escola* v. *Coca-Cola Bottling Co. of Fresno,*[409] was the manufacturer's superior capacity to absorb the risks of injury and to spread the costs either through insurance or through adjusting the prices of his products. 'The cost of an injury and the loss of time or health may be an overwhelming misfortune to the person injured, and a needless one, for the risk of injury can be insured by the manufacturer and distributed among the public as a cost of doing business.'[410] A second argument was based on the notion of the manufacturer's ability to control risk of defects arising, and the likelihood that strict liability would lead it to take additional precautions at the various stages of the production process.[411] In addition to these utilitarian or efficiency-based justifications, the courts rationalised strict liability in terms of general appeals to public protection. The ultimate consumer was normally unable to analyse or

---

[406] (1963) 377 P.2d 897.   [407] (1963) 377 P.2d 897, 901 (Traynor J).   [408] Ibid.
[409] (1944) 150 P.2d 436.   [410] *Escola* v. *Coca-Cola Bottling Co. of Fresno* (1944) 150 P.2d 436, 440.
[411] *Philips* v. *Kimwood Machine Co.* (1974) 525 P.2d 1033, 1041–2. This development was linked to the economic analysis of Guido Calabresi, and in particular the idea that the manufacturer's strict liability was based upon it being the 'least cost avoider': see G. Calabresi and J. Hirschoff, 'Towards a Test for Strict Liability in Torts' (1972) 81 *Yale LJ* 1054.

scrutinise the product for safety, and implicitly took it on trust that it would not be dangerous to life and limb.[412] Doctrinally this led to a new suggestion. The manufacturer could be seen as representing the safety of the product in question not only because of the kind of promotional activities which had given rise to liability in *Baxter* v. *Ford Motor Co.*[413] but also by virtue of the fact that he was putting the product on the market.[414]

There were also thought to be significant reasons relating to litigation and process costs for imposing strict liability. An action in tort making all those in the supply chain strictly liable could be seen as a means of 'short-circuiting' the successive actions for breach of contract of consumer against retailer, retailer against distributor, and so on, stretching back to the manufacturer. This process was not simply wasteful of resources; it was capable of being disrupted if at any point in the supply chain one of the parties was insolvent, out of the jurisdiction, or protected by an exclusion or limitation clause.[415] Secondly, tort liability extended the scope of potential plaintiffs in such a way as to remove some of the anomalies that had attached to liability for warranty. It was no longer necessary for the victim to have acquired title to the goods or to show reliance on the defendants' warranty of safety, and the artificial restraints of UCC section 2–318 were no longer applicable. This meant that not simply employees of the purchaser but also bystanders who were injured simply by virtue of being in the vicinity of the defective product could recover.[416] This was the consequence of the important change of emphasis brought about by framing the cause of action in tort:

If the philosophy of the strict liability is that all injured plaintiffs are to be compensated by holding the suppliers of products to strict liability for all the harm they do in the world, and in expecting them to insure against the liability and pass the cost on to society by adding it to the price, then there is no reason whatever to distinguish the pedestrian hit by an automobile with bad brakes from the injured driver of the car. If the supplier is to be held liable because of his representation of safety in marketing the goods, then the pedestrian stands on quite a different footing. He is not the man the supplier has sought to reach, and no implied representation has been made to him that the product is safe for use; nor has he relied on any assurance of safety whatever.[417]

Most American jurisdictions have now adopted the version of strict tort liability contained in section 402A of the *Restatement (Second) of Torts* which was first drawn up by the American Law Institute in 1965:

---

[412] *Jacob E. Decker & Sons* v. *Capps* (1942) 164 SW2d 828, 829. The same point can be put in economic terms: if the consumer is systematically unable to assess the degree of risk involved in the use of products, a strict liability regime which places the responsibility for risk assessment clearly on the producer is appropriate. See D. Dewees, D. Duff and M. Trebilcock, *Exploring the Domain of Accident Law* (1996), at 204.

[413] (1932) 12 P.2d 409, discussed above.

[414] *Jacob E. Decker & Sons* v. *Capps* (1942) 164 SW2d 828, 832–3; Prosser, 'The Assault on the Citadel', op. cit., 1123.

[415] Ibid., 1124.　　　　　　　　　　　　　　[416] *Piercefield* v. *Remington Arms Co.* (1965) 133 NW2d 129.

[417] Prosser, 'The Fall of the Citadel (Strict Liability to the Consumer)', (1966) 50 *Minn. LR* 791, 819.

Special Liability of Seller of Product for Physical Harm to User or Consumer

(1) One who sells any product in a defective condition unreasonably dangerous to the user or consumer or to his property is subject to liability for physical harm thereby caused to the ultimate user or consumer, or to his property, if

    (a) the seller is engaged in the business of selling such a product, and

    (b) it is expected to and does reach the user or consumer without substantial change in the condition in which it is sold.

(2) The rule stated in Subsection (1) applies although

    (a) the seller has exercised all possible care in the preparation and sale of his product, and

    (b) the user or consumer has not bought the product from or entered into any contractual relation with the seller.

The 'seller' here applies to all those engaged in handling the goods in a business capacity along the length of the supply chain; it therefore includes manufacturers, distributors, wholesalers, and retailers. As far as the range of plaintiffs is concerned, in imposing liability to the user or consumer section 402A apparently excludes an action brought by a mere bystander; however, this further extension has been accepted by the courts of several state jurisdictions, including California. In *Elmore* v. *American Motors Corp.*[418] the Supreme Court of California suggested that, 'if anything, bystanders should be entitled to greater protection than the consumer or user where injury to bystanders from the defect is reasonably foreseeable'. The reason was that bystanders have no opportunity of any kind to inspect for defects or to limit their purchases to those of reputable manufacturers.

The imposition of strict liability relieves the plaintiff of the burden of proving fault. However, it does *not* entail the manufacturer (or subsequent handler in the supply chain) becoming an automatic insurer for any damage caused by the product. Attention is shifted away from the quality of the defendant's conduct and from the scope of his duty of care towards the nature of the 'defect' and to the availability of defences. The central concept in section 402A is that of a product which reaches the consumer 'in a defective condition unreasonably dangerous'. This formulation is not equivalent to reading a requirement of negligence back into the section, since the test is whether the product is unreasonably dangerous from the point of view of the consumer, not whether the manufacturer was at fault in the process of producing it. Comment (*i*) to section 402A states that 'the article sold must be dangerous to an extent beyond that which would be contemplated by the ordinary consumer who purchases it, with the ordinary knowledge common to the community as to its characteristics'. This is the basis for the 'consumer expectation test' which courts in a number of American jurisdictions have applied. But at the same time the formulation used is designed to avoid a situation in which *absolute* liability, without the possibility of any defences, is imposed on the manufacturer. This has led some courts to develop a separate 'risk-utility defence' which seeks to measure the costs and benefits of product innovation, with particular reference to

[418] (1969) 451 P.2d 84, 89.

product design, in a way potentially more favourable to manufacturers.[419] Section 402A also makes provision for certain defences: in particular, the defendant will not be liable if the product left his hands in a safe condition and was subsequently mishandled by another.[420] It should also be noted that section 402A makes no reference to liability for pecuniary or 'pure economic' loss.

(iii) Directive 85/374/EEC and the Consumer Protection Act 1987   Proposals for a European Community Directive on Products Liability were first considered in the 1970s and, after slow progress, finally led to the adoption by the Member States of the present Directive in 1985. Independently of the Community the Council of Europe adopted a Convention on Product Liability in January 1977; this has remained unratified with the later development of the Community's proposal, but it provided a useful model for a harmonising measure. The Council of Europe Convention is stronger in that it does not contain any version of the 'state of the art' or 'development risks' defence that the Directive allows to Community Member States.[421] However, states such as Sweden and Finland, currently outside the EC, have chosen to use the Directive rather than the Convention as the basis for recent products-liability legislation.[422]

The Directive was the first significant attempt to achieve the harmonisation of an area of private law at Community level. The preamble seeks to justify the approximation of laws by arguing that divergences between the laws of different Member States 'may distort competition and affect the movement of goods within the common market and entail a differing degree of protection of the consumer'. In other words, different liability regimes may distort the market by subsidising producers in some states and penalising others. An argument directed more clearly to the kind of social-policy factors that influenced the American debate in the 1950s and 1960s is the assertion in the following paragraph of the preamble. According to this, 'liability without fault on the part of the producer is the sole means of adequately solving the problem, peculiar to our age of increasing technicality, of a fair apportionment of the risks inherent in modern technological production'.[423]

The Directive accordingly provides in its first article that 'the producer shall be liable for damage caused by a defect in his product'. The category of producer effectively includes all those in the supply chain from the manufacturer down (including the manufacturer of a component part). Also included is any person who 'presents himself as a producer' by putting his name, trademark, or other distinguishing feature on the product, as are other suppliers unless they can notify the consumer of the identity of the producer.[424] Those made responsible in this way are jointly and severally liable for damage caused.[425] In

---

[419] S. Birnbaum, 'Unmasking the Test for Design Defect: From Negligence [to Warranty] to Strict Liability to Negligence' (1980) 33 *Vanderbilt LR* 593, 600.

[420] *Restatement (Second) of Torts*, s. 402A, comment g. This and other defences are considered below.

[421] Art. 7(1)(e); see below.

[422] See D. G. Smith, 'The European Community Directive on Product Liability: A Comparative Study of its Implementation in the UK, France and West Germany' [1992] *Legal Issues in European Integration* 101, 103.

[423] See also the judgment of Advocate General Tesauro in Case C–300/95 *Commission v. United Kingdom* [1997] All ER (EC) 391, in particular at paras. 16–17.

[424] Art. 3.   [425] Art. 5.

addition, the person responsible for importing the product into the European Community (although not into the particular Member State, unless otherwise liable) will be deemed to be a producer for this purpose.[426] 'Products' include all movables except primary agricultural produce and game; electricity is also included in the Directive.[427]

The plaintiff is required to prove defect and damage and the causal link between them.[428] The definition of defect is contained in Article 6(1):

A product is defective when it does not provide the safety which a person is entitled to expect, taking all circumstances into account, including:

(a) the presentation of the product;
(b) the use to which it could reasonably be expected that the product would be put;
(c) the time when the product was put into circulation.

This reflects to some degree the 'consumer expectation' test developed under section 402A of the *American Restatement (Second) of Torts*. However, the reference to the reasonable expectation of the use to which the product would be put and to the time it was put into circulation also brings in elements associated with the 'risk–utility' test. Moreover, the Directive refers to the safety which 'a person', not necessarily the ultimate consumer, is 'entitled to expect'. This can be read as incorporating the risk–utility test for cases of defective design as opposed to defective manufacture (a product failing to match up to the intended specification).[429] None the less, the Directive is probably more favourable to the consumer than section 402A because it does not require him to prove that the product is both defective and 'unreasonably dangerous'.[430]

'Damage' under the Directive is defined as personal injury and death, on the one hand, and damage to property used for private use or consumption, on the other; 'pure economic loss' and business losses are thereby excluded. Damage to the product itself is also excluded and there is a 500-Ecu minimum threshold for property-damage claims, which is designed to prevent a flood of minor claims.[431] Contracting-out through exclusion or limitation clauses is prohibited.[432] A number of defences are spelled out: amongst others, these arise where the producer can prove that he did not put the product into circulation; that the defect did not exist when he put it into circulation; and that the defect arose out of his compliance with public regulations.[433] The Directive also contains a general exemption for non-business producers.[434]

The validity of the 'economic argument' for harmonising product liability law through a Directive has been called into question. Prior to the Directive, all the Member States had laws concerning product liability.[435] It is far from clear what the effects upon producer prices would be of moving to a general strict-liability regime; it is possible that the difference would be barely discernible.[436] Even on the assumption that a common strict liability standard might have a

---

[426] Art. 3(2).   [427] Art. 2.   [428] Art. 4.
[429] C. Newdick, 'The Future of Negligence in Product Liability' (1987) 103 *LQR* 288, 300.
[430] G. M. Whitehead and G. Scott, op. cit. (Select Bibliography), 172.   [431] Art. 9.
[432] Art. 12.   [433] Art. 7(1)(a), (b), and (d) respectively.   [434] Art. 7(1)(c).
[435] For a review, see F. Albanese and L. F. Del Duca (below, Select Bibliography).
[436] S. Whittaker, op. cit. (Select Bibliography), 235.

significant impact on prices, the Directive as drafted is most unlikely to achieve the desired levelling-out of the conditions of competition. One reason for this is that it does not seek to harmonise the remedies available to the consumer in the various Member States. The level at which damages are payable, in particular, is left up to Member States by virtue of a provision making it possible but not obligatory for national legal systems to impose a maximum limit on damages awards of 70 million Ecu.[437] Secondly, the Directive allows Member States two further derogations by providing that they may extend the scope of protection beyond industrial products to include agricultural products and game.[438] Member States may also make their own legislative provisions for a 'state of the art' defence.[439] According to this defence, a producer is exempted if he can show that the defect could not have been discovered given the state of scientific and technical knowledge at the time the product was put into circulation. Thirdly, the Directive does not seek to iron out significant potential differences between the laws of different Member States. It preserves existing principles of contractual or non-contractual liability already in force in Member States,[440] and permits but does not require the use of contributory negligence as a defence.[441] It explicitly preserves the existing national laws on contribution by joint tortfeasors.[442] Nor does the Directive address the matter of the different approaches taken by the Member States to the question of whether state social insurance institutions are subrogated to the claims of accident victims, differences which can substantially affect the level of damages payable by the defendant.[443] These divergencies raise the possibility of 'forum shopping' by plaintiffs seeking out the most advantageous jurisdiction in which to bring their action.[444]

Certain of these derogations were apparently included in the Directive as the price of gaining unanimous agreement for its adoption.[445] The power to make the Directive derives from Article 100 of the Treaty of Rome that, in contrast to the amendments made to the Treaty by the Single European Act of 1986, requires all the Member States to agree on the proposal in question.[446] With regard to the derogations, the Directive provides for a review procedure under which the Commission is required to submit a report to the Council of Ministers on the operation of the derogation provisions ten years after the adoption of the Directive.[447] The Directive itself acknowledges that the harmonisation it achieves 'cannot be total at the present stage, but opens the way

---

[437] Art. 16(1). [438] Art. 15(1)(a). [439] Art. 7(1)(e) and Art. 15(1)(b). [440] Art. 13.
[441] Art. 8(1). [442] Ibid.

[443] T. Weir, 'Governmental Liability' [1988] *PL* 40, 42; although under the scheme of recoupment contained in the Social Security Act 1989, s. 22 and Sch. 4, the position in English law is now closer to the position in systems which subrogate the state to the plaintiff's claim. See below, Chapter 8.

[444] Forum shopping is regulated by the rules of private international law and, within the European Community, by the Brussels Convention on Jurisdiction and Enforcement of Judgments in Civil and Commercial Matters of 1968. See R. Atree, 'Jurisdiction, Enforcement of Judgment and Conflicts of Laws', ch. 17 in P. Kelly and R. Atree (eds.), *European Product Liability Law* (1992).

[445] See D. G. Smith, op. cit. (Select Bibliography), 106–7.

[446] The Single European Act inserted a further provision, now Art. 100A of the Treaty of Rome, under which qualified majority voting (less than unanimity) will suffice for certain proposals.

[447] Art. 15(2).

towards greater harmonisation'.[448] This is a clear suggestion that the rationale for the Directive is not to ensure uniformity of laws throughout the Community, but to entrench a certain *minimum* level of social protection for consumers, below which no Member State will be permitted to fall. In due course the process of continuing harmonisation will see the scope for derogation at state level further limited. Yet it must also be recognised that this goal may potentially come into conflict with the economic argument for ensuring parity of producers' costs across the single market. With this economic goal in mind, the Directive could be interpreted as laying down *maximum* standards of protection; with all its limitations, it could paradoxically come to have a restrictive effect on the development of consumer-protection law in the Member States.[449]

The Directive was incorporated into English law by virtue of Part I of the Consumer Protection Act 1987. Earlier calls for the imposition of strict liability for defective products had been made in the aftermath of the Thalidomide affair, in which children were born with congenital disabilities after their mothers had taken the Thalidomide drug during pregnancy. The difficulties of proving negligence on the part of the company that had manufactured the drug gave rise to a wide public debate on the question of product liability. Both the English and Scottish Law Commissions made proposals for the introduction of strict liability and these were later echoed by the Pearson Commission in the late 1970s.[450] Some limited progress was made by the Consumer Safety Act 1978 which now, as amended,[451] forms Part II of the Consumer Protection Act 1987. This imposed certain regulatory requirements upon manufacturers in the area, in particular, of information and warnings relating to dangerous products put into circulation, and in addition to criminal sanctions provided for persons affected by a breach of the Act to bring a private action for breach of statutory duty.[452] However, this legislation fell a long way short of imposing a general private-law liability upon producers for dangerously defective products. It took the adoption of the Directive for the UK Parliament to introduce general liability of this kind, in the form of Part I of the Consumer Protection Act 1987.

The details of the Act are considered below; at this point certain features of its relationship with the Directive may be noted. The language used by the Act departs from that contained in the Directive in a number of respects. One justification for this could be the abstract and general quality of the language used in the Directive. However, there was an argument for leaving it up to the English courts (with appropriate guidance, where necessary, from the

---

[448] Preamble, final paragraph.

[449] See J. Stapleton, 'Three Problems with the New Product Liability', in P. Cane and J. Stapleton (eds.), *Essays for Patrick Atiyah* (1991); and for further discussion see Stapleton, *Product Liability* (1994), 60–5.

[450] Liability for Defective Products, Law Commission No. 82, Scots Law Commission No. 45, Cmnd. 6831, 1977; Royal Commission on Civil Liability and Compensation for Personal Injury, Cmnd. 7054, 1978, vol. 1, ch. 22.

[451] By the Consumer Safety (Amendment) Act 1986.

[452] Consumer Safety Act 1978, s. 6; see now, Consumer Protection Act 1987, s. 41(1); on breach of statutory duty generally, see Chapter 3, Section 4, above. The theoretical availability of this private action has had little impact on the development of consumer protection law. See the account of the law in A. Bell, 'Product Liability Damages in England and Wales' (1991) 20 *Anglo-Am. LR* 371.

European Court of Justice) to resolve any ambiguities of drafting.[453] As it is, not only does the Act make provision for the optional 'state of the art' or 'development risks' defence in Article 7(e) of the Directive, but it also appears significantly to expand its scope. Article 7(e) allows a defence where the producer shows that: 'the state of scientific and technical knowledge at the time when he put the product into circulation was not such as to enable the existence of the defect to be discovered.' Section 4(1)(e) of the Act, by contrast, provides for a defence where: 'the state of scientific and technical knowledge at the relevant time was not such that a producer of products of the same description as the product in question might be expected to have discovered the defect it if had existed in his products while they were under his control.' By apparently making the relevant standard that of the producer in the field and not the expectation of the consumer of the product, the Act has tilted the relevant test even further away from the consumer-expectation model towards the American risk–utility test, with its emphasis on adjusting the costs and benefits of innovation. The test is similar to that of negligence, except that the burden of proof is reversed.[454]

The possibility of the Act's incompatibility with the Directive raises the question of consumers claiming rights under the Directive itself. According to the doctrine of the direct effect of European Community law, a Directive is capable of directly conferring rights on individuals in national law only where the claim arises against a state body. This is known as 'vertical direct effect' to distinguish it from the more general 'horizontal' effect of a fundamental Treaty provision.[455] A particular Article of a Directive will only be accorded direct effect if it is clear and unconditional and capable of being given effect without further measures being taken either by the Community or the Member States. Claims under the Product Liability Directive will normally be brought against private or non-state producers, although a claim against an electricity producer is a possibility here. Electricity is within the scope of the Directive and the privatised, regulated utilities have been held to be within the scope of the doctrine of vertical direct effect.[456] Another possibility is that the Act will be interpreted in the light of the Directive. This is the doctrine of 'indirect effect' by virtue of which state legislation must be interpreted, so far as possible, in such a way as to bring about the aims of a relevant Directive in the same area.[457] The doctrine only applies where some ambiguity exists in the statute that is being interpreted; if its meaning is clear, there will be no scope for a contrary interpretation.[458] If the 1987 Act can be given an expansive interpretation by virtue of

---

[453] C. Newdick, 'Risk, Uncertainty and "Knowledge" in the Development Risk Defence' (1991) 20 *Anglo-Am. LR* 309, 326.

[454] Ibid., 310.

[455] *Marshall* v. *Southampton and South-West Hampshire Area Health Authority* Case 152/84 [1986] 1 CMLR 688.

[456] *Foster* v. *British Gas Corp.* [1991] ICR 84.

[457] *Von Colson and Kamann* v. *Land Nordrhein Westfalen* [1986] 2 CMLR 240. The principle has been recognised by the English courts: *Pickstone* v. *Freemans plc* [1989] AC 66; *Litster* v. *Forth Dry Dock & Engineering Co.* [1990] 1 AC 456. It also extends, according to the European Court, to legislation passed before a Directive covering the same area: *Marleasing SA* v. *Commercial International Alimentation SA* Case 106/89 [1992] 1 CMLR 305.

[458] *Webb* v. *EMO Air Cargo Ltd.* [1992] IRLR 116, CA.

this approach all plaintiffs will benefit and not simply those bringing claims against a state body. Mention should also be made of the possibility of a claim being brought against the state for damages for its failure properly to implement a Directive, under the principle first enunciated by the European Court of Justice in *Francovich* v. *Republic of Italy*.[459]

The principles of direct effect, indirect effect, and state liability all involve claims being brought by consumers themselves. It is also possible for the European Commission to bring infringement proceedings before the European Court of Justice under Article 169 of the Treaty of Rome, to clarify whether a Member State has complied with its obligations under a Directive. In the early 1990s the European Commission started infringement proceedings against the United Kingdom in respect of section 4(1)(e) of the 1987 Act,[460] but in 1997 the ECJ rejected the Commission's argument. The Court held that:

in order to have a defence under Art. 7(e) of the Directive, the producer of a defective product must prove that the objective state of scientific and technical knowledge, including the most advanced state of such knowledge, at the time when the product in question was put into circulation was not such as to enable the existence of the defect to be discovered. Further, in order for the relevant scientific and technical knowledge to be successfully pleaded against the producer, that knowledge must have been accessible at the time when the product was put into circulation.[461]

The Court went on to hold that section 4(1)(e) placed the burden of proof on the producer, as required by the Directive, and did not impose a limit on the state and degree of scientific knowledge to be taken into account. Nor did it make the defence dependent upon the subjective knowledge of the producer. Finally, the Court considered that any ambiguities in section 4(1)(e) could be resolved by national courts interpreting the Act in line with the wording and purpose of the Directive, as required by EC law.

Most, but not all, of the other Member States have adopted legislation incorporating the Directive (or seeking to do so) into their national legal systems. Of those states which have acted so far, all except Luxembourg make provision for the 'development risks' defence. However, the form of this defence is likely to be more restrictive in Germany, for example, than that contained in the UK's Consumer Protection Act. The relevant German legislation requires the state of knowledge of the defect to be judged by reference to objective, expert knowledge at the time and not that of the individual producer or, it would seem, of the 'reasonable producer' as the UK version implies.[462]

---

[459] [1992] IRLR 84.

[460] G. G. Howells, 'Europe's Solution to the Product Liability Phenomenon' (1991) 20 *Anglo-Am. LR* 205, 218.

[461] Case C–300/95 *Commission* v. *United Kingdom* [1997] All ER (EC) 391. For comment, see C. Hodges, 'Development Risks: Unanswered Questions' (1998) 61 *MLR* 560; M. Mildred and G. Howells, 'Comment on "Development Risks, Unanswered Questions"' (1998) 61 *MLR* 570.

[462] For reviews of the Directive's implementation, see Smith, 'The European Community Directive on Product Liability', op. cit.; P. Kelly and R. Atree (eds.), *European Product Liability* (1992). On Germany, see J. Zekell, 'The German Products Liability Act' (1989) 37 *Am. J. Comp. L.* 809; H. J. Dielmann, 'The New German Product Liability Act' (1990) *Hastings Int. & Comp. LR* 425; M. A. Veltins, 'The New Law of Product Liability in the Federal Republic of Germany' (1990) 3 *Transnational Lawyer* 83 and Markesinis, *The German Law of Obligations*, vol II, *The German Law of Torts*, (3rd edn., 1997).

Directive 85/374 has more recently been supplemented by Directive 92/59 on General Product Safety.[463] This is not concerned with extending the system of civil liability as such. However, it is possible that either the Directive or the implementing legislation that will in due course be enacted by the UK Parliament could give rise to actions for breach of statutory duty by individuals affected by non-compliance with their provisions.[464] Rather, the Product Safety Directive envisages regulations that will ensure that products in circulation comply with basic safety standards and that Member States set up bodies to monitor compliance with these standards. Of particular interest are the obligations placed upon producers to 'provide consumers with the relevant information to enable them to assess the risks inherent in a product throughout the normal or reasonably foreseeable period of its use, where such risks are not immediately obvious without adequate warnings, and to take precautions against those risks'; and to 'adopt measures commensurate with the characteristics of the products which they supply, to enable them to be informed of risks which those products might present and to take appropriate action including, if necessary, withdrawing the product in question from the market to avoid these risks'.[465] These measures appear to go beyond the more limited regulatory requirements that may be imposed upon producers under Part II of the Consumer Protection Act 1987.

(iv) Return to Negligence? As we have seen, the European Community Directive closely resembles the form of strict liability that has evolved in the United States. Somewhat ironically, the Directive's adoption and implementation have coincided with signs of a change of mood towards the strict liability principle in the United States. This is evident first of all in the growing use of the 'risk–utility test' in preference to the test of 'consumer expectation'. Thus, in *Barker* v. *Lull Engineering Co.*[466] the Supreme Court of California adopted a 'two-pronged' test under which the plaintiff, if she could not win on the basis of consumer expectations, could then try to establish that the manufacturer failed to pass the risk–utility test. In other words she was asked 'to prove, in light of the relevant factors, that on balance the benefits of the challenged design outweigh the risk of danger inherent in such design'.[467] The court denied that the risk–utility test was one which 'rings of negligence' in the sense of inviting the court to balance the cost of prevention against the magnitude of the harm and the risk of its occurring, as in the 'Hand test' for determining breach of duty.[468] It differed from negligence in that it 'explicitly focuses the trier of fact's attention on the adequacy of the product itself, rather than on the manufacturer's conduct, and places the burden on the manufacturer, rather than the plaintiff, to establish that because of the complexity of, and trade-offs implicit in, the design process, an injury-producing product should nevertheless not be found defective'.[469]

---

[463] The 1992 Directive is stated to be without prejudice to Directive 85/374.
[464] On breach of statutory duty, see Chapter 3, Section 4, above.
[465] Art. 3(2).
[466] (1978) 573 P.2d 443.
[467] 573 P.2d 443, 452.
[468] Above, Chapter 2; *United States* v. *Carroll Towing Co.* (1947) 159 F.2d 169, 173.
[469] 573 P.2d 443, 456.

None the less, courts have been at pains to point out that this test does not convert the manufacturer into an automatic insurer for consumer injury or damage, and in practice it may not be too difficult for a manufacturer to present enough evidence to meet the presumption against him. Moreover, courts in several jurisdictions have started to use the risk–utility test not as an alternative to consumer expectation, but as the principal determinant of liability in cases of defective design where, it is said, 'the consumer simply does not have adequate information to know what to expect'.[470] A recent review of the American case law suggested that in most jurisdictions consumer-expectation is retained only for cases of non-design defect (meaning products that are badly manufactured according to their specification, such as a car with faulty brakes). In some states the plaintiff had a choice of pursuing one route or the other. Some jurisdictions had also diluted the strict-liability element in the tests for applying the 'state of the art' defence, allowing manufacturers' compliance with the general practice of a particular industry to be advanced as a defence.[471]

A second area of contention in contemporary US law concerns awards of punitive damages against manufactures, which may dwarf the compensatory award paid to the consumer in respect of the costs of personal injury or property damage. Under English law the grounds for the award of punitive or exemplary damages are highly restricted.[472] The most significant category for present purpose concerns cases in which the defendant calculated that the gains he would make from committing a tort would outweigh compensatory damages he might have to pay to the plaintiff. By contrast, US jurisdictions recognised the possibility of punitive damages for a variety of purposes including the case of the 'calculating' defendant but also embracing the reckless or intentional commission of a wrong or malice against the plaintiff.[473] In the celebrated case of *Grimshaw* v. *Ford Motor Co.*[474] the defendants were aware of a design defect in one of their car models which rendered the vehicle liable to burst into flames when hit in the rear. Nevertheless, they declined to fix it because the costs of doing so were thought to outweigh the risk of litigation. They were held liable in a wrongful death action for punitive damages of $125 million (reduced on appeal to $3.5 million) as against compensation of nearly $3 million. There are numerous other cases in which punitive damages have far outstripped compensatory awards. In America the measure of damages is a jury matter, and appellate courts are reluctant, on the whole, to interfere with the jury's decision. In some states, legislatures have responded by passing Acts to limit both the availability of punitive damages and the scale on which they may

---

[470] *O'Brien* v. *Muskin Corp.* (1982) 463 A.2d 298, 308; see also discussion of the consumer-expectation test in *Dart* v. *Wiebe Manufacturing Inc.* (1985) 709 P.2d 876 and *Camacho* v. *Honda Motor Co.* (1987) 741 P.2d 1240; and see generally, S. Birnbaum, 'Unmasking the Test for Design Defect', op. cit.; C. Newdick, 'The Future of Negligence in Product Liability', op. cit.; N. P. Terry, 'State of the Art Evidence: From Logical Construct to Judicial Retrenchment' (1991) 20 *Anglo-Am. LR* 285.

[471] See N. P. Terry, op. cit.; *Feldman* v. *Lederle Laboratories* (1984) 479 A.2d 374.

[472] See the judgment of Lord Devlin in *Rookes* v. *Barnard* [1964] AC 1129, discussed in Chapter 8, Section 2(2)(d) below.

[473] G. C. Christie, 'Current Trends in the American Law of Punitive Damages' (1991) 20 *Anglo-Am. LR* 349.

[474] (1981) 119 Cal.App.3d 757.

be awarded. Defendants have also challenged high punitive awards on a variety of constitutional grounds, so far with little success.[475] Statutes limiting the operation of punitive awards have themselves been challenged on grounds of alleged unconstitutionality. Again the courts are generally reluctant to interfere, although there is a developing trend towards declaring such measures unconstitutional on the grounds of their potentially arbitrary effects in differentiating between the claims of different plaintiffs.[476]

Empirical research suggests that the courts are moving away from high damages claims of their own accord, and are at the same time taking a more restrictive view of the scope of manufacturers' liability. A study of judgments of appellate courts in product-liability cases carried out by Professors Henderson and Eisenberg found that the success-rate for plaintiffs began to fall in the early 1980s. This was largely because courts were setting an increasingly pro-defendant standard of responsibility and dismissing a larger number of claims at pre-trial hearings on questions of law, pre-empting the role of the jury which tends to be more strongly pro-plaintiff.[477] These findings cast doubt on the idea of a 'product liability crisis' in America, or at least indicate that the American courts are moving gradually towards their own solution to the initial mushrooming of liability following the strict-liability principle.

There are a number of justifications for moving away from the strict liability test back towards some kind of negligence standard. In the first place there is an economic argument as to which party, plaintiff or defendant, is best equipped to bear the damage or injury or the risk of it. Economic analysis suggests that the risk of loss should be imposed on the 'least cost avoider', that is to say, the person who can most effectively take steps either to avoid the risk of damage or to minimise its effects. The explicit assumption of the judges in such cases as *Henningsen* v. *Bloomfield Motors*[478] and *Greenman* v. *Yuba Products*[479] was that the manufacturer could most effectively avoid the defect through taking greater care in the process of production and that businesses throughout the length of the supply chain were better placed than the ultimate consumer to spread the costs of prevention either through insurance or through increased prices. This view has been challenged by arguments to the effect that manufacturers may, in certain circumstances, be no more able than consumers to assess the nature of certain risks.[480] Some risks are unavoidable, in particular in relation to hidden design defects. A strict liability regime which holds the

---

[475] The US Supreme Court has recently rejected such challenges under the excessive-fines clause of the US Constitution (*Browning-Ferris Industries of Vermont Inc.* v. *Kelco Disposal Inc.* (1989) 492 US 257) and under the due-process clause of the fourteenth amendment to the Constitution (*Pacific Mutual Life Insurance Co.* v. *Haslip* (1991) 111 S. Ct. 1032).

[476] E.g. by allowing punitive damages to be awarded only once, in effect favouring the first plaintiff to get judgment. The first plaintiff may be one of many if the defect caused a large-scale disaster or a string of accidents. See *McBride* v. *General Motors Co.* (1990) 737 F. Supp 1563, discussed by Christie, op. cit.

[477] 'The Quiet Revolution in Products Liability' (1991) 20 *Anglo-Am. LR* 188. See also the longer account, 'The Quiet Revolution in Products Liability: An Empirical Study of Legal Change' (1990) 36 *UCLA L. Rev.* 479, and for general discussion of American trends in this and related areas J. G. Fleming, *The American Tort Process* (1988).

[478] (1960) 161 A.2d 69.   [479] (1963) 377 P.2d 897.

[480] For a discussion and critique of the different economic theories, see Stapleton, *Product Liability*, ch. 5.

manufacturer automatically liable for the resulting harm may lead to manufacturers taking *excessive* amounts of care, pushing prices up beyond a level which reflects the potential costs to society of product defects, driving producers out of the market, or inhibiting innovation. It has also been suggested that product innovation may be stymied by the threat of high damages awards based on strict liability.[481]

Nor is it clear that the manufacturer is always best placed to take out the relevant insurance. Certainly as far as physical damage to property is concerned, the consumer, who has more information about the value of the property in question and the uses to which it is put, is in a better position to take out insurance covering the potential loss. Since household property is by and large covered by first-party or loss insurance, strict liability, by imposing upon the manufacturer what is in essence a requirement to carry third-party or liability insurance, may be creating the circumstances for a wasteful double-insurance of the loss in question. There are also signs that high damages awards have made it increasingly difficult for American producers to obtain the necessary liability insurance.[482]

These arguments do not seem so convincing in the case of personal injury, where the preventive or deterrent aim of strict liability may seem more clearly justified. However, if it is accepted that a certain level of risk is unavoidable as the price of product innovation, the interests of victims of injury are arguably better served by a system of collective health-care provision, buttressed by social-security benefits in relation to sickness and invalidity, than by a system which loads costs almost exclusively on to producers. In contrast to the United States, most European Community countries have some degree of collective health-care and social-insurance provision of this kind. It has thus been argued that for these countries strict product liability of the American kind, where compensation is assured through the costly court system, is both unnecessary and, in so far as it diverts economic resources from more worthwhile ends, undesirable.[483]

Whether these arguments will influence European courts and the European Community itself to weaken the strict-liability principle contained in the Products Liability Directive remains to be seen. The less desirable features of the American system may well be the result not of strict liability as such, but rather of the prominent role of the jury, the possibility of stratospherically high damages awards, and the incentive to litigation provided by the contingency-fee system.[484] In these respects, none of the product-liability regimes of the EC Member States is truly comparable to the American system. However, it may well be that the Product Liability Directive itself, through the test of defect which it provides and through its acknowledgment of a development-risks

[481] See Hodges, 'Development Risks: Unanswered Questions' (1998) 61 *MLR* 560.

[482] See the discussion of Howells, op. cit. (1990) 21 *Anglo-Am. LR* 204; Stapleton, *Product Liability*, in particular ch. 6.

[483] A. Bernstein, 'A Duty to Warn: One American View of the EC Products Liability Directive' (1991) 20 *Anglo-Am. LR* 224.

[484] See Fleming, *The American Tort Process*, op. cit.

defence, comes closer to setting a modified negligence standard than would appear at first sight.

2. The Causes of Action and Components of Liability

We now turn to a more detailed analysis of the components of liability under the different potential causes of action in contract, tort, and statute respectively. We will examine in turn the parties to the various actions; the types of products covered; the standard of care and of responsibility imposed upon the defendant and the availability of particular defences; the relevant principles of causation and remoteness; the concept of damage and the measurement of damages; and exclusion and limitation of liability.

(A) THE PARTIES TO THE ACTION

Here the fundamental point, referred to above, is the limited nature of the contract action for breach of warranty. Only a buyer who is in a direct contractual relation with a seller can sue for breach of an express or implied warranty of fitness. It is useful to distinguish here between 'vertical' contracts between businesses in the supply chain and 'horizontal' links involving consumers at the end of the chain (see Fig. 6.2).[485] Goods will normally pass through the hands of several commercial entities—the manufacturer, distributor(s), and retailer—before they reach the consumer. Each commercial supplier could have an action against the person or entity from which it bought the goods if it suffers loss as a result of a defect in the product. The last 'horizontal' contract between the retailer and the consumer will also contain, in addition to any express terms, the obligations of merchantable quality and fitness for the purpose intended which are implied by the Sale of Goods Act in any case of a sale made in the course of a business (although not to private sales).[486] Liability for breach of these obligations is strict, so the retailer will have no defence by claiming that the original defect was the responsibility of the manufacturer.

However, no contract action will arise if the person who purchased the product hands it on to a friend as a gift—as in *Donoghue* v. *Stevenson*[487]—or if the product injures another member of his household, as in *Priest* v. *Last*[488] where a husband bought a hot-water bottle which burst and scalded his wife. In that case he recovered damages only because he had met the expenses arising from her injuries. Still less will any contract claim arise if the injury or other loss is sustained by a bystander who has no relation of any kind with the person who bought the goods. Although a breach of contract has taken place in that defective goods have been supplied, the person suffering the loss is not the contracting party. The privity rule prevents the third party who has suffered the loss from bringing the action, on the grounds that he has not supplied the consideration for the contract in question.[489] Nor can the person who made the

---

[485] See Goode, *Commercial Law* (2nd edn.). [486] S. 14. [487] [1932] AC 562.
[488] [1903] 2 KB 148. [489] *Dunlop Pneumatic Tyre Co.* v. *Selfridge & Co. Ltd.* [1915] AC 847.

Fig. 6.2 Vertical and horizontal chains of supply

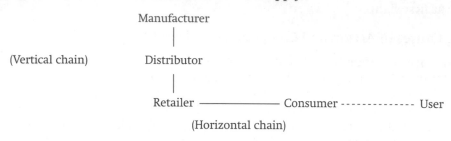

contract bring an action for the third party's loss, unless that loss in some way caused additional actionable damage to him.[490]

It might be possible for liability for the original defect to be transmitted back up the length of the supply chain. This could happen where a consumer (who is also the final purchaser) brings an action in contract against the retailer from whom he bought the product, and that retailer then sues the distributor for breach of contract, and so on back to the manufacturer. This, however, is an inefficient solution to the problem. For not only does it involve a multiplicity of parties and actions; more importantly it will not work if one of the parties in the chain is uninsured, insolvent, out of the jurisdiction, or protected by an exclusion clause. In that event, the liability will thus not get passed back up the chain.

Nor will it necessarily be possible for the retailer to leapfrog over an insolvent or unreachable supplier to one further up the supply chain or back to the manufacturer itself, by bringing an action in tort. Even if negligence can be established, the retailer's claim is classified as 'pure economic loss' because he has not suffered physical harm of any sort. The physical harm has been suffered by the consumer and the retailer's only damage is the pecuniary loss suffered by virtue of his liability in contract to the consumer. In *Lambert* v. *Lewis*[491] the Court of Appeal rejected such an action by a retailer against the manufacturer, on the grounds that under *Spartan Steel and Alloys Ltd.* v. *Martin & Co. (Contractors) Ltd.*[492] it was necessary to show that the economic loss arose directly out of physical damage to the plaintiff, that is to say, injury to the plaintiff or damage to goods in which he had a proprietary or possessory interest when they were damaged. The House of Lords rejected an appeal on different grounds, and in doing so stated that it was *not* deciding that economic loss could not be recovered in these circumstances. Since then, the decisions of the House of Lords in *The Aliakmon*[493] and *Murphy* v. *Brentwood District Council*[494] have further emphasised the exceptional nature of recovery in negligence for pure economic loss. There is a case for saying that where physical damage occurs at *some point* in the supply chain, it is artificial to regard the resulting economic losses of contractors higher up the chain as a case of 'pure economic loss'.[495]

---

[490] *Woodar Investment Development Ltd.* v. *Wimpey Construction UK Ltd.* [1980] 1 WLR 277. See the discussion of the Law Commission, op. cit., on the question of privity and liability for defective products.
[491] [1982] AC 225.   [492] [1973] 1 QB 27.   [493] [1986] AC 785.   [494] [1991] 1 AC 398.
[495] *The Kapetan Georgis* [1988] 1 Lloyd's Rep. 352, 356 (Hirst J).

But when a similar point was made in *The Aliakmon* the House of Lords responded unsympathetically to that suggestion.[496]

The manufacturer and consumer may be directly linked through contract if the retailer acts as the manufacturer's agent for the purposes of the sale to the consumer or, alternatively, as the agent of the consumer. Perfectly conceivable in principle, an agency relationship is unlikely in practice and will not be inferred by a court unless there is the clearest evidence of an intention to create it.[497] Alternatively, the manufacturer may make a representation direct to the consumer that gives rise to liability in contract. In *Carlill* v. *Carbolic Smoke Ball Co.*[498] the manufacturer's representation,[499] made through advertising, was taken to be a promise constituting an offer for a unilateral contract. The consumer accepted by taking the tablets for the period prescribed. This case, too, must be regarded as somewhat exceptional. It was not an action brought for misrepresenting the nature of the product as such, but a 'reward case' brought for the enforcement of the promise to pay the sum of money in the event that the tablets did not work.

Advertising statements will not normally give rise to legal liability for misrepresentation, on the grounds that they are just 'puffing up' the product.[500] Moreover, even when liability in damages for a misrepresentation can be established, for example, under section 2(1) of the Misrepresentation Act 1967, an action for damages will only lie if the statement in question induced a contract between the two parties. While an action for misrepresentation against the retailer is therefore entirely plausible,[501] it is unlikely to arise between the manufacturer and ultimate consumer. It is possible that a collateral contract might arise in an appropriate case, as in *Shanklin Pier Ltd.* v. *Detel Products Ltd.*[502] where the plaintiff bought the paint manufactured by the defendant following a visit from one of its representatives who made various statements about its qualities. The paint was bought from a retailer, and the act of entering into this separate contract of sale was seen as the consideration for a collateral contract containing the defendant's warranties as to the quality of the paint. However, this is a somewhat artificial solution about which the courts have traditionally been sceptical. And it will only be used where there is clear evidence of contractual intent on the part of the manufacturer,[503] which will normally be lacking when the statements are made through general advertising as opposed in a face-to-face meeting. In so limiting liability for misrepresentations English law is far more rigid than its American counterpart, which admits the possibility of liability for public misrepresentations, including advertisements, in the absence of privity.[504]

---

[496] See the discussion of this point in Chapter 2, Section 2(2)(b)(iv) above.

[497] On the circumstances in which an agency relationship will be implied from commercial dealings, see *New Zealand Shipping Co. Ltd.* v. *A. M. Satterthwaite & Co. Ltd., The Eurymedon* [1975] AC 154 (PC).

[498] [1893] 1 QB 256.

[499] That he would pay a sum of money to anyone who was not protected against influenza after taking its tablets for the duration of the prescribed course.

[500] *Dimmock* v. *Hallett* (1866) LR 2 Ch. App. 21.   [501] E.g. *Andrews* v. *Hopkinson* [1957] 1 QB 229.

[502] [1951] 2 KB 584; see also *Wells (Merstham) Ltd.* v. *Buckland Sand & Silica Co. Ltd.* [1965] 2 QB 170.

[503] *Heilbut Symons & Co.* v. *Buckleton* [1913] AC 30.

[504] *Baxter* v. *Ford Motor Co.* (1932) 12 P.2d 409; *Randy Knitwear Inc.* v. *American Cyanamid Co.* (1962) 181 NE2d 399; *Ford Motor Co.* v. *Lonon* (1966) 398 SW 2d 240.

It may, however, be possible to establish a separate duty of care in tort to avoid making careless statements that could endanger the consumer or otherwise cause his loss. Where the statement could cause the consumer physical harm, a duty of care is clearly established. Thus, liability has been imposed on the supplier of a volatile chemical in flasks whose labels carelessly failed to give an adequate warning of its properties;[505] on the distributor of a hair dye who gave a false assurance of its safety to a hairdresser, one of whose customers contracted dermatitis when it was applied;[506] and on a retailer who sold a cleaning fluid without testing to see if was correctly labelled.[507] Where economic loss is concerned, the plaintiff has the more difficult task of framing an action within the principles laid down by the House of Lords in *Hedley Byrne & Co. Ltd*. v. *Heller & Partners*,[508] with its limiting requirement of a pre-tort 'special relationship' between the parties.

Economic loss aside, the negligence action which the House of Lords recognised in *Donoghue* v. *Stevenson*[509] cut through the difficulties imposed by the privity rule by imposing a duty of care directly upon the manufacturer to the ultimate consumer, whether or not that person had any contractual rights against a retailer. Any person suffering physical injury or property damage can sue, including 'bystanders' and others not in a relation of any kind with the final purchaser, as long as the normal tests of causation and remoteness are satisfied. Nor are manufacturers the only potential defendants. Those who are responsible for assembling the different parts of a product[510] or who supply a defective component part are included.[511] Repair work[512] and installation work[513] may similarly give rise to liability, and it is also possible that a distributor[514] or a seller on hire purchase[515] may come under a duty of care in negligence to the consumer.

As we have seen, the principal difficulty in the negligence action concerns the need to show fault. This is difficult enough in an action against the original manufacturer, although the plaintiff is normally given the benefit of certain inferences in his favour.[516] For others in the supply chain, such as distributors and retailers, it may be impossible to prove negligence as they are not responsible for the production process itself, although it might be possible to hold them liable for failing to inspect the goods for obvious signs of defects. Strict liability independently of contract is needed if the consumer is to have the possibility of an action against all the business parties in the supply chain.

---

[505] *Vacwell Engineering Co. Ltd*. v. *BDH Chemicals Ltd*. [1971] 1 QB 88.
[506] *Watson* v. *Buckley, Osborne, Garret & Co*. [1940] 1 All ER 174; although cf. *Holmes* v. *Ashford* [1950] 2 All ER 76, where manufacturers were held to have given an adequate warning: see R. Bradgate, 'Misrepresentation and Product Liability in English Law' (1991) 20 *Anglo-Am. LR* 334, 341.
[507] *Fisher* v. *Harrods Ltd*. [1966] 1 Lloyd's Rep. 500.   [508] [1964] AC 465.
[509] [1932] AC 562.   [510] *Malfroot* v. *Noxal Ltd*. (1935) 51 TLR 551.
[511] *Barnes* v. *Irwell Valley Water Board* [1939] 1 KB 21.
[512] *Stennett* v. *Hancock and Peters* [1939] 2 All ER 578.
[513] *Hartley* v. *Mayoh & Co*. [1952] 2 All ER 525 (affirmed on a different point [1954] 1 QB 383).
[514] *Watson* v. *Buckley, Osborne, Garrett & Co. Ltd*. [1940] 1 All ER 174.
[515] *Andrews* v. *Hopkinson* [1957] 1 QB 229, 236 (McNair J).
[516] *Grant* v. *Australian Knitting Mills Ltd*. [1936] AC 85.

Under the Consumer Protection Act 1987, section 2(1), 'where any damage is caused wholly or partly by a defect in a product, every person to whom subsection (2) below applies shall be liable for the damage'. The Act does not spell out who may sue except in so far as this is implicit in the definition of 'damage' in section 5. 'Damage' means death, personal injury, or damage to property (but not business property), including land and excluding damage to the product itself.[517] Those suffering physical harm are, therefore, included, although it is possible that as with the tort of negligence and even in the case of American jurisdictions recognising strict liability, those who suffer injury as 'mere' bystanders will only recover if their presence was foreseeable. Users and consumers will come under the category of 'foreseeable plaintiffs' without much difficulty, but it is not clear how a court would deal with the problem of remoteness which arises where physical harm occurs in a *manner* which could not have been contemplated.[518] It is unclear whether the Act extends to 'nervous shock' recovery: section 45 of the Act provides that personal injury includes 'any disease and any other impairment of a person's physical or mental condition'. Although pure economic loss appears to be excluded this is not so obvious as it might be. These questions are discussed further below, in the analysis of 'damage'.

There is also difficulty over the definition of property damage. In the first place the aim of the Act (and of the Directive) is to prevent claims for damage to commercial property being brought under the strict-liability principle. This accords with the general orientation of products liability towards the protection of consumer interests as opposed to business interests. For property damage to be actionable, therefore, the property must first of all have been of a type ordinarily intended for private use and consumption. Secondly, it must actually have been intended by the person suffering the loss or damage to be used 'mainly for his own private use, occupation or consumption'.[519] The overall result of this is to exclude actions by business entities in respect of business losses. Consumers can sue, but only in respect of damage to property intended for 'private' use; 'private' use would appear to mean 'non-business' use. Where someone buys, for example, a car or a word processor for a mixture of personal and business uses, the court will have the task of identifying whether the product was intended 'mainly' for personal use. If not, the plaintiff will have to rely on common-law negligence to recover any property damage caused by the defective product.

The Act, following the Directive, provides for an extensive list of potential defendants.[520] First of all there is the category of *producers*:

'producer', in relation to a product, means—
(a) the person who manufactured it;
(b) in the case of a substance which has not been manufactured but has been won or abstracted, the person who won or abstracted it;

---

[517] S. 5(1).
[518] As in *Hughes* v. *Lord Advocate* [1963] AC 837. For discussion, see Whittaker (below, Select Bibliography), 264–5.
[519] S. 5(3)(a)–(b).   [520] S. 2(2).

(*c*) in the case of a product which has not been manufactured, won or abstracted but
      essential characteristics of which are attributable to an industrial or other process
      having been carried out (in relation to agricultural produce), the person who carried
      out that process . . .[521]

A product is defined as 'any goods or electricity' and includes a product,
whether a raw product or a manufactured component, which is included in
another product. The crucial point here is the extent to which the definition
extends beyond the obvious categories of industrial manufacturers. Products
'won or abstracted' under paragraph (*b*) could include, for example, minerals
(such as coal, gas, and oil) and water, so that mining and oil companies and
water companies are included under the Act. Farmers, however, are not
included since under section 2(4) there is an exemption for those who supply
agricultural produce ('any produce of the soil, of stock-farming or of fisheries')[522] before it undergoes industrial processing. The concept of an 'industrial or other process' under paragraph (*c*) is also important. The Directive refers
by contrast to 'products which have undergone initial processing'.[523] If paragraph (*c*) receives a purposive interpretation[524] to give effect to the clear intention of the Directive to maximise the number of potential defendants, it would
seem that any person who processes primary agricultural produce by, for
example, cleaning or packaging it with a view to consumption will be caught
by the Act. The only clear exemption that the Act and the Directive provide is
for the farmer or other 'primary producer' who does not himself process the
produce in this way.

The second group includes those who put their brand or trade mark on the
goods: 'any person who, by putting his name on the product or using a trade
mark or other distinguishing mark in relation to the product, has held himself
out to be the producer of the product.'[525] The purpose of extending liability in
this way is to catch those who represent the goods as their own, on the basis
that by doing so they should assume the same responsibility to the class of consumers as those who manufacture the goods.

The third group consists of those responsible for importing the goods into a
Member State of the Community, in the course of a business.[526] In so far as this
provision is designed to deal with the problem that the manufacturer and even
the 'brand-name' dealer may both be outside the jurisdiction of the consumer,
it does not do so very effectively. For the consumer may well have come into
contact with the product in a Community Member State other than the one
into which the product was initially imported. It would have been more effective had the Directive and the Act imposed liability on the person responsible
for importing the product into the Member State where the loss occurred or
where the consumer was domiciled.

Suppliers along the length of the vertical chain who do not fall into one of
these three categories will also be liable to the consumer unless they can iden-

---

[521] S. 1(2).   [522] Ibid.   [523] Art. 2.
[524] This is necessary under the doctrine of the 'indirect effect' of Directives: *Litster* v. *Forth Dry Dock &
Engineering Co. Ltd.* [1990] 1 AC 456.
[525] S. 2(2)(b).   [526] S. 2(2)(c).

tify to the consumer the person who supplied the goods to them. The consumer must make the request within a reasonable time of the damage occurring and at a time when it is not reasonably practicable for him to make the necessary identification.[527] For the supplier to escape liability, it is not necessary that the person he identifies be solvent or insured. This provision is therefore narrower than its equivalent in American law; section 402A of the Restatement imposes liability on suppliers without the possibility of this defence of 'identification' of the producer. Nor does the Act clearly cover repairers, installers, and others who work on a product. It would seem that actions against this group will have to be brought in contract or negligence as before.

As far as suppliers of components or of raw materials that go to form part of a defective product are concerned, the Act provides that they are not for this reason alone to be treated as supplying the product in question.[528] They also have a defence if they can show that the defect was not attributable to them but was wholly attributable to the producer of the subsequent product.[529] However, there is no defence where a component itself is defective and is then incorporated in a larger product. A supplier of faulty brakes that are incorporated into a car will be potentially liable along with the manufacturer of the car itself.

In common with the contractual and tortious forms of liability, the Act confines its liability to business producers and suppliers. This is the effect of section 4(1)(c) which provides a defence to suppliers who can show that the supply took place otherwise than in the course of their business. The same is true of producers, brand-namers, and importers who can show that the production or other such activity was 'done otherwise than with a view to profit'. This excludes the case of the producer of home-made cakes who gives them to her friends. The position of charities, however, is not so clear. If cakes are produced for and sold from a charity stall, are they supplied in the course of a business and produced with a view to profit? Where a producer distributes free samples to help generate trade, that is clearly within the Act. Governmental bodies are included within the Act by virtue of section 45, which defines business as including the activities of 'a local authority or other public authority', and the provisions of the Act concerning product liability bind the Crown.[530]

It may be noted, finally, that where more than one of these potential defendants is found liable, liability is joint and several.[531]

(B) THE 'PRODUCTS' COVERED

The Sale of Goods Act 1979 defines goods as 'personal chattels other than things in action and money', including growing crops but excluding real property (land).[532] The terms implied into a sale of goods contract by section 14 of the Act may equally well arise by implication in a contract to supply combined goods and services, as in the case of a building contract.[533] The categories of articles and substances to which a tort action in negligence has been applied

---

[527] S. 2(3).   [528] S. 1(3).   [529] S. 4(1)(f)(i).   [530] S. 9.   [531] S. 2(5).   [532] S. 61(1).
[533] See *Young & Marten Ltd.* v. *McManus Childs Ltd.* [1969] 1 AC 454.

are equally broad, if not broader. These include a tombstone,[534] underwear,[535] hair dyes,[536] motor vehicles,[537] lifts,[538] bottles,[539] and chemicals.[540]

Under the Consumer Protection Act, as we have seen, a product includes 'any goods or electricity and . . . includes a product which is comprised in another product, whether by virtue of being a component part or raw material or otherwise'.[541] Under section 45, goods include 'substances, growing crops and things comprised in land by virtue of being attached to it and any ship, aircraft or vehicle'. Manufactured drugs and other pharmaceutical products are therefore within the Act, but processed blood used for transfusions, for example, is not. The exemption for primary agricultural produce has already been noted. Land itself is not included in the definition of 'product'. Although the Act could be clearer on this point, it seems likely that plaintiffs suffering loss through defects in buildings will have to bring an action against the builder either under the Defective Premises Act 1972 or under common-law negligence.[542] The building itself, being an immovable, is part of the 'land' and not something simply attached to it. Where, however, the plaintiff is injured by a defective product which is incorporated into a house—such as bricks or roof tiles—he will have an action against the manufacturer of that product and others in the supply chain who fall within the definition of 'producer'. He will only rarely have an action against the builder. Although a builder will frequently contract to give title both to the land and to the materials which make up the building, section 46(4) of the Consumer Protection Act provides that where the supply of the materials takes the form of the disposal or creation of an interest in land, the supplier has a defence to any action under the Act. The builder will only be liable under the Act, therefore, in the event of supplying materials without also conferring title to the property.

(c) The Scope and Standard of Responsibility

Liability for breach of the implied terms in a contract for sale of goods is strict, enabling the buyer, under certain circumstances, to terminate the contract for breach of condition and return the goods, or alternatively to sue for damages.[543] Liability for misrepresentation is strict where the warranty in question is incorporated into the contract as a term, or forms a collateral contract; the buyer will have the normal range of contractual remedies. Where the misrepresentation is not incorporated into a contract in this way, damages are not available for a purely innocent misrepresentation (that is to say, one which is neither fraudulent nor negligent).[544] However, if the misrepresentor cannot show that he had reasonable grounds for making the statement he will be

---

[534] *Brown* v. *Cotterill* (1934) 51 TLR 21.
[535] *Grant* v. *Australian Knitting Mills Ltd.* [1936] AC 86.
[536] *Parker* v. *Oloxo Ltd.* [1937] 3 All ER 524.
[537] *Herschtal* v. *Stewart and Arden Ltd.* [1940] 1 KB 155.
[538] *Haseldine* v. *C. A. Daw Ltd.* [1941] 2 KB 343.
[539] *Hart* v. *Dominion Stores* (1968) 67 DLR (2d) 675.
[540] *Vacwell Engineering Co. Ltd.* v. *BDH Chemicals Ltd.* [1971] 1 QB 88.
[541] S. 1(2).
[542] On liability for defective buildings, see Chapter 3, Section 3(2)(g) above.
[543] Sale of Goods Act, s. 53.
[544] The buyer will, however, be able to rescind the contract and claim restitution and indemnity (or he may, alternatively, be awarded damages in lieu of rescission under section 2(2) of the Misrepresentation Act 1967), but the right to rescind may be lost by, for example, lapse of time (*Leaf* v. *International Galleries* [1950] 2 KB 86) or affirmation (*Long* v. *Lloyd* [1958] 1 WLR 753), or by resale of the goods to a third party.

liable for damages under section 2(1) of the Misrepresentation Act 1967. These will be calculated according to the measure for the tort of deceit.[545]

Liability in negligence rests, as we have seen, on proof of fault, normally without the benefit of *res ipsa loquitur*. Notwithstanding Lord Wright's willingness in *Grant* v. *Australian Knitting Mills*[546] to make an inference of negligence from the mere existence of contamination in the product, in other decisions the English courts have refused to find negligence simply from the fact that a product failed to conform to an expected standard of safety, or to the one advertised by himself. This can be seen in the case of a lemonade bottle which fractured when the plaintiff picked it up,[547] or the case of the car windscreen made of 'toughened safety glass' which shattered without warning.[548] Lord Atkin's original formulation in *Donoghue* v. *Stevenson* also emphasised the role of fault in that he would have imposed liability on a manufacturer who sold products 'in such a form as to show that he intends them to reach the ultimate consumer in the form in which they left him with no possibility of intermediate examination'.[549] In *Donoghue*'s case there was no possibility of intermediate examination as the bottle was opaque and concealed its contents. The courts soon tightened this aspect of the test, substituting 'probability' for 'possibility' of intermediate examination.[550] The failure of an intermediary to make an effective examination will not exempt the manufacturer if no such examination was anticipated.[551]

In *Donoghue* v. *Stevenson*,[552] however, clear limits were set to the manufacturer's responsibility in the sense that once he ceased to have 'control' of the item, he would cease to be liable for the consequences of its use. In *Evans* v. *Triplex Safety Glass*[553] the court was persuaded by an argument that the fault in the windscreen might have occurred when it was fitted, by a third party, and not during the process of manufacture. Where the product is mishandled by the consumer himself this does not, in itself, absolve the manufacturer, but it may provide a basis for a defence of contributory negligence.[554]

Under the Consumer Protection Act, liability is strict but, as under American law, this does not mean absolute or automatic liability. The boundaries to the producer's liability are set, above all, by the concept of 'defect' contained in section 3 of the Act, by the duties which are implicit in this definition, and by the defences which feature in section 4.

(i) The Concept of Defect There are, in principle, three kinds of possible defect. First are those that occur at the design stage, as in the production of a drug with unanticipated side-effects or a model of a motor vehicle with a tendency to swerve unexpectedly. Then we encounter those occurring in the process of manufacture itself which prevent the product complying with its

---

[545] *Royscot Trust Co.* v. *Rogerson* [1991] 3 All ER 294.   [546] [1936] AC 85.
[547] *Daniels* v. *R. White & Sons Ltd.* [1938] 4 All ER 258.
[548] *Evans* v. *Triplex Safety Glass Co. Ltd.* [1938] 1 All ER 283.   [549] [1932] AC 562, 599.
[550] *Paine* v. *Colne Valley Electricity Supply Co. Ltd.* [1938] 4 All ER 803, 808–9 (Goddard LJ).
[551] See *Clay* v. *A. J. Crump & Sons Ltd.* [1964] 1 QB 533; *Herschtal* v. *Stewart and Ardern Ltd.* [1940] 1 KB 155.
[552] [1932] AC 562; see in particular the judgment of Lord Macmillan.
[553] [1938] 1 All ER 283.   [554] *Farr* v. *Butters Brothers & Co.* [1932] 2 QB 606.

specification, such as the snail in the bottle in *Donoghue* v. *Stevenson*.[555] Finally, we have those deriving from a failure to give adequate warnings or instructions about the product, as in *Vacwell Engineering* v. *BDH Chemicals*.[556] The Act does not formally distinguish between the three types of defect. Instead, it simply states in section 3(1) that 'there is a defect in a product for the purposes of this Part if the safety of the product is not such as persons generally are entitled to expect; and for those purposes "safety", in relation to a product, shall include safety in relation to products comprised in that product and safety in the context of risks of damage to property, as well as in the context of risks of death or personal injury.' The crucial notion here is the standard of 'what persons generally are entitled to expect'. Section 3(2) broadly follows Article 6 of the Directive, but uses different language, by specifying that this standard shall be determined by reference to 'all the circumstances . . . including' the following three factors:

(a) the manner in which, and purposes for which, the product has been marketed, its get-up, the use of any mark in relation to the product and any instructions for, or warnings with respect to, doing, or refraining from doing, anything with or in relation to the product;

(b) what might reasonably be expected to be done with or in relation to the product; and

(c) the time when the product was supplied by its producer to another.

Section 3(2) also provides that a defect shall not be inferred from the mere fact that a safer product is put into circulation at a later date.

It will be recalled that the roughly parallel provision of American law, section 402A of the Restatement (Second) of Torts, refers to a 'defective condition unreasonably dangerous'. As we have seen, two tests have been adopted for the purposes of amplifying this definition, the consumer-expectation and risk–utility tests. The consumer-expectation test makes most sense when the defect takes the form of a defect in the manufacturing process: no reasonable or 'ordinary' consumer expects to find a snail in a bottle of ginger beer. Even here there are difficulties in terms of the different expectations which particular groups of consumers might have. How far should a manufacturer or distributor have to take into account the possibility of the product being used by a child or by a consumer who might suffer an allergic reaction? The sharpest criticism of the consumer-expectation test has come in the area of design defects. The test is said to be incoherent, since 'in many situations . . . the consumer would not know what to expect, because he would have no idea how safe the product could be made'.[557] The risk–utility test, by contrast, enables the court to engage in a balancing act, weighing the social utility of the product against the risk and seriousness of any injury that might occur from its use. More specifically, the test may be centred on the notion of the 'reasonably prudent manufacturer', enabling the court to take into account the manufacturer's capacity to eliminate the defect and his capacity to spread the risk through insurance or

---

[555] [1932] AC 562.   [556] [1971] 1 QB 88.

[557] Wade, 'On the Nature of Strict Tort Liability for Products' (1973) 44 *Miss. LJ* 825, cited by the Supreme Court of California in *Barker* v. *Lull Engineering Co.* (1978) 573 P. 2d 443, 454.

through price variations. Alternatively, it might take into account the role of the consumer by considering whether an alternative product was available, how far the consumer was aware of the danger in question, and how far he could have avoided it.[558] There is no uniform approach, as courts in different jurisdictions place different emphases on the various aspects of the test.

The Directive, and now the Act, do not unequivocally adopt one test or the other. The Act refers to the expectations which 'persons generally', not just consumers, are 'entitled' to have, not just those which they might happen to have. In this sense it is closer to risk–utility than to consumer-expectation. On the other hand, the manufacturer's expectations are not conclusive: the standard is therefore stricter than that implied by the foreseeability test used in the tort of negligence.

It is possible that the English courts will follow the American lead in setting a consumer-expectation standard for manufacturing defects and a broader risk–utility calculus for design defects. In judging whether a design innovation is defective for this purpose a court might take into account the utility of the drug[559] and weigh it against the harm arising from its use and the risk of this harm occurring.[560] Significantly, the Act directs attention to the packaging of a product and to the way it is presented and marketed. Expectations engendered by a product's promotion (for example, concerning the safety aspects of a vehicle design or of a new drug) will influence the standard to which the manufacturer is required to conform.

A question currently being addressed in the American courts is whether producers should bear liability for products which are inherently dangerous, for example, through over-consumption, but in respect of which full and adequate warnings have been given and no alternative is feasible. The Restatement (Second) of Torts acknowledges that 'many products cannot be made entirely safe for all consumption, and any food or drug necessarily involves some risk or harm, if only through over-consumption', but that 'good tobacco is not unreasonably dangerous merely because the effects of smoking may be harmful'.[561] This view has been challenged in litigation against cigarette companies by smokers who, while aware of the risks of smoking, nevertheless contracted diseases through long-term consumption of tobacco products; the matter has still to be clearly resolved.[562]

(ii) Special Duties: Duty to Warn and Post-Sale Duties   A duty to warn may arise as part of negligence. This may be limited by the circumstances of the original sale. This is the implication, at least, of *Hurley* v. *Dyke*[563] in which a car, sold at auction in a dangerously defective condition, was involved in an

---

[558]   See Birnbaum, 'Unmasking the Test for Design Defect', op. cit.; Whitehead and Scott (below, Select Bibliography).

[559] Was it designed to counter an otherwise intractable disease, such as AIDS or some forms of cancer, or to counter headaches, or was its purpose cosmetic?

[560] For instance, is there a risk of a serious physical kind, as in the Thalidomide affair?

[561] S. 402A, comment i.

[562] For a critical view of the Restatement position in this context, see *Dewey* v. *R. J. Reynolds Tobacco Co.* (1990) 577 A.2d 1239.

[563] [1979] RTR 265. See also *Kubach* v. *Hollands* [1937] 3 All ER 907.

accident in which a third-party passenger was injured. Because the car was sold 'as seen and with all its faults' the House of Lords held that the seller was not liable. The decision seems surprising in view of the possible danger to one who did not know the circumstances in which the car was sold. On the other hand, a manufacturer may come under a continuing duty to warn once the goods leave his hands, in particular if brand-naming or advertising concerning the product creates a misleading impression. This was the case in *E. Hobbs Farms Ltd. v. Baxenden Chemical Co. Ltd.*, where a manufacturer failed to correct a statement to the effect that insulation foam was 'self- extinguishing' after it became clear that this might not be the case. The customer succeeded in an action for negligent misrepresentation when the foam caught fire, causing extensive damage. According to Deputy Judge Ogden QC, 'a manufacturer who realises that omitting to warn past customers about something which might result in injury to them must take reasonable steps to attempt to warn them, however lacking in negligence he may have been when the goods were sold.[564] It should be borne in mind that the parties in this case had been in direct contractual privity, though.

The Consumer Protection Act's reference in section 3(2) to the promotion and packaging of the product impliedly creates a duty to warn consumers generally of possible dangers. A duty to warn is also implicit in the test of 'such safety as persons are entitled to expect'. This would certainly include a duty to warn about dangers that were either known to the manufacturer or reasonably foreseeable when the product was marketed; it could also include a duty to warn against foreseeable but unintended uses and misuses.[565] It is not clear, though, how far if at all this marks an improvement on the position in negligence.

Neither the Act nor the Directive spell out in any detail a post-sale duty to keep consumers informed about newly discovered defects in a product. It is possible that such an obligation could arise as part of the duty of care in negligence.[566] Section 3(2) of the Act requires the court to take into account the time when the product left the manufacturer's hands, that is to say, when he supplied it to another producer, not when it was supplied to the consumer. This is apparently designed to safeguard the manufacturer against liability brought about through wear and tear to the product. It could also be read as limiting the extent of any post-sale duty to warn where, for example, information concerning a defect comes to the manufacturers' attention some time after the product left the factory gate. Under these circumstances it is arguable that the manufacturer *should be* under a duty to issue a public warning about the product and, possibly, to pay the costs of withdrawing the product from the market and replacing those items sold to consumers. This is a developing area of liability in the United States.[567] It has only an implicit presence, at best, within article 3 of

---

[564] [1992] 1 Lloyd's Rep. 55, 65.

[565] Whitehead and Scott, op. cit. (Select Bibliography), 173.

[566] See *Rivtow Marine Ltd. v. Washington Iron Works* [1974] SCR 1189, where the Supreme Court of Canada discussed the liability of a crane manufacturer to inform the user of a possible danger arising after the sale.

[567] Discussed by Whitehead and Scott, op. cit. (Select Bibliography).

the Products Liability Directive. The more recent Product Safety Directive is more specific on this matter.[568] And Part II of the Consumer Protection Act 1987 is also important since it enables the Secretary of State to issue a duty to warn, requiring a manufacturer to issue a notice to warn consumers of a possible danger.[569] The Product Safety Directive will require the provisions of Part II of the 1987 Act to be extended, giving rise to the possibility of actions for breach of statutory duty being brought by consumers suffering loss or injury as a result of failure to comply with these provisions.

(iii) The Producer's Defences   Some of these are uncontroversial and closely follow the Directive. Thus, the producer will have a defence if he can show that the defect was attributable to compliance with a legal requirement;[570] that he did not at any point supply the product to another, as, for example, in a situation where it was put into circulation after being stolen from him;[571] that the defect did not exist when he parted with it;[572] and, in the case of a component supplier, that the defect was contained not in his component but in the final product and that it was the result either of the design of the final product or of compliance with instructions from the manufacturer of that product.[573]

Much more controversial is the so-called 'state of the art' or development-risks defence in section 4(1)(e). Inclusion of this was optional under the Directive.[574] Not only does the Act make provision for this defence, but it apparently widens its scope by providing that the producer will be exempted if he can show that 'the state of scientific and technical knowledge at the relevant time was not such that a producer of products of the same description as the product in question might be expected to have discovered the defect if it had existed in his products while they were under his control'. By contrast, the Directive provides a defence where 'the state of scientific and technical knowledge at the time when he put the product into circulation was not such as to enable the existence of the defect to be discovered'. The central difference is that the Act appears to set up as the relevant standard that of producers within the industry in question, whereas the Directive appears to envisage an external standard which could be set higher than that prevailing as a matter of practice within the industry at any given time. The Act can be read as injecting an element of subjectivity into the otherwise objective test laid down by the Directive. This may be defensible on the grounds that the court otherwise has no clear standard against which to judge the producer's liability.[575] The UK government took the view, during the passage of the Act, that the form of section 4(1)(e) was justified by the need to avoid restricting innovation in design. It could, however, be argued that where innovation has been chilled in America this is the result of high punitive damages awards and not strict liability as such. The German experience may well support this thesis.

In *Commission* v. *United Kingdom*,[576] the ECJ upheld section 4(1)(e) against a challenge mounted by the European Commission, and at the same time cast some light on the scope of the defence contained in Article 7(e) of the Directive.

[568] Art. 3(2).   [569] S. 13(1).   [570] S. 4(1)(a).   [571] S. 4(1)(b).   [572] S. 4(1)(d).
[573] S. 4(1)(f).   [574] Art. 15(1)(b).   [575] Newdick, op. cit., 310.
[576] Case C–300/95 [1997] All ER (EC) 391.

The Court took the view that section 4(1)(e) could not be read as establishing, as the relevant test, the subjective knowledge of the producer at the time the product was circulated. It was also confident that the UK courts would interpret section 4(1)(e) purposively, in line with both the wording and intent of the Directive. With regard to Article 7(e), the Court, following Advocate General Tesauro, held that the producer must be aware of the *most advanced* state of *accessible* scientific and technical knowledge in the relevant field at the point when the product was circulated. In many respects this is a stringent test. According to the Advocate General,

since [Article 7(e)] refers solely to the 'scientific and technical knowledge' at the time when the product was marketed, it is not concerned with the practices and safety standards in use in the industrial sector in which the producer is operating. In other words, it has no bearing on the exclusion of the manufacturer from liability that no one in that particular class of manufacturer takes the measures necessary to eliminate the defect or prevent it from arising if such measures are capable of being adopted on the basis of the available knowledge.[577]

The relevant knowledge is that of 'an expert in the sector', that is, the industry in question, but for this purpose knowledge may include even 'isolated opinions to the effect that [the product] is defective [even if] most academics do not take that view'. The justification for this extensive definition of scientific knowledge is that once the opinion has been put into circulation, even though it may not yet represent a scientific consensus, the risk of damage or injury is no longer unforeseeable.[578] The relevant knowledge must, on the other hand, be available in a language that is reasonably accessible and in a form that is subject to a reasonably high degree of circulation.[579]

The inclusion of a broad 'state of the art' defence aligns the apparently strict standard of the Act much more closely to that of negligence, albeit with the burden of proof reversed: the producer has the burden of showing that the defence is made out. An essential aspect of the strict liability standard in the United States is that it judges the product and not the producer. If this principle is observed, it is irrelevant that the producer did not know and could not have known about the defect at the time the product was put into circulation. Moreover, industry *practice* is less relevant than industry *capability*, or the potential for greater safety, in judging whether a 'state of the art' defence is made out.[580] Section 4(1)(e) puts this in doubt for English law. However, it should be borne in mind that the test of design defect in the tort of negligence might itself set a stringent standard for producers, requiring them to carry out research into the possible implications of design innovations. In *IBA* v. *EMI Electronics Ltd.*[581] the designer of a radio mast that collapsed in conditions of

[577] Advocate General's Opinion, at para. 20.
[578] Ibid., para. 22. For discussion, see Hodges, 'Development Risks: Unanswered Questions', op. cit., and the reply by Mildred and Howells, op. cit.
[579] Advocate General's Opinion, at para. 23.
[580] See the discussion of N. P. Terry, op. cit. Some recent US case law marks a retreat from the strict-liability standard in favour of a more explicit 'reasonably prudent manufacturer' test in the context of litigation over exposure to asbestos: *Feldman* v. *Lederle Laboratories* (1984) 479 A.2d 534.
[581] (1981) 14 *Building L. Rep.* 1.

high winds and ice was found liable for failing to investigate fully the possible effects of such conditions on the structure.

(D) CAUSATION AND REMOTENESS

The Act does not deal explicitly with the questions of causation and remoteness of damage and so it is likely that the English courts will apply the tests of but-for cause and 'legal cause' derived from general principles.[582] However, it is unclear how far principles that operate mainly in the context of negligence liability should be applied to a strict-liability tort. Section 2(1) states that a causal link between defect and damage must be established, impliedly putting the onus on the plaintiff. It seems unlikely that the courts would be willing to water down the requirement that the plaintiff has to establish but-for cause on the balance of probabilities under the tests recently reiterated by the House of Lords in *Wilsher* v. *Essex Area Health Authority*[583] and *Hotson* v. *East Berkshire Area Health Authority*.[584] However, given the policy of the Directive and of the Act there may be an argument for the use of principles of 'probabilistic cause', involving a partial reversal of the burden of proof,[585] if not the revolutionary 'market share' approach to apportioning liability.[586] In *Sindell* all those manufacturers who could have been responsible for producing a defective drug were held liable in proportion to their share of the relevant market at the time it was marketed. As far as remoteness is concerned, there is an argument for limiting the principle enunciated in *The Wagon Mound (No. 1)*,[587] namely that the defendant will not be liable if the damage was of a type of harm that was not reasonably foreseeable, to cases of negligence, since the idea that foreseeability should play a role in limiting the extent of the defendant's liability is out of place in a strict liability action. Alternatively, if the foreseeability test is to be applied there is a good case for ensuring that the relevant notion of 'type of damage' is broadly defined at least for cases of personal injury.[588]

Where damage is caused partly by a defective product and partly by the plaintiff's own fault the defence of contributory negligence will be available, by virtue of section 6(4) of the Act. Again, applying the defence of contributory negligence in a situation where the defendant may be liable without fault could be seen as contradictory.[589] As it is, where the defence applies the court will be able to make an apportionment of liability based not on relative blame but on the relative causal responsibility, for the damage in question, of plaintiff and defendant.

The Act's failure to clarify the way in which causation and contributory negligence will operate could pose a far more significant restriction, in practice, upon successful claims for compensation than even the inclusion of the 'state of the art' defence in section 4(1)(e).

---

[582] See above, Chapter 2, Section 4(1).   [583] [1988] AC 1074.   [584] [1989] AC 750.

[585] J. G. Fleming, 'Probabilistic Causation in Tort Law' (1989) 68 *Can. BR* 661; *Snell* v. *Farrell* (1990) 72 DLR (4th) 289; *Malec* v. *J. C. Hutton* (1990) 64 ALJR 316; see above, Chapter 2, Section 4(2)(a).

[586] Adopted in the California products-liability case of *Sindell* v. *Abbots Laboratories*, 607 P.2d 924 (1980).

[587] [1961] AC 388.   [588] S. Whittaker, op. cit. (Select Bibliography), 254.

[589] Ibid., 251–3.

(E) The Categories of Recoverable 'Damage'

Injury to the person and damage to the property of the consumer are recoverable both for breach of warranty under the Sale of Goods Act and under the common law of negligence. An example of a case in which the two actions were combined was *Grant* v. *Australian Knitting Mills*.[590] There, the plaintiff, who contracted dermatitis from a suit of underwear that had been contaminated in the process of manufacture, successfully sued both the manufacturer in the tort of negligence and the retailer for breach of contract.

The Consumer Protection Act defines damage in section 5(1) as 'death or personal injury or any loss of or damage to any property (including land)'. On normal principles, liability for personal injury includes liability for direct economic consequences, including loss of earnings. The Act limits the relevant scope of property damage to non-business property, that is to say property both ordinarily intended for private use, occupation, or consumption and actually used for these ends by the person suffering the loss or damage.[591] The effect is to allow recovery of the financial cost of replacing damaged property but to rule out claims for consequential losses such as lost profits. Small property claims are also excluded by section 5(4) which requires the plaintiff to have suffered property damage (excluding interest) amounting to more than £275.

The greatest uncertainty concerns recovery for 'pure' economic loss, that is to say economic losses that do not flow directly out of either personal injury to the consumer or damage to his property. For breach of warranty it is axiomatic that consequential economic losses of this kind *are* recoverable, subject to the normal rules of remoteness of damage in contract.[592] In negligence the scope for recovery of pure economic loss has been greatly reduced by the decision of the House of Lords in *Murphy* v. *Brentwood District Council*.[593] Although this case concerned defective property, the broad principles laid down by the House of Lords are entirely applicable to the question of defective products. The distinction drawn by the House of Lords between property which is in a dangerous state and that which is merely defective has been criticised as 'impossible', in particular in cases where the economic loss consists of steps taken to avoid a potential danger to life and limb.[594] The reader is referred to Chapter 2 above for a more detailed account of the issues arising out of *Murphy*. The only area in which pure economic loss is now clearly recoverable in negligence concerns liability for negligent misstatement under *Hedley Byrne & Co. Ltd.* v. *Heller & Partners*.[595] This could well be relevant in cases of product liability, where loss may be incurred as a result of misleading labels on articles or, more speculatively, through misleading advertising and promotion. The difficulty will lie in establishing the necessary proximity between the parties for a 'special relationship' to be established. Recent decisions are not encouraging in this regard.[596]

[590] [1936] AC 86.   [591] S. 5(3).

[592] *Hadley* v. *Baxendale* (1854) 9 Exch. 341: see Treitel, *Law of Contract* (9th edn., 1995), 870.

[593] [1991] 1 AC 398.   [594] Sir Robin Cooke, 'An Impossible Distinction?' (1991) 107 *LQR* 46.

[595] [1964] AC 465.   [596] In particular *Caparo Industries plc* v. *Dickman* [1990] 2 AC 605.

The Consumer Protection Act provides that damage to the 'product itself' as a result of the defect is not property damage within the meaning of the Act, so ruling out a claim in pure economic loss for a merely defective product.[597] The meaning of the 'product itself' here may give rise to the kind of difficulties encountered over the meaning of 'complex structure' prior to *Murphy* v. *Brentwood DC*, when the House of Lords did its utmost to restrict the use of the idea in that context.[598] The Act refers to there being no liability for 'the loss of or any damage to the product itself or for the loss of or any damage to the whole or any part of any product which has been supplied with the product in question comprised in it'. Is a car tyre, manufactured by a component supplier, 'comprised in' a motor vehicle so that if it bursts, causing the car to crash, the only damage is to the 'product itself'? If the car is not the 'product itself' but 'other property', recovery would seem possible. Are a defectively manufactured cork, supplied by a third party, and the wine in the bottle which is damaged by the cork's defectiveness part of the same property?[599] Given the House of Lords' scepticism as to the value of drawing fine distinctions between different components of a complex structure, it seems highly likely that the different parts will be seen as the same whole for this purpose, denying the consumer recovery for damage to the product as a whole.

Section 5(3) of the Consumer Protection Act requires there to be damage to property that the person suffering the loss intends for his own private use. It does not expressly require the person suffering the loss to have a proprietary or possessory right over the property at the moment it is damaged as the common law of negligence does. The categories of recoverable economic loss may therefore be broader under the Act than in cases arising under the common law such as *The Aliakmon*,[600] where the property was damaged before the plaintiff acquired (or resumed) ownership of the goods. In practice, however, the most significant limitation on the recoverability of pure economic losses is the exclusion of business property from the scope of the Act. While some economic-loss cases involve consumer interests, with *Murphy*[601] and its predecessors being the most obvious examples, the greater number tend to arise out of business losses of various kinds.

Damages for distress or unhappiness are rarely available for breach of warranty in the context of a sale-of-goods contract as opposed to a contract the purpose of which is to avoid distress or to provide some form of contentment.[602] In negligence the grounds of recovery for 'nervous shock' are limited in comparison with the general admission of recovery for physical harm.[603] Nervous shock is not mentioned as such in the Act, but the definition of personal injury in section 45 extends to 'any disease and any other impairment of a person's physical or mental condition'. The latter part of the definition would appear to correspond to nervous shock as it is currently defined by the courts for the

---

[597] S. 5(2). [598] See above, Chapter 2, Section 2(2)(b)(ii).

[599] See *M/S Aswan Engineering Establishment Co. Ltd.* v. *Lupdine Ltd.* [1987] 1 WLR 1, 23 (Lloyd LJ).

[600] [1986] AC 785. [601] [1991] 1 AC 398.

[602] See e.g. the recent case of *Hayes* v. *Dodd* [1990] 2 All ER 815, for the general approach in contract.

[603] See above, Chapter 2, Section 2(2)(c).

purposes of negligence, in the sense of a particular psychological condition.[604] Where the consumer suffers shock of this kind as a consequence of his own injury or as a result of damage to his property[605] then, by analogy with negligence, there should be recovery. Where a third party suffers shock as a consequence of witnessing an injury to another caused by a defective product, the matter is more difficult. In negligence the circumstances under which the third party can recover are strictly limited; there must normally be a close family or personal tie between the plaintiff and the injury victim, and the plaintiff must witness the accident or come on the scene shortly afterwards.[606] The Act makes no mention of these restrictions and it is entirely plausible to read it as imposing a general responsibility for psychological harm to a third party, as long as a causal link between such harm and the defect is established.[607]

Where a defective product causes death, the dependants of the deceased may bring an action for damages based on their economic dependency by virtue of section 6(1)(a) of the 1987 Act. This deems the death to have been caused by a 'wrongful act, neglect or default' for the purposes of section 1 of the Fatal Accidents Act 1976.[608] By extension it also becomes possible for an action of bereavement to be brought under section 1A of the 1976 Act. Again, a plaintiff born after receiving injuries while in the womb as a consequence of a defective product may bring an action under the Congenital Disabilities (Civil Liability) Act 1976, by virtue of section 6(3) of the 1987 Act.

(F) EXCLUSION AND LIMITATION OF LIABILITY

The availability of an exclusion clause in actions based on contract and tort is limited by the Unfair Contract Terms Act 1977, which is considered in more detail in Chapter 8 below.[609] A contract term excluding business liability for death or personal injury caused by negligence is void; a term covering property damage or economic loss must be 'reasonable'.[610] The Act is particularly protective of consumers in circumstances where they contract with business entities. A 'consumer' under the Act is one who does not contract in a business capacity or who does not hold himself out as doing so, where the other party is one who does contract in a course of a business.[611] Under section 3 exclusion and limitation clauses in business–consumer contracts must pass a test of reasonableness; this also applies between business entities where the contract is on written standard terms of the person protected by the clause. With specific regard to product liability, section 6 of the Act prevents a business entity excluding or limiting its liability to a consumer in regard to the implied terms of compliance with contract description, fitness for intended purpose, and merchantability under sections 13–15 of the Sale of Goods Act 1979 and to the cor-

---

[604] See *McLoughlin* v. *O'Brian* [1983] AC 410.   [605] *Attia* v. *British Gas Corp.* [1988] QB 304.

[606] *Alcock* v. *Chief Constable of South Yorkshire* [1993] 1 AC 310; see above, Chapter 2, Section 2(2)(c)(i).

[607] See the discussion of Whittaker, op. cit. (Select Bibliography), 273–4, suggesting that a requirement of proximity analogous to that prevailing under the common law of negligence should be adopted in the Act, a suggestion which was not taken up.

[608] See also Consumer Protection Act s. 6(2), dealing with the supplier's liability in the event of death.

[609] See Section 1(4).   [610] S. 2.   [611] S. 12.

responding terms implied into a hire-purchase contract.[612] Where two businesses contract with each other, any exclusion or limitation of these terms is subjected to a test of 'reasonableness'.[613]

The Consumer Protection Act, which as we have seen is concerned only with the liability of business entities to consumers, contains a clear policy of prohibiting exclusions or limitations: liability under the Act cannot be excluded or limited by any contract term, notice, or any other provision.[614]

The defence of *volenti non fit injuria*, or the plaintiff's voluntary assumption of risk, are only rarely available in claims based on the tort of negligence. This is because it is necessary to show not simply that the plaintiff was aware of a particular danger but that he consented to the defendant being careless in the sense of acting in breach of a duty of care.[615] The modern tendency has been for the courts to use contributory negligence to apportion responsibility between the parties rather than invoke the defence of *volenti*, which excludes the plaintiff's claim completely. It is likely that a similar approach would be taken under Part I of the Consumer Protection Act. It should be noted, however, that the plaintiff's conduct might be taken into account at the earlier stage of analysis when assessing whether the product is defective. For under section 3(2)(b), the court must consider 'what might reasonably be expected to be done with or in relation to the product'. If, therefore, the consumer uses a product that he knows to be dangerous, perhaps having received a warning to that effect from the producer, the product might no longer be regarded as defective for the purposes of the Act.[616]

(G) LIMITATION OF ACTIONS

The general principles of limitation of actions apply,[617] with two exceptions as far as the Consumer Protection Act is concerned.[618] In the first place, the limitation period for claims of damage to property under the Act is three years (the same as for personal injury) as opposed to the normal six-year period. Secondly, actions under the Act are subject to a special 'long-stop' of ten years (as opposed to the normal fifteen) from the time the producer in question supplies the goods to another. This long-stop is an absolute bar to liability. The additional restrictiveness of the limitation rules under the Act is another reason for supposing that negligence may continue to play a role in this area.

(H) CHOICE OF LAW

The complex rules concerning the applicable law for a particular tort or contract action are likely to be of great importance in practice. Actions under the Consumer Protection Act are classified as tort actions for this purpose.[619] The search by plaintiffs for the most advantageous jurisdiction is regulated within the European Community by the 1968 Brussels Convention on Jurisdiction and

---

[612] By ss. 9, 10, and 11 of the Supply of Goods (Implied Terms) Act 1973.
[613] For this purpose 'reasonableness' has the special meaning ascribed to it by Sch. 2 of the Act.
[614] S. 7.   [615] *Dann* v. *Hamilton* [1939] 1 KB 509.
[616] See, in the context of a discussion of Directive 85/374, Whittaker, op. cit. (Select Bibliography), 261.
[617] See Chapter 8 below, Section 1(9).
[618] See Limitation Act 1980 s. 11A, inserted by the Consumer Protection Act 1987.   [619] S. 6(7).

the Enforcement of Judgments, which was incorporated into English law by the Civil Jurisdiction and Judgments Act 1982 with effect from 1987.[620] An account of the effect of these Conventions, and of choice of law rules within the Member States of the European Community, lies outside the scope of this book.[621]

Conclusion

It may be useful to summarise the main points of this presentation of product liability law. We have seen how liability evolved from an initial position in which the law of negligence played a minor role in compensating victims of dangerously defective products, thanks largely to the 'privity of contract fallacy'. *Donoghue* v. *Stevenson*[622] put an end to this and ushered in the modern, all-embracing duty of care as far as physical injury and property damage are concerned. The major weakness of *Donoghue* v. *Stevenson* was that far from doing away with the need to show fault on the part of the producer, the judgments of the majority in that case (most notably Lord Macmillan) confirmed it by excluding the use of *res ipsa loquitur* to assist the plaintiff. While American courts developed a number of dynamic solutions to deal with this problem,[623] the English common law continued to be shaped by the traditional conceptual categories of civil liability, and in particular by a rigid demarcation between tort and contract.

With the adoption of Directive 85/374/EEC and its subsequent implementation in the form of the Consumer Protection Act 1987, a form of strict or 'stricter' liability based on the American model was incorporated into English law. In numerous respects the standard laid down by the Consumer Protection Act is closer to fault-based liability than might appear at first sight. The notion of 'defect' in section 3(1) and the wide defences made available to producers in section 4 make it clear that the producer is very far from being made an automatic insurer for losses caused by products put into circulation. Other restrictions on liability, such as the short limitation period and the confinement of recoverable damage to physical injury and non-business property losses, mean that the common law of contract and tort will continue to play a distinct and important role in this area. The introduction of the Act has not produced a conceptual synthesis.

Wider questions concerning the value and efficacy of product liability law are currently being posed. In the United States a reaction has set in against the expansion of civil liability which began in the late 1950s and continued for the next twenty-five years or so. Many of the features of American law which have given cause for concern, such as stratospheric levels of punitive

---

[620] And, to a lesser degree as far as products liability is concerned, by the Rome Convention on the Law Applicable to Contractual Obligations, which takes effect in English law by virtue of the Contracts (Applicable Law) Act 1990.

[621] For an account of this area see R. Atree, 'Jurisdiction, Enforcement of Judgments and Conflicts of Laws', ch. 17 in P. Kelly and R. Atree, op. cit. (Select Bibliography).

[622] [1932] AC 562.

[623] Ranging from the use of misrepresentation law and the notion of a transmissible warranty to the solution of strict liability in tort (adopted by 402A of the Second Restatement of Torts).

damages awarded against producers, would not apply to the forms of strict liability now found in the United Kingdom and other European countries. However, more general doubts about strict liability have led many American courts to curtail the use of the consumer expectation test in favour of the more open-ended risk–utility approach, in particular with regard to cases of defects in design, in what may be seen as at least a partial 'return to negligence'. The factors that have prompted this move include the concern that manufacturers are finding it increasingly difficult to obtain adequate third-party insurance cover and the fear that excessive liability is inhibiting innovation. Nor is it clear that the move to strict liability has led to any increase in the safety of products.[624] There is a perception that the best interests of both producers and consumers may not be served by a system which is so heavily reliant on civil litigation, and that it is necessary to find a more appropriate balance between civil liability and regulatory controls. It will be interesting to see how far these new tendencies towards judicial self-restraint will affect the approach of the English courts to the task of interpreting the Consumer Protection Act in coming years.

Select Bibliography

Symposium on Product Liability Law (1991) 20 (2) *Anglo-Am. LR.*

ALBANESE, F. and DEL DUCA, L., 'Developments in European Product Liability' (1987) 5 *Dickinson J. Int. Law* 193.

BORRIE, G., 'Product Liability in the EEC' (1987) 9 *Dublin University LJ* 82.

CALABRESI, G. and HIRSCHOFF, J., 'Towards a Test for Strict Liability in Torts' (1972) *Yale LJ* 1054.

GRIFFITHS, Lord, DE VAL, P. and DORMER, R. J., 'Developments in English Product Liability Law: A Comparison with the American System' (1988) 62 *Tulane LR* 353.

HOWELLS, G., *Comparative Product Liability* (1993).

HUBER, P., *Liability: the Legal Revolution and its Consequences* (1988).

KELLY, P. and ATREE, R. (eds.), *European Product Liability Law* (1992).

NEWDICK, C., 'The Future of Negligence in Product Liability' (1987) 103 *LQR* 288.

PRIEST, G., 'The Invention of Enterprise Liability: A Critical History of the Intellectual Foundations of Modern Tort Law' (1985) 143 *Jo. LS* 461.

PROSSER, W., 'The Assault upon the Citadel (Strict Liability to the Consumer)' (1960) 69 *Yale LJ* 1099.

—— 'The Fall of the Citadel (Strict Liability to the Consumer)' (1966) 50 *Minn. LR* 791.

SMITH, D., 'The European Community Directive on Product Liability: A Comparative Study of its Implementation in the UK, France and West Germany' [1992] *LIEI* 101.

STAPLETON, J., 'Products Liability Reform—Real or Illusory?' (1986) 6 *OJLS* 392.

—— 'Three Problems with the New Product Liability', in P. Cane and J. Stapleton (eds.), *Essays for Patrick Atiyah* (1991).

——'Product Liability (1994)

WADDAMS, S. J., 'The Strict Liability of Suppliers of Goods' (1974) 37 *MLR* 154.

---

[624] See Dewees, Duff and Trebilcock, *Exploring the Domain of Accident Law*, op. cit., ch. 4, for a review of the empirical evidence relating to the impact of product liability law.

WHITEHEAD, G. and SCOTT, G., 'A Comparison of Product Liability Law in the United States and the European Community' (1991) 2 *Eur. Bus. LR* 171.

WHITTAKER, S., 'The EEC Directive on Product Liability' (1985) 5 *Yearbook of European Law* 233.

7

Protection of Reputation and Privacy

1. DEFAMATION

1. Introduction

(A) THE MEANING OF 'DEFAMATORY'

No exhaustive definition of 'defamatory' emerges from the cases. This should come as no surprise for, as Lord Reid once said, it is not for the judges to 'frame definitions or to lay down hard and fast rules. It is their function to enunciate principles and much that they say is intended to be illustrative or explanatory and not to be definitive.'[1] One can nevertheless achieve a working description by combining two statements, namely: a defamatory statement is one which injures the reputation of another by exposing him to hatred, contempt, or ridicule, or which tends to lower him in the esteem of *right-thinking* members of society.[2]

In defamation the defendant need not have ascertained beforehand the likely effect of his words as long as his speech or writing was voluntary. What is relevant is that the words were understood by others in a defamatory sense. As Russell LJ put it: 'Liability for libel does not depend on the intention of the defamer; but on the fact of defamation.'[3] Courts treat the meaning of the words as a matter of construction rather than evidence, to be interpreted objectively in their context, with reference to the opinion of right-thinking members of society. Such a test is vague and unsatisfactory. In *Rubber Improvements Ltd.* v. *Daily Telegraph Ltd.*[4] Lord Devlin said that the test was the effect on the 'ordinary' and not the 'logical' man.[5] It has been decided, for instance, that a person alleged to be insane,[6] or a woman alleged to have been raped,[7] has been defamed, probably because such accusations lead them to being 'shunned and

---

[1] *Cassell & Co. Ltd.* v. *Broome* [1972] AC 1027, 1085. The Faulks Committee recommended the following definition: 'Defamation shall consist of the publication to a third party of matter which in all circumstances would be likely to affect a person adversely in the estimation of reasonable people generally.' This may well avoid some difficulties, but might give rise to others, so on balance it may be better to avoid any statutory definition.

[2] *Parmiter* v. *Coupland and Another* (1840), 6 M. & W. 105, 108; 151 ER 340, 342 (per Parke B), and *Sim* v. *Stretch* [1936] 2 All ER 1237, 1240 (per Lord Atkin). Italics supplied.

[3] *Cassidy* v. *Daily Mirror Newspapers Ltd.* [1929] 2 KB 331, 354.

[4] [1964] AC 234, 285 (henceforth referred to as *Lewis* v. *Daily Telegraph*).

[5] In *Hartt* v. *Newspaper Publishing plc* (*The Independent*, 27 Oct. 1989; CLY 1989, 2246) the court took the view that the yardstick should be the 'hypothetical reader who is not unduly suspicious, but who can read between the lines. He might think loosely, but is not avid for scandal, and will not select one bad meaning where other non-defamatory meanings are available.' See, also, *Skuse* v. *Granada Television* [1996] EMLR 278.

[6] *Morgan* v. *Lingen* (1863) 8 LT 800.

[7] *Youssoupoff* v. *Metro-Goldwyn-Mayer Pictures, Ltd.* (1934) 50 TLR 581.

avoided'. This sounds more like the reaction of a (very) 'ordinary' and not 'logical' person. But if 'ordinary' persons still think in this way, can they be described as 'right-thinking' members of society?

Various attempts have been made to explain what this last term means. Professor Street equates it with a 'substantial and respectable proportion of society'.[8] From a moral point of view the test is neither faultless nor convincing; but at least it is pragmatic, for the law largely depends on what the majority of people actually think, rather than on what they should think. In a modern pluralistic society, however, the designation of one or more sections as 'right-thinking' results in difficulties. For example, I call a workman a 'blackleg', a statement which would lower him in the eyes of his striking colleagues, but might raise him in the esteem of other members of the public who are inconvenienced by the strike. Is the test of defamation what right-thinking persons belonging to the class to which the statement is published think? Or right-thinking persons *generally*? The view, which has prevailed for some time now, is the latter one.[9] Two older cases bring this point clearly.

In *Byrne* v. *Deane*[10] automatic gambling machines, unlawfully kept by the defendants on their club premises, were removed by the police after someone informed them of their illegal presence. The following day someone put on the notice-boards of the club a typewritten paper containing a verse which ended with the lines: 'But he who gave the game away may he burn in hell and rue the day'—burn being originally spelt 'byrnn'. The issue was whether the plaintiff (named Byrne) was correct in alleging that the verse was defamatory of him in so far as it implied that he had been disloyal to the club. The Court of Appeal decided that 'to allege of a man . . . that he has reported certain acts, wrongful in law, to the police, cannot possibly be said to be "defamatory", because a "good and worthy subject of the King" would not regard such an allegation to be defamatory.'

In *R* v. *Bishop*[11] the appellant appealed against a criminal conviction for burglary on the ground that the jury were wrongly allowed to hear evidence in cross-examination of his previous convictions. Charged with burglary by stealing from X, the appellant sought to explain the presence of his fingerprints in X's premises by saying that he had entered on X's invitation for homosexual purposes. The prosecution applied for leave to ask the appellant questions relating to his previous convictions, relying on proviso (f)(ii) of section 1 of the Criminal Evidence Act 1898, which states: 'A person charged or called as a witness . . . shall not be asked . . . any question tending to show that he had committed or been convicted of . . . any offence other than wherewith he is then

---

[8] *Torts* (7th edn.), 304. Cf. the views of Mr Justice Holmes in the American case of *Peck* v. *Tribune*, 214 US 185 (1909), where reference was made to the reactions of '. . . a *considerable* and *respectable* class in [the plaintiff's] community' to test whether the plaintiff had been defamed. Interestingly enough, though the italicised words used by Holmes can be subjected to the same criticisms of Street's choice of words, they were inserted by the great American judge as a means of ensuring the opposite result namely, that 'liability [was not treated as] a question of majority vote.'

[9] Thus, see, *Tolley* v. *Fry* [1930] 1 KB 467 at 479 (per Greer LJ) and, more recently, *Gillick* v. *BBC* [1996] EMLR 267.

[10] [1937] 1 KB 818, esp. Slesser LJ at 833.   [11] [1975] QB 274.

charged . . . unless . . . (ii) . . . the nature of conduct of the defence is such as to involve imputations on the character of the prosecutor or the witnesses for the prosecution.' The request was granted and the appellant's previous convictions were revealed in cross-examination. On appeal, it was argued on his behalf that the jury was wrongly allowed to hear this evidence. For, after the enactment of section 1 of the Sexual Offences Act 1967, it is no longer an offence to commit a homosexual act in private with another consenting man over twenty-one. In the light of this, it was not an imputation on X's character to say that he was homosexual. Stephenson LJ, disagreeing with this argument, said that an allegation of conduct which is not illegal may still be an allegation of immorality:[12]

If Mr. Price were to sue the appellant in respect of his allegation if repeated outside a court of law, we venture to think that a submission that the words were incapable of a defamatory meaning would be bound to fail and a jury would generally be likely to find them defamatory . . . If this is still true, we are not behind the times in holding that Mr. Price's character was clearly impugned by the allegation of homosexual conduct made against him by the defendant.

It is submitted that the majority of the population would probably still consider an allegation of homosexuality as being defamatory. However, it is also clear that an (arguably) growing minority of citizens might not share such a view. Who in such a case are the 'right-thinking' members of society? If the view of the minority is preferred, is there not a danger here for the majority? Certainly in cases like *Byrne*, where *illegal* acts are involved, the attitudes of the average, law-abiding citizen should provide the proper yardstick for comparison.

But would the average, reasonable person treat a statement that he was 'hideously ugly' as defamatory? The actor and director Stephen Berkoff did; and was (unusually one is tempted to suggest) willing to chance litigation. A majority of the Court of Appeal was of the view that the words were capable of being defamatory and thought the matter should be left for a jury to decide.[13] Such a deferential attitude to the rights of juries seems unconvincing. This is partly because courts have, on other occasions involving more serious statements, taken a different view of their rights[14] but, mainly, because the judgment seems to place excessive limitations upon the desired ability to describe people or even to poke fun at them in every day life. It is submitted, therefore, that decisions such as *Berkoff* must be treated with suspicion. This is because of (*a*) the current and understandable wish (manifested mainly in the area of damage awards) to diminish the role of juries[15] and, (*b*), the tendency of our courts to

---

[12] Ibid., at 281.

[13] *Berkoff* v. *Burchill* [1996] 4 All ER 1008 (with a lengthy consideration of the various meanings of defamatory by Lord Justice Neill at 1011–17).

[14] Cf. *Shanson* v. *Howard* [1997] 4 CL 237; *Awa* v. *Independent News Auckland* [1995] 3 NZLR 701.

[15] Jury involvement in defamation cases is also likely to decrease as a result of the new "offer of amends" defence (ss. 4–6) and (possibly) the new summary procedure (ss. 8–10) introduced by the Defamation Act 1996. On the other hand, the new Act refused to adopt a frontal attack on the jury system that is still seen in this country (and the USA) as an important constitutional guarantee. Thus, see *Hansard*, HL Deb. 8 Mar., 1996, 592–5, 597–8. See, also, *Kirby-Harris* v. *Baxter* [1995] EMLR 516.

ascribe, especially under the growing influence of the European Convention of Human Rights, greater importance to free speech.

(B) LIBEL AND SLANDER

Defamation consists of libel and slander. The first is usually written, the second is oral. The distinction, unknown to Roman law, Scots law and the modern civilian systems, has a historical origin. Libel evolved out of statements considered in Tudor times to be prejudicial to the State. For this reason, they were criminally punished by the Court of Star Chamber. This, being a prerogative court, gave preference to the interests of the State. Governmental suspicion of the Press required that injurious publications should be suppressed at all costs.[16] On the other hand, the remedy for spoken words had been evolving in the common-law courts from an earlier time and represented a development from the older ecclesiastical jurisdiction. Indeed, the main peculiarity of slander—that it is actionable only upon proof of special damage (pecuniary loss)—provided the temporal justification for the common-law courts in taking over from the ecclesiastical courts. After the abolition of Star Chamber, libel was handed over to the common-law courts. The distinction between these two forms of defamatory statements remained too deeply ingrained to be discarded easily,[17] and, irrational though it is, we must begin by explaining them.

The main distinction is that libel consists of a defamatory statement or representation in 'permanent form', which, according to Professor Street,[18] must also be visible. Anything temporary and audible only is slander. Statements in books, articles, newspapers, letters are libels; and in *Monson* v. *Tussauds, Ltd.*[19] the making and placing of a waxwork of the plaintiff (a person prosecuted but not convicted for a criminal offence) near the 'Chamber of Horrors' was held to be a libel. Spoken words by themselves constitute slander. What if they are taped or included in a film reel? In *Youssoupoff* v. *Metro-Goldwyn-Mayer Pictures, Ltd.*[20] a Russian princess sued a film company, alleging that a film about Rasputin published pictures and words suggesting that he had seduced her. The company was held liable. However, it is doubtful whether the case conclusively decided whether permanency is the sole test of libel or whether the defamatory matter must be visible as well. Slesser J suggested that it is both:[21]

There can be no doubt that, so far as the photographic part of an exhibition is concerned, that is a permanent matter to be seen by the eye, and is the proper subject of an action for libel, if defamatory. I regard the speech which is synchronised with the photographic reproduction and forms part of one complex, common exhibition as an ancillary circumstance, part of the surroundings explaining that which is to be seen.

If this is so, then a defamatory anecdote in a film, heard but not accompanied by visible presentation, would be slander and not libel, although it is in permanent form; and the same would apply to a gramophone record.

---

[16] Suspicion is still reflected in criminal prosecutions for libel where truth is no defence.

[17] The Faulks Committee, unlike its predecessor (the Porter Committee), recommended the abolition of the distinction in civil proceedings: Cmnd. 5909, para. 91.

[18] *Torts*, 280.   [19] [1894] 1 QB 671.   [20] (1934), 50 TLR 581.

[21] Ibid., at 587. See also Street, *Torts*, 280–1.

Written and spoken words are clear illustrations of the distinction between libel and slander, but there are other examples. Broadcasting, radio, television, and theatrical performances used to pose nice problems, but they are now statutorily treated as publication in permanent form by section 1 of the Defamation Act 1952. Section 16(1) goes on to provide that 'words shall be construed as including a reference to pictures, visual images, gestures and other methods of signifying meaning'. Section 28 of the Cable and Broadcasting Act 1984 extends the same rule to cable programme services. Finally, in like vein, section 4(1) of the Theatres Act 1968 states that 'the publication of words in the course of a performance of a play shall . . . be treated as publication in permanent form'.

What of 'sky-writing' by an aeroplane, or dictating a telegram over the telephone? Perhaps the dictation is slander, while the reproduction in telegram form is libel for which the person dictating would be liable as he authorises its publication. The Faulks Committee suggested that sky-writing would be libel because the vapour takes some time to disperse.[22] Another possible argument in favour of this view might be the fact that sky-writing, in common with theatre or radio performances, can reach a very wide public. If this were to be considered as a decisive criterion then a plausible case could be made that this is a case of libel. Similar uncertainty apparently also surrounds records and taped recordings. The fact that their contents are in 'permanent' form would suggest that they should be treated (if defamatory) as libels even though they are not 'communicated' until they are played. On the whole, however, such distinctions do little credit to the law and civilian systems are no worse off for ignoring them.

Other differences between libel and slander are:

(i) Libel is both a tort and a crime, and the older limitation that it was criminal only where there was a danger of a breach of the peace appears to have been abandoned since the 1930s.[23] Slander is only a tort, though spoken words may, of course, constitute other crimes, for example sedition, blasphemy, criminal conspiracy.

(ii) Libel is actionable *per se*, whereas slander requires proof of special damage. Special damage here means material loss capable of estimation in money. Loss of marriage prospect, however,[24] and of consortium,[25] have been held to be 'special' damage. In four exceptional cases, which can again be explained by reference to history, slander is actionable *per se*. This is because they are 'either so obviously damaging to the financial position of the

---

[22] *Gulf Oil (GB) Ltd.* v. *Page* [1987] Ch. 327 came close to the imaginary example since it involved an aerial display of a sign defamatory of the plaintiffs. The libel/slander dichotomy was not considered as the legal dispute focused on the ability to obtain an interim injunction where there was a strong prima-facie case that the display of the material was part of a conspiracy to injure the plaintiff without just cause. The Court of Appeal granted an injunction, contrary, it would seem, to the long-standing practice not to grant interim injunctions in defamation cases.

[23] *R* v. *Wicks* [1936] 1 All ER 384, followed by *Goldsmith* v. *Pressdram Ltd.* [1977] QB 83. On this and related matters see Spencer in [1979] *CLJ* 60, 67 ff., and in *Reshaping the Criminal Law—Essays in Honour of G. L. Williams* (1978), 266 ff.

[24] *Speight* v. *Gosnay* (1891) 60 LJQB 231.   [25] *Lynch* v. *Knight* (1861), 9 HLC 577; 11 ER 854.

victim that pecuniary loss is almost certain; or so intrinsically outrageous that they ought to be actionable even if no pecuniary loss results'.[26]

The four cases are:

(*a*) Imputation of a criminal offence punishable with imprisonment in the first instance—the true basis of action being that allegations of such types of misconduct are likely to cause the person defamed to be shunned and excluded from society.[27]

(*b*) Imputation of un-chastity or adultery to a woman or girl. This was not actionable *per se* at common law, since immoral conduct used to come under the spiritual courts and the common-law courts insisted on proof of 'temporal loss'. Section 1 of the Slander of Women Act 1891, however, dispensed with this need for special damage. The Act does not go all the way, since imputation of immorality, provided that it falls short of the carnal knowledge, is without a remedy.[28]

(*c*) Imputation of certain diseases, which are exceedingly ill-defined. (Venereal diseases and leprosy are included but not smallpox. There is no clear authority of what the position is concerning 'new' diseases such as AIDS even though such allegations may have drastic consequences in, for example, the area of employment law. This heading of slander is so antiquated that it is better to avoid extending it. If, on the other hand, new forms of diseases such as AIDS do—for better or for worse—lead the average person to shun and avoid sufferers, then a case could be made for extending this heading to include them and thus 'deter' those persons who make such allegations.)

(*d*) Imputation 'calculated to disparage the plaintiff in any office, profession, calling, trade or business', so long as the calling or profession is lawful, no matter how humble. In *Foulger* v. *Newcomb*[29] it was held that a gamekeeper whose job it was to preserve foxes in a certain area could succeed against the defendant, who accused him of poisoning foxes. A qualification at common law was that it was not sufficient to show that the statement was likely to harm the plaintiff in his occupation; it had to be directed against him 'in the way of his calling'. Thus, an accusation that a schoolmaster had committed adultery on the school premises was held not to be actionable *per se*,[30] though an imputation of impropriety with a pupil might be.[31] After section 2 of the Defamation Act it now suffices that the words are likely to injure the plaintiff in his calling.

2. Elements of Liability

(A) The Allegation Must be Defamatory

Something has already been said about the meaning of 'defamatory'.[32] It should now be added that spoken words which are merely abusive, understood

---

[26] Per Asquith LJ in *Kerr* v. *Kennedy* [1942] 1 KB 409, 411.

[27] *Gray* v. *Jones* [1939] 1 All ER 798: 'You are a convicted person. I will not have you here. You have a conviction.'

[28] The main difficulty is defining 'un-chastity'. *Kerr* v. *Kennedy* [1942] 1 KB 409, 412, said that it includes lesbianism.

[29] (1867) LR 2 Ex. 327.   [30] *Jones* v. *Jones* [1916] 2 AC 481.

[31] *Thompson* v. *Bridges* (Ky. 1925) 273 SW 529, cf. *Hopwood* v. *Muirson* [1945] KB 313.

[32] Above, Section 1(a).

as vituperation, or uttered in a fit of temper, are not defamatory.[33] The reason is that abuse is only meant to give vent to one's own feelings rather than to injure the plaintiff. Also, abuse may damage the plaintiff's self-esteem. This is not the concern of defamation, which protects the esteem in which others hold him. The manner in which the words are spoken and the surrounding circumstances are crucial, and a speaker takes the risk that his audience may construe his words as defamatory. On the other hand, it is doubtful whether written words can ever be dismissed as mere abuse.

In most cases it is easy to decide whether words are defamatory. A straightforward allegation of dishonesty or immorality or other dishonourable behaviour raises few problems.[34] But other allegations might also affect the plaintiff's reputation in a prejudicial manner. As Lord Pearson put it:[35] 'words may be defamatory of a trader or businessman or professional man, though they do not impute any moral fault or defect of personal character. They can be defamatory of him if they impute lack of qualification, knowledge, skill, capacity, judgment or efficiency in the conduct of his trade or business or professional activity.'

Often the words used by the defendants may be innocuous in themselves but the general picture they paint of the plaintiff may damage his reputation. In *Liberace* v. *Daily Mirror Newspapers*[36] a journalist described Liberace, a well-known entertainer, as: 'the summit of sex—the pinnacle of masculine, feminine, and neuter. Everything that he, she or it can ever want to be . . . a deadly, winking, sniggering, snuggling, chromium-plated, scent impregnated, luminous, quivering, giggling, fruit flavoured, ice-covered heap of motherly love.' The judge held that these words, taken together, were capable, in their ordinary and natural sense, of meaning that Liberace was a homosexual, and the jury agreed that they were defamatory. The search is therefore for the meaning that words would convey to the ordinary man. This, as already stated, is a matter of construction, not evidence, but of construction in a non-technical sense. For the ordinary man does not live in an ivory tower and he is not inhibited by the knowledge of the rules of construction. So, though he is essentially a fair and reasonable person, he can and does read between the lines in the light of his general knowledge and experience of worldly affairs and is even allowed a certain amount of loose thinking.[37] In the ultimate analysis, therefore, the test of the 'ordinary man' is what the jurors think about the words published about the plaintiff.

---

[33] *Fields* v. *Davis* [1955] CLY 1543 (defendant calling the plaintiff, a married woman, a 'tramp').

[34] It is thus defamatory to refer to someone as a crook, coward, liar, hypocrite, a fanatic, a habitual drunkard, a drug addict or drug dealer, dishonest, a cheat. Authorities for the above, and many other instances are given in Gatley, 2.18 ff. (Select Bibliography).

[35] *Drummond-Jackson* v. *British Medical Association* [1970] 1 WLR 688, 698–9.

[36] *The Times*, 17 and 18 June 1959. According to RSC Ord. 33, r. 3 there is jurisdiction to try as a preliminary issue the question whether words complained of in an action for defamation are capable of having a particular meaning. This should be availed of where it is obvious that it would save costs without occasioning delay: *Keays* v. *Murdoch Magazines (UK) Ltd. and Another* [1991] 1 WLR 1184.

[37] *Lewis* v. *Daily Telegraph* [1964] AC 234, 258, per Lord Reid. For a more recent confirmation of this approach see: *Skuse* v. *Granada Television* [1996] EMLR 278. See, also, Lord Reid's views in *Morgan* v. *Odhams Press Ltd.* [1971] 1 WLR 1239 at 1245.

The reverse situation may also occur; namely, the plaintiff may be tempted to select libelous statements which are taken from a text which, however, as a whole, proves that there is no defamation. Thus, in *Charleston* v. *News Group Newspapers Ltd.*[38] the two plaintiffs, who played a 'respectable' married couple in a well known Australian soap opera, sued the *News of the World* for a photomontage which consisted of their faces superimposed on naked bodies performing sex. Though the photograph was accompanied by an eye-catching title, the supporting text made it clear that the pictures had been reproduced from a computer game in which the image of the plaintiffs had been used without their knowledge and consent. The plaintiffs complained that the picture and headline title was defamatory in so far that it implied that they had posed for the pictures. The action failed on the ground that the title and picture could not be seen in isolation and that the final decision as to whether the tort of defamation had been committed depended on the words being seen in the total context. Though this result is in tune with the prevailing tendency not to inhibit free expression, the actual result comes very close to giving tabloids a licence to hurt people through sensational reporting which is 'neutralised' or 'corrected' by a text invariably printed in smaller print.[39]

Matters become more complicated when the plaintiff argues that the words bear an inner meaning which render them defamatory; he says, in other words, that even if they are not defamatory on the surface they are so because of an innuendo. This depends on factors known to the recipient of the statement at the time of publication and is something which the plaintiff must plead and prove (if he does not do so, his pleadings will be struck out). Even if he fails to prove such facts to support an innuendo, he may still revert to the natural meaning of the words. It should be made clear, however, that when a defamatory meaning is derived from the words themselves, this is not an innuendo.[40]

Innuendoes form an important part of defamation. Thus, in *Tolley* v. *J. S. Fry & Sons, Ltd.*[41] the plaintiff, an amateur golfer, was pictured on a poster with a slab of the defendants' chocolate protruding from his pocket. The accompanying caddy in doggerel verse compared the excellence of the chocolate with the excellence of the plaintiff's stroke. The plaintiff alleged an innuendo by the defendants that he had agreed to the advertisement for gain and had thus prostituted his reputation as an *amateur* (i.e. not as professional playing for money) golfer. It was held that this was defamatory and that the plaintiff could recover.

It is immaterial whether or not the defendant knows of the external facts that transform an innocent statement into a defamatory one. We shall say more about unintentional defamation later, but for present purposes *Cassidy* v. *Daily Mirror Newspapers Ltd.*[42] can be given as an illustration. The defendants published a photograph of Mr Cassidy with Miss X and announced their engagement. In fact Mr Cassidy was already married, though he lived apart from his

---

[38] [1995] 2 All ER 313.

[39] Lord Nicholls was the only judge to draw attention to the dangers of such practice; ibid., at 320. It remains to be seen, however, whether his cautionary warning to news editors to avoid going down such a road will have any effect.

[40] *Lewis* v. *Daily Telegraph* [1964] AC 234.　　　　[41] [1931] AC 333.　　　　[42] [1929] 2 KB 331.

wife. The information on which the defendants based their statement came from Mr Cassidy himself, though they made no further attempt to ascertain its accuracy. Mrs Cassidy then brought an action alleging an innuendo that, since the paper had published the statement that Cassidy was unmarried, she must be regarded as his mistress. The court upheld her contention and awarded her £500.

It will be clear from the little that has already been said that the line between an ordinary meaning and an innuendo might not always be easy to draw. A derogatory implication may be so near the surface that it is hardly hidden at all or it may be more difficult to detect. If it is said of a man that he is a fornicator the statement cannot be enlarged by innuendo. If it is said of him that he was seen going into a brothel, the same meaning would probably be conveyed to nine men out of ten. But the lawyer might say that in the latter case a derogatory meaning was not a necessary one because a man might go to a brothel for an innocent purpose. An innuendo pleading that the words were understood to mean that he went there for an immoral purpose would not, therefore, be ridiculous.[43]

This last type of innuendo is the so-called 'false innuendo' and, as Lord Hodson put it in *Lewis* v. *Daily Telegraph*, 'it is no more than an elaboration or embroidering of the words used without proof of extraneous facts'. But then one could say that one saw X entering a named house, which could have a derogatory implication for anyone who knew that house was a brothel, but not for anyone who did not. This type of innuendo, known as a 'true' or 'legal' innuendo, is derived not from an elaboration of the words, but from extrinsic evidence associated with the statement. In the last example, therefore, the plaintiff has to prove that the person to whom the statement was made knew that the particular house was a brothel and understood the plaintiff was entering it for an immoral purpose. The distinction between these types of innuendo was once important for pleading purposes, but since 1972[44] it has ceased to be significant because a plaintiff now should give particulars of all such meanings.

Lewis v. *Daily Telegraph*[45] illustrates these points. The *Daily Telegraph* reported that the Scotland Yard Fraud Squad was inquiring into the affairs of the Rubber Improvement Co. Ltd. and its Chairman, Mr Lewis. They sued in defamation, claiming (*a*) that the words were defamatory in their ordinary and natural meaning, and (*b*) that the words meant or could be understood to mean that the plaintiffs were guilty of fraud and dishonesty. The defendants did not deny that the words in their ordinary meaning were defamatory, but pleaded justification. As to (*b*), they denied that the words meant or were capable of meaning that the plaintiffs were guilty of or suspected of fraud. The crux of the matter, therefore, was whether the words could be understood by an 'ordinary reasonable man' to bear the meaning alleged by the plaintiffs; or whether such defamatory meaning would be apparent only to readers who possessed special and additional knowledge of the question. The judge at first instance decided in favour of the first view and left the issue to the jury, which found for the

---

[43] *Lewis* v. *Daily Telegraph* [1964] AC 234, 278, per Lord Devlin.
[44] *Allsop* v. *Church of England Newspaper Ltd.* [1972] 2 QB 161.   [45] [1964] AC 234.

company and awarded it £100,000. The Court of Appeal and the House of Lords by a majority favoured the second view, namely that being investigated for fraud was not the same thing as being guilty of fraud, the latter requiring additional facts.[46] A new trial was thus ordered.

In his judgment Lord Reid considered how the judge should approach this task of deciding between a range of possible meanings:[47]

Ordinary men and women have different temperaments and outlooks. Some are unusually suspicious and some are unusually naive. One must try to envisage people between these two extremes and see what is the most damaging meaning they would put on the words in question . . . What the ordinary man, not avid for scandal, would read into the words complained of must be a matter of impression. I can only say that I do not think that he would infer guilt of fraud merely because an inquiry is on foot. And, if that is so, then it is the duty of the trial judge to direct the jury that it is for them to determine the meaning of the paragraph but that they must not hold it to impute guilt of fraud because as a matter of law the paragraph is not capable of having that meaning.

In the event, since the words used in the article could not be given a defamatory meaning otherwise than by 'some strained or forced or utterly unreasonable interpretation',[48] they could become defamatory *only* by pleading additional, extraneous facts known to the recipient of the statement[49] and showing that they were in fact understood in the sense claimed by the plaintiff. No such (true) innuendo was pleaded and no evidence adduced to this effect, so the judge was wrong in not telling the jury that, whatever the words meant, as a matter of law they did not mean that the plaintiffs were fraudulent.

This part of the case reveals that an innuendo constitutes a separate cause of action, which in the present context means that had it been pleaded and proved the plaintiffs would have succeeded in their action, even though the defendant had a defence on the first cause of action. Secondly, it follows that separate verdicts should be returned and separate damages should be assessed in respect of innuendoes.[50]

In *Lewis* the position with regard to false innuendoes was left open. In *Allsop* v. *Church of England Newspaper Ltd.*[51], however, it was made clear that the same rules should apply to both. Thus, where the words complained of have various meanings or overtones outside the dictionary definitions, it is desirable and necessary that the plaintiff should give particulars of all such meanings. Lord Denning MR offered two reasons for this:[52] 'in the first place, so that the defendant should know the case which he has to meet and to decide whether to plead justification or fair comment, or apologise: and, in the second place, so that the trial can be properly conducted.'

Pleading an innuendo is not only important for the defendant, it may also be important to the plaintiff. For when the plaintiff does not plead an innuendo

---

[46] See, also, *Mapp* v. *News Group, The Times* [1997] EMLR 397.
[47] [1964] AC 234, at 259–60.   [48] *Jones* v. *Skelton* [1963] 1 WLR 1362, 1370, per Lord Morris.
[49] At the time of publication for facts discovered after publication cannot support an innuendo: *Grappelli* v. *Derek Block (Holdings) Ltd.* [1981] 2 All ER 272.
[50] [1964] AC 234, 273, per Lord Hodson.   [51] [1972] 2 QB 161.
[52] Ibid., 167. See also *Fullam* v. *Newcastle Chronicle and Journal Ltd.* [1977] 1 WLR 651.

limiting the scope of possible defamatory meanings of the words complained of, the scope of the defence of justification is correspondingly widened. In *London Computer Operators Training Ltd.* v. *BBC*[53] the BBC was sued by the plaintiffs, who alleged that an entire broadcast concerning their operations at a computer operators' school had defamed them. The original defence was justification and fair comment, and the particulars pleaded were that students who had paid high fees had never been able to get a job, etc. At a subsequent date the BBC applied for leave to amend their defence by adding to the particulars of justification a certificate of the criminal record of the founder of the plaintiff company, which contained particulars of previous convictions for theft, larceny, and obtaining by false pretences. The Master granted leave, but the Judge in Chambers allowed only the part of the record that was relevant to the defence of justification. On further appeal the Court of Appeal restored the Master's decision. Since no innuendo had been pleaded, the court was entitled to examine the full width of the meanings that the jury might reasonably put upon the words. The greater the conceivable width, the greater the scope of the particulars of justification.[54]

Who decides whether a statement is defamatory or not—the judge or the jury? (Defamation actions can still be tried before a jury at the option of either party.) Since the passing of Fox's Libel Act in 1792 (which was meant to apply to criminal trials, but has also been followed in civil trials as well) the task of deciding whether words are defamatory is left to the jury, the judge merely directing or advising the jury. Indeed, the rationale of jury trial (such as it is) would disappear if the jurors were to cease being the final arbiters of meaning. In practice, however, the role is shared with the judge. For, whether the words in question are defamatory or not is for the jury to decide; but whether they are even 'capable' of bearing a defamatory meaning is for the judge to decide, and in this way he can exercise some control over the matter.[55] So (*a*) a judge may decide to leave the matter to the jury, in which case he must explain to them what defamation means in law. (*b*) If the words are obviously defamatory, he may indicate to them that the evidence submitted to the court can only be interpreted in one way. If, despite this, the jury finds for the defendant, a new trial may be ordered on appeal, though such a course will appear to be an interference with the functions of the jury and in practice has very rarely been taken. (*c*) If he believes that no reasonable man would consider the words to be defamatory, he must withdraw the case from the jury, but, once again, such a

---

[53] [1973] 1 WLR 424.

[54] Ibid., 428, per Cairns LJ. See also *S. & K. Holdings Ltd.* v. *Throgmorton Publications Ltd.* [1972] 1 WLR 1036.

[55] *Morgan* v. *Odhams Press Ltd.* [1971] 1 WLR 1239, 1251, per Lord Morris. In its recent Report (op. cit., Select Bibliography, 28), the Supreme Court Procedure Committee saw 'no reason . . . why all necessary rulings on whether the words are "capable" of any given meaning should not be dispensed of as early as possible, [for] in practice this would lead to earlier and cheaper settlements . . . ' Apparently, such a procedure already exists in Scots law. It is too early to predict what effect cases like *Keays* v. *Murdoch Magazines (UK) Ltd. and Another* [1991] 1 WLR 1184 will have on a future practice. In that case the Court of Appeal held that there was jurisdiction under Rules of Supreme Court, Ord. 33, r. 3 to try as a preliminary issue the question whether the words complained of were capable of bearing a particular meaning. This should be exercised where it was apparent that it would save costs without occasioning delay. See, now, *Mapp* v. *News Group Newspapers Ltd.* [1998] 2 WLR 260, esp. 265.

course will be taken only in very clear cases. In *The Capital and Counties Bank Ltd. v. G. Henty & Sons*[56] the defendants quarrelled with the manager of a branch of the plaintiff bank. They circularised some of their customers, who knew nothing of the dispute and who in turn showed the circular to others, informing them that the defendants would not receive in payment cheques drawn at any of the branches of the plaintiff. The latter claimed damages on the ground that the circular imputed insolvency. The House of Lords, after enunciating the principle just stated, proceeded to hold by majority that the words in question were not defamatory in their natural meaning and that the suggested innuendo was not one which any reasonable man would draw. Thus, despite the fact that the defendants' statement did cause a run on the plaintiff's bank, our highest court was of the view that the words that had caused such havoc did not warrant a referral to the jury. The defendants were thus entitled to judgment.[57]

(B) THE DEFAMATORY STATEMENT MUST REFER TO THE PLAINTIFF

The words have to be defamatory of the plaintiff and not of some other person, real or imaginary.[58] The identification of the plaintiff depends upon whether reasonable persons would believe that the words complained of referred to him.[59] The reasonable man, here as elsewhere in defamation, tends to be renamed the 'ordinary' man in order to take into account a 'certain amount of loose thinking'[60] and the inevitable tendency, especially when reading newspaper reports, to skim through the accounts without concentrated attention or second reading.

In *Morgan* v. *Odhams Press*[61] G, a journalist, while investigating a dog-doping conspiracy, came across Miss M, who was a kennel-maid at a greyhound track and was involved in the doping of the dogs. She confessed in the presence of the police and she was likely to be a key witness in any proceedings that might ensue. In the light of this, it was agreed that she would remain in the care of G. Later, while in G's company, she met the plaintiff and spent some time with him before being persuaded to return to G. Subsequently the *People* published the story, which included a photograph of Miss M. One day later, the *Sun* which, like the *People* was owned by the defendant company, produced a follow-up article stating that the 'dog-doping girl was kidnapped last week by members of the gang and kept in a house in Finchley'. Miss M, while staying with the plaintiff had on several occasions been seen in his company and his house was on the border of Finchley. He sued, alleging that his friends, on reading the second

---

[56] (1882) 7 App. Cas. 741.

[57] An analogous and more recent case—*Aspro Travel Ltd.* v. *Owners Abroad Group plc* [1996] 1 WLR 132—applied the same principle but on this point reached, it is submitted, the right result.

[58] *Bruce* v. *Odhams Press Ltd.* [1936] 1 KB 697, 705, per Greer LJ.

[59] If a statement does not refer to the plaintiff but a subsequent statement sheds light on the first and makes the identification clearer, then it may be taken into account. *Hayward* v. *Thompson* [1982] QB 47.

[60] Per Lord Reid in *Morgan* v. *Odhams Press Ltd.* [1971] 1 WLR 1239, 1245. See also Lord Pearson at 1269–70. See, also, *Skuse* v. *Granada Television* [1996] EMLR 278. In the case of two publications, where words used in the first are defamatory of the plaintiff and were understood to be aimed at him (even though they did not expressly identify him), the jury are allowed to look at the second publication to see to whom the first publication referred. *Hayward* v. *Thompson* [1982] QB 47.

[61] [1971] 1 WLR 1239.

article, had understood him to be one of Miss M's kidnappers. The key issue was whether the reasonable reader would understand the article as referring to the plaintiff. The Court of Appeal took the view that the case should not have been allowed to go to the jury. Two reasons were given for this. First, because the ordinary man must be envisaged as reading the article carefully, so that the discrepancies contained therein would prevent him from reading it as referring to the plaintiff; and secondly, because the article itself *must* contain some pointer indicating that it referred to the plaintiff. In the opinion of the court the article in question failed to satisfy both requirements. The House of Lords by a majority reversed the Court of Appeal and held that in determining the impression on the mind of the reader, regard should be had to the character of the article and the class of reader likely to read it. Lord Donovan once said that the ordinary sensible man reading an article in a popular newspaper is not expected to analyse it like a Fellow of All Souls.[62] The relevant impression to be taken into consideration was that which would be conveyed to an ordinary sensible man, having knowledge of the circumstances, reading the article casually, and not expecting a high degree of accuracy. Such a man could well reach the conclusion that the article referred to the plaintiff and hence the judge was right to leave the matter to the determination of the jury. Nor did their Lordships feel that it was necessary to discover a pointer referring to the plaintiff, though in this case it was felt that there was one.

The emphasis on how the ordinary man would interpret the defendant's statement means that at common law—now subject to what will be said below about 'unintentional defamation'—the latter's own knowledge of or intention to refer to the plaintiff are irrelevant. In *Newstead* v. *London Express Newspaper Ltd.*[63] the defendants' newspaper stated that 'Harold Newstead, a thirty-year old Camberwell man' had been convicted of bigamy. This was true of a Camberwell barman of that name, but not of the plaintiff, a barber, who was also aged about thirty and lived in Camberwell. The plaintiff's contention that the words were capable in law of being understood to refer to him was upheld, while the defendant's contention, that if words were true of one person they could not in law be defamatory of another, was rejected. In *E. Hulton & Co.* v. *Jones*[64] the defendants published a story of the discreditable doings in Dieppe of a fictitious character called Artemus Jones, who was said to be a churchwarden in Peckham. The plaintiff, who had been baptised Thomas Jones but called himself Thomas Artemus Jones (abbreviated to Artemus Jones), was a barrister not a churchwarden; he did not live in Peckham, nor had he visited Dieppe. He had, however, contributed articles to the very newspaper that published the fictitious story. He sued its proprietors for libel and was awarded £1,750, and the House of Lords upheld the decision.

Different problems arise when the defendant's statement refers to a class of people to which the plaintiff belongs. The question whether the words can be said to refer to him splits into two parts: one of law—are the words capable of

---

[62] Ibid., 1264.   [63] [1940] 1 KB 377.

[64] [1910] AC 20. The rigour of the common law, as exemplified by these two cases, is now modified by ss. 4–6 of the Defamation Act 1996.

referring to the plaintiff; one of fact—did reasonable people, who knew the plaintiff, believe the words to refer to him? It is generally accepted that the test for identification here is the same as for defamatory meanings: would a sensible ordinary reader identify the plaintiff as the person defamed?

In the leading case of *Knupffer* v. *London Express Newspaper Ltd.*[65] the defendants published an article about a Young Russian political party, which had a British branch consisting of twenty-four members led by the plaintiff. The party was an international one with several thousand members, and the article referred mainly to its activities in America and France. The plaintiff alleged that it was particularly applicable to Britain and, since the libel concerned the person responsible for the politics of the party, that it personally affected him. Rejecting this contention, the House of Lords laid down the general rule that where a class of persons is defamed, no one person can succeed unless he proves that the defamatory statement (*a*) was capable of referring to him, and (*b*) was in fact understood to refer to him. In the present case the plaintiff failed on (*a*). 'In deciding this question', said Lord Porter, 'the size of the class,[66] the generality of the charge and the extravagance of the accusation may well all be elements to be taken into consideration, but none of them is conclusive. Each case must be considered according to its own circumstances.'[67] The actual decision of the House of Lords in that case thus suggests an inclination to construe narrowly the first of these requirements. *Le Fanu* v. *Malcolmson*,[68] however, shows that a general statement or reference to a class may be actionable by a particular plaintiff if the words in the surrounding circumstances can be taken to refer to him. A local newspaper published a letter denouncing the alleged cruelty with which factory operatives were treated. The House of Lords upheld the verdict of the jury awarding damages to the owners of the factory, since there were special circumstances which enabled the jurors to identify the plaintiff's factory. To decide otherwise, it was said, 'would be opening a very wide door to defamation'.

Are the rules any different if the plaintiff is a legal (i.e. artificial) rather than a human entity? Since Lord Esher MR boldly asserted in *South Hetton Coal Co. Ltd.* v. *North-Eastern News Association Ltd.*[69] 'the law of libel is one and the same as to *all* plaintiffs', the answer has, in general terms,[70] been negative. Whether this

---

[65] [1944] AC 116.

[66] *Aspro Travel Ltd.* v. *Owners Abroad Group plc* [1996] 1 WLR 132 provides an illustration of this: allegations that a 'family' company was about to go bust were defamatory of its directors on the grounds that they were allowing it to trade though (apparently) insolvent. *Quare*, if the statement referred to the directors of a large, public company.

[67] Per Lord Porter at 124. For a more recent illustration see *Schloimovitz* v. *Clarendon Press*, *The Times*, 6 July 1973. But what if the defamatory statement refers to either one of two persons in the alternative? There seems to be no recent English authority on this point but, perhaps, the better solution is to say that both may sue.

[68] (1848) 1 HLC 637, 9 ER 910; *Orme* v. *Associated Newspapers Ltd.*, *The Times*, 4 Feb. 1981. (A critical article referring to the activities of the Unification Church (the Moonies) held by the judge to be capable of referring to their leader. After a 6-month trial the jury agreed, but also found that it was true.)

[69] [1894] 1 QB 133, 138 (italics supplied).

[70] For more details, see Duncan and Neill (below, Select Bibliography), ch. 9.

is correct is arguable.[71] For, authority apart, it is by no means obvious that the quite exceptional rules of defamation should be applicable to non-human entities. Defamation protects the esteem in which a victim is held in the eyes of others, which historically was the basis of the developing law and accounts for the rule that an individual's reputation is protected without him having to prove the falsity of the accusation or incurring any loss. (As we shall note further below the defendant can avoid liability if he can prove the accuracy of his statement.) It is arguable that when the rules are extended to institutions, they lose this justification. For example, to award (as the jury did) £100,000 to the Rubber Improvement Company is absurd, for it had no feelings to be injured nor any social relations that might have been impaired by the publication of the statement that its affairs were being investigated by the Fraud Squad. The only harm that it could have suffered, and which would have deserved compensation if it actually had been incurred, was harm to its commercial relations. 'Harm of that sort however, had it occurred, could be proved and therefore should be proved';[72] but it was not. All of which goes to show that what is here challenged is not an institution's right to compensation for loss resulting from a false statement made by the defendant and actionable under some such tort as injurious falsehood, but its right to take advantage of rules designed to protect *human* reputation and esteem.

It must be admitted, however, that whatever the merit of the above objections, they do not reflect the actual state of the law. For since the decision in *South Hetton Coal Co. Ltd.* v. *North-Eastern News Association Ltd.*[73] there is no doubt that a trading corporation and company can sue for defamation affecting its business or trading reputation. This, however, gives the corporation no right to sue for defamatory statements which reflect solely upon individual officers or members. The same rule was, in the 1970s, extended to non-trading corporations, such as local authorities.[74] However, this extension of the *South Hetton* rule to cover local councils (and, presumably, other government departments with corporate status such as the Secretaries of State for defence, education and science, energy, environment, and social services) rightly came to be seen as illogical and untenable. For this is not a simple extension of the rule from trading to non-trading corporations, but an unhappy assimilation of the notions of trading companies and government. For a local council is more than just a non-profit-making corporation; it is a kind of government department performing

---

[71] For criticism, see Weir 'Local Authority v. Critical Ratepayer—A Suit in Defamation' [1972] *CLJ* 238 ff., whose views are here adopted.

[72] Weir, ibid., 240. Cf. Lord Reid in *Lewis* v. *Daily Telegraph* [1964] AC 234, 262. 'A company cannot be injured in its feelings, it can only be injured in its pocket. Its reputation can be injured by a libel but that injury must sound in money. The injury need not necessarily be confined to loss of income. Its goodwill may be injured.'

[73] [1894] 1 QB 133.

[74] *Bognor Regis UDC* v. *Campion* [1972] 2 QB 169, 175, per Browne J In *Electrical, Electronic, Telecommunication and Plumbing Union* v. *Times Newspapers Ltd.* [1980] QB 585, O'Connor J held that a trade union could not sue for defamation. The earlier and opposite case of *National Union of General and Municipal Workers* v. *Gillian* [1946] KB 81, however, was not followed because of a technical point. In the opinion of the judge, the Trade Union and Labour Relations Act 1974 removed from unions the status of a separate legal personality.

public functions and a citizen's right to criticise its functioning should not be stifled by the technical rules of defamation which, in this case, impermissibly stifle political speech. Thus in *Derbyshire County Council* v. *Times Newspapers*,[75] the House of Lords overruled this line of reasoning. Lord Keith, speaking for all their Lordships, followed the decision in *Attorney-General* v. *Guardian Newspapers Ltd. (No. 2)*[76] (a case not of defamation but concerning confidentiality), and held that:

> . . . there are rights available to private citizens which institutions of central government are not in a position to exercise unless they can show that it is in the public interest to do so. The same applies . . . to local authorities. In both cases I regard it as right for this House to lay down that not only is there no public interest favouring the right of organs of government, whether central or local, to sue for libel, but that it is contrary to the public interest that they should have it. It is contrary to the public interest because to admit such actions would place an undesirable fetter on freedom of speech.[77]

This extract[78] suggests that in *Derbyshire* the House of Lords stopped short of according a similar immunity to statements criticising elected politicians[79] and other, unelected, officials who, presumably, can still sue their political tormentors (provided they can satisfy the usual elements of the tort). The rationale of *Derbyshire*, however, suggests that this could be the next step to be taken by our courts.[80] However, if our courts were minded to move in that direction, it might be preferable if they were to accord greater immunity to the *nature and content* of the speech (e.g. political speech v. titillating gossip) rather than make immunity hang on whether the person criticised was a politician or public (rather than a private) figure. For this would avoid the definitional difficulties which USA law has encountered as a result of adopting the second approach while also achieving the laudable aim of protecting political speech.

(c) PUBLICATION

In *Pullman* v. *W. Hill & Co. Ltd.*[81] Lord Esher MR described publication as: 'The making known the defamatory matter after it has been written to some person *other* than the person of whom it is written.'

If a statement is sent to the person of whom it is written, there is no publication of it, for one cannot publish a libel of a man to himself. Lord Esher's statement is equally true of spoken words. Communication to the plaintiff alone is thus insufficient to ground liability, because the law is concerned with

---

[75] [1993] AC 534.   [76] [1990] 1 AC 109.

[77] Ibid., at 458. Unlike the Court of Appeal [1992] 3 WLR 28, which reached the same result by boldly relying on the European Convention on Human Rights, their Lordships chose to place more faith on American materials as well as Lord Goff's judgment in *Attorney-General* v. *Guardian Newspapers Ltd. (No. 2)* [1990] 1 AC 109, 283–4, where the view was expressed that in the field of freedom of speech there was no difference in principle between English law on the subject and Art. 10 of the Convention.

[78] And, indeed, the wording of Lord Keith's judgment.

[79] But the *Derbyshire* reasoning applies to political parties and justifies withholding from them the right to sue: *Goldsmith* v. *Bhoyrul* [1998] 2 WLR 435, 438.

[80] In accord Neill (below, Select Bibliography), 14–15. See, also Lord Lester, 'Defaming Politicians and Public Officials' [1995] *PL* 1 ff.

[81] [1891] 1 QB 524, 527.

the esteem that *third* parties have of the plaintiff. In criminal libel, on the other hand, publication to the prosecutor alone will suffice.

Communication of the defamatory statement to one person (other than the defamed) will suffice. Typically, this takes place as a result of a positive act (writing or telling something to B about C) but, exceptionally, one may also be liable for not taking positive steps to prevent the publication by someone else. This, it will be remembered, was the case of the managers of the club in *Byrne* v. *Dean* who were held liable for not having removed the defamatory poem from the club's notice boards. (One might be tempted to draw an analogy between this rule and liability for 'adopting' a nuisance.)

A special rule is that a communication between spouses about a third party is not publication. This used to be explained by reference to the fiction of unity between husband and wife. It would, however, be better to accept that there is either an arbitrary rule that there can be no publication between spouses, or that there is a publication but that such communications are protected by absolute privilege. However, a communication by a third party to one spouse about the other is publication.[82] Another special rule is that by dictating a defamatory letter to his secretary an employer commits slander, though, as we shall see, he will probably be covered by the defence of qualified privilege. If she reads it back to him or hands it back typed, she is not making a fresh publication.[83] A statement not heard by the recipient because, for example, he is deaf, or is not understood because it is written in a language he does not know, or because it is not obviously referable to the plaintiff,[84] is not treated as having been published. Nor is a person liable if a third party on his own initiative hears or sees the defamation. However, he will be liable for statements which he intended a third party to know, or should have foreseen might come to his attention. So, in *Huth* v. *Huth*[85] the opening of a letter by a butler, acting out of curiosity and in breach of his duties, was held not to amount to publication by the defendant. But a defendant should anticipate that a husband might, at least in some circumstances, open his wife's letters.[86] Equally, a letter addressed to a businessman is likely to be opened by a secretary and, therefore, the correspondent will be liable for the resulting publication to the secretary unless the letter was clearly marked 'personal' or 'private'.[87] A guiding test given by Harman LJ in *Theaker* v. *Richardson*[88] was the following: 'The question of publication of a libel contained in a letter will depend on the state of the defendant's knowledge, either proved or inferred of the conditions likely to prevail in the place to which the libel is destined'.

The burden of proving publication rests on the plaintiff, but in many instances it is considerably eased by certain rebuttable presumptions of fact. An open postcard or 'telemessage', for example, is deemed to have been published to those who would normally see it in the course of transmission; spoken words

---

[82] *Theaker* v. *Richardson* [1962] 1 WLR 151.
[83] See *Osborn* v. *Boulter* [1930] 2 KB 226, 231; *Eglantine Inn Ltd.* v. *Smith* [1948] NI 29, 33.
[84] *Sadgrove* v. *Hole* [1901] 2 KB 1.   [85] [1915] 3 KB 32.
[86] Though in *Theaker* v. *Richardson* [1962] 1 WLR 151, 157, the court said that it would not treat this as normal practice and take judicial notice of it.
[87] *Pullman* v. *W. Hill & Co. Ltd.* [1891] 1 QB 524.   [88] [1962] 1 WLR 151, 157–8.

are deemed to have been published to persons within earshot. Equally, if it can be shown that a letter has been properly addressed, the publication to the addressee is presumed. In the case of defamatory innuendoes the plaintiff must prove that the words complained of were published to a specific person or persons possessed of the special facts which enabled them to understand the innuendo.

Interdepartmental 'memos' raise interesting questions with regard to publication. In *Riddick* v. *Thames Board Mills Ltd.*[89] the plaintiff was dismissed for incompetence with two months' salary. Then, as if he had been guilty of some misconduct, he was escorted by the two company officials who dismissed him to a waiting car, made to sit between them, and driven away. He brought an action for false imprisonment that was settled for £251. In the course of that action an interdepartmental memorandum of the *defendants* was disclosed. The document was the result of an inquiry made by R, the chief personnel manager, to his assistant F, and composed by F on the basis of information derived from the two people who had dismissed and escorted the plaintiff. F dictated his report to his secretary and sent it to R who, having read it, filed it away. As a result of this disclosure the plaintiff brought a second action for defamation based on this report. The jury found that the two persons who had dismissed the plaintiff in the first place and escorted him to the car had acted maliciously and had given a wrong account. They also found that the words in the memos, based on their account, were defamatory and awarded damages to the plaintiff. On appeal the decision was reversed. One ground on which the judges agreed was that a party (the company) disclosing a document on discovery should be entitled to the protection of the court against any use of it otherwise than in the action in which it was disclosed. However, the judges held different views on whether a report by one employee to another amounted to publication for the purposes of making the employer liable for defamation. Lord Denning MR argued that there was no publication, for the act of the employee making the report would be the act of the employer; and the act of the other employee in receiving it would also be the act of the employer. This would be, in effect, the employer making a publication to himself. Stephenson and Waller LJJ, on other hand, had disagreed and held that communications between employees, usually involving communications with secretaries, had for a long time been treated as publications. However, Stephenson LJ and Waller LJ disagreed between themselves on another point: Waller LJ felt that though there was publication the company was protected by qualified privilege, while Stephenson LJ felt that the defence did not apply. The only clear *ratio* of this unsatisfactory case is that relating to the disclosure of documents.

Difficult questions can arise with regard to repetition and republication by a third party. One thing seems reasonably clear: 'It is no justification to a person,

---

[89] [1977] QB 881. A written complaint made against a police officer under s. 49 of the Police Act 1964 (now Part IX of the Police and Criminal Evidence Act 1984) could be used by a police officer to found an action in defamation against the complainant, *Conerney* v. *Jacklin* [1985] Crim. LR 234. But statements made in the course of the investigation of the complaint would be protected from discovery; *Hehir* v. *Commissioner of Police for the Metropolis* [1982] 1 WLR 715.

in giving currency to that which is injurious to the character of another, for him to say that he heard the statement made by another person.'[90] More difficult is the question how far is the original publisher liable for subsequent repetitions?

The starting point must be clear: the original publisher is not liable for damage ensuing from republication of his statement if this is the voluntary act of a third party over which he has no control.[91] Where, however, he authorised the republication there is no doubt that he is liable for both the original publication and the republication;[92] and there is little doubt that the same would be true if the original publisher intended republication.[93] Even an unauthorised repetition, however, may make the original publisher liable. This would be whenever publication was made to a person who, to the knowledge of the original publisher, was under a legal or moral duty to repeat the words to a third person;[94] and, arguably, if repetition is the natural and probable consequence of the original publication.[95] Older cases used to treat voluntary republication as causally unconnected with the original statements; and, in principle, there is nothing to prevent a modern court from adopting a similar line if the facts of the particular case justify this. In general, however, it is unlikely that the original publisher will be absolved, at any rate for utterances whose repetition he had reason to anticipate. The recent decision of the Court of Appeal in *Slipper* v. *British Broadcasting Corporation*[96] could be taken to support this view. In that case the defendants made a film which dealt with the plaintiff's effort to get one of the great train robbers extradited from Brazil where he had sought refuge after he had escaped from an English jail. The plaintiff alleged that the film contained defamatory material about him and sued the BBC for damages that, he claimed, should take into account the fact that the reviews of the film in the national press essentially reproduced the sting of the libel. The defendants failed in their attempt to strike out the paragraph in the plaintiff's statement of claim that complained of the republication of the libel by the press. In Lord Justice Bingham's words:

Defamatory statements are objectionable not least because of their propensity to percolate through underground channels and contaminate hidden springs. Usually, in fairness to a defendant, such effects must be discounted or ignored for lack of proof. But here, where the further publications (although not republication) are provable and are said to have been foreseeable, natural, provable and perhaps even intentional results of the publication sued upon, I see no reason in logic or policy why those effects need be

---

[90] *Watkin* v. *Hall* (1868) LR 3 QB 396, at 403 (per Lush J). Cf., however, dicta in *Aspro Travel* v. *Owners Abroad plc* [1996] 1 WLR 132 (and discussion below of the defence of 'truth', Section 3(c)).

[91] Long line of cases starting with *Ward* v. *Weeks* (1830) 7 Bing 211, at 215.

[92] *Speight* v. *Gosnay* (1819) 60 LJQB 231 at 232 (per Lopes LJ). There may thus be two causes of action. However, the plaintiff may recover for both publications, even if he only sues for the first. See *Cutler* v. *McPhail* [1962] 2 QB 292, 299, per Salmond J.

[93] For a beautiful illustration taken from Sheridan's *School for Scandal*, Act 1, Sc. 1, see Clerk and Lindsell, no. 21–200, note 43.

[94] *Derry* v. *Handley* (1867) 16 LT 263; *Kendillon* v. *Maltby* (1842) Car. & M. 402 at 408 (per Lord Denman CJ).

[95] *Speight* v. *Gosnay* (1891) 60 LJQB 231; *Ward* v. *Lewis* [1955] 1 WLR 9 (dicta).

[96] [1991] 1 QB 283.

ignored if the factual premises are established. Nor do I see any threat whatever to freedom of expression, which (I accept) the courts must be vigilant to protect.[97]

In the court's view the question of republication is, essentially, one of *novus actus interveniens* and of a possible interruption in the chain of causation. Thus, *given appropriate facts* the repetition of the sting of a libel by an unauthorised third party may be treated as the 'natural' or the 'natural and probable' consequence of the original publication, so as to expose the original publisher to a claim for damages in respect of the repetition.[98]

Another point is that every repetition is a fresh publication that gives rise to a fresh cause of action against each successive publisher.[99] Thus, not only the author of an article, but the editor, printer, and publisher are also liable. Moreover, even mechanical distributors, such as bookstalls, could be liable. To avoid excessive harshness, however, the law distinguishes between republication and mere dissemination. Thus, in *Vizetelly* v. *Mudie's Select Library Ltd.*[100] the owners of a circulating library were liable for allowing people to use books which the publishers had asked them to return as they might contain libellous material. Romer LJ laid down the rule that distributors would not be liable if they proved the following points. First, that they were innocent of any knowledge of the libel contained in the work in question. Secondly, that there was no reason for them to be aware that the work contained libellous material. Thirdly, that they were not negligent in failing to know that the work was libellous. Scrutton LJ subsequently abridged the test when he restated by asking the question: 'Ought the defendant to have known the matter was defamatory?'[101] In *Goldsmith* v. *Sperrings Ltd.*[102] Lord Denning MR, relying on his own research, doubted the validity of the above. The fact that both parties had conducted the case on the assumption that secondary distributors can be sued (subject to the defence of innocent dissemination) was, in Lord Denning's view, irrelevant and

---

[97] [1991] 1 QB 283, 300.
[98] Ibid., 302 (per Slade LJ).
[99] *'Truth' (NZ) Ltd.* v. *P. N. Holloway* [1960] 1 WLR 997, 1002–3.
[100] [1900] 2 QB 170.
[101] *Sun Life Assurance Co. of Canada* v. *W. H. Smith & Sons Ltd.* (1934), 150 LT 211.
[102] [1977] 1 WLR 478, 487. The facts were as follows. Sir James Goldsmith sued *Private Eye* and 37 of its distributors for a series of defamatory articles. Actions against some of the distributors were settled on the understanding that they would no longer sell *Private Eye*. Negotiations with the others, including the publishers and editors, continued and the plaintiff agreed to discontinue all actions and not to impede the sales of the magazine once his terms had been accepted. The compromise negotiation failed and action against the remaining distributors continued. The question was whether this should be allowed, or whether the proceedings represented an abuse of the judicial process. For Lord Denning MR the latter was the correct view. This is partly because the learned judge refused to accept that an action lay against secondary distributors, but also because the plaintiff's predominant purpose in suing all the distributors was to shut off the channels of distribution and this would seriously affect the notion of freedom of the Press. Nor would the plaintiff derive any special benefit from such process except that it would be oppressive for the distributors. However, the majority of the Court of Appeal felt otherwise, taking the view that in an action for libel the plaintiff has a course of action against any distributor of the alleged libel. It would be a denial of justice to stay such an action at an interlocutory stage, unless there was strong evidence to show that the plaintiff's purpose in bringing these actions was not to protect and vindicate his reputation, but to destroy the paper. The evidence, particularly that relating to the terms on which the plaintiff had offered to settle his dispute, made it clear that his purpose was to vindicate his reputation and prevent further anticipated attacks upon it. If in doing these things a danger resulted for the freedom of the Press, then it was not the plaintiff's fault, but the result of a defect in the law which only Parliament could rectify.

the court should remedy the error. Scarman and Bridge LJJ, however, refused to accept this view. It was wrong for a judge to conduct his own researches, especially in interlocutory proceedings. More important, before such a view could be accepted it needed to be argued by counsel for both sides. Counsel for the defence had not been heard on this point and to decide it against him would violate the rule that both sides must be heard.

The harshness of the old rule (concerning distributors, sellers, broadcasters of live programmes and Internet operators), criticised by Lord Denning in the above case, has now been mitigated[103] by section 1 of the Defamation Act 1966. This gives the above 'type'[104] of (possible) defendants a statutory defence if they can show that they took all reasonable care in relation to the publication of the statement complained of and did not know (nor could have known) that what they did caused or contributed to the publication of a defamatory statement.

Publication through radio or television can give rise to nice problems. The tort is committed wherever the statement is heard or the programme received. The same, of course, is true of publications through newspapers and journals. This may give the plaintiff a chance to choose the most convenient forum to litigate. Factors that will influence this decision will include legal costs (contingent-fee system, availability of legal aid), likely measure of damages (as a general rule much higher in common-law than in civil-law jurisdictions), and the impact that the constitutional background may have on the likely success of the defamation action.[105] But simultaneous litigation in different countries is rightly discouraged; and damages awarded by the court of one country should, it is submitted, be taken into account whenever the same statement is the subject of litigation in more than one system.

3. Defences

Only the defences peculiar to defamation are discussed here; general defences which apply elsewhere as well are not included, though a brief reference will be made to 'consent'.

(A) Unintentional Defamation

It will be evident from the foregoing that at common law the fact that the maker of a statement was unaware of the circumstances making it defamatory does not absolve him from liability. Thus, in *Hulton* v. *Jones*[106] the defendants were liable for a statement which they believed was about a fictitious person. In *Newstead* v. *London Express Newspapers Ltd.*[107] the rule was extended to make a defendant liable for a libel which was true of one person and honestly aimed at

---

[103] But see Milmo in (1995) 145 *NLJ* 1340 and (1996) 146 *NLJ* 222, arguing that in one sense at least the position of potential defendants may have become worse.

[104] The full list is provided by the statute. But 'authors', 'editors' and 'publishers' are excluded from the purview of this defence and are thus subject to the normal common-law rules.

[105] E.g. in the United States the First Amendment provides preferential treatment to free speech at the expense of reputation.

[106] [1910] AC 20, especially Lord Loreburn at 23. Cf. the vigorous and attractive dissenting views of Fletcher-Moulton LJ in the Court of Appeal.

[107] [1940] 1 KB 377.

and intended for him, but which could reasonably be attributed to the plaintiff. Indeed one may go further and argue that if one combines these cases with dicta in *Morgans* v. *Odhams Press* we may have authority for the proposition that 'a person may be sued for making a true statement about X which anyone can, despite its terms, suppose to be a false statement about Y'.[108]

Cases like these added 'terror to authorship' and led to growing pressures for reform. This was attempted by section 4 of the Defamation Act 1952, which enabled a defendant to make an 'offer of amends' for an innocent defamation which, if accepted, would be the end of the dispute and, if not accepted, would provide a defence in any subsequent litigation. But the way the offer had to be made was hedged by so many qualifications[109] and technical requirements that the defence failed to assist many defendants; indeed, it would appear that only one case of significance was ever decided under this section.[110] While not entirely abandoning the mould of the earlier statute, sections 2–4 of the Defamation Act 1996[111] contain many novel features which are designed to breathe new life into the defence and remove some of the harshness of the common law.

An offer of amends must be in writing, expressed to be an offer under section 2 of the 1996 Act and state whether it is qualified or not.[112] According to section 2(4)

An offer to make amends under this section is an offer—
(a) to make a suitable correction of the statement complained of and a sufficient apology to the aggrieved party,

(b) to publish the correction and apology in a manner that is reasonable and practicable in the circumstances, and

(c) to pay to the aggrieved party such compensation (if any), and such costs, as may be agreed or determined to be payable.

Two important differences from the old section 4 must be noted thus far. First, unlike the old law, the new Act requires that the offer be accompanied by an offer of monetary compensation. This follows the views of the Neill Committee, which had rightly pointed out[113] that it would be

. . . unsatisfactory that defendants should have a defence available, based on their reasonable behaviour after publication, which would leave the plaintiff with no compensation at all, in respect to hurt feelings or injury to reputation, to take account of what was ex hypothesi a defamation. Indeed, it could well be a serious defamation, and we see no overriding public interest in depriving plaintiffs of all compensation merely because the defendants have seen the error of their ways.

Secondly, no time limit is any longer set on the making of the offer of amends. The old requirement that the offer be made promptly was thus discarded since it was seen as imposing on potential defendants an undesirable

---

[108] Weir, *A Casebook on Tort* (5th edn.), 446.   [109] Described in the previous edition of this book.
[110] *Ross* v. *Hopkinson*, *The Times*, 17 Oct. 1956.   [111] But they have not yet been brought into force.
[112] The offer may either be general (i.e. refer to the statement generally) or qualified to a specific defamatory meaning of the statement which the defendant accepts that it conveys.
[113] § VII. 17.

choice of either moving too quickly, even before a proper investigation of the matter, or loosing the right to invoke the defence (and thus avoiding litigation). The offer may thus be made at any time until the defendant has served a defence: section 2(5). The idea that once a defence has been served, the offer of amends procedure has, essentially, lost its *raison d'être*, can also be seen in section 4(4). This states that 'the person who made the offer need not rely on it [in the event that it is not accepted] by way of defence,[114] but if he does he may not rely on any other defence.' As a result of this arrangement, defendants may have to take some strategic decisions and decide whether to plead a defence (e.g. truth) which *if* it succeeds[115] will absolve them of all liability or go for the offer of amends which, though it may involve losing face, provides the comfort of limiting the financial consequences of their statement.

A further innovation of the new section 4 can also be seen in the consequences of the offer of amends being accepted or not. If it is, then, as with the old section 4, that will be the end of the matter and litigation will have been avoided or be brought to an end.[116] But if the offer *is not accepted*,[117] then the offer of amends will provide a defence to defamation proceedings subject to section 4(3) of the Act. This states that:

There is no such defence if the person by whom the offer was made knew or had reason to believe that the statement complained of—

(a) referred to the aggrieved party or was likely to be understood as referring to him, and

(b) was both false and defamatory of that party;

but it shall be presumed until the contrary is shown that he did not know and had no reason to believe that was the case.

(B) CONSENT

Consent is a general defence, in no way peculiar to the tort of defamation, and little need be said about it. Perhaps one example will suffice. In *Chapman* v. *Lord Ellesmere*[118] a horse-trainer was allowed by the stewards of the Jockey Club to train horses and his licence was subject to a number of conditions. One of these was that his licence might be withdrawn by the stewards—acting at their absolute discretion—and such withdrawal (or suspension) might be published in the *Racing Calendar*, the recognised organ of the Jockey Club, for any reason which might seem proper to them. At a subsequent race, a horse was found doped and was thus disqualified. This decision, as well as 'a warning' to its trainer, was published in the *Racing Calendar* and by *The Times*. The statement was held to involve a defamatory innuendo about the trainer, but its publication in

---

[114] But even if he does not rely on it as a defence he may use it in mitigation of damages: s. 4(5).

[115] And if it fails, land them with substantial costs.

[116] As against the person who made the offer. Thus, if the defamatory statement is contained in a book, an offer of amends made by the printer and accepted by the plaintiff will prevent him from proceeding against the printer but not against the author.

[117] The words are italicised in order to stress the fact that the requirements set out in s. 4(3) are only taken into account in cases where the offer is refused. It is irrelevant that the offeror does not satisfy these requirements if his offer is accepted.

[118] [1932] 2 KB 431; *Tadd* v. *Eastwood* [1985] ICR 132.

the *Racing Calendar* was not actionable because the plaintiff had consented to publication of the steward's decision in *that* journal. The fact that it was published in such a way as to carry a defamatory innuendo was a risk which the trainer, by consenting to a report of the decision being published, had elected to run. However, publication in *The Times* was without his consent, and as the law then stood,[119] was not covered by privilege; so it was actionable.

(C) JUSTIFICATION OR TRUTH

A peculiarity of the English (but not American) common law, which favours the plaintiff,[120] is that *he* does not have to prove that the statement complained of was false. If he proves that the allegations against him are defamatory then they will be *presumed* to be untrue. The burden is thus on the defendant to prove that the allegations are true; and, it would appear on the strength of Commonwealth authority[121] that there is no duty in negligence to take care *not* to publish injurious statements which are *true*.[122] One ludicrous side-effect of this rule is that a plaintiff may leave court with substantial compensation, but with his name not necessarily cleared. For this award does not necessarily imply that what the defendant said of him was false, but only that he (the defendant) failed to prove that it was true. A second and more general drawback is that it may inhibit free speech. For, as Lord Keith (among others) has observed:[123] 'Quite often the facts which would justify a defamatory publication are known to be true, but admissible evidence capable of proving those facts is not available.'

Truth is a defence because '. . . the law will not permit a man to recover damages in respect of an injury to a character which he either does not, or ought not to possess'.[124]

The defendant must establish the truth of the precise charge that has been made, which is ultimately a matter of interpretation of the facts. Repeating a rumour will not amount to justification, even if it is honestly believed. 'If you repeat a rumour you cannot say it is true by proving that the rumour in fact existed; you have to prove that the subject matter of the rumour is true.'[125]

In *Wakley* v. *Cooke and Healey*[126] the defendants called the plaintiff a 'libellous journalist' and proved that he had once been convicted of such a charge. The court took the view that these words did not mean 'that the plaintiff has been

---

[119] The publication might now be covered by s. 7 and Part II of the Schedule of the Defamation Act 1952.

[120] Less so now than in the past. See the concluding comments to the defamation section of this chapter.

[121] *Bell-Booth Group Ltd.* v. *A.G.* [1989] 3 NZLR 148.

[122] But the tort of Negligence has penetrated the tort of defamation where *untrue* statements are concerned made in the context of a negligently prepared reference. See: *Spring* v. *Guardian Assurance plc* [1994] 3 All ER 129.

[123] *Derbyshire County Council* v. *Times Newspapers Ltd.* [1993] 1 All ER 1011, 1018.

[124] *McPherson* v. *Daniels* (1829) 10 B. & C. 263, 272; 109 ER 448, 451; per Littledale J.

[125] *Cookson* v. *Harewood* [1932] 2 KB 478 at 485, per Greer LJ, approved by Lord Devlin in *Lewis* v. *Daily Telegraph* [1964] AC 234 at 283–4. *Stern* v. *Piper* [1996] 3 WLR 715 (containing an exhaustive discussion of the so-called 'repetition rule'). For the latest restatement and application of this rule see *Shah* v. *Standard Chartered Bank* [1998] 3 WLR 592, esp. at 610.

[126] (1849) 4 Exch. 511, 517; 154 ER 1316, 1318.

guilty, upon one occasion only, of having published a libel, but that he had been guilty of gross misconduct as a journalist, by the habit of libelling others'. The defence of truth accordingly failed. The Court of Appeal has also held[127] that the defendant may plead justification to any meaning of the published statement which a jury, properly directed, might reasonably find to be the real meaning of the words complained of and thus is not restricted to justifying the meaning pleaded by the plaintiff. The defendant must, however, plead his justification with sufficient particularity to enable the plaintiff to know precisely what case he has to meet.[128]

At common law, where a statement contained more than one charge,[129] and only part of the libel was justified, the defendant had to pay damages in respect of the part not justified.[130] That rule of partial justification has now been extended by section 5 of the Defamation Act, which provides that:

In an action for libel or slander in respect of words containing two or more distinct charges against the plaintiff, a defence of justification shall not fail by reason only that the truth of every charge is not proved if the words not proved to be true do not materially injure the plaintiff's reputation having regard to the truth of the remaining charges.

It is for the defendant who wishes to rely on this statutory defence to raise it, and the judge is under no obligation, when dealing with a defence of justification, to draw the jury's attention to section 5.[131]

If a statement carries a defamatory innuendo the defendant must prove the truth of this in order to escape liability. Statements to the effect that the plaintiff had committed a criminal offence used to create a difficulty because a conviction in the criminal trial was not prima-facie evidence for the purposes of the civil action, and guilt had to be proved over again. Section 13, subsection 2(A)[132] of the Civil Evidence Act 1968 has now altered the position so that in an action in which it is necessary to establish whether the *plaintiff* did or did not commit a criminal offence, proof of a previous conviction is conclusive evidence that he did commit the crime in question.

---

[127] *Prager* v. *Times Newspapers Ltd.* [1988] 1 WLR 77. If the words complained of are capable of a wider meaning than that pleaded by the plaintiff, the defendant is allowed to attempt to justify the words in that wider meaning. (The judgments of Purchas and Nicholl LJJ contain interesting pronouncements on justification.) See *Williams* v. *Reason* [1988] 1 WLR 96. (Evidence that the plaintiff, an amateur rugby player, had received 'boot money' (from Adidas, the manufacturers of sports equipment) was relevant to justifying the wider charge of 'amateurism').

[128] *Lucas-Box* v. *News Group Newspapers Ltd.* [1986] 1 WLR 147; *Prager* v. *Times Newspapers Ltd.* [1988] 1 WLR 77. The plaintiff, too, is under a similar obligation to be specific in his pleadings when the meaning of the words complained of is not clear.

[129] Where the words complained of are not several, or contain only one charge, the position is more complicated. Suppose, for example, that the defendant accuses the plaintiff of rape, whereas in fact he had been convicted only of indecent assault. Section 5 of the Defamation Act would clearly not avail the defendant. It would, however, be unfair to allow the plaintiff to recover damages as if he had not been convicted of any offence involving indecency at all. See Duncan and Neill, op. cit. (Select Bibliography). Another difficulty arrives whenever there are several defamatory allegations but all contain a 'common sting'. In such cases it will be enough to justify the sting: *Khashoggi* v. *IPC Magazines Ltd.* [1986] 1 WLR 1412; *Polly Peck* v. *Trelford* [1986] QB 1000.

[130] *Clarke* v. *Taylor* (1836) 2 Bing. (NC) 654, 665; 132 ER 252, 256; per Tindall CJ.

[131] *Moore* v. *News of the World Ltd.* [1972] 1 QB 441.

[132] Inserted by s. 12(1) of the 1996 Defamation Act.

One difference between justification and the two defences that follow used to be that even malice on a defendant's part did not deprive him of the defence of truth. This is no longer wholly true. For a modification has been introduced by the Rehabilitation of Offenders Act 1974, which provides that after certain periods of time, depending on the length of sentences imposed on offenders, their convictions are to be treated as 'spent' and, therefore, as if they had not occurred. Section 8(3), however, adds that in actions for defamation based on imputations of such offences, justification shall continue to be a defence by proof of the convictions except where 'the publication is proved to have been made with malice'. However, whether this rebuttal of the defence requires proof of spite or includes other improper motives, has not been decided.

(D) FAIR COMMENT

This defence stems from the belief that honest and fair criticism is indispensable in every freedom-loving society. The law weighs the interest of the plaintiff against freedom of speech and, on the whole, comes down in favour of the latter. It is for the judge to rule whether the matter is one of public interest,[133] and for the jury (ultimately) to decide whether the statement is one of fact or is an opinion, and if the latter, whether it is honest and fair. The requirements of this frequently invoked defence are as follows:

(i) Public Interest   The comment must refer to matters of public interest. In *London Artists Ltd.* v. *Littler*[134] Lord Denning MR said: 'Whenever a matter is such as to affect people at large, so that they may be legitimately interested in, or concerned at, what is going on; or what may happen to them or to others; then it is a matter of public interest on which everyone is entitled to make fair comment.' The reference to 'people at large' should not be taken to suggest that if the statement complained of refers to one person or a few persons only it can never be of public interest. Thus, in *South Hetton Coal Co.* v. *North-Eastern News Association Ltd.*[135] a colliery company owned most of the cottages in a certain village. The defendant published a long article describing some of the cottages owned by the plaintiff company as being, for the most part, unfit for habitation owing to a complete lack of decent sanitation, inadequate accommodation, and want of sufficient water-supply. It was held that the condition of these cottages was a matter of public interest, which would have given the defendants a defence, but that they had gone beyond the limits of fair and bona-fide comment. Here the public was legitimately *concerned*.

In *London Artists* v. *Littler* the public was legitimately *interested*.[136] The defendant, an impresario, wrote and published at a press conference a letter suggesting that the plaintiff organisers in the entertainment business had taken part in what appeared to be a plot to force the end of a successful play, which the defendant was producing, by arranging for four leading players to give identical notices to leave. This was likely to stop the play. The defendant's letter was written after he had received the players' notices simultaneously as

---

[133] *Telnikoff* v. *Matusevitch* [1990] 3 WLR 725, 730; [1992] 2 AC 343, 354–7, 363. Likewise, in the context of the defence of qualified privilege it is the judge who decides whether the occasion is privileged.

[134] [1969] 2 QB 375, 391.   [135] [1894] 1 QB 133.   [136] [1969] 2 QB 375.

well as a notice from the theatre-owners that they were planning to transfer another play to the theatre that he himself had rented from them. In the ensuing action for libel the defendant pleaded, *inter alia*, fair comment, but the trial judge held that the plea failed as the matter was not one of public interest. The defendant's appeal was dismissed, but on a different ground. His comments were, undoubtedly, on a matter of public *interest*, but 'fair comment', as we shall see, presupposes correct basic facts on which the comments and inferences are based.[137] In the present case one of the basic facts, which the defendant had failed to prove, was the existence of a plot between the plaintiffs to put an end to his play.

Matters of government, national or local, management of public and religious institutions, the conduct of foreign policy, etc., can obviously be brought under the heading of 'public interest'. Even the private behaviour of, for example, the prime minister or other ministers may fairly be commented on if this sheds light on matters of honesty and integrity, which are qualities of holders of public office. On the other hand, it has been held that the management by a parish clergyman of a charitable society is not necessarily the subject of public comment, so as to excuse the publication of injurious matter regarding the clergyman in relation to the charity.[138]

(ii) True Facts   The comment must be an opinion on true facts. There is, however, one instance where facts, though untrue, can be the subject of opinion and protected as fair comment. This is whenever the facts themselves, though untrue, are protected by privilege. Thus: 'If a statement made by a witness is fairly and accurately reported, and attributed to the witness who made it, then, no doubt, although the evidence given by the witness is afterwards shown to be false, the statement reported can be made the subject of fair comment.'[139]

The importance of ensuring that the facts are true can be seen from *London Artists Ltd. v. Littler*,[140] where, although the comment was in the public interest, the defence failed because the defendant could not prove the correctness of the underlying facts. These were that the theatre-owners (plaintiffs) wanted to get the defendant's play out of their theatre, that all the leading stars gave notice simultaneously, and that there was a plot between the owners and the actors to end the play. The first and second were proved, but not the last. There was some argument as to whether the allegation of a plot was a fact or a comment and the court took the view that, on balance, it was a fact. Even if this allegation were treated as comment, it would arguably not have helped the defendant since there were not enough facts to lead an honest man to have made such a comment.[141] Obviously the distinction is not clear-cut, as the next case demonstrates.

[137] On which see Lord Denning [1969] 2 QB 375, 391.
[138] *Gathercole v. Miall* (1846) 15 M. & W. 319; 153 ER 872.
[139] *Grech v. Odhams Press Ltd.* [1958] 2 QB 275, 287 per Jenkins LJ. See also *Mangena v. Wright* [1909] 2 KB 958, 977 per Phillimore J. It is for the defendant to prove that the statement was made on a privileged occasion and that his report of it was fair and accurate: *Brent Walker Group plc v. Time Out Ltd.* [1991] 2 QB 772.
[140] [1969] 2 QB 375.
[141] On which see Lord Denning MR's observations at 392–3.

In *Dakhyl* v. *Labouchere*[142] the plaintiff described himself as a 'specialist for the treatment of deafness, ear, nose and throat diseases', and the defendant described him as 'a quack of the rankest species'. Was this a comment (as the court was inclined to believe) or a statement of fact? Further, to say that A failed his examinations is an allegation of fact; to say that he is a fool because he failed is a comment on the fact. And what of a statement that the plaintiff is a 'sinner' or an 'immoral' person? There is no obvious answer to such questions; and in all cases it must depend on the facts which may, in appropriate circumstances, be gleaned from all the surrounding circumstances and not just discovered in the document complained of.[143]

Two qualifications should be added to what has been said. First, it is not always essential that:

the facts upon which the comment is based should themselves be stated in the alleged libel. The question is whether there is a sufficient substratum of fact stated or indicated in the words which are the subject-matter of the action and whether the facts or subject-matter on which comment is made, are indicated with sufficient clarity to justify comment being made. The substratum of fact, facts, or subject-matter may be indicated impliedly in the circumstances of the publication.[144]

In *Kemsley* v. *Foot*,[145] for example, the defendant published an article referring to one of the Beaverbrook newspapers and described it as 'lower than Kemsley' (Lord Kemsley being the owner of another group of papers). Was this an allegation of fact (in which case justification would be the right defence) or an expression of opinion? If the defendant states what some public man has done and then says that it is disgraceful, this is an expression of an opinion. But if he asserts that the plaintiff has been guilty of disgraceful conduct, and does not state what the conduct was, this is an allegation of fact. The same is true if he states an inference without the facts on which it is based, unless, as in this case, the basic facts are indicated in the words complained of. The House of Lords took the view that the defence of fair comment was available given that the conduct of the Kemsley Press was the fact on which the comment was made.[146]

Secondly, according to section 6 of the Defamation Act: 'In an action for libel or slander in respect of words consisting partly of allegations of fact and partly of expression of opinion, a defence of fair comment shall not fail by reason only that the truth of every allegation of fact is not proved if the expression of opin-

---

[142] [1908] 2 KB 325; cf. *Smiths Newspapers* v. *Becker* (1932) 47 CLR 279.

[143] In *Telnikoff* v. *Matusevitch* [1990] 3 WLR 725, 731, the Court of Appeal had, it is submitted more convincingly, taken the view that the facts should be gleaned from all the relevant surrounding circumstances. But this part of its judgment was reversed by the House of Lords: [1992] 2 AC 343 (Lord Ackner dissenting). The result in that case was that the decision whether the defendant's reply to a previously published article by the plaintiff in the same newspaper was fact or comment should be decided by looking at his letter alone and ignoring the earlier article. The final decision unduly restricts the defence of fair comment. It also produces the strange result that if the defendant pleads (as he had) fair comment as a defence, his reply would be read in isolation. But if he had also pleaded justification, his reply would have been looked at in conjunction with the earlier piece that had prompted his letter. This hair-splitting does not, it is submitted, inspire much confidence in the law! The decision is criticised by Mullis in [1991] *All ER Annual Rev.*, 390–1.

[144] Winfield and Jolowicz, *On Tort* (12th edn.), 326.   [145] [1952] AC 345.

[146] Provided, of course, that the jury felt that this was the type of comment an honest man might make.

ion is fair comment having regard to such facts alleged or referred to in the words complained of as are proved.'

From the above it will be clear that 'fair comment' differs from 'justification' in that it is directed to expressions of opinion, whereas justification applies to fact. In fair comment, the defendant must prove that the opinion was honestly held, whereas in justification honest belief is irrelevant. The two defences are, therefore, different and should be pleaded in the alternative.

(iii) **Fairness**   The comment must be fair: it is crucial that a jury could hold that it is one that an honest-minded person could make on the facts. However, it is not for the jury to substitute its own judgment as to what is fair. 'The question which the jury must consider', said Lord Esher in *Merivale* v. *Carson*,[147] 'is this—would any *fair man*, however prejudiced he may be, however exaggerated or obstinate his views, have said that which this criticism has said?'[148] Lord Denning MR appeared to put it more subjectively. For he said:[149] 'No matter that it was badly expressed so that other people read all sorts of innuendoes into it; nevertheless, he has a good defence of fair comment. His honesty is the cardinal test.' But the ambiguity seems to have been settled by the Court of Appeal in *Telnikoff* v. *Matusevitch*.[150] For the court took the view (and, in this context was approved by the House of Lords) that fairness is to be judged objectively (as defined in section (c), above), so that once the defendant has demonstrated this, then his comment will be presumed to be honest unless and until the *plaintiff* can then prove that it was motivated by malice.

The position may be different if the defendant attributes bad motives to the plaintiff rather than merely criticises his work. *Campbell* v. *Spottiswoode*[151] held that it was actionable to suggest, however honestly, that Dr Campbell, the editor of a religious magazine, in advocating a scheme for missions to the heathen, was an impostor and that his alleged aim of propagating the gospel was 'a mere pretext for puffing his obscure magazine'.

This approach, which is not without support from earlier authority,[152] implies that imputations of base or dishonourable motives can *never* be protected by fair comment. Other cases, however, can suggest that in these cases the test of fair comment is available, but applied more strictly in that the writer's opinion must not only be honestly held, but must also be a reasonable inference from the facts.[153] It is doubtful, however, whether this 'reasonableness' test is workable in

---

[147] (1888) 20 QBD 275, 281 (italics supplied): the test is objective—how the words would be understood, not how they were intended. Applied in *Cornwell* v. *Myskow* [1987] 1 WLR 630. The same case held that if justification is not pleaded by the defendant, evidence of the plaintiff's actual reputation at the date of the trial is irrelevant and should not be considered by the jury.

[148] The italicised words can cause some difficulties. For can a 'fair' man be obstinate and prejudiced? Many have thus argued that the defence should simply be called 'comment' the word 'fair' being dropped from the heading.

[149] *Slim* v. *Daily Telegraph Ltd.* [1968] 2 QB 157, 170.   [150] [1990] 3 WLR 725, 741.

[151] (1863) 3 B. & S. 769, esp. at 776–7: 122 ER 288, 290–1 per Cockburn CJ: 'A man has no right to impute to another, whose conduct may be fairly open to ridicule or disapprobation, base, sordid and wicked motives, unless there is so much ground for the imputation that a jury shall find, not only that he had an honest belief in the truth of his statements, but that his belief was not without foundation.'

[152] E.g. *Hunt* v. *The Star Newspaper Co. Ltd.* [1908] 2 KB 309, 320, per Fletcher-Moulton LJ.

[153] Buckley LJ in *Peter Walker & Sons Ltd.* v. *Hodgson* [1909] 1 KB 239, 253.

practice and is compatible with the general purpose of fair comment. Nowadays, therefore, it may be true to say that even imputations concerning motives are governed by the ordinary test and constitute fair comment when put forward as the expression of opinion. There is some authority for this,[154] especially if the test is the 'objective' one propounded by Lord Esher MR in *Merivale* v. *Carson.*[155]

(iv) Absence of Malice   The defence will be defeated by the plaintiff proving that the statement was made with malice which, in this instance, means evil motive or spite. In *Thomas* v. *Bradbury, Agnew & Co. Ltd.*[156] the Court of Appeal held that a book *reviewer*[157] for *Punch* was hostilely motivated against the plaintiff's books, which was evident not only by the review he wrote but also by his behaviour in the witness-box. His malice negated a plea of fairness. Malice will, of course, be difficult to establish, though it may be inferred from the words themselves, for example, if they are wholly disproportionate to the facts, or from the prior relationship between the parties. Wider dissemination of the statement than was necessary may also indicate malice.

(e) Privilege

There are two kinds of privilege: *absolute*, which is limited in scope but affords complete protection; and *qualified*, which is wider in its ambit but can be defeated by malice. The first category represents the triumph of speech rights over reputation.

(i) Absolute Privilege   Freedom of speech is so important on certain *occasions* that complete immunity is accorded to the maker of a statement, even if it is untrue and he was motivated by malice. Every communication on such occasions is protected. The occasions may be divided into three broad categories: parliamentary, judicial, and executive.

Parliamentary privilege: (1) Statements made in Parliament. Article 9 of the Bill of Rights 1688 states that 'the freedom of speech and debates or proceedings in Parliament ought not to be impeached or questioned in any court or place out of Parliament'.

In *Church of Scientology of California* v. *Johnson-Smith*[158] it was held that a plaintiff cannot even use statements in Parliament to show malice so as to defeat fair comment on statements made outside Parliament. Similar privilege extends to petitions to Parliament[159] and letters written *by* MPs to the Speaker[160] but not, it seems, letters written *to* MPs.[161]

Until recently, the effect of Article 9 of the Bill of Rights was that an MP's right to sue could be affected as much as the right to be sued for something he had said in Parliament. This problem came to a head when an MP brought a

---

[154] *Broadway Approvals Ltd.* v. *Odhams Press Ltd. (No. 2)* [1965] 1 WLR 805.

[155] (1888) 20 QBD 275, 281.   [156] [1906] 2 KB 627.

[157] The writer's malice may not, however, infect the publisher who, in such cases, will be allowed to plead the defence: *Lyon* v. *Daily Telegraph* [1943] KB 746.

[158] [1972] 1 QB 522.

[159] *Lake* v. *King* (1668) 1 Wms. Saund. 120; 85 ER 128.   [160] *Rost* v. *Edwards* [1990] 2 QB 460.

[161] *Rivlin* v. *Bilainkin* [1953] 1 QB 485.

defamation against *The Guardian*.[162] The action was stayed by the court because the newspaper's wish to plead justification, by reference to things said by the MP in the course of parliamentary proceedings, was prohibited by Article 9 of the Bill of Rights. The considerable debate that surrounded this issue[163] centred mainly on the idea that the purpose of the Bill of Rights was to prevent MPs being sued for opinions expressed during parliamentary proceedings, not from vindicating their own rights as plaintiff. So, in the end, the Defamation Act 1996,[164] while reaffirming the traditional immunity (s. 13(4)), also gives in section 13(1) MPs the right to waive Article 9 so that proceedings in Parliament can be used in evidence in court. Ironically, after the law was changed in the way described in the text the two MPs withdrew their libel actions!

(2) Reports, papers, proceedings, etc. ordered to be published by Parliament.[165]

Judicial privileges: (1) Statements by a judge, jury, advocates, or witnesses in any judicial or quasi-judicial proceedings.[166] As Fry LJ explained:[167] 'It is not a desire to prevent actions from being brought in cases where they ought to be maintained that has led to the adoption of the present rule of law; but it is the fear that if the rule were otherwise, numerous actions would be brought against persons who were merely discharging their duty.' Judicial proceedings means proceedings before any superior or inferior court, including county court, bankruptcy registrar, magistrate, professional disciplinary committees,[168] or tribunals exercising functions equivalent to those of an established court of justice,[169] so long as certain criteria are satisfied.[170]

(2) Communications between solicitor and client relating to judicial proceedings. The privilege is far-reaching and can even cover communications between (opposing) solicitors (when one makes a defamatory statement about the other's client) provided they have an 'immediate link' with possible legal or quasi-legal proceedings.[171] Communications that are not related to judicial

---

[162] *Hamilton v. Guardian, The Times,* 22 July 1995. See, also, *Allason v. Haines* [1995] EMLR 143.

[163] See, for instance, *Hansard* HL Deb., 7 May 1996, 24–52. An account of this incident, from the newspaper's angle, (with some interesting insights as to how s. 13(1) of the Defamation Act 1996 came about) can be found in Leigh and Vulliamy, *Sleaze: The Corruption of Parliament* (1997).

[164] An excellent illustration of the well-known principle that in English law a 'constitutional enactment' can be amended by ordinary legislation.

[165] Parliamentary Papers Act 1840, ss. 1 and 2.

[166] *Royal Aquarium and Summer and Winter Garden Society Ltd. v. Parkinson* [1892] 1 QB 431, 451 per Lopes LJ.

[167] *Munster v. Lamb* (1883) 11 QBD 588, 607. Cf. *Rondel v. Worsely* [1969] 1 AC 191, 269 per Lord Pearce.

[168] E.g. *Addis v. Crocker* [961] 1 QB 11.

[169] *O'Connor v. Waldron* [1935] AC 76, 81 per Lord Atkin. Evidence given at official conciliation proceedings does not attract absolute privilege: *Tadd v. Eastwood* [1985] ICR 132 (CA).

[170] What these criteria are is not entirely clear and there is ample authority as to what has to be considered under this heading. See *Shell Co. of Australia Ltd. v. Federal Commissioner of Taxation* [1931] AC 275; *Lincoln v. Daniels* [1962] 1 QB 237. Communications with the European Commission may attract absolute privilege: *Hasselblad (GB) Ltd. v. Orbinson* [1985] 2 WLR 1 and this even though the procedure adopted by the Commission to investigate complaints is more administrative than judicial in nature. Licensing justices, however, have not been included. See: *Attwood v. Chapman* [1914] 3 KB 275.

[171] Which the Court of Appeal thought did *not* exist in *Waple v. Surrey* [1998] 1 WLR 860. The court there stressed that one 'should be slow to extend the scope of this privilege'. See at 864–5 (per Brooke LJ).

proceedings are also privileged though it is uncertain whether this is of the absolute or qualified variety.[172]

(3) Fair and accurate newspaper reports of judicial proceedings publicly heard before any court specified by section 14(3) of the Defamation Act 1996[173] provided they are published *contemporaneously* with such proceedings. This privilege is now unequivocally treated as absolute, though qualified privilege would have served just as well.[174]

Executive privileges: Statements made by one officer of the State to another in the course of duty.[175] In *M. Isaacs & Sons Ltd.* v. *Cook*[176] it was made clear that it does not make any difference if the report in question is related to commercial matters. There is some doubt, however, about the scope of this privilege; in particular, how high-ranking the official has to be in order to claim immunity.[177]

(ii) Qualified Privilege   This defence, known in US law as 'conditional privilege', is, like fair comment, defeated by malice. It differs from absolute privilege in that here it is the communication that contains the statement complained of that is privileged, not the entire occasion on which the statement was made. Instances of this privilege, which may be very widely invoked, may be grouped under four heads; it can be said that they all share one characteristic—that is, they exist for 'the common convenience and welfare of society';[178] or as another judge put it:[179]

It was in the public interest that the rules of our law relating to . . . privilege communications were introduced because it is in the public interest that persons should be allowed to speak freely on occasions when it is their duty to speak, and to tell all they know or believe, or on occasions when it is necessary to speak in the protection of some (self or) common interest.

---

[172] *More* v. *Weaver* [1928] 2 KB 520 (absolute); cf. *Minter* v. *Priest* [1930] AC 558 (which left the matter open). The communication must be fairly referable to the relationship of solicitor and client.

[173] They include any court in the UK, the European Court of Justice (or any court attached to that court), the European Court of Human Rights, and any international criminal tribunal established by the Security Council or by an international agreement to which the UK is a party. See, also, Courts and Legal Services Act 1990, s. 69(2).

[174] Indeed, qualified privilege may still apply if the statutory requirements have not been fulfilled.

[175] *Chatterton* v. *Secretary of State for India* [1895] 2 QB 189. A different kind of privilege is the privilege against production of a document. In this case the claimant is not claiming protection against a possible defamation action but is attempting to prevent the publication of a confidential (usually official) document on which an action of defamation might be based. The matter is best discussed in books on evidence though one may remind the reader that since *Conway* v. *Rimmer* [1968] AC 910 the courts have clearly asserted their right to override ministerial objections and ask to inspect the relevant documents. This right, however, is sparingly exercised. See *Air Canada* v. *Secretary of State for Trade* [1983] 2 AC 394.

[176] [1925] 2 KB 391.

[177] Compare *Merricks* v. *Nott-Bower* [1965] 1 QB 57, and *Richards* v. *Naum* [1967] 1 QB 620. In *Fayed* v. *Al-Tajir* [1988] QB 712 internal documents of a foreign embassy were treated as attracting absolute privilege. The Vienna Convention on Diplomatic Relations may have played an important part in the outcome of this case.

[178] *Toogood* v. *Spyring* [1834] 1 CM. & R. 181, 193 (per Parke B); 149 ER 1044, 1049–50. It is for the judge to decide whether the occasion is privileged and the communication was made with reference to that occasion.

[179] *Gerhold* v. *Baker* [1918] W.N. 368 at 369 (per Bankes LJ). For a similar approach see *Henwood* v. *Harrison* (1872) LR 7 CP 606 at 622 (per Willes J).

The defendant has to establish the facts necessary to create the privilege; but whether the situation is one that attracts qualified privilege is for the judge to determine. As stated, this privilege will be lost if the plaintiff shows that the defendant was motivated by malice. Finally, the jury will have the last word as to whether the defendant acted in good faith. In short, all of the defamation protagonists (plaintiff, defendant, judge and jury) may have a role to play in this defence.

Matters of public interest: These included fair and accurate reports of Parliamentary proceedings. At common law this was finally settled in 1868 in *Wason* v. *Walter*[180] and is justified by the idea that the advantages of such publicity outweigh the possible injury to the plaintiff's reputation. However, as Lord Denning said in *Associated Newspaper Ltd.* v. *Dingle*,[181] if the newspaper 'adds its own spice and prints a story to the same effect as the parliamentary paper, and garnishes and embellishes it with circumstantial detail, it goes beyond the privilege and becomes subject to the general law'. Privilege will also be granted to a sketch of Parliamentary proceedings 'if it is made fairly and honestly with the intention of giving an impression of the impact made on the hearer'.[182]

The Parliamentary Papers Act 1840, section 3, as extended by section 9(1) of the Defamation Act 1952, confers a similar privilege on *extracts* or *abstracts* of reports or proceedings, etc., published by order of either House of Parliament.

Qualified privilege is also enjoyed by 'fair and accurate'[183] reports of judicial proceedings that the public may attend. Though this includes the proceedings of *any* court, the proceeding must be in public. No privilege extends to publication of obscene or prohibited matter. As regards proceedings in foreign courts, these, under the current regime, are privileged only so far as their matter is of legitimate interest to the public in *this* country.[184] Qualified privilege may also protect persons making statements to the proper authorities in order to procure the redress of public grievances. Finally, section 7 of the Defamation Act 1952 affords qualified privilege to numerous kinds of reports in newspapers and broadcasts of public meetings provided they were not made with malice. This section, and the Schedule of the Act, distinguish between statements privileged without any explanation or contradiction and statements privileged subject to explanation or contradiction. In the latter group the defence will be lost if it is shown that the defendant failed to publish in an appropriate manner any letter or statement offered by the plaintiff by way of explanation or contradiction of the remarks made by the defendant.

The above (mixed, i.e. common-law and statutory) regime, though not explicitly abrogated will, in practice, be overtaken by the regime envisaged by the Defamation Act 1996 (especially Sch. 1) when it comes into force. A detailed consideration (and comparison) of the wording of the lengthy (1952 and 1966)

---

[180] [1868] LR 4 QB 73.   [181] [1964] AC 371, 411.

[182] *Cook* v. *Alexander* [1974] QB 279, 288, per Lord Denning MR.

[183] The fairness and accuracy of the report is a matter to be decided by the jury, and the judge should decide this issue only in the most obvious of cases: *Kingshott* v. *Associated Kent Newspapers Ltd.* [1991] 1 QB 88.

[184] *Webb* v. *Times Publishing Co. Ltd.* [1960] 2 QB 535.

Schedules would not be appropriate to this book.[185] Still, one must note that the new regime, though it builds on the old (i.e. currently existing) scheme of things, also represents a rationalisation of it. Thus, first, section 14 of the 1996 Act will, as we have seen, accord *absolute* privilege to fair and accurate reports before a court to which this section applies, (i.e. mainly the UK courts and the two European Courts in Luxembourg and Strasbourg) if published contemporaneously with the proceedings. Secondly, qualified privilege will be granted by Schedule 1 of the 1996 Act to fair and accurate reports of proceedings in public of a legislature or court *anywhere in the world*. Thus, these reports need not be contemporaneous with the proceedings, nor are they limited to legislatures or courts 'in one of Her Majesty's dominions outside Great Britain' (as was the case with the 1952 Act). Nor, finally, is the statutory privilege under the 1966 Act limited (as it was under the old regime) to publications in newspapers and broadcasts. But, as is the case with the regime which the 1996 Act will replace,[186] the reports must be fair and accurate (though this does not mean that they must be *verbatim*); and the protection of the Schedule will not cover the publication of material prohibited by law.

Matters of interest to the publisher: In *Turner* v. *Metro-Goldwyn-Mayer Pictures Ltd*.[187] Lord Oaksey said:

There is . . . an analogy between the criminal law of self-defence and a man's right to defend himself against written or verbal attacks. In both cases he is entitled, if he can, to defend himself effectively, and he only loses the protection of the law if he goes beyond defence and proceeds to offence. That is to say, the circumstances in which he defends himself, either by acts or by words, negative the malice which the law draws from violent acts or defamatory words.

Thus, brewers who answered a complaint by a publican of poor-quality beer supplied to him, by voicing a suspicion that he had watered it, were covered by privilege.[188] In such cases not only is the business communication itself treated as being privileged, but also the incidents of the transmission and treatment of that communication, which are in accordance with the reasonable and usual course of business. This would include dictation to a secretary or typist.[189]

Matters of interest to others: There has to be a legal, moral, or social duty to make the statement *and* an interest in receiving it. To these standard 'tests' a third has been emerging recently and finds its most clear articulation in the lucid judgment of the Lord Chief Justice in *Reynolds* v. *Times Newspapers Ltd*.[190] According to this test—the learned judge calls it the 'circumstantial test'—the court must also ask itself the following question. 'Were the nature, *status* and source of the material, and the circumstances of the publication, such that the publication should in the public interest be protected in the absence of proof of

---

[185] For details, see *Gatley on Libel and Slander*, (9th edn.) chs 14 and 15.
[186] It should be noted that the new Act does not expressly abrogate any existing privileges (see s. 15(4)(b)) but simply makes most of them redundant in practice.
[187] [1950] 1 All ER 449, 470–1. [188] *Osborn* v. *Boulter* [1930] 2 KB 226.
[189] See ibid. and *Bryanston Finance* v. *de Vries* [1975] QB 703, below.
[190] [1998] 3 WLR 862, esp. 899 ff.

express malice?' 'Status' in this respect denotes 'the degree to which information on a matter of public concern may (because of its character and known provenance) command respect.' The Chief Justice continued: 'The higher the status of a report, the more likely it is to meet the circumstantial test. Conversely, unverified information from unidentified and unofficial sources may have little or no status and where defamatory statements of fact are to be published to the widest audience on the strength of such sources, the publisher undertakes a heavy burden in showing that the publication is "fairly" warranted by any reasonable occasion or exigency.' It was for this reason that the defendant/newspaper's plea of qualified privilege failed on this occasion.[191]

Privilege is accorded to such communications because: 'It is in the general interest of society that correct information should be obtained as to the character of persons in whom others have a legitimate interest.'[192] It follows that an inquiry about a person out of curiosity will not clothe the answer with privilege.[193] Communications made to the enquirer subsequent to the first reply—perhaps correcting or amplifying the contents of the latter in the light of new information available to the maker of the statement—will also be covered by the privilege.[194]

Common examples of the privilege discussed here are found in character-references given by former employees to prospective employers.[195] This heading is not free of difficulties. For example, though it will be easy for a judge to decide when there is a *legal* duty to communicate the defamatory matter, it may be less easy to decide if or when the defendant has a *moral* or *social* duty. Lindley LJ thought that 'the question of moral or social duty' is for 'each judge to decide as best he can for himself'.[196] But Scrutton LJ wondered whether in so doing a judge should merely 'give his own view of moral and social duty', or should 'endeavour to ascertain what view "the great mass of right minded men" would take'.[197] Perhaps a compromise between these two would be the right answer.

The limitation on this category of qualified privilege is illustrated by *Watt v. Longsdon*.[198] A director of a company informed the chairman of his suspicion that the plaintiff, an employee, was misbehaving with women; and he also informed the plaintiff's wife. It was held that communication to the chairman was privileged, but not to the wife, for although she had an interest in hearing about the allegation, he had no moral or social duty to inform her.

---

[191] The plaintiff, former Prime Minister of Ireland, sued *The Times* over a publication concerning the political crisis in Ireland in 1994. He claimed that the piece implied that he had deliberately misled the Irish Parliament by suppressing crucial information about the Irish Attorney-General, whose appointment to the Presidency of the High Court he had sought to promote. The jury found in his favour, but awarded 1p by way of damages. The paper's cross-appeal, concerning the applicability of the defence of qualified privilege, was rejected while the plaintiff's appeal was allowed and a new trial was ordered.

[192] *Whiteley v. Adams* (1863) 15 CB (NS) 392 (per Erle CJ).

[193] See, for instance, Hamilton LJ's dicta in *Greenlands v. Wilmshurst* [1913] 3 KB 507 at 541.

[194] *Gardner v. Slade* (1849) 18 LJQB 334 at 336 (per Lord Denman CJ and per Coleridge J).

[195] The rich casuistry is considered in Gatley, ch. 14.   [196] *Stuart v. Bell* [1891] 2 QB 341.

[197] *Watt v. Longsdon* [1930] 1 KB 130, 144. But in the case of newspaper publications 'public interest and public benefit are necessary . . . but not enough without more. There must be a duty to publish to the public at large and an interest in the public at large to receive the publication': per Stephenson LJ in *Blackshaw v. Lord* [1983] 3 WLR 283, 301 (italics supplied).

[198] [1930] 1 KB 130.

This part of the law of defamation, though still valid, must be constantly scrutinised against the expansion of the tort of negligence following the decision in *Spring* v. *Guardian Assurance plc*.[199] For though their Lordships were anxious to emphasise that the two torts occupy different grounds and cater for different interests, the new possibility of suing the referee in negligence may well overtake current practice.

Common interest: Qualified privilege also applies in cases where two parties have an interest in a statement about the plaintiff other than those falling under any of the above categories. Thus, it has been held that an employer and his employees have a common interest in the reason for the dismissal of an employee.[200] So, too, in *Watt* v. *Longsdon* the communication to the chairman of the company was privileged because both publisher and receiver had a common interest in the matter.

Is the dictation of a letter to a secretary covered by original privilege arising out of the dictation of the business letter? Or is it an ancillary privilege dependent upon whether privilege covers communication to the intended recipient? Lord Denning MR in *Bryanston Finance Ltd.* v. *de Vries*[201] thought that it is an original privilege because of the common interest in getting the letter written. This means that communications to secretaries do not depend upon whether or not the publication to the ultimate recipient of the letter would have been privileged. The converse is true if one accepts Lawton LJ's view[202] that the privilege is ancillary and depends upon whether the communication to the recipient was privileged or not. This second view does not exclude instances of common interest between employer and secretary so as to render such dictation privileged *per se*. Nowadays a great number of matters connected with the survival and prosperity of the business will be a matter for mutual concern for both employer and employee and in such cases all relevant communications will be privileged.

This, in fact, was a major issue in *Bryanston Finance* v. *de Vries*. The defendant and a colleague, who were involved in litigation over financial matters with a loan bank and its chairman, prepared a circular and letters accusing the chairman of the plaintiff company of various improprieties. They also threatened to send these documents to: (a) the shareholders of the plaintiff; (b) the Department of Trade and Industry; (c) the Stock Exchange; and (d) various other organisations, including the national Press, unless they reached a favourable settlement. Upon receipt of the letter and documents the chairman obtained an injunction to restrain their publication to the above-mentioned bodies, and then sued for libel. So far there had been publication only to the secretary, which the defendant claimed was privileged. The issue was whether it was original privilege, or depended upon communication to the recipients being privileged. If the second view is taken to be the common denominator of all three judgments, one would say that communication to the shareholders, Department of Trade, and the Stock Exchange would be privileged because of common interest, but communication to the Press would not be so.

---

[199] [1995] 2 AC 296.
[201] [1975] QB 703, 719.
[200] *Hunt* v. *Great Northern Railway Co.* [1891] 2 QB 189.
[202] Ibid., 736–8.

Watts v. *Times Newspapers*[203] recently highlighted a different difficulty. If a person makes a defamatory statement about X he may, as we saw, be led to publish an apology. This, indeed, was the situation in *Watts* where the defendant newspaper published two pieces concerning plagiarism by X, but to the second piece attached a photograph of Y (who had the same name as X). The paper agreed to publish a (neutral) apology. Unfortunately, it ended by publishing an apology which was largely drafted by Y's solicitor and which again made reference to the plagiarism by X. X then sued the newspaper for the contents of the apology, and the paper, in its turn, added Y's solicitor (the draftsman of the text) as a third party. Y's position (and that of his solicitor) was deemed to be covered by privilege since he was, essentially, responding to an attack made on him. But the paper, itself, did not share in the privilege. This was because it was the paper that had defamed Y and could thus not be seen to be taking advantage of his self-defence. But the court also held that the paper could not plead privilege (for the communication prepared by Y) since a simple, unembellished apology (without the references to X) would have been perfectly sufficient. The case thus suggests that though in some cases the defence of privilege may be available where an apology to A actually refers to B this will not always be so.[204]

Qualified privilege is defeated by malice. In addition to evidence of ulterior motive, malice may be established, for example, by showing that the defendant did not believe his own statement or exceeded the privilege by giving the statement wider publication than was necessary. Malice here may mean either (*a*) that the defendant did not honestly believe in the truth of what he said, or (*b*) use of a privileged occasion for an improper purpose, which is usually the case whenever the dominant desire is to injure the plaintiff. Lack of honest belief in his statement will deprive a defamer of his defence, provided, of course, that he acted intentionally or recklessly when publishing the defamatory matter. As Lord Diplock said in *Horrocks* v. *Lowe*,[205] despite the imperfection of the mental process by which the belief is arrived at (such as carelessness, impulsiveness, irrationality, prejudice, reliance on intuition), it may still be 'honest', that is, a positive belief that the conclusions one has reached are true. The law demands no more.

4. Damages

Subject to what will be said at the end of this section, damages are awarded by juries. Moreover, until recently, most lawyers (and, certainly, judges) would have agreed with Lord Hailsham who, in *Cassell & Co. Ltd.* v. *Broome*,[206] warned that the judiciary should avoid at any level to substitute itself for a jury, unless the award is manifestly too large or too small. In the years that have elapsed since that pronouncement was made juries have made some very substantial

---

[203] [1996] 2 WLR 427.

[204] This problem does not arise when the apology is made in open court for then it is covered by absolute privilege.

[205] [1975] AC 135, 150. On this see Duncan and Neill, op. cit. (Select Bibliography), ch. 18.

[206] [1972] AC 1027, 1065. See also *Blackshaw* v. *Lord* [1983] 3 WLR 283, 302 ff. *Cassell* is the leading case concerning punitive damages; and further guidance on their award in the context of defamation cases was given by the Court of Appeal in *Riches* v. *News Group Newspapers* [1986] QB 256.

awards which, coupled with high costs,[207] have led many (and, of course, not least the newspaper industry) to complain about the state of the law. The reasons why such high awards were made are not entirely clear. In part this may be because juries were not given any real guidance. The size of the awards may also have reflected a dislike of the tabloid press, totally unrestrained in our country by a patchy law of privacy (on which see below, Section 7). Discontent reached a peak in *Sutcliffe* v. *Pressdram Ltd.*,[208] when a jury awarded £600,000 to Sonia Sutcliffe, the wife of the 'Yorkshire Ripper', for a libel published by *Private Eye*. The judgments in the Court of Appeal offered interesting guidelines that could be used to direct juries in awarding *reasonable* amounts;[209] but the proposals seemed to have had little impact in practice, so Parliament was forced to intervene. As a result, section 8(2) of the Court and Legal Services Act 1990 states that 'rules of court may provide for the Court of Appeal, in such class of case as may be specified in the rules, to have power, in place of ordering a new trial, to substitute for the sum awarded by the jury such sum as appears to the court to be proper'. In *Rantzen* v. *Mirror Group Newspapers (1986) Ltd.*[210] the Court of Appeal was strongly influenced by article 10 of the European Convention for the Protection of Human Rights. It felt that 'the common law . . . requires the courts to subject large awards of damages to a more searching scrutiny than has been customary in the past'.[211] The reduction of the plaintiff's damages in that case from £250,000 to £110,000 was an obvious sign of the newly found confidence to intervene and reduce jury awards. But the situation was still not satisfactory in that it meant that additional time and expenditure had to be used in order to achieve a fairer result. Matters, it was thought, could be improved if the trial judge had the power—which superior courts had hitherto denied him—to give guidance to juries as to the right level of awards. This might include drawing their attention to levels of compensation found in personal injury (but not other defamation) cases. This last step was, indeed, taken by the Court of Appeal in *John* v. *Mirror Group Newspapers Ltd.*[212] and reduced the damages awarded to the singer Elton John for an allegation that he had been bulimic from £350,000 to £50,000.

---

[207] E.g. in 1987 the *Daily Star* had to pay Jeffrey Archer £500,000 after he won a libel action that cost an estimated £300,000. In the same year, Lieut. Cdr. Packard was awarded £450,000 in an action against a newspaper (which had sold a mere 40 copies in this country). In 1988 Koo Stark was awarded £300,000 in an action that cost an estimated £100,000 and in 1989 Count Tolstoy was ordered to pay Lord Aldington £1.5m. after prolonged hearings that were said to have cost close to £1m. These figures are small in comparison with those found in successful American libel actions, but they are huge in comparison with European standards; and until the (slow) introduction of structured settlements they meant that libel actions could often produce higher awards than many serious cases of physical injury. These huge awards, however, by no means constitute the norm, as a helpful appendix in Carter-Ruck on *Libel and Slander* (5th edn., 1997) shows, depicting all awards made between 1951 and 1997.

[208] [1991] 1 QB 153.

[209] Juries were thus asked to consider the weekly or monthly sum that a huge capital award would yield. Equally a large award would tempt defendants to appeal and thus cause plaintiffs delays, expenses, and anxiety. This is certainly true in many American cases where awards are often reduced as a result of remittiturs, appeals, or other post-trial settlements. But juries should not be given information about awards in (*a*) personal-injuries cases (because comparisons are 'inappropriate'); (*b*) other libel actions (since this might result in unseemly 'over' or 'under' bidding).

[210] [1993] 2 WLR 953.   [211] Ibid., 972.   [212] [1997] QB 586.

The damages awarded in defamation cases are also said to be 'at large'. Lord Hailsham explained this in the following way:

Quite obviously, the award must include factors for injury to the feelings, the anxiety and uncertainty undergone in the litigation, the absence of apology, or the reaffirmation of the truth of the matters complained of, or the malice of the defendant. The bad conduct of the plaintiff himself may also enter into the matter, where he had provoked the libel, or where perhaps he has libelled the defendant in reply. What is awarded is thus a figure which cannot be arrived at by any purely objective computation . . . In other words the whole process of assessing damages where they are 'at large' is essentially a matter of impression and not addition.

It follows that invariably, if not inevitably, such 'damages are in their nature punitive or exemplary in the loose sense' of the words. Since *Rookes* v. *Barnard*[213] there is in this country, as there has always been in America, a clear distinction between compensatory damages, which can include an enlarged award (aggravated damages) in cases of outrage, and punitive or exemplary damages, which go beyond compensation and attempt to 'punish the defendant'. One such case is where the defendant decides to publish a libel, calculating that possible damages will be outweighed by the profit accruing from the sale of, for example, the book and the publicity. This was the case in *Cassell* v. *Broome*, which was deemed to be a proper case for punitive damages in order to teach the defendant that tort does not pay. In such cases it is felt that over and above the figure awarded for loss of reputation an additional sum is needed to vindicate the strength of the law and act as a supplement to its strictly penal provisions.

The desirability of punitive elements in civil cases is a hotly disputed issue and is discussed more fully in Chapter 8, Section 2(2), below. In the context of defamation, however, this presents a further problem. This stems from the fact that they are often pleaded *in terrorem* in circumstances that do not really fit the strict criteria set out in the House of Lords cases of *Rookes* and *Cassell*. In such cases, however, it is not easy to persuade the court *in advance of the trial* that the case is so unarguable as to deserve striking out. As a result, a plaintiff may gain a considerable tactical advantage by 'threatening' criminal sanctions on a defendant without any of the safeguards that usually accompany criminal proceedings. No doubt some would find this a just counterpart, especially for media defendants who tend to be in a financially stronger position when compared to legally unaided plaintiffs. But if the scales of justice are unevenly tipped in defamation cases (first in favour of defendants and then, if plaintiffs turn out to be sufficiently resilient, in their favour), the balance should arguably be restored by other means than by resorting to the rather anomalous device of punitive awards.[214]

---

[213] [1964] AC 1129.

[214] Of the £350,000 originally awarded to Mr (now Sir Elton) John, £275,000 consisted of exemplary damages—a proportion which may show both how unguided the jury was but which could also be taken as a sign of the average juror's dislike of the behaviour of the tabloid press. This part of the award was reduced by the Court of Appeal to £5,000.

A further important point that must be made in this context is the following. Many, if not most, defamatory statements are published by one or more defendants in one or more newspapers, etc. Clearly, the plaintiff cannot be allowed to recover damages several times over. Section 12 of the Defamation Act provides: 'In any action for libel or slander the defendant may give evidence in mitigation of damages that the plaintiff has recovered damages, or had brought action for damages, for libel or slander in respect of the publication of words to the same effect as the words on which the action is founded, or has received or agreed to receive compensation in respect of any such publication.' Referring to the facts of *Lewis* v. *Daily Telegraph*,[215] where similar libels were published in two additional newspapers on the same day, each being dealt with by a different jury, Lord Reid said:

> I do not think it is sufficient merely to tell each jury to make such allowances as they may think fit. They ought, in my view, to be directed that in considering the evidence submitted to them, they should consider how far the damage suffered by the plaintiffs can reasonably be attributed solely to the libel with which they are concerned and how far it ought to be regarded as the joint result of the two libels. If they think that some part of the damage is the joint result of the two libels they should bear in mind that the plaintiffs ought not to be compensated twice for the same loss. They can only deal with this matter on very broad lines and they must take it that the other jury will be given a similar direction.

The above comments about the jury's role in assessing defamation awards will have to be read in conjunction with the new procedure for the summary disposal of defamation claims which is envisaged by sections 8, 9 and 10 of the Defamation Act 1996.[216] This innovative procedure, the brainchild of Lord Hoffmann, will be available to the court and allow it to 'dispose summarily' of the plaintiff's claim when it appears to have 'no realistic prospect of success.'[217] This could be either because there is no real likelihood that the cause of action will be established or because of the apparent strength of the merits of the defence. Reversly, however, section 8(3) of the 1996 Act also gives the court the power to give judgment for the plaintiff and grant him summary relief—which, according to section 9 can include damages of up to £10,000—if, in its view, 'there is no defence to the claim which has a realistic prospect of success and . . . there is no other reason why the claim should be tried.' This power to exclude juries from the award of damages, coupled with the aforementioned power to intervene with their awards, thus represents a further inroad to trial by jury and one which it is hoped will help streamline and expedite defamation trials in this country.

5. Mitigation of Damages

(A) APOLOGY

The making, or offer, of an apology is not a defence to liability, but goes towards mitigating damages. Section 1 of the Libel Act 1843 (Lord Campbell's

---

[215] [1964] AC 234, 261.   [216] But which are not (at the time of writing) yet in force.
[217] S. 8(2) of the Defamation Act 1996.

Act) enables a defendant in any action for defamation to give evidence that he has made, or offered, an apology either before, or as soon as possible after, the commencement of proceedings. But he must notify the plaintiff in writing of his intention to lead such evidence. In the case of publications in newspapers and periodicals, section 2 of the Act (as amended by the Libel Acts of 1845 and 1879) enables a defendant to plead that the libel was published without malice or gross negligence and that a full apology has been published. Such a plea must be accompanied by a payment into court by way of amends.

Apology is also relevant in making an 'offer of amends' for unintentional defamation under section 4(3) of the Defamation Act 1952 or, once it comes into force, the new defence of unintentional defamation. These were discussed earlier so we do not need to return to them again.

(B) PLAINTIFF'S REPUTATION

In mitigation of damages the defendant is entitled to adduce evidence of the plaintiff's *general* bad reputation prior to the publication of the libel. This is a controversial plea. In a leading modern case, *Plato Films* v. *Speidel*,[218] Viscount Simonds questioned why, if none of the other numerous and adequate defences is available, any further indulgence should be shown to a defendant; and the other judges were prepared to give this a measure of support. Despite their Lordships' reservations, the law was settled in 1882 in *Scott* v. *Sampson*[219] and none of them was prepared to disturb the long-standing rule. In that case Cave J said *obiter* that *general* evidence of bad reputation is in principle admissible, as immediately and necessarily connected with the question of damages. A plaintiff complains of loss of reputation,[220] and that he has been deprived of his character by the defendant. Why should not the defendant then be permitted to show that the plaintiff's character was previously tainted or that he had little character or reputation to lose? He then quoted Starkie on *Slander and Libel*:

> To deny this would be to decide that a man of the worst character is entitled to the same measure of damages with one of unsullied and unblemished reputation. A reputed thief would be placed on the same footing with the most honourable merchant, a virtuous woman with the most abandoned prostitute. To enable the jury to estimate the probable quantum of injury sustained a knowledge of the party's previous character is not only material but seems to be absolutely essential.

Only evidence showing the plaintiff's actual reputation prior to or at the time of publication of the libel can be submitted. Specific evidence revealing his character and disposition (i.e. of the reputation he ought to have) is not admissible. To put it differently: the defendant can lead evidence about the plaintiff's publicly known behaviour in order to show that the plaintiff did not have much reputation to lose. But he cannot lead evidence in order to remake

---

[218] [1961] AC 1090.   [219] (1881) 8 QBD 491, 503.

[220] In *Singh* v. *Gillard* (1988) 138 NLJ Reports 144, 145 Lord Donaldson MR stated that the defendant 'can prove that the plaintiff is of bad character and so has little or no reputation to be damaged. But the rules as to what evidence can be called in support of such a plea are highly restrictive' (relying on Neill LJ in *Pamplin* v. *Express Newspapers (No. 2)* [1988] 1 All ER 282, 286: 'an admitted master of the law and practice relating to claims for defamation'. Despite the date of the report, *Pamplin* was decided in Feb. 1985).

the plaintiff's reputation. For, it is said, it would be intolerable if a jury, learning long after of this or that discreditable episode in a person's life, could diminish his current public esteem. Other reasons have been given against the admission of evidence of *specific* instances of misconduct. If such allegations were allowed in evidence it would open the door to collateral issues, which have only an indirect bearing on the main question in the case. This would, inevitably, prolong the trial and tend to confuse the jury by distracting their attention from the main issue. The result might be that a trial in which the truth and falsity of one allegation was being investigated might degenerate into trials of the truth or falsity of other allegations not strictly relevant to the subject-matter of the trial, introduced by the defendants simply to mitigate damages. It would also place undue burden on the plaintiff, who would have to support with evidence his entire conduct through life rather than prove his general reputation. All these arguments against admitting evidence of particular facts concerning the plaintiff's life drew a great deal of support from the facts of *Plato* v. *Speidel*, though the case also brought out the deficiencies of the present law and the need for its reform.

In that case General Speidel claimed damages from the distributors of a film which depicted him as a party to the murder of King Alexander of Yugoslavia. The defendants pleaded justification and, alternatively, in mitigation of damages, allegations demonstrating that the general had been guilty of war crimes, persecuting the Jews, espionage while attached to the German Embassy in Paris in 1934, and so forth. The Court of Appeal struck out the plea and rephrased it as follows: 'Alternatively in mitigation of damages the defendants will at the trial of the action give evidence in chief that the plaintiff had a bad reputation as a man who was a party to and/or responsible for acts which were crimes against humanity and/or atrocities.' The defendants appealed, but the House of Lords, on the grounds already mentioned, upheld the Court of Appeal's refusal to allow evidence of specific facts concerning the general's past. What the defendants thus had to prove was that the plaintiff had a '*general* bad reputation', rather than that he committed acts A, B, and C, and the jury would be left to decide what reputation he deserved. In practice, this is notoriously difficult to achieve and that is why defendants can rarely use this weapon and, instead, choose to invoke one of the substantive defences including wide-ranging pleas of justification, sometimes based upon attaching imaginative or even ingenious meanings to the words complained of.

The position of the present law is thus unequivocal: it does not wish to hinder the plaintiff's attempt to vindicate himself by the fact that he has committed other misdemeanours or indiscretions not directly associated with the acts or omissions attributed to him in the words complained of. However, in the view of the Supreme Court Procedure Committee:[221] 'It is . . . not necessary for the purpose of effective vindication, nor consonant with justice, that a plaintiff who *has* misconducted himself in the same sector of his life as that to which the libel relates should recover damages on exactly the same generous basis as one

---

[221] *Report on Practice and Procedure in Defamation* (1991), 34.

who truly has an unblemished record in the relevant area of activity.' The Commission thus concluded[222] that it 'would be a significant improvement upon the present position if it were possible for defendants to rely upon specific instances of misconduct on the plaintiff's part, for the purpose of mitigating damages rather than by way of defence, provided that the allegations related to the same sector of the plaintiff's life (e.g. business probity, conduct towards his family, etc.) and provided proper and specific notice was given in the defence'.[223] The Commission's proposals were noted in the Defamation 1996 Bill but the relevant clause, which would have changed the law, was lost at the Committee stage of the House of Commons.

6. Epilogue

The complicated and controversial topic discussed in this chapter calls for some general concluding remarks, if only to force the reader to stand back somewhat and look at the wood and not just at the trees.

First, detailed criticism and proposals for reform are appropriate to a monograph, not a textbook. Yet defamation is such an unusual tort that it merits a limited exception. Indeed, 'archaic', 'odd', and 'complicated' may be better words for a tort which, though the subject of three Committee Reports in less than thirty years, is still considered to be so entangled, irrational, and capable of leading to such extraordinarily long court disputes[224] as to have, 'passed beyond redemption'.[225] For defamation still bears the traces of old battles between the ecclesiastical courts, Star Chamber, and the common-law courts, in their attempts to acquire jurisdiction. We may have buried the forms of action, but they do still rule us from their grave: Maitland could easily have had in mind the distinction between libel and slander when he made his famous aphorism. Yet the continuing distinction between libel and slander, unknown to the vast majority of legal systems, is the least-important peculiarity; others are more serious. Defamation is the only tort in which trial by jury is still widely used,[226] and in which the cause of action is extinguished with the death

---

[222] Ibid., 35.

[223] The committee accepted that, if accepted, its proposal would (as indicated in the text, above) lead to 'a widening of issues and . . . increase the length and cost of the inquiry'. However it regarded this as 'a legitimate price to pay for the avoidance of unduly high awards and, more importantly, for the avoidance of the court being allowed to assess the plaintiff's career and reputation on a false or misleadingly incomplete footing'. Ibid., 37.

[224] *McDonald* v. *Steel*, *The Times*, 16 June 1997—the trial lasted for 313 days which may be (partly) explained but is not excused by the fact that the (impecunious) defendants represented themselves in court.

[225] The citation, from Lord Diplock's judgment in *Slim* v. *Daily Telegraph Ltd.* [1968] 2 QB 157, 179, refers to 'the courts'. In *Singh* v. *Gillard* [1988] 138 NLJ Reports 144, Lord Donaldson MR said that 'the practice and procedure attendant upon the administration of justice in the context of claims for defamation is the last refuge of complexity and technicality in the law'.

[226] *Beta Construction* v. *Channel Four Television Co. Ltd.* [1990] 1 WLR 1042 contains some useful guidelines on which cases are suitable to be tried by judge alone under ss. 69(1) and (3) of the Supreme Court Act 1981. Jury trial should thus be avoided if (a) their involvement would entail a 'substantial' prolongation of the trial or (b) 'significantly' increase costs or (c) involve the jury in the examination of complicated or extensive documents (such as corporate accounts). S. 8 of the Courts and Legal Services Act 1990 may well, in due course, assist those who would like to see a reduction of jury involvement in defamation trials. So will s. 8 of the 1996 Act.

of either party. As a tort actionable *per se*, in certain circumstances it is not alone; but it is unique in so far as it makes it possible for a plaintiff to leave the court enriched because the defendant failed to prove that what he said of the plaintiff was true. In this connection it might be repeated that until comparatively recently some defamation awards were equal to, if not larger than, some awards for serious physical injury, besides leading our law to be held contrary to article 10 of the European Convention on Human Rights.[227] If this is objectionable in the case of human plaintiffs, it becomes even more so in the case of legal entities, which have been awarded enormous sums (£100,000 in the case of the Rubber Improvement Company) without having to prove any actual loss! If one adds to all this the intricacy and vagueness of some of the defences and the generally limited or unsuccessful nature of proposed or effected reforms, one can see why the tort has been described as the 'most difficult of all torts [and] certainly the oddest'.

Perhaps this is inevitable given the nature of the competing values—freedom of speech and protection of honour and reputation. This leads one naturally to the second and more general observation: how does one resolve such a clash?

Law, of course, is about competing values and how one can reconcile them when they clash. But here not only are the interests involved of the highest order; unfortunately, the protagonists who invoke them are often anything but attractive players in the legal game. For instance, it is now widely admitted that the late Robert Maxwell exploited the technicalities of the law to the full in order to stifle criticism against him. At the other end of the spectrum the sanctity of free speech has been invoked by a press—the distinction between tabloid and broad sheet is, alas, becoming blurred these days—which does not enjoy public esteem. It is thus difficult to choose one interest over another while totally ignoring the fact that those who invoke them are often cynical and shrewd manipulators of the law as well as of public opinion. Yet, when all is said and done, there is no doubt that the reforms of recent years have, for better or for worse, been progressively tipping the scales in favour of more free speech and less protection of reputation. The reduction of the role of jury involvement, the diminution of the limitation period from three to one years, the expansion of the defence of innocent defamation, the likelihood of greater predictability and moderation in damage awards, the changes wrought to the law as a result of cases like *Derbyshire*, are all working in favour of speech rights and the press. These changes must be heartily welcomed where political speech is concerned. Yet the scales must not be allowed to tip too far in the other direction, especially where the purpose of speech is general public titillation or gold-digging for the speaker, or the source of the information is from unverified or suspect sources.[228] The absence of a wider protection of privacy, to be discussed in the next section, still gives unacceptable powers to a press that has shown its willingness to abuse them for gain. And the spectrum of the American First

---

[227] *Tolstoy Miloslavsky* v. *United Kingdom* (1995) 20 *EHRR* 442. Contrast, however, Lord Bingham's views in *John* v. *MGN Ltd.* [1997] QB 586.

[228] See the valuable discussion of Lord Bingham in *Reynolds* v. *Times Newspapers Ltd.* [1998] 3 WLR 862.

Amendment, while attractive to some, is not welcome to others.[229] Indeed, the question is not just whether the American law in its entirety is better than ours. The question rather is whether our culture, which is much closer to that found on the Continent of Europe than many are ready to admit, can tolerate a legal regime which treats speech as sacrosanct and subordinates, almost absolutely, all other values to it. Thus posed, the question can, for us, only receive a negative answer. For it is a fact that our system has imposed restrictions on expression on grounds as varied as the protection of official secrets, the protection of minors, obscenity, contempt of court and such like which are much wider-ranging than the American parallels. Though the limits of these limitations are in our system capable of redefinition, refinement, and even liberalisation, on the whole they represent policy decisions that are consciously taken by us and by most European systems but not shared (at any rate to the same extent) by many of our American colleagues. So those who are pushing our law to move closer to the American model should be conscious that their reforming zeal should remain within realistic bounds if it is to succeed at all. The fate that has hitherto been reserved even to modest attempts to improve our law of privacy shows how easy it can be for an academic reformer to consign himself to being the perpetual *vox clamantis in deserto*. The true reformer is the successful reformer; and the successful reformer is, above all, a realist.

The widening of the debate to include within our purview modern civil law systems inevitably leads to the realisation that there exists more than one model to be inspired from. This brings us to our third and last general observation.

A branch of the law which is both complex and at the crossroads must be a prime candidate for comparative examination. Rich variations to our own practice can be found both in the common law and civil law systems. Our courts are beginning to take note of the richness of the available solutions. To be sure, their bias towards the common law jurisdictions remains obvious, not least because the common language gives the illusion that transplantability of idea is greater. Yet Europe is also a repository of fascinating ideas and solutions. One day we may well discover that 'Europe' is found not just in the decisions of the Courts of Luxembourg and Strasbourg but also in the decisions of the courts of France, Germany, the Netherlands, and Italy which have influenced so much the emergence of the new European jurisprudence. The excursus into American law, reproduced towards the end of this chapter, is thus a response to this growing interest in foreign law. It is also meant to remind observers that the other man's grass is not always greener though it may seem so to some on this side of the fence!

Select Bibliography

BARENDT, E., 'Libel and Freedom of Speech in English Law' [1993] *PL* 449.
CARTER-RUCK and STARTE, H. N. A., *On Libel and Slander* (5th edn., 1997).

---

[229] For a collection of essays on this topic see I. Loveland (ed.), *A Special Relationship* (1993).

DUNCAN, C. and NEILL, B., *Defamation* (2nd edn., 1983).

FLEMING, J. G., 'Retraction and Reply: Alternative Remedies for Defamation' 12 *UBCLR* 15 (1978).

GATLEY, *On Libel and Slander* (9th edn., 1998) by Patrick Milmo, W. V. H. Rogers and contributing editors.

HOLDSWORTH, Sir WILLIAM, 'Defamation in the 16th and 17th Centuries' (1925) 41 *LQR* 13.

JOHNSTON, I. D., 'Uncertainties in the Defence of Fair Comment' 8 *NZULR* 359 (1978).

KAYE, J. M., 'Libel and Slander—Two Torts or One?' (1975) 91 *LQR* 524.

KENNEDY, T. P. and REED, A., 'The Europeanisation of Defamation' (1996) *JEL* 5 (2) 201.

LLOYD, Lord, 'Law and the Press' (1966) 19 *CLP* 43.

—— 'Reform of the Law of Defamation' (1976) 29 *CLP* 183.

LOVELAND, I., 'Defamation of Government: Taking Lessons from America' (1994) *Legal Studies*, 206.

NEILL, Sir BRIAN, 'The Media and the Law' *Yearbook of Media and Entertainment Law* (1993) 1.

RUBENSTEIN, M. (ed.), *Wicked, Wicked Libels* (1972).

SHARLAND, A. and LOVELAND, I. 'The Defamation Act 1966 and Political Speech' [1997] *PL* 113.

Supreme Court Procedure Committee, *Report on Practice and Procedure in Defamation* (1991).

SYMMONS, C. R., 'The Problem of Hidden Reference in Defamation' (1974) 3 *Anglo-Am. LR* 98.

WATKINS, A., *A Slight Case of Libel* (1990).

WILLIAMS, K., ' "Only Flattery is Safe"; Political Speech and the Defamation Act 1996' [1997] 60 *MLR* 388.

2. INJURIOUS FALSEHOODS AND PASSING OFF[230]

The distinction between defamation and injurious falsehoods (a term coined by Salmond) is that in the former the defendant's allegation is against the plaintiff, whereas in the latter it is against his goods. Lord Esher MR said:[231] 'In such a case a jury would have to say which sense the libel really bore; if they thought it related to the goods only, they ought to find that it was not a libel; but, if they thought it related to the man's conduct of business, they ought to find it was a libel.' This statement shows that often it will be advisable for a plaintiff to sue on both grounds.[232] Indeed, the case of *Joyce* v. *Sengupta*[233] shows that if the

---

[230] This generic term covers different types of wrong. One of the older, 'slander of title', applies where property is for sale and the defendant falsely and maliciously alleges the existence of encumbrances or other impediments. This has covered miscellaneous allegations, such as that the plaintiff is selling in breach of copyright or patent (*Wren* v. *Weild* (1869) LR 4 QB 730; *Dicks* v. *Brooks* (1880) 15 Ch. D. 22—see now Patents Act 1977, s. 65). Or that the plaintiff's house was haunted (*Barrett* v. *Associated Newspapers Ltd.* (1907) 23 TLR 666). Another type, 'slander of goods', involves the malicious disparagement of the quality of the plaintiff's goods; *W. Counties Manure Co.* v. *Lawes Chemical Co.* (1874) LR 9 Ex. 218. It is important, however, to remember that mere 'business puffs', which are meant to assert that the defendant's wares are superior to those of the plaintiff, are not actionable: *White* v. *Mellin* [1895] AC 154. Nowadays the tort may be broad enough to encompass 'any damaging falsehood which interferes with prospective advantage'. For details see Fleming, *The Law of Torts* (8th edn.), 709–14.

[231] *South Hetton Coal Co. Ltd.* v. *North-Eastern News Association Ltd.* [1894] 1 QB 133, 139.

[232] E.g. *Griffiths* v. *Benn* (1911) 27 TLR 346, 350.　　　　　　　[233] [1993] 1 WLR 337.

facts will support an action under this heading the court will consider it even if the plaintiff's real aim to proceed under this tort was to obtain legal aid which, as we saw, is not available if the action is phrased in defamation. This is clearly an advantage as far as the plaintiff is concerned; but it may also deprive him of advantages that would be available to him if he were proceeding under defamation. Thus, in malicious falsehood, the plaintiff will have to prove the falsity of the words rather than enjoy the benefit (given to defamation plaintiffs) of placing on the defendant the onus of proving the truth of the statement. Moreover, in cases of malicious falsehood it is for the plaintiff to prove the defendant's malice (which, probably, means dishonest or improper motive),[234] and also show that he has suffered actual loss.[235] If, however, the plaintiff succeeds[236] on all of the above three points, an action will lie against the defendant or his estate (unlike defamation, where the cause of action is extinguished by death of either party).[237]

Passing off constitutes another form of unfair competition taking the form of a misrepresentation of the plaintiff's business. The following felicitous statement by Professor Fleming captures the essential difference to the tort described in the previous paragraph: 'While it is injurious falsehood for a defendant to claim that your goods are his, it is passing off for him to claim that his goods are yours.'[238] Many of the peculiarities of this tort must be sought in the common law; but its potential for growth, especially as it expands to encompass 'unfair trading' in general, suggests that it has as much of a future as it has a past.[239] It is not, however, discussed in traditional tort courses so its further consideration must be left to more specialised works.

3. PRIVACY

Besmirching the plaintiff's honour and reputation is not the only way one may interfere with his personality. Other invasions are possible, but they are less effectively prohibited by our legal order. And the gaps in our system, which are once again largely the result of the piecemeal and gradual development of our law, become more obvious when English law is compared with other legal systems such as those of the Federal Republic of Germany, France or the United States. This subject has always been sensitive to the competing forces of

---

[234] *Serville* v. *Constance* [1954] 1 WLR 487, 490. In *Joyce* v. *Motor Surveys* [1948] Ch. 252, the view seemed to be that an intention to injure without just cause or excuse would suffice.

[235] *Royal Baking Powder Co.* v. *Wright Crossley & Co.* (1901) 18 RPC 95, 99. The loss must also be monetary in nature; injured feelings will not be compensated through this tort: *Fielding* v. *Variety Incorporated* [1967] 2 QB 841. On the other hand, proof of a general loss of custom, rather than loss of identifiable customers, may be enough: *Ratcliffe* v. *Evans* [1892] 2 QB 524. The plaintiff's failure to prove pecuniary loss was the reason why in *Allason* v. *Campbell*, *The Times*, 8 May 1996, the claim in malicious falsehood failed.

[236] E.g. it is likely that all privileges that are recognised in the law of defamation are also relevant to this tort. Equally, liability may be avoided if the statements made are bona fide or are made pursuant to a duty imposed on their maker.

[237] The same difference exists with 'active transmissibility', that is, that in malicious falsehood the cause of action is inherited by the plaintiff's estate whereas in the case of defamation his right is extinguished by death.

[238] *The Law of Torts* (8th edn.), 714.   [239] Note, e.g., *Warnink* v. *Townend* [1979] AC 731.

openness and freedom of expression on the one hand and, on the other hand, the legitimate desire to keep away from public gaze certain aspects of one's private life. The subject has become even more troublesome given that in recent years our ability to collect, collate and disseminate information about individuals has been greatly increased as a result of technological advances. The brief account that follows, therefore, does little justice to the topic. It can, however, be stated from the outset that the law on privacy as it stands is underdeveloped, complicated, and fragmentary. The sketch that follows is divided into four sub-headings: (1) the difficulties of defining privacy; (2) the protection afforded by English law; (3) the drawbacks of solving privacy problems in a casuistic manner. Finally, in (4), we shall deal with some of the effects which the new Human Rights Act 1998 will have on this branch of the law.

1. Definitional Difficulties and Other Objections Against Recognising a Wider Protection of Privacy

The abundance of definitions could be taken to suggest that none of them is entirely satisfactory. Winfield, for example, who was one of the first academics in this country to urge the courts to make a tort of all offensive invasions of personal privacy, defined 'infringement of privacy' as an 'unauthorised interference with a person's seclusion of himself or of his property from the public'.[240] Earlier, a well-known American academic and subsequently judge—Thomas Cooley—coined the oft-quoted phrase 'the right to be let alone'.[241] Professor Westin, on the other hand, has provided a definition that includes legal entities. 'Privacy', he has argued, 'is the claim of individuals, groups, or institutions to determine for themselves when, how, and to what extent information about them is communicated to others.'[242] On the international level the Universal Declaration of Human Rights of 1948 provides in article 12 that 'no one shall be subjected to arbitrary interference with his privacy, family, home or correspondence . . .' No definition of privacy is given; but the interests protected are clearly envisaged in wide terms. Other attempts to define privacy can be found in the works given in the Select Bibliography. On the whole it is, perhaps, accurate to say that those who favour a *general* right of privacy have tried to supply a definition and are in a slight numerical majority over those who have opposed it.

Those who have opposed a general right of privacy have, as we shall see, had rather more success in showing that a workable definition may be difficult to frame than they have had in stopping the *gradual* expansion of the protected areas of human personality. This is not to say that legitimate concerns have not been voiced against an enlarged protection of privacy, especially if accomplished through the creation of a new, general rule. Dr Marshall, for example, referring to Judge Cooley's definition, has asked what the right to be let alone means: 'to go on battering the baby, or cheating the Inland Revenue, or poisoning the customers?'[243] His rhetorical question does more than challenge

---

[240] See below (Select Bibliography), 24.   [241] *Law of Torts* (2nd edn., 1888), 29.
[242] See below (Select Bibliography), 7.   [243] See below (Select Bibliography), 243.

a well-known definition; it reveals, through his examples, that the right of one person to stop revelations about his affairs may conflict with the right of another person to his freedom of expression and the right of the general public to be informed. Here, as in the law of defamation, this clash is the crux of the matter.

Yet the difficulty lies not so much in the kind of examples that Dr Marshall adduces in order to make his point against over-generalised definitions; none of them deserves to be protected against the glare of publicity. The value of Dr Marshall's point lies rather in the fact that it makes us aware of the undoubted difficulty of devising a test that defines what information must remain private. For, clearly, not everything that interests the public should be published in the public interest. But the difficulty in drawing lines in some marginal cases is not a reason for not trying to draw them at all, as the Press seems to suggest. Nor is the Press on higher ground when it asserts that it, alone, should be left with the task of regulating its conduct (in the sense of deciding what should be published and what the consequences of wrongful publication should be). For the argument that no one else (e.g. legislator, courts) can do the job better than it can do it itself is hardly convincing. Arguments such as these have, thus far, prevailed not because they are convincing but because our press has, especially by exploiting the 'sleaze culture' of the last decade, gained such an unhealthy stranglehold over our politicians.

Other objections, besides definitional difficulties, have been voiced against a general right to privacy. The fear that the recognition of a general right would trigger off endless litigation is another argument put forward by opponents of privacy. Empirical evidence, however, from countries (such as Germany) which recognise a general right of privacy do not support this assertion.[244] Why would the English public, which is notoriously known for its dislike of 'making a fuss', change its natural character. Indeed, why would it go a step further and resort to litigation, especially since this is not an area where legal aid applies and the costs of going to court can be notoriously high?

That the aforementioned objection, too, is not well founded can be seen by the fact that it is usually coupled with another one: the recognition of wider privacy rights would have a chilling effect on the Press.[245] This is an objection that deserves to be taken seriously for, in the words of Mr Justice Cardozo 'freedom of expression is the matrix, the indispensable condition of nearly every other form of freedom.'[246] However, foreign empirical evidence—and not just hearsay propaganda used by opponents of a privacy right—once again proves how fallacious this argument has proved to be in practice, at any rate in

---

[244] Nor is it convincing to say that privacy actions, though controllable in the Federal Republic of Germany, have got out of hand in the United States. Although it is true that in the American system there is a large corpus of case law under this heading, many of the cases could have been litigated under some other tort heading. And many other instances have, in fact, received even less protection than they do in Britain because of the preponderance given in American law to First Amendment rights (free expression). Nevertheless, as is pointed out below in the Excursus to this chapter, even the very liberal American law has been able to afford greater protection to plaintiffs in Mr Kaye's position than our courts were able to give (see the discussion of *Kaye* in Section 3 below).

[245] See, for instance, Lord Wakeham, *Hansard*, HL Deb., 24 Nov. 1997, 772.

[246] *Palko* v. *Connecticut* 302 US 319, 327 (1937).

countries such as ours. Germany, for instance, nowadays protects speech rights in a manner that is entirely comparable to that found in the United States[247] and certainly more effectively than we do through our law of defamation. That surely proves that a balance between the competing interests can be found by, for instance, giving preference to political speech but preferring privacy over salacious and titillating revelations or intrusions which mainly serve the financial interests of the publisher.

So the picture that emerges from this sketch is far less clear cut and convincing than opponents of privacy would like us to believe. The debate on the need for a general right of privacy is thus likely to continue until the newly enacted Human Rights Act 1998 (but not likely to come into force until the year 2000) gives the courts the occasion to reconsider the actual law. For present purposes, therefore, what we must now do is look at English law as it stands at present, note its shortcomings, and then speculate as to the changes that may come about in the next few years.

2. The Protection Afforded by English Law

Though many would regard this as being inadequate few would argue that it is limited, let alone non-existent. In fact, a combination of statutes and the common law have in their own pragmatic way gone a long way—especially in recent times—to close many of the most worrisome gaps. For didactic purposes the cases can be grouped under three broad headings: (*a*) privacy interests violated by intrusions into one's private sphere; (*b*) appropriation of personality and likeness; and (*c*) public disclosures of true private facts.

(A) Intrusions

The starting-point here is the idea that property carries for the owner the right to exclude others and, hence, from early times the torts of trespass and nuisance have proved sufficient to cope with most intrusions, however motivated. Indeed, such is the extent of protection afforded to the owner (but probably not to a licensee)[248] that the law, in the case of trespass, allows the plaintiff to succeed without proof of any damage[249] and, in appropriate cases, has even granted aggravated damages.[250] The narrow construction of police powers to

---

[247] See Markesinis, 'Privacy, Freedom of Expression, and the Horizontal Effect of the Human Rights Bill: Lessons from Germany', (1999 Winter Issue) *LQR*. American comparatists agree.

[248] The law on this may not be entirely clear. Is a guest in the home of his host entitled to rely on trespass to protect his privacy while in his room? Does a female employee of the master of the house have such rights? (Arguably yes, according to Lord Denman in *Lewis* v. *Ponsford* (1838) 8 Car & P 687; 173 ER 674). And what of an occupier of a hotel room or a hospital bed in circumstances such as those litigated in *Gordon Kaye* v. *Andrew Robertson and Sport Newspapers Ltd.* (reproduced in App. I of the Calcutt Report)?

The last two examples have not been tested in this country, though according to Mr Prescott, op. cit. (Select Bibliography), an action by the hospital authority in the *Kaye* case would have succeeded. Clearly, in such instances we are not talking of an action for damages (since the hospital has suffered none) but an action for an injunction restraining the publication of any photos or interviews.

[249] *Entick* v. *Carrington* (1765) 2 Wils. K. B. 275; 95 ER 807, 817 per Lord Camden CJ.

[250] *Merest* v. *Harvey* (1814) 5 Taunt. 442; 128 ER 761. There is, however, little modern authority on this point. Calculating damages in trespass actions would also present difficulties so, in many cases, the remedy might be an injunction restraining the publication of any photograph taken or recording made

enter and search premises has also been explained by Lord Denning in *Ghani* v. *Jones*[251] as depending on the individual's right that his 'privacy and his possessions . . . [be not] invaded except for the most compelling reasons'. The same privacy interests have been invoked by the courts as justification for a narrow construction of various statutes to prevent official searches of premises unless explicitly authorised.[252] But developments under the so-called 'Anton Piller' order,[253] giving the police under certain circumstances considerable powers of search and seizure in civil suits, represent, from a privacy point of view, an unfortunate retreat.[254]

Nuisance is another tort that could help a plaintiff whose privacy was interfered with by activities taking place outside his land. In *Walker* v. *Brewster*,[255] for example, the plaintiff sought to enjoin his neighbours from holding large fêtes on his adjoining grounds that attracted large crowds, destroying his privacy. *Constant* aerial surveillance has also been described as a 'monstrous invasion of privacy'[256] and might thus, in appropriate circumstances, amount to an actionable nuisance.

Privacy can also explain a series of statutory enactments such as the Post Office Act 1710[257] that imposed criminal penalties for the unauthorised opening of letters; and analogous enactments have imposed confidentiality requirements in the context of handling of telegraphic messages.[258] As late as 1979, however, Megarry VC rejected[259] the existence of a common-law remedy for interception of telephonic conversations, though the Interception of Communications Act 1985 created certain criminal offences as a result of *Malone* being successfully challenged before the European Court of Human Rights.[260]

(B) APPROPRIATION OF PERSONALITY

This may take such forms as an unauthorised use of another person's name, voice, or image, the last type of violation being the most common and, historically (in both the United States and the Federal Republic of Germany), one of the earliest types of privacy litigation to arise. *Sim* v. *H. J. Heinz Co. Ltd.*[261] is an example of an English case which had to deal with the unauthorised impersonation of Alistair Sim's characteristic voice in a television advertisement promoting the defendants' products. The plaintiff argued, *inter alia*, that his voice

---

during the 'intrusion'. The Calcutt proposals, discussed below, seem to offer a much clearer starting-point, unconnected with the technical rules of the ancient tort of trespass.

251 [1970] 1 QB 693, 708.

252 See *Inland Revenue Commissioners* v. *Rossminster Ltd.* [1980] AC 952; *Morris* v. *Beardmore* [1981] AC 446.

253 *Anton Piller KG* v. *Manufacturing Processes Ltd.* [1976] Ch. 55.

254 See also the powers of search and seizure granted the police by the Police and Criminal Evidence Act 1984, ss. 1, 8, 19.

255 (1876) LR 5 Eq. 25, 26.   256 *Bernstein* v. *Skyviews & General Ltd.* [1978] QB 479, 489 per Griffiths J.

257 Currently s. 14 of the Post Office Act 1969.

258 For fuller references see Seipp, op. cit. (Select Bibliography), 338 ff.

259 In *Malone* v. *Metropolitan Police Commissioner* [1979] Ch. 344.

260 If the interception is carried out by an unofficial person for unofficial purposes an action may lie for breach of confidence: *Francome* v. *Mirror Group Ltd.* [1984] 1 WLR 892.

261 [1959] 1 WLR 313.

as an actor was part of his stock-in-trade and, therefore, was something which he was entitled to protect as part of his goods. This was, in effect, an invitation to the court to extend analogically the remedy available for the tort of passing off. In the Court of Appeal Hodson LJ said that this was 'an arguable case'. But passing off has its own limitations, the remedy typically being available to persons engaged in some common field of activity. In the event, the plaintiff's request for an injunction was turned down. So the case, as far as English law is concerned, is really little more than an example of the ingenuity that legal advisers have to resort to in order to overcome the absence of well-accepted action in such cases.

The appropriation of one's likeness—typically by the use of a picture without permission—is, as stated, the commonest form of this type of privacy invasion. It involves no free-speech implications for the defendant and it should not be condoned by society, especially where the plaintiff's image is used to the commercial advantage of the defendant. In *Tolley* v. *Fry*[262] and in a number of other unreported cases in the 1930s[263] the English courts were able to make an ingenious use of the tort of defamation to combat the commercial appropriation of personality. Thus, as already noted, the plaintiff was able to succeed in his claim for damages because the court fastened on his 'amateur' status in order to assert that this was prejudiced by the innuendo that he had allowed his picture to be used 'for financial gain'. However, as we shall see, the overall protection accorded to victims of such violations is not sufficient and the claim for protection in such cases is strong. Many legal writers have supported this point of view,[264] and judicial systems such as those of the United States and the Federal Republic of Germany that have taken steps (by means of statutes, judicial decisions, or both) to deal with the problem do not appear to have suffered in any way.

(c) Public Disclosure of True Private Facts[265]

This is by far the most difficult though the most common category of invasion of privacy and the one that brings out most clearly the clash of one person's right to be let alone versus another person's right to speak and to be informed. It must be remembered, of course, that we are here envisaging cases involving the disclosure of private (not public)[266] facts which, moreover, are true (which, if anything, can make the disclosure even more painful to the victim). Further, the harm that these disclosures can cause to the affected individual has grown

---

[262] [1931] AC 333.   [263] Quoted by Fleming, *The Law of Torts* (8th edn.), 605, n. 44.

[264] E.g. Frazer, 'Appropriation of Personality—A New Tort?' (1983) 99 *LQR* 281; Prescott, op. cit. (Select Bibliography), at 456. The author, however, seems to limit the protection to cases where the likeness is used for 'promoting a commercial product or service'. This would mean that the use of one's image to promote a political party or other, non-contentious, cause might not be actionable and such a result would appear of dubious merit.

[265] The fullest discussion can be found in F. Gurry, *Breach of Confidence* (1985).

[266] This division is not as easy as it appears to be at first sight. For instance, something that happens at a party or in a restaurant may be witnessed by many people. In that sense it is public. But many systems (e.g. the German and French) have held that the fact that a number of people have witnessed an event does not, by itself, mean that it is in the public domain and can thus be repeated with impunity to the world at large.

as the modern ability to disseminate information has kept pace with our equally increased capacity to collect and collate information without the need of any physical intrusion.[267] Finally, this subject is further complicated by our system's apparent inability to distinguish in legal terms between those who seek publicity (politicians, actors) and those who have had publicity unwillingly thrust upon them.[268]

In order to prevent the disclosure of private information the courts have, once again, been obliged to make use of their ingenuity and have recourse to non-tort concepts. For example, in the middle of the last century in *Albert* v. *Strange*[269] the publication of some drawings made by the royal couple was enjoined on the grounds that the sanction was necessary to protect property rights in literary and artistic creations. Other instances are the notion of breach of an implied contract, as in the case where a photographer was stopped from using photographs taken of a customer without the latter's consent.[270] Alternatively, the device of breach of an implied obligation of confidence can be tried, as in *Argyll* v. *Argyll*[271] where a man was not allowed to disclose information given to him by his ex-wife during their marriage and concerning her private affairs.

Yet, the equitable remedies available for breach of confidence have their own limitations. In particular, they are limited by three requirements. First, that the information 'betrayed' must have the necessary quality of confidence about it. Secondly, that it must have been imparted in circumstances importing an obligation of confidence. And, finally, that it must have been used in an unauthorised way to the disadvantage of the person who had communicated it.[272] While there must, therefore, exist a relationship between the confider and the confidant, it need not amount to a pre-existing legal relationship. Recently Sir Nicolas Browne-Wilkinson VC held that where information relating to sexual conduct had been communicated to another person expressly in confidence, and that other person expressly disclosed that information to another, the court would intervene and enjoin such publications. The proposition that, in the absence of a legally enforceable contract or a pre-existing relationship, such as employer–employee or doctor–patient, it was not possible to enforce a legal duty of confidence was 'plainly wrong'.[273] Though this was a judgment delivered on a striking-out motion, and the Vice-Chancellor refused to be drawn into the question of where and how the borderlines should be

---

[267] E.g. through the use of telephoto lenses, parabolic microphones, or other 'listening' devices.

[268] Though there are dicta which suggest that '. . . those who seek and welcome publicity of every kind bearing upon their private lives so long as it shows them in a favourable light are in no position to complain of an invasion of their privacy by publicity which shows them in an unfavourable light.' Per Bridge LJ in *Woodward* v. *Hutchins* [1977] 1 WLR 760 at 765. The facts of the case (and examples from foreign jurisdictions) suggest, however, that these dicta should not be construed too strictly so as to deprive public figures of all protection of privacy.

[269] (1848) 2 De G. & S. 652; 64 ER 293.   [270] *Pollard* v. *Photographic Co.* (1888) 40 Ch. D. 345.

[271] [1967] Ch. 302.

[272] *Malone* v. *Commissioner of Police of the Metropolis (No. 2)* [1979] Ch. 344 at 375 (per Megarry VC). See, also, *Saltman Engineering Co. Ltd.* v. *Campbell Engineering Co. Ltd.* (1948) 65 RPC 203; *Coco* v. *A. N. Clark (Engineers) Ltd.* (1969) RPC 41, 47 per Megarry VC.

[273] *Stephens* v. *Avery and Others, The Times*, 1 Mar. 1988.

drawn, it is clearly a decision which shows that some judges at least are sensitive to the need to set limits to aggressive intrusions by the Press into private lives of individuals.

The popular Press's interest in raking up the past lives of individuals, often for no better reason than sensationalism and profit, has also prompted limited judicial and legislative interventions that have tried to put an end to such practices. The Rehabilitation of Offenders Act 1974, discussed earlier in this chapter, is an example of the latter kind, though by preserving the defence of truth the statute has only partially achieved the desired aim of allowing offenders— at least those guilty of lesser offences—to have their past forgotten. *Re X*,[274] on the other hand, offers an example of daring judicial creativity to achieve a highly laudable aim. The facts of this case were as follows. The case involved the child murderer Mary Bell who recently, again, made the headlines by accepting payment in order to collaborate with a writer who wrote about her story and her character. The facts of the litigation are described in full in the third edition of the book. Here suffice it to say that the court's ingenious employment of the wardship jurisdiction resulted in Mary Bell[275] being granted protection against disclosure of her present name for the sake of her child and (indirectly) herself.

Sections of the Press have shown equal insensitivity in another topic where, it is submitted, the plaintiff's right to be left alone should prevail over the public's interest to know. This involves the identification of victims of sexual offences.

The development of the law in this area is typical of the incremental growth of the common law. At first no anonymity whatsoever was granted to these unfortunate victims. Then section 4 of the Sexual Offences (Amendment) Act 1976 granted anonymity to victims of rape offences (as defined narrowly by s. 7(2) of the Act). Victims of 'lesser' sexual offences (such as unlawful sexual intercourse, incest, or buggery), anxious to be left alone to forget their traumatic experiences, were, in fact, left unprotected as far as their privacy was concerned. The Criminal Justice Act 1987 extended anonymity to cases involving conspiracy to rape and burglary with intent to rape; but in the House of Lords the minister from the Home Office thought that any further extension of the anonymity laws would be 'the thin end of the wedge'. The Calcutt Report disagreed, but the Home Office was, mysteriously it would seem, adamant. And then, quite unexpectedly and with very little publicity, the official attitude changed. The Sexual Offences (Amendment) Act 1991 made it possible to extend by statutory instrument anonymity to all cases of sexual offences; and Statutory Instrument 1336/1992 brought this protection into existence in October 1992. In this branch of the law, the incremental growth of English law has, surely, not been one of its strengths; and the adverse consequences that both the media and anonymous government circles feared would follow any extension of the anonymity laws have failed to materialise.

---

[274] [1984] 1 WLR 1422.

[275] Who since her release from prison had altered her name and concealed her past from all, including her child.

3. Solving Privacy Problems in a Casuistic Manner

From what has been said so far it will be obvious that English law affords extensive protection to various aspects of human privacy and personality. There is, indeed, a rich variety of available remedies matched only by a willingness to enlist tort, contract, crime, equity, common law, and statute to achieve the end-result. But the reverse side of this is a state of great complexity which, often, has some ludicrous results, dictated by historical accidents rather than flowing from rational criteria, and, worse still, also leaving some important legal gaps. A quick glance at some of the remedies we have mentioned in the previous subsection will substantiate these accusations.

Defamation can, at times, help the plaintiff. But *Tolley* v. *Fry*,[276] depending as it does on the innuendo based on the amateur status of the plaintiff, also shows its limitations. For what would the result be if the plaintiff were a professional? On the reasoning of that case the action would fail. Yet a professional, no less than an amateur, should be protected against such unwarranted invasion of his personality—especially where someone else stands to gain financially from it. Indeed, it will be the likeness of professionals which will be appropriated in practice and not that of 'ordinary' citizens which means that our law has developed a remedy for the unusual and not the typical case likely to give rise to complaints.

Trespass and nuisance also have their limitations, as the *Bernstein* case shows. For the owner of the land has no unlimited rights over the airspace above his property. And, of course, no remedy will lie if the photograph is taken from an angle so that it does not violate the protected part of the airspace over the land in question. Nor will the eavesdropping amount to trespass if it is carried out with the aid of a parabolic microphone and no wire-tapping or other invasion of the plaintiff's property takes place. Equally, nuisance will only succeed if the interference is over a prolonged period of time. And even then the remedy will be given only to those who have an interest in the land and will not include all those who happened to be on the land and affected by the photography. The attempt of a majority of the Court of Appeal in *Khorasandjian* v. *Bush*[277] to 'twist' the tort of nuisance was thus rejected by the House of Lords in *Hunter* v. *Canary Wharf Ltd.*[278]

The Rehabilitation of Offenders Act also has its limitations. Comparison with the California case of *Melvin* v. *Reid*[279] shows English law in a bad light. For some ex-criminals their past is never forgiven and forgotten. A day's sensational journalism may thus destroy a rehabilitation that would have taken years to accomplish. It is not only United States law that differs from English law in this

---

[276] [1931] AC 333. The limitations of this decision were revealed in *Gordon Kaye* v. *Andrew Robertson and Sport Newspapers*, reprinted in App. I of the Calcutt Report. The facts of the case are given below.

[277] [1993] QB 727.

[278] [1997] 2 WLR 684. Doctrinally the *Khorasandjian* (majority) judgment is suspect, as the dissenting judge (Sir Peter Gibson as he then was) was quick to point out. Yet in practice, the decision represents a laudable attempt to protect privacy—something which now may be (partly) achieved by the Protection from Harassment Act 1997 (on which see above, Chapter 4).

[279] 297 P. 91 (1931).

respect. The West German Constitutional Court handed down a classic judgment in the *Lebach* case,[280] stating that it is the function of the courts to weigh the value of free speech on the one hand against privacy on the other. That court then went on to lay down criteria that the lower courts should apply: e.g. purpose of publication (educational, prevention of crime, sensationalism); how long after the event does the disclosure take place; need to help reintegrate offenders into society; extent of publication, etc. Only the traditional insularity of common-law practitioners can explain why the experience of foreign systems, as casuistic in their approach as that of the common law, has failed to have been noticed by our courts.

Re X, the wardship case considered earlier, also shows the limits of the court's ingenuity. For it will be remembered that the mother's anonymity was only incidentally protected. Once the wardship ends—through the death of the child or its reaching the age of majority—the protection will disappear. Moreover, now that the recent furore over this case has shown that the child, for whom the anonymity was primarily granted, has become aware of its mother's past, the case of their privacy continuing to receive protection has become more dubious; had it been protected by a law of privacy the chances are that it would not have been lifted. But, being granted through the wardship jurisdiction it means that it will survive for a few more years until the child attains the age of majority.

The same limitations become obvious when we look at the actions based on breach of confidence. Since protection there depends largely on the acquisition of confidential information in the course of a confidential relationship, does it mean that it will not be granted where it is obtained as the result of some other reprehensible means? In *Hellewell* v. *Chief Constable of Derbyshire*[281] Sir John Laws had no doubt that the answer should be negative. But this, it is submitted, correct view was only *obiter* so we need a volunteer to risk litigation once again before we know for certain the final solution.

Nowhere, however, do we find more clearly the limitations of the casuistic approach than in the case of *Gordon Kaye (by Peter Froggatt his next friend)* v. *Andrew Robertson and Sport Newspapers Ltd.*,[282] a case which had a great impact on the contents of the Calcutt Report.

Mr Kaye's sufferings started with the 1989 winter storms. He was then severely injured by a detached piece from an advertisement hoarding. For three days after this incident he was on a life-support machine; another seven days followed in intensive care. His condition remained critical throughout this

---

[280] Reproduced in translation in Markesinis, *The German Law of Torts*, 390 ff. See also id., 'Conceptualism, Pragmatism and Courage: A Common Lawyer looks at Some Judgments of the Federal Supreme Court', 34 *Am. J. Comp. L.* 349 (1986).

[281] 'If someone with a telephoto lens were to take from a distance and with no authority a picture of another engaged in some private act, his subsequent disclosure of the photograph would, in my judgment, as surely amount to breach of confidence as if he had found or stolen a letter or diary in which the act was recounted and proceeded to publish it. In such a case, the law would protect what might reasonably be called a right of privacy, although the name attached to the cause of action would be breach of confidence.' [1995] 1 WLR 804, 807. In September 1998 the State of California passed an Act making such activities actionable as 'constructive trespasses'.

[282] [1991] FSR 62.

period. Visits were severely restricted, not least in order to limit the risk of infection. As is usual, complete calm and peace was ordered to facilitate recovery; and so as to ensure that those medical decisions were observed, a special notice was pinned on the door of his room to this effect.

The two defendants were the editor and owning company of the *Sunday Sport*—a weekly publication which the judge at first instance described as having 'a lurid and sensational style'. The photo of Mr Kaye lying asleep (or, probably, unconscious) in bed was printed on the same page as a photo of a scantily clad woman; but that only added to the bad taste of the contents of the front page.

Disregarding the notice on the door the defendants' agents entered Mr Kaye's hospital room where they photographed him with a flashlight and took an interview of sorts. At the trial the editor admitted—proudly one suspects—that his staff had achieved 'a great old-fashioned scoop'. He also accepted that other publications might well be willing to 'pay large sums of money for the privilege' of talking to and photographing Mr Kaye. Though the defendants claimed Mr Kaye had consented to all this, the available medical evidence suggested that he was, at best, only in very limited control of his faculties. Indeed, a quarter of an hour after the alleged 'voluntary' interview had taken place Mr Kaye had no recollection of the event. Though in the subsequent publication the defendants claimed to have been motivated by a desire to inform Mr Kaye's fans of the state of his health, the facts described above (and given more fully in the judgment) point in another direction. For the average reader this lurid and sensational journalism may well have had much baser motives.

Mr Justice Porter issued a series of orders, in effect banning the publication of the story (in its original form). The defendants appealed and Glidewell, Bingham, and Legatt LJJ essentially upheld the plaintiff's claim but, as a result of their careful review of our patchy law, had to issue a more restricted order. Basically, this allowed the defendants to publish some photos and their story provided they made it clear that neither had been obtained with Mr Kaye's consent. The reasoning of the learned justices as well as the reduced protection which, to their obvious regret, they were able to give to Mr Kaye, clearly reveal two points. First, the legal contortions which have to be made in order to protect deserving victims, and secondly, the need to establish some wider principle of privacy that will enable us to close unacceptable gaps in our law. Indirectly, the case and judgments also show how inadequate are the Press's current attempts to demonstrate that they can police themselves on this matter.

The leading judgment was delivered by Lord Justice Glidewell; but the other two Lord Justices delivered concurring opinions which present particular interest, not least because of their comparative content. In these judgments four causes of action were considered. In inverse order of likely success they were: passing off, trespass to the person, libel, and malicious falsehood.

Passing off was dealt with briefly. It was rejected since the case was not considered to be covered by the House of Lords' decision in *Warnink* v. *Townend and Sons*.[283] The plaintiff's claim seemed to have foundered mainly on the grounds

---

[283] [1979] AC 731.

that he was 'not in the position of a *trader* [italics supplied] in relation to his interest in his story about his accident'. True—but an extension of the tort could have been made, indeed, as already noted, was almost made in the case of *Sim* v. *Heinz*.[284] This case, which was not, apparently, cited to or by the court in either *Warnink* or *Kaye*, shows that an extension of this very 'commercial' tort could be attempted in order to avoid the 'grave defect in the law [of allowing one] party, for the purpose of commercial gain, to make use of the voice of another party without his consent'.[285] And if that could be done for the voice of an actor, why not for his image, especially when the appropriation of the likeness is used to enrich another person?

The attempt to use trespass to the person[286] to protect Mr Kaye did not fare much better. Two reasons were given, the first more convincing than the second. The first was that no case could be found to support the view that the taking of the flashlight photograph amounted to battery. The second was that there was no causal evidence to show that, as a result of their act, Mr Kaye had suffered distress and a setback in his recovery. In Lord Justice Glidewell's words there was 'no evidence that the taking of the photographs did in fact cause him [Mr Kaye] any damage'. The second point is, it is submitted, not very telling since battery is a tort actionable *per se* and will succeed without proof of any damage. But the first point presented a greater obstacle given that, apparently, 'there can be no battery unless there is *contact* with the plaintiff'.[287] Now, flashlight contact might be treated as sufficiently close to physical contact to justify, as Glidewell LJ was willing to entertain, an extension of the tort of battery. It must be noted, however, that in novel situations the current tendency is to resort to the tort of negligence rather than expand the older tort of battery and even to bypass the latter tort by having resort to criminal law. Why not then try negligence? This ever-growing tort, unlike battery, requires proof of the existence of a duty of care—something which would have caused no problem in the instant case; but it also requires proof of damage which, as stated, was not forthcoming. It may be thus that the two elements of the two torts were inadvertently telescoped into one. Clearly, the learned judge regarded this part of his judgment as secondary to the main thrust of his arguments that came in the remaining two causes of action: libel and malicious falsehood.

Libel was, according to Glidewell and Bingham LJJ, strongly arguable. *Tolley* v. *J. S. Fry and Sons Ltd*.[288] was the authority that persuaded the judge who heard the application at first instance; and it also appealed to the Appeal Court judges. If it was not used in the end, it was because of the rule in *Williams Coulson & Sons* v. *James Coulson and Co*.[289] which held that interim injunctions are to be used sparingly in libel actions—a rule confirmed in *Herbage* v. *Times Newspapers*

---

[284] [1959] 1 WLR 313. [285] *Sim* v. *Heinz* [1959] 1 WLR 313, 317.

[286] The tort of trespass to land was not considered. According to Mr Prescott (below, Select Bibliography), it could have been used if the hospital were willing to lend its name in the action. Damages would have been very difficult to estimate but an injunction to prevent publication of the so-called interview might have been granted. The new criminal offences recommended by the Calcutt Report (ch. 6) would, if implemented, make such activities actionable.

[287] Street on *Torts* (9th edn., 1992). [288] [1931] AC 333. [289] [1887] 3 TLR 846.

Limited and Others (unreported), despite the decision of the House of Lords in *American Cynamid* v. *Ethicon*.[290] So, though the judges felt that the publication was libellous, they also felt that a jury might well not take the same view and, in the circumstances, a general injunction should not be and was not granted.

But was the publication libellous on the authority of *Tolley* v. *Fry*? *Tolley* succeeded because an innuendo was discovered. It was, in 1931—but would it still be now?—defamatory for an amateur golfer to give the impression that he had 'prostituted his amateur status for gain'. But, as stated, the *ratio* of the case would not have covered a professional golfer even though he, too, needs (perhaps even more strongly than the amateur) to prevent the unauthorised use of his image. So where is the innuendo here? Given the nature of the publication in question, one could argue that any respectable member of society who appears to be associated with the *Sunday Sport* is, automatically, defamed. But the learned judge, hinting, perhaps, at this suggestion was right in taking the view that such 'a conclusion is [not] inevitable'. And if a jury were to decide that there was no defamation, that would be the end of Mr Kaye's interest to be left in peace in his hospital bed. Yet, as Lord Justice Bingham said: 'If ever a person has a right to be let alone by strangers with no public interest to pursue, it must surely be when he lies in hospital recovering from brain surgery and in no more than partial command of his faculties.' And yet this right, *de lege lata*, depends on the quaint facts of *Tolley* v. *Fry*; and the result, judging from the Court of Appeal judgment in *Tolley*[291] was not so obvious even in those halcyon days of the 1930s when sportsmen played for their sport and not for money.

In the end Mr Kaye succeeded by the skin of his teeth but then, again, only in a very limited way, because the judges were able to rely on the tort of malicious falsehood. This is not an easy tort, as any reading of a textbook will reveal; nor is it frequently used. But at least it avoided the injunction problems of *Coulson* v. *Coulson*. For in malicious falsehood the test of that case[292] applies only to the requirement that the plaintiff must show that the words are false; and the (original) statement by the *Sunday Sport* that the photos and interview were taken with Mr Kaye's consent were, clearly, false.

4. The Human Rights Act 1998[293]

In the summer of 1998 the Labour party's electoral promise to 'repatriate human rights'—a sound-bite slogan meant to stress the fact that Britain's failure to ratify the European Convention which it had helped draft forty years earlier was, finally, to be rectified—became a reality. Section 6 of the new Act makes it illegal for any 'public authority' to act in a way which is incompatible with the Convention while, in the event of such a violation, sections 7 and 8

---

[290] [1975] AC 395.   [291] [1930] 1 KB 467.   [292] [1887] 3 TLR 46.

[293] First reactions as to how it will work and what problems will be encountered can be found in Arden (below, Select Bibliography); Singh, 'Privacy and the Media: The Impact of the Human Rights Bill, in Markesinis (ed.) *Protecting Privacy*, (1998), ch. 7; Markesinis, 'Privacy, Freedom of Expression and the Horizontal Effect of the Human Rights Bill: Lessons from Germany', 1999 *LQR* (Winter Issue). See also Chapter 5, Section 5, above, for our discussion of the impact of the Act on governmental liability.

give the courts the right to make any order they think fit to put right the breach in question.[294]

Our courts are unlikely to create a new *general* cause of action. The Act does not authorise this; nor is it compatible with the way our judges see their role as interpreters of the law. But this does not mean that the new Act cannot have a profound effect on our law of privacy.[295] For, by including courts and tribunals within the phrase 'public authority', the new Act is, essentially, asking the courts when dealing with the common law to do so in a manner which is consistent with the Convention.[296] Moreover, in doing this our courts will have to take into account not only the text of the Convention but also of the case law of the Court in Strasbourg, (and to a lesser extent the national laws of the other European member states) since they have had such a defining influence on the Strasbourg jurisprudence. This will entail an as yet unnoticed revolution not only in our legal literature (which will have to become more international in its approach) but also in the judicial reasoning process. Mrs Justice Arden gave a hint of this recently when, speaking extra-judicially, she perceptively remarked:[297]

One thing that will influence the development of the law of privacy is an informed debate as to what the right of privacy should be . . . There are of course other factors that will influence the way that the courts develop the law, and they include previous decisions in England, decisions from other jurisdictions, Law Commission reports and other authoritative studies of which in this field there are many.

The bulk of this 'foreign' material is favourable to privacy; it starts from the premise that it must be balanced against free speech; it (invariably) gives political speech precedence; and it treats the many examples given earlier in this subsection as instances of a wider interest which is linked to the all-important interest of human dignity. These are all crucial ideas; but the significance of the last point should not be missed. For our judges, too, have for some time now been coming to realise that privacy (and, ultimately, human dignity) lies at the core of these cases. We thus noted how judges like Lord Denning saw the narrowness of police search powers as flowing from the need to protect privacy; and we saw how Mr Justice Laws admitted that privacy interests lie behind the inevitable trend to widen the law of breach of confidence. Indeed, four years before the Laws judgment Lord Keith had, essentially, made the same point in *A.-G.* v. *Guardian Newspapers*[298] when he said that 'breach of confidence involves no more than an invasion of privacy'. Even more recently, Lord Nicholls, in his judgment in *R* v. *Khan*[299] asked himself the question 'whether the present, piecemeal protection of privacy has now developed to the extent that a more comprehensive principle can be seen to exist.' Taken with other extra-judicial

---

[294] Section 8(1). This could include damages and accounts of profits—important remedies for the subject under consideration. Injunctive relief will also be available though our courts will have to take note of the Strasbourg jurisprudence that has adopted a sceptical stance towards any form of 'prior restraint'.

[295] See, for instance, the Lord Chancellor's remarks in *Hansard*, HL Deb., 3 Nov. 1997, 1229–30.

[296] Note that an amendment by Lord Wakeham intended as he, himself, put it (*Hansard*, HL Deb., 24 Nov. 1997, 772) to stifle this development was defeated. The parliamentary debates should thus encourage our judges to expand the right of privacy.

[297] Op. cit. (Select Bibliography).　　　[298] [1990] 1 AC 109, 205.　　　[299] [1977] AC 558, 583.

pronouncements from such eminent legal figures as the Lord Chief Justice,[300] these statements provide unmistakable signs that our judges are ready to move forward in three ways. First, incrementally to enlarge the domain of existing torts where justice—as defined above—requires this. Secondly, to do so by discovering the wider principle which underlies the rich case law. Thirdly, by breaking down gradually—as the Strasbourg Court, itself, is doing—the distinction which *appears* to be sanctioned by the Human Rights Act 1998 between one law of privacy informed by the Convention and applicable to public authorities and another law of privacy, more limited in its scope and less robust in its philosophical underpinnings, for violations of privacy by private entities, notably the Press.[301] These are not matters which can be discussed in a tort text-book; but the discerning reader of this brief exposé will, especially if he uses it with the accompanying further references, realise that new horizons have been opened to the alert advocate (and law student). As Lord Scarman put it in the House of Lords[302] the enactment of the new Human Rights legislation is 'the beginning of a new constitutional chapter' in the history of the United Kingdom. Only the most narrow-minded will fail to grasp this point.

Select Bibliography

ARDEN, Dame MARY, 'The Future of the Law of Privacy' Speech delivered at Kings College London on 26 Nov. 1997.

BINGHAM OF CORNHILL, Lord, 'Should There Be a Law to Protect Rights of Personal Privacy?' [1966] *EHRLR* 450.

BIRKS, P. B. H. (ed.) *Privacy and Loyalty* (1997).

CALCUTT, Sir DAVID, *Review of Press Self-Regulation*, Cmnd. 1102 (HMSO, 1990).

—— *Review of Press Self-Regulation*, Cmnd. 2135 (HMSO, 1993).

EADY, B., 'Opinion: A Statutory Right to Privacy' [1996] *EHRR* 243.

FELDMAN, D., 'The Developing Scope of Article 8 of the European Convention on Human Rights' [1997] *EHRLR* 266.

LORD CHANCELLOR'S DEPARTMENT AND THE SCOTTISH OFFICE, *Infringement of Privacy: a Consultation Paper* (1993).

LORENZ, W., 'Privacy and the Press—A German Experience', *Butterworth Lectures 1989–90* (1990), 79–119.

MACCORMICK, N., 'A Note Upon Privacy' (1973) 89 *LQR* 23.

MARKESINIS, B. S., (ed.) *Protecting Privacy* (1998).

—— 'The Right To Be Let Alone Versus Freedom of Speech' [1986] *PL* 67.

—— 'Subtle Ways of Legal Borrowing: Some Comparative Reflections on the Report of the *Calcutt* Committee "On Privacy and Related Matters" ', in *Festschrift für Werner Lorenz zum Siebzigsten Geburtstag* (1991), 717–37.

—— 'Our Patchy Law of Privacy. Time To Do Something About It' (1990) 53 *MLR* 802.

MARSHALL, G., 'The Right to Privacy: A Sceptical View' 21 *McGill LJ* 242 (1975).

[300] Op. cit. (Select Bibliography), at 461–2.

[301] That this horizontal effect is inevitable is argued by Sir William Wade in 'The United Kingdom's Bill of Rights' in *Constitutional Reform in the United Kingdom: Practice and Principles* (1998), 63. It is also supported, on the basis of comparative materials, by Markesinis, 'Privacy, Freedom of Expression and the Horizontal Effect of the Human Rights Bill: Lessons from Germany' (1999) *LQR*, (Winter Issue).

[302] *Hansard*, HL Deb., 3 Nov. 1997, 1256.

NAISMITH, S. H., 'Photographs, Privacy and Freedom of Expression' [1996] *EHRLR* 150.

PERRI 6, *The Future of Privacy*, 2 vols (Demos, 1998).

PRATT, W., *Privacy in Britain* (1979).

PRESCOTT, P., '*Kaye v Robertson*—A Reply' (1991) 54 *MLR* 451.

SEIPP, D. J., 'English Judicial Recognition of a Right to Privacy' (1983) *3 OJLS* 325.

WACKS, R., 'The Poverty of Privacy' (1980) 96 *LQR* 73.

—— *The Protection of Privacy* (1980).

WESTIN, A., *Privacy and Freedom* (1967).

WINFIELD, P., 'Privacy' (1931) 47 *LQR* 23.

YOUNGER, K., *Report of the Committee on Privacy*, Cmnd. 5012 (HMSO, 1972),

4. AN AMERICAN PERSPECTIVE[*]
by
Professor David A. Anderson

English and American Defamation Law Compared

Although the American law of defamation is descended from that of England, it has diverged so greatly that the resemblance is largely superficial. In practice the law works quite differently because of differences in the way defamation litigation is financed and conducted, and because of the impact in America of constitutional free-speech principles. The English preference for reputation over freedom of expression referred to above[304] is matched by an equally powerful American preference for free speech at the expense of reputation.

Doctrinally, the American law of defamation is far more protective of speech than the English law. It offers virtually all of England's common-law protections, plus a succession of constitutional restrictions designed to thwart suits that would survive the common-law barriers. But a reader of the Press of the two countries might wonder how much difference the doctrines make. Though successful libel suits undoubtedly are more frequent in England, they do not seem to produce the terror that libel inspires in much of the American press.[305] Ironically, the explanation may be that the doctrinal revolution designed to free American journalism from the fear of libel judgments has instead created a litigation quagmire that has itself become a source of terror. And the litigation difficulties that defamation victims face in England may give the Press some of the protection that doctrine denies them in that country.

The common law rules are similar. American law observes the English law's distinction between libel and slander and the related rules regarding slander *per se* and presumed harm. As in England, the essence of the tort is harm to reputation; insults and affronts to honour, actionable in some Continental legal systems, generally do not suffice in the United States. The same elaborate structure of absolute and conditional privileges protects many kinds of defamatory but socially useful communications.

[*] Thompson and Knight Centennial Professor, The University of Texas at Austin.
[304] See above, Section 1(2)(c).
[305] E. Barendt et al., *Libel and the Media: The Chilling Effect* (1997).

There are many minor differences, however, a few of which are significant enough to warrant mention here. The liberal pleading rules of American courts generally do not require plaintiffs to identify specifically the words of which they complain or the precise defamatory meaning they claim the words convey. Typically, the plaintiff merely alleges that he or she is defamed by the defendant's published article or broadcast. The defendant is then forced either to defend against all possible defamatory meanings that might be found in the material or engage in wasteful preliminary skirmishes attempting to pin down the plaintiff. The English rules requiring plaintiffs to plead innuendo go a long way toward eliminating such unnecessary confusion, and ought to be emulated in the United States.

A United States statute immunises on-line computer service providers from liability for defamatory messages posted on the Internet. American common law employs the same republication rules as the English common law.[306] Under these rules, a company that provides computer bulletin boards on which a subscriber posts a defamatory message accessible to all other subscribers is liable as a republisher, at least if the company is aware of the defamation. After a decision so holding,[307] the companies persuaded Congress to pass a statute stating that 'No provider or user of an interactive computer service shall be treated as the publisher or speaker of any information provided by another information content provider.'[308] This language protects a provider even if it is notified of a posting, knows that it is false and defamatory, and agrees that it should have been removed.[309] The statute may even protect a provider who induces a contributor to post defamatory matter.[310]

While the English courts require defendants to establish the precise truth of the defamatory accusation, the American courts usually accept a rough approximation. For example, evidence showing that the plaintiff, a journalist, had fabricated one story was held sufficient to preclude liability for a statement that the journalist had been fired for repeatedly fabricating stories.[311] This result is quite at odds with the very similar English case described above.[312]

These differences are minor, however, when compared with the differences introduced by American constitutional law. The American courts have concluded that the shared common-law principles do not give speech—or at least speech about matters of public concern—the degree of protection required under the free-speech and press clauses of the First Amendment to the US Constitution. They have created a body of federal constitutional defamation law that supplements, and in some instances supplants, the common law rules.

---

[306] See above Section 1(2)(c).

[307] *Stratton Oakmont, Inc.* v. *Prodigy Services Co.*, 1995 WL 323710 (N.Y. Supp. May 24, 1995).

[308] 47 U.S.C. s. 230 (1996).

[309] *Zeran* v. *America Online, Inc.*, 129 F.3d 327 (4th Cir. 1997), cert. denied 118 S.Ct. 2341 (1998).

[310] See *Blumenthal* v. *Drudge*, 992 F.Supp. 44 (D.C.D.C. 1998). This is a trial court decision that need not be followed by other courts.

[311] *Shihab* v. *Express-News Corp.*, 604 SW 2d 204 (Tex. App. 1980).

[312] See *Wakley* v. *Cooke and Healey* (1849) 4 Exch. 511, 517; 154 ER 1316, 1318. The case is described at Section 1(3)(c) above.

The effects are pervasive, introducing new rules with respect to fault, damages, burdens of proof, and appellate review.

(A) PUBLIC OFFICIALS

All of this constitutional development has taken place since 1964. Until then, the US Supreme Court adhered to the position that defamatory falsehoods 'are no essential part of any exposition of ideas'[313] and thus are 'not . . . within the area of constitutionally protected speech'.[314] The court abandoned that notion in *New York Times Co.* v. *Sullivan*,[315] one of the most dramatic and far-reaching decisions in American constitutional law. The effect of the common law on speech could not be ignored, even though truth was a complete defence, because 'would-be critics of official conduct may be deterred from voicing their criticism, even though it is believed to be true and even though it is in fact true, because of doubt whether it can be proved in court or fear of the expense of having to do so'.[316] These worries were likely to induce self-censorship inconsistent with America's 'profound national commitment to the principle that debate on public issues should be uninhibited, robust, and wide-open, and that it may well include vehement, caustic, and sometimes unpleasantly sharp attacks on government and public officials'.[317] The court quoted James Madison, the primary draftsman of the First Amendment: 'Some degree of abuse is inseparable from the proper use of every thing; and in no instance is this more true than in that of the press.'[318]

Although the rationale of *New York Times* v. *Sullivan* seemed to apply generally to libels occurring in discussions of public issues, the case did not require the court to go so far. Rather, the court fashioned a cluster of new constitutional defamation rules dealing only with libels against public officials. Sullivan was the elected official in charge of police in Birmingham, an Alabama city beset with racial violence. The *New York Times* published an advertisement by a group seeking to raise funds for civil rights demonstrators in the South. The advertisement accused the Birmingham police of brutal and unlawful treatment of Dr Martin Luther King Jnr. and other civil rights activists. It did not name Sullivan but he claimed he was necessarily implicated because only he had power to authorise the police actions alleged. The Alabama courts, applying common law principles similar to those of England and most of the other American states, awarded Sullivan $500,000 in damages against the *Times* and four black Alabama clergymen who had signed the advertisement.

The defendants urged the Supreme Court to hold that liability could never be imposed for criticism of the official conduct of a public official. Such liability, they argued, would be a species of seditious libel, which had been universally condemned in the United States since the notorious Alien and Sedition Acts expired in 1801. But the majority of the Justices were unwilling to go that far. Instead, they adopted a 'federal rule that prohibits a public official from recovering damages for a defamatory falsehood unless he proves that the statement

---

[313] *Chaplinsky* v. *New Hampshire*, 315 US 568, 572 (1942).
[314] *Beauharnais* v. *Illinois*, 343 US 250, 266 (1952).　　　[315] 376 US 254 (1964).　　　[316] Ibid., at 279.
[317] Ibid., at 270.　　　　　[318] Ibid., at 271, quoting 4 *Elliot's Debates on the Federal Constitution*, 571 (1876).

was made with "actual malice"—that is, with knowledge that it was false or with reckless disregard of whether it was false or not'.[319]

The court analogised this to a state-law rule, recognised only in a minority of the states, which expanded the common law privilege of fair comment to cover false statements of fact about the conduct of public officials. It soon became apparent, however, that the *Times* rule went beyond anything known to the common law anywhere. The 'actual malice' needed to satisfy the *Times* rule can be shown only by proving that the defendant published despite 'a high degree of awareness of probable falsity . . . There must be sufficient evidence to permit the conclusion that the defendant in fact entertained serious doubts as to the truth of his publication.'[320]

Had the court stopped with announcement of the 'actual malice' rule, the case would have gone back to Alabama for retrial. For all its stringency, the test would only have raised a jury issue, and had a new jury found that the *Times* published with the requisite subjective awareness of falsity, Sullivan might yet have won.

To prevent this, the court promulgated several rules ancillary to the 'actual malice' requirement. First, the court announced that 'actual malice' must be established with 'convincing clarity', rather than the preponderance of evidence usual in civil cases. Secondly, the court asserted that since the factual issue of 'actual malice' was one upon which constitutional rights depended, the jury's fact finding would be scrutinised more closely than usual. The court would '"make an independent examination of the whole record," so as to assure ourselves that the judgment does not constitute a forbidden intrusion on the field of free expression'.[321] Engaging in such a review of the Alabama trial record, the court concluded that a jury could not properly find that the *Times* published with knowing or reckless falsity, even though there was evidence that its secretary suspected that one of the allegations was false, and even though material in the *Times*'s own files would have shown several of the statements to be false. 'We think the evidence against the *Times* supports at most a finding of negligence in failing to discover the misstatements, and is constitutionally insufficient to show the recklessness that is required for a finding of actual malice.'[322] This language made clear that it would be futile to retry the case under the new 'actual malice' standard; the Supreme Court would ultimately hold the evidence insufficient.

Finally, the court drove a stake through the heart of Sullivan's lawsuit by holding unconstitutional his theory that criticism of his police officers defamed him. This theory smacked of seditious libel, 'transmuting criticism of government, however impersonal it may seem on its face, into personal criticism, and hence potential libel, of the officials of whom the government is composed'.[323]

Thus, although the 'actual malice' rule is usually thought of as the key holding in *New York Times* v. *Sullivan*, in fact the rule is the least of its products. Had the decision merely announced the 'actual malice' rule, the American courts probably would have continued to apply something very similar to the English

---

[319] 376 US at 279–80.
[321] 376 US at 285 (citation omitted).
[320] *St Amant* v. *Thompson*, 390 US 727, 731 (1968).
[322] Ibid., 288.
[323] Ibid., 292.

law of defamation, with an additional jury issue in public-official cases. What assured a decisive break with the English tradition was the court's demonstrated willingness to supervise the administration of state libel law, to make sure that the preference for 'wide open, robust debate' was observed in practice as well as in theory.

The decision in the *Times* case was not the only example of that commitment: in the next ten years, eleven libel cases were decided by the Supreme Court, and in only one of those was a judgment for the plaintiff able to surmount the substantive and procedural barriers erected by the court. Even with the more conservative bent of the court in recent years, it has adhered steadfastly to the basic principles of the *New York Times* case.[324]

The 'public official' category, of course, includes elected officials (local, state, and national) like Sullivan. But it also encompasses candidates for public office,[325] appointed officials,[326] and 'those among the hierarchy of government employees who have, or appear to the public to have, substantial responsibility for or control over the conduct of government affairs'.[327] Officers as lowly as the superintendent of the county motor pool[328] and a deputy sheriff[329] have been subjected to the *New York Times* rules.

(B) PUBLIC FIGURES

The primary rationale of *New York Times* v. *Sullivan* was the belief that citizen critics of government officials needed more freedom than the common law provided. But the court also expressed a more general concern to protect 'debate on public issues', which might well involve defamation of persons other than public officials. Thus, it seemed likely from the outset that at least some of the *Times* restrictions would be applied eventually to plaintiffs other than public officials. The opportunity first presented itself in two libel cases that the Supreme Court decided jointly in 1967.[330] One plaintiff, Wally Butts, was athletic director at a state university but was paid by a private alumni organisation. The other, General Edwin Walker, had retired from the army and was defamed in the course of activities he undertook as a private citizen after retirement. All members of the court agreed that, although neither was a public official, both were 'public figures', criticism of whom should receive some constitutional protection. Chief Justice Warren wrote that:[331] 'although they are not subject to the restraints of the political process, "public figures," like "public officials," often play an influential role in ordering society . . . Our citizenry has a legitimate and substantial interest in the conduct of such persons, and freedom of the press to engage in uninhibited debate about their involvement in public issues and events is as crucial as it is in the case of "public officials".' Although four members of the court would have adopted a somewhat

---

[324] See e.g. *Masson* v. *New Yorker Magazine, Inc.*, 111 S.Ct. 2419 (1991).
[325] *Monitor Patriot Co.* v. *Roy*, 401 US 263 (1961).   [326] *Henry* v. *Collins*, 380 US 356 (1965).
[327] *Rosenblatt* v. *Baer*, 383 US 75 (1966).   [328] *Clawson* v. *Longview Pub. Co.*, 589 P.2d 1223 (Wash. 1979).
[329] *Ammerman* v. *Hubbard Broadcasting Co.*, 91 NM 250, 572 P.2d 1258 (NM App. 1977), cert. denied 436 US 906 (1978).
[330] *Butts* v. *Curtis Pub. Co.* and *Walker* v. *Associated Press*, decided together at 388 US 130 (1967).
[331] 388 US at 164.

lower constitutional barrier for public figures, the majority voted to apply the same standards as in public official cases. The court voted five–four to affirm Butts's $460,000 judgment on the ground that he had met the constitutional burden, but unanimously reversed Walker's $500,000 award because he had not.

Determining whether a plaintiff is a public figure is not always easy. The lower courts generally have treated sports and entertainment celebrities as public figures, without much regard to their involvement in public issues.[332] Being classified as a public figure often goes unchallenged, even by the faintest of luminaries, so the applicability to celebrities of Chief Justice Warren's rationale for extending the *New York Times* rules to public figures has not been thoroughly explored.

The Supreme Court has not decided a celebrity case, but has tended to describe the public figure category somewhat more narrowly than the lower courts:[333]

That designation may rest on either of two bases. In some instances an individual may achieve such pervasive fame or notoriety that he becomes a public figure for all purposes and in all contexts. More commonly, an individual voluntarily injects himself or is drawn into a particular public controversy and thereby becomes a public figure for a limited range of issues. In either case such persons assume special prominence in the resolution of public questions.

The court has refused to treat as a public figure a prominent civil liberties lawyer,[334] a socialite involved in a notorious divorce case,[335] and a scientist who had received more than $500,000 in federal research funds.[336]

The public figure classification has both a geographical and a contextual dimension. A person who is well-known locally may be treated as a public figure for purposes of a publication circulated primarily in that locale, even though he is unknown nationally.[337] And a person may be a public figure in connection with discussion of her role in one activity but not another.[338]

As a result of the broad interpretations given to both the public official and public figure categories, the *New York Times* restrictions apply to a very large number—perhaps a majority—of American defamation cases. For these plaintiffs, success is very unlikely. One study showed that plaintiffs ultimately prevailed in only about 10 per cent of the media defamation cases in which the *New York Times* rules applied.[339]

(c) PRIVATE PLAINTIFFS

For a time it appeared that the Supreme Court would apply the *New York Times* rules to all plaintiffs defamed in connection with public affairs, even if they are

---

[332] E.g. *Carson* v. *Allied News Co.*, 529 F.2d 206 (7th Cir. 1976) (television entertainer); *Maule* v. *NYM Corp.*, 54 NY 2d 880 (1981) (sports writer).

[333] *Gertz* v. *Robert Welch Inc.*, 418 US 323, 351 (1974). [334] Ibid.

[335] *Time, Inc.* v. *Firestone*, 424 US 448 (1976). [336] *Hutchinson* v. *Proxmire*, 443 US 111 (1979).

[337] E.g. *Williams* v. *Pasma*, 656 P.2d 212 (Mont. 1982), cert. denied 461 US 945 (1983).

[338] E.g. *Vitale* v. *National Lampoon*, 449 F.Supp. 442 (ED Pa. 1978).

[339] See Franklin, 'Winners, Losers, and Why? A Study of Defamation Litigation' (1980) *Amer. Bar Found. Res. J.* 455.

neither public officials nor public figures. A number of lower courts had reasoned that 'uninhibited, robust, and wide-open' debate on public issues was
certain to produce defamation of private persons as well as public, and that
libel suits by the former were just as likely to cause self-censorship as those by
the latter.[340] The Supreme Court applied the *New York Times* rules to a private
plaintiff in one case, disallowing a $275,000 judgment won by a magazine dis-
tributor who had been defamed in reporting about his arrest on obscenity
charges. The case was *Rosenbloom* v. *Metromedia, Inc.*[341] Three justices agreed
with lower courts that: 'Drawing a distinction between "public" and "private"
figures makes no sense in terms of the First Amendment guarantees.'[342] But no
majority of the court ever fully embraced that view, and three years later the
court decided to draw precisely that distinction.

The case was *Gertz* v. *Robert Welch, Inc.*,[343] the second most important case in
the American law of defamation, after *New York Times* v. *Sullivan*. The plaintiff
was a lawyer who had been called a 'Communist-fronter' by a right-wing political group. His case had been decided by the trial court on the theory that since
he was not a public figure, he need not meet the *New York Times* requirements.
The United States Court of Appeals held that this was erroneous in light of
Rosenbloom. Gertz clearly had been defamed in the course of debate on a public
issue; the article claimed Communists were plotting to discredit American
police and that Gertz was involved. The Supreme Court, however, repudiated
Rosenbloom. The majority decided that applying *New York Times* to all those
defamed in discussion of public issues would entail too great a sacrifice of the
reputations of private persons. The latter deserve more protection from the
law, the court asserted, because (*a*) private individuals have not voluntarily
assumed a risk of public criticism by engaging in politics or achieving prominence in a particular field, and (*b*) they are less likely than public plaintiffs to
have access to media to rebut false charges.[344] Thus, while the free-speech
interest in encouraging robust debate might be the same whether the individuals affected were public or private, the countervailing reputational interest
was higher in the case of the latter, and a different balance was therefore
required.

This did not mean, however, that private plaintiff cases were to be free from
constitutional restraints. The court believed that the common law, with its
principles of strict liability tempered by numerous privileges and defences,
gives too little protection to speech, even in private plaintiff cases.

So the court promulgated a different set of constitutional rules for cases
where the discussion is about a matter of public concern but the person
defamed is private. First, the states may no longer impose strict liability in such
cases. There must be some showing of fault (presumably negligence) on the
part of the publisher; this spares private plaintiffs the difficulty of meeting the
New York Times test, 'yet shields the press and broadcast media from the rigors
of strict liability for defamation'.[345] Secondly, such plaintiffs may recover only

---

[340] See e.g. *Time, Inc.* v. *McLaney*, 406 F.2d 565 (5th Cir.), cert. denied 395 US 922 (1969).
[341] 403 US 29 (1971).   [342] Ibid., at 45.   [343] 418 US 323 (1974).   [344] Ibid., 344.
[345] Ibid., 348.

if they can show they have suffered actual injury. Unlike the common-law concept of special damages, which is limited to pecuniary losses, 'actual injury' may include humiliation and mental anguish. But it may not include presumed damages or punitive damages. The rationale is that the minimal fault requirement of *Gertz* strikes the proper balance between free speech interests and the legitimate interest in redressing private plaintiff's actual injury; a private plaintiff who wishes to recover more than that (i.e. presumed or punitive damages) must meet the higher constitutional requirement of actual malice.[346]

Since *Gertz* then, the American law of defamation has been subject to two different sets of constitutional restrictions. Suits by public officials and public figures are subject to the actual malice requirement, the 'clear and convincing' proof requirement, and aggressive judicial review of jury verdicts. Private plaintiffs face none of these requirements, but must show fault and actual injury, and are denied presumed and punitive damages unless they opt to proceed under the public plaintiff rules and prove actual malice. Obviously these divergent rules tend to make litigation quite complex, especially where the appropriate classification of the plaintiff is itself an issue. Most states have eased this difficulty somewhat by holding that whether the plaintiff is public or private is a question of law; it therefore can be decided by the judge before trial.[347] Where it is treated as a question of fact, the jury must be given alternative sets of instructions, the controlling set to be determined by the jury's decision on the public–private issue.[348]

In fact, the law is even more complicated than this, for two reasons. First, the Supreme Court has subsequently decided that at least some of the *Gertz* restrictions are applicable only to private plaintiffs who are defamed in discussion about matters of public concern.[349] The case involved a credit reporting agency that falsely reported to its private subscribers that the plaintiff corporation was bankrupt. The Vermont courts held that such purely private libels were not affected by *Gertz* and allowed the plaintiff to recover presumed and punitive damages without a showing of actual malice. The Supreme Court affirmed. The *Gertz* restrictions on damages were appropriate, the court said, where speech on issues of public concern might be chilled by the prospect of punitive and presumed damages. But in the case at hand, such damages properly could be awarded even without a showing of actual malice, 'in light of the reduced constitutional value of speech involving no matters of public concern'.[350] Since the private circulation of a credit report involved no subject of public concern, the *Gertz* rules on damages were not applicable. The court did not decide whether the *Gertz* rule on fault also would be inapplicable, because the Vermont courts had found the defendant negligent and the question therefore was not before the Supreme Court.

After *Times* and *Gertz*, the American constitutional law of defamation appeared to have two tiers, one for public officials and public figures, another

---

[346] Ibid., 349–50.
[347] See e.g. *Waldbaum v. Fairchild Publications, Inc.*, 627 F.2d 1287 (2d Cir.), cert. denied 449 US 898 (1980).
[348] Cf. *Nash v. Keen Pub. Corp.*, 214 NH 127, 498 A.2d 348 (1985).
[349] *Dun & Bradstreet, Inc.*, v. *Greenmoss Builders, Inc.*, 472 US 749 (1985).   [350] 472 US at 761.

for all other plaintiffs. Now it is clear that it has three tiers: one for public plaintiffs, one for private plaintiffs defamed in connection with public issues, and one for plaintiffs defamed in purely private contexts. It remains to be seen whether the court will ultimately decide that the latter must meet some constitutional minimum less than the full *Gertz* regime.

The second complicating factor is the Supreme Court's limited power in the American federal system. The court has no power to promulgate rules of tort law. That is the exclusive province of the state and federal legislatures and state courts. The Supreme Court's power is only negative. If a state permits liability to be imposed on a basis inconsistent with the constitutional rules announced by the Supreme Court, the court can invalidate the judgment but the effect of the court's decision is only to impose a set of constitutional restrictions on the existing body of state law, not to create a new federal law of defamation.

This has far-reaching consequences. Instead of supplanting contrary state law, the court's rules become a constitutional floor, defining a level of protection for defendants below which the states may not go. For example, in public plaintiff cases the federal constitutional rules do not prohibit punitive damages.[351] A number of state courts prohibit them in all defamation cases, however, as a matter of interpretation of their own state free-speech guarantees or as a result of their own more stringent interpretations of the federal constitution.[352] In private plaintiff cases *Gertz* requires only a minimal level of fault, but some of the states require more. *New York* requires a showing of 'gross irresponsibility'.[353] A few states require the same level of fault as would be required in a public plaintiff case: reckless or knowing falsehood.[354] Most states require the minimum permitted under *Gertz* negligence.[355] Though the federal constitutional restrictions do not necessarily apply to purely private libels, some states apply the *Gertz* rules to all defamation cases.[356] Before the Supreme Court intervened in 1964, the 'American' law of defamation consisted of fifty different bodies of law, derived from the English common law but each with its own variations. It is probably safe to say that, despite the imposition of a complex set of federal constitutional rules, there is less uniformity today than ever before.

(d) Truth and Falsity

No principle of the English common law was more fully accepted in the United States than the rule that the defendant had the burden of pleading and proving truth. The implication of the rule—that a statement is presumed to be false merely because it is alleged to be defamatory—might seem anathema to American ideas about free speech. But American courts, like the English,

---

[351] See *Curtis Pub. Co.* v. *Butts*, 388 US 130 (1967).

[352] See e.g. *Wheeler* v. *Green*, 286 Or. 99, 593 P.2d 777 (1979); *Stone* v. *Essex County Newspapers*, 367 Mass. 849, 330 NE 2d 161 (1975).

[353] *Chapadeau* v. *Utica Observer-Dispatch, Inc.*, 38 NY 2d 196, 379 NYS.2d 61, 341 NE 2d 569 571 (1975).

[354] See e.g. *Aafco Heating & Air Conditioning Co.* v. *Northwest Publications, Inc.*, 321 NE 2d 580 (Ind. App. 1974), cert. denied 424 US 913 (1976).

[355] See e.g. *Miami Herald* v. *Ane*, 458 So. 2d 239, 242 (Fla. 1984).

[356] E.g. *Jacron Sales, Inc.* v. *Sindorf*, 276 Md. 580, 350 A.2d 688 (1976).

believed the risk of unprovability ought to fall on the party who, by putting the defamatory words in circulation, has purported to know the facts. Despite its universal acceptance, however, the common-law rule probably was doomed from the day *New York Times* v. *Sullivan* was decided. Though that decision spoke of 'the defense of truth' and said nothing about shifting that burden, by requiring proof of knowledge of falsity or reckless disregard for truth the court made it a virtual necessity for public plaintiffs to prove falsity also. There remained a theoretical possibility of proving reckless disregard of falsity without proving the statement actually *was* false, but as a practical matter proof of the latter was usually a prerequisite to proving the former. After *Gertz* the same practical necessity faced private plaintiffs; one who could not show the defamation was false would have little hope of proving the defendant was negligent with respect to its falsity.

Nevertheless, it was not until 1986 that the Supreme Court explicitly shifted the burden of proving falsity to plaintiffs, and then only by a five–four vote. The case was *Philadelphia Newspapers, Inc.* v. *Hepps*.[357] Hepps was a private businessman accused by a newspaper of being connected with organised crime. The Pennsylvania Supreme Court had applied the traditional common law rule that truth was a defence to be pleaded and proved by the defendant. The US Supreme Court found that rule insufficiently protective of free speech. 'To ensure that true speech on matters of public concern is not deterred, we hold that the common law presumption that defamatory speech is false cannot stand when a plaintiff seeks damages against a media defendant for speech of public concern.'[358] The decision appears to apply to both public and private plaintiffs, but only if the defamation occurs in relation to matters of public concern. It is in terms limited to media defendants, but two members of the majority disavowed that limitation. Since the court has consistently refused to give media protection not enjoyed by other litigants, it is not likely to deny non-media defendants the benefit of the *Hepps* rule.

Despite the narrow vote, *Hepps* is a formidable precedent. Had the case been one where the plaintiff could prove falsity as easily as the defendant could prove truth, the decision might have left open a possibility that the burden would not be placed on plaintiffs for whom it would be onerous. But the facts of *Hepps* presented precisely the kind of case where the burden on the plaintiff is most difficult to meet. How is Hepps to prove that he does *not* have ties with organised crime? The defendant presumably has access to proof of the facts upon which its accusation is based. The plaintiff must undertake either to exonerate his associates or to exonerate himself from being associated with whomever the defendant believed to be criminals. For Hepps himself, the difficulty was compounded by the defendant's successful invocation of an evidentiary privilege to refuse to reveal the identity of confidential sources upon whose information the allegation was based. That the court was willing to shift the burden to a plaintiff who seemed to have so little chance of meeting it

[357] 475 US 767 (1986).
[358] Ibid., at 776–7. The court declined to decide whether falsity must be established with 'convincing clarity'.

extinguished any thought that the *Hepps* rule might be limited to cases in which it imposes no insuperable burden on the plaintiff.

(E) OPINION AND RHETORIC

The constitutional requirements also have implications for defamatory statements couched as opinion or hyperbole. The result is that some rhetorical excesses that would be actionable in England are absolutely protected in the United States.

As noted in the preceding subsection, the First Amendment requires libel plaintiffs to prove falsity. This implies that the statement complained of must be one that by its nature is capable of being proved true or false. In *Milkovich* v. *Lorain Journal*,[359] the Supreme Court rejected an argument that this necessarily means no statement of opinion can be actionable, but suggested that it does protect some statements of opinion that would be actionable at common law. The requirement that plaintiffs prove falsity 'ensures that a statement of opinion relating to matters of public concern which does not contain a provably false factual connotation will receive full constitutional protection'.[360]

A similar implication protects rhetorical hyperbole. If a statement cannot be reasonably interpreted as stating actual facts about the plaintiff, it is not capable of being proved false, and therefore cannot sustain liability. The court held that a pornographic magazine could not be held liable for publishing a parody that portrayed evangelist Jerry Falwell as a drunk who committed incest with his mother in an outhouse, because readers could not reasonably understand the publication to be an account of actual facts.[361] For similar reasons, a statement describing plaintiff as a 'blackmailer' cannot be actionable if the context makes clear that the term is meant rhetorically rather than literally.[362]

Some American lower courts have been willing to go even further, holding that all statements of opinion are absolutely protected. Among the statements held to be constitutionally protected opinion are an allegation that a university professor 'has no status within the profession'[363] and an assertion that a state official's criminal prosecution of an American Indian leader was motivated by personal revenge.[364]

These courts reject the common law proposition that a statement in the form of an opinion may be actionable if it implies the existence of undisclosed defamatory facts. Instead of focusing on the implications of such a statement these courts engage in a contextual analysis, looking at (*a*) the common usage of the language, (*b*) the verifiability of the statement, (*c*) the journalistic context in which the statement occurs (e.g. news report or commentary), and (*d*) the nature of the subject being discussed (e.g. political controversy).[365] Ultimately

---

[359] 497 US 1 (1990).   [360] Ibid., at 20.

[361] *Hustler Magazine, Inc.* v. *Falwell*, 485 US 46 (1988). This was not a defamation case but the Supreme Court has subsequently held that its principle is applicable to defamation. See *Masson* v. *New Yorker Magazine, Inc.*, 501 US 496 (1991).

[362] *Greenbelt Cooperative Publishing Ass'n.* v. *Bressler*, 398 US 6 (1970).

[363] *Ollman* v. *Evans*, 750 F.2d 970 (DC Cir. 1984) (*en banc*), cert. denied 471 US 1127 (1985).

[364] *Janklow* v. *Newsweek, Inc.*, 788 F.2d 1300 (9th Cir. 1986) (*en banc*).

[365] See *Ollman* v. *Evans*, op. cit.

the classification of the statement as 'fact' or 'opinion' seems to turn on an assessment of the likelihood that a reasonable reader would understand that the statement should not be taken as an assertion of literal fact. Statements that occur in political argument are likely to be treated as opinion even though on their face they appear to be factual assertions. The same is true of statements that appear in recognised forums for expression of opinion, such as newspaper editorials and letters-to-the-editor columns.[366]

The Supreme Court has now made clear that the First Amendment does not support such a sweeping rule, but some lower courts still interpret the rule broadly.[367] Moreover, the states are free to protect opinion more broadly than the federal constitution requires, and the highest court of New York has chosen to do so. That court held that the New York state constitution requires the four-step contextual analysis rejected by the Supreme Court in *Milkovich*.[368]

The 'opinion defence' enjoyed extraordinary success in the years preceding *Milkovich* and it has not disappeared despite that decision. One reason for its popularity may be that it gives courts a way of disposing of unmeritorious cases before trial. Whether a statement is to be characterised as opinion is a question of law.[369] The issue usually requires little development of a factual record, so defendants may move for dismissal or summary judgment at an early stage in the litigation. The doctrine is thus one of the few mechanisms in American defamation law that invites a speedy and inexpensive disposition before trial.

(F) THE LAW IN PRACTICE

At first blush, defamation law seems very protective of defendants in the United States and very favourable to plaintiffs in England. In practice, however, the difference is less than meets the eye, because of non-doctrinal factors. Litigation realities tend to work in favour of defendants in England and plaintiffs in America. Tort verdicts in general tend to be larger in the United States than in Britain, and libel verdicts tend to be even larger than other tort awards in the United States. One study, by the Libel Defense Resource Centre (a media-funded research institution) showed that the *average* verdict in libel cases against media defendants was almost $6 million and the median libel verdict was $590,000.[370] The largest affirmed judgment so far is $24 million,[371] but jury verdicts have gone as high as $220 million.[372]

The intricacy of the constitutional rules tends to make American defamation litigation complex and protracted, and the possibility of high stakes encourages both sides to spare no effort. A major case generates many thousands of pages of depositions, motions, and briefs before it ever reaches trial. Pre-trial battles,

---

[366] E.g. *Kotlikoff* v. *Community News*, 89 NF 62, 444 A.2d 1086 (1982); *Miskovsky* v. *Oklahoma Pub. Co.*, 654 P.2d 587 (Okla. 1982), cert. denied 459 US 923.

[367] See, e.g., *Dilworth* v. *Dudley*, 75 F.3d 307 (7th Cir. 1996); *Moldea* v. *New York Times Co.*, 22 F.3d 310 (2d Cir.) cert. denied 513 US 875 (1994).

[368] *Immuno A.G.* v. *Moor-Jankowski*, 77 NY 2d 235, 567 N.E.2d 1270, 566 NYS.2d 906, cert. denied 500 US 954 441 (1991).

[369] E.g. *Lewis* v. *Time, Inc.*, 710 F.2d 549 (9th Cir. 1983).

[370] See Libel Defense Resource Center Bulletin No. 1, Jan. 31, 1994.

[371] *Sprague* v. *Walter*, 441 Pa.Super. 1, 656 A.2d 890 (1995).

[372] *MMAR Group, Inc.* v. *Dow Jones Co.*, 987 F. Supp. 535 (S.D.Tex. 1997) (appeal pending).

trial, post-trial motions, and appeals invariably last for years. As a result, costs often run into seven figures. General William Westmoreland is reported to have spent more than $3 million before abandoning his libel suit against the Columbia Broadcasting System, and CBS reportedly spent $10 million on its defence. Although American libel defendants are less likely than their English counterparts ultimately to lose, the combination of expensive and protracted litigation and possible multi-million-dollar judgments in the United States makes libel a matter of no less concern.

In addition to the financial costs, libel defendants sometimes face intrusive pre-trial discovery procedures. A plaintiff is entitled to scrutinise defendant's records and question its employees, not only to find admissible evidence, but also to search for anything that might lead to the discovery of admissible evidence. In the case of media defendants, that gives their adversaries opportunities to probe newsroom practices and editing decisions and tie up personnel in protracted depositions and records searches. It is even possible in some cases for plaintiffs to compel disclosures of confidential news sources.[373] All of these factors tend to make libel suits a greater threat to the media than doctrine alone would lead one to suppose.

In England the media and other defendants enjoy several advantages. A defamation victim of modest means finds it difficult to initiate a libel suit in England. Legal aid is not available to defamation plaintiffs,[374] nor (in most instances) is the contingent-fee system by which American lawyers agree to represent tort plaintiffs for a percentage of the recovery.[375] Moreover, the libel plaintiff under 'the English rule' must be prepared, if he loses, to pay the opponent's legal costs in addition to his own, while the American plaintiff need not be concerned with any costs other than his own. Under some circumstances defendants in England can bring an early end to the proceedings by demanding that the plaintiff post security for costs. Together these factors mean that potential defendants in England need not worry much about being sued for libel by ordinary citizens; libel litigation is largely the preserve of the wealthy, or at least those well-connected enough to have someone to finance their litigation.

English defendants have a significant advantage in persuading plaintiffs to accept settlement. A defendant can make a 'payment in' to the court as a settlement offer. A plaintiff who rejects the offer may be required to pay all of the defendant's costs from the time of the payment onward, unless the plaintiff secures a judgment larger than the amount paid in.[376] This can be a potent weapon against a plaintiff who has unrealistic monetary expectations.

For unintentional defamation, English law allows a defendant who has been guilty of no negligence to escape liability altogether by making an 'offer of

---

[373] See e.g. *Miller* v. *Transamerican Press, Inc.*, 621 F.2d 721 (5th Cir. 1980), cert. denied 450 US 1041 (1981). In *Hepps* (op. cit.) a state statute prevented disclosure of the source.

[374] Legal Aid Act 1971, s. 7, Sch. 1, Part II(1).

[375] The Lord Chancellor has proposed that conditional fees (what Americans call contingent fees) be allowed in certain libel actions. See Alastair Brett, 'No Win, No Fee: No Free Press', *The Times*, 28 April 1998, at 18.

[376] Rules of the Supreme Court 1965, Ord. 22, R. 1.

amends'—a correction and apology and an offer to pay plaintiff's costs in initiating the action.[377] This provision is not as useful as it might be because of the burden placed on the defendant to show lack of negligence. None the less, it is more favourable than the American law of retraction, which typically allows defendants to mitigate damages but not to escape liability entirely.

The English Court of Appeal has power to control damages by substituting its own judgment for that of the jury in cases in which the court finds the jury's award excessive.[378] Courts in America have no such power, although through the device of remittitur they may require a plaintiff to choose between a reduced award and a new trial. As noted above,[379] the Court of Appeal appears to be willing to use this power to control excessive damage awards.

A few American courts have refused to enforce English defamation judgments. By statute, courts are obliged to honour foreign judgments when the winners seek to collect their judgments from assets located in the United States, but an exception allows them to refuse when the 'cause of action upon which the judgment is based is repugnant to the public policy of the state'. Some judgment debtors have argued that English defamation law is so unprotective of speech that it falls within the exception. The leading precedent holds that English law is inconsistent with Maryland public policy because it allows defamatory statements to be presumed false, allows qualified privileges to be overcome by proof of improper motive, and does not recognise the US constitutional limits relating to fault, opinion, and punitive damages.[380] The majority seemed to take no note of other differences that make English law more protective of defendants. A dissenting justice said this decision 'seems inclined to make Maryland libel law applicable to the rest of the world by providing a safe haven for foreign libel judgment debtors'. It cannot be doubted that American law gives defendants in defamation cases more protection than English law. But it hardly follows that the English resolution of the conflict between speech and reputation interests is wrong, let alone repugnant.

(G) INVASION OF PRIVACY

Although it has no counterpart in English law, the American tort law of invasion of privacy is related closely enough to defamation to deserve a brief mention here. Many libel suits in the United States are combined with claims for invasion of privacy. To some extent privacy law is an outgrowth of changes in the law of defamation. At one time a truthful statement made without adequate justification might have been actionable as defamation in either the United States or England, but as truth became an absolute defence, at least in the United States, the need for some other remedy became apparent.

'Invasion of privacy' is an umbrella term encompassing four distinct American torts. In addition, American law recognises other 'rights of privacy' that are not torts and are beyond the scope of this discussion. For example, a

---

[377] Defamation Act 1996, s. 2(4). [378] Courts and Legal Services Act 1990, s. 8(2).
[378] See above, Section 1(3)(e)(ii).
[380] *Telnikoff* v. *Matusevitch*, 347 Md. 561, 702 A.2d 230 (1997). See also *Bachchan* v. *India Abroad Publications*, 154 Misc. 2d 228, 585 NYS.2d 661 (NYSup. 1992).

constitutional 'right of privacy' protects against governmental interference in such personal matters as abortion and contraception,[381] and 'privacy' statutes restrict governmental acquisition and use of certain types of personal information.[382]

Of the four privacy torts, the one closest to the core of the privacy concept is the cause of action for public disclosure of embarrassing private facts. A person may recover damages for a disclosure that would be highly offensive to a reasonable person and is not of legitimate public concern.[383] Sexual activities and medical abnormalities are among the kinds of disclosures that are most often litigated. The matter need not have been completely secret before the defendant's disclosure. Even the most intimate secrets usually are known to one's closest friends and family, so it is enough that the defendant has disclosed publicly a matter that previously was known only to such a limited circle.[384] On the other hand, matters of official record may be disclosed with impunity, even if they were previously unknown by the public.[385]

The central issue is what facts are 'private', and the law has defined that term so narrowly—and the concept of legitimate public concern so broadly—that very few disclosures are actionable. Courts look to contemporary mores to determine what reasonable people would find highly offensive. From that point of reference, disclosures of such matters as one's income or net worth,[386] personal idiosyncrasies,[387] illegitimacy,[388] or medical diagnosis[389] usually are held not to be sufficiently offensive.

The concept of legitimate public concern is inspired by First Amendment values, and therefore is interpreted expansively. The public usually is held to have a legitimate interest in the identity of victims of crimes (including rape and other sex offences),[390] the sexual activities and medical problems of public officials,[391] and the marital difficulties of celebrities.[392] Courts are reluctant to second-guess an editor's judgment that a matter is of legitimate public concern; some judges have gone so far as to say they will defer to the editor's judgment unless it is one no rational editor could have made.[393]

In a society in which free flow of information is treated as a paramount value, judges find it difficult to impose liability for disclosing truth. The tort of

[381] *Roe* v. *Wade*, 410 US 113 (1973); *Griswold* v. *Connecticut*, 381 US 479 (1965).

[382] E.g. Privacy Act of 1974, 5 USC, s. 552a (1992).

[383] Restatement (Second) of Torts, s. 652D (1977).

[384] *Sipple* v. *Chronicle Publishing Co.*, 154 Cal.App.3d 1040, 201 Cal.Rptr. 665 (1984); *Dias* v. *Oakland Tribune, Inc.* 139 Cal.App.3d 118, 188 Cal.Rptr. 762 (1983); *Melvin* v. *Reid*, 112 Cal.App. 285, 297 P. 91 (1931).

[385] *Howard* v. *Des Moines Register & Tribune Co.* 283 NW 2d 289 (1979), cert. denied 445 US 904 (1980).

[386] *Wolf* v. *Regardie*, 553 A.2d 1213 (DC.App. 1989); *Schoneweis* v. *Dando*, 231 Neb. 180, 435 NW 2d 666 (1989).

[387] *Virgil* v. *Time, Inc.*, 527 F. 2d 1122 (9th Cir. 1975), cert. denied 425 UK.S. 998 (1976); *Sidis* v. *F.-R. Publishing Corp.*, 113 F.2d 806 (2nd Cir.), cert. denied 311 US 711 (1940).

[388] *Heath* v. *Playboy Enterprises Inc.*, 732 F.Supp. 1145 (1990).

[389] *Davis* v. *Monsanto Co.*, 627 F.Supp. 418 (1986); *Child Protection Group* v. *Cline*, 350 SE 2d 541 (1986); *Meetze* v. *Associated Press*, 230 SC 330, 95 SE 2d 606 (1956).

[390] *The Florida Star* v. *BJF*, 491 US 524 (1989); *Cox Broadcasting Corp.* v. *Cohn*, 420 US 469 (1975).

[391] *Hubert* v. *Harte-Hanks Texas Newspapers Inc.*, 652 SW 2d 546 (1983); *Kapellas* v. *Kofman*, 1 Cal.3d 20, 81 Cal.Rptr. 360, 459 P.2d 912 (1969).

[392] *Carlisle* v. *Fawcett Publications Inc.*, 201 Cal.App. 2d 733, 20 Cal.Rptr. 405 (1962).

[393] *Gilbert* v. *Medical Economics Co.* 665 F.2d 305 (10th Cir. 1981).

public disclosure of truthful but embarrassing private facts, therefore, exists more in theory than in practice; claims are numerous, but they almost never succeed.

The second American privacy tort is a cause of action for publications that depict a person in a false light. The falsehood need not be defamatory, but it must place the person in a false light that would be highly offensive to a reasonable person. For example, affixing plaintiff's byline to a sensational 'first-person' account that he did not write gave rise to a cause of action for false light invasion of privacy.[394]

The tort is a cousin to defamation, and is subject to many of the same state-law restrictions.[395] Similar constitutional restrictions also apply. A plaintiff who is a public official or public figure must show that the defendant published with reckless disregard of the possible falsity.[396] Private plaintiffs probably must prove at least that the defendant was negligent with respect to the falsity, and sometimes have been required to meet the same standard as a public plaintiff.[397]

Because of these restrictions and the necessity of showing a high degree of offensiveness, false light cases rarely succeed. Some states have refused to recognise the tort at all,[398] and there is considerable scholarly debate about its legitimacy.[399]

The two remaining privacy torts are of more practical significance. One is a cause of action for intentional and highly offensive intrusion into a person's private life. This tort supplements the law of trespass in two principal ways. First, it provides a remedy where the intrusion is physical but does not occur on plaintiff's premises. Thus, President Kennedy's widow was able to stop the famous 'paparazzo' Ron Galella from shadowing her and her children to photograph them in public parks, restaurants, and schools.[400] Secondly, it provides a remedy where the intrusion is accomplished without physical invasion, for example, by electronic surveillance or telescopic lenses.[401]

The intrusion branch of privacy provides a more effective remedy for media invasions of personal privacy than the other branches. In part, this is because the First Amendment provides less protection for newsgathering activities than for publication. An important California Supreme Court decision illustrates this. A television cameraman accompanied a helicopter rescue crew to the site of a highway accident, outfitted the flight nurse with a microphone, and filmed the rescue of a woman who was seriously and permanently injured in the wreck. The woman sued for both the intrusion and the subsequent broadcast of video showing her begging to be allowed to die. The court held that the First

---

[394] *Dempsey* v. *National Enquirer*, 702 F.Supp. 934 (D.Me. 1989).
[395] *Fellows* v. *National Enquirer Inc.*, 42 Cal.3d 234, 721 P.2d 97, 228 Cal.Rptr. 215 (1986).
[396] *Cantrell* v. *Forest City Publishing Co.*, 419 US 245 (1974).
[397] *Lovgren* v. *Citizens First National Bank*, 126 Ill.2d 411, 534 NE 2d 987 (1989).
[398] *Renwick* v. *The News and Observer Pub. Co.*, 310 NC 312, 312 SE 2d 405, cert. denied 469 US 858 (1984).
[399] See e.g. Diane Zimmerman, 'False Light Invasion of Privacy: The Light that Failed', 64 *NYULR* 364 (1989).
[400] *Galella* v. *Onassis*, 487 F.2d 986 (2nd Cir. 1973).
[401] *Dietemann* v. *Time Inc.*, 449 F.2d 245 (9th Cir. 1971).

Amendment barred the woman's claims for public disclosure of the sounds and images because those were a matter of legitimate public concern, but did not bar her claim for the TV crew's intrusion into a situation in which she had legitimate expectations of privacy. With two dissenting votes, the court rejected the defendants' argument that they had a First Amendment right to intrude to obtain information that was of legitimate public concern.[402]

This decision was based on common law, but the California legislature subsequently created a stronger statutory remedy. The statute makes it a tort to trespass or use a 'visual or auditory enhancing device'—e.g., a telephoto lens or a directional microphone—to film or record a person engaging in personal or familial activities under circumstances in which the person had a reasonable expectation of privacy. A person violating the statute is liable for up to three times the amount of special and general damages, plus punitive damages, and also may be enjoined.[403]

The final privacy tort, which generates more successful claims than the other three branches combined, provides a remedy for commercial exploitation of a person's name or likeness. It arose from the unconsented use of a person's photograph or testimonial in advertisements,[404] but it now extends to unauthorised use of a person's distinctive nickname,[405] slogan,[406] or costume,[407] or to the use of a model who looks like the plaintiff,[408] or a singer who imitates plaintiff's vocal style.[409]

This branch of the tort has produced an entire industry based on the value of celebrity endorsements, and often seems to have more to do with commerce than with personal privacy. Indeed, the interest it protects is sometimes called a 'right of publicity' rather than a right of privacy. Unlike the other privacy torts, which are personal to the victim and cannot be assigned or enforced after death, the right to control commercial exploitation is assignable *inter vivos*,[410] and in most jurisdictions is held to be a descendible interest enforceable at least for a number of years after the person's death.[411]

The tort is not conspicuously effective in protecting personal privacy because it covers only exploitation for commercial purposes, and most uses of personality for purposes even tangentially related to journalism or entertainment are not considered commercial. It is not actionable for a television station to use film of a bleeding accident victim to promote a documentary about emergency

---

[402] See *Shulman v. Group W Productions*, 18 Cal.4th 200, 74 Cal.Rptr. 843, 955 P.2d 469 (1998).

[403] See Cal.Civil Code s. 1708.8. The same remedies are available against a publisher or broadcaster who induces another person to violate the statute, and if the image or recording is published or broadcast, the plaintiff may recover the profits gained thereby.

[404] *Pavesich v. New England Life Insurance Co.*, 122 Ga. 190, 50 SE 68 (1905).

[405] *Hirsch v. S. C. Johnson & Son Inc.*, 90 Wis. 2d 379, 280 NW 2d (1979).

[406] *Carson v. Here's Johnny Portable Toilets Inc.*, 698 F.2d 831 (6th Cir. 1983).

[407] *Motschenbacher v. R. J. Reynolds Tobacco Co.*, 498 F.2d 821 (9th Cir. 1974).

[408] *Onassis v. Christian Dior-New York Inc.*, 122 Misc.2d 603, 472 NYS 2d 254 (trial court 1984), aff'd., 110 AD 2d 1095, 488 NYS 2d 943 (1985).

[409] *Midler v. Ford Motor Co.*, 849 F.2d 460 (9th Cir. 1988), cert. denied 503 US 951 (1992).

[410] *Factors Etc. Inc. v. Pro Arts Inc.*, 579 F.2d 215 (2nd Cir. 1978), cert. denied 440 US 908 (1979).

[411] *Martin Luther King Jnr., Centre for Social Change Inc. v. American Heritage Products Inc.*, 250 Ga. 135, 296 SE 2d 697 (1982).

medical treatment,[412] or for a magazine that had published photos of a sports hero to republish the photos in advertisements promoting the magazine.[413]

Thus, despite the existence of four rather elaborate privacy torts, American law rarely provides a remedy for persons who believe their privacy has been invaded by media or others. Many of the criticisms by Sir David Calcutt[414] and others of England's failure to protect privacy could be made of American law as well.

[412] *Anderson* v. *Fisher Broadcasting Co. Inc.*, 300 Or. 452, 712 P.2d 803 (1986).

[413] *Namath* v. *Sports Illustrated.*, 80 Misc.2d 531, 363 NYS 2d 279 (Sup. Ct. 1975), aff'd., 48 AD 2d 487, 371 NYS 2d 10, 352 NE 2d 584 (1976).

[414] Sir David Calcutt QC, op. cit. (Select Bibliography).

8

Defences and Remedies

1. DEFENCES

1. The Role of Defences in the Law of Torts

In Chapter 2 we examined the concept of duty of care and the ways by which the courts use it to set the boundaries to tort liability. The general defences that are the subject of Section 1 of this chapter perform a similar function. Historically, the defences of contributory negligence, consent (or assumption of risk) and common employment were of great importance in limiting the availability of personal injury claims to those injured at work or on the highway. The scope of these defences is now much reduced. This has been achieved by legislation which, in its way, has been just as important as the decision of the House of Lords in *Donoghue* v. *Stevenson*[1] in determining the nature of the contemporary tort system. Thus, formerly the contributory negligence of the plaintiff was a complete defence to a claim in negligence. Thanks to the Law Reform (Contributory Negligence) Act 1945, which gave the courts the power to apportion responsibility for damage between plaintiff and defendant and to adjust the plaintiff's damages accordingly, it is now a partial defence. The doctrine of common employment, which provided that an employee impliedly took the risk of any injuries at work caused by the negligence of a fellow employee, was also abolished by the Law Reform (Personal Injuries) Act 1948. The defence of consent survived these statutory changes unscathed, but the courts themselves ensured that it would have only a limited application in personal-injury cases.[2] Finally, in 1977 a further narrowing of the scope for defences occurred when Parliament enacted the Unfair Contract Terms Act, which restricted the use of contract terms and notices to exclude or limit tortious and contractual liability.

These defences are considered below, together with other defences which may be available to a defendant, including necessity and private defence, inevitable accident, authorisation, and limitation of action. The application of the defences in the context of the torts of interference with the person and interference with property have already been considered in earlier chapters. What follows is thus mainly concerned with their application to torts which require proof of damage in order to be actionable, and in particular with the tort of negligence.

2. Contributory Negligence

Contributory negligence provides a partial defence to a claim in tort in a case where the plaintiff's own carelessness was a material cause of his loss. Prior to

---

[1] [1932] AC 562.   [2] *Smith* v. *Charles Baker & Sons* [1891] AC 325; *Dann* v. *Hamilton* [1939] 1 KB 509.

the Law Reform (Contributory Negligence) Act 1945 the defence had the effect of excluding the plaintiff's claim completely. The 1945 Act displaced this common rule in favour of a provision enabling the court to apportion responsibility for the loss between plaintiff and defendant and to adjust the plaintiff's damages accordingly. It is in this sense that the defence now operates as a partial exclusion of liability, as opposed, for example, to the total exclusion that results from the application of the defence of consent.

The Act of 1945, as subsequently interpreted by the courts, greatly simplified the law. The common law had produced 'a vast proliferation of case law which added greatly to the hazards of litigation';[3] little of this now survives. None the less, certain conceptual and practical problems continue to surround the modern defence. These principally relate to the role of causation; the notion of the plaintiff's 'fault'; the position of certain special plaintiffs, such as children and rescuers; the process of apportionment; and the scope of the defence with regard to breach of contract and to torts other than negligence.

(A) CAUSATION AND CONTRIBUTORY NEGLIGENCE

The nature of the relationship between contributory negligence and causation was briefly considered in an earlier chapter.[4] Although the two areas are closely linked, contributory negligence is a defence in its own right. The general principles of causation underwent substantial modification prior to 1945, to produce the distinctive contributory negligence defence.[5] Since 1945 the approach of the courts to causation questions has been heavily influenced by the possibility of apportionment which the Act opened up.

The complete exclusion of liability under the old common law was difficult to explain on straightforward causation grounds. In *Butterfield* v. *Forrester*[6] the plaintiff collided with a pole which the defendant had negligently placed across the highway; the plaintiff was held to have been riding too quickly and to have been the sole cause of his injury. The case subsequently came to be treated as authority for the proposition that 'if there is blame causing the accident on both sides, however small that blame may be on one side, the loss lies where it falls'.[7] In other words, where any causal weight, no matter how small, could be attached to the plaintiff's fault, the defendant's fault ceased to matter.

The potential injustice of this approach led the courts to fashion an exception known as the 'last opportunity' rule, according to which the party who had the last chance of avoiding the accident in question was deemed to be solely responsible for the ensuing damage. In *Davies* v. *Mann*[8] the plaintiff carelessly let his donkey roam loose on the highway where it was struck by a cart driven by the defendant; the plaintiff recovered for the damage to the donkey notwithstanding his initial negligence. The last opportunity rule itself was hedged about with various kinds of exceptions and the area was further

---

[3] Glanville Williams, *Joint Torts and Contributory Negligence* (1951), 236.
[4] See Chapter 2, Section 4(3)(b).
[5] See Williams, op. cit., chs. 9 and 10, which contain a comprehensive review of the relevant case law.
[6] (1809) 11 East 60.
[7] *Cayzer, Irvine & Co.* v. *Carron Co.* (1884) 9 App. Cas. 873, 881 (Lord Blackburn).
[8] (1842) 10 M. & W. 546.

complicated by the decision of the Privy Council in *British Columbia Electric Railway* v. *Loach*.[9] This established the principle of 'constructive last opportunity', according to which responsibility would lie on the party who, but for his prior negligence, *would have had* the last chance avoiding the accident.

There are judicial dicta explaining the last opportunity rule in terms of causation and remoteness: thus the failure of the defendant to take due care was regarded as a *nova causa interveniens* which cancelled out the earlier carelessness of the plaintiff.[10] The plaintiff's carelessness was a cause in fact of his loss but it was not sufficiently proximate to the damage to be regarded as a cause in law.[11] Although the rule could therefore be seen as an application of the principles of remoteness, Glanville Williams argued convincingly against this view on the grounds that:

Except under the obscure doctrine of *Loach's* case,[12] the last opportunity rule in its heyday placed emphasis upon the act of negligence latest in time, whereas in the law generally 'the proximate cause is not necessarily the one that operates last.'[13] According to the one rule, it is the last straw that breaks the camel's back; according to the other, part of the blame is attributed to the weight of straws already lying there, which have placed the animal in such imminent peril.[14]

Moreover, the rule was not applied in cases having nothing to do with contributory negligence where the courts, as opposed to distinguishing between the relative fault of plaintiff and defendant, had the task of attaching responsibility to one or more of several co-defendants. In such cases it was acknowledged that joint and several liability could flow from concurrent causes, regardless of which one operated last in time.[15] In truth 'the law of last opportunity was introduced as a palliative for the crude common law rule allowing a wrong-doer's loss to lie where it fell',[16] and was not applied more generally in the law of torts.

The question is of more than just theoretical importance since it now affects the interpretation given to the Contributory Negligence Act 1945. If the last opportunity doctrine could be regarded as simply an illustration of the principles of causation and remoteness, it would be possible for it to survive the changes made by the Act. Under section 1(1),

Where any person suffers damage as the result partly of his own fault and partly of the fault of any other person or persons, a claim in respect of this damage shall not be defeated by reason of the fault of the person suffering the damage, but the damages recoverable in respect thereof shall be reduced to such extent as the court thinks just and equitable having regard to the claimant's share in the responsibility for the damage.

---

[9] [1916] 1 AC 719.

[10] *Radley* v. *London and North Western Railway* (1875) LR 10 Ex. 100, 108–9 (Denman J); see also *Swadling* v. *Cooper* [1931] AC 1, 8–9 (Viscount Hailsham) and *Caswell* v. *Powell Duffryn* [1940] AC 152.

[11] For the meaning of 'cause in fact' and 'cause in law' see the discussion in Chapter 2, above, at Section 4(1).

[12] [1916] 1 AC 719, above.

[13] *Yorkshire Dale SS Co.* v. *Minister of War Transport* [1942] AC 691, 698 (Viscount Simon LC).

[14] Op. cit., (n. 3 above), 244–5.

[15] E.g. *Grant* v. *Sun Shipping Co. Ltd.* [1948] AC 549.   [16] Williams, op. cit., 247.

The old rule derived from *Butterfield* v. *Forrester*[17] which let the loss lie where it fell is clearly ousted by the requirement that the plaintiff's claim 'shall not be defeated' by reason of his own negligence. Could it still be argued, however, that in a case where one party or the other had the last opportunity, he could be held *fully* responsible for the consequences of the accident? This would have the result of either allowing the plaintiff to recover in full or, in a case where his negligence was last in time, of defeating his claim completely, with no possibility of apportionment.

The Act does not purport to affect the normal common-law principles of causation. The retention of the last-opportunity doctrine has, none the less, been clearly rejected by the courts. In *Cakebread* v. *Hopping Bros.* (*Whetstone*) *Ltd.*[18] the Court of Appeal declined to apply 'last opportunity' to a case of an employer's breach of statutory duty in which the employee had had, on one interpretation, an adequate chance to avoid the danger posed by the employer's breach. The plaintiff's damages were apportioned. There was a similar result in a road-traffic case, *Davies* v. *Swan Motor Co.* (*Swansea*) *Ltd.*,[19] in which Denning LJ argued that last opportunity 'was dead before the Act, though it remained in use as a practical test. Since the Act, it is no longer a practical test and should disappear from the books.'[20] In *Jones* v. *Livox Quarries Ltd.*[21] he asserted that 'the doctrine of last opportunity is now obsolete'.[22] Since then, no court has seen fit to revive it. This is not surprising given the enormous complexity of the pre–1945 case law and the unsatisfactory distinctions between contemporaneous and successive acts of negligence to which it gave rise. To revive the doctrine would also frustrate the purpose of the Act by preventing apportionment from taking place in a large category of cases.

Apportionment under the Act gives the court a degree of flexibility which was not possible under the all-or-nothing approach of the common law. This greater flexibility has altered the approach of the courts to causation, making it unnecessary for them to absolve plaintiffs completely from blame in order to do justice in a particular case.[23] Some strained interpretations of what constitutes an operative cause have thereby been avoided. In *Jones* v. *Livox Quarries* the plaintiff rode on the back bumper of a traxcavator, contrary to his employer's express instructions, and was injured in a collision with a dumper caused by the negligence of the dumper driver (who was employed by a different employer). Lord Denning regarded the case as a 'good illustration of the practical effect of the Act of 1945': prior to the Act, 'the negligence of the dumper driver would have been regarded as the predominant cause. Now, since the Act, we have regard to all the causes, and one of them undoubtedly was the plaintiff's negligence in riding on the tow bar of the traxcavator. His share in the responsibility was not great—the judge assessed it at one-fifth—but, nevertheless, it was his share, and he must bear it himself.'[24]

---

[17] (1809) 11 East 60, above.   [18] [1947] KB 641.   [19] [1949] 2 KB 291.
[20] Ibid., 321.   [21] [1952] 2 QB 608.
[22] On the possibility that the doctrine was defunct anyway before the Act, see Lord Wright (1950) 13 MLR 2.
[23] *Stapley* v. *Gypsum Mines Ltd.* [1953] AC 663, 677 (Lord Porter).   [24] [1952] 2 QB 608, 617.

The flexibility provided by apportionment has not, however, relieved the court of the difficult task of identifying whether a particular act or omission is an operative cause in the first place. The Act refers to the damage being the 'result', in part, of the plaintiff's fault, and this has been taken to imply that the general principles of causation are relevant.[25] For the defence of contributory negligence to have any application at all, it must be shown, then, that the plaintiff's carelessness or other fault was a factual cause of his loss—in other words, that on the balance of probabilities the damage would not have occurred 'but for' his fault. But this is not sufficient on its own; as we have seen, it must also be shown that the plaintiff's fault was a legally proximate cause of his injury.[26] If the plaintiff's fault was a 'mere condition' of his injury, no defence will arise. In *Jones* v. *Livox Quarries* the plaintiff's carelessness in riding on the back of the traxcavator would have been irrelevant if, instead of being hit by another vehicle, he had been struck in the eye by a shot fired by a negligent sportsman.[27]

There must be a link, then, between the injury suffered and the risk which the plaintiff, through his carelessness, failed adequately to guard against. This causal link runs from fault to damage and not to the accident as such. If the plaintiff has contributed to the accident he will be taken to have contributed to his injuries as well if these were more likely than not to result from the accident. But he may also be contributorily negligent without having caused an accident in any way by, for example, failing to wear a seat-belt and as a consequence suffering much more extensive injuries than he otherwise would have done. As Lord Denning explained in *Froom* v. *Butcher*[28] in such cases 'the *accident* is caused by the bad driving. The *damage* is caused in part by the bad driving of the defendant, and in part by the failure of the plaintiff to wear a seat belt. If the plaintiff was to blame in not wearing a seat belt, the damage is in part the result of his own fault.'

The court's approach to analysing the legal effect of multiple causes in contributory negligence was considered in *The Volute*.[29] Lord Birkenhead's judgment makes it clear that the causal effect of an initial act of negligence will not be lost simply because the immediate cause of the damage occurs after a substantial interval of time. In some cases it would be clear that only the second event had any causative link to the damage. But 'there are cases in which the two acts come so closely together, and the second act of negligence is so much mixed up with the state of things brought about by the first act that the party secondly negligent . . . might . . . invoke the prior negligence as being part of the cause of the collision so as to make it a case of contribution'. This dictum was applied to the difficult facts of *Stapley* v. *Gypsum Mines Ltd*.[30] Two miners agreed to carry on working in dangerous conditions after failing to take the necessary

---

[25] S. 1; *Stapley* v. *Gypsum Mines Ltd*. [1953] AC 663, 677. [26] See Chapter 2, above, at Section 4(1).
[27] See the judgment of Denning LJ in *Jones* v. *Livox Quarries Ltd*. [1952] 2 QB 608.
[28] [1976] QB 286, 292.
[29] [1922] 1 AC 129. Admiralty law recognised the principle of apportionment for losses caused by maritime collisions before the more general adoption of the principle in the Contributory Negligence Act. See the Maritime Conventions Act 1911, s. 1.
[30] [1953] AC 663.

safety precautions as instructed by their employer. One of them was killed when the roof of the mine collapsed. His widow brought an action against the employer on the basis of its vicarious liability for the negligence and breach of statutory duty committed by the deceased's co-worker. The Court of Appeal held that the deceased had been responsible for his own death but the House of Lords allowed an appeal by a bare majority. Lord Reid held that the lack of care of each employee had been so bound up with that of the other that it was impossible to absolve the man who survived from all responsibility; damages were reduced by 80 per cent.

Although the possibility of apportionment has made it easier for the courts to avoid the need to find a 'sole cause', there are nevertheless cases in which the plaintiff's carelessness has been held totally to outweigh the negligence of the defendant. Such a case was *McKew* v. *Holland and Hannen and Cubitts (Scotland) Ltd.*[31] The plaintiff, who had earlier been injured by the defendants' negligence and forced to wear a cast on his leg as a result, fell down a flight of stairs when his leg gave way beneath him. His lack of care in venturing on to a steep flight of stairs without a handrail was held to have been a *nova causa interveniens* which broke the chain of causation, absolving the defendants of any responsibility for the further injuries he sustained as a result of his fall. The outcome has overtones of the now discredited 'last opportunity' rule, and the courts' failure to apply contributory negligence and apportion damages goes against the grain of most decisions in this area since the 1945 Act came into force.

(B) PLAINTIFF'S NEGLIGENCE

For apportionment to be possible under section 1 of the Contributory Negligence Act, the damage must result partly from the plaintiff's 'fault' and partly from that of the defendant. Under section 4, 'fault' is defined as 'negligence, breach of statutory duty or other act or omission that gives rise to liability in tort or would, apart from this Act, give rise to the defence of contributory negligence'. It has been suggested that the first part of this definition refers to the defendant's breach of duty and that the second part refers to the plaintiff's lack of care; otherwise, the definition makes little sense.[32] If this is so, the meaning of contributory negligence from the plaintiff's point of view is unchanged by the Act.

It is not necessary for the defendant to show that the plaintiff owed him a duty of care or that the plaintiff's carelessness caused him, the defendant, damage. Rather than providing a cause of action in its own right, 'contributory negligence is set up as a shield' against the plaintiff's claim.[33] It is possible that the defendant may bring a counter-claim based on damage caused to him by a separate breach of a duty of care by the plaintiff, but that is a different matter. The standard applied to the plaintiff in contributory negligence is the same as that

---

[31] [1969] 3 All ER 1621. The same approach has been taken in breach-of-statutory-duty cases: see *Rushton* v. *Turner Brothers Asbestos Co. Ltd.* [1960] 1 WLR 96; *Ginty* v. *Belmont Building Supplies Ltd.* [1959] 1 All ER 414; *Jayes* v. *IMI (Kynoch) Ltd.* [1958] ICR 155.

[32] Williams, op. cit. (n. 3 above), 318–19.

[33] *Nance* v. *British Columbia Electric Railway Co. Ltd.* [1951] AC 601, 611 (Viscount Simon).

of the 'reasonable person' in negligence liability generally. Here, as there, the test is not whether the damage or the accident was foreseeable but whether the plaintiff acted reasonably, that is to say, with the amount of self-care that a normal person would have exercised in the circumstances. This is clear from *Froom* v. *Butcher*: wearing a seat-belt is a sensible practice for all journeys no matter how short or whatever the conditions.[34] For even if the risk of an accident occurring is thought to be slight, the magnitude of the harm that might result is very great and the costs of preventing it by fastening the seat-belt are minimal. The same approach applies to the failure of motor-cyclists to wear crash-helmets.[35]

The fact that, in general, legislation makes it compulsory for seat-belts[36] and crash-helmets[37] to be worn by road-users is, without doubt, a useful indicator of what is 'reasonable'. Yet the presence of such a criminal regulation does not conclusively settle the issue as far as the defence of contributory negligence is concerned. Nor do the exceptions to these statutory requirements necessarily coincide with the courts' view of what might be 'reasonable' in a particular case. For example, it is possible that a woman in the advanced stages of pregnancy would be acting reasonably even if she had not fastened her seat-belt if this was physically impossible or highly uncomfortable. The fact that she did not have a medical certificate from her doctor for the purposes of obtaining exemption from the Road Traffic Act may thus be irrelevant.[38] A Sikh wearing a turban is exempted from the requirement to comply with the statutory requirement to wear a crash-helmet while driving a motor-cycle.[39] Whether he would also be able to escape the application of contributory negligence if his failure to do so resulted in him incurring greater injuries in the course of an accident is an open question. Although it might seem unfair that the defendant should be ordered to pay more because of the plaintiff's decision not to wear a crash-helmet, it should be remembered that damages awards of this kind will nearly always be met by liability insurance rather than from the personal resources of defendants. Drivers who drive vehicles which they know to be defective[40] and passengers who accept lifts with drivers whom they know to be drunk, or would have known but for their own drunkenness,[41] may be caught by the defence, as will those who go joy-riding.[42] In every case, though, 'whether this principle can be relied on successfully is a question of fact and degree to be determined in the circumstances out of which the issue is said to arise'.[43]

The standard expected of the plaintiff will be modulated in certain cases, just as it would be for the defendant if the normal standard of care were being

---

[34] [1976] QB 286, 293 (Lord Denning).

[35] *O'Connell* v. *Jackson* [1972] 1 QB 270; *Capps* v. *Miller* [1989] 1 WLR 839. See also *Platform Homes Ltd.* v. *Oyston Shipways Ltd.* [1998] Ch 466 (imprudent borrowing).

[36] Road Traffic Act 1988 s. 15; SIs 1982/1202, 1982/1342, and 1989/1219.

[37] Road Traffic Act 1988, s. 15.   [38] SI 1982/1201, reg. 5.

[39] Road Traffic Act 1988, s. 16(2).   [40] *Gregory* v. *Kelly* [1978] RTR 426.

[41] *Owens* v. *Brimmell* [1977] QB 859; *Ashton* v. *Turner* [1981] QB 137; *Meah* v. *McCreamer (No. 1)* [1985] 1 All ER 637.

[42] In that case, the defence of *ex turpi causa* or illegality may also apply: see *Pitts* v. *Hunt* [1991] 1 QB 24, discussed below.

[43] *Owens* v. *Brimmell* [1977] QB 859, 867 (Tasker Watkins J).

applied to his behaviour.[44] Children are held to a lower standard of self-protection than adults in regard to their use of the highway, although again it is a matter of degree in each case. In *Gough* v. *Thorne*[45] Lord Denning expressed the view that very young children 'cannot be guilty of contributory negligence', and that in the case of older children the extent to which they would be held to the same standards as adults was a question of degree. On the other hand, in *Morales* v. *Ecclestone*[46] an 11-year-old boy who was injured when he ran out into the road without looking was held to be 75 per cent to blame for his injuries. Rescuers and those who are placed in a situation of imminent danger and have to act in the heat of the moment are also unlikely to be held to have been contributorily negligent.[47]

Employees are not, as a group, held to any different standard from other potential plaintiffs. Yet the courts have, on occasion, recognised that long hours and the strain of working in noisy conditions, together with the fatigue caused by repetitive work, may mean that a lower standard is expected of those who regularly work in such conditions.[48] Where the employer is guilty of a breach of statutory duty it may have been the intention of the Act to ensure that a momentary lapse or inattention of the employee did not unduly endanger him. In such a case such a lapse would not amount to contributory negligence. For 'the purpose of imposing the absolute obligation is to protect the workman against those very acts of inattention which are sometimes relied upon as constituting contributory negligence so that too strict a standard would defeat the object of the statute.'[49] Nor, for the same reason, will it normally be possible in a breach of statutory duty case for the defendant to argue that the employee should have anticipated his own employer's carelessness.[50] Cases of statutory duty aside, however, such a failure, if unreasonable in the circumstances, could amount to contributory negligence,[51] just as a defendant's failure to anticipate certain careless behaviour of those to whom he owes a duty of care could, in principle, amount to a breach of that duty.[52]

(c) APPORTIONMENT

Once contributory negligence is made out, the court will reduce the plaintiff's damages 'to such an extent as [it] thinks just and equitable having regard to [his] share in the responsibility for the damage'.[53] Deductions for contributory negligence are extremely common in personal injury cases, but the tendency

[44] See the discussion in Chapter 2, above, Section 3(1)(a)(iii).   [45] [1966] 1 WLR 1387.

[46] [1991] RTR 151.

[47] *Jones* v. *Boyce* (1816) 1 Starkie 493 (passenger jumping from a coach); although cf. *Sayers* v. *Harlow Urban District Council* [1958] 1 WLR 623, where the plaintiff's actions in attempting to escape from a lavatory cubicle in which she had been trapped were held to have amounted to contributory negligence.

[48] *Caswell* v. *Powell Duffryn Associated Collieries Ltd.* [1940] AC 152.

[49] *Staveley Iron & Coal Co. Ltd.* v. *Jones* [1956] AC 627, 648 (Lord Tucker); although cf. *Caswell* v. *Powell Duffryn Associated Collieries Ltd.* [1940] AC 152, 164–7 (Lord Atkin).

[50] *Westwood* v. *Post Office* [1974] AC 1, 16 (Lord Kilbrandon).

[51] *Jones* v. *Livox Quarries Ltd.* [1952] 2 QB 608, 615 (Denning LJ).

[52] *Grant* v. *Sun Shipping Co. Ltd.* [1948] AC 549, 567; *London Passenger Transport Board* v. *Upson* [1949] AC 155, 173; see Chapter 2, above.

[53] Law Reform (Contributory Negligence) Act 1945, s. 1.

today is for them to be appealed only rarely. The appellate courts have the power to alter the judge's order but, according to Lord Denning, will only do so if the judge has misapplied the law, misapprehended the facts, or made a decision which is 'clearly wrong'.[54]

It had been thought prior to the decision of the Court of Appeal in *Pitts* v. *Hunt*[55] that there was nothing to prevent a court using the 1945 Act to make a deduction of 100 per cent in an appropriate case. However, in that decision Beldam LJ pointed out that this was not compatible with the requirement laid down by the Act. For in any case where both parties are 'at fault' (as defined in s. 1 and 4), the court should not allow the defence of contributory negligence completely to defeat the plaintiff's claim and 'to hold that he is himself entirely responsible for the damage effectively defeats his claim'.[56] It seems to follow as a matter of practice if, perhaps, not of law, that if the Act is to operate on the basis of apportionment as opposed to exclusion of damages the court should strive to avoid awarding a deduction *approaching* 100 per cent. In *Pitts* v. *Hunt* the plaintiff had been a passenger on a motor-cycle driven by the defendant and which was involved in a collision the immediate cause of which was the defendant's careless driving. Both were drunk at the time of the accident, the plaintiff knew that the defendant was uninsured and without a driving licence and the plaintiff had encouraged the defendant to drive in a dangerous manner. The plaintiff's action for damages against the estate of the defendant was defeated on the grounds of illegality. But the members of the Court of Appeal held that, had it been necessary, a deduction of 50 per cent for the plaintiff's contributory negligence in placing himself in danger would have been appropriate, reversing the judge's decision that the plaintiff had been 100-per-cent contributorily negligent.

Both the degree of the plaintiff's lack of care (fault) and the degree to which the damage can be attributed to his carelessness (causation) should be considered under the statutory formula. In *Froom* v. *Butcher*[57] Lord Denning repeated his view, expressed in *Davies* v. *Swan Motor Co.*[58] that 'consideration should be given not only to the causative potency of a particular factor, but also its blameworthiness'. Where the plaintiff could have avoided his injuries by wearing a seat-belt the reduction should only be 25 per cent, since the negligent driver took most of the blame for the accident. Where some injuries would have been sustained in any event, Lord Denning suggested a 15-per-cent deduction. Percentage reductions of this kind have been established in a number of contexts and tend to be followed as general guidelines to court practice; they do not produce strictly binding precedents since every case is likely to turn on its own facts. The scale of the deduction in *Froom* v. *Butcher* may be contrasted with Lord Reid's apportionment in *Stapley* v. *Gypsum Mines*,[59] where damages awarded to the widow of the deceased were reduced by 80 per cent. In that

---

[54] *Kerry* v. *Carter* [1969] 1 WLR 1372, 1376; cf. the extensive debate at appellate level in *Stapley* v. *Gypsum Mines Ltd.* [1958] AC 663, in which the Court of Appeal disagreed with the trial judge only to see the House of Lords substitute another ruling by a bare majority of 3–2.

[55] [1991] 1 QB 24.   [56] Ibid., 28.   [57] [1976] QB 286.   [58] [1949] 2 KB 291, 326.

[59] [1953] AC 633.

latter case, not only had the deceased been grossly negligent in the circumstances but his own carelessness was a substantial cause of the roof-fall.

(D) IDENTIFICATION

For certain purposes the plaintiff is identified with the contributory negligence of another person. This is the case, for example, with the derivative action of dependants of the deceased under the Fatal Accidents Act 1976.[60] The deceased's contributory negligence will reduce any damages the dependants are awarded. Under the Congenital Disabilities (Civil Liability) Act 1976 a child is identified with the contributory negligence of one of its parents, where the parent's carelessness caused the child to be born disabled. The damages are reduced by an amount the court considers appropriate 'having regard to the extent of the parent's responsibility'.[61]

(E) THE SCOPE OF THE DEFENCE AND OF THE CONTRIBUTORY NEGLIGENCE ACT

While it is self-evident that contributory negligence operates as a defence to the tort of negligence, its application to other torts and to other forms of civil liability is not always so clear.

Section 1 of the Contributory Negligence Act requires the court to apportion damages in any case where the plaintiff's 'damage' is the result partly of his own 'fault' and partly of the defendant's 'fault'. 'Damage' is defined as *including* loss of life and personal injury,[62] and so is not *confined* to these two categories. It is also well established that the Act covers property damage and there is no reason why it should not apply to pure economic loss either, although its application to such cases has been limited. As far as the principle enunciated in *Hedley Byrne & Co. Ltd.* v. *Heller & Partners Ltd.*[63] is concerned, the plaintiff may fail completely, on the grounds of causation, if it can be shown that he would have incurred the loss in question regardless of the defendant's advice.[64] On the other hand, in a case where the plaintiff succeeds in showing that his reasonable reliance on the misstatement was the cause of his loss the courts are reluctant to allow his failure to make additional inquiries to be regarded as contributory negligence.[65]

As we have seen, 'fault' is defined under the Act as meaning 'negligence, breach of statutory duty or other act or omission which gives rise to a liability in tort or would, apart from this Act, give rise to the defence of contributory negligence'.[66] This unsatisfactory provision only makes sense if the reference to the potential causes of action in the first limb refers to the defendant's fault and the reference to contributory negligence in the second limb refers to the plaintiff's. By adopting the common-law definition of contributory negligence

[60] S. 5.   [61] S. 1(7).   [62] S. 4.   [63] [1964] AC 465.

[64] *JEB Fasteners Ltd.* v. *Marks, Bloom & Co.* [1983] 1 All ER 583.

[65] See *Gran Gelato Ltd.* v. *Richcliff (Group) Ltd.* [1992] 1 All ER 865, 877 (Nicholls VC); although it should be noted that the authorities cited by the Vice-Chancellor for this approach, such as *Redgrave* v. *Hurd* (1881) 20 Ch. D. 1, pre-dated the Act of 1945 and were therefore concerned not with apportionment but with the possibility that the plaintiff's carelessness might defeat his claim completely.

[66] S. 4.

(the definition established 'apart from this Act'), the Act appears to be confining itself to changing the *remedial* aspects of the defence—substituting apportionment for the total exclusion of damages—without altering the scope of the defence. An alternative view is that apportionment is now applicable to all the causes of action listed in the first limb of the definition—negligence, breach of statutory duty, and all other acts and omissions giving rise to liability in tort. If this is correct, the Act has apparently widened the range of situations to which the defence can apply.

Certain cases are clearer. A separate Act excludes the defence in cases of conversion.[67] Under the common law contributory negligence did not operate as a defence to deceit;[68] in *Alliance and Leicester Building Society* v. *Edgestop Ltd.*[69] Mummery J decided that the passage of the 1945 Act had not led to any change in this rule. Conversely, there are indications from both before and after 1945 that the defence does apply to certain cases of nuisance,[70] and its application to the action for breach of statutory duty is well established.[71]

Its application to strict liability torts is unclear. If the defence does not apply, it could be said that a defendant who has not been at fault would be worse off than if he had been negligent, when the defence would clearly be relevant. To apply the defence, however, would mean that, questions of causation aside, the standard set by law would then be somewhat less than strict. A breach of sections 2–4 of the Animals Act 1971 has, nevertheless, been deemed by statute to constitute 'fault' by the defendant for the purposes of section 4 of the Contributory Negligence Act.[72] This is evidently intended to bring in the contributory negligence defence together with statutory apportionment, although it is not clear that it succeeds given the uncertainty surrounding the interpretation of the word 'fault' in the 1945 Act. There is no clear authority in English law on the application of the defence to liability under the rule in *Rylands* v. *Fletcher*, and Commonwealth authorities go both ways.[73]

As far as torts of intention are concerned, one might ask why should mere negligence be a defence to an interference on the part of the defendant which was by definition deliberate and therefore, on the face of it, more blameworthy? This argument has less force than it used to, since whereas the defence would once have excluded the defendant's liability it now serves simply to reduce damages. Moreover, relative blame is only one factor in the equation: the court might also wish to take into account the relative causal weight of the parties' actions. None the less, in *Lane* v. *Holloway*[74] the court rejected an argument that provocation by the victim of a savage blow constituted contributory negligence. In *Murphy* v. *Culhane*,[75] by contrast, where the plaintiff initiated a

---

[67] Torts (Inteference with Goods) Act 1977, s. 11(1); *Lipkin, Gorman* v. *Karpnale Ltd.* [1989] 1 WLR 1340, 1386 (Nicholls LJ).

[68] *Central Railway Co. of Venezuela* v. *Kisch* (1867) LR 2HL 99, 120 (Lord Chelmsford).

[69] [1994] 2 All ER 38.

[70] *Butterfield* v. *Forrester* (1809) 11 East 60 can be seen as a nuisance case; for more-recent authority see *Trevett* v. *Lee* [1955] 1 WLR 122.

[71] *Caswell* v. *Powell Duffryn Collieries Ltd.* [1940] AC 921; *Lewis* v. *Deyne* [1940] AC 921.

[72] Animals Act 1971, s. 10(1).   [73] See Fleming, *The Law of Torts* (8th edn., 1992), at 344–5.

[74] [1969] 1 QB 379.   [75] [1977] QB 94, 98–9.

criminal affray in the course of which the defendant struck him a fatal blow on the head, Lord Denning suggested that any damages awarded to the dead man's widow would be reduced for his contributory negligence. In the event the claim failed completely on the grounds of consent and *ex turpi causa*.[76] Although the use of contributory negligence in such cases remains theoretically possible, then, in practice it is likely to remain limited.

A particularly difficult question concerns the application of the Act to actions for breach of contract. It was not applied to such actions prior to the 1945 Act. The reference to 'negligence' in section 4 could, however, be read as covering breach of contract in cases where the relevant duty is expressed in terms of a standard to act with reasonable skill and care. In *Forsikring Vesta* v. *Butcher*[77] Hobhouse J distinguished between the following three categories:

(1) Where the defendant's liability arises from a contractual provision which does not depend upon negligence on the part of the defendant. (2) Where the defendant's liability arises from some contractual obligation which is expressed in terms of taking care (or its equivalent) but does not correspond to a common law duty of care which would exist in the given case independently of contract. (3) Where the defendant's liability in contract is the same as his liability in the tort of negligence independently of the existence of any contract.

The learned judge then went on to hold that only the third and final category was caught by the 1945 Act. His judgment was upheld by the Court of Appeal on the grounds that the reference to 'liability in tort' in section 4 meant that it only applied to actions originating in tort and not to actions for breach of a duty originating in contract. This was confirmed by the Court of Appeal in *Tennant Radiant Heat Ltd.* v. *Warrington Development Corp.*[78] According to Dillon LJ, a breach of covenant under a lease, being an obligation created by contract, 'does not fall within the definition of "fault" in section 4 of the 1945 Act'.[79] In *Barclays Bank plc* v. *Fairclough Building Ltd.* the Court of Appeal again refused to extend the scope of the defence. According to Beldam LJ, 'actions for breach of a strict contractual obligation would become unduly complex if contributory negligence were admitted as a partial defence by introducing an element of uncertainty into many straight forward commercial disputes and increasing the issues to be determined'.[80]

Since a number of decisions on the scope of duty of care in the tort of negligence have reduced the potential overlap between separate and concurrent tort and contract duties,[81] the scope to apply the Contributory Negligence Act to cases involving contractual relationships may now be highly restricted. Both

---

[76] See below, Section 5.

[77] [1986] 2 All ER 488, 508. The judgments of the Court of Appeal and House of Lords are reported at [1986] AC 852.

[78] [1988] 11 EG 71. See also the judgment of the Court of Appeal in *Barclays Bank plc* v. *Fairclough Building Ltd.* [1995] QB 214.

[79] See also *Lipkin, Gorman* v. *Karpnale Ltd.* [1989] 1 WLR 1340, 1360 (May LJ); *The Good Luck* [1989] 2 Lloyd's Rep. 238; P. Marshall and A. Beltrami, 'Contributory Negligence: a Viable Defence for Auditors?' [1992] *LMCLQ* 416.

[80] [1995] QB 214, 230.

[81] See the discussion of duty of care in Chapter 2, above.

the Scottish and English Law Commissions have recommended reform of the law to enable the defence to be applied generally to contract claims.[82] It is possible to use the doctrines of causation and mitigation of damages to defeat a claim for breach of contract by a plaintiff who was responsible for his own losses. It would, however, produce a 'more just and principled outcome' to allow apportionment by extending the scope of the 1945 Act, rather than by relying on 'all or nothing' outcomes.[83]

In *Gran Gelato Ltd.* v. *Richcliff (Group) Ltd.*[84] the question arose whether the 1945 Act applies to claims for damages under section 2(1) of the Misrepresentation Act 1967. According to Sir Donald Nicholls VC, section 2(1) is 'essentially founded on negligence',[85] with the result that the 1945 Act does apply to a case of concurrent claims for negligence in tort and under section 2(1). However, he went on to hold that it would not be just and equitable to order apportionment in a case where the plaintiff suffered loss as a result of relying on a misrepresentation which the defendant had intended him to regard as accurate. It was a 'well established principle' in cases of misrepresentation that 'carelessness in not making other inquiries provides no answer to a claim when the plaintiff has done that which the representor intended he should do'.[86]

3. Consent

The defence which is known variously as 'consent', 'assumption of risk', and '*volenti non fit injuria*' can operate as a total exclusion in respect of all forms of tort liability. However, the relevant principles operate rather differently in cases of negligence and strict liability than they do in respect of the torts of intentional interference. In negligence or strict liability, where the court is asking whether the plaintiff may be taken to have assumed the risk of damage flowing from the defendant's breach of duty, it is engaged in a process of allocating the risk of loss between the parties. In the intentional torts, where the question is whether the plaintiff can be said to have consented to the interference in question, the issues raise a set of ethical constitutional questions concerning the validity of such consent.

(A) Consent as a Defence to Negligence and Strict Liability

Two senses of consent may usefully be distinguished. According to the first, consent signifies the assumption of a particular risk of injury by the plaintiff; according to the second, the plaintiff agrees in advance to waive any claim he might have to compensation arising out of an injury. The classic consent defence refers to the first of these two senses. An assumption or risk, which may be express or implied by conduct, negatives a duty of care that would otherwise arise or, which amounts to the same thing in practice, negatives liability for breach of that duty. In *Dann* v. *Hamilton* Asquith J regarded *volenti* as 'a

---

[82] Scottish Law Commission No. 115 (1988); Law Commission No. 114 (1990).

[83] A. Burrows, 'Contributory Negligence in Contract: Ammunition for the Law Commission' (1993) 93 *LQR* 175, a note on *Schering Agrochemicals Ltd.* v. *Resibel NVSA* (Court of Appeal, 26 Nov. 1992; unreported).

[84] [1992] 1 All ER 865.   [85] Ibid., 875.   [86] Ibid., 876.

denial of any duty at all, and, therefore, of any breach of duty'.[87] While it is possible for the consent defence to arise in a case of implied waiver of claim,[88] this rarely occurs; the courts normally insist on finding an express waiver, based on an exclusion or limitation clause contained in a specific contract or notice. The interpretation of exclusion and limitation clauses and the application to such clauses of the Unfair Contract Terms Act 1977 give rise to specialised questions which require to be analysed separately from the general defence of consent.[89]

(i) **Consent as Assumption of Risk**   The plaintiff's claim will be defeated if he is taken to have consented to run the risk of being injured by the defendant's negligence. The same defence applies to certain strict-liability torts. Lord Diplock clarified the nature of the defence when he said that 'the consent that is relevant is not consent to the risk of injury but consent to the lack of reasonable care that may produce the risk'.[90] It is also the case that mere knowledge of the risk is not enough, and that the plaintiff's consent will not be inferred from his knowledge alone.[91] These two qualifications have substantially restricted the scope of the defence in modern personal-injury cases. A leading example of this trend is *Dann* v. *Hamilton*,[92] in which the plaintiff accepted a lift with the defendant whom she knew to be drunk. The defendant caused an accident in which he was killed and the plaintiff injured. Asquith J rejected the application of the *volenti* defence. 'The plaintiff, by embarking in the car, or re-entering it, with knowledge that through drink the driver had materially reduced his capacity for driving safely, did not impliedly consent to, or absolve the driver from liability for, any subsequent negligence on his part whereby the plaintiff might suffer harm.'[93]

If *volenti* and exclusion are now best regarded as separate defences, they nevertheless have common roots in the nineteenth-century use of express and implied contract terms to limit the liability of occupiers, employers, and others. In this respect they were both linked to a further defence, common employment, which has now been abolished by statute.[94] According to the doctrine of common employment, an employee (or 'servant', to refer to the term used by nineteenth-century judges) impliedly took the risk of any injury caused by the negligence of a fellow worker in the same employment. The employer, who would normally have been vicariously liable for the acts of an employee acting in the course of his employment, would thereby escape liability completely. The employer could only be made liable for a breach of his *personal* duty of care to ensure that there was a safe system and place of work and that the plaintiff's fellow workers were reasonably competent.[95] The basis of 'common employment'

---

[87] [1939] 1 KB 509, 512.

[88] See *Nettleship* v. *Weston* [1971] 2 QB 691, 701.

[89] See below, Section 4.

[90] *Wooldridge* v. *Sumner* [1963] 2 QB 43, 69–70.

[91] Hence it is said that the plaintiff must be *volens* and not merely *sciens* as to the risk: *Thomas* v. *Quatermaine* (1887) 18 QBD 685, 696 (Bowen LJ); *Nettleship* v. *Weston* [1971] 2 QB 691, 701.

[92] [1939] 1 KB 509.

[93] Ibid., 518.

[94] By the Law Reform (Personal Injuries) Act 1948, s. 1.

[95] The personal duty of care was fully recognised by the House of Lords in *Wilsons & Clyde Coal Co.* v. *English* [1938] AC 57, but there are indications of the doctrine in earlier cases and hints that it constituted an exception to the defence of common employment: see e.g. *Smith* v. *Charles Baker & Sons* [1891] AC 325, 343 (Lord Watson).

was a contract term which the judges regarded as an essential aspect of 'the mutual undertakings between the employer and employed to be implied from the relationship of master and servant constituted between them'.[96] The term was automatically implied into the contract of service on the grounds that 'when several workmen engage to serve a master in a common work, they know, or ought to know, the risks to which they are exposing themselves including the risks of carelessness, against which their employer cannot secure them, and they must be supposed to contract with reference to such risks'.[97] This produced some harsh results. Thus in one case two miners were killed when the cage in which they were travelling from the bottom of the pit failed to stop when it reached the top of the shaft. Claims for compensation against their employer were rejected on the grounds that the accident was due entirely to the carelessness of a third employee who was operating the cage at the time of the accident.[98]

The doctrine of common employment was never less than controversial. One judge thought that 'there never was a more useful decision, or one of greater practical and social importance in the whole history of the law'.[99] Not everyone, however took such a view. The Scottish courts thus found it 'a principle as distasteful as it is alien to Scottish jurisprudence'[100] and were only persuaded to follow it by House of Lords authority in the *Bartonshill* cases.[101] Common employment would have no application in a case where the injury to the plaintiff was caused by a person other than a fellow employee, such as the employee of a different employer. However, the same rationale of an assumption of risk could then be applied using the more general defence of *volenti non fit injuria*.

In *Woodley* v. *Metropolitan District Railway Co.*[102] the plaintiff, a workman employed by contractors who had been engaged by the defendant railway company, was struck by one of their trains while he was working in an unlit tunnel. He claimed damages for negligence based on the defendants' failure to provide a system to warn of the approach of trains. The Court of Appeal rejected his claim on the grounds that 'a man who enters on a necessarily dangerous employment with his eyes open takes it with its accompanying risks'. Cockburn CJ explained the scope of the *volenti* defence as follows:

If a man chooses the employment, or to continue in it with a knowledge of the danger, he must abide the consequences, so far as any claim to compensation against the employer is concerned. Morally speaking, those who employ men on dangerous work without doing all in their power to obviate the danger are highly reprehensible, as I certainly think the company were in the present instance. The workman who depends on

---

[96] *Johnson* v. *Lindsay & Co.* (1891] AC 371, 380 (Lord Herschell).

[97] *Bartonshill Coal Co.* v. *Reid* (1856) 3 Macq. 266, 295 (Lord Cranworthy). The basis of the doctrine was said to be the judgment of Lord Abinger in *Priestley* v. *Fowler* (1837) 3 M. & W. 1, but its rationale was first clearly articulated in the Massachusetts decision, *Farwell* v. *Boston Railroad Corporation* (1846) 4 Metcalf 49, and, in England, in *Hutchinson* v. *York, Newcastle and Berwick Railway Co.* (1850) 5 Exch. 343. The *Bartonshill* judgment in the House of Lords applied the doctrine to both English and Scots law.

[98] *Bartonshill Coal Co.* v. *Reid* (1856) 3 Macq. 266.

[99] Pollock CB in *Vose* v. *Lancashire and Yorkshire Railway Co.* (1858) 2 LJ Ex. 249.

[100] The expression of Lord Macmillan in *Radcliffe* v. *Ribble Motor Services Ltd.* [1939] AC 215, 235.

[101] *Bartonshill Coal Co.* v. *Reid* (1853) 3 Macq. 266, *Bartonshill Coal Co.* v. *Maguire* (1853) 3 Macq. 300.

[102] (1887) 2 Ex. D. 384.

his employment for the bread of himself and his family is thus tempted to incur risks to which, as a matter of humanity, he ought not to be exposed. But looking at the matter in a legal point of view, if a man, for the sake of the employment, takes it or continues it with a knowledge of its risks, he must trust to himself to keep clear of injury.

The growth in the size and financial stability of industrial undertakings and the greater availability of liability insurance gradually altered the perception that the employer was no better placed than his employees to ensure their safety at work. In 1880 Parliament passed the Employers' Liability Act which excluded the defence in a case where the plaintiff was injured by the negligence of a superior worker with supervisory or managerial responsibilities, as opposed to a fellow servant in general employment. This was only a partial restriction of the defence, but it nevertheless marked a turning point in the law of employers' liability. A short while later the House of Lords limited the scope of the *volenti* defence in the great case of *Smith* v. *Charles Baker & Sons*,[103] itself an appeal in an action for damages under the 1880 Act. The plaintiff was employed on the construction of a railway and was injured by a stone that fell from a crane that was being used to shift rock from a cutting. He had been aware for several months of the danger posed by the crane being swung, without warning, over his head, but had nevertheless continued in the employment. The House of Lords rejected an argument that consent could be inferred either at common law or under the Act from the fact of his staying at work. Lord Watson's formulation continues to be applicable:

In its application to questions between the employer and the employed, the maxim [*of volenti*] as now used generally imports that the workman had either expressly or by implication agreed to take upon himself the risks attendant upon the particular work which he was engaged to perform, and from which he has suffered injury. The question which has most frequently to be considered is not whether he voluntarily and rashly exposed himself to injury, but whether he agreed that, if injury should befall him, the risk was to be his and not his master's. When, as is commonly the case, his acceptance or non-acceptance of the risk is left to implication, the workman cannot reasonably be held to have undertaken it unless he knew of its existence and appreciated or had the means of appreciating its danger. But assuming that he did so, I am unable to accede to the suggestion that the mere fact of his continuing at his work, with such knowledge and appreciation, will in every case necessarily imply his acceptance. Whether it will have that effect or not depends, in my opinion, to a considerable extent upon the nature of the risk, and the workman's connection with it, as well as upon other considerations which must vary according to the circumstances of each case.[104]

Lord Bramwell, dissenting, argued that it was a 'question of bargain. The plaintiff here thought the pay worth the risk and he did not bargain for a compensation if hurt: in effect, he undertook the work, with its risks, for his wages and no more.'[105] It was this wide view of *volenti*, using the continuation of the contract as evidence of implied consent, which the majority ruling in *Smith* v. *Baker* decisively rejected. The implied term theory nevertheless lingered on for a further half-century, since the doctrine of common employment remained in

[103] [1891] AC 325.   [104] Ibid., 355.   [105] Ibid., 344.

place albeit in a form that became progressively more confined. In *Radcliffe* v. *Ribble Motor Services Ltd.*[106] an action was brought under the Fatal Accidents Act by the widow of a bus driver who was killed in an accident which happened to have been caused by another driver employed by the same company. The House of Lords held that for the defence of common employment to apply, the employees in question had to be employed not just by the same employer but also on 'common work', denoting a joint venture which necessarily exposed them to the risk of each other's negligence.

While this strained interpretation of the doctrine enabled the courts to avoid its application in the case in question, the House of Lords nevertheless felt unable to overturn the defence completely on the grounds that it had become too well established as a principle of the common law. It was thus left to Parliament to repeal it by section 1(1) of the Law Reform (Personal Injuries) Act 1948. This provided that 'It shall not be a defence to an employer who is sued in respect of personal injuries caused by the negligence of a person employed by him, that that person was at the time the injuries were caused in common employment with the person injured.' Section 1(2) of the Act renders void any contract term for the exclusion of an employer's liability to those employed by him in respect of injuries caused by the negligence of persons in common employment.

(ii) The Scope of the Modern Defence   The abolition of common employment and the conversion by statute of contributory negligence into a partial as opposed to a complete defence encouraged the courts further to limit the operation of *volenti*. In *Nettleship* v. *Weston*[107] Lord Denning said:

Now that contributory negligence is not a complete defence, but only a ground for reducing the damages, the defence of *volenti non fit injuria* has been closely considered and, in consequence, it has been severely limited. Knowledge of the risk of injury is not enough. Nor is a willingness to take the risk of injury. Nothing will suffice short of an agreement to waive any claim for negligence. The plaintiff must agree, expressly or impliedly, to waive any claim for any injury that may befall him due to the lack of reasonable care by the defendant.

In *Nettleship*'s case an amateur driving instructor was held not to have waived any claim which might arise out of the negligence of a learner driver whom he was supervising, since he specifically asked whether he would be protected by the car-owner's liability insurance policy.[108] Lord Denning's dictum, however, goes too far in suggesting that nothing short of an express or implied contract will suffice for the defence to apply. A contract or notice as such is not necessary. Nor is the defence confined to the case of an agreement to waive a future claim. Consent in the sense of a general assumption of risk can still prevent liability arising.

In *Dann* v. *Hamilton*[109] Asquith J distinguished two situations. In the first the defendant by his negligence creates a risk of physical danger which the plain-

---

[106] [1939] AC 215.   [107] [1971] 2 QB 691, 701.
[108] Salmon LJ dissented: see [1971] 2 QB 691, 704.
[109] [1939] 1 KB 509, 516–17; see also *Morris* v. *Murray* [1991] 2 QB 6, 14–15 (Fox LJ), 19–20 (Stocker LJ).

tiff, in full knowledge of the risk, chooses to accept. In the second, the plaintiff, by his words or conduct, is taken to consent to a subsequent act of negligence. It is more difficult to establish *volenti* in the second situation (as in *Dann's* case itself) since it is less plausible that the plaintiff would have given his consent to negligence in advance of it occurring. Nevertheless, Asquith J accepted that even then the defence would apply where 'the drunkenness of the driver at the material time is so extreme and so glaring that to accept a lift from him is like engaging in an intrinsically and obviously dangerous occupation, intermeddling with an unexploded bomb or walking on the edge of an unfenced cliff'. However, in holding that the plaintiff had not been *volens* even though she had made the apparently fatalistic remark that 'if anything is going to happen it will happen',[110] Asquith J appeared to have left very little scope for the defence to apply in passenger-driver cases. He later recorded that he would have accepted a plea of contributory negligence (which would then have been a complete defence), but none was made.[111] His approach was not followed in similar road-accident cases in Australia.[112]

More recently, in *Pitts* v. *Hunt*,[113] the plaintiff, who was injured when riding as a pillion passenger on a motor-cycle driven by the defendant, actively encouraged the defendant to drive in a dangerous manner and also knew that he was uninsured. Beldam LJ thought that the *volenti* defence would have applied but for the provision which is now section 149 of the Road Traffic Act 1988. This invalidates any agreement to limit or restrict the liability of a vehicle user to a passenger in circumstances where the user is required to be covered by a policy of insurance. It also provides that 'the fact that a person so carried has willingly accepted as his the risk of negligence on the part of the user shall not be treated as negativing any such liability on the part of the user'.[114] The other two members of the Court of Appeal took the same view of the application of the Act, and did not state an opinion on whether *volenti* would have been made out on the facts.

The Court of Appeal returned to the question of the application of the *volenti* defence in *Morris* v. *Murray*.[115] Plaintiff and defendant decided, after spending most of the day drinking alcohol, to go for a flight in the defendant's light aircraft. The defendant, who had consumed the equivalent of seventeen measures of whisky, crashed the plane shortly after take-off; he was killed and the plaintiff severely injured. The plaintiff brought an action against the defendant's estate. There was no question here of compulsory liability insurance and no equivalent to section 149 of the Road Traffic Act 1988. Fox LJ held that 'the volenti doctrine can apply to the tort of negligence, though it must depend upon the extent of the risk, the passenger's knowledge of it and what can be inferred as to his acceptance of it'. In this case the plaintiff had not been 'blind drunk' but simply 'merry' and hence knew what he was doing when he went on a flight with a pilot who had been drinking all afternoon. Accordingly, 'the

---

[110] [1939] 1 KB 509, 514. [111] See (1953) LQR 317.
[112] *Insurance Commissioner* v. *Joyce* (1948) 77 CLR 39; *Rogenkamp* v. *Bennett* (1950) 80 CLR 292.
[113] [1991] 1 QB 24. See also *Winnik* v. *Dick*, 1984 SLR 185. [114] Road Traffic Act 1988, s. 149(3).
[115] [1991] 2 QB 6.

wild irresponsibility of the venture is such that the law should not intervene to award damages and should leave the loss where it falls. Flying is inherently dangerous and flying with a drunken pilot is great folly. The situation is very different from what has arisen in motoring cases.'[116] This suggests that the defence could have had a wider application to passenger cases on the highway, but for its abrogation by the Road Traffic Act.

In *Morris* v. *Murray* Fox LJ suggested that 'volenti as a defence has, perhaps, been in retreat during this century—certainly in relation to master and servant cases'.[117] One reason for this is, it seems, an understandable reluctance on the part of the courts to be seen reviving in any form whatsoever the now-discredited defence of common employment. The *volenti* defence is only likely to apply in the most extreme of cases, such as *ICI* v. *Shatwell*.[118] Here two shot-firers (who happened to be brothers) decided to circumvent normal safety procedures, contrary to the express orders of their employer, in an attempt to finish a job more quickly. An explosion resulted in which both were injured; one brother then brought an action against the employer on the basis that it was vicariously liable for the negligence of the other brother. The House of Lords was unwilling to accept the proposition that if 'two men collaborate in doing what they know is dangerous and is forbidden and as a result both are injured, each has a cause of action against the other'. According to Lord Reid, 'there is a world of difference between two fellow servants collaborating carelessly, so that the acts of both contribute to cause injury to one of them, and two fellow servants combining to disobey an order deliberately, though they know the risk involved'.[119] The plaintiff's claim failed. By and large, however, the courts adhere to the view that in employment cases the defence should be applied 'with extreme caution'. Thus, 'it can hardly ever be applicable where the act to which the servant is said to be "volens" arises out of his ordinary duty, unless the work for which he is engaged is one in which danger is necessarily involved'.[120] Even then it is difficult to conceive of an employee working on a potentially dangerous site such as a North Sea oil-rig, for example, consenting in advance to run the risk of *negligence* on the employer's part, which is what the defence requires.

As with employment, so with occupiers' liability: although *volenti* is, in principle, available as a defence,[121] in the absence of an express exclusion of liability through contract or notice it is much more likely that the courts will use contributory negligence to apportion the loss.[122]

Similarly, *volenti* as such is rarely a defence to injuries sustained by sportsmen or spectators as a result of conduct that goes beyond the normal rules or

---

[116] [1991] 2 QB 6, 17. The need to show that the plaintiff was fully aware of the danger of a course of action led the Court of Appeal to reject a *volenti* plea in *Kirkham* v. *Chief Constable of Greater Manchester* [1990] 2 QB 283, where the plaintiff committed suicide in a police-cell while in an unbalanced state of mind. To similar effect is *Reeves* v. *Commissioner of Police of the Metropolis* [1998] 2 WLR 401.

[117] [1991] 2 QB 6, 17.   [118] [1965] AC 656.   [119] Ibid., 672.

[120] Goddard LJ in *Bowater* v. *Bowley Regis Corporation* [1944] KB 476, 480–1.

[121] The Occupiers' Liability Act 1957, s. 2(5), preserves the common law in this regard. See Chapter 3, Section 3(2)(c) above.

[122] See *Slater* v. *Clay Cross Co. Ltd.* [1956] 2 QB 264, 271 (Denning LJ); cf. *McGinlay* v. *British Railways Board* [1983] 1 WLR 1427.

conventions of the game. If liability is excluded it is more likely to be on the grounds that the defendant was not careless in the first place. This was the approach of Diplock LJ in *Wooldridge* v. *Sumner*,[123] in which a press photographer at the National Horse Show was injured by a horse which collided with him in the course of a round. The spectator accepts the risk of injury 'unless the participant's conduct is such as to evince a reckless disregard of the spectator's safety', but this is not because of *volenti* but because 'such an act involves no breach of the duty of care owed by the participant to him'.[124] It makes little difference how the result is explained, since it is exactly the same in each case. On the other hand, *volenti* was invoked in *Simms* v. *Leigh Rugby Football Club Ltd.*[125] where a rugby-league player whose leg was injured when he was thrown against a wall in the course of a tackle was held to have consented to the risk of such an injury occurring. Consent cannot normally be assumed where there is a foul, although the fact that the action is prohibited by the rules of the game will not, in itself, provide conclusive proof of negligence either.[126] A spectator or participant cannot be taken to have assented to an injury caused by an action which has nothing to do with the course of play, such as a golfer carelessly hitting a spectator with his club while demonstrating a stroke.[127]

In addition to applying to negligence under the circumstances noted above, the defence can also apply to strict-liability torts. The defence of 'common benefit' under *Rylands* v. *Fletcher* is essentially an application of consent,[128] and the defence is also preserved by section 5(2) of the Animals Act 1971. The application of the defence to breach of statutory duty is slightly more problematic. In principle, it is said not to be possible for the plaintiff to give his consent in advance to an act that amounts to a breach of a regulatory (frequently criminal) statute.[129] It would not seem to matter, for this purpose, whether the plaintiff is alleged to have assumed the risk or to have agreed to waive any future claim: the defence is excluded in either event. One of the principal merits of the action for breach of statutory duty for judges in the late nineteenth century was precisely its potential as a means of avoiding the defences of *volenti* and common employment in personal-injury cases. A possible exception was discussed by the House of Lords in *ICI* v. *Shatwell*,[130] namely the situation in which the employer is placed in statutory breach solely by virtue of his vicarious liability for the act of an employee of the same rank as the plaintiff. The plaintiff himself must also assent to and participate in the statutory breach. Some of the difficulties of this have already been pointed out:[131] it may not always be clear, for example, what is meant by an employee of a rank superior to the plaintiff, nor indeed that there is any useful purpose in drawing such a distinction. It may be that there are good reasons for applying the *volenti* defence to breach of statutory duty in the same way as it is applied to negligence, now that the scope of the defence has been greatly restricted. However, as long as breach of statutory

[123] [1963] 2 QB 43. [124] Ibid., 69. [125] [1969] 2 All ER 923.
[126] See *Condon* v. *Basi* [1985] 1 WLR 866; *Rootes* v. *Shelton* [1968] ALR 33.
[127] *Gleghorn* v. *Oldham* (1927) 43 TLR 465. [128] See Chapter 6, above.
[129] *Baddeley* v. *Earl Granville* (1887) 19 QBD 423; *Wheeler* v. *New Merton Board Mills Ltd.* [1953] 2 KB 669.
[130] [1965] AC 656, above. [131] See Chapter 3, Section 4(1).

duty is regarded as a tort which, being separate from common-law negligence, is based on failure to perform a duty imposed by Parliament, the courts are likely to proceed cautiously.

(B) CONSENT AS A DEFENCE TO TORTS OF INTENTIONAL INTERFERENCE

This question has already been analysed in earlier chapters, to which the reader is referred for a more detailed treatment.

Consent is, in principle, effective as a defence to the torts of assault and battery, but there have been suggestions that this is limited in some cases by an overriding principle of public policy which, for example, may prevent a person validly consenting to a serious battery.[132] A second problematic area concerns consent to medical treatment, where the courts have in effect obviated the need for formal consent in certain cases such as those involving children and patients in certain disabling physical conditions.[133] In general, though, consent to interference with the person must be clearly expressed; the circumstances under which the courts will infer consent from conduct are limited. In relation to false imprisonment, although consent may again be a defence, this runs up against the principle that it is not permissible to confine another simply for a breach of contract.[134] As far as trespass to goods and trespass to land are concerned, the defence is well established.[135]

4. Exclusion and Limitation of Liability

(A) THE NATURE OF THE DEFENCE

The defence of exclusion or liability through a contract term or notice raises similar issues to those that arise in relation to the defence of *volenti*, but if the two are 'analogous' they are nevertheless distinct. A formal exclusion may enable the defendant to avoid liability in a case where *volenti* has no application. In *White* v. *Blackmore*[136] the plaintiff's husband was killed following a freak accident while attending a day of jalopy races organised by the defendants. The cause of the accident was a vehicle becoming entangled with some safety ropes about a third of a mile away from where the plaintiff's husband had been standing; he became caught up in the ropes and sustained the injuries of which he later died. Buckley LJ noted that the deceased was not standing in a particularly dangerous place at the time of the accident and so could not have been said to have assumed a particular risk of injury from the alleged negligence of the course organisers. However, the defendants succeeded by virtue of an exclusion clause contained in a notice posted at the spectators' entrance.

The principle that occupiers of land can exclude or limit their liability to those who come on to their land as lawful visitors is well established in the law of occupiers' liability.[137] In *Ashdown* v. *Samuel Williams & Sons Ltd.*[138] the defendants knew that employees of a neighbouring employer, including the plain-

---

[132] See *Airedale NHS Trust* v. *Bland* [1993] 1 All ER 821, 895 (Lord Mustill).
[133] See Chapter 3, Section 1(3)(c)(i), above.   [134] See Chapter 4, Section 1(2), above.
[135] See Chapter 5, Section 1 at XXX (trespass to goods) and ibid., Section 2 at XXX (trespass to land).
[136] [1972] 2 QB 651.   [137] See Chapter 3, Section 3.   [138] [1957] 1 QB 409.

tiff, were used to taking a short-cut across their land to get to work. The short-cut crossed a railway track. When the plaintiff was taking the short-cut on her way to work one morning she was struck and injured by a railway wagon being shunted by the first defendants' employees, who were held to have been negligent in not keeping a look-out. It was held that the plaintiff had not been a trespasser—she had an implied licence to cross the defendants' land, based on their knowledge of the short-cut and its use. However, the defendants were absolved by a notice to the effect that those using their land did so at their own risk and were to have no claim for damages for injuries, whether or not it was the result of the defendants' negligence or breach of duty. 'It is not in dispute', said Jenkins LJ, 'that it is competent to an occupier of land to restrict or exclude any liability he might otherwise be under to any licensee of his, including liability for his own or his servants' negligence, by his conditions aptly framed and adequately made known to the licensee.'[139] In the circumstances the notice was deemed adequate and the plaintiff, who had read part of it, was bound by its terms. The decision was confirmed by section 2(1) of the Occupiers' Liability Act 1957, according to which the occupier is free to 'restrict, modify or exclude his duty to any visitor or visitors by agreement or otherwise'. If the occupier has the right to exclude others from his land, he also has the power to set conditions upon their lawful entry.[140]

(B) THE APPLICATION OF THE UNFAIR CONTRACT TERMS ACT

This power is now subject, however, to the provisions of the Unfair Contract Terms Act 1977, which regulates the use of exclusion or limitation clauses for the purposes of liability in both contract and tort.[141] The provisions of the Act have already been considered in the context of occupiers' liability. They apply only to 'business liability', that is to say, liability arising from things done in the course of a business or from the occupation of business premises.[142] Subject to this limitation, section 2(1) of the Act prohibits the exclusion or limitation of liability for personal injury or death caused by negligence. The exclusion or restriction of liability in negligence for other forms of loss (such as property damage or pure economic loss) is subjected to a test of reasonableness.[143] The fact that the plaintiff was aware of or agreed to the terms of any such contract term or notice 'is not to be taken as indicating his voluntary risk'.[144]

The orthodox view of exclusion clauses is that they take effect by means of an express or implied agreement between the parties, by which one or the other of them is exempted from liability for breach of a duty arising in contract

---

[139] Ibid.

[140] This, of course, must now be read in the light of the Unfair Contract Terms Act 1977. For further details see Chapter 3, above.

[141] Other important examples of the statutory regulation of exclusion clauses and the like are provided by s. 149 of the Road Traffic Act 1988 (discussed above) and s. 7 of the Consumer Protection Act 1987.

[142] More precisely, premises 'used for business purposes of the occupier': UCTA, s. 1(3).

[143] S. 2(2).

[144] S. 2(3). The Act also regulates exclusion clauses affecting certain contractual obligations, namely those in contracts for the sale or supply of goods (ss. 5–7), contracts between businesses and consumers, and contracts on the written standard terms of the party claiming the protection of the exclusion (s. 3). On the definition of 'consumer', see UCTA, s. 12.

or tort. To adopt language used by Lord Diplock,[145] they affect the 'secondary' obligations of the parties to pay damages for a breach of duty. But they do not affect the scope of that duty, that is to say the 'primary obligations' of performance in contract or the duty of care in the tort of negligence. A contrary view has been put by Professor Brian Coote, namely that exemption clauses are not always what they appear to be: in a given case, the correct analysis may well be to regard them as defining the nature of the initial obligations between the two parties to a contract.[146] This view could also be extended to certain duties of care in tort which depend upon the consent of one or both of the parties to the creation of a specific, pre-tort relationship. The occupier's common duty of care to lawful visitors is one such example, as is the duty of care under *Hedley Byrne & Co. Ltd* v. *Heller & Partners Ltd.*,[147] which rests upon the notion of a 'special relationship' between plaintiff and defendant. If this is correct, the effect of a notice or disclaimer is to exclude a duty of care in the sense of preventing one arising in the first place; and if there is no duty, there is no 'exemption clause' on which the Unfair Contract Terms Act can 'bite'.

The question was considered by the House of Lords in two consolidated appeals, *Harris* v. *Wyre Forest District Council* and *Smith* v. *Eric S. Bush.*[148] In each case the plaintiffs had purchased residential properties in reliance on mortgate valuations made by surveyors acting for the potential mortgagee. In *Smith* v. *Bush* the valuation was passed on by the building society to the plaintiff with a disclaimer to the effect that neither the building society nor the surveyors assumed any responsibility for its accuracy. In *Harris* v. *Wyre Forest DC* there was another disclaimer and the report was not even passed on to the plaintiffs. Nevertheless, they assumed, when the local authority proceeded to grant them the loan, that the surveyors had reported that the house was worth at least as much as the intended purchase price. In both cases the surveyors had negligently failed to report serious structural defects, with the result that the plaintiffs incurred serious financial losses of various kinds for which they were awarded damages at first instance.[149] In *Harris* the Court of Appeal reversed on the grounds that the surveyor's disclaimer prevented any duty of care arising under the principle in *Hedley Byrne* v. *Heller* (the point was not considered by the separate Court of Appeal which heard and rejected the appeal in *Smith* v. *Bush*). Kerr LJ thought that the judge had been wrong to characterise the disclaimer as an exclusion clause:

---

[145] In *Photo Production Ltd.* v. *Securicor Transport Ltd.* [1980] AC 827.

[146] B. Coote, *Exception Clauses* (1964). Two critics write: 'the thesis was elegantly formalistic, and ignored both the historical development of the problem, and the realities of the situation': J. Adams and R. Brownsword, 'The Unfair Contract Terms Act: A Decade of Discretion' (1988) 104 *LQR* 94, 95–6. See also E. Macdonald, 'Exclusion Clauses: The Ambit of s. 13(1) of the Unfair Contract Terms Act 1977' (1992) 12 *Leg. Stud.* 277.

[147] [1964] AC 465.   [148] [1990] 1 AC 831.

[149] In *Smith* v. *Bush* the loss—damage to the structure of the house caused by a chimney flue which collapsed—could conceivably be characterised as damage to property according to certain of the dicta in *Murphy* v. *Brentwood DC* [1991] 1 AC 398. In *Harris* v. *Wyre Forest DC*, by contrast, the loss was undoubtedly economic in the sense of a loss of value in the house once settlement was discovered. As the *Smith* and *Harris* cases preceded *Murphy*, and as they clearly came within the broad *Hedley Byrne* principle, nothing turned on the precise classification of the loss.

In order to decide the primary question whether or not the defendant owes any duty of care to the plaintiff it is not relevant to determine, on their true construction, the precise legal effect of the terms of any disclaimer or warning.[150] Considerations of the legal effect of any such provisions only arise if and when the existence of a duty of care has been established. However, in determining whether or not the circumstances warrant the inference that any such duty of care was owed by the defendant to the plaintiff, any disclaimer of responsibility and warning addressed by the defendant to the plaintiff may be of the greatest importance.

In this regard, Kerr LJ distinguished between cases 'where the existence of a duty of care is not open to doubt'—such as the duty of care owed by a driver of a motor vehicle to other users of the highway, which 'he necessarily assumes by driving'—and cases of misstatement in which 'the entirety of the statements made must be considered in order to determine whether or not the maker should be held to have assumed, or for some reason to be subjected to, a duty of care to the person addressed'.[151] There is some authority, albeit rather unclear, for this view in *Hedley Byrne* itself, where the defendants used their disclaimer to escape liability that the House of Lords would otherwise have imposed. Lord Reid said that 'the respondents never undertook any duty to exercise care in making their replies', and Lord Morris said that they 'effectively disclaimed any assumption of a duty of care'.[152]

Such a view, whatever its theoretical merit, would have had the effect of nullifying a large part of the effect of the Unfair Contract Terms Act 1977 (which, of course, could not have been anticipated in *Hedley Byrne* itself). Prior to *Harris* v. *Wyre Forest DC* most courts had taken a wide view of what constituted an exclusion clause: in *Phillips Products Ltd.* v. *T. Hyland and Hamstead Plant Hire Co. Ltd.* Slade LJ said that,

in applying section 2(2), it is not relevant to consider whether the form of a condition is such that it can aptly be given the label of an 'exclusion' or 'restriction' clause. There is no mystique about 'exclusion' or 'restriction' clauses. To decide whether a person 'excludes' liability by reference to a contract term, you look at the effect of the term.[153]

A good reason for taking this approach is provided by section 13(1) UCTA. This provides that to the extent that the Act prevents the exclusion or restriction of any liability, section 2 also prevents 'excluding or restricting liability by reference to terms and notices that exclude or restrict the relevant obligation or duty'. Allowing the appeal in *Harris* v. *Wyre Forest DC*, Lord Templeman noted that Kerr LJ's view of UCTA 'would not give effect to the manifest intention of the Act but would emasculate the Act'. He further argued that the proposed distinction between situations where the duty of care was 'inescapable' and other situations had no authority either under the Act or under the general law. According to his Lordship, the Act applied to 'all exclusion notices which would

---

[150] Let alone by the application of the Unfair Contract Terms Act 1977
[151] *Harris* v. *Wyre Forest DC* [1988] 1 QB 835, 853.
[152] [1964] AC 465, 483 and 504 respectively, cited by Caulfield J in the Court of Appeal in *Harris* v. *Wyre Forest DC* (n. 151 above), 849.
[153] [1987] 2 All ER 620, 626.

in common law provide a defence to an action for negligence'.[154] Lord Jauncey of Tullichettle concluded that the words of section 13(1) are

unambiguous and are entirely appropriate to cover a disclaimer which prevents a duty coming into existence. It follows that the disclaimers here given are subject to the provisions of the Act and will therefore only be effective if they satisfy the requirement of reasonableness.[155]

It may be, though, that the 'but-for' test adopted by the House of Lords goes too far in drawing into the scope of the Act *all* clauses which potentially modify a prima-facie duty of care. For this reason it has been suggested that in certain cases the courts should instead apply a test of 'reasonable expectations' according to which 'a clause should be regarded as an exclusion clause "in nature" if it would lead to the required contractual performance being less than that reasonably expected by the parties, when their expectations of performance are ascertained at the factual rather than the legal level'.[156] By extension this same approach could be applied to duties of care arising in tort, thereby offering a compromise between the 'all or nothing' approaches apparently adopted by the courts in the *Harris* v. *Wyre Forest* litigation.

The application of the test of 'reasonableness' is one of the most vexed questions to arise under the Act; it has been suggested that 'judicial development of the statutory discretion in commercial cases is both significant and difficult to predict'.[157] This development is surprising since the principal aim of the Act was to protect consumers in their dealings with businesses, although it is important to stress that the Act does also regulate relations between businesses in cases of negligence liability,[158] written standard form contracts,[159] and certain specialised exchanges such as contracts for the sale of goods and hire purchase.[160] As far as tort liability is concerned, the application of the Act to commercial cases will be rare. The *Hedley Byrne* duty of care in tort does not *normally* arise between two business parties.[161] The leading authority on the application of the reasonableness test in consumer cases is now the judgment of Lord Griffiths in *Smith* v. *Bush*.[162] Lord Griffiths suggested that four matters, in particular, should be considered. Were the parties of equal bargaining power? In the case of advice, could the advice have been easily obtained elsewhere? How difficult was the task for which liability is being excluded? And what would be the practical consequences—for example, for insurance—of the court's decision on the question of reasonableness? In this particular case, it had to be recognised that the purchasers of 'a dwelling house of modest value' were likely to be far less able to bear the risks attached to the property proving to be defective than the surveyors. For the latter could bear an incremental increase in their insurance premiums and, if necessary, pass part of the costs on to all house-purchasers through an increase in fees. This was not a situation in

---

[154] [1990] 1 AC 831, 848–9.

[155] Ibid., 873. Lord Griffiths cited Law Commission Report No. 69 in favour of the same interpretation: [1990] 1 AC 831, 857.

[156] Macdonald, op. cit. (n. 146 above), 287.

[157] Adams and Brownsword, op. cit. (n. 146 above), 92.   [158] S. 2.   [159] S. 3.   [160] Ss. 5–8.

[161] *Esso Petroleum Co.* v. *Mardon* [1976] QB 801 is a rare exception.   [162] [1990] 1 AC 831, 858 ff.

which adequate insurance cover was unavailable and it was also relevant that the surveyor and house-purchaser were not far removed from being in a direct contractual relation, when there would have been no question of the exclusion being reasonable.

In certain situations the interaction between express contract terms, duties of care in tort, and the legislation governing exclusion and limitation may give rise to complex problems which have yet to receive a clear doctrinal treatment. In *Johnstone* v. *Bloomsbury Health Authority*[163] the plaintiff, a junior hospital doctor, was employed under a contract of employment under which his standard working week was forty hours. On top of this he was required to be available for an additional forty-eight hours a week on average. He sought an injunction and declaration to the effect that he should not be required to work any longer than was compatible with maintaining his health and safety, and damages for ill health brought on by the excessive hours which he had been required to work. The defendant argued that the express contract term should prevail and sought to have the claim struck out on the grounds of failure to disclose a cause of action. This application failed, but the two judges making up the majority in the Court of Appeal gave different reasons for their decisions. Sir Nicolas Browne-Wilkinson VC agreed with the dissenting judge, Leggatt LJ, on the relationship between concurrent tort and contract duties. The effect of the express term governing working hours was to cut down the scope of the employer's duty of care in tort to have regard for the employee's health and safety. According to Sir Nicolas,

The approach adopted in the *Tai Hing* case[164] shows that where there is a contractual relationship between the parties their respective rights and duties have to be analysed wholly in contractual terms and not as a mixture of duties in tort and contract. It necessarily follows that the scope of the duties owed by one party to the other will be defined by the terms of the contract between them. Therefore, if there is a term of the contract which is in general terms (e.g. a duty to take reasonable care not to injure the employee's health) and another term which is precise and detailed (e.g. an obligation to work on particular tasks notwithstanding that they involve an obvious health risk expressly referred to in the contract) the ambit of the employer's duty of care for the employee's health will be narrower than it would be were there no such express term . . . The express and implied terms of the contract have to be capable of co-existence without conflict.[165]

Where Sir Nicolas disagreed with Leggatt LJ was in the interpretation of the relevant contract term. Sir Nicolas regarded the employer as having no absolute right to call on the employee to work the additional hours, but instead a right impliedly limited by the need to have regard for the employee's health.

Sir Nicolas's view that a contract between parties necessarily excludes or limits the scope of the relevant duty in tort appears to pay no regard to the need to ensure that the precise requirements of the defences of *volenti* or exclusion are made out in the circumstances. As Stuart-Smith LJ pointed out, the contract term in question could not be construed either as an express exclusion clause

---

[163] [1992] 1 QB 333; see also the discussion in Chapter 6, Section 3, above.
[164] *Tai Hing Cotton Mill Ltd.* v. *Liu Chong Hing Bank Ltd.* [1986] AC 80.   [165] [1992] 1 QB 333, 350.

or as tantamount to an assumption of risk in the sense required by *volenti non fit injuria*. Yet this was the effect of saying that the employee agreed, in effect, to take the risk of illness that arose from working long hours, even though it would foreseeably injure his health.[166] The use in this context of the dictum of Lord Scarman in *Tai Hing Cotton Mill Ltd. v. Liu Chong Hing Bank Ltd.*,[167] to the effect that the law would not search for liability in tort in a situation where the parties are in contractual relationship, seems misplaced. That latter instance involved a case concerning pure economic loss where the considerations are different. There is no authority for using contract, independently of the defences of *volenti* and exclusion, to cut down on a duty of care in tort which relates to physical health and safety, in particular now that legislation has abrogated the defence of common employment for cases of personal injury.

All three judges agreed that if the effect of the relevant contract term was to modify the employer's duty of care in tort, there was an arguable case that it was nullified by section 2(1) of UCTA.[168] It has not been conclusively established that UCTA applies to contracts of employment. It can be argued that the employer contracts in the course of his business and is therefore bound by section 2. Under paragraph 4 of Schedule 1 it is provided that 'section 2(1) and (2) do not extend to a contract of employment, except in favour of the employee': this would appear to indicate that the Act does indeed apply in the employee's favour. In addition, if the employee can only with difficulty be regarded as a consumer for the purposes of the 1977 Act, he may nevertheless be able to invoke section 3 in a case where the contract is concluded on the employer's standard written terms.

(c) Extending the Effect of Exemption Clauses to Third Parties

A separate issue arising from the interaction of tort and contract concerns the use of tort to extend the benefit of certain exclusion and limitation clauses to third parties external to the contract containing the clause in question. This issue arises, for example, in a case where the owner of a site enters into a contract with a builder for work to be carried out, part of which is then subcontracted.[169] The main contract may contain an exclusion or limitation clause that purports to protect both the main contractor and the subcontractor. According to the doctrine of privity of contract, the subcontractor is not in a position to take advantage of an exemption clause in a contract to which he is not a party; he may therefore have to bear the loss of any negligence in full. Another example is that of the liability of a stevedore who damages goods when unloading them at their destination.[170] There is usually an exemption clause in the contract between the carrier and the owner of the goods which limits the carrier's liability for damage to the goods and which purports to do the same for the stevedore. Again, the stevedore has difficulty taking advantage

---

[166] [1992] 1 QB 333, 343.   [167] T. Weir, 'Physician—Kill Thyself!' [1991] *CLJ* 397.
[168] See the analysis of Macdonald, op. cit. (n. 146 above), 285. An argument that the term could be struck down on the grounds of public policy was rejected, cf. the views of Weir, op. cit., 399.
[169] See e.g. *Norwich City Council v. Harvey* [1989] 1 WLR 828.
[170] See e.g. *Scruttons Ltd. v. Midland Silicones Ltd.* [1962] AC 446.

of a clause contained in a contract to which he is not a party. In a commercial context, where all parties know the risks in advance and will have taken out insurance accordingly, this possibility may upset the basis upon which the various risks were allocated when the contracts were drawn up. There is, accordingly, a strong argument from a practical point of view for ensuring that the subcontractor receives the benefit of the exemption.

One possibility would be to apply the defence of *volenti* against the plaintiff. Where he has had notice of the exemption, which he clearly has if it is contained in the main contract to which he is a party, the defence of *volenti* should apply to any claim he brings against the third-party defendant. This possibility was discussed by Lord Denning in *Scruttons Ltd.* v. *Midland Silicones Ltd.*[171] but rejected, for no very good reason, by the remainder of the House of Lords. One difficulty may be the problem of applying *volenti* to a limitation clause: it is normally a total defence to any claim and not one that has the effect of restricting the plaintiff's damages. On the other hand, the defence would appear to be flexible enough in principle to accommodate a situation like this.[172] In *The Eurymedon* the Privy Council came up with a different solution, namely an implied unilateral contract between (in this case) the owner of goods being shipped and the stevedore employed by the carrier to unload them.

In the building case of *Southern Water Co.* v. *Carey* this solution was described, with some justice, as 'uncomfortably artificial'.[173] Here various subcontractors were sued for negligence in design and in the supply of equipment in the completion of a sewerage scheme. The main contract contained a clause exempting both the main contractor and his subcontractors from liability in respect of such defects or damage. The judge rejected analyses extending the effect of the clause in contract, on the basis of agency and unilateral contract, in favour of a finding that the clause in question negatived the existence of any duty of care in tort for the damage in question. This finding was, perhaps, acceptable since the losses in question fell into the category of pure economic loss that, as we have seen, is rarely recoverable in the tort of negligence.[174] In *Norwich City Council* v. *Harvey*[175] the Court of Appeal reached the same outcome in a case where the subcontractor's negligence caused property damage to the site owner. The difficulty with this outcome is that, in contrast to pure economic loss, property damage is normally within the scope of the general duty of care in the tort of negligence. The negativing of the duty of care via the defence of *volenti* would have provided a better explanation. More generally, one reading of these cases 'is that they are really contract cases solved through tort', a route made necessary by the unduly restricted doctrine of privity of contract in

---

[171] Ibid., 488–9.

[172] See the judgment of Robert Goff LJ in *The Aliakmon* [1985] QB 350. His application of the doctrine of 'transferred loss' was rejected in the House of Lords [1986] AC 785. See Chapter 2, Section 2(2)(b)(v) above.

[173] [1985] 2 All ER 1077, 1084.

[174] *Murphy* v. *Brentwood DC* [1991] 1 AC 398; see also the use of the same rationale in *Pacific Associates Inc.* v. *Baxter* [1990] QB 993.

[175] [1989] 1 WLR 828.

English law.[176] Unless or until the English courts reassess this aspect of privity rule, there is unlikely to be quick progress towards a satisfactory doctrinal explanation.

5. Illegality

Illegality is rarely capable of being invoked as a defence to liability in tort. As Dillon LJ put it in *Pitts* v. *Hunt*,[177] 'it is clear for a start that the fact that a plaintiff was engaged in an illegal activity which brought about his injury does not automatically bring it about that his claim for damages for personal injury as a result of the negligence of the defendant must be dismissed'. Something more precise is needed. Two formulations of the defence have, from time to time, found favour with the courts. According to one, the defence is based on an overriding consideration of public policy: to compensate the plaintiff in certain cases would either affront the 'public conscience' or promote criminal acts or other behaviour deemed contrary to the general good. This point of view is expressed in the usage of the maxim *ex turpi causa non oritur actio*, which roughly translated means that no cause of action may be founded upon an immoral or illegal act.[178] According to the other formulation, the defence is based on a negation of liability in a situation where the plaintiff's participation in illegality makes it impossible for the court to assess the relevant standard of care. An example would be where both plaintiff and defendant are engaged in a joint illegal enterprise, such as robbing a bank or joy-riding in a stolen car.[179] This test is more precise and, in most contexts, easier to apply than the rather open-ended test of public policy.[180] However, it is unlikely that the defence can be confined to this second category. Its use may be uncommon, but the courts appear to treat it as a defence that may be kept in reserve for an appropriate case and have accordingly retained a loose approach to defining its scope and rationale.

Both formulations of the defence were adopted in various judgments of the Court of Appeal in *Pitts* v. *Hunt*.[181] The plaintiff, a passenger on a motor-bike being driven by the defendant, was seriously injured when the latter negligently collided with another vehicle. He was killed and the plaintiff brought an action for damages against his estate. The plaintiff knew when he set off on the journey that the deceased was uninsured and unlicensed. Both had been drinking alcohol for most of the evening; and the plaintiff had encouraged the deceased to drive in a recklessly dangerous manner, to the extent that the lives of other road-users had been put at risk. The court agreed unanimously that the defence was made out, but disagreed on its proper basis.

Balcombe LJ and, to certain extent, Dillon LJ, relied on the view of Mason J of the High Court of Australia in *Jackson* v. *Harrison*. There the view was taken that the denial of relief should not be based on the nature of the illegal activity in the sense of the degree of moral turpitude involved, but rather on the 'more

---

[176] Markesinis, 'Doctrinal Clarity in Tort Litigation: A Comparative Lawyer's Viewpoint' (1991) 25 *International Lawyer* 953, 963.

[177] [1991] 1 QB 24, 53.   [178] *Holman* v. *Johnson* (1775) 1 Cowp. 341, 343 (Lord Mansfield).

[179] *Jackson* v. *Harrison* (1978) 138 CLR 438.

[180] See C. A. Hopkins, 'Two Tales of Topers' [1991] *CLJ* 27, 28.   [181] [1991] 2 QB 25.

secure foundation' that 'the plaintiff must fail when the character of the enterprise in which the parties are engaged is such that it is impossible for the court to determine the standard of care which is appropriate to be observed'. This formulation was 'more limited in its application—and for that reason fairer in its operation'.[182] In applying this test, the High Court of Australia has denied recovery to plaintiffs injured in the course of joy-riding[183] while allowing a claim made by a plaintiff injured by the careless driving of one whom he knew to be disqualified at the time of the accident.[184] In this case, the disqualification had no bearing on the standard of care that the plaintiff could have expected of the defendant. Similarly, in the English case of *Ashton* v. *Turner*[185] a burglar who was injured while in the course of escaping from the scene of the crime in a get-away car was held to have no cause of action in negligence against the driver of the car, whose reckless driving caused the collision. In *Pitts* v. *Hunt* the involvement of the plaintiff in the reckless and dangerous driving of the deceased made it 'impossible to determine the appropriate standard of care', with the consequence, in Balcombe LJ's view, that the deceased owed the plaintiff no duty of care.[186]

Beldam LJ based his judgment, by contrast, on public policy, namely the policy enshrined in various Acts of Parliament of promoting road safety by creating the offences of causing death by reckless driving and driving when under the influence of drink and drugs. He rejected an argument to the effect that the law did not recognise the existence of a duty of care between the deceased and the plaintiff. The judge thus said: 'I am not convinced of the wisdom of a policy which might encourage a belief that the duty to behave responsibly in driving motor vehicles is diminished even to the limited extent that they may in certain circumstances not owe a duty to each other, particularly when those circumstances involve conduct which is highly dangerous to others.'[187]

The answer to the last point is that there is no reason why the relevant standard of care should be the same with regard to all road-users.[188] However, there are numerous other cases in which the courts have taken a similarly broad-brush approach to public policy. Lord Diplock referred on one occasion to a rule 'that the courts will not enforce a right which would otherwise be enforceable if the right arises out of an act committed by the person asserting that right ... which is regarded by the court as sufficiently anti-social to justify the court's refusing to enforce that right'.[189]

In some recent decisions the courts have taken the view that the public policy basis of the defence is founded on the need to deter illegal acts, rather than the looser notion of disallowing claims which affront the 'public conscience'. In *Clunis* v. *Camden and Islington HA*[190] the plaintiff, who had a history of mental

---

[182] *Jackson* v. *Harrison* (1978) 138 CLR 438, 455–6.

[183] *Smith* v. *Jenkins* (1970) 44 ALJR 78; *Bondarenko* v. *Summers* (1969) 69 SR (NSW) 269.

[184] *Jackson* v. *Harrison* (1978) 138 CLR 438.   [185] [1981] QB 137.   [186] [1991] 1 QB 25, 50–1.

[187] Ibid., 47.

[188] See Chapter 2, above, for discussion of this point in the context of breach of duty.

[189] *Hardy* v. *Motor Insurers' Bureau* [1964] 2 QB 745, 767.

[190] [1998] 2 WLR 902, doubting *Meah* v. *McCreamer (No. 1)* [1985] 1 All ER 367; see also *Murphy* v. *Culhane* [1977] QB 94; *Tinsley* v. *Milligan* [1994] 1 AC 340.

illness, was discharged from hospital and placed under the 'after-care' of the defendant health authority, a form of 'care in the community'. While in this situation, he committed an unprovoked attack upon a stranger in the London underground, killing him. He was then convicted of manslaughter. He sued the defendant in negligence on the grounds that the medical staff caring for him should have realised that he was a danger to others, and that had they treated him properly he would not have committed the assault for which he was imprisoned. The case was dismissed on various grounds, one of which was illegality: according to Beldam LJ, a manslaughter conviction ruled out the plaintiff's claim unless it could have been shown that he did not know what he was doing, which was not the case here. However, in *Reeves* v. *Commissioner of Police of the Metropolis*[191] a rather more flexible approach was taken. There, the deceased (on behalf of whose estate the action was brought) committed suicide while in police custody. It was held that the defendants had failed to take reasonable steps to prevent the deceased taking his own life. An illegality defence was rejected in part because, in the view of the Court of Appeal, the act in question—the deceased's suicide—was the very act which the defendants were under a duty to prevent.

Whichever test is adopted in a particular case, it is necessary to show that there was a causal link between the illegality in which the plaintiff was implicated and the loss of which he is now complaining. The 'cause' to be identified here is not simply the 'but-for' or 'factual cause'; the court may also be required to make a more complex judgment on the degree to which the plaintiff's illegality can be deemed to be a 'legal cause' of his loss. Thus:

If two burglars, A and B, agree to open a safe by means of explosives, and A so negligently handles the explosive charge as to injure B, B might find some difficulty in maintaining an action for negligence against A. But if A and B are proceeding to the premises which they intend burglariously to enter, and before they enter them, B picks A's pocket and steals his watch, I cannot prevail on myself to believe that A could not sue in tort ... The theft is totally unconnected with the burglary.[192]

A's presence at the scene of the crime is a 'mere condition' of his loss. Similarly, in *Saunders* v. *Edwards*[193] the plaintiff brought an action for fraudulent misrepresentation against the defendant over the sale to him of the defendant's flat. The two of them had previously agreed to undervalue the flat in favour of inflating the value of certain chattels included in the sale, with the aim of avoiding the payment of stamp duty. Since the fraud on the Inland Revenue was wholly unconnected with the fraud perpetrated by the defendant on the plaintiff, the latter's action was allowed to proceed.

In *Pitts* v. *Hunt* Dillon LJ considered that the plaintiff was barred from claiming damages since his loss arose 'directly ex turpi causa'.[194] A direct, causal connection in the sense described above is a necessary element of the defence, but

---

[191] [1998] 2 WLR 401; see also *Thackwell* v. *Barclays Bank plc* [1986] 1 All ER 676; *Saunders* v. *Edwards* [1987] 1 WLR 1116; *Euro-Diam* v. *Bathurst* [1990] 1 QB 1; *Kirkham* v. *Chief Constable of Greater Manchester* [1990] 2 QB 283.

[192] *National Coal Board* v. *England* [1954] AC 403, 428–9 (Lord Asquith of Bishopstone).

[193] [1987] 1 WLR 1116.   [194] [1992] 1 QB 24, 61.

it cannot be enough on its own: Dillon LJ's approach begs the question of exactly what is *turpi causa*. In making this assessment the courts can hardly avoid making some difficult value judgments about the degree of 'moral turpitude' of the plaintiff's act and balancing this against the nature and extent of the loss he sustained. In *Pitts* v. *Hunt* all three members of the Court of Appeal considered that the plaintiff's behaviour was indeed morally reprehensible—it had put the lives of other road-users at risk. The fact that the plaintiff himself suffered serious injuries, including permanent partial paralysis, did not weigh greatly in his favour. By contrast, the fraud against the Inland Revenue perpetrated by the plaintiff in *Saunders* v. *Edwards* was not considered sufficiently serious to bar him from suing the defendant for the consequences of *his* fraud; perhaps a rather surprising conclusion. But that decision is a reminder of how limited the defence of illegality is. As Bingham LJ put it, 'it is unacceptable that the court should, on the first indication of unlawfulness affecting any aspect of a transaction, draw up its skirts and refuse all assistance to the plaintiff, no matter how serious his loss nor how disproportionate his loss to the unlawfulness of his conduct'.[195]

6. Necessity

Certain applications of the defence of necessity have already been considered. Its principal significance is in relation to the torts of intentional interference or trespass: necessity can rarely justify negligence in the sense of a lack of care.[196] Necessity may be a defence to the torts of trespass to the person in the contexts of medical treatment and emergencies.[197] As far as the torts of trespass to goods and trespass to land are concerned, damage to property may be justified by the presence of an imminent danger to life and limb. 'The necessity for saving life has at all times been considered a proper ground for inflicting such damage as may be necessary upon another's property.'[198] In some cases, a countervailing threat to property will suffice, but here the scope of the defence is strictly limited. In each case the defendant must be shown to have acted reasonably in the circumstances.[199]

7. Inevitable Accident, Act of God

In the context of the tort of negligence, the plea of 'inevitable accident' is akin to saying that the defendant was not at fault, so this is not so much a defence as a denial of one of the main elements of liability. It only operates as a defence when *res ipsa loquitur* is pleaded and the defendant has to rebut what is akin to a reversal of the normal burden of proof. In cases of strict liability, where fault is irrelevant, inevitable accident may also constitute a defence.[200]

---

[195] [1987] 1 WLR 1116, 1134.
[196] See *Rigby* v. *Chief Constable of Northamptonshire* [1985] 1 WLR 1242, discussed in Chapter 5, above, at Section 2(2).
[197] See Chapter 4, Section 1(3).   [198] *Southport Corp.* v. *Esso Petroleum Co.* [1954] QB 182 (Devlin J).
[199] See the judgment of Lord Goff in *Re F* [1990] 2 AC 1, discussed in Chapter 4, and in Chapter 5, above.
[200] See *Southport Corp.* v. *Esso Petroleum Co. Ltd.* [1954] QB 182 (Devlin J).

'Act of God' amounts to a claim that an accident occurred as a result of natural forces outside the control of the defendant or anyone else; as such it may be a defence to a claim of liability under *Rylands* v. *Fletcher*.[201]

8. Authorisation

Authorisation is not, as such, a defence, but there are a number of instances in which lawful authority exists for persons to commit what would otherwise be torts. For example, police powers of search and arrest which are now largely defined by statute—that is, the Police and Criminal Evidence Act 1984—take priority over the common law in relation to the torts of trespass to the person and trespass to property.[202] Damage to property may be authorised by statute in the case of bodies set up to execute public works or to carry out public functions. Legal issues here concern the notion of negligence in the exercise of a statutory power[203] and the defence of statutory authority in the tort of nuisance.[204] One should also note the existence of the doctrine of 'act of state', according to which authorisation or subsequent endorsement by the Crown acts as a defence to an otherwise tortious act committed against a foreign citizen on foreign soil.[205]

9. Limitation of Action

It is a basic principle of the law of civil liability that actions should be barred after the passage of a certain period of time, in order to avoid both the administrative expense of examining 'stale claims' and potential injustice to defendants of reviving old wrongs. Limitation rules may also help to promote a degree of certainty in the allocation of liability, which is of assistance to insurance companies. Limitation Acts, the first dating from 1623, have accordingly required plaintiffs to initiate legal action within a specified time. The present limitation periods are mainly to be found in the Limitation Act 1980, as amended by the Latent Damage Act 1986 and by the Consumer Protection Act 1987. The basic principle is that actions in tort are subject to a limitation period of six years from the date on which the cause of action accrued.[206] But there are some important exceptions. Thus, in actions in tort for damages for personal injury, the relevant period is three years. This starts to run either from the date on which the cause of action accrued or from the date upon which the person injured first had knowledge of his injury, a concept that the Act then develops in greater detail.[207] This extension of the basic period is based on the notion of the 'discoverability' of the damage. A further exception incorporating a version of the discoverability test is provided for in cases of latent damage to property; this is examined in detail below.[208] The normal limitation period for claims

---

[201] See *Nicholls* v. *Marsland* (1876) 2 Ex. D. 1; *Greenock Corp.* v. *Caledonian Railway Co.* [1917] AC 556; Chapter 6, Section 1(3)(c)(iv), above.

[202] The details of police powers lie outside the scope of this book.

[203] See Chapter 3, above, at Section 5(2–3).   [204] See Chapter 5, above, at Section 3(5).

[205] *Buron* v. *Denman* (1848) 2 Ex. 167; *Johnstone* v. *Pedlar* [1921] 2 AC 262; *Walker* v. *Baird* [1892] AC 491; *Attorney-General* v. *Nissan* [1970] AC 179.

[206] Limitation Act 1980, s. 2.   [207] Ibid., ss. 11 and 14.

[208] Ibid., ss. 14A, 14B; Latent Damage Act 1986, ss. 1, 3–5.

under the Consumer Protection Act 1987, whether for personal injuries or for other forms of damage actionable under that Act, is three years,[209] and this period also applies to claims in defamation.[210]

A complete account of the details of limitation of actions lies outside the scope of his book.[211] However, certain features of the defence will be outlined here. The defence has become increasingly important as a source of case law on the nature of the cause of action in tort and on the interrelation of concurrent liabilities in contract and tort. Three issues in particular will be considered: the concept of the accrual of a cause of action; the limited statutory concessions made towards the discoverability test; and the problems raised in this context by two difficult cases of concurrent duties in contract and tort, namely those of defective buildings and professional negligence.

(A) THE ACCRUAL OF THE CAUSE OF ACTION

The basic rule that the limitation period begins to run from the date on which the plaintiff's cause of action accrued has, since the Limitation Act 1939, been subject to a power of the court to grant relief in certain cases such as deliberate concealment or other fraud by the defendant.[212] These limited provisions notwithstanding, the basic rule is capable of causing injustice in a case where the plaintiff's cause of action has accrued without him being aware of it. This will rarely arise in torts actionable *per se* (such as battery or conversion) because the plaintiff will normally be aware of the act of interference which constitutes the tort. A rare exception is *Stubbings* v. *Webb*,[213] in which the plaintiff brought an action for battery based on abuse suffered as a child, the memory of which she had unconsciously suppressed until early adulthood. In torts requiring damage, on the other hand, the cause of action accrues when the damage is *first* sustained, regardless of the plaintiff's knowledge. Although the damage may increase in scale and extent over time, the cause of action accrues when the damage first starts to occur and there will be no new cause of action unless a fresh causative factor is involved or a different kind of damage is sustained.

In *Cartledge* v. *E. Jopling & Sons Ltd.*[214] the plaintiff contracted pneumoconiosis by inhaling noxious dust at his place of work over a number of years. Pneumoconiosis is a disease which gradually destroys tissue in the lungs over a period of time, without the victim being immediately aware that this is happening. The employer had replaced the unsafe system of work which had caused the problem more than six years (then the relevant period) before the plaintiff issued his writ. The House of Lords held that the plaintiff's cause of action had accrued when the initial damage to the lung tissue took place, and that on this basis the claim was out of time. Lord Pearce, with whom the other Lords agreed, said that it was irrelevant that the extent of the damage was revealed only gradually: there can only be one cause of action in respect of a particular injury. Lord Pearce drew a distinction between the initial injury (or,

---

[209] Ibid., s. 11A.   [210] Administration of Justice Act 1985, s. 57.
[211] For a full account, see Clerk and Lindsell on *Torts* (17th edn., 1996), ch. 31.
[212] S. 26; see now Limitation Act 1980, s. 32(1), discussed below.   [213] [1993] AC 498.
[214] [1963] AC 758.

in property cases, defect) and the damage flowing from it, adopting the following dictum of Lord Halsbury in *Darley Main Colliery Co.* v. *Mitchell*:[215]

No one will think of disputing the proposition that for one cause of action you must recover all damages incident to it by law once and for ever. A house that has received a shock may not at once show all the damage done to it, but it is damaged none the less to the extent that it is damaged, and the fact that the damage only manifests itself later on by stages does not alter the fact that the damage is there; and so of the more complex mechanism of the human frame, the damage is done in a railway accident, the whole machinery is injured, though it may escape the eye or even the consciousness of the sufferer at the time, the later stages of suffering are but the manifestations of the damage done, and consequent upon the injury originally sustained.

The ruling of *Cartledge* also turned on a point of statutory interpretation: since Parliament had allowed an express exception to the basic rule in the case of fraud or concealment, to discover an implied exception based on the discoverability test would have amounted to judicial legislation. As Lord Reid put it, 'the necessary implication from [s. 26 of the Limitation Act 1939] is that, where fraud or mistake is not involved, time begins to run whether or not the damage could be discovered. So the mischief in the present case can only be prevented by further legislation.'[216]

Parliament duly responded by enacting through the Limitation Act 1963 a limited discoverability test for personal injury claims only,[217] the provisions of which are considered below. The issue of latent damage in non personal injury cases—cases of property damage and financial loss—was not addressed at this time. When it came before the House of Lords in *Pirelli General Cable Works Ltd.* v. *Oscar Faber & Partners*,[218] the House felt obliged to follow its earlier decision in *Cartledge*. In *Pirelli* the defendants, consulting engineers, contracted with the plaintiffs in 1969 to advise on the design and construction of a services block on their factory site. The block included a chimney. The defendants recommended as inner lining for the chimney a material, Lytag, which was relatively new and which turned out to be unsuitable for this purpose. The chimney was built in the summer of 1969 and it was found that cracks must have appeared in it not later than April 1970. The damage to the chimney was not, however, discovered until November 1977, whereupon it had to be repaired at the plaintiffs' expense. The plaintiffs sued the defendants for negligence in the design of the chimney and the judge allowed the claim on the basis that the relevant date for the purposes of limitation was the time at which the damage could, with reasonable diligence, have been discovered. He assessed this to have been some time in October 1972, so that the writ was issued within six years of time starting to run. The Court of Appeal, following its own earlier decision in *Sparham-Souter* v. *Town and Country Developments (Essex) Ltd.*[219] affirmed this judgment, but it was overturned in the House of Lords. Again, statutory interpretation was important: according to Lord Fraser of Tullybelton, 'it must . . . be taken that [in 1963] Parliament deliberately left the law unchanged'[220] so far as damage other

---

[215] (1886) 11 App. Cas. 127.
[217] Limitation Act 1963; see now Limitation Act 1980, ss. 11–14.
[219] [1976] QB 858.

[216] [1963] AC 758, 772.
[218] [1983] 2 AC 1.
[220] [1983] 2 AC 1, 15.

than personal injury was concerned. Lord Fraser thought that in cases of latent defects in property, the cause of action would accrue when the defect in question led to damage to the structure. This 'will commonly consist of cracks coming into existence as a result of the defect even though the cracks or the defect may be undiscovered and undiscoverable'.[221] It could even accrue earlier than this in a case where the 'defect is so gross that the building is doomed from the start', although such cases would be 'exceptional'. He also held that in a case of successive owners of the property, once time began to run against one owner it would start to run against them all: no purchaser could be in a better position than the person he bought from. Once again Parliament had to act to introduce a form of the discoverability test through the Latent Damage Act 1986 which, amongst other things, inserted sections 14A and 14B into the Limitation Act 1980.

(B) The Discoverability Tests under the Limitation Act 1980

As far as personal injury caused by negligence, nuisance, or other breach of duty (including contractual and statutory duties) is concerned, the 1980 Act now provides that the relevant limitation period is three years from *either* the occurrence of the damage *or* the 'date of knowledge' of the injured party.[222] Should the plaintiff die without initiating an action within this three-year period, the period is extended to a further three years either from his death or from the 'date of knowledge' of the personal representative.[223] Similarly with claims under the Fatal Accidents Act: there will be no claim if the plaintiff's own claim would have been time-barred, but if not, the deceased's dependants have three years to bring their Fatal Accidents Act claim either from his death or from their 'date of knowledge'.[224]

The 'date of knowledge' is defined by section 14(1) of the Act as the first date on which the plaintiff has knowledge of the following facts:

(a) that the injury in question was significant; and
(b) that the injury was attributable in whole or in part to the act or omission which is alleged to constitute negligence, nuisance or breach of duty; and
(c) the identity of the defendant; and
(d) if it is alleged that the act or omission was that of a person other than the defendant, the identity of that person and the additional facts supporting the bringing of an action against the defendant.

The plaintiff's knowledge (or lack of it) of his legal position, as opposed to his knowledge of the facts going to make up the cause of action, is irrelevant here. The Act goes on to say in section 14(2) that an injury is significant if the plaintiff 'would reasonably have considered it sufficiently serious to justify his instituting proceedings for damages against a defendant who did not dispute

---

[221] Ibid., 17.
[222] S. 11(2). By virtue of s. 11(1), this period applies to claims for personal injury arising from negligence, nuisance, or other breach of duty (including breach of contract and breach of statutory duty). On the meaning of 'damages in respect of personal injuries' in this context, see *Walkin* v. *South Manchester HA* [1995] 1 WLR 1543.
[223] See s. 11(4)–(6).   [224] Ss. 12–13.

liability and was able to satisfy a judgment'. The plaintiff is deemed to have certain knowledge, namely that which he might reasonably have been expected to acquire 'from facts observable or ascertainable by him' or from 'facts ascertainable by him with the help of medical or other appropriate expert advice which it is reasonable for him to seek'. As far as expert advice is concerned the plaintiff will have done enough it he has taken reasonable steps to obtain and, if necessary, to act on the advice.[225] In other words, as long as he does this he will not be deemed to know facts that the expert fails to ascertain or fails to report to him. None of this helps a plaintiff who receives bad legal advice as opposed to being badly advised on the facts of his claim. In the event of being poorly advised on the law, the plaintiff's only option is to have the court exercise its discretion to disapply the normal limitation rules[226] or to sue his advisers for negligence.

There is a separate regime for latent damage in cases of negligence leading to property or financial loss. Section 14A(4)(a) of the 1980 Act, as inserted by the Latent Damage Act 1986, begins by preserving the basic rule that the period of limitation starts with the accrual of the cause of action and runs for six years.[227] Paragraph (b) of that subsection then sets up an exception in the case of latent defects, in respect of which there is a three-year period from the 'earliest date on which the plaintiff or any person in whom the cause of action was vested before him had both the knowledge required for bringing an action for damages in respect of the relevant damage and a right to bring the action'. 'Knowledge' is defined in more or less the same way as it is for personal-injury cases (above). Section 14B of the 1980 Act then provides for a 'long-stop' according to which the plaintiff will necessarily be time-barred once fifteen years have elapsed from the defendant's breach of duty. In addition, section 3 of the Latent Damage Act 1986 provides that in the case of successive owners of property with a latent defect which has not yet been discovered, a fresh cause of action accrues each time a new purchaser acquires an interest. Hence the new purchaser will himself be able to take advantage of the discoverability period of three years. Finally, the 1986 Act provides that the provisions of sections 14A and 14B (1980) and section 3 (1986) do not affect causes of action accruing before the 1986 Act came into force (18 September 1986).[228]

Actions arising under the Consumer Protection Act 1987 are subject to a basic limitation period of three years and a 'long-stop' of ten years.[229]

(c) Limitation and Concurrent Duties in Contract and Tort

The context in which the courts have had the greatest difficulty in applying the rules of limitation concerns that of concurrent duties in contract and tort. The period of limitation in contract begins to run when the relevant breach of contract takes place and not, as in tort, when the damage is suffered. The problems

---

[225] S. 14(3). For recent applications of this provision, see *Stubbings* v. *Webb* [1993] AC 498 and *Broadley* v. *Guy Clapham & Co.* [1994] 4 All ER 439.

[226] S. 33(1); see e.g. *Ramsden* v. *Lee* [1992] 2 All ER 204.

[227] For discussion of these and other aspects of the 1986 Act see N. J. Mullany, 'Reform of the Law of Latent Damage' (1991) 54 *MLR* 349.

[228] Latent Damage Act 1986, s. 4.

[229] Limitation Act 1980, s. 11A.

this poses were explained by Mustill LJ in *Société Commerciale de Reassurance* v. *ERAS (International) Ltd.*:[230]

The different treatment for limitation purposes of claims in contract and in tort is . . . unsatisfactory because: (1) whatever the legal logic, the fact that claims in contract and in tort between the same parties arising out of the same facts become time-barred on dates which may well be years apart offends common sense; (2) the existence of different rules for what may really be the same claims forces the law into unnatural complications. Whatever the historical justification for holding that there are concurrent rights of action in contract and tort, nobody we believe would trouble nowadays to insist on the difference, but for the fact that one form of claim (usually the one in tort) offers procedural advantages. This is not a sound basis for the development of a practical and self-consistent law of negligence; (3) so far as limitation is concerned, the rules regarding the accrual of the cause of action tend to push the evolution of substantive law in the wrong direction. In most if not all cases a plaintiff will be better off by framing his action in tort whereas, in our judgment, if a contract is in existence this is the natural vehicle for recourse.

The Court of Appeal nevertheless felt obliged to hold that section 14A of the Limitation Act has no application to cases of breach of contract.[231] This is because section 14A simply refers to 'negligence' whereas section 11, which embodies the discoverability rule for personal-injury claims, specifically includes breach of contract within its scope. Under these circumstances the court concluded that the drafter had intended section 14A to be confined to latent damage caused by the *tort of negligence*, but the result is to exacerbate the tendency described by Mustill LJ, namely the divergence between the limitation periods governing contract and tort respectively.

Pirelli General Cable Works Ltd. v. *Oscar Faber & Partners*[232] was itself a case in which the parties had entered into a contractual relationship and in which the plaintiff's sole purpose in formulating the claim in tort was to take advantage of the extended limitation period. The significance of the *Pirelli* ruling and of the Latent Damage Act has been thrown into some doubt, however, by the later decision of the House of Lords in *Murphy* v. *Brentwood District Council*.[233] This is because Lord Fraser's judgment in *Pirelli* was based on the now-discredited theory, derived from *Anns* v. *Merton London Borough Council*,[234] that the loss suffered by the owner of the building is physical or property damage rather than, as *Murphy* decided, pure economic loss. In *Murphy* Lord Keith of Kinkel said of *Pirelli*:

If the plaintiffs had happened to discover the defect before any damage had occurred, there would seem to be no good reason for holding that they would not have had a cause of action in tort at that stage, without having to wait until some damage had occurred. They would have suffered economic loss through having a defective chimney upon which they required to expend money for the purpose of removing the defect. It would seem that in a case such as *Pirelli*, where the tortious liability arose out of a contractual

---

[230] [1992] 2 All ER 82. See also the comments of Mustill LJ in *Bell* v. *Peter Browne & Co.* [1990] 1 QB 495, 511.

[231] Confirming the approach of Deputy Judge Rokison QC in *Iron Trades Mutual Insurance Co. Ltd.* v. *J. K. Buckenham Ltd.* [1990] 1 All ER 808.

[232] [1983] 2 AC 1.   [233] [1991] 1 AC 398.   [234] [1978] AC 728.

relationship with professional people, the duty extended to take reasonable care not to cause economic loss to the client by the advice given. The plaintiffs built the chimney as they did in reliance on that advice. The case could accordingly fall within the principle of *Hedley Byrne & Co. Ltd.* v. *Heller & Partners Ltd.*[235]

If, as this passage indicates, *Pirelli* should now be regarded as a case of pure economic loss, the question arises as to when the cause of action under the principle in *Hedley Byrne* can be said to accrue. There are four possibilities:[236] the date on which the advice was given and relied upon; the date on which the chimney was built; the date of physical damage; and the date on which the economic loss was reasonably discoverable. The second and third possibilities are difficult to reconcile with various dicta in *Pirelli* and *Murphy*.[237] There is authority, on the other hand, to support the first hypothesis. In *Forster* v. *Oughtred & Co.*[238] the plaintiff was given negligent advice in reliance on which she mortgaged her property. It was held that she suffered financial loss as soon as the property was encumbered in this way. A similar decision was reached in *Bell* v. *Peter Browne & Co.*[239] In October 1977 the plaintiff consulted the defendants, a firm of solicitors, concerning the division of property between his wife and himself following their divorce. It was agreed that the title to the house, which they then held jointly, would be transferred to his wife, with the plaintiff to receive one-sixth of the sale proceeds in the event of a sale. In September 1978 the solicitors arranged for the transfer of title but negligently omitted to protect his continuing interest by a trust deed or mortgage. The plaintiff's wife subsequently sold the house without his knowledge and spent all the proceeds. The plaintiff found out in December 1986 and issued a writ against the solicitors in August 1987. The Court of Appeal held that the action was out of time: the cause of action in tort had accrued when the house was transferred to the plaintiff's wife without steps being taken to protect his interest in the property. According to Nicholls LJ, the plaintiff 'suffered [real] prejudice when the transaction was implemented without his having protection of a formal document'.[240] In *Iron Trade Mutual Insurance Co. Ltd.* v. *J. K. Buckenham Ltd.* the relevant principles were summarised as follows:

In cases where the damage alleged to have been sustained is financial loss, such loss, and therefore damage for the purposes of establishing this necessary ingredient of the tort of negligence, is established where as a result of the negligence of the defendant a contract is entered into by a plaintiff which affords the plaintiff lesser contractual rights, or exposes the plaintiff to a contingent loss or liability, the extent of which may well not materialise until a later date and which may depend on subsequent events, such as the

---

[235] [1991] 1 AC 398, 466.   [236] See E. McKendrick, 'Pirelli Reconsidered' (1991) 11 *Leg. Stud.* 326.
[237] See McKendrick, op. cit., at 333–5.   [238] [1982] 1 WLR 86.   [239] Ibid.
[240] [1990] 2 QB 495, 502. The court also held that the claim in contract was statute-barred, distinguishing the judgment of Oliver J in *Midland Bank Trust Co. Ltd.* v. *Hett, Stubbs and Kemp* [1979] Ch. 384, in which a continuing breach of contract was found. See, however, the judgment of the House of Lords in *Nykredit* v. *Edward Erdman & Co.* [1997] 1 WLR 1627, which, although not precisely on the limitation point, may require a reconsideration of the cases discussed in the text, since it holds that in a case of negligent valuation leading to a loan which is under-secured, the cause of action does not necessarily accrue as soon as the loan is made. For discussion, see A. Tettenborn, 'Accrual of a Cause of Action' (1998) 10 *Amicus Curiae* 19.

exercise of rights or options by a third party over which neither the plaintiff or the defendant has any control. In such cases damage is established at the date when the contract is entered into, even though its quantification may depend upon such subsequent events.[241]

The significance of these decisions for latent damage to buildings was considered by May J in *Nitrigin Eirreann Teoranta* v. *Inco Alloys Ltd*.[242] In June 1981 the defendants manufactured and supplied to the plaintiffs alloy tubing for use as part of a chemical-production plant. The tubing was supplied under a contract agreed by the two parties. In July 1983 the tubing was found to be cracked and on 27 June 1984 it ruptured completely, leading to an explosion which damaged the plant and caused it to be shut down for a period. The writ was issued on 21 June 1990. The judge held that the cause of action did not accrue until the explosion of June 1984, with the result that the action was in time. He rejected the defendant's argument that the cause of action accrued when the cracks first appeared in the tubing. He further concluded that *Pirelli* could no longer be read as authority for liability in negligence based on physical loss in such a case; because the piping was supplied in a defective condition the loss was properly characterised as purely economic. Although *Pirelli* could be explained by *Hedley Byrne*, this was not possible in the *Inco Alloys* case because there was no pre-tort special relationship between the parties: such a relationship, the judge held, cannot arise simply on the basis of a commercial contract of sale between the parties. However, he held that there was a cause of action for the damage caused to the rest of the plant by the explosion: this was physical damage to property other than the product which was supplied, and so fell within the scope of the general duty of care.

The effect of the misstatement cases on *Pirelli* could be to decide that a cause of action accrues when the advice in question is relied upon as, for example, in the case where a defective item of property (such as a house built on insecure foundations) is acquired for a price which is, unknown to the purchaser at the time, an overvalue. If this is so, the implications for limitation are considerable: many claims will be defeated as time will start to run well before the loss is discoverable. This is one possible interpretation of Lord Keith's remarks in *Murphy*.[243]

Another view is that no economic loss is suffered until the plaintiff becomes aware of the defect and of its financial consequences. This would bring forward the date of the accrual of the cause of action to the point at which most actions of this kind would no longer be caught by the limitation defence. This was the view of Deane J in the Australian case of *Sutherland Shire Council* v. *Heyman*. 'For so long as the inadequacy of the foundations is neither known nor manifest, no identifiable loss has come home; if the purchaser or the tenant sells the freehold or leasehold estate within that time, he or she will sustain no loss by reason of the inadequacy of the foundations.' It is only

[241] [1990] 1 All ER 808, 813 (Deputy Judge Rokison QC). [242] [1992] 1 All ER 854.
[243] R. O'Dair, 'Professional Negligence: Some Limiting Factors' (1992) 55 *MLR* 405, 406.

when the defect becomes known that the loss of market value in the property occurs.[244]

Deane J's approach in *Sutherland* would have the beneficial (if perhaps rather paradoxical) effect of harmonising the *Pirelli* test, which is based on the *occurrence* of damage, with the test of the *discoverability* of damage which seeks to avoid the situation in which the plaintiff's claim is eliminated before he even knows about it. The Latent Damage Act, however, is clearly based on the assumption that the cause of action in latent-defect cases accrues *before* the economic consequences of the defect are discovered; hence the need for the special statutory test of discoverability in sections 14A and 14B of the Limitation Act. As explained above, the Act has no application to claims arising before 1986 and so it is only slowly beginning to have an impact. As it does so, plaintiffs will benefit from a certain level of protection against the arbitrary loss of claims by virtue of limitation. But more generally the decision in *Murphy* and, in particular, Lord Keith's attempt to reclassify *Pirelli* as a *Hedley Byrne* case, have undercut the entire basis of the Act. Now that damage caused by defective buildings is classified as purely financial (unless the defect brings about personal injury or damage to *other* property) and now that *Murphy* has limited very substantially the scope of the duty of care with regard to such pure economic loss, far fewer plaintiffs in building cases will have a good cause of action. With the common law offering decreased protection, the Defective Premises Act 1972 becomes more important; but claims arising under this Act are outside sections 14A and 14B of the Limitation Act, as interpreted by the Court of Appeal in the *ERAS* case.[245] *Murphy* has made it imperative to consider further reform of the Limitation Acts which should involve a more complete reassessment of *Pirelli*. Courts in Canada, New Zealand, and Ireland have rejected *Pirelli* in favour of the *Sparham-Souter* test of discoverability, while in Australia its status is in doubt.[246]

(D) THE DISAPPLICATION OF THE NORMAL LIMITATION RULES

The court can grant relief from the normal limitation rules in a case where the plaintiff was under a disability of some kind at the point when the cause of action accrued,[247] and in cases of fraud, concealment, and mistake.[248] In addition, under section 33 of the 1980 Act the court has a wider power to 'disapply' the normal time-limits on actions in respect of personal injury and death. The

[244] (1985) 157 CLR 424, 505. See also *Hawkins* v. *Clayton* (1988) 164 CLR 539, 587–8 (Deane J), 600–1 (Gaudron J); McKendrick, 'Pirelli Reconsidered' op. cit., 335–6; Mullany, 'Limitations of Action and Latent Damage—An Australian Perspective' (1991) 54 *MLR* 216, 223–4, and 'Limitation of Actions: Where Are We Now?' [1993] *LMCLQ* 324. See also the judgment of the Court of Appeal in *First National Commercial Bank* v. *Humberts* [1995] 2 All ER 673, in which it was held that the limitation period in an action for damages in respect of a negligent valuation did not begin to run from the point when the loan was advanced, but from a later point when it became clear that the valuation had been negligently made.

[245] [1992] 2 All ER 82; see also *Warner* v. *Basildon Development Corp.* (1991) 7 Const. LJ 146, 154.

[246] *Kamloops* v. *City of Nielsen* [1984] 2 SCR 2 (Canada); *Bowen* v. *Mount Paramount Builders* (*Hamilton*) *Ltd.* [1977] 1 NZLR 394, *Mount Albert BC* v. *Johnson* [1979] 2 NZLR 234 (New Zealand); *Brian Morgan* v. *Park Developments Ltd.* [1983] ILRM 156 (Ireland); *Hawkins* v. *Clayton* (1988) 164 CLR 539; see Mullany, 'Limitation of Action', op. cit., 54 *MLR* 216, 219–23.

[247] See ss. 28, 28A, and 38(3).

[248] S. 32. See *Sheldon* v. *R.H.M. Outhwaite* (*Underwriting Agencies*) *Ltd.* [1996] AC 102.

Act lays down six guidelines for the exercise of this power. The length of and reasons for the plaintiff's delay; the extent to which the cogency of evidence adduced by either party might be affected by the delay; the defendant's conduct after the cause of action arose, including his response to requests by the plaintiff for information or inspection for the purpose of ascertaining relevant facts; the duration of a disability of the plaintiff after the cause of action arose; and the steps taken by the plaintiff to obtain expert advice and the nature of the advice he received.[249] The existence of this general power to disapply the limitation period, while no doubt a valuable device for overcoming injustices in particular cases, inevitably means that there is little certainty in the application of the limitation periods laid down by statute.

(e) THE EFFECT OF LIMITATION: PROCEDURAL OR SUBSTANTIVE?

The lapse of the limitation period only has the effect of barring the remedy; it does not extinguish the claim as such. Thus 'it is trite law that the English Limitation Acts bar the remedy and not the right, and furthermore, that they do not even have this effect unless and until pleaded';[250] their effects are said to be, accordingly, procedural rather than substantive. In practice not too many consequences follow from this, but one is that the plaintiff cannot recover a payment made in ignorance of his right to invoke the Limitation Act as a defence.[251] Exceptionally, the legislation provides that rights in conversion are extinguished by lapse of time[252] and the same applies to rights under the Consumer Protection Act 1987 which are barred by the ten-year long-stop under section 11A(3) of the 1980 Act.

(f) REFORM OF THE LAW RELATING TO LIMITATION OF ACTIONS

The Law Commission's Sixth Programme of Law Reform took the view that the law on limitation periods was 'uneven, uncertain and unnecessarily complex',[253] and a Consultation Paper published by the Law Commission in 1997[254] made a series of recommendations for reform. The central proposal was that for most civil actions, including the majority of actions in tort, 'there [should] be an initial limitation period of three years that would run from when the plaintiff knows, or ought reasonably to know, that he or she has a cause of action'. This would extend the principle of discoverability beyond its currently limited area of application, and would also aim, in the interests of greater certainty, to supply a general rule which, subject to specified exceptions, would apply to the most common types of civil claim. The Commission also proposed that there should be a general long-stop of thirty years for personal injury claims and ten years for all other claims, running from the date of the act or omission giving rise to the claim; that the long-stop could be extended by the plaintiff's disability and deliberate concealment by the defendant; and that the

---

[249] A substantial body of case law has built up around these provisions. For a full treatment, see Clerk and Lindsell, op. cit., ch. 31.

[250] *Ronex Properties Ltd.* v. *John Laing (Construction) Ltd.* [1983] QB 393, 404 (Sir John Donaldson MR).

[251] *Brize* v. *Dickason* (1786) 1 Term Rep. 285.   [252] Limitation Act 1980, s. 3.

[253] Law Com. No. 234 (1995), at 28.   [254] Law Com. No. 151 (1998), at para. 1.47.

courts should cease to have a discretion to disapply the limitation period in particular cases.[255] It remains to be seen whether these proposals will be the subject of legislative action.

Select Bibliography

ATIYAH, P. S., 'Causation, Contributory Negligence and *Volenti Non Fit Injuria*' 43 *Can. BR* 609 (1965).

BATES, F., 'Consenting to the Necessary' *Aust. LJ* 73 (1972).

BOHLEN, F. H., 'Incomplete Privilege to Inflict Intentional Invasions of Interest of Property and Personality' 39 *Harv. LR* 307 (1926).

CRAGO, N. H., 'The Defence of Illegality in Negligence Actions' 4 *MULR* 534 (1964).

DIAS, R. M. W., 'Consent of Parties and *Voluntas Legis*' (1966) *CLJ* 75.

FLEMING, J. G., 'Comparative Negligence at Last by Judicial Choice' 64 *Cal. LR* (1976).

FRIDMAN, G. H. L., 'The Wrongdoing Plaintiff' 18 *McGill LJ* 275 (1972).

GORDEN, D. M., 'Drunken Drivers and Willing Passengers' (1966) 82 *LQR* 62.

JAFFEY, A. J. E., '*Volenti Non Fit Injuria*' [1985] *CLJ* 87.

LAW COMMISSION, *Limitation of Actions*, Law Com. No. 151 (1998).

McKENDRICK, E., '*Pirelli* Reconsidered' (1991) 11 *Leg. Stud.* 326.

MULLANY, N. J., 'Limitations of Actions and Latent Damage—An Australian Perspective (1991) 54 *MLR* 216.

—— 'Reform of the Law of Latent Damage' (1991) 54 *MLR* 349.

—— 'Limitation of Actions—Where are We Now?' [1993] *LMCLQ* 34.

PAPE, G. A., 'The Burden of Proof of Inevitable Accident in Actions for Negligence', 41 *Ill. LR* 151 (1946).

WILLIAMS, G. L., *Joint Torts and Contributory Negligence* (1951).

—— 'The Defence of Necessity' [1953] *CLP* 216.

2. DAMAGES

1. The Notions of Damage and Damages[256]

Though one finds a great deal of case law and literature on *damages*, little effort has been devoted to defining *damage*. The common lawyer, unlike the civil lawyer, rarely asks himself the question 'what damage is redressable in a tort action?' since his system, for some time at any rate, has not concentrated on *damnum* but on *injuria*. The reason for this different emphasis is historical: damage awards lay, until comparatively recently, within the exclusive control of juries once the defendant's behaviour had been found to be tortious. Only

---

[255] Law Com. No. 151 (1998), at para. 1.47.

[256] This paragraph follows closely the account in Catala and Weir, 'Delict and Torts', 38 *Tulane LR* 663 ff. (1964), 667.

where damage was an element of tort itself could judges formulate rules in terms of *damage*. So the task of fixing the boundaries of liability had to be achieved through those concepts over which the judge had exclusive control. Remoteness and, later, duty were the obvious devices.

There are other reasons for this kind of attitude. The (English) law of tort has, as we have noted, functions other than that of compensation. In some instances it is used to vindicate private rights, and here the award of damages is not related to the plaintiff's loss (since often there may be none), but merely asserts his right. Thus in torts actionable *per se*, such as trespass to land, assault, false imprisonment, and libel, the plaintiff need not prove damage in order to succeed. The fact that no harm was suffered will not affect liability, though it may affect the quantum of damages. These torts illustrate the two meanings: damage and damages. The damage here is the interference with a legally recognised interest: whereas damages represent the sum awarded for the violation of such an interest.

Not all torts are actionable *per se*. In most torts some damage will have to be proved before there is a tort. Damage here forms the basis of the plaintiff's complaint; but, immediately, difficulties also arise. For we can see how judges could lay down rules about what kind of damage was suitable and the rules they laid down in fact differed according to the type of behaviour in question. Just as the most objectionable forms of behaviour (according to the early way of thinking, at any rate) were made actionable *per se*, we find that the less objectionable the behaviour, the stricter is the definition of the requisite damage. And for the least objectionable forms of damaging behaviour, such as the right to start legal proceedings and the right to speak, this strictness was extended for the definition of that damage to the prescription of the causal link between the behaviour and the damage. Thus, in an action for abuse of legal procedure the plaintiff fails unless *he* shows that because of the defendant's conduct he has suffered damage in the form of risk of imprisonment, risk to property, actual financial damage, or inevitable loss of reputation. Other types of 'injury', like anxiety or a tarnished reputation, will not suffice. Similarly, in all cases of slander, save the four exceptional categories which are actionable *per se*, the plaintiff has to show that he suffered special damage in the sense of damage which is capable of pecuniary estimation. Indeed, the cases suggest that a tight causal link will also be required, for it will not suffice to establish that the normal consequence of the words complained of was to make others think worse of the plaintiff. It will also have to be shown that the words complained of *directly* led others to deny the plaintiff some economic benefit. Finally, in negligence the plaintiff must prove damage. Where the harm is physical injury to person or property, the courts' main preoccupation has been with issues of duty and remoteness; and where the plaintiff's hurt has occurred invisibly in the form of shock or pure financial loss, they have encountered the greatest difficulties. Yet, a few cases apart, the courts have refused to deal with these problems under the rubric of 'damage' and have tried to use the concepts of duty and remoteness with which they are familiar. This brings us back to our opening remarks about the tendency of common-law judges to use remoteness or duty terminology where they are really expressing doubts as to the compensability of a particular type of damage.

2. Types of Damages

(A) GENERAL AND SPECIAL DAMAGES

We are not here concerned with special damage, which is what a plaintiff must prove as part of his cause of action in torts that are not actionable *per se*. We are not concerned with the actual awards made by courts, and the distinction turns upon whether the losses are precisely quantifiable or not. General damages are awarded in respect of damage which is 'presumed to flow' from the wrong complained of, and include pecuniary losses such as loss of future earnings, as well as non-pecuniary losses, such as damages for pain and suffering incurred before and after the trial. Obviously, general damages such as these must be averred to in the pleadings; but since they refer to inexact or unliquidated losses they need not be specifically pleaded. Special damages, on the other hand, are awarded for damage that the plaintiff must specify in his pleadings and prove. It is '. . . particular damage (beyond the general damage), which results from the particular circumstances of the case, and of the plaintiff's claim to be compensated, for which he ought to give warning in his pleadings in order that there may be no surprise at the trial'.[257] They include quantifiable lost earnings up to the trial, damaged property (e.g. clothing), and other out-of-pocket expenses. The distinction is thus of importance for pleading and evidential purposes, and also, as we shall see, for the purposes of calculating the rates of interest, but not so much from the point of view of the substantive law.

(B) NOMINAL AND SUBSTANTIAL DAMAGES

Where the tort is actionable *per se* the damages awarded will be nominal unless the plaintiff can prove loss or injury. As stated, the prime purpose of the law of tort is in these cases to vindicate rights that have been invaded.[258] Another reason given in favour of nominal damages is that they provide 'a . . . peg on which to hang costs'.[259] However, since the award of costs is nowadays left by section 51 of the Supreme Court Act 1981 (together with Order 62 of the Rules of the Supreme Court) to the *discretion* of the court, it is submitted that an undeserving plaintiff, who recovers nominal damages, should not be *automatically* regarded as a 'successful' plaintiff for the purposes of costs. In such cases the court may thus be well justified in refusing such a plaintiff's claim to unload on

---

[257] *Ratcliffe* v. *Evans* [1892] 2 QB 524, 528 per Bowen LJ.
[258] *Constantine* v. *Imperial Hotels Ltd.* [1944] KB 693, a case of unlawful discrimination where 5 guineas were awarded to the successful plaintiff. In *Alexander* v. *Home Office* [1988] 1 WLR 968 the Court of Appeal held that in cases of unlawful racial discrimination 'the prime objective of an award . . . is restitution . . . For the injury to feelings, however, for the humiliation, for the insult, it is impossible to say what is restitution . . . Awards should not be minimal . . . On the other hand, just because it is impossible to assess the monetary value of injured feelings, awards should be restrained . . . [nevertheless] even where exemplary or punitive damages are not sought, . . . compensatory damages may and in some instances should include an element of aggravated damages . . .', per May LJ at 975.
[259] *Beaumont* v. *Greathead* (1846) 2 CB 494, 499.

the 'losing side' all the costs of the litigation.[260] Substantial, or real, damages may also be awarded for actual loss and their measure is the value of the loss.

(c) Contemptuous and Aggravated Damages

Although a plaintiff may succeed, the court may indicate its disapproval of his behaviour by awarding him only a derisory amount[261] and, on occasion, he may even be refused costs, which can be a severe punishment for someone who has technically won his suit.

Aggravated damages, on the other hand, appear where the damages are general in the sense that they cannot be calculated precisely. Typically, this will occur in the case of certain torts such as defamation, false imprisonment, malicious prosecution, and, more recently, in cases of sexual and racial discrimination.[262] Factors such as the defendant's behaviour, his intentions and motives, his high-handed, malicious, or oppressive manner may be taken into account in assessing the aggravation of the injury to the plaintiff's *feelings of dignity and pride*,[263] thus producing additional sums which are normally quite moderate but which, in discrimination cases, can amount to several thousand pounds.[264]

Though the general principles applicable to this heading of damages are well established, their application in practice has not been without difficulties. For instance, in *Kralj* v. *McGrath*,[265]—a case of medical negligence involving a plaintiff subjected to a 'horrific' treatment—though requested, no such damages were awarded. The view taken by Woolf J was that the increased pain and suffering of the plaintiff should be reflected in the plaintiff's *general* damages. This approach was subsequently approved by the Court of Appeal in *AB* v. *South West Water Services*.[266] Yet, it is submitted, clarity (and transparancy) are evaded if the 'aggravated' element of the award is submerged in the general damages, so one must welcome a successful (if limited) attempt of a first instance judge to

---

[260] Cf. on this the interesting views of Devlin J in *Anglo-Cyprian Trade Agencies Ltd.* v. *Paphos Wine Ltd. Industries* [1951] 1 All ER 873, 874 (a contract case).

[261] *Kelly* v. *Sherlock* (1866) LR 1 QB 686. Such awards are more commonly made in libel actions.

[262] The statutory wrongs of sex and race discrimination are in many respects akin to torts. The relevant legislation provides that, in an appropriate case, compensation may be awarded according to the principles which would apply to a common law claim in tort, for the purposes of which it is declared 'for the avoidance of doubt' that damages may include compensation for injury to feelings: see Sex Discrimination Act 1975, ss. 65–66; Race Relations Act 1976, ss. 56–57.

[263] The words are italicised because they appear almost without fail in decisions awarding this kind of damages. That is why cases such as *Messenger Newspaper Group Ltd.* v. *National Graphical Association* [1984] IRLR 397, awarding aggravated damages to a corporation, seem unconvincing.

[264] See, for instance, *W* v. *Meah*; *D* v. *Meah* [1986] 1 All ER 935 where £2,500 were awarded in a case of vicious sexual assault. The plea for moderation—it is submitted hardly justified in cases like *W* v. *Meah*—can be found in a number of judgments, e.g. *Archer* v. *Brown* [1985] 1 QB 401 (a case of deceit) and *Alexander* v. *Home Office* [1988] 1 WLR 968 (a case of racial discrimination). In *Appleton* v. *Garrett* [1996] 5 PIQR P1 (discussed briefly below in the text) the judge assessed the 'aggravated' damages at 15% of the amount awarded for pain and suffering. In the racial discrimination case of *Armitage* v. *Johnson* [1997] IRLR 162 aggravated damages of £21,000 were awarded in respect of a systematic campaign of racial harassment directed at the complainant, a prison officer, by his colleagues, for whose conduct his employer was held responsible.

[265] [1986] 1 All ER 54.

[266] [1993] QB 507—a case of public nuisance brought against a nationalised corporation for contaminating drinking water and failing to warn the public properly.

distinguish the *South Water* ruling, at least in cases involving intentional torts.[267]

Notwithstanding these difficulties it is beyond doubt that aggravated damages, unlike punitive (exemplary) damages, are compensatory in nature since the emphasis is on the aggravated injury to the plaintiff which is being compensated. However, the interests affected are so incapable of precise monetary valuation that it is often difficult to say where 'satisfaction' for the plaintiff ends and punishment of the defendant begins[268]—hence the conceptual confusion with the next heading.

(D) PUNITIVE (OR EXEMPLARY) DAMAGES

The ambiguity that exists between this and the previous heading has led authors like Professor Street to argue that there are few, if any, cases dealing with punitive damages which cannot really be explained as instances of aggravated damages.[269] On the other hand, since the decision in *Rookes* v. *Barnard*,[270] there is little doubt that punitive damages do form an independent heading of damages. *Rookes* was a case of 'intimidation', a trade dispute, and its facts need not concern us here. However, in Lord Devlin's judgment[271] we find some of the clearest statements ever made about punitive damages. There, the learned judge accepted that the prime purpose of damages is to compensate the victim, whereas the purpose of punitive awards is to punish and deter the wrongdoer. In the latter case, therefore, the emphasis is not on the plaintiff and his hurt but on the defendant and his conduct. Because such awards blur the distinction between the civil and criminal functions of the law,[272] Lord Devlin felt that they should be limited to three kinds of cases.

The *first* category includes oppressive, arbitrary, or unconstitutional action by the servants of the government. The law's disapproval is, in these cases, directed against the unconstitutional act rather than focused on the effect it

---

[267] *Appleton* v. *Garrett* [1996] 5 PIQR P1 where Dyson J. awarded aggravated damages against a dentist who deliberately and persistently withheld from young patients information that the treatment he was administering was unnecessary. The same approach would probably be adopted in defamation cases where 'injury to the plaintiff's feelings and self-esteem is an important part of the damage for which compensation is awarded'.

[268] Hence, see the remarks of Lawton and Goff LJJ in *Drane* v. *Evangelou* [1978] 1 WLR 455. The most recent (and thorough) discussion of the subject can be found in *Thompson* v. *Comr. of Police of the Metropolis* and *Hsu* v. *Comr. of Police of the Metropolis* [1997] 3 WLR 403, yet even this reveals the closeness of the two notions. See also the Law Commission's Consultation Paper on *Aggravated, Exemplary and Restitutionary Damages* (1993), Law Com. No. 132, which recommended the abolition of aggravated damages as a separate head of damages, and their absorption into a 'strict compensatory model' (para. 8.18); see also Law Commission Report No. 247 (1997).

[269] See below (Select Bibliography), 30. See e.g. *Merest* v. *Harvey* (1814) 5 Taunt. 442; 128 ER 761; *Emblen* v. *Myers* (1860) 6 H. & N. 54; 158 ER 23. See, also, previous note.

[270] [1964] AC 1129.   [271] Ibid., at 1203 ff.

[272] The distinction seems further blurred by the fact that the Court of Appeal recently confirmed that there was, in principle, no argument of public policy prohibiting the defendants—a county council or police authority—from insuring themselves against the risk of them being held *vicariously* liable for punitive damages imposed because of the conduct of one of their servants (typically, false imprisonment or malicious prosecution committed by one of their constables): *Lancashire CC* v. *Municipal Mutual Insurance Ltd.* [1996] 3 WLR 493. It remains to be decided whether the same is true in the case of *personal* liability to pay punitive damages. It could be argued that insurability in such circumstances would erode further the 'punitive' element of the award.

has had on the plaintiff. It is thus irrelevant that the defendant was unconstitutionally detained for a very short time and, during his detention, treated in a civil manner.[273] The *fons et origo* of this common-law category is the famous case of *Wilkes* v. *Wood*[274] in which the legality of general warrants was successfully challenged in court.

Though Lord Devlin's judgment emphasises the exceptional nature of such awards, subsequent courts, in several instances, gave signs of more liberal tendencies. Thus, in *Holden* v. *Chief Constable of Lancashire*[275] exemplary damages were allowed in a case involving an unlawful arrest *without* any 'oppressive' behaviour on the part of the arresting officer. In *Bradford City Metropolitan Council* v. *Arora*[276] a local authority was ordered to pay (modest) punitive damages for practising race and sex discrimination in their hiring policy when filling senior posts in one of their teaching colleges since they were exercising 'a public function' when making these appointments. Such decisions, however, and certainly the *Arora* case, must now be viewed with suspicion given the more recent judgment of the Court of Appeal in *AB* v. *South West Water Services Ltd.*[277] For it was there said that punitive damages should not be awarded to torts that had not received punitive awards (or, *a fortiori*, had not been recognised as torts) at the time of *Rookes* v. *Barnard*. The result would thus seem to be that no punitive damages can now be awarded for negligence, public nuisance,[278] deceit,[279] sex or race discrimination,[280] patent infringments[281] or for violations of the Consumer Protection Act 1987. This highly formalistic approach, known as the 'cause of action' test, has been the subject of extensive criticism, not least from the Law Commission in its Consultation Paper and Report on *Aggravated, Exemplary and Restitutionary Damages*.[282]

Lord Devlin was also careful *not* to extend this category to oppressive actions by *private* individuals or corporations. The exclusion from the rule of private defendants has not pleased all academic commentators. Yet the distinction is supportable not only because it is compatible with the more modern trend to limit rather than expand the ambit of punitive damages in civil cases,[283] but also because 'the case of the government . . . is different, for the servants of the

---

[273] *Huckle* v. *Money* (1763) 2 Wils. KB 205; 95 ER 768.

[274] (1763) Lofft, 1; 98 ER 489; see also *A.-G. of St Christopher Nevis and Anguilla* v. *Reynolds* [1980] AC 637.

[275] [1986] 3 All ER 836; [1987] QB 380 (CA).   [276] [1991] 2 QB 507.   [277] [1993] QB 507, 518.

[278] *AB* v. *South West Water Services Ltd.* [1993] QB 507. But punitive damages might be appropriate in some instances of private nuisance. See: *Guppys (Bridport) Ltd.* v. *Brookling and James* (1984) 14 HLR 1—a case involving tenant harassment.

[279] The views of Sachs LJ in *Mafo* v. *Adams* [1970] 1 QB 548 at 555 has thus come to be preferred over that of Widgery LJ in the same case (ibid., at 558).

[280] *Deane* v. *Ealing LBC* [1993] ICR 329; *Ministry of Defence* v. *Cannock* [1994] IRLR 509. The Law Commission's Report on *Aggravated, Exemplary and Restitutionary Damages* (Law Com. No. 247, 1997) recommended that tribunals and courts should be given a power to grant exemplary damages in sex and race discrimination cases.

[281] *Catnic Components* v. *Hill & Smith Ltd.* [1983] FSR 512.

[282] Law Com. Nos. 132 (1993) and 247 (1997) respectively.

[283] In *AB* v. *South West Water Services Ltd.* [1993] 2 WLR 507, Lord Justice Stuart-Smith remarked (at 513) that 'this [i.e. the area of punitive damages] is *not* a developing field of the law' (emphasis added). Thus, in that case a nationalised Water Authority was not treated as an emanation of the State for the purposes of being included in Lord Devlin's second rule discussed in the text, above.

government are also the servants of the people and the use of their power must always be subordinated to their duty of service'.[284]

The *second* category includes cases in which the defendant's conduct was 'calculated' to make a profit for himself which could exceed the compensation payable to the plaintiff. The precise meaning to be attributed to the word 'calculated' has given rise to some judicial discussion. Thus, in *Broome* v. *Cassell* Lord Morris thought that 'the word "calculated" was [not to be] used to denote some precise balancing process.'[285] And in *Riches* v. *News Group Newspapers*[286]—a defamation case—it was made clear that the judge was entitled to leave the matter to the jury if there was evidence that the newspaper proprietors had felt that the economic benefits of publishing outweighed the risk of paying damages. More recently, the Court of Appeal returned to this issue in *John* v. *Mirror Group Newspapers Ltd.*[287] and repeated the view that no precise mathematical calculation need take place. What, instead, should be investigated is whether the defendant was aware of the fact that what he was planning to do was against the law (or had shown reckless disregard as to whether his proposed conduct was legal or illegal) *and* had, nonetheless, proceeded with his conduct in the belief that the prospect of material advantages outweighed the possibility of material loss. This kind of conduct is particularly likely to happen in libel cases, where Lord Devlin expressly said that 'one man should not be allowed to sell another man's reputation for profit'.[288] Thus, where the defendant with cynical disregard for the plaintiff's rights has calculated that the money to be made out of his wrongdoing will probably exceed the damages at risk, it is necessary for the law to show that it cannot be broken with impunity.[289]

This category is not confined to money-making in the strict sense. It extends to cases in which the defendant is seeking to gain at the expense of the plaintiff some object—perhaps some property which he covets—which he could either not obtain at all or not obtain except at a price greater than he wants to put down. Exemplary damages, in other words, are properly awarded when-

---

[284] *Rookes* v. *Barnard* [1964] AC 1129, 1226 (per Lord Devlin). McGregor, op. cit. (Select Bibliography), ss. 411, 415 provides a third, pragmatic, explanation. It is there suggested that the distinction between public and private sectors may have been 'motivated by the need to retain some scope for exemplary damages in order not to appear to be acting too cavalierly with the doctrine of precedent; in such a search, what better authorities to leave standing than those in which exemplary damages had originated?' These, however, may be academic speculations since in practice punitive damages under this heading are very rare. Thus, see *Holden* v. *Chief Constable of Lancashire* [1987] QB 380 (CA) and *A.-G. of St Christopher Nevis and Anguilla* v. *Reynolds* [1980] AC 637. Potentially more significant were Scott J's *obiter dicta* in *Columbia Picture Industries* v. *Robinson* [1987] Ch. 38, 87D–F; and they could be taken to support the view argued in the text that persons acting for the State can wield great and dangerous powers and must thus be subject to stringent controls.

[285] [1972] AC 1027, 1094.   [286] [1986] QB 256 (CA).

[287] [1996] 3 WLR 593. The same principles now apply to actions for malicious prosecution and false imprisonment where, according to s. 69(1) of the Supreme Court Act 1981, there is still a right to a jury trial. See: *Thompson* v. *Comr. of Police of the Metropolis* and *Hsu* v. *Comr. of Police of the Metropolis* [1997] 3 WLR 403 (with a most illuminating judgment from Lord Woolf MR)

[288] *Rookes* v. *Barnard* [1964] AC 1129, 1227. Yet in practice (and for different reasons) none of the litigated libel cases between *Rookes* and *Broom* yielded any punitive damages. Thus, see *McCarey* v. *Associated Newspapers* [1965] 2 QB 86; *Broadway Approvals* v. *Odhams Press* [1965] 1 WLR 805; *Manson* v. *Associated Newspapers* [1965] 1 WLR 1038.

[289] *Rookes* v. *Barnard* [1964] AC 1129, at 1227.

ever 'it is necessary to teach a wrongdoer that tort does not pay'.[290] The type of cases that gave rise to this litigation involved landlords who in various tortious ways were engineering the eviction of their protected tenants with a view to re-letting the premises at an unrestricted rent. Yet the plaintiffs in these cases fared unevenly, in some instances obtaining punitive awards[291] whereas in others failing to do so,[292] thus demonstrating that in practice and for various reasons the success of these claims is by no means assured.

Finally, the *third* category covers cases where exemplary damages are *expressly* authorised by statute, for example (arguably), section 97(2) of the Copyright, Designs and Patents Act 1988. Such statutes are in practice very rare and, since *Rookes* v. *Barnard*, no new statute authorising the award of punitive damages seems to have been enacted.

Though the preceding discussion emphasises the current (judicial) trend to bring punitive damages under control the theoretical debate as to whether they should be available at all has not abated. The main arguments for and against punitive awards in civil cases already appear in the speeches of Lord Wilberforce and Lord Reid in *Broome* v. *Cassell*;[293] and have been further elaborated since.[294]

What can we make from such diametrically opposed views and a rather unclear case law? There is little doubt that for the majority of authors all punitive awards are something of an anomaly since they repeatedly stress that retribution, deterrence, and rehabilitation are more appropriately pursued by the criminal law rather than by the law of torts. Yet the rejection of punishment in civil awards, purely on such an abstract and rigid demarcation of crime and tort, is hardly defensible, quite apart from the fact that it ignores existing realities. The true objections, therefore, must be sought elsewhere and Lord Reid's judgment provides some good clues. For example, by allowing punitive awards we may be violating such sacred principles as the *nullum crimen sine lege* rule, especially since such punitive awards can be made for any kind of conduct which can be described as 'high-handed', 'oppressive', or 'malicious'. Then there is no real limit to such punishment, except that these awards must not be unreasonable, which, however, is very vague. Punitive awards in civil actions may also be made by juries, notoriously susceptible to emotional and extra-legal considerations. What is more, the plaintiff's burden of proof is much lighter in a civil case than it is in a criminal case, so, in this context at least, it

---

[290] Ibid., 1227.

[291] *Drane* v. *Evangelou* [1978] 1 WLR 455 (CA); *Asghar* v. *Ahmed* (1984) 17 HLR 25 (CA); *McMillan* v. *Singh* (1984) 17 HLR 120 (CA)—all trespass cases. Cf. *Guppys (Bridport) Ltd.* v. *Brookling and James* (1983) 14 HLR 1 (CA) where the eviction was effected by means of a private nuisance.

[292] *Mafo* v. *Adams* [1970] 1 QB 548; *Millington* v. *Duffy* (1984) 17 HLR 232 (CA).

[293] [1972] AC 1027, 1112, and 1083 respectively.

[294] Thus, see, the debates in the House of Lords concerning the Administration of Justice Bill (HL, 6 May 1982, 1293 ff.) More recently Professor Peter Birks has adopted a more favourable position towards punitive damages in his 'Civil Wrongs: A New World', *Butterworth Lectures 1990–1991* (1992), esp. at 77–89. For the reasons given in the text, however, there are no signs that the courts are inclining to that view. See also *Supreme Court Procedure Committee Report on Practice and Procedure in Defamation* (1991), 39–43. One should, perhaps, add that the American experience does not seem to provide much comfort to those who favour punitive awards. See Fleming, *The American Tort Process* (1989), 214–24.

is in the defendant's interest to be tried by a criminal court. Finally, since tortious conduct which may result in punitive damages may also be subject to criminal sanctions, defendants may be exposed to both criminal and civil penalties for the same conduct. All these are serious, but not necessarily insurmountable, objections. Take, for example, the danger of excessive punitive awards. This has certainly materialised in the United States and has contributed to the present tort crisis (though it has also been pragmatically justified as a means of returning to the plaintiff part of his compensatory award that he will have to pay to his attorney under the there-prevailing contingency-fee system). But in this country the amounts awarded under this heading have been modest on the whole—about £1,000; though where the facts were particularly exceptional (as they were in *Cassell* v. *Broome*) larger amounts (£25,000) have been awarded. At present, therefore, as far as English law is concerned, this would appear to be a theoretical objection.

More serious is the possibility of the same conduct being punished twice by a civil and criminal court. This possibility was avoided in *Archer* v. *Brown*, with the judge refusing to impose additional punitive damages.[295] The principle of prohibiting punitive awards where the defendant has already been subjected to a criminal prosecution has received legislative sanction in some jurisdictions in the United States[296] and is a good one, though a number of details have still to be worked out.

All these correctives to the real or perceived drawbacks of punitive damages in the context of civil suits do not, however, address the real problem presented by this heading of damages. This, quite simply, is that whereas a case can be made for mulcting the bad defendant of the profits he has made from his tortious behaviour, there is no reason why this extra sum should then be given to the plaintiff, enriching him by a corresponding amount. (Had the punishment been a fine the money would have gone to the State.) In this context, an idea recently developed in some civil law systems may be worth some consideration. For in some of these systems the *practice* has developed whereby the additional punitive element of the award is given to charities (designated by the successful plaintiff) or, alternatively, could be channelled into, say, the legal-aid fund. On the whole, therefore, one is left with the impression that much thought still needs to be devoted by our system to this part of the law of damages. Until this is done, our courts are likely to remain hostile to claims for punitive damages when (*a*) they are based on causes of action for which prior to 1964 no such award was possible, and (*b*) they cannot be brought under one of the (two main) categories identified by Lord Devlin in his judgment in *Rookes* v. *Barnard*. When punitive damages *are* awarded, they are likely to be kept within reasonable bounds.[297]

---

[295] [1985] QB 401. But not all courts take this view. See *Messenger Newspapers Group Ltd.* v. *National Graphical Association* [1984] IRLR 397 where the judge refused to take into account a £675,000 fine imposed for contempt of court and ordered the defendant to pay an additional £25,000 as punitive damages.

[296] For the American position see Morris, 'Punitive Damages in Tort Cases', 44 *Harv. LR* 1173 (1931); 'Criminal Safeguards and the Punitive Damages Defendant' (Note), 34 *UCLR* 408 (1967).

[297] Thus, see *Thompson* v. *Commissioner of Police for the Metropolis* [1997] 3 WLR 403 as well as the earlier (but important) decision in *John* v. *MGN Ltd.* [1996] 3 WLR 593.

(E) COMPENSATORY DAMAGES

Compensation being a prime function of tort law, this heading deserves separate and more detailed treatment.

3. The Principle of Full Compensation

According to classical contract doctrine,[298] '. . . where a party sustains a loss by reason of a breach of contract, he is, so far as money can do it, to be placed in the same situation, with respect to damages, as if the contract had been performed.' Tort law, by contrast, seeks to put the victim in the position he was in before the tort. Where the victim's injury has been sustained by replaceable items of his property, the rule will thus be *restitutio in integrum*.[299] Where, on the other hand, the damage is to an irreplaceable item of property or consists of personal injury, exact return to the *status quo ante* is impossible. Lawyers then talk not of restitution but of 'fair compensation' (or, better, satisfaction) for harm which by its nature can never be accurately assessed. Even in such cases the basic principle is that of full and adequate compensation and, indeed, the tort system prides itself on placing such emphasis on the principle of complete compensation.

In personal injuries cases full compensation is achieved by making tort benefits earnings-related and by insisting that these represent, so far as possible, the full amount of the loss. The difference from social security compensation is thus marked *whenever* the latter tends to work on the basis of flat rates. For the tort system, more tailored as it is to the demands of individual plaintiffs rather than 'average models', such methods of compensation appear unfair. For flat-rate benefits, unlike earnings-related benefits, do not enable victims to maintain their pre-accident standard of living. For example, a man who has taken out a mortgage or entered into a number of hire-purchase agreements on the basis of his earnings will not be able to continue meeting his commitments if after his injury his compensation is unrelated to his pre-accident earnings but is, on the contrary, determined by pre-arranged flat rates. Moreover, flat-rate benefits, depending as they do on some single figure selected from all earners, are likely to lead to under-compensation for most and, perhaps, over-compensation for a few. The inadequacies of social security flat-rate benefits are, to some extent, avoided whenever certain additional payments are made on an earnings-related basis. But here, too, compensation is unlikely (in all cases) to be full, since ceilings tend to be imposed on earnings-related benefits.

However, the 100 per cent compensation principle, based on the victim's pre-accident earnings, also has its drawbacks, as many of its critics have pointed out.[300] The first is that, in so far as it leads to two persons involved in

---

[298] *Robinson* v. *Harman* (1848) 1 Exch. 850, 855; 154 ER 363, 365, per Parke B.

[299] See the oft-quoted passage in Lord Blackburn's judgment in *Livingstone* v. *Rawyards Coal Co.* (1880) 5 App. Cas. 25, 39.

[300] These criticisms are considered by Lord Steyn in *Wells* v. *Wells* [1998] 3 WLR 329, at 350–1. However, his Lordship concludes that '[n]ot only do these arguments contemplate a radical departure from established principle, but controversial issues regarding resources and social policy would be at stake. Such policy arguments are a matter for Parliament and not the judiciary'.

identical accidents being compensated differently, it helps to perpetrate the inequalities of wealth in our society. This argument, however, with all its political and ideological overtones, is unlikely to carry much weight so long as our market-orientated, private wealth system continues to prevail. In any event, it is not the role of tort damages to redress the economic imbalances that exist in life.

The second and (intellectually more interesting) objection is that such earnings-related benefits do not depend on any earnings-related contributions as some social-security benefits do.[301] In the case of a traffic accident, the rich man and the poor man will pay identical premiums if they represent identical risks (live in the same town, drive the same or approximately the same car, and have the same kind of driving experience and accident record). If they are injured, the rich person's compensation for his economic loss will be far greater than the poor person's, even though their injuries and the other conditions of the accident may be identical.[302] It could be said, therefore, that the rich person 'takes out of the system' more than he actually puts in. This objection, rather technical in nature, is valid but is less valid outside the context of road-traffic accidents. In any event, one could again say that a different solution would be unfair to the victim who would have to scale down his standard of living after the commission of the tort.

The third objection to the notion of full compensation that is related to pre-accident earnings is that it can encourage victims and their dependants not to return to work (where this is possible). A young childless widow, for example, who is compensated for her husband's death on the basis of his earnings and her dependency on them can, in theory, end up by being maintained at more or less the same pre-accident standard and need never return to work, even if she is well qualified to do so. This 'incentive argument' has a great deal of force if the full compensation is paid by means of periodic payments which can vary or even be terminated according to changing circumstances. But if the compensation takes the form of a lump sum, as it does at present, the full compensation is unlikely to discourage the recipient from returning to work if he is so inclined since, once paid, the compensation cannot be reduced or discontinued.

The fourth objection to the idea of full compensation is, potentially, the most important and, put simply, it is that, in practice, it can lead not just to full compensation, but to over-compensation. This appears to be widely accepted in the case of minor injuries which are (or could be) almost entirely covered by social-security benefits. But it can also be true in the case of larger awards, which can overlap with social security and other payments (from private insurance, pension funds, etc.), and may end by actually enriching the victim. That this is an anomaly, given that damages in tort are meant to compensate but not enrich the plaintiff, is beyond doubt. It will be noticed, however, that the anomaly is due rather to the fact that we lack an effective system of rules to deal with the

---

[301] This is true of most social insurance benefits (in particular social insurance benefits in respect of unemployment and invalidity) although not of benefits payable under the industrial injuries system.

[302] As far as non-pecuniary losses are concerned (e.g. pain and suffering, loss of amenity, etc.), if the injuries are identical, so will be their compensation.

interrelationships between the various methods of compensation than to the principle of full compensation. We return to this point later, where we shall note that if the relevant proposals of the Pearson Committee were to be implemented (which is unlikely), they would remove some of these problems. Before doing this, however, we should note that this proclaimed aim of full compensation is not always achieved in practice, since three factors seem to have watered it down.

The first is that when awards are made for future economic loss judges tend to 'discount' their awards to take into account a number of contingencies. The fact that our system of awards takes the form of a lump sum makes this inevitable since the court has to try to make an educated guess as to certain contingencies (possible life of the victim and his dependants, his future earnings, etc.) and the tendency, apparently, is to reduce awards too much rather than too little. Empirical studies that substantiate this argument are sadly lacking, though certainly cases can be cited where awards which appeared generous at the time of the trial have, with the passage of time proved to be inadequate.

The second factor that might lead to less than full compensation is the refusal of judges to calculate damages on systematic actuarial evidence. Though such evidence is admissible in court, the more rough-and-ready method of multiplier and multiplicand, which will be explained below, has always been preferred.[303] There is, however, no conclusive evidence to support this approach. What is more likely, however, is that damages tend to be less adequate in all cases where the period of expected future loss is great. This was clearly in the minds of the members of the Pearson Committee who, by a majority, proposed a 'modified multiplier' system. But Lord Hailsham LC informed the House of Lords[304] that consultations with the members of the legal profession had revealed great hostility to this complicated proposal, so the government was not going to recommend its acceptance.

The third and final factor undermining full compensation has been inflation. Courts tend to ignore it in their calculations except in the most extreme cases, and the reasons they have given, though not entirely convincing, are also not without value. Yet, it is a matter of fact that inflation, especially in the late seventies and early eighties when it reached record levels, did eat into awards which at the time that they were made, appeared generous, if not excessive.[305]

---

[303] For criticism by a leading actuary, see Prevett (1972) 35 *MLR* 140, 257. In *Mitchell* v. *Mulholland (No. 2)* [1972] 1 QB 65, 77, Edmund Davies LJ put it as follows: 'actuary and accountant may to a limited degree provide the judge with a means of cross-checking his calculations, and in arriving at the appropriate multiplier.' In *Auty* v. *National Coal Board* [1985] 1 All ER 930 Oliver LJ used even stronger language when he said: 'As a method of providing a reliable guide to individual behaviour patterns or to future economical and political events, the predictions of an actuary can be only a little more likely to be accurate (and will almost certainly be less interesting) than those of an astrologer' (at 939). See, however, the criticism of the traditional method by Thorpe LJ in *Wells* v. *Wells* [1997] 1 WLR 652.

[304] *Hansard* (HL) 1982, 621.

[305] For an earlier recorded instance see *Thurston* v. *Todd* (1966–7), 84 WN Pt. 1.

4. The Interrelationship of Tort and Other Compensation Systems

The Pearson Committee estimated[306] that every year in the United Kingdom some 3,000,000 people are injured and about 21,000 of them die of their injuries. Of these, only about 1,700,000 receive some financial assistance, but not all of them from the tort system. Indeed, only a very small minority, estimated at about 215,000, about 6 per cent of the grand total, received any compensation in the form of tort damages. For the remainder, social security, occupational sick pay, or private insurance represent the main if not sole sources of relief. But if tort victims represent only a small percentage of accident victims, their share of the aggregate value of compensation payments (estimated at £827 million at 1977 prices) amounted to just over £200 million, of that just over 6 per cent of the accident victims received some 25 per cent of the total compensation paid out. This category certainly includes a substantial percentage of the most serious types of injury, but even allowing for this, it is not disputed that tort victims fare rather better than the victims of other injuries. If these tort victims are allowed to pile on to their tort awards other benefits received from other systems of compensation (such as social security and private insurance), the danger is not only that they may end up by being over-compensated, but also that our overall compensation system may end up by being unduly costly and wasteful as regards some, and rather mean to others. Unfortunately, there is no easy solution to this problem of double compensation. Professor Atiyah, who has written extensively on this subject, has summed up the problem as follows:

If there was any rational pattern to the various compensation systems as a whole, it might have been possible to construct a 'hierarchy' of systems under which a man should be compensated by system A, if that were possible, and if not, he should then be relegated to systems B, C and D in turn. But this is not how things have developed. In fact, each system by and large decides whether it is willing to shoulder a burden, irrespective of other compensation available, or whether it wishes to push the burden on to another system, or whether it is willing to share the burden. But the whole process is one of almost unbelievable complexity.[307]

A victim of an accident may thus find himself receiving financial assistance from a wide variety of sources. He may, for example, have been prudent enough to take out first-party insurance against precisely such a possibility; or he may become entitled to an occupational pension paid by his employer; or he may benefit from the charitable disposition of his fellow human beings made either directly to him or, as is frequently the case these days, as a result of setting up some kind of 'disaster relief fund'. Finally, he may be eligible to receive one or more of a number of social-security benefits from the state. Legislation governs the relationship between tort and social security.[308] In other cases, it is up to the courts to decide whether a particular payment should be deducted

---

[306] Vol. i, para. 35 ff. There is no reason to believe that overall the picture has changed radically in the intervening twenty-odd years.

[307] Atiyah, *Accidents, Compensation and the Law* (4th edn.), 390.

[308] Social Security (Recovery of Benefits) Act 1997; see below.

from damages starting from the general principle that the purpose of the tort rules is to compensate the plaintiff and not, directly or indirectly, to allow him to make a gain from the tort. In principle, the law can take one of three options with regard to collateral benefits:[309] cumulation, under which the plaintiff is allowed to retain the benefit in question while being paid damages which represent his full loss; reduction, under which the collateral benefit is fully offset against the damages; and recoupment, whereby the third-party provider is given a right to recover the amount of the benefit through an action against the tortfeasor or, in some cases, the victim. At common law, the general approach is, in principle, to allow cumulation, but subject to a highly complex case law which attempts to distinguish (unconvincingly, in the eyes of many commentators) between those benefits which go to reduce the plaintiff's loss, and those which do not. The third option—recoupment—is seemingly barred at common law, but does operate in respect of certain social-security benefits, under a statutory régime which is now provided for by the Social Security (Recovery of Benefits) Act 1997. To analyse this body of law it is therefore necessary to consider separately the common-law rules and those applying to the statutory régime.

(A) Benefits not Covered by the Statutory Régime

The general starting-point against excessive compensation of the plaintiff has already been mentioned. But how do the courts decide when and why some of these (non-statutory) benefits should or should not be deducted from the tort award? Sometimes this comes down to the way in which the court calculates the plaintiff's loss. If an employee, for example, continues to receive part of his wages or salary from his employer during a period away from work, his loss is that much less than it would have been if he had not received these payments. By extension, the same rule applies to payments made by the employer in substitution for wages, such as sick pay; 'payments which correspond to wages must be taken into account when assessing loss of wages'.[310] In *Hussain* v. *New Taplow Paper Mills Ltd.*[311] the House of Lords held that the payment by the employer of a long-term sickness benefit fell into the same category as sick pay, and had to be deducted from the employee's claim for loss of earnings. Again, *if the plaintiff's employer is also the defendant in the tort action*, any *ex gratia* or voluntary payment that he makes to the employee will normally serve to reduce the extent of his liability.[312]

---

[309] See R. Lewis, 'Deducting Collateral Benefits from Damages: Principle and Policy' (1998) 18 *Legal Studies* 15 (Select Bibliography).

[310] Per Lord Templeman in *Smoker* v. *London Fire Authority* [1991] 2 All ER 449.

[311] [1988] AC 514.

[312] See *McCamley* v. *Cammell Laird Shipbuilders Ltd.* [1990] 1 WLR 963. But *obiter dicta* do exist which suggest that no deduction should be made for gratuitous payments made by the injured person's employer where he is *not* (also) the tortfeasor. The rationale behind this is, of course, the law's desire to encourage benevolence: see *Redpath* v. *Belfast and County Down Railway* [1947] NI 147. Moreover, no deduction will be made in respect of payments made to the plaintiff which are intended to be in the nature of a loan, to be returned in the event of damages being awarded against the tortfeasor: *Browning* v. *War Office* [1963] 1 QB 750, 770 (Diplock LJ).

The issue of deductibility, however, cannot always be resolved so straight-forwardly. Payments made to the plaintiff by third parties—whether they be insurance companies, charitable organisations, or (in the past) the State—will not necessarily be intended as direct replacements for lost earnings. While unemployment benefits and other forms of income replacement have been viewed in this way in the past,[313] charitable donations or insurance moneys may have a separate or a more general purpose. The same is true of certain pay-ments made by the plaintiff's employer. Disability pensions, for example, become payable after the employment has prematurely come to an end because of the injury, and so arguably should not be seen as equivalent to wages or salary, in contrast to sick pay which is paid while the employment is still continuing.[314] It can still be argued that all 'collateral benefits' of this kind, which the plaintiff would not have received but for the accident, should be taken into account (i.e. deducted from the tort award) when calculating his *net* loss. Some support for this view can be found in the House of Lords' decision in *British Transport Commission* v. *Gourley*,[315] which emphasised the importance of establishing the plaintiff's *net* loss by deducting from his claim for lost earnings an amount equivalent to the income tax which he would have paid had he stayed in employment. However, the courts have consistently rejected any gen-eral rule of this kind in the area of collateral benefits, and decisions following *Gourley* have restricted the ruling of that case to the limited question of the rela-tionship between taxation and lost earnings.[316]

The reasons given by the courts for rejecting a general rule of deduction are sometimes expressed in terms of causation; as Pigott B put it with regard to insurance moneys in *Bradburn* v. *Great Western Railway*:[317] 'he [the plaintiff] does not receive that sum of money because of the accident, but because he had made a contract providing for that contingency; an accident must occur to enti-tle him to it, but it is not the accident, but his contract, which is the *cause* of his receiving it.' Similarly, in *Parry* v. *Cleaver* Lord Pearson explained the application of tests of causation and remoteness to collateral benefits in the following terms:[318]

[313] On unemployment benefits, see *Parsons* v. *BNM Laboratories* [1964] 1 QB 95 (a wrongful dismissal case) and *Nabi* v. *British Leyland (UK) Ltd.* [1980] 1 WLR 529; on supplementary benefit and income support, *Lincoln* v. *Hayman* [1982] 1 WLR 488; on family income supplement and, by extension, family credit, *Gaskill* v. *Preston* [1981] 3 All ER 427; on statutory sick pay, *Palfrey* v. *GLC* [1985] ICR 437; and on redundancy pay-ments, *Colledge* v. *Bass Mitchells and Butlers Ltd.* [1988] ICR 125. The effect of these decisions has now largely been overturned by the legislation discussed in the next subsection in the text, above.

[314] *Parry* v. *Cleaver* [1970] AC 1 at 16 (per Lord Reid) and 42 (per Lord Wilberforce). The distinction between payments made during and after the end of the employment relationship was deemed to be cru-cial to the decision that a long-term benefit received by the plaintiff was akin to sick pay, and therefore deductible, in *Hussain* v. *New Taplow Paper Mills Ltd.* [1988] 1 AC 514.

[315] [1956] AC 185.

[316] See *Parry* v. *Cleaver* [1970] AC 1 at 13 (per Lord Reid) and 40 (per Lord Wilberforce); see also the review of the case law by Lord Templeman in *Smoker* v. *London Fire and Civil Defence Authority* [1991] 2 AC 502.

[317] (1874) LR 10 Exch. 1, 3 (emphasis added). It should be stressed that this is the rule for *personal* accident insurance. In the case of insurance for *property* damage no double compensation is allowed; so, in practice, the insurer compensates the insured and is then subrogated in his (the insured's) rights against the tortfea-sor. The rule in *Bradburn* was approved by both majority and minority in *Parry* v. *Cleaver* [1970] AC 1.

[318] [1970] AC 1, 49 (italics supplied). Cf. Lord Pearce's remarks to the effect that: 'Strict causation seems to provide no satisfactory line of demarcation'. *Ibid*, at 34.

I think the mental picture is this: here on one side is the accident with its train of *direct and natural consequences* happening in the ordinary course of events, and all these consequences are solely or predominantly *caused* by the accident: there on the other side is some completely collateral matter, outside the range of such consequences, having the accident as one of its causes but, on a fair view, *predominantly caused by some extraneous and independent cause*. It is clear from the decided cases that causation is an important factor in determining whether an item is too remote or not, though aspects of fairness and public policy also have a bearing.

On the other hand, the limits of the causation approach have frequently been pointed out, as for example, in the judgment of Windeyer J in the Australian case of *National Insurance Co. of New Zealand* v. *Espagne*.[319]

Causal considerations cannot be decisive of [this] question, unless there be a general rule of law that all benefits, or foreseeable benefits, received by an injured person because of, or as a consequence of, his injury, are to be set off against the damages he can recover from a wrongdoer. In my view, there is no such rule.

An alternative (and more convincing) policy reason for the non-deductibility of insurance payments is thus that the victim has 'paid for' the benefits which he now receives, whether through the payment of insurance premiums or occupational pension contributions, or simply through past service for his employer. At the very least, then, the benefit should not go to the tortfeasor (or his insurer) in the form of a reduced damages award. A broader policy justification (and one with much force) is that such a rule encourages potential accident victims to take out first-party insurance, or at least avoids discouraging them.[320] Similarly, by disregarding charitable or voluntary donations the courts simultaneously respect the benevolent intentions of the donors who, clearly, must have intended their generosity to benefit the victim and not the tortfeasor, at the same time as preserving the incentives of donors to make such payments. As Lord Reid put it in *Parry* v. *Cleaver*:[321]

It would be revolting to the ordinary man's sense of justice, and therefore contrary to public policy, that the sufferer should have his damages reduced so that he would gain nothing from the benevolence of his friends or relations or of the public at large, and that the only gainer would be the wrongdoer.

It is on these grounds that the courts have held that the only occasion upon which a voluntary or *ex gratia* payment will be set off against damages is when it is made by the tortfeasor himself. The instance of the employer/tortfeasor making *ex gratia* payments to his injured employee has already been mentioned.

---

[319] (1961) 106 CLR 569, 597. See also *Graham* v. *Baker* (1961) 106 CLR 340. In *Parry* v. *Cleaver* [1970] AC 1, 4 out of 5 judges involved in the House of Lords rejected the use of causation. One should, however, note that in all these cases our judges are thinking of cause in law. Cause in fact, in the sense of 'would the plaintiff have received the benefit but for the accident' is relevant in deciding whether to deduct the benefit from the tort award.

[320] D. R. Harris, *Remedies in Contract and Tort* (1988), 295.

[321] [1970] AC 1, 14. By parity of reasoning the same is true of free board and lodging, etc., received for relatives or friends. *Liffen* v. *Watson* [1940] 1 KB 556. See also *McCamley* v. *Cammell Laird Shipbuilders* [1990] 1 WLR 563.

Public policy featured strongly in the majority judgments in the House of Lords in the leading case of *Parry* v. *Cleaver*. In that case a policeman was injured by the negligence of a motorist and was obliged to leave the police force and take up less physically exacting employment elsewhere as a clerical worker. Upon his discharge from the police he became entitled, under his conditions of service, to an occupational disability pension, to which both he and his employer had contributed while he was employed. According to Lord Reid, there was 'no relevant difference between this and any other form of insurance',[322] with the result that it would not be taken into account when assessing the plaintiff's loss of earnings.[323]

Lords Morris and Pearson dissented from the main ruling on assessment on the grounds that a disability pension of this kind was a form of deferred pay and therefore analogous to wages or salary. In addition, Lord Morris drew a distinction between an insurance policy taken out by the plaintiff of his own accord, which was purely 'personal and private' to him, and a pension to which he was required to contribute as a condition of his employment. However, as already indicated, in *Smoker* v. *London Fire and Civil Defence Authority*[324] the House of Lords reaffirmed *Parry* v. *Cleaver* in a case where the employer paying a disability pension was also the defendant in the tort claim.

It is arguable that it should make no difference for this purpose whether the pension scheme under which the payment is made is a contributory one or not; even if the employee has not made individual contributions to the pension fund, he can be said to have earned the pension by his past service for the employer.[325] However, in *Hussain* v. *New Taplow Paper Mills*[326] the House of Lords held that payments akin to long-term sick pay were deductible from damages partly because the plaintiff had made no insurance contributions towards the scheme in question.

The single greatest difficulty in applying the law as it currently stands lies in distinguishing between sick pay, which is deductible on the grounds that it directly offsets the plaintiff's lost earnings, and disablement and invalidity pensions, which are not deductible under the rule in *Parry* v. *Cleaver*. In practice, it may be highly artificial to draw a clear distinction between these two categories. The Law Commission, in its Consultation Paper on *Damages for Personal*

---

[322] [1970] AC 1, 16. More recently, the Court of Appeal held that payment received by an injured employee under an accident insurance policy taken out for his benefit by his employer was not deductible from his tort award. In providing for his employees, the employer's motive was benevolence even though it had to be manifested through 'the use of an insurance policy': *McCamley* v. *Cammell Laird Shipbuilders Ltd.* [1990] 1 WLR 963.

[323] A complicated issue which *Parry* v. *Cleaver* left unclear concerned the relationship between a disability pension paid in respect of premature retirement, and loss of the retirement pension which the plaintiff would have expected to receive upon reaching pensionable age. In *Longden* v. *British Coal Corporation* [1998] IRLR 29 the House of Lords held that where the disability pension took the form of a lump sum, that part of the sum which represented payments which the plaintiff would have received post-retirement should be deducted from his damages. See R. Lewis, 'The Overlap between Damages for Personal Injury and Work Related Benefits' (1998) 27 *ILJ* 1 (see Select Bibliography), at 18.

[324] [1991] 2 All ER 449.

[325] Per Cohen LJ in *Payne* v. *Railway Executive* [1952] 1 KB 26, 35–6.

[326] [1988] AC 514, 532 (Lord Bridge); see R. Lewis, 'Damages for Personal Injury and Work Related Benefits', op. cit., at 13.

Injury: Collateral Benefits,[327] expressed the view that a 'disablement pension is compensation for lost earnings' and should therefore be deductible.

The courts have also considered the rights of the third-party provider of the collateral benefit to recover the sums in question from either the tortfeasor or the victim. At common law the third party provider has no general right of recoupment, by virtue of the decision of the Court of Appeal in *Metropolitan Police District Receiver* v. *Croydon Corp.*[328] This decision has been criticised by the Law Commission on the grounds that 'a tortfeasor is unjustly enriched at the expense of providers of collateral benefits who act under legal compulsion',[329] although the Law Commission also recognised that third-party providers could protect themselves contractually, by stipulating that the plaintiff should make the repayment in the event of a damages claim being successful.[330]

(B) Benefits Subject to the Statutory Régime

The modern Welfare State has established many types of benefits which are made to those whose earnings or other sources of income have been interrupted by injury or disease; these include unemployment benefits and benefits in respect of both short-term and long-term illness and disability. In practice, these benefits provide the bulk of financial support received by those without regular income or earnings, including those who are injured in tortious incidents. Only some of the victims of tortious events may also be lucky enough to obtain tort damages.[331] Over the years, opinion has hardened in favour of the view that plaintiffs should not be allowed to cumulate such damages with social security benefits in such a way as to receive double compensation.[332] But that is as far as agreement seems to have gone. How much deduction should be made, how, and by whom, have been subjects that have divided 'official' as well as academic opinion. The resulting legislation reflects this uncertainty; and coupled as it is by the usual verbosity favoured by English drafters, it has produced a régime that is as complex as it is intellectually contradictory. Moreover, legislative fine-tuning is still continuing. All attempts to simplify it, even for the purposes of presenting it to law students, are thus bound to produce fuzziness at the fringes. The reader has, accordingly, been warned!

One reason for the complexity is that we now have not one but several statutory régimes dealing with the question of deductibility of state-paid benefits, according to the date on which the cause of action accrued and the claim was made. This is the result of successive statutory changes to the system that was initially established by legislation in 1948. This 'old' régime was more fully

---

[327] Law Com. No. 147 (1997), at para. 4.67; see also paras. 4.5–4.60, where the arguments traditionally put in favour of non-deduction of collateral benefits are subjected to a rigorous (and largely critical) analysis.

[328] [1957] 1 QB 154.   [329] Law Com. No. 147, para. 5.6.

[330] Ibid., para. 5.13. The Law Commission also considered whether there should be a general right of third parties to recover collateral benefits from the victim; such a matter should, in its view, be left up to the development of the common law rather than be made the subject of statutory intervention (ibid., para. 5.26).

[331] See our discussion in Chapter 1, above.

[332] Although, as we have seen, a different view is taken with regard to private and/or employer-based insurance.

described in the third edition of this book. At its core lay section 2(1) of the Law Reform (Personal Injuries) Act 1948 which provided that in the case of certain specified benefits[333] there should be a *partial* deduction from damages for personal injury, amounting to *half* the social-security payments made to the plaintiff up to a maximum period of five years from the cause of the action. Benefits both paid and likely to be paid after the judgment were deductible, but in calculating future benefit entitlement no account was taken of likely increases in the levels of payment. The courts read the Act as implying that beyond the five-year period no deduction was to be made in respect of the specified benefits.[334] Legislation also limited the scope of deductibility in two significant ways both of which favoured the plaintiff. The first (and most important) restricted deductibility to the portion of damages representing loss of future earnings, and secondly by providing that the statutory set-off should be made before any reduction in the victim's award for contributory negligence. This 'old' régime still applies to torts which occurred before 1 January 1989 and which have not, somehow, been affected by the law on limitation periods, but, clearly, it is of decreasing importance.

The Social Security Act 1989 replaced the 'old' régime with a new scheme of state 'recoupment' of social-security benefits from damages awards which exceed a threshold of £2,500. This scheme, which we may call the 'new' régime, was further amended with effect from 6 October 1997 by the Social Security (Recovery of Benefits) Act 1997. The basic principle is now that the court must disregard receipts of certain specified social security benefits when making its assessment of damages. However, the *tortfeasor* must then pay to the Department of Social Security the full amount of any of the relevant benefits that the plaintiff has received in respect of his injury or accident.[335] The Department of Social Security is not formally subrogated to the plaintiff's claim, but the effect is similar. Hence the tortfeasor must now pay in full, but the plaintiff is worse off than he was (when the 1948 Act applied) since a *complete* (and not 50 per cent) deduction of benefits takes place. The justification for recoupment is the argument that the previous system had the effect of 'subsidising' the activities of tortfeasors, as well as giving rise to double compensation of plaintiffs. Although a full account of the scheme is outside the scope of this book, a number of points concerning its operation may be noted.

First, the deduction is made only against certain heads of damages: these are compensation for lost earnings, for cost of care and for loss of mobility.[336] This

[333] The 1948 Act did not cover a number of significant statutory payments, including unemployment benefit, income support (previously supplementary benefit), redundancy compensation, and attendance allowance; in these cases the courts decided that benefits paid should be deducted in full. The leading case is *Hodgson* v. *Trapp* [1989] AC 807.

[334] *Haste* v. *Sandell Perkins* [1984] QB 735; *Jackman* v. *Corbett* [1987] 2 All ER 699.

[335] The courts have had to consider the complex situation which arises where the plaintiff was, prior to the accident, in receipt of non-recoupable social security benefits. In such a situation, the plaintiff may not be able to prevent the recoupment of benefits received after the accident (see *Hassall* v. *Secretary of State for Social Security* [1995] 1 WLR 812), but in so far as he is thereby left financially worse off than he would have been had he continued to receive the non-recoupable benefit, he may have a claim for the difference, as special damages, against the tortfeasor (*Neal* v. *Bingle* [1998] 2 WLR 57).

[336] See Social Security (Recovery of Benefits) Act 1997, ss. 1(1)(a), 1(4)(b) and 29, and Sch. 2, Column 1.

is a change made by the 1997 Act. For claims in respect of torts committed between 1989 and 1997, the deduction could be made in respect of all heads of loss. The thinking behind the change made in 1997 is that social security benefits do not provide compensation for heads of loss such as pain and suffering; therefore, recoupment is inappropriate in these cases. This marks a partial return to the Act of 1948. However, it is still the case, under the new régime, that no account is taken of contributory negligence. Recoupment of benefits and reductions for contributory negligence will therefore have a cumulative impact in diminishing the plaintiff's award.

Secondly, the range of social-security benefits in respect of which deduction must be made is now reasonably comprehensive; the drafter appears to have sought to include all benefits which could be payable in respect of one of the heads of damage to which the deduction rule applies. Hence there is little scope for the common law rules to apply as they did to certain social-security payments under the 1948 Act.[337]

Thirdly, there are certain exemptions.[338] These include payments made under specified statutory schemes (such as the Criminal Injuries Compensation Scheme, which has its own rules relating to recoupment) and charitable trusts. Claims made under the Fatal Accidents Act 1976 are also excluded.[339] The Act also grants the Secretary of State the power to adopt regulations exempting payments below a certain amount,[340] but at the time of writing this power has not been exercised. By contrast, between 1989 and 1997, the relevant legislation provided for 'small payments' of below £2,500 to be subject to a modified version of the 'old' régime under the Act of 1948, and this system still applies to compensation payments made in the period between when the 1989 Act (as later consolidated in the Social Security Administration Act 1992) was in force.

Fourthly, the maximum period for which benefits may be taken into account remains five years, but it may now be shortened to less than that if the payment is made before the five years have expired. In that case no account will then be taken of benefit paid or payable after receipt of the compensation. This appears to be an attempt to encourage early settlements.[341]

Fifthly, the introduction of compulsory recoupment has made it necessary to institute a complex and potentially intrusive scheme of state administration of the process of making personal injury payments. The compensator (who would normally be the tortfeasor's insurance company) must not make any payment to the victim until he has applied for and has received a certificate of recoverable benefits from the Secretary of State, specifying the amount to be deducted. The Compensation Recovery Unit of the Department of Social Security has the task of processing these applications. In the last resort the Secretary of State

---

[337] The 'listed benefits' are those contained in Sch. 2, Column 2 of the 1997 Act. Should a court be required to consider a benefit falling outside this list, it seems most likely that the residual common-law rule of reduction of damages in respect of social security benefits would be applied (*Hodgson* v. *Trapp* [1989] AC 807).

[338] Social Security (Recovery of Benefits) Act 1997, Sch. 1, Part I, and SI 1197/2205, reg. 2.

[339] Social Security (Recovery of Benefits) Act 1997, reg. 2(2)(a).

[340] Ibid., Sch. 1, Part 2.   [341] Social Security (Recovery of Benefits) Act 1997, s. 3.

can initiate proceedings against a compensator who fails to apply for a certificate. Both alleged tortfeasors and recipients of state benefits are under a duty to provide the Compensation Recovery Unit with information concerning the claim.[342]

Whatever its other merits, the recoupment scheme has done little to clarify the law of collateral benefits. The distinctions between different types of benefits are as arbitrary as they were before. For example, the rationale for the exclusion from the scheme of Fatal Accidents Act cases is unclear. The new régime has in effect achieved a partial levelling down of the compensation of tort victims so that they are now at less of an advantage compared to accident victims who are wholly dependent on social security. However, the savings made do not appear to be substantial enough to produce significant improvements in the levels of social security benefits paid to all accident victims, in particular when account is taken of the cost of administering the recoupment scheme. Moreover, accident victims with the benefit of private or occupational insurance continue to receive full compensation without deduction. This preferential treatment of private, as opposed to social, insurance has no clear rationale.[343]

5. Miscellaneous Matters

(a) LUMP SUMS (AND ALTERNATIVE OPTIONS)

The first thing to note is that in tort actions damages must be awarded[344] once only in respect of each cause of action and they take the form of a lump sum.[345] The English courts have no power to order the payment of damages in periodic sums unless the parties agree.[346] Accordingly, they often have to include compensation for future damage that is likely to accrue, in addition to compensation for damage that has already accrued. This is easier to decide in theory than to apply in practice. The problems become apparent in personal-injury cases, where the judge has to try to guess not only what would have happened to the victim if he had not been injured, but also what is now likely to happen to him

---

[342] See SI 1997/2205, regs. 3–6.

[343] It should also be noted in this regard that under the common law, private insurers are not subrogated to the personal injury claims of plaintiffs taking out first party life and accident insurance, Fleming, *Tort* (8th edn., 1992) at 367.

[344] *Miliangos* v. *George Frank (Textiles) Ltd.* [1976] AC 443 abolished the old rule that damages must be expressed in sterling. Thus, see, *The Despina R.* [1979] AC 685. But the sterling rule still applies to non-pecuniary damages such as damages for pain and suffering and loss amenity: *Hoffman* v. *Sofaer* [1982] 1 WLR 1350.

[345] This rule against successive actions has to be qualified in at least two major respects. First, it does not apply to continuing torts (e.g. continuing trespass) and, secondly, it does not apply whenever two different rights have been violated: *Brunsden* v. *Humphrey* (1884) 14 QBD 141. For a more recent illustration see *Barrow* v. *Bankside Agency Ltd.* [1996] 1 WLR 257 and note that the doctrine of *res iudicata* may be relevant in such cases.

[346] *Fournier* v. *Canadian National Railway* [1927] AC 167. At common law it was not clear whether the courts would have the power even if the arrangement was agreed to by the parties themselves (see *Metcalfe* v. *London Passenger Transport Board* [1938] 2 All ER 352 at 355); however, the Damages Act 1996, s. 2, now provides that '[a] court awarding damages in an action for personal injury may, with the consent of the parties, make an order under which the damages are wholly or partly to take the form of periodical payments'.

as a result of the accident. This 'guessing game' is further aggravated by the fact that it takes place against a number of imponderables, some of which are related to the victim (e.g. the nature of his injury, its likely complications, and pre-trial anxiety—known as 'compensation neurosis'—which can postpone complete recovery and complicate the task of assessment of the loss); while others are linked with wider economic factors (e.g. inflation, rates of taxation, etc.) but may affect particularly harshly a victim who, because of the tort, may have reduced earning capacity. The great disadvantage of lump-sum awards is not only that they make such estimates of future developments little more than educated guesses, but also that they are not open to subsequent correction. In *Lim v. Camden and Islington Area Health Authority*[347] Lord Scarman was frank about this danger when he said:

Sooner or later . . . if the parties do not settle, a court (once liability is admitted or proved) has to make an award of damages. The award, which covers past, present and future injury and loss, must under our law be a lump sum assessed at the conclusion of the legal process. The award is final; it is not susceptible to review as the future unfolds, substituting fact for estimate. Knowledge of the future being denied to mankind, so much of the award as is to be attributed to future loss and suffering—in many cases the major part of the award—will almost surely be wrong. *There is really only one certainty: the future will prove the award to be either too high or too low.*

These remarks were prompted by Lord Denning MR's attempt in the Court of Appeal[348] to change or, at least, adapt the existing practice and to enable an award of damages in cases such as the one before the court to be regarded as an interim award, allowing the court to make further adjustments in the future. The idea, according to Lord Scarman, was

an attractive, ingenious suggestion—but . . . unsound. For so radical a reform can be made neither by judges nor by modification of rules of court. It raises issues of social, economic and financial policy not amenable to judicial reform which will almost certainly prove to be controversial and can be resolved by the legislature only after full consideration of factors which cannot be brought into clear focus, or be weighed and assessed, in the course of the forensic process.[349]

The alternative to the lump-sum method of payment of damages is the annuity system which is adopted (in theory, though not rigidly in practice) by a number of European systems such as, for instance, the French and the German. Its main advantage is its ability to adapt the award downwards or upwards depending on whether the victim's condition and other circumstances become better or worse. In a number of instances—for example, in cases of fatal accidents where the chances of remarriage of the surviving spouse have to be considered—this method of payment of the damage award helps avoid awkward or embarrassing guessing exercises. But annuities also have crucial weaknesses. For example, they require that the cases are 'kept open' and insurance companies, who meet most of the claims, understandably prefer to pay (if they have

---

[347] [1980] AC 174, 182–3 (emphasis added).   [348] [1979] QB 196, 214 ff.

[349] [1980] AC 174, 183. See also Lord Steyn's highly critical comments on the present systems of lump sum payments in *Wells* v. *Wells* [1998] 3 WLR 329, 351.

to pay) and 'close their books'. A mechanism must also be devised to allow for the adjustment of the sums paid, and this can involve costs and delays. Victims also tend to prefer to receive their compensation in one large amount even though the unexpected receipt of large sums may lead them to spend their awards in a very short time and then leave them without adequate financial resources to maintain themselves. Last but by no means least, lawyers are more likely to receive their remuneration without complaints and expeditiously if the client/victim receives a large sum rather than modest, periodic payments. For a variety of practical reasons, therefore, the lump-sum method of payment of the damage award may not be as bad as some of its critics believe; and for practical reasons it seems unlikely to be replaced.

In the future, therefore, the search for better solutions is likely to turn towards mixed systems which, so far as possible, will attempt to combine the advantages of the two extreme solutions—namely, the lump sum versus the system of annuity payments. The emerging practice of 'structured settlements', described in subsection (*iv*), addresses these problems in the case of damages for serious injuries; but three further ways of improving the position of deserving plaintiffs must also be considered here. They are: (*i*) postponed or split trials; (*ii*) interim awards; and (*iii*) provisional damages.

(i) Postponed or Split Trials It has already been noted why the lump-sum method of payment of damages raises serious difficulties in the calculation of the right level of the award, especially where the extent of the injury is not yet fully determined. One way around this difficulty is to postpone the trial or settlement of the claim until a clearer picture about the victim's position has emerged. Unfortunately, such a solution presupposes that such a delay will make the prognosis of the future easier, which is not always the case. Moreover, this way of proceeding adds to the delays of the tort process, which has always been one of the major weaknesses of the system. Finally, such delays may trigger off in susceptible plaintiffs the so-called problem of 'compensation neurosis' and thus further delay their rehabilitation.

As a result of these limitations the different corrective device of 'split trials' was proposed by the Court of Appeal in 1974 in *Coenen* v. *Payne*.[350] This, as the name suggests, entails separating 'liability' which can be resolved (or admitted) as soon as possible after the accident (when recollections of witnesses are still (relatively) clear), from the 'quantum' of damages, which in most serious cases could be postponed until a clear prognosis could be attempted. Once again, however, there is no certainty that postponement makes prognosis easier; and, under existing law (and subject to what is said below), when the award is made it is final. In any event, this method of proceeding can only have its full effect if it is combined with the possibility of interim damages. Both these ideas, however, have met with little enthusiasm in practice and are mentioned here for the sake of completeness rather than as oft-used procedures in the compensation process.

---

[350] [1974] 1 WLR 984, now covered by the Supreme Court Rules, Order 33, rule 4(2A) and by the County Court Rules, Order 13, rule 2(2)(c).

(ii) Interim Damages The idea of awarding interim damages is even older. It can be traced back to the Winn Committee report of 1968 and is nowadays regulated by Part II of Order 29 of the Rules of the Supreme Court, rule 11. Such an order can be made at the discretion of the court where 'need' can be shown by the plaintiff.[351] The money is meant to cover the plaintiff's interim pecuniary losses (such as loss of earnings, medical expenses, and the like) and cannot include a percentage of his (possible) general damages. For a variety of reasons this procedure, too, seems to be under-used in practice. Some of the reasons for this seem to be purely technical;[352] and, nowadays, the operation of the Social Security (Recovery of Benefits) Act 1997 (described above in Section 4) may also have an adverse effect in so far as there is the danger that the new scheme might swallow up all interim payments, especially in those cases involving smaller sums. So this device, too, has been of limited use to plaintiffs.

(iii) Provisional Damages Provisional damages provide the third, comparatively recent, innovation that aims to improve the position of the deserving victim of personal injury. They were made possible by section 6 of the Administration of Justice Act 1982 which empowers the courts 'to make a provisional award in cases where the medical prognosis is particularly uncertain and where there is a *chance*,[353] falling short of probability, that some *serious* disease or *serious* deterioration in the plaintiff's condition will accrue at a later date'.[354]

In the debates in the House of Lords the Lord Chancellor, Lord Hailsham, did not envisage that frequent use would be made of this provision;[355] and events have proved him right. The example he gave of a case suitable to be brought under this heading, was of a young child whose skull was fractured in an accident and who, at the trial, may appear to have made full recovery. Yet in cases of cranial injuries there is always a chance of subsequent epilepsy. Section 6 will now enable the court to award nothing in respect of the feared event but to give damages later if the feared event materialises. This procedure will avoid trying to evaluate the possibility of the feared event materialising and then awarding for this 'chance' a smaller sum that may end by being too low or too high. Unlike the Pearson proposals on this point, it is not obligatory for the court to adopt this procedure on its own; it will be for the plaintiff to claim that a provisional damages award be made; and the interests of the defendant will also have to be given due weight. The case of *Willson* v. *Ministry of Defence*[356] has, as already stated, revealed how conservative the approach of the courts has been.

The provision of section 6 of the Administration of Justice Act 1982 was brought into force in July 1985.[357] Under the new régime, as it was judicially

---

[351] *Schott Kem Ltd.* v. *Bentley* [1991] 1 QB 61.

[352] They are discussed in the Law Commission Consultation Paper No. 125, 71–2.

[353] In *Willson* v. *Ministry of Defence* [1991] 1 All ER 638 the trial judge was of the view that section 32A of the Supreme Court Act 1981 was concerned with measurable not fanciful chances, thus further limiting the opportunity of using this procedure.

[354] It will be noticed that this section applies to contingencies due to medical reasons.

[355] *Hansard* (HL) 1982, 28. [356] [1991] 1 All ER 638, 641.

[357] Rules of the Supreme Court, Ord. 37, rs. 7–12.

explained in *Willson*'s case, three requirements will have to be fulfilled before use of this procedure can be sanctioned. First, there must be a *chance* of the feared event materialising at some later date. The chance may be slim but, as stated, it must be measurable. Secondly, there must be a serious deterioration of the plaintiff's physical (and, presumably, also mental) condition and not just an ordinary deterioration or progression of the injury or illness. This is a matter of fact and degree but the facts of *Willson*'s case suggest that the courts are taking a conservative (arguably over-conservative) attitude on this requirement. Finally, the judge must be persuaded that the case before him justifies the exercise of his discretion to give the plaintiff the right to return at a later date for more; or, on the contrary, that it is one that is best resolved by a once-and-for-all award of damages. In his decision, the judge will also, normally, specify the period within which the application for further damages must be made, though nowadays there seems to be a preference for not setting a limit at all.[358]

The tort victim may not just get worse as a result of his injuries; he may also die. If a provisional award has been made to him prior to the death, how will this affect the legal position of his dependants? The answer is now to be found in section 3 of the Damages Act 1996 which does not preclude his dependants from bringing a lost dependency claim. Wisely, however, the Act adds that any part of the provisional award that was 'intended to compensate him for pecuniary loss in a period that in the event falls after his death shall be taken into account in assessing the amount of any loss of support' suffered by the dependants.

For most commentators the régime described above seems to be unduly restrictive. Their arguments can be found in the specialised literature; and they are also conveniently summarised and discussed critically in the Law Commission Consultation Paper No. 125.[359] Here it is enough to note two of the most doubtful limitations and, also, add an observation of wider import.

First, one must recall that the feared event must be specified by the plaintiff's lawyers in the original action in considerable detail. As we have seen, the courts seem to take an overly narrow view on the question whether the subsequent event is a serious deterioration or an ordinary deterioration or development of the injury or illness.

Secondly, the right to return to the court and have the award adjusted arises only once and this may cause injustice in some cases. For example, suppose that the plaintiff is injured in his legs and runs the risk of subsequently developing arthritis. Since it is the disease that must be specified by the plaintiff's application and not the parts of his body that are susceptible to it, what will happen to the plaintiff who develops arthritis in one of the injured legs? It would be unfair to suggest that he would have to wait until the other leg was also affected by the disease; but it would be equally unfair to limit his subsequent increase of damages to include the arthritis in the one leg.

Finally, one may use this opportunity to ask a wider a question concerning the attitudes of our (conservatively inclined) legislators. For, having identified

---

[358] See Bragg, 'Provisional Damages' (1992) 136 *SJ* 654, 5.   [359] At 76–84.

an area of the law that needs reform, why do they then feel such an irresistible urge to circumscribe the reforming rules to such an extent as to make them almost useless? The tendency is obvious in other parts of the law of torts;[360] and readers inclined towards speculating about more general matters might wish to ponder over this question. In the meantime, however, and as far as this particular topic is concerned, all one can say is that the institution of provisional damages is, over ten years after its introduction, still in its formative stages. One must, therefore, hope that the courts will be responsive to calls to liberalise their present position on this issue before judicial accretions (such as *Willson*) make this task truly impossible.

(iv) Structured Settlements[361]   To cure some of the defects of the lump sum which, as we have noted, tend to be aggravated in cases of serious physical injuries, the practice of 'structured settlements' emerged in the late 1980s, following roughly the model established earlier in the United States and Canada. To the extent that they form part of 'an out of court settlement' process they have nothing to do with court awards which are the subject of this chapter. Yet even a book such as this cannot fail to give an account of their existence. For their emergence constitutes one of those fascinating examples of 'bargains in the shadow of the law' in the sense that structured settlements represent a 'corrective' to existing practices, worked out by practitioners (lawyers, actuaries, and insurers) rather than being introduced by legislation[362] or the courts, and finally made viable through the active co-operation of the Inland Revenue. The latter's intervention was crucial and came in the form of a 1987 interpretation of an earlier court judgment[363] in a way that allows payments to be made to the plaintiff in the form of an annuity to be treated, in certain circumstances, as payments of capital (and thus not subject to tax) rather than payments of income. This led to four 'model agreements' being reached between the Inland Revenue and the Association of British Insurers which make the new method of payment of awards attractive to all the parties in the dispute. For, by treating

---

[360] For instance, the old s. 4 of the Defamation Act 1952 dealing with 'unintentional defamation'.

[361] A thorough discussion of the practice and its weak points can be found in R. Lewis, *Structured Settlements: the Law and Practice* (1993) (see Select Bibliography), and in the Law Commission's Consultation Paper No. 125, *Structured Settlements and Interim and Provisional Damages*, and the Law Commission's Report No. 224 of the same name. For shorter but just as interesting discussions see: Allen, 'Structured Settlements' (1988) 104 *LQR* 448; Edwards, 'Structured Settlements' (1989) *The Law Society's Gazette*, 32; Hulls, 'Structuring Personal Injury Awards' (1990) *The Law Society's Gazette*, 27; Lewis, 'Pensions Replace Lump Sum Damages: Are Structured Settlements the Most Important Reform of Tort in Modern Times?' (1988) 15 (4) *J. Law Soc.* 392; Lewis, 'Structured Settlements in Practice' (1991) *Civil Justice Quarterly* 212; Lewis, 'Legal Limits on the Structure of Settlement of Damages' [1993] *CLJ* 470; Rifkind, 'The Nuts and Bolts of Structured Settlements' (1992) *The Lawyer* 6; Upenicks, 'Structured Settlements: Are They Here to Stay?' (1982) 3 (4) *Advocates Quarterly* 393; Whitfield, 'The Basics and Tactics of Structured Settlements' (1992) 142 *New LJ* 135.

[362] Though now the subject is to some extent covered by the Damages Act 1996—especially ss. 2 and 4—which came into force on 24 September 1996. Before that Act, certain amendments to tax legislation had been made to encourage structured settlements (see Finance Act 1995, s. 142, and further changes made by the Finance Act 1996).

[363] *Dott* v. *Brown* [1936] 1 All ER 543. It has been argued by Francis, 'Taxation of Structured Settlements' [1991] *British Tax Review* 56, that this interpretation may be, partially at least, wrong. Since it is unlikely, however, that anyone other than the Revenue has *locus standi* to challenge this interpretation, the practical significance of this doubt may be nil, as the author of the article readily admits.

the periodic payments as non-taxable capital, liability insurers who adopt one of the four model agreements can pay out less and yet end up by funding payments to the injured plaintiff that are greater than if he had received from them a lump sum and then invested it directly producing taxable, annual income.

The way structured settlements work is as follows.

First, the parties to the dispute work out through their advisers the amount that would be payable if the conventional lump sum was used. Part of that amount is then paid to the plaintiff as 'up-front monies' to cover such items as expenses already incurred. The bulk of the agreed amount is then used by the insurer covering the liability involved to purchase an annuity or annuities for the benefit of the injured person. The amounts paid out can be varied, or 'structured' over a period of time which may equal the plaintiff's lifetime or even exceed it by a fixed period. Payments can be protected against inflation, released in fixed amounts, or even arranged in such a way as to provide for larger sums to be made available at pre-set intervals in order to take care of larger than usual, exceptional, or one-off, expenditure (e.g. educational payments, or purchase of a car or a house or special equipment, etc.). Such contingencies, however, must be carefully planned in advance and must conform with the terms of one of the model agreements with the Revenue, for the settlements, once agreed, cannot be revised or adapted at a later time.[364] Since payments thus made are not, as already stated, subject to tax, the insurer is allowed to invest (for the purposes of the annuity) a sum which is smaller than that which the plaintiff himself would have to invest to obtain a similar amount, since in his case the annual return would be subject to tax. This represents a 'saving' for the insurer; and though there seem to be no clear rules as to how its size is estimated,[365] in practice it tends to represent something in the order of 10 per cent of the cost of the entire settlement. For the plaintiff, of course, the saving by not paying tax on the annual payment is, currently, of the order of 25–40 per cent.

The four types of annuity allowed by the agreement are the following: (*a*) Basic Terms, allowing pre-set payments for a fixing period; (*b*) Indexed Terms, similar to the above, but making payments inflation-proof; (*c*) Terms of Life, providing for pre-set payments to be made until the claimant's death (or, in the event of an early death for the claimant's estate or dependents); and (*d*) Indexed Terms of Life, which are similar to the previous category but are protected against inflation.

The above can be made clearer by Tables 8.1 and 8.2, which were compiled by a specialist on this subject,[366] utilising figures from the first judicially approved settlement in this country in the case of *Kelly* v. *Dawes*.[367] On the basis

---

[364] In this sense they 'suffer' from the same defect which affects lump sum awards.

[365] In *Kelly* v. *Dawes* (*The Times*, 27 Sept. 1990) the discount was 5.8% of the amount that was structured. In *Everett* v. *Everett and Norfolk County Council* (Unreported) 4 June 1991, the discount was 13.75%, and in *Grimsley* v. *Grimsley and Meade* (Unreported) 28 Jan. 1991, the discount reached 33%. The Law Commission speculated that the amount may in part 'reflect the difficulties in the plaintiff's case and the desire to settle', op. cit. at 60, n. 98.

[366] Lewis, op. cit. (Select Bibliography).   [367] *The Times*, 27 Sept. 1990.

Table 8.1 The Terms of the Settlement in *Kelly* v. *Dawes*

Agreed lump sum damages if conventional method used		£427,500
Plaintiff actually received:		
(1) 'Up-front monies' (A lump sum for special damages already incurred and to provide for unforeseen circumstances)	£110,000	
(2) Benefits from an annuity purchased for capital sum of (Annuity produces £25,760 p.a., RPI linked)	£300,000	
Total capital value of settlement	£410,000	£410,000
Discount for the insurer		£17,500

of the above, the balance-sheet on this new development would probably be as in Table 8.1.

On the positive side we note first that more money can be awarded to the plaintiff at a lower cost to the defendant and his insurer. Secondly, we see that the burden and anxiety of investing the tort award is removed from the shoulders of the plaintiff and squarely placed on those of the defendant's insurer and other experts. Thirdly, the feared dissipation (by the plaintiff) of the tort award is avoided or, at least, considerably reduced, since the award is no longer payable in one large lump. Fourthly, since this type of payment can only take place through a negotiated process and it cannot be judicially imposed, there is at least the possibility that a number of these complicated cases will be resolved outside the court-room thereby saving the time and cost of a full-blown trial.

The following might be considered to be drawbacks of the new practice.

First, we have seen that as things stand at present such settlements can only be negotiated by the parties but cannot be judicially imposed. For some this may be a weakness of the existing system.[368]

Secondly, the new device seems to work best in the case of large awards which are appropriate in the more serious types of injuries but may be prohibitively expensive to operate in the majority of cases which involve minor injuries and thus lesser awards.

Thirdly, since the bulk of tort litigation is concerned with minor injuries, the saving of judicial time that structured settlements may bring in their wake may thus be exaggerated. Fourthly, there exist some technical drawbacks in the system as currently operated which, apparently, result largely from specialised Revenue rules. These are reviewed in more detail in the Law Commission Paper No. 125 and the interested reader is referred to paragraphs 3.22 to 3.97 of the Report for further details.

---

[368] On this see the Law Commission Consultative Paper No. 125, paras. 3.71 ff.

Table 8.2 Comparison of the benefits of a structured settlement and a
traditional lump sum award (£)[369]

A Years from trial or settlement	B Annual sum produced by the structured settlement	C Interest on balance of lump sum at 9.25% gross	D Interest net of tax and administration charges	E Amount withdrawn from balance of lump sum	F Balance of £300,000 lump sum remaining
0	25,526	27,750	16,545	−9,017	290,983
1	26,591	15,916	15,970	−10,871	280,112
3	29,591	24,718	14,489	−15,102	252,116
6	34,256	19,840	11,289	−22,976	119,520
9	39,655	12,596	6,619	−33,036	103,025
12	45,906	2,253	−1,004	−46,910	−22,556

Based upon a lump sum of £300,000 as in *Kelly* v. *Dawes*.
Assumptions: inflation at 5% p.a. and present tax levels.

(B) Duty to Mitigate

The principle of compensation means that the plaintiff can only claim damages
for losses that he has actually sustained.[370] So, damages for lost income resulting from a tortiously inflicted injury which resulted in the plaintiff losing his
job will be reduced by any amount earned from alternative employment. If the
plaintiff's loss could have been minimised by accepting an alternative employment then he will, normally, be expected to do this; and he must also undergo
'reasonable' medical treatment, made necessary by his injuries, if this is likely
to improve his employment chances or decrease his loss.[371] But the courts will
not ask the plaintiff to undergo a surgical operation that involves a substantial
risk;[372] nor will a mother's wrongful birth claim be affected by her failure to
have an abortion (as a way of mitigating her loss).[373] What is 'reasonable' will,
obviously, depend largely on the circumstances of each case; and most authorities leave it to the defendant to prove that the plaintiff has failed to mitigate
his loss.[374]

[369] This table is compiled from those contained in Frenkel Topping's report to the court in *Kelly* v.
Dawes. It reveals that after year 12, whereas the lump sum (in col. F) is exhausted, the structured settlement payment (in col. B) can continue, inflation-linked, for the rest of the plaintiff's life. The lump sum
would be exhausted earlier if inflation or tax levels increased.

[370] *Bellingham* v. *Dhillon and Another* [1973] 1 QB 304. But see *Gardner* v. *Marsh & Parsons* [1997] 3 All ER 871
(where the court had to consider whether a benefit which accrued after the tort/breach of contract and
benefited the plaintiff should be taken into account in assessing his damages).

[371] *McAuley* v. *London Transport Executive* [1957] 2 Lloyd's Rep. 500; *Morgan* v. *T. Wallis* [1974] 1 Lloyd's Rep.
165.

[372] *Savage* v. *Wallis* [1966] 1 Lloyd's Rep. 357.   [373] *Emeh* v. *Kensigton A.H.A.* [1985] QB 1012.

[374] Since *Roper* v. *Johnson* (1873) L.R. 8 CP 167. See, also, *Steele* v. *Robert George and Co. Ltd.* [1942] AC 497,
at 501, 503, 506, and 508; *Richardson* v. *Redpath, Brown and Co. Ltd.* [1944] AC 62, 72, 73, 75; *Garnac Grain Co.
Inc.* v. *H. M. F. Faure and Fairclough Ltd.* [1968] AC 1130. The contrary view, therefore, of the Privy Council in
Selvanayagam v. *University of the West Indies* [1983] 1 WLR 585—(criticised by McGregor in 46 *MLR* 758)—placing on the plaintiff the burden of proof that he acted reasonably, must be regarded as *per incuriam* and, in
any event, as not binding on English courts.

(C) ITEMISATION OF AWARDS

In most cases of personal injury a victim suffers two distinct kinds of damage which are always discussed under two headings. The first includes such items as are capable of direct translation into money terms: for example, loss of earnings, medical expenses, and other out-of-pocket expenses. For these items, as stated, the rule is *restitutio in integrum*. Non-pecuniary losses, on the other hand, include all such immeasurable elements as pain and suffering, or loss of an eye or a limb, which can clearly not be valued accurately in money terms; and for these the guiding principle is 'fair compensation'. This not only indicates the inability to value these losses precisely, but only approximately; it also suggests the underlying idea that there should be some measure of uniformity in the sum awarded for such losses, otherwise great injustice could result.

In this context three major changes in the practice of the courts must be mentioned. Growing realisation of the need for consistency and comparability in awards led the Court of Appeal in *Ward* v. *James*[375] to rule that juries should no longer be used for the assessment of damages save in very exceptional cases.[376] Lord Denning MR, delivering the judgment of the full Court of Appeal, justified this as follows:

. . . recent cases show the desirability of three things. First *assessability*: In cases of grave injury, where the body is wrecked or the brain destroyed, it is very difficult to assess a fair compensation in money, so difficult that the award must basically be a conventional figure, derived from experience or from awards in comparable cases. Secondly, *uniformity*: There should be some measure of uniformity in awards so that similar decisions are given in similar cases; otherwise there will be great dissatisfaction in the community, and much criticism of the administration of justice. Thirdly, *predictability*: Parties should be able to predict with some measure of accuracy the sum which is likely to be awarded in a particular case, for by this means cases can be settled peaceably and not brought to court, a thing very much to the public good. None of these three is achieved when the damages are left at large to the jury.

It will be noticed that while the first two reasons given for the change are related to what could be called the 'fairness' of the awards, the last is a purely 'administrative' argument, though no less important for that. For it is this consistency which makes it possible to proceed to settlement out of court and thus expedites the administration of justice.

The second change came with *Jefford* v. *Gee*,[377] where it was held that judges must assess separately damages payable: (*i*) for accrued pecuniary loss; (*ii*) for

---

[375] [1966] 1 QB 273, 299–300.

[376] There is, according to s. 69(1) of the Supreme Court Act 1981 a prima-facie right to a jury trial in cases of fraud, malicious prosecution, false imprisonment and, of course, defamation. But s. 69(3) has been seen as strengthening further this presumption against jury trial since it gives a judge the right to deny a jury trial if the case will require a 'prolonged examination of documents or accounts or any scientific . . . investigation which cannot be made with a jury'. See *H* v. *Ministry of Defence* [1991] 2 QB 103. Recent decisions of the Court of Appeal to intervene in jury awards have struck a further blow to the unfettered powers which juries enjoyed in the past. See, in particular, Lord Woolf's judgment in *Thompson* v. *Comr. of Police of the Metropolis* and *Hsu* v. *Comr. of the Police of the Metropolis* [1997] 2 All ER 762, where clear and thorough guidelines where given on the matter of jury instruction.

[377] [1970] 2 QB 130.

non-pecuniary damages; and (*iii*) for damages for loss of future earnings. This threefold division was largely dictated by the passing of the Administration of Justice Act 1969, which made it obligatory for courts to award interest in any case in which judgment[378] was given for more than £200, all or part of which consisted of damages in respect of personal injury or the death of a person. *Jefford* v. *Gee* was, therefore, the case that elaborated the principles of the award of interest, and it did so by dividing the damages headings as above. After some hesitation, these principles were confirmed in *Pickett* v. *British Rail Engineering Ltd.*,[379] and the position is as follows: (*i*) special damages (i.e. pre-trial losses) carry interest at half the usual short-term rate; (*ii*) for non-pecuniary damages the interest on damages is on a more modest rate—currently 2 per cent;[380] finally (*iii*) future pecuniary losses carry no interest since they have not materialised at the time of the trial.

The final change was firmly established in *George* v. *Pinnock*,[381] where it was accepted that the parties themselves had a right to know how the judge arrived at his final figure. The older practice, therefore, of allowing an appeal only where the total figure was erroneous, was deemed to be incorrect. Nowadays, therefore, the most common ground for overturning an award is if there is an error in one of its component parts; and this, typically, consists in the trial judge having failed to consider whether there is an overlap between different headings of damages with the result that the plaintiff has been enriched.[382]

6. Pecuniary Losses

(A) MEDICAL (AND OTHER) EXPENSES

The plaintiff may recover as part of the special damages any medical (e.g. medical fees, transport to and from the hospital, etc.) or other related *reasonable*[383] expenses incurred as a result of his injury. What amounts to a reasonable expense (causally related to the injury) can vary enormously, and includes such items as expenditure for appliances or equipment (needed to cope with the injuries), greater expense for a holiday, or heating the home, and, in these days of greater numbers of cases of brain damage leading to mental disability, the

---

[378] This power of the court to award interest on a judgment meant that if the defendant paid his debt any time between the commencement of the proceedings and the giving of judgment he escaped having to pay interest at all. Now, however, as a result of s. 15 and Sch. 1 of the Administration of Justice Act 1982 the courts are given power to award interest on any debt outstanding when the writ is issued.

[379] [1980] AC 136.

[380] *Birkett* v. *Hayes* [1982] 1 WLR 816; *Wright* v. *British Railways Board* [1983] 2 AC 773.

[381] [1973] 1 WLR 118.

[382] Thus, see, *Harris* v. *Harris* [1973] 1 Lloyd's Rep. 445 CA (future loss of earnings and loss of marriage prospects); *Clarke* v. *Rotax Aircraft Equipment Ltd.* [1975] 1 WLR 1570 (loss of earning capacity and loss of future earnings). It is doubtful, but probably not finally settled, whether there can be an overlap between pecuniary and non-pecuniary losses. See Lord Scarman's *obiter* in *Lim Poh Choo* v. *Camden and Islington Area Health Authority* [1980] 174 at 192.

[383] This crucial condition is implied by s. 2(4) of the Law Reform (Personal Injuries) Act 1948. See, also, *Cunningham* v. *Harrison* [1973] QB 942. Thus, having treatment in New York rather than London has been treated as reasonable: *Winkworth* v. *Hubbard* [1960] 1 Lloyd's Rep. 150. And being treated at home may be reasonable even if it would be cheaper to be treated in a private institution: *Rialas* v. *Mitchel* (1984) 128 SJ 704 CA. The factual context of each case is, however, paramount and the precedental value of these decisions must not be exaggerated.

fees payable to the Court of Protection which often manages the sums awarded as damages.[384] For illustrations of these headings, often totalling large sums, specialist literature should be consulted.[385] There is also much authority to support the view that an injured housewife is entitled to claim the cost of employing domestic help;[386] and a Canadian decision recently awarded such a plaintiff the cost of her husband doing some of this work (even though the minority objected that the tasks performed by the husband were not, really, performed for his wife but for the household which they shared).[387] The cost of adapting the victim/plaintiff's home should, in some circumstances, be allowable; but the *total* cost of acquiring new accommodation (e.g. moving from a two-storey house into a bungalow) is, it is submitted rightly, viewed with disfavour.[388] The Court of Appeal was recently also unwilling to treat as a related expense (and thus allow it to the victim) the sums that the victim was ordered to pay in matrimonial proceedings that followed the breakdown of her marriage as a result of her injury.[389] The decision, apparently based on considerations of public policy, is not, however, convincing; and the earlier contrary decision of *Jones* v. *Jones*[390] seems preferable.

Prospective medical expenses will be estimated as accurately as possible[391] and will be awarded as part of the general damages. Moreover, in accordance with section 2(4) of the Law Reform (Personal Injuries) Act 1948, failure to use the facilities of the National Health Service will not affect the 'reasonableness' of the plaintiff's expenses. As Slade J put it in *Harris* v. *Brights Asphalt Contractors Ltd.*,[392] '. . . when an injured plaintiff in fact incurs expenses which are reasonable, that expenditure is not to be impeached on the ground that, if he had taken advantage of the facilities under the National Health Service Act, 1946, these reasonable expenses might have been avoided.' But if advantage is in fact taken of the Health Service, then the plaintiff will not be allowed to claim what he would have had to pay if he had contracted for such services or facilities. In a society like ours the victim's right to be compensated for private hospitalisation is understandable, though some feel that this should not be allowed since even private hospitalisation is nowadays subsidised by the State.[393] What is less easy to justify, however, is the victim's right to claim such compensation, take advantage of free Health Service facilities, and use the award for other

---

[384] Substantial sums can be awarded under this heading. See e.g. *Jones* v. *Jones* [1985] QB 704 (CA) (£28,000 including the Official Solicitor's administration costs).

[385] *Hoffman* v. *Sofaer* [1982] 1 WLR 1350 and *Housecroft* v. *Burnett* [1986] 1 All ER 332 are good examples.

[386] *Daly* v. *General Steam Navigation Ltd.* [1981] 1 WLR 120; *Shaw* v. *Wirral H.A.* [1993] 4 Med. LR 275.

[387] *Kroeker* v. *Jansen* (1995) 123 DLR (4th) 652.

[388] Cf. *Cunningham* v. *Harrison* [1973] QB 942 and *Moriarty* v. *McCarthy* [1978] 1 WLR 155, 163.

[389] *Pritchard* v. *J. H. Cobden Ltd.* [1987] 2 WLR 627.

[390] [1985] QB 704 (where, however, the defendant had conceded the point).

[391] *Lim* v. *Camden and Islington Area Health Authority* [1980] AC 174.

[392] [1953] 1 QB 617, 635. The Law Commission's Consultation Paper on *Damages for Personal Injury: Medical, Nursing and other Expenses* (Law Com. No. 144, 1996) recommended the retention of s. 2(4) of the 1948 Act, and also proposed that the NHS should be able to bring a claim against tortfeasors for the costs of caring for their victims (see paras. 4.2 and 4.3).

[393] The Pearson Committee (Cmnd. 7054–1, paras. 339–42) felt that such expenses should be recoverable only if private treatment was reasonable on medical grounds. Note, also, s. 5 of the Administration of Justice Act 1982, discussed below.

purposes. This point, however, rarely arises in practice as far as the pre-trial medical expenses are concerned since at this stage plaintiffs are never sure that defendant's insurers will pay and, therefore, rarely risk incurring the expenses themselves.

(b) THIRD PARTIES TAKING CARE OF PLAINTIFF'S NEEDS

Not infrequently, relatives or friends come to the assistance of a victim and thereby incur *financial* loss (e.g. of wages) or expenses. The usual reason for this is to ensure that the plaintiff/victim receives proper medical and nursing care. To do this, the third party may have to give up his or her paid job. In such cases these third parties cannot claim these losses in their own name, for as against them the tortfeasor has committed no tort. The question thus arises whether the 'primary' or 'direct' victim[394] can recover these sums and, if so, is he under a legal or (merely) moral duty to reimburse his benefactor (the third party)? In *Roach* v. *Yates*[395] the Court of Appeal had no difficulty in awarding such compensation to the 'primary' victim since 'he would naturally feel he ought to compensate [in that case his wife and sister-in-law, who had given up their employment in order to nurse him] for what *they* had lost'. The italicised words could be taken to suggest that the loss in question was, in fact, the third party's (benefactor's) though, for technical reasons, it was claimed by what we have called the 'primary' or 'direct' victim of the tort. Indeed, this position was adopted by Lord Denning in *Cunningham* v. *Harrison*[396] where he also added the rider that the sum thus collected (by the 'primary' victim/plaintiff) would then be held on trust for the third party (benefactor). By a strange coincidence, however, one day later, in *Donnelly* v. *Joyce*,[397] a differently constituted Court of Appeal reached the same final result (i.e. that the torteasor should pay the loss of the third party/benefactor) but via a different route. This was, quite simply, that the loss was that of *the primary (direct) victim* and it consisted not of the expenditure, itself, but of the *need* for the nursing services.

The *Donnelly* v. *Joyce* ruling, which won the day for the next twenty years, was probably prompted by the desire to put an end to uncertainties which had crept into the practice of the law and concerned how the award thus gained by the 'primary' victim should be handled (i.e. kept by him or held in trust in the name of the benefactor, and should the latter course be open only when there was a formal agreement to such effect between the 'primary' victim and the third party). These difficulties were, apparently, avoided by making it clear that the claim for the award was that of the 'primary' victim and not the third party/benefactor and it was then entirely for him to decide how, in fact, the

---

[394] In what follows, we refer to the injured person/plaintif as the 'primary' or 'indirect' victim to distinguish him from the volunteer who comes to his aid (usually giving up his job in order to nurse him) since, in a sense, he too is a victim (albeit indirect) of the tort.

[395] [1953] 1 QB 617, 635.　　　　　　[396] [1973] QB 942.

[397] [1974] QB 454. In *Donnelly* v. *Joyce* the young plaintiff claimed the cost of special boots, which he needed as a result of the accident and which had been bought for him by his parents, and for his mother's lost earnings as a result of her giving up her job to look after him. The defendant conceded the first claim but contested the second on the ground that the plaintiff was under no legal obligation to reimburse his mother.

money would be used. But as Lord Bridge put it in *Hunt* v. *Severs*,[398] the decision which terminated the reign of the *Donnelly* judgment:

By concentrating on the plaintiff's [primary victim's] need and the plaintiff's loss as the basis of an award . . . the reasoning in *Donnelly* diverts attention from the award's central objective of compensating the voluntary carer. Once this is recognised it becomes evident that there can be no ground in public policy or otherwise for requiring the tortfeasor to pay to the plaintiff, in respect of services which he himself has rendered, a sum of money which the plaintiff must then repay to him.

One reason why the House of Lords felt obliged to return to the Denning rationale (that what at issue here is the benefactor's and not the 'primary' victim's loss) were the unusual facts of the case which revealed a basic flaw in the *Donnelly* approach, and which clarify the last sentence of Lord Bridge's statement. For in the *Hunt* case the volunteer offering the services (and suffering the loss) was the plaintiff's husband who was also the defendant tortfeasor in the action! So, if the *Donnelly* reasoning had applied, the plaintiff (wife) would have claimed the loss suffered by her husband who gave up his job to look after her. But the husband, it will be recalled, was also the tortfeasor who had injured her in the first place so, on this kind of reasoning, he would be paying damages for his own loss. The House of Lords was able to avoid this result in the instant case while preserving intact the basic principle that in the more run-of-the-mill kind of case plaintiffs will still be able to recover for the gratuitous provision of services by third parties.

The logic of *Hunt* v. *Severs* is clear enough, but the House of Lords' decision gives rise to numerous problems in the case where the defendant is also the provider of care for the plaintiff.[399] One is that the ruling apparently does not apply if the victim and the carer enter into a contract under which the latter becomes obliged to render the services in question, in return for agreed remuneration. The courts have consistently taken the view that it would be undesirable to place the victim and carer in the position of being required to make a contract of this kind,[400] yet that is precisely the effect of *Hunt* v. *Severs*. The ruling also provides a disincentive for accident victims to accept gratuitous care from close relatives who may be in the best (and most cost-effective) position to provide it for them. These were among the considerations that led the Law Commission, in its Consultation Paper on *Damages for Personal Injury: Medical, Nursing and other Expenses*,[401] to recommend that *Hunt* v. *Severs* should be reversed by statute, in favour of a rule to the effect that the defendant's liability for the plaintiff's nursing care should be unaffected by any liability which the plaintiff might incur to pay those damages back to the defendant.

It could also be said that there is an air of artificiality to the reasoning in *Hunt* v. *Severs*: in practice, it is not the defendant who would have to pay the damages

---

[398] [1994] 2 All ER 385 at 394.

[399] See D. Kemp, 'Voluntary Services Provided by Tortfeasor to his Victim' (1994) 110 *LQR* 524; A. Reed, 'A Commentary on Hunt v. Severs' (1995)15 *OJLS* 133.

[400] See, in particular, *Donnelly* v. *Joyce* [1974] QB 454, at 463–4 (Megaw LJ); *Hunt* v. *Severs* [1993] QB 815, at 831 (Sir Thomas Bingham MR).

[401] Law Com. No. 144 (1996), at para. 3.68.

in question (and then have them repaid by the plaintiff), but the defendant's insurance company. The effect of the House of Lords' judgment, then, was that 'plaintiff and defendant were unable collectively to call upon the proceeds of the defendant's indemnity insurance to cover the cost of caring for the plaintiff'.[402] Both the House of Lords[403] and the Law Commission[404] rejected this line of argument, on the traditional grounds that the courts should not be influenced, in setting the extent of the defendant's liability, by the fact that the defendant was carrying third party insurance in respect of the loss in question. While this approach may be correct in principle, in a case like *Hunt* v. *Severs* it runs the risk of producing a result that is both unjust to the parties immediately concerned and perverse in the incentives it creates for future parties in the same position.

The assessment of the award for the services given to the plaintiff by these third parties has also posed a difficult dilemma. The dilemma is this: should these services (of the third party) be valued at nil (which is what happened prior to *Donnelly*) or at their full—and hence high—commercial rate? The Court of Appeal's compromise suggestion can be found in *Housecroft* v. *Burnett*.[405] There the measure of the loss was said to be 'the proper and reasonable cost' of taking care of the plaintiff's needs. In practice this means the relative's lost earnings (where he or she is engaged in gainful employment), with the commercial rate applicable to such services serving as an upper limit. But where this 'caring' relative does not give up paid employment, the commercial rate will be inappropriate.[406]

Finally, in this context, section 5 of the Administration of Justice Act 1982 should be noted. This provides that any saving to the injured person which is the result of his being wholly or partly maintained at public expense in a hospital or nursing home or other institution should be set off against any income lost by him as a result of his injuries.

American, Canadian, and German courts have also been called to address a complicated variation of the *Donnelly* problem where what is in issue is not financial loss but physical injury sustained by the third party/volunteer in the interests of the 'primary' victim. Typically, in these cases a person has had a kidney negligently removed in hospital. Unfortunately (for everyone concerned) this 'primary' victim turns out to have one kidney only—apparently something that occurs in 1 out of 100 people—and thus is in need of an immediate transplant or else he will die. So a close relative (e.g. father/the benefactor) is asked and agrees to donate one of his kidneys in order to save the life of the 'primary' victim. Can the 'primary' victim claim for such harm suffered by the third party/volunteer? The fact that the volunteer's (relative's) loss was the result of his own, voluntary act can present legal difficulties; and the decision to donate an organ, coming after due deliberation, distinguishes these cases from the typical rescue cases (where the intervention is on the spur of the moment and unaccompanied by the certainty of hurt) which, otherwise, would

---

[402] Law Comm. No. 144 (1996), at para. 3.65. [403] [1994] 2 AC 350, at 363 (Lord Bridge).
[404] Loc. cit. [405] [1986] 1 All ER 332, at 343 per O'Connor LJ.
[406] *McCamley* v. *Cammell Laird Shipbuilders* [1990] 1 WLR 963, 966–7.

appear the closest legal concept which could be used as a starting-point in the reasoning process. Yet despite these difficulties, the Canadian and German courts have allowed for the compensation of the donors—a much better solution (it is submitted) than by channelling the claim through the child/primary victim.[407] It must be hoped that if, or rather when, such a case comes before our courts they will be willing to take note of the rich foreign case law on this topic.

(C) LOSS OF EARNINGS:[408] ACTUAL AND PROSPECTIVE

Where the actual loss of earnings can be proved, then, whatever the class of earnings in question, the plaintiff is entitled to recover them. So, damages may be awarded for loss of wages, loss of salary, and, in the case of professional men and women, loss of fees. Compensation may also be given for failure to realise other gains such as company profits[409] or prize money.[410] In *Moriarty* v. *McCarthy*[411] a 24-year-old woman was seriously injured in a car accident. The court took the view that as a result of the accident her chances of marriage were 'grossly reduced' and, in economic terms, that also meant a reduction in her 'chances of finding a man who is prepared to take her on and support her'. This was a perfectly legitimate heading of future economic loss that should be compensated by the courts—a result which subsequent decisions have effected in a somewhat odd manner.[412] In similar vein, a man who was disfigured and suffered a severe personality change which led to his abandonment by his wife, was awarded the costs of home help for the care of his children.[413]

Financial losses accruing down to the date of the trial are part of 'special damages' so they must be specifically pleaded and proved. Their calculation will normally cause little difficulty and they will be made by reference to the plaintiff's pre-accident earnings and the period of disability and proceed on the assumption that, but for the accident, the plaintiff would have continued to earn at the same rate. The assessment of general damages for the loss of future

---

[407] Thus, *Urbanski* v. *Patel* [1978] 84 DLR (3d) 650 (Canada); BGH JZ 1988, 150 (Germany) (English translation in Markesinis, *The German Law of Obligations, vol. II, The German Law of Torts* (3rd edn., 1997), 632; cf. *Sirianni* v. *Anna* 285 NYS (2d) 709 (1967); *Moore* v. *Shah* 458 NYS (2d) 33; *Ornelas* v. *Fry* 727 P.2d 810.

[408] In some cases the plaintiff may, despite his injury, retain his employment. His injuries, however, make it unlikely that he will be able to keep his job and in that case one often refers to a reduction (or loss) of his earning capacity. In *Moeliker* v. *A. Reyrolle Ltd.* [1977] 1 All ER 9, the court took the view that an award could be made under this heading where there was a real and substantial risk that the plaintiff would lose his job prematurely. The term 'loss of earning capacity' may also be more appropriate where the injured person is young and has no earnings yet—for instance *Joyce* v. *Yeomans* [1981] 1 WLR 549 and, most recently, *Dhaliwal* v. *Personal Representatives of Hunt* [1995] 4 PIQR Q56. However, in the subsequent case of *Foster* v. *Tyne and Wear CC* [1986] 1 All ER 567 the court took the view that loss of earning capacity was not really a heading of damages different to that of loss of future earnings. So no substantive point turns on the different terminology. The discussion in the text proceeds on this basis which, incidentally, was also shared by the Pearson Committee, Cmnd. 7054-1, para. 338.

[409] *Lee* v. *Sheard* [1956] 1 QB 192.   [410] *Mulvane* v. *Joseph* (1968) 112 SJ 927.

[411] [1978] 1 WLR 155, 161.

[412] I.e. by not reducing, as they would otherwise have done, the multiplier they would have used if the victim had been a man: see *Hughes* v. *McKeown* [1965] 1 WLR 963; *Housecroft* v. *Burnett* [1986] 1 All ER 332. A number of reasons, it is submitted not all very convincing, have been given for reducing the multiplier for female victims: *viz.* the likelihood of marriage, and the possibility of the woman giving up her work, at least for a period of time, in order to bring up children.

[413] *Oakley* v. *Walker* (1977) 121 SJ 619.

(prospective) earnings is, inevitably, less precise and fraught with difficulties to which we have already alluded.

These are largely due to the number of imponderables, such as: how long would the plaintiff live? How long would he continue working and at what rate? Would he be promoted to get a rise? Conversely, might he lose his job? What will the rate of inflation be in the future? Would there be any significant change in his personal tax status? Though actuarial techniques can be used to assist courts in their task and, apparently, 'figure more prominently [these days] in the evidence on which courts rely'[414] judges have shown a consistent preference[415] for the multiplicand and multiplier method.[416] This tries to discover so far as possible the net annual loss suffered by the victim (the 'multiplicand') and arrive at a figure for the award of lump-sum damages by applying to this a 'multiplier', which must reflect not only the predicted number of years for which the loss will last but also the elements of uncertainty contained in that prediction and the fact that the plaintiff will receive a lump sum immediately, which he is expected to invest. Two factors above all are liable to complicate this process: inflation and taxation. The trend of recent decisions has been strongly in the direction of ignoring the effects of both when computing damages awards.

The guiding principle is that the damages must be assessed on the basis that the total sum awarded will be exhausted at the end of the period contemplated and that during that period the plaintiff will be expected to draw upon both the income derived from the investment of the sum awarded *and* upon part of the capital itself. Any other calculation which did not require the simultaneous use of income plus capital would result in part of the capital remaining intact at the end of the contemplated period and, consequently, in over-compensation of the plaintiff. This method of calculation, however, also means that the chosen multiplier will be considerably less than the number of years taken as the period of the loss.

For many years the courts assumed that the lump sum would be invested in equities which, on average, yield a rate of return of around 4–5 per cent per annum, and reduced the multiplier accordingly. In *Wells* v. *Wells*[417] the House of Lords, in a decision which one expert commentator described as 'the most important decision in personal injury litigation since the Second World war',[418] overturned this approach. The former practice had been based on the assump-

---

[414] Per Lord Bridge in *Hunt* v. *Severs* [1994] 2 All ER 385 at 396.

[415] Thus in *Hunt* v. *Severs* [1994] 2 All ER 385 at 396, Lord Bridge stated: '. . . before a judge's assessment of the appropriate multiplier for future loss, which he has arrived at by the conventional method of assessment and which is not attacked as being wrong in principle, can properly be adjusted by an appellate court by reference to actuarial calculations, it is essential, in my judgment, that the particular calculation relied on should be precisely in point and should be seen as demonstrably giving a more accurate assessment than the figure used by the judge.'

[416] An excellent illustration of how this is used by judges can be found in Lord Pearson's judgment in *Taylor* v. *O'Connor* [1971] AC 115, 144.

[417] [1998] 3 WLR 329 (reversing the Court of Appeal [1997] 1 WLR 652).

[418] David Kemp, 'Damages for Personal Injury: a Sea Change', 114 (1998) *LQR* 571 and which the press of the time thought would bring an unprecedented increase in the level of awards (*The Times*, 17 July 1998).

tion that the victim should be taken to be in the same position as any other ordinary prudent investor. However, as Lord Lloyd explained:

Granted that a substantial proportion of equities is the best long-term investment for the ordinary prudent investor, the question is whether the same is true for these plaintiffs. The ordinary investor may be assumed to have enough to live on. He can meet his day-to-day requirements. If the equity market suffers a catastrophic fall, as it did in 1972, he has no immediate need to sell. He can abide his time and wait until the equity market recovers.

The plaintiffs are not in the same happy position. They are not 'ordinary' investors in the sense that they can wait for long-term recovery, remembering that it was not until 1989 that equity prices regained their old pre–1972 level in real terms. For they need the income, and a portion of the capital, every year to meet their current care.[419]

His Lordship concluded that it was more appropriate for the court to assume that the victim would invest most of the lump sum in index-linked government securities. These offer a guarantee of protection against future inflation but, in part because of this protection against inflation, also offer a lower rate of return than equities. On this basis, the multiplier should be calculated on the assumption of a rate of return of 3 per cent per annum instead of the hitherto 4 or 4.5 per cent, a change which is almost certainly likely to lead to an inflation in the size of awards. Section 1 of the Damages Act 1996 confers a power upon the Lord Chancellor to set by order the expected rate of return which the courts should follow in such cases, in the interests of achieving greater certainty and consistency of practice; however, at the time of writing the power has not been exercised.

The multiplier will also be affected by the age of the victim at the time of the tort. Clearly, the older the victim the smaller the multiplier, the younger the victim the greater the multiplier. In practice it will rarely exceed the figure 16, with a maximum of 18.[420] It is equally obvious that this method of calculation, despite the tendency to itemise awards, will in the end only lead to approximate compensation for future pecuniary loss. In fact, the number of imponderables in the calculation makes it likely that, the longer the period of the expected future loss, the less adequate the damages. Of the many imponderables, inflation is probably most to blame though in these days of reduced inflation levels this is not likely to be as great a concern as it was in the late 1970s.

Economists and politicians are not alone in having to tackle this problem. A system of periodic and index-linked payments would avoid many of the difficulties which lawyers have to face. But, as stated, periodic payments have their own problems and, in any event, are not likely to take over our present lump-sum system. Unfortunately, once the lump sum is fixed it becomes immutable apart from the exception, already discussed, of section 6 of the Administration of Justice Act 1982. Inflation can thus eat into the award as it does with everything else, and the victim's or his dependants' ability to resist it or make alternative provisions will, almost by definition, be even more restricted than the victim's ability before the accident to counterbalance its effects. With this in

---

[419] [1998] 3 WLR 329, at 335.   [420] *Graham v. Dodds* [1983] 1 WLR 808, 816 ff.

mind Lord Reid in *Taylor* v. *O'Connor*[421] argued that it would be useless and wrong to try to ignore the problem of inflation. To do so would be only on the basis that a return to a period of stable inflation was imminent (which, only now, seems *likely* to happen); or due to an inability to recognise the possibility of a change for the worse. Recognising the effects of inflation could, according to this school of thought, be reflected in an increased multiplier and, therefore, a larger award. But the House of Lords was not unanimous on this point. There was also another school of thought, which as early as 1968 had found in Lord Diplock a powerful advocate. Admittedly, at that time inflation was at single figures and thus the problem was less pressing. But Lord Diplock's basic assumption, that inflation could not be isolated from other factors which may falsify predictions, was sound enough. Incomes policy, tax rates, and the structure of interest rates were also susceptible to changes and these changes, too, could falsify the general predictions on which the assessment of damages was based. Besides, inflation affected everyone and many felt that plaintiffs cannot find themselves in a class that is shielded from the effect of inflation with which their fellow citizens have to battle. The lines were thus drawn and for the next six or seven years the picture became obscured.[422]

What could be termed the 'Diplock approach' finally prevailed. The courts' justification and the means they have suggested to minimise the effects of inflation were carefully considered in *Cookson* v. *Knowles*[423] and *Lim* v. *Camden & Islington Area Health Authority*.[424]

It is now clear that inflation beyond the date of the trial is not taken into account when determining the multiplicand. In *Cookson* v. *Knowles* the Court of Appeal held, and the House of Lords subsequently agreed, that for the purposes of calculating the dependency in fatal accident cases, as well as for the purposes of calculating loss of earnings in non-fatal cases, the loss should be divided into two parts, the first from the date of the death (or injury) to the date of trial, and the second from the date of trial into the future. In determining the rate of earnings of the deceased (or plaintiff) for the assessment of the first part of the loss, any increase in earnings due to inflation, which he would have received but for the death (or injury), should be taken into account. So, if a plaintiff was earning the net sum of £3,000 per annum at the time of his death (or injury) in, say, 1970, and if at the time of trial, say in 1975, he would have had net earnings (but for his death or injury) of £5,000, then the average between these two figures should be used as the multiplicand for this period (accident to trial). So, this part of the award could incorporate without much guessing the changes that would have taken place during this period, including changes in earnings and inflation. As to the second part of the loss, i.e. from the trial onwards, this should be assessed on the basis of the assumed rate of earnings at the time of

---

[421] [1971] AC 115.

[422] See *Mitchell* v. *Mulholland (No. 2)* [1972] 1 QB 65; *Young* v. *Percival* [1975] 1 WLR 17; *Moriarty* v. *McCarthy* [1978] 1 WLR 155.

[423] [1977] QB 913, approved by the House of Lords in [1979] AC 556.

[424] [1980] AC 174 and reiterated more recently by the Court of Appeal in *Auty* v. *National Coal Board* [1985] 1 WLR 784.

the trial (in our example, £5,000), with no addition for further inflationary increases in the future.

Nor will the multiplier, which in personal-injury cases is calculated at the time of the trial,[425] normally be increased to take into account the possible future effects of inflation. Although experience has shown that the effects of inflation cannot always be offset by investment in equities or growth stocks, a high rate of interest is obtainable by investment in fixed-interest-bearing securities; and by using multipliers suitable to a period of stable currency, inflation is taken care of in a rough-and-ready way by the higher rates of interest which are obtainable as one of its own consequences.[426]

In *Lim* v. *Camden & Islington Area Health Authority*[427] the judge at first instance was given evidence that the plaintiff would be subject to substantial taxation and took the view that this was a proper case to try to protect her against inflation. The Court of Appeal, having seen the earlier speeches in the House of Lords, accepted this increase of the multiplier as a proper case to be included in the exceptional circumstances envisaged by Lord Fraser. In the House of Lords Lord Scarman took a similar line when he said:[428] 'The law appears to be now settled that only in exceptional cases, where justice can be shown to require it, will the risk of future inflation be brought into account in the assessment of damages for future loss.' He concluded as follows:[429]

The correct approach should be, therefore, in the first place to assess damages without regard to the risk of future inflation. If it can be demonstrated that, upon the particular facts of a case, such an assessment would not result in a fair compensation . . . some increase is permissible. But the victims of tort who receive a lump sum award are entitled to no better protection against inflation than others who have to rely on capital for their future support. To attempt such protection would be to put them into a privileged position at the expense of the tortfeasor, and so impose upon him an excessive burden, which might go far beyond compensation for loss.

As far as taxation is concerned, when calculating the multiplicand the court will look to the net annual earnings of the plaintiff, i.e. the figure arrived at after making a deduction for the tax that he would have paid. This rule was clearly established by the House of Lords in *British Transport Commission* v. *Gourley*.[430] In *Gourley*'s case the injured plaintiff was a high earner who, but for the accident, would have had annual earnings of £37,000. Had he earned this sum he would have paid tax and in the end, he would have been left with £3,000 net. The House of Lords reasoned that if the full sum had been paid it would not have attracted tax in the plaintiff's hands, as damages for personal

---

[425] *Pritchard* v. *J. H. Cobden* [1987] 1 All ER 300. Note, however, that in fatal-accident cases the appropriate multiplier is selected at the date of death. See Lord Fraser in *Cookson* v. *Knowles* [1979] AC 556; *Graham* v. *Dodds* [1983] 1 WLR 808.

[426] See Lord Fraser in *Cookson* v. *Knowles* [1979] AC 556, 577.   [427] [1980] AC 174.

[428] Ibid., 193.   [429] Ibid., 193–4.

[430] [1956] AC 185. Deductions from gross earnings are also made for social security contributions (*Cooper* v. *Firth Brown Ltd.* [1963] 1 WLR 418) and for occupational pension contributions (*Dews* v. *National Coal Board* [1987] 2 All ER 545). *Gourley* was distinguished in *Deeny* v. *Gooda Walker Ltd.* (*in liquidation*) (*No. 2*) [1996] 1 WLR 426, HL, on the grounds that the damages in this case, which were awarded to Lloyd's Names, would be taxable under Schedule D.

injury are not taxable. The plaintiff, it was argued, would thus be left substantially better off than if he had received this sum as earnings. The purpose of the tort action being compensation rather than the enrichment of the plaintiff, the House of Lords felt that the award for lost earnings should be reduced to the net loss. The *Gourley* case is consistent with the principle that the plaintiff should not be over-compensated; however, it is open to attack on a variety of grounds.

In the first place, it might be argued that future rates of income taxation cannot be predicted with any greater confidence than the likely future effects of inflation. The result of *Gourley* is to project into the future the rate that happens to prevail at the time of the trial; according to what subsequently happens, the plaintiff may be under- or over-compensated as the case may be. Secondly, the *Gourley* case may result in double taxation of the plaintiff. As Lord Oliver explained in *Hodgson* v. *Trapp*,[431] if the plaintiff invests the damages award as he is meant to do, he will pay standard rate tax on the investment proceeds, 'so that it may fairly be said that the plaintiff suffers tax twice, first by having the notional tax deducted from his earnings for the purpose of computing the award and then again by suffering the actual tax which is deducted from the income earned by the award'. One answer to this is that in setting the multiplier, the courts normally assume a rate of return on the invested award which is net of standard rate tax.[432] But this merely compounds one complicating factor with another and requires the court to make a difficult and perhaps artificial calculation, when it might be more straightforward to take the view that the one form of taxation will largely offset the other, and ignore the effects of both. A further criticism is that *Gourley* results in a fiscal subsidy to tortfeasors, which is reflected in lower insurance premiums. In the light of this it has been suggested that the question of damages and taxation is best dealt with not by the law of tort but by taxation law, and that the courts are in effect undermining Parliament's decision to make a damages award itself non-taxable. The *Gourley* deduction means that the benefits of taxation go to the tortfeasor and not the plaintiff, as Parliament must have intended.[433] Despite these criticisms the *Gourley* rule is now probably too well entrenched to be reversed by the courts.

In *Hodgson* v. *Trapp*[434] the House of Lords rejected an argument that in certain circumstances the multiplier should be increased to make up for the likely incidence of higher rate income tax on the proceeds derived from investment of the damages award. Although Lord Oliver left open the possibility of making allowance for high rates of future taxation in exceptional cases, his judgment suggests that such cases will be rare. The trial judge had arrived at a multiplier of eleven years in respect of lost earnings and one of twelve for future nursing costs; in each case he then added a further year to make up for the likely effects of higher rate tax. In rejecting this approach Lord Oliver argued that:[435]

---

[431] [1989] AC 807, 828.
[432] *Thomas* v. *Wignall* [1987] QB 1098, 1112, per Lloyd LJ; Burrows (1989) 105 *LQR* 366, 370.
[433] Bishop and Kay, 'Taxation and Damages: The Rule in Gourley's Case' (1987) 103 *LQR* 211.
[434] [1989] AC 807, overruling *Thomas* v. *Signall* [1987] QB 1098.   [435] [1980] AC 807, 834.

The system of multipliers and multiplicands conventionally employed in the assessment takes account of a variety of factors, none of which is or, indeed, is capable of being worked out scientifically, but which are catered for by allowing a reasonably generous margin in the assumed rate of interest on which the multiplier is based. There is, in my judgment, no self-evident justification for singling out this particular factor and making for it an allowance which is not to be made for the equally imponderable factor of inflation.

These dicta make the *Gourley* rule seem even more anomalous; after all, the effect of that is precisely to make special provision for the (uncertain) effects of future taxation when computing the multiplicand.

(D) REDUCTION OF EXPECTATION OF LIFE

There may be instances where the plaintiff's injuries are such that he can no longer expect to survive for the span of his pre-accident anticipated working life. In that case, will the plaintiff's 'lost years' be taken into account when calculating his damages for lost future earnings? In 1962 the Court of Appeal in *Oliver* v. *Ashman*[436] unanimously held that damages for future loss of earnings could be awarded only in respect of the period during which it was anticipated that the plaintiff would survive his accident; nothing was thus recoverable for the 'lost years'. The decision was seriously criticised,[437] yet the result on the facts was not, it is submitted, wrong. For there the plaintiff who was claiming compensation, about two years old at the time of the accident and not quite five at the time of the trial, would normally have lived until the age of sixty-six, but was now expected to die at around thirty-six. He claimed what he would have earned during the thirty years of which the defendant had deprived him, but his claim was rejected. As stated, on these facts, the decision was right. For it is ludicrous to award a child the money he might have *saved* sixty years later. And we are talking of the money he might have saved and not the money he would have used for his living expenses since, *ex hypothesi*, there would be none during the 'lost years'. Furthermore, the same rule operates correctly in the case of an adult without dependants. For surely if we replaced his lost earnings by an annuity, which would cease on his death, we would not increase its annual amount on the ground that his earning life has been shortened. Not to apply the rule in *Oliver* v. *Ashman* to the adult without dependants would really give him more to spend than he would have earned during the spending period of his life. Alternatively, it would swell the bonus which his estate would confer on persons financially unharmed by his death. Though *Oliver* v. *Ashman* produced no injustice in the case of a child or adult *without dependants*, it operated harshly in the case of a victim with dependants, who was kept alive for long enough to deprive his dependants of their dependency. For, as we shall see,[438] under the Fatal Accidents Acts they cannot sue if the victim's action has been satisfied, settled, or statute-barred; and he, as a result of *Oliver* v. *Ashman*, could

---

[436] [1962] 2 QB 210.
[437] But also defended by Weir (see below, Select Bibliography), 15–16. On the whole question of lost years, see Fleming in 50 *Cal. LR* 598 (1962).
[438] Below, Section 8.

not claim (while still alive) for his lost years and then pass on these sums to his dependants via his estate.[439] The pressure to change the law thus grew and various ways were proposed to achieve this end. In the event the House of Lords in *Pickett* v. *British Rail Engineering Ltd.*[440] overruled *Oliver* v. *Ashman* and allowed a *living* plaintiff to recover the value of his lost earnings during his lost years, minus his living and other expenses during that period.[441] This right, however, is now limited to living plaintiffs and does not survive under the Law Reform Act 1934 for the benefit of his estate.[442]

7. Non-Pecuniary Losses

We now come to the kinds of damages that are particularly vague and difficult to quantify. There is also some controversy as to what function these damages aim to achieve and whether, as in some states in the United Sates, they should be subject to 'caps', i.e. upper limits. Moreover, though different headings do exist, and we shall try to present the law under them, it is evident that clear distinctions between them cannot be maintained. It is thus not always easy to keep strictly separate headings such as pain and suffering and loss of amenities, which is why one must always guard against the risk of 'double compensation'. These definitional overlaps have also been one reason why the various legislative proposals for reform have not, in the case of non-pecuniary damages, recommended the type of elaborate itemisation which they felt was necessary in the case of damages for pecuniary losses.

(A) PAIN AND SUFFERING

A plaintiff is entitled to recover for his pain and suffering—the two terms have never been clearly distinguished by the courts—actual and prospective, resulting from the tortfeasor's conduct or from medical or surgical treatment made necessary as a result of the tortious conduct. This will include his nervous shock[443] and any other recognised psychiatric symptoms,[444] but not sorrow or grief.[445] The point was affirmed in *Hinz* v. *Berry*;[446] but, in practice, the distinction is not always easy to draw, leaving room for some creative advocacy (and

---

[439] *Murray* v. *Shuter* [1976] QB 972 is a case which reveals the potential injustice of the rule and the measures the courts had to take to avoid it.

[440] [1980] AC 136.

[441] For judicial elaborations on the meaning of 'living expenses' and the problems this may give rise to in the context of the interrelationship between the Fatal Accident Act and the Law Reform Act, see *Benson* v. *Biggs Wall & Co. Ltd.* [1983] 1 WLR 72, 75 ff.; *Harris* v. *Empress Motors Ltd.* [1983] 1 WLR 65; *Clay* v. *Pooler* [1982] 3 All ER 570.

[442] S. 4, Administration of Justice Act 1982, overruling *Gammell* v. *Wilson* [1982] AC 27, where the House of Lords had reluctantly decided that a claim for the income which would have accrued to the plaintiff during the 'lost years' survived for the benefit of his estate. This led to potential double compensation as explained and criticised by Markesinis and Tettenborn in (1981) 131 *New LJ* 869. Happily, all these complications now belong to history.

[443] E.g. *Hinz* v. *Berry* [1970] 2 QB 40.

[444] Such as 'compensation neurosis'. See, *James* v. *Woodall Duckham Construction Co. Ltd.* [1969] 1 WLR 903.

[445] Though sometimes the courts can ingeniously link the two and provide some (monetary) solace to the plaintiff. See *Kralj* v. *McGrath* [1986] 1 All ER 54 and contrast *Kerby* v. *Redbridge Health Authority* [1994] PIQR Q1.

[446] [1970] 2 QB 40.

judgments). No award for this type of damage is, however, made if the plaintiff is permanently unconscious and thus not in any pain.[447] Despite some earlier doubts it is now accepted that the plaintiff's economic and social position is irrelevant as far as this heading of damages is concerned.[448] Nor may damages for pain and suffering be awarded in a case where death occurs instantaneously.[449]

(B) Loss of Amenities

If the plaintiff's injuries deprive him of the capacity to engage in sport or other pastimes, which he enjoyed before his injury, then this must be compensated. Other losses compensated under this heading include: impairment of one of the five senses;[450] sexual life;[451] diminution of marriage prospects (an item which is additional to the pecuniary loss that may result from such an event); destroyed holiday;[452] inability to play with one's children;[453] and many others.

Until fairly recently, it was uncertain whether this head of damage was separate from or merely part of any award for pain and suffering. In other words, what was unclear was whether the damages are awarded in respect of the *objective loss of amenities*, or in respect of the subjective mental suffering which comes with the appreciation of such loss. In *Wise* v. *Kaye*[454] the plaintiff was rendered immediately unconscious and remained so at the time of the trial three-and-a-half years later. Though she had suffered an almost complete loss of her faculties, she had no knowledge whatever of this loss. For Diplock LJ this was a good reason for awarding her a comparatively small sum under this heading. However, the majority of the Court of Appeal thought otherwise, and two years later in *West* v. *Shephard*[455] the House of Lords agreed with this view. As Lord Morris put it, the fact of unconsciousness

is . . . relevant in respect of and will eliminate those heads or elements of damage which can exist only by being felt or thought or experienced. The fact of unconsciousness does not, however, eliminate the actuality of the deprivation of the ordinary experiences and amenities of life which may be the inevitable result of some physical injury.

This majority view was reaffirmed in *Lim* v. *Camden Health Authority*,[456] where Lord Scarman said that the cases

draw a clear distinction between damages for pain and suffering and damages for loss of amenities. The former depend upon the plaintiff's personal awareness of pain, her capacity for suffering. But the latter are awarded for the fact of deprivation—a substantial loss, whether the plaintiff is aware of it or not.

[447] *Wise* v. *Kaye* [1962] 1 QB 638. This is so even if the result of lack of consciousness or pain is due to drugs or anaesthetics: *West* v. *Shephard* [1964] AC 326. The greater availability of pain-killing drugs may well reduce further these awards and, perhaps, lead the courts into making larger awards under the heading of loss of amenity.
[448] *Fletcher* v. *Autocar and Transporters* [1968] 2 QB 322, 340–1 (per Diplock LJ) and 364 (per Salmon LJ).
[449] See *Hicks* v. *Chief Constable of South Yorkshire* [1992] 2 All ER 65.
[450] E.g. taste and smell: *Cook* v. *J. L. Kier and Co.* [1970] 1 WLR 774.   [451] Ibid.
[452] *Ichard* v. *Frangoulis* [1977] 1 WLR 556.   [453] *Hoffman* v. *Sofaer* [1982] 1 WLR 1350.
[454] [1962] 1 QB 638.
[455] [1964] AC 326. The vigorous dissents of Lords Reid and Devlin repay careful study.
[456] [1980] AC 174.

Nevertheless, his judgment leaves one with the impression that an important reason for accepting this view was his desire not to disturb what had become an established rule, since it has influenced both judicial awards and extra-judicial settlements for many years.[457]

(c) Damages for Bereavement

When the plaintiff's life expectancy is reduced by an injury and this causes him mental suffering this will be taken into account when assessing his damages for pain and suffering and loss of amenity. This was always so and is now embodied in section 1(*b*) of the Administration of Justice Act 1982. In 1935, however, the Court of Appeal in *Flint* v. *Lovell*[458] held that there existed an independent heading of damages for loss of expectation of life, and the House of Lords, two years later in *Rose* v. *Ford*,[459] held that this right also survived for the benefit of the deceased's estate. Four years later, however, the House of Lords, in a judgment[460] that often touched on the metaphysical, decided that the sums to be awarded under this heading should be modest conventional figures.[461] As the Pearson Committee observed, such damages were of little significance for living plaintiffs, for where the injuries were serious enough to reduce life expectancy these damages formed only a small part of the total award. In the case of death the only real function these damages performed was to give the parents of young children killed in accidents a small sum which they would otherwise not have obtained under the Fatal Accidents legislation.[462]

Loss of expectation of life was abolished by section 1(*a*) of the Administration of Justice Act 1982, and was replaced by a new claim, 'bereavement', which gives a fixed sum by way of damages to a spouse for the loss of the other spouse and to parents for the loss of a child. The amount was fixed by the Act at £3,500, but is capable of being increased by order. Since April 1991 the figure has been £7,500.

---

[457] [1980] AC 189. A second reason given was that this reform would be best effected by means of comprehensive legislation. Other jurisdictions have not adopted this rule; and the Pearson Committee recommended its abolition: Cmnd. 7054–1, vol. i, para. 398. The highest awards for pain and suffering and loss of amenities are around the £100,000 mark; £95,000 was, for instance, awarded in *Brightman* v. *Johnson* (quoted by Kemp and Kemp, *The Quantum of Damages*, vol. 2, para. 1–010) whereas in *Housecroft* v. *Burnett* [1986] 1 All ER 332, O'Connor LJ thought £75,000 was an appropriate guideline for the average incident of tetraplegia. Faced with similar (and, often, much larger) awards, various systems (e.g. Canada, Eire, and a number of jurisdictions in the USA) have opted for judicially or legislative imposed maxima for non-pecuniary losses. The idea has much to commend it—especially in the case of unconscious plaintiffs (who still receive substantial awards for loss of amenities). On the other hand, see Law Commission Report No. 225, *Personal Injury Compensation: How Much is Enough?* (1994) (suggesting that the current levels may be insufficient).

[458] [1935] 1 KB 354.   [459] [1937] AC 826.   [460] *Benham* v. *Gambling* [1941] AC 157.

[461] By 1982, when this heading of damages was abolished, the sum was about £1,250.

[462] This is because soon after the first Fatal Accidents Act in 1846 the court held in *Blake* v. *The Midland Railway Co.* (1852) 18 QB 93; 118 ER 35, that only financial loss (and not bereavement) was compensatable under the new statute. In the case of the death of a young child, therefore, its parents could recover nothing. Since it could not earn anything its 'value' to its parents was 'nil'. Like Oscar Wilde's cynic, English law knew the 'price' of everything but the 'value' of nothing. Through the medium of damages for loss of expectation of life 'the meanness of refusing parents damages for their grief was neutralized by the absurdity of giving the dead child a claim for being killed' (Weir, op. cit. (Select Bibliography), 12).

As the Parliamentary debates show, the acceptance of this new right raises many problems, philosophical as well as legal. In the first place, the very principle of paying a sum for bereavement is doubtful. As the Lord Chancellor put it: 'there is no sum of money at all that one can nominate which is not an insult to the bereaved person, whether it is £10 million or £10.' Having said this, he also accepted that others, perhaps the majority, might think otherwise, hence his willingness to propose this heading. But the sum should, he felt, be fixed. It would be unattractive, if not invidious, for courts to have to calculate a person's grief in money terms. This may explain why the sum is a conventional one, but it does not explain why a similar right was not given to children for the loss of one or both parents. Awards by way of *solatium* are disapproved of by many lawyers, but to award them in one case and not in another will only strengthen the belief that these awards are arbitrary, and therefore objectionable on this score as well. The Lord Chancellor's reason for denying children damages for the loss of a parent was more technical. He felt that a minor child's dependency damages would already be substantial and the bereavement damages would add little or nothing. Certainly, as we shall see, courts are conscious of the problem involved here, and have in recent years tried to increase dependency damages by awarding children something more than just the cost of hiring 'substitute service'. It is therefore tempting to suggest that bereavement damages should have been either avoided altogether or awarded to both these types of claimants.

(D) Damages for the Injury Itself

Finally, the injury itself will also be compensated. In the more serious cases of injury, the injury and its consequences will not be easily distinguished and the sums awarded under the injury heading will cover both these items. There may, however, be minor injuries, for example the loss of a toe, which may leave no residual disability and cause no loss of amenity. The award of a minimum sum for pain and suffering may here be inadequate and an additional sum may be called for. A slight disfigurement, particularly in the case of a woman, may also affect such things as her chance of marriage, and, once again, the courts may make appropriate awards.

8. Death in Relation to Tort

(A) Survival of Causes of Action

The death of a person can have effects on tortious liability in two ways: (*a*) it may affect an existing right of action or liability, or (*b*) it can create a new liability towards the dependants of the victim. In this section we are concerned with the former, i.e. transmissibility of the cause of action after death.

If a tort has been committed and the plaintiff or the defendant dies, does the action survive? At common law personal actions died with the party, which was expressed in the maxim *actio personalis moritur cum persona*. The result was not altogether unfair, at any rate after 1846. For a right to sue was of little use to the dead victim. And since the Fatal Accidents Act of 1846, enacted as a result of increased numbers of deaths in the wake of the railway revolution, the victim's surviving spouse and children were given an *independent* right to sue for their lost dependency.[463] The railway revolution was itself overtaken by the car revolution, one consequence of which was that often the tortfeasor, too, was killed along with his victim. It therefore became necessary not only to provide for the victim's dependants, as the 1846 Act had done, but to make sure that this right survived against the estate of the tortfeasor. The Law Reform (Miscellaneous Provisions) Act of 1934 ensured that the tortfeasor's insurance[464] company *remained*[465] liable to the victim's dependants. Having removed half of the common-law rule, and having thereby made the tortfeasor's liability transmissible to his estate, the Act went on to remove the rest of the common-law rule and allowed the deceased victim's estate to carry on his action. The only exception relates, as we have noted, to the tort of defamation, where the cause of action dies with either the injured person or the wrongdoer (s. 1(1)). The disappearance of the cause of action with the death of the *defamed* person is understandable once it is accepted that the tort action in defamation *primarily* protects a non-pecuniary interest (the defamed person's reputation). But the 1934 legislator seems to have been carried away in his reforming zeal and, it is submitted, unconsciously and wrongly excluded the reverse right: the living victim's right to claim against the *defamer's* estate.

Where the prospective defendant (wrongdoer) dies, the normal rules apply to the measure of damages, and the ordinary periods of limitation also apply by virtue of section 1 of the Proceedings against Estates Act 1970. Where the prospective plaintiff (wronged person) dies, the damages recovered for the benefit of the deceased's estate will include all the normal headings discussed above, except that exemplary damages cannot be recovered for the benefit of the deceased's estate even if he himself would have been entitled to them.[466] On the other hand, funeral expenses, which of course would not have been recoverable had the victim lived, are recoverable by the estate.[467] Though section 1(2)(c) of the 1934 Act does not expressly state this, the case law clearly implies that only reasonable funeral expenses will be allowed.[468]

It should also be noted that according to section 1(2)(c) of the 1934 Act damages recoverable for the benefit of the estate should be calculated without reference to any loss or gain to the estate consequent on his death. The kind of

---

[463] The law, in force until then, was embodied in the rule of *Baker* v. *Bolton* (1808) 1 Camp. 493; 170 ER 1033.

[464] Compulsory third-party insurance for road accidents was introduced in 1930. If the 1934 Act had not been passed the victim's insurers would have earned an undeserved windfall.

[465] S. 1(1). So *vested* rights against the tortfeasor *survived* against his estate. S. 1(4), however, also created one exception: if the tortfeasor died at the same time as his victim, the right of action is 'deemed' to have subsisted before the death and thus the victim can still sue the tortfeasor's estate.

[466] S. 1(2)(a).

[467] S. 1(2)(c). Since *Morgan* v. *Scoulding* [1938] 1 KB 786, it has been accepted that the cause of action is completed by the injuries and is vested in the deceased at the moment of the death. In practice this means that in such cases the estate will be able to claim only the funeral expenses. If there is an interval between accident and death, then the estate will be able to claim all pecuniary and (appropriate) non-pecuniary items of damage for that period.

[468] See e.g. *Hart* v. *Griffiths-Jones* [1948] 2 All ER 729 and *Gammell* v. *Wilson* [1982] AC 27 where it was suggested that the cost of a headstone is allowable but the cost of a memorial monument is not.

typical gain that could ensue would come from the proceeds of an insurance policy and these amounts will thus not be taken into account when calculating the amount of damages. The same goes for losses consequent upon death. Thus, if the deceased was a tenant for life of a valuable property the loss of the life interest would be excluded from any calculation of damages awarded to his estate. Similarly, this provision would exclude the loss of an annuity ceasing on death. On the other hand, section 1(5) of the Act states that the rights conferred by it are in addition to and not in derogation of any rights conferred by the Fatal Accidents Act which, as we shall see, provides a remedy where death is caused by the wrongful act, neglect, or default of another person.

(B) DEATH AS CREATING A CAUSE OF ACTION

(i) Introduction   The rule in *Baker* v. *Bolton*[469] denied any claim by the dependants of the deceased victim of a tort. As already stated, this rule was altered in 1846 by the Fatal Accidents Act, which granted a remedy mainly to widows and orphans.[470] In the years that followed, subsequent Acts and decisions widened the categories of possible claimants.[471] The law, consolidated in the Fatal Accidents Act of 1976, was again substantially amended by the Administration of Justice Act 1982. Section 1(1) runs:

If death is caused by any wrongful act, neglect or default which is such as would (if death had not ensued) have entitled the person injured to maintain an action and recover damages in respect thereof, the person who would have been liable if death had not ensued shall be liable to an action for damages, notwithstanding the death of the person injured.

A hypothetical question has to be asked: at the time of his death could the deceased have maintained action against the tortfeasor? If he could not, because either the action had been statute-barred,[472] or there had been accord and satisfaction,[473] or there had been judgment,[474] then the dependants cannot bring an action either. If the deceased could have brought an action himself then, and only then, does the cause of action come into existence. In *Pigney* v. *Pointer's Transport Services Ltd.*[475] the deceased committed suicide while in a condition of acute neurotic depression induced by the accident. It was held that in the circumstances his death did not amount to a *novus actus* and thus his widow

---

[469] (1808) 1 Camp. 493; 170 ER 1033, reinforced in a different context in *Admiralty Commissioners* v. *SS America* [1917] AC 38.

[470] The full list of possible claimants, given in ss. 2 and 5, included wives, husbands, parents, grandparents, step-parents, children, grandchildren, and stepchildren.

[471] Further extensions took place in 1934, 1959, and 1982. McGregor (see below, Select Bibliography), 971, rightly draws attention to the more liberal position that prevails in France, Belgium, Switzerland, and the Scandinavian countries where elaborate lists are replaced by the requirement that a relationship of dependency upon the deceased be shown and concludes that these systems have experienced no real difficulties in 'casting the ambit of recovery as widely as this and dispensing with lists'. Some judicial support for this now appears in *Shepherd* v. *The Post Office, The Times*, 15 June 1995. The statement, however, was made in the context of cohabitees, discussed below, and was probably not intended to be as broad as Dr McGregor's.

[472] *Williams* v. *Mersey Docks* [1905] 1 KB 804.

[473] *Read* v. *The Great Eastern Railway Co.* (1868) LR 3 QB 555.

[474] *Murray* v. *Shuter* [1972] 1 Lloyd's Rep. 6.   [475] [1957] 1 WLR 1121.

was successful in her action. The date of the decision is important because it is clear that it was decided under the influence of the *Re Polemis* rule.[476] Whether the same result would nowadays be reached under the *Wagon Mound* rule has been doubted.[477] Whatever the answer, the case illustrates the role of causation under the Fatal Accidents Act and the Law Reform Act. For under the former, what had to be shown was that the defendant caused the death of the bread-winner, whereas under the latter, death is only a factor which makes a pre-existing action transmissible to the deceased's estate. In *Pigney*'s case, therefore, the point whether the suicide was a *novus actus* was relevant to the widow's claim under the Fatal Accidents Act, but was not relevant for the Law Reform Act claim of his own estate. For such claims, how the death has come about is irrelevant.[478] The only point one might arguably make is that it is against public policy to allow the deceased's estate to recover from an act of self-destruction. In *Beresford* v. *Royal Insurance Co.*[479] this point was successfully argued, and money due under a life-insurance policy was withheld when the death of the insured was caused by his own act. But *Beresford* and *Pigney* are distinguishable since liability to pay under a life-insurance policy is *created* by the death of the insured and *Beresford* held that it is against public policy for such liability to be *created* by an act of self-destruction; whereas in the claim under the Law Reform Act, Pigney's suicide did not create liability, but only made pre-existing liability *transmissible* to the estate.

Related to the above is the question of contributory negligence on the part of the *deceased*. Section 5 of the Fatal Accidents Act 1976 (as amended by s. 3(2) of the Administration of Justice Act 1982) decrees that:

where any person dies as the result partly of his own fault and partly of the fault of any other person or persons, and accordingly if an action were brought for the benefit of the estate under the Law Reform Act 1934 the damages recoverable would be reduced under section 1(1) of the Law Reform (Contributory Negligence) Act 1945, and damages recoverable in an action under this Act shall be reduced to a proportionate extent.

Dodds v. *Dodds*[480] clarified a related problem. The father was killed in a car accident caused not by his own negligence, but by that of his wife. An action was brought under the Fatal Accidents Acts with the wife and child as dependants and it was held that, though the widow herself had no claim, the child did, and that there should be no reduction of *his* award. The remedy given under the Acts is given to dependants *individually* and not as a group, and therefore each dependant is regarded as a separate plaintiff. However, it should be

---

[476] The result of this remarkable case must, surely, represent one of the high-water marks in the application of the *Polemis* rule; but it may also embody some sympathy on the part of the court for the plaintiff, and dependant of the victim of the original tort. While there is no evidence to support this view and, indeed, a subsequent case (see next note) has shown that such sympathy will not always be shown for dependants, the supposition advanced herein could be tested by asking what would have happened if Mr Pigney had tried unsuccessfully to kill himself and, in the process, increased his original injuries and the cost of their treatment. Would the court have still refused to treat the attempted suicide as a *novus actus* and made the original tortfeasor liable for such extra medical and other costs?

[477] *Farmer* v. *Rash* [1969] 1 WLR 160, which is post-*Wagon Mound (No. 1)*, went the other way, but in his short judgment the judge did not go into the problems of causation.

[478] Except with regard to the claim for funeral expenses.   [479] [1938] AC 586.

[480] [1978] QB 543.

made clear that the reduction or elimination of the dependant's claim in such circumstances is not the result of the Acts, but of his own contributory negligence.

This interrelationship of the dependant's claim with the possible action that the deceased could have brought should not conceal the fact that the cause of action given to the dependants is a completely new one. In Lord Blackburn's words,[481] it is 'new in its species, new in its quality, new in its principle, in every way new'.

(ii) Who Brings the Action   Although the right of action under the Acts exists for the benefit of the dependants, the action must be brought by and in the name of the executor or administrator. If, however, the executor or administrator does not bring the action six months after the death, or if there is no executor or administrator, all or any of the dependants may bring the action. Section 2 of the 1976 Act, which ordains the above, goes on to say in subsection 3 that not more than *one* action shall lie for and in respect of the same subject-matter or complaint, so there is no room for consideration of a dependant not named in the proceedings. Such a dependant may, therefore, apply before judgment to be brought into the proceedings. After judgment dependants excluded from the action have no claim against the dependant, though they may have some legal or equitable remedy against the representative. According to section 2B(3) of the Limitation Act 1975 the action must be brought within three years of the deceased's death (or, in certain cases, from the moment the dependants knew they had a cause of action). That is assuming, of course, that the deceased died possessed of this right of action. In principle, he will have lost his right of action if three years have lapsed from the moment the cause of action accrued or he acquired relevant knowledge, whichever is the later.

Section 1(2) stated that the action shall be for the benefit of the dependants of the deceased. This means that a person must a be a *dependant in law*, i.e. one included in the list given in section 1(3) of the 1976 Act, as amended by the Administration of Justice Act 1982, as well as a *dependant in fact*, a requirement discussed below. Dependants in law are the following: the wife or husband (or former wife or husband) of the deceased; *any* of his ascendants or descendants; any person *treated* by the deceased as his parent or child or other descendant; any person who is, or is the issue of, a brother, sister, uncle, or aunt of the deceased. Subsection 4 adds that, for the purposes of the previous subsection,

any relationship of affinity shall be treated as a relationship of consanguinity, any relationship of the half blood as a relationship of the whole blood, and the stepchild of any person as his child, and an illegitimate person shall be treated as the legitimate child of his mother and reputed father.

Adopted children are also entitled to claim following paragraph 3(1) of Schedule 1 to the Children Act 1975. The same is true of a child *en ventre sa mère* at the time of the injury but born after the death of the victim.[482]

---

[481] *The Vera Cruz* (1884), 10 App. Cas. 59, 70–1.   [482] *The George and Richard* (1871) LR 3 A. and E. 466.

This list now includes *all* ascendants (and not, as previously, only parents or grandparents) and former spouses, which, section 1(4) states, includes persons whose marriage with the deceased has been annulled or declared void, as well as those whose marriage with the deceased has been dissolved.

After some hesitation expressed in the debates in the House of Lords,[483] the Administration of Justice Act 1982, section 3, has enlarged the categories of dependants in law by including 'any person living with the deceased as husband (or wife)'. Most commonly this will refer to the deceased's partner,[484] who will now be given a Fatal Accident claim if the following (fairly stringent) requirements are satisfied. *First,* the plaintiff was living in the same household before the death, *secondly,* had been so living for at *least* two years before that date, and *thirdly* had been living during the whole[485] of that period *as* the husband or wife of the deceased. A more radical widening has been recommended by the Law Commission, which in its Consultation Paper on *Claims for Wrongful Death* suggested that 'the statutory list should be abolished and replaced by a test whereby any individual has a right of recovery who had a reasonable expectation of a non-business benefit from continuation of the deceased's life, or a test whereby any individual has a right of recovery who was or, but for the death, would have been dependent, wholly or partly, on the deceased'.[486]

A claimant need not only be a dependant in law, he must also be a dependant in fact, which means that he must have been financially dependent on the deceased. Thus, if no pecuniary dependency is proved, the defendant will succeed. Section 3(1) of the 1976 Act contains the basic rule. It states:[487] 'In the action such damages may be awarded as are proportioned to the injury resulting from the death to the dependants respectively.' No further statutory guidance as to the damages recoverable is given, save that a sum may be awarded for the funeral expenses of the deceased if they were in fact borne by the persons for whose benefit the action is brought (but see s. 3(4)). The Administration of Justice Act 1982 has now added a new section (1A) to the Fatal Accidents Act, creating a claim for damages for bereavement in favour of one spouse for the death of another, or parents for the death of a minor, unmarried child. The damages here are not at large but are fixed at £3,500, and are to be shared equally whenever the claim is made by both parents for the death of their child. Apart from the claim for bereavement, either the lost pecuniary advantage must have actually been derived from the deceased prior to his death or, alternatively, there must have been a reasonable expectation of pecu-

---

[483] *Hansard* (HL) 8 Mar. 1982, 42 ff.

[484] Mistress has been the most commonly used term to refer to the partner of a male breadwinner, but English law has experienced as much embarrassment with the terminology as it has with the institution. See Allot, *The Limits of the Law* (1980), ch. 8. The increase in the number of extra-marital cohabitations may alter such coy attitudes.

[485] Though see *Pounder* v. *London Underground Ltd.* [1995] PIQR P217 where it was held that in the context of a ten-year relationship a brief absence during the said two-year period did not affect the claim.

[486] Law Com. No. 148 (1997), para. 4.6.

[487] S. 3(2) provides that such damages shall be divided among the dependants in such shares as may be directed. This is an important power given to the court and likely to be exercised whenever there are doubts about the mother's ability to look after dependent children.

niary benefit as of right or otherwise.[488] Thus, in *Berry v. Humm*[489] a widower was held to have an expectation of pecuniary benefit from the continued performance of domestic services by his wife for which he would otherwise have to pay. In *Taff Vale Railway v. Jenkins*[490] the deceased was an intelligent girl of sixteen, who had almost completed her apprenticeship as a dressmaker. The jury's verdict was in favour of her parents, notwithstanding that she had not as yet earned anything and had so far conferred upon them no pecuniary benefit. There was a clear inference that she would have done so in the future and that was sufficient.

It is also essential to show that the benefit that the dependant has lost was derived from the familial relationship subsisting between the deceased and the dependant. In *Burgess v. Florence Nightingale Hospital for Gentlewomen*[491] a husband claimed in respect of his wife, who was also his professional dancing partner, but Devlin J held that, though he was entitled to recover damages for pecuniary loss due to the death of his wife, he could not recover for the loss of earnings caused from the interruption of the professional relationship.

The claim for bereavement has another aspect. What happens when a young child is deprived of the care of its parents, particularly its mother? The Administration of Justice Act 1982 has given no claim for bereavement in this case and the result appears harsh. The reason is that the dependency award for the child will usually be substantial. But in the past the courts have not felt so and have striven to find ways to increase children's dependency awards. One was by recognising that the services of a wife or mother have a pecuniary value for the loss of which damages may be recovered even if no actual expenditure is incurred in replacing them. In *Hay v. Hughes*,[492] for example, substantial damages were awarded under this head to two young boys whose parents had been killed, even though the boys' grandmother was looking after them and was prepared to continue doing so indefinitely without expecting any financial reward. The damages were, in fact, assessed on the basis of evidence of the cost of employing a nanny housekeeper. In *Mehmet v. Perry*[493] the children's health justified their father giving up his employment after the death of their mother, in

---

[488] The expected pecuniary benefit, however, must not result from crime: *Burns v. Edman* [1970] 2 QB 541. Will this result be applied to all types of immoral or illegal transactions?

[489] [1915] 1 KB 627.   [490] [1913] AC 1.

[491] [1955] 1 QB 349; cf. *Malyon v. Plummer* [1964] 1 QB 330.

[492] [1975] QB 790. In *Spittle* v. *Bunney* [1988] 1 WLR 847 the Court of Appeal watered down somewhat the effect of *Hay* v. *Hughes* by taking the view that in assessing damages for the loss of a mother's services the court should take into account the decreasing level of dependency as the child grew older and he became less in need of looking after. The court gave as an example the need to be taken to school which, after a certain age had been reached, would disappear. But though this type of commercial service may change, the emotional dependency might well increase. The courts' emphasis on the former aspect must surely be the result of their inability to fix a 'price' on the latter.

[493] [1977] 2 All ER 529. See also *Regan* v. *Williamson* [1976] 1 WLR 305 where the court spoke of a special 'qualitative factor', recognising the extra value of maternal (over nanny) care and justifying a modest increase in the award. In *Creswell* v. *Eaton* [1991] 1 WLR 1113, the deceased mother was employed prior to her death and so was only a 'part-time carer'. By contrast, the children's aunt, who commendably (in the opinion of the court) gave up her job in order to look after them, became a 'full-time carer'. Simon Brown J took the view (ibid., at 1121) that where 'a claim is based in large part upon a relative's actual loss of earning reasonably incurred, modest discount [in the instant case calculated at 15%] only should be made to reflect the part-time nature of the deceased mother's care'.

order to look after them. It was there held that his actual loss of wages, not the hypothetical cost of employing a housekeeper, provided the correct measure of damages payable.

K. v. JMP Co. Ltd.[494] presented a different and more acute problem. The children in that case were illegitimate, so their mother herself had no claim under the Fatal Accidents Act. Her union, however, with the deceased was very stable and he had looked after all of them in an exemplary manner, providing, *inter alia*, for their holiday expenses, etc. The Court of Appeal took the view that the children should be compensated not only for the amounts that the father spent on them (which were taken to include the rent, washing-machine instalments, and electricity bills), but also for any diminution in the value of their mother's services resulting from their father's death. Thus, though no award was made for the mother's loss, it was held that her expenses for holiday travel could be claimed since this was an item the father would have paid in order to enable his children to enjoy their holidays. By holding it to be a loss to the children it was thus held to be recoverable. These methods of increasing the dependency awards of minors must, on the whole, be encouraged in the interests of proper compensation; and they are likely to be continued by the courts in the face of Parliament's refusal to extend to them the new right of damages for bereavement.

(iii) The Assessment of the Award   The loss here being the loss of an expectation of a future *pecuniary*[495] advantage, it follows that in trying to calculate the award a court must take into account a number of imponderable factors referring both to the dependants and the deceased. As far as the former are concerned, the dependants' own expectation of life is a material factor. In the case of a widow, for example, this may be very material, and evidence of her own expectation of life as well as the state of her health will be admissible in court. If she has actually died before the trial the damages awarded to her estate must be for the period of her survival only and should not be calculated on the basis of her life expectancy as it was at the time of her husband's death.[496]

Remarriage raises problems of the assessment both of the widow's dependency and of that of her children. If the widow remarries and her new husband accepts her children as members of his household, he is under a legal obligation to support them. This means that their damages should not be calculated on the basis that they have lost the support of a father, but only so as to compensate them for the risk of loss in the future. Thus, in assessing the damages payable to a child for his father's death, the court is bound to take into account

---

[494] [1976] QB 85.

[495] Non-pecuniary losses—e.g. for mental suffering—were, despite the neutral wording of the 1846 Act, excluded almost from the start: see *Blake* v. *Midland Ry.* (1852) 18 QB 93. American jurisdictions, though they initially followed the English rule, have, in recent years, moved in a more liberal direction. Megaw J in *Perec* v. *Brown* (1964) 108 *SJ* 219, however, felt that this was not possible under the Fatal Accidents Act. The claim for bereavement thus is the only (statutory) exception.

[496] *Williamson* v. *Thornycroft* [1940] 2 KB 658. Likewise in the event of remarriage: *Lloyds Bank and Mellows* v. *Railway Executive* [1952] 1 TLR 1207; *Mead* v. *Clarke Chapman* [1956] 1 WLR 76. The same is true if remarriage has taken place after adjudication but before an appeal is heard: *Curwen* v. *James* [1963] 1 WLR 748. The wider implications of these cases are not affected by the 1971 Act.

the fact or the prospects of the mother's remarriage;[497] and the same is true when assessing the damages of a widower in respect of his wife's death. In 1971, however, the Law Reform (Miscellaneous Provisions) Act enacted that, in assessing the damages payable to a *widow* in respect of the death of her husband, 'there shall not be taken into account the remarriage of the widow or her prospect of remarriage', and this rule has now been embodied in section 3(2) of the 1976 Act. This reversal of the common-law rule (which conformed with the basic principle that damages under the Fatal Accidents Act were awarded for actual pecuniary loss) was accepted because women's organisations resented as much as judges the evaluation of the widow's remarriage prospects. However well-intentioned the reform may have been, it has none the less created an anomaly in the law in so far as it allows a widow who has actually remarried and who is supported by her second husband to receive damages for the continuing loss of support of the first husband; and it has also resulted in the second anomaly that claims of widows and widowers are no longer treated alike. Indeed, even a widow's prospects of remarriage must still be considered when the claims of the children are in issue. So, this basic anomaly should either be abolished or, perhaps, be extended to cover widowers and children as well.

In assessing the lost dependency, by far the most difficult part of the calculation is that referring to the deceased. The basic aim is to provide dependants with a sum of money that will afford them material benefits of the same standard and for the same period of time as would have been provided by the deceased had he not been killed. This means that the total value of the dependency must be assessed and a capital sum arrived at that will enable the dependants to spend each year, free of tax, a sum equal to the pre-accident dependency.

More specifically, the starting-point for the assessment of damages will be the amount of the dependency, which in straightforward situations will be ascertained by deducting from the earnings of the deceased the estimated amount of his own personal and living expenses. The deceased's earnings will be calculated not just on the basis of a single figure, but on the basis of all the surrounding circumstances, including the possibility of a variation in his rate of earnings. This approach, however, cannot be used where the pecuniary benefit was in kind rather than in money; where the deceased had not yet started to earn any money; and where the deceased was not the breadwinner of the family but, say, the wife. In these cases different and, perhaps, more speculative methods will be adopted, but here we shall restrict our comments to the most typical case, the death of the breadwinner.

Once the dependency figure is reached it will be capitalised by the application of an appropriate multiplier which, in fatal-accident cases unlike personal-injury cases will be determined at the time of the death.[498] This is for the court to fix on the basis of innumerable vague calculations connected with the likely duration of the dependency, the deceased's pre-accident life-expectancy, his rate of earnings, and so on. As in the case of the future lost earnings of a living

---

[497] *Thompson* v. *Price* [1973] QB 838.
[498] *Cookson* v. *Knowles* [1979] AC 556; *Graham* v. *Dodds* [1983] 1 WLR 808.

plaintiff, here too the multiplier must be such that the capital sum awarded, together with the income it generates, will be exhausted at the end of the period intended to be covered. The calculation is thus made on the assumption, not always supported in real life, that the dependants will spend each year part of the capital as well as the whole of the income which they receive from so much of the capital as remains. Once again, therefore, the multiplier will be considerably lower than the expected duration of the dependency.

The period of dependency, and thus the multiplier, must of course be reckoned from the date of the death. But in *Cookson* v. *Knowles*[499] the House of Lords introduced the following more precise method of calculation. In place of a single lump sum, the damages should be divided into two main parts, the first covering the loss to the dependants from the date of the death until the date of the trial, and the second their loss from the date of the trial for the future. The first part of the damages should be calculated like the special damages for loss of earnings in an action for personal injury and should be based on an average of the deceased's rate of earning as it was at his death and the rate as it would have been at the date of the trial. The second part of the damages should be based upon the latter rate, using as a multiplier a figure equivalent to the period of dependency as estimated at the date of the death, less the period which has already elapsed between the death and the trial.

(iv) Pecuniary Gains and Other Deductions and the Question of Duplication of Damages During the nineteenth century judges restricted the scope of the application of the fatal-accidents legislation in any way they could. One was by interpreting the word 'injury' to mean financial loss only; another was by insisting that the dependants should set against their award any pecuniary advantage accruing to them as a result of the death of the victim. Pensions and insurance moneys were the two most usual benefits received by dependants and, until the Fatal Accidents Act 1959, they had to be accounted for. The move away from that direction has since gained pace. The law now is in section 3(4) of the Fatal Accidents Act 1976, as amended by the Administration of Justice Act 1982, which states: 'In assessing damages in respect of a person's death in an action under this Act, benefits which have accrued or will or may accrue to any person from his estate or otherwise as a result of his death shall be disregarded.' Compensation payments made under the Fatal Accidents Act are also excluded from the statutory recoupment provisions of the Social Security (Recovery of Benefits) Act 1997.[500]

The formula adopted in the 1976 Act excludes from the assessment of damages all the pecuniary gains a dependant is likely to receive as a result of the death, including insurance money, return of premiums, gratuities, as well as all benefits from the estate which accrue to the dependants. Thus, in *Pidduck* v. *Eastern Scottish Omnibuses Ltd.*[501] the Court of Appeal held that a widow's allowance, which became payable to her upon her husband's death and which was a pension entitlement of his, should be disregarded from the assessment of

---

[499] [1979] AC 556, approved by the House of Lords in *Graham* v. *Dodds* [1983] 1 WLR 808, 815.
[500] See SI 1997/2205, reg. 2(2)(a).   [501] [1990] 1 WLR 993.

her lost dependency. The reason for this was section 4 which, in the words of one of the judges,[502] was meant 'to produce an exception to the common law rules for calculating quantum of damages, namely to prevent the deduction of a benefit which would otherwise have to be deducted in order to arrive at the true loss on a common law basis'. In the later case of *Stanley* v. *Saddique (Mohammed)*,[503] the same judge gave the word 'benefit' in section 4 a wider meaning. For in that case, one of the defendant's contentions was that section 4 excludes, for the purposes of assessing damages for lost dependency, only direct *pecuniary* benefits. In that case, however, the plaintiff had benefited from exceptional services from his stepmother, which he would not have received from his own (unreliable) mother. This, according to the defendants, was not a *pecuniary* benefit and should thus be taken into account and reduce his claim for lost dependency. The court, however, refused to adopt such a view and held that 'the benefits accruing to the plaintiff as a result of his absorption into the family unit consisting of his father and stepmother and sibling should be wholly disregarded for the purposes of assessing damages'.[504] On the other hand, it has been held that the adoption of an infant who has lost his parents in an accident will affect the quantification of his 'lost dependency'. So in *Watson* v. *Willmott*[505] Garland J held that *vis-à-vis* the deceased father, the infant's lost dependency would be worked out by awarding him the difference (if any) between the lost dependency of his (deceased) *natural* father minus his dependency on his *adoptive* father. *Vis-à-vis* the mother, the court took the view that the adoption replaced the non-pecuniary dependency on the deceased mother and thus the non-pecuniary dependency on the natural, deceased mother would be assessed only up to the date of the adoption.

The above would suggest that the wording of the Fatal Accidents Act 1976 may still give some grounds for doubt (and litigation); but the trend towards *not* deducting from awards made under the 1976 Act sums received as a result of the death is still continuing. This may, indirectly, lead towards over-compensation of plaintiffs; but to the extent that this is considered as a disadvantage *in the kind of circumstances that tend to be litigated under this heading* it is, arguably, counterbalanced by the simplification that it is bringing into the law.

9. Damage to Property

Generally speaking, property damage receives similar treatment to personal injuries, though assessment of loss in the former is easier when compared with the problems that arise in the latter. For exposition purposes it might be helpful to deal with loss (destruction) and damage separately adding, perhaps, that the bulk of the relevant case law comes from the area of negligence and is concerned mainly with damage or loss of ships and motor vehicles.

With regard to loss, the principal heads under which damages are awarded are found in *Liesbosch Dredger* v. *SS Edison*,[506] which was discussed earlier in

---

[502] Ibid., at 998, per Purchas LJ.
[503] [1991] 2 WLR 459 containing an excellent summary of the legislative history of s. 4.
[504] Ibid., at 468–9; cf. *Hayden* v. *Hayden* [1992] 1 WLR 986.   [505] [1990] 3 WLR 1103.
[506] [1933] AC 449; above, Chapter 2, Section 4(3)(c).

Chapter 2. These are the market value of the property (at the place and time of destruction); cost, if any, of transporting a substitute to the place in question; loss of profit to a foreseeable extent; and to these should be added loss of use before replacement or other expenses made necessary as a result of the tort.[507] With regard to the market value of the thing destroyed, the estimate is of loss, not the cost of restoration. In *Moss* v. *Christchurch Rural District Council*[508] the plaintiff's cottage, which was let, was destroyed by a spark from the defendant's steamroller. The measure of damages was the difference between his interest before and after the fire. Sometimes the loss is equivalent to the cost of restoration;[509] and it can also happen that loss exceeds the cost of restoration, as with the destruction of a historic mansion. The loss to a plaintiff who has only a limited interest in a thing is the value of his interest.[510] Loss of profit may be actual or estimated.[511] If the market value of the thing in question is calculated so as to include its profitable use, no further loss of profit is recoverable.[512]

Where property is damaged and not destroyed, the broad rule is that a plaintiff's loss is the reduction in its value. Where land has been damaged, its reduction in value has to be estimated according to the facts. If part of it has been severed, a distinction is drawn between the defendant's intentional and unintentional wrongdoing. If the severance was intentional, the plaintiff may choose between claiming in respect of the lessened value of his land or the value of the part severed.[513] If it was unintentional, only the lessened value is recoverable.[514]

When a chattel is damaged, the reduction in value is often the reasonable cost of repair.[515] Sometimes the depreciation in value of a thing because of the very fact that it has had to be repaired exceeds the cost of repair; in which case the plaintiff recovers his loss.[516] The cost of repair is normally calculated as at the time of the damage, except where the damage was not discoverable until later, or where it was reasonable for the plaintiff to have postponed repair.[517] Repair means reasonable repair, not meticulous restoration.[518] The cost of unreasonable repair is not recoverable, but it is not always easy to determine what is reasonable. At one end of the spectrum stands a case which decided that a plaintiff who was sentimentally attached to his car could not recover the cost of repair, which far exceeded its market value, and the technical reason given for this was the rule about the need to take reasonable steps to mitigate

---

[507] E.g. hiring a car, equivalent to the one destroyed, until the delivery of a new one: *Moore* v. *DER Ltd.* [1971] 1 WLR 1476.

[508] [1925] 2 KB 750. See also *Nor-Video Services Ltd.* v. *Ontario Hydro* (1978) 84 DLR (3d.) 221, where electrical interference forced the plaintiffs to stop a whole television channel, but they did not lose subscribers or income. The cost of restoring the channel was about $200,000. It was held that the measure of damages was the loss, not restoration.

[509] *J. & E. Hall Ltd.* v. *Barclay* [1937] 3 All ER 620.

[510] Torts (Interference with Goods) Act 1977, ss. 7 and 8.

[511] *The Fortunity* [1961] 1 WLR 351.   [512] *The Llanover* [1947] P. 80.

[513] *Peruvian Guano Co. Ltd.* v. *Dreyfus Brothers & Co.* [1892] AC 166.

[514] *Townend* v. *Askern Coal and Iron Co.* [1934] Ch. 463.

[515] *The London Corporation* [1935] P. 70, 77 (per Greer LJ).   [516] *Payton* v. *Brooks* [1974] RTR 169.

[517] *Martindale* v. *Duncan* [1973] 1 WLR 574; *Dodd Properties Ltd.* v. *Canterbury City Council* [1980] 1 WLR 433.

[518] *Dodd Properties*, preceding note.

the damage.[519] At the other end stand cases dealing with damage to unique items where the courts are prepared to sanction the recovery of high repair costs.[520] What of cases falling between these two extremes? The owner of a damaged vintage car has been held entitled to recover the higher repair costs because of the 'legitimately sentimental value'[521] of the damaged article. If so, should not the owner of a treasured but valueless pet, which has been injured through the defendant's negligence, be able to claim the higher cost of cure than the market value, which is nil, or the cost of acquiring a substitute? These are interesting questions, which, however, cannot receive a universal answer beyond restating that a plaintiff's right to be restored to the *status quo ante* has always to be weighed against the duty to do what is reasonable to mitigate the cost to the defendant. It is of interest to note that in a case where a plaintiff was induced to pay more for a house than it was worth because of a negligent report by the defendant surveyor, damages for vexation and inconvenience were included in the award.[522]

A plaintiff may also recover in respect of the loss of use of his thing during repair.[523] But unlike some foreign systems (e.g. German) a claim for the cost of a substitute hire cannot be made if no such hiring has taken place. Thus, in our system, the cost of actual hiring must be strictly pleaded and proved as special damage;[524] and, of course, it must be reasonable.[525] If the profit that would have been earned by the chattel is lower than the cost of hiring the substitute, only the former amount can be claimed. And, conversely, the plaintiff must account for any extra profit that the hired chattel enabled him to make.[526] The fact that he had a substitute ready to hand, so that his activities were not impaired, is irrelevant; what is estimated is the loss of use of the damaged thing.[527] Loss of use can be measured with reference to the hire of a substitute, which is special damage and, as such, has to be pleaded and proved.[528] Damages may also be claimed for the damage of a non-profit earning chattel.[529] As Earl Halsbury LC memorably put it:[530] 'Supposing a person took away a chair out of my room and kept it for twelve months, could anybody say you had a right to diminish the damages by showing that I did not usually sit in that chair, or that there were plenty of other chairs in the room?'

In recent times negligent valuations of property have given rise to differences of opinion as to how the plaintiff's loss should be estimated. Typically, the plaintiff will be a lender of money who lent money to the borrower on the

---

[519] *Darbishire* v. *Warran* [1963] 1 WLR 1067.

[520] *O'Grady* v. *Westminster Scaffolding* [1962] 2 Lloyd's Rep. 238.

[521] Fleming's expression, *Torts*, 225.   [522] *Perry* v. *Sidney Phillips & Son* [1982] 1 WLR 1297.

[523] *Macrae* v. *Swindells* [1954] 1 WLR 597; *The Hebridean Coast* [1961] AC 545.

[524] *SS Strathfillan* v. *SS Ikala* [1929] AC 196.

[525] *Moore* v. *DER Ltd.* [1971] 1 WLR 1476. Thus, the owner of a damaged Rolls-Royce can claim the cost of hire of a substitute Rolls-Royce while his car is being repaired: *HL Motorworks (Willesden) Ltd.* v. *Alwahbi* [1977] RTR 276.

[526] *The World Beauty* [1969] P. 12.   [527] *The Mediana* [1900] AC 113.

[528] *The Hebridean Coast* [1961] AC 545.

[529] Though the calculation here will vary according to the circumstances, and the courts have refused to adopt a single method of assessment.

[530] *The Mediana* [1900] AC 113, 117.

basis of a valuation of the property carried out by a professional valuer. It is important to realise that in these cases two things can go wrong. First, the valuer may (because of his negligence) produce a wrong valuation (typically, an over-valuation) in which case the lender has a diminished security for his loan. In the second case, the value of the property may go down, for instance because of changed market conditions. These two events (which may be combined in practice) may produce widely differing figures; and the problem faced by our courts was to determine the extent of the liability of the valuer where the borrower defaults and the value of the security is insufficent to satisfy the lender's demands. The leading decision now is now found in three consolidated appeals found under the name of *South Australia Asset Management Corp.* v. *York Montague Ltd.*[531]

Lord Hoffmann's leading judgment in that case is notable for its clarity and perceptiveness. This is largely because he commenced his inquiry by making a fundamental distinction: in some cases a professional was hired to provide information (in this case on the value of the land in question) leaving it to someone else (in this case the lender) to decide upon a course of action—a decision which will be taken on the basis of multiple commercial and financial factors available to the lender. In other cases, however, the professional is hired to advise someone on what to do. The crucial question was thus to determine the precise scope and ambit of the valuer's duty and this should be done in the

best way giving effect to the express obligations assumed by the valuer, neither cutting them down so that the lender obtains less than he was reasonably entitled to expect, nor extending them so as to impose on the valuer a liability greater than he could reasonably have thought he was undertaking.[532]

In the instant case, the valuers were hired to provide information which, along with other factors, would enable the lenders to decide whether to make the loan. He was not asked to advise about the financial merits of entering into the deal or the borrower's creditworthiness. The correct principle as far their liability was concerned was thus, for such cases, generalised as follows:

It is that a person under a duty to take reasonable care to provide information on which someone else will decide upon a course of action is, if negligent,[533] not generally regarded as responsible for all the consequences of that course of action. He is responsible only for the consequences of the information being wrong. A duty of care which imposes upon the informant responsibility for losses which would have occurred even if the information which he gave had been correct is not in my view fair and reasonable as between the parties. It is therefore inappropriate either as an implied term of a contract or as a tortious duty arising from the relationship between them.[534]

---

[531] [1996] 3 All ER 365. See also *Nykredit Mortgage Bank plc.* v. *Edward Erdman Group Ltd.* (*No. 2*) [1997] 1 WLR 1627; *Platform Home Loans Ltd.* v. *Oyston Shipways Ltd.* [1998] Ch 466.

[532] Ibid., at 371.

[533] Lord Hoffmann carefully limited his comments to negligent valuations and said nothing about fraudulent valuations. In this latter type of case, however, the 'advisee' might be able to claim his full losses.

[534] Ibid., at 372.

In the *South Australia* case the property in question was valued at £15 million and the lender advanced £11 million. In fact the property was only worth £5 million; and because of a market drop, it was sold at £2.5 million. The lender could thus claim his full loss, i.e. £11 million (loan) minus £2.5 million (price realised from the sale of property).

Select Bibliography

ATIYAH, P. S., *The Damages Lottery* (1997).
—— 'Loss of Earnings or Earning Capacity?', 45 *Aust. LJ* 228 (1971).
—— 'Collateral Benefits Again' (1969) 32 *MLR* 397.
BISHOP, W. and KAY, J., 'Taxation of Damages: the Rule in Gourley's Case' (1987) 104 *LQR* 211.
BURROWS, A., *Remedies for Torts and Breach of Contract* (2nd edn., 1994).
CANE, P., *Atiyah's Accidents, Compensation and the Law* (5th edn., 1993).
FLEMING, J. G., 'Damages: Capital or Rent?', 19 *UTLJ* 295 (1969).
—— 'Impact of Inflation on Tort Compensation' 26 *Am. J. Comp. L.* 51 (1978).
—— 'The Collateral Source Rule and Loss Allocation in Tort' 54 *Cal. LR* 1478.
HARRIS, D. et al., *Compensation and Support for Illness and Injury* (1984).
KEMP, D. (ed.), *Damages for Personal Injury and Death* (5th edn., 1993).
—— 'The Overlap Between Damages for Personal Injury and Work Related Benefits' (1998) 27 *ILJ* 1.
LAW COMMISSION, *Structured Settlements and Interim and Provisional Damages*, Law Com. No. 125 (1992).
—— *Aggravated, Exemplary and Restitutionary Damages*, Law Com. No. 132 (1993).
—— *Damages for Personal Injury: Medical, Nursing and Other Expenses*, Law Com. No. 144 (1996).
—— *Damages for Personal Injury: Collateral Benefits*, Law Com. No. 147 (1997).
—— *Claims for Wrongful Death*, Law Com. No. 148 (1997).
—— *Structured Settlements and Interim and Provisional Damages*, Law Com. No. 147 (1997).
LEWIS, R., *Structured Settlements: the Law and Practice* (1993).
—— 'Deducting Collateral Benefits from Damages: Principle and Policy' (1998) 18 *Legal Studies* 15.
MCGREGOR, H., *On Damages* (16th edn., 1997).
MUNKMAN, J., *Damages for Personal Injuries and Death* (10th edn., 1996).
REPORT OF THE ROYAL COMMISSION, *On Civil Liability and Compensation for Personal Injury* (The Pearson Committee Report) (Cmnd. 7054–1, 1978).
STAPLETON, J., *Disease and the Compensation Debate* (1986).
WEIR, J. A., *Compensation for Personal Injuries and Death; Recent Proposals for Reform*, The Cambridge-Tilburg Lectures (1978).

3. Other Remedies[535]

Actions for the recovery of land and chattels have been explained earlier.[536] Apart from processes at law, certain forms of self-help are allowed, although they are not actively encouraged by the law; these too have been analysed earlier.[537]

1. Injunctions

An action for damages lies after a tort has been committed. An injunction is sought to prevent the continuance of a tort, or in anticipation of a threatened tort. It is an order commanding the discontinuance of some activity or forbidding the causing of damage. In the nature of things it applies to intentional or continuing acts, so it has no application to negligence.[538] The injunction historically arose in equity and the grant of this remedy is still governed by equitable principles and is hence discretionary, unlike damages that are awarded as of right. In principle an injunction cannot be granted unless it is based on some actual or potential cause of action in tort, contract, breach of trust, or otherwise.[539] Courts have on occasion granted injunctions in defence of 'property rights',[540] broadly defined, and to prevent certain breaches of the criminal law in circumstances where it is not clear that any civil-law action for damages would have been available.[541] If these cases are evidence of a wider principle of liability for illicit interference with trade or livelihood that spans existing categories of civil wrong, such a principle has yet to be adequately rationalised.[542]

(A) Prohibitory Injunctions

An injunction may be issued to restrain a threatened act that, unless restrained, is likely to be repeated, with the result that the plaintiff will then have an action based on a civil law wrong. The court will nearly always grant the plaintiff such an injunction, unless he had acquiesced in some way in the activity or had misled the defendant or the court.[543] If the harm is trivial an injunction may not be granted.[544] On the other hand, the defendant is not to be allowed to 'buy' the right to continue his infringement of the plaintiff's interest at the cost of paying nominal damages each time an interference occurs.[545] Nor, in

---

[535] Sections 3 and 4 of this chapter draw on material prepard by R. W. M. Dias for the second edition of this book.

[536] See Chapter 5, Section 2(1) and Section 1(3).

[537] Recovery of chattels, above, Chapter 5, Section 1; expulsion of trespassers and re-entry on land, above, Chapter 5, Section 2; distress damage feasant, above, Chapter 6, Section 2; abatement of nuisance, above, Chapter 5, Section 6(3)(6); self-defence, above, Chapter 4, Section 1(3)(b).

[538] *Miller* v. *Jackson* [1977] QB 966, 980 (Lord Denning MR).   [539] *White* v. *Mellin* [1895] AC 154, 163–4.

[540] *Springhead Spinning Co.* v. *Riley* (1868) LR 6 Eq. 551 (damage to business); *Gee* v. *Pritchard* (1818) 2 Swans. 402 (privacy).

[541] *Ex parte Island Records* [1978] Ch. 122; see above, Chapter 5, Section 5(3)(a)(iv).

[542] See previous note.   [543] *Armstrong* v. *Sheppard and Short Ltd.* [1959] 1 QB 384.

[544] Ibid., 396–7 (Lord Evershed MR).

[545] *Woollerton and Wilson Ltd.* v. *R. Costain Ltd.* [1970] 1 WLR 411, 413 (Stamp LJ); cf. *Charrington* v. *Simons & Co. Ltd.* [1971] 1 WLR 598, 603.

principle, should a court refuse to grant an injunction and award damages instead simply because the injunction will affect the public at large, since this would be to dilute the content of the private rights which it is the role of the court to protect.[546] An injunction may be refused if compliance with it would be impossible or illegal (although a mere breach of contract will not normally prevent the order being made). A court may postpone the coming into force of an injunction in order to give the defendant time to rectify the situation.[547]

(B) Mandatory Injunctions

The court may order the defendant to perform some act, for example, to abate a nuisance.[548] Such injunctions are issued only rarely, and even then only in cases where the defendant has acted deliberately or unreasonably.[549] In *Redland Bricks Ltd.* v. *Morris*[550] the defendant's excavations withdrew support from the plaintiff's land, making further subsidence likely. The House of Lords refused an interlocutory injunction, partly on the ground that the trial judge's order had been too imprecise and partly on the ground that the cost of restoration far exceeded the market value of the land in question. Lord Upjohn stated the following principles governing the grant of an injunction: (*i*) there must be a very strong probability of grave damage; (*ii*) the nature of the injury must be such that damages would be inadequate; (*iii*) the cost to the defendant must be taken into account, as should his behaviour in the sense that the court should determine whether he had tried to 'steal a march' on his neighbour or whether his behaviour had been reasonable; and (*iv*) it must be possible for the defendant to know exactly what he has to do.

(C) Quia Timet Injunctions

Normally an injunction is sought in order to prevent the continuance or repetition of a tort. Where damage has been done, a prohibitory injunction may be issued with reference to the future, ordering the defendant to cease carrying on the activity, or a mandatory injunction may be issued ordering him to put matters right. Where damage is only threatened, or the cause of action is not yet complete, the injunction sought is known as a *quia timet* action alleging that the plaintiff fears that a tort will be committed. He has to show a high probability of substantial damage and that damages will be insufficient or inadequate. In *Redland Bricks Ltd.* v. *Morris*[551] Lord Upjohn said that a *quia timet* injunction will lie (*i*) where the defendant is threatening and intending to do acts which will cause irreparable harm to the plaintiff, and (*ii*) in cases where the plaintiff has received compensation for his loss but alleges that earlier acts of the defendant will lead to future actionable damage.

---

[546] See *Shelfer* v. *City of London Electric Lighting Co.* [1895] 1 Ch. 287; *Miller* v. *Jackson* [1977] QB 966; *Kennaway* v. *Thompson* [1981] QB 88; Chapter 5, Section 3(6)(a) above.

[547] *Pride of Derby and Derbyshire Angling Association Ltd.* v. *British Celanese Ltd.* [1953] Ch. 149.

[548] *Kelsen* v. *Imperial Tobacco Co. Ltd.* [1957] 2 QB 334.   [549] *Daniel* v. *Ferguson* [1981] 2 Ch. 27.

[550] [1970] AC 652, 665–6.   [551] Ibid., 665.

(D) Interlocutory Injunctions

An interlocutory or provisional injunction is designed to restrain the commission or continuance of an activity pending the settlement of either the legal or factual basis of the plaintiff's claim, thereby enabling the *status quo* to be preserved. Since a defendant may suffer through being restrained in this way, the plaintiff is usually required to give an undertaking to pay damages to the defendant in the event of the injunction being discharged at a full trial of the action. It was held in *Patel v. W. H. Smith (Eziot) Ltd.*[552] that an interlocutory injunction could be issued to restrain a trespass on land even though there was no special damage.

Prior to the decision of the House of Lords in *American Cyanamid Co. v. Ethicon Ltd.*[553] it was generally understood that the plaintiff had to show a prima-facie case that he would succeed at the full trial of the action if he was to succeed at the interlocutory stage. However, in that case Lord Diplock laid down a new, two-stage test. At the first stage the plaintiff need show, not a prima-facie case, but simply that there is a serious issue to be tried. At the second stage the court will then decide whether an injunction should be granted on the balance of convenience between the parties. This test greatly favours the *status quo* and has given rise to considerable controversy, not least in the context of the economic torts, where Parliament has intervened to modify its effect on the trade-dispute immunities.[554] Interlocutory injunctions are hardly ever granted in defamation cases, *Cyanamid* notwithstanding.[555] An interlocutory injunction may be issued in the context of an action for nuisance, as in *Burris v. Azadani*,[556] where the purpose of the order was to restrain threats of violence and harassment of the plaintiff by the defendant.

2. Damages in Lieu of an Injunction

Where a court could issue an injunction, but decides against doing so,[557] it may award damages in lieu. This power was originally conferred by section 2 of the Chancery Amendment Act 1858 (Lord Cairns' Act) and has been continued by later legislation.[558] In *Shelfer v. City of London Electric Lighting Co.*[559] A L Smith LJ suggested that the power to grant damages could be exercised where (*i*) the injury to the plaintiff is small, (*ii*) it can be expressed in monetary terms, (*iii*) monetary compensation would be adequate in the circumstances, and (*iv*) it would be oppressive to the defendant to issue the injunction. The defendant must put forward the case for awarding damages as opposed to an injunction. In later cases courts have interpreted the *Shelfer* guidelines flexibly and have taken into account other considerations, such as the seriousness and persistence of the interference, the behaviour of the two parties, and the wide public

---

[552] [1987] 1 WLR 853.　　　　[553] [1975] AC 396.

[554] Trade Union and Labour Relations (Consolidation) Act 1992, s. 221. See Chapter 5, Section 5(5) above.

[555] *Bestobell Paints Ltd.* v. *Gigg* (1975) 119 SJ 678.　　　　[556] [1995] 1 WLR 1372.

[557] *Hooper* v. *Rogers* [1975] Ch. 43, 48 (Russell LJ).　　　　[558] Supreme Court Act 1980, s. 50.

[559] [1895] 1 Ch. 287, 322–33.

interest. The matter is very much one for the judge's discretion.[560] It has been said that damages awarded in this way should represent a 'proper and fair price' for the continuation of the activity.[561]

Select Bibliography

GRAY, C., 'Interlocutory Injunctions since *Cyanamid*' [1981] *CLJ* 307.
JOLOWICZ, J. A., 'Damages in Equity—A Study of Lord Cairns's Act' [1975] *CLJ* 224.

4. JOINT AND CONCURRENT LIABILITY

1. Joint and Concurrent Liability Distinguished

Where several tortfeasors cause different damage to one plaintiff, the torts are independent and each person is liable for the damage he inflicts. Where tortfeasors cause the *same* damage they may either be *joint tortfeasors* or *several concurrent tortfeasors*. Tortfeasors are 'joint' in cases of express authorisation or instigation; principal and agent; vicarious liability; the liability of an employer and an independent contractor (where the former is under a personal, non-delegable duty of care); the liability of tortfeasors who act in breach of a joint duty; and tortfeasors who act in pursuance of a common design.[562] Several concurrent tortfeasors are those who, acting independently of each other, combine in their actions to cause damage to the plaintiff, for example, when two careless motorists collide and injure a pedestrian.[563]

In joint liability each tortfeasor is liable for the full amount of the plaintiff's loss, but there is only one tort and so the cause of action against each one is the same and is supported by the same evidence. The common law took the view that since there is only one tort, judgment against one tortfeasor, even if unsatisfied, barred further action against the other or others.[564] Only if judgment against one defendant only partially satisfied the plaintiff would successive actions lie.[565] This rule was changed by statute in 1935[566] and the relevant provisions are now found in section 3 of the Civil Liability (Contribution) Act 1978.

2. Successive Actions

Section 3 of the 1978 Act states that judgment against any one person shall not be a bar to an action, or its continuance, against any other person jointly liable

---

[560] See e.g. *Sampson* v. *Hodson-Pressinger* [1981] 3 All ER 710, 715 (Eveleigh LJ).

[561] *Bracewell* v. *Appleby* [1975] Ch. 408, 419–20. This means that in an appropriate case, damages in lieu of an injunction may compensate the plaintiff for loss of a bargaining opportunity in respect of the activity: see *Wrotham Park Estates Co. Ltd.* v. *Parkside Homes Ltd.* [1974] 1 WLR 798; *Jaggard* v. *Sawyer* [1995] 1 WLR 269.

[562] On the latter, see *Brooke* v. *Bool* [1928] 2 KB 578; *CBS Songs Ltd.* v. *Amstrad Consumer Electronics plc* [1988] AC 1013.

[563] *Drinkwater* v. *Kimber* [1952] 2 QB 281; *Thompson* v. *LCC* [1899] 2 QB 840.

[564] *Brinsmead* v. *Harrison* (1872) LR 7 CP 547.   [565] *The Koursk* [1924] P. 140.

[566] The Law Reform (Married Women and Joint Tortfeasors) Act 1935.

in respect of the same damage.[567] This provision applies both to joint and to several concurrent tortfeasors. It is possible that a plaintiff may recover damages in a second action over and above those which he was awarded in the first, for example, if he had underestimated his damage. Section 4, however, states that a plaintiff who brings another action against a joint or concurrent tortfeasor shall be refused costs in the later action unless he satisfied the court that there was a reasonable ground for bringing it. If joint or concurrent tortfeasors are sued at the same time there will be judgment for a single sum, which they will share between them; the plaintiff must not be over-compensated for his loss. A controversial rule is that the plaintiff will be awarded the lowest sum for which any one defendant could be held liable.[568] This can create unfairness to the plaintiff in the event of exemplary, punitive, or aggravated damages being awardable against one defendant. Although the rule is designed to protect the innocent defendant from being made to pay a greater amount than he could personally be held responsible for, it is arguable that he could shift his loss by seeking contribution from the guilty defendant.

Following the abolition of the bar against successive actions, the only remaining distinction between joint and several liability concerns the effect of release of tortfeasors. In joint torts the release of one tortfeasor, whether by accord and satisfaction or under seal, automatically releases the other or others;[569] this is because there is only one obligation resting on all of them, and if this is extinguished with regard to one it is extinguished for all.[570] In contrast, the liabilities of concurrent tortfeasors are separate, with the result that a release of one does not necessarily release the others. An agreement not to sue is not the same as a release for this purpose, in the sense that it does not extinguish the obligation; it merely gives the other party to the agreement a defence should a claim be brought.[571] Such an agreement does not therefore extinguish the cause of action against the rest. This distinction has been called arid, technical, and without any merits;[572] accordingly, a court has held that even a release will not extinguish the claim against the others if there is an express or implied reservation of the right of action against them.[573] Nor will it release the other tortfeasors in a case where the settlement does not meet the full value of the plaintiff's claim for damages.[574]

3. Contribution and Apportionment

The common law did not provide for contribution between joint or concurrent tortfeasors,[575] unless the tort was clearly illegal in itself and the party claiming contribution acted in the belief that it was lawful or, if the tort was clearly ille-

---

[567] See *Wah Tat Bank Ltd.* v. *Chan* [1975] AC 507; *Bryanston Finance Ltd.* v. *de Vries* [1975] 1 QB 703; *Birse Construction Ltd.* v. *Haite Ltd. (Watson and Others, Third Parties)* [1996] 1 WLR 675.

[568] *Cassell & Co. Ltd.* v. *Broome* [1972] AC 1027.

[569] *Thurman* v. *Wild* (1840) 11 A. & E. 453.   [570] *Duck* v. *Mayeu* [1892] 2 QB 511, 513.

[571] *Apley Estates Co. Ltd.* v. *de Bernales* [1947] Ch. 217.

[572] *Bryanston Finance Ltd.* v. *de Vries* [1975] QB 703, 723 (Lord Denning MR).

[573] *Gardiner* v. *Moore* [1969] 1 QB 55.

[574] *Jameson* v. *Central Electricity Generating Board (Babcock Energy Ltd., Third Party)* [1997] 3 WLR 151.

[575] *Merryweather* v. *Nixon* (1799) 8 Term Rep. 186.

gal, the party claiming contribution was held vicariously liable for the wrong-doing of another which he had not authorised.[576] Provision for contribution again had to be made by statute. Section 1(1) of the Civil Liability (Contribution) Act 1978 now states that 'any person liable in respect of any damage suffered by another person may recover contribution from any other person liable in respect of the same damage (whether jointly with him or otherwise)'. The Act is not limited to actions in tort; it extends to all forms of civil liability, whether based on tort, breach of contract, breach of trust, or otherwise.[577]

The party seeking contribution must be liable, actually or hypothetically: section 1(6) refers to 'liability which has been or could be established in an action'. The wording used here rules out a claim for contribution by a defendant whose liability cannot be established because the period of limitation has elapsed. A contribution may, however, be claimed from a defendant against whom an action has simply been stayed, for example, because, thanks to an exclusive jurisdiction clause, they must be sued in another jurisdiction.[578]

Where, on the other hand, the claimant has paid the plaintiff, section 1(2) preserves the right to contribution against a joint or concurrent tortfeasor, even though the claimant is no longer liable to the original plaintiff 'since the time when the damage occurred, provided that he was so liable immediately before he made or was ordered or agreed to make the payment in respect of which the contribution is sought'. At the time contribution is sought the claimant may no longer be liable because of settlement or compromise. Under section 1(4) a party who made a payment under a bona-fide settlement or compromise may claim contribution 'without regard to whether or not he himself is or ever was liable in respect of the damage, provided, however, that he would have been liable assuming that the factual basis of the claim against him could be established'. The provision is oddly phrased: would a defendant motivated to enter into a compromise as a result of legal as opposed to factual doubts about liability be covered by it?[579] Section 1(4) was enacted in order to clarify this area in the light of *Stott* v. *West Yorkshire Road Car Co. Ltd. and Another, Home Bakeries Ltd. and Another, Third Parties*.[580] Here, one defendant made an out-of-court settlement with the plaintiff without admitting liability, and then sought contribution. It was held that he could recover, provided that the other defendant was liable and provided that the claimant would have been liable had he been sued to judgment.

With regard to the person from whom contribution is claimed, section 1(3) of the 1978 Act provides that

a person shall be liable to make contribution . . . notwithstanding that he has ceased to be liable in respect of the damage in question since the time when the damage occurred, unless he ceased to be liable by virtue of the expiry of a period of limitation or

---

[576] *Adamson* v. *Harris* (1827) 4 Bing. 66; *Lister* v. *Romford Ice and Cold Storage Co. Ltd.* [1957] AC 555.

[577] S. 6(1).

[578] See *R. A. Lister & Co. Ltd.* v. *E. G. Thomson (Shipping) Ltd. and Another (No. 2)* [1987] 1 WLR 1614.

[579] See A. M. Dugdale, 'Civil Liability (Contribution) Act 1978' (1979) 42 MLR 182, 184, and cf. the position of the builder who compromised in *Dutton* v. *Bognor Regis UDC* [1972] 1 QB 373.

[580] [1971] 2 QB 651.

prescription which extinguished the right on which the claim against him in respect of the damage was based.

Limitation does not normally extinguish the action as such[581]—conversion is an exception is this regard.[582] Let D1 signify the defendant seeking contribution and D2 the defendant from whom the contribution is sought. By virtue of section 1(3), the fact that the plaintiff's claim may be statute-barred against D2 will not now prevent D1 from bringing a claim for contribution against D2 (as long as the limitation rules do not protect D1 himself from an action by the plaintiff, in which case section 1(6) rules out his claim for contribution). The problem used to arise where certain classes of defendants were protected by special limitation rules which placed them at an advantage as compared to others: as in the case of *George Wimpey & Co. Ltd.* v. *British Overseas Airways Corporation*;[583] or in a case where the plaintiff initiated an action against D1 within the period of limitation but, by the time D1 sought contribution against D2, this period had elapsed, meaning that D2 would have had a defence against any claim brought by the plaintiff.[584]

Section 1(5) provides that judgment in an action by the original plaintiff against the party from whom contribution is sought 'shall be conclusive in the proceedings for contribution as to any issue determined by that judgment in favour of the person from whom contribution is sought'. This should be read as meaning 'any issue on the merits'; otherwise it might cancel out the effect of section 1(3) by reintroducing the possibility that a limitation defence available to D2 in an action brought by the plaintiff would indeed prevent D1 from seeking contribution.[585]

The question of the effect upon the right of contribution of a limitation defence available in an action brought by the plaintiff must be distinguished from the limitation of the period within which the contribution claim itself must be brought. This period is two years from the date when the right of contribution accrues,[586] which is either the date of judgment against the defendant seeking contribution or, in the event of a compromise, the date of the agreement to pay the sum in question.

Under section 2(1) of the Act, the amount of contribution which a party will have to make depends on what the court considers is 'just and equitable having regard to the extent of that person's responsibility for the damage in question'. The court has power to exempt a party completely or, conversely, to order him to pay a complete indemnity.[587] Contribution can only be assessed between parties before the court; no account is to be taken of the possible responsibility of other persons.[588] With regard to the phrase 'responsibility for the damage', here, as under the Law Reform (Contributory Negligence) Act 1945, 'responsi-

---

[581] See above, Section 1(9)(d).   [582] Limitation Act 1980, s. 3.
[583] [1955] AC 169. S. 1(3) effectively reverses the outcome in this case.
[584] As in *Ronex Properties Ltd.* v. *John Laing Construction Ltd.* [1983] QB 398.
[585] *Nottingham Health Authority* v. *City of Nottingham* [1988] 1 WLR 903, 908 (Balcombe LJ).
[586] Limitation Act 1980, s. 10.
[587] Civil Liability (Contribution) Act 1978, s. 2(2). For a case of complete indemnity, see *Williams* v. *Trimm Rock Quarries* (1965) 109 SJ 454.
[588] *Maxfield* v. *Llewellyn* [1961] 1 WLR 1119.

bility' implies both causal responsibility and the relative degree of fault of the parties: 'the investigation is concerned with "fault", which includes blameworthiness as well as causation. And no true apportionment can be reached unless both these factors are borne in mind.'[589]

The relationship between contribution and contributory negligence was clarified by the House of Lords in *Fitzgerald* v. *Lane*.[590] The plaintiff was seriously injured when he tried to cross a pedestrian crossing against the lights. He was struck by the car of the first defendant and thrown into the path of the car of the second. Both defendants had been driving too quickly and were held liable in negligence. The trial judge assessed the responsibility of the plaintiff and the two defendants as a third each. On this basis he made a deduction of one-third of the plaintiff's damages (under the Contributory Negligence Act) and then held (under the Contribution Act) that each defendant, being equally to blame with the other, should pay half of the resulting sum. The Court of Appeal overturned this judgment on the basis that since the plaintiff was equally to blame with the defendants considered *as a group*, he should only recover *half* of his damages. The House of Lords reversed on the law, pointing out that the correct procedure was that adopted by the judge: the court should first of all assess the extent of the plaintiff's responsibility under the Contributory Negligence Act, and only then consider the apportionment of responsibility between the defendants. However, the order of the Court of Appeal was upheld as the House of Lords came to a different conclusion on the extent of the plaintiff's responsibility for the accident, assessing this at 50 per cent and not just a third.

Under section 2(3) the amount of contribution assessed by the court against D2 must not exceed the amount which a court either has or might have awarded the plaintiff in an action against him for the loss in question, if that amount has been limited either by an enactment or a prior agreement or by virtue of section 1 of the Contributory Negligence Act. As far as prior agreement is concerned, it should be borne in mind that a limitation clause or notice that has this effect will be subject to the Unfair Contract Terms Act 1977.[591] The reference to the Contributory Negligence Act can produce some odd effects given that the Act does not apply to claims for breach of contract (other than those overlapping with the tort of negligence).[592] Consider, for example, the common situation in which liability for damage caused by a defective product is passed back up the chain of supply. If the retailer is sued for breach of contract, any contributory negligence on the part of the plaintiff will not be taken into account. Should the retailer then seek contribution from the manufacturer, he will find that the manufacturer's responsibility will be limited. For any action by the plaintiff against the manufacturer would have been in tort and not contract, the latter could have invoked the defence of contributory negligence to limit his liability, and this reduced sum will set the limit to any contribution he will be required to pay under the Contribution Act.

---

[589] *Miraflores* v. *George Livanos* [1967] 1 AC 826, 845 (Lord Pearce).   [590] [1989] AC 328.
[591] See above, Section 1(4)(a–b) of this chapter.   [592] *Forsikring Vesta* v. *Butcher* [1989] AC 852 (CA).

4. Indemnity

It remains possible to obtain an indemnity separately from the Contribution Act. Agreements for indemnity, such as liability insurance, are common. Such contracts are lawful if the aim is to indemnify the wrongdoer against the consequences of his own carelessness,[593] although not if they seek to indemnify him against intentional wrongdoing unless this was induced by the fraud of another or the act was not obviously wrong.[594]

An example of an implied right to indemnity arises in the context of the employment relationship. In *Lister* v. *Romford Ice and Cold Storage Co. Ltd.*[595] the House of Lords held that an employer who is made vicariously liable for a tort committed by an employee in the course of his employment can recover an indemnity from the employee by virtue of a term implied into the contract of employment. The decision flatly contradicts most of the purposed justifications for imposing vicarious liability on the employer—for example, the arguments that the employer's 'deep pockets' enable it to bear the costs and spread the risk of liability more effectively and that the employer, as the party who takes the profits from the enterprise, should also bear liability for certain risks arising from its operation. In practice the pressure to recover this indemnity will come, if at all, from the employer's liability insurer who will be subrogated to any claim the employer will have against the employee. As a result of a 'gentlemen's agreement' the insurance companies almost invariably do not pursue their subrogation rights to an indemnity against the employee, as *Lister* would allow them to do.

5. Secondary Civil Liability

The English law of tort apparently does not contain a general principle of secondary civil liability, that is to say liability as an accessory to the commission of a civil wrong on a par with the equivalent and well-recognised principle in the criminal law. The existence of such liability, separate from the established categories of joint tortfeasors and liability for the active inducement or procurement of wrongful acts such as is found in the economic torts,[596] was recently doubted in the Court of Appeal.[597] However, Glanville Williams considered that the criminal law definition of an accessory could be 'used in tort to indicate a joint tortfeasor',[598] and there is also academic support for the existence of a wider principle of secondary civil liability, distinct from the concept of joint torts, which has tended to be obscured by the modern-day division of obligations law between contract, tort, and equity. Philip Sales has argued that:

---

[593] See *Hardy* v. *Motor Insurers' Bureau* [1964] 2 QB 745; *Gardner* v. *Moore* [1984] AC 548. Intention was stretched to include gross negligence in *Askey* v. *Golden Wine Co. Ltd.* [1948] 2 All ER 35, but in *Tiline* v. *White Cross Insurance Association Ltd.* [1921] 3 KB 327 a motorist found guilty of manslaughter on the basis of 'criminal negligence' was able to recover an indemnity under his liability insurance policy.

[594] *W. H. Smith & Son* v. *Clinton* (1908) 99 LT 840, 841.

[595] [1957] AC 555; *Morris* v. *Ford Motor Co. Ltd.* [1973] QB 792; see above, Chapter 6, Section 4(4).

[596] See Chapter 5, Section 4, above.

[597] *CBS Songs Ltd.* v. *Amstrad Consumer Electronics plc* [1986] FSR 159, 212 (Slade LJ).

[598] *Joint Torts and Contributory Negligence* (1951), at 11.

There are two main principles that emerge from the cases. First, liability may be imposed on a person who induces or procures the commission of a civil wrong against the plaintiff by a third party. Second, liability may be imposed on a person who assists a third party to commit a civil wrong against the plaintiff. There is a substantial body of authority in support of the first of these principles, and in support of its general applicability throughout the civil law. The second principle is less well recognised, but is also supported by authority in particular areas and should be accepted as a principle of general application along with the first.[599]

The first category of cases referred to by Sales contains examples of liability which are familiar and not particularly controversial: these consist of the economic torts of inducing breach of contract;[600] inducing breach of fiduciary duty;[601] and inducing breach of statutory duty;[602] and the principle of liability as a joint tortfeasor for authorising or joining in the tortious act of another.[603] The second category is much more contentious. Here Sales refers to the well-established liability for knowing assistance in a dishonest breach of trust[604] and to cases in which the notion of joint torts has been extended to cover assistance in the commission of a tort.[605] There is no clear authority, however, for a tort of assisting in a breach of contract (or a breach of statutory duty); nevertheless, it is argued that:

the dividing line between inducing a third party to commit a wrong and assisting in its commission is so fine as to be non-existent. Often the offering of assistance is itself an inducement to the third party to act wrongfully. Moreover, the connection between the loss suffered by the plaintiff and the assistance provided to the third party wrongdoer by the defendant may be as strong as that between the loss and the wrong committed by the third party.[606]

What is proposed here is a unifying principle of liability[607] which, in the context of the law of tort, would involve at the very least a clarification and more probably an extension of the category of joint tortfeasors; it would also involve taking another look at the economic torts.[608] A contrary view is taken by Tony Weir and stresses the limits of the economic torts. The correct distinction in the tort of inducing breach of contract is 'between getting a man not to perform his contract and causing him not to',[609] there being no liability in the second case unless unlawful means are used and the defendant aimed to injure the plaintiff. It seems likely that this difficult area will continue to receive the

---

[599] 'The Tort of Conspiracy and Civil Secondary Liability' [1990] *CLJ* 491, 503.
[600] *Lumley* v. *Gye* (1853) 2 E. & B. 216.   [601] *Midgley* v. *Midgley* [1893] 3 Ch. 282.
[602] *Meade* v. *Haringey LBC* [1979] 1 WLR 637.
[603] See Williams, op. cit. at 9–16. Sales adds a third category of procuring a contempt of court: *Seaward* v. *Paterson* [1897] 1 Ch. 545. As he says, this could be regarded as quasi-criminal in nature, although he is prepared to argue that 'such secondary liability is a product of the common law which arises out of the civil obligations of the principal contemnor, which are reinforced but are not extended by the order of the court' [1990] *CLJ* 491, 505.
[604] *Barnes* v. *Addy* (1874) LR 9 Ch. App. 244.   [605] [1990] *CLJ* 491, 508.
[606] Sales, op. cit. [1990] *CLJ* 491, 507–8.
[607] The case for the existence of such a principle is made by D. Cooper, 'Secondary Liability in Civil Wrongs', Ph.D. Thesis, University of Cambridge, 1995.
[608] Above, Chapter 5, Section 5.
[609] *Casebook on Tort* (8th edn., 1996), at 609. See also Weir, *Economic Torts* (1997), at 38.

attention of the courts and that academic writings will inform the approach of the practising Bar and of the Bench.

Select Bibliography

ATIYAH, P. S., 'Causation, Contributory Negligence and *Volenti Non Fit Injuria*' (1965) 43 *Can. BR* 609.

GREGORY, C. O., 'Contribution Among Joint Tortfeasors: A Defence', 54 *Harv. LR* 1170 (1941).

JAMES, F., 'Contribution Among Joint Tortfeasors: A Pragmatic Criticism', ibid., 1156.
—— 'Replication', ibid., 1178.

SALES, P., 'The Tort of Conspiracy and Secondary Civil Liability' [1990] *CLJ* 491.

WILLIAMS, G. L., *Joint Torts and Contributory Negligence* (1951).

Index